Studies
In The
Scriptures

1943-1944

Volume 12 of 17

Studies
In The
Scriptures

1943 - 1944

Volume 12 of 17

Arthur W. Pink

Sovereign Grace Publishers, Inc.
P.O. Box 491
Mulberry, Indiana 46058

Studies In The Scriptures 1943 - 1944
Hardback Edition
Volume 17 of 17 Volumes
Copyright © 2013
By SGPBooks.com, Inc..

ISBN 1-58960-224-2

Studies in the Scriptures -- 1943
Index

Studies in the Scriptures
1944 Index

Vol. XXII   JANUARY, 1943.   No. 1

STUDIES IN THE SCRIPTURES

" Search the Scriptures."   John 5:39.

Publisher and Editor—ARTHUR W. PINK,
27 Lewis Street,
Stornoway, Isle of Lewis,
Scotland.

NEW YEAR'S COMFORT.

As we launch out into another year there is little visible prospect of a smooth and pleasant voyage. To the natural eye the clouds are dark and fierce storms seem imminent. The very uncertainty of what the morrow may bring forth fills many with uneasiness and trepidation. But how different should be the state of God's children: an all-sufficient Object is presented to the eyes of their faith from which unbelief derives no comfort. If the poor worldling is concerned with *what* lies before him, it is the blessed privilege of the believer to be occupied with *Who* goes before him—the One who is his Captain, his Guide, his Forerunner. "The Lord! HE it is that doth go before thee" (Deut. 31:8). What a difference that makes! O that writer and reader may be enabled to lay hold of this grand Truth as we enter another period of time and keep it steadily in mind throughout the coming days!

1. The Lord has gone before you in the grand decree of His *predestination.* Last year was one of suspense and sorrow, of trial and trouble and perhaps you tremble at what this one has in store. Well, here is solid comfort. Your future has all been marked out for you. You shall not tread a step which is not mapped on the grand chart of God's foreordination. All your circumstances have been Divinely ordered for you. Ah, Christian reader, what an immense difference this makes that you are not a child of chance, that your lot is not decided by the caprice of fickle fortune. Infinite wisdom and infinite love have arranged everything. You will go nowhere during 1943 but where God has decreed, His "goings forth have been from of old, from everlasting" (Micah 5:2), planning your path, your life. A predestinating God has appointed "the bounds of your habitation" (Acts 17:26). You may be thrust into the furnace of affliction, yet you will not be deserted. You may be brought low, yet it will be for your future blessing. You may be chastened, yet the rod is in the hand of your Father.

> "Your times of trial and of grief,
> Your times of joy and sweet relief,
> All shall come and last and end
> As shall please your heavenly Friend."

2. The Lord has gone before you in the preparations of His *Providence.* "My god [God] shall supply all your need" (Phil. 4:19): full provision has *already* been made for it. Jehovah does not have to improvise. No unexpected emergency can overtake Him:

IMPORTANT NOTICES

Please advise promptly of change in address, otherwise copies will be lost in the mails.

We are glad to send a sample copy to any of your friends whom you believe would be interested in this publication.

This magazine is published as "a work of faith and labour of love," the editor and his wife gladly giving their services free. There is no regular subscription price, as we do not wish the poor of the flock to be deprived. This does not mean that those looking for something for nothing may "help themselves." Those getting this Magazine, who are financially able and who receive spiritual help from its pages, are expected to gladly contribute towards its expenses; otherwise, their names are dropped from our lists.

Will those forwarding International Money Orders please have them made out to us at Stornoway, Isle of Lewis, Scotland. Checks (Cheques-Eng.) made out on U.S.A. Banks are not negotiable here, so please do not send them.

CONTENTS

THE SERMON ON THE MOUNT.

25. *False Prophets.* Matt. 7:15.

Our last two articles of this series were devoted principally to showing the relation of good works unto final salvation, this being both pertinent and needful, forasmuch as many of the "false prophets" of our day expressly repudiate all that we therein insisted upon. They dogmatically affirm that "believing the Gospel is *all* that is needed to ensure Heaven for any sinner." And is it not so? Certainly not. First, it requires to be pointed out that there is an *order* in presenting the Gospel and it is the business of those who preach to observe that order: unless they do so nothing but *disorder* will ensue and spurious converts will be the issue of their labours. If due attention is paid to the Word of God it will not be difficult to discover what that order is: the proclamation and enforcing of the Divine Law *precedes* the publication of the Divine Gospel. Broadly speaking the Old Testament is an exposition of the Law, while the New Testament sets forth the substance and benefits of the Gospel.

The Gospel is a message of "good news." To whom? To sinners. But to what sort of sinners? To the giddy and unconcerned, to those who give no thought to the claims of God and where they shall spend eternity? Certainly not. The Gospel announces no good tidings to *them*: it has no music in it to *their* ears. They are quite deaf to its charms, for they have no sense of their need of the Saviour. Only those who have their eyes opened to see something of the ineffable holiness of God and their vileness in His sight—who have learned something of His righteous requirements and of their criminal neglect to meet those requirements—only those who are deeply convicted of their depravity, their moral inability to recover themselves, whose conscience is burdened with an intolerable load of guilt and who are terrified by their imminent danger of the wrath to come—only those who know that unless an all-mighty Redeemer saves them they are doomed—only those are qualified to appreciate and welcome the Gospel. "They that are whole need not a physician, but they that are sick."

Now the natural man has no realization of the desperate sickness of his soul. He is quite unconscious of what spiritual health consists of, namely, personal holiness. Never having sincerely measured himself by the Divine Standard, he knows not how far, far short he comes of it at every point. God has no real place in his thoughts and therefore he fails to comprehend how obnoxious he is in His sight. Instead of seeking to glorify the One who made and sustains him, he lives only to please himself. And what is the means for enlightening him? What is the sure "line and plummet" (Isa. 28:17) for exposing the crookedness of his character? The preaching of God's *Law,* for that is the unchanging Rule of conduct and standard of righteousness. "By the Law is the knowledge of sin" (Rom. 3:20)—its nature, as rebellion against God; its exceeding sinfulness as contrariety to Divine holiness; its infinite evil, as deserving of eternal punishment.

"I had not known sin, *but by the Law*" (Rom. 7:7) declares one who formerly had prided himself in his integrity and righteousness. God's Law requires inward conformity as well as outward: it addresses itself to the motions of the heart as well as prescribes our actions. We are sinless or sinful just in proportion as we conform or fail to conform to the Law both internally and externally. Just so far as we have false ideas of God's Law do we entertain false estimates of our character. Just so far as we fail to perceive that the Law demands perfect and perpetual obedience shall we be blind to the fearful extent of our disobedience. Just so far as we realize not the spirituality and strictness of the Law, that it pronounces a lascivious *imagination* as adultery and causeless anger against a fellow-creature to be *murder*, shall we be unaware of our fearful criminality. Just so far as we hear nothing of the awful thunders of the Law's curse shall we be insensible to our frightful danger.

It has been rightly said that "The Gospel has such respect to the Law of God and the latter is so much the reason and ground of the former, so essential to the wisdom and glory of it, that it cannot be understood by him who is ignorant of the Law. Consequently, our idea and apprehension of the Gospel will be erroneous and wrong just so far as we have wrong notions of God's Law" (S. Hopkins). The excellence of the Mediator cannot be recognized until we see that the Law demands flawless and undeviating obedience on pain of eternal damnation and that such a demand is right and glorious. We must see that *sin* is infinitely criminal and heinous. The essential work of the Mediator was to honour and magnify that Law and make atonement for the wrongs done to it by His people. And they who repudiate this Law or who view it not in its true light, are and must be totally blind to the wisdom and glory of the Gospel. For while they never see sin in its real odiousness and true ill-desert they are incapable of realizing or perceiving their deep need of the Divine remedy.

That salvation which Christ came here to purchase for His people consists first in the gift of His Spirit to overcome their enmity against God's Law (Rom. 8:7) and produce in them a love for it (Rom. 7:22). It is by this we may discover whether or not we have been regenerated. Second, to bring them to a cordial consent to the Law, so that each genuine Christian can say, "So then with the mind I myself serve the Law of God" (Rom. 7:25). Third, to deliver them from the curse of the Law by dying for their sins of disobedience against it, Himself bearing its penalty in their stead (Gal. 3:13). Consequently, they who are experimentally ignorant of God's Law, who have never heartily assented to it as "holy, just and good," have never been sensible of sin in its true hideousness and demerits. They have never been subject to a supernatural work of grace within them—are yet in nature's darkness—strangers to Christ, still in their sins, having felt neither the strength of sin nor the power of the Gospel.

Again—the order which is to be observed in the presentation of the Gospel is exemplified in the appointment of *John the Baptist*. He was the forerunner of Christ, going before to "prepare His way" (Isa. 40:3). John came "in the way of righteousness" (Matt. 21:32), crying, "Repent ye" (Matt. 3:2). A saving faith in Christ must be preceded by and accompanied with a heart-felt sense of the true odiousness and ill-desert of sin. An impenitent heart is no more able to receive Christ than a shuttered window is capable of letting in the rays of the sun. None but the humbled, contrite, broken-hearted penitent is ever comforted by the Lord Jesus, as none but such will ever desire Him or seek after Him. This is the unchanging order laid down by Christ Himself: "repent and (then) believe the Gospel" (Mark 1:15): ye "repented not afterward that ye might believe" (Matt. 21:32) was His solemn affirmation. First "repentance toward God and (then) faith toward our Lord Jesus Christ" (Acts 20:21) was what the Apostle testified to Jews and Gentiles alike.

It has often been said that nothing more is required of the sinner than that he come to Christ as an empty-handed beggar and receive Him as an all-sufficient Saviour. But that assertion needs clarifying and amplifying at two points lest souls be fatally misled thereby. To come to Christ empty-handed signifies not only that I renounce any fancied righteousness of mine but also that I relinquish my beloved idols. Just so long as the sinner holds fast to the world or clings to any fond sin, he cannot thrust forth an *empty* hand. The things which produce death must be dropped before he can "lay hold on eternal life." Furthermore, Christ cannot be received in part but only in the entirety of His Person and office: He must be received as "Lord and Saviour" or He cannot be savingly received at all. There must be a submitting to His authority, a surrendering to His sceptre, a taking of His yoke upon us, as well as a trusting in His blood, or we shall never find "rest unto our souls."

"But as many as received Him, to them gave He power to become the sons of God" (John 1:12). This verse is often *quoted* by the self-appointed "evangelists" of our day but it is rarely *expounded.* Instead of throwing all the emphasis on "received," attention rather needs to be directed unto "received *Him.*" It is not "received it"—a mental proposition or doctrine, nor even received "His"—some gift or benefit; but "Him," in the entirety of His Person as clothed with His offices, as He is proposed in the Gospel. Such a "receiving" as is here spoken of implies an enlightened understanding, a convicted conscience, renewed affections—the exercise of love, an act of the will—choice of a new Master, the acceptance of His terms (Luke 14:26, 27, 33). It is at the last point that so many balk: "why call ye Me, Lord, Lord, and do not the things which I say?" (Luke 6:46). And therefore is the inquirer bidden to "sit down first and count the cost" (Luke 14:28). The order is first the Person of Christ and then His gifts (Rom. 8:32): thus God bestows and thus we receive.

Those, then, who declare that a bare believing of the Gospel is all that is needed to ensure Heaven for any sinner are "false prophets," liars and deceivers of souls. It also requires to be pointed out that saving faith is not an isolated act but a *continuous* thing. When the Apostle contrasted genuine saints with apostates, he described them as "them that believe to the saving of the soul" (Heb. 10:39). Note well the tense of the verb: not "them that believed" one day in the past but "them that believe" with a faith which is operative in the present. In this he was holding fast, "the form of sound words" (2 Tim. 1:13) employed by his Master, for Christ, too, taught: "as Moses lifted up the serpent in the wilderness, even so must the Son of man be lifted up, that whosoever *believeth* in Him should not perish but have everlasting life" (John 3:15, 18, 36; 5:24 etc). In like manner another Apostle says, "If so be ye have tasted that the Lord is gracious, to whom (*not,* ye "came," but) *coming*, as unto a living Stone" (1 Peter 2:4)— coming daily, as needy as ever.

Saving faith is not an isolated act which suffices for the remainder of a person's life, rather is it a living principle which continues in activity, ever seeking the only Object which can satisfy it. Nor is it a thing apart, but a *productive principle* which issues in good works and spiritual fruits. "Faith, if it hath not works, is dead, being alone" (James 2:17). A faith which does not bring forth obedience to the Divine precepts is not the faith of God's elect. Saving faith is something radically different from a mere mental assent to the Gospel, believing that God loves me and that Christ died for me. The demons assent to the whole compass of Divine revelation but what does it advantage them? Nor is the "faith" advocated by the false prophets of any more value or efficacy. Saving faith, my reader, is one which "purifieth the heart" (Act 15:9), which "worketh by love" (Gal. 5:6), which "overcometh the world" (1 John 5:4). And such faith man can neither originate nor regulate. Has such a faith been Divinely communicated to *you*?

Now it is in their opposition to those aspects of the Truth we have been concerned with above, that the false prophets may be identified. Not that their preaching is all cast in the same mold: far from it. As the servants of God are variously gifted—one to evangelize, another to indoctrinate, another to exhort and admonish—so Satan accommodates his emissaries to the different types of people they meet with. On the one hand, Romanists and other legalists teach that salvation is by obedience to the Law, that repentance and good works are meritorious. On the other, Plymouth Brethren and other Antinomians insist that the Law is entirely Jewish, that the Gentiles were never under it and have nothing to do with it. But just as the Pharisees, the Sadducees and the Herodians differed widely the one from the other yet made common cause in antagonizing Christ, so the false prophets, though far from being uniform in their heterodoxy, nevertheless are one in opposing the Truth. Conversely whatever are their distinctive gifts and spheres of service, the true ministers of God are always identifiable by their fidelity to the Faith once for all delivered to the saints.

It is particularly the Antinomian kind of false prophets we are here seeking to expose and warn against. For the last two or three generations they have swarmed in Christendom, especially in the so-called "evangelical" and "orthodox" sections of it. Almost all the "evangelists," "Bible teachers" and leaders among the "Fundamentalists" were and are "wolves in sheep's clothing." They have deceived multitudes by their very seeming soundness in the Faith. They have denounced "Higher Criticism" and Evolutionism, Christian Science and Russellism. They have affirmed the Divine Inspiration of the Scriptures and have made much of the mercy of God and the atoning blood of Christ. But they have falsified God's way of salvation. Christ bade His hearers "strive" (agonize) to enter in at the "strait gate" (Luke 13:24)—these men declare such striving to be altogether unnecessary. Christ affirmed, "except ye repent, ye shall all likewise perish." They say that sinners may be saved without repentance. Scripture asks, "If the righteous scarcely be saved, (with difficulty), where shall the ungodly and the sinner appear?" (1 Peter 4:18): these men aver that salvation is easy for anyone. Scripture uniformly teaches that unless the believer perseveres in holiness he will lose Heaven: but these men insist he will merely forfeit some "millennial crown."

As one of the Puritans quaintly, yet truly, expressed it, "The face of error is highly painted and powdered so as to render it attractive to the unwary." The false prophets, whether of the Papist or the Protestant order, make a great show of devotion and piety on the one hand and of zeal and fervour on the other, as did the Pharisees of old with their fasting and praying and who "compassed sea and land to make one proselyte" (Matt. 23:15). They are diligent in seeking to discredit those truths they design to overthrow by branding them "legal doctrines" and denouncing as "Judaisers" those who are set for the defense of them. "With goods words and fair speeches they deceive the heart of the simple" (Rom. 16:18). They speak much about "grace," yet it is not that *Divine* grace which "reigns through righteousness" (Rom. 5:21), nor does it effectually teach men to deny "ungodliness and worldly lusts" (Titus 2:11, 12). With "cunning craftiness" they "lie in wait to deceive" (Eph. 4:14) souls who have never been established in the Truth and beguile with "enticing words" (Col. 2:4), making a great show of quoting Scripture and addressing their converts as "beloved brethren."

Many of the false prophets of Protestantism have popularized themselves by granting their deluded followers the liberty of preaching. As any reader of ecclesiastical history knows, it has been a favourite device of false prophets in all ages to spread their errors through the efforts of their converts, flattering their conceits by speaking of their "gifts" and "talents." By multiplying lay preachers they draw after them a host of disciples. Such incompetent novices are themselves ignorant of the very essentials of the Truth, yet in their egotism and presumption deem themselves qualified to explain the deepest mysteries of the Faith. A great deal safer and more excusable would it be to put an illiterate rustic into a dispensary to compound medicines out of drugs and spirits he understands not and then administer the same unto his fellows, than for young upstarts with no better endowment than self-confidence to intrude themselves into the sacred office of the ministry—the one would poison men's bodies—but the other their souls.

"But such are false apostles, deceitful workers, transforming themselves into the Apostles of Christ. And no marvel, for Satan himself is transformed into an angel of light" (2 Cor. 11:13, 14). In all opposition to the Truth there is an agent at work which belongs to the office of the Spirit of Truth to discover and unmask. If "another Gospel" (Gal. 1:6) be preached rather than the Gospel of Christ it is the fruit of Satanic energy, the minds and wills of its promulgators being led captive by the devil. Satan is the archdissembler, being the prince of duplicity as well as of wickedness. When he had the awful effrontery to tempt the Lord Jesus he came with the Word of God on his lips saying, "It is written" (Matt. 4:6)! Though Satan's kingdom be that of darkness, yet his craft is the mimicry of light and thus it is that his agents work by deception. They claim to be the "apostles (or "missionaries") of Christ," but they have received no call or commission from Him. Nor should we marvel at their pretence when we remember the hold which the father of lies has over men.

"Therefore it is no great thing if his ministers also be transformed as the ministers of righteousness, whose end shall be according to their works" (2 Cor. 11:15). They are "deceitful workers" for they pose as champions of the Truth and as being actuated by a deep love for souls. As sin does not present itself to us *as sin* nor as paying death for its wages but rather as something pleasant and desirable, and as Satan never shows himself openly in his true colours, so his "ministers" put on the cloak of sanctity, pretending to be dead to the world and very self-sacrificing. They are crafty, specious, tricky, hypocritical. What urgent need, then, is there to be on our guard that we be not imposed upon by every mealy-mouthed and "gracious" impostor, who comes to us, Bible in hand. How we should heed that injunction, "Prove all things" (1 Thess. 5:21). Certain it is, my reader, that any "preacher" who rejects God's Law, who denies repentance to be a condition of salvation, who assures the giddy and godless that they are loved by God, who declares that saving faith is nothing more than an act of the will which every person has the power to perform, is a false prophet and should be shunned as a deadly plague.—A.W.P.

THE MISSION AND MIRACLES OF ELISHA.

1. *Introduction.*

That which occupies the central and dominant place in what the Spirit has been pleased to record of the life of Elisha are the *miracles* performed by and connected with him. Far more miracles were wrought by him or were granted in answer to his prayers than by any other of the Old Testament Prophets. In fact the narrative of his history consists of little else than a record of supernatural acts and events. Nor need this at all surprise us, though it is strange that so few seem to grasp the implication and signification of the same. The character of Elisha's mission and ministry was in thorough keeping with Israel's condition at that time. The very fact that these miracles were *needed* by them indicates the state into which they had fallen. Idolatry had held sway for so long that the true and living God was no longer known by the nation. Here and there were individuals who believed in and owned the Lord but the masses were worshippers of idols. Therefore by means of drastic interpositions, by awe-inspiring displays of His power, by supernatural manifestations of His justice and mercy alike, God forced even the skeptical to recognize His existence and subscribe to His supremacy.

In our introductory article on the life of *Elijah* we pointed out what is implied and denoted by the *prophetic* office and mission. We think now it is fitting that we should make a few remarks upon the reason for and meaning of *miracles*. The two partake of much the same nature, for prophecy is really an oral miracle, while miracles are virtually prophecies (forthtellings of God) in action. As God only sends forth one of His Prophets in a time of marked declension and departure of His people from Himself, so miracles were quite unnecessary while the sufficiency of His Word was practically recognized. The one as much as the other lies entirely outside the ordinary line or course of things, neither occurring during what we may term normal times. Which of the Patriarchs, the priests or the kings performed any miracles? How many were wrought during the lengthy reign of Saul, David or Solomon? Why, then, were so many wonders done during the ministry of Elijah and still more so during that of Elisha?

The mission and ministry of Elisha was the same in character as that which God did in Egypt by the hand of Moses. There Jehovah was unknown: entirely so by the Egyptians, largely so by the Israelites. The favoured descendants of Abraham had sunk as low as the heathen in whose midst they dwelt, and God by so many remarkable signs and unmistakable interventions brought them back to that knowledge of Himself which they had lost. Unless the Hebrews in Egypt had been thoroughly convinced by those displays of Divine power that Moses was a Prophet sent from God, they had never submitted to him as their leader—how reluctantly they owned his authority on various occasions! So also in the conquest of Canaan, God wrought four miracles in favour of His people: one in the *water* of Jordan; one in the *earth,* in throwing down the walls of Jericho; one in the *air,* in destroying their enemies by hail; and one in the *heavens,* by slowing the course of the sun and the moon. Thereby the nations of Canaan were furnished with clear proof of Jehovah's supremacy, that the God of Israel possessed universal dominion, that He was no local Deity but the Most High reigning over all nature.

But, it may be asked, how do the miracles wrought by Christ square with what has been said above? Surely they should present no difficulty. Pause and ask the question, *Why* did He work miracles? Did not His teaching make clearly evident His Divine mission—the very officers sent to arrest Him having to acknowledge, "Never man spake as this man"? Did not the spotless holiness of His life make manifest the heavenliness of His Person—even Pilate being forced to testify, "I find no fault in Him"? Did not His conduct on the Cross demonstrate that He was no impostor—the centurion and his fellows owning "truly this was the Son of God" (Matt. 27:54)? Ah, but men must be left without the shadow of an excuse for their unbelief: the whole world shall have it unmistakably shown before their eyes that Jesus of Nazareth was none other than "God manifest in flesh." The Gentiles were sunk in idolatry—Judaism was reduced to a lifeless formality and had made void the Word of God by their traditions and therefore did Christ reveal the wisdom and power of God as none other before or since by a series of miracles which warranted Him saying, "he that hath seen Me hath seen the Father."

Thus it will be seen that there is another characteristic which links closely together prophecy and miracles: the character of the times in which they occur supplying the key both to their implication and their signification. Both of them may be termed abnormalities, for neither of them are given in the ordinary course of events. While conditions are relatively decent God acts according to the ordinary working of the laws of creation and the operations of His Providence. But when the Enemy comes in like a flood, the Spirit of the Lord lifts up a more apparent and noticeable standard against him, coming out as it were more into the open and obliging men to take cognizance of Him. But there is this difference: the one intimates there is a state of grievous departure from God on the part of His people—the other indicates that the knowledge of the true and living God has publicly disappeared—that He is no longer believed in by the masses. Drastic diseases call for drastic remedies.

The missions of Elijah and Elisha form two parts of one whole, the one supplementing the other, though there was a striking contrast between them. Therein we have an illustration of the spiritual signification of the number *two.* Whereas *one* denotes there is no other, *two* affirms there is another and therefore a *difference.* That difference may be for good or for evil and therefore this number bears a twofold meaning according to its associations. The second that comes in may be for opposition or for support. The two, though different in character, may be one in testimony and friendship. "The testimony of two men is true" (John 8:17 and cf. Num. 35:30). Thus two is also the number of *witness,* and the greater the contrast between the two witnesses the more valuable their testimony when they agree therein. Hence it is that all through the

Scriptures we find two persons linked together—to present a contrast: as in such cases as Cain and Abel, Abraham and Lot, Ishmael and Isaac, Jacob and Esau—or two bearing witness to the Truth—as Enoch and Noah, Moses and Aaron, Caleb and Joshua, Naomi and Ruth, Ezra and Nehemiah, the sending forth of the Apostles by twos (Mark 6:7 and cf. Rev. 11:3).

This linking together of two men in their testimony for God contains valuable instruction for us. It hints broadly at the *twofoldness* of Truth. There is perfect harmony and unity between the two great divisions of Holy Writ, yet the differences between the Old and New Testaments are apparent to every thoughtful reader of them. It warns against the danger of lopsidedness, intimating the importance of seeking to preserve the balance. The chief instruments employed by God in the great Reformation of the sixteenth century were Luther and Calvin. They took part in a common task and movement, yet how great was the difference between the two men and the respective parts they were called upon to play. Thus with Elijah and Elisha: there are manifest parallels between them, as in the likeness of their names, yet there are marked contrasts both in their missions and their miracles. It is in the observing of their respective similarities and dissimilarities that we are enabled to ascertain the special teaching which they are designed to convey to us.

At first glance it may appear that there is a much closer resemblance than antithesis between the two men. Both of them were Prophets, both of them dwelt in Samaria, and they were confronted with much the same situation. The falling of Elijah's mantle upon Elisha seems to indicate that the latter was the successor of the former, called upon to continue his mission. The first miracle performed by Elisha was identical with the last one wrought by his master: the smiting of the waters of the Jordan with the mantle, so that they parted asunder for him (2 Kings 2:8, 14). At the beginning of his ministry Elijah had said unto Ahab king of Israel, "As the LORD God of Israel liveth, before whom I stand" (1 Kings 17:1). And when Elisha came into the presence of Ahab's son he also declared, "As the LORD of hosts liveth, before whom I stand" (2 Kings 3:14). As Elijah was entertained by the widow of Zarephath and rewarded her by restoring her son to life (1 Kings 17:25), so Elisha was entertained by a woman at Shunem (2 Kings 4:8-10) and repaid her by restoring her son to life (4:35-37).

Striking as are the points of agreement between the two Prophets, yet the contrasts in their careers and works are just as vivid and certainly more numerous. The one appeared suddenly and dramatically upon the stage of public action without a word being told us of from whence he sprang or how had previously been engaged—but of the other the name of his father is recorded and an account of his occupation at the time he received his call into God's service. The first miracle of Elijah was that for the space of three and half years there should be neither dew nor rain according to his word, whereas the first public act of Elisha was to heal the springs of water (2 Kings 2:21, 22) and to produce an abundance of water (3:20). One of the most noticeable features of Elijah's life was his loneliness, dwelling apart from the apostate masses of the people; but Elisha seems to have spent most of his life in the company of the Prophets, presiding over their schools. The different manner in which their earthly careers terminated is even more marked: the one being taken to Heaven in a chariot of fire and the other falling sick in old age and dying a natural death.

The principal contrast between the two Prophets appears in the character of the miracles wrought by and connected with them. The majority of those performed by Elijah were associated with death and destruction, whereas by far the greater of those attributed to Elisha were works of healing and restoration. If the former was the Prophet of judgment, the latter was the Prophet of grace—if the course of one was fittingly closed by a "whirlwind" removing him from this scene, a peaceful dove would be the more appropriate emblem of the other. Elisha's ministry consisted largely of Divine interpositions in a way of mercy, interventions of sovereign goodness, rather than judicial dealings. He commenced his mission by a miracle of blessing, healing the death-dealing springs of water—what immediately followed was the establishing of his authority, the symbol of his extraordinary office. The work of Elijah was chiefly a protest against evil, while the work of Elisha was an almost continuous testimony to the readiness of God to relieve the distressed and respond to the call of need wherever that call came from a contrite and believing heart.

Unto many it may seem really astonishing that a ministry like that of Elisha should immediately follow after Elijah's, for in view of the desperate defiance he encountered we would naturally suppose the *end* had been reached, that the patience of God was at last exhausted. But if we take into account what has been before us above on the signification of miracles, we shall be the less surprised. As we have pointed out, a state of general infidelity and idolatry forms their background and thus the reason for and purpose of them breaking through the darkness and making Himself manifest to His people who know Him not. Now since God is "light" (1 John 1:5), that is, the ineffably Holy One, it necessarily follows that when revealing Himself He will do so as the Hater and punisher of sin. But it is equally true that God is "love" (1 John 4:8), that is, the infinitely Benevolent One and consequently, when appearing more evidently before the eyes of His creatures it is in wondrous works of kindness and benignity. Thus we have the two sides of the Divine character revealed in the respective ministries of Elijah and Elisha: deeds of vengeance and deeds of mercy.

While their two missions may certainly be considered separately, yet Elisha's ministry should be regarded primarily as the complement of Elijah's. The two, though dissimilar, make one complete whole—and only subordinately a thing apart. On the one hand Elijah's mission was mainly of a public character; on the other Elisha's was more in private. The former had to do principally with the masses and those who had led them astray and therefore his miracles consisted chiefly of judgments, expressive of God's wrath upon idolatry. The latter was engaged mostly with the Lord's Prophets and people and consequently his acts were mainly those of blessing, manifestations of the Divine mercy. The comforting and assuring lesson in this for Christians today is that even in a season of apostasy and universal wickedness, when His rod is laid heavily upon the nations, the Lord will neither forget nor forsake His own but will appear unto them as "the God of all grace." Things may become yet worse than they now are: even so the Lord will prove Himself to be "a very present help" to His people.

Coming now to the subordinate viewpoint and considering Elisha's career as the sequel to Elijah's, may we not find in it a message of hope in this dark, dark hour? Those with any measure of spiritual discernment cannot fail to perceive the tragic resemblance there is between the time in which Elijah's lot was cast and our own sad day. The awful apostasy of Christendom, the appalling multiplication of false prophets, the various forms of idolatry now so prevalent in our midst and the solemn judgments from Heaven which have been and are being visited upon us and the blatant refusal of the multitudes to pay any heed to them by mending their ways all furnish an analogy which is too plain to be missed. There is therefore a real temptation to conclude that the end of all things is at hand—some say an end of the age, others the end of the world. Many thought the same when Napoleon was desolating Europe and again in 1914-18, but they were wrong and it is quite likely that they who think the same today will have their conclusions falsified. There is at least hope for us here: Elijah was followed by Elisha! Who can tell what mercy God may yet show to the world?

We must be on our guard against missing the consolation which this portion of Scripture may contain for us. The darkest night is followed by the morning's light. Even though the present order of "civilization" is doomed to destruction, we know not what favours from God await this earth in generations to come. Of necessity there will be a time when this world and all its works will be burned up and that event may be very near. On the other hand that event may be thousands of years away and if such is the case then black as is the present outlook and blacker as it may become, yet the clouds of Divine judgment will again disperse and the Sun of Righteousness arise once more with healing in His wings. More than once have the times of Elijah been substantially duplicated even during this Christian era, yet each time they were followed by an Elisha of mercy. Thus it may be again, yea, will be, unless God is now on the point of ringing down the curtain upon human history.

Very little, indeed, seems to have been written upon the life of Elisha, yet this is not difficult to account for. Though there is almost twice as much recorded about him than his predecessor, his history is not given in one connected piece or consecutive narrative, but rather is disjointed, the current of his life being crossed again and again by references to others. The scattered allusions to the Prophet's career do not lend themselves so readily to biographical treatment as do the lives of Abraham, Jacob or David. Why is this? for there is nothing meaningless in Scripture, perfect wisdom directing the Holy Spirit in every detail. May it not be that we have a hint here of the method which will be followed by the Lord in that era which will possibly succeed the period of Christendom's history foreshadowed by Elijah's life? May not the broken and disconnected account of Elisha's deeds presage the form God's dealings will take in a future generation: that instead of being a regular stream they will be occasional showers of blessing at intervals?—A.W.P.

DOCTRINE OF SAINTS' PERSEVERANCE.

6. *Its Blessedness.*

In an earlier article we dwelt upon the deep importance of this doctrine. Here we wish to show something of its great preciousness. Let us begin by pointing out the opposite. Suppose that the Gospel proclaimed only a forgiveness of all sins up to the moment of conversion and announced that believers must henceforth keep themselves from everything unworthy of this signal mercy. What if it declared that means are provided, motives supplied, and warnings given of the fatal consequences which would surely befall those who failed to make a good use of those means and diligently respond to those motives. And that whether or not he should ultimately reach Heaven is thus left entirely in the believer's own hands Then what? We may well ask what would be the consequences of such a dismal outlook: what would be the thoughts begotten and the spirit engendered by such a Gospel? what effect would it produce upon those who really believe it? Answers to these questions should prepare us to more deeply appreciate the converse.

It hardly requires a profound theologian to reply to the above queries. They have only to be carefully pondered and the simplest Christian should be able to perceive for himself what would be the inevitable result. If the Christian's entrance into Heaven turns entirely upon his own fidelity and his treading the path of righteousness unto the end of his course, then he is far worse off than was Adam in Eden, for when God placed him under the Covenant of Works he was not heavily handicapped from the beginning by indwelling sin. But each of his fallen descendants is born into this world with a carnal nature which remains unchanged up to the moment of death. Thus the believer would enter into the fight not only without any assurance of victory but face almost certain defeat. If such a Gospel were true then those who really believed it would be total strangers to peace and joy, for they must inevitably spend their days in a perpetual dread of Hell. Or the first time they were overcome by temptation and worsted by the Enemy, they would at once abandon the fight and give way to hopeless despair.

"I will not turn away from them, to do them good" (Jer. 32:40). "I will never leave thee nor forsake thee" (Heb. 13:5). "Nothing whatever can or shall be able to separate us from the love of God which is in Christ Jesus our Lord" (Rom. 8:39). "He will keep the feet of His saints" (1 Sam. 2:9). How immeasurable the difference between the vain imaginations of men and the sure declarations of God! It is the contrast of the darkness of a moonless and starless midnight from the radiance of the midday sun. "Of them which Thou gavest Me have I lost none" (John 18:9) affirmed the Redeemer. Is not that inexpressibly blessed! Everyone of the redeemed shall be brought safely to Heaven. The final apostasy of a believer is an utter impossibility, not in the nature of things but by the Divine constitution. No one who has once been received into the Divine favour can ever be cast out thereof. God has bestowed on each of His children a life that cannot die, He has brought him into a relationship which nothing can change or effect, He has wrought a work in him which lasts "forever" (Eccl. 3:14).

It is sadly true that multitudes of empty professors have "wrested" this truth to their destruction, just as many of our fellows have put to an ill use some of the most valuable of God's temporal gifts. But because foolish gluttons destroy their health through intemperance is no reason why sane people should refuse to be nourished by wholesome food; and because the carnal pervert the doctrine of Divine Preservation is no valid argument for Christians being afraid to draw comfort from the same. Most certainly it is the design of God that His people should be strengthened and established by this grand article of the faith. Note how in John 17 Christ mentions again and again the words "keep" and "kept" (vv. 6, 11, 12, 15). And His reason for so doing is clearly stated: "these things I speak in the world that they may have My joy fulfilled in them" (v. 13). He would not have them spend their days in the wretchedness of doubts about their ultimate bliss, uncertain as to the issue of their fight. It is His revealed will that they should go forward with a song in their hearts, praising Him for the certainty of ultimate victory.

But the joy which issues from a knowledge of our security is not obtained by a casual acquaintance with this Truth. Christ's very repetition, "I kept them . . . those that

Thou gavest Me I have kept" (John 17:12) intimates to us that we must meditate frequently upon this Divine preservation unto eternal life. It is to be laid hold of in no transient manner but should daily engage the Christian's heart till he is warmed and influenced by it. A few sprinklings of water do not go to the roots of a tree but frequent and plentiful showers are needed. So it is not an occasional thought about Christ's power to keep His people safe for Heaven which will deeply affect them but only a constant spiritual and believing pondering thereon. As Jacob said to the Angel, "I will not let thee go except thou bless me" (Gen. 32:26), so the believer should say to this truth, I will not turn from it until it has blessed me.

When our great High Priest prayed, "Holy Father, keep through Thine own name those whom Thou hast given Me" (John 17:11) it was not (as the Arminians say) that He asked merely that they might be provided with adequate means by the use of which they must preserve themselves. No, my reader, it was for something more valuable and essential. The Saviour made request that faith should be continually wrought in them by the exceeding greatness of God's power (Eph. 1:19) and where that is, there will be works of sincere (though imperfect) obedience and it will operate by responding to the holiness of the Law so that sins are mortified. The Father answers that prayer of the Redeemer's by working in the redeemed "both to will and to do of His good pleasure" (Phil. 2:13), fulfilling in them "all the good pleasure of His goodness and the work of faith with power" (2 Thess. 1:11) preserving them "through faith unto salvation" (1 Peter 1:5). He leaves them not to their feeble and fickle wills but renews them in the inner man "day by day" (2 Cor. 4:16).

That Christ would have His redeemed draw comfort from their security is clear again from His words, "Rejoice because your names are written in Heaven" (Luke 10:20). To what purpose did the Lord Jesus thus address His disciples but to denote that infallible certainty of their final salvation by a contrast from those who perish: that is, whose names were written only "in the earth" (Jer. 17:13) or on the sands which may be defaced. Surely He had never spoken thus if there were the slightest possibility of their names being blotted out. "Rejoice because your names are written in Heaven"— is not the implication both necessary and clear as a sunbeam?—such rejoicing would be premature if there were any likelihood of final apostasy. This call to rejoice is not given at the moment of the believer's death as he sees the angels about to convoy him to the realm of ineffable bliss but while he is still here on the battlefield. Those name are written by none other than the finger of God, indelibly inscribed in the Book of Life, and not one of them will ever be erased.

Take again His words in the parable of the lost sheep: "I say unto you that likewise joy shall be in Heaven over one sinner that repenteth" (Luke 15:7). "Such exalted hosannas would not resound on these occasions among the inhabitants of the skies if the doctrine of final perseverance was untrue. Tell me, ye seraphs of light; tell me, ye spirits of elect men made perfect in glory why this exuberance of holy rapture on the real recovery of a sinner to God? Because ye know assuredly that every true conversion is (1) a certain proof that the person converted is one of the elect number and (2) that he shall be infallibly preserved and brought to that very region of blessedness into which ye yourselves are come. The contrary belief would silence your harps and chill your praises. If it be uncertain whether the person who is regenerated today may ultimately reign with you in Heaven or take up his eternal abode among apostate spirits in

Hell, your rejoicings are too sanguine and your praises too presumptuous. You should suspend your songs until he actually arrives among you and not give thanks for his conversion until he has persevered unto glorification" (A. Toplady).

1. What encouragement is there here for *the babe in Christ!* Conscious of his weakness he is fearful that the flesh and the world and the Devil may prove too powerful for him. Aware of his ignorance, bewildered by the confusion of tongues in the religious realm, he dreads lest he be led astray by false prophets. Beholding many of his companions who made a similar profession of faith so quickly losing their fervour and going back again into the world, he trembles lest he make shipwreck of the faith. Stumbled by the inconsistencies of those called "the pillars of the church," chilled by older Christians who tell him he must not be too extreme, he is alarmed and wonders how it can be expected that he shall hold on his way almost alone. But if these fears empty him of self-confidence and make him cling closer to Christ, they are blessings in disguise for he will then prove for himself that "underneath are the everlasting arms," and those arms are all-mighty and all-sufficient.

The babe in Christ is as much a member of God's family as is the mature "father" (1 John 2:13) and the former is as truly the object of Divine love and faithfulness as is the latter. Yea, the younger ones in His flock are more the subjects of the Shepherd's care than are the full-grown sheep: "He shall gather *the lambs* with His arm and carry them in His bosom" (Isa. 40:11). The Lord does not break the bruised reed nor quench the smoking flax (Matt. 12:20). He gave proof of this in the days of His flesh. He found some "smoking flax" in the nobleman who came to Him on behalf of his sick son: his faith was so weak that he supposed the Saviour must come down to his house and heal him ere he died—as though the Lord Jesus could not recover him while at a distance or after he had expired (John 4:49): nevertheless He cured him. So, too, after His ascension He took note of a "little strength" (Rev. 3:8) and opened a door which none can shut. The highest oak was once an acorn and God was the maintainer of its life.

When we affirm the final perseverance of every born-again soul we do not mean that saints are not *in themselves* prone to fall away, nor that at regeneration such a work is wrought in them once and for all that they now have sufficient strength of their own to overcome sin and Satan. Nor do we declare there is no likelihood of their spiritual life decaying. So far from it, we hesitate not to declare that the very principle of grace (or "new nature") in the believer considered abstractedly in itself—apart from the renewing and sustaining power of God—would assuredly perish under the corruptions of the flesh and the assaults of the Devil. No, the preservation of the Christian's faith and his continuance in the paths of obedience lies in something entirely *external to himself* or his state. Wherein lay the impossibility of any bone of Christ being broken? Not because they were in themselves incapable of being broken, for they were as liable to be broken as His flesh to be pierced but solely because of the *unbreakable decree of God.* So it is with the mystical Body of Christ: no member of His can perish because of the purpose, power and promise of God Himself.

How important it is, then, that the babe in Christ should be instructed in *the foundation of* Christian perseverance, that the ground on which his eternal security rests is nothing whatever in himself but wholly outside. The preservation of the believer depends not upon his continuing to love God, believe in Christ, tread the highway of holiness, or make diligent use of the means of grace, but on the Covenant-engagements entered into between the Father and the Son. That is the basic and grand Cause which produces as a necessary and infallible effect our continuing to love God, believe in Christ and perform sincere obedience. O what a sure foundation is that! What firm ground for the soul to rest upon! What unspeakable peace and joy issues from faith's apprehension of the same! Though fickle in ourselves, the Covenant is immutable. Though weak and unstable as water we are, yet *that is* "ordered in all things and sure." Though full of sin and unworthiness, yet the sacrifice of Christ is of infinite merit. Though often the spirit of prayer is quenched in us, yet our great High Priest ever lives to make intercession for us. Here, then, is the "anchor of the soul" and it is "both sure and steadfast" (Heb. 6:19).

Here concluding this subdivision it is necessary to point out in such days as these that it must not be inferred from the above that because the grace, the power and the faithfulness of God insures the preservation of the feeblest babe in Christ that henceforth he is relieved of all responsibility in the matter. Not so—such a blessed truth has not been revealed for the purpose of encouraging slothfulness but rather to provide an impetus to use the means of preservation which God has appointed. Though we must not anticipate too much what we purpose to bring before the reader under a later division of our subject when (D.V.) we shall consider at more length the safeguards which Divine wisdom has placed around this truth, yet a few words of warning, or rather explanation, should be given here to prevent a wrong conclusion being draw from the preceding paragraphs.

The babe in Christ is weak in himself, he is left in a hostile world, he is confronted with powerful temptations both from within and from without to apostatize. But strength is available unto faith, armour is provided against all enemies, deliverance from temptations is given in answer to prevailing prayer. But he must *seek* that strength, *put* on that armour, and *resist* those temptations. He must fight for his very life, and refuse to acknowledge defeat. Nor shall he fight in vain, for Another shall gird his arm and enable him to overcome. The blessedness of this doctrine is that he shall not be left to himself nor suffered to perish. The Holy Spirit shall renew him day by day, quicken his graces, move him to perseverance and make him "more than conqueror through Him that loved him."—A.W.P.

THE UNKNOWN WAYS OF LOVE
C.H. Spurgeon—1876

"Jesus answered and said unto him, What I do thou knowest not now; but thou shall know hereafter" (John 13:7).

These words of our Lord were spoken in answer to Peter's exclamation of surprise, "Lord, dost Thou wash my feet?" It was a very natural expression of astonishment and one which deserved no censure. But at the same time it was not a very wise remark, for, albeit that it was a marvelously condescending action for the Lord Jesus to wash His disciples' feet, He had already performed a greater condescension by coming upon the earth at all in the form of a man. For the Son of the Highest to dwell among mortals in a human body, capable of being girt about with a napkin and able to take a basin and pour water into it, is a far greater marvel than that He should, being a man, leave the supper table and act as a menial servant by washing His disciples' feet. Had Peter understood also what his Master had prophesied and explained to him, namely, His approaching sufferings and death, he would have seen that for his Master to take a towel and basin was little compared with His having our iniquities laid upon Himself and being a sacrifice for *sin*.

If it surprises you to see the Lord of Glory wear a towel, does it not amaze you still more to see Him clad in the purple robe of mockery? Are you not still more astonished to see His vesture stripped from Him and to hear Him cry upon the Cross, "I may tell all My bones: they look and stare upon Me" (Psa. 22:17)? It is wonderful that He should take the basin in the upper room but surely it was more extraordinary that He should take the cup in the garden and drink in its full bitterness till He sweat as it were great drops of blood falling to the ground. To wash the disciples' feet with water was certainly a surprising action but to pour out His heart's blood to wash *us* was far greater— for this involved His death, His making His grave with the wicked and His being numbered with the transgressors.

The expression of Peter is thus seen to be very natural but not very profound. Dear Brethren, do you not think it very likely that our pretty pious speeches which strike us as very proper and seem to our friends to be very commendable, will one of these days appear to be mere baby prattling and do even now appear so to the Lord Jesus? Those choice sayings and holy sentences which we have read with admiration and greatly valued—even those are not like the words of Jesus for solid intrinsic weight and worth—but may in other lights appear far less beautiful than they now do. I have myself proved in different humours and frames of mind that the very things which struck me being so very deep and gracious have at other times appeared to be one-sided, shallow, or questionable. We know in part and prophesy in part: our highest attainments here are those of little children and even for the close student, the deeply experienced Christian, the venerable man of years and the graciously anointed instructor of the churches, there is no room for boasting.

Note next that our Saviour answered Peter's speech in the words of the text, which are as admirable for their tone as for their matter: which should we admire most in this reply, its meekness or its majesty? To Peter's ignorant simplicity how gentle He is! "What I do thou knowest not now; but thou shalt know hereafter." And yet how royally He confronts Peter's forward objection and how distinctly His majestic personality puts down the too conspicuous individuality of Peter! "What I do thou knowest not now." How perfect the blending of the majesty and the meekness. Who shall tell which of the colours is best laid on? This is ever the way of our Lord Jesus. You shall find through life, beloved, that whenever Jesus Christ comes to rebuke you, He will do so powerfully but gently; He will speak as a friend, and as a king; you will feel both His love and His authority and own the power both of His goodness and His greatness. His smile shall not make you presume, nor shall His royal glance cause you to tremble. You will find His left hand supporting you while in His right you see His imperial sceptre. Blessed Saviour, are You more meek or more majestic? We cannot tell, but certainly to our hearts You are both kind and kingly, sweet and sovereign, gracious and glorious.

Let us now come to the words themselves. We have looked at the occasion of them and at the manner of them and we will now weigh their matter. The words have suggested to me many thoughts: first, in *our Lord's doings* that there is much which we cannot understand. Our text is not merely true about the washing of the feet but also all that our Lord does: "What I do thou knowest not now." We may know the external part of what He does, or think we do, but there is more in His actions than any of us can conceive. The external is not all—there are wrapped up within the mercies which we perceive other and yet greater mercies as yet unknown to us. You traverse the soil of Canaan and you drink of its rivers and are refreshed by its corn and wind but the goodly land has hidden riches. Its stones are iron and out of its hills you may dig brass. The brooks of which you drink derive their cool waters from springs which have tapped "the deep which lieth under." If you know in some measure what Jesus does, yet the mystery is not altogether laid bare to your eye; there are folds of His manifold grace which are as yet unopened. The work of Jesus is beyond you: it is lower than your fall, higher than your desire; it surpasses you, and is altogether too high for you. Who can, by searching, find it out unto perfection?

Our want of knowledge of the Divine doings is a wide subject, and I shall not attempt to explore its hithermost boundaries but shall restrain myself to the text. Brethren, there are many things that God does which we cannot understand now and probably never shall. For instance, why *He permitted evil* at first and tolerates it still. To this inquiry the Divine answer would be, "What I do thou knowest not." Leave that alone. It is our highest wisdom to be ignorant where God has not enlightened us. It is great folly to pretend to know when we do not—and there lives not a man, nor ever will live a man who has even an approximation to an understanding of the dread mystery—the existence of moral evil. The bottom of this abyss no mind can reach and he is foolhardy who ventures on the plunge. Let this dread secret alone! You cannot endure the white heat which burns around it. Many a man has lost the eyes of his reason while trying to peer into this fiery furnace. What have you to do with that which God conceals from you? It is God's business not yours. The thing was done ere you were born and He who permitted it can answer to Himself if He cares so to do.

So also with regard to *predestination.* That God ordains all things and had before His eye the chart of everything that has been, is, or shall be, is most true. But who knows the depths of foreknowledge and destiny? To sit down and pluck the eternal purposes to pieces, to question their justice and impugn their wisdom is both folly and audacity. Here the darkness thickens and out of it comes forth the oracle, "What I do thou knowest not." The things which are revealed belong to us and to our children; and as to the unrevealed, if it is to the glory of God to conceal a thing, let it be concealed. Christ has rent the veil of the holy place and into the secret of Divine love you may now freely enter. But other veils which He rends not you may not touch. Some truths are closed up from our understanding, even as the ark of the covenant was shut against prying eyes: let us not violate their sanctity lest we meet the doom of the men of Bethshemesh. Rather let us zealously guard them as priceless treasure that we may obtain the blessing which rested upon the house of Obededom. The same remark applies to the great designs of God in *Providence.* He is pleased in prophecy often to tell us what He has meant by His Providence, and perhaps it will be one of the enjoyments of the future state to see the hand of God in the whole current of history—but while incidents are occurring we must not expect to understand their drift and bearing. The wonderful tapestry of human history, all woven in the loom of God's infinite wisdom, will astonish both men and angels when it is complete. But while it is yet unfinished it will not be possible for us to imagine the completed pattern. From between those wheels of Providence, which are full of eyes, I hear a voice which says, "What I do thou knowest not now."

But we will confine ourselves to the loving acts of the Lord Jesus Christ, since what the Lord was doing with Peter was not very mysterious, nor a deed of transcendent power, nor of stern justice. He was humbly girding Himself with a towel and pouring water into a basin to wash His followers' feet. It was a very simple matter and evidently a very gracious, kind, and condescending act; but yet, even concerning *that* Jesus said, "What I do thou knowest not now."

My Brethren, even the acts of our Lord Jesus Christ in His loving condescension we do not fully understand. Ah, think a minute: how can we? Does not our Lord's love always surpass our knowledge, since He Himself is the greatest of all mysteries? Let me read these words to you: "Jesus knowing that the Father had given all things into His hands, and that He was come from God and went to God; He riseth from supper, and laid aside His garments; and took a towel and girded Himself" (John 13:3, 4). Do you understand the higher and the lower points of this transaction? You must comprehend them both before you can see what He has done. "Jesus knowing that the Father had given all things into His hands." Can you see the glory of this? Jesus our Lord was conscious that His Father had made Him Head over all things to His church. That He had laid the government upon His shoulder and given Him the key that He might open and no man shut and shut and no man open. He knew assuredly that at His girdle swung the keys of Heaven and death and Hell and that having fulfilled the commission of the eternal God He was about to return to His throne. Have you grasped the idea? Do you perceive the glory of which Jesus was conscious? If you have done so, then descend by one long sweep—He, this Lord of All, having all things in His hand, takes off His garments, foregoes the common dress of an ordinary man and places Himself in the undress of a servant—and wears a towel that He may do service to His own disciples. Can you follow Him from such a height to such a depth!

A superior in the East never washes an inferior's feet: Christ acts as if He were inferior to His friends, inferior to those poor fishermen, inferior to those foolish scholars who learn so slowly, with whom He had been so long a time and yet they did not know Him and who soon forgot what they knew and needed line upon line and precept upon precept. Having loved them to the end, He stoops to the extreme of stooping and bows at their feet to cleanse their defilements. Who, I say, can compute the depth of this descent? You cannot know what Christ has done for you, because you cannot conceive how high He is by nature. Neither can you guess how low He stoops in His humiliation and death. With an eagle's wing you could not soar so high as to behold Him as God over all blessed forever, sitting at the right hand of the Father, the adored of cherubim and seraphim: nor could you dive, even if you dared to take a plunge into the abyss, until you reached the depth of "My God, My God, why hast Thou forsaken Me." And yet you must somehow know the interval. I was about to say the infinity, between these two points of height and depth before you could know what Jesus has done for you.

Moreover, think awhile. Was anything that Jesus did understood *while He was doing it*? He is born a babe in Bethlehem but who knew what He did in the manger? A few shepherds and sages and two or three favoured saints discerned the Saviour in the Babe. But to the mass of mankind He was unknown God came on earth and angels sung His advent, but O earth, your Lord might have said to you, "What I do thou knowest not now." He lived here the life of a mechanic's son: that life was the most august event in all human history, but men knew not what it was or what it meant. "The world knew Him not." He came forward to preach the Gospel: did they know who it was that spake as never man spake? Did they comprehend what He spake? Ah, no. He was hid from their eyes. At last He laid aside the life He had so strangely taken—who knew the reason of His death upon the Cross? Did even His disciples know though He had told them? When earth shook and graves were opened by His last cry, did even His own followers understand what a sacrifice had been offered? No, until the Spirit was poured upon them from on high they did not comprehend that "It behooved Christ to suffer." He could say to each of His own disciples, of all that He had done, "What I do thou knowest not now."

This is true, too, of every separate gift which our Lord's love has given to His people. You have been justified in Jesus Christ, but do you fully know the wondrous righteousness with which justification by faith has endowed you? You are accepted in the Beloved, but do any of you realize what it is to have full acceptance with the Father? I know you have realized the fact and rejoiced in it, but have you known, ay, *can* you know the full sweetness of its meaning? You are one with Christ and members of His body: comprehend you that? You are the joint-heirs with Christ: know you the full significance of that? He is betrothed unto you in an everlasting marriage: know you what that means? Ah, no. These wonders of His love, we hear of them, and we believe them, but "What I do" saith He, "thou knowest not now."

Our Lord is doing great things by way of preparing us for a higher state of existence. We shall soon be rid of this vile body, and released from this narrow world. We are going to a sphere more suited for our Heaven-born life, where we shall be the comrades of angels and commune with the spirits of the just made perfect! We shall serve the Lord day and night in His temple but what the glory shall be we do not know—for the ear has not heard it, nor the eye beheld it, nor the heart conceived it. As for the preparations which are going on within us to make us ready for this sublime condition, we know that they are being carried on but we cannot as yet see their course, their separate tendencies, and their ultimate issues. The instrument does not comprehend the tuner: the tuner fetches harsh sounds from their disordered strings but all those jarring notes are necessary to the harmonious condition which he is aiming to produce. If the discords were not discovered now, the music of the future would be marred. My Brethren, concerning all that Christ has done it is true, "What I do thou knowest not now." Oh, if His worth were little we could measure it, if His love were scanty we could know it, if His wisdom were finite we could judge it—but where everything is past finding out, who can pretend to know? Remember that in our salvation Christ Himself is the sum and substance, in it every attribute of His deity is brought into exercise to the full. He makes it His glory counting our salvation to be His coronet and crown jewels; and therefore it is not at all marvellous that we not know what He does.

Our want of understanding does not prevent the efficacy of our Lord's work. Peter does not know what Christ is doing when He washes his feet but the Master washes them just as clean whether Peter understands it or not. Jesus did not say, "There, Peter, you do not understand what I am doing by washing your feet. So I shall not wash them until you do." No—He moves on with the basin and towel and washes them clean, though Peter does not know why. Is not this a great mercy, Brethren, that the blessings which Christ bestow upon us are not dependent for their efficacy upon our capacity to understand them? Just look out in the world and see how true this is. A mother has her little child on her lap and she is washing its face. The child does not like the water and it cries. Ah, babe, if you could understand it you would smile. The child cries and struggles in the mother's arms but it is washed all the same. The mother waits not for the child to know what she is doing but completes her work of love. So is the Lord often exercising Divine acts upon us and we do not appreciate them, nor are we pleased. Perhaps we even strive against His work of love—but for all that He perseveres and turns not away His hand because of our crying.

Does the tree understand pruning, the land comprehend plowing? yet pruning and plowing produce their good results. The physician stands at the bedside of the patient and gives him medicine, medicine which is unpalatable and which in its operation causes the patient to feel worse than he was before. This the sufferer cannot understand and therefore he draws unhappy conclusions—but the power of the medicine does not depend upon the patient's understanding its qualities—and therefore it will do him good, though it puzzles him by its strange manner of working.

If a fool eats his dinner, it will satisfy his hunger as much as if he were a philosopher and understood the processes of digestion. This is a great mercy, for the most of men can never become philosophers. It is not necessary for the man to be learned in the nature of caloric in order to be warmed by the fire or comforted by a greatcoat. A man may be ignorant of the laws of light and yet be able to see; he may know nothing of acoustics and yet be quick of hearing. A passenger who does not know a valve from a wheel enters a carriage at the station and he will be drawn to his journey's end by the engine as well as if he were learned in mechanics. It is the same in the spiritual as in the natural world. The efficacy of spiritual forces does not depend upon our capacity to understand them.

I have mentioned this very simple fact because it really is necessary for us to remember it. We are so knowing, or think we are—we think it so essential that we should form a judgment of what the Lord is doing. Ah, dear Brethren, there are more essential things than this. It is better to trust, to submit, to obey, to love, than to know. Let the Lord alone. He is doing rightly enough, be sure of that. Is He to be questioned and cross-examined by us? Are we to judge His judgments? Dare we demand answers to our impertinent enquiries and say, Why this, why that, and why the other? Were He a God if He would submit to such examination? If we call ourselves His disciples, how can we justify a spirit which would arraign our Lord? Be still and know that He is God. What more would you know?

Remember that the things which you understand are for your good, but they can only bring you a small amount of benefit because they must be in themselves small, or you would not be able to measure them. When a great, deep good is coming to you, you will not be able to comprehend it, for your comprehension is narrow: yet it will be none the less but all the more a blessing because you know it not. Joseph is gone, and here is his bloody coat! "Without doubt he is torn in pieces! All these things are against me. O how my heart is broken with the loss of my darling child, I cannot understand it; it cannot be right" (Gen. 42:36). So talks poor Jacob, but it was right, all the same for that. Joseph was on the sure road to Pharaoh's throne and to providing for his brethren in the land of Egypt. So it is with you, my Brethren, under your present trial and affliction. You cannot understand it now but that does not make a penny worth of difference—it is working out for you a far more exceeding and eternal weight of glory. Be content to let faith rule and knowledge wait and what you know not now you shall know hereafter. *(completed in the February issue).*

DIVINE HEALING.

A number of friends who appreciated our recent articles on this subject have written to us expressing the desire for a few words on James 5:14-16. We respond to their wish with a certain amount of diffidence, for we are not sure in our own mind either as to its interpretation or application. This is a passage which has long been an occasion of controversy and debate and those who took part therein found—as is often the case—that it was easier to refute the argument of their opponents than to establish their own position. When we are uncertain about the meaning of Scripture we usually remain silent thereon but in this instance we will give the leading views which have been expressed and state how we feel toward them.

First, Romanists insist that this "anointing with oil" is a standing ordinance in the church and James 5:14, 15 is the principal passage appealed to by them in support of their dogma and practice of "extreme unction." But here, as everywhere, the papists go contrary to the Scriptures, for instead of anointing the sick as a healing ordinance, they only administer it to those at the point of death. We have no hesitation in denouncing their *perversion* as a mere hypocritical pageantry. The "unction" they use must be oil— olive mixed with balsam—consecrated by a bishop, who must nine times bow the knee, saying thrice "Ave sanctum oleum" (Hail, holy oil), and thrice, "Ave sanctum chrisma" (Hail holy chrism) and thrice more, "Ave, sanctum balsamum" (Hail, holy balsam). The members anointed are the eyes, ears, nose, mouth and for the extremities the reins and feet: in women, the navel. The design thereof is the expulsion of the relics of sin and to equip the soul for its conflicts with the powers of evil in the moment of death. One has but to mention these things to reveal the absurdity!

Second, the position generally taken by the Reformers and Puritans, was that this anointing the sick with oil was not designed as a sacrament, there being but two in number: baptism and the Lord's Supper. They pointed out that so far from this being a standing rite, the Apostles themselves seldom used oil in the healing of the sick: they wrought cures by a touch (Acts 3:7), by the shadow (Acts 5:15), by handkerchiefs (Acts 19:12), by laying on of hands (Acts 28:8), by speaking (Acts 9:34). Nor does it appear that they were permitted to employ this gift indiscriminately—no, not even among Brethren in Christ dear to them, or why should Paul leave Trophimus at Miletum sick (2 Tim. 4:20)? or sorrow so much over the illness of Epaphroditus (Phil. 2:27)? In this, too, God exercised His sovereignty. But what is more to the point, this supernatural endowment was only of brief duration: "But that grace of healing has disappeared, like all the other miraculous powers, which the Lord was pleased to exhibit for a time, that He might render the power of the Gospel which was then new, the object of admiration forever" (Calvin).

A list of the "charismata" or supernatural gifts which obtained during the apostolic period is found in 1 Corinthians 12: "to another faith, by the same Spirit; to another the gift of healing by the same Spirit; to another the working of miracles; to another prophecy; to another discerning of spirits; to another divers kinds of tongues; to another the interpretation of tongues" (vv. 9, 10). They were designed chiefly for the authenticating of Christianity and to confirm it in heathen countries. Their purpose, then, was only a *temporary* one, and as soon as the Canon of Scripture was closed they were withdrawn. As 1 Corinthians 13 plainly intimates, "whether there be prophecies (inspired messages from God) they shall cease (to be given any more); whether there be tongues, they shall cease, whether there be (supernatural) knowledge, it shall vanish away" (v. 8). It was the view of Matthew Henry, Thomas Manton, John Owen and in fact nearly all of the Puritan divines, that James 5:14, 15 refers to the exercise of one of those supernatural gifts which the church enjoyed only in the first century.

Among the leading arguments advanced in support of this contention are the following. First, the "anointing with oil" clearly appears to look back to Mark 6:13 where we are told of the twelve, they "anointed with oil many that were sick, and healed them." Second, the positive promises of healing, verse 15, seems to be an unconditional and general one, as though no exceptions, no cases of failure, were to be looked for. Third, "healing" was certainly one of the miraculous gifts specified in 1 Corinthians 12. Moreover, it hardly seems likely that the "faith" here mentioned is an ordinary one: though whether it differed in kind or only in degree is not easy to determine. There was the "faith of miracles" either to work them or the expectation of them on the part of those who were the beneficiaries, as is clear from Matthew 21:21, Mark 11:24, 1 Corinthians 13:2. The "anointing with oil" after the praying over the sick is regarded as a seal or pledge of the certainty of healing or recovery.

On the other side, we find such a deeply-taught man and so able an expositor as Thomas Goodwin (1600-1680,) insisting for the contrary. He pointed out, first, that James 5:14 is quite different from Mark 6:13, for here the anointing with oil is joined with prayer, whereas prayer is not mentioned there—but only the miraculous gift. Second, the ones to be sent for were not specified as men endowed with the gift of healing, but the "elders," and there is nothing to show that all of them possessed that *gift*. The "elders" were standing *officers* who were to *continue*. Third, the ones to be healed are the "sick" or infirm but extraordinary healing would have extended further—to the blind, the deaf and dumb and would have reached to unbelievers instead of being restricted to church members: cf. 1 Corinthians 14:22. Fourth, the means commanded: oil and prayer on all such occasions, whereas the extraordinary gift of healing was not so confined, but was frequently effected without any means at all, by mere word of mouth.

Third, rather more than a century ago, a certain Edwin Irving, founder of the "Catholic Apostolic church," propounded the theory that the supernatural gifts which existed in the early Church had been lost through the unbelief and carnality of its members and that if there were a return to primitive order and purity, they would again be available. Accordingly he appointed "apostles" and "prophets" and "evangelists." They claimed to speak in tongues, prophesy, interpret and work miracles. There is little doubt in our mind that this movement was inspired by Satan and probably a certain amount of abnormal phenomena attended it, though much of it was explainable as issuing from a state of high nervous tension and hysteria. Irving's theory, with some modifications and some additions, has been popularized and promulgated by the more recent so-called "Pentecostal movement," where a species of unintelligible jabbering and auto-suggestion cum mesmerism is styled "speaking in tongues," and "faith healing." Many of their devotees and dupes attempt to carry out James 5:14, 15, but with very meager and unsatisfactory results.

Concluded in the February issue.

Continued from back page

good thing from them that walk uprightly. Whatever tomorrow may hold, the Divine promises assure the Christian that the Lord has gone before and made every provision for him. No dire situation, no pressing emergency, no desperate peril can possibly arise but what there is one of the "exceeding great and precious promises" (2 Peter 1:4) exactly suited to our case. Their value lies in the fact that they are the word of His who cannot lie and "this God is our God forever and ever: He will be our Guide even unto death" (Psa. 48:14).

6. The Lord has gone before you into *Paradise*. Did He not expressly announce ere He left this scene, "In My Father's House are many mansions: if it were not so I would have told you: I go to prepare a place for you" (John 14:2)? Not for Himself but for His redeemed: nor would He entrust this task unto the angels. How it tells of the love of the Bridegroom for His Bride! Christ has entered Heaven on our behalf, taking possession thereof in our name: "whither the Forerunner is for us entered, even Jesus" (Heb. 6:20). His entry ensures ours. "Father," He says, "I will that they also whom Thou hast given Me, be with Me where I am, that they may behold My glory which Thou hast given Me". (John 17:24).

> "He and I in one bright glory
> Endless bliss shall share:
> Mine, to be forever with Him,
> His, that I am there."

Here, then, is real substantial comfort, and what shall be my response thereto? "The LORD, He it is that doth go before thee" (Deut. 31:8). Then, first, my eye should be constantly fixed upon Him: "*looking unto* Jesus" (Heb. 12:2)—looking away from all else, trusting none other. Second, then it is my business to follow Him—for what other purpose is a Guide?—"When He putteth forth His own sheep, He goeth before them, and the sheep follow Him" (John 10:4). And as they do, so they find that He makes them to lie down in green pastures, that He leads them beside the still waters. Ah, who would not follow such a Shepherd! O that the Lord may say of us as He did of Caleb, "he hath followed Me fully" (Num. 14:24).

Third, then *fear* should be entirely *banished* from my heart. And will it not be so if faith really lays hold of this: "The LORD, HE it is that doth go before thee, He will be with thee, He will not fail thee, neither forsake thee; fear not, neither be dismayed" (Deut. 31:8).

7. The Lord has gone before *the preacher.* This little message would hardly be complete if we failed to include a special word for the minister of the Gospel. Nor has God overlooked him at this very point. "Behold HE goeth before *you*" (Matt. 28:7), is addressed immediately unto the servants of Christ and it is for their faith to appropriate the same. According as they do so will their hearts and hands be strengthened. If you are really the servant of Christ, your Master has not called you to draw a bow at a venture but has appointed your specific place in His vineyard and has ordered everything in connection therewith. That does not mean all will be smooth sailing. It did not mean that for the Apostles, as the book of Acts shows. But it *did* mean that they were not left without a Pilot. HE not only went before them but gave assurance, "Lo, I am *with you,* alway, even unto the end of the world" (Matt. 28:20). That is the grand consolation of this writer. May it be yours, too.—A.W.P.

"known unto God are all His works from the beginning of the world" (Acts 15:18). Therefore is it written, "And it shall come to pass that before they call I will answer" (Isa. 65:24). Before we reach a place, God has provided for us wherever the road leads, all has been made ready. "Who went in the way *before you,* to search you out a place to pitch your tents in" (Deut. 1:33); and He will not do less for His people today. Canaan was fully prepared for Israel long before they arrived there: "when the LORD thy God shall have brought thee into the land which He sware unto thy fathers, to Abraham, to Isaac, and to Jacob, to give thee great and goodly cities, which *thou buildest not,* and houses full of good things which thou filledst not, and wells digged which thou diggedst not, vineyards and olive trees which thou plantedst not" (Deut. 6:10, 11). Here is comfort for the preacher too: "The LORD, *He* it is that doth go before thee," to prepare hearts for the message, for the reception of the Truth.

3. The Lord has gone before you *in Person.* The path which He calls you to tread has first been traversed by Himself. None other than the Lord of Glory became incarnate, entered this world of ours and tabernacled here for thirty-three years in the flesh, that He might be the Captain of our salvation (Heb. 2:10). "When He putteth forth His own sheep, He goeth *before* them" (John 10:4). Are they required to tread the way of obedience? Well, their Shepherd has Himself preceded them therein. Are they required to deny themselves and take up their cross? Well, He Himself did nothing less. Are they called upon to be buffeted, not for their faults but when they do well, to be persecuted for righteousness' sake? Well, "Christ also suffered for us, leaving us an example that ye should follow His steps" (1 Peter 2:21). What comfort is there here: that the trials we endure for the Truth's sake, that the unkind treatment we meet with from professing brethren because we dare not compromise are an essential part of the process of our being conformed to the image of God's Son! Shall we be called upon to pass through the valley of the shadow of death? Well, the Christian has nothing to fear, for Christ has gone before Him and extracted the sting of death.

4. The Lord has gone before you in the directions of His *Precepts.* "Thy Word is a lamp unto my feet and a light unto my path" (Psa. 119:105), revealing the way of peace and blessing through this dark world. Especially is that true of its preceptive portions, for they make known the paths of righteousness which we are to tread. Ignorance of God's will concerning the way we should go is inexcusable, for He has already clearly and definitely made known His will. The highway of holiness does not have to be made by us: it is there plainly enough before us in the Word and it is ours to walk in it. "Thou shalt guide me with Thy counsel and afterward receive me to glory" (Psa. 73:24). A "guide" is one who goes before us, directing our course and the "counsel" of our Divine Guide is contained in His prohibitions and commandments and according as we heed them shall we escape the dangers around us and be kept in the narrow way which leadeth unto Life.

5. The Lord has gone before you in the provisions of His *promises.* What are the Divine promises but so many anticipations of our varied needs and guarantees that God stands pledged to supply them? They are so many proofs of His omniscience which foresaw what would meet our requirements. They are so many tokens of His lovingkindness to manifest His tender concerns for us long before we had any historical existence. They are so many evidences of His faithfulness that He will withhold no

(*continued on proceeding page*)

VOL. XXII.   FEBRUARY, 1943.   NO. 2

STUDIES in the SCRIPTURES

" Search the Scriptures." John 5:39.

Publisher and Editor—ARTHUR W. PINK,
27 Lewis Street,
Stornoway, Isle of Lewis,
Scotland.

A SEARCHING QUESTION.

"For what dost thou make request" Nehemiah 2:4.

Nehemiah was a man whom many would envy. His environment was attractive and he occupied a position of prominence and honour. He dwelt "in the palace" (1:1) and was "the king's cupbearer" (1:11). Nevertheless he was far from being happy. Ah, my reader, material things cannot satisfy—neither wealth nor dignities supply contentment to their possessors. But Nehemiah was stricken with something more than natural discontent: his spirit was grieved because of the dishonour which had been done the Lord, because of the reproach which lay upon His cause, because of the woeful condition of His people. Jerusalem was in ruins: the temple was desolate. Israel were captives in a strange land, suffering because of the sins of their fathers. Nehemiah was deeply exercised, so that he "sat down and wept and mourned certain days and fasted" (1:4). Then he poured out his heart in contrite prayer and earnest supplication (1:5-11). Having prevailed with God, chapter 2 shows us how he prevailed with the king of Persia.

When Nehemiah appeared again before the king to serve him with wine, his countenance reflected the anguish of his soul. Whereupon his royal master inquired as to the cause of his sadness. For a moment Nehemiah was affrighted, sought the help of God, and then, like a man, told the king the cause of his grief. So far from being angry, the king asked, "For what dost thou make request?" The privilege of offering petition unto me is yours: what is it thou wouldest have me to do for thee? God touched the heart of this monarch showing that "the king's heart is in the hand of the LORD, as the rivers of water: He turneth it whithersoever He will" (Prov. 21:1). The Lord had given His servant favour in the eyes of this august ruler. Beautiful is it to behold the sequel. Nehemiah refused to take personal advantage of such an opportunity and seek his own aggrandizement. Instead of asking for higher honours and emoluments for himself, he sought that which was for the glory of God and the good of His people.

"For what dost thou make request?" It is surely not a straining of this passage to apply it to the subject of prayer. Doing so, we may observe here, first, a call to *solemn consideration* when we are about to engage in this holy exercise. It is not an equal you are approaching, but the Majesty of Heaven. It is the Most High, the King of kings, the ineffably Holy One you are going to address. A realization of that fact should deeply

IMPORTANT NOTICES

Please advise promptly of change in address, otherwise copies will be lost in the mails.

We are glad to send a sample copy to any of your friends whom you believe would be interested in this publication.

This magazine is published as "a work of faith and labour of love," the editor and his wife gladly giving their services free. There is no regular subscription price, as we do not wish the poor of the flock to be deprived. This does not mean that those looking for something for nothing may "help themselves." Those getting this Magazine, who are financially able and who receive spiritual help from its pages, are expected to gladly contribute towards its expenses; otherwise, their names are dropped from our lists.

Will those forwarding International Money Orders please have them made out to us at Stornoway, Isle of Lewis, Scotland. Checks (Cheques-Eng.) made out on U.S.A. Banks are not negotiable here, so please do not send them.

CONTENTS

THE SERMON ON THE MOUNT.

25. *False Prophets:* Matthew 7:15-20.

"Beware of false prophets, which come to you in sheep's clothing, but inwardly they are ravening wolves" (v. 15). No idle or needless warning was this, but one which should be seriously taken to heart by all who have any concern for the glory of God or value their eternal interests. Our danger is real and pressing, for "false prophets" are not few in number but "many" (1 John 4:1) and instead of being found only in the notoriously heretical sects have "crept in" among saints until they now dominate nearly all the centres of orthodoxy. If we are deceived by them and imbibe their lies the result is almost certain to be fatal, for error acts upon the soul as deadly poison does on the body. The very fact that these impostors assume "sheep's clothing" and pose as the servants of Christ greatly increases the peril of the unwary and unsuspicious. For these reasons it is imperative that we should be on our guard. But to be properly on our guard requires that we should be informed, that we should know how to recognize these deceivers. Nor has our Lord left us unfurnished at this vital point, as the succeeding verses show.

"Ye shall know them by their fruits." Three questions are suggested by this statement, to which it is necessary we should obtain correct answers if this rule here laid down by Christ is to be used by us to good advantage. First, what sort of knowledge is it that is mentioned? Is it relative or absolute? Is it the forming of a credible and reliable judgment of the teachers we sit under and whose writings we peruse, or is it an unerring discernment which precludes us from making any mistake? Second, how is this knowledge obtained? Is it a Divine endowment or a human acquirement? Is it one of the spiritual gifts which accompanies regeneration, a sense of spiritual perception bestowed upon the Christian, or is it something after which we must labour, which can be procured only by our own diligence and industry. Third, what are the "fruit's" brought forth by the false prophets? Are they their character and conduct or is something else intended? Really, it is this third question which is the principal one to be pondered but we will say a little upon the first two before taking it up.

The answer to the first question should be fairly obvious, for even in the day of human deification we have heard of none laying claim to infallibility except the arch-humbug at Rome. But though the knowledge here predicated is not an inerrant one, yet it is something much superior to a vague are uncertain one. In those words our Lord lays down a rule, and like all general rules we may make mistakes—both favourable and unfavourable—in the application of it. The knowledge which Christ here attributes to His people is such a persuasion as to inform them how they should act toward those who appear before them as preachers and teachers, enabling them to test their claims and weigh their messages. Though it does not always enable its possessor to penetrate the disguise worn by impostors, yet it is sufficient to arouse his suspicion and if acted on to preserve him from falling a prey to deceivers. It is a knowledge which fortifies the Christian from being beguiled by religious seducers.

And how is this knowledge procured? It is both obtained and attained from God, attained by practice. Spiritual discernment is one of the accompaniments of the new birth: necessarily so, for regeneration is a being brought out of darkness into God's marvellous light. In that light the Christian is able to perceive things which previously were hidden from him, yet he must perforce walk with Him who is light if he is not to recede into the shadows. There are degrees of light, and the measure of our spiritual illumination decreases as distance increases between us and "the Sun of righteousness." Moreover, sight is as essential as light for clear vision. The faculty of spiritual perception belongs to each soul renewed by the Spirit, yet faculties unemployed soon become useless to their possessors. When the Apostle was contrasting unhealthy saints with the healthy (Heb. 5:11-14) he described the latter as "those who by reason of *use* have their senses *exercised* to discern both good and evil." The more we walk in the light and the more we exercise our spiritual faculties the more readily shall we perceive the snares and stumbling stones in our path.

"Ye shall know them by their fruits." False prophets are to be identified by what they produce. By their "fruits" we understand, principally, their creed, their character, and their converts. Is it not by these three thing that we recognize the true Prophets? The genuine servants of God give evidence of their Divine commission by *the doctrine* they proclaim: their preaching is in full accord with the Word of Truth. The general tenor of their lives is in harmony wherewith, so that their daily walk is an example of practical godliness. Those whom the Spirit quickens and edifies under their preaching bear the features of their ministerial fathers and follow the lead of their shepherds. Conversely, the ministers of Satan though feigning to be the champions of the Truth oppose and corrupt it: some by denying its Divine authority, some by mingling human tradition with it, others by "wresting" it or by withholding vital portions thereof. Though their outward conduct is often beyond reproach, their inward character, the spirit which actuates them, is that of the *wolf*—sly, cruel, fierce. And their converts or disciples are like unto them.

The true Prophet accords God *His rightful place.* He is owned as the King of kings and Lord of lords, as the One who "worketh all things after the counsel of His own will." He is acknowledged to be the sovereign Ruler of Heaven and earth, at whose disposal are all creatures and all events, for whose pleasure they are created (Rev. 4:11), whose will is invincible and whose power is irresistible. He is declared to be God in *fact* as well as in name. He is the One whose claims upon us are paramount and incontestable. The One who is to be held in the utmost reverence and awe—the One who is to be served with fear and rejoiced in with trembling (Psa. 2:11). Such a God the false prophets neither believe in nor preach. On the contrary, they prate about a "God" who wants to do this and who would like to do that but cannot because His creatures will not permit it. Having endowed man with a free will, he must neither be compelled nor coerced and while Deity is filled with amiable intentions He is unable to carry them out. Man is the architect of his fortunes and the decider of his own destiny and God a mere Spectator.

The true Prophet gives *Christ His rightful Place,* which is very much more than to be sound concerning His Person. Romanists are more orthodox about the Deity and humanity of Christ than are multitudes of Protestants, yet the former as much as the latter are grossly heterodox upon His official status. The true Prophet proclaims the Lord Jesus as *the Covenant Head* of His people, who was set up before the foundation of the world to fulfill all the terms of the Covenant of Grace [Everlasting Covenant] on their behalf and to secure for them all its blessings. He sets forth Christ as the "Surety" and "Mediator" of the Covenant (Heb. 7:22; 8:6); as the One who came here to fulfill His Covenant engagements: "Lo, I come, to do Thy will, O God" (Heb. 10:9)—it was a voluntary act, yet in discharge of a sacred agreement. All that Christ did here upon earth and that which He is now doing in Heaven was and is the working out of an eternal compact. Everything relating to the Church's salvation was planned and settled by Covenant stipulation between the Eternal Three. Nothing was left to chance, nothing remained uncertain, nothing was rendered contingent upon anything the creature must do. About this glorious and fundamental Truth the false prophets are completely silent.

It was to fit Him for His Covenant engagements the Surety became incarnate. It was to redeem His people from the curse of the Law that Christ was made under it, fulfilled its terms, endured its penalty in the place and stead of His Covenant people. It was for them and no others He shed His precious blood. Because He faithfully and perfectly discharged His covenant obligations, the Father has sworn with an oath that all for whom He acted shall be eternally saved, that not one of them should perish, solemnly declaring that "He shall see of the travail of His soul and be satisfied" (Isa. 53:11). God has made with Christ and His people in Him, "an Everlasting Covenant, ordered in all things and *sure*" (2 Sam. 23:5). But the false prophets reverse all this. They misrepresent the redemptive work of Christ as being a vague, indefinite, general promiscuous thing, rendering nothing sure. They believe Christ shed His blood for Judas equally with Peter and for Pilate as truly as Paul. They preach a salvation which is uncertain and contingent, as though it were for anybody or nobody as the caprice of men shall decide: Christ provided it and if we accept it, well and good; if not, He will be disappointed.

The true Prophet *puts man in his proper place.* He declares that man is a depraved, ruined and lost creature, dead in trespasses and sins. He points out that man is alienated from God, that his mind is enmity against Him, that he is an inveterate rebel against Him. He shows this is true not only of those in heathendom but equally so of those born in Christendom: that "there is none righteous, no not one; there is none that understandeth, there is none that seeketh after God" (Rom. 3:10, 11). He makes it clear that man is a total wreck, that no part of his being has escaped the fearful consequences of his original revolt from his Maker: that his understanding is darkened, his affections corrupted, his will enslaved. Because of what transpired in Eden man has become the slave of sin and the captive of the Devil. He has no love for the true and living God. He has instead a heart that is filled with hatred against Him—so far from desiring or seeking after Him, he endeavours by every imaginable means to banish God from his thoughts. He is blind to His excellency, deaf to His voice, defiant of His authority and unconcerned for His glory.

The true Prophet goes still further. He not only portrays the sinner as he actually is but he announces that man is utterly unable to change himself or better his condition one iota. He solemnly announces man to be "without strength," that he *cannot* bring himself into subjection to the Divine Law or perform a single action pleasing to God (Rom. 8:7, 8). He insists that the Ethiopian can change his skin or the leopard his spots more readily than they who are accustomed to do evil can perform that which is good (Jer. 13:23). In short, he declares that man is hopelessly and irremediably lost unless a sovereign God is pleased to perform a miracle of grace upon him. But it is the very opposite with the false prophets. They speak "smooth things" and flatter their hearers, persuading them that their case is very far from being as desperate as it really is. If they do not expressly repudiate the Fall, or term it (as the Evolutionists) a "fall upward," they greatly minimize it, making it appear to be only a slight accident which may be repaired by our own exertion, that man is little affected by it, that he still has "the power to accept Christ."

According as the Fall of man be viewed and preached so will be the conceptions of men concerning the need and nature of redemption. Almost every Gospel Truth will necessarily be coloured by the light in which we view the extent of the Fall. Take the Truth of *Election*: which is the deciding factor? God's will or mine? Why, if I be in possession of freedom of will and am not on probation, everything must turn on the use I make of this all-important endowment. But can this be made to square with the Scriptures? Yes, by a little wresting of them. It is true that false prophets hate the very word "election," but if they are pressed into a corner they will try and wriggle out of by saying those whom God elected unto salvation are the ones whom He foreknew would be willing to accept Christ and that explanation satisfies ninety-nine per cent of their hearers. The truth is God foreknew that if He left men to their pleasure *none would* ever accept Christ (Rom. 9:29), and therefore He made a sovereign and unconditional selection from among them. Had not God eternally chosen me, I certainly had never chosen Him.

The same holds true of *regeneration*. If the sinner is spiritually impotent and his case hopeless so far as all self-effort and help is concerned, then he can no more quicken himself than can a rotten corpse in the tomb. A dead man is powerless and that is precisely the *natural* condition of every member of the human race, religious and irreligious alike: "*dead* in trespasses and sin." The individual concerned in it contributes no more to his new birth than he did to his first. This was expressly insisted upon by Christ when He declared, "which were born not of blood (by descent from godly parents), nor of the will of the flesh (by his own volition), nor of the will of man (by a persuasive preacher), but of God" (John 1:13). There must be an act of *Divine* creation before anyone is made a new creature in Christ. But the false prophets represent man to be merely "bruised" or at most crippled by the Fall and insist that he may be born again simply by accepting Christ as his personal Saviour—a thing which none can do until he is brought from death unto life.

The genuine Prophet trumpets forth with no uncertain sound the grand Truth of *justification*. Rightly did Luther declare that, "Justification by faith is the doctrine of a standing or falling church," for those who pervert it corrupt the Gospel at its very heart. In view of man's fallen and depraved condition, in view of his being a transgressor of the Divine Law, lying beneath its awful condemnation, the question was asked of old, "How then, can man be justified with God?" (Job 25:4). To be "justified" is very much more than being pardoned: it is the declaration by the Divine Judge that the believer is *righteous* and therefore entitled to the *reward* of the Law. But how is this possible when man has no righteousness of his own and totally unable to produce any? The answer is that Christ not only bore in His own body the sins of God's elect but He rendered to the Law a perfect obedience in their place—the moment they believe in Him His obedience is reckoned to their account, so that each can say, "in the LORD have I righteousness and strength" (Isa. 45:24). But the false prophets deny and ridicule this basic truth of the imputed righteousness of Christ.

The true Prophet gives the *Holy Spirit His rightful place*, not only in the Godhead, as co-eternal and co-equal with the Father and the Son but in connection with salvation. Salvation is the *gift* of the Triune God: the Father planned it, the Son purchased it, the Spirit communicates it. The genuine servant of God is very explicit in declaring that the work of the Holy Spirit is as indispensable as the work of Christ: the One serving *for* His people, the Other acting *in* them. It is the distinctive office of the Spirit to illumine the understanding of God's elect, to search their conscience and convict them of their ruined and guilty condition. It is His office to work repentance in them, to communicate faith unto them and to draw out their hearts unto Christ. The most sound and faithful preaching in the world will avail nothing unless the Holy Spirit applies it in quickening power. The most winsome offers and persuasive appeals will be useless until the Spirit bestows the hearing ear. The true Prophet knows this and therefore he has no confidence in his own abilities but humbly seeks and earnestly prays for the power of the Spirit to rest upon him. But how different is it with deceivers of souls!

The genuine servant of God not only realizes the truth of that word, "Not by might, nor by power, but by My Spirit, saith the LORD of Hosts" (Zech. 4:6) in connection with the fruitage of his labours. And he is also deeply conscious of his own need of being personally *taught* by the Spirit. He has been made to feel his utter insufficiency to handle sacred things and to realize that if he is to enter into the spiritual meaning of the Word he must be Divinely taught in his own soul. A mere intellectual study of the letter of Scripture cannot satisfy one who longs for a deeper experimental knowledge of the Truth, nor will he be content with simply informing the minds of his hearers. As it is a tender conscience and a fuller heart-acquaintance with God and His Christ that he covets for himself, so it is to the conscience and heart of his *hearers* he addresses himself. It is the opposite with the false prophets: they are occupied solely with the letter of Scripture, with outward profession: there is no deep probing, nothing searching in their messages, nothing to disturb the religious worldling.

Another mark by which many of the false prophets may be recognized is the disproportionate place they give to prophecy in their preaching and teaching. This has ever been a favourite device of religious charlatans as those versed in ecclesiastical history are well aware. Nor should any observer of human nature be surprised at this. God has placed an impenetrable veil upon the future, so that none can know "what a day may bring forth" (Prov. 27:1). But man is intensely curious about coming events and gives a ready ear to any who pretend to be able to enlighten him. If on the one hand the irreligious will flock to palmists, astrologers and other fortune-tellers, the religious will crowd around anyone who claims to be able to explain the mysterious content of the Apocalypse. In times of war and national calamity the curious are easily beguiled by men with charts on the book of Daniel. The express prohibition of our Lord, "It is not for you to know the times or the seasons" (Acts 1:7) should deter His people from giving ear to those who claim to have "light" thereon.

In this article we have not dealt with false prophets generally but have confined ourselves to those who wear "sheep's clothing," whose attacks are made upon the flock of Christ. These are men who boast of their soundness in the Faith, and obtain a hearing among those who regard themselves as the cream of orthodoxy. Thus far we have dwelt upon their creed, of what they believe and teach. Next month (D. V.) we shall describe some of the distinguishing traits of their characters and then point out that the type of converts they make also serves to identify them by the "fruit" they produce. Our design in entering into such detail is that young Christians may be furnished with a full-length photo of these deceivers and to make it clear we are not condemning such because they differ from us on one or two minor matters, but are thoroughly corrupt in doctrine. Furthermore, in all that has been before us it should be clear that we should labour diligently to become thoroughly acquainted with God's Word for ourselves, or how shall we be fitted to detect these seducers of souls? Ponder Acts 17:11.—A.W.P.

THE MISSION AND MIRACLES OF ELISHA.

2. *His Call.*

In our introductory article we sought to point out the close connection there is between the missions and ministries of Elijah and Elisha—let us now consider the personal relation that existed between the two Prophets themselves. This is something more than a point of interest: it throws light upon the character and career of the latter, and it enables us to discern the deeper spiritual meaning which is to be found in this portion of the Word. There was a twofold relation between them: one official and the other more intimate. The former is seen in 1 Kings 19:16 where we learn that Elijah was commanded to "anoint Elisha to be Prophet," and it is worthy of note that while it is generally believed all the Prophets were officially "anointed" yet Elisha's case is the only one expressly recorded in Scripture. Next we learn that immediately following his call Elisha "went after Elijah and ministered unto him" (19:21), so the relation between them was that of master and servant, confirmed by the statement that he "poured water on the hands of Elijah" (2 Kings 3:11).

But there was more than an official union between these two men: the ties of affection bound them together. There is reason to believe that Elisha accompanied Elijah during the last ten years of his earthly life, and during the closing scenes we are shown how closely they were knit together and how strong was the love of the younger man to his master. During their lengthy journey from Gilgal to the Jordan, Elijah said to his companion, again and again, "Tarry ye here, I pray thee," but nothing could deter Elisha from spending the final hours in the immediate presence of the one who had won his heart or make him willing to break their communion: so they "still went on, and talked" (2 Kings 2:11). Observe how the Spirit has emphasized this: first "they went down to Bethel" (v. 2), but later "they *two* went on" (v. 6), "they two stood by Jordan" (v. 7), "they two went on dry ground" (v. 8), refusing to be separated. And when they *must* be, Elisha cried, "My father! my father" (v. 12)—a term of endearment. And in token of his deep grief "took hold of his own clothes and rent them in two pieces."

As the invariable rule of Scripture, it is the *first* mention which supplies the key to all that follows: "Elisha, the son of Shaphat, of Abelmeholah shalt thou anoint to be Prophet in *thy room*" (1 Kings 19:16). Those words signify something more than that he was to be his successor. Elisha was to take Elijah's place and act as his accredited representative. This is confirmed by the fact that when he found Elisha, Elijah "cast his mantle upon him" (v. 19), which signified the closest possible identification. It is very remarkable to find that when Joash, the king of Israel, visited the dying Elisha he uttered the self-same words over him as the Prophet had used when Elijah was departing from this world. Elisha cried "My father! my father! the chariot of Israel and the horsemen thereof"—the real defense of Israel (2 Kings 2:12). And Joash said, "O my father! my father! the chariot of Israel and the horsemen thereof" (2 Kings 13:14): that not only marked the identification of Elisha with Elijah, but the identification as actually *owned* by the king himself.

Another detail which serves to manifest the relation between the two Prophets is found in the striking reply made by Elisha unto the question of his master: "Ask what I shall do for thee before I be taken from thee," namely, "I pray thee, let a double portion of thy spirit be upon me" (2 Kings 2: 9). That his request was granted appears clear from the sequel: "if thou see me when I am taken from thee, it shall be so unto thee," and verse 12 assures us, "and Elisha saw it." Moreover, when the young Prophets saw him smite the waters of the Jordan with his master's mantle so that they "parted hither and thither, they exclaimed, "The spirit of Elijah doth rest on Elisha" (v. 15). The "double portion" was that which pertained to the firstborn or oldest son and heir: "But he shall acknowledge the son of the hated for the firstborn, by giving him a *double* portion of all that he hath: for he is the beginning of his strength: the right of the firstborn is his" (Deut. 21:17), and cf., 1 Chronicles 5:1.

Elisha, then, was far more than the historical successor of Elijah: he was appointed and anointed to be his *representative*—we might almost say his "ambassador." He was the man who had been called by God to take Elijah's place before Israel. Though Elijah had left this scene and gone on High, his ministry was not to cease: true, he was no longer here in person but he would be so in spirit. Elisha was to be in "his room" (1 Kings 19:16), for the starting point of his mission was the ascension of his master. Now what, we may ask, is the spiritual significance of this? What is the important instruction to be found in it for us today? Surely the answer is not far to seek. The relation between Elijah and Elisha was that of *master* and *servant*. Since the anointing of Elisha into the prophetic office is the only case of its kind expressly recorded in Scripture, are we not required to took upon it as a representative or *pattern* one? Since

Elijah was a figure of Christ, is it not evident that Elisha is a type of those servants specially called to represent Him here upon earth?

The conclusion drawn above is manifestly confirmed by all the preliminary details recorded of Elisha ere he entered upon his life's work. Those details may all be summed up under the following heads: his call, the testing to which he was submitted and from which he successfully emerged, the oath he was required to follow, and the special enduement which he received equipping him for his service. The closer these details are examined and the more they be prayerfully pondered, the more evidently will it appear to anointed eyes that the experiences through which Elisha passed are those which substantially each genuine servant of Christ is required to encounter. Let us consider them in the order named. First, the call of which he was the recipient. This was his induction into the sacred ministry. It was a clear definite call by God, the absence of which makes it the height of presumption for anyone to invade the holy office.

The summons which Elisha received to quit his temporal avocation and henceforth devote the whole of his time and energies to God and His people is noted in, "So he departed thence, and found Elisha the son of Shaphat, who, plowing with twelve yoke of oxen before him, and he was with the twelfth; and Elijah passed by him and cast his mantle upon him" (1 Kings 19:19). Observe how that here, as everywhere, God took the initiative: Elisha was not seeking unto God. But the Lord through Elijah sought him out. Elisha was not found in his study but in the field, not with a book in his hand, but at the plow. As one of the Puritans said when commenting thereon, "God seeth not as man seeth, neither does He choose men because they *are* fit, but He fits them because He hath chosen them." Sovereignty is stamped plainly upon the Divine choice, as appears also in the calling of the sons of Zebedee while "mending their nets" (Matt. 4:21), of Matthew while he was "sitting at the receipt of custom" (Matt. 9:9), and Saul of Tarsus when persecuting the early Christians.

Though Elisha does not appear to have been seeking or expecting a call from the Lord to engage in His service, yet it is to be noted that he was *actively engaged* when the call came to him, as was each of the others alluded to above. The ministry of Christ is no place for idlers and drones who wish to spend much of their time driving around in cars or being entertained in the homes of their members and friends. No, it is a vocation which calls for constant self-sacrifice, which entails the burning of the midnight oil and which demands tireless devotion to the performance of duty. Those, then, who are most likely to be sincere and energetic in the ministry are those who are industrious and business-like in their temporal avocation. Alas, how many who wish to shirk their natural responsibilities and shelve hard work have entered the ministry to enjoy a life of comparative ease.

"Elisha" means "God is Saviour" and his father's name "Shaphat" signifies "judge." "Abelmeholah" is literally "meadow of the dance" and was a place in the inheritance of Issachar, at the north of the Jordan valley. Elisha's father was evidently a man of some means for he had "twelve yoke of oxen" engaged in plowing, yet he did not allow his son to grow up in idleness as so often is the case with the wealthy. It was while Elisha was usefully engaged in the performance of duty, undertaking the strenuous work of plowing, that he was made the recipient of a Divine call unto special service. This was indicated by the approach of the Prophet Elijah and his casting his mantle—the insignia of his office—upon him. It was a clear intimation of his own investiture of the Prophetic office. This call was accompanied by Divine power, the Holy Spirit moving Elisha to accept the same, as may be seen from the promptness and decidedness of his response.

Before we look at his response let us consider the very real and stern *test* to which Elisha was subjected. The issue was clearly drawn: to enter upon the prophetic office, to identify himself with Elijah meant a drastic change in his manner of life. It meant the throwing up of a lucrative worldly position—the leaving of the farm—for the servant and soldier of Jesus Christ *must not* "entangle himself with the affairs of this life" (2 Tim. 2:4)—Paul's labouring at "tent-making" was quite the exception to the rule and a sad reflection upon the parsimoniousness of those to whom he ministered. It meant the breaking away from home and natural ties. Said the Lord Jesus, "he that loveth father or mother more than Me is not worthy of Me, and he that loveth son or daughter more than Me is not worthy of Me" (Matt. 10:37): if such immoderate affection was an effectual bar to Christian discipleship (Luke 14:26) how much more so from the Christian ministry? The test often comes at this very point: it did so with the present writer, who was called to labour in a part of the Lord's vineyard thousands of miles from his native land, so that he saw not his parents for the space of thirteen years.

There was first, then, the testing of Elisha's affections, but he shrank not from the sacrifice he was now called upon to make. "And he left the oxen and ran after Elijah." Note the alacrity, the absence of any reluctance. And he said, "Let me, I pray thee, kiss my father and my mother and I will follow thee." Observe his humble spirit: he had already taken the *servant's* place, and would not even perform a filial duty without first receiving permission from his master. Let any who may be exercised in mind as to whether or not they have received a call to the ministry search and examine themselves at this point, to see if such a spirit has been wrought in them. The nature of Elisha's request shows clearly that he was not a man devoid of natural feelings, but an affectionate son, warmly attached to his parents. So far from being an excuse for delaying his obedience to the call, it was a proof of his promptness in accepting it and of his readiness to make a deliberate break from all natural ties.

"And he (Elijah) said unto him, Go back again: for what have I done to thee?" (v. 20). It was as though the Prophet said: Do not act impulsively, but sit down and count the cost ere you definitely commit yourself. Elijah did not seek to influence or persuade him: it is not to me but to God you are accountable—it is *His* call which you are to weigh. He knew quite well that if the Holy Spirit were operating He would complete the work and Elisha would return to him. O that the rank and file of God's people would heed this lesson! How many a young man, never called of God, has been pressed into the ministry by well-meaning friends who had more zeal than knowledge? None may rightly count upon the Divine blessing in the service of Christ unless he has been expressly set apart thereto by the Holy Spirit (Acts 13:2). One of the most fearful catastrophes which has come upon the churches (and those terming themselves "assemblies") during the past century has been the repetition of what God complained of old: "I have not sent these prophets, yet they ran" (Jer. 23:21). To intrude into the sacred office calls down Heaven's curse (2 Sam. 6:6, 7).

But Elisha's acceptance of this call from God not only meant the throwing up of a comfortable worldly position and the breaking away from home and natural ties. It also involved his following or casting in his lot with one who was very far from being a popular hero. Elijah had powerful enemies who more than once had made determined attempts on his life. Those were dangerous times, when persecution was not only a possibility but a probability. It was well, then, for Elisha to sit down and count the cost: by consorting with Elijah he would be exposed to the malice of Jezebel and all her priests. The same is true in principle of the Christian minister. Christ is despised and dejected of men, and to be faithfully engaged in His service is to court the hostility not only of the secular but of the religious world as well. It was on religious grounds that Jezebel persecuted Elijah, and it is by the false prophets of Christendom and their devotees that the genuine ministers of God will be most hated and hounded. Nought but love for Christ and His people enable him to triumph over his enemies.

"And he returned back from him and took a yoke of oxen and slew them and boiled their flesh with the instruments of the oxen and gave unto the people and they did eat" (1 Kings 19:21). This farewell feast was a token of joy at his new calling and an expression of gratitude to God for His distinguishing favour. The burning of the oxen's tackle was a sign that he was bidding a final adieu to his old employment. Those oxen and tools of industry, wherein his former labours had been bestowed, were now gladly devoted to the celebration of the high honor of being called to engage in the service of God Himself. Those who rightly esteem the sacred ministry will freely renounce every other interest and pleasure, though called upon to labour amid poverty and persecution; yea, they who enter into the work of our heavenly Master without holy cheerfulness are not at all likely to prosper therein. Levi the publican made Christ "a great feast in his own house" to celebrate his call to the ministry, inviting a great company thereto (Luke 5:27-29).

"Then he arose and went after Elijah." See here the power of the Holy Spirit! The evidence of God's effectual call is a heart made willing to respond thereto. Divine grace is able to subdue every lust, conquer every prejudice, surmount every difficulty. Elisha left his worldly employment, the riches to which he was heir, his parents and friends, and threw in his lot with one who was an outcast here. Thus it was with Moses, who "refused to be called the son of Pharaoh's daughter, choosing rather to suffer affliction with the people of God than to enjoy the pleasures of sin for a season; esteeming the reproach of Christ greater riches than the treasures in Egypt: for he had respect unto the recompense of the reward" (Heb. 11:24-26). Love for Christ and His saints, faith in His ultimate "Well done," were the motive-springs of his actions. And such must actuate one entering the ministry today.

"Then he arose and went after Elijah and ministered unto him" (1 Kings 19:21). That was the final element in this initial test. Was he prepared to take a subordinate and lowly place, to become a servant, subjecting himself to the will of another? That is what a servant is: one who places himself at the disposal of another, ready to take orders from him, desirous of promoting *his* interests. He who would be given important commissions must prove himself. Thus did God approve of Stephen's service to the poor (Acts 6:5) by later permitting him to address the leaders of the nation (Acts 7:1, 2). Because Phillip "disdained not to serve tables" (Acts 6:2, 5) he was advanced to the rank of missionary to the Gentiles (Acts 8:5, 26). On the other hand, Mark was discontented to be merely a servant of an Apostle (Acts 15:37, 39) and so lost the opportunity of being trained for personal participation in the most momentous missionary journey ever undertaken. Elisha became the servant of God's servant, and we shall see (D. V.) how he was rewarded.— A.W.P.

DOCTRINE OF SAINTS' PERSEVERANCE.

6. *Its Blessedness.*

2. What comfort is there here *for fearing saints*! All Christians have a reverential and filial fear of God and an evangelical horror of sin. Some are beset with legal fears and most of them with anxieties which are the product of a mingling of legal and evangelical principles. These latter are occasioned more immediately by anxious doubts, painful misgivings, evil surmisings of unbelief. More remotely, they are the result of the permissive appointment of God, who has decreed that perfect happiness must be waited till His people get home to Heaven. Were our graces complete, our bliss would be complete, too. In the meantime it is needful for the Christian traveler to be exercised with a thorn in the flesh and that "thorn" assumes a variety of forms with different believers. Whatever its form, it is effectual in convincing them that this earth is not their rest or a mount whereon to pitch tabernacles of continuance. In many instances that "thorn" consists of anxious misgivings, as the frequent "fear not" of Scripture intimates: the fear of being completely overcome by temptation, of making shipwreck of the faith, of failing to endure unto the end.

Once again we would quote those words of Christ, "Of them whom Thou gavest Me have I lost none" (John 18:9). Is not that inexpressibly blessed! That every one of the dear children whom the Father has entrusted to the care and custody of the Mediator shall be brought safely to Glory! The feeblest as much as the strongest, those with the least degree of grace as those with the most, the babes as truly as the full grown. Where true grace is imparted, though it be as a grain of mustard seed, it shall be quickened and nourished so that it shall not perish. This should be of great consolation to those timid and doubting ones who are apt to think it will be well with Christians of great faith and eminent gifts but that such frail creatures as they know themselves to be, will never hold out, who dread that Satan's next attack will utterly vanquish them. Let them know that the self-same Divine protection is given to all the redeemed. It is not because one is more godly than another but because both are held fast in the hand of God. The tiny mouse was as safe in the ark as the ponderous elephant.

What encouragement is there here for the godly, who, when they view the numerous Amaleks in the way and hear of the giants and walled cities before them, are prone to dread their meeting with them. How many a one has trembled as he has pondered that word of Christ, "Verily I say unto you, That a rich man shall hardly enter into the kingdom of Heaven. And again I say unto you, It is easier for a camel to go through the eye of a needle than for a rich man to enter into the kingdom of God" (Matt. 19:23, 24) and said the Apostles, "Who then can be saved?" (v. 25). If it be such a difficult matter to get to Heaven, if the gate be so strait and the way so narrow—and so many of those professing to tread it turn out to be hypocrites and apostates, what will become of me? When thus exercised, remember Christ's answer to the astonished disciples, "with God all things are possible" (v. 26). He who kept Israel on the march for forty years without their shoes wearing out, can quite easily preserve you, O you of little faith.

"Thou has a mighty arm: strong is Thy hand, and high is Thy right hand" (Psa 89:13). Grandly is that fact displayed in creation. Who has stretched out the heavens with a span? Who upholds the pillars of the earth? Who has set limits to the raging ocean, so that it cannot overflow its bounds? Whose finger kindled the sun, the moon and the stars, and kept those mysterious lamps of the sky alight all these thousands of years? Whose hand has filled the sea with fish, the fields with herds and made the earth fertile and fruitful? So, too, the mightiness of the Lord's arm is manifest in *Divine Providence.* Who directs the destinies of nations and shapes the affairs of kingdoms? Who sets the monarch upon his throne and casts him from it when it so pleases Him? Who supplies the daily needs of a countless myriad of creatures so that even the sparrow is provided for when the earth is blanketed with snow? Who makes all things work together for good—even in a world which lies in the Wicked one—to them that love Him, who are the called according to His purpose?

When a soul is truly reconciled to God and brought to delight in Him, it rejoices in all His attributes. At first it is apt to dwell much upon His love and mercy but as it grows in grace and experience it delights in His holiness and power. It is a mark of spiritual understanding when we have learned to distinguish the manifold perfections of God, to take pleasure in each of them. It is a proof of more intimate communion with the Lord when we perceive how adorable is the Divine character, so that we meditate upon its excellences separately and in detail and praise and bless Him for each of them. The more we are given to behold all the varied rays of His pure light, the more we are occupied with the many glories of His crown, the more shall we bow in wonderment before Him. Not only shall we perceive how infinitely He is above us, but how there is everything in Him suited to our need—grace to meet our unworthiness, mercy to pardon our sins, wisdom to supply our ignorance, strength to minister to our weakness. "Who is like unto Thee, O LORD, among the gods! who is like Thee, glorious in holiness, fearful in praises, doing wonders!" (Exo. 15:11).

How this glorious attribute of God's power ensures the final perseverance of the saints! Some of our readers have passed through sore trials and severe tribulations, yet they prevailed not against them: they shook them to their foundations but they did not overthrow their faith. "Many are the afflictions of the righteous, but the LORD delivereth him out of them all" (Psa. 34:19). Fierce were the foes which many a time gathered against you and had not the Lord been on your side you would have quickly been devoured. But in Him we find a sure refuge. The Divine strength has been manifested in our weakness. Is it not so, my brother, my sister: that such a frail worm as yourself has never been crushed by the weight of opposition that has come upon you?—ah, "underneath *were* the everlasting arms." Though you trembled at your feebleness, yet "out of weakness were made strong" (Heb. 11:34) has been your case, too. Kept alive with death all around you, preserved when Satan and his hosts encompassed you. Must you not say "strong is Thy right hand"!

3. What comfort is there here for souls who are *tempted to entertain hard thoughts of God*! The awful corruptions of the flesh which still remain in the believer are ever ready to complain at the difficulties of the way and murmur against the dispensations of Divine Providence. The questionings of unbelief constantly ask, Has God ceased to be gracious? How can He love me if He deals with me thus? These questions are sufficient in themselves to destroy the soul's peace and quench its joy. But when to these are added the infidelities of Arminianism which declare that God takes no more care of His children than to suffer the Devil to enter in among and devour them, that the Lord Jesus, that great Shepherd of the sheep, affords no more security to His flock than

to allow wolves and lions to come among and devour them at their pleasure—how shall the poor Christian maintain his confidence in the love and faithfulness of the Lord? Such blasphemies are like buckets of cold water poured upon the flames of his affection for God and are calculated only to destroy that delight which he has taken in the riches of Divine grace.

The uninstructed and unestablished believer is apt to think within himself, I may for the present be in a good state and condition but what assurance is there that I shall *continue* thus? Were not the apostate angels once in a far better state and more excellent condition than mine? They dwelt in Heaven itself but now they are cast down into Hell, being "reserved in everlasting chains under darkness unto the judgment of the great day" (Jude 6)! Adam in Paradise had no lusts within to tempt and seduce him, no world without to oppose and entangle, yet being in honour he continued not but apostatised and perished. If it was not in *their* power to persevere much less so in mine, who is "sold under sin" and encompassed with a world of temptations, what hope is there left to me? Let a man be exercised with such thoughts as these, let him be cast back solely upon himself and what is there that can give him any relief or bring his soul to any degree of composure? Nothing whatever, for the so-called "power of free will" availed not either the angels which fell or our first parents.

And what is it which will deliver the distressed soul from these breathings of despair? Nothing but a believing and laying hold of this grand comfort: that the child of God has an infallible promise from his Father that he shall be preserved unto His heavenly kingdom, that he shall be kept from apostasy, that the intercession of his great High Priest prevents the total failing of his faith. So far from God's being indifferent to the welfare of His children and failing in His care for them, He has sworn, "I will not turn away from them to do them good" (Jer. 32:40). So far from the good Shepherd proving unfaithful to His trust, He has given express assurance that not one of His sheep shall perish. Rest on those assurances, my reader, and your hard thoughts about God will be effectually silenced. As to the stability and excellency of the Divine love, is it not written, "The LORD thy God in the midst of thee is mighty, He will rejoice over thee with joy; He will rest in His love, He will joy over thee with singing" (Zeph. 3:17)? What can more endear God to His people than that?! How it should fix their souls in their love to Him.

Well might Stephen Charnock say of Arminians, "Can these men fancy Infinite Tenderness so unconcerned as to let the apple of His eye be plucked out, as to be a careless Spectator of the pillage of His jewels by the powers of Hell, to have the delight of His soul (if I may so speak) tossed like a tennis ball between himself and the Devil?" He that does the greater thing for His people shall He not also do the less: to regenerate them is more wonderful than to preserve them, as the bestowal of life exceeds the maintaining of it. The reconciliation of enemies is far harder than dealing with the failings of friends: "while we were yet sinners, Christ died for us. *Much more then*, being now justified by His blood, we shall be saved from wrath though Him. For if, when we were enemies, we were reconciled to God by the death of His Son, much more, being reconciled, we shall be saved by His life" (Rom. 5:8-10). If there were such efficacy in the death of Christ, who can estimate the virtue of His resurrection! "He ever liveth to make intercession for us" (Heb. 7:25).

4. What comfort is there here for *aged pilgrims*! Some perhaps may be surprised

at this heading, supposing that those who have been longest in the way and have experienced most of God's faithfulness have the least need of consolation from this truth. But such a view is sadly superficial to say the least. No matter how matured in the faith one may be, or how well acquainted with the Divine goodness, so long as he is left down here he has no might of his own and is completely dependent upon Divine grace to preserve him. Methuselah stood in as much need of God's supporting hand during the closing days of his pilgrimage as does the veriest babe in Christ. Look at it from the human side of things: the aged believer, filled with infirmities, the spiritual companions of his youth all gone, perhaps bereft of the partner of his bosom, cut off from the public means of grace—looks forward to the final conflict with trepidation.

"And even to your old age I am He, and even to hoar hairs will I carry you" (Isa. 46:4). Why has such a tender and appropriate promise been given by God if His aged saints have no need of the same? They, any more than the young, are not immune from Satan's attacks. He is not slow to tell the tottering believer that as many a ship has foundered when in sight of port, so the closing storm of life will prove too much for him: that though God has borne long with his unbelief and waywardness, even His patience is now exhausted. How then is he to meet such assaults of the Fiend? In the same way as he has done all through his course—by taking the shield of faith, wherewith he shall be able to quench all the fiery darts of the Wicked one (Eph. 6:16)—by having recourse to the sure promise of Him who has said, "Lo, I am with you alway, even unto the end" (Matt. 28:20).

Ah, my aged friend, how often have you proved in your experience the truth of those words, "thine enemies shall be found *liars* unto thee" (Deut. 33:29). What a shameless liar the Devil is! Did he not tell you in some severe trial, "The hand of the Lord is gone out against you: He has forsaken you and will no more be gracious to you. He has deserted you as He did Saul the king and now you are wholly given up unto the powers of evil: the Lord will no more answer you from His holy oracle; He has utterly cast you off"? Yet you found that God had not deserted you after all and this very day you are able to join the writer in thanking Him for His lovingkindness and to testify of His unfailing faithfulness. How often has your own unbelief whispered to you, "I shall one day perish at the hand of this foe who seeks my life: my strength is gone, the Spirit withholds His assistance, I am left alone and must perish"? Yet year after year has passed and though faint you are still pursuing, though feeble you will hold on your way, by His grace!

Has not Satan often told you in the past, "Your profession is a sham, iniquities prevail over you, the root of the matter is not in you. You were a fool to make a profession and cast in your lot with God's people: there is no stability in you. You are certain to apostatise and bring reproach upon the cause of Christ"? And did not your own doubts second his motion, telling you that your experience was but a flash in the pan, some evanescent emotion which like a firebrand would die out into black ashes? Unbelief has whispered a thousand falsehoods into your ear, saying this duty is too difficult, this toil will prove too great, this adversity will drown you. What madness it was to lend an ear to such lies! Can God ever cast away one on whom He has fixed His everlasting love? Can He renounce one who was purchased by the blood of Christ? Thus will it prove of your last fears: "Thine enemies shall be found liars unto thee."

5. What comfort is there here *for preachers*! Many a rural minister views with

uneasiness the departure into cities of some of his young converts. And may well he be exercised at the prospect of them leaving their sheltered homes to be brought into close contact with temptations to which they were formerly strangers. It is both his duty and privilege to give them godly counsel and warning, to follow them with his prayers, to write them: but if they be soundly converted he need not fear about their ultimate wellbeing. Servants of God called to move into other parts are fearful about the babes in Christ which they will leave behind, yet if they really be such they may find consolation in the blessed fact that the great Shepherd of the sheep will never leave nor forsake them.—A.W.P.

THE UNKNOWN WAYS OF LOVE.
C.H. Spurgeon—1876
Conclusion
"Jesus answered and said unto him, What I do thou knowest not now;
but thou shalt know hereafter" (John 13: 7).

III. Our not being able to know what the Lord does *should never shake our confidence in Him.* I hope, dear brethren, our faith in Christ does not rest upon our capacity to understand what He does: if so, I fear it is not faith at all, but a mere exercise of self-conceited carnal reason. Some things which the Lord has done bear upon their very fore-front the impress of His infinite love, but I hope you know enough of Him now to be able to believe that where there are no traces of love apparent to you, His love is surely there. I rejoice in that part of my text which runs thus: "What I do." This washing of the feet was not being done by Bartholomew or Nathaniel: it was the personal act of the Lord Himself. Now, when the Master and Lord is the Actor, who wants to raise a question or to suggest inquiry? It must be right if *He* does it: to question His conduct would be an insult to His majestic love.

Do you know Christ? Then you know the character of His deeds. Do you know your Lord? Then you are sure that He will never act unkindly, unbecomingly, or unwisely. He can never send a needless sorrow, or wantonly cause a tear to flow. Can He? Here, then, is the question, not why is it done—but who is doing it? And if the Lord is doing it, we can have no doubt about the excellence of His design. We believe that He is right when we cannot see that He is so. If we do not trust Him far beyond what we know, it will show that our confidence in Him is very limited. When a person only obeys another because he chooses to obey and sees it a proper thing to do, he has not the spirit of implicit obedience at all. And when a person only confides in another as far as he can see that he is safe, he is a stranger to implicit confidence. Confidence has its sphere beyond the boundaries of knowledge: where judgment ceases, faith begins. "What I do thou knowest not now." Ah, You best beloved of our souls, in that You speak truly, but we can reply to You that we know and are sure that what You do is supremely good.

IV. Our want of understanding as to what our Lord does generally shows itself most in reference to *His personal dealings with us.* "What I do thou knowest not now" refers to His washing Peter's feet. Brethren, if there is anything which we are not likely to understand thoroughly, it is that which has to do with ourselves. We are too close home to see clearly. In this case the looker-on sees more than the player. We generally form a better opinion of the character, position, and needs of another than we do concerning ourselves. It is said of Moses' face that everyone saw it shine but one man, and that was Moses, for he could not see his own countenance. So also if a man's face is black it is black to everybody but himself: he does not see his own spots. We cannot form accurate estimates of ourselves and so we must not expect when Christ is personally dealing with us that we should be able to understand what He does to us.

If the Lord is dealing with us in an afflicting way we are generally in an unfavourable state of mind for forming any judgment at all, being, as a rule, too disturbed in mind by the affliction itself. When an hospital patient is under the knife he is a poor judge of the necessity of the operation or the skill of the surgeon. In after days, when the wound is healed he will judge better than he can do when the knife is just cutting through nerves and sinew and bone. Judge nothing before the time. You are not in a right condition to judge, and therefore do not attempt it. When you are smarting under the rod, your opinions and estimates and forecasts are about as much to be depended upon as the whistling of the wind or the dashing of the waves. Cease from judging, calculating and foreboding, and believe that He who ordains our lot orders all things in kindness and wisdom.

I do not wonder that Peter was puzzled and could not understand his Lord's procedure, for it is always a hard thing for an active and energetic mind to see the wisdom of being compelled to do nothing. Here is a man who can drag a net to the shore full of big fishes, and instead of using his strength he is made to sit still and do nothing! Peter, the hardy, vigorous worker, must sit down like a gentleman or a cripple and do nothing. He cannot make it out. He has been very useful and he thinks he could be useful now; he could at any rate wait at the table, or carry the basin, or wash his fellows' feet, if it must be done. But he is bound to sit still and do nothing and does not understand it. Brethren, the hardest work a man ever has to do who wants to serve the Lord Jesus is to stand aside in forced inactivity and take no share in what is going on. It is hard to be put on the shelf among the cracked crockery and to be of no more use than a broken vessel, while you feel you could be useful if you had but strength to leave your chamber. The proud idea that you have been wonderfully useful tempts you to repine at being laid among the lumber and you feel it to be a very mysterious business.

Then what is worse, Peter not only cannot do anything, he is *receiving from others* and must be waited on by them, and chiefly by his Master, who he at other times loved to serve. To have his feet washed must have appeared to a hardy fisherman like Peter a strange luxury. He would say, "Cannot I do it myself? I am not used to being waited on." To sit there and while doing nothing, to be also engrossing the care of another must have been a singular position to him. It is very unpleasant to an active man to be unable to work and to be dependent upon others for every little detail and necessity of life. To borrow other people's strength and tax other people's care is not desirable. To stand in need of anxious prayers and to arouse pitying thoughts seem strange to those who have been accustomed to do rather than to suffer. "Why," you seem to say, "I have prayed for them, I have worked for them: are they now to pray and work for me? I have fed the sheep; are the sheep going to feed me? I have washed the saints' feet; are they going to wash mine? Am I to be dependent upon others and not to be able to lend a hand or lift a finger?" Ah, well, we must not ask questions, but we are very apt to do so. We do not know and we become inquisitive, but the Saviour says, "What I do thou knowest not now."

All the while there is very prominent in our mind a sense of insignificance and unworthiness, which makes our receipt of favours the more perplexing. "What," says Peter, "I, I unworthy Peter, shall I be washed by the Lord Jesus Christ?" So it seems to us unworthy sinners. Why should God's people be thinking about me, and careful about me? Why has the Lord Himself deigned to make my bed in my sickness? Why has His blessed Spirit condescended to be my Comforter, applying precious promises to me? Whence is this to me? We do not comprehend it. We are lost in wonder, and it is no marvel that we are.

That we greatly need the sacred purging of Jesus is not so wonderfully mysterious after all, for we *need* purging and cleansing love for the removal of daily defilement. Sometimes trials in business, sad bereavements, acts of ingratitude, pains of sickness, or depressions of spirit are just the basin and the water and the towel with which our Lord is washing our feet. We are clean through the blood of Jesus, but the daily cleansing we still need. It is a wonder that some of us are ever out of the furnace, for our dross is so abundant. I shall not be surprised if I find myself often under the flail, for the straw and the chaff are plentiful in me. Some metals are so apt to rust that it is no wonder they are so often burnished. Some soils need a deal of plowing; they are very apt to cake and grow hard and therefore must be broken up. So it is with us, there is a need be for what the Lord is doing.

In Peter's case there was a need of fellowship, for our Lord said, "If I wash thee not thou hast no part with Me." You cannot have fellowship with Christ except He does this or that for you, nay, especially except He tries you; for how shall you know the suffering Saviour except you suffer yourself? Communion with the afflicted Redeemer is promoted by our personal afflictions. There was a need yet again for Peter and the rest to learn the lesson of washing their brethren's feet by seeing the Lord wash theirs. No man can rightly wash another's feet till his own feet have been washed by his Saviour. It is in the kingdom of Christ a law that there must be experience before there can be expertness. You must be comforted or you cannot comfort; you must find mercy yourself or you cannot lead others in the search. You must be washed or you cannot wash. Thus there were good reasons for our Lord's act but they were not seen by Peter, nor do the motives for our Lord's dispensations toward us always appear upon the surface. When Jesus Himself is dealing with us, especially if it is in a way of trial, we do not understand it and He has need to say, "What I do thou knowest not now."

V. Upon this point and upon many others *we shall one day be informed.* "What I do thou knowest not now, but thou shalt know *hereafter.*" That "hereafter" may be very soon. Peter knew within a few minutes what Jesus meant, for He says to him, "Know ye what I have done unto you? If I your Lord and Master have washed your feet, ye ought also to wash one another's feet." Thus the light was not long in breaking. Why are you in such a hurry when you are in trouble to begin spelling out a naughty reason for God's dealings, when if you will but wait you shall know the right reason in a short time? A child is in an ill temper because there has been a rule made by the father and not explained. And so it sits down and sulks and thinks of some unkind, ungenerous motive, on the father's part. In a minute or two after it understands it all and has to eat its own words, and confess, "How bad of me to impute such unkindness to my dear father, who is always seeking my good." If you will get reasoning in haste about your Lord's dispensations, you will have to take all your reasonings back and you will have to afflict your soul for being so hasty. Therefore wait a while, for "thou shalt know hereafter," and that "hereafter" may be very near.

Peter understood his Master's washing his feet better after his sad fall and three-fold denial. I should not wonder that when the Lord turned and looked upon Peter and he went out and wept bitterly, the penitent disciple said to himself, "Now I begin to see why my Lord washed my feet." When he perceived how sadly he needed washing, he would prize the token which his Lord had given him. He saw his own frailties and imperfections as he had not seen them before, for he had said, "Though all men should be offended, yet will I never be offended." But after his sad denial he knew himself to be as apt to err as the rest of the others were. At a certain point of your experience you will possibly discover the explanation of your present adversity. After the Lord had met with Peter at the sea and had said to him, "feed My sheep" and "feed My lambs" another method of explanation was open to him. When Peter began to be a pastor and to deal with the souls of others, he would clearly see why his Master washed his feet, for he would find that he had much to do of the same kind of service. Often does our work for Christ unfold the work of Christ and we know our Lord by being called to follow His steps.

Yonder in Heaven, best of all, Peter understands why the Master washed his feet and surely sometimes Peter must inwardly smile to think of what he once thought and said. Peter sings amid the heavenly throng, "Unto Him that loved us and washed us from our sins in His own blood," and then he thinks to himself, "In my folly in the days of my flesh I said unto Him, 'Thou shalt never wash my feet.' I loved Him when I said it, but what monstrous folly lay in my speech." Ah, he understands it now and we shall soon understand as he does. All things will be clear when we once pass into the region of light.

I anticipate the blessed confidences of Heaven. How blessed will be those familiar revelations of mysteries so long obscure! What sweet communications there will be between God and His people in the world to come. I look forward to the time when we shall see the knots untied and the riddles all explained: then shall we see the good of apparent evil and the life which lay in the bosom of death. Could we hear the stories of pilgrims who have reached Home they would run like this—"I was traveling a pleasant road, blessing God for so delightful a pilgrimage but suddenly a huge rock fell across my path and I had with regret to turn back and traverse a more rugged road. I never understood why until I came Home to Heaven and now He tells me, 'Child, there was a precipice but a little way in front, and you would have been dashed to pieces and therefore I blocked up your way.' "

Another who has reached the desired haven will tell us, "The vessel in which I sailed was wrecked; she struck upon a rock, and on a broken fragment of her timbers I swam to shore. I could never comprehend the reason for this calamity till now. For now I learn that the boat was being steered by crafty hands to a shore whereon I should have been made a slave and kept in lifelong captivity—and there was no way of deliverance but by dashing the boat to shivers and landing her passengers where they would be free."

Brethren, you will probably bless God in Heaven more for your sorrows than for your joys. When you once ascend the celestial hills you will see that the best blessings came to you in the roughest garments; your pearls were found n oyster shells and your jewels were brought out of Egypt. Sickness, trial, adversity, bereavement and pain have been more truly angels of God to you than your wealth, your health, your strength, your comfort—infinitely more so than your laughter and your ease. O brothers and sisters, we shall know hereafter. Well, as we shall know hereafter we may leave the knowing till then, and give all our attention to the obeying and the trusting.

I have done when I have addressed a warning to those out of Christ. There are some in this congregation who do not know my Lord. I have been much exercised in my mind about you while I have been confined to my chamber and unable to address you. My prayer has been that the Holy Spirit would bless to your conversion the messages of my brethren who have kindly occupied this pulpit. If you still remain unconverted, I would like to say that you do not know what God has been doing with you, or what He is doing with you now—but you will know hereafter. You have Sabbath-Days, but you do not know their value: you will value them differently by and by, when you lie dying and especially when you are called before the judgment seat of God.

You have your Bible, and you neglect it. You do not know that God has sent a love letter to you in that form—you will know it when you stand before His awful bar. Some of you have been pleaded with very often and earnestly entreated to lay hold on eternal life. The Lord has backed up our entreaties by sending sickness to you and personal trouble. Well, you have not known much about it and you have not wished to know—but you will have to know hereafter. If you die without Christ you will wake up in eternity and cry, "Ah me, that ever the Lord should call me and I refuse, that He should stretch out His hand and I should disregard."

In Hell it will be an awful discovery, "I was the subject of Gospel invitations, I was the object of earnest expostulations but I continued in my sin and here I am eternally lost." What I earnestly desire should happen would be that you should this morning find out what the Lord has done for you and you should understand it and open your eyes and say, "Here am I, a man who has lived long in sin and I have been spared on purpose that God might save me ere I die."

Or perhaps it will take this form: "Here I am, a young man and I came in here this morning with no precise motive, little knowing what God was about to do with me but I know it now—He has brought me hither that I may, this morning, believe in Jesus and give my heart to Him." O hearers of the Gospel, if you once come to know what God has really done with you and for you, you will hardly forgive yourselves for your conduct towards Him! You will say, "Did He really love me so, redeem me with such a price and have I been so unkind and thoughtless towards Him?" You will upbraid yourselves and chasten yourselves, and grieve to think you should have treated so good a Friend so ill. O may the Divine Spirit this morning open your eyes to know what the Lord Jesus does unto you! May His grace be magnified in you. Amen and Amen.

DIVINE HEALING.

Fourth, there is the grotesque idea of the Dispensationalists. These are a class of men who pose as being exceptionally enlightened and under the guise of "rightly dividing the Word of Truth" arbitrarily partition the Scriptures. They affirm "*this* is not for us," "*that* does not pertain to this present era of Grace," "*that* relates to the Tribulation period," "*this* will be fulfilled in the Millennium." Because the opening verse of James reads, "To the twelve tribes which are scattered abroad, greetings," these robbers of God's children declare this Epistle is "entirely Jewish." As well might they reason that the first Epistle of Paul is designed only for Papists because it is addressed to "all that be in Rome" (Rom. 1:1). The Epistle of James belongs to all the "beloved brethren," to all born-again souls (1:16, 18). It is surely striking that the very passage we are here considering (5:14-16) comes right between a reference to Job (a Gentile) who endured patiently his affliction and found the Lord to be "pitiful and of tender mercy" (v. 11) and to Elijah who is described as "a man subject to like passions as we are" yet mighty in prayer (v. 17)—as though the Spirit was anticipating and refuting this mad notion.

Now where such widely different interpretations are given of a passage it usually follows that the true one ties somewhere between the two extremes and such we believe is the case here. We are very loath to regard our passage as being an obsolete one, that it refers to something which pertained only to the apostolic age and relates not at all to us. When referring to the Popish travesty of this "anointing with oil" Thomas Goodwin said: "The Reformed churches seeing that such a sacrament could not be and this must needs be a perversion of it, did justly reject it, only in rejecting it (as in some other things) they went too far, even denying it to have that use of restoring the sick as a seal of the promise and an indefinite means to convey that blessing which God in mercy hath appointed it to be." We are strongly inclined to agree with this eminent Puritan that the churches which grew out of the Reformation went too far when they set aside this passage as containing Divine directions to be followed by Gospel churches throughout this Christian era. Such a sweeping conclusion needs qualifying.

The knotty point to be settled is, how far and at which points is this qualification to be made? Personally we believe the general principle and promise of the passage holds good for all generations—seasons of great spiritual declension and deadness only excepted. In normal times it is the privilege of the saint—when seriously ill, or suffering great pain— and not on every light occasion to send for the "elders" (pastors, ministers) of the local Gospel church to which he belongs. They who preach God's Word to him should surely be the fittest to spread his case before Him: cf. Job 42:8. They are to pray over him, commending him to the mercy of God and seeking recovery for him if that is according to the Divine will. Whether or not the "anointing with oil" should accompany the praying is a detail on which we are not prepared to state dogmatically. But where the sick one desires it, his request should be complied with. The kind of oil is not specified, though most likely olive was used in the first century.

It should be pointed out that those promises of God which relate to temporal and eternal mercies are quite different from those pertaining to spiritual and eternal things—the former being general and indefinite and not unconditional and absolute as are many of the latter—and therefore as God reserves to Himself the freedom to make them good when, as, and to whom He pleases, we must ask in full submission to His sovereign pleasure. To illustrate: if I am starting out on a journey I ask God to preserve me from all harm and danger if that be His holy will (Rom. 1:10). But I make no such proviso when requesting Him to deliver me from those who assault my soul (2 Tim. 4:18). Thus the "Prayer of faith" here is not a definite expectation that God will heal but a peaceful assurance that He will do that which is most for His glory and the sick one's good. That the promise of James 5:15 is an indefinite and not an absolute one is clear from this consideration: if it were not so, he could continually claim the promise and so never die—the "and IF he have committed sins" further confirms the indefiniteness of what is here in view.

Some are likely to object against what has been pointed out in the last paragraph and say, But faith must have a foundation to rest upon and it has none other than the Word of God: if then there be here no definite promise to lay hold of and plead before God, the "prayer of *faith*" is impossible, for there is no assurance the sick one will be healed. That may sound very plausible and pious, yet it is wrong. There *is* a faith of reliance and submission as well as a faith of *expectation*. There is no higher, no stronger, no grander faith than one which has such confidence in the wisdom and goodness of God as leads me to present my case to Him and say, "Do as seemeth Thee good." It is always a help when we can plead a promise but God is greater than all His promises and where some specific need or emergency is not covered by some express promise, faith may count upon the mercy and power of God Himself—this is what Abraham did: Hebrews 11:19!

Personally we greatly fear that there are very few "elders" now left on earth whom it would be any good to send for in an emergency: only those living close to God and blessed with strong faith would be of any use. This is a day of "small things." Nevertheless the Lord remains unchanged and ready to show Himself strong on the behalf of those who walk uprightly. Though there be no spiritual elders available, yet *God is* accessible; seek unto Him and if He grants you the "prayer of faith" then healing is certain either by natural means or supernatural intervention. "The Lord is undoubtedly present with His people to assist them in all ages and when necessary He heals their diseases as much as He did in ancient times. But He does not display those miraculous powers or dispense miracles by the hands of Apostles, because that gift was only of temporary duration" (Calvin).

"Confess your faults one to another, and pray one for another, that ye may be healed" (James 5:16). Here the scope of our passage is widened: in verse 13 the afflicted or tried one is to pray for himself; in verse 14 the ministers are to pray for the one seriously sick, now fellow-Christians are to pray for each other. But first they are bidden to confess their faults one to another, which does *not* mean revealing the secrets of their hearts or acquainting their brethren with that which is suited only for the ear of God—but cases where they have tempted or injured *one another* or consented to the same evil gossiping, for example. A mutual acknowledgement of those faults which cause coldness and estrangement, exciting one another to repentance for the same, promotes the spirit of prayer and fellowship. The "healing" here is also wider, referring primarily to that of the soul (Psa. 41:4) and breaches (Heb. 12:13), being the term used in 1 Peter 2:24, yet also includes removal of physical chastisements.

A few brief observations on our passage In conclusion, 1. Personal prayer (James 5:13) is enjoined before ministerial (v. 14) and social (v. 16): individual responsibility cannot be shelved. 2. God is not indifferent to the sickness of His people (v. 14), but cares for their bodies as well as their souls. 3. Are not ministers too free in visiting the sick and praying over them, instead of waiting until they are sent for (v. 14)? 4. If none but "elders" (ministers) were to anoint with oil, surely they alone are eligible to administer Baptism and the Lord's Supper! 5. All sickness is not occasioned by *sin* or the "if" of verse 15 would be meaningless. 6. Yet God *does* sometimes visit with physical chastisements as the "if" denotes. 7. The mutual confession of verse 16 refutes the Popish error of "auricular confession," for the priest does *not* confess *his* sins to those revealing to him the secrets of their souls!—A.W.P.

STRENGTH RENEWED.

"They that wait upon the LORD shall renew their strength" (Isa. 41:31). What a blessed promise is this for those conscious of their feebleness! But it must be personally appropriated if we are to enjoy the good of it: faith must lay definite hold of the same and humbly but earnestly plead it before God. Nor should we regard it as restricted to the reviving of our *souls*: it includes also the reenergizing of our bodies, as not a few can testify. It is blessedly true that those who trustfully wait upon the Lord shall have their graces quickened, their spiritual strength renewed. But it is equally true that the greater includes the less and that if we confidently count upon His doing so, the Lord will renew our physical strength. "Through faith also Sarah herself received strength" (Heb. 11:11), and as the remainder of the verse shows, it was physical strength—but it was received "through faith"!

"The LORD shall renew their strength." On many occasions has this writer—when preaching six times a week (rarely for less than an hour, usually seventy-five to ninety minutes) in the heat of Australia, journeying here and there to do so—returned home at 10 p.m. feeling worn and weary and pleading this promise expectantly and partaking of light refreshment, sat down for four hours' hard study and writing an article for this magazine. So also has his wife, born of parents who died before she was ten and herself of frail constitution, found this one of her chief stand-by's for many years past and proven for herself those words, "out of weakness were made strong" (Heb. 11:34). And why should not you also, Christian reader? Read carefully Isaiah 40:28-31 and turn it into believing prayer: but remember the strength must be used in the performance of duty and not frittered away! As prevention is better than cure, so is the renewing of our vitality more desirable than "faith healing."—A.W.P.

(continued from back page)

For what *ought* I to make request? What should be the chief burden of my petitions? Is not the reply furnished in the two prayers of the Lord Jesus: the one which He gave to His disciples (Matt. 6), and the other which He offered Himself (John 17)? A pondering of them in the light of our present inquiry reveals three things. First, that we should make the honour of God our chief concern, that His glory might be more and more manifested in us and by us and through us. That is where our Redeemer began: "When ye pray say, Our Father which art in Heaven, hallowed be Thy name" (Matt 6:9) and "Father the hour is come, glorify Thy Son that Thy Son also may glorify Thee" (John 17:1) This is what lay nearest His heart and should it not ours, too? Second, that we should supplicate for the whole Household of Faith. The prayer which He taught His disciples is the *Family* Prayer: all its pronouns are in the plural number. It is not "*my* Father" but "*our* Father." It is not "give *me* and forgive *me*," but "give *us* and forgive *us*." Our hearts are to take in and go out to all our brothers and sisters. We behold the same thing in the petitions of our great High Priest: "I pray for *them*: I pray not for the world" (John 17:9). Six times over in that prayer we find Him making mention of the company "given to Him": it was (and is) for the whole election of grace He intercedes. Third, that we should ask chiefly, though not solely, for spiritual blessings upon our fellow-saints. Only one of the petitions of Matthew 6 relates to the supply of temporal needs. In John 17 Christ prays for the preservation (v. 12), the joy (v. 13), the sanctification (v. 17), the unification, (v. 21), the perfecting (v. 23) and the glorification (v. 24) of the elect.—A.W.P.

(continued from front page)

impress the soul. Even though I am a real Christian, that gives me no license to rush into the Lord's presence with unbecoming familiarity and unholy irreverence. If Nehemiah was afraid in the presence of Artaxerxes, how much more cause have I to tremble before the Almighty: not with the trembling of servile dread but with the awe of His sovereignty, His infiniteness, His omniscience. Far be it from God's children to offer the "sacrifice of fools" unto Him before whom the very seraphim veil their faces. This searching question, then, bids us remove the shoes of carnality, approach with humility, and weigh beforehand the petitions we propose to present. Is my request suited to the character of Him whom I supplicate?

"For what dost thou make request?" Second, this is a call to *definiteness*. May we not legitimately take this as the King of Zion making similar inquiry of us? You seek unto His Throne of Grace: you desire an audience with His sacred Majesty—for what purpose? Why, to unburden your heart before Him, to obtain grace to help in time of need. But if you are not to insult Him and if your quest is not to be profitless, He requires definiteness. He stops you, as it were, on the threshold with this challenge: "for what dost thou make request?" Vague and undefined desires, indefinite and general petitions will get you nowhere. It is very necessary that we should put this question to ourselves ere we bow the knee before the Lord—exactly what is it I am going to ask for? Suppose that you were limited to a single request, for what would it be? If you might ask for one thing only, what would you select? Much of our praying fails because of *lack of* this definiteness. Can you remember the chief thing for which you supplicated even yesterday? If not, is there any wonder your praying accomplishes so little?

"For what dost thou make request?" Third, this is a test of *the state of our souls.* That for which we make request supplies an index to our inward condition, for "out of the abundance of the heart the mouth speaketh." The natural man will ask for natural (material) things, the selfish for that which will minister to his own gratification—he asks amiss that he may "consume it upon his own lusts." But the spiritual will ask for spiritual mercies that he may honour God and glorify Christ. He will ask for a heart that hates sin and loves holiness. He will ask for the subjugation of that which rises up in rebellion against the Lord. That He will "subdue his iniquities." He will ask for God's love to be shed more abundantly in his heart and His Law to be written more deeply in his mind. He will ask for the strengthening of his graces: "quicken me according to Thy Word." He will beg the Divine Husbandman to make him a more fruitful branch of the Vine.

"For what dost thou make request?" Fourth, this puts to the proof the *breadth of our affections.* The prayers of a genuine Christian are by no means restricted to the supply of his own personal need, but are concerned with those of his brothers and sisters in Christ. Thus our requests not only reveal the state of our hearts but the breadth of them. How we need to pray "Lord, enlarge my heart" (Psa. 119:32): deliver me from a selfish and sectarian spirit. What a word is that: "Praying always with all prayer and supplication in the Spirit, and watching thereunto with all perseverance and supplication for all saints" (Eph. 6:18). "We know that we have passed from death unto life, because we love the brethren" (1 John 3:14), many of whom we have never seen in the flesh and are not even acquainted with their names! And how do we evidence our love for them? Because we find they are laid on our hearts: because we make their cause and welfare our own: because we daily make request for their blessing.

VOL. XXII.   MARCH, 1943.   NO. 3

STUDIES IN THE SCRIPTURES

" Search the Scriptures." John 5:39.

Publisher and Editor—ARTHUR W. PINK,
27 Lewis Street,
Stornoway, Isle of Lewis,
Scotland.

IN THE POTTER'S HOUSE.

"The word which came to Jeremiah from the LORD, saying, Arise, and go down to the potter's house, and there I will cause thee to hear My words. Then I went down to the potter's house, and, behold, he wrought a work on the wheels. And the vessel that he made of clay was marred in the hand of the potter: so he made it again another vessel, as seemed good to the potter to make it" (Jer. 18:1-4). This is a passage which has presented difficulty to not a few, or probably it would be more correct to say that (in most cases at least) it has been *made* to present difficulty. Enemies of the Truth have grievously "wrested" these verses and even the interpretations of its friends have not always succeeded in removing the mists which have beclouded the minds of those influenced by error. Because of this and also as we hope to write upon some later portions in this chapter, a comment or two on its opening verses may not prove unacceptable.

Arminians have appealed to this passage in support of their horrible and God-dishonouring tenet that the Creator may be thwarted by the creature, that puny man is able to bring to nought the designs of the Most High. If such a dreadful calamity were possible, then, to be consistent, they should carry such a premise to its logical conclusion, and avow

"The universe He fain would save,
But longs for what He cannot have!
We therefore worship, praise and laud,
A disappointed, helpless God!"

Such a blasphemous caricature of Deity is repugnant and repellent to the last degree unto every renewed heart, yet is it one which finds more or less acceptance today in professedly "Christian" quarters. The natives of dark Africa manufacture idols with their hands but the heathen in Christendom fashion a "God" out of their Satan-blinded minds.

A disappointed and defeated God! What a concept! What a contradiction in terms! How can He be the great Supreme if man is capable of check-mating Him? How can He be the Almighty if lacking in ability to carry out His will? Who would render homage unto One who is thwarted by His creatures? How vastly different is the God of Holy Writ, who has but to speak and it is done—who commands and it stands fast (Psa. 33:9)! Jehovah is no pasteboard Monarch. No, "our God is in the heavens: He hath done *whatsoever* He hath pleased" (Psa. 115:3). "Whatsoever the LORD pleased, that

IMPORTANT NOTICES

Please advise promptly of change in address, otherwise copies will be lost in the mails.

We are glad to send a sample copy to any of your friends whom you believe would be interested in this publication.

This magazine is published as "a work of faith and labour of love," the editor and his wife gladly giving their services free. There is no regular subscription price, as we do not wish the poor of the flock to be deprived. This does not mean that those looking for something for nothing may "help themselves." Those getting this Magazine, who are financially able and who receive spiritual help from its pages, are expected to gladly contribute towards its expenses; otherwise, their names are dropped from our lists.

Will those forwarding International Money Orders please have them made out to us at Stornoway, Isle of Lewis, Scotland. Checks (Cheques-Eng.) made out on U.S.A. Banks are not negotiable here, so please do not send them.

CONTENTS

THE SERMON ON THE MOUNT.

25. *The False Prophets*: Matthew 7:15-20.

During the days of His earthly ministry the Lord Jesus furnished full proof that He was the perfect Preacher as well as the model Man. That fact has not received the attention which it deserves, especially among those responsible for training the future occupants of our pulpits. We have perused numerous works on homiletics, but never came across one which attempted to analyze and summarize the methods followed by Christ in His public and private discourses. If the believer finds it necessary and beneficial to ponder the prayers of the Saviour in order that his devotional life may be directed and enriched thereby, surely the minister of the Gospel should feel it both essential and helpful to make a close study of how He approached and addressed both sinners and saints. If he does so he will discover the use Christ made of the Scriptures, the wealth of illustration He drew from the simplest objects of nature, the particular aspects of Truth on which He threw the most emphasis, the variety of motives to which He appealed, the different parts of man's complex constitution to which He addressed Himself, the repetitions He deemed needful, the searching questions He so often asked, the homely comparisons He made, and the sharp contrasts He drew.

Even if the student confines his attention to the Sermon on the Mount he will perceive how wide was the range of this single Address, how numerous were the themes covered, how diverse the characters dealt with, and thus how many-sided is the work of the ministry. First the Lord depicted those upon whom the benediction of God rests, describing them according to their character and conduct. Next He defined the function and purpose of His servants: they are the salt of the earth and the light of the world. Then He declared His attitude unto the Law and the Prophets and inculcated the basic law of His kingdom (Matt. 5:20). Next He expounded the spirituality of the Law and showed it demands conformity of heart as well as of action, displaying the high and holy standard which God will in no wise lower. This was followed by a warning against hypocrisy, especially in connection with prayer and fasting. Treasures in Heaven were contrasted from those on earth, and the futility of seeking to serve two masters shown. Expostulation was made against covetousness and carking care. The subject of judging others was opened up, spiritual ambition encouraged, and the golden rule enunciated. The ways of death and of life were faithfully drawn.

This brief summary brings us to our present passage, which opens with a solemn warning. It is not sufficient to enforce the Law and expound the Gospel. Nor has the pulpit completed its task by setting before believers their various duties and calling to the discharge thereof. There are enemies to be warned against. Doubtless it is a far more delightful task to expatiate upon the riches of Divine grace and the excellencies and glories of the Redeemer, but there are also other matters which need attention. If the example of Christ and His Apostles is to be followed the saints are to be put on their guard against those who would seduce them, who with "cunning craftiness lie in wait to deceive" (Eph. 4:14). Salvation is obtained by coming to the knowledge of the Truth (1 Tim. 2:4), and they who are deluded into believing a lie shall be dammed (2 Thess. 2:11, 12). The very fact that eternal destiny is involved by what we believe is sufficient to show the deep seriousness of the issue here raised. He who has the care of souls must spare no pains in sounding the alarm.

"Beware of false prophets, which come to you in sheep's clothing, but inwardly they are ravening wolves" (Matt. 7:15). Herein we behold their "cunning craftiness." They do not appear in their true colours but are cleverly disguised. They pose as true friends of the Lord's people, when in reality they are their deadliest foes. They proclaim themselves to be genuine Christians, whereas in truth they are the emissaries of Satan. They feign themselves to be the teachers of the Truth, but their aim is to instill falsehoods. They work not outside in the profane world, but among the assemblies of the saints pretending to be deeply taught of God, the champions of orthodoxy, men filled with love earnestly seeking the good of souls. Beware of them, says the great Shepherd of the sheep, for inwardly they are ravening wolves—fierce, merciless, seeking the destruction of the flock. Let that fact alarm you, arouse you to your danger and make you vigilant in guarding against it. Suffer not yourselves to be imposed upon.

And what is the best course to take in order to heed this solemn warning? What is the wisest policy to follow so as to be safeguarded from these murderers of souls? How shall we obtain the needed wisdom that we may be enabled to detect and identify these subtle dissemblers? Vitally important is it that we should obtain right answers to these questions. First, let us duly note *the place* where this warning occurs in our Lord's sermon. It is found not at the beginning but near its close. Is there not both instruction and comfort in that? Does it not intimate that if we have really taken to heart Christ's teaching in the former sections we shall be fortified against the danger He here warns against? Does it not tell us that if we earnestly heed His preceding exhortations—if we diligently seek to cultivate inward holiness and endeavour to walk according to the rules given by our Master—that if *we* ourselves have a personal and experimental knowledge of what it is to be a real disciple of His, then we shall have little difficulty in recognizing the false ones?

"The light of the body is the eye: if therefore thine eye be single, thy whole body shall be full of light" (Matt. 6:22). That clearly states the principle to which we have alluded above. Our Lord's language here is parabolic but its meaning is quite clear and simple. The activities of the body are directed according to the light received through the eye, and when that organ is sound and functioning properly—perceiving objects as they really are—the whole body is illuminated and enabled to discharge its duties. We can then move with safety and circumspection. In like manner the faculties of the soul are principally directed by the dictates of the *understanding*, and where that is enlightened by the Holy Spirit and dominated by the Truth we shall be preserved from the snares of Satan and the stumbling-stones of the world. A "single eye" has but one object—God—the pleasing and glorifying of Him. "But if thine eye be evil, thy whole body shall be full of darkness." Thus the "single" eve is a holy one, being contrasted from that which is evil or carnal.

When the "eye" is occupied with Him who is Light, its possessor is able to distinguish between the things which differ and to form a sound and right judgment both of persons and things. Our estimation of values is determined by whether our minds are Divinely illuminated or still in nature's darkness. Where the soul is regulated by the Truth it will be endowed with a wisdom which enables its possessor to distinguish between good and evil. The understanding then becomes a faculty which discerns between the genuine and the spurious. "Thou through Thy commandments hast made me wiser than mine enemies" (Psa. 119:98). Habitual submission to the Divine authority brings its own reward in this life—part of which is a spiritual discretion which preserves from impostures.

When the understanding is dominated by the Word the whole soul is "full of light," so that all its faculties are under its beneficent influence: the conscience being informed, the affections turned to their legitimate object, the will moved in the right direction. In God's light we "see light" (Psa. 36:9), perceiving the difference between good and evil, the things to be sought and those to be avoided.

"If any man will to do His will, he shall know of the doctrine, whether it be of God" (John 7:17). The fundamental condition for obtaining spiritual knowledge, discernment and assurance, is a genuine determination to carry out the revealed will of God in our daily lives. "A good understanding have all they that do His commandments" (Psa. 111:10). Capacity to distinguish Truth from error consists not in vigour of intellect nor in natural learning, but in a sincere willingness and earnest desire to yield ourselves unto the Divine will. Where there is a genuine subjection to the Divine authority and a deep longing to please the Lord, even though it appears to be directly against our temporal interests and worldly prospects, and even though it involves fierce opposition from enemies and ostracism by our professed friends, there will be both spiritual discernment and assurance. Where the heart puts the glory of God before everything else it will be raised above and delivered from the prejudices of pride, self-love, carnal fears, and fleshly aspirations which cloud and bias the understanding of the unregenerate. "Then shall we know if we follow on to know the LORD" (Hosea 6:3), is the sure promise.

Bagster's Interlinear gives a more literal translation of John 7:17: "If anyone desire His will to practice he shall know concerning the teaching, whether from God it is." The Greek word rendered "desire" signifies no fleeting impression or impulse but a deep-rooted determination. Certainty may be arrived at in connection with the things of God, but in order thereto the heart must first be right toward Him, that is, surrendered to Him. When there is a resolution to perform God's will at all costs, there will be a capacity and an enablement to discern and embrace the Truth and to detect and refute error. It is the state of our souls which makes us receptive to or repellent against the temptations and lies of the Enemy: when the heart is yielded to God and conformed to His will, we have no difficulty in seeing through the deceits of Satan. It is those who are governed by self-will and devoted to self-pleasing who fall such easy victims to "seducing spirits and doctrines of devils" (1 Tim. 4:1). The Truth frees from deception, but only as the Truth is appropriated and assimilated.

"Ye shall know them by their fruits" (Matt. 7:16). Ah, but note well *to whom* this is said. The Lord does not predicate this of all who make a bare profession of faith: it is very far from being a knowledge common to all in Christendom. The "ye" is definitely restricted to God's own people, to those who have entered the strait gate and are walking in the narrow way of the immediate context. True, even they need to be on their guard, but if they give heed to the warning of Christ, as assuredly they will, they shall at once recognize these impostors. *Ye* shall know them: but none others will. It is because the sheep "follow" the good Shepherd that "they know His voice," and because they know His voice "a stranger will they not follow, but will flee from him for they know not the voice of strangers" (John 10:4, 5). It is the obedient ear, and that only, which distinguishes between the voice of the true and the false shepherds. If the ear be attuned to the precepts of Scripture it will reject the sophistries of religious charlatans.

"Ye shall know them by their fruits. Do men gather grapes of thorns or figs of thistles? Even so every good tree bringeth forth good fruit, but a corrupt tree bringeth forth evil fruit. A good tree cannot bring forth evil fruit, neither can a corrupt tree bring forth good fruit. Every tree that bringeth forth not good fruit is hewn down, and cast into the fire. Wherefore by their fruits ye shall know them" (Matt. 7:16-20). In these words our Lord intimates that His people should have no difficulty in recognizing the false prophets: if they do but exercise ordinary precaution they will detect the imposture which is sought to be played upon them. The masqueraders are to be identified by their "fruits." At a distance, trees look very much the same, but a closer inspection of them enables us to distinguish the fruitful from the fruitless ones, and whether the fruit is wholesome or injurious. In like manner there needs to be a careful examination of those who appear before us as the servants of God, that the true ones may be distinguished from the counterfeit.

Last month we suggested that there is a three-fold reference in the "fruits" produced by the false prophets, namely, their creed, their character, and their converts. Having dwelt therein at some length on the first let us say a few words now upon the second and third. The character of these men is clearly indicated by Christ's descriptive words, "inwardly they are ravening wolves." It was none other than the Lord of Love who employed what this supercilious generation would term "harsh language." Love is faithful as well as gentle, and it was love to His own which moved Christ to tear off the disguise and reveal these enemies of His flock in their real character. He who denounced the scribes and Pharisees as "hypocrites" and "blind guides," and termed Herod "that fox" (Luke 13:32), hesitated not to brand these subtle deceivers as "ravening wolves." When a bottle of deadly poison is placed among others containing healing lotions it needs to be plainly labeled: that is why we definitely mention the "Plymouth

Brethren" when warning against the false prophets of our day.

That Christ here left an example for His servants to follow appears clearly from the instance of the Apostle Paul. When taking leave of the elders of the Ephesian church, he warned them, "after my departure shall grievous wolves enter in among you, not sparing the flock. Also of your own selves shall men arise, speaking perverse things to draw away disciples *after them*" (Acts 20:29, 30). In that last clause we have another mark of the false prophets. They are inveterate proselytizers. They continually obtrude themselves upon people's attention. They are ever creeping into houses "leading captive silly women led away with divers lusts" (2 Tim. 3:6). They are continually coaxing and wheedling folk to come to their meetings. But the true Prophet never attempts guile or presses anyone to attend his services. No, he is content to follow his Master's practice: "he that hath ears to hear let him hear," and there he leaves it. When a place receives them not they "go their ways" (Luke 10:10) instead of pleading and arguing and seeking to draw disciples "after them."

"But inwardly they are ravening wolves" (Matt. 7:15). What a solemn but suggestive and revealing word is that. The wolf, like the fox, is tricky and treacherous, subtle and sly, hence the words "cunning craftiness" in connection with the purveyors of error who "lie in wait to deceive" of Ephesians 4:14. They scruple not to employ the most dishonourable tactics and resort to tricks which honest men of the world would scorn to use. The wolf is cruel and merciless: so are these deceivers of souls. They prate about love, but they are full of hatred toward those who expose them. They are greedy, having voracious appetites, and false prophets are men of insatiable ambition, hungry for applause, avaricious. Jeremiah 23:32 speaks of their "lightness" or irreverence and Zephaniah 3:4 also says, "their prophets are light and treacherous." So far from being sober and solemn they are frivolous and frothy: it cannot be otherwise, for the fear of God is not upon them.

"By their fruits ye shall know them" (Matt. 7:20). Not by their profession, nor their sanctimoniousness, nor their zeal—but their "fruits"—we understand, thirdly, *the converts* they make. The parent is more or less reproduced in his children. In Jeremiah 23:16 it is said of those who give ear to the false prophets "they make you vain." Egotistical themselves, their disciples are also conceited. They are proud of their letter-knowledge of the Scriptures, boastful of their orthodoxy. They claim to have light which those in the "man-made systems" are without. But their walk betrays them—no traces of humility, no mourning over sin, no experimental acquaintance with the plague of their hearts. They loudly boast of their assurance but produce not the evidences on which Scriptural assurance is based. They prate about eternal security but refuse to examine their hearts and see whether they are in the faith. They have much to say about their peace and joy but are strangers to the groanings of Romans 7. They boast they are "not under the Law" and give proof thereof in their characters and conduct.

In conclusion, let us anticipate a question: why does God permit these false prophets which work such havoc in Christendom? This is a very solemn question and we must restrict ourselves to what the Scriptures say by way of reply. "Thou shalt not hearken unto the words of that [false] prophet, or the dreamer of dreams, for the LORD your God proveth you to know whether ye love the LORD your God with all your heart and with all your soul" (Deut. 13:3). From those words it is clear that God suffers teachers of error for the same reason as He does persecutors of His people—to test their love, to try their fidelity, to show that their loyalty to Him is such that they will not give ear unto His enemies. Error has always been more popular than the Truth, for it lets down the bars and fosters fleshly indulgence. And for that very reason it is obnoxious to the godly. The one who by grace can say, "I have chosen the way of Truth" will be able to add, "I have *stuck unto* Thy testimonies" (Psa. 119:30, 31), none being able to move him therefrom.

"For there must be also heresies among you, that they which are approved may be made manifest among you" (1 Cor. 11:19). Error serves as a flail, separating the chaff from the wheat. Let some plausible and popular preacher come forward with an old error decked out in new clothes and empty professors will at once flock to his standard—but not so with those who are established in the faith. Thus, by means of the false prophets God makes it appear who are the ones who hold the Truth in sincerity. They are faithful to Him despite all temptations to turn away unto a "broader-minded" way. The genuine gold endures every test to which it is subjected. Thus, too, are the unregenerate "converts" revealed—the counterfeit gold will not withstand the fire. Those who are attracted by a novelty do not last but are soon carried away by some newer innovation. "They went out from us, but they were not of us; for if they had been of us, they would have continued with us: but they went out that they might be made manifest that they were *not* all of us" (1 John 2:19). Thus, they who turn away from orthodoxy to heterodoxy must not be regarded as real Christians.

The false prophets are also ordained of God for the punishment of those who receive not the love of the Truth. "For this cause God shall send them strong delusion that they should believe a lie, that they all might be damned, who believed not the Truth, but had pleasure in unrighteousness" (2 Thess. 2:11-12). Ahab could not endure Elijah and Micaiah the servants of God, therefore he was suffered to follow the priests of Baal unto his destruction.

It is very clear from Matthew 24:5, 11, etc., that Israel's rejection of Christ was followed by the appearing of many false christs in their midst who fatally deceived large numbers of the Jews. It was not until primitive and genuine Christianity had been jettisoned that the religious world was plagued by the monster of Romanism. A very large proportion of those found in the false cults of our day were once members of or regular attendees at churches which were more or less sound in the Faith. Beware, my reader, if you despise God's Truth you will fall in love with Satan's lies.—A.W.P.

THE MISSION AND MIRACLES OF ELISHA.

3. *His Testing.*

Last month we pointed out that the peculiar relation which existed between Elijah and Elisha foreshadowed that which pertains to Christ and His servants, and that the early experiences through which Elisha passed are those which, substantially, each genuine minister of the Gospel is called upon to encounter. All the preliminary details recorded of the Prophet ere his mission commenced must have their counterpart in the early history of any who is used of God in the work of His kingdom. Those experiences in the case of Elisha began with a definite call from the Lord, and that is still His order of procedure. That call was followed by a series of very real testings, which may well be designated a preliminary course of discipline. Those testings were many and varied.

They were seven in number, which at once indicates the thoroughness and completeness of the ordeals through which Elisha went and by which he was schooled for the future. If we are not to ignore here the initial one there will of necessity be a slight overlapping between this section and what was before us last month.

First, the testing of his *affections*. This occurred at the time he received his call to devote the whole of his time and energies to the service of God and His people. A stern test it was. Elisha was not one who had failed in temporal matters and now desired to better his position, nor was he deprived of those who cherished him and so anxious to enter a more congenial circle. Far from it. He was the son of a well-to-do farmer, living with parents to whom he was devotedly attached. Response to Elijah's casting of the prophetic mantle upon him meant not only the giving up of favourable worldly prospects but the severing of happy home ties. The issue was plainly drawn. Which should dominate?— zeal for Jehovah or love for his parents? That Elisha was very far from being one of a cold and unfeeling disposition is clear from a number of things. When Elijah bade him remain at Bethel, he replied, "I will not leave thee" (2 Kings 2:2). And when his master was caught away from him he evidenced his deep grief by crying out, "my father! my father" and by rending his garments asunder (v. 12).

No, Elisha was no stoic, and it cost him something to break away from his loved ones. But he shrank not from the sacrifice demanded of him. He "left the oxen" with which he had been plowing and "ran after Elijah" asking only, "Let me, I pray thee, kiss my father and my mother, and then I will follow thee" (1 Kings 19:20). Permission being granted, a hasty and farewell speech was made and he took his departure. The sacred narrative contains no mention that he ever returned home even for a brief visit. Dutiful respect, yea tender regard, was shown for his parents, but he did not prefer them before God. The Lord does not require His servants to callously ignore their filial duty, but He does claim the first place in their hearts. Unless one who is contemplating an entrance into the ministry is definitely prepared to accord Him that, he should at once abandon his quest. No man is eligible for the ministry unless he is ready to resolutely subordinate natural ties to spiritual bonds. Blessedly did the spirit prevail over the flesh in Elisha's response to this initial trial.

Second, the testing of his sincerity. This occurred at the outset of the final journey of the two Prophets. "And it came to pass when the Lord would take up Elijah into Heaven by a whirlwind that Elijah went with Elisha from Gilgal. And Elijah said unto Elisha, Tarry here, I pray thee" (2 Kings. 2:1, 2). Various reasons have been advanced by the commentators as to why the Tishbite should have made such a request. Some think it was because he wished to be alone, that modesty and humility would not suffer that his companion should witness the very great honour which was about to be bestowed upon him. Others suppose it was because he desired to spare Elisha the grief of a final leave-taking. But in view of all that follows and taking this detail in connection with the whole incident, we believe these words of the Prophet bear quite a different interpretation, namely, that Elijah was now making proof of Elisha's determination and attachment to him. At the time of his call Elisha had said, "I will follow thee," and now he was given the opportunity to go back if he were so disposed

There was one who accompanied the Apostle Paul for awhile, but later Paul had to lament, "Demas hath forsaken me, having loved this present world and is departed into Thessalonica" (2 Tim. 4:10). Many have done likewise—daunted by the difficulties of the way, discouraged by the unfavourable response to their efforts, their ardour cooled and they concluded they had mistaken their calling. Or, because only small and unattractive fields opened to them, they decided to better themselves by returning to worldly employment. To what numbers do those solemn words of Christ apply: "No man having put his hand to the plow and looking back is fit for the kingdom of God" (Luke 9:62). Far otherwise was it with Elisha. No fleeting impression had actuated him when he declared to Elijah, "I will follow thee," and when he was put to the proof as to whether or not he was prepared to follow him to the end of the course, he successfully stood the test and gave evidence of his unwavering fidelity. "As the Lord liveth, and as thy soul liveth, I will not leave thee," was his unflinching response. O for like stability!

Third, the testing of his *will* or resolution. From Gilgal Elijah and his companion had gone on to Bethel, and there he encountered a subtle temptation, one which had prevailed over any whose heart was not thoroughly established. "And the sons of the Prophets that were at Bethel came forth to Elisha and said unto him, Know thou that the LORD will take away thy master from thy head today?" (2 Kings 2:3). Which was as much as saying, Why think of going on any further, what is the use of it, when the Lord is on the point of taking him from thee? And mark it well, they who here sought to make him waver from his course were not the agents of Jezebel but those who were on the side of the Lord. Nor was it just one who would deter Elisha, but apparently the whole body of the Prophets endeavoured to persuade him that he should relinquish his purpose. It is in this very way God tries the metal of His servants—to make evident to themselves and others whether they are vacillating or steadfast, whether they are regulated wholly by His call and will or whether their course is directed by the counsels of men.

A holy independence is to mark the servant of God. Thus it was with the chief of the Apostles: "I conferred not with flesh and blood" (Gal. 1:16). Had he done so, what trouble would he have made for himself! Had he listened to the varied advice the other Apostles would proffer, what a state of confusion his own mind had been in! If Christ is my Master, then it is from Him, and from Him alone, I must take my orders. Until I am sure of His will I must continue to wait upon Him. Once it is clear to me, I must set out on the performance of it and nothing must move me to turn aside. So it was here. Elisha had been Divinely called to follow Elijah and he was determined to cleave to him unto the end, even though it meant going against the well-meant advice and offending the whole of his fellows. "Hold ye your peace" was his reply. This was one of the trials which the present writer encountered over thirty years ago when his pastor and Christian friends urged him to enter a theological seminary, though they knew that deadly error was taught there. It was not easy to take his stand against them, but I am deeply thankful I did so.

Fourth, the testing of his *faith*. "And Elijah said unto him, Elisha, tarry here I pray thee, for the LORD hath sent me to Jericho" (2 Kings 2:4). "Tarry *here*." They were at Bethel, and this was a place of sacred memories. It was here that Jacob had spent his first night as he fled from the wrath of his brother. Here he had been favoured with that vision of the ladder whose top reached unto Heaven and beheld the angels of God ascending and descending on it. Here it was Jehovah had revealed Himself and given him precious promises. When he awakened, Jacob said, "Surely the LORD is in this place....this is none other but the house of God and this is the gate of Heaven" (Gen. 28). Delectable spot was this: the place of Divine communion. Ah, one which is supremely attractive to those who are spiritually-minded and therefore one which such are entirely loath to leave. What can be more desirable than to abide where such privileges and favours are enjoyed! So felt Peter on the holy mount. As he beheld Christ transfigured and Moses and Elijah talking with Him, he said, "Lord, it is good to be here: if Thou wilt, let us make here three tabernacles: one for Thee, and one for Moses, and one for Elijah"—let us remain and enjoy such bliss. But that could not be.

God still tests His servants at this very point. They are in some place where the smile of Heaven manifestly rests upon their labours. The Lord's presence is real, His secrets are revealed to them and intimate communion is enjoyed with Him. If he followed his own inclinations he would remain there, but he is not free to please himself—he is the servant of Another and must do *His* bidding. Elijah had announced, "the LORD hath sent me to Jericho." And if Elisha was to "follow" him to the end, then to Jericho he, too, must go. True, Jericho was far less attractive than Bethel, but the will of God pointed clearly to it. It is not the consideration of his own tastes and comforts which is to actuate the minister of Christ but the performance of duty—no matter where it leads to. The mount of transfiguration made a powerful appeal unto Peter, but at the base thereof there was a demon-possessed youth in dire need of deliverance (Matt. 17:14-18)! Elisha resisted the tempting prospect, saying again, "I will not leave thee." O for like fidelity!

Fifth, the testing of his *patience.* This was a two-fold one. When the two Prophets arrived at Jericho the younger one suffered a repetition of what he had experienced at Bethel. Once again "the sons of the Prophets" from the local school accosted him, saying, "Knowest thou that the LORD will take away thy master from thy head today?" Elijah himself they left alone, but his companion was set upon by them. It is the connection in which this occurs that supplies the key to its meaning. The whole passage brings before us Elisha being tested first in one way and then at another. That he should meet with a repetition at Jericho of what he had encountered at Bethel is an intimation that the servant of God needs to be specially on his guard at this point. He must not put his trust even in "princes," temporal or spiritual, but cease entirely from man, trusting in the Lord and leaning not unto his own understanding. Though it was annoying to be pestered thus by these men, Elisha made them a courteous reply, yet one which showed them he was not to be turned away from his purpose: "Yea, I know it, hold ye your peace."

"And Elijah said unto him, Tarry I pray thee here, for the Lord hath sent me to Jordan" (2 Kings 2:6). This he said to prove him, as the Saviour tested the two disciples on the way to Emmaus when He "made as though He would have gone further" (Luke 24:29). Much ground had been traversed since they had set out together from Gilgal. Was Elisha growing tired of the journey or was he prepared to persevere unto the end? How many grow weary of well-doing and fail to reap because they faint. How many fail at this point of testing and drop out when Providence appears to afford them a favourable opportunity of so doing. Elisha might have pleaded: I may be of some service here to the young Prophets, but of what use can I be to Elijah at the Jordan? Philip was being greatly used of God in Samaria (Acts 8:12) when the angel of the Lord bade him arise and go south "unto Gaza, which is *desert*" (v. 26). And he arose and went, and God honoured his obedience. And Elisha said to his master, "I will not leave thee," no, not at the eleventh hour—and great was his reward.

Sixth, the testing of his *character.* "And it came to pass, when they were gone over (the Jordan) that Elijah said unto Elisha, Ask what I shall do for thee, before I be taken away from thee" (2 Kings 2:9). Here is clear proof that Elijah had been making trial of his companion when he had at the different stopping places bade him, "Tarry here," or remain behind, for certainly he had extended no such an offer as this had he been disobedient and acting in self-will. Clearly the Tishbite was so well-pleased with Elisha's devotion and attendance that he determined to reward him with some parting blessing: "Ask what I shall do for thee." If this was not the most searching of all the tests certainly it was the most revealing. What was his heart really set upon? What did he desire above all else? At first glance it seemed surprising that Elijah should fling open so wide a door and offer to supply anything his successor should ask. But not only had they spent several years together, Elisha's reaction to the other testings convinced him that this faithful soul would ask nothing which was incongruous or which God could not give.

"And Elisha said, let a double portion of thy spirit be upon me." He rose above all fleshly and worldly desires, all that the natural heart would crave, and asked for that which would be most for the glory of God and the good of His people. Elisha sought neither wealth nor honours, worldly power or prestige. What he asked for was that he might receive that which marked him out as Elijah's firstborn, the heir of his official patrimony (Deut. 21:17). It was a noble request. The work to which he was called involved heavy responsibilities and the facing of grave dangers, and for the discharge of his duties he needed to be equipped with *spiritual* power. That is what every servant of God needs above everything else—to be "endued with power from on high." The most splendid faculties, the ablest intellect, the richest acquirements count for nothing unless they are energized by the Holy One. The work of the ministry is such that no man is naturally qualified for it: only God can make any man meet for the same. For that endowment the Apostles waited upon God for ten days. To obtain it Elisha had to successfully endure the previous testings, pass through Jordan and keep his eye fixed steadily upon his master.

Seventh, the testing of his *endowment.* When we ask God for something it is often His way to test our earnestness and importunity by keeping us waiting for it, and then when He grants our request, to put our fidelity to the proof in the *use* we make of the same. If it is faith that is bestowed, circumstances arise which are apt to call into exercise all our doubts and fears. If it is wisdom which is given, situations soon confront us where we are sorely tempted to give way to folly. If it is courage which is imparted, then perils will have to be faced which are calculated to make the stoutest quake. When we receive some spiritual gift, God so orders things that opportunity is afforded for the exercise of it. It was thus with Elisha. A double portion of Elijah's spirit was granted him and the Prophetic mantle of his master fell at his feet. What use would he make of the sane? As this comes before us **next month**, suffice it now to say that he was confronted by the Jordan—he was on the wrong side of it and no longer was there any Elijah to divide asunder its waters!

We turn now from the testings to which Elisha was subjected unto *the course* which he had to take: the spiritual significance of his journey has also to receive its counterpart in the experiences of the servant of Christ. That journey began at *Gilgal* (2 Kings 2:1) and none can work acceptably in the kingdom of God until his soul is acquainted with what that place stands for. It was the first stopping-place of Israel after they entered Canaan, and where they were required to tarry ere they set out on the conquest of their inheritance (Josh. 5:9). It was there that all the males who had been born in the wilderness were circumcised. Now "circumcision" speaks of separation from the world, consecration to God, and the knife's application to the flesh. Figuratively it stood for the cutting off of the old life, the rolling away of "the reproach of Egypt." There is a circumcision "of the heart" (Rom. 2:29) and it is that which is the distinguishing mark of God's spiritual children as circumcision of the flesh had identified His earthly people. Gilgal then, is where the path of God's servant must necessarily begin: not until he unsparingly mortifies the flesh, separates from the world and consecrates himself unreservedly to God is he prepared to journey further.

From Gilgal Elisha passed on to "Bethel" which means "the house of God." As we have seen, it was originally the place of hallowed memories, but in the course of time it had been grievously defiled. Bethel had been horribly polluted, for it was there that Jeroboam set up one of his golden calves, appointed an idolatrous priesthood and led the people into terrible sin (1 Kings 12:28, 33; Amos 3:3-5). Elisha must visit this place so that he might be suitably affected with the dishonour done unto the Lord. History has repeated itself. The House of God, the professing Church, is defiled and the servant of Christ must take to heart the apostate condition of Christendom today if his ministry is to be effective. From Bethel they proceeded to Jericho: a place that was under God's curse (Josh. 6:26; 1 Kings 16:34). The servant of God needs to enter deeply into the solemn fact that this world is under the curse of a holy God. And what is that "curse"? Death (Rom. 6:23), and it is of that the Jordan (the final stopping-place) speaks. That, too, must be passed through in the experience of his soul if the minister is to be effectual.—A.W.P.

DOCTRINE OF SAINTS' PERSEVERANCE.
7. *Its Perversion.*

Nowhere is the depravity of man and the enmity of their minds against God more terribly displayed than in the treatment which His Holy Word receives at their hands. By many it is criminally neglected, by others it is wickedly wrested and made to teach the most horrible heresies. To slight such a revelation, to despise such an inestimable treasure, is an insult which the Most High will certainly avenge. To corrupt the sacred Scriptures, to force from them a meaning the opposite of what they bear, to handle them deceitfully by picking and choosing from their contents is a crime of fearful magnitude. Yet this, in varying measure, is what all the false cults of Christendom are guilty of. Unitarians, Universalists and those who teach the unconsciousness of the soul between death and resurrection and the annihilation of the wicked, single out certain snippets of Scripture but ignore or explain away anything which makes against them. A very high percentage of the errors propagated by the pulpit are nothing more or less than Truth itself, but the Truth distorted and perverted.

Broadly speaking the doctrine which we have been expounding in this series has been perverted by two main classes. First, by open Arminians, who expressly repudiate most of what has been advanced in the preceding articles. With them we are not here directly concerned. Second, by what we can only designate "mongrel Calvinists." This class deny the sovereign and unconditional election of God and also the limited or particular redemption of Christ. They are one with Arminians in believing that election is based on God' foreknowledge of those who would believe the Gospel, and they affirm Christ atoned for the sins of all of Adam's race, and yet they term themselves "Calvinists" because they hold the eternal security of the saints, or "once in grace, always in grace." In their crude and ill-balanced presentation of this doctrine they woefully pervert the Truth and do incalculable damage unto those who give ear to them. As they do not all proceed along exactly the same line to distort the Truth at the same particular point, we will divide this branch of our subject so as to cover as many errors as possible.

1. It is perverted by those who affirm mere professors with what pertains only to the regenerate. Here is a young man who attends a service at church where a "special evangelistic campaign" is being held. He is not seriously inclined, in fact rarely enters a place of worship, but is visiting only now to please a friend. The evangelist makes a fervent emotional appeal and many are induced to "go forward" and be prayed for—our young man among them—again to please his friend. He is persuaded to "become a Christian" by signing a "decision card." And then he is congratulated on the "manly step" he has taken. He is duly "received into the church," and at once given a class of boys in the "Sunday School." He is conscious there has been no change within and though somewhat puzzled supposes the preacher and church-members know more about the matter than he does. *They* regard him as a Christian and assure him he is now safe for eternity.

Here is another young man who is passing a "Gospel Hall" on a Lord's Day evening; attracted by the hearty singing, he enters. The speaker expatiates at length on John 3:16 and similar passages. He declares with much vigour that God loves everybody and points out in proof thereof that He gave His Son to die for the sins of all mankind. The unsaved are urged to believe this and are told that the only thing which can now send them to Hell is their unbelief. As soon as the service is over the speaker makes for our young man and asks him if he is saved. Upon receiving a negative reply, he asks, "Would you like to be, here and now?" Acts 16:31 is read to him and he is asked, "Will you believe?" If he says yes, John 5:24 is quoted to him and he is told that he is now eternally secure. He is welcomed into the homes of these new friends, frequents their meetings and is addressed as "Brother."

The above are far more than imaginary cases: we have come into personal contact with many from both classes. And what was the sequel? In the great majority of instances the tide of emotion and enthusiasm soon subsided, the novelty quickly wore off, attending "Bible readings" soon palled, and the dog returned to its vomit and the sow to her wallowing in the mire. They were then regarded as "backsliders" and perhaps told, "The Lord will bring you back again into the fold." And some of these man-made converts are foolish enough to believe their deceivers and assured that "once saved, saved forever." They go on their worldly way with no trepidation as to the ultimate outcome. They have been fatally deceived. And what of their deceivers? They are guilty of perverting the Truth, they have cast pearls before swine, they have taken the children's bread and thrown it to the dogs. They gave to empty professors what pertained only to the regenerate.

2. It is perverted by those who fail to insist upon *credible evidences of regeneration,* as is the case with the above examples. The burden of proof always rests upon the one who affirms. When a person claims that he is a Christian, that claim does not make him one, and if he is mistaken, it certainly is not kindness on my part to confirm him in a delusion. A church is weakened spiritually in proportion to the number of its unregenerate members. Regeneration is a *supernatural* work of *grace* and therefore it is a great insult to the Holy Spirit to imagine that there is not a radical difference between one who has been miraculously quickened by Him and one who is dead in trespasses and sins— between one who is indwelt by Him and one in whom Satan is working (Eph. 2:2). Not until we see clear evidence that a supernatural work of grace has been wrought in a soul are we justified in regarding him as a brother in Christ. The tree is known by the fruit it bears: good fruit must be manifested on its branches ere we can identify it as a good tree.

We will not enter into a laboured attempt to describe at length the principal birthmarks of a Christian. Instead we will mention some things which, if they are absent, indicate that "the root of the matter" (Job 19:28) is not in the person. One who regards sin lightly, who thinks nothing of breaking a promise, who is careless in the performance of temporal duties, who gives no sign of a tender conscience which is exercised over what are commonly called "trifles," lacks the one thing needful. A person who is vain and self-important, who pushes to the fore seeking the notice of others, who parades his fancied knowledge and attainments, has not learned of Him who is "meek and lowly in heart." One who is hyper-sensitive, who is deeply hurt if someone slights them, who resents a word of reproof no matter how kindly spoken, betrays the lack of a humble and teachable spirit. One who frets over disappointments, murmurs each time his will is crossed and rebels against the dispensations of Providence exhibits a will which has not been Divinely subdued.

That a person belongs to some "evangelical church" or "assembly" and is regular in his attendance there, is no proof that he is a member of the Church which is Christ's (mystical) body. That a person goes about with a Bible in his hand is no guaranty that the Divine Law is within his heart. Though he may talk freely and fluently about spiritual things, of what worth is it if they do not regulate his daily walk? One who is dishonest in business, undutiful in the home, thoughtless of others, censorious and unmerciful, has no title to be regarded as a new creature in Christ Jesus, no matter how saintly his pose be on the Sabbath Day. When the Pharisees and Sadducees came to Christ's forerunner to be baptized of him, he said, "Bring forth therefore fruits meet for repentance" (Matt. 3:8): I must first see some signs of godly sorrow for sin, some manifestations of a change of heart, some tokens of a transformed life. So we must demand the evidences of regeneration before we are justified in crediting a Christian profession, otherwise we endorse what is false and bolster up one in his self-deceit.

3. It is perverted by those who sever the cause from its *necessary effect.* The cause of the believer's perseverance is one and indivisible, for it is Divine and nothing whatever of the creature is mingled with it; yet to our apprehension, at least, it appears as a compound one and we may view its component parts separately. The unchanging love, the immutable purpose, the Everlasting Covenant and the invincible power of God are conjoint elements in making the saint infallibly secure. But each of those

elements is active and brings forth fruit after its own kind. God's love is not confined to the Divine bosom but is "shed abroad" in the hearts of His people by the Holy Spirit (Rom. 5:5), from whence it flows forth again unto its Giver: "we love Him because He first loved us" (1 John 4:19). Our love is indeed feeble and fluctuating, yet it *exists,* and cannot be quenched, so that we can say with Peter, "Thou knowest that I love Thee." "I know My sheep and (though imperfectly) am known of Mine" (John 10:14) shows the response made.

The preacher who has much to say upon the love of God and little or nothing about the believer's love to Him is partial and fails in his duty. How can I ascertain that I am an object of God's love but by discovering the manifest effects of His love being shed abroad in my heart? "If any man *love God* the same is known of God" (1 Cor. 8:3). "All things work together for good to *them that love God,* to them who are the called according to His purpose (Rom. 8:28). It is by their love for Him they give proof they are the subject of His effectual call. And how is genuine love for God to be identified? First, *by its eminency:* God is loved above all others so as He has no rival in the soul: "whom have I in heaven but Thee, and there is none upon earth that I desire beside Thee" (Psa. 73:25). All things give way to His love: "Because Thy lovingkindness is better than life, my lips shall praise Thee" (Psa 63:3). The real Christian is content to do and suffer anything rather than lose God's favour, for that is his all.

Second, true love for God may be recognized *by its component parts.* Repentance is a mourning love, because of the wrongs done its Beloved and the loss accruing to ourselves. Faith is a receptive love, thankfully accepting Christ and all His benefits. Obedience is a pleasing love, seeking to honour and glorify the One who has set His heart upon me. Filial fear is a restraining love which prevents me offending Him whom I esteem above all others. Hope is love expecting, anticipating the time when there shall be nothing to come between my soul and Him. Communion is love finding satisfaction in its Object. All true piety is the expression and outflow of love to God and those who bear His image. Hungering and thirsting after righteousness is love desiring more of God and His holiness. Joy is the exuberance of love, delighting itself in its all-sufficient portion. Patience is love waiting for God to make good His promise, moving us to endure the trials of the way until He comes to our relief. Love "beareth all things, believeth all things, hopeth all things, endureth all things" (1 Cor. 13:7).

Third, real love for God expresses itself in *obedience.* Where there is genuine love for God it will be our chief concern to please Him and fulfill His will. "He that hath My commandments and keepeth them, he it is that loveth Me" (John 14:21). "This is the love of God, that we keep His commandments" (1 John 5:3). Inasmuch as it is the love of an inferior to a superior it must show itself in a respectful subjection, in the performance of duty. God returns love with love: "I love them that love Me" (Prov. 8:17 and cf. John 14:21). "A Christian is rewarded as a lover rather than as a servant: not as doing work, but as doing work out of love" (Manton). If we love God we shall do His bidding, promote His interests, seek His glory. And this not sporadically but uniformly and constantly; not in being devout at certain set times and the observance of the Lord's Supper, but respecting His authority in all the details of our daily lives. Only thus does love perform its function and fulfill its design: "whoso keepeth His Word, in him verily is the love of God perfected (attains its proper goal): hereby know we that we *are* in Him" (1 John 2:5).

From what has been pointed out in the last three paragraphs it is clear that those who dwell upon the love of God for His people to the virtual exclusion of their love for Him do pervert the truth of the security of the saints, as the individual who persuades himself that he is the object of God's love without producing the fruit of his love for Him is treading on very dangerous ground. This divorcing of the necessary effect from its cause might be demonstrated just as conclusively of the other elements or parts, but because we entered into so much detail with the first we will barely state the other three. The immutability of God's purpose to conduct His elect to Heaven must not be considered as a thing apart; the means have been predestinated as much as the end, and they who despise the means perish. The very term "covenant" signifies a compact entered into by two or more persons, wherein terms are prescribed and rewards promised: nowhere has God promised covenant blessings to those who comply not with covenant stipulations. Nor have I any warrant to believe the saving power of God is working in me unless I am expressly proving the sufficiency of His grace.

4. It is perverted by those who *lose the balance of Truth* between Divine preservation and Christian perseverance. We may think it vastly more honouring unto God to write or say ten times as much about His sovereignty as we do upon man's responsibility, but that is only a vain attempt to be wise above what is written, and therefore is to display our own presumption and folly. We may attempt to excuse our failure by declaring it is a difficult matter to present the Divine supremacy and human accountability in their due proportions, but with the Word of God in our hands it will avail us nothing. The business of God's servant is not only to contend earnestly for the Faith but to set forth the Truth in its Scriptural proportions. Far more error consists in misrepresenting and distorting the Truth than in expressly repudiating it. Professing Christians are not deceived by an avowed infidel or atheist, but are taken in by men who quote and requote certain portions of Holy Writ, and are silent upon all the passages which clash with their lop-sided views.

Just as we may dwell so much upon the Deity of Christ as to lose sight of the reality of His humanity so we may become so occupied with God's keeping of His people as to overlook those verses where the Christian is bidden to keep himself. The incarnation in nowise changed or modified the fact that Christ was none other than Immanuel tabernacling among men, that "God was manifest in flesh," nevertheless we read, "Wherefore in all things it behooved Him to be made like unto His brethren" (Heb. 2:17), and again, "Jesus increased in wisdom and stature and in favour with God and man" (Luke 2:52). The theanthrophic person or the Mediator is grossly caricatured if either His Godhead or manhood be omitted from consideration. Whatever difficulty it may involve to our finite minds, whatever mystery which transcends our grasp, we must hold fast to the fact that the Child born, the Son given, was "the mighty God" (Isa. 9:6); nor must we suffer the truth of God's garrisoning of His people to crowd out the necessity of their discharging their responsibility.

It is perfectly true there is a danger in the other side and that we need to be on our guard against erring in the opposite direction. Some have done so. There are those who consider the humanity of Christ could not be true humanity in the real sense of that word, arguing that His temptation was nothing more than a meaningless show unless

He was capable of yielding to Satan's attacks. One error leads to another. If the last Adam met the Devil on the same plane as did the first Adam, simply as a sinless man and if His victory (as well as all His wondrous works) is to be attributed solely to the power of the Holy Spirit, then it follows that the exercise of His divine prerogatives and attributes were entirely suspended during the years of His humiliation. Hence we find that those who hold this fantastic view endorse the "kenosis" theory interpreting the "made Himself of no reputation" of Philippians 2:7 as the temporary setting aside of His omniscience and omnipotence.

Contending for Christian perseverance no more warrants the repudiation of Divine preservation than insisting on the true manhood of Christ justifies the impugning of His Godhood. Both must be held fast: on the one hand reasoning must be bridled by refusing to go one step further than Scripture goes. On the other hand faith must be freely exercised, receiving all that God has revealed thereon. That which is central in Philippians 2:5-7 is the position Christ entered and the character in which He appeared. He who was "in the form of God" and deemed it not robbery "to be equal with God" took upon Him "the form of a servant" and was "made in the likeness of men." He laid aside the robes of His incomprehensible glory, divested Himself of His incommunicable honours, and assumed the mediatorial office instead of continuing to act as the universal Sovereign. He descended into the sphere of servitude, yet without the slightest injury to His Godhead. There was voluntary abnegation of the exercise of full dominion and sovereignty, though He still remained "The Lord of Glory" (1 Cor. 2:8). He "became obedient unto death" but He did not become either feeble or fallible. He was and is both perfect man and "the mighty God."

As the Person of the God-man Mediator is falsified if either His Godhead or manhood be denied, or perverted if either be practically ignored, so it is with the security of the saints when either their Divine preservation or their own perseverance is repudiated, or perverted if either be emphasized to the virtual exclusion of the other. Both must be maintained in their due proportions. Scripture designates our Saviour "the true God" (1 John 5:20), yet it also speaks of Him as "the man Christ Jesus" (1 Tim. 2:5). Again and again He is denominated "the Son of Man," yet Thomas owned Him as "my Lord and my God." So, too, the Psalmist affirmed, "He will not suffer thy foot to be moved: He that keepeth thee, will not slumber...The LORD shall preserve thee from all evil: He shall preserve thy soul. The LORD shall preserve thy going out and thy coming in from this time forth and for evermore" (121:3, 7, 8); nevertheless, He also declared, "By the Word of Thy lips I *have* kept me from the paths of the destroyer" (17:4), and again, "I have kept the ways of the Lord...I have kept *myself* from mine iniquity (18:21, 23). Jude exhorts believers, "keep yourselves in the love of God," and then speaks of Him, "that is able to keep you from falling" (21:24). The one complements, and not contradicts, the other.—A.W.P.

AN HONEST HEART.

If there is one thing more than another which we seek to keep in mind while preparing articles for these pages it is the need for and importance of preserving the *balance* of Truth, for we have long been convinced that untold harm has been done to souls through failure at this point. If the preacher gives a disproportionate place in his ministry to the Divine Law, relegating the Gospel to the background, not only are his hearers in danger of forming a one-sided concept of the Divine character but the Christian is deprived of that which is most needed for the establishing and growth of his faith in Christ. On the other hand if the Divine Law be virtually shelved so that its strictness, its breadth and its spirituality are not made known, light thoughts upon sin and superficial views of the holiness of God will be the inevitable result. Both the Law and the Gospel must be expounded and enforced if souls are to be acquainted with God as "light" (1 John 1:5) and as "love," and if they are to render unto Him that which is His due.

In like manner there needs to be proportionate attention paid to both doctrinal and practical teaching, the one relating to instruction and the other concerning deportment. It is an essential part of the pulpit's office to open up the foundational truths of the Christian Faith, for only thus will souls be fortified against error. It is ignorance of the Truth which causes so many to fall easy victims to Satan's lies. Such doctrines as the Divine Inspiration of the Scriptures, the Holy Trinity, the Sovereignty of God, the Fall of man, the Everlasting Covenant, the Person and Office of the Mediator, the design and nature of the Atonement, the Person and Work of the Holy Spirit, the Justification and Sanctification of the believer must be systematically taught if the minister would discharge his duty. Yet he must not confine himself to doctrine: they who feed on rich food and then take little or no exercise become sickly and useless—true alike naturally and spiritually. Faith must produce works if it be worth anything. Well-nurtured branches of the vine are for fruitfulness and not ornamentation. Christians are to "adorn the doctrine of God" (Titus 2:10) by a daily walk which glorifies Him and is a blessing to their fellows.

Once more—if the balance is to be preserved the preacher must see to it that he is careful to maintain a due proportion between the objective and subjective sides of the Truth. He fails miserably in the discharge of his duty if he neglects to probe the professor and search the conscience of his hearers. He needs to remind them frequently that God requires Truth "in the *inward* parts" (Psa. 51:6), that His Law must be written "upon the heart" (Heb. 8:10) if it is to exert any effectual power in the life. He is required to call his hearers to "examine yourselves whether ye be in the faith" (2 Cor. 13:5)—yea urge them to pray with David, "Search me, O God, and know my heart; try me and know my ways" (Psa. 139:23). Multitudes of professing Christians mistake an intellectual assent to the letter of Scripture for a saving faith, and most of what they hear in so-called evangelical circles is only calculated to bolster them up in a false hope. He who is faithful in dealing with souls will frequently remind his hearers of Christ's statement, "Not everyone that saith unto Me, Lord, Lord, shall enter into the kingdom of Heaven: but he that *doeth* the will of My Father which is in Heaven" (Matt. 7:21).

But the preacher needs to be much on his guard lest he overdoes what is termed "experimental preaching." If he virtually confines himself to the lines specified in the preceding paragraph his hearers will become too introspective, too busily engaged in looking within, and instead of their assurance being strengthened, genuine Christians will be filled with doubts and questions about their state. To counteract that tendency the objective side of the Truth must also be emphasized. Christ in all the wonders and glories of His peerless Person, in the perfections of His mediatorial office, in the sufficiency of His atoning work, must be held up to view, so that the hearts of His redeemed may be drawn out to Him in faith, in love, in worship. They must be encouraged to "look unto Jesus" (Heb. 12:2) and "consider the Apostle and High Priest of their profession" (Heb. 3:1), for only thus will they be furnished with both incentives and strength to run the race that is set before them.

What has been pointed out above applies as much to the editor of a magazine as to the occupant of the pulpit. He must beware of being a "hobbyist"—always harping upon a favourite theme. Side by side with pressing the precepts of Scripture he must dwell upon the exceeding great and precious promises of God. Messages of exhortation must be balanced by messages of consolation. Articles which rebuke and lay low need to be followed by subjects which comfort the mourner and lift up the soul in praise to God. If on the one hand we read that the Lamb is to be eaten with "bitter herbs" (Exo. 12:8), right after we are told of the "tree" being cast into the bitter waters of Marah so that they were made sweet (Exo. 15:25). If the Word of God be likened to a "hammer" which breaks in pieces the hard heart (Jer. 23:29) and a sword to pierce even to "the dividing asunder of soul and spirit" (Heb. 4:12)—we also find it being compared with "honey and the honeycomb" (Psa. 19:10). He who is wise will observe these things and seek grace to be regulated accordingly.

At present we are engaged with a particularly searching portion of the Sermon on the Mount, and one design we have in dwelling upon it in such detail is the testing and exposing of formal professors. It is therefore expedient that we should accompany these articles with a message that is intended to help (under God's blessing) those of the unestablished saints who are liable to draw a false conclusion therefrom. If empty professors are ready to greedily devour that Bread which is the peculiar portion of God's little ones, it is also true that not a few regenerate souls are prone to appropriate unto themselves that which applies only to hypocrites. If on the one side there are unregenerate people who firmly believe themselves to be real Christians, on the other side there are genuinely renewed souls who greatly fear they are not Christians at all— they who now conclude the profession of faith made by them, sincerely, in the past, was based on a delusion, and that after all they have been deceiving themselves and others—that they are hypocrites.

It is indeed a fearful thing for a soul to be living in "a fool's paradise," persuading one's self all is well while in reality the wrath of God abides on him. But is it anything less tragic (even though less dangerous) for a child of God to live in "the slough of despond," passing sentence of Divine condemnation upon himself when in fact God has blotted out his transgressions? Why allow Satan to rob me of all rest of soul when peace and joy are my birthright and legitimate portion? Perhaps, the reader replies, because I cannot help myself, the Enemy is too powerful for me. But my friend, Satan obtains his hold *by lies*, and his hold is broken as soon as we meet him with the Truth. He succeeds in seducing men into sinful acts by promising them pleasure and profit therefrom; but the child of God meets his evil suggestions by reminding himself that if he sows to the flesh he must of the flesh reap corruption. In the light of what God says are the fearful and certain consequences of sin, the lie of Satan is exposed and rendered powerless. Once you have good and solid reason to believe a work of grace has been wrought within you, pay no attention to the doubts which Satan seeks to cast thereon.

But something much graver and more grievous is involved than an act of folly when a child of God accredits Satan's lie that he is but a deceived soul and hypocrite: he dishonours and insults *the Holy Spirit! A* genuine Christian would be horrified at giving place to the delusion that the redemption of Christ is imperfect and inadequate, that His atoning blood is not sufficient to cleanse from sin, that it must be plussed with something from the creature. And ought he not to be equally horrified at calling into question the reality and efficacy of the Spirit's work in regeneration, supposing it is not to be credited unless it is regularly confirmed by certain feelings of which we are the subjects? Is it any less a sin to deny or even doubt the work of the Holy Spirit than it is to deny or doubt the sufficiency of the finished work of Christ? Are we as diligent in seeking to guard against the one as much as the other? It is much to be feared that few even among the saints regard these sins as being equally grave. Ah, my reader, it is a vile thing for me to affirm that I am unregenerate if there is clear proof—obtainable by comparing myself with God's unerring Word—that the blessed Spirit of God has quickened me into newness of life. Plain warning against this enormity has not been sufficiently given by the pulpit.

What is meant, it may be asked, by the "clear proof" which God's Word presents to the renewed of their regeneration? That is a most important question, for ignorance thereon or a mistaken conception of the nature of that proof has kept many a quickened soul from enjoying that spiritual peace and assurance to which he was justly entitled. Unless I know what are the principal features of a born-again soul, how can I compare or contrast myself with them? If I form my own idea of what it is which fundamentally and experimentally distinguishes a Christian from a non-Christian, or if I derive my concept from the ideas and confessions of fellow mortals instead of allowing it to be molded by the teaching of Holy Writ, then I am certain to err. How many, for example, suppose that regeneration consists of a radical change of the old nature, a transforming of the flesh into the beauty of holiness—and then because they discover there is still a sink of iniquity within and sin now rages even more fiercely than it did formerly, draw the conclusion that most certainly no miracle of grace has been wrought within them?

Now in the parable of the Sower, the first recorded one of Christ's, we find what should be of great comfort to the fearing and trembling ones of the flock, for if they will carefully compare themselves with the different characters which are depicted in that parable, they ought to be able to perceive *which of them* portrays their *own* case and describes their own condition, and thus ascertaining which company they really belong. But in order to this there must be a genuine and frank looking of facts in the face. On the one hand, there must be no undue eagerness to believe the best of themselves, refusing to recognize their own features if the mirror of the Word reflects them as ugly ones. And on the other hand there must be no stubborn determination to go on believing the worst of themselves, declining to identify their picture even when it is drawn by the heavenly Artist, simply because it depicts their countenance as made comely by the operations of Divine grace. Mock humility and feigned modesty are as much a sin as pride and presumption. David was not boasting when he said, "How love I Thy Law," nor was Paul when he said, "I have fought a good fight." Each spoke the truth, but gave God the glory for his experience.

In the parable of the Sower our Lord sets before us the reception which the preaching of God's Word meets with. He likens the world to a field, which He divides into four parts according to the different kinds of its ground or soil. In His interpretation of the parable Christ explained those different soils as representing various classes of those who hear the Word. They may be termed the hard-hearted, the hollow-hearted, the half-hearted, and the honest-hearted. The importance of this particular parable appears in the fact that it is recorded by Matthew, Mark and Luke, and all three narratives should be carefully compared in order to obtain the complete pictures set forth. In this parable Christ is speaking not from the standpoint of the Divine counsels, for there can be no failure there—but from that of human accountability. What we have here is the Word of the Kingdom addressed to man's responsibility, the effect it has on him, his response thereto, and the reasons why the outcome is unfruitfulness or fruitfulness.

The first class are the wayside hearers. In eastern countries the public highway often runs right through the centre of a field, and because of the traffic constantly passing over it is beaten down, packed, and becomes hard and unyielding. Such is the heart of all those who are given up to the commerce, the pleasures and fashions of this world. They may from various motives attend the house of prayer, but the preaching of the Word has no effect upon them: they are unresponsive thereto. They do not go there seeking a blessing and their souls are unaffected by what they hear. They do not cry unto God, "that which I see not teach Thou me" (Job 34:32), for they are not concerned for His glory or their own eternal welfare. They have no real personal interest in spiritual things and are quite unimpressed by the most solemn representations and unmoved by the most winsome appeals. Their bodies are in the pews but their minds are elsewhere, their thoughts are upon the things that perish, their affections set on things below. They are not there to worship God and are glad when the service is over.

Now let us notice the two things which are said of this class. First, "when anyone heareth the Word of the kingdom, and understandeth it not" (Matt. 13:19). How could the message have any effect upon him when he failed to grasp its purport? And how could he expect to enter into its meaning when his attention was not concentrated thereon, when his interest was elsewhere? He has none but himself to blame. If he prays not for light, whose fault is it that he remains in darkness!? Second, "then cometh the Wicked One and catcheth away that which was sown in his heart." Where there has been no meditation upon the Word heard or read, no understanding thereof, and so, no impression made upon the heart, it is an easy matter for the great Enemy of God and man to catch away the good Seed or crowd out of the mind that which obtained a superficial entrance, so that there will not even be serious reflection thereon. Now my reader, are you prepared to solemnly and definitely affirm that you have no understanding of the Word of God, that it is entirely to you as if written in an unknown tongue, that Satan has so caught it away it has no place in your thoughts?

The second-class are the stony-ground hearers. The type of ground referred to here is that where the bed or base is of rock yet with a thin layer of earth over it. Into this shallow soil the seed is received but the result is most superficial and evanescent. It cannot be otherwise, for as our Lord points out, "they had no deepness of earth, and when the sun was up they were scorched, and because they had no root they withered away." Those who belong to this class are what may be termed the emotional type. They are very impressionable, easily moved, quickly stirred. Yet it is all on the surface. They make good resolutions and quickly break them. They hear the Gospel and are carried away by the eloquence of the preacher and leap into Christ as it were in a moment, and profess an instantaneous faith in Him. Their faces are radiant and their joy is exuberant. They are the ones who come "forward" at Revival meetings and rush into church membership, but their future history is most disappointing.

Let us take note of the three things said of this class. First, "the same is he which heareth the Word and anon (instantly) with joy receiveth it." The emotions have been stirred, but the conscience has not been searched. There was no awe of soul in realizing Who it is with whom we have to do, no heart-rending horrors of the sinfulness of sin, no alarm at the wrath to come—no-thing but a sudden, yet transient, joy. Second, "yet hath he no root in himself." It was only a surface effect, a mere passing sentiment. There has been no plowing up of the soul, no Law-work producing deep and lasting convictions. Third, "but dureth for a while: for when tribulation or persecution ariseth because of the Word, by and by he is offended" (Matt. 13:20, 21). Their "goodness is as a morning cloud and as the early dew that goeth away" (Hosea 6:4) The scoffs of the ungodly, the cold shoulder from old friends prove too much for them, and the churches know them no more. Now my reader, test yourself at this point: has your experience stood the test of time or have you abandoned your profession and returned to your wallowing in the mire?

The third class are the thorny-ground hearers. The type of ground here referred to is where the soil seems to be more fertile and favourable, for it is neither so beaten down as to have an impenetrable surface nor so shallow that there is no room for root. But it is inimical to a desirable crop, for weeds and thistles, thorns and briars choke and crowd out the good seed so that an harvest is prevented. This is admittedly the most difficult class to diagnose. The seed has taken root and a shoot springs up and promises well, but it is surrounded by hostile weeds. However, it survives and puts forth an ear, but it is so festooned with briars that the sunshine cannot reach it—its life is choked, and it comes to nothing. They who belong to this class attempt to serve two masters. They are very pious on the Lord's Day, but thoroughly impious on the other days. They sing the songs of Zion, are members of a church, but make no serious attempt to regulate their daily lives by the precepts of Holy Writ.

Let us take note of Christ's interpretation of the thorns. In Matthew 13:22 they are defined as "the cares of this world and the deceitfulness of riches." The one who has made a Christian profession is young. He has a growing family, his position in this world is not yet secured and therefore he cannot be expected to be out and out for the Lord. Once he "makes good in life" he will have more leisure for spiritual things and more to give to the cause of Christ. Meanwhile temporal anxieties weigh him down. Suppose he "makes good"—does the Lord *now* have the first place in his affections and thoughts? Far from it—riches are deceitful and cumber their possessor. He feels he must live in accord with his improved position, do more entertaining, send his children to college. Mark 4:19 adds "the lust of other things entering in"—perhaps he aspires to civic office or membership in Parliament, and how can he spirituality thrive in politics! Luke 8-14 gives "the pleasures of this life." These are the thorns which choke so many, and they "bring no fruit to perfection" or completion. Would you say, my readers, that the "thorns" have so choked the Word of God in you that you have brought no fruit to completion?

The fourth class are the good-ground hearers. This is soil which not only receives the seed and has depth to give it root, but where it springs up, bears fruit and actually brings forth a goodly yield, so that the husbandman is well-rewarded for his labours.

Let us take careful note then of what is here predicated of the good-ground hearer. First, it is, "he that heareth the Word and *understandeth it.*" He has taken pains so to do. He has "searched the Scriptures daily" (Acts 17:11) to ascertain whether or not the things to which he has listened are really according to the Divine Oracles, for he feels there is far too much at stake to take any man's say-so for it. Mark 4:20 adds, "and *receive* it." He has prayerfully pondered what he has heard and personally appropriates it as God's message to his own soul. However unpalatable to the flesh, however searching and humbling, he refuses it not. Luke 8:15 adds "and *keep* it and bring forth fruit *with patience.*" He holds fast the Word because it is treasured up in his heart as his most cherished possession, and though he is much discouraged by the slowness of his growth he perseveres in crying to God for the increase.

But there is one word said concerning this fourth class which we wish to particularly observe: they are the ones who receive the Word "In an *honest* and good heart." This is the only time in the parable that our Lord defines the kind of heart which received the Word. It is here we have disclosed the decisive factor, that which fundamentally distinguishes those belonging to the fourth class from all the others. Thus it is of prime importance we should seek to ascertain exactly what is connoted by "an honest and good heart" (Luke 8:15), and diligently search ourselves whether or not we possess such. Clearly the terms used here by Christ are in designed contrast from Jeremiah 17:9—"the heart is deceitful above all things and desperately wicked," which describes that which every descendant of Adam is born with. "An honest and good heart" then is not the natural heart, but one which Divine grace has imparted.—A. W. P.

(continued from back page)

In like manner we must learn to distinguish between God when we perceive the dual relationship of Christ to the Father: as the Son and as God-man Mediator. The perfect accord of the two passages is evident when we perceive the dual relationship of Christ to the Father: as the Son and as God-man. In like manner we must learn to distinguish between God speaking as absolute sovereign and as the Enforcer of human responsibility—as the One who deals with men according to their condition.

Now in the verses at the beginning of this article there is not even an apparent difficulty: men must read into it what is not there before they encounter a stumbling stone. The Lord does *not* affirm therein that He is represented by "the potter" (vv. 5-10 are considered in our next), and if we suppose He *is*, then we shall be rightly confounded. Jeremiah was sent to a "potter's house" that he might receive instruction from what he saw. While there he witnessed a vessel of clay "marred" in the hand of the potter. Most assuredly that cannot picture man's fall, for his Creator pronounced him "very good" when he left His hands. Nor can it picture the experience of any since the Fall, for the hand of God is the place of safety and not of injury. Further, we are told this potter "made it (the marred vessel) again another vessel." But God never mends what man has marred, but displaces with something altogether *new:* the old covenant was set aside for the New (Heb. 8:8), the old creation for a New (2 Cor. 5:17), the present Heaven and earth by a New (Isa. 65:17). Rather is the "as seemed good to the potter to make it" the particular similitude fastened upon (v. 6).—A.W.P.

(continued from front page)

did He in Heaven and in the earth, in the seas and all deep places" (Psa 135:6). "This is the purpose that is purposed upon the whole earth, and this is the hand that is stretched out upon all the nations. For the LORD of hosts hath purposed, and who shall disannul? and His hand is stretched out, and who shall turn it back?" (Isa. 14:26, 27). "I am God, and there is none like Me, declaring the end from the beginning and from ancient times the things that are not yet done, saying, My counsel *shall* stand and I will do *all* My pleasure" (Isa. 46:9, 10).

But are there not other passages which speak of God in quite another strain? Suppose such be the case, then what? Why, would these not oblige us to modify our conception of the absoluteness of God's supremacy as predicated in the verses cited above? Certainly not. The Holy Scriptures are not a "nose of wax" (as Papists have wickedly affirmed) which man may twist as he pleases. They are the inspired Word of God, without flaw or contradiction; yet we need wisdom from the Holy Spirit if we are to *interpret* them aright. "God is Spirit" (John 4:24), incorporeal, and therefore "invisible" (Col. 1:15), "whom no man hath seen nor can see" (1 Tim. 6:16). Must we, forsooth, modify this representation of His ineffable Being because we read of His "eyes" (2 Chron. 16:9), His "hands" (Psa. 95:5) and "feet" (Exo. 24:10)? "He that keepeth Israel shall neither slumber nor sleep" (Psa. 121:4): is that negated by the statement, "Then the Lord awaked as one out of sleep" (Psa. 78:65), or because He represents Himself as "rising up early" (Jer. 7:13)?

When Scripture affirms that God's "dominion is an everlasting dominion, and His kingdom is from generation to generation: And all the inhabitants of the earth are reputed as nothing: and He doeth according to His will in the army of Heaven, and among the inhabitants of the earth: and *none* can stay His hand" (Dan. 4:34,35), are we obliged to place limitations upon such supremacy when we hear Him saying elsewhere, "I have called, and ye refused; I have stretched out My hand, and no man regarded; but ye have set at nought all My counsel, and would none of My reproof" (Prov. 1:24, 25)? Of course not. Then how are we to avoid such an expediency? By distinguishing between things that differ: by discriminating between God's secret will and His revealed will, between His eternal decree and the rule which He has given us to walk by. The latter passage speaks of men scorning the Word of God, which it is their responsibility to obey. The former passage affirms the sovereign supremacy of God over all, whose eternal purpose is accomplished in and by men, not because of their willing compliance but in spite of their enmity and rebellion—as was the case with Pharaoh.

Settle it in your mind once and for all, my reader, that the true and living God is King of kings and Lord of lords, the Almighty, whom neither man nor devil can defeat or successfully resist—for such is the plain and positive teaching of His word. The churches may no longer proclaim such a God. The vast majority of those who still pose as His people may no longer believe in such an One, but that alters not the fact that He *is so*: "Let God be true and every man a liar" (Rom. 3:4). Settle it in your mind likewise that Holy Writ cannot contradict itself, and therefore if the meaning of some passages are not clear to you, humbly look to their Author to enlighten you—for the obscurity is in your mind and not in His Word. When Christ affirmed, "I and My Father are one" (John 10:30), He spake according to His absolute Deity. But when He declared, "My Father is greater than I" (John 14:28), He spake as the God-man Mediator. The perfect accord of the two passages is evident man

. *(continued on proceeding page)*

VOL. XXII.   APRIL, 1943.   NO. 4

STUDIES IN THE SCRIPTURES

" Search the Scriptures." John 5:39.

Publisher and Editor—ARTHUR W. PINK,
27 Lewis Street,
Stornoway, Isle of Lewis,
Scotland.

IN THE POTTER'S HOUSE.

"Then the word of the LORD came to me, saying, O house of Israel, cannot I do with you as this potter? saith the LORD. Behold, as the clay is in the potter's hand, so are ye in Mine hand, O house of Israel. At what instant I shall speak concerning a nation, and concerning a kingdom, to pluck up, and to pull down, and to destroy it; if that nation, against whom I have pronounced, turn from their evil, I will repent of the evil that I thought to do unto them. And at what instant I shall speak concerning a nation, and concerning a kingdom, to build and to plant it; if it do evil in My sight, that it obey not My voice, then I will repent of the good, wherewith I said I would benefit them" (Jer. 18:5-10).

A superficial reading of those verses may suggest they contain that which supports the Arminian's conception of God, yet a more careful pondering should show there is nothing whatever in them which militates against the "immutability of His counsel" (Heb. 6:17). The Lord does not here say to Israel "ye have become marred in My hand"—ye have defeated My purpose concerning you," nor does He declare, "I will repair and make another vessel of you"—revise My intention and try again. Rather does He affirm His sovereignty and supremacy over them: "as the clay is in the potter's hand so are ye in Mine hand." Again, it is to be carefully noted that God is not here speaking of the spiritual and eternal destiny of individuals, but of the earthly and temporal fortunes and misfortunes of kingdoms (Jer. 18:7) In this passage the Most High is viewed as the Governor of the nations, as the Dispenser or Withholder of eternal blessings, and not as the Predestinator of His Church to everlasting glory. God deals with kingdoms on a very different footing from what He does His dear children, and unless that be clearly recognized we shall be without the master-key which opens scores of passages

The favour which the Lord shows unto a nation is an altogether different thing from the love which He bears unto His elect, and he who is blind to such a distinction is utterly unqualified to expound Holy Writ. God's favour unto a nation is merely the outward dispensing of good things, which favour is forfeited when they turn their backs upon Him. But His love for the elect is an eternal and unchanging purpose of grace which effectually works in them, ceasing not to do them good and securing their everlasting felicity with regard to the former. He may pluck up and pull down what His

IMPORTANT NOTICES

Please advise promptly of change in address, otherwise copies will be lost in the mails.

We are glad to send a sample copy to any of your friends whom you believe would be interested in this publication.

This magazine is published as "a work of faith and labour of love," the editor and his wife gladly giving their services free. There is no regular subscription price, as we do not wish the poor of the flock to be deprived. This does not mean that those looking for something for nothing may "help themselves." Those getting this Magazine, who are financially able and who receive spiritual help from its pages, are expected to gladly contribute towards its expenses; otherwise, their names are dropped from our lists.

Will those forwarding International Money Orders please have them made out to us at Stornoway, Isle of Lewis, Scotland. Checks (Cheques-Eng.) made out on U.S.A. Banks are not negotiable here, so please do not send them.

CONTENTS

THE SERMON ON THE MOUNT.

26. *Profession Tested*: Matthew 7:21-27.

"Not everyone that saith unto me, Lord, Lord, shall enter into the kingdom of Heaven; but he that doeth the will of my Father which is in Heaven" (Matt. 7:21). With these words of our Lord commenced the twelfth and final division of this notable Sermon. It was perhaps the most searching and solemn section in it. Here the One who cannot be imposed upon by any deceit makes known His inexorable demand for reality. Here the One who shall yet officiate as the Judge of all the earth declares that at the Grand Assize all who have deceived themselves and deluded others will stand forth in their real characters. Here the One who knows every thought and imagination of the heart, before whose omniscient eye all things are naked and opened, makes it crystal clear that lip service is worthless and that even the most imposing deeds count for nothing where vital and practical godliness are lacking. The more this passage be thoughtfully pondered the less surprised are we that so many seek to get rid of this Sermon by terming it "Jewish" and insisting "it is not for this dispensation."

If it be true that Matthew 5-7 is more hated by our moderns than any other portion of God's Word, it is equally true that none is more urgently needed by them. Never were there so many millions of nominal Christians on earth as there are today, and never was there such a small percentage of real ones. Not since before the days of Luther and Calvin, when the great Reformation effected such a grand change for the better, has Christendom been so crowded with those who have "a form of godliness" but who are strangers to its transforming power. We seriously doubt whether there has ever been a time in the history of this Christian era when there were such multitudes of deceived souls within the churches who verily believe that all is well with their souls when in fact the wrath of God abideth on them. And we know of no single thing better calculated to undeceive them than a full and faithful exposition of the closing verses of our Lord's Sermon on the Mount.

The relation of this passage to the context is easily determined. Taking the more remote one, this final section forms a fitting conclusion to the whole address, which be it remembered was delivered in the hearing of the multitude (5:1; 7:28), though more immediately to His "disciples." It was a most suitable climax. Christ had commenced by delineating the character of those who are approved of God, and He finished by describing those upon whom eternal judgment will fall. Herein we may see how the chief of the Apostles patterned his ministry after the example of his Master. If on the one hand "love" constrained him, on the other hand it was by "the terror of the Lord," that he sought to persuade men. Thus, when standing before Felix, "he reasoned of righteousness, temperance and judgment" so that the governor "trembled" (Acts 24:25). Alas, how little of this faithful dealing with souls is there in this degenerate day—how little probing of the conscience—how little plain speaking of the awful doom awaiting the ungodly! How little shaking them out of their fatal complacency!

If we look at the more immediate context we shall be increasingly impressed with the appropriateness of this solemn peroration. Our Lord had just uttered a warning against the false prophets who are to be recognized by the "fruits" which they bear, or in other words, by the "converts" which they make—the disciples they draw after them. It is the Antinomian beguiled who are there more especially in view, as is clear from our Lord's words "who come to you in sheep's clothing," thereby concealing their real character. In like manner their adherents assume a sanctimonious pose and employ the most pious language, carrying a Bible with them wherever they go and being able to quote it freely. They refer to the Redeemer in most reverent terms, being particular to accord Him His title of "Lord." Nevertheless, when weighed in the balances they are found wanting, for they are lacking in vital godliness. Their hearts are not renewed, their wills are not surrendered to God, their conduct corresponds not with their high pretensions.

It is the juxtaposition of Matthew 7:19 and 7:20 which enables us to clearly perceive the scope of the latter. Though the Saviour had said in verse 16, "Ye shall know them by their fruits," He repeats this identifying mark of these deceivers of souls in verse 19, and then immediately adds, "Not everyone that saith unto Me, Lord, Lord, shall enter into the kingdom." The intimate connection, then, between these two sections of His address is too plain to miss—converts made by the false prophets are big talkers but little doers. They claim to be devoutly attached to Christ but their claim is invalid, being unsupported by the evidence which is necessary to give it credibility. The fine talk is not corroborated by a Christian walk, and therefore it is insufficient to obtain for them an entrance into His kingdom. If the blind follow the blind both fall into the ditch. It takes something more than "sheep's clothing" to make one a servant of Christ, and something more than lip service needed before He will own anyone as a true disciple of His. It is empty and windy professors whom He here exposes.

"Not everyone that saith unto Me, Lord, Lord, shall enter into the kingdom of Heaven: but he that doeth the will of My Father which is in Heaven." Let us consider first the application of these words to those who were immediately addressed. Many of the Jews were so impressed by the miracles wrought by Christ that they were disposed to be His disciples while ignorant of, and in fact, strongly opposed to His doctrine concerning salvation and the requirements of the kingdom of God. "Now when He was in Jerusalem at the Passover, in the feast day, many believed in His name, when they saw the miracles which He did. But Jesus did not commit Himself unto them" (John 2:23, 24). Nicodemus expressed the attitude of some of the more influential when he said, "Rabbi, we know that Thou art a teacher come from God, for no man can do these miracles that Thou doest except God be with him" (John 3:2). But so far from allowing Nicodemus to entertain the idea that an acknowledgement of Him as a "Teacher sent from God" would secure for him the blessings He came to bestow, He told him frankly that except he were born again he could neither see nor enter the kingdom of God.

When Christ had fed the great multitude from the five loaves and two small fishes, so deeply were they impressed that we are told: "Then those men, when they had seen the miracle that Jesus did, said, This is of a truth that Prophet that should come into the world." Yet, "when Jesus therefore perceived that they would come and take Him by force, to make Him a king, He departed again into a mountain Himself apart alone" (John 6:14, 15). This it was which directly occasioned the searching declaration of the section which is now before us. Very far was He from taking advantage of a temporary and superficial bias of men in His favour. Plain speaking and honest dealings characterized the whole of His transactions with His countrymen. It was to prevent them from imagining that their owning Him as Prophet or even acknowledging Him as the Messiah in the sense that they understood the term was sufficient, that He here pressed upon His hearers they must be actually and personally *doers* of God's will before they were qualified to participate in the blessings of His spiritual and eternal kingdom.

While the verses before us were addressed first and locally to the Jews of Christ's day, yet it is obvious that they have a far wider application—that they belong to the Gentiles of our day. As we have proceeded through this Sermon section by section, we have endeavoured to point out again and again and make clear the force and relevance of our Lord's words as they respected His immediate hearers and also their pertinence unto and bearing upon ourselves. There was nothing provincial or evanescent in the teaching of Christ: it was designed for all nations and for all generations, and by it all men will yet be judged (John 12:48). This declaration of Christ's, then, is full of important instruction to all in every country and every age, wherever the Gospel is presented to the examination and reception of men. It was true at the beginning, it is just as true today, and it will continue so as long as the world lasts, that some, yea, many, will go no further than a mere lip profession, and consequently will be excluded from the kingdom—and that only those who really perform the Divine will shall enter into the enjoyment of the blessings of Christianity.

This expression, "the kingdom of Heaven," need not detain us very long, for we have explained its meaning in previous articles. As it is employed here it is synonymous with "the kingdom of God" in John 3:3, as a comparison of Matthew 18:3 and Luke 18:17 clearly proves. It had reference to the new order of things introduced by the Messiah, being a contrast from and the successor of Judaism. That new order of things may be contemplated as beginning in this present life and perfected in the life to come, they being two aspects of the one economy. We designate the former the kingdom of grace and the latter the kingdom of glory. Most of the older commentators understood "the kingdom of Heaven" in the verse now before us as referring to the second aspect, and therefore as being equivalent to the state of celestial blessedness, but personally we see no reason for this restriction. A mere lip profession fails to secure even a present participation in the peculiar privileges of Christianity, for it obtains neither reconciliation with God, the forgiveness of sin, nor an enjoyment of that holy happiness which is the portion now of those truly converted. It inevitably follows that those who enter not the kingdom of grace on earth will never enter the kingdom of glory in Heaven.

"Not every one that saith unto Me, Lord, Lord, shall enter into the kingdom of Heaven" or as we find it in Luke 6:46, "Why call you Me, Lord, Lord?" This expression is equivalent to acknowledging Christ as "Teacher and Master," even owning Him as the Son of God, the alone Saviour of sinners. There is a designed emphasis in the "Lord, Lord," for it is meant to express not merely profession, but a decided, open, habitual profession. Thus Christ here declares that a merely verbal acknowledgment of the truth concerning His Person or a lip profession that we are His disciples and prepared to accept His teaching—however explicit, public, and often repeated that profession is made—does not open the way to the enjoyment of the special blessings of His kingdom—unless it is proved to be the result of true repentance and sound conversion and unless it is accompanied with a corresponding course of conduct in doing the will of the Father. An outward profession of the most orthodox religion is useless if it be joined not with vital godliness and sincere obedience. Even the demons owned Him as the "Son of God" (Matt. 8:29), but what did it avail them!?

It scarcely needs to he pointed out that no entrance into the kingdom of God is possible unless Christ is owned as "Lord." Unitarians and those "Modernists" who deny that Christ is anything more than the ideal Man, are certainly outside the pale of salvation. "The words before us obviously imply what is very distinctly stated in other parts of Scripture, that a profession of discipleship, and acknowledgment of our submission in mind and heart to Christ Jesus, is absolutely necessary in order to our enjoying the privileges of discipleship. No person who does not call Christ 'Lord, Lord' can enter into the kingdom of God: no man who is ignorant of His claims, who treats these claims with neglect, who rejects these claims, or who, though he may be all but persuaded that these claims are just, yet from worldly motives does not acknowledge them—no such person can participate in the peculiar blessings of His disciples, either on earth or in Heaven" (John Brown, to whom we are indebted for some things above and in what follows). "Ye call Me Master and Lord, and ye say well, for so I am" (John 13:13). "Whosoever transgresseth and abideth not in the doctrine of Christ, hath not God" (2 John 1:9).

But while the necessity of owning Christ as Lord is clearly implied in His words here, the truth which they more directly teach is that profession however necessary in connection with faith and obedience cannot of itself secure a participation in the spiritual blessings of the new economy. No matt how loudly a man avows his acceptance of the teachings of Christ, unless he be a *doer* of the Word his avowals count for nothing. He who requires the heart will not be put off with shadows for the substance, the mere semblance for the reality, words instead of works. Empty compliments are not worth the breath which utters them. They who trust in a form of godliness which is devoid of its power are building their hopes upon a foundation of sand. Not only is a bare profession insufficient for the saving of the soul, but it is an insult to Christ Himself. It is a horrible mockery to call Him Lord while we continue to do only that which is pleasing to ourselves, to profess to obey Him while we treat His commands with contempt. It is *obedience* which marks men as His disciples and distinguishes them from the subjects of Satan.

Let us now describe the different types of professors. First, there are those who are simply *nominal* ones. They bear the name of "Christians" and that is all. They happen to have been born in a country where Christianity is the prevailing religion and where it is regarded as a mark of respectability to give some recognition and assent to it. A few drops of water were sprinkled upon them in infancy by a preacher and possibly they received some kind of instruction in the rudiments of religion during the days of their childhood. But after reaching maturity, except for an occasional visit to a church, probably at "Christmas" or "Easter" that is as far as they go. Yet if asked to declare themselves they readily affirm they are "Christians," but that means little or nothing more than that they are not Jews, pagans or open infidels. Such persons usually are grossly ignorant of the very fundamentals of the Faith and often the lives of respectable heathens would put theirs to shame. Surely such people are outside the kingdom of God. They cannot participate in its blessings either on earth or in Heaven—if they could, its blessings would not he spiritual ones.

Second, *formal* professors. This class is made up of those who regard themselves as much in advance of the ones in the former. They are able to repeat some catechism, or at least can give a fairly intelligent account of both the doctrine and the laws of Christ. If not members of a church they are at least "adherents" and regular attendees at its services. They claim to be submissive to Christ's authority and observe all the outward acts of worship which characterize His follower, but they know nothing of the blessedness of communion with the Lord nor is His joy their strength. Their religion is but a mental assent to an orthodox creed and going through a round of external observances. They evince no desire for the Truth to have a dominating power over their affections and wills, and most of them regard as deluded enthusiasts and canting hypocrites those who regard experimental godliness as the only genuine Christianity, and who pant after a deeper acquaintance with God. It is plain that these, too, are outside the kingdom, being strangers to those operations of the Spirit which alone make us meet for it.

Third, *deceived* professors. "There is a generation that are pure in their own eyes, and yet is not washed from their filthiness" (Prov. 31:12). Those in this class look with pharisaical pity upon these described above. These deem themselves better taught. They place no reliance upon infant sprinkling, no subscription to the soundest confession of faith, rather do they pride themselves upon an intellectual assent to the letter of Holy Writ. They are quite sure that Christ died for them and that they have accepted Him as their personal Saviour. None can shake their assurance. Yet meekness and lowliness characterize them not. Forbearing one another and forgiving one another they are strangers to the fruit of the Spirit and practical godliness is missing from their daily lives. Their associates address them as "Brother" or "Sister" and that suffices. But what does it profit me to have the reputation of being a wealthy man if I have not the wherewithal to purchase the necessities of life? What avails it to call me a healthy person if disease be eating away my very vitals? If Christ bars the door of the kingdom against me, no personal assistance will give me entrance.

Fourth, *hypocritical* professors. The number in this class we are fain to believe is much smaller than in the preceding ones. For the former there is some hope while life lasts, but for these we can see none. Hypocritical professors are those who deliberately assume a role—they are consciously playing a part. They know that they are not Christians, but for one reason or other are anxious to make their fellows believe they are so. Some of them belonged formerly to one of the other groups, of the third especially, then they discovered the emptiness of their profession or that they had been deceived. They are too dishonest to disclaim themselves as Christians so they take increased pains to persuade others of their piety. Not content with a dull formal round of duties, they put the appearance of a deep interest in the things of God and of zeal in seeking to promote His cause. This is incomparably the vilest of the four classes we have sketched. Such conduct is no less contemptible than irrational. God cannot be imposed upon and no affronts are likely to be more severely punished than dishonour done to His omniscience. The hypocrite's portion will be the "outer darkness" where there is wailing and gnashing of teeth.

Fifth, the *genuine* professor. This is the real Christian, who enjoys the blessings of the kingdom of grace here and shall be admitted to the bliss of the kingdom of glory hereafter. He is described here according to his conduct and actions: "but he that doeth the will of My Father which is in Heaven." Two points need determining: what is here signified by the Father's will? And what is meant by the doing of it? "The fundamental part of doing the will of God is revealed in these words: 'This is My beloved Son in whom I am well pleased, hear ye Him' (Matt. 17:5). Where this is complied with, everything else follows" (J. Brown). The will of the Father is perfectly made known by the incarnate Word, for He is the final spokesman of God (Heb. 1:1, 2), all judgment being committed unto Him (John 5:22). The will of the Father is that we should forsake our sins, trust in His Son, take His yoke upon us, and follow Him; to do less and yet call Him our Lord is most horrible mockery. So perfect and intimate is the oneness of the Father and the Son that Christ goes on to say, "Whosoever heareth these sayings of *Mine* and doeth them" is like one who builds his house upon a rock" (Matt. 7:24 and cf. Luke 6:48).

What is meant by doing the Divine Will? Obviously it does not connote a perfect or flawless performance thereof, for there is no Christian who has ever attained to such excellence in this life, though nothing short of this is the standard set before us (Matt. 5:48). It means that I have surrendered my heart and will to the claims of Christ, so that I truly desire Him to "reign over me" (Luke 19:14) and order my life. It means that I have subjected myself to His authority and that it is the prevailing bent of my mind and constant endeavour to please and honour Him in all things. It means that I genuinely aim to be both internally and externally conformed to His holy image, and that it is my greatest grief when I do those things which displease Him. It means I truly seek that my thoughts, affections and actions are regulated by His precepts. It is not a sinless obedience which is here in view, but it is a sincere one. It is not a forced one, but prompted by love. It is not merely an external compliance with the Divine commands but a "doing the will of God from the heart" (Eph. 6:6).—A. W. P.

THE MISSION AND MIRACLES OF ELISHA.

1. *First Miracle.*

The relation between Elijah and Elisha was that of master (2 Kings 2:16) and servant (2 Kings 3:11), and thus it set forth that which exists between Christ and His ministers. For some time Elijah himself occupied the stage of action, but upon the completion of his mission and after a miraculous passage through Jordan he was supernaturally removed to Heaven. Thus it was with the One whom he foreshadowed: when the Saviour had finished the work given Him to do and had risen in triumph from the grave, He ascended on high. But men were appointed by Him to serve as ambassadors in the world from which He departed, to act in His name and perpetuate His mission. So it was with His type. Elisha was to succeed Elijah and carry forward what he had inaugurated. In order thereto he had been called by him. We saw last month how Elisha was subjected to a series of tests, which shadowed forth the disciplinary experiences by which the servant of Christ approves himself and through which he is schooled for his life's work. Then we viewed the path which Elisha was required to tread and pointed out briefly the spiritual significance thereof in connection with the preparatory history of the minister of the Gospel. One other preliminary feature remains for our consideration, namely, *the enduement* Elisha received.

It will be remembered that when Elijah had put to his companion that searching question, "Ask what I shall do for thee, before I be taken away from thee," Elisha had replied, "I pray thee, let a double portion of thy spirit be upon me." This, we believe, betokened three things. First, it revealed his modesty and humility, being an acknowledgment of his weakness and insufficiency. He was conscious of his unfitness for his mission and felt that nothing but a plentiful supply of the Spirit which had rested upon the Tishbite would avail for the tasks confronting him. Happy the young servant of Christ who is aware of his own impotency, for in felt weakness lies his strength. Happy the one who has experimentally learned the force of that word, "Not by might, nor by power, but by My Spirit saith the Lord" (Zech. 4:6). Second, if Elisha was to take Elijah's place at the head of the schools of the Prophets, then he needed a superior endowment to theirs—a double supply of the Spirit of wisdom and power. Third, as the accredited servant of God he needed more than the rank and file of His people: not only the Spirit indwelling, but also the Spirit resting upon him.

We have only to turn to the final discourse of our Lord unto His Apostles, recorded in John 14-16, to discover the part which the Holy Spirit must play if His servants are to be duly equipped for their work. First, He declared he would pray the Father that another Comforter should be given them, who would abide with them forever (14:16). Then He promised this blessed Comforter, sent in His name, would teach them all things (15:26). It was by means of the Spirit of Truth given unto them that they would be enabled to bear testimony unto their Master (15:26, 27). He would guide them into all Truth, show them things to come, and glorify Christ by a fuller revelation to them of the mystery of His Person, office and work (16:13-15). In the book of Acts we see how those promises were made good. They were already *indwelt* by the Spirit of life (John 20:22) but the "power of the Holy Spirit was to come *upon* them" (Acts 1:8). This took place on the day of Pentecost, when "there appeared unto them cloven tongues like as of fire and it sat upon each of them. And they (the Apostles—1:26) were all filled with the Holy Spirit" (2:4, 5).

This, then, is the deep need of the servant of Christ: that he be endowed by the Spirit, for without such an anointing his labours can only prove ineffectual. It was thus that Christ Himself was furnished: Matthew 3:16; Acts 2:38, and the disciple is not greater than his Lord. Much has been said and written on this subject of the minister being endowed and empowered by the Holy Spirit and varied, indeed, are the directions given as to what must be done in order to enter into this blessing. Personally we have long been convinced that the position occupied by the Apostles was an entirely unique one, and therefore we are certainly not warranted in praying and looking for any supernatural enduement such as they received. On the other hand we must be careful of going to an opposite extreme and concluding there is no special and distinct anointing by the Spirit which the servants of God need today. Elisha shows otherwise, for his case is, we believe, a typical and representative one.

Taking it for granted, then, that most of our readers will concur in the last remarks, we proceed to the important question—What is required of the minister if he is to enjoy a double portion of the Spirit? In answering this inquiry we will restrict ourselves to what is recorded of Elisha. In his case there were two things: first, the passage through Jordan, for it is to be duly noted that Elijah did not ask him, "what shall I do for thee," until they had gone through its divided waters! Now the Jordan stands for death (Jer. 12:5), and death must be experimentally passed through before we can know the power of resurrection. The minister has to *die to self,* to all self-pleasing and self-seeking before the Spirit of God will use him. Second, the Prophet had to keep his eye fixed steadily upon his master if his desire was to be realized (2 Kings 2:10). It is all summed up in those words of Paul, "not I, but Christ" (Gal. 2:20). Just in proportion as self is set aside and the magnifying of Christ be our aim and goal of my ministry, is Holy Spirit likely to use me.

"And it came to pass as they still went on and talked that behold, there appeared a chariot of fire and horses of fire and parted them asunder; and Elijah went up by a whirlwind to Heaven, and Elisha saw it" (2 Kings 2:11, 12). Of course he did—God never disappoints those who renounce self and are occupied solely with Christ. Elijah had made the granting of Elisha's request upon this very thing: "if thou *seest me* when I am taken from thee it shall be so unto thee." Additional incentive, then, had the young Prophet to keep his gaze steadfastly on his master. Those who follow on to know the Lord, will press forward in the race set before them. They will suffer nothing to turn them aside from fully following Christ. They are given to behold things which are hidden not only from the world but also from their half-hearted brethren. A view of the unseen is ever the reward which God grants unto faith and fidelity. It was so with Abraham (John 8:56), with Moses (Heb. 11:27), with Stephen (Acts 7:55), with John (Rev. 1:1).

But something more than spiritual vision was granted unto Elisha, namely, spiritual perception—he not only saw, but *understood* the significance of what he beheld. "And Elisha saw, and he cried, My father! my father! the chariot of Israel and the horsemen thereof!" (2 Kings 2:12). Only as we ponder carefully the words of that sentence will the force of it be apparent. He did say, "the chariot of *fire,*" nor even, "the chariot of *God,*" but "the chariot *Israel.*" What did he mean? And why preface that explanation with the "My father! my father!"? He was interpreting for us the wondrous vision before him, the supernatural phenomenon described in the preceding verse. There was a Divine suitability in Elijah's being removed from this scene in a chariot of fire driven by horses of fire. No other conveyance could have been more suitable and suggestive, though we have met no writer who appears to have grasped the significance of it. Why did God send a fiery chariot to conduct His servant to Heaven? Let us endeavour to find the answer to that question.

Scripture interprets Scripture and if we turn to other passages where "chariots" and "horses" are mentioned we shall obtain the key which opens to us the meaning of the one here before us. "Some trust in chariots and some in horses, but we will remember the name of the LORD our God" (Psa. 20:7). Good reason had Israel for saying that. Go back to the beginning of their national history. Behold them in their helplessness before the Red Sea as "Pharaoh's horses, his chariots, and his horsemen" (Exo. 14:23) menaced their rear. Ah, but behold the sequel! They are all safe on the other side, singing, "The LORD is a man of war: the LORD is His name. Pharaoh's chariots and his host hath He cast into the sea....the depths have covered them....Thy right hand, O LORD, is become glorious in power: Thy right hand, O LORD, hath dashed in pieces the enemy" (Exo. 15:3-6). The ungodly may look to such things as horses and chariots for protection and prowess, but the saints will find their sufficiency in the name of the Lord their God.

Sad indeed is it to see how woefully the favoured nation of Israel failed at this very point. "They soon forgot His works," yea, they "forgot God their Saviour" (Psa. 106:13, 21) and relied upon the arm of flesh. They even sought alliances with the heathen until one of their Prophets had to cry, "Woe to them that go down to Egypt for help and stay on horses, and trust in chariots, because they are many; and in horsemen, because they are very strong; but they look not unto the Holy One of Israel, neither seek the LORD" (Isa. 31:1). Now set over against this our present passage and is not its meaning clear? As Elisha beheld that awe-inspiring sight his soul perceived the significance thereof: "My father! my father! the chariot of Israel and the horsemen thereof" (2 Kings 2:12). *Thou* my master, hast been in the hand of the Lord, Israel's *real* chariot and horses, their true defense against Jezebel and Baal's prophets which are bent on their destruction. The nation was too carnal, too much given to idolatry to recognize what they were losing in the departure of Elijah. But Elisha realized it was "the chariot of Israel" which was being taken from them.

This brings us then to *the time* when Elisha performed his first miracle. It was what men generally would deem a most unpropitious one, when the Prophet's spirits were at their lowest ebb. His beloved master had just been taken from him and deeply did he feel the loss. "He took hold of his own clothes and rent them in two pieces" (v. 12). That action was emblematic of his grief, as a comparison of Genesis 37:34 and Joshua 7:6 shows. Yet it was a temperate sorrow, a controlled sorrow, and not an inordinate one: he only rent his garment in two pieces—had he done more they would have been wastefully ruined. His action may also have betokened Israel's rejection of Elijah (cf. 1 Sam. 15:26-28). But severe as was his loss and heavy as must have been his heart, Elisha did not sit down in despair and wring his hands with inconsolable dejection—repining over the loss of eminent ministers accomplishes no good to those left behind, but rather enfeebles them. Man's extremity is God's opportunity. The darkest hour of all is the best time to prove His sufficiency. This is what Elisha did now.

Second, consider now *the object* on which it is wrought. A formidable one it was, none less than the river Jordan. He had friends, the Prophets at Jericho, on the other side. The problem was how to come to them. Probably he was unable to swim, or surely he had done so, as miracles are not wrought where there is no urgent need for them. There was no boat to take him over—how then was he to cross it? A very real difficulty confronted him. Let us note that he looked the difficulty squarely in the face: he "went back and stood by the bank of the Jordan" (v. 13), instead of foolishly playing the part of ostrich, which buries its head in the sand when menaced by danger. To close our eyes to difficulties gets us nowhere, nor is anything gained by the under-estimating or belittling of them. The Jordan was a challenge to Elisha's faith. So he regarded it and so he dealt with it. That is why God suffers His servants and saints to be confronted with difficulties: to try them and see of what mettle they are made.

Third, the *instrument* and means for it. "And he took up also the mantle of Elijah that fell from him, and went back and stood by the bank of Jordan" (v. 13). When his master's mantle fluttered to his feet he knew beyond doubt that Heaven had granted his request: not only had he seen Elijah at the moment of his departure, but the gift of his prophetical garment was an additional token of receiving a double portion of his spirit. And now came the test: what use would he make of his master's mantle! Testing always follows the bestowment of a Divine gift. After Solomon had asked the Lord for "an understanding heart" that he might judge His people wisely and well and "discern between good and bad," he was quickly confronted by the two women each claiming the living child as hers (1 Kings 3:9, 16). No sooner did the Spirit of God descend upon Christ than He led Him into the wilderness to be tempted of the Devil. Scarcely had the Apostles been endued with power from on high and begun to speak with other tongues, than they were charged with being "full of new wine." So here: Elijah's mantle fell at his feet, but before Elisha stretched the Jordan!

Fourth, the *mode* of it. This is of deep interest and importance, for it inculcated a truth of the greatest possible moment. "And he took the mantle of Elijah that fell from him and smote the waters" (2 kings 2:14). That was what the mantle had been given to him for: not to be idolized as a venerable memento but to be made practical use of. "Unto him that hath shall more be given" (Luke 8:18), which means unto him that has in reality, who evidences it in improving the same by putting it out to interest. By cleaving so steadfastly to his master, Elisha had already given proof that he was indwelt by the Spirit and now the double portion became his. This, too, he used, and used in the right way—he followed strictly the example his master had left him. In the context we are told, "Elijah took his mantle and wrapped it together and smote the waters" (v. 8). Now his disciple did precisely the same thing. Is not the lesson for us as though it were written with a sunbeam? If the servant of Christ would work miracles, his ministry must be patterned closely after his Master's example.

Fifth, the *meaning* of it. In view of all that had been before us this should now be apparent. As we have sought to show, Elisha is to be regarded as through the piece as the representative servant, as a figure of the ministers of Christ—in their call, their testings, the path they must tread, their spiritual enduement. The miracles he performed are not to be taken as exception to the rule. What then is the meaning and message of this first miracle—the smiting of and dividing asunder the waters of the Jordan? Clearly it is victory over death, *ministerial victory.* The servant of Christ is sent forth to address those who are dead in trespasses and sins. What an undertaking! How is he to prevail over the slaves and subjects of Satan? As Elisha did over the Jordan! He must be Divinely equipped: he must obtain a double portion of the Spirit. By acting as Elijah did: using what has been given him from above. When Elisha smote the waters in the exercise of faith, he said, "Where is the LORD God of Elijah?"—give proof that Thou art with me, too.

Sixth, the *value* of it. "And when he also had smitten the waters they parted hither and thither: and Elisha went over" (2 kings 2:14). There was the proof that though Elijah was not present, the *God* of Elijah was! There was the proof that he had received a double portion of his master's spirit. There was the proof that by using the same means as his master had employed, God was pleased to honour his faith and grant the same result. There was the proof of his power over death. Three times in Scripture do we read of a miraculous crossing of the Jordan—see Joshua 3:17 for the first— typifying, we believe, the victory of Christ over the gave, the deliverance of the Church from spiritual death, and the resurrection of their bodies in the day to come. Here then is how the minister of the Gospel furnishes proof of his calling and commission: by preaching the Word (the appointed means) in the power of the Spirit so that souls are born again. Such fruit is evidence that God is with him, granting him victory over death.

Seventh, the *recognition* of it. "And when the sons of the Prophets which were to view saw him, they said, The spirit of Elijah doth rest on Elisha. And they came to meet him and bowed themselves to the ground before him" (2 Kings 2:15). The miracle they had witnessed convinced them, and they owned him as the successor or representative of Elijah. The parted waters of Jordan demonstrated the presence of the Holy Spirit. So the regeneration of souls make manifest that the servant of God has been endowed with power from on high, and those with spiritual perceptions will own and honour him as such, for faithful ministers are to be "esteemed very highly in love for their work's sake" (1 Thess. 5:13). If Romanists have gone to one extreme in unwarrantably exalting the priesthood and making it a barrier to prevent the individual Christian having direct dealings with God Himself, the democratic spirit of our day has swung so far to the other side as to level all distinctions. Those who have received a double portion of the Spirit are to "be counted worthy of double honour" if they "rule well" (1 Tim. 5:17).—A.W.P.

DOCTRINE OF SAINTS' PERSEVERANCE.

7. *Its Perversion.*

5. It is perverted by those who divorce the purpose of God *from the means* through which it is accomplished. God has purposed the eternal felicity of His people and that purpose is certain of full fruition—nevertheless it is not effected without the use of means on their part, any more than a harvest is obtained and secured apart from human industry and persevering diligence. God has made promise to His saints that "bread shall be given" them and their "water shall be sure" (Isa. 33:16), but that does not exempt them from the discharge of their duty or provide them with an indulgence to take their ease. The Lord gave a plentiful supply of manna from Heaven, but the Israelites had to get up early and gather it each morning, for it melted when the sun shone on it. So His people are now required to *labour for* "that meat which endureth unto everlasting life" (John 6:27). Promises of Divine preservation are not made to sluggards and idlers but those called unto the use of means for the establishing of their souls in the practice of obedience. Those promises are not given to promote idleness but are so many encouragements to the diligent, assurances that sincere endeavours shall have a successful issue.

God has purposed to preserve believers *in holiness* and not in wickedness. His promises are made to those who strive against sin and mourn over it, made to those who take their full thereof and delight therein. If I presume upon God's goodness and count upon His shielding me when I deliberately run into the place of temptation, then

I shall be justly left to reap as I have sown. It is Satan who tempts souls to recklessness and to the perverting of the Dive promises. This is clear from the attack which he made upon the Saviour. When he bade Him cast Himself from the pinnacle of the temple and to rely upon the angels to preserve Him from harm, it was an urging Him to presume upon the end by disdaining the means. Our Lord stopped his mouth by pointing out that, notwithstanding His assurance from God and of His faithfulness concerning the end, yet Scripture requires that the means tending to that end be employed, the neglect of which is a sinful tempting of God. If I deliberately drink deadly poison I have no ground for concluding that prayer will deliver me from its fatal effects.

The Divine preservation of the saints no more renders their own activities, constant care and exertions superfluous than does God's gift of breath make it unnecessary for us to breathe. It is their own preservation in faith and holiness which is the very thing made certain. They themselves, therefore, must live by faith and in the practice of holiness, for they cannot persevere in any other way than by watching and praying. They must carefully avoid the snares of Satan and the seductions of the world, resisting and mortifying the lusts of the flesh, working out their own salvation with fear and trembling. To neglect those duties, to follow a contrary course, is to "draw back unto perdition" and *not* to "believe to the saving of the soul" (Heb. 10:39). He who argues that since his perseverance in faith and holiness is assured he needs exercise no concern about it or trouble to do anything toward it, is not only guilty of a palpable contradiction but gives proof that he is a stranger to regeneration and has neither part nor lot in the matter. "Make me to go in the path of Thy commandments, for therein do I delight" (Psa. 119:35) is the cry of the renewed.

6. It is perverted by those who deny the truth of *Christian responsibility.* In this section we shall turn away from the "mongrel Calvinists" to consider a serious defect on the part of "hyper-Calvinists," or as some prefer to call them, "fatalists." These people not only repudiate the general offer of the Gospel, arguing that it is a virtual denial of man's spiritual impotency to call upon the unregenerate to savingly repent and believe, but they are also woefully rent in exhorting believers unto the performance of Christian duties. Their favorite text is, "without Me ye can do nothing," but they are silent upon, "I can do all things through Christ which strengtheneth me" (Phil. 4:13). They delight to quote the promises wherein God declares, "I will" and "I shall," but they ignore those verses which contain the qualifying "if ye" (John 8:31) and "if we" (Heb. 3:6). They are sound and strong in the truth of God's preservation of His people, but they are weak and unsound on the correlative tone of the saints' perseverance. They say much about the power and operation of the Holy Spirit, but very little on the method He employs or the means and motives He makes use of.

"As many as are led by the Spirit of God they are the sons of God" (Rom. 8:14). He does not compel but inclines: it is not by the use of physical power but by the employment of moral suasion and sweet inducements that He leads, for He deals with the saints not as stocks and stones but as rational entities. "I will instruct thee and teach thee in the way which thou shalt go: I will guide thee with Mine eye" (Psa. 32:8). The meaning of that is more apparent from the contrast presented in the next verse: "Be ye not as the horse (rushing where it should not) or as the mule (stubbornly refusing to go where it should) which have no understanding: whose mouth must be held in with bit and bridle." God does not drive His children like unintelligent animals, but guides by enlightening their minds, directing their inclination, moving their wills. God led Israel across the wilderness by a pillar of cloud by day and a pillar of fire by night: but they had to respond thereto, to *follow* it. So the Good Shepherd goes before His sheep, and they follow Him.

It is true, blessedly true, that God "draws," yet that drawing is not a mechanical one as though we were machines, but a *moral* one in keeping with our nature and constitution. Beautifully is this expressed in Hosea 11:4, "I drew them with cords of a man, with bands of love." Every moral virtue, every spiritual grace, is appealed to and called into action. There is perfect love and gracious care on God's part toward us. There is the intelligence of faith and response of love on our part toward Him—and thereby He keeps us in the way. Blessed and wondrous indeed is the inter-working of Divine grace and the believer's responsibility. All the affections of the new creature are wrought upon by the Holy Spirit. He draws out our love by setting before us God's love: "We love Him, because He first loved us" (1 John 4:19), but we *do* love Him, we are not passive, nor is love inactive. He quickens our desires and revives our assurance, and we "rejoice in hope of the glory of God" (Rom. 5:2). He brings into view "the prize of the high calling" and we "press toward the mark, forgetting those things which are behind and reaching forth unto those things which are before" (Phil. 3:13, 14).

It is very much like a skilled musician and a harp: as his fingers touch its strings they produce melodious sounds. God works in us and produces the beauty of Holiness. But how? By setting before our minds weighty considerations and powerful motives, and causing us to *respond* thereto. By giving us a tender conscience which is sensitive to His still small voice. By appealing to every motive-power in us: fear, desire, love, hatred, hope, ambition. God preserves His saints not as He does the mountain pine which is enabled to withstand the storm without its own concurrence, but by calling into exercise and act the principle that was imparted to them at the new birth. There is the working of Divine grace first, and then the outflow of Christian energy. God works in His people both to will and to do of His good pleasure, and they work out their own salvation with fear and trembling (Phil. 2:12, 13). And it is the office of God's servants to be used as instruments in the hands of the Spirit. It is their task to enforce the responsibility of the saints, to admonish slothfulness, to warn against apostasy, to call unto the use of means and the performance of duty.

If the hyper-Calvinist preacher compares the method he follows with the policy pursued by the Apostles he should quickly perceive the vast difference there is between them. True, the Apostles gave attention to doctrinal instruction, but they also devoted themselves to exhortation and expostulation. True, they magnified the free and sovereign grace of God and were careful to set the crown of glory upon the One to whom alone it belonged, yet they were far from addressing their hearers as so many paralytics or creatures who must lie impotent till the waters be moved. "No," they said, "Let us not sleep, as do others" (1 Thess. 5:6), but "awake to righteousness and sin not" (1 Cor. 15:34). They bade them "run with patience the race that is set before us" (Heb. 12:1) and not sit down and mope and hug their miseries. They called upon them to "resist the Devil" (James 4:7), not take the attitude they were helpless in the matter.

They gave direction, "keep yourselves from idols" (1 John 5:21) and did not at once negate it by adding, "but you are unable to do so." When the Apostle said, "I think it meet, as long as I am in this tabernacle, to *stir you up* by putting you in remembrance" (2 Peter 1:13), he was not usurping the prerogative of the Spirit but was enforcing the responsibility of the saints.

7. It is perverted by those who use the doctrine of justification to crowd out the companion doctrine of sanctification. Though they are inseparably connected, yet they may be and should be considered singly and distinctly. Under the Law, the ablutions and oblations, the washings and sacrifices were together, and justification and sanctification are blessings which must not be disjoined. God never bestows the one without the other, yet we have no means of knowing we have received the former apart from the evidences of the latter. Justification refers to the relative or legal change which takes place in the status of God's people. Sanctification to the real and experimental change which takes place in their state, a change which is begun at the new birth, developed during the course of their earthly pilgrimage and is made perfect in Heaven. The one gives the believer a *title* to Heaven, the other a *meetness* for the inheritance of the saints in light. The former clears him from the guilt of sin, the latter cleanses from sin's defilement. In sanctification something is actually *imparted* to the believer, whereas in justification it is only *imputed*. Justification is based entirely on the work which Christ wrought for His people but sanctification is principally a work wrought in them.

By our Fall in Adam we not only lost the favour of God but also the purity of our nature, and therefore we need to be both reconciled to God and renewed in our inner man, for without personal holiness "no man shall see the Lord" (Heb. 12:14). "As He which hath called you is holy, so be ye holy in all manner of conversation (behaviour); because it is written, Be ye holy for I am holy" (1 Peter 1:15, 16). God's nature is such that unless we be sanctified there can be no intercourse between Him and us. But can persons be sinful and holy at one and the same time? Genuine Christians discover so much carnality, filth and vileness in themselves that they find it almost impossible to be assured they are holy. Nor is this difficulty solved, as in justification, by recognizing that though completely unholy in ourselves we are holy in Christ, for Scripture teaches that those who are sanctified by God are holy *in themselves* though the evil nature has *not been removed* from them.

None but "the pure in heart" will ever "see God" (Matt. 5:8). There must be that renovation of soul whereby our minds, affections and wills are brought into harmony with God. There must be that impartial compliance with the revealed will of God and abstinence from evil which issues from faith and love. There must be that directing of all our actions to the glory of God by Jesus Christ, according to the Gospel. There must be a spirit of holiness working within the believer's heart so as to sanctify his outward actions if they are to be acceptable unto Him in whom "there is no darkness." True, there is perfect holiness in Christ for the believer, but there must also be a holy nature received from Him. There are some who appear to delight in the imputed obedience of Christ who make little or no concern about personal holiness. They have much to say about being arrayed in "the garments of salvation and covered with the robe of righteousness" (Isa. 61:10), who give no evidence that they are "clothed with humility" (1

Peter 5:5) or that they have "put on....bowels of mercies, kindness, humbleness of mind, meekness, longsuffering, forbearing one another and forgiving one another" (Col. 3:12, 13).

How many there are today who suppose that if they have trusted in Christ all is sure to be well with them at the last, even though they are not personally holy. Under the pretence of honouring faith, Satan, as an angel of light, has deceived and is now deceiving multitudes of souls. When their "faith" is examined and tested, what is it worth? Nothing at all so far as insuring an entrance into Heaven is concerned: it is a powerless, lifeless, fruitless thing. The faith of God's elect is unto "the acknowledging of the truth which is after godliness" (Titus 1:1). It is a faith which purifies the heart (Acts 13:9), and it grieves over all impurity. It is a faith which produces an unquestioning obedience (Heb. 11:8). They therefore do but delude themselves who suppose they are daily drawing nearer to Heaven while they are following those courses which lead only to Hell. He who thinks to come to the enjoyment of God without being personally holy, makes God out to be an unholy God, and puts the highest indignity upon Him. The genuineness of saving faith is only proved as it bears the blossoms of experimental godliness and the fruits of true piety.

Sanctification consists of receiving a holy nature from Christ and being indwelt by the Spirit so that the body becomes His temple, setting apart unto God. By the Sprit's giving me vital union with "the Holy One" I am "sanctified in Christ Jesus" (1 Cor. 1:2). Where there is life there is growth, and even when growth ceases there is a development and maturing of what has grown. There is a living principle, a moral quality communicated at the new birth, and under sanctification it is drawn out into action and exercised in living unto God. In regeneration the Spirit imparts saving grace, in sanctification He strengthens and develops it—the one is a *birth*, the other a *growth*. Therein it differs from justification: justification is a single act of grace—sanctification is a continued work of grace. The one is complete, the other *progressive*. Some do not like the term "progressive sanctification" but the thing itself is clearly taught in Scripture. "Every branch that beareth fruit, He purgeth it that *it may bring forth more fruit*" (John 15:2). "I pray that your love may abound yet *more and more* in knowledge and all judgment" (Phil. 1:9). That you "may *grow up into Him* in all things" (Eph. 4:15) is an exhortation thereto.

8. The doctrine of the Saints' perseverance is perverted by those who fail to accord the *example of Christ* its proper place. Few indeed have maintained an even keel on this important matter. If the Socinians have made the exemplary life of Christ to be the whole end of the incarnation, others have so stressed His atoning death as to reduce His model walk to comparative insignificance. While the pulpit must make it clear that the main and chief reason why the Son of God became flesh was in order that He might honour God in rendering to the Law a perfect satisfaction on behalf of His people, yet it should also make equally plain that a prominent design and important end of Christ's incarnation was to set before His people a pattern of holiness for their emulation. Thus declares the Scriptures: "He hath left us an example that we should follow His steps" (1 Peter 2:21), and that example imperatively obligates believers unto its imitation. Though some have unduly pressed the example of Christ upon unbelievers, others have woefully failed to press it on believers. Because it has no place in the justification of a

sinner, it is a serious mistake to suppose it exerts no influence upon the sanctification of a saint.

The very name "Christian" intimates that there is an intimate relation between Christ and the believer. It signifies "an anointed one," that he has been endued with a measure of that Divine unction with his Master received "without measure" (John 3:34). And as Flavel, the Puritan pointed out, "Believers are called 'fellows' or co-partners (Psa. 45:7) of Christ from their participation with Him of the same Spirit. God gives the same spirit unto us which He more plentifully poured out upon Christ. Now where the same Spirit and principle is, there the same fruits and operations must be produced according to the proportions and measures of the Spirit of grace communicated....Its nature also is *assimilating*, and changes those in whom it is, into the same image with Christ, their heavenly Head (2 Cor. 3:18)." Again—believers are denominated "Christians" because they are disciples of Christ (Matt. 28:19 margin, Acts 11:26), that is, learners and followers of His, and therefore it is a misuse of terms to designate a man a "Christian" who is not sincerely endeavouring to mortify and forsake whatever is contrary to His character—to justify his name he must be Christ-like.

Though the perfect life of Christ must not be exalted to the exclusion of His atoning death, neither must it be omitted as the believer's model. It may be true that no attempt to imitate Christ can obtain a sinner's acceptance from God. It is equally true that the emulating of Him is imperatively necessary and absolutely essential in order to the saints' preservation and final salvation. "Every man is bound to the imitation of Christ under penalty of forfeiting his claim to Christ. The necessity of this imitation convincingly appears from the established order of salvation, which is fixed and unaltered. Now conformity to Christ is the established method in which God will bring many souls to glory. 'For whom He did foreknow, He also did predestinate to be conformed to the image of His Son, that He might be the First among many brethren' (Rom. 8:29). The same God who has predestinated men to salvation, has in order thereto, predestinated them unto conformity to Christ, and this order of Heaven is never to be reversed. We may as well think to be saved without Christ, as to be saved without conformity to Christ" (John Flavel).

In Christ God has set before His people that standard of moral excellence at which He requires them to aim and strive after. In His life we beheld glorious representation in our own nature of the walk of obedience which He demands of us. Christ conformed Himself to us by His abasing incarnation. How reasonable, therefore, is it that we should conform ourselves to Him in the way of obedience and sanctification. "Let this mind be in you which was in Christ Jesus" (Phil. 2:5). He came as near to us as was possible for Him to do. How reasonable then is it that we should endeavour to come as near as it is possible for us to do. "Take My yoke upon you, and learn of Me" (Matt. 11:29). "Even Christ pleased not Himself" (Rom. 15:3). How reasonable is it that we should be required to deny ourselves and take up our cross and follow Him (Matt. 16:24), for without so doing we cannot be His disciples (Luke 14:27). If we are to be conformed to Christ in glory how necessary that we first be conformed to Him in holiness: "He that saith he abideth in Him ought himself so to walk even as He walked" (1 John 2:6). "Let everyone that nameth the name of Christ depart from iniquity" (2 Tim. 2:19)—let him either put on the life of Christ or drop the name of Christ.—A.W.P.

AN HONEST HEART.

"But that on the good ground are they, which in an honest and good heart, having heard the Word, keep it, and bring forth fruit with patience" (Luke 8:15). Let it be duly considered that as it is not the falling of the seed into the ground which makes it good, so it is not the Word of God which makes the heart honest. The soil itself must be rich or there will be no satisfactory crop, and the heart itself must first be honest if the Word is to be received and bear fruit. But such a heart no man has by nature—instead it is deceitful above all things and desperately wicked. "By nature we are a lie and in our best estate vanity. The old nature is a lie, a mere falsity, something contrary to that nature God created. It was first introduced by a lie of the Devil (Gen. 3:5) and therefore a fancy that God had lied in His command. Therefore our old nature is no better than a lie, and we cannot serve God with it" (Stephen Charnock, the Puritan). The heart of fallen man is radically and essentially dishonest, feeding on lies, loving deceits, producing hypocricies; and he can no more effect any alteration in it than the Ethiopian can change his skin. Nor does he even desire to do so—he is totally unconscious of its rottenness.

"The preparation (or disposings) of the heart in man....is from the LORD" (Prov. 16:1). It is by the regenerative operations of the Holy Spirit that the heart is made honest. Honesty of heart is the grand distinction between the genuine Christian and all other men. We do not regard it as a separate grace, like purity or humility, but rather is the regulator of all the graces: thus we read of "*unfeigned* faith" (2 Tim. 1:5) and "unfeigned love" (1 Peter 1:22). As holiness is the glory of all the Divine perfections, so honesty is what gives colour and beauty to all the Christian's graces. Holiness is the distinctive glory of the Godhead: as Howe termed it, "an attribute of attributes, casting lustre upon the others." "As God's power is the strength of His perfections, so His holiness is the beauty of them: as all would be weak without almightiness to back them, so all would be uncomely without holiness to adorn them" (Charnock). This it is on a lower plane: without honesty to regulate them, the graces of the Christian would be worthless.

As honesty of heart is that which distinguishes the genuine Christian from all other men, so it is the grand feature which is common to all the children of God, none of them being without it. Different saints are eminent for various graces: Abraham for his faith, Moses for his meekness, Phineas for his zeal, Job for his patience or endurance. But honesty is that which characterizes and regulates all of them, so that to speak of a dishonest Christian is a contradiction in terms. An honest heart is an "upright" heart (Psa. 7:l0): it is a "single" (Col. 3:22) or "undivided" one (Hosea 10:2). An honest heart is a "sound" one (Prov. 14:30), a "true" one (Heb. 10:22). The marks and fruits of an honest heart are candor, genuineness, truthfulness, integrity, righteousness, fidelity, sincerity—in contrast from dissimulation, guile, deceitfulness, pretense, treachery. An honest heart hates all shams. But passing from generalizations let us point out some of the more specific and fundamental workings and manifestations of an honest heart.

1. An honest heart *loves the Truth,* and none other does. "This is condemnation that light is come into the world and men loved darkness rather than light, because their deeds were evil" (John 3:19), and that is true—a description of all men the world over. What a fearful state to be in: not only in the dark, but loving the darkness. And why? Because it is congenial to their depraved hearts, it is their native element. Hence the

passage goes on to say, "for everyone that doeth evil hateth the light, neither cometh to light, lest his deeds should be reproved" (v. 20). Many excuses are made why they turn away from plain and faithful preaching and why they do not read God's Word in private, but the real reason is because they hate the Light—exposure, even to themselves, is the very last thing of all they desire. In sharp contrast therefrom: "But he that doeth truth cometh to the light, that his deeds may be made manifest, that they are wrought in God" (v. 21). This is the man with an honest heart: so far from hating the Light, he welcomes it, wanting to be searched and discovered by it.

An honest heart is open to the Word, not merely to certain portions only, but to the Word as a whole. Such an one sincerely wants the Truth, the whole Truth and nothing but the Truth. He does not wish the preacher to please or flatter him, but to be frank and faithful. The language of the unregenerate is, "Speak unto us smooth things, prophesy deceits" (Isa. 30:10). They desire to hear of an easy and flesh-pleasing road to Heaven, one which does not demand the denying of self and forsaking the world. They want to be at ease in their sins and assured they are the children of God while free to serve the Devil. But it is the very opposite with one having an honest heart. He is fearful of being imposed upon, and thinking more highly of himself than he has a right to do. If he is deceived, he ardently longs to be undeceived; if he is building his house upon sand, he wants to know it. He is willing to be tested and searched, and therefore he "cometh to the Light"—does so repeatedly and continuously, as the tense of the verb denotes.

An honest heart, then, is a Truth-loving heart, one which genuinely desires to know the mind of God, one which is ready for his creed, his character and his conduct to be searched by the light of the Sanctuary. He wants to know the truth about *God*, the One with whom he has to do, the One before whom he must yet appear and render an account. He will not be put off with any superficial and sentimental representations of the Divine Character, he determines at all costs to acquaint himself with God as He actually is. He wants to know the truth about *himself*, whether his soul be only slightly disposed or whether his case be so desperate as to be altogether beyond help. He is anxious to determine whether he has only a head or intellectual knowledge of things that matter most or whether he has been given a heart or spiritual knowledge of them. He wants to make certain of how he stands with regard to God and eternity, and he dare not take any man's opinion or say-so with regard thereto.

2. An honest heart *accepts the Divine diagnosis* of fallen man's condition and bows to the Divine verdict passed upon him. That diagnosis is that which is sinful, depraved, corrupt in every part of his being; that his understanding is darkened, his affections perverted, his will enslaved. The Divine Physician declares that, "from the sole of his foot even unto the head there is *no* soundness in him" (Isa. 1:6). It explains why this is so: because man, every man, is "shapen in iniquity" and "conceived in sin" (Psa. 51:5), and therefore "the wicked are estranged from the womb: they go astray as soon as they be born, speaking lies" (Psa. 58:3). So far from allowing that there is something spiritually good in every man, which only needs to be carefully cultivated in order to bring it to fruition, the Divine Physician declares, the "imagination of man's heart is evil from his youth" (Gen. 8:21), and in the flesh, "there dwelleth no good thing" (Rom. 7:18). And the honest heart quarrels not with that diagnosis, but receives it as true of himself.

Because fallen man is what he is he stands condemned before his Judge. The Divine Law pronounces him guilty. It declares that he is a rebel against God, that he has followed the desires of his own heart and disregarded the claims of his Maker. It declares that there is, "no fear of God" before his eyes (Rom. 3:18), that he has conducted himself as though there is no Day of reckoning to be faced. It declares that he has "set at nought all God's counsel and would none of His reproof" (Prov. 1:25). It declares that "the wrath of God abideth on him" (John 3:36). It declares that, in the searching light of the Divine holiness, his best performances, his religious actings, his very righteousnesses are as "filthy rags" (Isa. 64:6). Now because the *honest* heart welcomes the Light, because it sincerely desires to know the worst about himself, it bows to the Divine verdict and "sets to his seal that God is true" (John 3:33). An honest heart acknowledges, "I am vile" (Job 40:4), "without excuse" (Rom. 1:20), a Hell-deserving sinner; and none but an honest heart sincerely does so.

3. An honest heart causes its possessor to take his place *before God in the dust.* How can it be otherwise if he accepts the Divine diagnosis and condemnation of his condition? As the penitent thief on the Cross acknowledged, "we indeed justly, for we receive the due reward of our deeds" (Luke 23:41), so the one who truly bows to God's verdict owns that the everlasting burnings are his legitimate due. Thus pride receives its death-wound, all pretensions to goodness are repudiated, and with the publican of old he smites upon his breast crying, "God be merciful to me a sinner." Instead of seeking to extenuate his transgressions, he wonders at God's longsufferance toward him. Instead of asking, What have I done to deserve eternal damnation? he marvels that he is not in Hell already. He perceives clearly that if such a wretch as himself is to receive salvation it must be by grace alone, and that God has the full right to withhold such grace if He so pleases.

4. An honest heart *ceases fighting against God,* which is only another way of saying that he repents of his evil past, for true repentance is a taking sides with God against myself. He who loves the Truth is influenced and regulated by it; and therefore is he brought to renounce whatever is opposed to it. As light and darkness are opposites, so uprightness and crookedness, honesty and sin have nothing in common. Where there is an honest heart repentance and conversion necessarily follow. And repentance is not only a sorrowing for sin but also a turning away from it, the throwing down of the weapons of our warfare against God. To love the light is to love God, for He is light (1 John 1:5), and if we love God we shall forsake our sins, abandon our idols and mortify our lusts. An honest soul cannot do otherwise: anything short of that would be hypocrisy. "If we say that we have fellowship with Him and walk in darkness we lie and do not the Truth" (1 John 1:6). The upright man is the one who "feareth God and escheweth evil" (Job 1:8).

5. An honest heart *seeks to please God* in all things and offend Him in none. That is why this honesty is termed "simplicity (the single eye) and godly sincerity" (2 Cor. 1:12), for it desires and seeks the approbation of God above everything else. An honest heart refuses to accept the plaudits of men on anything for which conscience would condemn him. "God is a Spirit and they who worship Him must worship Him in spirit and in truth" (John 4:24). He cannot be imposed upon by pious words or a sanctimonious demeanor. He must be approached with

"a true heart" (Heb. 10:22): all dissimulation and pretense has to be set aside in our dealings with Him who "trieth the heart and the reins" and whose eyes are "a flame of fire." When the heart beats true toward God there is a deep desire to please Him, not in some things only, but in *all* things, so that without reserve it asks, "Lord, what wilt Thou have me to do?" (Acts 9:6). True, that desire is not fully realized in this life, but the genuineness of it is evidenced when we can truly say, "I hate *every* false way" (Psa. 119:104).

6. An honest heart *feigns not wisdom,* but is very conscious of and frankly owns up to great ignorance. Even though he is well acquainted with the letter of Scripture and thoroughly familiar with all the external means of grace, that contents him not: there is a longing for a spiritual, an experimental, an efficacious knowledge of the Truth. Such an one feels himself to be the veriest babe in Divine things, which is indeed a healthy sign, for it is under such the mystery of godliness is revealed (Matt. 11:25). Such an one cries daily, "that which I see not teach Thou me" (Job 34:32), for he longs to know the way of the Lord more perfectly—not only in the letter but chiefly in the power thereof. So conscious is he of his ignorance that he prays with David, "make me to understand the way of Thy precepts" (Psa. 119:27)—how to walk in them, the way to keep them. And again, "Teach me Thy statutes"—observe well how this is repeated again and again (Psa. 119:12, 26, 64, 68, 124, 135), for it is in *this* the upright realize themselves to be more deficient.

7. An honest heart *makes conscience of sin.* Necessarily so if he sincerely desires to please God. Therefore he does not willfully and habitually ally himself in any known sin, against the light and stirrings of conscience, for "the highway of the upright is to depart from evil" (Prov. 16:17). As one of the lesser known Puritans said, "A righteous man hates all sins, even the ones he cannot conquer; and loves all the Truth, even that which he cannot understand" (Anthony Burgess). He makes conscience of what the world calls peccadilloes or trifling faults, praying, "Take us the foxes, the *little* foxes that spoil the vines" (Song. 2:15), yea, "cleanse Thou me from secret faults" (Psa. 19:12)—the sins of ignorance of which I am not conscious, but which defile before the thrice Holy One. Consequently, an honest heart makes it a point of confessing all known sins to God, even those of which his fellows know nothing. Sin is his heaviest burden and greatest grief.

8. An honest heart *welcomes godly reproof.* "Grace will teach a Christian to take those potions which are wholesome, though they be not toothsome" (Geo. Swinnock, 1660). "Rebuke a wise man and he will love thee" (Prov. 9:8), but hypocrites will resent it and fools rage at thee. An honest heart prefers the bitters of gracious company to the dainties of the ungodly: he would rather be smitten by a saint than flattered by the unregenerate. He not only gives a permit to faithful admonition but, when in his right mind, invites to, "*Let* the righteous smite me: it shall be a kindness; and let him reprove me, it shall be an excellent oil, which shall not break my head" (Psa. 141:5). "As oil refreshes and perfumes, so does reproof, when fitly taken, sweetens and renews the heart. My friend must love me well if he tells me my faults: there is an unction about him if he points out my errors" (C. H. Spurgeon) and about me also if I heed him. "Faithful are the wounds of a friend, but the kisses of an enemy are deceitful" (Prov. 27:6)—only the upright will subscribe to that.

9. An honest heart *is impartial.* "Now therefore are we all present before God, to hear *all things* that are commanded thee of God" (Acts 10:33). These words of Cornelius were the language of sincerity. How very rare is such a spirit. The average church-member wishes to hear only that which accord with "*our* doctrines" and when he reads the Bible it is through theologically-tinted glasses. Here is where so many preachers are handicapped: they are bound by a detailed creed and know that if they departed therefrom they would lose their position. Bias, prejudice, sectarian shibboleths quench the spirit of honesty. To desire the Truth for *Truth's* sake is rare indeed. But an honest heart is impartial, refusing to pick and choose and is not swayed by denominational prejudices.

An honest heart values the Divine precepts equally with the promises, appropriates the admonitions and threats as well as the comforting portions of Scripture, acknowledges himself in the wrong and his opponent who has the Truth on his side to be right, and admires and owns the image of Christ when he sees it in one belonging to another company.

10. An honest heart is *chiefly concerned with the inner man.* In His solemn denunciations of the Scribes and Pharisees Christ said, "Woe unto you, Scribes and Pharisees, hypocrites! for ye make clean the outside of the cup and of the platter, but within they are full of extortion and excess...Woe unto you, Scribes and Pharisees, hypocrites! for ye are like unto whited sepulchers, which indeed appear beautiful outward, but are within full of dead men's bones, and of all uncleanness. Even so ye also outwardly appear righteous unto men, but within ye are full of hypocrisy and iniquity" (Matt. 23:25, 27-28). It is at this point especially that the genuine Christian is distinguished from the formal religionists. One with an honest heart makes conscience of wandering thoughts, evil imaginations the workings of unbelief, the risings of pride and rebellion against God. He seeks grace to mortify his lusts and prays to be cleansed from "secret faults." He cries daily, "Create in me a clean heart, O God, and renew a right spirit within me" (Psa. 51:10); "Unite my heart to fear Thy name" (Psa. 86:11); "Incline my heart unto Thy testimonies and not to covetousness" (Psa. 119:36). He makes much of *heart work* and endeavours to keep it with all diligence (Prov. 4:23).

Probably most of our readers are ready to exclaim, Alas, this quite cuts me off: I freely admit that such honesty of heart as has been described ought to be found in me, but to my shame and sorrow I must confess that much to the contrary is still operative in my soul. But cannot you see that is the last thing you world frankly own if you were dishonest?! The fact is that no soul is conscious of the workings of unbelief until God has *given* faith, is not troubled about the swellings of pride until humility is *bestowed*, mourns not over coldness until love is *communicated*, and is not exercised over deceitfulness before he is *made* sincere. We best learn to know things by their opposites. It would be a great mistake to insist that there is such a thing as perfect and unmixed honesty in this life, so that there is no guile or falsehood joined with it. We not only know in part, but our faith and love are weak and unstable, and honesty of heart has to contend with much that is opposed to it. If we can plead before God uprightness of intentions and if we grieve over all crookedness within us, that is sure proof we are no longer under the dominion of hypocrisy.

There are two distinct and mutually-hostile principles at work within the Christian, each bringing forth after its own kind, and it is by *what* each one brings forth that its presence may be ascertained. The "works of the flesh" are manifest (Gal. 5:19, etc.), but "the fruit of the Spirit" (v. 22, etc.) is equally identifiable. A detailed description of "the fruit of the Spirit" should not be understood to mean that "the flesh" has ceased to exist. And a portrayal of the workings of an honest heart must not be taken to signify that all which is contrary thereto has been expelled. David was an upright man, yet he found it needful to pray, "Remove from me the way of lying" (Psa. 119:29). The disciples of Christ had been given honest hearts, yet their Master deemed it requisite to bid them, "be not as the hypocrites" (Matt. 6:5). It is the regenerate who are exhorted, "wherefore laying aside all malice, and all guile and all hypocrisies" (1 Peter 2:1), which would obviously be quite meaningless if those evils had been eradicated from their beings. "Who can understand his errors! Cleanse Thou me from secret faults" (Psa. 19:12). There is more deceit and more deceit and self-ends operating in all of us than we perceive. If you prize an honest heart above a good name and value a clear conscience before God beyond a high reputation among men you are no hypocrite.—A.W.P.

(continued from back page)

Jeremiah 18:7, 8 simply means that many of the judgments which God pronounces against kingdoms are not absolute declarations or infallible predictions of what is about to surely take place, but rather ethical intimations of His sore displeasure on account of sin and solemn threats of what must inevitably follow if there be no change for the better in those denounced. Whether or not the impending judgments become historical events is contingent upon their refusal to heed the warning. In like manner Jeremiah 18:9 has reference to no absolute promise of God: it is no unqualified declaration of what He would certainly do, but rather an intimation of His readiness to bless and prosper, accompanied by a warning that such blessing will be forfeited if obedience gives place to disobedience. God never signified in any promise of national blessing that the promise held good under *all* circumstances. See Deuteronomy 28:2 and 15! God ever presses upon men the fundamental distinction between sin and holiness. It was the fatal mistake of the nation of Israel to regard God's promises to them as absolute, supposing the fulfillment was certain regardless of their degeneracy.

We must, then, distinguish sharply between God's decrees and His denunciations, between His absolute purpose and His conditional promises, between His bestowment of spiritual gifts and temporal mercies, between the administration of the Covenant of Grace and the dispensations of His providence. We must distinguish between the ground on which Jehovah deals with His Church and with a nation, for the former is in Christ and the latter out of Christ. There was a radical and vital difference between Christ shedding tears over Jerusalem because the Jews stubbornly refused to enter into the benefits of a temporal covenant (Matt. 23:37) and His shedding His blood for His brethren that they might receive the blessings of the Everlasting Covenant (Heb. 13:20, 21). Changes in God's material favours unto a nation do not imply that the eternal purpose of spiritual grace is liable to alteration, any more than the removal of a local "candlestick" (Rev. 2:5) argues that He may take away His Spirit from any regenerate soul. The "wills" and "shalls" of Divine immutability and fidelity are never jeopardized by the "ifs" of human responsibility.—A.W.P.

(continued from front page)

providence has planted and set up, but to the elect, His assurance is, "He which hath begun a good work in you will finish it" (Phil. 1:6). From the former He may withdraw what He has bestowed, but to the latter, "the gifts and calling of God are without repentance" (Rom. 11:29). Nor do the variations of the Divine dispensations with a kingdom argue any fickleness in His character, rather do they demonstrate His stability—as long as a nation's ways please Him He gives proof of His approbation. When displeasing He evidences His disapprobation.

God may act in mercy with a nation today and in wrath tomorrow without the least "shadow of turning" or change of character, and so far from that being any alteration of His eternal decree it is through these multifarious dispensations it is accomplished, for He foreordained *all* that comes to pass. There is therefore no proportion whatever between the fluctuations of His temporal bestowments on a kingdom and the peculiar love and special grace of the Everlasting Covenant wherein God assures His saints of their eternal security on the ground of His immutability. The decrees of God, as to their execution are suspended on no condition in man. If they were, it would destroy alike His wisdom, independence and fidelity. On the other hand, when He declares, "them that honour Me, I will honour, and them that despise Me shall be lightly esteemed" (1 Sam. 2:30), God is enunciating a moral law according to which He governs the race. His decrees are His irresistible determinations. His laws reveal the duty of men and the issues thereof according to their response.

The Lord approves of obedience and righteousness wherever it is found and rewards the same with temporal blessings without the least saving grace. Conversely, He disapproves of sin and unrighteousness and sooner or later visits His anger upon them in this world. But even when the dark clouds of His judgments hang over a kingdom, calamity may be averted by national humiliation before God and reformation of conduct. But that no more implies fickleness in the Divine character that it denies His foreknowledge. The history of God's judgments on Egypt is a case in point: each time her monarch humbled himself in any measure, the Divine rod was lifted. Nevertheless, God had foreordained the destruction of Pharaoh and suited His dispensations in great variety and with many changes to bring it about. He plagued and freed him, freed and plagued him again, yet there was not the least alteration in God, all being so many effects of His power suited to the accomplishment of His unalterable purpose.

God's governmental dealings make more or less evident to men the proportion there is between their conduct and His attitude toward them—the correspondence is such as to convey impressions of His goodness, justice and mercy. The character of God's dominion is seen to be such that where righteousness and morality obtain He blesses "in basket and store," but where wickedness is obstinately indulged in it inevitably entails a doom of evil. Yet if sin is forsaken that doom is avoided and a heritage of prosperity is entered into. But such alterations as these in the Divine administration, so far from making God to be capricious in His ways or unstable in the principles of His government, rather demonstrates that He is unalterably the same. It is because His procedure is marked by undeviating righteousness that He must change His dealings with men when their relation or attitude to Him involves a change. Consequently when God is said to "repent" it connotes no change in His purpose or mind, but only in the matter of His treating with men.

VOL. XXII.   MAY, 1943.   NO. 5

STUDIES IN THE SCRIPTURES

" Search the Scriptures."   John 5:39.

Publisher and Editor—ARTHUR W. PINK,
27 Lewis Street,
Stornoway, Isle of Lewis,
Scotland.

GOD GOVERNING THE NATIONS.

"*If* that nation, against whom I have pronounced, turn from their evil I will repent of the evil that I thought to do unto them" (Jer. 18:8). Then is no "if" in connection with what God has foreordained, and the history of nations has been as truly and definitely predestinated as the destiny of each individual. "Known unto God are all His works from the beginning of the world" (Acts 15:18), and they are known to Him because they were decreed by Him. Now if God decreed an event He either foresaw what would be the issue of it or He did not. If He did not, where is His infinite wisdom and understanding? On the other hand, if He foresaw an event would not be, why did He purpose it should be? If God purposed a thing, then either He is able to bring it to pass by His wisdom and power, or He is not. If not, where is His omniscience and omnipotence? From the horns of that dilemma there is no escape. If God be *God* then there can be no failure with Him "The counsel of the LORD standeth forever, the thoughts of His heart to all generations" (Psa. 33:11).

"If that nation, against whom I have pronounced, turn from their evil I will repent of the evil that I thought to do unto it." There is always an "if" in connection with human responsibility, for man is as "unstable as water" being influenced by many things both from within and without; nevertheless he is held strictly accountable unto God. Nations, equally with Christians, are responsible: the Lord is their Maker, their Ruler, their God. His Moral Law is as binding upon kingdoms as it is upon the Church. *If* the rulers of the nations acknowledge God in the discharge of their office, if their laws be equitable and beneficent, maintaining a balance between justice and mercy, if the Sabbath be duly enforced, if the Lord be owned in prosperity and sought unto in adversity, *then* the smile of Heaven will be upon that people. But if He be slighted and defied His frown will be experienced. As effects are dependent upon the operation of causes, and the character of the one determines the nature of the other, so a course of obedience is followed by very different consequence from one of disobedience, be it the case of a nation or individual.

"Righteousness exalteth a nation: but sin is a reproach to any people" (Prov. 14:34) expresses a foundational principle and an unchanging fact. Right doing or walking according to the Divine Rule is the basic condition of national prosperity. A righteous administration of government and the public worship of God gives an ascendancy to a people

IMPORTANT NOTICES

Please advise promptly of change in address, otherwise copies will be lost in the mails.

We are glad to send a sample copy to any of your friends whom you believe would be interested in this publication.

This magazine is published as "a work of faith and labour of love," the editor and his wife gladly giving their services free. There is no regular subscription price, as we do not wish the poor of the flock to be deprived. This does not mean that those looking for something for nothing may "help themselves." Those getting this Magazine, who are financially able and who receive spiritual help from its pages, are expected to gladly contribute towards its expenses; otherwise, their names are dropped from our lists.

Will those forwarding International Money Orders please have them made out to us at Stornoway, Isle of Lewis, Scotland. Checks (Cheques-Eng.) made out on U.S.A. Banks are not negotiable here, so please do not send them.

CONTENTS

THE SERMON ON THE MOUNT.

26. *Profession Tested.* Matthew 7:21.

"Not everyone that saith unto Me, Lord, Lord, shall enter into the kingdom of Heaven; but he that doeth the will of My Father which is in Heaven." Last month we sought to provide an exposition of this verse: explaining the meaning of its terms, pointing out its bearing upon the Jews of that day, and its application unto our own. On this occasion we propose to deal with it more in a *topical* manner. Obviously the theme of this verse is the inadequacy of a mere lip profession of Christian discipleship, and since so many are fatally deceived at this very point we deem it advisable to devote another article to the subject. We shall now endeavour to show something of the attainments possible to the formalist and how near he may come to the kingdom of Christ without actually entering it. It is the third class of professors, the *deceived* ones, that we have chiefly in view. We shall seek to examine and test them at four simple but essential points and show of each one wherein they come short of that which is the experience and portion of the regenerate.

1. *Knowledge.* It is plain from the teaching of Holy Writ that there are two distinct orders or types of knowledge of spiritual and Divine things, and that the difference between them is not merely one of degree but of kind, a radical and vital difference. There is a knowledge of God and of His Word which is a saving one, but there is also a knowledge of the same Objects which—though it may be accurate and extensive—is a non-saving one. Thus it is of vast importance that everyone who values his soul should be properly informed as to the essential differences between these two kinds of knowledge, so that he may diligently examine himself and ascertain *which* of them is *his*. That the above distinction is no arbitrary one, no imaginary one of ours, is evident from many passages. When the Apostle declared that the Colossian saints "*knew* the grace of God *in truth*" (1:6), he was employing discriminating language, for there

are others who know the grace of God only in *theory.* "This is life eternal, that they might know Thee the only true God, and Jesus Christ, whom Thou hast sent" (John 17:3), which is a saving knowledge. "When they knew God they glorified Him not as God," but became idolaters and were abandoned of Him (Rom. 1: 21-24): that was a non-saving knowledge of God.

"Though I have the gift of prophecy, and understand all mysteries, and all knowledge . . . and have not charity (love), I am nothing" (1 Cor. 13:2). Nor is that an altogether unlikely case. Far from it. It is possible for the natural man to acquire a much fuller and more intelligent grasp of the Truth than that which is possessed by the majority of genuine Christians. If he be endowed with competent intellect, if he has received a good education, if he closely applied himself to the study of Scripture (as he might to one of the arts or sciences), then he may become expertly proficient in a letter knowledge and notional understanding of the same. By patient industry he may master the Hebrew and Greek languages in which they were originally written. By reading and rereading sound theological works he may secure a comprehension of the whole doctrinal system of Truth. By consulting able commentators he may obtain light upon perplexing passages. He may even arrive at an understanding of the "mysteries" of iniquity and of godliness, so that he is quite sound in the Faith. And if he is a fluent speaker, he may discourse upon Divine things so that none may legitimately take issue with his orthodoxy, yea, many, may find his preaching instructive and helpful.

There are also very many unregenerate listeners who by waiting upon the ministry of the Word may obtain a wide knowledge thereof. A considerable number are possessed with an insatiable curiosity, or appetite for the acquisition of religious information, and who by regular attendance at church, close attention to what they hear and the aid of retentive memories, become well instructed in spiritual things, especially where this is supplemented by the reading of a considerable amount of devotional literature. Though unregenerate, they obtain clear views of the whole Gospel scheme and those gifted with clear minds often grasp more of the profounder aspects of Truth than many of God's own children are capable of understanding (for "not many wise men after the flesh" 1 Cor. 1:26, are among His elect). They often dig more deeply into the mines of Truth and make greater discoveries than do the saved. They may apprehend things so clearly as to satisfy their judgment and express their notions so distinctly to others as to convince, yea, to defend, their beliefs so tellingly and argue about the same to such effect as to silence any who differ from them.

Nor is this knowledge limited to the doctrinal side of the Truth. They may attain unto well-proportioned conceptions of the Divine character and perfections and correct views of the Person and work of Christ and the office and operations of the Holy Spirit. By sitting under the faithful preaching of God's servants and by reading articles of a searching nature they may secure a good understanding of the experimental side of things. They may be quite clear upon the miracle of regeneration and be able to draw the lineaments of the new creature so true to life as though they had the image thereof in their own souls. They may be able to describe the work of grace as accurately as though they had an experience of it in their own hearts. They may depict the conflicts between the flesh and Spirit as though such opposition were taking place within themselves. They may speak as glowingly of the Christian's graces as if they were the possessors of them. They may narrate the actings of certain graces and such-and-such a temptation as though they were recounting their own history. They may have the exact idea and true notion of all these things in their heads when there is nothing whatever of them in their hearts.

Yet in spite of all that we have predicated above of these unregenerate yet orthodox preachers and hearers, authors and readers, they are those who are "ever learning and never able to come to the knowledge of the Truth" (2 Tim. 3:7), that is to say, they do not and cannot arrive at the *saving* knowledge of it. And why is this so? Because they lack the necessary faculty for its entrance. "The natural man receiveth not the things of the Spirit of God, for they are foolishness unto him; neither can he know them, because they are spiritually discerned" (1 Cor. 2:14). A saving knowledge of the Truth is impossible unto the unregenerate. There must be a suitability between the instrument and its task, between the agent and that which is to be apprehended. An animal is incapable of entering into what the human intellect may comprehend, and one who has no spiritual faculty is unable to receive spiritual things in a *spiritual* way. The natural man may acquire a theoretical and notional knowledge of things, but he cannot obtain a spiritual or saving knowledge of them, for he is totally devoid of spiritual life.

Let us now attempt to answer the question, What is the essential difference between these two kinds of knowledge? wherein does a natural and notional knowledge of Divine things come short of a spiritual and saving knowledge of them? Consider the following: "I have heard of Thee by the hearing of the ear, but now mine eye seeth Thee" (Job 42:5). We give not an exposition of those words, but use them illustratively of this contrast. One may listen for years to sermons but when the soul actually has Christ revealed *in* him (Gal. 1:16) he learns the tremendous difference there is between a hearsay knowledge of Him and a spiritual perception as He stands manifested to the soul as a living Reality. Let us endeavour to still further simplify by a human analogy. A child is born with such a filament over his eyes that he is quite blind. He receives a good education and loved ones seek to use their eyes on his behalf and take pains in describing to him some of the beauties and wonders of Nature—by their word pictures he obtains clear concepts of many objects. But suppose a specialist performs a successful operation and vision is vouchsafed him: how vastly different his own sight of a glorious sunset from the previous notion he had formed of it!

No matter how carefully and accurately his friends have described a sunset to him, how vivid the contrast when he beheld one for himself! Equally real, equally radical, equally vivid is the difference between a second-hand knowledge of the Truth and a personal acquaintance and experience of its power. Following out the analogy a little further—while blind that man may have thought his friends exaggerated the grandeur of a sunset, but as soon as he has seen one for himself he knows that neither poet's tongue, nor artist's brush could possibly do it justice. He may even have entertained doubts as to the thing itself, wondering if his friends were but drawing upon their imagination and seeking to amuse him with a fairy tale, but now all uncertainty is at an end. So with the regenerate soul and Christ: once his sin-blinded eyes are opened to behold the Lamb, he exclaims with one of old, "I *know* that my Redeemer liveth." A saving knowledge of Christ ravishes the soul and so draws the heart unto Him as to esteem all else as dross in comparison with the excellency of the knowledge of Him (Phil. 3:8).

A Laplander may have read about honey, but not until he has eaten some does he really know what it is like. Nor does the soul truly know the Lord until he has "*tasted that He is gracious*" (1 Peter 2:3). The formalist knows God is omniscient, the Christian has an inward experience thereof, by His detecting to him the heart's deceitfulness and discovering secret sins. The former knows God is all-mighty, but the latter has felt His omnipotence working within him enabling him to believe (Eph. 1:19), subduing his lusts, overcoming the world. The one kind of knowledge then is speculative, the other practical; the one is merely notional, the other experimental; the one is acquired second-hand, the other is communicated directly. He "hath shined in our hearts to give the light of the knowledge of the glory of God in the face of Jesus Christ" (2 Cor. 4:6). Natural knowledge puffs up, but spiritual humbles and makes the soul painfully conscious of its spiritual ignorance: observe how in the 119th Psalm David prays no less than eight times, "Teach me." Natural knowledge produces no spiritual fruit, and it is vain to boast of spiritual learning if it be not accompanied with a holy life.

2. *Repentance.* There are four principal acts and exercises in repentance—confession of sin, hatred of sin, sorrow for sin, resolution against sin—and each of these may be and has been performed by the unregenerate. Cain cries out at the weight and grievousness of his sin, saying, "my punishment (or "iniquity") is greater than I can bear" (Gen. 4:13). Pharaoh acknowledged his sin and condemned himself for it (Exo. 9:27), so did Israel when they had provoked the Lord (Num. 14:40), so did Saul (1 Sam. 15:14), so did Judas (Matt 27:3). As to hatred of sin, Jehu detested the idols of Baal and destroyed them, yet his heart was not upright (2 Kings 10:26-28, 31). After their lengthy captivity in Babylon Israel were delivered from their love of idolatry, so that the Spirit said, "thou that abhorrest idols" (Rom. 2:22). Many there are who hate injustice and oppression, lying and dishonesty. Concerning sorrow for sin: Israel mourned after their worship of the golden calf (Exo. 33:4) and "mourned greatly" (Num. 14:39) after they had sorely provoked the Lord, and yet continued in their provocations (v. 44). As to resolution against sin, a strong case of such is seen in Balaam (Num. 22:18, 38).

If the unregenerate may go thus far in a way of repentance, wherein do they fall short? If theirs be not "repentance unto life" (Acts 11:18) where is it to be found? Saving repentance proceeds from sorrow for sin, whereas the sorrow of the formalist is defective at many points. First, they *mourn not for sin itself,* but over its *consequences.* Not as their deeds are contrary to God, a violation of His Law, opposed to His holy will, but because they involve unpleasant effects. Second, not for consequences in reference to God, but themselves, not because He is dishonoured. His authority spurned, and the creature preferred above Him. If they mourn because of His displeasure it is rather for the effects of His anger. They care nothing about Satan being gratified and the cause of Christ reproached so long as they are not afflicted in their persons or estates. Third, they mourn not for all its consequences in reference to themselves: not as it defiles the soul, keeps at a distance from God, hardens the heart and renders it more incapable of holy duties: but only as it deprives mercies and produces miseries.

Their *hatred of sin* is defective. It is not extended to all sin: they cannot say, "I hate every false way." They may hate gross sin such as the State penalizes but wink at lesser ones. They may hate open wickedness but not secret faults. They may abominate theft and uncleanness, yet make no conscience of pride and self-righteousness. They may hate those things which are cried down by people among whom they now live, and yet enter into the same heartily if they move to another part of the earth. They may hate an unprofitable sin, but refrain not from those which bring them in a revenue. They may hate a sin which is contrary to their peculiar temperament, but not that which is agreeable to their constitution. They may hate others' sin rather than their own, as Judas complained at the prodigality of Mary; but such hatred is directed rather against the persons than the sins of others. Their hatred is superficial. It is not with all their heart: it reaches not to the corruptions of their nature, nor is it accompanied with mortifying endeavours.

Their *resolutions against sin* are defective. In their *rise*. They issue not from a renewed heart, from a principle of holiness and love to Christ, but from apprehensions of unpleasant effects and future damnation. Or from the restraining power of God, which keeps them from purposing to sin rather than moves them to full resolution against it: so that their resolutions are negative rather than positive. Thus it was with Balaam, he said not, "I will not," but "I cannot" (Num. 22:18, 38)—he had a mind to, but the Lord prevented him. In its *continuance*. Their good resolutions are not followed out to full execution, but are quickly broken. The cause from which they proceed is not constant, and therefore the effects are evanescent. They flow no longer when the spring from which they issue runs dry. That spring is but a momentary anguish or flash of fear, and when that vanishes their resolutions fail. Their goodness is but as "the morning cloud" and "early dew" (Hosea 6:4) which quickly disappears. David feared the danger of this when he prayed, "Keep this forever in the imagination of the hearts of Thy people, and *stablish* their hearts unto Thee" (1 Chron 29:18).

3. *Faith*. We read of those who "stay themselves (rely upon) the God of Israel," yet it was "not in truth or in righteousness" (Isa. 48:2), for they were obstinate and their neck "as an iron sinew." There are those who have a faith which is so like unto a justifying one that they themselves take it to be the very same and even Christians regard it as the faith of God's elect. Simon Magus, for example, "believed" (Acts 8:13), and gave such a profession of it that Philip and the local church received him into their fellowship and privileges. Those that received the Seed into stony ground did for a "while believe" (Luke 8:13), and according to its description it differed nothing from saving faith except in its root—the difference not being evident but lying under ground. The unregenerate may have a faith which receives unquestioningly the Bible as the Word of God, for the Jews entertained no doubts that the Scriptures were the very Oracles of God. Agrippa believed in the veracity of the Prophets and received their testimony without question (Acts 26:26, 27). They may have a faith which leads to the owning of Christ as their Lord and worshipping Him as such (Matt. 7:21). They may even have a faith which produces strong assurance: those who opposed Christ were quite sure they were "the seed of Abraham" and not the slaves of Satan (John 8: 33, 34).

Wherein does this faith come short of a saving one? wherein is it defective? It is merely an intellectual assent to the letter of Scripture and not "with the heart" (Rom. 10:10) so as to bring Christ *into* it (Eph. 3:17), just as one may read and accredit an historical work and no spiritual effect be produced thereby. It is a faith which is "alone" (James 2:17) for it is unaccompanied by other graces, whereas a saving faith has as its concomitants love, meekness, holiness, perseverance, etc. Such a faith consents not to take a whole Christ: it will embrace Him as a Saviour but is not willing for Him to reign over them as King. Those with such a faith desire Christ's pardon but not His sceptre,

His peace but not His yoke. They will accept Him to deliver them from Hell, but not to sanctify and cast out of their temples whatever God abominates. They are not willing to subscribe to Christ's terms of discipleship, which are the denying of self, the taking up of the Cross, and following Him whithersoever He leads: such terms they consider harsh and unnecessary.

The faith of the formalist and empty professor is a lifeless and barren one. "As the body without the spirit is dead so faith without works is dead" (James 2:26). In that chapter the Apostle points out, first, the worthlessness of a bare profession of charity. To give good words to a brother in need, bidding him, "Depart in peace, be warmed and filled," yet withholding those things needful to him, is cruel hypocrisy (vv. 15, 16). Equally so to say we believe the Holy One and a Day of judgment and yet live impiously is such a mockery of faith (v. 17). Second, such faith is inferior to that of the demons for they "believe and tremble" (v. 19), whereas empty professors are not afraid to mock God. Third, such a faith is radically different from that possessed and exercised by the father of all who believe, for he rendered unreserved obedience unto the Divine commands (vv. 21-24). A faith which does not purify the heart (Acts 15:9), work by love (Gal. 5:6), overcome the world (1 John 5:4), and bring forth fruit acceptable to God, will not conduct anyone to Heaven.

4. *Good works.* The unregenerate may make an exceedingly fair show of the practical side of religion, that is in their deportment, both in their addresses to God and dealings with men, in public and private alike. They may go far in their external conformity to the rule of righteousness and visible compliance with the revealed will of God, both as to moral and positive precepts. The outward carriage of the Pharisees, by Christ's own testimony, was "beautiful" (Matt. 23:27) and among their fellows they were esteemed as exceptionally holy men. Such may not only abstain from all gross sins but meet all the external requirements of morality and piety. Paul declares that, while unconverted, he was "blameless" as to his observance of the Law (Phil. 3:6). The rich young ruler affirmed of the Commandments, "all these have I kept from my youth up" (Luke 18:21), nor did Christ charge him with idle boasting. They may practice great austerities in order to mortify the flesh, as some of the Gnostics had for their rule, "Touch not, taste not, handle not" (Col. 2:21). A spirit of fanaticism may induce some of them to suffer martyrdom (1 Cor. 13:3).

Wherein lies the defectiveness of the works of the unregenerate? First in the state of the persons performing them. They are not reconciled to God, and how can He accept aught from His enemies! The individual must first be reconciled to God before He will receive anything at his hands: "the Lord had respect to Abel *and* to his offering" (Gen. 4:4). Second, in the root from which their actions proceed: their fruits are but the wild grapes of a degenerate vine: they must be renewed in the inner man before anything spiritual can be borne. Third, in the motive which prompts them, which is either servile or a spirit of legality rather than love; a dread of Hell, or an attempt to gain Heaven instead of from gratitude. Fourth, in the end which they have in view which is a selfish one instead of seeking to promote the Divine honour: it is to pacify God rather than glorify Him. Fifth, in the absence of Christ's merits their works are neither wrought for Christ's sake nor offered in His name, and since none may come unto the Father but by Him (John 14:6) all their works are refused, as Cain's offering was.—A.W.P.

THE MISSION AND MIRACLES OF ELISHA.

5. *Second Miracle.*

"And they said unto him, Behold now, there be with thy servants fifty strong men; let them go, we pray thee, and seek thy master: lest peradventure the Spirit of the LORD hath taken him up and cast him upon some mountain or into some valley" (1 Kings 2:16). Two things must be borne in mind in connection with this request, lest we be too severe in our criticism of those who made it. First, these young Prophets had known that Elijah was to be removed from Elisha that day, as is clear from their words to him on a former occasion: "Knowest thou that the LORD will take away thy master from thy head today?" (v. 5). As to how they had learned of this we cannot be sure, nor do we know how full was their information, yet it seems clear they knew nothing more than the general fact that this was the day which would terminate the earthly career of the renowned Tishbite.

Second, in verse 7 we are told, "And fifty men of the sons of the Prophets went and stood to view afar off; and they two (Elijah and Elisha) stood by Jordan" (v. 7). Here again we cannot be certain what it was or how much they actually beheld. Perhaps some are ready to exclaim, If they were definitely on the lookout, they must have seen the remarkable translation of Elijah, for the "chariot of fire and the horses of fire" in mid-air would surely have been visible to them. Not necessarily so: probably that "fire" was very different from any that we are acquainted with. Moreover we must bear in mind that on a later occasion, "the mountain was full of horses and chariots of fire round about Elisha" yet his own personal attendant saw them not until the Prophet asked "LORD, I pray Thee, open his eyes, that he may see" (2 Kings 6:17)! We are therefore inclined to believe that as these young Prophets watched, Elijah suddenly and mysteriously disappeared from their view without their actually beholding his miraculous translation to Heaven. Consequently they felt that something unprecedented and supernatural had taken place, and they ascribed it to a Divine intervention, as their reference to "the Spirit of the LORD" intimates.

Though they must have realized that an event quite extraordinary had occurred, yet they were uneasy, fearful that something unpleasant had befallen their teacher. They were deeply concerned, and veneration and love for Elijah prompted their petition. Let us seek to put ourselves in their place and then ask, Had we acted more intelligently? At any rate, was their request any more foolish than Peter's on the Mount of Transfiguration when he said to Christ, "if Thou wilt, let us make here three tabernacles: one for Thee, and one for Moses, and one for Elijah" (Matt. 17:4)! Moreover it should be observed that they did not rashly take matters into their own hands, but respectfully submitted their request unto Elisha. Before criticizing them too harshly let us make sure that *our* hearts are as warmly attached to God's servants as theirs, and that we are as troubled over their departure as they were.

Elisha tersely refused their request: "Ye shall not send." But why did he not explain to them the uselessness of such a quest, by informing them exactly what had happened to Elijah? Probably because he concluded that if the Lord had intended them to know of His servant's miraculous exit from this scene, He had opened their eyes to behold what himself had been permitted to see—not all of the Twelve witnessed Christ's transfiguration! Moreover, is there not hint here as to why this privilege had been withheld from them, in the statement that, "they stood to view *afar off*"—not so Elisha, who followed his master fully: it is only those who "draw near" that enjoy the highest privileges of grace. Finally we may learn from Elisha's reticence that there are some experiences which are too sacred to describe unto others. O for more of such holy reserve and modesty in this day of curiosity and vulgar intruding into one another's spiritual privacy.

"And when they urged him till he was ashamed, he said, Send. They sent therefore fifty men, and they sought three days, but found him not" (v. 17). Let it not be forgotten that up to this time only one individual from all mankind has gone to Heaven without passing through the portals of death, and it is very doubtful if the contemporaries of Enoch (or those who lived later) knew of his translation, for the words "he was not found" (Heb. 11:5) intimate that search was also made for him. By Elisha's being "ashamed" we understand that he felt if he were to continue refusing them they would likely think that he was being influenced by an undue desire to occupy Elijah's place of honour. "And when they came again to him (for he tarried at Jericho) he said unto them, Did I not say unto you, Go not?" (2 Kings 2:18). Now *they* must have felt ashamed. "This would make them the more willing to acquiesce in his judgment another time" (Matthew Henry).

This brings us to Elisha's next miracle. First, let us consider the *order* of it. It was Elisha's second one and the Scriptural significance of that numeral casts light upon this point. *One* expresses unity and sovereignty. It stands all alone, but where there are *two* another has come in. So in the first miracle Elisha acted alone and none contributed aught thereto. But here in this one Elisha is not alone: a second party is seen in connection with it—the "men of Jericho," and they were required to furnish a "new cruse" with "salt therein" before the wonder was performed. Probably this very fact will prove a serious difficulty to the thoughtful reader. Those who have followed closely the preceding articles of this series will remember how we pointed out again and again that Elisha is to be regarded as a representative character, as a figure of the servants of Christ. Some may conclude the type fails us at this point, for it will be said, Surely you do not believe that ministers of the Gospel demand something at the hands of sinners in order to their being saved! Our answer will be given under the meaning of this miracle.

Second, let us take note of *the place* where this occurred: it was at Jericho. This, too, is very illuminating. Jericho had been the first city of the Canaanites to defy the children of Israel, for it was closed and barred against them (Josh. 6:1). Whereupon it was pronounced "accursed" and orders were given that Israel should not appropriate anything in it unto themselves: "And ye, in any wise keep yourselves from the accursed thing, lest ye make yourselves accursed, when ye take of the accursed thing" (v. 18). By the power of Jehovah, Jericho was overthrown, following which His people "burnt the city with fire and all that was therein" (v. 24). After which the fearful denunciate went forth, "Cursed be the man before the LORD that riseth up and buildeth this city Jericho" (v. 26). But both of those Divine prohibitions were flouted. The first by Achan, who "saw among the spoils a goodly Babylonian garment and two hundred shekels of silver and a wedge of gold" (7:21), which he covet and stole, for which he and his family were stoned to death and their bodies destroyed by fire.

The second prohibition was broken centuries later, in the reign of the apostate Ahab: "In his days did Hiel the Bethelite build Jericho" (1 Kings 16:34). Thus Jericho was the city of *the curse*. It was the *first* place in Canaan where defiance of the Lord and His people was displayed. It was there that Israel, in the person of Achan, committed their *first* sin in the land of promise. A fearful curse was denounced against the man who should have the nerve to rebuild the city. That there is an unmistakable parallel between these things and what occurred in *Eden* scarcely needs pointing out: but we must not anticipate. That which is now before us is the fact that, in defiance of the Divine threat, Jericho had recently been rebuilt—probably the attractiveness of its locality was the temptation to which Hiel yielded (as the pleasantness of the fruit in Eve's eyes induced her to partake: Gen. 3:6), for we are told, "And the men of the city said unto Elisha, Behold, I pray thee, the situation of this city *is pleasant*" (2 Kings 2:19).

Third, the *objects* of it, namely the springs of water. "And the men of the city said unto Elisha, Behold, I pray thee, the situation of this city is pleasant, as my lord seeth, but the water is naught and the ground is barren" (v. 19). Herein God had evidenced His displeasure on that accursed rebuilding of Jericho by making its water unwholesome and the ground barren, or as the margin gives, "causing to miscarry." The Jewish commentators understood this to mean that these waters caused the cattle to cast their young, the trees to shed their fruit before it was mature, and even the women to be incapable of bearing children. The Hebrew word which is rendered "the water is *naught*" ("ra") is a much stronger one than the English denotes. In the great majority of cases it is translated "evil" (as in Gen. 6:5; Prov. 8:13), "bad" (as Gen. 24:50, etc) and "wicked" no less than thirty-one times. Its first occurrence is in "the tree of knowledge of good and evil" (Gen. 2:9)! But it signifies not only evil but that which is harmful or injurious to others, being translated "the *hurtful* sword" (Psa. 144:10).

Jericho, then, was pleasant for situation but there was no good water for its inhabitants or their flocks and herds. This was a serious matter, a vital consideration, for the Israelites were an essentially pastoral people—observe how often we find mention of the "wells" in their early history: Genesis 16:14; 21:25; 26:15, 22; 29:2; Numbers 21:16-18, etc. These men of Jericho then lacked the one thing needful. How this reminds us of another and later incident in the career of Elisha: "Now Naaman, captain of the host of the king of Syria, was a great man with his master, and honourable, because by him the LORD had given deliverance unto Syria: he was also a mighty man in valour, *but* he was a leper" (2 Kings 5:1). In spite of his exalted position, his endowments, his exploits, he lacked the one thing needful—health. He was a leper and that neutralized, spoilt everything else. And thus it is with every man in his natural condition, however favoured by creation and by providence—the springs of his life are defiled.

Fourth, the *means used*: "And he said, Bring me a new cruse and put salt therein. And they brought it to him. And he went forth unto the springs of water, and cast the salt in there" (2 Kings 2:20, 21). The appropriateness of this particular means for counteracting the effects of the curse is at once apparent. Salt is the grand purifier and preserver. It is by means of the salty vapours which the rays of the sun distil from the ocean that the atmosphere of our earth is kept healthy for its inhabitants—that is why the sea breezes act as such a tonic to the invalid and the convalescent. Salt prevents putrefaction, hence after the backs of prisoners were scourged salt was rubbed into the wounds—though extremely painful it prevented blood poisoning. Salt is the best seasoning for how insipid and unsavoury are many foods without a sprinkling of it. Salt is the emblem of Divine holiness and grace, and so we read of the "covenant of salt" (Num. 18:19; 2 Chron. 13:5). Hence also the exhortation "Let your speech be always with grace, seasoned with salt" (Col. 4:6)—with the savour of true piety. The ministers of Christ are therefore denominated "the salt of the earth" (Matt. 5:13).

Fifth, the *instrument* of it. Obviously the salt itself could not heal those unwholesome waters, any more than the "rods" or twigs of the trees with their "white streaks" that Jacob pilled in them and set before the flocks were able to cause the cattle to bring forth young ones that were "ringstreaked, speckle and spotted" (Gen. 30:37-39). Though the men of Jericho were required to furnish the salt and though the Prophet now cast the same into the springs, yet he made it clear this would avail nothing unless the blessing of Jehovah accompanied the same. *His* power must operate if anything good was to be accomplished, therefore we find that as Elisha cast in the salt he declared, "Thus saith the LORD, I have healed the waters, there shall not be from thence any more death or causing to miscarry" (2 Kings 2:21). Thereby the Prophet disclaimed any inherent power of his own: yet he was instrumentally employed of God, for the very next verse says, "So the waters were healed unto this day, according to *the saying* of Elisha which he spake"! "I have planted, Apollos watered (they were the instruments); but *God* gave the increase" (1 Cor. 3:6).

Sixth, the *meaning* or typical significance of it. The first key to this is found in the *order* of it. Under that point we intimated that probably some readers would find a difficulty in the men of Jericho being required to furnish the salt and be inclined to object, Surely the minister of the Gospel (for as figure of such Elisha is here to be viewed) does not demand anything at the hand of sinners in order to their being saved. But such a difficulty—like most, if not all others—is self-created, and that through entertaining vague and general concepts instead of distinguishing sharply between things that differ. When we speak of "salvation," we refer to something that is many-sided. If on the one hand we must guard most carefully against the error of man's contributing anything unto his regeneration, on the other we must watch against swinging to the opposite extreme and denying that man is required to concur with God in connection with his reconciliation, preservation, etc. The typical picture which is here set before us is Divinely perfect, yet we need to view it closely if we are to see its details in their proper perspective.

The first miracle, the smiting of the Jordan, adumbrates the ministerial power of the evangelist over death, and in connection with the new birth man contributes nothing whatsoever unto it: see John 1:13. But this second miracle images a *later,* the second experience in the history of those truly converted. This miracle at Jericho speaks of neutralizing the effects of the curse, overcoming the power of innate depravity; and here the minister of the Gospel acts not alone, for in this matter there is the conjunction of both the Divine and the human elements. Thus the second key to its meaning lies in the *place* where it occurred. It is true that the conjunction of the Divine and human elements of conversion cannot be so closely defined as to express the same in any theological formula, nevertheless the reality of those two elements can be demonstrated both from Scripture and experience. We do not like the expression "man co-operating with God" for that savours too much of a dividing of the honour, but man's "concurring with God" seems to be both permissible and necessary.

The third key is contained in the fact that these men of Jericho are represented as taking the initiative, coming unto Elisha, acquainting him with their need, supplicating his assistance! Apparently they knew from his dress that Elisha was a Prophet and as he no doubt still carried Elijah's mantle, they hoped he would use his power on their behalf. The servant of God ought to be readily identified by his (emblematic) "garments" or spiritual graces, easily accessible and approachable, one to whom members of a community will gladly turn to in their troubles. Elisha did not repulse them by saying this lay outside his line of things, that his concern lay only with the young Prophets. Instead he at once intimated his willingness to help. Yet something was required of them: compare 4:41 and 5:10 for further illustrations of the same principle. *They* were told to provide the "new cruse" with salt therein. That put them to the proof: it was a test as to whether they were willing to follow the Prophet's instructions. They promptly heeded—how different from many who disregard the directions of God's servants!

This miracle, then, does not give us a history of the servant of God going unto those who are utterly unconcerned, dead in trespasses and sins, but rather that of awakened souls, seeking help, acquainting the minister with their need. In the first miracle it is God acting in sovereign power, enabling His servant to ministerially triumph over death: here it is His servant addressing human responsibility. In bidding awakened and inquiring sinners provide a "new cruse and put salt therein" he is but saying to them, "Cast away from you all your transgressions whereby ye have transgressed, and make you a new heart and a new spirit" (Ezek. 18:31 and cf. James 4:8). These men of Jericho could not have procured the new cruse and the salt unless God had first placed it at their hands, and the sinner cannot bring a responsive and obedient heart unto the minister until God has previously quickened him. That this miracle is, instrumentally, attributed to the "saying of Elisha"—the Hebrew term (dabar) is rendered "word" in 1 Kings 17:2, 8—denotes that awakened sinners are delivered from the effects of the curse as they obey the instructions of God's faithful servants.

Seventh, the *permanency* of it. "Thus saith the LORD, I have healed these waters: there shall not be from thence any more death or causing to miscarry: so the waters were healed unto this day, according to the word of Elisha which he spake" (1 Kings 2:21, 22). It was no superficial and temporary change that was wrought, but an effectual and permanent one. "I know that whatsoever God doeth, it shall be forever: nothing can be put to it, nor anything taken from it" (Eccl. 3:14). Herein we see again the appropriateness of the *salt,* the emblem of incorruption—hence, used in the covenant to express its perpetuity. Placed in a "new cruse" and then cast into "the springs of water" we have a figure of the new and honest heart, out of which are "the issues of life" (Prov. 4:23). The nature of fallen men, even the most attractive specimens, is like unwholesome water and barren soil: it must be renewed by God before any good works can be produced—make the tree good and its fruit will be good. The miracle is attributed, instrumentally, not to the faith or the prayer of Elisha (though there was both), but to his *word*. By His response God avouched His Prophet and sustained his testimony in Israel.—A. W. P.

DOCTRINE OF SAINTS' PERSEVERANCE.

8. *Its Safeguards.*

There may be some who will at once take exception to the employment of this term in such a connection, affirming that the Truth of God requires no safe-guarding at the hands of those called by Him to expound it: that their business is to faithfully preach the same and leave results entirely to its Author. We fully agree that God's eternal Truth stands in no need of any carnal assistance from us, either in the way of dressing it up to render it more attractive or in toning it down to make it less offensive. We heartily subscribe to the Apostle's dictum that, "we can do nothing against the Truth, but for the Truth" (2 Cor. 13:8)—God overrules the opposition of those who hate it and makes the wrath of His enemies to praise Him. Nevertheless in view of such passages as Mark 4:33; John 16:12; 1 Corinthians 3:2, and Hebrews 5:12 it is clear that our presentation of the Truth needs to be regulated by the condition of those to whom it is ministered. Moreover, this raises the question, What is *faithfully* presenting the Truth? Are there not other modifying adverbs which are not to be omitted?

The Truth should not only be preached "faithfully" but wisely, proportionately, seasonably as well. There is a zeal which is not according to knowledge nor tempered by wisdom. There is an unbalanced presentation of the Truth which accomplishes more harm than good. We read of "the present Truth" (2 Peter 1:12) and of "a word in due season" (Prov. 15:23 and cf. Isa. 50:4), which implies there is such a thing as speaking unseasonably, even though it be the Truth itself which is spoken and that "faithfully." What is a "word in season"? Is it not a timely and pertinent one, a message suited to the condition, circumstances and needs of the persons addressed? In His a wisdom and goodness God has provided cordials for the faint and comfort for those who mourn, as He has also given exhortations to the slothful, admonitions to the careless, solemn warnings to the reckless, and fearful threats to those who are defiant. Discrimination needs to be used in our appropriation and application of the Scriptures. As it would be cruel to quote terrifying passages to one who is already mourning over his sins, so it would be wrong to press promises of Divine preservation upon a professing Christian who is living a carnal and worldly life.

"Watch and pray that ye enter not into temptation: the spirit indeed is willing, but the flesh is weak" (Matt. 26:41). Those words furnish an illustration of a "word in due season." The disciples (not Peter only) had boasted, "though I should die with Thee, yet will I not deny Thee." They were so confident and temporarily blind to their own instability. Their Lord therefore bade them guard against self-reliance and seek grace from above, and though they were quite sincere in their avowal, yet were they much too feeble to resist Satan's attacks in their own strength. They thought themselves immune from such a horrible sin as denying their Master, but instead of bolstering them up in their sense of security, He warned them of their danger. Another example of a seasonable word is the Apostle's exhortation to the one who claims that he "standeth by faith," namely, "Be not high-minded, but fear. For if God spared not the natural branches, take heed lest He also spare not thee. Behold therefore the goodness and severity of God: on those that fell, severity; but toward thee, goodness, *if* thou continue in His goodness: otherwise thou also shalt be cut off" (Rom. 11:20-22).

But it is rather those safeguards by which God Himself has hedged about the subject of the everlasting security of His people that we would now particularly consider, those defenses which are designed to shut out unholy trespassers from this garden of delights; or to change the figure, those descriptions of character and conduct which serve to make known the particular persons to whom alone His promises belong. Last month we dwelt at some length on how this blessed doctrine is misrepresented by Arminians and perverted by Antinomians. To use a term employed by an Apostle, it has been grievously "wrested," torn from its setting, disproportionately contorted, divorced from its qualifying terms, detached from the necessary means by which it is attained, applied unto those to whom it does not belong. Hence our present object is to direct attention unto some of the principal bulwarks by which this precious truth is protected and which must be duly emphasized and continually pressed by the servants of God if it is to be portrayed in its true perspective and if souls are not to be fatally misled. Only thus shall we "faithfully" present this truth.

1. By insisting that it is the preservation of *saints* and not everyone who deems himself a Christian. It is of deep importance to define clearly and sharply the character of those who are Divinely assured of being preserved unto the heavenly kingdom— that God be not dishonoured, His Truth falsified, and souls deceived. "He preserveth the souls of His *saints*" (Psa. 97:10), but of none others. It is so easy to appropriate (or misappropriate) such a promise as, "Thou shalt guide me with Thy counsel and afterward receive me to glory" (Psa. 73:24), but before so doing, honesty requires that I ascertain whether the experiences of the one described in the context are those of *mine.* Asaph confesses to being envious at the prosperity of the wicked (vv. 3, 12) until he felt he had cleansed his own heart and hands "in vain" (v. 13). But he checks himself, tender lest by such murmuring he should stumble God's children (v. 15), recording how his "heart was grieved" and his conscience pricked at giving way to such foolish repinings, until he owned unto God, "I was as a beast before Thee" (v. 22). The recollection of God's gracious forbearance (v. 23) moved him to say, "it is good for me to draw near to God" (v. 28).

When I can find such marks *in myself* as the Psalmist had, such graces operating in my heart as did in his, then—but not before—am I warranted in comforting myself as he did. If I challenge the utterances of my mouth as to whether or no they are likely to offend God's little ones, if I make conscience of envying the prosperity of the wicked and mourn over it, if I am deeply humbled thereby, if I realize "my steps had well nigh slipped" (v. 2) and that it was a longsuffering God who had "holden me by my right hand," alone preserving me from apostasy; if this sense of His sovereign goodness enables me to affirm, "Whom have I in Heaven but Thee? and there is none upon earth that I desire besides Thee" (v. 25)—if all of this produces in me such a sense of my utter insufficiency as to own, "My flesh and my heart faileth, but God is the strength of my heart" (v. 26), then am I justified in saying, "Thou shalt guide me with Thy counsel and afterward receive *me* to glory." Yes, God "preserveth the souls of His saints," but what avails that for me unless I be one of them!?

Again—how many there are who eagerly grasp at those words of Christ concerning His sheep, who have only the vaguest idea of the ones whom He thus designates: "And I give unto them eternal life, and they shall never perish; neither shall any pluck them out of My hand" (John 10:28). The very fact that the verse opens with "and" requires us to ponder what immediately precedes, and because His flock is but a "little" one (Luke 12:32) it behooves each one who values his soul to spare no pains in seeking to ascertain whether *he* belongs to it. In the context the Saviour says, "My sheep hear My voice, and I know them, and they follow Me." Observe diligently the three things which are here predicated of them. First, they *hear* Christ's voice. Now to hear His voice means far more than to be acquainted with His words as they are recorded in Scripture—more than believing they *are* His words. When it was said unto Israel, "the LORD will not hear you in that day" (1 Sam. 8:18) it signified that He would not heed their requests or grant their petitions. When God complained, "When I spake, ye did not hear," it was not that they were physically deaf but their hearts were steeled against Him, as the remainder of the verse indicates: "But did evil before Mine eyes, and did choose that wherein I delighted not" (Isa. 65:12).

When God says, "This is My beloved Son in whom I am well pleased: *hear ye Him*" (Matt. 17:5), He is requiring something more of us than that we simply listen respectfully and believingly to what He says: He is demanding that we submit ourselves unreservedly to His authority, that we respond promptly to His orders, that we obey Him. In Proverbs 8:33 "hearing" is contrasted from refusing, and in Hebrews 3:15 we read, "If ye will hear His voice harden not your hearts." When Christ declares of His flock, "My sheep hear My voice" it signifies they *heed* it—they are not intractable but responsive, doing what He bids. Second, He declares, "and I know them," that is, with a knowledge or approbation. Third, "and they *follow Me*": not the bent of the flesh, not the solicitations of Satan, not the ways of the world, but the example which Christ has left them (1 Peter 2:21). Of them it is said, "they follow the Lamb whithersoever He goeth" (Rev. 14:4). But in order to follow Christ, self has to denied and the cross taken up (Matt. 16:24). Only those who thus "hear," are "known" of Christ, and who "follow" Him, shall "never perish."

2. By insisting that no person has any warrant to derive comfort from the doctrine of Divine Security until he is sure that he possesses *the character or conduct* of a saint. This naturally grows out of the first point, though we have somewhat anticipated what should be said here. Not everyone who bears the name of Christ will enter Heaven, but only His sheep. It is therefore folly that only those bearing the marks of such have any claim upon the promise made to that favoured company. And the burden of proof always rests upon the one who affirms. If one answers some advertisement from an employer for labour for a skilled workman, he is required to give evidence of his qualifications by well-accredited testimonials. If a person puts in a claim to an estate he must produce proof that he is a legitimate heir and satisfy the court of his bona fides. If a captain requires an additional hand for his ship he demands that the applicant show his papers or give demonstration that he is a fully qualified seaman. Before I can procure a passport I must produce my birth certificate. And one who avers himself a saint must authenticate his profession and evidence his new birth before he is entitled to be regarded as such.

God's saints are distinguished from all other people, not only by what He has done for them but also by what He has wrought in them. He set His hand upon them from all eternity, having loved them "with an everlasting love" (Jer. 31:3) and therefore were they "blessed with all spiritual blessings in the heavenlies in Christ," chosen in Him before the foundation of the world, predestinated "unto the adoption of children by Jesus Christ to Himself," and "accepted in the Beloved" (Eph. 1:3-6). It is true that they fell in Adam and became guilty before God, but an all-sufficient Redeemer was provided for them, appointed to assume and discharge all their liabilities and make full reparation to the broken Law on their behalf. It is also true that they are "by nature the children of wrath even as others" being born into this world "dead in trespasses and sins" (Eph. 2:1-3); but at the ordained hour a miracle of grace is performed within them so that they become "new creatures in Christ Jesus" (2 Cor. 5:17) and their bodies are made "the temple of the Holy Spirit" (1 Cor. 6:19). Faith and holiness have been communicated to them, so that though they are still in the world they are not of it (John 17:14).

The saints are endowed with a new life, with a spiritual and supernatural principle or "nature" which affects their whole souls. So radical and transforming is the change wrought in them by this miracle of grace that it is described as a passing from death unto life (John 5:24), from the power of darkness into the kingdom of God's dear Son (Col. 1:13), from "having no hope and without God in the world," to being "made nigh by the blood of Christ" (Eph. 2:12, 13), from a state of alienation to one of reconciliation (Col. 1:21), out of darkness into God's marvellous light (1 Peter 2:9). Of them God says, "This people have I formed for Myself: they shall show forth My praise" (Isa. 43:21). Obviously such a tremendous change in their state and standing must effect a real and marked change in their character and conduct. From rebellion against God they are brought unto subjection to Him, so that they throw down their weapons of opposition and yield to His sceptre. From love of sin they are turned to hate it, and from dread of God they now delight in Him. Formerly they thought only of gratifying self, now their deepest longing is to please Him who has shown them such amazing grace.

The saints are those who enter into *a solemn covenant* with the Lord, unreservedly dedicating themselves unto Him, making His glory their paramount concern. "Formerly soldiers used to take an oath not to flinch from their colours, but faithfully to cleave to their leaders; this they called sacramentum militare, a military oath; such an oath lies upon every Christian. It is so essential to the being of a saint, that they are described by this: 'gather My saints together unto Me; those that have made a covenant with Me' (Psa. 50:5). We are not Christians till we have subscribed this covenant, and that without any reservation. When we take upon us the profession of Christ's name we enlist ourselves in His muster-roll, and by it do promise that we will live and die with Him in opposition to all His enemies . . . He will not entertain us till we resign up ourselves freely to His disposal, that there may be no disputing with His commands afterwards, but, as one under His authority, go and come at His word" (W. Gurnall, 1660).

3. By insisting that perseverance is *an imperative necessity.* Adherence to the Truth no matter what opposition is encountered, living a life of faith in and upon God despite all the antagonism of the flesh, steadfastly treading the path of obedience in face of the scoffs of the world, continuing to go forward along the highway of holiness notwithstanding the hindrances of Satan and his emissaries is not optional but obligatory. It is according to the unalterable decree of God: no one can reach Heaven except by going along the only way that reaches there—Christ "endured the Cross" *before* He received the crown. It is according to the irreversible appointment of God: "For we are His workmanship, created in Christ Jesus unto good works, which God hath before ordained that we should walk in them" (Eph. 2:10). It is according to the established order of God, "that ye be not slothful but followers of them who through faith and patience (the Greek word may be rendered, "perseverance" with equal propriety) inherit the promises" (Heb. 6:12): It is according to the design of the Atonement, for Christ lived and died that He might "purify unto Himself a peculiar people zealous of good works" (Titus 2:14).

Assurance of Divine preservation no more renders less imperative the saint's own perseverance than God's informing Hezekiah he should live a further fifteen years abolished the necessity of his eating and drinking, resting and sleeping, as hitherto. "The elect are as much chosen to intermediate sanctification on their way as they are to that ultimate glorification which crowns their journey's end, and there a no coming to the one but through the other. So that neither the value, nor the *necessity*, nor the practical value of good works is superseded by this glorious truth . . . It is impossible that either the Son of God who came down from Heaven to propose and make known His Father's will; or that the Spirit of God, speaking in the Scriptures and acting on the heart, should administer the least encouragement to negligence and unholiness of life. Therefore that opinion that personal holiness is unnecessary to final glorification is in direct opposition to every dictate of reason, to every declaration of Scripture (Augustus Toplady). Alas, the attitude of multitudes of professing Christians is, "Soul, thou hast much good laid up . . . take thine ease" (Luke 12:19), and the doom of the fool will be theirs.

Concerning the imperativeness of perseverance C. H. Spurgeon said in the introductory portion of his sermon on, "The righteous also shall hold on his way" (Job 17:9), "The man who is righteous before God has a way of his own. It is not the way of the flesh, nor the way of the world; it is a way marked out for him by the Divine command, in which he walks by faith. It is the king's highway of holiness, the unclean shall not pass over it: only the ransomed of the Lord shall walk there, and these shall find it a path of separation from the world. Once entered upon the way of life, the pilgrim must persevere in it or *perish,* for thus saith the Lord, 'If any man draw back, My soul shall have no pleasure in him.' Perseverance in the path of faith and holiness is a *necessity* of the Christian, for only 'he that endureth to the end shall be saved.' It is in vain to spring up quickly like the seed that was sown on the rock, and then by-and-by to wither when the sun is up; that would but prove that such a plant has no root in itself, but 'the trees of the Lord are full of sap' and they abide and continue and bring forth fruit, even in old age, to show that the Lord is upright.

"There is a great difference between nominal Christianity and real Christianity, and this is generally seen in the failure of the one and the continuance of the other. Now, the declaration of the text is that the truly righteous man *shall* hold on his way: he shall not go back, he shall not leap the hedges and wander to the right hand or the left, he shall not lie down in idleness, neither shall he faint and cease to go upon his journey; but he 'shall hold on his way.' It will frequently be very difficult for him to do so, but he will have such resolution, such power of inward grace given him, that he will hold on his way with stern determination, as though he held on by his teeth, resolving never to let go. Perhaps he may not always travel with equal speed; it is not said that he shall hold on his *pace,* but he shall hold on his *way.* There are times when we run and are not weary, and anon when we walk and are thankful that we not faint; ay, and there are periods when we are glad to go on all fours and creep upwards with pain; but still we prove that 'the righteous shall hold on his way.' Under all difficulties the face of the man whom God has justified is steadfastly set towards Jerusalem, nor will he turn aside till his eyes shall see the King in his beauty."—A. W. P.

BEHOLDING THE CRUCIFIED CHRIST.

"They crucified Him....and sitting down they watched Him there" (Matt. 27:35, 36). The reference is to the Roman soldiers, as is clear from John 19:23, confirmed by Matthew 27:54. They were the ones authorized to carry out the death sentence which had been passed by Pilate, and into their hands the governor had delivered the Saviour (Matt. 27:26, 27). With coarse scurrility they executed their task. Adding insult to injury they exposed the Lord Jesus unto the indignities of a mock coronation: robing Him in scarlet, crowning Him with thorns, hailing Him as King of the Jews. Giving full expression to their enmity they spat upon Him, smote Him with a reed, mocked Him.

Restoring to Him His raiment, they conducted Him to Golgotha and affixed Him to the Cross. Having gambled for His garments, they sat down to watch Him—to frustrate any attempt at rescue which His friends might make, and to wait until life was extinct. By way of introduction let us briefly take note of three things.

First, *the circumstances.* The initiative had been taken by the religious leaders of Israel, for there "assembled together the chief priests and the scribes, and the elders of the people, unto the palace of the high priest, who was called Caiaphas, and consulted that they might take Jesus by subtlety and kill Him" (Matt. 26:3, 4). How many of the foulest crimes which have blackened the pages of history were perpetrated by ecclesiastical dignitaries? Yet the common people were in full accord with their leaders, for "the multitude" (Mark 15:8) requested Pilate to adhere to his custom of releasing a prisoner unto them, and when he gave them the choice between Christ and Barabbas, they preferred the latter; and when the governor asked what was their pleasure concerning the former, they cried "Crucify Him" (Mark 15:13). And it was to "content the people" Pilate released Barabbas (v. 15). When Pilate expostulated with them "all the people said, His blood be on us and on our children" (Matt. 27:25). And Pilate, the administrator of the Roman law, which boasted of justice, acceded to their unjust demands.

Second, *the scene.* This was the outskirts of Jerusalem, a city more memorable than either Rome, London or New York. This was the residence of David, the royal city, the seat of Israel's kings. It had witnessed the magnificence of Solomon's reign. It was here the temple stood. It was here the Lord Jesus had taught and wrought miracles, and into which He had ridden a few days earlier seated upon an ass, the multitudes crying, "Hosanna to the Son of David! Blessed is He that cometh in the name of the Lord; Hosanna in the highest" (Matt. 21:9)—so fickle is human nature! Israel had rejected their King and therefore He was conducted beyond the bounds of the city, so that He "suffered without the gate" (Heb. 13:12). The actual place of the crucifixion was Golgotha which signified "the place of a skull." Nature had anticipated the awful deed, the very contour of the ground resembling a death's head. Luke gives the Gentile name "Calvary" (23:33), for the guilt of that Death rested on both Jew and Gentile, as its saving efficacy was to be experienced by each.

Third, *the time.* This was as significant and suggestive as the historical and topographical associations of the place itself. Christ was crucified on the fourteenth of Nissan or about the beginning of April. It was the first of Israel's great national feasts, the most important season in the Jewish year. It was the Passover, when solemn celebration was made of that night when all the firstborn sons of the Hebrews were spared from the angel of death in the land of Egypt. At this season Jerusalem was thronged by immense multitudes, for it was one of the three annual occasions when every male Israelite was commanded to appear before Jehovah in the temple (Deut. 16:16). Thus, huge crowds had journeyed thither from all parts of the land. It was in no obscure corner nor in secret that the Great Sacrifice was offered up to God. And the fourteenth of Nissan was the day appointed for it, for the Lord Jesus was the antitypical Lamb—"Christ our Passover is sacrificed for us" (1 Cor. 5:7). On no other day *could He* be slain: at an earlier date they "sought to take Him: but no man laid hands upon Him, because His hour was not yet come" (John 7:30).

"They crucified Him....and sitting down they watched Him there." My divisions will be simple: what they saw; what I see; what do you see?

I. What they saw.

1. They beheld *the most amazing event* of all history, the most awe-inspiring spectacle ever set before the eyes of men, the most tragic and yet the most glorious deed ever performed on this earth. They beheld God incarnate taken by wicked hands and slain, yet at the same time the Redeemer voluntarily laying down His life for those who have forfeited every claim upon Him. To those soldiers it was an ordinary event: the execution of a criminal. And thus it is with most of those who hear the Gospel: it falls upon their ears as a religious commonplace. To those Roman soldiers, at least for awhile, Christ appeared to them only as a dying Jew. Thus it is with the multitude today: to them the Lamb of God possesses neither form nor comeliness and when He is set before them in the mirror of the Word they see in Him no beauty that they should desire Him. His peerless Person attracts them not. His righteous claims are disregarded—His sceptre is flouted—for His atoning blood they feel no need.

2. They beheld *the incomparable perfections of the crucified One.* How immeasurably different the mien of the suffering Saviour from what they had witnessed from others in similar circumstances! No cursing of His lot, no reviling of His enemies, no maledictions upon themselves. The very reverse—His lips are engaged in prayer! "Father," He says, "forgive them, for they know not what they do" (Luke 23:34). How amazed they must have been as they heard that Blessed One on the tree making "intercession for the transgressors" (Isa. 53:12). The two thieves who were crucified with Him mocked the Redeemer (Matt. 27:44), but at the eleventh hour one of them was "granted repentance unto life" (Acts 11:18) and turning to Jesus he said, "Lord, remember me when Thou comest into Thy kingdom" (Luke 23:42). The Lord did not decline his appeal and say he had sinned beyond the reach of mercy but answered, "Verily, I say unto thee, Today shalt thou be with Me in Paradise" (v. 43). Thus they witnessed an unparalleled display of sovereign grace unto one of the greatest of sinners.

3. They beheld *most mysterious phenomena.* They had sat down to "watch Him," but after a while they were no longer able to do so. At midday it suddenly became as midnight: "from the sixth hour (after sunrise) there was darkness over all the land unto the ninth hour" (Matt. 27:45). It was as though the sun refused to shine on such a scene, as though nature itself was mourning over such a sight! During those three hours there took place a transaction between Christ and God which was infinitely too sacred for finite eyes to gaze upon—a mystery which no mortal mind can fully enter into. As soon as the Saviour committed His spirit into the hands of the Father, "Behold, the veil of the temple was rent in twain from the top to the bottom; and the earth did quake and the rocks rent, and the graves were opened, and many bodies of the saints which slept arose" (Matt. 27:51, 52). No ordinary sufferer was this. It was the Creator of Heaven and earth, and Heaven and earth here expressed their sympathy.

4. They beheld and heard *that which was blessed to their conviction and conversion.* Pharaoh witnessed the moat remarkable display of God's power in the plagues which He sent upon Egypt, but so far from inclining him to repentance he continued to harden his heart. Thus it ever is with the unregenerate while then are left to themselves: neither the most astonishing tokens of God's goodness nor the most awe-inspiring of His judgments melt or move them. But in the case before us God was pleased to soften the callous hearts of these Roman soldiers and illumine their heathen minds, for we are informed, "Now when the centurion and they that were with him, watching Jesus, saw

the earth quake and those things that were done, they feared greatly, saying, truly this was the Son of God" (Matt. 27:54). Personally we regard this as another of the miracles which took place at Calvary—a miracle of amazing grace, and it is our expectation to meet in Heaven the very man who hammered the nails into the Saviour's hands and feet and thrust the spear into His side: God's answer to Christ's prayer, "Father, forgive them." Thus there is hope for the vilest sinner out of Hell if he will surrender to the Lordship of Christ and trust in His all-sufficient blood.

II. What I see.

I perceive here *an unveiling of the character of man.* "Now all things that are discovered (margin) are made manifest by the light: for whatsoever doth make manifest is light" (Eph. 5:13). Now Christ is "the true light" (John 1:9)—the essential, Divine, all-revealing light; consequently all men and all things stood exposed in His presence. The worst things predicated in Scripture of fallen human nature were verified and exemplified in the days of Christ. God says that the heart of man is "desperately wicked" (Jer. 17:9), and it was demonstrated to be such by the treatment meted out to His beloved Son. Scarcely was He born into this world than a determined effort was made to slay Him. Though He constantly went about doing good, relieving the distressed and ministering to both the souls and bodies of the needy, yet so little was He appreciated that He had to say, "The foxes have holes and the birds of the air nests, but the Son of Man hath not where to lay His head" (Matt. 8:20). On one occasion, "they besought Him that He would depart out of their coasts" (Matt. 8:34).

But not only was Christ unwelcome here, men *hated Him* and that "without a cause" (John 15:25). He gave them every reason to admire and adore Him, but they had an inveterate aversion for Him. The Word of Truth declares that "the carnal mind is enmity against God" (Rom. 8:7). Men do not believe it, in fact most of them affect the very opposite; nevertheless, at Calvary they gave proof of it. Multitudes go through the form of paying homage to God, but it is a "god" of their own imagination. They hate the true and living God, and were it possible would rid the universe of His existence. This is clear from their treatment of Christ, for He was none other than "God manifest in flesh" (1 Tim. 3:16) and Him they hated and hounded to death, and nothing short of death by crucifixion would appease them. Here at Calvary the real character of man was revealed and the desperate wickedness of his heart laid bare. There it was shown that he was capable of the blackest of all crimes. Then let us not be surprised that the history of mankind is written in tears and blood.

2. I perceive here air *unveiling of sin.* Sin! that "abominable thing" which the Lord hates (Jer. 44:4), but which is regarded so lightly by those who commit it. Sin! which caused our first parents to be banished from Eden and which is responsible for all the want and woe that is in the world. Sin! which produces strife and bloodshed and has turned this "land of the living" into a mammoth cemetery. Sin! that hideous monster we so much dislike hearing about and which we are so ready to gloss over and excuse. Sin! over which Satan employs all his subtle arts to render attractive, setting it forth in the most appealing colours and winsome garbs. One of the great designs of the Incarnation was to bring to light the hidden things of darkness. The personal presence here of the Holy One acted like a brilliant light being turned on in a long-neglected room, revealing its squalor and filth. "If

I had not come and spoken unto them, they had not had sin, but now they have no cloak for their sin" (John 15:22).

In the passage just quoted Christ was speaking *comparatively.* Evil as man had shown himself all through his history, the coming of Immanuel to this earth brought sin to such a head that all that which had gone before was relatively but a trifling thing when compared with the monstrous wickedness which was done against Love incarnate. In the treatment which the Son of God received at the hands of men we see sin in its true colours, stripped of a disguise, exposed in its hideous reality, revealed in its true nature as contempt of God, rebellion against Him. Here at Calvary we behold the climax of sin and the fearful and horrible lengths to which it is capable of going. That which germinated in Eden culminated in the crucifixion. The first sin occasioned spiritual suicide, the second took the form of fratricide (Cain murdering his brother), but here at Calvary it issued in Deicide—the slaying of the Lord of Glory. We see also the fearful wages which sin pays—death, departure from God. Since Christ hung there as the Sin-bearer of all who believe in Him, He received the punishment which was due unto them.

3. I perceive an *unveiling of the character of God.* The heavens declare His glory and the firmament shows His handiwork, but nowhere are His perfections more awfully and illustriously displayed than at the Cross. See here His *ineffable holiness.* The holiness of God is the delight He has in all that is pure and lovely, and therefore does His nature abominate and burn against whatever is evil. God hates sin wherever it is found and He made no exception of Christ when He beheld it lying by imputation upon His beloved Son. There God had "laid on Him the iniquity of us all" (Isa. 53:6)—that is, all His people — He dealt with Him accordingly, pouring out His holy wrath upon Him. God is "of purer eyes than to behold evil, and canst not look on iniquity" (Hab. 1:13) and therefore did He turn His back upon the Sin-bearer. "My God, My God, why hast Thou forsaken Me?" the suffering Saviour cried, and then answered His own query: "Thou art holy" (Psa. 22:1, 3).

See here God's *inflexible justice.* The pronouncement of His Law is, "the soul that sinneth it shall die" (Ezek. 18:4), and no deviation from it can be made, for Jehovah has expressly declared that He, "will by no means clear the guilty" (Exo. 34:7). But will He not make an exception of that One whom He testifies is the Lamb "without spot and without blemish" (1 Peter 1:19)? No, for though Christ was sinless both by nature and by action yet because the sins of His people had been laid upon Him, God "spared not His own Son" (Rom. 8:32). Because sin was transferred to Him punishment must be visited upon Him, and therefore did God cry, "awake O sword against My Shepherd, against the Man that is My Fellow, saith the LORD of hosts, smite the Shepherd" (Zech. 13:7). God would not abate one iota of His righteous demand or allow sentiment to sully the fair face of His government. He claims to be par excellence the Judge who is "without respect of persons" and fully was that demonstrated at Calvary by refusing to exempt the Person of His Beloved, the One in whom His soul delighted (Isa. 42:1), when occupying the place of the guilty.

See here God's *amazing grace.* "God commendeth His love toward us (His people) in that while we were yet sinners, Christ died for us" (Rom. 5:8). Had He so pleased, God could have consigned the whole of Adam's race to everlasting woe. That is what each of us richly deserve. And why should He not do so? By nature we are depraved and corrupt; by practice incorrigible rebels—with no love for Him and no concern for His glory. But out of His own goodness and benignity He determined to save a people from their sin, to redeem them by Christ, "to the praise of the glory of His grace" (Eph. 1:6). He determined to pluck them as brands from the burning, that they might be the eternal monuments of His mercy. And because it was wholly outside of their power to make atonement for their fearful crimes, He Himself provided an all-sufficient Sacrifice for them. He is "the God of all grace" (1 Peter 5:10) and innumerable tokens and proofs has He given of this, but nowhere were the "riches of His grace" so lavishly and so wondrously displayed as at Calvary.

See here God's *manifold wisdom.* The Word of Truth declares, "There shall in nowise enter into it anything that defileth, neither worketh abomination" (Rev. 21:27), then how is it possible that I can ever gain admittance into the heavenly Jerusalem? How can it be that one so completely devoid of righteousness as I am and so filled with unrighteousness could ever receive the Divine approbation? The Law says, "The soul that sinneth it shall die" and I have sinned and broken the Law—how then can I escape its penalty? Since I am a spiritual pauper how can the necessary ransom be procured? Those are problems that no human intelligence can solve. Nor is the knot to be cut by an appeal to the bare mercy of God, for His mercy is not an attribute which overrides His justice and integrity. But at the Cross the Divine perfections shone out in glorious unity like the blending of the colours in the rainbow: there "mercy and truth met together, righteousness and peace have kissed each other" (Psa. 85:10). God's justice was satisfied by Christ and therefore His mercy flows freely to all who repent and believe. God's grace reigns "through righteousness," and Christ's blood can cleanse the foulest. The wisdom of God appears in creation and Providence but nowhere so grandly as at the Cross.

4. I see myself. What? Yes, as I turn my gaze to the Cross I behold myself, and so does each other who looks with the eyes of faith. Christ hung there as the Sponsor and Surety of His people, and there cannot be representation without identification—Christ identified with those whose sins He bears—believers identified with Him. In the sight of God they are one. Christ took my place and faith appropriates that fact. In the Person of my Substitute I satisfied every requirement of God's Law. In the Person of Christ I paid the full price which Divine justice demanded. In the Person of Christ I stand approved before God, for I am clothed with His meritorious perfections (Isa. 61:10). The whole ransomed Church of God can say of Christ, "He was wounded for our transgressions and bruised for our iniquities" (Isa. 53:5), "Who His own self bare our sins in His own body on the tree" (1 Peter 2:24). And faith individualizes it and declares, "I am crucified with Christ....who loved me and gave Himself *for me*" (Gal. 2:20). Hallelujah! What a Saviour.

III . What do you see ?

I mean those of you who are unsaved. 1. You behold One whom you *despise and reject.* Perhaps you deny it, saying your attitude is merely negative—indifference. You err. If you are not the friend of Christ you are His enemy—there is no third class. "He that is not with Me is against Me" (Matt. 12:30) is His own verdict, and from that there is no appeal. You have despised His authority, flouted His laws, treated His claims with contempt. You reject His yoke and sceptre, refusing to be ruled by Him. Thus you unite with those who cast Him out and hounded Him to death.

2. You behold One who is *presented as Saviour.* Yes, despite your wicked treatment of Him hitherto. He is set before you in the Gospel as One willing and able to heal

the wounds that sin has made and save your souls from eternal death. If you will throw down the weapons of your warfare against Him, surrender to His Lordship and trust in His redeeming blood, He will accept you now—"him that cometh to Me I will in no wise cast out" (John 6:37). But if you refuse to do so, then—

3. You behold the One who is to be *your Judge.* Come to Him now as a repentant sinner, as a spiritual pauper, casting yourself upon His grace, and He will pardon your iniquities and give you a royal welcome. "Come unto Me all ye that labour and are heavy laden, and I will give you rest" (Matt. 11:28) is His own invitation and promise. But continue turning your back upon Him and He shall yet say to you, "Depart from Me ye cursed into everlasting fire, prepared for the Devil and his angels" (Matt. 25:41).with those who cast Him out and hounded Him to death.

2. You behold One who is *presented as Saviour.* Yes, despite your wicked treatment of Him hitherto. He is set before you in the Gospel as One willing and able to heal the wounds that sin has made and save your souls from eternal death. If you will throw down the weapons of your warfare against Him, surrender to His Lordship and trust in s redeeming blood, He will accept you now—"him that cometh to Me I will in no wise cast out" (John 6:37). But if you refuse to do so, then—

3. You behold the One who is to be *your Judge.* Come to Him now as a repentant sinner, as a spiritual pauper, casting yourself upon His grace, and He will pardon your iniquities and give you a royal welcome. "Come unto Me all ye that labour and are heavy laden, and I will give you rest" (Matt. 11:28) is His own invitation and promise. But continue turning your back upon Him and He shall yet say to you, "Depart from Me ye cursed into everlasting fire, prepared for the Devil and his angels" (Matt. 25:41).

[A sermon—slightly revised—preached by the editor in Colorado in 1911.]

(continued from back page)

Israel (1) did evil in the sight of the LORD and forgat the LORD their God, and served Baalim and the groves. Therefore (2) the anger of the LORD was hot against Israel and He sold them into the hand of Chushanrishathaim and the children of Israel served Chushanrishathaim eight years. And (3) when the children cried unto the LORD, the LORD raised up a deliverer to the children of Israel, who delivered them" (Judges 3:7-9). The same order—sin, punishment, penitence and merciful deliverance—is repeated again and again in the book of Judges.

That these principles of the Divine administration apply to the Gentiles, equally with the Jews, is unmistakably clear from the case of Nineveh a heathen city, concerning which the Lord said "their wickedness is come up before Me" (Jonah 1:2). Unto the vast metropolis the Prophet was sent, crying, "Yet forty days and Nineveh shall be overthrown" (3:4). But note well the sequel: "So the people of Nineveh believed God, and proclaimed a fast and put on sackcloth, from the greatest of them even to the least of them... And he (the king) caused it to be proclaimed . . . Let neither man nor beast, herd or flock, taste anything: let them not feed nor drink water . . . let them cry mightily unto God: yea, let them turn every one from his evil way and from the violence that is in their hands. Who can tell if God will turn and repent, and turn away from His fierce anger, that we perish not? And God saw their works, that they turned from their evil way; and God repented of the evil that He had said that He would do unto them, and He did it not" (Jonah 3:5-10).—A.W.P.

(continued from front page)

over those where such things prevail not. Nothing so tends to uphold the throne, elevate the mind of the masses, promote industry, sobriety and equity between man and man, as does the genuine practice of piety, the preservation of the virtues and suppression of vice, as nothing more qualifies a nation for the favour of God. Righteousness is productive of health, of population, of peace and prosperity. But every kind of sin has the contrary tendency. "The prevalence of vice and impiety is a nation's reproach, conduces to disunion, weakness and disgrace, and exposes any people to the wrath and vengeance of God" (Thomas Scott). When sin has become a public "reproach" then ruin is imminent.

We repeat, then, that Jeremiah 18 portrays not Jehovah as the Determiner of eternal destiny but rather as the Dispenser of temporal benefits, not as decreeing the hereafter of individuals but as distributing the portions of the kingdoms. "Thou art the God, even Thou alone, of all the kingdoms of the earth" (2 Kings 19:15), and as such He governs them on the basis of His moral Law and in accordance with the discharge of their responsibilities thereto. Jeremiah 18 reveals to us the fundamental principles which sibilities thereto. Jeremiah 18 reveals to us the fundamental principles which regulate the dealings of the Most High with the nations and the relations which He sustains to them. First, He is shown as an absolute Sovereign over Israel in particular and over all peoples in general: "as the clay is in the potter's hand, so are ye in Mine hand, O house of Israel"

(v. 6). Jehovah has the most incontestable and immediate power over them. This shows the infinite ease with which He can deal with the most fractious. "He increaseth the nations and destroyeth them: He enlargeth the nations and straiteneth them" (Job 12:23).

Second, the Lord is here depicted as the righteous Governor of the nations, dealing with them according to their deserts. In the exercise of His high and unchallengeable authority the Most High is pleased to act according to the principles of goodness and equity. There is no arbitrary caprice in the infliction of punishment: "the curse causeless shall not come" (Prov. 26:2). The Lord "doth not afflict willingly ("from the heart," margin) nor grieve the children of men" (Lam. 3:33), but only because they give Him occasion to and because the honour of His name requires it. "O that thou hadst hearkened to My commandments, then had thy peace been as a river and thy righteousness as the waves of the sea" (Isa. 48:18) is His own avowal. Yea, had they respected His authority "I should soon have subdued their enemies and turned My hand against their adversaries" (Psa. 81:14) He declares. Let it be definitely recognized that God's dealings with the nation of Israel illustrate His administration of the nations today.

Third, the justice of God is tempered with mercy in His government of the nations. "The Lord is of great mercy" (Num. 14:18) and "plenteous in mercy" (Psa. 86:5), and therefore, "His tender mercies are over all His work" (Psa. 145:9). Consequently, when the dark clouds of Divine wrath gather over a kingdom, yea even when His thunderbolts have begun to be launched, genuine repentance will check the storm. When a people humble themselves beneath God's almighty hand, evidencing the genuineness of their repentance by turning away from their wickedness and doing that which is pleasing in His sight, His judgments are turned away from them. "And the children of

. (continued on proceeding page)

VOL. XXII.   JUNE, 1943.   NO. 6

STUDIES IN THE SCRIPTURES

" Search the Scriptures." John 5:39.

Publisher and Editor—ARTHUR W. PINK,
27 Lewis Street,
Stornoway, Isle of Lewis,
Scotland.

GOD GOVERNING THE NATIONS.

"Repent ye, and believe the Gospel" (Mark 1:15): "repentance toward God, and faith toward our Lord Jesus Christ" (Acts 20:21). Unless there be both repentance and faith there is no forgiveness of sins for any soul, yet there are comparatively few passages in which both of them are expressly *mentioned.* In Luke 13:3; Acts 2:38 and 17:30 "repentance" alone is inculcated. In John 3:15; Romans 1:16 and 10:4 only "believing" is specified. Why is this? Because the Scriptures are not written as lawyers draw up documents, wherein terms are needlessly repeated and multiplied. Each passage of the Word must be interpreted in the light of and consistently with "the Analogy of Faith" (Rom. 12:6, Greek)—the general tenor of Scripture—and none made exceptional to the general rule. Thus concerning the above references: where only "repentance" is mentioned, "believing" is implied, and when "believing" is found alone, "repentance" is presupposed. The same principle applies to all other subjects: for example, prayer, "Ask, and ye shall receive" (Matt. 7:7) is not to be taken without qualification: if we are to "receive, we must "ask" *aright*—believingly (Heb. 11:6), according to God's will (1 John 5:14), in the name of Christ (John 14:13), and so on.

Our object in beginning with the above was to pave the way for an explanatory word on what was before us last month. Not a few have been puzzled over Jonah's positive and unqualified declaration, "Yet forty days and Nineveh shall be overthrown" (3:4), for such an announcement of disaster appeared to hold out no hope of escape. This affords a striking example of the necessity for interpreting each passage in the light of and in harmony with the Analogy of Faith. Now it is one of the established maxims of Scripture that where there is genuine repentance and reformation God will show mercy and stay His judgments. This is plainly stated in such places as Leviticus 26:40-42; 1 Kings 8:33-36, yet it is not formally expressed in every chapter or even every book. When God's Prophets were sent forth to announce judgments it was (except in extreme cases) with the proviso that the people threatened would be spared if they forsook their wickedness and returned to the paths of virtue. It was unnecessary to always *state* this because it was plainly revealed in the general rule.

Thus, when Jonah proclaimed the overthrow of Nineveh, though he specified not the *means* by which judgment could be arrested, yet they were understood—a reprieve would be granted if there were true repentance. Consequently his proclamation was no

IMPORTANT NOTICES

Please advise promptly of change in address, otherwise copies will be lost in the mails.

We are glad to send a sample copy to any of your friends whom you believe would be interested in this publication.

This magazine is published as "a work of faith and labour of love," the editor and his wife gladly giving their services free. There is no regular subscription price, as we do not wish the poor of the flock to be deprived. This does not mean that those looking for something for nothing may "help themselves." Those getting this Magazine, who are financially able and who receive spiritual help from its pages, are expected to gladly contribute towards its expenses; otherwise, their names are dropped from our lists.

Will those forwarding International Money Orders please have them made out to us at Stornoway, Isle of Lewis, Scotland. Checks (Cheques-Eng.) made out on U.S.A. Banks are not negotiable here, so please do not send them.

CONTENTS

THE SERMON ON THE MOUNT.

26. *Profession Tested:* Matthew 7:22-23.

There are few passages in all the Word of God which are more solemn than Matthew 7:21-23 and which are more calculated to induce the sober believer to work out his own salvation with fear and trembling. Certainly this writer regards it as much too important to skim over hastily. In these verses the Lord makes it known that there are those who regard themselves as genuine Christians merely because they have certain resemblances to the children of God, and who are even looked upon as such by others simply because of their outward conformity to the principles and ordinances of Christianity, and yet are denounced by Christ as "ye that work iniquity." So presumptuous are they that they are firmly convinced Heaven is theirs, yea, they are here represented as complaining to their Judge when He closes the door against them, putting in a plea for their claim at the bar of justice and arguing as though it were unfair that they should be excluded from the everlasting bliss of the righteous. Thus it is clearly implied that they lived and died in the full assurance they were the objects of God's approbation, that they were completely secured from the wrath to come.

Nor is this fatal delusion cherished by a comparative few, for our Lord here gives plain intimation that there are "many" who have implicit confidence in their salvation, but who will nevertheless hear from His lips those terrible words, "depart from Me." How is their infatuation to be explained? The general answer would be the deceitfulness of the human heart plus the sophistries of Satan. But on so deeply a serious matter as this we need something more than generalizations. When a thoughtful person learns that some dangerous disease is menacing the community, he wants to learn all he can about its nature, its symptoms, and especially the best means of prevention, of safeguarding himself against it. If we deem no pains and care too much in fortifying ourselves against a bodily disease, will the reader complain at the slowness of the writer's progress if he endeavours to give a more specific and detailed answer to this weighty question?—how shall we account for such a fatal confidence? We will seek to point out the grounds on which such a delusion rests, that we may avoid this woeful mistake.

1. *Ignorance.* Last month we showed at some length the insufficiency of a mere intellectual acquaintance with the letter of Scripture, but let it not be concluded therefrom that a notional knowledge of the Truth is of no value because it falls short of a saving one, still less derive encouragement for slothfulness. It is in the use of *means* that God is often pleased to meet with souls, and while they are reading and meditating on His Word, to shine into their hearts. Scripture places no premium upon ignorance or indolence. Instead of saying, If such knowledge will not bring a man to Heaven to what purpose is it to labour after knowledge? rather ask yourself, How far must I be from Heaven if I lack even that knowledge?! What we brought out on the subject of a notional knowledge of the Truth last month, instead of affording comfort to the ignorant should rather strike them with fear and trembling. If so much knowledge will not secure salvation, then how much worse is my case when I am destitute of what even he possesses? If those who come so near to the kingdom as to be able to view it and yet not enter, then what hope is there for those who are content to remain far off from it?

So near are the ignorant to Hell that they are within the very shadow of it. "Darkness and the shadow of death" are joined together in Scripture (Matt. 4:16). Ignorance is spiritual darkness, the very shadow of eternal death. There is but a thin partition between those immersed in spiritual ignorance and Hell itself. Hell is termed "the *outer* darkness" (Matt. 8:12), because ignorance is the inner darkness, the next room as it were to Hell itself. Sad, indeed, is the condition of such. If those who come so near to Canaan as to obtain a taste of its wondrous fruits and yet fall in the wilderness so that they never entered in, how can they expect to enter Canaan who refuse to stir out of Egyptian darkness? One with much knowledge may possibly perish, but one who is quite ignorant of spiritual things shall *certainly* perish. When God makes mention of "a people of no understanding," He at once adds, "therefore He that made them will not have mercy on them" (Isa. 27:11). "Where ignorance is bliss 'tis folly to be wise," certainly does not hold good here.

We do not have to go so far afield today as what is termed heathendom, there are millions within Christendom, yea, countless thousands of church goers and members who know not what is necessary to bring a soul to Heaven. They know not that regeneration is imperative, that "except a man be born again he cannot see the kingdom of God," that as a fish cannot live out of water because away from its own element, so man is totally unfit for communion with the Holy One until he be renewed within. They know not that there must be a new creation, a miracle of grace wrought in the soul to make fallen man a new creature, so that it can be said of him, "old things are passed away, behold all things are become new" (2 Cor. 5:17). The new Jerusalem is for new creatures. They know not that God must communicate to the heart a principle of holiness before there can be any holy affections, motions or fruits. Without holiness no man shall see the Lord (Heb. 12:14) and by nature man does not have the least grain of it.

So ignorant are the vast majority of those even in places reputed to be sound and orthodox that they know not there must be the denying of self before anyone can become a follower of Christ: a repudiation of our own wisdom, righteousness, strength, desires, will, and interests. They know not there must be a renunciation of the world before anyone can be a follower of Him who left the glories of Heaven and entered the manger of Bethlehem: that we must be crucified unto the world and the world unto us or we shall never enter into the benefits and blessings purchased by the crucifixion of Christ. They know not that there must be a plucking out of right eyes and a cutting off of right hands, a mortifying of the flesh with its affections and lusts, so that we die daily. They know not that there must be a taking up of the cross if any man will come after Christ, which will cost him the loss of godless companions, the scorn of professors, many a tear and groan. They know not that the Christian life is a fierce wrestling (Eph. 6:12), a continual fight, a race that has to be run with all our might if the crown is to be obtained. If they really knew these things, they would not be nearly so confident of Heaven when they are total strangers to the very things required of all those for whom Heaven is intended.

2. *Negligence and slothfulness.* Those who *do* have a vague and general idea of the things mentioned above are too indolent to lay them to heart, make them their chief concern and prayerful meditation, that they many understand them more clearly. Even if they know them they will not take the pain to seriously examine their state by them: they will not go to the trouble of comparing their hearts with the Divine rule. So little interested are they in the eternal welfare they will not spare a few hours to solemnly inquire whether or not they measure up to what the Word of God requires of them. Alas for the wretched carelessness of the vast majority concerning their souls and everlasting state. They conduct themselves as atheists, acting as though there is no God, no day of reckoning, no lake of fire. They carry themselves as madmen, chasing shadows, playing with dynamite, sporting on the edge of the Pit. They are indeed beside themselves (Luke 15:17), devoid of "the spirit of a sound mind" (2 Tim. 1:7). If they were sane they would study God's Word to discover its directions concerning salvation and would test themselves by those directions.

Their very indifference and carelessness demonstrates the mass of our fellows to be practical atheists and spiritual lunatics. If they were sane they would be deeply concerned whether Heaven or Hell was to be their eternal abode. They would deem no trouble too great to ascertain which they were journeying unto, which their personal condition fitted them for. They would snatch a few of their swiftly passing hours and devote them to diligent inquiry and self-examination. They would not proffer idle excuses and postpone the task, but would promptly and earnestly set about. it. Only those bereft of spiritual sense and reason would neglect a matter the issue of which is either everlasting life or everlasting death. But no—rather than seriously trouble themselves, they will complacently assume all is well with them and take it on trust they are bound for Heaven, when the only grounds they have for such trust are the lies of Satan and that which their own deceitful hearts prompt. They thus rest the whole weight of eternity upon a cobweb and pin the everlasting concern of their souls upon a shadow!

What makes it more inexcusable is the fact that these same people are quite competent and painstaking over their *temporal* affairs. If a new position be offered them they make careful inquiries before committing themselves. If they purpose making an investment, they go to much trouble in ascertaining the soundness of it. If they think of purchasing a property they make full investigation as to its title-deeds and value. But when it comes to *eternal* things they are dilatory and slipshod, half-hearted and lazy. They make no serious preparation to meet their God, and when His call comes it finds them wanting. They are sluggards and therefore the sluggard's portion and doom will be theirs. Thus, when men and women are so slack and careless about their souls, when they will not make serious and solemn inquiry about their state, we need not wonder that so many are so woefully mistaken as to promise themselves Heaven when in reality nothing but Hell is reserved for them.

3. *Misapprehensions of God.* Where people are in ignorance and where they are too sottish to make any real and serious effort to dispel their ignorance, false conceptions of the Divine character are certain to obtain. True, there are degrees of ignorance and therefore there are considerable differences in the erroneous ideas men form of God. But those formed by the *unregenerate*, whether they be the gross ones of the heathen or the more refined ones of Christendom, are alike false. Viewing God through the blurred lens of depraved hearts and minds they fashion Him as one suited to their corrupt inclinations. They invent a God who treats sin lightly, who looks with indulgence upon their waywardness, who is willing to accept a few religions performances as sufficient compensation for all their debt. "Thou thoughtest that I was altogether such an one as thyself" is the charge which He prefers against them, but adds, "I will reprove thee and set them in order before thine eyes" (Psa. 50:21).

They do not believe that God is inexorably just so that He will "by no means clear the guilty," but that every transgression and disobedience must receive a due recompense of reward unless a sinless Substitute make atonement for them. They do not believe it is impossible to mock God with impunity, that as men sow they reap, so that if they sow to the flesh they must of necessity reap corruption. They do not believe that God is omniscient, that "His eyes are in every place, beholding the evil and the good," for if they did it would act as a curb upon them. They do not believe God is so strict that He will call us to account for "every idle word" and that He "weigheth the spirits" (Prov. 16:2)—the springs of action, the motives which prompt. They do not believe He is ineffably holy, so that sins of thought as well as deed, of omission as well as of commission, are hateful to Him. They do not believe that God is "a consuming fire" (Heb. 12:29) so that this world and all its works will be burned up and that everyone whose name is not written in the Book of Life will be cast into the Lake of Fire. They do not believe that God is absolute sovereign, so that "He hath mercy on whom He will have mercy, and whom He will He hardeneth" (Rom. 9:18).

Even where there is sufficient light and conviction as to reveal to sinners that they come short of the Divine rule, and where they perceive that what the Word insists is necessary to salvation is not found in them, instead of abandoning their false hopes they persuade themselves that God is more merciful than the Scriptures represent Him to be. It is true, says the sinner, in such a case that the way to Heaven is a narrow one and that God's kingdom can only be entered "through much tribulation" (Acts 14:22), but God will save me even though I fail here and there and I be lacking in this and that. It is true that God *is* merciful, yet for *one sin* He banished our first parents from Eden! It is true that God is merciful, but for *one sin* His curse descended upon Ham and his posterity. It is true that God is merciful, but for *one sin* Lot's wife was turned into a pillar of salt, Achan and his family were stoned to death, Gehazi was smitten with leprosy, Ananias and Sapphira became corpses. God is merciful, yet He sent the flood upon the world of the ungodly, rained fire and brimstone upon the cities of the plain, sent His angel and slew all the firstborn of Egypt and destroyed Pharaoh and his hosts at the Red Sea.

Though they allow themselves in this sin and that, though they are thoroughly self-willed and self-pleasing, they tell themselves that God is lenient. Though they ignore God's righteous claims upon them and make no effort to meet His holy requirements, they comfort themselves with the thought that He is gracious. They refuse to allow that He is as strict and rigid as His faithful servants declare Him to be. They petulantly ask, Even though I be not precise and puritanical as some are, shall I not be saved even as they? Though I come not up to their standard, yet God is very pitiful and knows how weak we are, and therefore He will lower the standard for me so that I may be saved as well as the best of them. Poor deluded souls: if that be all their hope, their case is indeed hopeless. Will God be so merciful as to contradict Himself and go contrary to His Word? Must He show them so much mercy as to despise His own Truth and make Himself a liar!? What cause have they to tremble who have nothing to bear up their hopes of Heaven but downright blasphemy.

4. *Self-love and self-esteem.* This is as prolific and powerful a cause of self-deception as any of those mentioned above. Sinners compare themselves with their fellows and award themselves the first prize every time. He who is immoral regards himself as better than those who grind the poor and rob the widow. He who is a liar and a thief prides himself that he is no murderer. He who is outwardly religious deems himself vastly superior to the openly profane. Each one discovers some cause or other to say with the self-righteous Pharisee, "I thank God that I am not as this publican." This is because they measure themselves by a wrong standard. Even a soiled handkerchief looks comparatively clean if it is placed on a miry road, but were it laid on newly-fallen snow its uncleanness would soon be evident. So it is with those who are blind to their deplorable condition. Men are possessed with such a high estimate of themselves and entertain such a good opinion of their soul's condition that even if they can be induced to measure themselves by the rule of God's Word and examine their state, they come to the work prepossessed, prejudiced in their own favour. Self-love will not suffer them to deal impartially with their souls.

When they read some condemnatory passage of Scripture they refuse to appropriate it: when they hear a particularly solemn and searching sermon they take it not home to themselves but apply it to some of their fellows. If they be awakened in some measure to the awfulness of sinning against God and alarmed at the fearful punishment reserved for such, this mood is only fitful and fleeting—they quickly reassure themselves that no such guilt rests upon them. Sudden death may strike down some of their companions, but self-delusion blinds them to their own peril. A manifest judgment from God may fall upon their community, but they persuade themselves they are in no danger of the wrath to come. The fact is that there are very few, indeed, who abandon all hope, give way to utter despair and conclude *they will* experience the everlasting burnings, and yet there is only a very little company who will escape them. The multitudes continue defying God, sinning with a high hand, and go on walking along the road which leads to the Pit, and yet by one means or another each persuades himself he shall not enter there. "For he flattereth himself in his own eyes, until his iniquity be found to be hateful" (Psa. 36:2).

Yes, the sinner "*flattereth himself* in his own eyes." If he did not, he would be in terrible distress and anguish. He would not go on so cheerfully and gaily if he really believed himself in danger of Hell. But he has too good an estimate of himself for that:

he does not think he has ever done anything worthy of such a doom. He is sure he is not bad enough for such a place. Men convince themselves they do not live in vice but are decent citizens and good neighbours. They can see no reason why God should be angry with them. They do not take His name in vain nor scoff at religion. Yea, they flatter themselves they have done much to commend themselves to Him and obtain His approbation. They read their Bibles occasionally and say their prayers. They attend church and contribute to its upkeep. They send their children to the Sabbath-School. They resolve that later on they will be even better, out and out for Christ, but meanwhile they want to enjoy the world a little longer, "trust in themselves that they are righteous" (Luke 18:9) and are comparatively clean in their own sight, and yet they are not washed from their filthiness (Prov. 30:12).

There are others, many such, who flatter themselves they are genuine Christians. They persuade themselves that they have repented of their past, believed the Gospel, and that their sins are forgiven. Consequently when they hear or read anything solemn it makes no impression upon them. Self-love and self-esteem blind them to their true condition. They are Laodiceans who say, "I am rich (spiritually) and increased with goods (have made considerable progress and grown in grace) and in need of nothing," but as the Lord declares, "and knowest not that thou art wretched, and miserable, and poor, and blind, and naked" (Rev. 3:17). And nothing shakes them out of their self-complacency. They continue flattering themselves "until their iniquity be found to be hateful"—until they are disillusioned in Hell. As a blind man cannot judge of colours, so prejudiced in their own favour are the self-righteous that it is impossible for them to judge of the complexion of their souls, whether the image of God or the image of the Devil be stamped upon it. As one has well said, "Satan blinds one eye and self-love closes the other, and the deceitfulness of sin seals both," and thus they assure themselves they are on the way to Heaven when they are on the high road to Hell. Doubtless a number of such will read this very article and be quite unsearched by it, sure that it pertains not to *their* case.

A closing word to Christian readers. Since the four things described above are the principal ones among the more immediate causes of deceit concerning the state of the soul, then how sincerely ought the regenerate examine themselves at these points and seek to make sure they are not imposing on themselves. How they should "cease from man" and search the Scriptures without bias to ascertain the general tenor of their teaching as to *what God requires* if they are to dwell with Him forever, not confining themselves to such verses as John 3:16 and Romans 10:13, but comparing such as Isaiah 55:7; Acts 3:19; Hebrews 5:9, etc, so as to obtain a full answer to the question, "What must I do to be saved?" How cautiously and conscientiously should we examine ourselves, testing the grounds of our hope, determining whether or not there really is in us that which meets God's terms, whether or not our righteousness exceeds that of the religious formalist (Matt. 5:20). Nor can such a task be discharged hurriedly: "*Give diligence* to make your calling and election sure" (2 Peter 1:10)—with what earnestness should we give ourselves to this work!

"Thus saith the LORD, Let not the wise man glory in his wisdom, neither let the mighty man glory in his might, let not the rich man glory in his riches: but let him that glorieth glory in this, that he understandeth and knoweth *Me,* that I am the LORD which exercise lovingkindness, judgment and righteousness in the earth" (Jer. 9:23,

24). Yes, "knoweth Me," the living God, and not a fantasy which your own sentiment has devised. To believe in a God which has no existence save in their own imagination is the case with multitudes in the churches today. "Acquaint now thyself with Him and be at peace" (Job. 22:21). To cherish the image of a fictitious God entails a fictitious peace. Eternal life is "to know Thee the only *true God*, and Jesus Christ, whom Thou has sent" (John 17:3). How we should labour after such a knowledge of Him! Finally if self-love and esteem effectually hinder an impartial examination of myself, if it be the case with a host of my fellows that "a deceived heart hath turned him aside, that he cannot deliver his soul nor say, Is there not a lie in my right hand?" (Isa. 44:20) how earnestly should I cry to God to grant me an honest heart which desires to know the truth and nothing but the truth about my case.—A.W.P.

THE MISSION AND MIRACLES OF ELISHA.

6. *Third Miracle.*

"And he went up from thence unto Bethel: and as he was going up by the way, there came forth little children out of the city and mocked him, and said unto him, Go up thou bald head, go up thou bald head. And he turned back and looked on them, and cursed them in the name of the Lord. And there came forth two she bears out of the wood and tare forty and two children of them" (2 Kings 2:23, 24). In seeking to give an exposition of this miracle let us observe, first, its *connection.* It will be noted that our passage opens with the word "And" and as there is nothing meaningless in Scripture it should be duly pondered. Nor is its force difficult to perceive, for it evidently intimates that we should observe the relation between what we find here and that which immediately precedes. The context records the wonders which God wrought through Elisha at the Jordan and at Jericho. Thus the truth which is here pointed by the conjunction is plain: when the servant has been used by his Master he must expect to encounter the opposition of the Enemy.

There is an important if unpalatable truth illustrated here, one which the minister of Christ does well to take to heart if he would be in some measure prepared for and fortified against bitter disappointment. After a season of blessing and success he must expect sore trials. After he has witnessed the power of God attending his efforts he may count upon experiencing something of the rage and power of Satan, for nothing infuriates Satan so much as beholding his victim delivered from spiritual death and set free from that which he occasioned in Eden. Elisha had been signally favoured both at the Jordan and at Jericho, but here at Bethel he hears the hiss of the Serpent and the roaring of the lion against him. Ah, the minister of the Gospel is fully aware of this principle, yea often reminds his hearers of it. He knows it was the case with his Master, for after the Spirit of God had descended upon Him and the Father had testified to His pleasure in Him, He was at once led into the wilderness to be tempted of the Devil. Yet how quickly is this forgotten when *he* is called to pass through this contrastive experience.

It is one thing to know this truth theoretically and it is quite another to have a personal acquaintance with it. The servant of Christ is informed that the smile of Heaven upon his labours will arouse the enmity of his great Adversary, yet how often is he taken quite unawares when the storm of opposition bursts upon him! It ought not to be so, but so it usually is. "Think it not strange concerning the fiery trial which is to try you" (1 Peter 4:12). Various indeed are the ups and downs which are encountered by those who labour in the Christian vineyard. What a striking contrast is here presented to our view! At Jericho Elisha is received with respect: the young Prophets render obeisance to him and the men of the city seek his help; here at Bethel he is contemptuously ridiculed by the children. At Jericho, the city of the curse, he is an instrument of blessing; at Bethel, which signifies "the house of God" and where blessings might therefore be expected, he solemnly pronounces a curse upon those who mock him.

Second, its *occasion*. This was the insulting of God's servant. As Elisha was approaching Bethel, "there came forth little children out of the city and mocked him." Upon reading this incident it is probable that some will be inclined to say, It seems that children then were much like what they are now—wild, rude, lawless, totally lacking in respect for their seniors. From this analogy the conclusion will be drawn: therefore we should not be surprised nor unduly shocked at the present day delinquency of our youth. But such a conclusion is entirely unwarranted. It is true there is "nothing new under the sun" and that fallen human nature has been the same in every age. But it is not true that the tide of evil has always flowed uniformly, and that each generation has witnessed more or less of the appalling conduct which now mark the young in every part of Christendom. No, very far from it.

When there was an ungrieved Spirit in the churches the restraining hand of God was held upon the baser passions of mankind. That restraint operated largely through parental control—moral training in the home, wholesome instruction and discipline in the school, and adequate punishment of young offenders by the State. But when the Spirit of God is "grieved" and "quenched" by the churches, the restraining hand of the Lord is removed, and there is a fearful moral aftermath in all sections of the community. When the Divine Law is thrown out by the pulpit there inevitably follows a breakdown of law and order in the social realm, which is what we are now witnessing all over the so-called "civilized world." That was the case to a considerable extent twenty-five years ago, and as the further an object rolls down hill the swifter becomes it momentum, so the moral deterioration of our generation has proceeded apace. As the majority of parents were godless and lawless it is not to be wondered at that we now behold such reprehensible conduct in their offspring.

Older readers can recall the time when juveniles who were guilty of theft, wanton destruction of property, and cruelty to animals, were sternly rebuked and made to smart for their wrong-doing. But a few years later such conduct was condoned and "boys will be boys" was used to gloss over a multitude of sins. So far from being shocked, many parents were pleased and regarded their erring offspring as "smart," "precocious" and "cute." Education authorities and psychologists insisted that children must not be suppressed and repressed but "directed" and prated about the evils inflicted on the child's character by "inhibitions," and corporal punishment was banished from the schools. Today the parent who acts according to Proverbs 13:24; 19:18; 22:15 and 23:1 will not only be called a brute by his neighbours but is likely to be summoned before the courts for cruelty, and instead of supporting him the magistrate will probably censure him. The present conduct of children is not normal but abnormal. What is recorded in our passage occurred in the days of Israel's *degeneracy!* Child delinquency is one of the plain marks of a *time of apostasy*—it was so then, it is so now.

Third, its *location*. As with the former miracles, the place where this one happened also throws much light upon that which occasioned it. Originally Bethel was called "the house of God" (Gen. 28:16-17), but now it had become a habitation of the

Devil, one of the principal seats of Israel's idolatry. It was here that Jeroboam had set up one of the calves. Afraid that he might not be able to retain his hold upon those who had revolted from Rehoboam, especially if they should go up to Jerusalem and offer sacrifices in the temple, he "made two calves of gold, and said unto them, It is too much for you to go up to Jerusalem: behold thy gods, O Israel, which brought thee up out of the land of Egypt. And he set the one in Bethel, and the other put he in Dan . . . And he made a house of high places and made priests of the lowest of the people which were not of the sons of Levi. And Jeroboam ordained a feast for the eighth month, on the fifteenth day of the month, like unto the feast that is in Judah and he offered upon the altar. So did he in Bethel, sacrificing unto the calves that he had made: and he placed in Bethel the priests of the high places which he had made" (1 Kings 12:28-32).

Thus it will be seen that so far from Bethel being a place which basked in the sunshine of Jehovah's favour it was one upon which His frown now rested. Its inhabitants were no ordinary people, but high-rebels against the Lord, openly defying Him to His face, guilty of the most fearful abominations. This it was which constituted the dark background of the scene that is here before us: this it is which accounts for the severity of the judgment which fell upon the youngest of its inhabitants: this it is which explains why these children conducted themselves as they did. What occurred here was far more than the silly prank of innocent children: it was the manifestation of an inveterate hatred of the true God and His faithful servant. Israel's worship of Baal was far more heinous than the idolatry of the Canaanites, for it had the additional and awful guilt of apostasy. And apostates are always the fiercest persecutors of those who cleave to the Truth, for the very fidelity of the latter is a witness against and a condemnation of those who have forsaken it.

Fourth, its *awfulness*. The fearful doom which overtook those children must be considered in the light of the enormity of their offense. Our degenerate generation has witnessed so much condoning of the greatest enormities that they may find it difficult to perceive how this punishment fitted the crime. The character of God has been so misrepresented by the pulpit, His claims so little pressed, the position occupied by His servants so imperfectly apprehended, that there must be a returning to the solemn teaching of Holy Writ if this incident is to be viewed in its proper perspective. Of old God said, "Touch not Mine anointed and do My Prophets no harm" (Psa. 105:15): they are His messengers, His accredited representatives, His appointed ambassadors, and an insult done to them is regarded by Him as an insult against Himself. Said Christ to His ministers, "He that receiveth you receiveth Me, and he that receiveth Me receiveth Him that sent Me" (Matt. 10:40). Conversely, he that despiseth and rejecteth the one sent forth by Christ despiseth and rejecteth Him. How little is this realized today! The curse of God now rests on many a place where His ministers were mocked.

"And he went up from thence unto Bethel; and as he was going up by the way, there came forth little children out of the city and mocked him, and said unto him, Go up, thou bald head" (2 Kings 2:23). After the vain search which had been made for Elijah (v. 17), it is likely that some inkling of his supernatural rapture was conveyed to the Prophets at Jericho, and from them to their brethren at Bethel (v. 3), and hence we may conclude that his remarkable translation had been noised abroad—received with scepticism and ridicule by the inhabitants of Bethel. In their unbelief they would mock at it, as the apostate leaders of Christendom do not believe that the Lord Jesus actually rose again from the dead and that He ascended to Heaven in a real physical body, as they make fun of the Christian's hope of his Lord's return and of being caught up to meet Him in the air (1 Thess. 4:16, 17). Thus in saying, "Go up, thou bald head" they were, in all probability, scoffing at the tidings of Elijah's translation—scoffs put into their mouths by their elders.

"They had heard that Elijah was 'gone up to Heaven' and they insultingly bade Elisha follow him, that they might be rid of him also, and they reviled him for the baldness of his head. Thus they united the crimes of abusing him for a supposed bodily infirmity, contemptuous behaviour towards a venerable person, and enmity against him as the Prophet of God. The sin therefore of these children was very heinous: yet the greater guilt was chargeable on their parents, and their fate was a severe rebuke and awful warning to them" (Thomas Scott). How true it is that "the curse causeless shall not come" (Prov. 26:2). "And he turned back and looked on them" which indicates he acted calmly, and not on the spur of the moment. "And he cursed them in the name of the Lord"—not out of personal spite, but to vindicate his insulted Master. Had Elisha sinned in cursing these children Divine providence had not executed it. This was fair warning from *God* of the awful judgment about to come upon Israel for their sins.

Fifth, its *ethics*. The passage before us is one which infidels have been quick to seize upon, and lamentable, indeed, have been many of the answers returned to them. But the Scriptures have survived every opposition of its enemies and all the purile apologies of its weak-kneed friends. Nor are the Scriptures in any danger whatever from this skeptical and blatant age. Being the Word of God they contain nothing which His servants have any need to be ashamed of, nothing which requires any explaining away. It is not our province to sit in judgment upon Holy Writ: our part is to tremble before it (Isa. 66:2), knowing that one day we shall be judged by it (John 12:48). As Jehovah was able to look after the sacred Ark without the help of any of His creatures (1 Sam. 6:10-12) so His Truth is in need of no carnal assistance from us. It is to be received without question and believed in with all our hearts. It is to be preached and proclaimed without hesitation or reservation: holding back no part of it.

Certain so-called "Christian apologists" have replied to the taunts of infidels by a process of what is termed "toning down" the passage, arguing that it was not little children but young men who were cursed by the Prophet and torn to pieces by the bears: but such an effeminate explanation is as senseless as it is needless. We quite agree with Thomas Scott when he says, "Some learned men have endeavoured to prove that these offenders were not young children but grown-up persons, and no doubt the word rendered 'children' is often used in that sense. The addition, however of the word 'little' seems to clearly evince they were not men, but young boys who had been brought up in idolatry and taught to despise the Prophets of the Lord." Others hesitate not to roundly condemn Elisha, saying he should have meekly endured their taunts in silence and that he sinned grievously in cursing them. Sufficient to point out that his Master deemed otherwise: so far from rebuking His servant, he sent the bears to fulfill his curse, and there is no appeal against *His* decision!

The passage before us is one that Dispensationalists have sought to make capital out of, supposing that it furnishes a convincing illustration and demonstration of the line they draw or rather the gulf they would make between the Old and New Testaments. Trading on the ignorance and credulity of their hearers, most of whom will readily accept the dogmatic assertions of any who pose as men with "much light," these teachers have insisted that many of the actions of the Prophets were entirely foreign to and actuated by a radically different spirit from that which was inculcated and exemplified by Christ and His Apostles. They argue that Elijah's slaying of the prophets of Baal and Elisha's cursing of the children evidences the vast difference there is between the dispensations of the Law and of Grace, and the unlearned and unwary are deceived by such clap trap. Sufficient to remind such people that Ananias and Sapphira fell dead at the denunciation of Peter and that Elymas was smitten with blindness by Paul (Acts 13:8-11)!

How blind these dispensationalists are. During the very course of why they term this "era of grace" God is even now giving the most awe-inspiring and wide-reaching proof of His wrath against those who flout His Law, visiting the earth with sorer judgments than any He has sent since the days of Noah. The New Testament equally with the Old teaches "it is a righteous thing with God to recompense tribulation to them that trouble you" (2 Thess. 1:6). In the incident before us God was righteously visiting the sins of the fathers upon the children, as He was by the death of their children also smiting the parents in their tenderest parts. At almost the end of the Old Testament era we read that Israel "mocked the messengers of God and despised His words and *resisted His Prophets*, until the wrath of the LORD arose against His people till there was no remedy" (2 Chron. 36:16). Here at Bethel God was giving a warning, a sample of His coming wrath, unless they reformed their ways and treated His servants better.

Sixth, its *meaning*. At first glance it certainly appears that there can be no parallel between the above action of Elisha and that which should characterize the servants of Christ, and many are likely to conclude that it can only be by a wide stretch of the imagination or a flagrant wresting of this incident that it can be made to yield anything pertinent for this age. But it must be remembered that we are not looking for a *literal* counterpart but rather a *spiritual* application, and viewing it thus our type is solemnly accurate. Ministers of the Gospel are "unto God a sweet savour of Christ in them that are saved *and* in them that perish. To the one they are the savour of death unto death and to the other the savour of life unto life" (2 Cor. 2:15, 16). Certainly the evangelist has no warrant to anathematize any who oppose him but he is *required* to pronounce accursed of God those who love not Christ and who obey not His Law (1 Cor. 16:22; Gal. 3:10).

Seventh, its *sequel*. This is recorded in the closing verse of 2 Kings 2. "And he went from thence to mount Carmel, and from thence he returned to Samaria." In the violent death of those children as the outcome of Elisha's malediction we behold the stating of the Prophet's Divine authority, the sign of his extraordinary office, and the fulfillment of the prediction that he should "slay" (1 Kings 19:17). After his unpleasant experience at Bethel the Prophet betook himself to Carmel, which had been the scene of Elijah's grand testimony to a prayer-answering God (1 Kings 18). By making for the mount this servant of God intimated his need for the renewing of his strength by communion with the Most High and by meditation upon His holiness and power. Samaria was the country where the apostate portion of Israel dwelt, and by going thither Elisha manifested his readiness to be used of his Master as He saw fit in that dark and difficult field of labour.

There is only space left for us to barely mention some of the more outstanding lessons to be drawn from this solemn incident. First, "Behold therefore the goodness and severity of God" (Rom. 11:22): if the previous miracle exemplified His "goodness," certainly this one demonstrated His "severity"; and the one is as truly a Divine perfection as the other! Second, the words as well as actions of children, even "little children," are noticed by God! They should be informed of this and warned against showing disrespect to God's servants. Third, what must have been the grief of those parents when they beheld the mangled bodies of their little ones! But how much greater the anguish of parents in the Day of Judgment when they witness the everlasting condemnation of their offspring if it has been occasioned by their own negligence and evil example. Fourth, sooner or later God will certainly avenge the insults shown His ministers: this writer could relate more than one example of a horrible death overtaking one and another of those who opposed and slandered him.—A.W.P.

THE RISEN CHRIST AND THOMAS.

"But Thomas, one of the twelve, called Didymus, was not with them when Jesus came" (John 20:24). It is remarkable that one of the disciples should have been absent from the assembly on such an interesting occasion as when Christ appeared among them after His resurrection. What was the cause of his absence it would be worse than useless to conjecture. But the intention of Divine Providence in it is obvious. It was to display the natural unbelief, as to the things of God, that is in the heart of man; and to teach us the kind of evidence that God accounts sufficient for His saving Truth.

Why was one of the disciples absent? Why was this disciple Thomas? The narrative itself affords an answer to both questions. Divine Providence intended to give us a specimen of unbelief even in His own people. Thomas was peculiarly incredulous; therefore he was the person fitted to act the part designed for him on this occasion. If Thomas was afterwards convinced, there is no room left for captiousness to allege that the fact of Christ's resurrection was received by the disciples on slight grounds, without sufficient evidence and caution.

The unbelief of Thomas was unreasonable and sinful in a degree beyond expression. Why did he not believe the united testimony of the other Apostles? He should have received the testimony of any one of them. Unbelief justly exposed him to eternal condemnation. Has Thomas a license for unbelief more than any other of the human race? Must he not be liable to condemnation on the same ground with the rest of mankind? Must he be satisfied in his own whims with respect to the evidence of this fact? "Except I shall see in His hands the print of the nails, and put my finger into the print of the nail and thrust my hand into His side, I will not believe." Did ever any infidel express a more unreasonable demand for the evidence of Christ's resurrection and the truth of the Christian religion? The demands of skeptics are moderate and sober compared to this intemperance of unbelief. The most unreasonable of them demand only that a particular revelation of the Gospel should be made to every man. This falls far short of the extravagance of unreasonableness of the unbelief of Thomas.

But there is wisdom in this madness. If Thomas is unreasonable God uses his unreasonableness to effect a great purpose. By this means, in the satisfaction given to Thomas, we have the fact of the resurrection established on evidence beyond all suspicion. The possibility of delusion is removed; and the reality that it was Jesus whom the Apostles saw, rests not merely on the testimony of *their* eyes, but of the hands of the most unreasonable unbeliever that ever was in the world. Of all the infidels that ever existed, Thomas was the most extravagant. Voltaire and Hume are men of moderation compared to the prince of infidels. Nothing will satisfy this philosopher but the handling of the prints of the nails in his Master. Was it not possible that the risen body of Jesus should have had no scars? Was not this the most likely thing to be expected? That the Almighty power which could raise Him, could raise Him without a mark of His crucifixion? But Thomas was in all respects unreasonable that through this Jesus might exhibit Himself with evidence of His resurrection the most extravagant incredulity could presume to demand.

By this providential fact the Lord teaches us that His own disciples believe in Him not because they are naturally more teachable or less incredulous than others. It is God only who overcomes their unbelief. They are not only by nature the children of wrath even as others; but after they are brought to faith and life, the only security of their perseverance is the favour and love of God in Christ. They are kept by faith, and that faith is not of themselves, but is the gift of God. The strongest of all the disciples of Christ would not abide in the faith for a single day, if, like Peter or like Thomas, they were to be given up to their own unbelief. But if the strongest would not stand in their strength, the feeblest will not be plucked from the hand of the heavenly Father. After the fearful example of Peter and of Thomas, let no disciple of Christ trust in his own steadfastness. We are strong only when, seeing our own weakness, we have strength in the Rock of our salvation.

The world in general and philosophers in particular look upon Christians as a weak-minded people who are prone to believe without sufficient evidence. The man of science, even when he can find no fault with the man of God, still thinks himself justifiable in considering him as utterly below himself in mental powers. He thinks there must be a soft place in his head somewhere. The best that he can find to say is, that he is "an amiable enthusiast." The Truth however, is far otherwise. Whether the believer is a man of strength of intellect, or feeble in mind, he would be equally an unbeliever with the most talented of his enemies, were he left to himself. Yea, the weakest would likely be the most presumptuous and rash, and blasphemous in the extravagance of their complaints against the Gospel. Thomas would not be behind Paine in the rashness of his demands and assertions. The Christian is made a little child by the Word and Spirit of God, but by nature he receiveth not the things of the Spirit, for they are to him, as well as to others, foolishness, until his eyes are opened to discover them, by the grace of God.

It is a matter of fact, worthy of particular attention, that the simplest of the men of God make a more correct and more scientific estimate of the philosopher, than the philosopher can make of him. The philosopher, with all his knowledge, knows not God by his philosophy. He knows not, then, the correct and enlightened views of the man of God on the highest of all sciences. The philosopher, not appreciating the value of the soul, nor the amount of the unspeakable glory of the heavenly inheritance, as well as of the danger of overlooking condemnation, sees not the wisdom of the conduct of the man of God. He has no way to judge him but by himself; and therefore as he himself is wise, the other must be a fool. The pleasure of knowledge and the glory of fame are, with the philosopher, the very essence of the happiness of the third heavens. In all this, the man of God, even the weakest of them, can enter into the feelings and sentiments of the men of science, for, by nature, he is such a one himself. And he still finds, in his very best moments, that if he should lose sight of Heaven, and be left of God, he would make his paradise with the philosophers, or, at least, according to his taste, with some group of those who are, in different ways, in pursuit of earthly joys.

The Christian is not amazed that men seek the praise of man more than that of God; and that they pursue the things of this world rather than the things of God. He is rather amazed that God has turned himself out of this course, and enables him to resist the temptations which he daily meets in the world. To him there is no mystery in the character and choice of the philosopher, of the sensualist, of the men of the world. In them he sees himself as he is by nature. It is with new eyes that he sees spiritual things in a correct manner. "The natural man receiveth not the things of the Spirit of God: for they are foolishness unto him; neither can he know them, because they are spiritually discerned. But he that is spiritual judgeth all things, yet he himself is judged of no man" (1 Cor. 2:14, 15). The Christian is the true philosopher. He not only has knowledge of the most sublime of all the sciences, of which the wise men of this world are as destitute as the wild ass of the wilderness, but he has that discernment of human views and character which human wisdom never has attained. The Christian knows the philosopher better than the philosopher knows himself. Of all the sciences, the science of mind is the most sublime; and Christians have a knowledge of the mind of man which no mere philosopher can obtain by his art. The philosopher gives an account of himself and of others, and of his own notions and views which every Christian can detect as delusive and unreal.

In this providential fact we see the forbearance and condescension of Christ to His people, even when they are unreasonable. He graciously removes the doubts of Thomas, though He might justly have left him to perish in his presumptuous unbelief. From this we may be assured that, in one way or other the Lord will remove the doubts of His people with respect to the evidence of the Gospel. He will not give them that evidence which extravagance many rashly demand, He will keep them from such extravagance, or remove their doubts by opening their eyes to understand the proper evidence. This will be the same thing with presenting to their view and to their touch His hands and His side. He will assuredly overcome the unbelief and hardness of heart of the most obstinate of His chosen ones.

If He were not provoked to give up Thomas, His patience cannot meet with a more extravagant case of incredulity. He could call a Saul of Tarsus in the midst of his furious enmity to Him, and He did overcome the unbelief of the incredulous and obstinate Thomas. What a consolation is this for the believer! What thoughts of unbelief arise in the heart! And how Satan could perplex the mind of the highest saint on earth, none but the believer can have any conception of. If we were for a few minutes, from a state of the most assured faith, to be given into the hands of Satan to sift us as wheat, how would our faith fail us! Who knows what effect the fiery darts of the wicked one would have upon our minds, if they were not quenched? And quenched they cannot be but on the shield of faith: and in the case God permits that faith to fail—what then, will support us? How shall we without dismay look into an eternal world? But though God may for a moment suffer us to be tried by the tempter, He will not suffer us to be tempted above what we are able, but will with the temptation make a way of escape, that we may be able to bear it. Our constant prayer to God ought to be that He would not give us into the hands of Satan, or that He will continue to give us the shield of faith.

In matters of so great moment, the mind, particularly at death, naturally looks for and wishes every evidence of the Truth, and sometimes demands unreasonable evidence. Nothing but the blood of Jesus should be before our eye and we should always remember that we glorify God, not by doubting, but by believing His Word. Were not Christ present with His people in the time of their trial, and especially at the time of their death, nothing could deliver them from horror. That they are not only saved from fear, but enabled to rejoice and triumph in death, is the surest evidence that the Gospel is true. It is not surprising that persons ignorant of the character of God, of their own character and of the consequences of sin, should be stupidly unconcerned at death. But the Christian knows too much to be kept from the very agonies of Hell if he had not the life of Heaven, when he passes through the dark valley and shadow of death. In the removal of the doubts of reason, let us gain confidence that the Lord will not forsake us in the time of our need. To a Christian, who is deeply acquainted with his own weakness, Hell itself is not a greater object of horror than to be given up without assistance from God, to wrestle with the prince of this world at the hour of death.

It is remarkable that the Lord, though He complied with the unreasonable demand for evidence in the case of Thomas, yet He would not listen to the request of the rich man in Hell, for the conviction of his relations on earth. "Then he said, I pray thee, therefore, father, that thou wouldest send him to my father's house; for I have five brethren; that he may testify unto them lest they also come into this place of torment" (Luke 16:27, 28). Did Abraham yield to the proposal and admire the plan? No. "Abraham saith unto him, They have Moses and the Prophets; let them hear them. And he said, Nay, father Abraham: but if one went unto them from the dead, they will repent. And he said unto him, if they hear not Moses and the Prophets, neither will they be persuaded though one rose from the dead" (vv. 29-31). Our skeptics are still calling for more or better evidence. If the Gospel is true, they allege it should have evidence against which no man could find objection. Let them alone. Press on them the evidence that God has given of the truth of His Gospel. If they believe not this, it will be found, in the Day of Judgment, that they have not rejected it from its own insufficiency, but from their own enmity to the Truth. Testimony is a sufficient ground of evidence; and if they reject the testimony of God by His Apostles, they will justly perish.

And the same thing will hold true with respect to the denial of the testimony of God with regard to any particular doctrine or part thereof. The enemies of the doctrine, or fact recorded, will allege a want of proof; and, on the authority of philosophical doctrines, will take on them to modify the testimony of God. They make the dogmas of human science an authority paramount to the testimony of God in the Scriptures. This is the boldness, the blasphemy of infidelity. If God has given His testimony on any part, it is evidence paramount in authority to every other. To prove the truth alleged on such authority, nothing is necessary but to show that it is the result of the fair exposition of the laws of language. Let God be true, and let all men be liars. Against the testimony of God the philosopher is not to be heard more than a convicted perjurer. Our Lord, even though, for His own wise purposes, indulged Thomas, yet did not approve of his unbelief, nor of his demand.

He did not ascribe his incredulity to greater talents or greater caution, or greater concern about the Truth, than were discovered by his brethren. On the contrary, He shows that they rather are blessed who will believe without such evidence as Thomas demanded. There are two extremes, equally to be avoided, into which men are prone to fall. Some believe without evidence, believe against all evidence, believe what all evidence, capable of being submitted to the mind of men, shows to be absurd and impossible. On the other hand, there are some who unreasonably refuse evidence that is sufficient, evidence which God has pronounced sufficient, and look on themselves as manifesting greater intellect or greater wisdom in demanding evidence of another kind which God has not appointed. "Thomas, because thou hast seen Me, thou hast believed: blessed are they that have not seen, yet have believed."—Alexander Carson.

DOCTRINE OF SAINTS' PERSEVERANCE.

8. *Its Safeguards.*

4. By insisting on *continuance* in well-doing. It is not how a person commences but how he ends which is the all-important matter. We certainly do not believe that one who has been born of God can perish, but one of the marks of regeneration is its *permanent* effects, and therefore I must produce those permanent fruits if my profession is to be credited. Both Scripture and observation testify to the fact that there are those who appear to run well for a season and then drop out of the race. Not only are there numbers induced to "come forward" and "join the church" under the high-pressure methods used by the professional evangelists who quickly return to their former manner of life, but there are not a few who enter upon a religious profession more soberly and wear longer. Some seem to be genuinely converted: they separate from ungodly companions, seek fellowship with God's people, manifest an earnest desire to know more of the Word, become quite intelligent in the Scriptures, and for a number of years give every outward sign of being Christians. But gradually their zeal abates, or they are offended at some wrong done them, and ultimately they go right back again into the world.

We read of a certain class "who for a while believed, and in time of temptation fall away" (Luke 8:13). There were those who followed Christ for a season, yet of them we read, "From that time many of His disciples went back and walked no more with Him" (John 6:66). There have been many such in every age. All is not gold that glitters, and not everyone who makes a promising start in the race reaches the goal. It is therefore incumbent upon us to take note of those passages which press upon us the necessity of continuance for they constitute another of those safeguards which God has placed around the doctrine of the security of His saints. On a certain occasion "many believed on Him" (John 8:30), but so far from Christ assuring them that Heaven was now their settled portion, we are told, "Then said Jesus to those Jews which believed on Him, IF *ye continue* in MY word then are ye My disciples indeed" (v. 31). Unless we abide in subjection to Christ, unless we walk in obedience to Him unto the end of our earthly course, we are but disciples in name and semblance.

We read of certain men who, "when they were come to Antioch, spake unto the Grecians, preaching the Lord Jesus." The power of God accompanied them and richly blessed their efforts, for, "The hand of the Lord was with them: and a great number believed and turned unto the Lord" (Acts 11:20, 21). Tidings of this reached the church at Jerusalem, and mark well their response: they sent Barnabas to them, "who, when he came and had seen the grace of God, was glad, and exhorted them all that with purpose of heart they would *cleave unto* the Lord" (vv. 22, 23). Barnabas was not one of those fatalistic hyper-Calvinists who argued that since God has begun a good work in them all would be well—that the Holy Spirit will care for, instruct, and guard them, whether or not they be furnished with ministerial nurses and teachers. Instead, he recognized and discharged his own Christian responsibility, dealt with them as accountable agents, addressed to them suitable exhortations, pressed upon them the indispensable duty of their cleaving to the Lord. Alas that there are so few like Barnabas today.

At a later date we find that Barnabas returned to Antioch accompanied by Paul, and while there they were engaged in "confirming the souls of the disciples, exhorting them *to continue* in the faith" and warning them that "we must through much tribulation enter into the kingdom of God" (Acts 14:22). How far were they from believing in a mechanical salvation, reasoning that if these people had been genuinely converted they would necessarily "continue in the faith"! Writing to the Corinthians, the Apostle reminded them of the Gospel he had preached unto them and which they had received, yet failing not to add, "By which also ye are saved IF ye *hold fast* that which I preached unto you, unless ye have believed in vain" (1 Cor. 15:2). In like manner he reminded the Colossians that they were reconciled to God and would be preserved unblameable and unreproveable "IF ye *continue* in the faith, grounded and settled, and be not moved away from the hope of the Gospel" (1:23). There are those who dare to say there is no "if" about it, but such people are taking direct issue with Holy Writ.

Even when writing to a minister of the Gospel, his own "son in the faith," Paul hesitated not to exhort him, "Take heed unto thyself and unto the doctrine; continue in them," adding, "for in doing *this* thou shalt both save thyself (from apostasy) and them that hear thee" (1 Tim. 4:16). To the Hebrews he said, "But Christ as a Son over His own house, whose house are we, IF we hold fast the confidence and the rejoicing of the hope firm *unto the end*" (3:6). And again, "For we are made partakers of Christ IF we hold the beginning of our confidence steadfast unto the end" (3:14). How dishonestly has the Word of God been handled by many! Such passages as these are never heard from many pulpits from one year's end to another. It is much to be feared that many pastors of "Calvinistic" churches are afraid to quote such verses lest their people should charge them with Arminianism. Such will yet have to face the Divine indictment "Ye have not kept My ways, but have been *partial* in the Law" or Word (Mal. 2:9).

We find precisely the same thing in the writings of another Apostle. James though addressing those whom he terms, "my beloved brethren," calls upon his readers, "But be ye doers of the Word, and not hearers only, deceiving your own selves. For if any be a hearer of the Word, and not a doer, he is like unto a man beholding his natural face in a glass: for he beholdeth himself, and goeth his way, and straightway forgetteth what manner of man he was (that is, nothing but a superficial and fleeting effect is produced upon him). But whoso looketh into the perfect Law of liberty, and *continueth* therein, he being not a forgetful hearer, but a doer of the work, this man shall be blessed in his deed" (1:22-25). The word for "beholdeth" is a metaphor taken from those who not only glance at a thing but bend their bodies towards it that they may carefully scrutinize it—used in Luke 24:12, and 1 Peter 1:12; denoting earnestness of desire, and diligent enquiry. To "continue therein" signifies a persevering study of the Truth, and abiding in the belief of and obedience to the same, thereby evidencing our *love* for it. Many have a brief taste for it, but their appetite is quickly quenched again by the things of this world.

It is perfectly true, blessedly true, that there is no "if," no uncertainty, from the *Divine* side in connection with the Christian's reaching Heaven: everyone who has been justified by God shall without fail be glorified. Those who have been Divinely quickened will most assuredly continue in the faith and persevere in holiness unto the end of their earthly course. This is clear from 1 John 2:19, where the Apostle alludes to some in his day who had apostatized, "They went out from us, but they were not of us"—they belonged not to the family of God, though for awhile they had fraternized with some of its members.

"For" adds the Apostle, "if they had been of us (had they really been one in a personal experience of the regenerating power of the Spirit) they would have *continued* with us"— nothing could have induced them to heed the siren voice of their seducers. "But they went out from us that they might be made manifest that they were *not* all of us"—but merely temporary professors, stony-ground hearers, nominal Christians, members of a totally different family. Previously they had every appearance of being the genuine article, but by their defection they were exposed as counterfeits. No, there is no "if" from the Divine side.

Nevertheless, there is an "if" from the *human* side of things, from the standpoint of our responsibility, in connection with my making sure that I am one of those whom God has promised to preserve unto His heavenly kingdom. Continuance in the faith, in the path of obedience, in denying self and following Christ, is not simply desirable but indispensable. No matter how excellent a beginning I have made, if I do not continue to press forward I shall be lost. Yes, lost, and not merely miss some particular crown or millennial honours as the deluded dispensationalists teach. It is persevere or perish: it is final perseverance or perish eternally—there is no other alternative. Romans 11:22 makes that unmistakably clear: "Behold therefore the goodness and severity of God: on them that fell (the unbelieving Jews) severity: but toward thee (saved Gentiles, v. 11), goodness, IF thou *continue* in His goodness: *otherwise* thou also shalt be cut off." The issue is plainly drawn: continuance in God's goodness or being "cut off." To continue in God's goodness is the opposite of returning to our badness. The evidence that we are the recipients of God's goodness is that we continue in the faith and obedience of the Gospel. The end cannot be reached apart from the appointed means.

But I cannot see the consistency between what has been set forth in the last two paragraphs, some will exclaim. What of it: who are you? who am I? Merely short-sighted creatures of yesterday, upon whom God has written "folly and vanity." Shall human ignorance set itself against Divine wisdom? Does any reader dare call into question the practice of Christ and His Apostles: *they* pressed the "if" and insisted upon the needs-be for this "continuing"; and those ministers who fail to do so—no matter what their standing or reputation—are no servants of God. Can you see the consistency between the Apostle affirming so positively of those who have received the Holy Spirit from Christ "ye *shall* abide ("continue"—the same Greek word as in all the above passages) in Him," and then in the very next breath exhorting them, "And now, little children, *abide* ("continue") in Him" (1 John 2:27, 28)—if you cannot it must be because of theological blinkers. Can you see the consistency of David asserting so confidently, "The LORD will perfect that which concerneth me: Thy mercy O LORD, endureth forever," and then immediately after praying, "forsake not the works of Thine own hands" (Psa. 138:8)—if you cannot then this writer places a big question-mark against your religious profession.

5. By insisting that there are *dangers to guard against.* Here again there will be those who object against the use of this term in such a connection. What sort of dangers, they will ask: dangers of the Christian's severing his fellowship with God, losing his peace, spoiling his usefulness, rendering himself unfruitful?—granted, but not of missing Heaven itself. They will point out that safety and danger are opposites and that

one who is secure in Christ cannot be in any peril of perishing. However plausible, logical, and apparently Christ-honouring that may sound, we would ask, Is *that* how Scripture represents the case? Do the Epistles picture the saints as being in no danger of apostasy? Or, to state it less baldly: are there no sins warned against, no evils denounced, no paths of unrighteousness described, which if persisted in do not certainly terminate in destruction? And is there no responsibility resting on me in connection therewith? Apostasy is not reached at a single bound, but is the final culmination of an evil process, and it is against those things which have a tendency unto apostasy against which the saints are repeatedly and most solemnly warned.

One who is now experiencing good health is in no immediate danger of dying from tuberculosis, nevertheless if he recklessly exposes himself to the wet and cold, if he refrains from taking sufficient nourishing food which supplies strength to resist disease, or if he incurs a heavy cough on his chest and makes no effort to break it up, he is most likely to fall a victim to consumption. So while the Christian remains spiritually healthy he is in no danger of apostatizing, but if he starts to keep company with the wicked and recklessly exposes himself to temptation, if he fails to use the means of grace, if he experiences a sad fall, and repents not of it and returns to his first works, he is deliberately heading for disaster. The seed of eternal death is still in the Christian: that seed is sin, and it is only as Divine grace is diligently and constantly sought for the thwarting of its inclinations and suppressing of its activities, that it is hindered from developing to a fatal end. A small leak which is neglected will sink a ship just as effectually as the most boisterous sea. And as Spurgeon said on Psalm 19:13, "Secret sin is a stepping stone to presumptuous sin, and *that* is the vestibule of 'the sin which is unto death' " (Treasury of David).

Did no dangers menace Israel after Jehovah brought them out of Egypt with a high hand and by His mighty arm conducted them safely through the Red Sea? Did all who entered upon the journey to Canaan actually arrive at the promised land? Perhaps some one replies, *They* were under the old covenant and therefore supply no analogy to the case of Christians today. What says the Word? This, they "were all baptized unto Moses in the cloud and in the sea; and did all eat the same spiritual meat, and did all drink the same spiritual drink, for they drank of that spiritual Rock that followed them, and that Rock was Christ" (1 Cor. 10:2-4). What analogy could be closer than that? Yet the passage goes on to say, "But with many of them God was not well pleased: for they were overthrown in the wilderness" (v. 5). And what is the use which the Apostle makes of this solemn history? Does he say that it has no application unto us? The very reverse: "Now these things were our examples, to the intent that we should not lust after evil things as they also lusted . . . neither let us tempt Christ, as some of them also tempted and were destroyed of serpents" (vv. 6-9). Here is a most deadly danger for us to guard against.

Nor did the Apostle leave it at that. He was still more definite, saying, "Neither murmur ye as some of them also murmured, and were destroyed of the Destroyer. Now all these things happened unto them for examples, and they are written for our admonition upon whom the ends of the world are come," making this specific application unto Christians, "Wherefore let him that thinketh he standeth take heed lest *he* fall" (vv. 10-12). Paul was no fatalist but one who ever enforced moral responsibility. He inculcated no mechanical salvation, but one which must be worked out "with fear and trembling." Charles Hodge of Princeton was a very strong Calvinist, yet on 1 Corinthians 10:12 he failed not to say: "There is perpetual danger of falling. No degree of progress we have already made, no amount of privileges which we may have enjoyed, can justify the want of caution. 'Let him that thinketh he standeth,' that is, who thinketh himself secure . . . neither the members of the church nor the elect can be saved unless they persevere in holiness, and they cannot persevere in holiness without continual watchfulness and effort," i.e., against the dangers menacing them.

The above is not the only instance when the Apostle made use of the case of those Israelites who perished on their way to Canaan to warn New Testament saints of *their danger.* After affirming that God was grieved with that generation, saying, "They do alway err in their heart and they have not known (loved) My ways, so I sware in My wrath, They shall not enter into My rest," Paul added, "Take heed, brethren, lest there be in any of you an evil heart of unbelief in departing from the living God. But exhort one another daily, while it is called Today, lest any of you be hardened through the deceitfulness of sin" (Heb. 3:12, 13). We are not here warned against an imaginary peril but a real one. "Take heed" signifies watch against carelessness and sloth, be on the alert as a soldier who knows the enemy is near, lest you fall an easy prey. Those here exhorted are specifically addressed as "brethren" to intimate there are times when the best of saints need to be cautioned against the worst of evils. An "evil heart of unbelief" is a heart which dislikes the strictness of obedience and universality of holiness which God requires of us.

After referring again to those "whose carcasses fell in the wilderness" to whom God sware, "they shall not enter into My rest, because of their unbelief" or "disobedience" (3:16, 19), the Apostle said, "Let us therefore *fear* lest a promise being left us of entering into His rest, any of you should seem to come short of it" (Heb. 4:1). "Fear" is as truly a Christian grace as is faith, peace or joy. The Christian is to fear temptations, the dangers which menace him, the sin which indwells him, the warnings pointed by others who have made shipwreck of the faith and the severity of God in His dealings with such. He is to fear the threats of God against sin and those who indulge themselves in it. It was because Noah was "moved with fear" at the warning he had received from God that he took precautions against the impending flood (Heb. 11:7). God has plainly announced the awful doom of all who continue in allowed sin, and fear of that doom will inspire caution and circumspection, and will preserve from carnal security and presumption. And therefore are we counselled, "passing the time of your sojourn here in *fear*" (1 Peter 1:17)—not only in exceptional seasons, but the whole of our time here.

We can barely glance at a few more of the solemn cautions addressed not merely to formal professors but to those who are recognized as genuine saints. "Be sober, be vigilant, because your adversary the Devil, as a roaring lion walketh about seeking whom he may devour. Whom resist steadfast in the faith" (1 Peter 5:8, 9). Obviously such a warning would be meaningless if the Christian were not threatened with a most deadly danger. "Ye therefore, beloved, seeing ye know these things before, *beware* lest *ye also,* being led away with the error of the wicked, fall from your own steadfastness" (2 Peter 3:17). This warning looks back to the false prophets of (2:1, 2)—and what is said of them in verses 18-22? The "error of the wicked" here cautioned against includes both doctrinal and practical, especially the latter—forsaking of the "narrow way" the highway of holiness which alone leads to Heaven. "Hold that fast which thou hast, that no man take thy crown" (Rev. 3:11)—cling tenaciously to the Truth you have received, the faith which has been planted in your heart, in the measure of grace given you.

But how do you reconcile the Christian's danger with his safety? There is nothing to reconcile, for there is no antagonism. Enemies and not friends need reconciling, and warnings are the Christian's friend, one of the safeguards which God has placed around the Truth of the security of His people, preventing them from wresting it to their destruction. By revealing the certain consequences of total apostasy Christians are thereby cautioned and kept from the same: a holy fear moves their hearts and so becomes the *means of preventing* the very evil they denounce. A lighthouse is to warn against recklessness as mariners near the coast so that they will steer away from the fatal rocks. A fence before a precipice is not superfluous, but is designed to call to an halt those journeying in that direction. When the driver of a train sees the signals change to red he shuts off steam, thereby preserving the passengers under his care. The danger signals of Scripture to which we have called attention are heeded by the regenerate and therefore are among the very means appointed by God for the preservation of His people, for it is only by attending to the same they are kept from destroying themselves.—A.W.P.

SOLOMON'S TEMPLE.

[What follows is not designed for the careless and casual reader who hurriedly skims these pages merely to ascertain what is in them, but for refined minds that can appreciate the sublime and who will deem themselves well repaid for rereading this piece more slowly and thoughtfully. We can say this the more freely inasmuch as it is no composition of ours—nor is our pen capable of reaching such heights—but rather that of one who wrote almost two centuries ago: James Hervey, a rector in a small parish in Northamptonshire. No one denomination can claim a monopoly of God's most faithful and eminent servants, nor have they been confined to Nonconformity. Some of His choicest ministers were bestowed upon the Church of England, as such men as Toplady, Berridge, John Newton, and a host of others since them prove.]

With immense charge and exquisite skill Solomon had erected the most rich and finished structure that the sun ever saw. Yet, upon a review of his work and a reflection on the transcendent perfections of the Godhead, how he exalts the one and abases the other! The building was too glorious for the mightiest monarch to inhabit, too sacred for unhallowed feet even to enter, yet infinitely too mean for the Deity to reside in. It was, and the royal worshipper acknowledged it to be, a most marvellous vouch-safement in uncreated excellency to "put His Name there." The whole passage breathes such a delicacy and is animated with such a sublimity of sentiment: "But will God indeed dwell on earth? Behold! the Heaven and Heaven of heavens cannot contain Thee, how much less this house that I have builded!" (1 Kings 8:27).

"But will"—a fine abrupt beginning, most significantly describing the amazement and rapture of the royal Prophet's mind. "*God*": he uses no epithet, where writers of inferior discernment would have multiplied them; but speaks of the Deity as an incomprehensible Being, whose perfections and glories are exalted above all praise. "Dwell"—to bestow on sinful creatures a propitious lock, to favour them with a transient visit of kindness, even this were an unutterable obligation. Will He then vouchsafe to *fix* His abode among them and take up His stated residence with them? "Indeed"—a word in this connection peculiarly emphatic, expressive of a condescension, wonderful and extraordinary almost beyond all credibility. "Behold"!—intimating the continued, or rather the increasing surprise of the speaker, and awakening the attention of the hearer. "Behold! the Heaven"—the spacious concave of the firmament: that wide extended azure circumference, in which worlds unnumbered perform their revolutions, is too scanty an apartment for the Godhead. "Nay: the Heaven of heavens"—those vastly higher tracts, which lie far beyond the limits of human survey, to which our very thoughts can hardly soar; even these (unbounded as they are) cannot afford an adequate Habitation for Jehovah; even these dwindle into a point when compared with the Infinite of His Essence; even these "are as nothing before *Him*." "How much less"—proportionate is this poor diminutive speck (which I have been erecting and embellishing) to so august a Presence, so immense a Majesty!

We are apt to be struck with admiration at the stateliness and grandeur of a masterful performance in architecture. And perhaps on a sight of the ancient sanctuary should have made the superficial observation of the disciples: "What manner of stones!" and "what buildings are here!" But what a nobler turn of thought and more just plane of things does it discover to join with Israel's king in celebrating the condescension of the Divine Inhabitant! That the high and lofty One who fills immensity with His glory, should, in a peculiar manner fix His abode there! Should there manifest an extraordinary degree of His benedictive Presence, permit sinful mortals to approach His Majesty, and promise "To make them joyful in His house of Prayer!" This should more sensibly affect our hearts than the most curious arrangement of stones can delight our eyes

Nay, the everlasting God does not disdain to dwell in *our souls* by His Holy Spirit, and to make even our *bodies* His temple! Tell me, ye that frame critical judgments and balance nicely the distinction of things, Is this most astonishing or most rejoicing? He humbleth Himself, the Scriptures assure us, ever to behold the things that are in Heaven (Psa. 113:6). 'Tis a most condescending favour if HE pleases to take the least approving notice of angels and archangels when they bow down in homage from their celestial thrones. Will He then graciously regard, will He be united, most intimately united to poor polluted man, breathing dust?—unparalleled honour! invaluable privilege! Be *this* my portion, and I shall not covet crowns nor envy conquerors.

(continued from back page)

their Messiah ere Jerusalem was razed to the ground. Well nigh six thousand years have gone since the Fall of our first parents, and yet human history has not closed! The Lord is "slow to anger," yet that slowness is neither indifference to evil nor slackness in dealing with the same—rather is it a proof that He "bears with much longsuffering the vessels of wrath fitted to destruction."

Still another purpose is served by the slowness of God unto anger and the interval between a nation's degeneracy and the execution of Divine judgment upon it, and that is, it serves to test more completely human responsibility and make manifest how richly deserved is the retribution which overtakes evildoers. If God's slowness to anger evidences His forbearance, how the general response of men thereto displays the inveteracy of their wickedness. "Because sentence against an evil work is not executed speedily, therefore the heart of the sons of men is fully set in them to do evil" (Eccl. 8:11). Because God keeps silent they imagine He is altogether such an one as themselves (Psa. 50:21). "Let favour be shown to the wicked, yet will he not learn righteousness" (Isa. 26:10). Despising the riches of God's goodness and longsuffering, after the hardness of his impenitent heart, man treasures up unto himself wrath against the day of wrath (Rom. 2:4, 5). And June, 1943 Studies in the Scriptures thus is it made apparent that he is "without excuse" and that his "damnation is just."— A.W.P.

(continued from front page)

heralding of God's inexorable fiat but rather the sounding of an alarm which operated as a means of moral suasion. Had Nineveh obstinately persisted in her sins, she would certainly have been promptly overthrown; but because she ceased from being a city where every form of wickedness ran riot and became a place where the name of God was feared and His authority respected, her doom was averted. Jonah was not disclosing the Divine decree, but rather spoke ethically, addressing himself to human responsibility. And when it is said that, "God repented of the evil that He had said that He would do unto them," He deigned to use a familiar form of speech. There was no change in His eternal purpose but an alteration in His *bearing* toward them because their conduct had changed for the better.

That our explanation of Jonah 3:4-10 is no mere plausible attempt or subtle device of getting out of a "tight place" should be quite evident from Jeremiah 18. "At what instant I should speak concerning a nation and concerning a kingdom to pluck up, and to pull down, and destroy it; *if* that nation against whom I have pronounced (not "decreed"!), turn from their evil, I will repent of the evil that I thought to do unto them" (vv. 7, 8). Though the threat be genuine and the danger real, yet the announcement of judgment is not an absolute one, but *qualified*, and when the qualification is not expressed it is *implied*. The implied reserve that God will deal in mercy with those who genuinely put right that which displeases Him and will not destroy such was perceived and appealed to by Abram when he said, "That be far from Thee to do after this manner, to slay the righteous with the wicked: and that the righteous should be as the wicked, that be far from Thee: Shall not the Judge of all the earth do right?" (Gen. 18:25).

Even though no particular notice be taken of other passages and attention be entirely confined unto what is recorded in Jonah 3, will not the thoughtful reader be struck by the very terms of the Prophet's announcement: "Yet forty days and Nineveh shall be overthrown"? Had the guilt of Nineveh been so great and her course in evil so long confirmed, why was any intimation of her destruction at all necessary? If her doom was fixed, if God had purposed her overthrow, then why send one of His Prophets to declare the same? Further, why pronounce Nineveh's judgment almost six weeks before it should be executed? Ah, did not that very interval suggest that a door of hope stood open if her people would humble themselves and avail themselves of it? Was not that very interval an intimation of mercy in reserve? Was it not as much as though God said, "I gave her space to repent" (Rev. 2:21)? But if we compare Scripture with Scripture (and we are ever the losers by failing to do so) then the "forty days" confirms the conclusion we have drawn, for forty is the number which expresses probation and testing: see Deuteronomy 8:2-4; Acts 7:30; Matthew 4:2, etc.

How what above has been before us exemplifies the wondrous patience and forbearance of God! How it demonstrates that His anger is not like ours—a violent passion which ebbs and flows—but rather the calm and deliberate expression of His insulted holiness upon those who despise His authority and refuse to seek unto His mercy. God warns before He smites, expostulates ere He punishes, gives ample time and opportunity for an escape from His judgments. Enoch and Noah preached for many years before the flood destroyed the world. Prophet after Prophet was sent unto Israel before God banished them into captivity. Almost forty years passed after the Jews crucified

. *(continued on proceeding page)*

VOL. XXII. JULY, 1943. NO. 7

STUDIES IN THE SCRIPTURES

" Search the Scriptures." John 5:39.

Publisher and Editor—ARTHUR W. PINK,
27 Lewis Street,
Stornoway, Isle of Lewis,
Scotland.

GOD'S VOICE IN JUDGMENTS.

"Now therefore go to, speak to the men of Judah, and to the inhabitants of Jerusalem, saying, Thus saith the LORD; Behold, I frame evil against you, and devise a device against you: return ye now every one from his evil way, and make your ways and your doings good" (Jer. 18:11). As the "therefore" denotes, practical application is here made of what has been before us in the context. The Prophet had been called upon to witness an object-lesson set before him in the potter's house. Then the Lord had made known to him the relations which He sustains unto nations, viz., Sovereign, Ruler and Judge over them, and the principles which regulate His dealings with them: authority and power, righteousness and mercy. A specific yet illustrative example of such is here shown us . . . Israel had long provoked God to His face, and though He had been slow to anger, the time had now arrived when He would take them to task and deal with them for their wickedness. The dark clouds of His wrath were suspended over them, yet even at this late hour if they genuinely departed from their evil ways and walked the paths of virtue, mercy should "rejoice against judgment."

God speaks to us not only through His word (both personal and written) but also through His works and ways. "The heavens declare the glory of God; and the firmament showeth His handiwork. Day unto day uttereth speech, and night unto night showeth knowledge. There is no speech nor language, where their voice is not heard. Their line is gone out through all the earth, and their words to the end of the world" (Psa. 19:1-4). Creation testifies to the excellencies of the Creator. The Divine providences, too, are vocal: "I spake unto thee in thy prosperity" (Jer. 22:21)—My bounties declared My goodness and should have melted your hearts. God's judgments also carry with them a definite message: that is why we are exhorted to "hear ye the rod, and who hath appointed it" (Micah 6:9)—observe how the verse opens with "the LORD'S voice crieth unto the city." His "rod" bids us consider the Hand that wields it and calls upon us to forsake our sins.

When God speaks in judgment it is the final warning that He is not to be trifled with. When the Almighty is roused to fury who can stand before Him? Nations are no more able to successfully resist Him than can the clay hinder the fingers of the potter who shapes it; yea they are counted as "the small dust of the balance" (Isa. 40:15), which signifies utter insignificance. May we exclaim, "who would not fear Thee, O

(continued on back page)

IMPORTANT NOTICES

Please advise promptly of change in address, otherwise copies will be lost in the mails.

We are glad to send a sample copy to any of your friends whom you believe would be interested in this publication.

This magazine is published as "a work of faith and labour of love," the editor and his wife gladly giving their services free. There is no regular subscription price, as we do not wish the poor of the flock to be deprived. This does not mean that those looking for something for nothing may "help themselves." Those getting this Magazine, who are financially able and who receive spiritual help from its pages, are expected to gladly contribute towards its expenses; otherwise, their names are dropped from our lists.

Will those forwarding International Money Orders please have them made out to us at Stornoway, Isle of Lewis, Scotland. Checks (Cheques-Eng.) made out on U.S.A. Banks are not negotiable here, so please do not send them.

CONTENTS

THE SERMON ON THE MOUNT.

26. *Profession Tested*: Matthew 7:22, 23.

What is the relation between our present verses and the one immediately preceding? Matthew Henry gives the following as his analysis of verses 21-23. "1. Christ here shows by a plain remonstrance that an outward profession of religion, however remarkable, will not bring us to Heaven, unless there be a correspondent conversation. 2. The hypocrite's plea against the strictness of this law, offering other things in lieu of obedience. 3. The rejection of this plea as frivolous." Personally we think William Perkins perceived more clearly the connection between verses 22, 23 and verse 21: "In these two verses Christ returns to explain and confirm the first conclusion of the former verse concerning those professors that shall not be saved. The words contain two parts: first, a description of the persons by their behaviour; secondly, a declaration of their condemnation." For our own part we regard the verses which are now to be before us as containing an exemplification and amplification of what had been affirmed in the preceding one, showing that the most gifted and eminent professors will not be treated as exceptions if they fail to meet the fundamental requirement of God's kingdom.

In the previous verse Christ had declared, "Not everyone that saith unto Me, Lord, Lord, shall enter into the kingdom of Heaven, but he that doeth the will of My Father which is in Heaven." Something far more important and radical than a mere lip profession is needed in order to participate in spiritual blessings, even a full surrendering of ourselves unto Christ and a performing of the Divine will from the heart. But now the Lord went on to affirm something still more solemn and searching: "Many will say to Me in that day, Lord, Lord, have we not prophesied in Thy name? and in Thy name have cast out devils? and in Thy name done many wonderful works? And then will I profess unto them, I never knew you: depart from Me ye that work iniquity." Here it is not simply the rank and file of those claiming to be the followers of Christ who are in view, but the most influential ones among them, their *leaders and preach-*

ers. Nor does He single out a few exceptional cases, but declares there are "many" who have occupied positions of prominence and authority, who wrought mighty works in His name, but so far from enjoying His approbation are denounced by Him as workers of iniquity.

First, it should be pointed out that the gifts and works of these men are described according to the nature of those which obtained in Bible times. Strictly speaking there is no such thing as "prophesying" today, nor has there been for eighteen centuries past. A Prophet was the mouthpiece of God. Under inspiration of the Holy Spirit he gave forth a Divine revelation. In other words, he spoke by Divine inspiration. It was not an ordinary and natural gift, but an extraordinary and spiritual one. It was withdrawn when the Canon of Scripture was completed, for in His written Word we now have the Divine will fully revealed, containing as it does a complete and perfect Rule of faith and practice (2 Tim. 3:16, 17). Consequently, any person who now poses as a Divine Prophet, claiming to have a special message from God, is either an impostor or fanatic: an emissary of Satan seeking to beguile the unwary, or a neurotic who suffers his enthusiasm to run away with him, or an egotist who desires to direct attention to himself and occupy the limelight.

Because a man spoke by Divine inspiration in Bible times it was no proof that he was regenerate. Here, as everywhere else, God exercised His sovereignty, employing as His mouthpieces whom He pleased. Thus we find Balaam the soothsayer uttered some remarkable predictions concerning Israel, the Messiah Himself, and the judgments which should overtake various nations—all of which were fulfilled. We are told that "the LORD put a word in Balaam's mouth" (Num. 23:5), that he "knew the knowledge of the Most High" and "saw the vision of the Almighty" (Num. 24:16), yet he "loved the wages of unrighteousness" (2 Peter 2:15) and perished amid the enemies of the Lord (Num. 31:8). So also of the apostate king of Israel it is written, "the Spirit of God came upon him and he prophesied," so that it became a proverb, "Is Saul also among the Prophets?" (1 Sam. 10:10, 11). More remarkable still is the case of Caiaphas, the man who delivered up the Redeemer into the hands of Pilate, for of him we are told: "And this spake he not of himself (but by Divine inspiration): but being high priest that year, he *prophesied* that Jesus should die for that nation; and not for that nation only, but that also He should gather together in one the children of God that were scattered abroad" (John 11:51, 52).

"And in Thy name have cast out devils" or "demons" (Matt. 7:22). This was another of the supernatural gifts or powers bestowed upon men at the beginning of the Christian era, and yet it was not confined to the regenerate. It is at least open to doubt whether the man mentioned in Luke 9:49 was such, for there we are told that, "John answered and said, Master, We saw one casting out demons in Thy name and we forbade him, because he followeth not with us." But a clearer case to the point is that of the betrayer of our Lord. In Matthew 10:1 we are expressly told that, "when Christ had called unto Him His twelve disciples He gave them power over unclean spirits, to cast them out" and one of that company was Judas Iscariot! Had Judas failed to perform this feat his fellow Apostles had at once had their suspicions aroused and when the Saviour announced, "One of you shall betray Me," instead of asking, "Lord, is it I?" had at once known He referred to Judas. "And in Thy name done many wonderful works" or "works of power," miraculous works—the Greek word occurring again in

Matthew 11:20 in connection with Christ's "mighty works." This power, too, was conferred upon Judas.

If it should be asked, Why should God so remarkably endow the unregenerate, even using them as His mouthpieces? several answers may be returned. First, as has been intimated above, in order to exemplify God's uncontrollable sovereignty over and ownership of all men. He can employ His creatures as He pleases and elect as His agents and instruments whom He will, and none can say Him nay. Second, to display His invincible power. "The king's heart is in the hand of the LORD, as the rivers of water: He turneth it whithersoever He will" (Prov. 21:1), and if the king's heart, so every man's; but how little is that realized today. Balaam was but a puppet in His hands, unable to resist His will. Caiaphas was the enemy of Christ and yet compelled to utter a remarkable prophecy about Him! Third, to evince that supernatural gifts and endowments—though highly esteemed among men—are not the most precious of His bestowments: something infinitely more valuable is reserved for the objects of His everlasting love. What comparison is there between Balaam's prophecy and the "new song" in the mouths of the redeemed, between the miracles performed by Judas and being made meet for the inheritance of the saints in light!

Our Lord thus plainly intimates that men may conduct themselves as His commissioned servants—acting in His name—that they may be endowed with the most remarkable gifts, that they may perform supernatural works, and yet not be saved. It was so at the beginning of this dispensation; it is so now. It would be a great mistake to draw the conclusion that because our Lord describes these unregenerate professors according to the terminology of the first century, when ministers were endowed with extraordinary gifts and exercised supernatural powers, that it has no direct hearing on leaders among professing Christians in this twentieth century. Because verse 22 depicts conditions which no longer obtain in kind, that is no proof that it has no immediate application unto men of prominence in the religious realm today. Rather should we reason that if such a fearful warning was needed at the beginning of this era when men were so wonderfully gifted, how much more pertinent is it to those of lesser talents and abilities in this degenerate generation!

The modern equivalent of prophesying in the name of Christ would be *preaching* in His name: the casting out of demons would find its present counterpart in the deliverance of Satan's slaves chronicled by our "city missions"—such as the reforming of drunkards, reclaiming of fallen women, recovering of drug addicts—while the "wonderful works" may be taken as referring to the costly buildings termed "churches" with their huge membership, and the sensational achievements of "missionaries" in heathen lands. Not that we wish to imply that all engaged in such activities are unregenerate, nevertheless after close observation and personal contact with many of these workers, we seriously doubt whether more than a small percentage of them have really been born again. Nor should this at all astonish us. Our Lord Himself distinctly declared of "many" of those serving in His name, "I never knew you" and if that were true of those who wrought during the early days of the Christian era, why should it be thought strange that such a state of affairs pertains now that Christendom is so apostate?

Here, then, is what is most solemn of all in this awe-inspiring passage: that there will be many preachers, Christian leaders and workers—and in view of our Lord's use of the word in verse 13, probably the great majority of them—who will be shut out of

Heaven. Sad and awful as this is, yet from our observation in many sections of Christendom and from what generally obtains, we cannot say this surprises us. Among the young men accepted as students for the ministry, is there any larger percentage of regenerate ones than of the young men making a Christian profession who enter not the ministry? We are far from believing they are all hypocrites. Doubtless there are many thousands who select the ministry as their avocation because of the social prestige and financial remuneration it affords. But large numbers of youths who receive the Word "with joy" (Matt. 13:20) mistake their religious enthusiasm and fervour for a call from God and love for souls, and having more zeal than knowledge and friends who encourage rather than counsel caution, they make the great mistake.

Once the young man is accepted as a student for the ministry his regeneration is (with very rare exceptions) tacitly assumed. And what is there, then, which is in anywise calculated to open his deceived eyes? Some of the denominations require him to spend years at a university in order to obtain a degree, and there his time and energies are strenuously occupied with subjects that contain nothing whatever for the soul, but only that which is apt to foster intellectual conceit. One who has mistaken carnal ambition and enthusiasm for a call from God is not likely to find a course in sociology, psychology, logic, philosophy, etc., likely to disillusion him. And even when the young man is not required to enter a university, he has to take a course in "divinity." In other words he is introduced to the sacred study of theology as a subject on which to exercise his intellectual powers, as a text book over which he must pore and whose contents he must master in order to successfully pass examinations thereon. The result is, in the vast majority of cases, he is so sickened therewith that after his ordination he never again opens a theological treatise.

Nor is there any more hope, humanly speaking, that his eyes may be opened to his lost condition after he has been ordained and called to a charge. If he is to "make good" therein, such a multitude of duties demand his attention that there is little opportunity for the careful examination of his own soul. There are so many departments of the church he has to superintend, so many sermons and addresses he must prepare each week, so many calls to make, that he has little leisure for self-introspection. He is so occupied with the concerns and needs of others, that attention to the ministerial injunction, "take heed *unto thyself*" (1 Tim. 4:16) is crowded out. It is greatly to be feared that thousands of ministers today have ground to lament, "they made me the keeper of the vineyards, but *mine own vineyard* have I not kept" (Song. 1:6). But whatever be the contributing causes and occasions of this tragic fatality, the fact remains that the Divine Judge is yet going to say unto many of those who preached and wrought in His name, "I never knew you."

"And then will I profess unto them, I never knew you: depart from Me ye that work iniquity" (Matt. 7:23). There are five things here which claim our attention, though utterly insufficient is any mortal to do them justice. First, the time-mark: "then." Second, the character in which Christ is here viewed: as the Judge of men. Third, the solemn verdict announced: "I never knew you." Fourth, the fearful sentence imposed: "depart from Me." Fifth, the real character of religious formalists: "ye that work iniquity." It would not be possible to assemble together five things of greater gravity and moment than these. And what human pen is competent to comment upon subjects so awesome? Oh that both writer and reader may approach the same with becoming reverence and solemnity!

"And *then*" looks back to the "in that day" of the previous verse. It is the Day of final retribution, when "every man's work shall be made manifest: for the Day shall declare it, because it shall be revealed with fire and the fire shall try every man's work of what sort it is" (1 Cor. 3:13). It is "the day of wrath and revelation of the righteous judgment of God" (Rom. 2:5), "because He hath appointed a Day, in the which He will judge the world in righteousness by that Man whom he hath ordained" (Acts 17: 31). Who can conceive of the consternation which will possess the hearts of impenitent rebels, of unmasked hypocrites, of disillusioned formalists, as they are compelled to stand with an assembled universe before the dread Tribunal? Then will the books be opened, the secrets of all hearts disclosed, the hidden things of darkness brought to light. Then shall each one who has trampled upon the Divine Law, rejected the only Mediator, and done despite to the Spirit of grace, stand forth in his true colours, stripped of the disguise with which he imposed upon his fellow creatures. "The Heaven shall reveal his iniquity and the earth shall rise up against him" (Job 20:27). They will be speechless with guilt, utterly overwhelmed, unable to "stand in the judgment" (Psa. 1:5).

"And then will I profess unto them, I never knew you, depart from Me, ye that work iniquity" (Matt. 7:23). The Speaker is the Lord Jesus yet not as presenting Himself as the Saviour of sinners, but rather officiating as their Judge, pronouncing their doom. In this solemn passage our Lord gave plain intimation that He was more than Man, that He is none other than the Arbiter of every man's eternal state, from whose decision there can be no appeal. Amazing, indeed, was the contrast between His lowly appearance and external circumstances and this language of conscious majesty and power. While delivering this sermon on the mount Christ appeared before men's eyes as a Galilean peasant, yet both the tone and tenor of it proclaimed Him to be none other than Immanuel, God manifest in flesh. No wonder we are told that, "when Jesus had ended these sayings, the people were astonished at His doctrine, for He taught them as one having authority and not as the scribes" (vv. 28, 29). And it is before this very Judge that both writer and reader must yet appear!

"I never knew you" (v. 23). This does not mean that Christ was totally unacquainted with their persons, that He was not cognizant of their character and conduct. No, rather does it signify that He did not approve of or accept them. When it is said "The LORD *knoweth* the way of the righteous" (Psa. 1:6) it is to be understood that He is pleased with the same. Here, then, is the awful verdict: "I never knew you"; no, not even when you were preaching and working in My name. You may have deceived yourselves and those to whom you ministered, but it was impossible to impose upon Me. In His, "I will *profess* unto them," He seems to speak ironically: you have professed much, made free use of My name, maintained your standing as leaders in the church—so now hear *My* profession! "I *never* knew you" makes it quite clear they were not such as had fallen from grace, as it also looks back to eternity past: they had *never* been born again, never evangelically repented, never believed *savingly*, and had not been among the favoured company upon whom His approbation rested before the foundation of the world.

"Depart from Me" (Matt. 7:23). Here is the fearful sentence imposed. They may have been highly respected in the churches, but they are objects of abhorrence to the Lord Christ. They frequently had His name on their lips, but since He dwelt not in their hearts they are totally disqualified for the celestial courts. "If the most admired and useful preacher on earth had no better evidence of his conversion than his abilities and success as a preacher, he would preach to others and be himself a castaway" (Thomas Scott). "Depart from Me" is the announcement of their just condemnation. They had been near to Him by their profession and by the position they held in the church, but now they must go to the only place for which they are fitted, which is banishment from the Holy One. Herein we discover the force of that terrible expression "the second death" (Rev. 21:8): it is not extinction of being or the annihilation of the soul, but eternal separation from Christ, alienation from the life of God; it is a being "punished with everlasting destruction *from* the presence of the Lord and the glory of His power" (2 Thess. 1:9), cut off forever from the Bestower of blessing, tormented in the Lake of Fire.

"Ye that work iniquity" (Matt. 7:23). How different is the Divine estimate from the human! These preachers and leaders pleaded that they had wrought many "wonderful works" but because they had not proceeded from renewed hearts, because they had been done to win the applause of their fellows, rather than for the glory of God, the One who cannot be imposed upon declares they are "works of iniquity." Ah, my reader, we may look upon and admire the outward show, but the One who will yet judge us "looketh on *the heart*" (1 Sam 16:7), and therefore, "that which is highly esteemed among men is abomination in the sight of God" (Luke 16:15)—even the righteousnesses of the natural man are but "filthy rags" in His sight.

> *Deeds of greatness as we deemed them*
> *He will show us were but sin;*
> *Cups of water we'd forgotten*
> *He will tell us were for Him.*

Not only the gross external crimes, but pride and presumption, and the religious performances of hypocrites are "works of iniquity."

In view of the articles preceding this one there is no need for us to make a lengthy application here. The chief lesson for us to take to heart from the above is the utter insufficiency of the most imposing gifts. Yet how many there are who suppose that the exercise of unusual abilities in the church is evidence of great spirituality. As uncommon natural endowments are by no means always accompanied with moral worth, so the presence of abnormal powers is no proof of regeneration. We must learn to distinguish between the performing of wonderful works and the possession of spiritual graces, for the former is no guarantee of the latter. Showy talents may raise a man above his fellows, even above genuine Christians, but unless he is indwelt by the Spirit of God, what are they worth? "Though I have the gift of prophecy and understand all mysteries . . . and have not charity (love), I am nothing" (1 Cor. 13:2). Then let us search ourselves and see whether or not we have something better than those to whom Christ will yet say, "I never knew you." A principle of holiness within evidenced by a godly walk without is infinitely to be preferred above the power to cast out demons and heal the sick. To commune with God in private is an inestimably grander privilege than to speak with tongues in public.—A.W.P.

THE MISSION AND MIRACLES OF ELISHA.

7. *The Fourth Miracle.*

First, its *background.* It has pleased the Holy Spirit in this instance to provide a somewhat lengthy and complicated one, so it will be the part of wisdom for us to patiently ponder the account He has given of what led up to and occasioned this exercise of God's wonder-working power. Just as a diamond appears to best advantage when placed in a suitable setting, so we are the more enabled to appreciate the works of God when we take note of their connections. This applies equally to His works in creation, in providence and in grace. We are always the losers if we ignore the circumstances which occasion the varied actings of our God. The longer and darker the night, the more welcome the morning's light, and the more acute our need and urgent our situation, the more manifest the hand of Him that relieves and His goodness in ministering to us. The same principle holds good in connection with the Lord's undertaking for our fellows, and if we were not so self-centered we should appreciate and render praise for the one as much as for the other.

2 Kings 3 opens by telling us, "Now Jehoram the son of Ahab began to reign over Israel in Samaria the eighteenth year of Jehoshaphat king of Judah, and reigned twelve years. And he wrought evil in the sight of the LORD; but not like his father, and like his mother: for he put away the image of Baal that his father had made. Nevertheless he cleaved unto the sins of Jeroboam the son of Nebat, which made Israel to sin; he departed not there from" (vv. 1-3). Five things are taught us in these verses about that "abominable thing" which God "hates" and which is the cause of all the suffering and sorrow that is in the world, namely, sin. First, that God Himself personally *observes* our wrongdoing: it was "in the sight of the Lord" that the guilty deeds of Jehoram were performed. How much evil doing is perpetrated secretly and under cover of darkness, supposing none are witness thereto. But though evil doing may be concealed from *human* gaze, it cannot be hidden from the omnipresent One, for "the eyes of the LORD are in every place (by night as well as by day) beholding the evil and the good" (Prov. 15:3). What curb this ought to place upon us.

Second, that God *records* our evil deeds. Here is a clear case in point. The evil which Jehoram wrought in the sight of the Lord is set down against him, likewise that of his parents before him, and further back still, "the sin of Jeroboam." Unspeakably solemn is this: God not only observes but registers against men every infraction of His Law. They commit iniquity and think little or nothing of it, but the very One who shall yet judge them has noted the same against them. It may all be forgotten by them, but nothing shall fade from what God has written, and when the dead, both small and great, stand before Him the "books" will be opened, and they will be "judged out of those things which were written in the books, according to their works" (Rev. 20:12). And my reader, there is only one possible way of escape from receiving the awful wages of your sins, and that is to throw down the weapons of your warfare against God, cast yourself at the feet of Christ as a guilty sinner, put your trust in His redeeming and cleansing blood, and God will say, "I have *blotted out,* as a thick cloud, thy transgressions" (Isa. 44:22).

Third, that God recognizes *degrees* in evil doing, for while Jehoram displeased the Lord, yet it is said, "but not like his father and like his mother." Christ declared unto Pilate, "he that delivered Me unto thee (Judas) hath the greater sin" (John 19:11); and again we are told, "He that despised Moses' law died without mercy under two or three witnesses: of how much sorer punishment suppose ye, shall he be thought worthy who hath trodden under foot the Son of God" (Heb. 10:28, 29). There are many who ignore this principle and suppose that since they are sinners it makes no difference how much wickedness they commit. They madly argue, "I might as well be hung for a sheep as a lamb," but are only "treasuring up unto themselves wrath against the day of wrath"

(Rom. 2:5), for "every transgression and disobedience" will yet receive "a just recompense of reward" (Heb. 2:2).

Fourth, that God observes whether our reformation be *partial* or complete. This comes out in the fact that we are told Jehoram "put away the image (or statue) that his father had made," but he did not destroy it, and a few years later Baal worship was restored. God's Word touching this matter was plain: "thou shalt utterly overthrow them and quite break down their images" (Exo. 23:24). Sin must be dealt with by no unsparing hand, and when we resolve to break therefrom we must "burn our boats behind us" or they are likely to prove an irresistible temptation to return unto our former ways. Fifth, that God duly notes our *continuance* in sin, for it is here recorded of Jehoram that he not only "cleaved unto the sins of Jeroboam" but also that "he departed not therefrom" which greatly aggravated his guilt. To enter upon a course of wrong-doing is horrible wickedness, but to deliberately persevere therein is much worse. How few heed that word "break off thy sin by righteousness" (Dan. 4:27).

"And Mesha king of Moab was a sheepmaster, and rendered unto the king of Israel an hundred thousand lambs, and an hundred thousand rams, with the wool. But it came to pass, when Ahab was dead, that the king of Moab rebelled against the king of Israel" (2 Kings 3:4, 5). In fulfillment of Balaam's prophecy (Num. 24:17) David had conquered the Moabites so that they became his servants (2 Sam. 8:2), and they continued in subjection to the kingdom of Israel until the time of its division, when their vassalage and tribute were transferred to the kings of Israel, as those of Edom remained to the kings of Judah. But upon the death of Ahab they revolted. Therein we behold the Divine Providence crossing his sons in their affairs. This rebellion on the part of Moab should be regarded in the light of, "when a man's ways please the LORD, He maketh even his enemies to be at peace with him" (Prov. 16:7)—but when our ways displease Him, evil from every quarter menaces us. Temporal as well as spiritual prosperity depends entirely upon God's blessing. To make His hand more plainly apparent God frequently punishes the wicked after the similitude of their sins. He did so to Ahab's sons—having turned from the Lord—Moab was moved to rebel against them.

Having dwelt upon the Divine side of Moab's revolt, let us offer one remark upon the human side. As we ponder this incident we are made to realize that "there is no new thing under the sun." Discontent and strife, jealousy and bloodshedding, have characterized the relations of one nation to another all through history. Instead of mutual respect and peace, "living in malice and envy, hateful and hating one another" (Titus 3:3) have marked them all through the piece. How aptly were the great empires of antiquity symbolized by "four great *beasts*" (Dan. 7:4-7)—and wild, ferocious and cruel ones, at that! Human depravity is a solemn reality, and neither education nor legalization can eradicate or sublimate it. What, then, are the ruling powers to do? Deal with it with a *firm* hand: "For rulers are not a terror to good works but to the evil . . . he beareth not the sword in vain: for he (the governmental and civil ruler) is the minister of God (to maintain law and order), a revenger (to enforce law and order) upon him that doeth evil" (Rom. 13:4)—to strike terror into them, and not pamper—to punish the lawbreaker—not attempt to reform him.

"And it came to pass when Ahab was dead that the king of Moab rebelled against the king of Israel" (2 Kings 3:5). The Moabites were the descendants of the son which

Lot had by his elder daughter. They occupied a territory to the southeast of Judah and east of the Red Sea. They were a strong and fierce people—"the mighty men of Moab" (Exo. 15:15). Balak—who sent for Balaam to curse Israel—was one of their kings. Even as proselytes they were barred from entering the congregation of the Lord unto the tenth generation. They were idolaters (1 Kings 11:33). For the space of no less than a hundred and fifty years they had apparently paid a heavy annual tribute, but upon the death of Ahab they had decided to throw off the yoke and be fined no further.

"And king Jehoram went out of Samaria the same time, and numbered all Israel" (2 Kings 3:6). There was no turning to the Lord for counsel and help. He was the One who had given David success and brought the Moabites into subjection, and unto Him ought Jehoram to have turned now that they rebelled. But he was a stranger to Jehovah; nor did he consult the priests of the calves, so that apparently he had no confidence in them. How sad is the case of the unregenerate in the hour of need; no Divine Comforter in sorrow, no unerring Counsellor in perplexity, no sure Refuge when danger menaces them. How much men lose even in this life by turning their backs upon the One who gave them being. Nothing less than spiritual madness can account for the folly of those who "observe lying vanities" and "forsake their own mercies" (Jonah 2:8). Jonah had to learn that lesson in a hard school. Alas, the vast majority of our fellows never learn it, as they ultimately discover to their eternal undoing. Will that be the case with you, my reader?

"And he went and sent to Jehoshaphat the king of Judah, saying, The king of Moab hath rebelled against me: wilt thou go with me against Moab to battle" (2 Kings 3:7). Both Thomas Scott and Matthew Henry suppose that it was merely a political move on the part of Jehoram when he "put away the image of Baal that his father had made." That this external reformation was designed to pave the way for obtaining the help of Jehoshaphat, who was a God-fearing, though somewhat vacillating man. The words of Elisha to him in verses 13, 14 certainly seem to confirm this view, for the servant of God made it clear that he was not deceived by such a device and addressed him as one who acted the part of a hypocrite. Any student of history is well aware that many religious improvements have been granted by governments simply from what is termed "State policy" rather than from spiritual convictions or a genuine desire to promote the glory of God. Only the One who looks on the heart knows the real motives behind much that appears fair on the surface.

"And he said I will go up: I am as thou art, my people as thy people, and my horses as thy horses" (v. 7). It seems strange that such an one as Jehoshaphat was willing to unite with Jehoram in this expedition, for he had been severely rebuked on an earlier occasion for having "joined affinity with Ahab" (2 Chron. 18:1-3), for Jehu the Prophet said unto him, "Shouldest thou help the ungodly and love them that hate the LORD? therefore is wrath upon thee from before the LORD" (2 Chron. 19:2). How, then, is his conduct to be explained on this occasion? No doubt his zeal to heal the breach between the two kingdoms had much to do with it, for 2 Chronicles 18:1-3 intimates he was anxious to promote a better spirit between Judah and Israel. Moreover, the Moabites were a common enemy, for we learn from 2 Chronicles 20:1 that at a later date the Moabites, accompanied by others, came against Jehoshaphat to battle. But it is most charitable to conclude that Jehoshaphat was deceived by Jehoram's reformation. Yet we should mark the absence of his seeking directions from the Lord on this occasion.

Second, its *urgency.* "And he said, Which way shall we go up? And he answered, The way through the wilderness of Edom. So the king of Israel went, and the king of Judah, and the king of Edom: and they fetched a compass of seven days' journey: and there was no water for the host, and for the cattle that followed them. And the king of Israel said, Alas! that the LORD hath called these three kings together, to deliver them into the hand of Moab!" (2 Kings 3:8-10). We must abbreviate our remarks. Note that Jehoram was quite willing for the king of Judah to take the lead, and that he made his plans without seeking counsel of God. The course he took was obviously meant to secure the aid of the Edomites, but by going so far into the wilderness they met with a desert wherein was no water. Thus the three kings and their forces were in imminent danger of perishing. This struck terror into the heart of Jehoram and at once his guilty conscience smote him— unbelievers know enough of the Truth to condemn them! "The foolishness of man perverteth his way: and his heart fretteth against the LORD" (Prov. 19:3)—what an illustration of that is furnished by the words of Jehoram on this occasion.

"But Jehoshaphat said, Is there not here a Prophet of the LORD, that we may inquire of the LORD by him? And one of the king of Israel's servants answered and said, Here is Elisha the son of Shaphat, which poured water on the hands of Elijah. And Jehoshaphat said, The word of the LORD is with him. So the king of Israel and Jehoshaphat and the king of Edom went down to him" (2 Kings 3:11-12). Here we see the difference between the righteous and the unrighteous in a time of dire calamity: the one is tormented with a guilty conscience and thinks only of the Lord's wrath; the other has hope in His mercy. In those days the Prophet was the Divine mouthpiece, so for one the king of Judah made inquiry; and not in vain. It is blessed to observe that as the Lord takes note of and registers the sins of the reprobate, so He observes the deeds of His elect, placing on record here the humble service which Elisha had rendered to Elijah—not even a cup of water given to one of His little ones shall pass unnoticed and unrewarded! Appropriately was Elisha termed "the chariot of Israel and the horsemen thereof" (2 Kings 13:14)—their true *defense* in the hour of danger; and to him did the three kings turn in their urgent need.

Third, its *discrimination.* "And Elisha said unto the king of Israel, What have I to do with thee? get thee to the prophets of thy father and to the prophets of thy mother" (2 Kings 3:13). Mark both the dignity and fidelity of God's servant. So far from feeling flattered because the king of Israel consulted him, he deemed himself insulted and hesitated not to let him know he discerned his true character. It reminds us of the Lord's words through Ezekiel, "These men have set up their idols in their hearts and put the stumblingblock of their iniquity before their face: should I be inquired of at all by *them*?" (14:3). "And the king of Israel said unto him, Nay: for the LORD hath called these three kings together to deliver them into the hands of Moab," (2 Kings 3:13), as much as to say, "Do not disdain me: our case is desperate." "And Elisha said, As the LORD of hosts liveth, before whom I stand, surely, were it not that I regard the presence of Jehoshaphat the king of Judah, I would not look toward thee, nor see thee" (v. 14). Little do the unrighteous realize how much they owe, under God, to the presence of the righteous in their midst—as soon as Lot was removed from Sodom that city was destroyed!

Fourth, its *requirement.* "But now bring me a minstrel" (v. 15). In view of 1 Samuel 16:23, Thomas Scott and Matthew Henry conclude that his interview with Jehoram had perturbed Elisha's mind and that soothing music was a means to compose his spirit, that he might be prepared to receive the Lord's mind. Possibly they are correct, yet we believe there is another and more important reason. In the light of such passages as, "Sing unto the LORD with the harp; with the harp and the voice of a psalm" (Psa. 98:5), and "Jeduthun, who prophesied with a harp, to give thanks and to praise the LORD" (1 Chron. 25:3 and cf. v. 1), we consider that Elisha was here showing regard for and rendering submission to *the order* established by God. The Hebrew word for "minstrel" signifies "one who plays on a stringed instrument"—as an accompaniment to the Psalm he sang. Thus it was to honour God and instruct these kings that Elisha sent for the minstrel. "And it came to pass *when* the minstrel played, that the hand of the LORD (cf. Ezek. 1:3; 3:22) came upon him" (2 Kings 3:15)—the Lord ever honours those who honour Him.

Fifth, its *testing.* "And he said, Thus saith the LORD, Make this valley full of ditches. For thus saith the LORD, Ye shall not see wind, neither shall ye see rain; yet that valley shall be filled with water, that ye may drink, both ye, and your cattle, and your beasts" (vv. 16, 17). A pretty severe test was this, when all outward sign of fulfillment was withheld. It was a trial of their faith and obedience, and entailed a considerable amount of hard work. Had they treated the Prophet's prediction with derision, they would have scorned to go to so much trouble. It was somewhat like the order Christ gave unto His Apostles as He bade them make the multitudes "sit down" when there was nothing commensurate in sight to feed so vast a company—only a few loaves and fishes. The sequel shows they heeded Elisha and made due preparation for the promised supply of water. As Matthew Henry says, "They that expect God's blessings must prepare room for them."

Sixth, its *meaning.* The very number of this miracle helps us to apprehend its significance. It was the fourth of the series, and in the language of Scripture numerics it stands for the earth—cf. the four "seasons" and the four points of the compass, etc. What we have in this miracle is one of the Old Testament foreshadowments that the Gospel was not to be confined to Palestine but would yet be sent forth throughout the earth. Prior to His death Christ bade His Apostles, "Go not into the way of the Gentiles, and into any city of the Samaritans enter ye not; but go rather to the lost sheep of the house of Israel" (Matt. 10:5, 6 and cf., John 4:9); but after His resurrection He said, "Go ye therefore and teach *all* nations" (Matt. 28:19). But there is more here. "Salvation is of the Jews" (John 4:22), and "their debtors" we Gentiles are (Rom. 15:26, 27). Strikingly is this typified here, for it was solely for the sake of the presence of Jehoshaphat this miracle was wrought and that the water of life was made available for the Samaritans and the Edomites! Thus it is a picture of the minister of the Gospel engaged in *missionary* activities that is here set forth.

Seventh, its *timing.* "And it came to pass in the morning when the meat offering was offered up, behold, there came water by the way of Edom, and the country was filled with water" (2 Kings 3:20). This hour was chosen by the Lord for the performing of this miracle to intimate to the whole company that their deliverance was vouchsafed on the ground of the sacrifices offered and the worship rendered in the temple in Jerusalem. It was at the same significant hour that Elijah had made his effectual prayer on

Mount Carmel, (1 Kings 8:36), when another notable miracle was wrought. So, too, it was at the hour "of the evening oblation" that a signal blessing was granted unto Daniel (9:21). Typically, it teaches us that it is through the merits of the sacrifice of Christ that the life-sustaining Gospel of God now flows forth unto the Gentiles.—A.W.P.

DOCTRINE OF SAINTS' PERSEVERANCE.

8. *Its Safeguards.*

In the foregoing volume we devoted four articles to a setting forth of the principal springs from which the final perseverance of the saints (in their cleaving unto the Lord, their love of the Truth, and their treading the path of obedience) does issue, or the grounds on which their eternal security rests. It is therefore fitting, if the balance of Truth is to be duly observed by us, that we should give equal space unto a presentation of some of the safeguards by which God has hedged about this doctrine, thereby forbidding empty professors and presumptuous Antinomians from trespassing upon this sacred ground. We have already dwelt upon five of these safeguards and we now proceed to point out others. In such a day as this it is the more necessary to enter into detail upon the present branch of our subject that the mouths of certain enemies of the Truth may be closed, that formalists may be shown they have no part or lot in the matter, that hyper-Calvinists may be instructed in the way of the Lord more perfectly, and His own people stirred out of their lethargy.

6. By insisting on the necessity for *using the means of grace.* There are some who assert that if God has regenerated a soul he is infallibly certain of reaching Heaven whether or no he uses the means appointed, yea that no matter to what extent he fails in the performance of duty or how carnally he lives, he cannot perish. Now we have no hesitation in saying that such an assertion is a grievous perversion of the Truth, and in view of Satan's words to Christ, "If Thou be the Son of God cast Thyself down (from a pinnacle of the temple), for it is written, He shall give His angels charge over Thee, and in their hands they shall bear Thee up" (Matt. 4:6) , there is no room for doubt as to who is the author of such a lie. It is a grievous perversion because a tearing asunder of what God Himself has joined together. The same One who has decreed the end has also ordained the means necessary unto that end. He has promised certain things unto His people, but He requires to be inquired of concerning them; and if they have not, it is because they ask not.

Even among those who would turn away with abhorrence from the extreme form of Antinomianism mentioned above, there are those who regard the use of means quite indifferently in this connection, arguing that whatever be required in order to preserve from apostasy the Lord Himself will attend unto, that He will so work in His people both to will and to do of His good pleasure that it is quite unnecessary for ministers of the Gospel to be constantly addressing exhortations unto them and urging to the performance of duty. But such a conclusion is thoroughly defective and erroneous, for it quite loses sight of the fact that God deals with His people throughout as moral agents, enforcing their responsibility. Whether or not we can see the consistency between the Divine foreordination and the discharge of human accountability, between the Divine decree and the imperativeness of our making use of the means of grace, is entirely beside the point. Christ exhorted and admonished His Apostles, and they in turn the churches; and that is sufficient. It is vain to pit our puny objections against their regular practice.

Just as God has ordained material means for the accomplishment of His pleasure in the material realm, so He has appointed that rational agents shall use spiritual means for the fulfilling of His will in connection with spiritual things. He could make the fields fertile and the trees fruitful without the instrumentality of rain and sunshine, but it has pleased Him to employ secondary causes and subordinate agents in the production of our food. In like manner He could cause His people to grow in grace, make them fruitful unto every good work, and preserve them from everything injurious to their welfare, without requiring any industry and diligence on their part; but it has not so pleased Him to dispense with their concurrence. Accordingly we find Him bidding them, "Work out your own salvation with fear and trembling" (Phil. 2:12), "*Labour* therefore to enter into that rest, lest any man fall after the same example of unbelief" (Heb. 4:11). Promises and precepts, exhortations and threats, suitable to moral agents are given to them, calling for the employment of those faculties and the exercise of those graces which He has bestowed upon them.

It is a serious mistake to suppose that there is any conflict between one class of passages which contain God's promises of sufficient grace unto His people, and another class in which He requires of them the performance of their duty. In his exposition of Hebrews 3:14 John Owen pointed out that the force of the Greek rendered "if we hold the beginning of our confidence firm unto the end" denotes "our utmost endeavour to hold it fast and to keep it firm and steadfast"; adding, "Shaken it will be, opposed it will be, kept it will *not be*, without our utmost diligence and endeavour. It is true our persistency in Christ doth not, as to the issue and event, depend absolutely on our own diligence. The unalterableness of our union with Christ, on the account of the faithfulness of the covenant, is that which doth and shall eventually secure it. But yet our own diligent endeavour is such an indispensable means for that end that *without it,* it will *not* be brought about." Our diligent endeavour is necessitated by the precept which God commands us to make use of, and by the order He has established in the relations of one spiritual thing to another.

The older writers were wont to illustrate the consistency between God's purpose and our performance of duty by an appeal to Acts 27. The ship which carried the Apostle and other prisoners encountered a fearful gale and it continued so long and with such severity that the inspired narrative declares, "all hope that we should be saved was then taken away" (v. 20). A Divine messenger then assured the Apostle, "Fear not Paul, thou must be brought before Caesar; and to you God hath given thee all (the lives of) them that sail with thee," and so sure was the Apostle that this promise would be fulfilled, he said unto the ship's company, "Be of good cheer, for there shall be no loss of life among you, but of the ship, for I believe that it shall be even as it was told me" (vv. 22-25). Yet next day, when the sailors feared they would be smashed upon the rocks and started to flee out of the ship, Paul said to the centurion, "except these abide in the ship, ye *cannot* be saved" (v. 31)!

Now *there* is a nice problem which we would submit to the more extreme Calvinists: how can the positive promise, "there shall be no loss of life" (v. 24) and the contingent "except these abide in the ship ye cannot be saved" (v. 31) stand together? How are you going to reconcile them according to your principles? But in reality there is no difficulty: God made no absolute promise that He would preserve those in the ship regardless of their use of appropriate means. They were not irrational creatures He would safeguard, but moral agents who must discharge their own responsibility, and neither be inert nor act presumptuously. Accordingly we find Paul bidding his companions "take meat," saying

"This is for your health" (v. 34), and later the ship was lightened of its cargo (v. 38) and its main-sail hoisted (v. 40), which further conduced to their safety. The certainty of God's promise was not suspended upon their remaining in the ship, but it was a making known of the means whereby God would effect their security.

Reverting to Owen's exposition of Hebrews 3:14, he said: "Our persistency in our subsistence in Christ is the emergence and effect of our acting grace unto that purpose. Diligence and endeavours in this matter are like Paul's mariners when he was shipwrecked at Melita. The preservation of their lives depended absolutely on the faithfulness and power of God, yet when the mariners began to fly out of the ship Paul tells the centurion that unless his men stayed therein they could not be saved. But why need he think of the shipmen when God took upon Himself the preservation of them all? He knew full well that He would preserve them; but yet that He would do so in and by the use *of means*. If we are in Christ, God has given us the lives of our souls, and hath taken upon Himself, in His covenant, the preservation of them. But yet we may say, with reference unto the means that He hath appointed, when storms and trials arise, *unless* we use our own diligent endeavours we cannot be saved." Alas that some who profess to so greatly admire this Puritan and endorse his teachings have wandered so far from the course which he followed.

If it be asked, Did the purpose of God that Paul and his companions should all reach land safely depend upon the uncertain will and actions of men? The answer is, No, as a cause from which the purpose of God received its strength and support. But Yes, as a means, appointed by Him, to secure the end He had ordained, for God has decreed the subordinate agencies by which the end shall be accomplished as truly as He has decreed the end itself. In His Word, God has revealed a conjunction of means and ends, and there is a necessity lying upon men to use the means and not to expect the end without them. It is at our peril that we tear asunder what God has joined together and disrupt the order He has appointed. The same God who bids us believe His promises, forbids us to tempt His providences (Matt. 4:7). Even though the means may appear to us to have no adequate connection with the end, seeing God has enjoined them, we must use the same. Naaman must wash in the Jordan if he would be cleansed of his leprosy (2 Kings 5:10) and Hezekiah must take a lump of figs and lay it on his boil if he is to be recovered (2 Kings 20:4-7).

They are greatly mistaken who suppose that since the preservation of believers is guaranteed in the Covenant of Grace that this renders all means and motives, exhortations and threats, useless and senseless. Not so. The doctrine of the everlasting security of the saint does not mean that God will preserve him whether or no he perseveres, but rather that He has promised to give him all needed grace for him to continue in the path of holiness. This supposes that believers will be under such advantages and have suitable aids used with them in order to this, and that they shall have motives constantly set before them which induce and persuade unto obedience and personal piety and to guard them against the contrary. Hence the propriety and usefulness of the ordinances of the Gospel, the instructions and precepts, the promises and incentives which are furnished us to perseverance without which the purpose of God that we should persevere could not be effected in a way suited to our moral nature.

Christians are indeed "kept by the power of God" (1 Peter 1:5), yet it needs to be pointed out that they are not preserved mechanically, as a child is kept in the nursery from falling into the fire by a tall metal fender or guard, or as the unwilling horse is held in by bit and bridle; but spiritually so by the workings of Divine grace in them and by means of motives and inducements from without which call forth that grace into exercise and action. We quite miss the force of that declaration unless we complete the verse: "Who are kept by the power of God *through faith,* unto salvation ready to be revealed in the last time." It is not "for" or "because of faith" but "through faith" yet not without it, for faith is the hand which, from a sense of utter insufficiency and helplessness, clings to God and grasps His strength—not always firmly, but often feebly—not always consciously, but instinctively. Though the saint be "kept by the power of God" yet he himself has to fight every step of the way. If we read of "this *grace* wherein we stand" (Rom. 5:2), we are also told "for by *faith* ye stand" (2 Cor. 1:24).

Viewing the event from the standpoint of the Divine decree it was not possible that Herod should slay Christ in His infancy, nevertheless God commanded Joseph to use means to prevent it, by fleeing into Egypt. In like manner, from the standpoint of God's eternal purpose it is not possible that any saint should perish, yet He has placed upon him the necessity of using means to prevent apostasy and everything which has a tendency thereto. True, he must not trust in the means to the exclusion of God, for those means are only efficacious by His appointment and blessing; on the other hand, it is presumption and not faith which talks of trusting God while the means are despised or ignored. **Nor have we said anything in this article** which warrants the inference that Heaven is a wage that we earn by our own industry and fidelity, rather do the means appointed by God mark out the course we must take if we would reach the desired Goal. It is "*through* faith and patience" we "inherit the promises" (Heb. 6:12): our glorification will not be bestowed in return for them, yet there can be no glorification to those devoid of these graces.

The sun shines into our rooms *through* their windows: those windows contribute nothing whatever to our comfort and enjoyment of the sun, yet are they necessary as means for its beams to enter. The means and mediums which God has deigned for the accomplishment of His ends concerning us are not such as to be "conditions" on which those ends are suspended in uncertainty as to their issue, but are the sore links by which He has connected the one with the other. Exhortations and warnings are not so much the means whereby God's promises are accomplished as the means by which the *things* promised are wrought. God has promised His people sufficient grace to enable and cause them to make such a use of the means that they will be preserved from fatal sins or apostasy, and the exhortations, consolations, admonitions of Scripture are designed for the stirring up into exercise of that grace. The certainty of the end is assured not by the nature or sufficiency of the means in themselves considered, but because of God's ordination in connection therewith.

God has assured His people that His grace shall be all-sufficient and that His strength shall be made perfect in their weakness, but nowhere has He promised a continuance of His love and favour unto dogs returning to their vomit or to sows which are content to wallow in the mire. If our thoughts on this subject be formed entirely by the teaching of God's Word (and not partly by carnal reason), then we shall expect perseverance only in that wherein God has promised it, and that is by availing ourselves of the helps and advantages He has provided, especially the study of and meditation upon His Word and the hearing or reading the messages of His servants. Though God has promised grace unto His people, yet He requires them to—sincerely, believingly, earnestly—seek it: "Let us therefore come boldly unto the Throne of Grace, that we may obtain mercy and find grace to help in time of need" (Heb. 4:16). And that grace we are constantly in need of as long as we are left here—"Day by day the manna fell," O to learn that lesson well.

Much confusion has resulted on this and other points through failure to distinguish between implication and application, or what Christ purchased for His people and God's actually making over the same unto them according to the order of things He has established. As faith is indispensable before justification so is perseverance before glorification, and that necessarily involves the use of means. True, our faith adds nothing whatever to the merit of Christ in order to our justification, yet until we *believe* we are under the curse of the Law; nor does our perseverance entitle us to glorification, yet only those who *do* persevere unto the end will be glorified. Now as God requires obedience from all the parts and faculties of our souls, so in His Word He has provided motives to the obedience required, motives suited unto "all that is within us"—that love, fear, hope, etc., may be called into action of ourselves—we are not sufficient to make a good use of the means, and therefore we beg God to work in us that which He requires: Colossians 1:29.

God has promised to repair the spiritual decays of His people and to heal their backslidings freely, yet He will do so in such a way as wherein He may communicate His grace righteously to the praise of His glory. Therefore are duties, especially that of confession of sins to God, prescribed to us in order thereto. "He that covereth his sins shall not prosper, but whoso confesseth and forsaketh them shall have mercy" (Prov. 28:13). "I will heal their backsliding" (Hosea 14:4): there is the promise and the end. But first "Take with you words, and turn to the LORD: say unto Him, Take away all iniquity and receive us graciously" (v. 2): there is the duty and the means unto that end. Although repentance and confession be not the procuring cause of God's grace and love, from where alone our healing or recovery proceeds, yet are they required in the appointed method of God's dispensing His grace.

It must be insisted upon that the Christian's concurrence with the Divine will by no means warrants the horrible conclusion that he is entitled to divide the honours with God. How could this possibly be, seeing that if he does what he is bidden he remains but an "unprofitable servant"? How could it be, when to whatever extent he does improve the means, it is only the power of Divine grace which so enabled him? How could it be, when he is most sensible in himself that far more of failure than success attends his efforts? No, when the redeemed have safely crossed the Jordan and are safely landed on the shores of the heavenly Canaan they will exclaim with one accord, "Not unto us, O LORD, not unto us, but unto Thy name give glory, for Thy mercy, for Thy Truth's sake" (Psa. 115:1).

To sum up. The doctrine of the perseverance of the saints, in the pursuit and practice of holiness as it is set forth in God's Word, provides no shelter for either laziness or licentiousness: it supplies no encouragement for us to take our regeneration and glorification for granted, but bids us "give diligence to make your calling and election sure" (2 Peter 1:10). Exhortations and threats are not made unto us as those already assured of final perseverance, but as those who are called to the use of means for the establishment of our souls in the ways of obedience, being annexed to those ways of grace and peace which God calls His saints unto. Perseverance consists in a continual exercise of spiritual graces in the saints, and exhortations are the Divinely appointed means for stirring those graces into action and for a further increase of them. Therefore those preachers who do not press upon the Lord's people the discharge of their duties and are remiss in warning and admonishing them, fail grievously at one of the most vital points in the charge committed to them.—A.W.P.

THE DESTRUCTION OF DAGON. (SERIES PART 1)

The opening chapters of the first book of Samuel bring before us some sad incidents, making evident the deplorable condition into which the favoured Nation had fallen, for they treat of a portion of that time covered by the Book of Judges, when "in those days there was no king in Israel; every man did that which was right in his own eves" (21:25). First, we have Hannah, in bitterness of soul praying unto and weeping before the Lord, and Eli the high priest so lacking in discernment as to suppose she was drunk (Chap. 1). Concerning Eli's sons we read that they were "sons of Belial" who "knew not the LORD" (2:12). Though engaged in the sacred office of the priesthood, they conducted themselves in a most horrible manner. First, we are told that they misappropriated for their own use portions of the sacrifices, for they "abhorred the offering of the LORD" (2:13-17), thereby being guilty of the fearful sin of sacrilege. Moreover, they committed immorality, and that at the very "door of the tabernacle" (2:22). Later, we find the Lord making known unto their father (2:27-34) and unto Samuel (3:11-14) the judgment which He would execute upon the house of Eli.

"And the word of Samuel came to all Israel. Now Israel went out against the Philistines to battle, and pitched beside Ebenezer: and the Philistines pitched in Aphek. And the Philistines put themselves in array against Israel: and when they joined battle, Israel was smitten before the Philistines: and they slew of the army in the field about four thousand men" (1 Sam. 4:1-2). Jehovah was no longer fighting for His people, and without Him they suffered defeat at the hands of the enemy. The Lord will not show Himself strong on the behalf of those who displease and dishonour Him. As He announced through one of His Prophets at a later date, "The LORD is with you while ye be with Him: and if ye seek Him He will be found of you; but if ye forsake Him, He will forsake you" (2 Chron. 15:2). The same principle is repeated in the New Testament: James 4:8-10.

"And when the people were come into the camp, the elders of Israel said, Wherefore hath the LORD smitten us today before the Philistines? Let us fetch the ark of the covenant of the LORD out of Shiloh unto us, that, when it cometh among us, it may save us out of the hand of our enemies" (1 Sam 4:3). See here the blindness and the folly of the religious leaders. They were oblivious to the fact that the nation was ripe for judgment, and refused to consider that the defeat which had just been experienced was a call from the Lord unto humiliation, repentance and reformation. How absurd the expedient suggested. True, wonders had indeed happened in the past when the ark had gone before the people, but it had been by the Divine command the sacred coffer was in the vanguard, and not at the caprice of men. Tokens of the Lord's power were granted at a time when the nation, generally speaking, was walking in obedience to Him, and not when He was being openly defied. Those things made all the difference.

The expedient resorted unto by those "elders" has often been repeated in

principle. There has usually been a large proportion of those who nominally profess to be the people of God, that are so deluded as to believe no matter how sinful
and worldly their lives be, they are entitled unto Divine help. Total strangers to
vital godliness, supposing that a half-hearted attention to external forms will satisfy the Lord, in the hour of emergency they call upon Him in hope. To indulge the
conceit because a "day of prayer" is appointed for a people who are "lovers of
pleasure more than lovers of God" (2 Tim. 3:4), He will promptly put forth His
mighty arm on their behalf, is the modern parallel to Israel's making an idol of the
ark and concluding it would save them from their enemies. Rightly did Thomas
Scott say of those hypocrites, they "dishonoured Him more in attending of His
ordinances than they could do by neglecting them, so that He abhors those services for which they expect His favour." Let the reader ponder such passages as
Isaiah 29:13-14; Malachi 1:12-14.

"So the people sent to Shiloh (where the tabernacle then abode) that they
might bring from thence the ark of the covenant of the LORD of Hosts, which
dwelleth between the cherubim: and the two sons of Eli, Hophni and Phinehas,
were there with the ark of the covenant of God" (1 Sam. 4:4). What a spectacle:
that which symbolized the throne of Jehovah in Israel's midst being borne by these
sons of Belial! But have no unholy men handled the sacred things of Christ during
the past fifty years? Are there no Hophnies and Phinehases in Christendom today?
Are the Scriptures never publicly read, prayers made, the ordinances of Christian
Baptism and the Lord's Supper administered, by men whose beliefs and ways evince
that they "abhor the offering of the Lord"? Well did Thomas Scott say of Eli's
sons, "being hardened to their destruction, they were left to venture presumptuously into the holy of holies and to carry the ark into the army and thus, without
any proper call, they were found within the reach of the sword of the Philistines,
by which they were destined to be destroyed."

"And when the ark of the covenant of the LORD came into the camp all
Israel shouted with a great shout, so that the earth rang again" (v. 5). How much
seeming zeal there is for the ark of the Lord while the Lord of the ark is despised!
Poor deluded souls; like parched travelers in the desert having false hopes raised
by a mirage of water. Mistaking the shadow for the substance, they thought that
all would now be well with them. Their shouting was but the infatuation of the
flesh and not an inspiration of the Spirit. It went beyond what our moderns would
term "wishful thinking": it was heralding the victory before the enemy was so
much as engaged. Carried away by an act of awful presumption they gave expression to hilarious joy as though they had already triumphed over the Philistines.
Has mankind become any wiser with the passing of the centuries? Is our own
"enlightened generation" too discreet to count their chickens before they are
hatched? It hardly looks like it with all this ambitious and utopian post-war planning.

"And when the Philistines heard the noise of the shout they said, What meaneth
the noise of this great shout in the camp of the Hebrews? And they understood that the
ark of the LORD was come into the camp. And the Philistines were afraid; for they
said, God is come into the camp: And they said, Woe unto us! for there hath not been
such a thing heretofore" (vv. 6, 7). Such ignorance and superstition was excusable on

the part of the Philistines. They had heard something of the wonders which the God of Israel had wrought for His people in the past, and as they listened to the acclamations of the Hebrews they were filled with dismay. But not for long. Their leaders called upon them to, "Be strong and quit you like men, O ye Philistines, that ye be not servants unto the Hebrews, as they have been to you: quit yourselves like men and fight" (v. 9). It was not the "fear of the Lord" but only a fleeting natural alarm which had overtaken them, and they quickly threw it off. Had Jehovah actually been with Israel how different things would have been.

"And the Philistines fought and Israel was smitten, and they fled every man to his tent: and there was a very great slaughter, for there fell of Israel thirty thousand footmen. And the ark of God was taken, and the two sons of Eli, Hophni and Phinehas, were slain" (vv. 10, 11). Israel had regarded the ark as a fetish—as many now consider a meaningless "mascot" or a golden "cross" which has been "blest" by some Papist, will afford its possessor protection in the hour of danger—but it availed them not when the enemy struck. They had given a premature shout of victory, but now their army suffered a sevenfold worse defeat than the previous one. The sons of the high priest had personally accompanied the sacred coffer, and now they lay cold in death. God's threats are not idle words, but sure predictions of what is in store for evil-doers. The fearful judgments which had been announced to Eli and Samuel were now literally executed. And, my reader, each of us, individually, and the nation to which we belong, has to do with the same God. He will not be mocked with impunity. Though He be slow to anger, yet His wrath is the more terrible when it does strike.

Tidings of this fearful disaster were speedily conveyed unto the high priest. He was seated by the wayside in sore suspense, "For his heart trembled for the ark of God" (v. 13). When the news was broken to him, it was too much for the aged Eli, so that he "fell from off the seat backward by the side of the gate and his neck was broken and he died" (v. 18). His daughter-in-law was in childbirth and when she learned of the national catastrophe and the death of her father-in-law and husband, she, too, expired, but not until after naming her son "Ichabod" saying "the glory is departed from Israel, for the ark of God is taken" (vv. 19-22). It may strike some as strange that God suffered the ark to fall into the hands of the Philistines, but considering all the circumstances it had surely been much more strange had His *blessings* attended the superstitious expediency of the rebellious Israelites.—A.W.P.

WELCOME TIDINGS.

"And it came to pass when Moses held up his hand that Israel prevailed, and when he let down his hand Amalek prevailed. But Moses' hands were heavy: and thy took a stone and put it under him, and he sat thereon; and Aaron and Hur stayed up his hands, the one on the one side and the other on the other side; and his hands were steady until the going down of the sun" (Exo. 17:11, 12). From earliest times the Lord's people have looked upon this as an example of the efficacy of importunate prayer. Rightly so, we believe. In fact the Chaldee paraphrase of verse 11 actually expresses it, "when Moses held up his hand in prayer." But more: this incident supplies a blessed illustration of a servant of God being upheld in his work by the instrumentality of others. Even the Apostle Paul recognized his need of the saints' help in this direction, for again and again we find him asking for their prayers on his behalf.

During the past few months an unusual number of letters from readers of this magazine, many of whom we have never met in the flesh (though undoubtedly we have contacted them in spirit before the Throne of Grace), have made mention that they pray daily for the editor and his wife. This is a great encouragement to us, and we trust we are duly grateful for the same. How much we owe personally to their supplications, and to what extent the fruitfulness of this written ministry is due thereto, only the Day will declare. Certain we are that if it had not been for the co-operation and help of our spiritual partners, this publication had ceased long ago. Prayer is one of the Divinely-appointed channels through which the blessings of Heaven flow down to this earth.

Once again it is our privilege and pleasure to give our friends some indication of how the Lord has graciously heard their prayers on our behalf, and how He has deigned to make this little monthly messenger a help to some of His scattered sheep in this dark day. Only a few extracts are possible from the letters received. May they encourage all of us and stimulate unto more earnest and definite intercession.

"We are rejoicing before the Lord in still preserving to us such a faithful witness and ministry in these times of spiritual decay. We have to praise His great name for thus providing food convenient for our souls. He does indeed feed us with the finest of the wheat. It is cause for humbling ourselves before Him, that He should deign still to remember us so lovingly, notwithstanding our backsliding and our utter unworthiness. He continually reminds us it is not for anything in us, but simply to promote His own honour and glory, and we can truly realize this when we look within and behold what manner of creeping things we are, in contrast with what manner of persons we ought to be in all holy conversation and godliness" (Australia). "Thank you very much for sending me the magazines so regularly. They have searched me and refreshed me" (Scotland). "We are thankful to receive the Studies and the teaching that is in them and that the great sins of our own day are taken notice of" (New reader).

"Many thoughts in your Studies help me and give comfort, some frighten me, nevertheless I look forward for your magazine coming. So far I have received all copies" (Australia). "Your magazine has been blessed to me. Often I have felt as if I were not in God's mind at all: everything seemed to be against me. Then I would find something in them that would clear the mist away and I would feel so happy, for things did not seem so bad after all (Aged Pilgrim). "Please find enclosed a small token of my appreciation for the Studies throughout another year. To me they have been a real help and blessing, while very often, too, they have caused heart searchings" (One in the Navy).

"When the Studies come in such a wonderful way it would be a very dull heart that failed to return thanks and praise to Him to whom all praise belongs. He doeth all things well. I know of no one around here with whom I can have fellowship in spiritual things. The 'Doctrine of Man's Impotency' was not altogether pleasant reading, but I am thankful you had the courage to take it up. The dignity of man has been preached for so long that we needed a reminder of what by nature we really are. Your Studies stir me up to make more diligent use of the means of grace and to seek more earnestly those things that belong to my peace" (Australia). "I continue to find the Studies very helpful, and experience a blessing in perusing their pages. Nothing I have ever read has revealed my shortcomings in the life of grace more than your writings. May the Lord whom you try to serve bless your labours in these dark days. We know not what lies ahead, but the Lord changeth not, and in Him lies our only hope as individuals and as a nation. I wonder if it is a mark of grace when one seeks and searches to make still more and more sure that one's feet are on the Rock? To whom can we go except to Him who has the Words of Eternal Life? O to be sure that I had a saving interest and covenant right in Him" (Scotland). O that there were more who sought to make sure.

"We are still not only enjoying but profiting from your Studies. You are certainly making a great contribution to the edifying of the saints. Your numerous quotations from the writings of the Puritans are making many conscious of the real value of their works. I know that for my own part their writings are having a great influence on my ministry" (Young Preacher). "I am glad you are able to continue the publication of your Studies, which are always illuminating and spiritually profitable" (Anglican Minister). "Thank you for your Studies during 1942. Your writings have helped me more than I can say, and I very seldom speak in public without drawing on them for some of their good things" (England).

"I do appreciate the Studies and trust you are able to continue. I read them more than anything else, and am not able to convey to you how much help they have been to me from time to time. Only yesterday I spent hours reading your expositions. It was the Lord's Day, and often I am quite alone and never go outdoors. I do not want to seem as if I am better than others, but O I am very much alone in spiritual matters! Although I have quite a lot of Christian friends, it is a rare thing if they ever speak of Scriptural topics" (Canada). "How glad I am to be able to send a tiny gift towards the printing of the magazine. They are indeed most helpful and seem to become more so than ever as the years go by. They contain just that which one's soul longs for, but at the same time it reveals to my own heart, at any rate, the empty teaching of today. Were it not that one has the precious Word of God to go to at all times, I don't know what I should do" (England).

"I want to express to you again my deep gratitude for the spiritual instruction, counsel and blessing your ministry has been to me through another year. May God richly bless you both and grant you the needed strength and wisdom for the task which lies before you. O that there was more such ministry in the world today! Many thanks, too, for the extra copies you have been sending. I appreciate them much and have forwarded them to a poor but worthy family in the northern part of our state" (U.S.A.). "Truly I have to confess that the Studies have been the means from the Lord in sustaining my soul many a time. After I read them, I always want to go back to them, and am seldom, if ever, disappointed in getting something fresh and good. I thank the Lord that He still has a faithful few in this sinful world who are not ashamed to hold forth the words of Truth. May the Lord prosper your work greatly for His own glory" (Scotland). "Thank you for the Studies which it has been my privilege, in the mercy of the Lord, to receive during this year. Your choice of subjects has been, I verily believe, God-given, and have been most searching and edifying. 'Doctrine of Saints Perseverance' and 'Christian Resurrection' have been specially helpful. Thanking the Lord for His gracious care of you both and ever praying that you may be kept to provide that which is truly food for His people in these difficult times" (Wales).

"I feel constrained to write and thank you for the Studies. Every article in them seems to be rich with good wholesome food, and undoubtedly written with the object of producing a good inward constitution capable of digesting the same. The articles on 'Divine Healing' appeared, so far as I am concerned, at a particularly suitable time," (Scotland). "Your articles on Divine Healing have been of much help to me. I could not agree with much of the 'Divine-healers' doctrine, yet I could not give the reason why. How I need to thank God for His patience with such a stupid ignorant creature" (U.S.A.). "The reading of your Studies during the past year has been of great blessing and profit to me, and valued far beyond the wealth and riches of the world. To a youth of twenty years of age, living in a grim world at war, with corruption and apostasy all around us, the truths contained in your magazine have been strengthening and confirmed my faith" (Philadelphia).

"Personally, in reading your Studies, I have sometimes been edified, instructed, and encouraged; and at others, searched, reproved, and stirred up to confession and prayer. I trust, therefore, I can without presumption say that they have been to me a source of spiritual teaching and gracious profit. May the Lord continue to bless you with much of His spirit and grace in the work, and favour you with many inward encouragements, as well as outward testimonies, that this 'labour of love' is not in vain" (England).

(continued from back page)

France, as she is responsible for Eire's refusal to grant us naval bases, of Vichy's steady opposition, of the French Canadian's disloyalty, and of many other hostile factors and forces; but *who* is permitting the "Mother of Harlots" to employ her powerful influence thus? None other than the Lord of Hosts. He is righteously using Rome as a rod on the back of an apostate Protestantism.

We cannot expect the unbelieving nations to look beyond Hitler and his fellows, but it is the privilege of Christians to "look unto *the LORD*" (Micah 7:7). It is the very nature of faith to be occupied with its Author. It is the duty of faith to "set the LORD always before" it (Psa. 16:8). When the Ammonites and Moabites came up against Judah, Jehoshaphat turned unto God and said, "we have no might against this great company that come against us; neither know we what to do: but our eyes are *upon Thee*" (2 Chron. 20:12). This is the first message to His own people which the voice of the Lord has in His judgments: look above the human scourges and behold *My* hand in righteous retribution. And it is the business of God's servants at such a time to urge upon the saints to "consider in thine heart that the LORD He is God in Heaven above and upon the earth beneath: there is none else" (Deut. 4:39). O that it may be the experience of both writer and reader—"Unto Thee lift I up mine eyes, O Thou that dwellest in the heavens" (Psa. 123:1) and then shall we prove for ourselves "they looked unto Him, and were lightened" (Psa. 34:5).—A.W.P.

(continued from front page)

King of nations!" (Jer. 10:7). No spiritual warrant whatever has any people to put their trust in human greatness, the sire of their armies, the excellency of their equipment, the strength of their defenses. God has but to blow upon them and they are immediately overthrown, entirely demolished. Mark how this is emphasized in Jeremiah 18, "At what *instant* I shall speak concerning a nation, and concerning a kingdom, to pluck up and to pull down and to destroy it" (v. 7): it is done in a moment—suddenly, swiftly, invincibly.

"Behold I frame evil against you." It is the evil of punishment about to be inflicted on the evil of sin. It is no momentary outburst of uncontrollable anger, but dispassionate and deliberated retribution, and when the almighty "frames" or devises that evil against a kingdom, no power can deliver it. Though Lucifer himself says, "I will ascend above the heights of the cloud: I will be like the Most High" (Isa. 14:14), yet is his proud boast seen to be an empty one, for the Lord says, "yet thou shalt be brought down to Hell, to the sides of the Pit" (v. 15). "Damascus is waxed feeble and turneth herself to flee, and fear hath seized on her: anguish and sorrows have taken her as a woman in travail" (Jer.

49:24)—suddenly, sorely, irresistibly, from which there is no escape. How this should make the wicked to tremble and depart from their evil ways! God turneth "a fruitful land into barrenness, for the wickedness of them that dwell therein" (Psa. 107:34).

"Behold *I* frame evil against you." Calamities and judgments come not by chance, nor are they originated by inferior agents or secondary causes. Though He may be pleased to make use of human instruments, yet the Lord is the Author of and principal Agent in them. Before the Assyrians fell upon apostate Israel Jehovah declared, "I will send him against a hypocritical nation, and against the people of My wrath will I give him a charge, to take the spoil, and to take the prey, and to tread them down like the mire of the streets" (Isa. 10:6). The Lord moved him, though he was in no wise conscious of any Divine impulse or commission. And when God had finished making use of the Babylonians and raised up the Medes and Persians to humiliate them into the dust, He declared of Cyrus "thou art *My* battle-axe and weapons of war: for with thee will I break in pieces the nations, and with thee will I destroy kingdoms" (Jer. 51:20). Cyrus was as truly God's "servant" as Moses or any of the Prophets: see Isaiah 45:1; Ezra 1:1. Curses as much as blessings, calamities as much as boons, judgments as truly as favours proceed from the Almighty, and it is but a species of atheism to deny the fact.

"Behold I frame evil against you." How this word needs to be pressed upon this evil and adulterous generation, which is occupied with anyone and anything rather than the living God. In a land where Bibles are so plentiful we are without excuse when we look no higher than the agencies now threatening us. Yea, it is a grievous sin for us to throw the blame of our present trials and troubles upon human instruments instead of upon our national iniquities, and refuse to see *God* employing those instruments against us. Hitler is but a scourge in the hand of the Almighty. Nor are they helping any to fix their gaze on the supreme Framer of Evil who constantly direct attention to the machinations of the pope and his longing to see the British empire destroyed. Doubtless the papacy was behind the entrance of Italy into active conflict and the perfidy of

. (continued on proceeding page)

VOL. XXII.   AUGUST, 1943.   NO. 8

STUDIES IN THE SCRIPTURES

" Search the Scriptures." John 5:39.

Publisher and Editor—ARTHUR W. PINK,
27 Lewis Street,
Stornoway, Isle of Lewis,
Scotland.

GOD'S VOICE IN JUDGMENTS

"Thus saith the Lord, Behold, I frame evil against you and devise a device against you" (Jer 18:11). That is the language of God unto a kingdom whose overthrow is threatened by His judgments, to whom the dispensations of his providence announce impending ruin. The dark clouds of calamity overhead testify to God's disapproval of a nation's sins. Under such solemn presages of the impending storm of Divine wrath proud spirits ought to be tamed and the masses brought to realize what a vain thing it is to fight against the Almighty and how fearful are the consequences of flouting His authority and treading underfoot His laws. The effects of evil doing are termed by the Spirit "gall and wormwood," but it is not until God brings a nation into external miseries they are made to realize the truth thereof. "Thine own wickedness shall correct thee and thy backsliding shall reprove thee: know therefore and see that it is an evil and bitter thing that thou hast forsaken the Lord thy God and that My fear is not in thee, saith the Lord of hosts" (Jer 2:19).

"Behold, I frame evil against you." The speaker is the Most High and "none can stay His hand or say unto Him what doest thou?" He framed evil against the antediluvians. "The earth was filled with violence...all flesh had corrupted his way upon the earth" (Gen 6:11,12). Warnings of impending doom were given by Enoch (Jude 14,15) and Noah, but none heeded. Then the storm burst: "all the fountains of the great deep were broken up, and the windows of heaven opened" (Gen 7:11). And what could men do to help themselves? Nothing whatever. God "framed evil" against Sodom and Gomorrah and what could their inhabitants do when He "rained fire and brimstone" upon them (Gen 18:24). They were powerless to withstand it. God "framed evil" against Egypt. Her haughty monarch exclaimed "who is the Lord that I should obey His voice?" (Exo 5:2), but discovered that He was not to be defied with impunity when He "took off their chariot wheels" and drowned him and his hosts in the Red Sea.

When the Almighty sends a devastating earthquake, what can puny man do? When He withholds the rain and famine ravages a land, who can resist Him? When He visits with a pestilence which cuts off millions in the prime of life, as the "flu" did in 1918, who can say Him nay? When He unleashes the dreadful hounds of war, who can turn them back? Is there, then, no hope? Yes, if the masses will truly humble them-

(continued on back page)

IMPORTANT NOTICES

Please advise promptly of change in address, otherwise copies will be lost in the mails.

We are glad to send a sample copy to any of your friends whom you believe would be interested in this publication.

This magazine is published as "a work of faith and labour of love," the editor and his wife gladly giving their services free. There is no regular subscription price, as we do not wish the poor of the flock to be deprived. This does not mean that those looking for something for nothing may "help themselves." Those getting this Magazine, who are financially able and who receive spiritual help from its pages, are expected to gladly contribute towards its expenses; otherwise, their names are dropped from our lists.

Will those forwarding International Money Orders please have them made out to us at Stornoway, Isle of Lewis, Scotland. Checks (Cheques-Eng.) made out on U.S.A. Banks are not negotiable here, so please do not send them.

CONTENTS

THE SERMON ON THE MOUNT

26e. Profession tested: Matthew 7:24, 25

Verses 24-27 form the conclusion of our Lord's Address. Upon them Spurgeon said, "These were the closing words of our Saviour's most famous sermon upon the mount. Some preachers concentrate all their powers upon an effort to conclude with a fine thing called a peroration, which being interpreted, means a blaze of rhetorical fireworks, in the glory of which the speaker subsides. They certainly have not the example of Christ in this discourse to warrant them in the practice. Here is the Saviour's peroration, and yet it is as simple as any other part of the address. There is an evident absence of all artificial oratory. The whole of His hill-sermon was intensely earnest, and that earnestness was sustained to the end, so that the closing words are as glowing coals, or as sharp arrows of the bow. Our Lord closes not by displaying His own powers of elocution, but by simply and affectionately addressing a warning to those who, having heard His words, should remain satisfied with hearing, and should not go forth and put them into practice."

"Therefore whosoever heareth these sayings of Mine, and doeth them, I will liken him unto a wise man, which built his house upon a rock: and the rain descended, and the floods came, and the winds blew, and beat upon that house; and it fell not: for it was founded upon a rock" (vv 24,25). Simple as that language is, yet many have misunderstood its meaning and missed its import. No two of the commentators give a uniform exegesis of theses verses, and though there is more or less substantial agreement with the older and soundest expositors, yet even among them there is considerable difference of opinion. When we consult more recent writers thereon, especially those who may be broadly classed as belonging to the "Fundamentalist School," while there is much more of a saying of the same thing yet we are personally convinced it is a saying of the *wrong* thing. A critical examination of the view they have taken obliges one to point out that they have read into this passage what is not there, that they have utterly failed to bring out what is there, and this because they have missed the scope of our passage through ignoring its context.

According to the Antinomian interpretation of this passage our Lord ought to have said, "Whosoever believeth the Gospel and trusts in My atoning blood, I will liken him unto a wise man who built his house upon the Rock; and every one who endeavours to heed My precepts and then trusts in his own good works to obtain for him acceptance with God, I will liken unto a foolish man who built his house upon the sand." But in the verses before us Christ said nothing of the sort. And why? Because He was dealing with something more solemn and searching than what constitutes the ground of a sinner's acceptance with God. It is perfectly true, blessedly true, that every sinner who exercises a saving faith in the Sacrifice of Christ is a wise man, and that he is eternally secure; as it is equally true that any one who relies upon his own obedience to the Divine commandments in order to obtain a passport into everlasting bliss is a fool, as he will prove in the day of testing. But we say again, Christ is not here speaking of either the object or ground of saving faith but of something far more probing and revealing, and we throw everything into the utmost confusion if we confound the two things.

Before we are ready to weigh the terms of our passage we must first ascertain and determine its scope, and that calls for a careful noting of its context. In the verses immediately preceding it is clearly the testing of profession which is in view, the making evident of the reality which lies behind all surface appearances, and in this closing section Christ continues to show what it is which distinguishes the genuine and living Christian from a nominal and lifeless one. In some passages the "house" or home is a figure of the place of affection and rest, but here it is viewed as a shelter and refuge from the storm. The stability and security of a house depends ultimately on the strength of its foundation. For if that be faulty, no matter how good the materials of which it is composed or how reliable the workmanship of those engaged in its construction, when a hurricane strikes it will fall. This obvious fact has been grasped by all the commentators, but as to what our Lord signified by the "rock" foundation there is wide difference of opinion.

Probably the passage which occurs most readily to the minds of many of our readers in this connection is Isaiah 28:16, "Thus saith the Lord God, Behold I lay in Zion for a foundation a Stone, a tried Stone, a precious cornerstone, a sure foundation," and from Acts 4:11 and 1 Peter 2:5-7 we know that the precious "Stone" and "Sure Foundation" is Christ Himself. Yet we make great mistake if we suppose that *every* NT passage containing the word "foundation" looks back to Isaiah 28:16 or refers to the same thing. Not so "The foundation of God standeth sure, having this seal, The Lord knoweth [loveth, and therefore preserveth] them that are His" (2 Tim 2:19): as the contrast from the preceding verse denotes, the "foundation" here signifies the Divine decree or foreordination, which cannot be overthrown. "Built upon the foundation of the apostles and prophets, Jesus Christ Himself being the chief cornerstone" (Eph 2:20) refers to the ministerial foundation, the Truth proclaimed. Hebrews 6:1 speaks of "the foundation of repentance from dead works," for one has not made a start in practical godliness until that has been laid. Thus there is a need for the teacher here who is qualified to distinguish between things that differ.

There is one other passage which it is important to consider in this connection, namely, "Charge them that are rich in this world that they be not high minded, nor trust in uncertain riches, but in the living God, who giveth us richly all things to enjoy: that they do good, that they be rich in good works, ready to distribute, willing to communicate, laying up in store for themselves a good foundation against the time to come, that they may lay hold on eternal life" (1 Tim 6:17-19). Why is this passage so infrequently cited and still more infrequently expounded and enforced? For every time allusion is made to it, "For other foundation can no man lay than that is laid, which is Jesus Christ" (1Co 3:11) is quoted twenty times. Is that handling the Word honestly? No, it is not, and the churches have suffered greatly because of such unfaithfulness in the pulpit. This passage, be it noted, is addressed to the minister of the Gospel, specifying one of the duties his office obligates him to perform, but has one preacher in a hundred, during the past fifty years, conscientiously discharged it? have not the vast majority toadied to their wealthy members and withheld from them that which they most needed!

But does this passage teach that we are required to perform deeds of charity for the purpose of acquiring "merit" before God and thereby purchase for ourselves His favourable regard? or, as one has expressed it "raise a cloud of gold-dust which will waft us to Heaven." Certainly not: there is nothing here which fosters the fatal delusion of Papists. Nevertheless, there is important instruction which we cannot afford to ignore. It is *Christians* that are "rich in this world" who are to be thus charged: "Be not high minded"— affecting yourselves to be superior to the poor of the flock; "nor trust in uncertain riches"—which may speedily disappear; "but in the living God"—who changeth not, and is your true Portion. "Who giveth us richly all things to enjoy"—but not to squander on over-indulgence. "That they do good" with what God has loaned to them, faithfully discharging their stewardship. "Laying up for themselves a good foundation" in their conscience, a reliable basis for their hope, a sure ground of assurance, thereby confirming their personal interest in Christ, for "good works" are the evidences of the genuineness of our faith.

"Laying up in store for themselves [not 'before God'!] a good foundation against the time to come": whether it be adversity that overtakes you through financial reverses, so that those you have aided will be the readier to assist you; or a bed of lingering illness, so that you may not have the additional anguish of a conscience accusing you of selfishness and callousness; or the hour of death itself, that you may have the comfort of knowing you have discharged your stewardship faithfully and that the poor call you blessed; or the Day to come, when "they that have done good" will come forth "unto the resurrection of life" (John 5:29) and their "good works" will be owned and rewarded by the Judge of all the earth. "That they may lay hold on eternal life" obtaining a firmer conscious grip on the same, for the "good works" of the Christian are so many testimonies of his portion in Heaven. Having our affections set upon Christ and our true riches in Him, let us act like wise merchants, not grasping at shadows and uncertainties, but suing for His glory and the good of our fellows what He has entrusted to us, thereby laying up for ourselves "treasures in Heaven" (Matt 6:20) and acquiring additional confirmation that we already possess the "earnest" of "eternal life." The "house" of *such* an one is built upon a *"rock"*!

It will be seen from the last four paragraphs that the term "foundation" is found in widely different connections, that it is not always used to denote precisely the same thing, and therefore that its significance in a particular verse must be sought by ascertaining the scope and meaning of the passage in which that verse occurs; and that is no task for the "novice" but rather for the experienced expositor. What, then, is the *scope* (the dominating subject and design) of Matthew 7:24, 25? As already stated, it is the *testing of profession*, a furnishing proof of the reality or worthlessness of the same. Rightly did Andrew Fuller point out, "Our Lord is not discoursing on our being justified by faith, but on our being judged according to our works, which, though consistent with the other, is not the same thing, and must not be confounded with it. The character described is not the self-righteous rejector of the Gospel, but one who though he may hear it and profess to believe it, yet brings forth no corresponding fruit. It is not a passage suited to expose the errors of Romanists, but one which needs to be pressed upon Antinomians—they who hold 'only believe, and all is well.'"

Our passage opens with the word "Therefore," which indicates our Lord was drawing a conclusion from what He had just been saying. In the preceding verses He was certainly not describing work-mongers, those who trusted in their good deeds and religious performances to gain them acceptance with God. Rather is He there calling upon His hearers to enter in at the strait gate (vv 13,14), warning against false prophets (vv 15-20), denouncing an empty profession. In the verse immediately before (23), so far from presenting Himself as the Redeemer, tenderly wooing sinners, He is seen as the Judge, saying to the hypocrites "depart from Me, ye that work iniquity." Thus to say the least, this would be a very strange point in His discourse at which to abruptly introduce the Gospel of the grace of God and announce that His own finished work is the only saving foundation for sinners to rest their souls upon: this would give no meaning whatever to the opening "therefore." Moreover, in what at once follows, instead of speaking of our need of trusting in His atoning blood, Christ shows how indispensable it is that we render obedience to His precepts.

John Brown, the renowned Scottish expositor, brought out quite clearly the force of our Lord's "Therefore" both in reference to what preceded and to what follows. "Surely, 'if not every one who calls Christ Lord, Lord, shall enter into the kingdom of heaven, but he only who does the will of His Father which is in heaven'; if to all workers of iniquity, even although they shall have 'prophesied and cast out devils, and done many wonderful works in the name of Christ,' it shall at last be said by our Lord, declaring by His judgment the final state of men, 'depart from Me: I never knew you'; then it certainly follows that he who hears and does our Lord's sayings is a wise man, and that he who hears them and does them not is a fool. The one saves, the other loses, the salvation of the soul, the happiness of eternity." As Matthew Henry also pointed out, "The scope of this passage teaches us that the only way to make sure work for our souls and eternity is to hear and do the sayings of the Lord Jesus." They who think they are savingly trusting in the blood of Christ while disregarding His commands are fatally deceiving themselves.

In many respects Matthew 7:24-27 is closely analogous to 25:1-12. Both passages treat of professing Christians. In each case those professors are divided into two classes, called the "wise" and the "foolish." In each case these radically different characters had something in common: in the former, both are likened unto builders and each erect a house: in the latter, both are termed "virgins" and both go forth to meet the Bridegroom with lamps in their hands. In each case the latter class is found wanting when put to the proof and meet with irretrievable disaster: in the former when the storm bursts the house of the fool falls, in the latter when the Bridegroom arrives the fool faces a closed door. In each case the difference between the two classes was nothing external, but that which lay *out of sight*—the faulty "foundation" of the former and the lack of oil "in their vessels" with the latter. We have compared these two passages together not only to note the interesting correspondence which exist between them, but chiefly because the latter throws light upon the former and helps to fix its interpretation.

Let us duly note what Christ does *not* here say of the one He terms wise: "he that heareth these sayings of Mine and understandeth them," nor even "he that heareth these sayings of Mine and *believeth in Me*" what He *did* say goes much further than that. There are multitudes who believe in Christ who do not put His precepts into practice. In the same way that there are millions in India who believe in Buddha, millions in China who believe in Confucius, millions in Africa who believe in Mahomet, so vast numbers in Christendom believe in Christ. And because they "believe in Christ" they suppose that all is well with them and that when they die they will go to Heaven. Nor are there many now left on earth who are likely to disillusion them. The great majority of the preachers in this apostate age are only adding to the number of the deceived, by telling them that all God requires of them is to believe the Gospel and receive Christ as their personal Saviour. They quote such passages as John 3:16 and Acts 16:31 which contain the word "believe," but are guiltily silent on the many verses which insist on repentance, forsaking of sins, denying of self, and which call to obedience.

How often, for example, we hear quotes "For in Christ Jesus neither circumcision availeth anything nor uncircumcision, but a new creater" or "creation" (Gal 6:15), especially by those who (rightly) wish to show that neither the ceremonial ordinances of Judaism nor the baptism and Lord's supper of Christianity are of any worth in the justifying of sinners before God. So too, though not quite so frequently, we are reminded that "For in Jesus Christ neither circumcision availeth anything nor uncircumcision, but faith which worketh by love" (Gal 5:6), that is, out of gratitude to God for His unspeakable Gift and not from a legal motive which works only for what it may obtain. But how very rarely is this one ever mentioned: "Circumcision is nothing and uncircumcision is nothing, but *the keeping of the commandments of God*" (1Co 7:19). That which concerns our submission to the Divine authority, our walking in subjection to His will, is studiously kept in the background: such partiality is most reprehensible. It is only by placing these three verses side by side that we obtain a complete and balanced view. We are not vitally united to Christ unless we have been born again; we are not born again unless we possess a faith which "worketh by love"; and we have not this saving faith unless it is evidenced by a "keeping of God's commandments."

No wonder there is now so much dishonesty among those in the pew when there has been such dishonesty in the pulpit. The unsaved are frequently told "Whosoever shall call upon the name of the Lord shall be saved" (Rom 10:13), but who is faithful enough to tell them that none ever did or could savingly "call upon" Him out of an *impenitent* heart; fewer still will remind them that Christ is "the Author of eternal salvation unto all them that obey Him" (Heb 5:9). In like manner, when addressing those who profess to be Christians, how many preachers give great prominence to the comforting promises of God, but say little about His holy requirements. There is also a certain class of Calvinists who are fond of citing "Greater love hath no man than this that a man lay down his life for His friends," but they fail to add "ye are My friends IF ye *do* whatsoever I command you" (John 15:13,14) which is the surest identifying mark of those for whom Christ died. There are thousands who glibly talk of their love for Christ, but how rarely are they reminded "and hereby we do know that we know Him, IF we *keep* His commandments. He that saith I know Him, and keepeth not His commandments is a liar, and the truth is not in him" (1Jo 2:3,4).

In the passage before us Christ continues to insist upon the imperative necessity of practical godliness. The regard or disregard which we pay to His precepts in this life He likens unto building our house on a sound or a worthless foundation, and the issue thereof in the Day of testing is compared to a tempest which puts to the proof our labours. Only those who have actually done that which He enjoined, who have rendered sincere obedience to His laws, will endure the test. He who has heard Christ's sayings and talked about repentance but has never repented, he who has admired the statutes issued by Christ but never rendered personal submission to them, shall be put to utter confusion in the hour of crisis. For the last time in this sermon our Lord enforced what may be termed its text: "except your righteousness shall exceed that of the scribes and Pharisees, ye shall in no case enter into the kingdom of heaven." It is not sufficient to eulogise the practical righteousness which He taught: it must be embodied and expressed in our personal character and conduct. Saving faith is a practical persuasion of the truth of Christ's teaching which is followed by a whole-hearted obedience to His authority. —AWP

THE MISSION AND MIRACLES OF ELISHA
8. Fifth Miracle

In creation we are surrounded with both that which is useful and that which is ornamental. The earth produces a wealth of lovely flowers as well as grain and vegetables for our diet. The Creator has graciously provided things which charm our eyes and ears as well as supply our bodies with food and raiment. The same feature marks God's Word. The Scriptures contain something more than doctrine and precept: there are wonderful types which display the wisdom of their Author and delight those who are able to track the merging of the shadow into the substance, and there are mysterious prophecies which demonstrate the foreknowledge of their Giver and minister pleasure to those granted the privilege of beholding their fulfillment. These types and prophecies form part of the internal evidence which the Bible furnishes of its Divine inspiration, for they give proof of a wisdom which immeasurably transcends that of the wisest of mortals. Nevertheless one has to turn unto the doctrinal and perceptive portions of Holy Writ in order to learn the way of salvation and the nature of that walk which is pleasing to God.

In our earlier writings we devoted considerable attention to the types and prophecies, but for the last decade we have concentrated chiefly upon the practical side of the Truth. Observation taught us that many of those who were keenly interested in a Bible reading on some part of the tabernacle or an attempt to explain some of the predictions of Daniel, appeared quite bored when we preached upon Christian duty or deportment: yet they certainly needed the latter for they were quite deficient therein. A glorious sunset is an exquisite sight, but it would supply no nourishment to one that was starving. The perfumes of a garden may delight the senses, but they would be a poor substitute for a good breakfast to a growing child. Only after the soul has fed upon the doctrine of Scripture and put into practice its precepts is it ready to enjoy the beauties of the types and explanations of the mysteries of prophecy.

This change of emphasis in our writings has lost us hundreds of readers, yet if we could relive the past fifteen years we would follow the same course. The solemn days through which we are passing demand, as never before, that first things be put first. There are plenty of writers who cater to those who read for intellectual entertainment; our longing is to minister unto those who yearn for a closer walk with God. What would be thought of a farmer who in the spring wasted his time in the woods listening to the music of the feathered songsters, while his fields were allowed to remain unploughed and unsown? Would it not be equally wrong if we dwelt almost entirely on the typical significance of the miracles of Elisha, while ignoring the simpler and practical lessons they contain for our hearts and lives? Balance is needed here as everywhere, and if we devote more space than usual on this occasion to the spiritual meaning of the miracle before us (and similarly in the "Dagon" articles) it will not be because we have made or shall make a practice of so doing.

First, its *connection*. "Great service had Elisha done in the foregoing chapter for the three kings: to his prayers and prophesies they owed their lives and triumphs. One would have expected that the next chapter should have told us what honours and what dignities were conferred on Elisha for this: that he should have been immediately preferred at court, and made prime-minister of state; that Jehoshaphat should have taken him home with him and advanced him in the kingdom. No, the wise man delivered the army, but no man remembered the wise man (Eccl 9:15). Or, if he had preferment offered him, he declined it: he preferred the honour of doing good in the schools of the prophets, before that of being great in the courts of kings. God magnified him and that sufficed him: magnified him indeed, for we have him here employed in working no less than five miracles" (Matthew Henry). He who has, by grace, the heart of a true servant of Christ, would not, if he could, exchange places with the monarch on his throne or the millionaire with all his luxuries.

Second, its *beneficiary*. "Now there cried a certain woman of the wives of the sons of the prophets unto Elisha, saying, Thy servant my husband is dead, and thou knowest that thy servant did fear the Lord: and the creditor is come to take unto him my two sons to be bondmen" (2 Kings 4:1). The one for whom this miracle was wrought was a woman, "the weaker vessel" (1 Peter 3:7). She was a widow, a figure of desolation: "how doth the city sit solitary that was full of people! how is she become as a widow!" (Lam 1:1)— contrast the proud boast of corrupt Babylon: "I sit a queen and am no widow, and shall see no sorrow" (Rev 18:7). Not only was she bereft of her husband but she was left destitute: in debt and without the means of discharging it. A more pitiable and woeful object could scarcely be conceived. In her sad plight she betook herself to the servant of Jehovah and made known unto him her dire situation. Her husband may have died while Elisha was absent with the kings in their expedition against the Moabites, and thus he be unacquainted with her troubles.

Third, its *urgency*. The situation confronting this poor widow was indeed a drastic one. Her human provider and protector had been removed by the hand of death. She had been left in debt and had not the wherewithal to discharge it—a burden that would weigh heavily on a conscientious soul; and now she was in immediate danger of having her two sons seized and taken from her by the creditor to serve as bondmen to him. Observe that in the opening words of 2 Kings 4 it is *not* said "now there *came* a certain woman of the wives of the sons of the prophets unto Elisha," but "there *cried* a certain woman," which indicates the pressure of her grief and the earnestness of her appeal unto the prophet. Sometimes God permits His people to be brought very low in their circumstances, nor is this always by way of chastisement because of their folly. We do not think that such was the case here. The Lord is pleased to bring some to the end of their own resources that His delivering hand may be the more plainly seen acting on their behalf.

One of the outstanding characteristics of the regenerate is that they are given honest hearts (Luke 8:15), and therefore is it their careful endeavour to "provide things honest in the sight of all men" and to "owe no man anything" (Rom 12:17; 13:8). They are careful to live within their income and not to order an article unless they can pay for it. It is because so many hypocrites under the cloak of a Christian profession have been so dishonest in financial matters and so unscrupulous in trade, that reproach has so often been brought upon the churches. Yet, in certain exceptional cases, even the most thrifty and upright may run into debt. It was so here. The deceased husband of this widow was a man who "did fear the Lord" (v 1), nevertheless he left his widow in such destitution that she was unable to meet the claims of her creditor. There has been considerable speculation by the commentators as to the cause of this unhappy situation, most of which this writer finds himself quite unable to approve. What then is his own explanation?

In seeking the answer to the above question three things need to be borne in mind. First, as we pointed out in our introduction to the life of Elijah series, the prophet was an abnormality, that is, there was no place for him, no need of him in the religious life of Israel during ordinary times—it was only in seasons of serious declension or apostasy that he appears on the scene. Thus, no stated maintenance was provided for *him*, as it was for the priests and levites under the law. Consequently the prophet was dependent upon the gifts of the pious or the productions of his own manual labours, and judging from the brief records of Scripture one gathers the impression that most of them enjoyed little more than the barest necessities of life. Second, for many years past Ahab and Jezebel had been in power, and not only were the pious persecuted but the prophets went in danger of their lives (1 Kings 18:4). Third, it seems likely to us that this particular prophet obtained his subsistence from the oil obtained from an olive grove, and that probably there had been a failure of the crop during the past year or two—note how readily the widow obtained from her "neighbours" not a few "*empty vessels*."

"And Elisha said unto her, what shall I do for thee?" Possibly the prophet was himself momentarily non-plussed, conscious of his own helplessness. Possibly his question was designed to emphasise the gravity of the situation: it is beyond *my* power to extricate you. More likely it was to make her look above him: I too am only human. Or again it may have been to test her: are you willing to follow my instructions? Instead of waiting for her reply, the prophet at once proceeded to ask a second question: "Tell me, what hast thou in the house?" (v 2). Perhaps this was intended to press upon the widow the seriousness of her problem, for the prophet must have known that she possessed little or nothing, or why should she have sought unto him? Or, in the light of her answer, its force may have been an admonition not to despise small mercies. Her "not anything save a pot of oil" reminds of Andrew's "but what are these among so many" (John 6:9). Ah, do not we often reason similarly!

Fourth, its *test*. "Then he said, Go borrow thee vessels abroad of all thy neighbours, even empty vessels, borrow not a few" (v 3). It was a test both of her faith and her obedience. To carnal reason it would appear that the prophet was only mocking her, for of what possible service could a lot of empty vessels be to her? But if her trust was in the Lord then she would be willing to submit herself unto and comply with His word through His servant. And are not His thoughts and ways ever the opposite of ours? Was it not so when He overthrew the Midianites? What a word was that unto Gideon: "The people that are with thee are too many for Me to give the Midianites into their hands, lest Israel vaunt themselves against Me, saying, Mine own hand hath saved me" (Judg 7:2). And in consequence, his army was reduced from over twenty-two thousand to a mere three hundred (vv 3-7); and when that little company went forth it was with trumpets and "*empty* pitchers" and lamps inside the pitchers in their hands (v 16)! Ah, my reader, we have to come before the Lord as "empty vessels"—emptied of our self-sufficiency—if we are to experience His wondering working power.

Fifth, its *requirement*. "And when thou art come in thou shalt shut the door upon thee and upon thy sons, and shalt pour out into all those vessels, and thou shalt set aside that which is full" (v 4). This was to avoid ostentation. Her neighbours were not in the secret, nor should they be permitted to witness the Lord's gracious dealings with her. It reminds us of Christ's raising of the daughter of Jairus: when they arrived at the house it was filled with a skeptical and scoffing company, and the Saviour "put them all out" (Mark 5:40) ere He went in and performed the miracle. The same principle obtains to-day in connection with the operations of Divine grace: the world is totally ignorant of this mystery—God's filling of empty vessels: "the Spirit of Truth, whom the world cannot receive, because it seeth Him not, neither knoweth Him" (John 14:17). Yes, she must shut the door "that in retirement she and her sons might the more leisurely ponder and adore the goodness of the Lord" (T. Scott).

Sixth, its *means*. This was the "pot of oil" which appeared to be so utterly inadequate to meet the demands of the widow's creditor. It *was* so in itself, but under the blessing of God it proved amply sufficient. The "five barley loaves and the two small fishes" (John 6:9) seemed quite useless for feeding a vast multitude with, but in the hands of the Lord they furnished "as much as they would," and even "when they were filled" there remained a surplus of twelve baskets full. Ah, it is the little things which God is pleased to use. A pebble from the brook slung by faith is sufficient to overthrow the Philistine giant. A "little cloud" was enough to produce " a great rain" (1 Kings 18:44,45). A "little maid" was used as a missionary in Syria (2 Kings 5:2). A "little child" was employed by Christ to teach His disciples humility (Matt 18:2). A "little strength" supplied by the Spirit enables us to "keep Christ's Word and not deny His name" (Rev 3:8). O to be "little" in our own sight (1 Sam 15:17). It is blessed to see this widow did not despise the means, but promptly obeyed the prophet's instructions, her faith laying hold of the clearly-implied promise in the "*all* those vessels" (v 4).

Seventh, its *significance*. In this miracle we have a most blessed, striking and remarkable typical picture of the grand truth of *redemption*, a subject which is we fear rather hazy in the minds even of many Christians. The Gospel is preached so superficially today, its varied glories are so lost in generalizations, that few have more than the vaguest idea of its component parts. Redemption is now commonly confused with atonement: the two are quite distinct, one being an effect of the other. The sacrifice which Christ offered unto Divine holiness and justice was "that He might bring us to God (1 Peter 3:18)—a comprehensive expression covering the whole of our salvation both in the removal of all hindrances and in the bestowal of all requisites. In order to bring us to God it was necessary that all enmity between them should be re-moved— that is *reconciliation*; that the guilt of their transgression should be cancelled—that is *remission* of sins; that they should be delivered from all bondage—that is *redemption*; that they should be made, both experimentally and legally, *righteous*—that is regeneration and justification.

Redemption, then, is one of the grand effects or results of the Atonement, the satisfaction which Christ rendered unto the Law. God's elect and debtors to the Law, for they have broken it; and they are prisoners to His justice, for they are "by nature the children of wrath even as others" (Eph 2:3). And our deliverance ("or salvation") is not a mere manumission without price, that is, a simple discharge by an act of clemency, without an adequate compensation being made. No, while it is true our redemption is of grace and effected by sovereign power, yet it is so because a ransom is offered, a price paid, in every way equivalent to the discharge secured. In the words "I will *ransom* them from the power of the grace, I will *redeem* them from death" (Hosea 13:14) we are taught that the latter is the consequence of the former. Ransom is the paying of the price required, redemption is the setting free of those ransomed, and this deliverance is by the exercise of Divine power. "Not accepting deliverance" (Heb 11:35): the Greek word "deliverance" here is commonly rendered "redemption"—they refused to accept it from the afflictions on the dishonourable terms (apostasy) demanded by their persecutors.

Redemption necessarily presupposes *previous possession*. It denotes the restoration of something which has been lost, and that, by the paying of a price. Hence we find Christ saying by the Spirit of prophecy "I *restored* that which I took not away" (Psa 69:4)! This was strikingly illustrated in the history of Israel, who on the farther shores of the Red Sea sang, "Thou in Thy mercy hast led forth Thy people which Thou hast redeemed" (Exo 15:13). First in the book of Genesis, we see the descendants of Abraham sojourning in the land of Canaan. Later, we see the chosen race in cruel servitude, in bondage to the Egyptians, groaning amid the brick-kilns, under the whip of the taskmasters. Then a ransom was provided in the blood of the pascal lamb following which, the Lord by His mighty hand brought them out of serfdom and brought them into the promised inheritance. That is a complete picture of redemption.

There are many who perceive that Christians were a people in bondage, lost to God, but recovered and restored to Him; yet who fail to perceive they belonged to the Lord *before* Christ freed them. The elect belonged to Christ long before He shed His blood to ransom them, for they were chosen in Him before the foundation of the world (Eph 1:4) and made over to Him as the Father's love-gift (John 17:9). But they too fell and died in Adam, and therefore did He come to seek and to save that which was lost.

Christ "purchased the church of God" with His own blood (Acts 20:28) and therefore does the Father say to Him "by the blood of Thy covenant I have sent forth *Thy* prisoners out of the pit where is no water" (Zech 9:11)— He has a legal right to them. There is no unavailing redemption: all whom Christ purchased or ransomed shall be redeemed, that is, delivered from captivity, set free from sin. Judicially they are so now, experimentally too in part (John 8:36), but perfectly so only when glorified—hence the future aspect in Luke 21:28; Romans 8:23.

Now observe how all the leading features of redemption are typically brought out in 2 Kings 4.

1. The object of it is a widow. She had not always been thus. Formerly she had been married to one who "feared the Lord," but death had severed that happy bond and left her desolate and destitute—apt figure of God's elect, originally in union with Him, and then through the fall "alienated" from Him (Eph 4:18).

2. Her creditor was enforcing his demands, had actually come to seize her sons "to be bondmen." The Hebrew word rendered "creditor" in 2 Kings 4:1 signifies "one who exacteth" what is justly due to him, and is so translated in Job 11:6. It looks back to "And if thy brother that dwelleth with thee be waxen poor and be *sold* unto thee, thou shalt not compel him to serve as a bond-servant, but as a hired servant, as a sojourner, he shall be with thee and shall *serve* thee unto the year of jubilee" (Lev 25:39,40). Our Lord had reference to this practice in His parable of Matthew 18:23-25. Thus the "creditor" of 2 Kings 4:1 who showed no mercy to the poor widow is a figure of the stern and unrelenting Law.

3. As the widow was quite unable to pay her creditor, so we are utterly incompetent to satisfy the demands of the Law or effect our own redemption.

4. She, like us, was shut up to the mere favour of God: "being justified freely by His *grace* through the redemption which is in Christ Jesus" (Rom 3:24) and that is exactly what we should expect to find in this miracle, for five is the number of grace: see Gen 43:34; 45:22; Exo 13:18 margin, 1Co 14:19, etc. Hence too the means used, the "oil" multiplied—figure of the grace of God (Psa 23:5; Isa 61:3) superabounding.

5. Yet it was a grace that wrought "through righteousness" (Rom 5:21), for it obtained the freedom of the widow's sons by meeting the full due of her creditor.

6. Both aspects of redemption are seen here: by price—"sell the oil and pay thy debt" (v 2); and by power—the miraculous supply of oil.

7. Nor was it a general and promiscuous redemption, but a definite and particular one: for a "widow"—special object of God's notice (Deut 24:19; Psa 68:5; James 1:27)—and not her neighbours. Christ purchased "the Church of God" (Acts 20:28) and not a mere abstraction of "freewillism." —AWP.

THE DOCTRINE OF SAINTS' PERSEVERANCE
8d. Its Safeguards

7. *By enforcing the threatenings of Scripture.* The One with whom we have to do is ineffably holy and therefore does He hate sin wherever it is found. He will not ignore sin in His own children when it is unjudged and unconfessed any more than He will in those who are the children of the Devil. The pope and his underlings may traffic in their vile "indulgences" and "special dispensations," but the Lord God never lowers His standard, and even those in Christ are not exempted from bitter consequences if

they pursue a course of folly. But God is also merciful and faithful, and therefore He threatens before He punishes and warns before He smites. In His Word He has described those ways which lead to disaster and destruction, that we may shun them, yet those who deliberately follow them may know for certain that they shall receive the due reward of their defiance. It is therefore incumbent upon the minister of the Gospel to press the Divine threatenings, as it is the part of wisdom for his hearers or readers to take the same to heart.

"If ye forgive not men their trespasses, neither will your Father forgive your trespasses" (Matt 6:15). "And that servant which knew his Lord's will and prepared not himself, neither did according to His will, shall be beaten with many stripes" (Luke 12:47—spoken to Peter: v. 41). "Behold, thou art made whole: sin no more, lest a worse thing come unto thee" (John 5:14). "If a man abide not in Me, he is cast forth as a branch and is withered, and men gather them and cast into the fire and they are burned" (John 15:6— spoken to the eleven apostles). "For if ye live after the flesh, ye shall die; but if ye through the Spirit do mortify the deeds of the body, ye shall live" (Rom 8:13). "Be not deceived, God is not mocked: for whatsoever a man soweth, that shall he also reap. For he that soweth to his flesh, shall not the flesh reap corruption; but he that soweth to the spirit, shall of the spirit reap life everlasting" (Gal 6:7,8). Have such passages as these been given due place in the preachings and writings of the orthodox during the past fifty years? No indeed: *why?*

There are three particular passages which claim a fuller notice from us in this connection, passages which are among the most solemn and frightful to be found in all the Word of God, yet which are nevertheless addressed immediately unto the people of God. Before citing the same we would preface our remarks upon them with this general observation: they have not received the attention they ought in the practical ministrations of God's servants. The minister of the Gospel has only discharged half his duty when he cleans these verses of the false glosses which his opponents have placed upon them. It is quite true that Arminians have made an altogether unwarrantable and wrong use of them, but probably God suffered His enemies to thereby bring them into prominent notice because His friends ignored them. The Christian teacher must not only show there is no conflict between these passages and such verses as John 10:28 and Philippians 1:6, but he must also bring out their positive meaning and the solemn bearing which they have upon Christians themselves.

"For it is impossible—for those who were once enlightened, and have tasted of the heavenly gift, and were made partakers of the Holy Spirit, and have tasted the good Word of God, and the powers of the world to come, if they shall fall away—to renew them again unto repentance; seeing they crucify to themselves the Son of God afresh, and put Him to an open shame. For the earth which drinketh in the rain that cometh oft upon it, and bringeth forth herbs, meet for them by whom it is dressed, receiveth blessing from God. But that which beareth thorns and briers is rejected, and is nigh unto cursing whose end is to be burned" (Heb 6:4-8). Those words are addressed to "holy brethren, partakers of the heavenly calling" (3:1), and their connection is as follows. In 5:11-14 the apostle had reproved the Hebrews for being slow in their apprehension of the Truth and in walking suitably thereto, and after this exhortation of 6:1-3 he warns them of the awful danger of continuing in a slothful state—"*For* it is impossible."

But, it may be objected, Surely it is not the intention of our Heavenly Father to terrorize His own dear children. No, certainly not; yet He would have them suitably affected thereby. Though such threatenings are not designed to work in Christians a fear of damnation, yet they should beget in them a holy care and diligence of avoiding the evils denounced. There is no more incongruity between a Christian's being comforted by the Divine promises and alarmed by the Divine threatenings, than there is between his living a life of joyful confidence in God and also one of humble dependence upon Him. We must distinguish between things that differ: there is a fear of caution as well as of distrust, a fear that produces carefulness and watchfulness as well as one which fills with anxiety. There is a vast difference between a thing that is meant to weaken the security of the flesh and the confidence that faith has in Christ. Assurance of perseverance is quite consistent with and ought ever to be accompanied by "fear and trembling" (Phil 2:12,13).

In his opening remarks on Hebrews 6:4-6 John Owen said, It "is a needful and wholesome commination (denunciation) duly to be considered by *all* professors of the Gospel." And in the course of his masterly exposition pointed out, "For not to proceed in the way of the Gospel and obedience thereto is an untoward entrance into a total relinquishment of the one and the other. That they therefore may be acquainted with the danger hereof, and be stirred up to avoid that danger, the apostle gives them an account of those who, after a profession of the Gospel, beginning at a non-proficiency under it, do end in apostasy from it. And we may see that the severest comminations are not only useful in the preaching of the Gospel, but exceeding necessary towards persons that are observed to be slothful in their profession." Scripture nowhere teaches that the saint is so secure that he needs not to be wary of himself, nor unmindful of the defection of those who for a time seemed to run well.

Another of the Puritans said on this passage, "Certainly all of us should stand in fear of this heavy judgment of being given up to perish by our apostasy, to an obstinate heart, never to reconcile ourselves by repentance, *even the children of God*; for he proposeth it to them…The apostle saith, It is impossible they should be saved, because it is impossible they should repent. This is a fearful state, and yet, as fearful as it is, it is not unusual: it is a thing we see often in some that have made a savoury profession of the name of God, and afterwards have been blasted. O, then, you that have begun and have had a taste of the ways of God, and to walk closely with Him, you should lay this to heart! Therefore this is propounded to *believers*, that they should keep at a very great distance from such a judgment, lest we grow to such an impenitent state as to be given up to a reprobate mind and vile affections" (Thomas Manton). The best preventative is a conscience kept tender of sin, which mourns over and confesses to God our transgressions, and seeks grace to mortify our lusts.

"For if we sin willfully after that we have received the knowledge of the Truth, there remaineth no more sacrifice for sins; but a certain fearful looking for of judgment and fiery indignation, which shall devour the adversaries. He that despised Moses' law died without mercy under two or three witnesses; of how much sorer punishment, suppose ye, shall he be thought worthy who hath trodden under foot the Son of God, and hath counted the blood of the covenant wherewith He was sanctified an unholy thing, and hath done despite unto the Spirit of grace? For we know Him that hath said, Vengeance belongeth unto Me, I will recompense, saith the Lord. And again, The Lord shall judge His people. It is a fearful thing to fall into the hands of the living God" (Heb

10:26-31). It is outside our present design to give an exposition of these verses (which we did when going through that Epistle), as we shall not now expose the Arminian errors thereon (which we hope to very shortly) rather do we now direct attention unto them as another example of the fearful threatenings which are directly addressed to Christians, and which it is madness and not wisdom to scoff at.

The scope of the above passage is easily grasped: Hebrews 10:23 gives an exhortation, vv. 24, 25 announce the means of continuing in that profession while vv. 26-31 declare what will befall those who relinquish the Truth. In his comments J. Owen points out, "The apostle puts himself among them ("if *we* sin" etc.), as is his manner in comminations: both to show that there is no respect of persons in this matter, but that those who had equally sinned shall be equally punished; and to take off all appearances of severity towards them, seeing he speaks nothing of this nature but on such suppositions as wherein if he were himself concerned he pronounceth it against himself also. The word 'willingly' signifies, of choice—without surprisal, compulsion or fear...If a voluntary relinquishment of the profession of the Gospel and the duties of it be the highest sin, and be attended with the height of wrath and punishment, we ought earnestly to watch against everything that inclineth or disposeth us thereto."

J. Owen concluded his remarks on these verses by saying, "This therefore is a passage of Holy Writ which is much to be considered, especially in these days wherein we live, wherein men are apt to grow cold and careless in the profession, and to decline gradually from what they had attained unto. To be useful in such a season it was first written, and it belongs unto us no less than unto them to whom it was first originally sent. And we live in days wherein the security and contempt of God, the despite of the Lord Christ and His Spirit are come to the full, so as to justify the truth that we have insisted on." In the pressing of this passage on the attention of all professing Christians was deemed so necessary in the balmy days of the Puritans, how much more so in the dark times in which our lot is cast! How woefully remiss, then, are those preachers who not only fail to devote a whole sermon to these verses, but who never so much as quote them from one years' end to another, except it be to refute the Arminians in such a manner that empty professors are made to believe there is nothing for them to fear.

"For if after they have escaped the pollutions of the world through the knowledge of the Lord and Saviour Jesus Christ, they are again entangled therein, and overcome, the latter end is worse with them than the beginning. For it had been better for them not to have known the way of righteousness than after they have known it, to turn from the holy commandment delivered unto them. But it is happened unto them according to the true proverb: The dog is turned to his own vomit again, and the sow that was washed to her wallowing in the mire" (2 Peter 2:20-22). At the close of his remarks on this passage Matthew Henry says, "If the Scriptures give such an account of Christianity on the one hand and of sin on the other as we have in these verses, we certainly ought highly to approve of the former and persevere therein, because it is a 'way of righteousness' and a 'holy commandment,' and to loathe and keep the greatest distance from the latter because it is set forth as offensive and abominable." Far better never to make a profession, than make a fair one and then sully and repudiate it.

"He that being often reproved hardeneth his neck, shall suddenly be cut off, and that without remedy" (Prov 29:1). The solemn threatenings of Scripture are so many discoveries to the Church in particular and to the world in general of the severity of

God against sin and that He adjudges them worthy of eternal destruction who persist therein. If professing Christians turn a deaf ear to exhortations, admonitions and warnings, if they steel their hearts against entreaties and threatenings, and determine to follow a course of self-will and self-pleasing, they place themselves beyond the hope of mercy. It is therefore the imperative duty of the servant of Christ to faithfully warn God's people of the fearful danger of backsliding and of what awaits them if they remain in that state: to definitely point out the connection which God has established between sin and punishment, between apostasy and damnation, so that a holy fear may be instilled to preserve them from making shipwreck of the faith, and to prevent carnal professors from indulging the vain hope of once in grace always in grace.

8. *By holding up the rewards*. Many preachers have failed to do so, allowing the fear of man to withhold from God's children a portion of their necessary bread. Because certain enemies of the Truth have wrested this subject, they deemed it wisest to be silent thereon. Because Papists have grievously perverted the teaching of Scripture upon "rewards," insidiously bringing in their lie of creature-merits at this point, not a few Protestants have been chary of preaching thereon, lest they be charged with leaning toward Romanism. Rather should this very abuse move them to be the more diligent and zealous in presenting their right and true meaning and use. Threatenings and rewards: does not the one naturally suggest the other? The former to act as deterrents, the latter as stimulants: deterrents against evil doing, stimulants or incentives unto the discharge of duty. But if the one has been shelved in the pulpit, the other has received scant attention even in orthodox quarters. We can but briefly touch upon the subject here, but hope to devote a separate article to it in the next issue.

In Scripture "eternal life" is presented both as a "gift" and as a "reward"—the reward of perseverance. To some it may appear that such terms and concepts are mutually opposed. Yet is not prayer *both* a privilege and a duty? Is not the natural man startled when he finds that God bids His people to "rejoice with trembling"—what a seeming paradox! The apparent difficulty is removed when it is seen that the "rewards" which God has promised His people are not those of justice but of bounty; that they are not a *proportioned* remuneration or return for the duties which we perform or the services we have rendered, but the end to which our obedience is suited. Thus the rewards proposed unto us by God are not calculated to work in His people a legal spirit but are designed to support our hearts under the self-denials to which we are called, to cheer us amid the sufferings we encounter for Christ's sake, and to stir us to acts of obedience meet for what is promised. Certainly Moses was inspired by no mercenary spirit when "he had respect unto the recompense of the reward" (Heb 11:26).

That eternal life and glory *is* set forth in God's Word as the reward and end of perseverance which await all faithful Christians is clear from Hebrews 10:35, to cite no other passages now: "Cast not away therefore your confidence which hath great recompense of reward." On those words Matthew Henry said, "He exhorts them not to cast away their confidence, that is, their holy courage and boldness, but to hold fast the profession for which they had suffered so much before, and borne those sufferings so well. Second, he encourages them to this by assuring them that the reward of their holy confidence is very great: it carries a present reward in it, in holy peace and joy and much of God's presence and power visited upon them; and it shall have a great recompense of reward hereafter." While the Christian sincerely endeavours to walk obediently and mix faith with God's promises the Spirit comforts and witnesses with his spirit that he is a child of God; but when he becomes careless of duty, and neglects the means of grace, He not only withholds His witness but suffers the threatenings of Scripture to so lay hold of him that Psalm 38:2, 3 becomes his experience.

9. *By insisting on steadfastness.* "Let us hold fast the profession of our faith without wavering" (Heb 10:23). Press forward along the path of holiness, no matter what obstacles and opposition you meet with. Your very safety depends upon it, for if you deny the faith either by words or actions, you are "worse than an infidel" who never professed it. The very fact that we are here bidden to "hold fast" our Christian profession implies that it is no easy task assigned us, that there are difficulties to be overcome which call for the putting forth of our utmost strength and endeavours in the defence and furtherance of it. "Without wavering" means, with unvarying and un-flinching constancy. Sin is ever seeking to vanquish the Christian; the world is ever endeavouring to draw him back into its seductive embraces; the Devil, like a roaring lion, is ever waiting to devour him. Therefore the call to him is "be ye steadfast, unmoveable, always abounding in the work of the Lord"—the duties He has assigned (1Co 15:58).

The need for pressing such exhortations as the above appears from the solemn warning addressed to those whom the apostle calls "beloved" in 2 Peter 3:17: "Beware lest ye also being led away with the error of the wicked fall from your own steadfastness." Upon this Matthew Henry says, "We are in great danger of being seduced and turned away from the Truth. Many who have the Scriptures and read them do not understand what they read, and too many of those who have a right understanding of the sense and meaning of the Word are not established in the belief of the Truth, and all these are liable to fall into error. Few attain to the knowledge and acknowledgement of doctrinal Christianity; and fewer find so as to keep in the way of practical godliness which is the narrow way which only leadeth unto life. There must be a great deal of self-denial and suspicion of ourselves, and submitting to the authority of Christ Jesus our great Prophet, before we can heartily receive all the truths of the Gospel, and therefore we are in great danger of rejecting the Truth." Ministers of Christ, then, need to insist much upon the imperativeness of steadfastness and constancy.

10. By *withholding from backsliders* the comfort of the truth of eternal security. After all that has been said under the previous heads there is little need for us to enlarge upon this point. Any preacher who encourages the slothful and the un-dutiful is doing great harm to souls. To tell those who have deserted the paths of righteousness that because they once believed in Christ all will come out well with them in the end, is to put a premium on their carnality. To assure those who have forsaken the means of grace and gone back again into the world that because they formerly made a credible profession God will recover and restore them, is to say what Scripture nowhere warrants. A griping purgative and not rich and savoury viands is what is needed by one whose system is out of order. The Divine threatenings and not the promises need to be pressed upon those who are follow-ing the desires and devices of their own hearts. Only by heeding the ten things mentioned in these articles is the precious truth of the eternal security of the saints safeguarded from profanation. —AWP

DAGON DESTROYED

We resume at the point where we left off: "And she said, The glory is departed from Israel, for the ark of God is taken" (1 Sam 4:22). Such was the dying lament of the daughter-in-law of Eli, the high priest of Israel. The sacred chest, the lid of which was "the mercy-seat" that constituted the throne of Jehovah in the midst of His people and where the Shekinah glory abode, had been removed from its appointed place in the holy of holies and conducted to the field of battle, in the hope that it would overthrow the enemies of the Hebrews. But their presumptuous expectation had not been realized. So far from it, Israel had been utterly routed, the sons of the high priest slain, and the ark of the covenant captured by the Philistines. Before expiring, the daughter-in-law of Eli named the son to which she had just given birth "Ichabod," saying "the glory is departed from Israel." The name of her son memorialized the fearful catastrophe which had overtaken the favoured nation, and described the spiritual desolation which had fallen upon it.

That which is described in 1 Samuel 4 is something more than an historical event which happened in the remote past: it illustrated and adumbrated certain basic and unchanging principles in the governmental dealings of God, which have been made manifest again and again in the course of history. Subsequently the ark of the covenant was restored to Israel and when Solomon erected the temple and the ark was set in its appointed place we are told that "the cloud [the Shekinah] filled the house of the Lord, so that the priests could not stand to minister because of the cloud: for *the glory* of the Lord had filled the house of the Lord" (1 Kings 8:10,11). But history repeated itself: the Lord was again despised, those who bore His name trampled upon His law, conformed to the ways of the heathen, worshipped false gods, and refused to heed the expostulations of His prophets. Carnality and idolatry became rampant, and though God bore long with the waywardness of his people, giving many warnings and solemn threatenings before He smote them in His wrath, the time eventually came when His awful vengeance fell.

Nearly four hundred years after Solomon the Lord delivered Israel into the hands of Nebuchadnezzar, many being carried away to Babylon: yet even that calamity produced no national repentance. Among the captives was Ezekiel and if we turn to his prophecies we obtain light on the spiritual situation as it then existed, particularly in connection with the departure of the Shekinah—the visible and awe-inspiring emblem of Jehovah's presence in the midst of Israel. In chapter 8 we find the prophet brought in vision "to Jerusalem" and he tells us "Behold, the glory of the God of Israel was there" (v 4). In 9:9 we find Jehovah complaining "The iniquity of the house of Israel and Judah is exceeding great, and the land is full of blood, and the city full of perverseness." Then in 10:4 we read "the glory of the Lord went up from the cherubim and stood over the threshold of the house," and in 10:18 "the glory of the Lord departed from off the threshold of the house." Finally, in 11:23 we are told, "The glory of the Lord went up from the midst of the cherubim and stood upon the mount which is upon the east side of the city." Slowly and gradually as though reluctant to leave, the Shekinah glory had departed and once more "Ichabod" described their sad state.

There is no intimation that the Shekinah ever returned unto Israel during the remainder of the OT period. Another temple was built in the days of Ezra and Nehemiah, and though God owned it as His house yet nothing is said of "the glory of the Lord filling it." But at the beginning of the NT era something yet more wonderful and blessed took place. As John declares in his Gospel, "The Word was made [or "became"] flesh and dwelt ["tabernacled"] among us, and we beheld *His glory*—the glory as of the Only-begotten of the Father—full of grace and truth" (1:14). Once again Israel was put upon trial: their long-promised Messiah appeared in their midst, making unmistakable demonstration of His divine credentials. He preached to them the Gospel, went about doing good, healed their sick. But they had no heart for Him. He bade them repent, but they refused. He came unto His own, and His own received Him not. They despised and rejected Him. Then it was He said unto them "O Jerusalem, Jerusalem, that killest the prophets and stonest them which are sent unto thee, how often would I have gathered thy children together, even as a hen gathereth her chickens under her wings, and ye would not. Behold your house is *left* unto you *desolate*" (Matt 23:37,38). Once again "Ichabod" was written over Israel.

Has the above no meaning and message for us? Is the history of Christendom without anything approaching a parallel? A literal duplication, not but something strictly analogous, yes. The outstanding characteristic of this dispensation and the climacteric gift of God unto His people is the presence of the Holy Spirit in their midst. That brings before us a many-sided theme, but we must confine ourselves unto that which is germane to our present inquiry. The Spirit of God indwells the Church corporately and the saint individually. He sustains a special relation to the servants of Christ, enduing them with power and making their labours fruitful. Normally, He is therefore in the midst of "Christendom," that is, the whole body of Christian profession, for even the unregenerate are made "partakers" of His presence and blessings while in outward fellowship with the saints (Heb 6:4), as they are bidden to "hear what the Spirit saith unto the churches" (Rev 3:22) and hence they are guilty of doing "despite unto the Spirit of grace" (Heb 10:29) when they refuse to hear Him and apostatize from their profession.

It is to be noted that one of our statements in the above paragraph is qualified: under *normal* conditions the Spirit of God is in the midst of Christendom generally and in the local churches (which have always contained a mixture of believers and unbelievers) particularly. But because He is the *Holy* Spirit He may be "grieved" (Eph 4:30) and "quenched" (1Th 5:19). He is "grieved" by the individual Christian when his conversation is unbecoming, and then He withholds His comforts. He is "quenched" or put out by the corporate body when His ministrations are "despised" (1Th 5:20), that is, when unbelievers are allowed to predominate in the local assembly, or if it becomes carnal and worldly, or if false doctrine be tolerated, or if a Scriptural discipline be not maintained. Any impartial reader of ecclesiastical history is aware that at various periods the Spirit was "quenched" and His power and blessing withdrawn from Christendom as a whole. Only those who are determined to call bitter sweet and darkness light, or who apply a wrong standard of measurement, will take exception to that assertion.

The Holy Spirit was certainly "quenched" at the beginning of the fourth century, when Constantine adopted Christianity as the state religion, when the simplicity of spiritual worship was superceded by an imposing and elaborate ritual, when those who professed to be "strangers and pilgrims" in this scene (1 Peter 2:11) sought after worldly prestige and emoluments and when vast multitudes were compelled to be "baptized" at the point of the sword. The insignificant minority who had eyes to see were painfully conscious that God had written "Ichabod" over Christendom, that the Holy Spirit, grieved and quenched, had withdrawn, no longer working in their midst. True, God still maintained unto Himself a "remnant"—raising up an isolated witness for Himself here and there, and little companies of His people meeting in secret for prayer and the ministry of the Word; but the collective system, the corporate body, was indeed a House now left unto them "desolate," as was evident from the "dark ages" which followed, when Rome completely dominated things.

It is not our purpose now to review the whole past nineteen centuries and trace the revivals and declensions that have followed each other: rather would we come much closer to our own times and observe the present application of what has been before us above. One has only to read the writings of C. H. Spurgeon—perhaps God's most valuable gift unto His people since the days of the Puritans—from 18801890 to discover the terrible departure from the truth and practical godliness which had taken place even then. Plainly and pointedly did that faithful minister denounce the "Downgrade Movement" in the churches, and when the leaders refused to right things, withdrew his "tabernacle" from the "Baptist Union." During 1890-1910, which falls within the memory of this writer, the decline accelerated rapidly: there was scarcely a theological seminary in Germany, Britain or the USA, which was not a hotbed of heresy. Ministers vied with each other in preaching "higher criticism," the "evolutionary hypothesis" and the so-called "new theology," and only here and there was a feeble voice raised in outcry.

In thousands of instances "churches" became little better than social clubs and places of entertainment. Well do we remember, some forty-odd years ago, the innovation and popularization of the "Pleasant Sunday afternoon" services, when worldly vocalists and instrumentalists tickled the ears of the audiences with semi-sacred and then downright secular items of music. And the so-called "Christian Brotherhoods" to whom the pastor gave a talk on "Christian Socialism" or the local member of parliament was invited to air his political views before them. And the multiplication of "bazaars" opened by the "mayoress," "socials," "whist drives," charades and plays to attract and "hold the young people." Even the pretence of requiring creditable evidence of regeneration before one was received into church-fellowship was dropped, and the maintenance of Scripture discipline ceased. Such was the awful sowing: now we are reaping the horrible harvest. How could it be otherwise, then, that the Holy Spirit should be grieved and quenched by such a travesty—conducted in the name of Christ!

Today all who have eyes to see cannot fail to perceive that "Ichabod" has once more been written over a degenerate Christendom, though only those with honest hearts will acknowledge it. The glory of God— the token and evidence of His presence—has "departed." The Spirit of God has withdrawn His unction and blessing, and their House is left unto them "desolate." The temple remained standing in Jerusalem for forty years *after* Christ pronounced the awful sentence of Matthew 23:28 before Titus destroyed it in AD 70: the priesthood continued to function and its services were perpetuated, but God no longer owned it. Thus it is with Christendom: the body still exists, but it is lifeless; the "form of godliness" has not yet entirely disappeared, but its power has.

Even the smaller groups who came out from the apostate mass, though some of them have preserved "the landmarks of the fathers," yet they are so pharisaical that the Spirit of God is quenched there too. Pride is as hateful to God as worldliness and false doctrine, and those who boast "the temple of the Lord are these" (Jer 7:4), "the Testimony of God is with *us*," "all others have departed from the Truth except *our* party"; are too lacking in spiritual discernment to perceive their own sad condition. Lookers-on generally see most!

Except for a few details there is little original in the above, the ground having been frequently gone over. But we have never heard or read anything along the line of what follows, namely, that which happened unto the ark *after* it was captured by the Philistines, and its present bearing upon and application unto our own times. Others have recognized that the Holy Spirit has departed from Christendom—not absolutely and entirely so, but from the corporate body and in withdrawing the manifestations of His presence. Personally we have no doubt that what is recorded in 1 Samuel 5, equally with the preceding chapter, illustrates and adumbrates fundamental principles in the ways of God with that people who are called by His name. Yea, we cannot get away from the conviction that our own generation has witnessed and is witnessing a solemn repetition of what took place in the house of Dagon. The striking incidents narrated in 1 Samuel 5 supply a description of literal historical facts, yet which, we believe, possess an allegorical signification. As to how little or how far we have succeeded in interpreting the same in this and the following article (D.V.) we leave to the judgment of our readers.

"And the Philistines took the ark of God and brought it from Ebenezer unto Ashdod. When the Philistines took the ark of God they brought it into the house of Dagon and set it before Dagon" (1 Sam 5:1,2). Elated over such a capture, they placed it in their temple in honour of Dagon, the god whom they worshipped (Judg 16:23). But "the triumphing of the wicked is short and the joy of the hypocrite for a moment" (Job 20:5). And so it proved here, for the next thing we are told is, "And when they of Ashdod arose early on the morrow, behold, Dagon was fallen on his face to the earth before the ark of the Lord. And they took Dagon and set him in his place again. And when they arose early on the morrow morning, behold Dagon was fallen upon his face to the ground before the ark of the Lord; and the head of Dagon and both the palms of his hands were cut off upon the threshold, only the stump of Dagon was left to him" (vv 4,5).

What would constitute the modern form or equivalent of "Dagon"? In seeking the answer to that question we must be governed by the information which Scripture supplies about him, or it, and all the accompanying details. First, let us consider more definitely what the ark stands for in this connection, and because it possesses a manifold significance we must follow a process of elimination. Let it be duly noted at this point that never once in 1 Samuel 5 or 6 is "the glory of the Lord" mentioned: it is utterly unthinkable that the Shekinah, emblem of the Holy Spirit, should enter a heathen shrine. The ark was the basis of the mercy-seat, the throne of God in Israel's midst, and a blessed type of the person and work of Christ; but in none of these respects do we think it should here be contemplated. Rather it is as "the ark of *testimony*" (Exo 25:16) we regard it. It was repeatedly designated thus because of the "testimony" (Exo 25:16,21) deposited therein, namely, the two tables of stone on which were inscribed the ten commandments (1 Kings 8:4).

Thus, in this Christian era we regard *the Truth of God* as the antitype of the "ark of testimony." And the sacred ark had fallen into the hands of the uncircumcised! Does it strike the ears of our readers as an incongruous statement to speak of God's holy and eternal Truth being delivered unto His enemies? Surely it should not, when the Lord Himself makes use of the expression "Truth is fallen in the street" (Isa 59:14). Perhaps it may not appear so strange and startling if we next consider *who* it was that had captured the ark.

It was neither the Ammonites, the Moabites, or the Midianites; but the *Philistines*. And who were they? Their origin and genealogy is given in Genesis 10. They were the descendants of Ham (v 6), and Ham is, as his name denotes, the "black one" or sun-burnt. He is a symbol and picture of the man who has turned away from God—the Light. He portrays those who have received the Light, but hated and rejected it. But though the Truth enlightens them not, yet it must have some effect, namely to darken them; and the more light received and refused, the darker they become.

Ham begat "Mizraim" (Gen 10:6), who gave his name to the country of Egypt—the house of bondage to God's people (cf. Isa 31:1). Mizraim begat "Casluhim" (Gen 10:14), which signifies "folly"—that which issues from turning away from Wisdom: see Romans 1:22, 23, where we have described the descent of the religious man of the earth, getting further and further away from God. From Casluhim came the Philistines, which means the "migrators" or "wanderers," so named because they left Egypt and settled in Canaan, "Palestine" deriving its name from them—they dwelt in its southwest part, on the sea coast. The Philistine is never seen outside the land of Canaan. Although he was no true "pilgrim" or "sojourner" as were Abraham, Isaac and Jacob (Heb 11:9,13), yet he claimed a home in the domain of faith. Thus we must not look for his modern counterpart in heathendom as such, nor in the openly-defiant and profane world, but rather inside Christendom itself: they are children of the flesh, yet with pretensions to the blessings of faith.

Everything recorded of the Philistines in Scripture helps to identify their successors. In Genesis 26:14,15 we find them making trouble for Isaac and his herdmen, by stopping up the walls which his father had digged—figure of depriving God's people of the Water of Life. One of their women infatuated Samson the Nazarite, figure of one consecrated to God, and brought about his ruin (Judg 14). In that same chapter we find him propounding a riddle to thirty of her companions, but after pondering it for seven days they were unable to declare its meaning—no Philistine is let into the secret of how (contrary to nature) a devourer can yield meat: they know nothing of how God comes in and makes everything serve His purpose, bringing blessing to His people out of their strongest foe. Their guile, treachery and cruelty are seen in the treatment which they meted out to Samson. Their haughty demeanour and contempt of those who dare to oppose them appeared in Goliath's attitude and language unto David. The final reference made to them in Holy Writ is found in Jehovah's solemn announcement "I will cut off the pride of the Philistines" (Zech 9:6).

The Pharisees were the Philistines of our Lord's day. Firmly entrenched in Immanuel's land they hotly contested every attempt made to eject them. Plainly stamped upon them were the features of Ham. Though they held the lead in the religious realm, yet were they in gross darkness. For when the Light of the world appeared in their midst, the "true," bright Light shining before their eyes, they asked Him for a "sign" (Matt 12:38). What proof was that of their blindness, for it was like asking for a candle at noonday! They were the ones figured by the "elder son" in Luke 15:28, etc., —the real "Wanderer," never at home with God. And wherever phariseeism has been found during the last nineteen centuries there was the moral embodiment of the Philistine: chiefly, of course, in Romanism, but that abominable mother has many children. Many theological professors and doctors of divinity, prating of their superior scholarship and riding roughly over any who opposed them, bore the stamp of the Philistine. (Part of the above we have culled from a work, now out of print, by F. C. Jennings on Judges.)

The limited space here at our disposal precludes us from now taking up other collateral considerations, so in the closing of this article let us bring together the two points already considered and notice a striking omission. In view of the great importance of the ark, one had naturally supposed that the loss of it would have made the deepest possible impression on Israel, that they had made the most desperate efforts to recover it from the Philistines; or that they had unitedly humbled themselves before the Lord and with fastings and prayers besought Him to intervene and remove the grievous dishonour cast upon His name. But apart from the grief of Eli and his daughter-in-law, there is no hint of any perturbation in the Nation. They appear to have been stolidly indifferent. And has not the same grievous lack of zeal and concern for God's glory characterized Christendom? When British and American professors echoed the infidelity of the German neologians, when almost every cardinal doctrine of the Christian faith was denied by the very men who had taken solemn ordination vows to defend it, was not their wicked perversion of the Divine Testimony met, generally, with callous apathy! How none of the churches followed Spurgeon's example when he withdrew from the corrupt system. And though here and there an individual protested and walked out, the majority complacently tolerated or approved. —AWP

---

have not grieved; Thou hast consumed them, but they have refused to receive correction; they have made their faces harder than a rock" (Jer 5:3).

"We will walk after our own devices." We are quite resolved to continue in sin, and no preaching can change us. We are fully determined to do so, no matter what it may cost us. Of old God sent a shortage of food on Israel, but it produced no reformation: "yet have ye not returned unto Me, saith the Lord." He smote them with blasting and mildew so that their gardens and vineyards were destroyed, but it moved them not: "yet have ye not returned unto Me, saith the Lord." He sent pestilence among them and slew their young men, but they continued impenitent: "yet have ye not returned unto Me, saith the Lord." He destroyed some of them by fire, but they persisted in their sins: "yet have ye not returned unto Me, saith the Lord" (Amos 4:6-10). And history has repeated itself! It is still doing so before our very eyes. The perversity of ancient Israel finds its counterpart in the contumacy of modern Christendom. God has given Britain "space to repent," alas, it has to be added "and she *repented not*" (Rev 2:21), nor is their the slightest indication she will yet do so. —AWP

(continued from front page)

selves beneath the Hand that has begun to smite them. God's judgments are articulate: they call upon all to throw down the weapons of their high-handed rebellion against Heaven. God takes away their peace and comforts that they may put away their idols. Calamities are sent upon evil-doers that they should depart from their wickedness. God is able to destroy the mightiest kingdom in the twinkling of an eye, but usually He spreads His judgments over a period, as in the ten plagues upon Egypt, granting space for repentance and allowing an interval between the announcement of His having "framed evil," and the actual and full execution thereof.

Thus it is here in Jeremiah 18:11: after declaring He had devised a device against a nation God adds, "Return ye now everyone from his evil way, and make your ways and your doings good." Conversion ought to be the immediate outcome of God's judgments, whether they be threatened or in actual course of fulfillment. If men would forsake their sins God would soon lay aside His rod. But observe the urgency of the Call: "return ye *now* every one from his evil way." There is no time for delay: God will not be trifled with. Men are very prone to procrastinate: they put off the day of repentance and defer their reformation. They hope and resolve, yet postpone the same, and the longer they do so the harder their hearts become and the more completely the Devil obtains possession of them. Agrippa was "almost persuaded," but that was as far as he went: his lusts held him fast. "*Today* if ye will hear His voice, harden not your hearts" (Psa 95:7): if ever there was a time when it was imperative to heed that exhortation it is now.

"And they said, There is no hope" (Jer 18:12). There are three possible interpretations of those words. First, they may be regarded as the language of despair: there is no hope for us *in God*, we have sinned beyond the reach of mercy. But that would necessarily presuppose they were deeply convicted of their guilt, and the remainder of the verse definitely precludes any such concept. Second, "there is no hope" might be the language of confessed helplessness. There is no hope *in us*: we are too besotted to reform, too wedded to our sins to break from them; but the remainder of the verse is flatly against this too. Third, "there is no hope" was the language of blatant defiance. There is no hope *for you*: it is useless to preach to us, our minds are fully made up, we are determined to have our own way, and nothing you say can change us. "We will walk after our own devices and we will every one do the imagination of his evil heart" they declared. It was the language of open rebellion, whether expressed in words or in deeds.

That this is the obvious meaning of their "there is no hope" is clear not only from the words which immediately follow but also from other passages in Jeremiah. "But they hearkened not nor inclined their ear, but walked in the counsels and in the imagination of their evil heart, and went backward and not forward" (7:24); "thou saidst, *I will not hear*: this hath been thy manner from thy youth that thou obeyedst not My voice" (22:21 and see 44:16,17). They declined to be affected by the heavy clouds of judgment over their heads. They refused to forsake their evil ways. They were determined to persist in their disobedience. They openly defied the Almighty. They were impervious to all expostulations and admonitions. Their hearts were fully set in them to drink their fill of iniquity. "For the people turneth not unto Him that smiteth them neither do they seek the Lord of Hosts" (Isa 9;13). "Thou hast stricken them, but they

. *(continued on proceeding page)*

VOL. XXII.   SEPTEMBER, 1943.   NO. 9

STUDIES IN THE SCRIPTURES

" Search the Scriptures." John 5:39.

Publisher and Editor—ARTHUR W. PINK,
27 Lewis Street,
Stornoway, Isle of Lewis,
Scotland.

THE WORD OF HIS GRACE

Various reasons may be suggested why the Scriptures should be so designated: Acts 20:32. Among them the following. *First,* it is most in accord with His gracious character that their Author should communicate with His people. In view of all that we know of His perfections it is inconceivable that God should hold Himself aloof in unbroken silence: a dumb Deity would be no more winsome than the inarticulate idols of the heathen. If a human parent writes to his sons and daughters when they are absent from home, shall our heavenly Father withhold a like proof of His love for His dear children? We are told that "it *became Him* [the Father], for whom are all things and by whom are all things, in bringing many sons unto glory to make the Captain of their salvation perfect through sufferings" (Heb 2:10): that is to say, it accorded with His perfections and redounded to His glory that the whole plan of redemption should be as He designed it. Then may it not be said, reverently, it *became* the Triune God to give us a written revelation, that since He is in Himself "the God of all grace" (1 Peter 5:10) He should bestow upon us the Word of His grace? To make such a communication graces or adorns His character. The Psalmist declares of God "Thou hast magnified Thy Word above all Thy name" (138:2), that is, above every other revelation of himself.

Second, yet the gift of His Word is an act of pure benignity on His part. There was nothing whatever outside of God which *required* Him to grant His creatures a written revelation. No indeed: the great I AM finds within Himself the springs of all His actions. He takes counsel with none (Rom 11:34) and gives not account of any of His matters (Job 33:13). God is exalted high above all, fulfilling His own sovereign pleasure, working all things after the counsel of His own will. He is the one absolutely Free Agent in the universe: under no restraint. All creatures are under infinite obligations unto Him, but He is obligated to none. If then He vouchsafes us a communication it proceeds from His mere condescension and magnanimity: it is an act of pure grace. It must be so, for we were not entitled to it, and could do nothing to earn or merit it; no, not in our unfallen state. The holy angels are dependent creatures, maintained in being and sustained in holiness by their Maker, and therefore it is impossible for them to do anything which brings the Most High into their debt. His Word, then, has issued not from the requirements of justice but proceeds freely from His sovereign grace.

(continued on back page)

IMPORTANT NOTICES

Please advise promptly of change in address, otherwise copies will be lost in the mails.

We are glad to send a sample copy to any of your friends whom you believe would be interested in this publication.

This magazine is published as "a work of faith and labour of love," the editor and his wife gladly giving their services free. There is no regular subscription price, as we do not wish the poor of the flock to be deprived. This does not mean that those looking for something for nothing may "help themselves." Those getting this Magazine, who are financially able and who receive spiritual help from its pages, are expected to gladly contribute towards its expenses; otherwise, their names are dropped from our lists.

Will those forwarding International Money Orders please have them made out to us at Stornoway, Isle of Lewis, Scotland. Checks (Cheques-Eng.) made out on U.S.A. Banks are not negotiable here, so please do not send them.

CONTENTS

THE SERMON ON THE MOUNT

26f. Profession Tested: Matthew 7:24, 25

A pondering of Matthew 7:24-27 suggests the need of our seeking to supply answers to the following questions. First, what is the force of the opening "Therefore"? Second, who are represented by the "wise" and the "foolish" men? Third, what is denoted by the "rock" and the "sand" on which they build? Fourth, what is signified by the "house" which each one erects? Fifth, what is portrayed by the hurricane which bursts upon the "house" and tests its security? Simple as these questions are the replies returned thereto will determine the soundness or unsoundness of any exposition given to the passage. In seeking our answers recourse must also be had unto the parallel passage in Luke 6:47-49, which supplies a number of additional details. The best analysis of these verses we have met with was furnished by one of the earliest of the Puritans, W. Perkins, 1590. He focused attention on three things: the duty inculcated—obedience; the property of this duty—wisdom; the reward—security. The three parts of this wisdom lay in digging deep, in securing a rock foundation, and in building thereon.

First, the force of the opening "Therefore." In addition to the more general remarks made thereon in the previous article let us now point out that, Christ was here drawing a plain but searching conclusion from His solemn statement in vv. 21-23. There He had declared that, Not every one who renders lip-service to His Lordship shall enter into the kingdom of heaven, but only he that does the will of the Father as made known by the Son; yea, that the many who substitute preaching and performing wonderful works for actual obedience to His commands, He will yet say unto such "Depart from Me, ye that work iniquity." Then He at once added, *"Therefore* whosoever heareth these sayings of mine and doeth them, I will liken him unto a wise man, which built his house upon a rock." Is not the connection, then, between the two passages unmistakably indicated? Is not our Lord's design and meaning in the verses now before us crystal clear? In vv. 21-23 Christ is viewed in His office of Judge, testing professors, making known unto us who it is that will survive the fiery trial of that dread Day; and in vv. 24-27 He reveals the path which must be trod if that Day is to be wisely and successfully anticipated.

In the Day of testing not what we have said, but what we have *done* in obedience to the Divine will, shall alone be accepted as evidence: not the profession we have made, but the verification we have given of it in our Christian walk; not the doctrines we believed, but the fruits they bore in our daily lives. It will be useless to plead that we possessed extraordinary gifts and employed them in "Christian service," that we were leaders in the churches and did much in the name of Christ, if we wore not His yoke and followed not the example He has left us. Real practical godliness is the only thing which will be approved in that Day. Personal holiness is little esteemed here, but it will be everything there (Heb 12:14). In that Day the Judge of all the earth will "give to every man according as his *work* shall be" (Rev 22:12). Therefore the man who acts wisely now is the one who makes conscience of the commandments of Christ, who regulates his conduct by them; conversely, the one who disregards the revealed will of God and follows a course of self-pleasing, no matter what garb of religion he wears, is playing the part of the fool, as he will yet discover to his eternal undoing.

The answer to our *second* question has largely been anticipated in what we wrote in the preceding article. The "wise" man is the one who "heareth these sayings" of Christ, who "cometh to" Him (Luke 6:47), which involves turning his back upon the world and forsaking the service of Satan, and who "doeth them." "These sayings of Mine" is emphatic, having particular reference to the principles Christ had enunciated and the precepts He had inculcated in the previous sections of this Sermon on the mount. We have to go unto other parts of the NT to learn Christian *doctrine*, but here we have described Christian *practice*. Some, like Tolstoi, have magnified this Sermon to the disparagement of the Epistles; others, like the Dispensationalists, have exalted the Epistles above the Sermon: the one is as reprehensible as the other. One part of Scripture must not be pitted against another part. Both this Sermon and the Epistles are essential parts of the revealed will of God. "Who have, in every age, uprightly and unreservedly, obeyed these sayings of our Lord, except they who have firmly believed the doctrines of the Gospel as more clearly and fully revealed in the apostolic epistles"? (T. Scott).

The "wise" man, then, is the one who cometh to Christ, heareth His instructions and doeth them. To *do* that which He has commanded includes, first, a believing of them, that is, a definite appropriation of His precepts, a taking of them home to myself. It involves an understanding of them, and that calls for humility and meekness of mind rather than keenness of intellect, a meditating upon Christ's words and a crying unto Him "that which I see not teach Thou me." It involves a making conscience of them, the realization theses sayings of Christ contain not only good counsel which it is my wisdom to heed, but that they are His imperative requirements which I disregard at my peril. It involves an actual putting of them into practice so that I abstain from those things which He forbids and perform those duties which He specifies: "If ye know these things, happy are ye if ye do them" (John 13:17). "*All* the sayings of Christ: not only the laws He has enacted, but the truths He has revealed must be done by us. They are a light not only unto our eyes, but to our feet, and are designed to not only *in*form our judgments but to *re*form our hearts and lives" (Matt. Henry).

We regard the word "doth" as the all-important one in our present passage, and care needs to be taken lest we improperly limit its meaning. To "do" our Lord's sayings includes very much more than the mere outward performance of those actions which He requires. Our whole inner and outer man must be conformed to them; our character must be moulded by them, our affections must be regulated, our wills governed, and our habits of thought dominated by them, as well as our actions being in accord with them. The Word of Christ must "dwell in" us, and that "richly" (Col 3:16), and that calls for a definite process of spiritual horticulture. We must "lay apart all filthiness and superfluity of naughtiness" if we are to "receive with meekness the ingrafted Word which is able to save our souls" (James 1:21). Note well that expression "the *ingrafted* Word": that which is addressed to us must be rooted in us, planted in the soul, drawing all the sap of the stock to itself—"all that is within us" serving the Word. Thereby we are "transformed by the renewing of our mind" (Rom 12:2). This, and nothing short of this, is what constitutes a genuine "conversion."

From what has been said above it will appear how intimately related are the several answers unto those questions we formulated in the opening paragraph, how that they necessarily grow naturally out of each other. Cannot the reader now decide for himself what is denoted by this "rock" on which our Lord represents the wise man as building his house? Bearing in mind the scope of our passage and its relation to the context, does not the first half of v. 24 furnish a decisive index to the meaning of the second half? It is "these sayings" of Christ, understood, believed and obeyed, which is the "rock" here. "These sayings are the dictates of eternal truth and righteousness, and the everlasting mountains shall be sooner rooted up than any one of these shall be falsified. This is the foundation on which the wise builder places his edifice: not his own conjectures or reasonings, nor the arguments and reasonings of other men, but the 'true and faithful sayings of God'" (J. Brown)—to which may be added, and not following the carnal desires of our own hearts. If the reader still insists that the "rock" here is Christ Himself, we reply, If so, Christ considered as Prophet and not as Priest, as Lord, and not as Saviour, as *Teacher* and not Redeemer.

There should be little difficulty in determining *what* is signified by the "house" which the builder erects upon the "rock" or "sayings" of Christ, though a certain latitude should be allowed as to *how* it be stated. The principle definitions made by the best of the expositors are: the *profession* he makes, the *character* that is formed, the *hope* which is cherished. When analysed these three expressions or things differ little in essence. The profession made is only valid if it be verified by a character which is formed by the whole range of Christ's teaching in this Sermon, a character which is displayed by conduct in accordance therewith. So too the hope cherished by the believer, the assurance he possesses, that God has accepted him in the Beloved, is but presumption, a mere carnal confidence, unless it be grounded upon this "rock," that is, unless the one claiming such a hope be possessed of that character which alone warrants the expectation of everlasting bliss. Furthermore, the cherishings of a good hope, the possession of a peaceful assurance that I am a child of God, is an essential part of a character which is formed by an appropriation and assimilation of the "sayings" of Christ.

This figure of the building of a house to represent the formation of a Christian's character under the teaching of Christ is employed frequently in the

Acts and Epistles. When taking leave of the elders of Ephesus Paul commended them to God and the Word of his grace "which is able to *build you up*" (Acts 20:32). The Colossian saints were exhorted "As ye have therefore received Christ Jesus the Lord, so walk ye in Him, rooted and built up in Him" (2:7,8); while Jude bade the saints be "building up yourselves on your most holy faith" (v 20). The same word here rendered "built" is also translated "edify." Thus, "Follow after the things which make for peace and things wherewith one may edify another" (Rom 14:19); "Let every one of us please his neighbour for his good to edification" (Rom 15:2). "Let no corrupt communication proceed out of your mouth, but that which is good to the use of edifying" (Eph 4:29). "Wherefore comfort [or "exhort"] yourselves together, and edify one another, even as also ye do" (1 Thess 5:11). Timothy was instructed "Neither give heed to fables and endless genealogies which minister questions, rather than godly edifying which is in faith" (1 Thess 1:4). How careful we should be in our converse with each other that what we say be of a spiritually constructive character and not destructive.

The "house," then, may be taken first for the profession made, which is yet to be put to the proof in the day of testing. Or more definitely it represents the character of the one making a Christian profession; and by "character" we include the whole frame of his beliefs, sentiments, affections, and active habits. Having by the faith of the Truth found the only sure foundation, he erects on it an edifice of thoughts, feelings and volitions. He is moulded according to "that form of doctrine whereto he was delivered" (Rom 6:17). He is not regulated by his own carnal desires, nor the opinions and examples of his fellows, but by the sure and authoritative precepts of Christ. Accordingly he cherishes a "hope of eternal life" (Titus 1:2) and it is "a good hope through grace" (2 Thess 2:16), for it is based upon a reliable foundation, grounded on the precepts and promises of the Lord; which precepts have been laid hold of and translated into practice, and which promises have been mixed with faith and made our own. Such a hope will prove both "sure and steadfast" in the hour of testing.

From all that has been before us on the different points it will be seen that everything goes back to and turns upon the word "doeth": *that* strikes the keynote of the verse, and therefore its dominant theme is, our practical compliance with the Divine will. The importance which God attaches to and the value which He places upon *obedience* comes out plainly in the words of His prophet, "Behold, to obey is better than sacrifice and to hearken than the fat of rams" (1 Sam 15:22). To keep strictly to the path of the Divine commandments is more pleasing unto God than any of the outward forms of religion or the most liberal contributions to His earthly cause. Well did T. Scott point out with regard to the Levitical sacrifices, "their value was entirely from the appointment of God, and they were not acceptable except offered in obedience to Him, and with a penitent, believing and pious mind. When therefore they were substituted in the place of true piety or trusted in as meritorious; when the means were used to compensate for the neglect of the end, they became an abomination, however costly and numerous they were." So now.

The same insistent emphasis upon obedience was made by Christ. When interrupted in His talking to the people by one who informed Him that His mother and brethren stood without, desiring to speak with Him, He made answer by stretching forth His hand "toward His disciples" and saying, "Behold My mother and My brethren. For whosoever shall *do* the will of My Father which is in heaven, the same is My brother and sister and mother" (Matt 12:46-50). It was as though He said, those that are nearest and dearest to Me, spiritually speaking, are My "disciples," and they are described as the ones who *comply with* the Divine will. Again; when a certain woman said to Him, "Blessed is the womb that bare Thee and the paps which Thou hast sucked," He replied "Yea, rather, blessed are they that hear the Word of God and keep it" (Luke 11:27,28). The ones on whom the benediction of God rests are they who *keep* His Word—in their hearts, as their most precious possession; in their minds, by frequent meditation; in their lives, as the rule of practice.

Conscientious souls are likely to be troubled at this point, sensible that their obedience is so imperfect and faulty. It remains therefore that we should endeavour to set their fears at rest and attempt to show more definitely what Christ did *not* signify and what He *did* imply by "whoso heareth these sayings of Mine and *doeth* them." Our Lord did not mean that His disciples perpetually and flawlessly perform His precepts, for He neither removes from them the carnal nature at their regeneration, nor does He grant them such a measure of his grace in this world as to enable them to render a sinless obedience. God could have done both had He thought well, but it has pleased Him to exalt imputed righteousness rather than inherent in this life. Not only does every saint fail to render that obedience which is required by God's Law as a whole, but he does not obey any single commandment perfectly, for every duty we perform, yea, our highest act of worship, is marred by sin. In the most holy men corruption deprives them of the purity that ought to be there, and lusts fight against the perfect holiness they desire and strive after (Rom 7:18-21; Gal 5:17).

Christians perform the sayings of Christ *sincerely* though not perfectly, in spirit and in truth, though not in the letter and full execution. When Christ said to the Father of His apostles, "They *have kept* Thy Word" (John 17:6), He did not mean they had done so as flawlessly and excellently as He had Himself done. And when we read "hereby we do know that we know Him if we keep His commandments" (1 John 2:3), consistency requires us to understand it that, as we only "know Him" in part in this life (1 Cor 13:12) so we only "keep His commandments" *in part*. Where there is a *genuine willingness* (Rom 7:18; Heb 13:18; 1 Tim 6:18), God accepts it for the deed (2 Cor 8:12). Because His people have His Law written in their hearts (Heb 10:16), because they delight in it with their inner man (Rom 7:22), because they truly desire to obey it fully (Psa 119:5), and pray earnestly to that end (Psa 119:35), and repent of and confess their disobedience (Psa 32:5), God is pleased—according to the terms of the Covenant of Grace, and for Christ's sake—to accept their imperfect obedience and account it as a keeping of His Law.

To prevent wrong conclusions being drawn from the last paragraph two things need to be pointed out. *First,* it must *not* be inferred that God has lowered His standard in order to meet our infirmities: that standard is par excellence and shall never be altered. But the Surety of God's people fully conformed to it and His perfect obedience is reckoned to the account of those who savingly believe on Him, so that imputatively they are flawlessly righteous in the sight of the Law. Inherently they are righteous in the sense that they fully approve of the Law, delight in it, and sincerely set themselves to an unreserved obedience of the whole of it; and thus "the righteousness of the Law *is* fulfilled *in* them" (Rom 8:4). Yet because of their remaining depravity they fail to realize their desires (Phil 3:12), mourn over and confess their sinful failures, and are forgiven for Christ's sake. In this life they are more active in seeking from God the remission of their failures than they are in offering to Him that which is faultless. Some of the old writers were wont to say, the present perfection of a Christian consists in a penitential acknowledgement of his imperfection.

Second, the nature and scope of this sincere but imperfect obedience needs to be amplified and honestly stated.

1. The Christian's compliance with "these sayings" of the Lord is *internal and spiritual* as well as external. If any man should respond to every positive and negative precept of Christ in his outward conduct and yet his inner man be not affected and influenced by them, it would be like a body minus a soul—a corpse. As some one has aptly expressed it; obedience of soul is the soul of obedience. It is at this point, especially, the righteousness of the saint exceeds that of the scribes and pharisees, for while they rested wholly on their outward obedience of the Law, within they were full of unmortified lusts. The Law is "spiritual" (Rom 7:14) and requires spiritual compliance thereto. The only worship God will accept is that which is "in spirit and in truth" (John 4:24). Nevertheless, our obedience is not to consist solely of spiritual meditation and contemplating the mortification of our lusts and the cultivation of our graces: there must be an external walking in the Truth also.

2. Sincere obedience is *impartial*, extending to the whole Law as it is explained in the precepts and exhortations of both the OT and the New. To affect much devotion unto the things pertaining to God and then evince an utter lack of conscience and equity in things pertaining to man, is horrible hypocrisy. The pharisees were notorious in this: they made long prayers, yet devoured widows houses; they fasted twice a week, yet laid burdens on their disciples grievous to be borne; they thithed, yet taught that neither father nor mother was to be relieved if men had placed their substance under a vow to God. O my reader, thy attendance at "early morning communion" or "the breaking of bread" is a vile mockery if you are unscrupulous and grasping in your dealings with men. Your psalm singing and lauding of the person and perfections of Christ is a stench in God's nostrils if you lie and thieve. On the other hand, however honest and truthful with your fellows, if you rob God of the submission, devotion and praise which are His due, your heart is rotten. Of the parents of the Baptist it is written, "They were both righteous before God, walking in *all* the commandments and ordinances of the Lord blameless" (Luke 1:6).

3. Sincere obedience is *universal*, by which we mean, it includes the things to be *believed* as well as practiced, and hence it is termed "the obedience of faith" (Rom 1:5). God's commandments must not be limited to the prohibition of wickedness, but extended also to false doctrines. If the Epistles be read attentively it will be found that the apostles were as emphatic and stern in their denunciation of teachers of error as of lascivious livers, and that they pressed the necessity of a sound and holy faith as vehemently as they did a good and pure conscience. A sincere heart is set against heresies as definitely and diligently as against sinful conduct, and sinful conduct as heresies. One who is opposed to ungodliness but indifferent about false doctrines, may justly suspect the soundness of his heart; while one who denounces false doctrine but tolerates wickedness in himself or his family has serious reason to question the validity of his profession. Christians are given no more licence in matters of faith than of deportment. Stubborn heretics are to be cast out of the church equally with the openly immoral.

This article is already long enough, so we must postpone our answer to the fifth question—What is portrayed by the hurricane which bursts upon the "house" and tests its security?—till we consider (D.V.) v. 27. —AWP

THE MISSION AND MIRACLES OF ELISHA
9. Sixth Miracle

First, we shall take notice of *its connection.* Our present narrative opens with the word "And" which intimates that the incident described here is closely related to what was before us in our last, though we must not conclude that this by any means exhausts its force. Sometimes the Spirit of God has placed two things in juxtaposition for the purpose of comparison, that we may observe the resemblances between them; at other times, it is with the object of pointing a contrast, that we may consider the points of dissimilarity. Here it is the latter: note the following antitheses. In the former case the woman's place of residence is not given (v 1), but here it is (v 8). The one was a widow (v 1), this woman's husband was alive (v 9). The former was financially destitute, this one was a woman of means. The one sought out Elisha, the prophet approached the other. Elisha provided for the former, this one ministered unto him. The widow had "two sons," whereas the married woman was childless. The one was put to a severe test (vv 3,4), the other was not.

Second, a word on *its location.* The place where this miracle was wrought cannot be without significance, for there is nothing meaningless in Holy Writ, though in this instance we confess to having little or no light. The one who was the beneficiary of this miracle resided at Shunem, which appears to mean "uneven." This place is mentioned only twice elsewhere in the OT. First, in Joshua 19:18 from which we learn that it was situated in the territory allotted to the tribe of Issachar. Second, in 1 Samuel 28:4, where we are told it was the place that the Philistines gathered themselves together and pitched in battle array against Israel, on which occasion Saul was so terrified that, after inquiring in vain of the Lord, he sought unto the witch of Endor. Matthew Henry tells us that "Shunem lay in the road between Samaria and Carmel, a road which Elisha was accustomed to travel, as we gather from 2:25." It seems to have been a farming district, and in this pastoral setting a lovely domestic scene is laid.

Third, its beneficiary. "And it fell on a day, that Elisha passed to Shunem, where was a great woman" (2 Kings 4:8). The Hebrew word ("gadol") is used in very varied connections. In Genesis 1:16, 21 and many other passages it refers to material or physical greatness. In Exodus 32:21, "great sin," it has a moral force. In 2 Kings 5:1, Job 1:3, Proverbs 25:6 it is associated with social eminence. In Psalm 48:1 and numerous other places it is predicated of the Lord Himself. This woman was one of substance or wealth, as is intimated by the servants her husband had and their building and furnishing a room for the prophet. God has "His own" even among the rich and noble. This woman was also "great" spiritually. She was great in hospitality, in discernment—perceiving that Elisha was "a holy man of God," in meekness—by owning her husband's headship, in thoughtfulness for others—the care she took in providing for the prophet's comfort, in contentedness (v 13), in wisdom—realising Elisha would desire retirement and quietness; and, as we shall see, in faith—confidently counting upon God to show Himself strong on her behalf and work a further miracle.

"And it fell on a day that Elisha passed to Shunem, where was a great woman, and she constrained him to eat bread." Elisha seems to have resided at or near mount

Carmel (2:25; 4:25): but went his circuit through the land to visit the seminaries of the prophets and to instruct the people, which probably was his stated employment when not sent on some special service. At Shunem there lived a woman of wealth and piety, who invited him to come to her house, and with some difficulty prevailed" (Thos. Scott). Several practical points are suggested by this. The minister of the Gospel should not be forward in pressing himself upon people, but should wait until he is invited to partake of their hospitality, least of all should he deliberately court the intimacy of the "great," except it be with the object of doing them good. "Mind not high things, but condescend to men of low estate" (Rom 12:16) is one of the rules God has given His people to walk by, and His servant should set them an example in the matter.

The Lord's servants, like those to whom they minister, have their ups and downs, not only in their inward experience but also in external circumstances. Yes, they have their "ups" as well as their "downs." They are not required to spend all their days in caves or sojourning by brooks. If there are those who oppose, God also raises up others to befriend them. Was it not thus with our blessed Lord when He tabernacled here? Though for the most part He "had not where to lay His head," yet there were many women who "ministered unto Him of their substance" (Luke 8:2,3), and the home at Bethany welcomed Him. So with the apostle Paul: though made as the offscouring of all things to the Jewish nation, yet the saints loved and esteemed him highly for his work's sake. If he was cast into prison, yet he also makes mention of "Gaius mine host" (Rom 16:23). It has ever been thus. The experience of Elisha was no exception, as the present writer can testify, for in his extensive journeyings the Lord opened the hearts and homes of many of His people unto him.

"Given to hospitality" (Rom 12:13) is required of the saints, and of God's servants too (1 Tim 3:2; Titus 1:8), and that "without grudging" (1 Peter 4:9), and this held good equally under the OT era. It is to be noted that this woman took the initiative, for she did not wait until asked by Elisha or one of his friends. From the words "as often as he passed by" we gather that she was on the look-out for him. She sought occasion to do good and bought up her opportunities. Nor was her hospitality any formal things, but earnest and warm-hearted. Hence it may strike us as all the more strange that the prophet demurred and that she had to constrain him to enter her home. This intimates that the servant of God should not readily respond to every invitation received, especially from the wealthy: "seekest thou great things for thyself? seek them not" (Jer 45:5) is to regulate his conduct. Elisha responded to her importunity and after becoming better acquainted with her, never failed to partake of her kindness whenever he passed that way.

"And she said unto her husband, Behold now, I perceive that this is a holy man of God, which passeth by us continually. Let us make a little chamber, I pray thee, on the wall; and let us set for him there a bed, and a table, and a stool, and a candlestick: and it shall be, when he cometh to us, that he shall turn in thither" (vv 9,10). Herein we have manifest several other features of her moral greatness. Apparently she was the owner of this property, for her husband is not termed a "great man," yet we find her conferring with him and seeking his permission. Thereby she took her proper place and left her sisters an admirable example. The husband is "the head of the wife, even as Christ is the head of the Church," and therefore the command is "wives, submit yourselves unto your own husbands, as unto the Lord" (Eph 5:22,23). Instead of taking matters into her own hands and acting independently, this "great woman" sought her husband's consent and cooperation. How much domestic strife would be avoided if there was more of this mutual conferring.

This great woman was endowed with spiritual discernment, for she perceived that Elisha was a holy man of God. The two things are not to be separated: it is those who walk in subjection to the revealed will of God who are granted spiritual perception: "he that is spiritual discerneth all things" (1 Cor 2:15) and the spiritual person is the one who is regulated by the precepts of Holy Writ, who is humble and meek and takes the place which the Lord has appointed. "If therefore thine eye be single thy whole body shall be full of light" (Matt 6:22): it is acting in self-will which beclouds the vision. "I understand more than the ancients," said David. And why so? "Because I keep Thy precepts" (Psa 119:100). It is when we forsake the path of obedience that our judgment is clouded and our perception dimmed.

While admiring the virtues and graces of this woman, we must not overlook the tribute she paid unto Elisha. Observe how she refers to him. Not as a "charming" or "nice man": how incongruous such an appellation for a servant of God! No, it was not any such carnal or sentimental term she employed. Nor did she allude to him as a "learned man," for scholarship and spirituality by no means always go together. Rather as "a *holy* man of God" did she designate the prophet. What a description! what a searching word for every minister of the Gospel to take to heart. It is "holy men of God" who are used by the Spirit (2 Peter 1:21). And how did she perceive the prophet's holiness? Perhaps by finding him at prayer, or reading the Scriptures. Certainly from the heavenliness of his conversation and general demeanour. Ah, my reader, the servant of God should need no distinctive manner of dress in order for people to identify him: his walk, his speech, his deportment ought to be sufficient.

Returning to the "great woman" let us next take note of her *constancy*. The inviting of Elisha into her home was actuated by no fleeting mood of kindness, which came suddenly upon her and as suddenly disappeared, but rather was a steady and permanent thing. Some are mere creatures of impulse. But the conduct of those is stable who act on principle. How often a church is elated when a minister is installed, and its members cannot do too much to express their appreciation for him; but how soon such enthusiasm often cools off. The best are spasmodic if not fickle, and need to bear in mind the injunction "let us not be weary in well doing" (Gal 6:9). It is blessed to see this woman did not tire of ministering to God's servant but continued to provide for his need and comfort, and at considerable trouble and expense.

Fourth, we turn now to *the occasion* of this miracle. "And it fell on a day that he came thither and turned into the chamber and lay there. And he said to Gehazi his servant, Call this Shunammite. And when he had called her, she stood before him" (vv 12,13). Elisha did not complacently accept the loving hospitality which had been shown him as a matter of course, as though it were something which was due him by virtue of his office. No, he was truly grateful and anxious to show his appreciation. In this he differed from some ministers we have met, who appeared to think they were fully entitled to such kindness and deference. While resting from his journey, instead of congratulating himself on his "good fortune," he thought upon his benefactress and wondered how best he could make some return. But how? She was in no financial need: apparently she lacked none of the good things of this life—what then should be done for her? He was at a loss to know: but instead of dismissing the thought, he decided to interrogate her directly.

Fifth, its peculiarity. "And he said unto him, Say now unto her, Behold thou hast been careful for us with all this care, what is to be done for thee? Wouldest thou be spoken for to the king or to the captain of the host? And she answered, I dwell among mine own people" (v 13). This miracle differed from most of those we have previously considered in that it was *unsought*; proposed by the prophet himself. He suggested that royal honours might be bestowed on herself or husband if she so desired. "Elisha had no doubt acquired considerable influence with Jehoram and his captains by the signs deliverance and victory obtained for him (3:4-27), and though he would ask nothing for himself, he was willing to show his gratitude on behalf of his kind hostess by interposing on her behalf, if she had any petition to present" (Thos. Scott). Yet we feel that the prophet knew her too well to imagine her head was set upon such trifles as earthly dignities, and that he gave her this opportunity to declare herself more plainly.

"And she answered, I dwell among mine own people" (v 13). It looks as though the prophet's offer to speak unto the king for her, intimated that positions of honour could be procured for her and her husband in the royal household. Her reply seems to show this, for it signified, I am quite satisfied with the portion God has given me: I desire no change or improvement in it. How very rare is such *contentment*! She was indeed a "great woman." Alas that today there are so few like her. As Matthew Henry points out "It would be well with many, if they did but know when they are well off." But they do not. A roving spirit takes possession of them, and they suppose they can improve their lot by moving from one place to another, only to find as the old adage says, "A rolling stone gathers no moss." "The wicked are like the troubled sea when it cannot rest" (Isa 57:20), but it should be far otherwise with the people of God. It is much to be thankful for when we can contentedly say, "I dwell among mine own people."

Sixth, its nature. "And he said, What then is to be done for her? And Gehazi answered, verily she hath no child, and her husband is old. And he said, Call her. And when he had called her, she stood in the door. And he said, About this season, according to the time of life thou shalt embrace a son. And she said, Nay, my lord, thou man of God, do not lie unto thine handmaid. And the woman conceived and bare a son at that season that Elisha had said unto her" (v 14-17). Observe the prophet's humility: in his perplexity he did not disdain to confer with his servant. He was no pleased to use his interests in the Court of heaven, which was far better than seeking a favour from Jehoram. It should be remembered that in OT times the giving of a son to those who had long been childless was a special mark of God's favour and power, as the cases of Abraham, Isaac, Manoah, and Elkanah go to show. We are not sure whether her language was that of unbelief or of overwhelming astonishment; but having received a prophet in the name of a prophet she received "a prophet's reward" (Matt 10:41).

Seventh, its meaning. This may be gathered from the miracle preceding. There we had before us a typical picture of redemption, a setting free from the exactions of the Law, a deliverance from bondage. What then is the sequel of this? Surely that which we find in the lives of the redeemed, namely, their bringing forth *fruit* unto God. This order of cause and effect is taught us in "being made free from sin...ye have your fruit unto holiness" (Rom 6:22 and cf. 1 Cor 6:20). But it is not the products of the old nature transformed, for the "flesh" remains the same unto the end, bringing forth after its own evil kind. No, it is altogether supernatural, the "fruit of the spirit," the manifestation of the graces of the new nature communicated by God at the new birth. Accordingly we have here the fruit of the womb, yet not by the ordinary workings of nature, but, as in the case of John the Baptist (Luke 1:7,57), that which transcends nature, which issues only from the wonder-working power of God.

It is to be carefully noted in this connection that the beneficiary of our miracle is designated a "great woman." As we have pointed out in a previous paragraph, this appellation denotes, more immediately, that she was one upon whom Divine providence had smiled, furnishing her liberally with the things of this life. But she was also morally and spiritually "great." In both respects she was an appropriate figure of that aspect of salvation which is here before us. Redemption finds its object, like the widow of the foregoing miracle, in distress—poor, sued by the Law, unable to meet its demands. But redemption does not leave its beneficiaries thus. No, God deals with them according to "the riches of His grace" and they can now say "He hath made us kings and priests unto God and His Father" (Rev 1:6). The righteousness of Christ is imputed to them, and they are "great" indeed in the eyes of God—"the excellent, in whom is all My delight" (Psa 16:3) is how He speaks of them. Such are the ones in whom and by whom the fruits of redemption are brought forth.

Everything recorded of this woman indicates that she was one of the Lord's redeemed. She honoured and ministered unto one of His servants, in a day when they were far from being popular. Moreover, Elisha accepted her hospitality, which he surely had not done unless he discerned in her the marks of grace. The very fact that at first she had to "constrain" him to partake of her kindness—the margin renders it "laid hold of him"—indicates he would not readily receive favours from anybody and everybody. But having satisfied himself of her spirituality, "as oft as he passed by, he turned in thither to eat bread." Let it be remarked that that expression to "eat bread" means far more to an Oriental than to us. It signifies an act of communion, denoting there is a bond of fellowship between those who eat a meal together. Thus by such intimacy of communion with the prophet this woman gave further evidence of being one of God's redeemed.

As the procuring of our redemption required miracles (the Divine incarnation, the death of the God-man, His resurrection), so the application of it unto its beneficiaries cannot be without supernatural operations, both before and after. Redemption is received by faith, but before saving faith can be exercised the soul must be quickened, for one who is dead unto God cannot move toward Him. The same is true of our conversion, which is a right about-face, the soul turning from the world unto God, which is morally impossible until a miracle of grace has been wrought upon us: "turn Thou me, and I shall be turned" (Jer 31:18). Such a miracle as regeneration and conversion, whereby the soul enters into the redemption purchased by Christ, is necessarily followed by one which shows forth the miraculous *fruits* of redemption. Such is the case here, as we see in the child bestowed upon the great woman. Remarkably enough that gift came to her unsought and unexpected. And is it not thus in the experience of the Christian? When he came to Christ as a sin-burdened soul, redemption was all that he thought about: there was no asking for or anticipation of subsequent fruit. —AWP

THE DOCTRINE OF SAINTS' PERSEVERANCE
9. Its Opposition

It has been shown at length in earlier articles that the concept of a total and final apostasy of a regenerated soul is not according to Truth. To postulate the eternal destruction of one to whom Divine grace has been savingly communicated to the soul is contrary to the whole tenor of the Covenant of redemption, to the attributes of God engaged in it, to the design and work of the Redeemer in it, to the Spirit's mission and His abiding with God's children "forever" (John 14:16). One who is indwelt by the Triune God shall not and cannot so fall from holiness and serve sin as to give himself wholly to its behests. One who has been delivered from the power of darkness and translated into the kingdom of God's dear Son shall never again become the willing subject of Satan. One who has been made the recipient of a supernatural experience of the Truth shall never be fatally deceived by the Devil's lies. True, his will is mutable, but God's promise is unchangeable; his own strength is feeble, but God's power is invincible; his prayers are weak, but Christ's intercession is prevalent.

Yet in all ages this doctrine of the final perseverance of the saints has been opposed and denied. Satan himself believed in the apostasy of Job and had the effrontery to avow it unto Jehovah (Job 1:8-11). We need not be surprised then to find that the supreme imposture of the religious realm repudiates most vehemently this precious truth and pronounces accursed all who hold it. The merit-mongers of Rome are inveterately opposed to everything which exalts free grace. Moreover, they who so hotly deny unconditional election, particular redemption, and effectual calling, must, in order to be consistent, deny the eternal security of the Christian. Since Papists are such rabid sticklers for the "free will" of fallen man, logically, they must deny the indefectibility of all who are in Christ. If I have by an act of my own volition brought myself into a state of grace, then it clearly follows that I am capable of forsaking the same. If the "free will" of the sinner first inclines him to exercise repentance and faith, then obviously he may relapse into a state of confirmed impenitence and unbelief.

But Rome has by no means stood alone in antagonizing this blessed article of the Faith. Others who differ widely from her in many other respects have made common cause with her in this. Considerable sections of "Protestantism," whole denominations which claim to take the Word of God for their *sole* Rule of faith and practice, have also strenuously and bitterly fought against those who maintained this truth. These are what are known as Arminians, for James Arminius or Van Harmin, a Dutchman of the sixteenth century, was the first man of any prominence in orthodox circles who opposed the theology taught by John Calvin—opposed it covertly and slyly and contrary to the most solemn and particular promise and pledge which he gave to the Classis before he was installed as professor of divinity at Leyden in 1602. Since then, for the purpose of theological classification, non-Calvinists and anti-Calvinists have been termed "Arminians." The one man who did more than any other to popularize and spread Arminianism in the English-speaking world was John Wesley.

We shall now make it our business to examine the attacks which Arminians have made upon this truth of the final perseverance of the saints and the leading arguments they employ to prejudice and overturn it. But let us say at the outset, it is not because we entertain any hope of delivering such people from their errors that we are now writing, still less that we are prepared to enter the lists against them. No, it is useless to argue with those whose hearts are set against the Truth: convince a man against his will and he is of the same opinion still. Moreover God's eternal Truth is infinitely too sacred to be made the matter of carnal debate and wrangling. Rather is it our design to help those of God's people who have been harassed by the dogs who yapped at their heels and show that their bark is worse than their bite. We write now with the object of delivering the "babes" from being "corrupted from the simplicity that is in Christ" (2 Cor 11:3).

1. By misrepresenting and misstating the truth for which we contend.

It is a favourite device of Arminians to set up a "man of straw" and because *he* is incapable of withstanding their assaults, pretend they have overthrown the Calvinistic tenet itself. To caricature a doctrine and then hold up that caricature to ridicule, to falsify a doctrine and then denounce that falsification as a thing of evil, is tantamount to acknowledging that they are unable to overthrow the doctrine as it is held and presented by its friends. Yet this is the very practice of which Arminian dialecticians are guilty. They select a single part of our doctrine and then take it up as though it were the whole. They sever the means from the end and claim we teach that the end will be reached irrespective of the means. They ignore the safeguards by which God has hedged around this part of His Truth, and which His true servants have ever maintained, and then affirm that such a doctrine is injurious, dangerous, inimical to the promotion of practical godliness. In plain language, they seek to terrify the simple by a bogey of their own manufacture.

That we have not brought an unjust and unfair charge against Arminians will appear from the following citation. "The common doctrine that perseverance requireth and commandeth all saints or believers to be fully persuaded, and this with the greatest and most indubitable certainty of faith, that there is an absolute and utter impossibility either of a total or a final defection of their faith: that though they shall fall into ten thousand enormities and most abominable sins and lie wallowing in them like a swine in the mire, yet they should remain all the while in an estate of grace, and that God will by a strong hand of irresistible grace bring them off from their sins by repentance before they die." Those were the words of one of the most influential of English Arminians in the palmy days of the Puritans, issuing from the pen of one, John Goodwin, a nephew of the pious and eminent expositor, Thomas Goodwin. In the light of what we have written in previous articles of this series few of our readers should have much difficulty in perceiving the sophistry of this miserable shift.

No well-instructed scribe of Christ ever set forth the doctrine of the saints perseverance in any such distorted manner and extravagant terms as the above, yet such is a fair sample of the devices employed by Arminians when engaged in assailing this truth: they detach a single element of it and then render repugnant their one-sided misrepresentation of the whole. The perseverance which we contend for, and which the operations of Divine grace effectually provide for and secure, is a perseverance of *faith and holiness*, —a continuing steadfast in believing and in bringing forth all the fruits of righteousness. Whereas as any one can see at a glance, the travesty presented in the above quotation is a preservation in spite of and in the midst of perseverance *in wickedness*. To speak about falling "into ten thousand enormities and most abominable sins and lie wallowing in them like a swine in the mire (i.e. quite at home in such filth and content therewith), and yet they shall remain all the while in an estate of grace" is a palpable contradiction of terms, for an "estate of grace" is one of subjection and obedience to God.

Again, Goodwin makes out the Calvinist to say in God's name, "You that truly believe in My Son, and have been made partakers of the Holy Spirit, and therefore are fully persuaded and assured from My will and command given unto you in that behalf, yea, according to the infallible Word of Truth you have from Me, that you cannot possibly, no, not by the most horrid sins and abominable practices, that you shall or can commit, fall away either totally or finally from your faith; for in the midst of your foulest actings and courses there remains a seed in you which is sufficient to make you true believers, and to preserve you from falling away finally, that it is impossible you should die in your sins; you that know and are assured that I will by an irresistible hand work perseverance in you, and consequently that you are out of all danger of condemnation, and that heaven and salvation belong unto you, and are as good as yours already, so that nothing but giving of thanks appertains to you."

The incongruity of such a fiction should at once be apparent. First, as true saints do not have a firm and comfortable assurance of their perseverance many of them are frequently beset by doubts and fears. Second, it is by means of God's promises and precepts, exhortations and threatenings, that they are stirred up to the use of those things by which perseverance is wrought and assurance is obtained. Third, no rightly-taught saint ever expected his perseverance or the least assurance of it under such a foul supposition as falling into and continuing in "horrid sins and abominable practices." Fourth, the promises of eternal security are made to those in whose mind God writes His laws and in whose hearts He places His holy fear, so that they shall not depart from Him: they are made to those who "hear" the voice of the good Shepherd and who "follow" the example He has left them. Fifth, so far from "nothing but giving of thanks" appertaining to them, they are bidden to work out their own salvation with fear and trembling, to run with patience the race set before them, to make their calling and election sure by adding to their graces and bringing forth the fruits of righteousness.

Let us say once more, and it cannot be insisted upon too frequently and emphatically in this degenerate age, that the perseverance of saints which is depicted in Holy Writ is not a simple continuance of Christians on this earth for a number of years after regeneration and faith have been wrought in them and then their being admitted as a matter of course to Heaven, *without* any regard to their moral history in the intervening period. No, though *that* may be how incompetent novices have portrayed it, and how Antinomians have perverted it, yet such a concept is as far removed from the reality as darkness is from light. The perseverance of the saints is a steady pressing forward in the course on which they entered at conversion—an enduring unto the end in the exercise of faith and in the practice of holiness. The perseverance of the saints consists in a continuing to deny self, to mortify the lusts of the flesh, to resist the Devil, to fight the good fight of faith;

and though they suffer many falls by the way, and receive numerous wounds from their foes, yet, if "faint," they "hold on their way."

2. By insisting that this doctrine encourages loose living.

We have heard numbers of Arminians declare "If I were absolutely sure that Heaven would be my everlasting portion, then I would drop all religion and take my fill of the world," to which we replied, Perhaps *you* would, but the regenerate feel quite different: they find their delight in One who is infinitely preferable to all that can be found in this perishing world. Yet Arminians never tire of saying that this article of the non-apostasy of the saints is a vicious and dangerous one, affording great encouragement unto those who believe themselves to be Christians to indulge themselves in iniquities, such as Lot, David, Solomon and Peter committed. It is granted that those who commit such sins and die without repentance for them and faith in the blood of the Lamb have no inheritance in the kingdom of God and Christ. It is also a fact that God visited the transgressions of those men with His rod and recovered them from their falls. Nor are such instances recorded in the Word to encourage us in sin, but rather to caution us against and make us distrustful of ourselves.

Such a gross view as is propounded in the above objection loses sight entirely of the nature of regeneration, tacitly denying that the new birth is a miracle of grace, effecting a radical change within, renewing the faculties of the soul, giving an entirely different bent to a person's inclinations. To talk of a child of God falling in love again with sin is tantamount to suggesting that there is no real difference between one who has passed from death unto life, who has had the principle of holiness communicated to him, who is indwelt by the Spirit of God, and those who are unregenerate. That one who has been merely intellectually impressed and emotionally stirred to temporarily reform his outward conduct may indeed return to his former manner of life, is readily conceded; but that one who has experienced a supernatural work of grace within, who has been made "a new creature in Christ Jesus," can or will lose all relish for spiritual things and becomes satisfied with the husks which the swine feed on, we emphatically deny.

3. By asserting our doctrine deprives God's people of the sharpest bit which He has given for curtailing the flesh in them.

It is affirmed by many Arminians that the most effectual means for restraining their evil inclinations, alike in the regenerate and the unregenerate, is the fear of the everlasting burnings, and from this premise they draw the conclusion that when a person is definitely assured he has been once and for all delivered from the wrath to come, the strongest deterrent against carnality and lasciviousness has been taken from him. There would be considerable force in this objection if God had not communicated to His children that which operates in them more mightily and effectually than the dread of punishment, and since He *has*, then the argument has little point or weight to it. Whatever influence the fear of Hell exerts in curtailing the lusts of the flesh, certain it is that the righteous are withheld from a life of sin by far more potent considerations. Faith purifieth the heart (Acts 15:9), faith overcometh the world (1 John 5:4) but Scripture nowhere ascribes such virtues to a dread of the Lake of fire. An unruly horse needs to be held in by a bridle, but one that is well broken in is better managed by a gentler hand than a biting bit.

The case of the saint would certainly be a perilous one if there was no stronger restraint upon his lusts than the fear of Hell: how far does such fear restrain the ungodly! As the nature of a cause determines the nature of its effects, and as a man's conduct will be determined by the most powerful principle governing him, so a slavish fear can produce only slavish observance and surely God requires something better than *that* from His people. Such service as the fear of Hell produces will be weak and wavering, for nothing more unsettles the mind and enervates the soul than alarms and horrors. Nabal's heart "died within" him for fear (1 Sam 25:37), and the soldiers that kept the sepulchre "became as dead men" for fear (Matt 28:4): thus any obedience from thence can only be a dead obedience. Moreover, it will be fickle and fleeting at the best: Pharaoh relaxed his persecution of the Hebrews when no longer tormented by God's plagues, and even gave them permission to leave Egypt; but soon after he repented of his leniency, chiding himself for it, and pursued them with murder in his heart (Exo 14:5). Those hypocrites whom "fearfulness" surprised, remained hypocrites still (Isa 33:14).

It is true that believers are bidden to "fear Him which is able to destroy both body and soul in Hell" (Matt 10:28), yet it should be pointed out that there is a vast difference between fearing *God* and dreading eternal punishment, in the parallel and fuller passage Christ added, "yea, I say unto you, Fear *Him*" (Luke 12:5)— not fear Hell! One of the covenant promises which God has made concerning His elect is, "I will put My fear in their hearts, that they shall not depart from Me" (Jer 32:40), and that is a filial fear, a respect for His authority, an awesome veneration of His majesty; whereas the fear of the unregenerate is a servile, anxious and tormenting one. The holy fear of the righteous causes them to be vigilant and watchful against those ways which lead to destruction, but the fear of the wicked is occupied only with the destruction itself: the one is concerned about the evils which occasion God's wrath, the other is confined to the effects of his wrath. But the exercise of faith and the operations of filial fear are not the only principles which regulate the saint, the love of Christ constrains him, gratitude unto God for His wondrous grace has a powerful effect upon his conduct. —AWP

DAGON DESTROYED

We closed our last article by calling attention to a striking omission: that in the closing verse of 1 Samuel 4 and the opening ones of 5 there is no hint that the Nation was filled with consternation at their loss of the sacred ark or that they made any attempt to recover it, or that they cried unto the Lord to intervene. Instead, they seemed to have been quite unmoved by such an unprecedented calamity, and taking the line of least resistance remained inert. Yet if we take into consideration all the attendant circumstances we should not be surprised. Consider the *time* when it occurred. It was at some point within the period covered by the book of Judges, and in that book we are told four times "In those days there was no king in Israel," and twice it is added "every man did that which was right in his own eyes," which is ever the case when there is no strong central authority. But more: the *priesthood* had failed, yea, was abominably corrupt (1 Sam 2:12-17,22), and thus Israel was without competent leaders either spiritual or civil. What then could be expected of the rank and file of the people!

"When the Philistines took the ark of God they brought it into the house of Dagon, and set it by Dagon" (1 Sam 5:2). In their most recent form we regard the

Philistines as the "Modernists," the "Rationalists," the "Higher Critics," who captured the majority of the seminaries and theological institutions; dominated religious literature, gained possession of almost all the most influential pulpits, and thereby secured control of the public Testimony of God, corrupting the ministerial springs at their source. And what are we to understand by "Dagon" in this connection? It was the "god" of the Philistines, the idol to which they paid homage (Judg 16:23). That idol was a monstrosity, being fashioned after a fish in its lower half but after the human form in its upper (1 Sam 5:4, margin): thus it portrayed the worship of man plus something inferior in the scale of being. Unto such "strong delusion" were they given up as to worship a nonentity, a figment of their own imagination, something resembling the fabled "mermaid."

And was not "Evolution"—the theory that man has come from the animals and they from fishes—the grand idol of all the apostate professors and teachers! And what grew out of it? A logical corollary of the Evolutionary theory was the flesh-pleasing idea of *the progress of man* and his wonderful achievements. These were crystallized in the imposing expression "Civilisation," or "our Christian civilisation," or more recently "our twentieth-century civilisation." Pulpit and press, politicians and educational authorities have united in lauding "the steady march of progress," the tremendous "advance" which has been made, and the utopia which would soon be established in the world. God allowed almost a century to pass for the full development of the modern "Dagon," that the pride and folly of its deluded devotees might the more plainly appear, for it was in 1848 Charles Darwin's "Origin of Species" appeared—popularised for the masses by Henry Drummonds "The *Ascent* of Man." Yet side by side with the trumpeting forth of progress and advancement there has been an ever increasing and more widely spread spiritual deterioration and moral degeneracy.

If our memory serves us correctly it was in the 1908 issues of "Things to Come," a monthly edited by E. W. Bullinger, there appeared some striking articles from the pen of P. Mauro, entitled "The state of the crops," being a topical excursus on the words "The harvest of the earth is ripe" (Rev 14:15). In them he pointed out how results showed that the natural efforts and attainments of man had already reached their limits, that whether in literary productions, musical compositions, painting or forms of architecture nothing was now being achieved which excelled the fruits of previous generations, that the best being brought forth in these fields of human industry were but replicas or inferior imitations of what our fathers and forefathers possessed. But if the summit of attainment had already been reached by 1908, how far has the world traveled down the incline on the farther side since then!

Some one has said, "The popular taste is a good index to the health of society." Apply that dictum to our own times and it will quickly appear how the mental and moral health of society has declined. The vast majority now prefer such minor poets as Yeates and Bottomley to the superior excellency of Wordsworth and Tennyson; the crude and hideous sculptures of Robin and Epstein to those of the ancient Greeks; the grotesque and crazy productions of the "cubist" and "surrealist" schools to the masterpieces of Raphael and Turner; the jazz of the jungle and the crooning of Harlem to the strains of Beethoven; the ethical standards of Shaw to Shakespeare's; the modern "thriller" to the more wholesome fiction of Thackeray and Scott. No matter in which direction we turn it is the ugly and the vulgar which is preferred to the beautiful and refined. What a commentary on our so-called "progress."

This "progress" which has been so much advertised and acclaimed has been merely a mechanical one and not a spiritual and moral. The past century has indeed witnessed some remarkable inventions, but how far have they contributed to the real good of mankind? Electricity and incandescent gas has replaced the candles and oil-lamps of our forebears, but has there been a corresponding increase of spiritual illumination among the people? Steam and petrol power have largely superceded carriages and drays drawn by horses but have they issued in any moral elevation? The present generation has taken to flying in the air, but there is no evidence of increased heavenly mindedness. On the lowest ground, these inventions have failed to produce more contentment and mental serenity. And do not the losses entailed by these modern devices far outweigh any gains? Witness the appalling "toll of the road": in America and Britain tens of thousands killed and hundreds of thousands maimed every year! Witness the towns and cities of Europe blasted into ruins from the air! Would it not be a mercy if the clock of "progress" could be pushed back a hundred years?

It matters not which aspect we consider of modern "Progress" for its thin veneer of delusion is easily seen though if the examination be made coolly and critically. For example, how proud the boastings of a generation or so ago about our "Prison Reforms" and our more enlightened treatment of crime when in reality a maudlin sentimentality was allowed to oust a sense of justice. The eugenist contemplates morals principally from a utilitarian viewpoint. The modern scientist virtually denies the responsibility of the criminal, contending that he is the helpless victim of heredity and environment. "Social workers" affirm that society and not the criminal is to blame. In consequence the retributive element in punishment has been more and more displaced by the reformative. Short sentences became increasingly popular and prisoners increasingly petted. A premium was practically placed upon crime by making the lot of the culprit pleasanter, certainly more secure, than that of the average workman. It makes no difference to these theorists that the virtuous (though outnumbered) are to be met with in the slums, while some of the most vicious spring from good parents and excellent homes.

Instead of asking the question, what harvest could be expected from such a sowing? we would push our inquiry further back and ask, Was this highly praised movement actuated by nobler or inferior principles to those which have regulated our fathers? It is a simple matter for the objector to reply, this generation is more tempered by mercy than were previous ones. It is equally simple for us to deny it. But let us ask, Is the criminal the only one entitled to mercy? what of *his victims*—the thousands of comparatively poor people robbed by swindlers and tricksters. Is it lack of mercy which seeks to throw a wall of protection around the weak and gullible, by imposing such penalties as are likely to deter those who would prey upon them? Then prisons ought not to be made so attractive that they cease to be a deterrent to crime. Is it unmerciful to qass the death-sentence on a slayer if an hundred potential murderers are curbed by such an example? Let justice be tempered by mercy, but not a mercy which closes its eyes to the essential difference between right and wrong.

Suffer us to allude unto one other aspect of our twentieth-century progress, namely, the enormous efforts which have been made by the state to raise the "standard of life" for the labouring classes. Fabulous sums have been spent during the last twenty years in "doles," "pensions," and "family allowances." Even the unprecedented cost of the present war was not allowed to curtail the colossal upkeep of the "social services." And *has* the "standard of life" been raised at all? The answer to that question depends upon your standard of measurement. Better fed and better housed working-men certainly have not produced better workmanship! As the majority of impartial and competent observers foresaw, the "dole" has been most demoralizing, destroying in many the incentive to earn their bread honestly by the sweat of the brow. Nor has it produced more contentment: the more they be given, the more they expect—demand. What proportion of the huge sums spent in doles and allowances found its way into the pockets of publicans, brewers, distillers, dog-racing proprietors, and amusement caterers.

To return unto 1 Samuel 5. The sacred ark had been captured by the Philistines and Israel tamely submitted to their loss. It looked as though the Lord Himself was indifferent, for He put no obstacle in the way of His enemies and even permitted them to conclude that Dagon was greater than Himself. That is why, after recounting the calamities recorded in 1Samuel 4—see 78:60-65—the Psalmist uses those striking figures of speech: "Then the Lord awaked as one out of sleep, like a mighty man that shouteth by reason of wine" (78:65). Jehovah now took into His own hands the work of avenging His outraged honour and vindicating His great name. God is a jealous God: He had shown Himself such by severely chastising His friends, because they had long tolerated unjudged evils in their midst. And now the fierceness of His jealousy should be felt by His foes. He made bare His right arm and smote His insulting adversaries, and He continued to smite until they were compelled to recognize *Who* it was that was dealing with them.

"And when they of Ashdod arose early on the morrow, behold, Dagon was fallen upon his face to the earth before the ark of the Lord" (1 Sam 5:3). Once more we express our conviction that the history of Dagon contains an allegorical significance, that it portrays what has occurred again and again in the lives of different nations and empires, yea that it gives us a pattern of what has been and is taking place in the world before our own eyes. It is a revelation of the unchanging principles in the governmental dealings of God, and therefore is fraught with important spiritual instruction. The "Dagon" worshipped by our moderns is the so-called "Christian Civilisation." And what happened *to it*, my reader, during 1914-1918? when the most "cultured" and "highly civilised" of the nations engaged each other in a contest of such gigantic dimensions and ruthless ferocity, employed such diabolical means and methods and sacrificed the flower of their manhood to such an appalling extent, that the whole range of human history supplies no parallel. Man has prated of his ascent from the animal, and it was left to the disciples of such a philosophy to demonstrate how beastly they still were. Proud "civilisation" was shaken to its foundations, humiliated into the dust, flung on its very face in 1914-1918.

And what was the Philistines' response to their humiliating experience? Did they acknowledge the Hand that had overturned their idol? Did they own their insensate folly and confess they were vainly fighting against Heaven? No, they did not, for the next thing we read of is that "they took Dagon and set him in his place again" (v 3). They were still determined that Dagon should be their "god." See the blinding and besotting power of self-will. How true it is that "they that make them [the senseless idols] are like unto them" (Psa 115:8)! And what effect did the frightful tragedy of 1914-1918 have upon the nations of Christendom? Was there a general turning unto God and an humbling of themselves before Him? No, in the language of Isaiah 26:10, 11 it had to be said "They *will not* behold the majesty of the Lord. Lord, when Thy hand is lifted up, they *will not see*." Neither the goodness of God nor the severity of God made any impression: they continued to harden their hearts and followed out their mad dreamings.

May we not see in the institution of the League of Nations with the wonderful benefits it was going to confer upon mankind in the restablising and securing of "Civilisation" the setting up again of "Dagon"? Was not the widely preached "Universal Brotherhood of Man" now to receive practical expression by the nations of the earth banded together as they never had been before. Might was now to give place to right, force to reason. In future, disputes should be justly but amicably settled by arbitration and war would be rendered impossible. The world would now be "made safe for democracy." Civilisation would at last stand upon a firm basis and the steady march of progress which had been so rudely interrupted, could be resumed with an ever-brightening prospect. Such in brief were the promises made and the hopes inspired by that wonderful production of twentieth-century politicians and diplomats. And what a will 'o the wisp it proved!

The "march of progress" from 1920 onwards, was, if measured by the standards of righteousness and decency, steadily downwards and not upwards. During the fifteen years that followed, "Civilised Britain" became more and more a "Continentalised Britain," a "Paganised Britain." That which our fathers had so carefully erected their children took pleasure in tearing down. Everything which had ennobled the "Victorian" era was sneered at and jettisoned. Those with the least sense of decency were determined to drag down into the gutter the whole of the rising generation. An orgy of licentiousness was widely entered into. Night-clubs were multiplied, dog-racing tracks opened all over the country, gambling spread like wild fire among the young people and cocktail parties abounded on every side. The beaches lowered their bathing restrictions and modesty became a thing of the past. Youth was allowed to have its fling unrestrained. The sanctity of the Sabbath totally disappeared, the Lord's day being devoted to pleasuring and carousing.

Mayfair became another Harlem and other places emulated their very example or attempted to "go one worse." The novels and magazines of the last decade have been filled with obscenities and blasphemies. A friend of ours engaged in the publishing business years ago recently wrote us, "Today we have shops stacked with books which, had they been published when we were boys the authors and publishers would have been put in jail." Censorship has long since been reduced to a farce. The great majority of the children never entered either a "Sunday school" or "church" in the years between 1920-38 and their ideas were formed by the pictures they saw at the "movies" and the debasing productions of a degenerate press. As a recent writer said "the Evangelical Christian," "The best sellers of today are more often than not books whose morals are of the barnyard, whose language is of the sewer and whose ethics are of the pit. The ghastly thing is that you will find such novels prominently displayed and often commended by large Church publishing houses."

And what was the sequel to the Philistines setting up again of their idol? This, "And when they arose early on the morrow morning, behold, Dagon was fallen upon his face to the ground before the ark of the Lord; and the head of Dagon and both the palms of his hands were cut off upon the threshold; only the fishy part was left to him" (v 12). Thus did Jehovah again stain their pride and write folly across that which they were so determined to honour. This time Dagon was not only overturned but dashed to pieces, losing its head and hands—the members which speak of wisdom and power—so that nothing but the stump remained. In its present application the realization of this is not to be looked for in any particular act or event, but in a process of decay and demolition. As the recent withdrawal of the Spirit in Christendom was gradual, covering an interval of several years; as the overturning of Dagon was most noticeable during 19141918; so the final destruction of Dagon, though the pace of deterioration has greatly increased, may be extended over a longer or shorter period.

There is no doubt in this writer's mind that the present generation is even now witnessing and will continue to witness the smashing up of the much-vaunted modern Dagon. It was surely significant that the three men occupying the most prominent and influential positions in modern life, namely, Mr. N. Chamberlain, the prime-minister of Great Britain, Mr. F. Roosevelt, the president of the USA, and the pope from the Vatican all placed themselves on record in public statements in 1938, that if the threatened war of Europe eventuated it would mean and entail "The end of Civilisation as we know it." No doubt they alluded more especially to the material and financial structure, for most of the ethical and spiritual elements, the best features of our corporate life, that which made for refinement and elevation of the mind, had well-nigh disappeared from the world when those men made their pronouncements. How dreadfully everything has gone from bad to worse since then may be gathered from the newspapers, though in their present abbreviated form only a small part of the tragedy is being chronicled.

The breakdown and breakup of "Civilisation" appears in such things as the decay of the sanctity of marriage—as evidenced by the multiplication of divorces, the abandonment of such numbers of babies, the fearful increase of bigamy; juvenile delinquency and of immorality and disease among the young, the vandalism which is now so rife, such widespread pilfering, the appalling amount of absenteeism in all sections of labour, and the supine efforts of the authorities to deal with such evils. English law carries a penalty of seven years for the crime of bigamy, yet guilty ones rarely receive more than three months. Thousands of culprits who ought to be sent to prison are given nominal fines. Recently an ARP chief in a big London borough, when deploring the wanton injury inflicted on the "shelters," complained that "We have had fines as low as 1/- (25 cents) against young hooligans caught damaging shelter equipment." Law and order is almost reduced to a farce. The chief officer for the LMS railway stated, "In the past year 8,600 carriage windows had been broken; 19,300 door-straps removed, 40,000 electric lamps removed." The head of Dagon is already broken off!

It is said "the war is responsible for theses evils." Not so: war conditions have merely brought things to a head and caused the scum to rise to the surface. "He that is an hireling...seeth the wolf coming, and leaveth the sheep, and fleeth…The hireling fleeth because he *is* a hireling" (John 10:12,13) reveals the principle. We do what we do because we are what we are. There is ever a rigid consistency between character and conduct. When the testing time comes each one reveals what he is by what he does. Character is most revealed by our conduct in the *crises* of life. When did the "hireling" flee? When he saw the wolf approaching: that was not what made him an hireling, but *discovered him* as such— one with no love for the sheep. Present conditions have caused the masses to drop all pretence and come out in their true colours. The thin coating of "civilised" varnish has worn off and twentieth-century character stands exposed.

But even when Dagon was destroyed something yet more drastic was required to bring the Philistines to their senses. "The hand of the Lord was heavy upon them of Ashdod and He destroyed them, and smote them with emerods" (v 6). They removed the ark to Gath, and "a very great destruction" smote the men there also (v 9). They sent it to Ekron and its inhabitants were so terrified they demanded that the ark be retruned to Israel (v 11). Thus did God avenge Himself and make the wrath of man to praise Him. Never did a boastful people undergo so deep a dishonour in the eyes of their neighbours, to whom they became a laughing stock; and never did an idol suffer a worse disgrace than that which befell Dagon. Afterwards the ark was restored again to Israel, and if history continues, in God's appointed time, after His judgments have accomplished their designed work, the Spirit will return to a purged Christendom and the Testimony of God be established again in its midst. —AWP

---

seat. The dais upon which the Mediator is now seated is the Throne of Grace and Therefore are His subjects invited, "Let us therefore come boldly unto the throne of grace, that we may obtain mercy and find grace to help in time of need" (Heb 4:16). It is written "But He giveth more grace," and if we find ourselves straitened the fault is entirely ours and not because of any reluctance in Him to bestow. Nor is the particular fault or cause of our lack difficult to determine: "God resisteth the proud, but giveth grace unto the humble" (James 4:6). "He hath filled the hungry with good things and the rich He hath sent empty away" (Luke 1:53). It is the poor in spirit, those who feel themselves to be utterly dependent upon the Divine bounty, and not the self-righteous and self-satisfied, who are enriched by the heavenly Donor.

Seventh, because it is itself the chief means of grace. It not only instructs us where grace is to be found and how further supplies of it are to be obtained, but it is the principal medium through which grace is actually imparted to the soul. As its sacred pages are reverently perused the mind is instructed, the conscience enlightened, the affections warmed, and the will moved. As its exceeding great and precious promises are meditated upon and treasured up in the heart new strength is imparted to the soul. As its holy precepts are turned into earnest prayer help is obtained for the discharge of duty. As its timely warnings and admonitions are heeded, temptations lose their power and the snares of Satan are avoided. As its cheering revelation of what God has prepared for them that love Him is received by faith, new hope is kindled in the breast and the trials of life are borne with greater fortitude. As the end of the journey is neared death loses its terrors and the call to remove hence becomes more desirable. —AWP

(continued from front page)

Third, hence the gift of His Word is one of unmerited and undeserved goodwill on God's part. If unfallen creatures are entirely incapable of bringing the Most High under any obligation to them, how much less so those who have revolted from His scepter and repudiated His government over them. What claim can rebels have upon Him whose laws they defiantly trample underfoot? To what favourable consideration are insurrectionists entitled from their Sovereign? None whatever. Their very enmity calls for His wrath and not His mercy, for sentence of judgment rather than expressions of lovingkindness. Then let amazement be rekindled in our hearts as we contemplate afresh this marvel of the Divine clemency. Be astonished O ye heavens and earth, that instead of annihilating the apostate race of Adam Jehovah was pleased to address them in overtures of grace, calling upon them to throw down the weapons of their warfare and be reconciled to Him, making known to them the way of recovery and restoration to His favour. That was indeed grace—grace "fathomless as the sea."

Fourth, it is so denominated because it is the chief instrument employed by His Spirit. In Hebrews

10:29 we find the Holy Spirit is called "the Spirit of grace," and He is so designated there in connection with His ministration and operation in the assemblies of the saints. The Word and the Spirit are so intimately conjoined that we are scarcely warranted in thinking of the one without the other. The Word does not operate without the Spirit's agency and the Spirit works not apart from the Word. It was by the Spirit's inspiration that the Word was first given, for "holy men of God spake moved by the Holy Spirit" (2 Peter 1:21). It is by the Spirit we are enlightened (Eph 1:17,18), yet the Word is the means He employs. It is by the Spirit we are sanctified (Rom 15:16), yet not apart from the Truth (John 17:17). It is by the Spirit we are strengthened (Eph 3:16) as He causes the Word to dwell in us richly (Col 3:16). It is by the Spirit we are comforted (Acts 9:31) as He applies the Divine promises to our hearts. How appropriate, then, that the grand Instrument employed by the Spirit of grace should be termed "the Word of His grace."

Fifth, in His Word God has disclosed to us the wondrous "riches of His grace." Therein is set forth the incarnate Word "full of grace and truth" (John 1:14), the One who "came to seek and to save that which was lost," the "Friend of publicans and sinners" (Luke 7:34), the One who fed the hungry, healed the sick, cleansed the leper, raised the dead. Therein is revealed the "Gospel of the grace of God" bringing "good tidings of great joy," for it proclaims rest for the weary, pardon to the guilty, justification to the ungodly, adoption to the outcast, treasures in heaven for spiritual paupers. Its terms are "Ho! every one that thirsteth, come ye to the waters, and he that hath no money; come ye buy, and eat; yea, come, buy wine and milk without money and without price" (Isa 55:1). Such good news is not to be confined to the cloister but freely proclaimed to "every creature." The twentieth century needs it as urgently as did the first, and its music is just as welcome to ears opened by the Spirit of grace. It is "the poor, the maimed, the lame, the blind" who are to be called to the feast which grace has spread (Luke 14:13).

Sixth, it is called the Word of his grace because therein we are informed how grace is to be obtained, namely, by coming as empty-handed beggars to the Mercy-

. *(continued on proceeding page)*

VOL. XXII.   OCTOBER, 1943.   NO. 10

STUDIES IN THE SCRIPTURES

"Search the Scriptures." John 5:39.

Publisher and Editor—ARTHUR W. PINK,
27 Lewis Street,
Stornoway, Isle of Lewis,
Scotland.

THE WORD OF TRUTH

One of the many titles given to the Holy Scriptures is "the Word of Truth" (2Ti 2:15). They are such because a communication from "the God of Truth" (Isa 65:16), a revelation from Him "that cannot lie" (Tit 1:2). O the privilege of possessing such a boon! Do we definitely and thankfully realize when we take up the Bible to read that it is nothing less than a message from Heaven, reliably translated into our mother tongue? What a priceless treasure! "The Word of Truth": no errors or fables in it, nothing to mislead or deceive; but inerrant and absolutely trustworthy. How grateful is this writer that from the cradle he was trained to receive the Sacred Scriptures as the Word of Truth, and that his parents in their turn had received the same pious teaching in their infancy. True, that training had been lost upon him unless God had been pleased to sanctify the same and in His appointed time to grant him a personal and saving knowledge of the Truth. Yet it is His way to honour those who honour Him (1Sa 2:30), though He reserves to Himself the sovereign right to do so in whatever manner pleases Him.

The Word of Truth: what a peerless and priceless treasure is this! Not a production of the Church nor even the composition of the holy angels, but the Word of *God Himself*. It is a "light that shineth in a dark place" (2Pe 1:19). It is a life-giving Stream for parched pilgrims as they journey through this "wilderness of sin." It is the Word of Truth in pointed contrast from all "science falsely so-called" (1 Tim 6:20) and "philosophy and vain deceit" (Col 2:8). Living as we are in a world of shams and make-beliefs, of exaggeration and prevarication, of fiction and falsity, how inestimably valuable is this "Thus saith the Lord"! Well may we say of the Scriptures "More to be desired are they than gold, yea, than much fine gold" (Psa 19:10). In the midst of so much conflicting opinion, speculation and uncertainty, where should we be if the Word of Truth had not been vouchsafed to us? We should be mariners upon the sea of life without chart or compass. We should be ignorant alike of our origin, our duty, and our destiny.

What a blessing it is when all doubt as to their Divine Authorship is removed and we are favoured with a definite assurance that the Holy Scriptures *are* "the Word of Truth"! One of the chief elements in "the faith of God's elect" (Tit 1:1) is a deep

(continued on back page)

IMPORTANT NOTICES

Please advise promptly of change in address, otherwise copies will be lost in the mails.

We are glad to send a sample copy to any of your friends whom you believe would be interested in this publication.

This magazine is published as "a work of faith and labour of love," the editor and his wife gladly giving their services free. There is no regular subscription price, as we do not wish the poor of the flock to be deprived. This does not mean that those looking for something for nothing may "help themselves." Those getting this Magazine, who are financially able and who receive spiritual help from its pages, are expected to gladly contribute towards its expenses; otherwise, their names are dropped from our lists.

Will those forwarding International Money Orders please have them made out to us at Stornoway, Isle of Lewis, Scotland. Checks (Cheques-Eng.) made out on U.S.A. Banks are not negotiable here, so please do not send them.

CONTENTS

THE SERMON ON THE MOUNT
Profession Tested: Matthew 7:26, 27.

"And everyone that heareth these sayings of Mine, and doeth them not, shall be likened unto a foolish man which built his house upon the sand: and the rain descended and the floods came and the winds blew, and beat upon that house, and it fell, and great was the fall of it" (vv 26,27). It is scarcely necessary to point out that our Lord was here using parabolic language, but what is the force of the figure He employed? what is signified by this building a house upon the sand? Clearly He had in view those who claim to be His followers, but whose profession has no reality behind it: a class of people who expect to go to Heaven, but whose hopes rest upon a faulty foundation; those who trust in something which will fail them in the hour of testing. Unspeakably solemn, then, are these verses, containing that which should cause every reader who values his or her soul to tremble at them, and to reexamine himself with sevenfold thoroughness, to discover whether or no they describe his own perilous condition.

For the last time in this Sermon our Lord enforced the text on which it is based: "For I say unto you, that except your righteousness shall exceed the righteousness of the scribes and Pharisees, ye shall in no case enter into the kingdom of heaven" (5:20). Wherein lay the defectiveness of their "righteousness"? First, there was a total neglect of their internal condition: "Woe unto you scribes and Pharisees hypocrites! for ye are like unto whited sepulchers, which indeed appear beautiful outward, but are within full of dead men's bones and of all uncleanness" (Mat 23:27)—there was no mortification of their lusts. Second, they failed to put first things first: "Ye pay tithes of mint and anise and cumin, and have omitted the weightier matters of the Law—judgment, mercy and faith" (23:23). Third, they wrought for their own glory, from a principle of self-interest: "but all their works they do for to be seen of men" (23:5) and not for the purpose of obeying and honouring God. Fourth, they practiced not what they preached: "they say, and do not" (23:3)—their talk was all right, but their walk was all wrong.

Spirituality of soul, purity of heart, integrity of conduct, the scribes and Pharisees had no regard for. They were forward in fasting, praying at street corners, and giving of alms ostentatiously, but it was all done with the object of enhancing their reputation among men. And in *their* religion we have an exemplification of what is the natural persuasion of men the world over namely, that a religion of external performances will suffice to ensure a blissful eternity. Undoubtedly there are many who would in words deny this, but who in their works substantiate it. They bring their bodies to the house of prayer, but not their souls; they worship with their mouths, but not "in spirit and in truth." They are sticklers for immersion or early morning communion, yet take no thought about keeping their hearts with all diligence. They boast of their orthodoxy, but disregard the precepts of Christ. Multitudes of professing Christians abstain from external acts of violence, yet hesitate not to rob their neighbours of a good name by spreading evil reports against them. They contribute regularly to the "pastor's salary," but shrink not from misrepresenting their goods and cheating their customers, persuading themselves that "business is business." They have more regard for the laws of man than those of God, for *His* fear is not before their eyes.

After dwelling at such length in the previous articles on the "wise" build there should be little difficulty in identifying the various groups which are commonly classified as the "foolish." They are all those, no matter what their profession and pretensions, who *do not* the "sayings" of Christ. Even F. W. Grant in his brief notes on this passage said, "He who puts His sayings livingly into practice shall build a house that will endure the storm. No one else and nothing else will": though we are very much afraid that scarcely two out of a hundred of those wont to read his "Numerical Bible" really believe any such thing. In Luke's account of the "wise" builder an additional item is added: "Whosoever cometh to Me, and heareth My sayings, and doeth them I will show you to whom he is like. He is like a man which built a house and *digged deep*, and laid the foundation on a rock" (6:47,48). The "foolish ones" *failed* to "dig deep." As this is the vital point which distinguishes the two classes let us endeavour to show what is signified by this "digging deep."

If ever there was a time when these words "digged deep" needed to be pressed upon the notice of professing Christians it is today. We are living in an age which is characterized by superficiality and shallowness, when religion itself has degenerated into a mere surface thing. There is no deep ploughing, no spade work, no foundation exercises, no brokenness of heart. If I have never mourned over my waywardness, I have no solid ground for rejoicing. "Want of depth, want of sincerity, want of zeal in religion—this is the way of our times. Want of an eye to God in religion, lack of sincere dealing with one's soul, neglect of using the lancet with our hearts, neglect of the searing warrant which God gives out against sin, carelessness concerning living upon Christ; much reading about Him, much talking about Him, but too little feeding upon His flesh and drinking of His blood— these are the causes of tottering professions and baseless hopes." If Spurgeon found occasion of making such complaint as far back as 1870 how sadly conditions have worsened since then!

A saving apprehension or laying hold of Christ is not the simple thing so many suppose. Man must be humbled into the dust before he will, as a beggar, betake himself to the Redeemer. The Divine Law is the appointed school-master to drive sinners to Christ, but so many people play truant—run away from school. Not a few attempt to build upon Christ but there has been no proper foundation-work, and so in the day of testing the floods of opposition and persecution come in between their hearts and Christ, and temptations part them to the overthrow of their profession. By nature our hearts are so filled with self-love and self-pity there is no room for Christ. Many are willing to receive Him for His benefits who have no love for His person and no resolution to bow to his Lordship, which is like a woman marrying a man solely for his money. Observe Paul's order: "For whom I have suffered the loss of all things, and do count them but dung, that I may win Christ, and be found in Him; not having mine own righteousness which is of the law, but that which is through the faith of Christ, the righteousness which is of God by faith" (Phi 3:8,9)—first Christ Himself and then His righteousness!

1. He "digs deep" who does not enter upon a Christian profession hurriedly and lightly, but instead "sits down and counts the cost" (Luk 14:28). There are some who say they are saved before they have any feeling sense that they are lost. There are others who profess to receive Christ who yet have no realisation of the claims of His scepter. There are those who present themselves for baptism who know nothing about the terms of Christian discipleship. Such people rush into a profession of religion, and in most cases rush out of it again. They receive the Word "with joy" rather than with painful convictions of sin, but they have "not root in themselves" and so "dureth for awhile only" (Mat 13:20,21). Hence it was that when one said unto Him "I will follow Thee whithersoever Thou goest" Christ told him that he had not "where to lay His head"; and when another lightly said "I will follow Thee" He answered "No man, having put his hand to the plough [and ploughing is no easy work!] and looking back, is fit for the kingdom of God" (Luk 9:58-62); while to His apostles He gave the warning "remember Lot's wife" (Luk 17:32).

2. He "digs deep" who labours to be emptied of self-righteousness, self-esteem, and self-sufficiency. The sinner needs first to be convicted of his utter inability *to come* to Christ—that God must give him a heart which is willing to receive Him as King to rule over him. Observe how the Lord Himself pressed this fact upon His hearers: "No man can come to Me except the Father which hath sent Me draw him" (Joh 6:44)—but who believes that today when the "free will" of man is so much cried up! "They that be whole need not a physician, but they that are sick" (Mat 9:12). Why should I seek unto the great Physician for strength when I have no consciousness of my weakness, for cleansing while I am quite unaware of my foulness? Only God can subdue our innate pride and self-complacency, and in order thereto there must needs be ardent wrestlings of soul with Him that He would graciously put forth His power and overcome that in me which rises up against Him.

3. He "digs deep" who strives after an experimental and inward knowledge of the Truth. A mere notional or theoretical acquaintance with it will not suffice him. He longs to have a practical knowledge of the Truth so that it becomes deeply rooted within him, so that it finds a home in the "hidden parts" (Psa 51:6). Truth has to be bought (Pro 23:23), and the wise builder is quite willing to pay the necessary price—sacrificing worldly interests so to do. As Spurgeon said, "seek an inwrought experi-

ence of Divine Truth. Ask to have it burnt into you. Why is it that people give up the doctrines of grace if they fall in with eloquent advocates of free will? Why is it they renounce the orthodox creed if they meet with smart reasoners who contradict it? Because they have never received the Word in the power of the Holy Spirit so as to have it sealed in their hearts…It is one thing to have a creed it is quite another thing to have the Truth graven upon the tables of the heart. Many fail here because Truth was never made experimentally their own."

4. He "digs deep" who baulks not at the work of mortification, who follows Christ as the grand Exemplar of mortification. What the Saviour suffered in His pure flesh by way of expiation, those who would be saved must suffer in their corrupt flesh by way of mortification. It is true the flesh in us is reluctant, as was the holy humanity of Christ, saying "let this cup pass from Me," but the spirit is willing, crying "Father, Thy will be done" even in the crucifixion of my dearest lusts. Christ died a violent death, and sin must not die an easy and comfortable one. His body was nailed to the tree till His soul was separated from it, and the body of sin must be so nailed till the soul of sin—the will and love of it—depart. Christ died a tormenting death, in pains and agonies, and we must so die to sin that we "suffer in the flesh" (1Pe 4:1). Christ died a lingering death, and so does sin languish little by little, mortification upon mortification, dying "daily." Alas how few dig deep enough to come to the denying of self!

5. He "digs deep" who endeavours to hide God's Word in his heart so that he may be kept from sinning against Him (Psa 119:11). By "hiding" is not here meant concealing but treasuring, so that it may be preserved. To so "hide" means first, to obtain a spiritual understanding of it—and for that diligence and labour are required (Pro 2:1-4). Only then does "wisdom" enter the heart and knowledge become pleasant unto the soul (Pro 2:10). Second, when it is assented unto by faith, otherwise it will quickly vanish. "The Word preached did not profit them not being mixed with faith in them that heard it" (Heb 4:2). Third, when it is kindly entertained: Christ complained to the Jews "ye seek to kill Me because My word has no place in you" (Joh 8:37). Fourth, when it is deeply rooted, settled in the affections, so that it becomes the "ingrafted Word" (Jam 1:21). The Word must not be studied out of curiosity, or for the object of teaching others, nor for our comfort, but with this prime end in view: that it may deliver us from sin—storing our minds with what is holy, resisting Satan's temptations with an "It is written," its promises sustaining us in times of trial.

6. He "digs deep" who sincerely endeavours to have his heart sensibly affected by the exceeding sinfulness of sin. Since sin be that abominable thing which God hates, that which occasioned the death of Christ, and that which is the cause of all his own misery, the believer seeks to obtain a deep horror for and hatred of sin. To this end he frequently reminds himself and meditates upon the fearful tragedy which the first sin introduced into Eden, how that it corrupted at its source the stream of human nature. He constantly ponders the fact that all the sorrow and suffering in the world are the immediate effects of sin. He essays to view sin in the light of eternal punishment. "When I meet with professors who talk lightly of sin, I feel sure that they have built without a foundation. If they had ever felt the Spirit's wounding and killing sword of conviction, they would flee from sin as from a lion. True forgiven sinners dread the appearance of evil as burnt children dread the fire. Superficial repentance always leads to careless living. Pray earnestly for a broken heart" (Spurgeon).

7. He "digs deep" who makes diligent search and thorough examination within to make sure that God has written His Word on his heart (2Co 13:5; 2Pe 1:10). He is so concerned about his eternal welfare, so aware of the deceitfulness of the human heart, that he dare not take anything for granted. He is determined to "prove" his own self, that a supernatural work of grace has been truly wrought within him. He spares no pains to measure himself by the Word to see whether the fruits of regeneration are really being brought forth in the garden of his soul. He earnestly seeks the Divine assistance in this all-important matter, crying to God, "Examine me, O Lord, and prove me; try my reins and my heart" (Psa 26:2): let me not be mistaken, but graciously make known to me my real condition, and if I be one of Thy redeemed cause Thy blessed Spirit to bear witness with my spirit that I am a child of Thine. And if the seeker be sincere and importunate his quest will not be in vain, neither will his request fall upon deaf ears.

Let us now describe several kinds of "foolish" builders. First, they build on the "sand" whose hope is based upon a round of religious performances. The one who counts upon church-membership, church-attendance, the saying of prayers and the reading of the Bible, as being all that is needed to ensure for him an entrance into the Everlasting Kingdom is resting on a broken reed. That was the case with the pharisees. They fasted and tithed, made long prayers and were most punctilious in attending to ceremonial rites, but they were outside the pale of God's mercy. "Except a man be born again he cannot see the kingdom of God" (Joh 3:3) no matter how zealous he be in attending "communions," how liberal in supporting "missionaries," or how "faithful to the cause." Until I have a heart which receives Christ as my Prophet, Priest and King, which unfeignedly loves Him, which obeys Him, there is no hope for me.

Second, they build on "the sand" whose hope is based on visions, dreams and happy feelings. There is a class in Christendom, larger than some suppose, whose trust reposes in those very things. Ask them to tell you their experience, inquire what ground they have for concluding that God has met with them in saving grace, and they will relate to you some mysterious vision, some remarkable dream, some voice which spoke to them, many years ago, saying "thy sins be forgiven thee," which produced an ecstasy of joy and assurance which nothing can shake. Now we will not positively affirm that they were deluded into imagining such things, yet we would point out that Satan transforms himself as an "angel of light" and can produce remarkable impressions. Whatever remarkable experience you met with in the past, unless you are *now* trusting in the blood and righteousness of Christ and sincerely endeavouring to *perform* His precepts, you are trusting in what will fail you in the Day to come.

Third, they build "on the sand" whose hope is based on a "faith in Christ" which produces no obedience to Him. Unto such He searchingly says, "Why call ye Me, Lord, Lord, and do not the things which I say?" (Luk 6:46). A mere intellectual assent to the Gospel or a belief in the historical Christ is worthless, for it brings forth no spiritual fruits. To hear and acquiesce and then perform not is a mocking of God. As there were many who "believed in His name when they saw the miracles which He did" to whom the Saviour *"did not* commit Himself" (Joh 2:23,24), so there are thousands today who non-savingly "believe in Christ" yet have not "the root of the matter" (Job 19:28) within them. The faith of God's elect is one which in a vital and practical way is "the acknowledging the Truth which is after godliness" (Tit 1:1), which issues in "purifying the heart" (Act 15:9), which "worketh by love" (Gal 5:6) and which "overcometh the world" (1Jo 5:4). Only *such* a faith will suffice for time and eternity.

Fourth, they build "on the sand" whose hope rests on a merely intellectual knowledge of the Truth. The difference between theoretical and practical knowledge is one both of kind and of degree. Theoretical knowledge is fluctuating and evanescent, constantly subject to alteration; but practical knowledge is deep-rooted and permanent. Once I have experienced the burning effects of fire no sophistical arguments can persuade me it is harmless. Once I have tasted that the Lord is gracious none can convince me that He is not. The difference between the two is apparent also from the effects produced. Pilate had a theoretical knowledge that it was contrary to the evidence before him to condemn Christ to death, but when the issue of his own interests with Caesar was raised (Joh 19:12) his practical judgment determined him to save his prestige. One who has a theoretical acquaintance with the precepts may talk well about them, but only one with a practical knowledge will walk according to them. One with a theoretical knowledge of the Truth may admire it, but only one with a practical knowledge thereof would die for it.

Fifth, they build "on the sand" who make not conscience of confessing sin. There is a radical difference between the unregenerate and the regenerate in this matter. The former, being dead toward God and having but light thoughts upon sin, are not weighed down by it; but to the latter it is their heaviest burden, and therefore are they thankful to unbosom themselves unto the Lord. Christ has bidden them pray to their Father "forgive us our sins" (Luk 11:4). Scripture warns them "he that covereth his sins shall not prosper" (Pro 28:13), and so David proved: "When I kept silence; my bones waxed old through my roaring all the day long"; but eventually he said "I will confess my transgressions unto the Lord, and Thou forgavest the iniquity of my sin" (Psa 32:3,5). After his sad fall, Peter went out and "wept bitterly." Read through the second half of Romans 7 and observe how keenly distressed Paul was by indwelling corruption. The believer has a sensitive conscience and keeps short accounts with God; but the conscience of the unbeliever is calloused, and he neither mourns over nor confesses his sins.

To sum up. No matter what experience I have had, or what be the character and strength of my faith, or how deep and steady be my assurance, or how eminent my gifts, unless any or all of these issue in a life of practical obedience to Christ they will avail nothing when death overtakes me. And that is no harsh verdict of ours, but the decision of the Son of God: "Everyone that heareth these sayings of Mine, and *doeth them not*, shall be likened unto a foolish man who built his house upon the sand." Not that the Christian will "do" them perfectly—"for in many things we all offend" (Jam 3:2)—though he ought to, and must not excuse but rather mourn over and confess his failure. No, the obedience of the Christian is not a faultless one, yet it is real and actual. It is not flawless, yet it is sincere. It is the genuine desire, resolution and endeavour of the Christian to please Christ in *all* things, and it is his greatest grief when he displeases Him. Lord, "*Make me to go* in the path of Thy commandments, for therein do I delight" (Psa 119:35). —AWP

THE MISSION AND MIRACLES OF ELISHA
10. Seventh Miracle

"And the woman conceived, and bare a son at that season that Elisha had said unto her, according to the time of life" (2Ki 4:17). As Matthew Henry pointed out, "We may well suppose, after the birth of this son, that the prophet was doubly welcome to the good Shunammite: he had thought himself indebted to her, but from henceforth, as long as she lives, she will think herself in his debt, and that she can never do too much for him. We may also suppose that, the child was very dear to the prophet, as the son of his prayers, and very dear to the parents as the son of their old age." What is more attractive than a properly trained and well behaved child! And what is more objectionable than a spoilt and naughty one? From all that is revealed of this "great woman" we cannot doubt that she brought up her boy wisely and well, that he added to the delightfulness of her home, that he was a pleasure and not a trial to visitors. Alas that there are so few of her type now left. Godly and well-conducted homes are the choicest asset which any nation possesses.

"And when the child was grown, it fell on a day that he went out to his father to the reapers" (v 18). The opening clause does not signify that he was now a fully-developed youth, but that he had passed out of infancy into childhood. This is quite obvious from a number of things in the sequel. When he was taken ill, a "lad" carried him back home (v 19); for some time he "sat on her knees" (v 20), and later she—apparently unaided—carried him upstairs and laid him on the prophet's bed (v 21). Yet the child had grown sufficiently so as to be able to run about and be allowed to visit his father in the harvest field. While there he was suddenly stricken with an ailment, for "he said unto his father, My head, my head!" (v 19). It is hardly likely that this was caused by a sunstroke, for it occurred in the morning, a while before noon. Seemingly the father did not suspect anything serious, for instead of carrying him home in his own arms, he sent him back by one of his younger workers. How incapable we are of fore-seeing what even the next hour may bring forth!

"And when he had taken him and brought him to his mother, he sat on her knees till noon" (v 20). What a lovely picture of maternal devotion! How thankful should each one be who cherishes the tender memories of a mother's love, for there are tens of thousands in this country who were born of parents devoid of natural affection, who cared more for the public house and the movies than for their offspring. But powerful as true mother love is, it is impotent when the grim reaper draws near, for our verse adds "and then died." Death strikes down the young as well as the old, as the tombstones in our cemeteries bear ample witness. Sometimes he gives more or less protracted notice of his gruesome approach, at others, as here, he smites with scarcely any warning. How this fact ought to influence each of us!—to put it on its lowest ground, how foolish to make an idol of one who may be snatched away at any moment. With what a light hand should we grasp all earthly objects. Here, then, is first, *the occasion* of this miracle: the death of the child.

Second, a word upon *its mystery*. How often the Lord's dealings seem to us as passing strange. Hopes suddenly blighted, prospects swiftly changed, loved ones snatched away. "All flesh is grass" (Isa 40:6), and that "today is and tomorrow is cast into the oven" (Mat 6:30). Thus it was here. The babe had survived the dangers incident to infancy, only to be cut down in childhood. That morning apparently full of life and health, trotting merrily off to the harvest field: at noon a corpse on his mother's knee. But in her case such a visitation was additionally inexplicable. The boy had been given to her by the Divine bounty because of the kindness she had shown to one of God's servants, and now, to carnal reason, it looked as though He was dealing most unkindly with her. A miracle had been wrought in bestowing the child and now that miracle is neutralized. Yes, God's ways are frequently "a great deep" unto human intelligence: yet let the Christian never forget, those ways are ever ordered by infinite love and wisdom.

It is indeed most blessed to observe how this stricken mother conducted herself under her unexpected and severe trial. Here, as throughout the whole of this chapter, her moral and spiritual greatness shines forth. There was no wringing her hands in despair, no giving way to inordinate grief. Nor was there any murmuring at Providence, any complaint that God had ceased to be gracious unto her. It is in such crises and by their demeanour under them that the children of God and the children of the Devil are manifest. We do not say that the former always conduct themselves as the great woman, yet they sorrow not as do others who have no hope. They may be staggered and stunned by a crushing affliction, but they do not give way to an evil heart of unbelief and become avowed infidels. There may be stirrings of rebellion within, and Satan will seek to foster hard thoughts against God, but he cannot induce them to curse Him and commit suicide. Divine grace is a glorious reality, and in his measure every Christian is given to prove the sufficiency of it in times of stress and trial.

Third, *its expectation*. "And she went up and laid him on the bed of the man of God, and shut the door upon him, and went out" (v 21). This must be pondered in the light of her subsequent actions if we are to perceive the meaning of her conduct here. There was definite purpose on her part, and in view of what immediately follows it seems clear that these were the actions of faith. She cherished the hope that the prophet would restore her son unto her. She made no preparations for the burial of the child, but anticipated his resurrection by laying him upon Elisha's bed. Her faith clung to the original blessing God, by the prophet's promise and prayers, had given him unto her, and now she takes the dead child to God (as it were) and goes to seek the prophet. Her faith might be tried even to the straining point, but in that extremity she interpreted the inexplicable dealings of God by those dealings she was sure of, reasoning from the past to the future, from the known to the unknown. The child had been given unto her unasked, and she refused to believe it had now been irrecoverably taken away from her.

Her faith was indeed put to a severe test, for not only was her child dead but at the very time she seemed to need him the most, Elisha was many miles away! Ah, that was no "accident" but wisely and graciously ordered by God. How so? That there might be fuller opportunity for bringing forth the evidences and fruits of faith: a faith which does not triumph over discouragement and difficulties is not worth much. The Lord often causes our 'circumstances' to be most 'unfavourable' in order that faith may have the freer play and rise above them. Such was the case here. Elisha might be absent, but she could go to him. Most probably she had heard of the raising of the widow's son, Zarephath (1Ki 17:23) by Elijah, and she knew that the spirit of Elijah now rested on Elisha (2Ki 2:15), and therefore with steadfast confidence she determined to seek him.

That she *did* act in faith is clear from Hebrews 11:35, for that chapter which chronicles the achievements of faith of the OT saints says "through *faith*...women received their dead raised to life again"—there were but two who did so, and the "great woman" of Shunem was one of them.

"And she called unto her husband and said, send me I pray thee one of the young men, and one of the asses, that I may run to the man of God, and come again" (v 22). While faith triumphs over difficulties, it does not act unbecomingly by forcing a way through them and setting aside the requirements of propriety. Urgent as the situation was, yet she did not rush away without informing her husband of her intention. The wife should have no secrets from her partner, but take him fully into her confidence: failure at this point leads to suspicions, and where they exist love is soon chilled. Nor did this stricken mother content herself with scribbling a hurried note, telling her husband to expect her return within a day or so. No, once again she took her proper place and owned her subjection to him: though she made known to him her desire, she demanded nothing, but respectfully sought his permission, as her "I pray thee" plainly shows. Faith is bold and venturesome, but it does not act unseemly and insubordinately.

"It is happy and comely when harmony prevails in domestic life: when the husband's authority is tempered with affection, and unsuspecting confidence; when the wife answers that confidence with deference and submission, as well as fidelity, and when each party consults the other's inclinations, and both unite in attending on the ordinances of God and supporting His cause" (Thomas Scott). But such happiness and harmony is attainable and obtainable only as both husband and wife seek grace from God to walk in obedience to His precepts, and as family worship is duly maintained. If the wife suffers herself to be influenced by the very *un-*'feminine' spirit which is now so rife in the world and refuses to own the lordship of her husband (1Pe 3:6), or if the husband acts as a tyrant and bully, failing to love, nourish and cherish his wife (Eph 5:25,29) and "giving honour unto the wife as unto the weaker vessel" (1Pe 3:7), then the smile of God will be forfeited, their prayers will be "hindered," and strife and misery will prevail in the home.

"And he said, Wherefore wilt thou go to him today? it is neither new moon nor Sabbath. And she said, It shall be well" (v 23). While admiring *her* virtues, her husband appears in a much less favourable light. His question might suggest that he was still ignorant of the death of his son, yet that scarcely seems likely. If he had made no inquiry about the child he must have been strangely lacking in tender regard for him, and his wife's desire to undertake an arduous journey at such a time ought to have informed him that some serious emergency had arisen. It is difficult to escape the conclusion that his language was more an expression of irritability, that he resented being left alone in his grief. At any rate, his words served to throw light upon another praiseworthy trait in his wife: that it was her custom to attend the prophet's services on the feast days and the Sabbath. Though a "great woman" she did not disdain those unpretentious meetings on mount Carmel. No genuine Christian, however wealthy or high his station, will consider it beneath him to meet with his poorer brethren and sisters.

Those words of her husband's may be considered from another angle, namely, as a further testing of her faith. Even where the deepest affection obtains between husband and wife there is not always spiritual equality, no, not even where they are one in the Lord. One may steadily grow in grace, while the other makes little or no progress. One may enter more deeply into an experimental acquaintance with the Truth, which the other is incapable of understanding and discussing. One may be given a much increased measure of faith without the other being similarly blest. None can walk by the faith of another, and it is well for those of strong faith to remember that. Certainly there was no cooperation of faith in this instance: rather did the husband of our "great woman" seem to discourage than encourage her. She might have reasoned with herself, perhaps this is an intimation from God that I should not seek unto Elisha: but faith would argue, this is but a further testing of me, and since my reliance is in the Lord I will neither be daunted nor deterred. It is by our reactions to such testings that the reality and strength of our faith is made evident. Faith must not expect a smooth and easy path.

"And she said, It shall be well": that was the language of firm and unshaken confidence. "Then she saddled an ass, and said to her servant, Drive and go forward, slack not thy riding for me, except I bid thee" (v 24). Her husband certainly does not shine here. Had he discharged the duties of love *he* had undertaken this tiring journey instead of his wife, or at the very least offered to accompany her. But he would not exert himself enough to saddle the ass for her, but left her to do that. How selfish many husbands are! how slack in bearing or at least sharing their wives' burdens! Marriage is a partnership or it is nothing except in name, and the man who allows his wife to become a drudge and does little or nothing to make her lot lighter and brighter in the home, is not worthy to be called "husband." Nor is it any sufficient reply to say, It is only lack of thought on his part: inconsiderateness and selfishness are synonymous terms, for unselfishness consists largely in thoughtfulness of others. The best that can be said for this man is that he did not actually forbid his wife starting out for Carmel.

We know not how far distant Shunem was from Carmel, but it appears that the journey was a considerable and hard one—in a mountainous country. But love is not quenched by hardships and faith is not rendered inoperative by difficulties, and in the case of this mother both of these graces were operative within her. Love can brook no delay and thinks not of personal discomfort as her language to the servant shows. It is also the nature of faith to be speedy and look for quick results—patience is a distinct virtue which is only developed by much hard schooling. An intense earnestness possessed the soul of this woman, and where such earnestness is joined with faith it refuses a denial. While our faith remains a merely mental and mechanical thing it achieves nothing, but when it is intense and fervent it will produce results. True, it requires a deep sense of need, often the pressure of an urgent situation to evoke this earnestness, and that is why faith flourishes most in times of stress and trial, for it then has its most suitable opportunity to declare itself.

"So she went and came unto the man of God to mount Carmel. And it came to pass, when the man of God saw her afar off, that he said to Gehazi his servant, Behold, yonder is that Shunammite" (v 25). There are several things of importance to be noticed here. First, like his predecessor, Elisha was the man of the mount: 2:25—symbolical of his spiritual elevation, his affections set upon things above. Second, but mark how he conducts himself not in haughty pride of fancied self-superiority: he waited not for the woman to reach him, but dispatched his servant to meet her, thereby evidencing his solicitude. Third, was it not a gracious token from the Lord to cheer her heart near the close of a trying journey: how "tender" are God's mercies. Fourth, "that Sunammite" denotes either that she was the only pious person in that place or that she so over-towered her brethren and sisters in spirituality that such an appellation was quite sufficient for the purpose of identification.

"Run now, I pray thee, to meet her, and say unto her, Is it well with thee? is it well with thy husband? is it well with the child? And she answered, It is well" (v 26). Incidentally, this shows that younger men engaged in the Lord's service and occupying lowlier positions are required to execute commissions from their seniors: compare 2 Timothy 4:11-13. We do not regard the woman's "it is well" as expressing her resignation to the sovereign will of God, but rather as the language of trustful expectation. She seems to have had no doubt whatever about the outcome of her errand. It appears to us that, throughout the whole of this incident, the "great woman" regarded the death of her child as a trial of faith. Her "it is well" looked beyond the clouds and anticipated the happy issue. Surely we must exclaim, O woman, great is thy faith. Yes, and great too was its reward, for God never puts to confusion those who really count upon Him showing Himself strong on their behalf. Let us not forget that this incident is recorded for *our* learning and encouragement.

"And when she came to the man of God to the hill, she caught him by the feet: but Gehazi came near to thrust her away. And the man of God said, Let her alone, for her soul is vexed within her, and the Lord hath hid it from me and hath not told me" (v 27). Our minds at once revert to the two women who visited the Lord's sepulchre and when He eventually met them saying, All hail "came and held Him by the feet and worshipped Him" (Mat 28:9). In the case before us, the "great woman" appears to have (rightly) viewed Elisha as the ambassador of God, and to have humbly signified that she had a favour to ask of him. In the rebuffing from Gehazi we see how her faith met with yet another trial. And then the Lord tenderly interposed through His servant and rebuked the officious attendant. The Lord was accustomed to reveal His secrets unto the prophets (Amo 3:7), but until He did so *they* were as ignorant and as dependent upon Him as others, as this incident plainly shows.

Here was still a further test of faith: the prophet himself was in the dark, unprepared for her startling request. But the Lord has just as good a reason for concealing as for revealing. In the case before us it is not difficult to perceive why He had withheld from Elisha all knowledge of the child's death: He would have him learn from the mother herself, and that, that she might avow her faith. "Then she said, Did I desire a son of my lord? did I not say, Do not deceive me?" (v 28). Those were powerful arguments to move Elisha to act on her behalf. "As she did not impatiently desire children, she could not think that her son had been given her, without solicitation, merely to become the occasion of her far deeper distress" (T. Scott). The second question evidenced that her dependence was entirely upon the word of God through His servant: "However the providence of God may disappoint us, we may be sure the promise of God never did, nor ever will deceive us: hope in *that* will not make us ashamed" (Matthew Henry). And here we must pause. —AWP

DOCTRINE OF SAINTS' PERSEVERANCE
9b. Its Opposition

4. By declaring it *neutralises the force of exhortations*. The argument used by Arminians on this point may be fairly stated thus: if it be absolutely certain that all regenerated souls will reach Heaven then there can be no real need to bid them tread the path that leads thither, that in such case it is meaningless to urge them to run with patience the race set before them; but since God *has* uttered such calls to His people, then it follows that their final perseverance is by no means sure, the less so seeing that failure to heed those calls is threatened with eternal death. It is insisted upon that exhortations to effort, watchfulness, diligence etc., clearly imply the contingency of the believer's salvation, that all such calls to the discharge of these duties signify that security is conditional upon his own fidelity, upon the response which he makes unto these demands of God upon him. It should be a sufficient reply to point out that if this objection were really valid then no Christian could have any firm persuasion of his everlasting bliss so long as he was left upon earth: hence the inference drawn by Arminians from the exhortations must be an erroneous one.

What strange logic is this: because I am persuaded that God loves me with an unchanging and unquenchable love therefore I feel free to trample upon His revealed will, and have no concern whether my conduct pleases or displeases Him. Because I am assured that Christ, at the cost of unparalleled shame and suffering, purchased for me eternal redemption, an inalienable inheritance, therefore I am encouraged to forsake instead of to follow Him, vilify rather than glorify Him. That might be the theology of devils, and those they possess, but it would be repudiated and abhorred by any one renewed by the Holy Spirit. How preposterous to argue that because a person believes he shall persevere to the end, that he will therefore despise and neglect everything that promotes such perseverance. Such an argument as the above is tantamount to saying that because God has regenerated a soul He now requires no obedience from him, whereas one of the chief ends for which he is renewed is to capacitate him for obedience, that he may be conformed to the image of His son.

So far from the absolute promises of God concerning the everlasting safety of His people weakening the force of motives to righteousness, they are the very means made use of by the Spirit to stir up the saints, and to encourage them in the practice of righteousness and engage them in the continuance thereof. Most certainly the apostles perceived no inconsistency or incongruity between the Divine promises and the precepts. They did not judge it meaningless to argue from such blessed assurances to the performance of the duties of holiness. One of them said "Having therefore these promises, dearly beloved, let us cleanse ourselves from all filthiness of the flesh and spirit, perfecting holiness in the fear of God" (2Co 7:1). Those promises were, "I will dwell in them and walk in them, and I will be their God and they shall be My people: I will be a Father unto you and ye shall be My sons and daughters"(6:16, 18), and on them he based his exhortation. After saying, ye "are kept by the power of God through faith unto salvation" another apostle proceeded to urge, "Wherefore gird up the loins of your mind, be sober and hope to the end...And if ye call on the Father...possess the time of your sojourning here in fear" (1Pe 1:5, 13, 17)—apparently it never occurred to him that such exhortations had been neutralised or even weakened by the doctrine before advanced.

5. *By appealing to cases* and examples which, though plausible, are quite inconclusive. In order to prove their contention that a real child of God may so backslide as to lose all relish for spiritual things, renounce his profession and die an infidel, Arminians are fond of referring to alleged illustrations of this very thing. They will point to certain men and women who have come before their own observation, people who were genuinely and deeply convicted of sin, who earnestly sought relief from a burdened conscience, who eventually believed the Gospel, put their faith in the atoning blood of Christ and found rest unto their souls. They will tell of the bright profession made by these people, of the peace and joy which was theirs, of the radical change made in their lives, and how they united with the church, had blessed fellowship with the saints, lifted up their voices in praise and petition at the prayer meetings, were diligent in speaking to their companions of their eternal welfare, how they walked in the paths of righteousness and caused the saints to thank God for such transformed lives. But alas these bright meteors in the religious firmament soon faded out.

It is at this point that the Arminian seeks to make capital out of such cases. He tells of how, perhaps in a few months, the religious ardour of these "converts" cooled off. He relates how the temptations of the world and lusts of the flesh proved too strong for them, and how like dogs they returned to their vomit. The Arminian then alleges that such cases are actual examples of men and women who have "fallen from grace," who have apostatized from the faith, and by appealing to such he imagines he has succeeded in overthrowing the doctrine of the final perseverance of the saints. In reality, he has done nothing of the sort. He has merely shown how easily Christians may be mistaken, and thus pointed a warning for us not to be too ready to indulge in wishful thinking and imagining all is gold which glitters. Scripture plainly warns us there is a class whose "goodness is as a morning cloud and as the early dew it goeth away" (Hos 6:4). Christ has told us of those who received the Word with joy, yet had not root in themselves (Mat 13:20,21). The foolish virgins carried the lamp of their profession, but they had no oil in their vessels. One may come "near" to the kingdom yet never enter it (Mar 12:34).

In order to make good his objection the Arminian must do something more than point to those who made a credible profession and afterwards falsified and renounced it: he must prove that a person who is truly regenerated, born from above, made a new creature in Christ, then apostatised and died an apostate. This he cannot possibly do, for none such ever existed or ever will. The fact is that while there are many who, in varying degrees, adopt the Christian religion, there are very few indeed who are ever born of the Spirit, and the *only* way in which we may *identify* the latter is by their *continuance in holiness*. He who does not persevere to the end was never begotten by God. Nor is that statement a begging of the question at issue: it is insisting upon the teaching of Holy Writ. "The righteous also shall hold on his way" (Job 17:9): observe that it is not "he ought to" nor merely that "he may do so," but a positive and unqualified "shall." Therefore any one who fails to "hold on his way," be he a religious enthusiast, a professing Christian, or zealous church-member, was never "righteous" in the sight of God.

We will labour this point a little further because it is probably the one which has presented more difficulty to our readers than any other. Yet it should not, for when resolved by the Word all is clear as a sunbeam. "I know that whatsoever God doeth, it shall be *forever*: nothing can be put to it nor anything taken from it: and God doeth it, that men should fear before Him" (Ecc 3:14). This is one of the distinctive marks of the Divine handiwork: its indestructibility, its permanency, and therefore it is by *this* mark we must test both ourselves and our fellows. "The orthodox doctrine does not affirm the certainty of salvation because we once believed, but certainty of perseverance in holiness if we have truly believed, which perseverance in holiness, therefore, in opposition to all weaknesses and temptations, is the only sure evidence of the genuineness of past experience or of the validity of our confidence as to our future salvation" (A. A. Hodge). "Whosoever liveth and believeth in Me shall never die" (Joh 11:26) said Christ, for the life that He giveth is an "eternal" one, which the Devil himself cannot destroy (see Job 2:6!). Thus, unless we acknowledge our mistake in concluding the apostates were once regenerate, we give the lie to the Word of God.

6. By asserting that this doctrine *makes all warnings and threatenings pointless*. Arminians argue that if the believer be eternally secure in Christ he cannot be in any peril, and that to caution him against danger is a meaningless performance. First, let it be said that we have no quarrel with those who insist that most solemn warnings and awful threatenings *are* addressed immediately to the children of God, nor have we the least accord with those who seek to blunt the point of those warnings and explain away those threatenings: so far from it, in both the June and August articles of this series we have shown that God Himself has safeguarded the truth of the final perseverance of His people by these very measures, and have insisted there are very real dangers they must guard against and genuine threatenings they are required to heed. So long as the Christian is left in this world he is beset by deadly dangers, both from within and from without, and it would be the part of madness to ignore and trifle with them. It is faith's recognition of the same which causes him to cry out "Hold Thou me up, and I shall be safe"(Psa 119:117).

Yet what we have just admitted above in no way concedes that there is any conflict between the promises and warnings of God: that the one assures of preservation while the other forecasts destruction. For what is it that God has promised unto His people? This: that they "shall not depart from Him" (Jer 32:40), that they shall "hold on their way" (Job 17:9), and that to this end He will "work in them both to will and to do of His good pleasure" (Phi 2:13), granting unto them all-sufficient grace (2Co 12:9), and supplying all their need (Phi 4:19). In perfect accord with these promises are the warnings and threatenings addressed to them, by which God has made known the inseparable connection there is, by His appointment, between a course of evil and the punishment attending the same. Those very threatenings are used by the Spirit to produce in Christians a holy circumspection and caution, so that they are made the means of preventing their apostacy. Those warnings have their proper use, and efficacy in respect of the saints, for they cause them to take heed to their ways, avoid the snares laid for them, and serve to establish their souls in the practice of obedience.

Whether or not we can perceive the consistency between the assurances God has made His people and the grounds He has given them to tremble at His Word, between the comforting promises and the stirring exhortations, between the witnesses to their safety and the warnings of their danger, certain it is that Scripture abounds with the one as much as with the other. If on the one hand the Christian is warranted in being fully persuaded that "neither principalities nor powers" shall be able to separate him from the love of God in Christ Jesus, and that God shall tread Satan under his feet shortly (Rom 8:38,39; 16:20): on the other hand, he is bidden to "put on the whole armour of God, that ye may be able to stand against the wiles of the Devil. For we wrestle not against flesh and blood, but against principalities and powers" (Eph 6:12,13), and "Be sober, be vigilant, because your adversary the Devil, as a roaring lion, walketh about seeking whom he may devour" (1Pe 5:8). Yet though the believer is warned "Let him that thinketh he standeth take heed lest he fall," it is immediately followed by the declaration "but God is faithful, who will not suffer you to be tempted above that ye are able" (1Co 10:12,13). Then let us beware of being wise in our own conceit and charging the Almighty with folly.

Because the enemies of the Christian are inveterate, subtle, and powerful, and the exercise of his graces inconstant, it is salutary that he should live under a continual remembrance of his weakness, fickleness and danger. He needs to be ever watchful and prayerful lest he enter into temptation, recalling what befell the self-confident Peter. Because indwelling corruption remains a part of himself, while he is left in this scene, it behooves him to keep his heart with all diligence, for he who trusteth in his own heart is a fool (Pro 28:26), unmindful of his best interests. We are only preserved from presumption while a real sense of our own insufficiency is retained. The consciousness of indwelling sin should cause every child of God to bend the suppliant knee with the utmost frequency, humility and fervour. Let not the Christian mistake the field of battle for a bed of rest. Let him not indulge in a slothful profession or carnal delights, while his implacable foes, the flesh, the world, and the devil are ever seeking to encompass his ruin. Let him heed the warnings of a faithful God and he will prove Him to be an unerring Guide and invincible Guard.

7. *By drawing a false inference from the Divine righteousness.* Arminians are fond of quoting that "God is no respecter of persons," from which they argue that His justice requires Him to apportion the same retribution unto sinning Christians as He does unto non-Christians who transgress; and since our doctrine gives no place to the eternal punishment of a saint, it is said we charge God with partiality and injustice. That the Lord "is righteous in all His ways and holy in all His works" (Psa 145:17) is contended for as earnestly for by us as by our opponents; but what the Arminian denies is maintained by the Calvinist, and that is, the absolute sovereignty of God. That the Most High is obliged to apportion equal punishment to equal faults and equal rewards to equal deservings, cannot be allowed for a moment. Being above all law, the Framer and not the subject of it, God's will is supreme, and He doeth whatsoever pleaseth Him. If God bestows free grace and pardoning mercy to those in Christ and withholds it from those out of Christ, who shall say unto Him, What doest Thou? Has He not the right to do what He chooses with His own: to give a penny to him who labors all day and the same to him that works but one hour (Mat 20:12-15)!

To argue that because God is no respecter of persons that therefore He must deal with Christians and non-Christians alike is to ignore the special case of the former. They sustain a nearer relation to Him than do the latter. Shall a parent treat a refractory child as he would an insubordinate employee—he would dismiss the one from his service, must he turn the other out of his home? The Scriptures teach that God the Father is tender to His own dear children, recovering them from their sins and healing their backslidings, while He suffers aliens to lie wallowing in their rebellions and pollutions all their lives. Furthermore a Surety stood for them and endured in their stead the utmost rigor of the Law's sentence, so that God is perfectly righteous in remitting their sins. Nevertheless, so that they may know He does not look lightly upon their disobedience, He "visits their transgressions with the rod and their iniquity with stripes" (Psa 89:32). Finally, they are brought to sincere repentance, confession, and forsaking of their sins, and thereby they obtain the relief provided for them, which is never the case with the children of the Devil.

8. By alleging our doctrine makes its believers *proud and presumptuous*. That the carnal may wrest this doctrine, like other portions of the Truth, to their own destruction, is freely admitted (2 Peter 3:16); but that any article of the Faith which God has delivered unto His saints has the least tendency unto evil, we indignantly deny. In reality, the doctrine of the saints' perseverance in holiness, in humble dependence upon God for supplies of grace, lays the axe at the very root of the proud and presumptuous conceits of men, for it casts down their high thoughts and towering imaginations concerning their own native ability to believe the Gospel, obey its precepts, and continue in the faith and practice thereof. We rest wholly on the goodness and faithfulness of God, the merits of Christ's blood and the efficacy of His intercession, the power and operations of the Spirit, having "no confidence in the flesh" (Phi 3:3). Only the Day to come will reveal how many who "trusted in themselves" and were persuaded of their inherent power to turn unto God and keep His commandments, were thereby hardened and hastened to their eternal ruin.

Let any candid reader ponder the following question. Which is the more likely to promote pride and presumption: extolling the virtues and sufficiency of man's "free-will," or emphasizing our utter dependence upon God's free grace? Which is more apt to foster self-confidence and self-righteousness: the Arminian tenet that fallen man has the power within himself to turn unto God when he chooses and do those things which are pleasing in His sight, or the Calvinist's insistence upon the declarations of Scripture that even the Christian has no strength of his own, that apart from Christ he can "do nothing" (Joh 15:5), that we are "not sufficient of ourselves" to so much as "think anything as of ourselves" (2Co 3:5), that "all our springs" are in God (Psa 87:7), and that because of our felt weakness and acknowledged helplessness, God graciously keeps our feet and preserves us from destruction? It is just because our doctrine is so flesh-abasing and pride-mortifying that it is so bitterly detested and decried by the pharisees.

9. By pretending our doctrine *renders the use of means superfluous*. If Christians are secure in the hand of God and He empowers them by His Spirit, why should they put forth their energies to preserve themselves? But such reasoning leaves out of account that, throughout, God deals with His people as moral agents and accountable creatures. Rightly did Calvin point out, "He who has fixed the limits of our life, has also entrusted us with the care of it; has furnished us with means and supplies for its preservation; has also made us provident of dangers, and, that they may not oppress us unawares, has furnished us with cautions and remedies. Thus it is evident what is our duty." Grace is not given to render our efforts needless but to make them effectual. To say that assurance of final salvation cuts the nerve of enterprise is contrary to all experience: who will work the harder, the man without hope or even a half-expectation, or one who is sure that success will crown his labors.

10. By arguing that our doctrine *makes "rewards" meaningless*. If it be God who preserves us, then there is no room left for the recognition of our fidelity or owning of

our efforts. If there be no possibility of the saint falling away finally, then is his perseverance incapable of reward by God. Answer: Heaven is not something which the Christian earns by his obedience or merits by his fidelity, nevertheless, everlasting felicity is held before him as a gracious encouragement, as the goal of his obedience. Let it be recognized that the reward is not a legal one but rather one of bounty, in accord with the tenor of the Covenant of Grace, and all difficulty should vanish. Let this point be decided in the light of our Surety's experience: was it not impossible that Christ should fail of His obedience? yet did not God reward Him (Phi 2:9-11)! So, in our tiny measure, because of the "joy set before us" we despise our cross and endure suffering for Christ's sake.

And now a word by way of application. Since this article of Faith be so much criticised and condemned as a thing fraught with evil tendencies, let the Christian make it his studied business that his conduct gives the lie to the Arminian's objections. Let him make it his constant concern to "adorn the doctrine of God our Savior in all things" (Tit 2:10), by taking heed to his ways, giving no licence to the flesh, attending to the Divine warnings, and rendering glad and full response to His exhortations. Let him show forth by his daily life that this preservation is a continuance in faith, in obedience, in holiness. Let him see to it that he evidences the reality of his profession and the spirituality of his creed by growing in grace and bringing forth the fruits of righteousness. Let him earnestly endeavour to keep himself in the love of God, and to that end avoid everything calculated to chill the same, and thereby he will most effectually "put to silence the ignorance of foolish men" (1Pe 2:15). —AWP

REWARDS

To the infidel much in the Scriptures seems so inconsistent and inharmonious that he charges them with "abounding in contradictions." That there should be no variableness or shadow of turning with God, yet that He is frequently said to "repent"; that He claims to be omnipotent and invincible, yet complains "ye have set at nought all My counsel" (Pro 1:25); that He is love, yet abhors the wicked (Psa 5:6); that He is of tender mercy, yet has appointed an eternity of torment for all those whose names are not written in the book of life—to mention no others— appear to the sceptic as irreconcilable teachings. To the natural man the Christian life appears to be a mass of bewildering paradoxes. That the poor in spirit and those who mourn should be pronounced happy, that we have to be made fools in order to become wise, that it is when we are weak we are strong, that we must lose our life in order to save it (Mat 16:25), and that we are bidden to "rejoice with trembling" (Psa 2:11) transcend his comprehension. Yet none of these things present any insuperable difficulty unto those who are taught of God.

In like manner there is not a little in the teaching of Holy Writ which perplexes the theologian. As he studies and ponders its declarations, one doctrine—for a time, at least—seems to clash with another. If God has predestinated whatsoever cometh to pass, then what room is left for the discharge of human responsibility and free agency? If the Fall has deprived man of all spiritual strength, then how can he be held blameworthy for failing to perform spiritual duties? If Christ died for the elect only, then how can He be offered freely to "every creature"? If the believer be Christ's "freeman," then why is he required to take upon him His "yoke"? If he has been set at "liberty" (Gal 5:1) then how can he be "under the Law" (1Co 9:21). If the believer be preserved by God, then how can his own perseverance be necessary in order to the attainment of everlasting bliss? if he be secure, how can he be in danger? If he has been delivered from the power of darkness and translated into the kingdom of God's dear Son, why does he so often have occasion to cry "O wretched man that I am"? If sin does not have dominion over him, why do "iniquities prevail against" him (Psa 65:3)? Real problems are these.

We have commenced this article thus because the subject which is here to engage our attention seems to many to clash with other articles of the Faith. In ordinary speech the word "reward" signifies the recognition and requital of a meritorious performance, the bestowment of something to which a person is justly entitled. But what can the creature merit at the hands of the Creator, to what—save disapprobation and punishment—is a sinful creature entitled from a holy God? If salvation be "by grace" and eternal life is a "free gift" then what place is left for the recompensing of human effort? Yet whatever difficulties may be involved, the fact remains that Scripture has not a little to say about God's rewarding the obedient and crowning the overcomer. The Dispensationalists (among them most of the so-called "Fundamentalists") have realized there is a knot here, but instead of patiently seeking to untie they have summarily cut it, by asserting that rewards have a place only under the Legal Dispensation and are entirely excluded from the Age of Grace; yet the very Epistles which, as they allow, belong to the present Era, contain many passages postulating "rewards." Verily, "the legs of the lame are not equal" (Pro 26:7).

Our present subject is by no means a simple one, and certainly it is not suited for a novice to take up and descant upon. Not that the teaching of Scripture thereon is at all obscure or hard to be understood, but rather that much wisdom is needed in the *handling of it*, so as to avoid conveying false impressions, weakening the force of other articles of the Faith, and failing to preserve the balance of the Truth. Very little attention was given to the subject of Divine rewards either by the Reformers or the Puritans (less by the latter than the former)—probably they felt that most of their energies needed to be devoted unto counteracting the evil leaven of Romanism, with its strong emphasis upon creature "merits" and salvation by works. Yet in avoiding one error there is always the danger of going to the opposite, and even where that is avoided, it is usually at the price of depriving God's children of some portion of their needed and Divinely-provided Bread. Whatever be the explanation, the fact remains that our present theme is a much-neglected one for comparatively little has been said or written upon it. We are therefore the more cast back upon God for help.

The servant of God must not suffer the fear of man to muzzle him, as he will if he deems it wisest to remain silent on the subject lest he be charged with "leanings towards Romanism": *their* very perversion of this truth renders it all the more necessary and urgent that *he* should give a plain and positive exposition of the same. On the other hand, the fact that Papists have so grievously wrested it should warn him that great care needs to be exercised in the way he presents it. He needs to make it crystal clear that it is utterly impossible to bring God under obligation to us or make Him in any wise our Debtor. In like manner it must be shown that the creature cannot acquire any merit by the most self-sacrificing or benevolent deeds he performs. By so doing he will preclude the laying of any foundation for pharisaic pride. Nevertheless, he must see to it that he does not so whittle away the passages holding up "rewards" to believers, as to render them meaningless and valueless, for they are among the motives, encouragements, incentives, and consolations which God sets before His people.

In a brief and incidental statement upon this doctrine Calvin beautifully preserved the balance when in his "Institutes" (bk. 3, chap. 15) he said: "The Scripture shows *what* all our works are capable of meriting, when it represents them as unable to bear the Divine scrutiny, because they are full of impurity; and in the next place, what would be merited by the perfect observance of the Law, if this could anywhere be found, when it directs us 'when ye have done all those things which are commanded you, say, We are unprofitable servants' (Luk 17:10), because we shall not have conferred any favour on God, but only have performed the duties incumbent on us, for which no thanks are due. Nevertheless, the good works which the Lord has conferred on us, He denominates our own, and declares that He will not only accept, but also reward them. It is our duty to be animated by so great a promise, and to stir up our minds that we 'be not weary in well doing' (2Th 3:13) and to be truly grateful for so great an instance of Divine goodness.

"It is beyond a doubt, that whatever is laudable in our works proceeds from the grace of God, and that we cannot properly ascribe the least portion of it to ourselves. If we truly and seriously acknowledge this truth, not only all confidence, but likewise all idea of merit, immediately vanishes. We, I say, do not, like the sophists, divide the praise of good works between God and man, but we preserve it to the Lord complete, entire, and uncontaminated. All that we attribute to man is, that those works which were otherwise good are tainted and polluted by impurity. For nothing proceeds from the most perfect man which is wholly immaculate. Therefore let the Lord sit in judgment on the best of human actions, and He will indeed recognize in them His own righteousness, but man's disgrace and shame. Good works, therefore, are pleasing to God, and not unprofitable to the authors of them; and they will moreover receive the most ample blessings from God as their reward: not because they merit them, but because the Divine goodness has freely appointed them this reward." Let us attempt to offer some amplification of these excellent remarks.

First, no creature is rewarded by God because he justly deserves what is bestowed upon him, as a hired labourer who has performed his duty is entitled to the wage he receives. For, in this sense, even the angels in heaven are incapable of a reward: according to strict justice, they merit no favour. They are no hirelings, for God has a natural, original, undisputed right in them, as much as He has in the sun, moon and stars; and these, therefore, deserve to be paid for their shining, as much as the angels do for their service. If the angels love God it is no more than He infinitely deserves. Moreover, the angels do not profit God, and so lay Him under no obligation, any more than the birds profit the risen sun by their morning songs or render that luminary under obligation to shine all day upon them. "Can a man be profitable unto God as he that is wise may be profitable unto himself? Is it any pleasure to the Almighty that thou art righteous? or is it gain to Him that thou makest thy ways perfect?" (Job 22:2, 3).

It is most essential that this should be insisted upon, more especially in these days, that the Most High may be accorded His due place in our thoughts, His awful majesty, exalted independency and self-sufficiency preserved in their integrity. That the creature may be allotted his proper place: as being not only a creature, but as less than nothing in the sight of Him that gave him being and is pleased to maintain his existence. That the axe may be laid at the very root of self-righteousness. Papists are far from being alone in indulging the flesh-pleasing conceit that even a fallen and sinful creature is capable of performing meritorious deeds, which entitle him to favourable regard by the Lord God. Unless Divine grace has given our pride its death-wound, every one of us secretly cherishes the belief—though we may not be honest enough to openly avow it—that we deserve a reward for our good works; and hence we are apt to think that God would be very hard and severe, if not cruel and unjust, were He to take no notice of our *best* endeavours and damn us because of our sins. "Wherefore have we fasted, say they, and Thou seest not?" (Isa 58:3).

But, second, The fact remains that Scripture abounds in declarations that God has promised to reward the fidelity of His people and compensate them for the sufferings they have endured in His service. "The recompense of a man's hands shall be rendered unto him" (Pro 12:14). "Whoso despiseth the Word shall be destroyed, but he that feareth the commandment shall be rewarded" (Pro 13:13). "Blessed are ye when men shall revile you and persecute you, and shall say all manner of evil against you falsely for My sake. Rejoice and be exceeding glad, for great is your reward in heaven" (Mat 5:11,12). "His Lord said unto him, Well done, good and faithful servant; thou hast been faithful over a few things, I will make thee ruler over many" (Mat 25:23). "When thou makest a feast call the poor, the maimed, the lame, the blind and thou shalt be blessed; for they cannot recompense thee, for thou shalt be recompensed at the resurrection of the just" (Luk 14:13,14). "Every man shall receive his own reward according to his own labour" (1Co 3:8). "Whatsoever good things any man doeth the same shall he receive of the Lord" (Eph 6:8). Now these, and all similar passages, must be allowed their legitimate force and given a due place in our minds and hearts.

The principal difficulty which this subject presents to the thoughtful Christian is, What have I done which is meet for reward? and even though I had, how could reward consist with free grace? The solution to this problem is found in noting the grounds on which God bestows rewards. First, in order to manifest His own excellencies. It is in His office as moral Governor that He exercises this function, in which office He evidences His holiness, goodness and benevolence, as well as His sovereignty and justice. As the Ruler of all it becomes Him to manifest His approbation of righteousness, to put honour upon virtue, and to display the bountifulness of His nature. Though according to strict justice the angels in Heaven deserve nothing at His hands, yet God is pleased to reward their sinless obedience in testimony of His approbation of their persons and service. God rewards them not because they do Him any good, nor because they are entitled to anything from him, but because He delights in that which is amiable and because He would demonstrate to the universe that He is a Friend of all that are morally excellent, He liberally recompenses them. Since they love Him with all their hearts and strength, He deems it fitting that they should be made eternally blessed in the enjoyment of Himself.

Second, in the case of His people who fell in Adam and who have also themselves sinned and come short of the glory of God, they neither merit anything good at His hands, nor is it fitting that their persons and conduct—considered merely as they are in themselves—should be approved; nay, so much corruption still indwells them and so much impurity is attached to all that proceeds from them, that the Divine Law condemns them. Thus it must be on quite a different ground that God considers them suited to reward. What that is, the Gospel of the grace of God makes known. It is on account of the believer's interest in the righteousness and worthiness *of Christ* that his person and performances are accepted and peculiar favours are shown unto and bestowed upon him. He is "accepted in the Beloved" (Eph 1:6), and his consecration (Rom 12:1), his gifts or benevolences (Phi 4:18) and his worship are "acceptable to God by Jesus Christ" (1Pe 2:5); yea, his prayers ascend up before God only because the "much incense" of Christ's merits is added to them (Rev 8:3,4).

Third, in showing His approval of the service of His saints God is, at the same time, owning the Spirit's work in them, for it is by His gracious operations and power that they are enabled to perform such service. Thus far all is plain and simple: it is when the good works which God rewards are viewed as the saints' own that many are likely to encounter difficulty. But that difficulty is greatly relieved if it be definitely understood that God's rewarding of our efforts is solely a matter of *bounty* on His part, and not in any wise because we have rendered a *quid pro quo* and have earned the recompense. The reward bestowed upon us is not an acknowledgement that the same was due us by way of debt, but rather is the reward itself given out of pure and free grace. If an earthly parent promises his child the gift of a new Bible when he has correctly memorized the Ten Commandments, that child did not bring his parent under obligation nor did he merit the book: the book is freely given by way of bounty, yet by constituting it a "reward" or "prize" for an effort of memory it became an incentive and inducement to the child to succeed in his task.

Scripture itself makes the distinction between rewards of justice and rewards of bounty, yea it shows how a thing may be, at the same time, *both* a "free gift" and a "reward." "Now to him that worketh [i.e. earns, so that he has ground to be self-complacent, see v 2] is the reward not reckoned of grace, but of debt" (Rom 4:4), which certainly signifies there are two very different kinds of reward, or rather, that they are bestowed on radically different grounds. That a thing may be at the same time both a free gift and a reward appears by a comparison of Matthew 5:46 and Luke 6:32. In the former Christ asks, "For if ye love them which love you, what *reward* have you?" but in the latter "For if ye love them that love you, what *thank* have you?"—the Greek word ("charis") here rendered "thank" signifies "favour," being translated "grace" more than one hundred times. Clearer still is Colossians 3:22-24: "Servants, obey in all things your masters according to the flesh...fearing God...knowing that of the Lord ye shall receive the reward of the inheritance"—what can be freer or more unearned than an "inheritance"? yet the eternal inheritance is here styled a "reward" as an incentive to obedience unto God.

The same inheritance which is called a reward in Colossians 3:24 is designated "the purchased possession" in Ephesians 1:14—purchased for the saints by Christ. In like manner, in Romans 6:22 we read "Being now made free from sin and become servants of God, ye have your fruit unto holiness and the end [that at which you aim, that which will abundantly compensate your serving of God] everlasting life," yet in the very next verse that everlasting life is said to be "the gift of God through Jesus Christ our Lord." Just as the Saviour exhorted the Jews to "labour—not for the meat which perisheth, but—for that which endureth unto everlasting life," yet He at once added "which the Son of man shall *give* unto you" (Joh 6:27). The same apostle who taught that the saints are "accepted in the Beloved" (Eph 1:6), hesitated not to say "wherefore we labour [or "endeavour"], whether present or absent, we may be accepted of Him" (2Co 5:9); and though he insisted that "By grace are ye saved through faith, and that not of yourselves: it is the gift of God; not of works, lest any man should boast" (Eph 2:8,9), he also exhorted his hearers to "labour therefore to enter into" the rest God has promised His people (Heb 4:11).

J. Owen said, "I grant that eternal life may be called the reward of perseverance, in the sense that Scripture uses that word." After stating it is procured neither as the deserving cause, nor proportioned unto the obedience of them by whom it is attained, but withal the free gift of God and an inheritance purchased by Jesus Christ, Owen declared it is "a reward by being a gracious encouragement as the end of our obedience." That the reward is not a proportioned remuneration or return for the duties performed and service rendered is clear from the words of Christ, when He declared that "whosoever shall give to drink unto one of these little ones a cup of cold water only in the name of a disciple, verily I say unto you, he shall in no wise lose his reward" (Mat 10:42). So also when Abraham had made enemies of the kings of Canaan by rescuing Lot out of their hands, and then refused to be enriched by the king of Sodom, what proportion was there between his actions and Jehovah's response, when He said to him "Fear not, Abraham, I am thy shield and thy exceeding great Reward" (Gen 15:1)? There was a *connection* between the two things, but *no proportion*.

"Be not deceived, God is not mocked: for whatsoever a man soweth, that shall he also reap. For he that soweth to the flesh shall of the flesh reap corruption, but he that soweth to the spirit shall of the spirit reap life everlasting" (Gal 6:7,8). The sorrows and joys of the future life bear a similar relation to what is wrought in this as the harvest does to the sowing, one being the consequence, the fruit, or reward of the other. There is a definite relation subsisting between sowing to the spirit and reaping everlasting life, between what is done unto Christ in this life and the joys of the life to come. This relation is just as *real* as that between sowing to the flesh and reaping corruption, despising and defying Christ and the torments of Hell, though it is not in all respects the same. —AWP

and holding fast that which is good (1Th 5:21). One reason why God permits so much disputing and doctrinal differences is that His own people may be stirred up to the more diligent search for Truth itself. Even though I have chosen the way of Truth I shall still need to pray, "Remove from me the way of lying" (Psa 119:29), to which the flesh is ever prone. "Lead me in Thy Truth" (Psa 25:5), must be my daily cry.

Best of all is it when we are found "*walking in* the Truth" (2Jo 4), for it is then God is most glorified. His Word is given to us for this very purpose: to be a lamp unto our feet and a light unto our path—to direct our conduct and regulate our deportment. In proportion as our daily life is ordered by the Word do we evince the sincerity and reality of our profession. The extent to which we actually walk in the Truth will determine the measure of our enjoyment of God's approbation: "If a man love me, he will keep My words: and My Father will love him, and We will come unto him and make Our abode with him" (Joh 14:23). "His Truth shall be thy shield and buckler" (Psa 91:4): our defence and protection—panoplied in "the whole armour of God" the Christian is safe in the day of battle. By walking in the Truth we find rest unto our souls (Jer 6:16). —AWP

(continued from front page)
conviction, an unshakable confidence, that the Bible is a Divine revelation. Neither the arguments of men nor the assaults of Satan can move its possessor from what has been rightly termed this "impregnable rock." The Christian *knows* it is the Word of God for it has spoken to his heart in a way nothing else has or can. It would make no difference to him if every one else on earth was a sceptic or infidel, for his faith stands not in the wisdom of men but in the power of God, and neither human sophistry nor Satanic malice can destroy it. How could they, when God has given him to "know *the certainty* of the words of Truth" (Pro 22:21). Hence it is that he can exclaim with one of old "Thy words were found, and I did eat them; and Thy Word was unto me the joy and rejoicing of mine heart" (Jer 15:16).

What an unspeakable mercy it is when we are given a *love* of the Truth! By nature both writer and reader are liars. "The wicked are estranged from the womb, they go astray as soon as they be born, speaking lies" (Psa 58:3). No child has to be taught to lie—it comes naturally to him; nor does he have to be corrupted by contact with others—he is born corrupt at the core of his being. This is the just entail of the Fall. Our first parents preferred the Devil's lie to God's Truth, and all of their descendants inherit the poisonous virus which then entered into them. In consequence "the whole world lieth in the wicked one" (1Jo 5:19) and he is "a liar and the father of it" (Joh 8:44). Thus by nature we have no love for the Truth, but instead a strong antipathy and resistance against it. The unregenerate do not want to know the truth about themselves: no, they wish to be flattered and encouraged to entertain a good opinion of themselves. Hence, the Lord Jesus declared "Because I tell you the Truth, ye believe not" (Joh 8:45)—had He told them lies they had welcomed Him.

Since the whole world lieth in the wicked one and he is the arch-liar, we should not be surprised at the world being so full of pretence and hum-buggery and that the Truth of God is so bitterly hated. A striking illustration of this solemn feature, now spread before us on a lower plane, appears in the outlook of most of our fellows toward the war. The great majority do not want to know the truth but wish to hear fairy tales. The popular speaker or writer is the one who airily announces that victory is just round the corner and who heralds each minor success as proof that the end of the awful conflict is near at hand. Such a statement is likely to be hotly challenged, yet while many say and probably think they want to be told the real facts and know the worst, deep down in their hearts they do not. They pride themselves on being optimists and denounce as pessimists any who differ from them. Since this be the case in connection with temporal things, who is likely to tolerate the truth concerning Eternity! The fact is that "Truth is fallen in the street" (Isa 59:14) and is now being ruthlessly trampled on on every side.

How thankful we should be if we can honestly say "I have *chosen the way of Truth*" (Psa 119:30). The religious realm is a veritable "babel" or confusion of tongues, wherein are innumerable controversies and doubtful disputations, all varnished with specious pretence, until many are at their wit's end and the "unlearned and unstable" are in despair. But not so the one who is resolved to be directed by the Word of God and who brings all he hears and reads to the touchstone of the Truth, proving all things

. *(continued on proceeding page)*

VOL. XXII.   NOVEMBER, 1943.   NO. 11

STUDIES IN THE SCRIPTURES

" Search the Scriptures." John 5:39.

Publisher and Editor—ARTHUR W. PINK,
27 Lewis Street,
Stornoway, Isle of Lewis,
Scotland.

THE WORD OF FAITH

"The Word of Faith that we preach" (Rom 10:8). We shall not here attempt an exposition of that interesting passage, but rather deal with this expression topically, suggesting different reasons why the Word of God is so termed. First, because faith is the principal thing required by the Word. Being a Divine revelation nothing less than our hearty acceptance of it is its manifest due. Being the Word of Him that cannot lie it is fully entitled to our credence. It is not a mark of wisdom or superior mental acumen, but of spiritual imbecility, to discredit and disdain this celestial communication: "O fools and slow of heart to believe all that the Prophets have spoken" (Luke 24:25). The Scriptures are "worthy of all acceptation." Faith in its simplest form is receiving "the witness of God" (1 John 5:9). God has spoken, and faith cannot doubt or question what He has said. The soul that reverently and confidently accepts the Divine testimony "hath set to his seal that God is true" (John 3:33), and until he does so, his skepticism makes out God to be a liar (1 John 5:10). Faith, then, is its legitimate demand.

Second, because it is *the foundation* on which faith rests. However black may be my record, however vile I appear in my own eyes or those of my fellows, when faith appropriates that word "Him that cometh to Me I will in no wise cast out" (John 6:37,38) it has firm ground to stand upon. Faith rests upon the promise of the faithful and immutable God. Faith builds upon His sure Word, knowing that He will never alter one thing which has gone forth from His mouth. Said David, "And now, O Lord God, Thou art that God and Thy words be true, and Thou hast promised this goodness unto Thy servant" (2 Sam 7:28): he knew that such an One would neither deceive nor fail him. "Whosoever believeth on Him shall not be confounded" (Rom 9:33). When God has promised a thing it is infallibly certain of accomplishment, and we may rest thereon in the greatest perplexities and extremities. When faith "lays hold of the hope set before us" it becomes "as an anchor of the soul, both sure and steadfast" (Heb 6:18,19).

Third, because it is *the sphere* in which faith operates. Faith has nothing to do with feelings, impulses, or the dictates of carnal reason: the Word of God is the realm in which it lives, moves, and has its being. Faith soars high above the opinions of the world, or "the voice of the Church": it moves within the circle of Divine revelation. It recognizes no duty except what Holy Writ enjoins. It cherishes no desires save those

(continued on back page)

IMPORTANT NOTICES

Please advise promptly of change in address, otherwise copies will be lost in the mails.

We are glad to send a sample copy to any of your friends whom you believe would be interested in this publication.

This magazine is published as "a work of faith and labour of love," the editor and his wife gladly giving their services free. There is no regular subscription price, as we do not wish the poor of the flock to be deprived. This does not mean that those looking for something for nothing may "help themselves." Those getting this Magazine, who are financially able and who receive spiritual help from its pages, are expected to gladly contribute towards its expenses; otherwise, their names are dropped from our lists.

Will those forwarding International Money Orders please have them made out to us at Stornoway, Isle of Lewis, Scotland. Checks (Cheques-Eng.) made out on U.S.A. Banks are not negotiable here, so please do not send them.

CONTENTS

THE SERMON ON THE MOUNT

26h. Profession Tested: Matthew 7:25, 27

It now remains for us to ascertain what is signified by the hurricane which struck the "house" of the "wise" and of the "foolish" builder. Concerning that of the former it is said, "And the rain descended, and the floods came, and the winds blew, and beat upon that house; and it fell not: for it was founded upon a rock" (v. 25). Identically the same thing is narrated in connection with the latter, except in regard to the outcome: "it fell, and great was the fall of it." After having entered into such detail concerning the "wise" and the "foolish" man, the "digging deep" of the former and this fatal omission by the latter, the foundation of "rock" and that of "sand," and the "house" which each one erected, there should be little difficulty in discovering the general drift of what is denoted by the storm: though the language used be figurative, its purport is obvious. By means of the storm the strength and stability or the weakness and insecurity of the "house" was demonstrated.

The hurricane was that by which the work of each man was put to the proof and his wisdom or folly made evident. Thus it is clear that once more, what is here before us is the *testing of profession* and the making manifest of its worth or worthlessness. This had been the dominating theme of our Lord's Sermon from 7:13, onwards. The "strait gate" and "the narrow way" correspond to the "digging deep" and the foundation of rock, while the "wide gate" and "broad way" correspond to the omission of digging deep and the foundation of "sand." In like manner we may see in the "wise" builder the "good tree" which bringeth forth "good fruit," and in the "foolish" builder the "corrupt tree" with its "evil fruit." In the "he that doeth the will of My Father which is in heaven" we have the one whose house stands firm, while in the many to whom Christ will say, "I never knew you, depart from Me, ye that work iniquity" we have those whose building is overthrown by the storm.

We must not, however, conclude that nothing more is signified by our Lord in this figure of the storm bursting upon the house than the testing of Christian profession, though scarcely any of the commentators seem to have seen anything further in it. Surely due attention to the immediate setting, to say nothing of the more remote or general context, requires us to enlarge our viewpoint. Consider the *outcome* of the storm. In the case of the "wise man" it beat upon his house in vain: in spite of all its fury, his building stood firm. And why? Because it was founded upon a "rock." And what did that purport? Why, that the wise man was something more than a hearer of the Word, namely, a *doer* of it, one who heeded its warnings, who responded to its exhortations, who performed its precepts, whose character and conduct was moulded and regulated by its teachings. This, and nothing but this, is what Christ insists upon at the beginning of our passage: "Whosoever heareth these sayings of Mine and *doeth* them, I will liken him unto a wise man which built his house upon a rock."

Among the "sayings" of Christ are some peculiarly distasteful to flesh and blood, yea, at direct variance with the inclinations of fallen human nature. To pluck out right eyes and cut off right hands, to love our enemies, bless them which curse us, do good to them that hate us, and pray for them which despitefully use and persecute us, is not so simple as it may sound—see, then, the appropriateness of our Lord's similitude of "digging deep" when portraying such tasks. To distribute our alms and perform our devotions in secret, to expressly ask the Father to forgive us our debts *as* we forgive our debtors—being told that if we forgive not neither shall we be forgiven; to take no anxious thought for the morrow but to have a heart freed from carking care, to have such confidence in the providential bounty of God that we trustfully count upon Him supplying our every need, are duties which will tax our abilities to the utmost. True, but we shall not be the losers by practicing such precepts.

"And it *fell not*, for it was founded upon a rock": that is what we desire to lay hold of in this connection. Here is *encouragement* indeed. Instead of being so occupied with the narrowness of the way, cast your eyes forward to the glorious goal to which it conducts you—even Life. Instead of being so concerned about the painfulness of the work of mortification, think rather of what it is the appointed means of saving you from –even from being "cast into *Hell*" (5:29). Instead of complaining about the difficulties of obedience, consider its rich compensation. God has definitely assured us that in the keeping of His commandments "there is great reward" (Ps. 19:11), such as "the answer of a good conscience," peace of soul, the enjoyment of His approbation. It is *this* aspect of the Truth which Christ is here pressing upon our attention: the one who *does* His "sayings" is assured of *safety* in the day of testing and trial. The "house" of such an one will not, cannot be overthrown by the storm. Is not *that* a recompense well worth striving for?

Throughout this Sermon on the mount the Lord Jesus had presented a most exalted and unique standard of morality and spirituality, one which calls for real self-sacrifice on the part of those who sincerely endeavour to measure up to it and perform the duties it enjoins. But here He shows how great is the reward of those who submit themselves unto His yoke. In the stability and security of the wise man's "house" we have depicted one of the principal fruits of an obedient walk: the actual doing of these "sayings" of Christ delivers from the fatal assaults of the Devil, the world and the flesh. This consideration ought to move us to perform obedience readily and gladly, for this is a benefit which no human monarch can bestow. Neither wealth, education nor social prestige can confer security on the soul—rather do such things generally occasion destruction to their possessors. Neither human wit nor strength of resolution can procure preservation in the hour of trial and tribulation: nothing but the keeping of Christ's Word will obtain it, but that *does*. How this promise should encourage us and stimulate unto unreserved obedience!

The force of the figure which was here used by Christ would be more impressive to His immediate hearers than to those of us who live in strong houses and in those parts of the earth where devastating floods and tornadoes are seldom or never experienced. "In Judea, as in other oriental countries, the rains are periodical. When they descend, they often descend in torrents, and continue to do so, with unabated violence, for a number of days. In consequence of this the most trifling mountain brook becomes a mighty river—a deluge rushing down with dreadful impetus from the high grounds to the plains, converting them into one wide waste of waters. The huts of the inhabitants, generally formed of clay hardened in the sun, are exposed to great danger. They are often literally melted down by the heavy rains or overturned by the furious gusts of wind; and when not founded on the solid rock, undermined and swept away by the resistless torrent. In such a country, it is the part of a wise man to take good care that the foundation on which he builds his habitation be solid. He who attends to this precaution is likely to find the advantage of doing so, and he who neglects this precaution is likely to pay dear for his folly" (J. Brown).

Spurgeon was right when he said, "Whether your religion be true or false, it will be *tried*; whether it be chaff or wheat the fan of the great Winnower will surely he brought into operation upon all that lies on the threshing floor. If thou hast dealings with God, thou hast to do with a 'consuming fire.' Whether thou be really or nominally a Christian, if thou comest near to Christ He will try thee as silver is tried. Judgment must begin at the house of God, and if thou darest to come into the house of God, judgment will begin with thee." It is God's will that whosoever taketh upon him the profession of His name shall be tried and proved. Adam and Eve were tempted and tried by Satan. God made trial of Abraham when He bade him take his only and dearly-beloved son and offer him up for a burnt offering on mount Moriah (Gen. 22). For the trial of his faith and patience He gave Job and all that he had, except his life, into Satan's hand. God left Hezekiah to himself to try him and make known what was in his heart, when the ambassadors of Babylon came to inquire of him what wonders God had done in the land of Israel (2 Chron. 32:31).

It will be gathered from the above that we do not accept the view of those who *restrict* this trial of the "house" to the hour of death or the day of judgment. It is true that at death "the spirit shall returneth unto God that gave it" (Eccl. 12:7) and that it then enters Paradise or is consigned to the abode of the damned. At the Grand Assize the worth or worthlessness of the profession will be made manifest to an assembled universe. But we can see nothing in our present passage which requires us to limit the meaning of this storm unto the final testing, while on the other hand there is much in Scripture which makes it clear that both real and empty profession is, in a variety of ways but in different degrees, put to the proof in *this* life. When our Lord announced of His apostle, "Satan hath desired to have you, that he may sift you as wheat" (Luke 22:31), which desire was granted, He expressed that which applies to all His people. It is as requisite that the faith of the saints should be tried by afflictions as gold is tried in the fire (1 Pet. 1:7).

When the apostle said to believers, "Beloved, think it not strange concerning the fiery trial which is to try you, as though some strange thing happened unto you" (1 Pet. 4:12), he was referring unto an experience which is met with in this life, and one which, as his language denotes is by no means exceptional. For example: for a Jew belonging to an orthodox family to make public profession of the Christian faith, has always involved dishonor and disgrace; his family disinherit and disown him, and in the sight of all his brethren he is regarded as "the offscouring of all things." In the first two centuries A.D., being a Christian frequently involved forfeiture of citizenship, the "spoiling of his goods" and being cast unto the lions, or at least, living in caves "destitute and afflicted." Yet notwithstanding such trials, the faith of God's elect remained unshaken. During the past century the Lord's people, and especially His servants, have been tested in a more subtle manner: they have had to suffer the reproach of credulity and simple-mindedness, of being hopelessly behind the times, because they refused to believe the agnostic scientists and the theories of "modern scholarship"—sensitive natures find such reproaches harder to bear than physical sufferings. In this day, the test is to resist the seductions of an alluring world, to refuse to compromise.

Having generalized so much upon the verses before us, it is time that we turned to examine more closely their several details. First, "And the rain descended." This may be taken as a figure of the providential trials and adverse dispensations by which those bearing the name of Christ are put to the proof. "These rains typify *afflictions from Heaven*. God will send you adversities like showers, tribulations as many as the drops of the dew. Between now and Heaven, Oh, professor, you will feel the pelting storm. Like other men, your body will be sick; or if not, you shall have trial in your house: children and friends will die, or riches will take to themselves wings and fly like an eagle. You must have trials from God's hand, and if you are not relying on Christ, you will not be able to bear them. If you are not by real faith one with Christ, even God's rains will be too much for you" (C. H. Spurgeon). The response of the heart, the manner in which we act in times of adversity, reveals our state: if unregenerate, our unbelieving heart will betray itself by acting as the worldling does—seeking to drown our sorrow amid carnal pleasures, or sinking in despair.

Second, "and the floods came," or as Luke 6:48, says, "the floods *arose*." Thus it is a thing of the earth which is here in view, namely *opposition from the world*. By this also must the professor be tested, to demonstrate whether or no his claim to being a Christian is genuine. It is true that in former days the floods of persecution raged more furiously than they do now; nevertheless, they are far from having totally subsided. The world's opposition assumes many forms: sometimes it is ridicule—and how often have the gibes and sneers of the ungodly tumbled down the "house" of those who made a fair show in the flesh! Cruel mockings are still used against the people of God. In other cases it is reproach and slander, the "cold shoulder," boycotting, and only those who have a rock foundation will bear up under them. Not that the ones exposed always drop their profession entirely: far from it—often they retain the *name* of Christian, but compromise and walk arm-in-arm with the world to escape its persecutions.

Third, "and the winds blew and beat upon the house." Here it is "the Prince of the power of the air" (Eph. 2:2) who is at work: in other words, it is *Satan assaulting* the one who claims to be saved. At times he will cast a cloud of despondency over the human spirit, assailing with artful insinuations and blasphemous suggestions, particularly so when God's providences seem to be all against us, seeking to fill the soul with doubts of the Divine goodness and faithfulness. At other times he seeks to beguile with error, and only those established in the Truth will withstand him. He employs various tactics, according as he approaches in the form of a serpent or seeks to terrify as the roaring lion. He attracts by the world, appeals to the carnal nature, and only those whose "treasure" is really in Heaven scorn his gilded baubles. He suggests a compromise, the making the best of both worlds, the serving of two masters, and none save they who have truly "received Christ Jesus *the Lord*" (Col. 2:6) resist him.

The Lord plainly teaches us in this passage that he who takes upon him the Christian profession must expect a stormy passage through this world. He who is Truth incarnate painted no false and flattering picture of what Christian discipleship involves, but faithfully warns us that severe testings and trials await those who profess to he His followers. So far from being carried to Heaven on "flowery beds of ease," they may expect to meet with fierce opposition from the world, the flesh and the Devil. He who was despised and rejected of men, tempted of the Devil, hated by the world, opposed by the religious leaders, deserted by those who should have stood by Him, has said, "the disciple is not above his Master." "We must through much tribulation enter into the kingdom of God" (Acts 14:22), and they who deny this are false prophets. "All that will live godly in Christ Jesus shall suffer persecution" (2 Tim. 3:12), yet that very persecution shall be made to work together for their good.

"And it fell not." Here are consolation and compensation indeed. Severely assaulted and shaken their "house" may be, but overthrown it shall not be. And why? "For it was founded upon a rock," that is to say, the profession was a *genuine* one, and therefore one which endures and survives every testing. It is no comfortable thing to live through such an experience as this hurricane: ah, but dwell upon the happy issue. It is no pleasant experience to meet with the sneers of acquaintances, the loss of friends, the opposition of the world and the enmity of Satan, but is it not worth all these and much more if, like the three Hebrews, we come forth from the fires unharmed? While I *do* Christ's "sayings," Satan can gain no advantage over me: while I practice the Divine precepts the world cannot overcome me: while I tread the path of obedience the "flesh" is denied and cannot bring about my ruin. Neither in this life, the hour of death, nor the day of judgment will the "house" of such an one fall.

"And the rain descended, and the floods came, and the winds blew, and beat upon that house: and it fell, and great was the fall of it" (v. 27). Here is the solemn contrast. Here is the fearful outcome for the one who erects his house upon the sand. Here is the certain fate of all who rest their hope and base their confidence on a worthless foundation. Here is the fearful ruin which overtakes the empty professor. He who makes no conscience of Christ's "sayings," joins not practice to profession, who refuses to walk in the path of the Divine commandments, is headed for eternal damnation. An empty professor may withstand the lighter gusts of opposition in days of peace and prosperity, but he is not at all likely to survive the temptations of the times in which our lot is cast, as witness the multitudes now making shipwreck of the faith they once affirmed. And even those who continue to call themselves Christians but refuse the

Master's yoke will find in the hour of death that they have no refuge from the judgment awaiting them.

Some times God exposes those who have made an eminent profession by sending them such anguish of conscience and foretastes of Hell that at the end they are exposed to all around them. A notable example of this was Francis Spira in the seventeenth century. For weeks he lay groaning on his couch, not from physical pain but from anguish of soul, and though numbers of God's servants spoke to and prayed with him, no relief was obtained. Said he to the ministers and friends around his bed, "Take heed of relying on that faith which worketh not a holy and unblamable life, worthy of a believer. Credit me, it will fail. I have tried it. I presumed I had gotten the right faith. I preached it to others. I had all places of Scripture in memory that might support it. I thought myself sure, and in the meantime lived impiously and carelessly. And behold now the judgment of God hath overtaken me: not to correction, but to damnation." He felt the fires of God's wrath burning in his soul as few have ever experienced them in this world, and expired thus. His house "fell" and great was the fall of it.

What has been before us should dispel the influence of the world, move us to self-judgment, and warn us against a superficial use of God's Word. If we allow Satan's world to so ensnare us that, for the sake of enjoying it, we consent to ignore Christ's rules for separation from evil and holiness of life, then dire will be the consequences. Such a passage as this ought to bring home to us both the heinousness and madness of our acts of disobedience, cause us contritely to confess the same, and entreat the Lord's pardon while it may yet be obtained. Finally, we would press upon our readers that the will of God, the standard He has appointed, cannot be known by mere casual and occasional glances at the Bible. Too many are but text-mongers, singling out favorite passages which appeal to them. It is only by carefully and earnestly searching the Scriptures, by a systematic and continuous pondering of them, that we can discover "all the counsel of God." Those who do so will have their souls sustained by grace and upheld by the power of Christ in the day of trial, and will have no regrets for so employing their time and energies when the hour of death is upon them. —AWP

THE MISSION AND MIRACLES OF ELISHA

11. Seventh Miracle

In the last we dwelt, first, upon the *occasion* of this miracle, namely, the death of the "great woman's" son. Second, upon the *mystery* of it. To all appearances, the child had been quite well and full of life in the morning, yet by noon he was a corpse. In her case such a disaster was doubly inexplicable, for the son had been given to her by the Divine bounty because of the kindness she had shown to one of God's servants; and now, to carnal reason, it looked as though He was dealing most unkindly with her. Furthermore, the wonder-working power of God had been engaged in bestowing a son upon her, and now this miracle was neutralized by suddenly snatching him away. Third, upon its *expectation*. It is inexpressibly blessed to behold how this stricken mother reacted to the seeming catastrophe; throughout the whole narrative it is made evident that she regarded this affliction as a trial of her faith, and grandly did her confidence in God triumph over it. Continuing our study of the miracle which follows, we note.

Fourth, its *means*. "Then he said to Gehazi, gird up thy loins and take my staff in thine hand, and go thy way: if thou meet any man, salute him not; and if any salute thee, answer him not again: and lay my staff upon the face of the child" (2 Kings 4:29). Some think the prophet believed that the child was only in a swoon, yet we can hardly conceive of the mother leaving the boy under such circumstances—rather had she sent a message by one of her servants: nor is it likely that Elisha's instructions to the servant would be so peremptorily expressed if such had been the case. Matthew Henry says "I know not what to make of this." Another of the Puritans suggests that, "It was done out of pure conceit, and not by Divine instinct, and therefore it failed of the effect." Thomas Scott acknowledged, "It is difficult to determine what the prophet meant by thus sending Gehazi. He had divided Jordan by using Elijah's mantle, and perhaps he thought that his own staff would be sufficient." Personally we are inclined to think that the prophet's design was to teach Gehazi a much-needed lesson. However, this much seems clear from the incident: no servant of God should delegate unto another that which it is his own duty to do.

"And the mother of the child said, As the Lord liveth, and as thy soul liveth, I will not leave thee. And he arose, and followed her" (v. 30). It is clear from these words of hers, that, whatever was or was not the prophet's design in ordering his servant to make all speed to where the child lay, she regarded his action as another testing of her faith. She evidently had no confidence in Gehazi, or in Elisha's staff as such. She was not to be put off in this way. Her language was both impressive and emphatic, signifying, I swear that I will not return home unless thou dost personally accompany me: the situation is desperate, my expectation is in thee as the Lord's ambassador, and I refuse to take any No. Here we behold the boldness and perseverance of her faith. Whether there was any unwillingness on Elisha's part to set out on this journey, or whether he was only putting her to the test, we cannot be sure, but such earnestness and importunity won the day and now stirred the prophet to action.

"And Gehazi passed on before them, and laid the staff on the face of the child: but there was neither voice nor hearing. Wherefore he went again to meet him, and told him saying, The child is not awaked" (v. 31). Young's concordance gives as the meaning of the name Gehazi "Denier." If the various references made to him be carefully compared it will be seen that his character and conduct were all of a piece and in keeping with his name. Why Elisha should have had such a man for his personal attendant we know not, yet in view of there being a Judas in the apostolate, we need not be unduly surprised. First, we see him seeking to officiously thrust away the poor mother when she cast herself at his master's feet (v. 27). Here we note the absence of prayer unto the Lord, and the nonsuccess of his efforts. Later, we find him giving expression to selfish unbelief, a complete lack of confidence in the power of Elisha (v. 43). Finally, his cupidity masters him and he lies to Naaman, and is stricken with leprosy for his pains (5:20-27). Thus in the verse before us we have a picture of the unavailing efforts of an unregenerate minister, and his failure made manifest to others.

"And when Elisha was come into the house, behold, the child was dead, laid upon his bed" (v. 32). In previous paragraphs we have dwelt much upon the remarkable faith of the mother of the child, yet we must not allow it to so occupy our attention as to obscure the faith of the prophet, for *his* was equally great. It was no ordinary demand which was now made upon him, and only one who was intimately acquainted with God would have met it as he did. The death of this child was not only quite unexpected by him, but must have seemed bewilderingly strange. Yet though he was in the dark as to the reason of this calamity, he refused to accept it as final. The mother had taken her stand upon the Divine bounty and kindness, expecting an outcome in keeping with God's grace toward her, and no doubt the prophet now reasoned in the same way. Though he had never before been faced with such a desperate situation, he knew that with God all things are possible. The very fact that the dead child had been placed upon his bed was a direct challenge to his faith, and nobly did he meet it.

"He went in therefore, and shut the door upon them twain, and prayed unto the Lord" (v. 33). We are not quite clear whether "them twain" refers to himself and the child or to the mother and Gehazi who had most probably accompanied him, but whichever it was, his action in closing the door denoted his desire for privacy. The prophet practiced what he preached to others. In the miracle recorded at the beginning of our chapter, Elisha had bidden the widow "shut the door upon" herself and her sons (v. 4) so as to avoid ostentation, and here Elisha follows the same course. Moreover, he was about to engage the Lord in prayer, most urgent and special prayer, and *that* is certainly something which calls for aloneness with God. The minister of the Gospel needs to be much on his guard on this point, precluding everything which savors of advertising his piety like the pharisees did: see Matthew 6:5-6. Here, then, was the means of this miracle: the unfaltering faith of the mother and now the faith of the prophet, expressed in prayer unto his Master— acknowledging his own helplessness, humbly but trustfully presenting the need to Him, counting upon His all-mighty power and goodness.

Fifth, its *procedure*. "And he went up, and lay upon the child, and put his mouth upon his mouth, and his eyes upon his eyes, and his hands upon his hands; and he stretched himself upon the child, and the flesh of the child waxed warm" (2 Kings 4:34). The means used by the prophet and the policy he followed are so closely linked together that they merge into one another without any break, the faith of Elisha finding expression in prayer. Considering the extraordinary situation here, how that act of the prophet's serves to demonstrate that he was accustomed to count upon God in times of emergency, to look for wondrous blessings from Him in response to his supplications, that he was fully persuaded nothing was too hard for Jehovah and therefore no petition too large to present unto Him. The more faith looks to the infinite power and all-sufficiency of the One with whom it has to do, the more is He honored. Next, the prophet stretched himself on the body of the little one, which was expressive of his deep affection for him, and his intense longing for its restoration, as though he would communicate his own life and thereby revive him.

Those who are familiar with the life and miracles of Elijah will at once be struck with the likeness between Elisha's actions here and the conduct of his predecessor on a similar occasion, in fact so close is the resemblance between them it is evident the one was patterned after that of the other—showing how closely the man of God must keep to the Scripture model if he would be successful in the Divine service. First, Elijah had taken the lifeless child of the Zarephath widow, carried him upstairs and laid him on his own bed, thereby preventing any human eyes from observing what transpired. Next, he "cried unto the Lord" and then "he stretched himself upon the child" (1 Kings 17:19-21). In addition to what had been pointed out in the foregoing paragraph, we believe this stretching of the prophet on the one for whom he prayed signified an act of *identification*, and it was a proof that he was putting his whole soul into the work of supplication. If we are to prevail in interceding for another, we must perforce make his or her case *ours*, taking his need or burden upon our own spirit, and then spreading it before God.

"Then he returned, and walked in the house to and fro" (v. 35). Let it be noted that even the prayer of an Elisha did not meet with an immediate and full answer: why then should *we* be so soon disheartened when Heaven appears to be tardy in responding to our crying! God is sovereign in this, as in everything else; by which we mean that He does not deal uniformly with us. Sometimes our request is answered immediately, at the first time of asking, but often He calls for perseverance and persistence, requiring us to "wait patiently for Him." We have seen how many rebuffs the faith of the mother met with, and now the faith of the prophet is tested too. It is true that he had been granted an encouragement by the "waxing warm" of the child's body—as the Lord is pleased to often give us "a token for good" (Ps. 86:17) ere the full answer is received; but as yet there was no sign of returning consciousness, and the form of the little one still lay silent and inert before him. And *that* also has been recorded for *our* instruction.

"Then he returned, and walked in the house to and fro, and went up and stretched himself upon him"

(v. 35). This pacing up and down seems to denote a measure of perturbation of mind, for the prophets were "subject to like passions as we are" (James 5:17) and compassed with the same infirmities. But even if Elisha was now at his wit's end, he did not give way to despair and regard the situation as hopeless. No, he continued clinging to Him who is the Giver of every good and perfect gift, and again stretched himself upon the child. Let us lay this important lesson to heart and put it into practice, for it is at this point so many fail: it is the *perseverance* of faith which wins the day: see Matthew 7:7. Scott has pointed out, "It is instructive to compare the *manner* in which Elijah and Elisha wrought their miracles, especially in raising the dead, with that of Jesus Christ. Every part of their conduct expressed a consciousness of inability and an entire dependence upon Another, and earnest supplication for His intervention; but Jesus wrought by His own power: He spake, and it was done: 'Young man, I say unto thee arise; Talitha cumi; Lazarus come forth.'" In all things *He* has the pre-eminence.

Sixth, its *marvel*. This was nothing less than the quickening of the child, the restoring "a dead body to life" (8:5). After the prophet had again stretched himself upon the child we are told that he "sneezed seven times, and the child opened his eyes" (v. 35). See how ready God is to respond to the exercise of real faith in Himself! In this case neither the mother nor the prophet had any definite or even indefinite promise they could plead, for the Lord had not said the child should be preserved in health or recovered if he fell ill. But though they had no promise, they laid hold of the known *character* of God: since He had given the child unasked, Elisha would not believe He would now withdraw His gift and leave his benefactress worse off than she was before. Elisha knew that with the Lord there is "no variableness, neither shadow of turning" (James 1:17), and he clung to that. True, it makes prayer easier when there is some specific promise we can plead, yet it is a higher order of faith that lays hold of God Himself. There was no promise that God would pardon a penitent murderer, and no sacrifice was appointed for such a sin, yet David appealed not in vain to the "multitude of His tender mercies" (Ps. 51:1).

"And the child opened his eyes" (v. 35). See what a prayer-hearing, prayer-answering God is ours! Hopeless as our case may be so far as all human aid is concerned, it is not too hard for the Lord. But we must "ask *in faith*, nothing wavering: for he that wavereth is like a wave of the sea, driven with the wind and tossed," and therefore is it added let not that man think he shall obtain anything from the Lord" (James 1:6-7). No, rather it is the one who declares with Jacob, "I will not let Thee go, except Thou bless me" (Gen. 32:26) who obtains his request. What must have been Elisha's delight when he saw the child revive and obtain this further experience of God's grace in hearkening to his petition and delivering him from his grief! How great must have been his joy as he called for Gehazi and bade him summon the mother, and when he said to her, "Take up thy son"! Blessed is it to behold her silent gratitude—too full for words—as she "fell at his feet," and in worship to God, "bowed herself to the ground." "And she took up the son and went out" (v. 37), to get alone with God and pour out her heart in thanksgiving to Him.

Seventh, its *meaning*. Some help is obtained therein by noting that this passage which sets before us the seventh miracle of our prophet opens with the connective conjunction (v. 18). That "And" not only intimates the continuity of the narrative, notes a striking contrast between the two principal divisions of it, but also indicates there is an intimate relation between them. As we have pointed out on previous occasions, the word "and" is used in Scripture sometimes with the purpose of linking two things together, but at other times with the object of placing two objects or incidents in juxtaposition in order to display the contrasts between them. In the present instance it appears to be used for *both* reasons. As we hope to show, light is thrown on the typical significance of this miracle by carefully noting how it is immediately linked to the one preceding it. When we look at the respective incidents described, we are at once struck with the antitheses presented. In the former we behold Elisha journeying to Shunem, in the latter it is the woman who betakes herself to him. There it was the woman befriending the prophet, here he is seen befriending her. In that a son is miraculously given to her, in this he is taken away.

The typical meaning of that does not appear on the surface, and therefore it will not be a simple matter for us to make it clear unto the reader. Only the regenerate will be able to follow us intelligently, for they alone have experienced in their spiritual history that which is here set forth in figure. That which is outstanding in this incident is the mysteriousness of it: that a child should be miraculously given to this woman, and then that the hand of death should be laid upon him! That was not only a sore trial to the poor mother, but a most perplexing providence. To carnal reason it seemed as though God was mocking her. But is there not also something equally tragic, equally baffling, in the experience of the Christian? In the last miracle we were shown a picture of the fruit of redemption, and here death appears to be written on that fruit. Ah, my reader, let it be clearly understood that we are as dependent upon God for the *maintenance* of that fruit as we were for the actual bestowal of it.

And *what is* the "fruit of redemption" as it applies to the individual? From the side which looks God-ward: reconciliation, justification, sanctification, preservation. But from the selfward side, what a list might be drawn up. Peace, joy, assurance, fellowship with God and His people, delight in His Word, liberty in prayer, weanedness from the world, affections set upon things above. O the inexpressible sweetness of our "espousals" (Jer. 2:2) and of our "first love" (Rev. 2:4). But, in many cases, how soon is that joy dampened and that love is "left"! How wretched then is the soul: like Rachel mourning for her children, we "refused to be comforted." How sore the perplexity! How Satan seeks to take advantage and persuade such an one that God has "ceased to be gracious." How passing strange that such a blight should have fallen upon the "fruit of the spirit"! How deeply mysterious the deadness which now rests upon the garden of God's planting, causing the soul to say with the poet,

> Where is the blessedness I knew
> When first I saw the Lord;
> Where is the soul-refreshing view
> Of Jesus and His Word?
> What peaceful hours I once enjoyed!
> How sweet their memory still,
> But now I feel an aching void
> The world can never fill.

Yes, it does indeed seem inexplicable that the child of God's own workmanship should pine away, and to a sense, lie cold and lifeless. Ah, but we must not stop there. We must not sit down in despair and conclude that all is lost. The incident before us does not end at that point: the death of the child was not the final thing! There is "good hope" for us here, important instruction to heed. That "great woman" did not give away to dejection and assume that all hope was gone. Very far from it. And if the Christian who is sensible of spiritual decays, of languishing graces, of his dire need of being renewed in the inner man, would experience a gracious reviving, then he should emulate this mother and do as she did. And again we would point out that she did not faint in the day of trouble and indulge in self-pity: she did not bemoan her helplessness and say, What can I do in the presence of death? And if *she* did not, why should *you*!

Mark attentively what this stricken woman did. 1. She regarded this inexplicable and painful dispensation as a testing of her faith, and she acted accordingly. 2. She moved promptly: without delay she carried the child upstairs and laid him on the prophet's bed—in anticipation of the Lord's showing Himself strong on her behalf. 3. She vigorously bestirred herself, going to some trouble in order to obtain relief, starting out on an arduous journey. 4. She refused to be deterred when her own husband half-discouraged her. 5. She sought unto the one who had promised the son in the first instance: the soul must turn to God and cry "*quicken* Thou me according to Thy Word" (Ps. 119:25). 6. She clung to the original promise and refused to believe that God had ceased to be gracious (v. 28). 7. She declined to be put off by the unavailing intervention of an unregenerate minister (vv. 29-30). 8. She persisted in counting upon the power of Elisha, who was to her the representative of God. And gloriously was her faith rewarded.

Regarding the typical meaning of this miracle in connection with Elisha himself, it teaches us the following points. 1. The servant of God must not be surprised if those in whose conversion he has been instrumental should later experience a spiritual decay, especially when he is absent from them. 2. If he would be used to their restoration, no half measures will avail, nor may he entrust the work to a delegate. 3. Prayers, believing, expectant, fervent prayer, must be his first recourse. 4. In seeking to revive a languishing soul, he must descend to the level of the one to whom he ministers (v. 34) and not stand as on some pedestal, as though he were a superior being. 5. He must not be discouraged because there is not an immediate and complete response to his efforts, but should persevere therein. 6. No cold and formal measures will suffice: he must throw himself into this work heart and soul. 7. The order of recovery was renewed circulation (v. 34), sneezing, eyes opened: the affections warmed, the head cleared (understanding restored), vision. —AWP

DOCTRINE OF SAINTS' PERSEVERANCE

9c. Its Opposition

In our last two articles we sought to show how pointless is *the reasoning* of Arminians in the opposition which they make to this blessed article of the Faith: in this one and in that which follows we shall seek to demonstrate that their use of Scripture is equally unhappy. If the charges they bring against this doctrine be baseless, if the inferences they draw and the conclusions they make upon it are wide of the mark, certainly their interpretations and applications of Holy Writ concerning this subject are quite erroneous. Nevertheless they *do* appeal directly to God's Word and attempt to prove from its contents that one and another of the saints renounced the Faith, went right back again into the world, and died in their sins; that certain specific cases of such are there set before us of men who not only suffered a grievous fall by the way or entered into a backslidden state, but who totally, finally and irremediably apostatised. In addition to these specific examples, they quote various passages which they contend teach the same fearful thing. It is therefore incumbent upon us to examine attentively the cases they point to and weigh carefully the passages they cite.

Before entering immediately into this task, however, one or two general remarks need to be made that the issue between Calvinists and Arminians may be the more clearly drawn. First, it must be laid down as a broad principle that God's Word cannot contradict itself. It is human to err and the wisest of mortals is incapable of producing that which is without flaw, but it is quite otherwise with the Word of Truth. The Scriptures are not of human origin, but Divine, and though holy men were used in the penning of them, yet so completely were they controlled and moved by the Holy Spirit in their work that there is neither error nor blemish in the Sacred Volume. That affirmation concerns, of course, the original manuscripts: nevertheless we have such confidence in the superintending providence of God, we are fully assured He has guarded His own holy Word with such jealous care, that He has so ordered the translation of the Hebrew and Greek into our mother tongue that all false doctrine has been excluded. Since then the Scriptures are Divinely inspired, they cannot teach in one place it is impossible the child of God should be eternally lost, and in another place that he may be, and in yet another that some have been so.

Second, it has been shown at length in previous sections that God's Word clearly teaches the final perseverance of His saints, and that, not in one or two vague and uncertain verses but in the most positive and unequivocal language of many passages. It has been shown that the eternal security of the Christian rests upon a foundation that "standeth sure," which Satan and his emissaries cannot even shake; that his everlasting felicity depends, ultimately upon nothing in or from himself, but is infallibly secured by the invincibility of the Father's purpose, the immutability of His love, and the certainty of His covenant faithfulness; that it is infallibly secured by the Surety engagements of Christ, by the sufficiency of His atonement, and by the prevalency of His unceasing intercession; that it is infallibly secured by the regenerating work of the Holy Spirit, by His abiding indwelling, and by the efficacy of His keeping power. The very honor, veracity, and glory of the Triune Jehovah is engaged, yea, pledged in this matter. In order "more abundantly to show unto the heirs of promise the immutability of His counsel" the Most High has gone so far as to "confirm it by an *oath*" (Heb. 6:17). Thus, the indefectibility of the Church is made infallibly certain, and no "special pleading" of men, however subtle and plausible, can have the slightest weight in the balance against it.

Third, in view of what has been pointed out in the last paragraph it should be patent to all honest and impartial minds that the cases cited by Arminians as examples of children of God apostatising and perishing must be susceptible of being diagnosed quite differently, and that the Scriptures they appeal to in support of their contention must be capable of being interpreted in full harmony with those which clearly affirm the opposite. It is a basic principle of exegesis that no plain passage of the Word is to be neutralized by one whose meaning appears to be doubtful or ambiguous, that no explicit promise is to be set aside by a parable the significance of which is not readily determined, that no doctrinal declaration is to be nullified by the arbitrary interpretation of a figure or type. That which is uncertain must yield to what is simple and obvious, that which is open to argument must be subordinated to what is beyond any debate. True, the Calvinist must not resort to any subterfuges to avoid a difficulty, nor wrest a passage adduced by his opponents so as to make it teach what he wants. If he be unable to explain a verse he must honestly admit it, for no single man has all the light; nevertheless, we must believe there *is* an explanation, and that, in full accord with the Analogy of Faith, we must humbly wait upon God for further light.

Fourth, in order to disprove the doctrine of the final perseverance of the saints the Arminian is bound to do two things: produce the case of one who was truly born again, and then demonstrate that this person actually died in a state of apostasy, for unless he can do *both* his example is not to the point. It is not sufficient for him to bring forward one who made a credible profession and then repudiated it, for Scripture itself shows emphatically that such a person was never regenerate: the man who "dureth for a while" only, and then in a season of temptation or persecution is "offended" and falls away, is described by Christ as one who "hath not root in himself" (Matt. 13:21)—had the "root of the matter" (Job 19:28) been in him he had survived the testing. To the same effect the apostle declares of such "they went out from us, but they were not of us; if they had been of us, they would have continued with us"(1 John 2:19). Nor is it sufficient for the Arminian to point to genuine children of God who backslide or meet with a grievous fall: such was the experience of both David and Peter, yet so far from being abandoned of God and suffered to die in that state, each was graciously brought to repentance and restored to communion with the Lord. Let us now look at the examples advanced.

1. *The case of Adam.* Here is one who was the immediate workmanship of God's own hands, created in His image and likeness, "blessed" by the Lord and pronounced

"very good" (Gen. 1:28,31). Here is one who had no sinful heredity behind him and no corruption within him, instated in the Divine favor, placed in a garden of delights and given dominion over all terrestrial creatures. Yet he abode not in that fair estate, but fell from grace, disobeyed his Maker, and brought upon himself spiritual death. When he heard the voice of the Lord God, instead of fleeing to Him for mercy, he hid himself; when arraigned before Him, instead of penitently confessing his sin he sought to brazen it out, seeking to throw the blame upon Eve and casting the onus upon God for giving her to him. In the sequel his awful doom is plainly intimated, for the Lord God "drove out the man" from Eden and barred his way back to "the tree of life" by stationing around it "cherubim and a flaming sword" (Gen. 3:24). Now, say our opponents, what could be more to the point! Adam certainly had "the root of the matter" within him, and it is equally certain that he apostatised and perished. If sinless Adam fell then obviously a Christian who still has sin indwelling him may fall and be lost.

How, then, is the fatal fall of Adam to be explained consistently with the doctrine of the final perseverance of the saints? By calling attention to the immeasurable difference there was between him and them. What does the case of Adam make manifest? This: the defectibility of man when placed in the most favorable and advantageous circumstances. This: that creaturehood and mutability are correlative terms: "man being in honor abideth not" (Ps. 49:12). This: that if the creature is to be kept from committing spiritual suicide a power outside of himself must preserve him. The case of Adam supplies the dark background which brings out more vividly the riches of Divine grace which it is the glory of the Gospel to exhibit. In other words, it serves to demonstrate beyond any peradventure of a doubt the imperative necessity of *Christ* if the creature—be he fallen or unfallen—is to be saved from himself. *There* is the fundamental, tremendous, vital difference between the case of Adam and that of the Christian: he was never in Christ, whereas they are; he was never redeemed by blood of infinite worth, they have been; there was none to intercede for him before God, there is for them.

"Howbeit that was not first which is spiritual, but that which is natural; and afterward that which is spiritual" (1 Cor. 15:46). Though the immediate application of these words be unto the bodies of believers, yet they enunciate a general and basic principle in the ways of God with men, in the manifestation of His purpose concerning them. Adam appears on the earth before Christ: Cain was given to Eve before Abel; Ishmael was born before Isaac and Esau before Jacob: the elect are born naturally before they are born again supernaturally. In like manner, the Covenant of Works took precedence over the Covenant of Grace, so far as its revelation was concerned. Thus Adam was endowed with a natural power, namely, that of his own free will, but the Christian is endowed with a spiritual and supernatural power, even God's working in him "both to will and to do of His own good pleasure." Adam was given no promise of Divine preservation, but the saints are. Adam stood before God in dependence upon his own creature righteousness, and when that was lost, all the blessings and virtues arising from it were lost; whereas the believer's righteousness is *in Christ*: "in the Lord have I righteousness and strength" (Isa. 45:24) is his joyous confession, and since his righteousness is in Christ it is an unassailable and non-forfeitable one.

Adam was placed under a covenant of works: do this and thou shalt live, fail to do and thou must die. It was a covenant of strict justice, unmixed with mercy, no provision being made for any failure. The grace or strength or power with which Adam was endowed, was entrusted to himself and his own keeping. But with His saints God has made a "*better* covenant" (Heb. 8:6), of which Jesus is the "Surety" (Heb. 7:22) and *in Him* are treasured up inexhaustible supplies of grace for them to draw upon. This "better covenant" is one in which justice and mercy harmoniously blend together, wherein "grace reigns through righteousness." In this "better covenant" God has promised to keep the feet of His saints, to put His fear in them so that they "shall not depart from" Him (Jer. 32:40). In this covenant God has made provision for our failures, so that "if we confess our sins He is faithful and just to forgive us our sins and to cleanse us from all unrighteousness" (1 John 1:9). Thus our state by redemption and regeneration is far, far better than was that of our first parents by creation, for we are given what unfallen Adam had not, namely, confirmation of our wills in holiness—though not every *act* is such—for He "works in us that which is well pleasing in His sight through Jesus Christ" (Heb. 13:21), which He never did in Adam. We may add that most of what has been said above applies to the case of the angels who fell.

2. *The case of King Saul.* It is affirmed by Arminians that this king of Israel was a regenerate man. In support of this contention they appeal to a number of things recorded about him. First, that the prophet Samuel "took a vial of oil and poured it upon his head and kissed him" (1 Sam. 10:1). Second, because it is said that "God gave him another heart" (v. 9). Third, because we are told "the Spirit of God came upon him and he prophesied" (v. 11). Then it is pointed out that Saul acted in fearful presumption and disobedience (1 Sam. 13:9,13), thereby displeasing the Lord so that it was announced the kingdom should be taken from him (vv. 13,14). That because of God's displeasure "the Spirit of the Lord departed from Saul and an evil spirit from the Lord troubled him" (16:14). That later, when menaced by the Philistines, he "enquired of the Lord" but "the Lord answered him not" (28:6). Finally, how that he had recourse to a witch and ultimately fell upon the field of battle sorely wounded, and ended his life by taking a sword and falling upon it (31:4), thereby sealing his doom by the unpardonable act of suicide.

In reply thereto we would say: we grant the conclusion that Saul passed out into an eternity of woe, but we do not accept the inference that he was ever a regenerate man. At the outset it must be remembered that the very installation of Saul upon the throne expressed the Lord's *displeasure* against Israel, for as He declared to the prophet "I gave thee a king in Mine anger (cf. 1 Sam. 8:5,6) and took him away in My wrath" (Hos. 13:11). Concerning the three things advanced by Arminians to show that Saul was a regenerate man, they are no proofs at all. Samuel's taking of the vial of oil and kissing him were simply symbolic actions, betokening the official status that had been conferred upon Saul: this is quite clear from the remainder of the verse, where the prophet explains his conduct, "Is it not because the Lord hath anointed thee to be captain over His inheritance?" (10:1)—*not* because "The Lord delighteth in thee" or because thou art "a man after His own heart." It is not said the Lord gave Saul "a *new* heart," but "another." Moreover, the Hebrew word (haphak) is never translated "gave" elsewhere, but in the great majority of instances "turned": it simply means the Lord turned his heart from natural timidity (see 1 Sam. 10:21,22) to boldness (cf. 1 Sam. 11:1-7; 13:1-4). That the Spirit of God came upon him so that he prophesied is no more than is said of Balaam (Num. 22:38; 24:2) and Caiaphas (John 11:51).

3. *The case of Solomon.* This is admittedly the most difficult one presented in Scripture, and it is our belief that God meant it to be such. His history is such a solemn one, his fall so great, his backsliding so protracted, that had his spiritual recovery and restoration to fellowship with the Lord been made unmistakably plain, a shelter would be provided for the careless and presumptuous. In Solomon the monarchy of Israel reached its zenith of splendor, for he reaped the harvest of glory for which David both toiled and suffered, entering into such a heritage as none else before or since has ever enjoyed. But in Solomon, too, the family of David entered *its decline*, and for his sins the judgments of God fell heavily on his descendants. Thus he is set before us as an awful *warning* of the fearful dangers which may surround and then overthrow the loftiest virtues and most dazzling mundane greatness.

That Solomon was a regenerate man we doubt not: that he enjoyed the favor of God to a most marked degree the inspired narrative makes plain. That he suffered a horrible decline in character and conduct is equally evident. Neither the special wisdom with which he was endowed, the responsibilities of the exalted position he occupied, nor the superior privileges which were his, rendered him proof against the temptations he encountered. He fell from his first estate and left his first love. His honor and glory were sadly eclipsed, and so far as the historical account of the books of Kings and Chronicles is concerned, he was buried in shame, the dark shadows of a misspent life and wrecked testimony shrouded his grave. Over the fate of Solomon there rests such a cloud and silence that many good men conclude he was lost: on the other hand there are those who do not believe that he so fell as to lose the favor of God and perish eternally.

With others, it is our own conviction that before the end of his earthly pilgrimage Solomon was made to repent deeply of his waywardness and wickedness. We base this conviction upon three things. First, the fact that he was the writer of the book of Ecclesiastes (1:1) and that it was penned at a later period of his life than the Proverbs and Canticles (see 1 Kings 4:32). Now to us it seems impossible to ponder Ecclesiastes without being struck with its prevailing note of sadness and without feeling that its writer is there expressing the contrition of one who has mournfully returned from the paths of error. In that book he speaks out the bitter experiences he had gone through in pursuing a course of folly and madness and of the resultant "vexation of spirit"—see especially 7:2, 3, 26, 27 which is surely a voicing of his repentance. Second, hereby God made good His express promise to David concerning Solomon: "I will be his Father and he shall be My son. If he commit iniquity, I will chastise him with the rod of men, and with the stripes of the children of men: but My mercy shall not depart away from him, as I took it from Saul" (2 Sam. 7:14,15). Third, centuries after his death the Spirit declared, "Did not Solomon king of Israel sin by these things? *yet* among many nations was there no king like him, who was *beloved* of his God" (Neh. 13:26).

4. *The case of Judas.* Though his be not nearly so difficult of solution, nevertheless it is admittedly a very mysterious one, and there are features about it which pertain to none other. But that which more immediately concerns us here is to show there is nothing in this awful example which militates in the least against the doctrine for which we are contending. That Judas is eternally lost there is no room to doubt: that he was ever saved there is no evidence whatever to show. Should it be said that the Lord would never have ordained a bad man to be one of His favored apostles, the answer is, that

God is not to be measured by *our* standards of the fitness of things: He is sovereign over all, doing as He pleases and giving no account of His matters. Moreover, He has told us that our thoughts and ways are not as His. The mystery of iniquity is a great deep, yet faith has full confidence in God even where it cannot understand.

That Christ was in nowise deceived by Judas is clear from John 6:64, "For Jesus knew from the beginning who they were that believed not, and who should betray Him." Furthermore, we are told that He declared on this solemn occasion, "Have not I chosen you twelve, and one of you is a devil" (v. 70). Notably and blessedly did that act make manifest the moral excellency of the Saviour. When the Son became incarnate He averred "Lo I come to do Thy will, O God" (Heb. 10:7), and God's will for Him was revealed "in the volume of the Book." In that Book it was written that a familiar friend should lift up his heel against Him (Ps. 41:9). This was a sore trial, yet the perfect Servant balked not at it, but complied therewith by calling a "devil" to be one of His closest attendants. Christ rendered full obedience to the Father's pleasure though it meant having the son of perdition in most intimate association with Him for three years, constantly dogging His steps even when He retired from His carping critics to be alone with the twelve.

Appeal is made by the Arminians to John 17:12, "While I was with them in the world, I kept them in Thy name: those that Thou gavest Me I have kept, and none of them is lost but the son of perdition, that the Scripture might be fulfilled." Yet there is nothing here which supports their contention. Judas was "given to" Christ and "chosen" by Him as an *apostle*, but he was never given to Him by a special act of grace, nor "chosen in Him" and united to Him as a member of Him, as the rest of the apostles and as all the election of grace are. This is clear from His words in John 13:18, "I speak not of you all (cf. vv. 10,11): I know whom I have chosen"; that is chosen unto eternal life, for otherwise He had chosen Judas equally with the others. Let it be carefully noted that in John 17:12 Christ says *not* "none of them is lost *except* the son of perdition." In using the disjunctive "but" He sharply contrasted Judas from the rest, showing he belonged to an entirely different class: compare Matthew 12:4; Acts 27:22; Revelation 21:27, where the "but" is in direct opposition to what precedes.

Christ's statement in John 17:12 was designed to show that there had been no failure in the trust committed to Him, but rather that He had complied with His commission to the last detail. It also served to assure the eleven of this, that their faith might not be staggered by the perfidy of their companion. It gave further proof that He had not been deceived by Judas, for before he betrayed Him, He terms him "the son of perdition." Finally, it declared *God's* hand and counsel in it: Judas perished "that the Scripture might be fulfilled." Among the reasons why God ordered that there should be a Judas in the apostolate, we suggest it was in order that an impartial witness might bear testimony to the moral excellency of Christ: though in the closest possible contact with Him by day and night, he could find no flaw in Him, but confessed "I have betrayed the *innocent* blood" (Matt. 27:4). It was not from saving grace Judas "fell," but from "ministry, and apostleship" (Acts 1:25). —AWP

LOVE REPROVING

Some time ago we received the following inquiry from one of our readers: "Do you think it possible to be too critical of Christians (?) nowadays? The reason I put a question-mark after 'Christians' was because I wondered if some of them really are born again of the Spirit. We cannot always tell, can we? Are we not, at all events, to speak the Truth in love? This is a very practical question with us just now." It is a practical question for *all* who (by grace) really desire to conduct themselves according to the revealed will of God and follow the example which Christ Himself has left us. The wording of these questions indicates that the inquirer does not have in mind the matter of how I should act toward one who has wronged me personally, but rather, what is my duty unto professing Christians with whom I come into contact and whose ways grieve me and whose walk causes me to doubt their regeneration? As others of our readers may be exercised upon these points, we will here amplify the answer given to our friend.

First, let us turn the light of Holy Writ upon this matter: "Thou shalt not hate thy brother in thine heart: thou shalt in any wise rebuke thy neighbour, and not suffer sin upon him" (Lev 19:17). There are three things which call for our prayerful response. First, this is a plain precept bidding us to rebuke an erring brother: it is not optional but obligatory; the words "in any wise" signify that this duty must not be omitted under any pretence. God requires His people to uphold the demands of righteousness. *He* will not wink at sin, nor must *they*. Second, God would also correct our innate self-centredness. We are so occupied with our own wellbeing as to be in danger of neglecting the good of our neighbour. This verse plainly denotes it is a lack of love for others if we see them commit sin with indifference and make no effort to bring them to repentance and forsake their evil course. A mild, plain, and seasonable reproof is the best way of expressing our solicitude for an erring brother, though it be distasteful to us and unwelcome to him. Third, the marginal rendering "that thou bear not sin for him" means that thou become not an accessory of the act. Silence gives consent: if I rebuke not, I condone evil and share the guilt.

The basic issue which is here raised narrows down to this: *what is it* for a Christian to "act in love" towards others, particularly the wayward? Few words have been employed more inaccurately and loosely in recent years than has "love." With a great many people it is but a synonym for moral laxity, weakness of character, a taking the line of least resistance, a quiet tolerating of what is felt to be wrong. Multitudes of parents have supposed they were treating their children "lovingly" when they overlooked their folly, made excuses for their wildness, and refused to discipline them for disobedience. They have prided themselves on being "kinder" toward their offspring than the "stern measures" which were meted out to them in their own youth. But it is *laxity* and not love which allows a child to have its own way: "he that spareth his rod *hateth* his son: but he that loveth him chasteneth him betimes" (Prov 13:24). Let those of our readers who have young children ponder Proverbs 19:18; 22:15; 23:13, 14; 29:15, 17, and remember those are the words of Him who *is* Love!

That which we have referred to in the above paragraph has been by no means confined to home life: the same evil has held sway in the "churches." Leniency and weakness have overridden righteousness and faithfulness. Instead of maintaining and enforcing the discipline which God's Word enjoins the great majority of the "churches" have winked at even glaring offences, refusing to deal with those who walk disorderly. And this reprehensible laxity was misnamed "love." A maudlin sentimentality which shrank from "hurting the feelings" of others ousted all concern for the glory of Christ and the honour of His "house." This was one of the inevitable effects of the one-sided preaching of the pulpit, where the love and grace of God were constantly proclaimed while His justice and wrath were studiously ignored. God is "light" (1 John 1:5) as well as "love" (1 John 4:8), holy as well as merciful, severe as well as good (Rom 11:22), and unless the balance be preserved between those *two sides* of the Divine character, not only will He be grievously misrepresented, but the most serious results will follow.

"Beloved, let us love one another, for love is of God: and every one that loveth is born of God and knoweth God" (1 John 4:7). Christian love is not a thing of nature, but is entirely supernatural. It is not a part of our "personality" or anything which issues from our "disposition," but is a Divine communication received at the new birth. It is neither a sentiment, emotion, nor passion, but a holy principle which is spiritual in its origin, its nature, its characteristics, its manifestations. But alas, many of God's own children are today so ill-taught, so ignorant, so carnal, that they are unable to recognize true brotherly love when they see it in exercise. Their thinking is so much coloured by the world, they are so much corrupted by mingling with hollow professors, that they mistake pleasantries and cordiality for spiritual love. They forget that some who make no profession at all are naturally genial, kindly, warm-hearted, courteous, sympathetic. Christian love is neither the milk of human kindness nor creature good-will perfected by grace. Much that passes for it is merely the amiability and affability of the flesh.

How are we to know when we truly "love one another"? When we feel our hearts drawn out to them because of their affableness, their charming demeanour, their "sweet" ways? No, for appearances are deceptive. A winsome smile, a hearty hand-shake, a kiss, is no sign of the new nature, as Judas' kissing of Christ demonstrated. Nor does a suave style or honeyed-mouth expressions prove anything to the point: rather does the Christian need to be doubly on his guard in the company of those who flatter him: ponder Proverbs 20:19; 26:28; Psalm 12:3. Then how are we to know when we "love one another" and when they love us? When we truly seek their highest good: when they aim at our spiritual wellbeing. The one who evidences the most spiritual love for me is he who is ever seeking to promote my eternal interests by wise counsels, by salutary warnings, by timely rebukes, by godly encouragements; and if I be spiritual I shall love him in return for his piety, his heavenly-mindedness, his faithfulness.

"Open rebuke is better than secret love. Faithful are the wounds of a friend, but the kisses of an enemy are deceitful" (Prov 27:5,6). Ah, my reader, little as you may like it, the one who "wounds" you the most may be the best friend you have, who has the most spiritual love for you. But the one who winks at your faults, is silent about your sins, and refuses to rebuke you for what is dishonouring to God, is your enemy and *hates* you! Alas, what a low plane even the people of God are now living upon. Many of them are so easily ruffled that, the least criticism of them and they are "hurt," offended; which shows they have more self-love than the love of God in them. O for grace to say with the Psalmist, "Let the righteous smite me, it shall be a kindness; and let him reprove me, it shall be an excellent oil, which shall not break my head" (141:5). "Rebuke a wise man, and he will love thee" (Prov 9:8)—how few of the "wise" are now left!

"By this we know that we love the children of God, when we love God and keep His commandments" (1 John 5:2). Go back to the previous verse for the connection: "Whosoever believeth that Jesus is the Christ is born of God, and every one that loveth

Him that begat loveth him also that is begotten of Him." We love the brethren because they have been made "partakers of the Divine nature": it is *that*, and nothing pertaining to the old creation, which is the uniting bond. How that lifts us entirely out of the realm of nature, into the spiritual sphere! It is love for God which produces love for those who bear His image. And what is the touch-stone of my love to God? Not rapturous feelings, nor beautiful words of devotion, nor heartily singing His praises, but by keeping His commandments: John 14:15, 21, 24; 15:10. The strength of my love for God is to be gauged by the measure of my obedience to His Word. The same principle holds good in my relations with the brethren: love to them will be manifested by efforts to encourage them in the path of obedience—and that necessarily involves rebuking them for disobedience.

To come more immediately to the opening questions. "Is it possible to be too critical of Christians (?) nowadays?" Why the qualifying "nowadays"? Has God lowered His standard to meet these evil times? Is it permissible or expedient for me to compromise because the present generation is so lax and carnal? Do not the days in which our lot is cast call for a clearer drawing of the line between the Church and the world? If so, should not this help to determine my conduct toward the individual? We are not unmindful that large numbers hold the view that God requires less from people in degenerate times, but we know of nothing in His Word which supports them. Rather are such days the very time when the Christian most needs to show his colours, when shallowness and hollowness marks the religious profession all around there is greater urgency for us to make manifest the reality that we are "strangers and pilgrims" in this scene. The Scriptures are just as much the Rule and the sole rule, for *us* to walk by, as they were for our more godly forebears and in the Day to come *we* shall be judged by them as truly as they will be. It is never right to do wrong—nor to condone wrong.

John, the apostle of love, began his third epistle with these words, "The elder unto the well-beloved Gaius, whom I love *in the Truth*." What a needed word is this for today, when so much that passes for love, even in avowedly Christian circles, is nothing but a sickly sentimentality at the expense of the Truth. One of the outstanding cries in the religious world is to this effect though we have differed in our beliefs and practices let us now sink our differences and come together in love. When pastor of a church in Sydney we were regarded as a narrow-minded bigot because on what Rome calls "good Friday" we refused to take part in a "united Communion service," where Fundamentalists and Modernists, Trinitarians and Unitarians, Creationists and Evolutionists were invited to gather together and thereby express "fraternal love" for one another. What a travesty and mockery! The wisdom which is from above is "*first* pure, *then* peaceable" (James 3:17). The more I am walking in the Truth and the more my brother is doing the same, the more cause have we to love one another.

It may be helpful to answer the opening question by changing the form of it: Is it possible to be too critical *of myself*? May I permit myself a certain amount of indulgence, exclude some part of my life from the control of God, be less strict about some matter than others? In the light of such verses as "Take us the foxes, the *little* foxes, that spoil the vines" (Song of Sol 2:15), "grow up into Him in *all* things, which is the Head, even Christ" (Eph 4:15), "*whatsoever* ye do, do all to the glory of God" (1 Cor 10:31) is there any difficulty in answering that question! If not, am I justified in countenancing a lower standard for others than I seek to apply to myself? Am I not required to love my neighbour as myself? And am I doing so if I gloss over something in him which I know to be against his or her spiritual interests and can only work ill for him? If it be my plain duty to warn him against physical evils, then on what ground am I justified in being silent when I see spiritual danger menacing him?

But let it be pointed out that I certainly am not warranted in being "critical" about the conduct of others, unless I am accustomed to unsparingly judge *myself*. It is the very worst species of hypocrisy to point the finger of condemnation at another while I am guilty of something equally bad. I must first cast out the beam from mine own eye before I am qualified to perform so delicate an operation as seeking to remove a mote from my brother's eye. Since there has been a "beam" in mine own eye that is cause for humility, and if the humility be real and deep it will preserve me from acting proudly and haughtily when seeking not to "criticise," but—*help* my brother. Nothing is more un-Christianlike than for me to berate an erring one in a spirit of self-righteousness and in tones of self-superiority, rather than in the spirit of "consider thyself, lest thou also be tempted" (Gal 6:1). If I am to wash my brother's feet from the defilements of the way, then I must needs take the place of lowliness in order to serve him.

On the other hand, we must guard against going to an opposite extreme. If pride and haughtiness are to be reprehended, mock humility or even an undue occupation with our own frailty and faultiness is not to be commended. If we must wait until we are blameless then there are many precepts of Scripture we cannot act upon; if we must tarry until our own character and conduct be faultless then we are disqualified from rebuking anybody. We greatly fear that many have created their own difficulty or deterrent through a wrongful appropriation of those words "he that is without sin among you, let him first cast a stone at her" (John 8:7). How often have we heard professing Christians say, when it had become their manifest duty to admonish another, Who am I to cast stones at others? It should be remembered that John 8:7 was not spoken to conscientious saints, jealous of the honour of the Lord, anxious to promote the good of others, but to hypocritical pharisees, who were deliberately seeking to ensnare Christ.

Is it possible to be too critical of Christians? It is certainly possible to expect too much from them and then be irritated because they fail to produce what we look for. If our thoughts be governed by Scripture, which declares "in many things we all offend" (James 3:2), if we bear in mind the frailties—some of them glaring ones—of the most eminent characters mentioned in the Word, if we constantly remind ourselves of how far short *we* come of the standard God has set before us, then we ought to be preserved from looking for anything approaching perfection in Christians. They too are men and women of "like passions" as ourselves. Hence the force of "*forbearing* one another in love" (Eph 4:2): yet that must not be twisted into "winking at one another's faults" or condoning sin under the pretence of love.

No, we cannot "always tell" whether a professing Christian be a regenerate or unregenerate person, and therefore it behoves us to be cautious and conservative, lest we be guilty of giving that which is holy unto dogs (Matt 7:6). It is a very serious and solemn matter to encourage a deluded soul in his deception, as we *do* when we lead him to believe *we* regard him as a Christian. But how is this to be avoided? By a withholding the tokens of fellowship—for example, refusing to address as "Brother" or "Sister"—from all whom we stand in doubt of, especially from those whose walk is manifestly worldly and contrary to the precepts of Scripture. While we cannot read the hearts of those we mix with, we can test their outward life by the Word, and if its general tenor be opposed to the requirements of holiness and be contrary to the example of Christ, we certainly are not warranted in regarding them as children of God.

Certainly we should be "loving in rebuking sin." It is in love God chastens His people, that they "might be partakers of His holiness" (Heb 12:6,10). We are bidden to "speak the Truth in love," and Christ was doing so as truly when denouncing the pharisees in Matthew 23 as when He was comforting His disciples in John 14, but does that mean His countenance, the tone of His voice, or His general bearing was the same? He ever spoke the Truth in love, but if some would reread the four Gospels with this particular thought in mind it might cause them to revise, or at least modify their present conception of what speaking "in love" really is. Something depends upon the fault committed: mole-hills are not to be magnified into mountains. There are times when it is fitting to rebuke "sharply" (Titus 1:13), as Christ did in Luke 24:25, but for the most part it should be done in "the spirit of meekness" (Gal 6:1). There is a happy medium between harshness and firmness, as there is between sentimentality and tenderness.

We know of a small church, far removed from these parts, the pastor and members of which are seeking to act one toward another in a spirit and manner which we deem highly commendable. Its minister tells us "I have never seen a congregation more pliable to the Word of God, more willing to rectify wrongs,— endeavouring to walk as Christ would have them walk. Each member is interviewed by the joint-elders-group concerning their position listed in the church discipline; and further, each one applying for membership specifies that it is his desire to have a pastor who will deal with the sin problems of that member as a shepherd would the problems of the sheep." That admirably expresses our own convictions: love ministering to the needy as a shepherd to the sheep. —AWP

(continued from back page)

preach to or lead in prayer before a mixed congregation, which is forbidden by 1 Timothy 2:12; 1 Corinthians 14:34. The Spirit quickens and empowers, but He never prompts to anything contrary to Scripture. "He that hath an ear, let him hear what the Spirit saith unto the churches" (Rev 2:7), i.e. as it is recorded in the alone Rule of Faith.

Seventh, because faith is *the key* which opens the Scriptures. Yet how little is this realized. The chief hindrance to our lack of perception of spiritual things is neither mental dullness nor lack of what the world terms "education." Proof of that is seen in the fact that men endowed with the keenest of intellect and equipped by the highest standards of "modern scholarship" find the Word of God a sealed book to them. Many an illiterate rustic possesses far more spiritual understanding of the things of God than do thousands of those who possess a M.A. or D.D. degree. It is *unbelief* which prevents admittance into the Temple of Truth. The Word of God obtains no entrance into minds which are closed by self-conceit and prejudice, nor into hearts blocked by indifference or distrust. "The entrance of Thy words giveth light," and it is faith which opens the door to admit them. When faith receives the first three chapters of Genesis it has more light upon creation and the course of human history than all the pseudo scientists and false philosophers put together. The miracles which stumble the sceptic present no difficulty to the humble believer. "Lord, increase our faith" (Luke 17:5). —AWP

(continued from front page)

which the Divine Oracles inspire. It realizes that to act without an express "thus saith the Lord" is to act either presumptuously or in blind credulity. In prayer its language is "Remember the word unto Thy servant upon which Thou hast caused me to hope" (Psa 119:49): concerning which Matthew Henry pertinently said, "Those that make God's promises their portion, may with humble boldness make them their plea." However opposed its dictates to human wisdom, the language of faith is "nevertheless at Thy word I will let down the net" (Luke 5:5). When God speaks that is enough; where He is silent, faith refuses to move.

Fourth, because it is *the means* by which faith is informed. Faith is not self-sufficient, but dependent. It is like a dutiful but ignorant child who desires to please his father, yet knows not how until his will is made known. If we had not the Word of God in our hand faith would be completely at a loss—like a mariner without chart or compass. This is not sufficiently realized. It is true that unless the Word be mixed with faith it profits us not; it is equally true that faith cannot function aright unless informed by the Word. Faith is the eye of the spirit: but something more than sight is needed—light is equally essential, for the keenest vision is useless in a darkened room. Hence the Psalmist declares "The entrance of Thy words giveth light: it giveth understanding unto the simple" (119:130), that is, to the one who receives them with childlike simplicity, which is exactly what faith does. The Scriptures, then, are the Word of Faith because they instruct it. "For the Commandment is a lamp and the Law is light" (Prov 6:23); "the Commandment of the Lord is pure, enlightening the eyes" (Psa 19:8).

Fifth, because it is *the food* by which faith is nourished. Faith is a creature, or at any rate a part of the new creation, and like every other creature it stands in need of that which will minister to its maintenance. Since God be its Object, His words are what it feeds upon. Said one of the prophets, "Thy words were found, and I did *eat* them, and Thy Word was unto me the joy and rejoicing of mine heart" (Jer 15:16). That was not only the language of faith, but it describes both the means and the process by which faith is nourished. Faith makes a personal *appropriation*, taking unto itself what God has said. Faith proceeds to a *mastication* of what is placed before it. God's Word is made up of words, and on them faith ruminates and meditates. Faith issues in *assimilation*, so that the Word is actually taken up into the soul, and strength and energy is supplied thereby. Thus will faith aver "I have esteemed the words of His mouth more than my necessary food" (Job 23:12). And thus also do we read of being "nourished up in the words of faith" (1 Tim 4:6).

Sixth, because it is *the Rule* by which it is directed. Though this approximates closely to what was considered under our fourth point, yet it is to be distinguished from it. The Word of God is more than informative: it is authoritative, and therefore is it designated "The Faith which was once [for all] delivered unto the saints" (Jude 3), which they are exhorted to "earnestly contend for." The Word is the alone Rule which faith has to walk by. But is not the Christian also prompted and guided by the Spirit? Such a question betrays sad confusion of thought and much harm has been wrought among those giving place to it. How often we have heard different ones make the claim that the Spirit moved them to perform such and such an act—for example, a woman to

. *(continued on proceeding page)*

VOL. XXII.   DECEMBER, 1943.   NO. 11

STUDIES IN THE SCRIPTURES

"Search the Scriptures." John 5:39.

Publisher and Editor—ARTHUR W. PINK,
27 Lewis Street,
Stornoway, Isle of Lewis,
Scotland.

THE WORD OF RIGHTEOUSNESS

At no point does the uniqueness of the Divine Oracles appear more strikingly and conspicuously than in their teachings concerning righteousness. Those teachings are at direct variance with the beliefs and conceits of men the world over: in fact so radical and unpalatable are its pronouncements on this subject that many of those who profess to receive the Scriptures as a Divine revelation have exhausted their ingenuity in attempting to explain away some of its plainest statements. The sweeping assertion that among the sons of men "there is none righteous, no, not one," but that "all the world" stands "guilty before God" (Rom. 3:10,19), is one which never had its origin in any human brain. The declaration that "all our righteous-nesses are as filthy rags" (Isa. 64:6) is too distasteful to the proud heart of fallen man to have been invented by "the Church." The question, how can the unrighteous become righteous before the Divine Judge? is one which, when duly weighed, defies solution by human wisdom. If he had no other evidence for the inspiration of the Scriptures than their teaching upon righteousness, they would suffice to convince this writer of their Divine Authorship.

"The Word of righteousness" (Heb. 5:13). The word righteousness is a forensic one, being the antithesis of guiltiness. Reduced to its simplest form it means righteous, or up to the required standard. It therefore presupposes a rule by which conduct is measured, and that Rule is the will of God as revealed in His Word. The will of God for man is summed up in the Divine Law, and righteousness is nothing more or less than a perfect conformity to the Law in heart and life. Hence we find the Lord saying "Judgment also will I lay to the line, and righteousness to the plummet" (Isa. 28:17), that is, all shall yet be measured by the immutable standard of His Law. Thus we may say, in the first place, that the Word of God is given this particular title because righteousness itself has no other *Rule* to be regulated by. "All Scripture is given by inspiration of God, and is profitable for doctrine, for reproof, for correction, for *instruction in righteousness*" (2 Tim. 3:16).

Second, the Word is so denominated because righteousness is its prime and inexorable *demand*. The Law is inflexible and implacable. It makes no favourable allowance for human infirmities, constitutional weaknesses, or personal defects. All possibility of misapprehension on this score is excluded if we weigh its solemn declaration,

(continued on back page)

IMPORTANT NOTICES

Please advise promptly of change in address, otherwise copies will be lost in the mails.

We are glad to send a sample copy to any of your friends whom you believe would be interested in this publication.

This magazine is published as "a work of faith and labour of love," the editor and his wife gladly giving their services free. There is no regular subscription price, as we do not wish the poor of the flock to be deprived. This does not mean that those looking for something for nothing may "help themselves." Those getting this Magazine, who are financially able and who receive spiritual help from its pages, are expected to gladly contribute towards its expenses; otherwise, their names are dropped from our lists.

Will those forwarding International Money Orders please have them made out to us at Stornoway, Isle of Lewis, Scotland. Checks (Cheques-Eng.) made out on U.S.A. Banks are not negotiable here, so please do not send them.

CONTENTS

THE SERMON ON THE MOUNT
27. Conclusion: Matthew 7:28, 29

Once more we have been permitted and enabled to complete a lengthy though pleasant task, for after writing sixty-four articles on Matthew 5-7 our present business is to pen the closing one. Those three chapters record what is commonly designated our Lord's sermon on the mount. Really, it is far more than a sermon, being what might well be termed the Messiah's manifesto, the magna charta (or "constitution"), of His kingdom, for therein He unfolded the laws and conditions under which alone we can enter His kingdom. In our second article we pointed out that, in keeping with its character and design, this address had twelve divisions— the *governmental* number. They may be expressed thus: 1. The character of those on whom the Divine blessing rests: 5:3-11. 2. The ministerial office: 5:12-16. 3. The spirituality and authority of the Moral Law: 5:17-48. 4. Practical righteousness or good works: 6:1-19. 5. Warning against covetousness: 6:20-34. 6. Unlawful judgment: 7:1-5. 7. Unlawful liberality: 7:6. 8. Seeking grace: 7:7-11. 9. The golden rule: 7:12.10. The way of salvation: 7:13, 14. 11. False prophets: 7:15-19. 12. Profession tested: 7:20-27.

In the verses which are to be before us we are informed of the effect which our Lord's sermon had upon the large concourse that heard it. This writer often closes his eyes and seeks to visualize the various scenes presented in Holy Writ. On this occasion, the incarnate Son of God, but known only as "Jesus of Nazareth" to the Jews at that time, sat down upon the mountain side—perhaps on some slight eminence, that all might see and hear Him the better. Follow Him then throughout the whole of Matthew 5-7 and attempt to enter into the feelings of His audience. Remember there was no halo of glory about His head, that to their eyes He appeared simply as a Galilean peasant. Yet again and again He sets over against "Ye have heard that it was said by them of old time" His imperative and imperial "But *I* say unto you." He denounced the Pharisees as "hypocrites." He declared that in the Day to come, He would say unto the empty professors "I never knew you: depart from Me, ye that work iniquity." He closed by insisting that men's eternal destiny would be regulated by how they complied with "these sayings of Mine."

"And it came to pass, when Jesus had ended these sayings, the people were astonished at His doctrine for He taught them as one having authority, and not as the scribes" (7:28,29). Here is made known to us the impression which our Lord's discourse produced upon its auditors. They were amazed, and well they might be. The Speaker had not graduated from the Rabbinical schools, nor had He been granted a "preaching license" by the sanhedrim; yet He declared, "Think not that I am come to destroy the Law or the Prophets: I am not come to destroy but to fulfil." Then He added "For I say unto you, That except your righteousness exceed the righteousness of the scribes and pharisees ye shall in no case enter into the kingdom of heaven." He went on to declare that causeless anger was insipient murder and that those who indulged in lustful glances were guilty of adultery. He bade them love your enemies, bless them that curse you, do good to them that hate you. He made it evident that it was not merely good advice or salutary counsel He was offering them, but rather was issuing peremptory demands. It was as the King of righteousness He spoke.

The crowd was astonished both at the matter and manner of His preaching, for He spoke with a weight, a majesty, an earnestness which carried conviction. They were filled with a temporary wonderment: yet it is not said that they repented or believed on Him or became His disciples. We too admire the matchless wisdom of His discourse, maintaining as it did throughout a perfect balance of Truth. We are made to marvel at its scope: that He covered so much ground in so brief a space, containing that which was suited to all classes and conditions of men, be they lost or saved, babes or fathers in Christ. We are made to tremble at the fearful solemnity of its utterances: the repeated reference to "Hell" and "Hell fire." We are solemnized as we learn from its final section that in the great Assize the Preacher of this sermon will personally officiate as the Judge of men, pronouncing sentence of doom upon those who conform not to the Divine will. No wonder, that on another occasion, the officers sent by the pharisees to arrest Christ, returned without Him saying "never man spake like this Man" (John 7:46).

"The people were astonished at His doctrine." Have we not good reason to be astonished that they were not much more than "astonished"? Ought they not to have been brought to His feet in worship, perceiving it was more than man who addressed them? Ought they not to have been convicted and converted by His teaching: made deeply sensible of how far, far short they fell of such a standard of holiness, turning to Him in contrition and crying out for mercy? Alas, what is man, even when he hears the Truth from the lips of Truth incarnate! Capable of being impressed by a Divine message when it falls on his ears from without, but incapable of perceiving his own inward depravity and wretchedness in the light of that message. How true it is that "except a man be born from above he cannot see the kingdom of God" (John 3:3), no, not even when it is brought nigh to him by the King Himself. Then let us not be surprised when only temporary effects are produced under the most faithful and earnest preaching; rather let us be deeply thankful if the Message has found an abiding home in *our* heart.

It may be asked, Why did not Christ put forth His Divine power and turn the hearts of His hearers unto Himself? If three thousand were converted under the Pentecostal sermon of Peter (Acts 2:41), why were not a similar number at least brought from death unto life by this address of the Saviour's? Most certainly He could, had He so pleased, have imparted to the whole of that multitude a saving knowledge of the Truth. Then why was He not pleased to do so? why should the apostles perform "greater works" (John 14:12) than He wrought? Because He had taken upon Him the "form of a *servant*" (Phil. 2:7), and therefore did He aver, "I came down from heaven not to do Mine own will, but the will of Him that sent Me" (John 6:38). The exercise of His Divine attributes was entirely subordinated unto the will of the Father. Not only did He refuse to work miracles on His own behalf (Matt. 4:3,4), but He only put forth His power for the good of others as He had orders to do so from Above. This lovely perfection of Christ's, which is the glory of His mediatorial holiness, has not received anything like the attention which it justly calls for.

The obedience of Christ was the absolute conformity of His entire spirit and soul to the mind and will of the Father, His ready and cheerful performance of every duty and every thing which God commanded Him. As He Himself declared, "My meat is to do the will of Him that sent Me" (John 4:34). Familiar as are these words to the saints, how few have perceived the *fulness* of Christ's obedience or recognised that His *every act* during the thirty-three years He tabernacled among men was distinctly and designedly an act of submission to God. But this will be the more plainly seen if the reader traces through the four Gospels that oft-repeated expression "that it might be fulfilled which was spoken by— the prophet," and then ponders the import of those words. The whole of Christ's course had been marked out for Him. Thus it was that "He came and dwelt in Capernaum" (Matt. 12:12-14). It was not the force of circumstances which drove the Lord Jesus to select that place as His ministerial headquarters, nor was it out of personal inclination: that town had been selected by God for Him long before He came to earth, and it was in subjection to the Divine will that He went there. Christ made obedience to the Father the one great business of His life.

His miracles of mercy were wrought in obedience to the Father's revealed will. "When the even was come they brought unto Him many that were possessed with demons: and He cast out the spirits with His word and healed all that were sick *that it might be fulfilled* which was spoken by Isaiah the prophet" (Matt. 8:16). How striking is the particular aspect of Truth here made known to us! Christ was tender, sympathetic, full of compassion, yet the first and deepest motive which moved Him to heal the sick was that the will of God might be done. In the volume of the Book it was written of Him, and therefore did He say, "I delight to do Thy will, O God" (Ps. 40:7,8). A striking and beautiful illustration of this is found in John 11. Lazarus is taken seriously ill, and his sisters sent the Saviour an urgent message, saying: "Lord, behold, he whom Thou lovest is sick" (v. 3). Then we read, "Now Jesus loved Martha, and her sister, and Lazarus," yet the very next thing recorded is "when He had heard therefore that Lazarus was sick, He abode two days still in the same place where He was." Mysterious delay! But the mystery was solved by His own declaration, "this sickness is not unto death, but for the glory of God" (v. 4). Not even His affection for those sorely-tried souls would move Him to respond to their appeal until the Father's hour had arrived.

In like manner, Christ's saving of sinners was in order to the rendering of obedience to God. "All that the Father giveth Me shall come to Me and him that cometh to Me I will in no wise cast out; *for* I came down from heaven not to do Mine own will but the will of Him that sent Me" (John 6:37,38). What a view does this present to us of the redemptive work of Christ! How it magnifies His blessed submission unto the One who had commissioned Him! Here then is the explanation why He put not forth His own Divine power to convert the whole of His hearers by this sermon on the mount: because He had no word from the Father so to do. Admire then and adore the Lord of glory as He so perfectly discharged His office as Servant. What an example of entire submission to God has He left us. Does the reader desire that we press the question a stage further back and ask, Why was it the Father's pleasure that His incarnate Son should so often suspend the exercise of His Divine attributes and refrain from putting forth His own power? Surely if no other answer was available than what has been pointed out above, *it* would be sufficient: to display the perfect oneness between the Son and the Father, to evidence that the Former would not act independently of the Other, to manifest His moral perfections and thereby leave His people an example.

But there were other reasons why it was fitting that a vail should be cast over the Divine glory of the incarnate Son. This was the season of His humiliation, when He came not to rule over the earth as King of kings and Lord of lords, but to "have not where to lay His head." He had entered the place of subserviency, of obedience, yea, He had become "obedient unto death, even the death of the cross" (Phil. 2:8). And in order thereto it was necessary that He should come unto His own and that "His own receive Him not" (John 1:11), yea, that He should be "despised and rejected of men." He had descended from Heaven to earth in order that He should be "taken and by wicked hands crucified and slain" (Acts 2:23), yet at the same time offer Himself as a sacrifice to God, as a sin-offering on behalf of His people. It was not then the season for Him to convert men en masse, to overthrow Satan's kingdom and deliver his captives. The Corn of wheat must fall into the ground and die before the fruit thereof is brought forth (John 12:24). In due time God would exalt Him "with His right hand to be a Prince and a Saviour, for to give repentance to [the spiritual] Israel, and forgiveness of sins" (Acts 5:31), for then would "the rod of His strength" go out of Zion and His people be made willing "in the day of His power" (Ps. 110:2,3).

Again, by cloaking His Divine power yet at the same time acting as "a Minister of the circumcision for the Truth of God, to confirm the promises made to the fathers and that the Gentiles might glorify God for His mercy" (Rom. 15:8,9) an admirable test was made of men. Though He stopped short of renewing their hearts, yet by acting as the final Spokesman of God (Heb. 1:1,2), by speaking to men as they had never been spoken to before, Christ addressed Himself to the responsibility of His hearers. The Light shone in midday splendor, but the darkness comprehended it not. And why? Because men loved darkness rather than light. Thereby their real character was unmistakably revealed: as incorrigibly and inveterately opposed to God, steeled against Him even when speaking to them through His own Son. Nor could they plead lack of clear evidence that Christ was the Messiah Himself, for the miracles He wrought unequivocally established His credentials. Thus in their not being converted by such a Sermon as this, they were left "without excuse." Christ, then, put not forth His power to regenerate them, first, because He had no commission from the Father so to do; second, because it was not the time for Him to exercise His royal prerogative; third, because by leaving His auditors to the exercise of their own wills, their accountability was put to the proof and their utter depravity demonstrated.

But further: the Father was pleased that His Son should restrain the power of His Godhead even from His public ministry that it might be more clearly evidenced when His term of obedience had expired, that He was vested with all-sufficient unction and invincible might. After His resurrection Christ affirmed "all power is given unto Me in heaven and in earth" (Matt. 28:18), and on the day of Pentecost after the public descent of the Holy Spirit Peter announced, "Let all the house of Israel know assuredly, that God hath made that same Jesus whom ye have crucified both Lord and Christ" (Acts 2:36), where "made" has *not* the force of "constituted" but signifies *made manifest*, for it was from Christ the Spirit had been given (v. 33). God would have it made known unto His people that the Mediator, being ascended, was not only "set down on the right hand of the Majesty on high," where He is "upholding all things by the word of His power" (Heb. 1:3), ruling as King in His royal office, but also that He governs His Church by His Word and Spirit (Rev. 3:1). It was for this reason, when promising the apostles that they should do "greater works" than He had wrought, that He added by way of proof "because I go unto My Father" (John 14:12)—there to rule His people and remain until His enemies are made His footstool.

Finally, it appears to us there is yet another and more solemn reason why (so far as the inspired narrative informs us) not one soul was born again through the instrumentality of this Sermon. We cannot shake off the conviction that here in Matthew 5-7 we have, as it were, a miniature tableau, a typical representation and anticipation of the great Assize. Christ seated on the mount was a figure of His taking His place on the throne of judgment. Encircled by His disciples and the "multitudes" before Him gives a picture of the dread Day to come. The contents of this Sermon reveal both the order of procedure which will then be followed and the grounds on which the verdicts will be passed: "His own" vindicated by the benediction (the "Blessed are ye") pronounced upon them, and all the others weighed and found wanting in the balance of the very laws which He here enunciated. The effect upon the people will be the same. For though the visible appearance of Christ in that Day will be very different, though He will be seen with "His eyes as a flame of fire" and wearing "many crowns" (Rev. 19:12), yet none shall he brought to repentance and faith by such a sight. "Astonished" they may well be as they learn *Who* it is they despised and rejected, overwhelmed with horror they will be as they hear His "Depart from Me ye cursed into everlasting fire," but saved by such a spectacle and sentence none will be.

"For He taught them as one having authority and not as the scribes." Apparently no deeper impression was made on the people than a sense of wonderment, which caused them to draw an invidious distinction between Christ and the scribes, who dwelt mainly on "the traditions of men" and such matters as tithing mint and cummin and the ceremonial washings of pots and pans. That Christ should teach with authority was intimated in prophecy, when it was announced that Jehovah would put His own words in His mouth and that He should speak unto Israel all that had been commanded Him (Deut. 18:18). It is remarkable that even His enemies bore witness, "Master, we know that Thou art true, and teachest the way of. Truth, neither carest Thou for any man" (Matt. 22:16). "Though Christ were here in a mean and base state, yet He would not suffer His calling to be condemned, but gets grace thereto" (W. Perkins, 1590, to whom we have been indebted in the course of these expositions). Herein Christ has left His servants an example, for the minister of the Gospel is bidden to "exhort and rebuke with all *authority*" (Titus 2:15), which he can do only as he cleaves closely to the Word and exhorts in the name of Christ.

Let our closing reflection be this: the words of "authority" in Matthew 5-7 are addressed as directly *to us* as to those who first heard them! By its precepts and rules our conduct must be directed: by its promises and encouragements our souls are to be sustained, for in these very scales shall *we* be weighed in the Day of testing and adjudication. To us this Sermon comes with even greater authority than to those who heard it preached in Palestine, for in moving His apostle by the Spirit to register the same as a permanent record of His will He speaks to us from Heaven. Hence the force of that exhortation, "See that ye refuse not Him that [not 'hath spoken' but] *speaketh*: for if they escaped not who refused Him that spoke on earth, much more shall not we escape if we turn away from Him that speaketh from heaven" (Heb. 12:25). Then let us earnestly seek grace to be something more than "astonished" with this Sermon, namely receive it into our hearts and minds and incorporate it into our daily walk. —AWP

THE MISSION AND MIRACLES OF ELISHA
12. Eighth Miracle

The passage which is to be before us (2 Kings 4:38-41) has in it practical instruction as well as spiritual lessons for us, for the Scriptures make known the evils and dangers which are in this world as well as the glory and bliss of the world to come. Elisha was visiting the school of the prophets at Gilgal, instructing them in the things of God. At the close of a meeting he gave orders that a simple meal should be prepared for them, for though he was more concerned about their spiritual welfare he did not overlook their physical. It was a time of "dearth" or famine, so one went out into the field to gather herbs, that they might have a vegetable stew. He found a wild vine with gourds and securing a goodly quantity, he returned and shred them into the pot of pottage, quite unconscious that he was making use of a poisonous plant. Not until after the broth was poured out was the peril discovered, for when they began eating the men cried out "there is death in the pot." How little we realise the many and varied forms in which death menaces us, and how constantly we are indebted to the preserving providence of God.

The effects of the curse which the Lord God pronounced upon the sin of Adam have been by no means confined unto the human family. "Cursed is *the ground* for thy sake" (Gen. 3:17) was part of the fearful sentence, and as Romans 8:22 informs us "the whole creation groaneth and travaileth in pain together until now." No matter where one looks, the observant eye can behold the consequences of the Fall. No section of creation has escaped: even the fields and the woods bring forth not only thistles and thorns, but that which is noxious and venomous. Some of the most innocent-looking herbs and berries produce horrible suffering and death if eaten by man or beast. Yet for the most part, in fact with rare exceptions, God has mercifully provided the sentient creature with adequate protection against such evils. The instinct of the animals and the intelligence of men causes each of them to leave alone that which is harmful: either the eye discovers, the nostril detects, or the palate perceives their evil qualities, and thereby they are guarded against them.

It scarcely needs to be pointed out that what we have alluded to above in the material world adumbrates that which obtains in the religious realm. Among that which is offered for intellectual and spiritual food how much is unwholesome and vicious. The fields of Christendom have many "wild gourds" growing in them, the use of which necessarily entails "death in the pot," for fatal doctrine acts upon the soul as poison does upon the body. This is clear from that apostolic declaration, "their word will eat as doth a canker" or "gangrene" (2 Tim. 2:17), where the reference is to the evil doctrine of heretical teachers. But just as God has mercifully endowed the animals with instincts and man with sufficient natural intelligence to avoid what is injurious, so He has graciously bestowed upon His people spiritual "senses" which if exercised "discern both good and evil" (Heb. 5:14). Thus they instinctively warn against unsound writings and preachers, so that "a stranger will they not follow, but will flee from him; for they know not the voice of strangers" (John 10:5).

The mercy of the Creator appears not only in the protecting "senses" with which He has endowed His creatures so that they may recognize and avoid most if not all of the things around them which are inimical to their well being, but also in providing them with suitable remedies and effective antidotes. If there be herbs which are injurious and poisonous there are others which are counteracting and healing. If the waters of Marah are bitter and undrinkable, there was a tree at hand which when cut down and cast into the waters renders them sweet (Ex. 15:25). If we read at the beginning of the sacred Volume of a tree the eating of whose fruit involved our race in disaster and death, ere that Volume is closed we are told of another Tree the leaves of which are "for the healing of the nations" (Rev. 22:2). This fact, then, holds good in both the material and the spiritual realms: for every evil God has provided a remedy, for every poison an antidote, for every false doctrine a portion of the Truth which exposes and refutes it. With these introductory observations we may now consider the details of Elisha's eighth miracle.

First, *its location.* "And Elisha came again to Gilgal, and there was a dearth in the land" (2 Kings 4:38). It will be remembered that it was from this place that Elisha had started out with his master on their final journey together ere Elijah was raptured to heaven (2 Kings 2:1), where his sincerity had been put to the proof by the testing "Tarry here, I pray thee." From Gilgal they had passed to Bethel (2:2), and from thence to Jericho, and finally to the Jordan. It is striking to note that our hero wrought a miracle at each of these places though in the inverse order of the original tour or journey. At the Jordan he had divided its waters so that he passed over dry-shod before the wondering gaze of the young prophets (2:14,15). At Jericho he had healed the evil waters (2:19-22). At Bethel he had cursed the profane children in the name of the Lord and brought about their destruction (2:23-25). And now here at Gilgal Elisha exercises the extraordinary powers with which God had endowed him. Wherever he goes the servant of God should, as opportunity affords, exercise his ministerial gifts.

"And Elisha came again to Gilgal, and there was a dearth in the land." Gilgal was to the east of Jericho, close to the Jordan, where there would be more moisture and vegetation than further inland. It was a place made memorable from the early history of Israel. It was there that the Nation had set up twelve stones as a monument to God's gracious intervention, when he had caused them to pass through the river dry-shod (Josh. 4:18-24). It was there too that they had circumcised those who had been born in the wilderness wanderings, thereby rolling away the reproach of Egypt from off them, evidencing their separation from the heathen, as being God's peculiar people—type of the "circumcision of the *heart*" (Jer. 4:4; Rom. 2:29), which is the distinguishing mark of God's spiritual children. It was there also that they had first partaken of "the old corn of the land" (5:11) so that miraculous supplies of manna ceased. Yet even such a favored spot as this was affected by the dearth, for great wickedness had also been perpetrated there (1 Sam.15:21-23 and cf. Hosea 9:15).

Second, *its occasion*: "there was a dearth in the land." The Hebrew word for "dearth" (raab) signifies a famine, and is so rendered in 1 Kings 18:2. This is one of the "four sore judgments" which the Lord sends when He expresses His displeasure against a people: "the sword and the famine and the noisome beast and the pestilence" (Ezek. 14:21). In this dispensation the "famine" with which a righteous God afflicts a land is one far more solemn and serious than that of dearth of material food, as that threatened in Amos 8:11: "Behold, the days come saith the Lord God, that I will send a famine in the land, not a famine of bread nor a thirst for water, but of hearing the words of the Lord." Such a "famine" is upon Christendom today. It has not yet become quite universal, but almost so. Thousands of places dedicated to Divine worship became social centres, political clubs, ritualistic playhouses, and today they are heaps of rubble. The vast majority of those still standing provide nothing for people desiring soul food, and even in the very few where the Word of God is ostensibly ministered it is no longer so in the power and blessing of the Spirit. It is this which gives such pertinency to our present passage.

"And Elisha came again to Gilgal, and there was a dearth in the land: and the sons of the prophets were sitting before him." What a blessed and beautiful conjunction of things was this. How instructive for the under-shepherd of Christ and for His sheep in a day like this. Though God was acting in judgment the prophet did not consider that warranted him ceasing his labors until conditions became more favorable. So far from it, he felt it was a time when he should do all in his power to "strengthen the things that remain that are ready to die" (Rev. 3:2), and encourage those who are liable to give way to dejection because of the general apostasy. "Preach the Word; be instant in season, out of season" (2 Tim. 4:2) is the injunction which God has laid upon His ministers. In seasons of "dearth" the servant of Christ needs to be particularly attentive to the spiritual needs of young believers, instructing them in the holiness and righteousness of a sin-hating God when His scourge is upon the nation, and also making known His faithfulness and sufficiency unto "His own" in the darkest hour, reminding them that "God is our refuge and strength, a very present help in trouble" (Ps. 46:1).

See here what a noble example Elisha has left those called by God to engage in proclaiming His truth. The prophet was not idle: he did not wait for needy souls to come to him, but took the initiative and went to them. Times of national distress and calamity do not exempt any from the discharge of spiritual duties or justify any slackness in employing the appointed means of grace. Nor did these "sons of the prophets" raise the objection that Elisha sought unto them at an inopportune time and make the excuse they must needs busy themselves looking after their temporal interests. No, they gladly availed themselves of their golden opportunity, making the most of it by attentively listening to the instructions of Elisha. Their "sitting before him" betokened respect and attentiveness. It reminds us of Mary who "sat at Jesus' feet, and heard His word" (Luke 10:39), which Christ designated that "good part," the "one thing needful" (v. 42). And though many today no longer may *hear* the Word preached, they can still sit and *read* it: be thankful for the printed page if it contains that which strengthens faith and promotes closer walking with God.

Third, *its beneficiaries*. "And he said unto his servant, Set on the great pot, and seethe [boil or concoct] pottage for the sons of the prophets" (v. 38). The order of action in this verse is significant for it shows how the needs of the soul take precedence over those of the body. Elisha saw to it that they had spiritual food set before them ere arranging for material. On the other hand, the prophet did not conduct himself as a fanatic and disdain their temporal needs. Here, as everywhere in Scripture, the balance is rightly preserved. Attention to and enjoyment of fellowship with God must never be allowed to crowd out the discharge of those duties pertaining to the common round of life. As Christ thought of and ministered to the bodily needs of the hungry multitudes after He had broken unto them the Bread of Life, so His servant here was concerned about the physical well being of these students: a plain and simple meal in either case in the one bread and fish, in the other vegetable stew.

"And one went out into the field to gather herbs and found a wild vine, and gathered thereof wild gourds his lap full, and shred them into the pot of pottage: for they knew them not" (v. 39). Apparently this person took it upon himself to go out and gather herbs in the field: no doubt his intention was good, but so far as the narrative is concerned it records no commission from Elisha to act thus—a clear case where the best intentions do not warrant us to act unless we have a definite word from God, and to use only those means He has appointed. It is possible this person may have returned thanks unto God when his eye fell upon those gourds and felt that his steps had been directed by Him to the place where they were growing: if so, a warning how easily we may misunderstand the Divine providences when we are acting in self-will and interpret them in a way which justifies and apparently sanctifies the course we have taken. When Jonah fled from the command the Lord had given him, to "flee unto Tarshish" and went down to Joppa, he "found a ship going" to that very place (1:3)!

Seasons of "dearth" are peculiarly dangerous ones. Why so? Because in times of famine, food is scarce, and because there is less to select from we are very apt to be less particular and act on the principle of "Beggars cannot be choosers." Certainly there is a warning here to be careful about what we eat at such times, and especially of that which grows wild. The Hebrew word here rendered "wild" means uncultivated, and is generally connected with "wild beasts," which were not only ceremonially unclean under the Mosaic law but unfit for human consumption. It is to be duly noted that there was a plentiful supply of these "wild gourds" even though there was a "dearth in the land." So it is spiritually: when there is a "famine" of hearing the words of the Lord, Satan sees to it that there is no shortage of spurious food witness the number of unsound tracts and poisonous booklets which are still being freely circulated in this day when there is such a scarcity of paper, to say nothing of the vile literature in which the things of God are openly derided.

Yet though these gourds were "wild" they must have borne a close resemblance to wholesome ones or he who gathered them had not been deceived by them, nor would it be said of those who stood by while he shred them into the pot of pottage that "they knew them not." This too has a spiritual counterpart, as the Enemy's "tares" sown among the wheat intimates. Satan is a subtle imitator: not only does he transform himself "into an angel of light" but his "deceitful workers" transform themselves "into the apostles of Christ" (2 Cor. 11:13,14) for they come preaching Jesus and His Gospel, but as the Holy Spirit warns us it is "another Jesus" and "another Gospel" than the genuine one (2 Cor. 11:4). Those who looked on while this person was shredding the wild gourds into the pot raised no objection, for they were quite unsuspicious, instead of carefully examining what they were to eat. What point this gives to the apostolic exhortation "*Prove* ALL things, hold fast that which is good" (1 Thess. 5:21), and if we refuse to do so, who is to blame when we devour that which is injurious?

Fourth, *its need*. "So they poured out for the men to eat. And it came to pass as they were eating of the pottage, that they cried out and said, O thou man of God, there is death in the pot. And they could not eat thereof" (v. 40). It was not until the eleventh hour that they discovered their peril, for the deadly danger of these "wild gourds" was not exposed until they had begun actually to eat of the same; not only had their appearance deceived them, but they had no offensive or suspicious odor while cooking. The case was particularly subtle, for seemingly it was one of their own number who had gathered the poisonous herbs. Ah, note how the apostle commended the Bereans for carefully bringing *his* teaching to the test of Holy Writ (Acts 17:11): much more do *we* need to do so with the preachings and writings of uninspired men. We need to "consider diligently" what is set before us by each ecclesiastical ruler (Prov. 23:1 and cf. Matt. 24:45), for though they be "dainties" and "sweet words" yet are they usually "deceitful meat" (Prov. 23:2,8). How we need to make Psalm 141:4 our prayer!

It was when the sons of the prophets began to eat the pottage that they discovered its deadly character. Ah, my reader, are you able to discriminate between what is helpful to the soul and what is harmful? Is your spiritual palate able to detect error from Truth, Satan's poison from "the sincere [pure] milk of the Word?" Do you really endeavor so to do, or are you lax in this matter? "Hear my words O ye wise men, and give ear unto me ye that have knowledge, for the ear *trieth* words as the mouth tasteth meat" (Job 34:2,3). But let us not miss the moral link between what is said in verse 40 and that which was before us in verse 38: it was those who had just previously been sitting at the feet of Elisha who now discovered the poisonous nature of these gourds. Is not the lesson plain and recorded for our learning: it is those who are instructed by the true servant of God who have most spiritual discernment, and a better judgment than others not so favored. Then "take heed what ye hear" (Mark 4:24) and what ye read.

Fifth, *its nature*. "They cried out and said, O thou man of God, there is death in the pot. And they could not eat thereof." What made them aware of their peril we know not. Nor is the child of God always conscious of it when some secret repression or unseen hand prevented him from gratifying his curiosity and turned his feet away from some "synagogue of Satan" where there is "death in the pot" being served in that place. Have not all genuine Christians cause to say with the apostle, "Who delivered us from so great a death, and doth deliver: in whom we trust that He will yet deliver us" (2 Cor. 1:10). From that pot of death., Elisha, under God, delivered them.

Sixth, *its means*. "But he said, Then bring meal. And he cast it into the pot, and he said, Pour out for the people that they may eat. And there was no harm [margin 'evil thing'] in the pot" (v. 41). The "meal" we regard as the Word of God: either the written or the personal Word one of the great types of Christ is seen in the "meat" (i.e. 'meal') offering of Leviticus 2. It is only by the Word we are safeguarded from evil. See how graciously God provided for "His own": though there was a "dearth in the land" yet these sons of the prophets were not without "meal"! How thankful we should be for the Word of God in our homes in such a day as this. Though someone else fetched the meal, "he [Elisha] cast it into the pot"!

Seventh, *its meaning*. Much of this has been intimated in what has already been pointed out, and consideration of space has obliged us to abbreviate these closing paragraphs. Let it not be overlooked that verse 38 begins with "And": after a reviving be careful where you go for your food! If you are suspicious of the soundness of a religious publication take counsel of a competent "man of God." Let not a time of spiritual "dearth" render you less careful of what you feed upon. In seasons of famine the servant of God should be diligent in seeking to strengthen the hands of *young* believers. Only by making the Word of God our constant guide shall we be delivered from the evils surrounding us. —AWP

DOCTRINE OF SAINTS' PERSEVERANCE

9d. Its Opposition

We turn now to look at some of those Scriptures appealed to by Arminians in support of their contention that those who have been born of the Spirit may fall from grace and eternally perish. We say "some of them," for were we to expound every passage cited and free them from the false meaning attached thereto, this section would be extended to an undue and wearisome length. We shall therefore single out those verses which our opponents are fondest of quoting, those which they regard as their chief strongholds, for if *they* be overthrown we need not trouble with their weaker defences. It is hardly necessary to say that there is not one passage in all the Word of God which expressly states the dogma the Arminians contend for, and therefore they are obliged to select those which abound in figurative expressions, or which treat of national and temporal destruction, or those relating to unregenerate professors, thereby deceiving the unwary by the mere sound of words and wresting the Scriptures by straining fragments divorced from their contexts.

John Wesley in his "Serious Thoughts" on the apostasy of saints framed his first proposition thus: "That one who is holy and righteous in the judgment of God Himself may nevertheless so fall from God as to perish everlastingly." In support of this he quoted, "But when the righteous turneth away from his righteousness and committeth iniquity and doeth according to all the abominations that the wicked man doeth, shall he live? All his righteousness that he hath done shall not be mentioned: in his trespass that he hath trespassed and in his sin that he hath sinned, in these shall he die" (Ezek. 18:24). That the founder of Wesleyan Methodism understood this to refer to eternal death is evident from the purpose for which he adduced it. As this passage is generally regarded by Arminians as "unanswerable and unassailable" we will consider it at more length.

This construing of "shall he die" as "shall perish eternally" is contrary to the entire scope and design of Ezekiel 18, for this chapter treats not of the perseverance or apostasy of the saints, neither of their salvation nor damnation. Its sole aim is to vindicate the justice of God from a charge that He was then punishing the Jews (temporally) not for their own sins but for the sins of their forebears, and therefore there was manifest unfairness in His dealings with them. This chapter has nothing whatever to do with the spiritual and eternal welfare of men. The whole context concerns only the house of Israel, the land of Israel, and their conduct in it, according to which they held or lost their tenure of it. Thus it has no relevancy whatever to the matter in hand, no pertinency to the case of individual saints and their eternal destiny.

Again, though the man here spoken of is indeed acknowledged by the Lord to be "righteous," yet that righteousness by which he is denominated only regards him as an inhabitant of the land of Palestine and as giving him a claim to the possession and enjoyment of it, but not as justifying him before God and giving him title to everlasting life and felicity. For this "righteousness" is called "his" (v. 24) and not Another's (Isa. 45:24; Jer. 23:6), that which *he* had "done" (v. 24 and cf. vv. 5-9) and not what Christ had done for him (Rom. 5:19); it was a righteousness of works and not of faith (Rom. 4:5, Phil. 3:9). This man was "righteous" legally but not evangelically. Thus, if a thousand such cases were adduced it would not militate one iota against the eternal security of all who have been constituted righteous before God on the ground of Christ's perfect obedience being reckoned to their account and who have been inwardly sanctified by the Spirit and grace of God.

Let the reader carefully peruse the whole of chapter 18. The mission of the prophet Ezekiel was to call Israel to repentance. He pointed to the awful calamities which had come upon the nation as proof of their great guilt. They sought to escape that charge by pleading "The fathers have eaten sour grapes and the children's teeth are set on edge." The prophet answers, that, though in His governmental and providential dealing God often visits the father's sin on sinful children, yet the guilt of sinful fathers is never in His theocracy (according to the covenant of Horeb) visited on righteous children. He went further, and reminded them that temporal prosperity was restored to the Nation as soon as an obedient generation succeeded a rebellious, and that as soon as a rebellious individual truly repented he was forgiven, just as when a righteous man became wicked he was plagued in his body or estate.

"Then the Lord of that servant was moved with compassion, and loosed him and forgave him the debt . . . And his lord was wroth and delivered him to the tormentors" (Matt. 18:27,34). This is quoted to prove that "persons truly regenerated and justified before God, may through high misdemeanors in sinning, turn themselves out of the justifying grace and favor of God, quench the spirit of regeneration, and come to have their portion with hypocrites and unbelievers." Arminians are not the only ones who wrest this passage, for Socinians quote verses 24-27 to disprove the atonement of Christ, arguing therefrom that God freely forgives sins out of His "compassion," without any satisfaction being rendered to His broken Law. Both of these erroneous interpretations are the consequence of ignoring the scope and design of this passage: Christ was not there showing either the ground on which God bestows pardon or the doom of apostates.

The scope and intention of Matthew 18:23-35 is easily perceived if the following details be attended to. 1. Christ is replying to Peter's "how often shall my brother sin against me, and I forgive him? (v. 21). 2. It is a parable or similitude of "the kingdom of heaven" (v. 23), which has to do with a *mixed* condition of things, the whole sphere of profession, in which the tares grow together with the wheat. 3. From Christ's application in v. 35 we see that He was enforcing Matthew 6:14, 15. On account of the mercy and forgiveness which the Christian has received from God in Christ, he ought to extend forgiveness and kindness to his offending brethren (Eph. 4:32). Failure so to do is threatened with awful vengeance. "IF" I forgive not from my heart those who offend me, then I am only an unregenerate professor. Note how Christ represented this character at the beginning: no quickened soul would boast "I will pay Thee all" (v. 26)!

Luke 11:24-26, appealed to by Arminians, need not detain us, for the last clause of Matthew 12:45 proves it is a parable about the nation of Israel—freedom from the spirit of idolatry since the Babylonian captivity, but possessed by the Devil himself when they rejected Christ and demanded His crucifixion. Nor should John 15:6 occasion any serious difficulty. Without proffering a detailed exposition, it is sufficient to point out that the "Vine" is not a figure of vital relationship (as is "the Body": 1 Cor. 12:11; Col. 1:24), but only of external and visible. This is clear from such passages as Psalm 80:8-14; Jeremiah 2:21; Hosea 10:1; Revelation 14:18,19. Thus there are both fruitful and fruitless "branches" (as "good" and "bad" fishes Matt. 13:48): the latter being in Christ only by profession—hence the "*as* a branch." Confirmatory of this the Father is here designated "the Husbandman" (v. 1)—a term having a much wider scope than "the Dresser" of His vineyard (Luke 13:9).

"For if God spared not the natural branches, take heed lest He also spare not thee" (Rom. 11:21). But such a passage as this (vv. 17-24) is nothing to the purpose. The "natural branches" were the unbelieving portion of the Jews (v. 20), and they were "broken off" from the position of witness for God in the earth, the "kingdom" being taken from them and given to others: Matthew 21:43. What analogy is there between these and the supposed case of those united to Christ and later becoming so severed from Him as to perish? None whatever: a much closer parallel would be found in a local church having its candlestick "removed" (Rev. 2:5): set aside as Christ's witness on earth. True, from their case the apostle points a solemn warning (v. 22) but that warning is *heeded* by the truly regenerate, and thus is made a means of their preservation.

"Through thy knowledge shall the weak brother perish for whom Christ died?" (1 Cor. 8:11). 1. It is not affirmed that the weak brother *had* "perished"! 2. From the standpoint of God's purpose and the sufficiency of His keeping power, the feeblest of His children *will not* perish. 3. But the strong Christian is here warned of and dehorted from a selfish misuse of his "liberty" (v. 9) by pointing out the horrible *tendency* of the same. Though Christ will preserve His lambs, that does not warrant me in casting a stumblingstone before them. No thanks were due the Roman soldier that not a bone of Christ's body was broken when he thrust his spear into the Savior's side, and the professing Christian who sets an evil example before babes in Christ is not guiltless because God preserves them from becoming infidels thereby. My duty is to so walk that its influence on others may be good and not bad.

First Corinthians 9:27 simply informs us of what God required from Paul (and all His servants and people), and what by grace he did in order to escape a possible calamity. 2 Corinthians 6:1 refers not to saving grace but to ministerial as verse 3 shows: as laborers together in Christ's vineyard they are exhorted to employ the gifts bestowed upon them. "Ye are fallen from grace" (Gal. 5:4) is to be interpreted in the light of its setting. The Galatians were being troubled by Judaisers who affirmed that faith in Christ was not sufficient for acceptance with God, that they must also be circumcised. The apostle declares that if they should be circumcised with the object of gaining God's favor then Christ would profit them nothing (v. 2), for they would thereby abandon the platform of grace, descending to fleshly ceremonies; in such case they would leave the ground of free justification for a lower and worthless plane.

"Holding faith and a good conscience, which some having put away, concerning faith have made shipwreck; of whom is Hymeneus and Alexander" (1 Tim. 1:19,20). So far from these being regenerated men who spiritually deteriorated, Hymeneus was a profane and vain babbler, who increased from one degree of impiety "unto more ungodliness" (2 Tim. 2:16,17); while Paul said of Alexander that he did him "much harm" and "greatly withstood his preaching" (2 Tim. 4:14,15). Their "putting away" a good conscience does not necessarily imply they formerly had such, for of the unbelieving Jews who contemptuously refused the Gospel (Acts 13:45,46) it is said—the same Greek word being used—that they "put it from" them. They made shipwreck of the Christian Faith they professed (cf. 1 Tim. 1:19) for they denied a future resurrection (2 Tim. 2:18), which resulted in overthrowing the doctrinal faith of some of their hearers; but as 2 Timothy 2:19 shows this was no apostasy of real saints.

Hebrews 6:4-8. There are two sorts of "enlightened" persons: those who are savingly illuminated by the Holy Spirit, and those intellectually instructed by the doctrine of the Gospel. In like manner, there are two kinds of "tasting" of the heavenly gift, the good Word of God, and the powers of the world to come: those who under a fleeting impulse merely sample them, and those who from a deep sense of need relish the same. So there are two different classes who become "partakers of the Holy Spirit": those who only come under His awe-inspiring and sin-convicting influences in a meeting where His power is manifest, and those who receive of His grace and are permanently indwelt by Him. The "repentance" of those viewed here is but that of Cain, Pharaoh and Judas, and those who openly repudiate Christ become hopelessly hardened, given up to a reprobate mind.

The description furnished of the above class at once serves to identify them, for it is so worded as to come far short of the marks of the children of God. They are not spoken of as God's elect, as those redeemed by Christ, as born of the Spirit. They are not said to be justified, forgiven, accepted in the Beloved, or "made meet for the inheritance of the saints in light." Nothing is said of their faith, love, or obedience. Yet *these* are the very things which distinguish the saints from all others! Finally, the description of this class in terms which fall below what pertains to the regenerate is employed again in verse 9: "But [not 'and'], beloved, we are persuaded better things of you [in contrast from them] and things which [actually] accompany salvation."

Hebrews 10:26-29. The apostle says nothing here positively of any having actually committed this fatal sin, but only supposes such a case, speaking conditionally. This particular "sin" referred to here must be ascertained from the Epistle in which this passage occurs: it is the deliberate repudiation of Christianity after being instructed therein and making a public profession thereof and going back to an effete Judaism—the condition of such would be hopeless. The nearest approach to such sin today would be for one who had been taught the Truth and intelligently professed to the same, renouncing it for, say, Romanism, or Buddhism. To renounce the way of salvation set forth by the Gospel of Christ is to turn the back on the only Mediator between God and men. "There remaineth no more sacrifice for sins" for those who prefer "calves and goats" (Judaism) or "Mary and the saints" (Romanism) rather than the Lamb of God.

"Now the just shall live by faith, but if any man draw back My soul shall have no pleasure in him" (Heb. 10:38). This also is purely hypothetical, as the "if" intimates: it announces what would follow should such a thing occur. To quote what is merely suppositionary rather than positive, shows how weak the Arminian case is. That there is nothing here whatever for them to build upon is clear from the very wording and structure of the sentence: it is *not* "Now the just shall live by faith *and* if any man draw back." The "but if any man draw back" places him in opposition to the class spoken of in the first clause. This is further evident in what immediately follows: "But we are not of them that draw back unto perdition, but of them that believe to the saving of the soul" (v. 39). Thus, so far from this passage favoring the total apostasy of real saints, it definitely establishes the doctrine of their final perseverance.

"There shall be false teachers among you, who privily shall bring in damnable heresies, even denying the Lord that bought them" (2 Peter 2:1). Any seeming difficulty here is at once removed if attention be carefully paid to two things. First, it is not said they were *redeemed*, but only "bought." The first man was given "dominion" over all things terrestrial (Gen. 1:28), but by his fall lost the same, and Satan took possession by conquest. Christ does not dispossess him by the mere exercise of Divine power, but as the Son of man He secured by right of purchase all that Adam forfeited. He "buyeth that field" (Matt. 13:44) which is "the world" (v. 39)—i.e. the earth and all in it. Second, it is not said they were bought by Christ, but "the Lord," and the Greek word is not the customary "kurios" as in verses 9, 11, 20, but "Despotes," which signifies dominion and authority—translated "masters" in 1 Timothy 6:1, 2; Titus 2:9; 1 Peter 2:18. It was as a Master He bought the world and all in it, acquiring thereby an unchallengable title (as God-man) to rule over it. He therefore has the right to demand the submission of every man, and all who deny Him that right, repudiate him as the Despotes. 2 Peter 2:20-22. There are none of the distinguishing marks of God's children ascribed to the characters mentioned in this passage, nothing whatever about them to show they were ever anything more than formal professors. Attention to the following details will clarify and simplify these verses. 1. The "pollutions of the world" here "escaped" are the gross and outward defilements (in contrast from the inward cleansing of the regenerate), as is clear from the "again *entangled* therein." 2. It was not "through faith in" but "through the knowledge of the Lord and Savior" that this reformation of conduct and amendment of walk was effected. 3. These are not said to have "loved the way of righteousness" (Ps. 119:47,77,159), but merely to have "known" it: there is a twofold knowledge of the Truth: natural and spiritual, theoretical and vital, ineffectual and transforming—it is only the former the apostates had. The heart of stone was never taken from them. 4. They were never "saints" or "sheep" but "dogs" domesticated and "swine" externally washed.

"These are spots in your feasts of charity, when they feast with you, feeding themselves without fear; clouds they are without water, carried about of winds; trees whose fruit withereth; without fruit, *twice dead*, plucked up by the roots" (Jude 12). It is the words in italics which the Arminian fastens upon, but we have quoted the whole verse that the reader may see that it is couched in the language of imagery. A manifestly figurative expression is taken literally: if "twice dead," it is argued they were twice alive—the second time by the new birth, the life from which they had killed. The Epistle in which this expression occurs supplies the key to it. Its theme is Apostasy: of the Israelites (v. 5), angels (v. 6), and lifeless professors in Christendom (vv. 8-19), from which the saints are "preserved" (v. 1) and "kept" (v. 24).Those of verse 12 were dead in sin by nature, and then by apostasy—by defection from the faith, they once professed. "I *will not* blot out his name" (Rev. 3:5) is a promise to the overcomer, every believer (1 John 5:4). —AWP

REWARDS

We closed our previous article on this subject by quoting Galatians 6:7, 8, pointing out that the joys and sorrows of the future life bear the same relation to what is wrought in this as the harvest does to the sowing, one being the consequence, the fruit or reward of the other. There is a definite relation subsisting between sowing to the spirit and reaping life everlasting, between what is done unto Christ in this life and the crowning in the life to come. This relation is just as real as that between sowing to the flesh and reaping corruption, despising and defying Christ and the torments of Hell, though it is not in all respects the same. The portion allotted the wicked is that of due and personal desert, but that bestowed on the righteous is not so, it being entirely of grace, a matter of largess, for it is impossible to lay God under obligation to us or make Him our Debtor. Eternal life is bestowed upon the believer as the reward of Christ's undertaking, because of what He wrought in his stead and on his behalf. Yet that is not the only angle from which the bestowal of eternal life is viewed in Scripture: it is also represented as the end or outcome of our bearing "fruit unto holiness" in the service of God (Rom. 6:22).

Before amplifying the last sentence let us point out the fundamental difference between the "sowing" of the wicked and that of the righteous. All the works of the wicked are essentially their own, having no higher rise than their corrupt nature: issuing from their evil hearts produced of themselves; and as bitter waters can only proceed from a bitter fountain, so their own works are polluted and sinful. But it is quite otherwise with the good works of the righteous: they proceed not from the depraved principle of the flesh, but from the "spirit" or new nature which was communicated to them at regeneration. They are the product of God's working in them both to will and to do of His good pleasure, and therefore does He aver "from Me is thy fruit" (Hosea 14:8). Even the water of the purest fountain is no longer pure when it flows through an impure channel, and because the flesh in the Christian defiles those good works he performs, but of which God is the Author and Spring, they could not be accepted and rewarded by Him were they not also cleansed by the blood of Christ and perfumed with His merits. Thus we have no ground for boasting or self-gratulation.

Whenever we think or speak of the grace of God we must bear in mind that it reigns "through righteousness" (Rom. 5:21). Grace does not override any of the other attributes of God, but is always exercised in perfect harmony therewith and also in full accord with His governmental ways. Therein we behold the "manifold wisdom of God" by displaying in the same act both His mercy and justice, His bounty and His holiness. Therefore we find the Word expressly affirming "For God is *not unrighteous* to forget your work and labour of love which ye have showed toward His name, in that ye have ministered to the saints and do minister" (Heb. 6:10). It is indeed an act of infinite condescension upon His part that He should even deign to take notice of our trifling performances: it is equally an act of pure grace that He should be pleased to reward the same, for no matter how self-sacrificing or arduous those performances, they were naught but the bare discharge of our bounden duty: nevertheless it is also an act of righteousness when He approves of our services and richly recompenses the same both in this life and the life to come.

It is no more erroneous or inconsistent to affirm that the *future* reward will be bestowed upon the Christian both for Christ's sake (primarily and meritoriously) and because of his own obedience (according to the terms of the new covenant and the governmental principles of God), than it is to say that our *present* peace and joy flow directly from the mediation of Christ, and subordinately yet truly so from our own obedience and fidelity. "Great peace have they which love Thy Law" (Psa. 119:165 and Isa. 58:13,14). Those who deny themselves for Christ's sake and the Gospel's are assured of a rich recompense: "a hundredfold now in this time" as well as "in the world to come eternal life" (Mark 10:30). "Godliness is profitable unto all things, having promise of the life that now is and of that which is to come" (1 Tim. 4:8). Though our obedience be not meritorious, yet God deems it (as the fruit of His Spirit) virtuous and amiable and meet for His approbation, and as a Being of perfect rectitude and benevolence it becomes Him to cordially own the same. If *future* rewards clashed either with Divine grace or the merits of Christ then *present* ones must do the same, for a difference in place or time can make no difference as to the nature of things themselves.

In a recent article on the Perseverance of the Saints we pointed out that the subject of rewards needs to be given its due place in connection with that doctrine. And this for a twofold reason. First, to arouse the careless and expose the formalist. This is one of the many safeguards by which God has hedged about the precious truth of the everlasting bliss of His people. That bliss is not awaiting triflers and sluggards. If there be no sowing to the spirit in this life, there will be no reaping of the spirit in the life to come. This requires to be pressed upon all who claim to be Christians—never more so than in this day of vain pretentions, when hollow professors abound on every side. A faith which produces no good works is a worthless one. A branch in the Vine that bears not fruit is doomed to be burned (John 15:6). The man who hides his talent, instead of improving the same, is cast into "outer darkness" (Matt. 25:24-30). If the cross be avoided there will be no crown. "If we suffer [for Christ's sake] we shall also reign with Him; if we deny Him, He also will deny us" (2 Tim. 2:12).

Second, this subject of rewards should be set before God's people as an incentive to perseverance, as an encouragement to fidelity. How often have we heard one and another say, The more I try to do that which is right, the worse things seem to become; the harder I endeavour to please God, the more circumstances appear to combine against me. Ah, that may be for the testing of your faith. But whether it be for that end or no, seek grace to lay hold of that word "And let us not be weary in welldoing; for in due season we shall *reap*, if we faint not" (Gal. 6:9). Here is the very application which the apostle made of what he had said in the previous verses upon sowing and reaping, as the opening "And" shows. Here is part of that Bread which God has provided for His children when they are dejected and enervated by the difficulties and discouragements of the way. God has provided a bountiful recompense for our labours and this should stimulate us in the performance of duty.

Not only is the promise of reward set before the saints as an incentive to activity, but also as consolation in sorrow, to enable them to endure the oppositions encountered. "Blessed are they that are persecuted for righteousness' sake, for theirs is the kingdom of heaven. Blessed are ye when men shall revile you and persecute you, and shall say all manner of evil against you falsely for My sake. Rejoice and be exceeding glad, for great is your reward in heaven" (Matt. 5:10-12). This is the manner in which Christ proffers comfort to His sorely-pressed servants: by assuring them of the grand compensation awaiting them on High. Then let us not pretend to a wisdom superior to His, and withhold from His children this part of their Bread because, forsooth, we imagine that to act thus is to impugn the grace of God. As Matthew Henry rightly says upon Matthew 5:12 "Heaven, at last, will be an abundant recompense for all the difficulties we meet with in our way. This is that which hath borne up the suffering saints in all ages."

"For ye had compassion of me in my bonds, and took joyfully the spoiling of your goods, knowing in yourselves that ye have in heaven a better and enduring substance" (Heb. 10:34). Here is a pertinent example of the powerful and beneficial influence which a believing view of the promised recompense exerts upon sorely-pressed Christians. These Hebrews had been cruelly despoiled of their earthly possession, and most remarkable had been their deportment under such a trial. So far from giving way to bitter lamentations and revilings, which is the ordinary thing with worldlings on such occasions, or even enduring their loss fatalistically and stoically, they took it cheerfully and gladly. And why? how was such victory over the flesh made possible? Because their faith and hope were in lively exercise; they viewed the promised reward, their inheritance on High; with their bodily eyes they beheld their temporal affliction, but with the eyes of their souls the eternal glory prepared for them. That recompense is here called an "enduring substance" as elsewhere "weight of glory" (2 Cor. 4:17), in contrast from everything down here which is but a shadow, a mirage which vanishes away.

This was the motive which inspired Abraham: "By faith he sojourned in the land of promise as in a strange country, dwelling in tents [not erecting a castle or palace] with Isaac and Jacob, the heirs with him of the same promise. *For* he looked for a city which hath foundations, whose Builder and Maker is God" (Heb. 11:9,10). *That* was the grand inducement which made him keep on conducting himself as a stranger and pilgrim in this transient scene. That was what braced him to endure all the hardships of the way: his heart was occupied not with Canaan but with Heaven—he looked beyond the toilsome sowing to the blissful reaping. In like manner this was the motive which actuated Moses; "when he was come to years [he] refused to be called the son of Pharaoh's daughter, choosing rather to suffer affliction with the people of God than to enjoy the pleasures of sin for a season; esteeming the reproach of Christ greater riches than the treasures in Egypt." And why? "for he had respect unto the recompense of the reward" (Heb. 11:24-26). His great renunciation in the present was prompted by faith's laying hold of the grand remuneration in the future.

But a far greater than Abraham or Moses is presented as our Exemplar in this, as in all things else. Of none less than the Redeemer is it recorded "who for the joy that was set before Him endured the cross, despising the shame, and is set down at the right hand of the throne of God" (Heb. 12:2). A variety of motives moved the Saviour to endure the cross—love for His Father (John 14:31), the glory of His Father (John 12:27,28), love for His Church (Eph. 5:25)—but among them was the prospect of future recompense. In the previous verse we are exhorted to lay aside every weight and the sin which doth so easily beset us, and run with patience the race that is set before us, and the supreme inducement so to do is, "looking unto Jesus...who for the joy that was set before Him endured." Whether that "joy" consisted in the answer to His prayer in (John 17:5), the exaltation of Him above all creatures (Eph. 1:20-22; Phil. 2:9), or His seeing of the travail of His soul and being satisfied (Isa. 53:11) when He shall present the Church to Himself a glorious Church (Eph. 5:27), or all three, yet the fact remains that *this* was an essential motive or reason which prompted the Lord Jesus to do and suffer—that future "joy" was ever before the eye of the Captain of our salvation as He ran His race and finished His course: the prize was kept steadily in view.

It should be pointed out that promises of reward are not restricted to those engaged in the public service of God but are also made to the rank and file of His people. We call attention to this lest humble saints should allow Satan to deprive them of their legitimate portion on the ground that they are "not worthy" to appropriate the same— personal worthiness or unworthiness does not at all enter into the question, as the greatest of the apostles has made quite evident (1 Cor. 15:9,10). It is true there are distinctive promises made unto and rewards reserved for the ministers of the Gospel (1 Peter 5:1-4), nevertheless, there are not a few made unto the whole family of God: Ephesians 6:8 etc. Note how jealously Paul guarded this very point, for after declaring he had fought a good fight, finished his course and kept the faith, he said, "Henceforth there is laid up for me a crown of righteousness, which the Lord, the righteous Judge, shall give me at that day," he immediately added, "and not to me only, but unto *all them also* that love His appearing" (2 Tim. 4:8).

Said Paul, "Brethren I count not myself to have apprehended, but this one thing I do: forgetting those things which are behind, and reaching forth unto those things which are before, I press toward the mark for the prize of the high calling of God in Christ Jesus" (Phil. 3:13,14). Here we behold the saint running for the "prize": that is what inspired his self-disciple and strenuous endeavours, that was the inducement or incentive. But the prize will not be accorded him for the merit of his running, but because of the worthiness of Christ: yet without such pressing onward, the prize would not be secured. It is sovereign grace which has appointed this prize for the runner, yet unless the "mark" or goal be actually reached, it is not obtained. The prize or "reward" or "glory" is set before us in the Word for faith to lay hold of and for hope to enjoy in confident (not doubtful) expectation, as a motive to stir us unto the use of those means leading thereunto and to make us more fervent in those duties without the performance of which it cannot be reached.

We will close by briefly considering two objections. There will probably be those ready to charge us with inculcating creature deserts, that what we have written is nothing else than an adoption of the Romish heresy of human merits. Our reply is that we have advanced nothing but what is clearly taught in Holy Writ itself. If due attention be paid to the *connections* in which the term "reward" is found this at once rules out of court the Papish conceit. Take its first occurrence: God said to Abraham "I am thy exceeding great Reward" (Gen. 15:1): what had the patriarch done to *entitle* him to such a Portion? Where the question of desert is raised, justice requires a due ratio between the performance and the remuneration, but there is *no* proportion between the works and sufferings of the Christian and the "exceeding and eternal weight of glory" promised him. Mark the use of the term in Matthew 6:8 and then ask, On what ground does God recompense our prayers? Certainly it is not for any worth which is in them. There cannot possibly be any merit in begging at the Throne of Grace!

Again; it is objected that to present rewards as an inducement unto fidelity is to foster a mercenary spirit, to reduce the Christian unto a mere hireling—performing his labours for the sake of gain. This is quite an unwarrantable, conclusion. Sordidness lies not in aiming at a reward in general, but in subordinating piety to self-interests, as they who followed Christ for the loaves and fishes (John 6:26). A mercenary spirit actuates him who performs duty solely for the sake of remuneration, or at least, principally for it. We are to view the reward not as a debt due us, but as that which the grace of God has promised, and which His bounty deems suited unto our obedience. Rewards are presented to us as an incitement to gracious activity, to cheer us under self-denials, to strengthen our hearts when meeting opposition. It is the minister's task not only to urge believers unto the performance of duty, but also to hold before them the promised recompenses. That eyeing of the reward in nowise signifies a lack of love for God is clear from the case of Christ Himself (Heb. 12:2). —AWP

OUR ANNUAL LETTER

"Beware lest thou forget the Lord" (Deut. 6:12).

It is sadly apparent that a greatly increasing number of our fellows are doing this very thing: and are not *we* in danger of the same? The very fact that this warning is addressed to God's people shows they are prone unto this fearful sin. Are we ever mindful of His omniscience, that His eyes are in every place, beholding the evil and the good (Prov. 15:3)? Are we never oblivious that He records our conversations when we speak one to another (Mal. 3:16)? When trouble comes without warning, when suddenly confronted with an emergency, are we promptly occupied with His sufficiency? During the last half of this month or the first week of next the world goes mad over an orgy of feasting and fleshly indulgence: how the Christian needs to "Beware lest he forget the Lord" in such seasons of mirth and merry making.

There are countless thousands of young people who were accustomed to attend the public means of grace on the Sabbath day who are now in the forces and services, and much watchfulness and prayerfulness is called for on their part if they are not to "forget the Lord." It needs to be borne in mind by them that though their circumstances have changed, there is no change in God: either in His just claims upon us, His abhorrence of sin, or His readiness to hear the cry of the humble. They may be far away from home and loved ones, yet they still have God's Word by them and His throne of grace is ever accessible to the needy. To you, in an especial way, sounds out this warning: "Beware lest thou forget the Lord." Your peril, your need of His help and strength is greater now than ever it was before.

But most of our readers are still in civilian life, yet many of them in greatly altered circumstances, amid subnormal and abnormal conditions, undergoing heavy strain, encountering acute anxieties, subject to new forms of temptation. How is it with you? Are you casting all your care upon Him, knowing that He careth for you (1 Peter 5:7)? Suffer not circumstances and conditions to crowd God out of your minds: things must not be allowed to supplant *Him*. Unless this humble messenger is helping you to prove that "the Lord is a very present help in trouble" it is of little service to you. Unless you find in these pages, under God, that which nourishes your soul, strengthens your faith, and is making you a more fruitful branch of the Vine, its articles are of little or no value. Intellectual information is profitless unless the Divine precepts and promise are becoming more practical and precious.

This issue completes one more volume, which means that writer and reader are another twelve months nearer *eternity* than when it was commenced! Solemnising thought: how we need to pray "So teach us to number our days that we may apply our hearts unto wisdom" (Psa. 90:12). O that we may be enabled to offer this petition sincerely, understandingly and expectantly. Throughout another year we have been favoured with daily manifestations of God's goodness and faithfulness: granting us light from His Word, a goodly measure of health and strength, encouragements along the way, freely supplying our every need. Despite increased difficulties our printers have been enabled to procure paper and do their work for us. Despite the intensified dangers on the sea, we have heard of no copies or gifts being lost in transit. Despite considerable increase in expenses we close another year with a balance to the good.

We thank those of the friends who have made a real effort to obtain new readers for us: they were urgently needed to take the place of old ones who had dropped out. A decreasing circulation is still our greatest trial: each letter telling of blessing received from this monthly messenger makes us yearn to reach more of the hungry sheep. As it now costs us 5/- to mail this magazine to each person for a year, we trust those sending in this or a smaller amount will not expect a written acknowledgment—your continuing to receive the "Studies" (D.V.) will indicate your donation has come to hand. We are still gladly, sending to a number not in the position to contribute unto costs of publishing, as well as to chaplains and missionaries.

The Sermon on the Mount articles will (D.V.) be followed by a series on the "Prayers of the Apostles": we know of no book dealing with them, so will be cast back the more upon the Lord. We have nearly completed our exposition of the Final Perseverance of the Saints, and purpose taking up next the little-attended-to doctrine of Reconciliation. We hope to also write at some length on Spiritual Growth, a subject which is by no means free of difficulty—due to our dullness of perception and the weakness of our faith. If the Lord be pleased to conduct us into these green pastures and permits us to drink from these Waters of Life, seasons of refreshing will be the portion of both writer and reader. Pray to this end.

Once more, in the mercy of God, we have promise that the twelve issues of 1943 "Studies" will be available in bound form by the end of the year, for those desiring the same in a more suitable condition for permanent use. The price will be 5/6 ($1.25) postpaid. Unless they were printed at the same time as the loose copies, we could not sell at anything like this figure. The quantity is limited, so first come first served.

Asking for a continued place in your prayers, and with Christian greetings,

Yours by Divine Mercy, A. W.and Vera E. Pink

(continued from back page)

tion from the righteousness of all creatures whatsoever" (James Hervey). But more: it is the "righteousness of God" because God the Father devised it from all eternity, God the Son wrought it out here upon earth, and God the Holy Spirit makes it good to us by working in us a faith which appropriates the same. To sum up Romans 1:16, 17 and 3:21, 22: salvation is by righteousness, righteousness is found in Christ, that righteousness becomes ours by faith.

In Romans 4 the apostle proceeded to illustrate his doctrine by two notable examples. Abraham, who was the most eminent of the patriarchs, the most illustrious pattern of piety among the O.T. saints, the "friend of God" (James 2:23). David, who was the most zealous of the kings, the "sweet Psalmist of Israel," a "man after God's own heart" (1 Sam. 13:14). How then were *they* justified before God? Not as upright beings who could claim it, but as sinful creatures who must implore it; not by their own obedience, but by faith in the promised Messiah. Abraham "worked not" with a view to obtaining justification, but "believed on Him that justifieth the ungodly" (vv. 1-5). How was David justified? By his zeal for God's glory or by his noble services for his fellow-men? No, by a righteousness imputed, even the righteousness of Christ, that blessed redemption through which "iniquities are forgiven and sins are covered" (vv. 6-8).

Fourth, the Word is so designated because righteousness is its *chief bestowment.* "Think not that I am come to destroy the Law or the Prophets: I am not come to destroy, but to fulfil" (Matt. 5:17) said Christ. He fulfilled the Law by rendering to it a personal, perfect and perpetual obedience as the Surety of His people, and the moment they savingly believe in Him *His obedience* is reckoned to their account and becomes their legal righteousness before God (Rom. 4:24; 5:19). The perfect righteousness of Christ is "upon all them that believe" (Rom. 3:22). It is their "wedding garment" (Matt. 22:12) the "best robe" (Luke 15:22) by which they are covered. And thus may each one say, "In the Lord have I righteousness and strength" (Isa. 45:24). Now can he declare "I will greatly rejoice in the Lord, my soul shall be joyful in my God; for He hath clothed me with the garments of salvation, He hath covered me with the robe of righteousness" (Isa. 61:10). A righteous nature is also communicated, which produces righteous conduct: "everyone that doeth righteousness is born of God" (1 John 2:29). Righteousness imputed, righteousness imparted, constitute our salvation. Then let us unite with the Psalmist in exclaiming, "My mouth shall show forth Thy righteousness and Thy salvation all the day...I will go in the strength of the Lord God. I will make mention of Thy righteousness, even of *Thine only*" (Psa. 71:15,16). —AWP

(continued from front page)

"Cursed is every one that continueth not in all things which are written in the Book of the Law to do them" (Gal. 3:10). "Cursed is every one"—without any exception of persons, without any regard to pleas of human weakness or violent temptations. "That continueth not": it is not sufficient to observe those holy commandments in the general tenor of our lives: our course of conduct must be without the slightest intermission from the earliest dawn of reason to the final breath we draw. In *all* things: we must refrain from every sin forbidden and the least approach to them, and practice every virtue enjoined and every duty enforced. The Law insists upon an obedience which is perfect in its principle, perfect in all its parts, perfect in every degree, and in each of these respects, *perpetual*; and pronounces a curse on the slightest failure.

The spirituality and strictness of such a Law reveals the ineffable purity and immaculate righteousness of its Author. It shows that His nature is so holy and His will so immutable that He will not tolerate the least sin nor spare the slightest transgression. It tells us that those sins in which the light of nature could discern but little turpitude, that those faults which the light of reason is ready to excuse as mere trifles, are unspeakably odious and intolerably loathsome in the eyes of Jehovah. Only when the soul is made acutely aware of this does it cry out with the Psalmist, "my flesh trembleth for fear of Thee and I am afraid of Thy judgments" (119:120). It is because of their sottish insensibility of this that the vast majority of our fellows are sleeping in a false security and dreaming in presumptuous hope, instead of crying to God for mercy and fleeing from the wrath to come. It is because of their willful ignorance and excuseless blindness that the religious crowd knows not that "by the deeds of the Law there shall no flesh be justified in His sight" (Rom. 3:20).

Third, the Word is so denominated because righteousness is its *grand revelation*. Thousands of years ago the questions raised "How then can man be justified with God?" (Job 25:4) and that perplexity had remained unresolved until the end of time had not God Himself supplied the solution. In the Scriptures He has made known a perfect righteousness provided for the unrighteous. It was for that reason the apostle declared, "I am not ashamed of the Gospel of Christ—however it may be deemed foolishness by the sophisticated Greeks or prove a stumbling-block to the carnal Jews—for it is the power of God unto salvation": the grand Instrument which He has ordained for that purpose, and which He will certainly crown with the success He has appointed. And wherein lies the chief and distinguishing glory of the Gospel? "For therein is the *righteousness* of God revealed, from faith to faith" (Rom. 1:16,17): not demanded of impotent sinners, but made ready for their free acceptance—held aloft by a promising God, appropriated by believing souls.

After furnishing conclusive proof that Jew and Gentile alike are destitute of righteousness, the apostle went on to say "But now the righteousness of God without the Law is manifested, being witnessed by the Law and the Prophets, even the righteousness of God which is by faith of Jesus Christ unto all and upon all them that believe" (Rom. 3:21,22). It is a perfect righteousness, which obliterates all guilt and bestows an inalienable title to eternal life. "It is styled the righteousness of God by way of superlative preeminence in opposition to any righteousness of our own and in contradistinc

. *(continued on proceeding page)*

VOL. XXIII.   JANUARY, 1944.   NO. 1

STUDIES ɪɴ ᴛʜᴇ SCRIPTURES

"Search the Scriptures." John 5:39.

Publisher and Editor—Aʀᴛʜᴜʀ W. Pɪɴᴋ,
27 Lewis Street,
Stornoway, Isle of Lewis,
Scotland.

A PROSPEROUS NEW YEAR

This is our desire both for our readers and for ourselves. But the mere wishing or desiring of it will not bring the same to pass. What more is necessary? Only God can grant us prosperity either spiritual or temporal, and we must submit to his good pleasure. True, but He is not capricious in this. Prosperity or the absence of it is not a fortuitous thing, nor is it the product of a blind and inexorable fate. If we enjoy not prosperity the fault is entirely our own, and we are dishonest if we ascribe it solely unto the sovereignty of God. "In returning and rest shall ye be saved, in quietness and in confidence shall be your strength: and *ye would not*" (Isa. 30:15)—had it not been flagrantly dishonest if they attributed their disquietude and fears to the sovereign will of God? "O that thou hadst hearkened to My commandments! then had thy peace been as a river" (Isa. 48:18)—then how wicked to charge God with being responsible for their lack of peace.

If we consult the Scriptures we shall find definite teaching on this subject: that there are clearly-revealed laws which *we* must observe, conditions which we are required to meet, if we are to enjoy prosperity. Let us first consider one or two things which *hinder* prosperity. "Why transgress ye the commandments of the Lord that ye cannot prosper" (2 Chron. 24:20). Ah, here is the cause of all our troubles; disobedience, for "the way of transgressors is hard" (Prov. 13:15). Observe how emphatically and absolutely it is expressed: "ye cannot prosper"—a holy God will not place a premium on insubordination. He may suffer "the wicked" to flourish as a green bay tree, for he is like a beast being fattened for the slaughter; but not so with those who profess His name. Disobedience, then, chokes the channel of blessing. "He that covereth his sins shall not prosper" (Prov. 28:13). Unconfessed sin in the heart of a believer is like a worm at the root of prosperity. "If I regard iniquity in my heart, the Lord will not hear me" (Psa. 66:18)— prayer is then futile. Unless we keep short accounts with God we shall not enjoy His smile. Jeremiah 10:21 tells us what prevents "pastors" from prospering: self-sufficiency, failing to be cast entirely upon the Lord.

"This Book of the Law shall not depart out of thy mouth; but thou shalt meditate therein day and night, that thou mayest observe to do according to all that is written therein: for *then* shalt thou make thy way prosperous, and *then* thou shalt have good

(continued on back page)

IMPORTANT NOTICES

Please advise promptly of change in address, otherwise copies will be lost in the mails.

We are glad to send a sample copy to any of your friends whom you believe would be interested in this publication.

This magazine is published as "a work of faith and labour of love," the editor and his wife gladly giving their services free. There is no regular subscription price, as we do not wish the poor of the flock to be deprived. This does not mean that those looking for something for nothing may "help themselves." Those getting this Magazine, who are financially able and who receive spiritual help from its pages, are expected to gladly contribute towards its expenses; otherwise, their names are dropped from our lists.

Will those forwarding International Money Orders please have them made out to us at Stornoway, Isle of Lewis, Scotland. Checks (Cheques-Eng.) made out on U.S.A. Banks are not negotiable here, so please do not send them.

CONTENTS

THE PRAYERS OF THE APOSTLES

1. Introduction

Much has been written upon what is usually called "The Lord's Prayer" but which we prefer to term "The Family Prayer," and much upon the High Priestly prayer of Christ in John 17, but very little upon the prayers of the apostles. Personally we know of no book devoted to the same, and except for a booklet on the two prayers of Ephesians 1 and 3 have seen scarcely anything thereon. It is not easy to explain this omission, for one had thought the apostolic prayers had such importance and value for us that they had attracted the attention of those who wrote on devotional subjects. While we very much deprecate the efforts of those who would have us believe the prayers of the Old Testament are obsolete and unfitted to the saints of this dispensation, yet that there is a peculiar suitability unto Christians of the prayers recorded in *the epistles* seems evident. Excepting only the prayers of the Redeemer, in them alone are the praises and petitions specifically addressed unto "the Father," in them alone are they offered in the name of the Mediator, and in them alone do we find the full breathings of the Spirit of adoption.

How blessed it is to hear some aged saint, who has long walked with God and enjoyed intimate communion with Him, pouring out his heart before Him in adoration and supplication. But how much more blessed should we esteem it could we have listened to the utterances of those who had companied with Christ in person during the days when He tabernacled in this scene. And if one of the apostles was still here upon earth what a high privilege we should deem it to hear him engage in prayer! Such a high one, that methinks most of us would be quite willing to go to considerable inconvenience and travel a long distance in order to be thus favoured. And if our desire was granted how closely we would listen to his words, how diligently we should seek to treasure them up in our memories. Well, no such inconvenience, no such journey is required: it has pleased the Holy Spirit to record quite a number of the apostolic prayers for our instruction and satisfaction. Do we evidence our appreciation of such a boon? Have we ever made a list of them and meditated upon their import?

In our preliminary task of surveying and tabulating the recorded prayers of the apostles two things impressed us: one, which at first seems quite surprising, the other which was to be expected. That which is apt to strike us as strange—to some of our readers it may be almost startling—is the book of Acts, which supplies us with most of the information we possess about the apostles, has not a single prayer of theirs in its twenty-eight chapters. Yet a little reflection should show us that this omission is in full accord with the special character of that book, for the Acts is much more historical than devotional, consisting far more of a chronicle of what the Spirit wrought through the apostles than in them. It is the public deeds of Christ's ambassadors which is there made prominent, rather than their private exercises. True, they are shown to be men of prayer, as is seen by: "We will give ourselves continually to prayer and to the ministry of the Word" (Acts 6:4), and again and again we behold them engaged in this holy exercise (9:40; 10:9; 20:36; 21:5; 28:8), yet we are not told what they *said*, the nearest approach being 8:15, yet their words are not re-corded—we regard the prayer of 1:24 as that of the hundred and twenty, and that of 4:24-30 as that of "their own company."

The second feature which impressed us while contemplating the field which is to be before us, was that the great majority of the recorded prayers of the apostles issued from the heart of *Paul*; and this, as we have said, was really to be expected. If it be asked, why so, several reasons may be returned. He was, preeminently, the apostle unto the Gentiles. Peter, James, and John ministered principally to Jewish believers (Gal. 2:9), and, even in their unconverted days *they* had been accustomed to bow the knee before the Lord. But the Gentiles had come out of heathenism and it was fitting that their spiritual father should also be their devotional exemplar. Moreover, he wrote twice as many epistles as all the other apostles added together, nevertheless there are eight times as many prayers in his epistles as in all of theirs. But chiefly, we call to mind the first thing said of Paul after his conversion; "Behold, he *prayeth*" (Acts 9:11): it is as though that struck the keynote of his subsequent life, that he would be, to an especial degree, marked as a man of prayer.

It is not that the other apostles were devoid of this spirit, for God does not employ prayerless ministers, as He has no dumb children. To "cry day and night unto Him" is given by Christ as one of the distinguishing marks of His elect (Luke 18:7). Yet certain of His servants and some of His saints are permitted to enjoy closer and more constant fellowship with the Lord than others, and such was obviously the case (excepting John) with the man who on one occasion was even caught up into Paradise. A special measure of "grace and supplications" (Zech. 12:10) was vouchsafed him, so that he appears to have been favoured with a spirit of prayer above even his fellows, which dwelt in him to a remarkable degree. Such was the fervor of his love for Christ and the members of His mystical Body, such was his intense solicitude for their spiritual wellbeing and growth, that there continually gushed from his soul a flow of prayer to God for them, and of thanksgiving on their behalf. If we are permitted to proceed with these expository meditations, many illustrations of what has just been said will come before us, examples of where ebullitions of devotion broke forth in the midst of his doctrinal and practical instructions.

Ere proceeding further it should be pointed out that in this series of articles I do not propose to confine myself to the petitionary prayers of the apostles, but rather to take in a wider range. In Scripture "Prayer" includes much more than making known our requests unto God, and this is something which His people now need reminding of—some of them instructing, in these days of superficiality and ignorance. The very verse that presents to us the privilege of spreading our needs before the Lord emphasises this very thing: "in everything by prayer and supplication *with thanksgiving* let your requests be made known unto God" (Phil. 4:6) unless gratitude be expressed for mercies already received and thanks be given for granting us the continued favor of petitioning our Father, how can we expect to obtain His ear and to receive answers of peace. Yet prayer, in its highest and fullest sense, rises above thanksgiving for gifts vouchsafed: the heart is drawn out in contemplating the Giver Himself so that the soul is prostrated before Him in worship and adoration.

In the above paragraph our pen traveled faster than it should have done. Though we ought not to digress from our immediate theme and enter into the subject of prayer in general, yet it should be pointed out that there is yet another aspect which needs to take precedence of those referred to above, namely self-abhorrence and confession of our own unworthiness and sinfulness. The soul must solemnly remind itself of *Who it is* that is to be approached, even the Most High, before whom the very seraphim "veil their faces" (Isa. 6:2). Though Divine grace has made the Christian a "son," nevertheless he is still a *creature*, and as such at an infinite and inconceivable distance below the Creator and therefore it is fitting he should both deeply feel and acknowledge this by taking his place before Him in the dust. Moreover, we need to remember *what we are*, namely, not only creatures, but (considered in ourselves) *sinful* creatures and thus there needs to be both a sense and an owning of this as we bow before the Holy One. Only thus can we, with any meaning and reality, plead the mediation and merits of Christ as the ground of our approach.

Thus, broadly speaking, "prayer" takes in or includes confession of sin, petitions for the supply of our needs, and the homage of our hearts unto the Giver Himself. Or, we may say its principal branches are humiliation, supplication and adoration. Hence we hope to embrace within the scope of this series not only passages like Ephesians 1:16-19 and 3:14-21, but also single verses such as 2 Corinthians 1:3 and Ephesians 1:3. That "blessed be God," is itself a form of prayer is clear from Psalm 100:4, "Enter into His gates with thanksgiving, and into His courts with praise: be thankful unto Him, bless His name"—other references might be given, but let this suffice. The "incense" which was offered in the tabernacle and temple consisted of various spices compounded together (Exod. 30:34,35), and it was the blending of one with another that made the perfume so fragrant and refreshing. The incense was a type of the intercession of our great High Priest (Rev. 8:3,4) and of the prayers of saints (Mal. 1:11). In like manner there should be a proportioned mingling of humiliation, supplication, and adoration in our approaches to the throne of grace, not one to the exclusion of the others but a blending of them together.

The fact that so many prayers are found in the New Testament epistles calls attention to an important aspect of *ministerial duty*. The preacher's obligations are not fully discharged when he leaves the pulpit, for he needs to water the Seed which he has sown. As this magazine is now being sent to quite a number of young preachers we will enlarge a little upon this point. It has already been seen that the apostles devoted themselves "continually to prayer and to the ministry of the Word" and therein have they left an excellent example to be observed by all who follow them in the sacred vocation. Observe the order, and not only observe but heed and practice the same. The most laborious and carefully-prepared sermon is likely to fall unctionless on the hearers unless it has been born out of travail of soul before God. Unless the sermon be the product of earnest prayer we must not expect it to waken the spirit of prayer in those who hear it. As we have pointed out, Paul mingled supplications with his instructions. It is our privilege and duty to retire to the secret place after we leave the pulpit and beg God to write His Word on the hearts of those who have listened to us, to prevent the Enemy snatching away the Seed, to so bless our efforts that they may bear fruit to His eternal praise.

Luther was wont to say "There are three things that go to the making of a successful preacher: supplication, meditation, and tribulation." This was taken down by one of his students from his "Table talks." We know not what elaboration the great Reformer made, but suppose he meant that, prayer is necessary to bring the preacher into a suitable frame to handle Divine things and to endue him with power; that meditation on the Word is essential in order to supply him with material for his message; and that tribulation is required as ballast for his vessel, for the minister of the Gospel needs trials to keep him humble, as the apostle was given a thorn in the flesh that he might not be unduly exalted by the abundance of the revelations granted to him. Prayer is the appointed medium of receiving spiritual communications for the instruction of our people. We must be much with God before we can be fitted to go forth and speak in His name. The Colossians were reminded that their master was "always labouring fervently for you in prayers, that ye may stand perfect and complete in all the will of God." Could your church be truthfully told that of *you*?

But let it not be thought that this marked characteristic of the epistles points a lesson for preachers only. Far from it. These epistles are addressed to God's children at large, and everything in them is both needed by and suited to their Christian lives. Believers too should pray much not only for themselves but for *all* their brethren and sisters in Christ, and especially according to these apostolic models, petitioning for the particular blessings they specify. We have long been convinced there is no better way— no more practical, valuable, and effective way—of expressing solicitude and affection for our fellow saints than by bearing them up before God in the arms of our faith and love. It is by studying these prayers in the epistles and pondering them clause by clause that we may learn more clearly what blessings we should desire for ourselves and others—what spiritual gifts and graces we most need to ask for. The very fact that these prayers, inspired by the Holy Spirit, have been placed on permanent record in the Sacred Volume intimates that the particular favors are to be sought and obtained from God.

We will conclude these preliminary and general observations by calling attention to a few of the more definite features of the apostolic prayers. Observe then, *to Whom* these prayers are addressed. While there is not uniformity of expression but rather appropriate variety in this matter, yet the most frequent manner in which the Deity is addressed therein is as: "the Father of mercies" (2 Cor. 1:3); "the God and Father of our Lord Jesus Christ" (Eph. 1:3; 1 Peter 1:3); "the Father of glory" (Eph. 1:17); "the

Father of our Lord Jesus Christ" (Eph. 3:14). In this we may see of how the holy apostles had heeded the injunction of their Master, for when they requested of Him saying, "Lord, teach us to pray," He responded thus: "When ye pray, say, our *Father which art in heaven*" (Luke 11:1,2) an example of which He also set before them in John 17:1, 5, 11. This too has been recorded for our learning. We are not unmindful of how many have unlawfully and lightly addressed God as "Father," yet their abuse does not warrant our non-use of owning this blessed relationship. Nothing is more calculated to warm the heart and give liberty of utterance as a realisation that we are approaching our "Father." If we have received "the Spirit of adoption" (Rom. 8:15) let us not quench the same.

Next, we note their *brevity*. The prayers of the apostles are short ones: not some, or even most, but all of them are exceedingly brief, most of them comprised in but one or two verses, and the longest in only seven verses. How this rebukes the lengthy, lifeless and wearisome prayers of many a pulpit. Wordy prayers are usually windy ones. I quote again from Martin Luther, this time from his comments on the Lord's prayer to simple laymen: "When thou prayest let thy words be few, but thy thoughts and affections many, and above all let them be profound. The less thou speakest the better thou prayest...External and bodily prayer is that buzzing of the lips, that outside babble that is gone through without any attention, and which strikes the ears of men; but prayer in spirit and in truth is the inward desire, the motions, the sighs, which issue from the depths of the heart. The former is the prayer of hypocrites and of all who trust in themselves: the latter is the prayer of the children of God, who walk in His fear."

Observe too their *definiteness*. Though exceedingly brief yet their prayers are very explicit. There were no vague ramblings or mere generalisations, but specific requests for definite things. How much failure there is at this point. How many prayers have we heard that were so incoherent and aimless, so lacking in point and unity, that when the Amen was reached we could scarcely remember one thing for which thanks had been given or request had been made, only a blurred impression remaining on the mind and a feeling that the supplicant had engaged more in a form of indirect preaching than direct praying. But examine any of the prayers of the apostles and it will be seen at a glance that theirs are like those of their Master's in Matthew 6:9-13 and John 17—made up of definitive adorations and sharply-defined petitions. There is no moralising and uttering of pious platitudes, but a spreading before God of certain needs and a simple asking for the supply of them.

Consider also *the burden of them*. In the apostolic prayers there is no supplicating God for the supply of temporal needs and (with a single exception) no asking Him to interpose on their behalf in a providential way. Instead, the things asked for are wholly of a spiritual and gracious nature. That the Father may give unto us the spirit of understanding and revelation in the knowledge of Himself, the eyes of our understanding being enlightened so that we may know what is the hope of His calling, the riches of the glory of His inheritance in the saints, and the exceeding greatness of His power to usward (Eph. 1:17-19). That He would grant us according to the riches of His glory to be strengthened with might by His Spirit in the inner man, that Christ may dwell in our hearts by faith, that we might know the love of Christ which passeth knowledge, and be filled with all the fullness of God (Eph. 3:16-19). That our love may abound more and more, that we might be sincere and without offence, and be filled with the fruits of righteousness (Phil. 1:9-11), walk worthy of the Lord unto all pleasing (Col. 1:10), that we might be sanctified wholly (1 Thess. 5:23).

Note also the *catholicity* of them. Not that it is either wrong or unspiritual to pray for ourselves individually, any more than it is to supplicate for temporal and providential mercies; rather are we directing attention to where the apostles placed all their emphasis. In one only do we find Paul praying for himself, and rarely for particular individuals. His general custom was to pray for the whole Household of Faith. In this he adheres closely to the pattern prayer given us by Christ, and which we like to think of as the *Family* prayer. All its pronouns are in the plural number: "give us" (not only "me"), "forgive us" etc. Accordingly we find the apostle exhorting us to be making "supplication for *all* saints" (Eph. 6:18), and in his prayers he sets us an example of this very thing. He asked that the Ephesian church might "be able to comprehend with *all* saints what is the breadth and length, and depth, and height, and to know the love of Christ which passeth knowledge" (3:18). What a corrective for self-centeredness! If I am praying for "all saints" I include myself!

Finally, let us point out a striking *omission*. If all the apostolic prayers be read attentively it will be found that in none of them is any place given to that which occupies such prominence in those of Arminians. Not once do we find God asked to save the world or to pour out His Spirit on all flesh. The apostles did not so much as pray for the conversion of the city in which a particular Christian church was located. In this they conformed again to the example set for them by Christ: "I pray not for the world," said He, "but for them which Thou hast given Me" (John 17:9). Should it be objected that the Lord Jesus was there praying only for His immediate apostles or disciples, the answer is that when He extended His prayer beyond them it was not for the world, but only for His believing people unto the end of time: see verses 20, 21. It is true the apostle exhorts that prayers, "be made for all [classes of] men: for kings and all that are in authority" (1 Tim. 2:1)—in which duty many are woefully remiss—yet it is not for their salvation, but "that *we* may live a quiet and peaceable life in all godliness and honesty" (v. 2). There is much to be learned from the prayers of the apostles. —AWP

THE MISSION AND MIRACLES OF ELISHA

13. Ninth Miracle

It seems strange so very few have perceived that a miracle is recorded in 2 Kings 4:42-44, for surely a careful reading of those verses makes it evident that they describe the wonder-working power of the Lord, for no otherwise can we explain the feeding of so many with such a little and then a surplus remaining. It is even more strange that scarcely any appear to have recognised that we have here a most striking foreshadowment of the only miracle wrought by the Lord Jesus which is narrated by all the four Evangelists, namely, His feeding of the multitude from a few loaves and fishes. In all of our reading we have not only never come across a sermon thereon, but so far as memory serves us, not so much as a quotation from or allusion to this striking passage. Thomas Scott dismisses the incident with a single paragraph, and though Matthew Henry is a little fuller, he too says nothing about the supernatural character of it. We wonder how many of our readers, before turning to this article, could have answered the question, Where in the Old Testament is described the miracle of the feeding of a multitude through the hands of a man?

First, *its occasion*. Though there was a "dearth [famine] in the land" (2 Kings 4:38) yet we learn from the first verse of our passage that it was not a total or universal one: some barley had been grown in Baalshalisha. In this we may perceive how that in wrath the Lord remembers mercy. Even where the crops of an entire country are a complete failure—an exceedingly exceptional occurrence—there is always food available in adjoining lands. Therein we behold an exemplification of God's goodness and faithfulness. Of old He declared "While the earth remaineth, seedtime and harvest, and cold and heat, and summer and winter, and day and night *shall not cease*" (Gen. 8:22). Though more than four thousand years have passed since then, each returning one has furnished clear evidence of the fulfillment of that promise—a demonstration both of the Divine veracity and of God's continuous regulation of the affairs of earth. As we have said, it is very rare for there to be a total failure of the crops in any single country, for as the Lord declares "I caused it to rain upon one city and caused it not to rain upon another city: one piece was rained upon and the piece whereon it rained not withered" (Amos 4:7).

Second, *its contributor*. "And there came a man from Baal-shalisha and brought the man of God bread of the first fruits" (2 Kings 4:42). Let us begin by observing how naturally and artlessly the conduct of this unnamed man is introduced. Here was one who had a heart for the Lord's servant in a time of need, who thought of him in this season of scarcity and distress, and who grudged not to go to some trouble in ministering to him. "Shalisha" adjoined "mount Ephraim" (1 Sam. 9:4) and probably a journey of considerable distance had to be taken in order to reach the prophet. Ah, but there was more behind this man's action than meets the eye: we must look deeper if we are to discover the springs of his deed. It is written "the steps are ordered of the Lord" (Ps. 37:23). And thus it was in the case before us: this man now befriended Elisha because God had worked in him "both to will and to do of His good pleasure" (Phil. 2:13). It is only by comparing Scripture with Scripture we can discover the fullness of meaning in any verse.

Ere passing on let us pause and make application unto ourselves of the truth to which attention has just been called. It has an important bearing on each of us, and one which needs the more to be emphasised in this day of practical atheism. The whole trend of things in our evil generation is to be so occupied with what are termed "the laws of Nature," that the operations of the Creator are lost sight of; man and his doings are so eulogised and deified that the hand of God in providence is totally obscured. It should be otherwise with the saint. When some friend comes and ministers to your need, while being grateful to him for the same, look above him and his kindness to the One who has sent him. I may pray, "Give us this day our daily bread" and then, because I am so absorbed with secondary causes and the instruments which He may employ fail to see my Father's hand as He graciously answers my petition. God is the Giver of every temporal as well as spiritual thing, even though He uses human agents in the conveying of them.

"And there came a man from Baal-shalisha." This town was originally called "Shalisha" but the evil power exerted by Jezebel had stamped upon it the name of her false god, as was the case with other places—(compare "Baal-hermon," 1 Chron 5:23). But even in this seat of idolatry there was at least one who feared the Lord, who was regulated by His law, and who had a heart for His servant. This should be a comfort to the saints in a time of such fearful and widespread declension as now obtains. But however dark things may get, and we believe they will yet become much darker before there is any improvement, God will preserve to Himself a remnant. He always has, and He always will. In the antediluvian world there was a Noah, who by grace was upright in his generations and walked with God. In Egypt, when the name of Jehovah was unknown among the Hebrews, a Moses was raised up, who "refused to be called the son of Pharaoh's daughter." So now there is one here and there as "a voice in the wilderness." Though the name of this man from Shalisha is not given, we doubt not it is inscribed in the Book of Life.

"And there came a man from Baal-shalisha and brought the man of God bread of the first fruits." Again we point out that there is more here than meets the careless eye or is obvious to the casual glance. Other passages which make mention of the "firstfruits" must be compared if we are to learn the deeper meaning of what is here recorded and discover that this man's action was something more than one of thoughtfulness and kindness to Elisha. "The first of the firstfruits of thy land thou shalt bring into the house of the Lord thy God" (Ex. 23:19—repeats in 34:26). The "firstfruits," then, belonged to the Lord, being an acknowledgment both of His goodness and proprietorship: a fuller and very beautiful passage thereon is found in Deuteronomy 26:1-11. From Numbers 18:8-13 we learn that these became the portion of the priests: "whatsoever is first ripe in the land, which they [the people] shall bring unto the Lord, shall be thine [Aaron's and his sons] every one that is clean in thine house shall eat of it" (v. 13). The same holds good in the rebuilt temple: "the first of all the firstfruits... shall be the priest's" (Ezek. 44:30).

This man from Shalisha then, was, in principle, acting in obedience to the Divine Law. We say "in principle," because it was enjoined that the firstfruits should be taken into "the house of the Lord" and that they became the priest's portion. But this man belonged to the kingdom of Israel and not of Judah: he lived in Samaria and had no access to Jerusalem, and even had he gone there, entrance to the temple had been forbidden. In Samaria there were none of the priests of the Lord, only those of Baal's. But though he rendered not obedience to the letter, he certainly did so in the spirit, for he recognised that these firstfruits were not for his own use; and though Elisha was not a priest he was a prophet, a servant of the Lord. It is for this reason, we believe, that it is said he brought the firstfruits not to "Elisha" but to "the man of God." That designation occurs first in Deuteronomy 33:1 in connection with Moses, and is descriptive not of his character but of his office—one wholly devoted to God, his entire time spent in His service. In the Old Testament it is applied only to the prophets and extra-ordinary teachers: 1 Samuel 2:27, 9:6; 1 Kings 17:18 etc., but in the New Testament it seems to belong to all of God's servants: 1 Timothy 6:11; 2 Timothy 3:17.

What has been pointed out above should throw light on a problem which is now exercising many conscientious souls and which should provide comfort in these evil days. The situation of many of God's people is now much like that which obtained when our present incident occurred. It was a time of apostasy, when everything was out of order. Such is the present case of Christendom. It is the clear duty of God's people to render obedience to the letter of His Word wherever that is possible, but when it is not they may do so in spirit. Daniel and his fellows could not observe the Passover feast in Babylon, and no doubt that was a sore grief to them. But that very grief signified their desire to observe it, and in such cases God accepts the will for the deed. For many years past this writer and his wife have been unable to conscientiously celebrate the Lord's supper, yet (by grace) we do so in spirit, by remembering the Lord's death for His people in our hearts and minds. "Not forsaking the assembling of *ourselves* together" (Heb. 10:25) is very far from meaning that the sheep of Christ should attend a place where the "goats" preponderate, or where their presence would sanction what is dishonoring to their Master.

Ere passing on we should point out another instructive and encouraging lesson here for the humble saint. As this man from Shalisha, acting in the spirit of God's Law, journeying with his firstfruits to where Elisha was, he could have had no thought in his mind that by this action he was going to be a contributor unto a remarkable miracle. Yet such was actually the case, for those very loaves of his became the means under the wonder-working power of God of feeding a large company of people. And this is but a single illustration of a principle which, by the benign government of God, is of frequent occurrence, as probably most of us have witnessed for ourselves. Ah, my reader, we never know how far-reaching may be the effects and what fruits may issue for eternity from the most inconspicuous act done for God's glory or the good of one of His people. How often has some obscure Christian, in the kindness of his heart, done something or given something which God has been pleased to bless and multiply unto others in a manner and to an extent which never entered his or her mind.

"And brought the man of God bread of the firstfruits, twenty loaves of barley, and full ears of corn in the husk thereof." How it appears that it delighted the Holy Spirit to describe this offering in detail. Bearing in mind that a time of serious "dearth" then obtained, may we not see in the varied nature of this gift thoughtfulness and consideration on the part of him that made it. Had the whole of it been made up in the form of "loaves" some of it might have gone moldy before the whole of it was eaten: at best it would need to be consumed quickly: to obviate that, part of the barley was brought in the husk. On the other hand, had all been brought in the ear time would be required for the grinding and baking thereof, and in the meanwhile the prophet might be famished and fainting. By such a division both disadvantages were prevented. From the whole, we are taught that in making gifts to another or in ministering to his needs we should exercise care in seeing that it is in a form best suited to his requirements. The application of this principle pertains to spiritual things as well as temporal.

Third, *its generosity*. Before noting the use to which Elisha put this offering, let us observe that, gifts sometimes come from the most unexpected quarters. Had this man come from Bethel or Shunem there would be no occasion for surprise, but that one from Baal-shalisha should bring God's servant an offering of his firstfruits was certainly not to be looked for. Ah, does not each of God's servants know something of this experience! If on the one hand some on whose cooperation he had reason to count failed and disappointed him, others who were strangers have befriended him. More than once or twice have the writer and his wife had this pleasant surprise: we cherish their memory, while seeking to forget the contrasting ones. Joseph might be envied and mistreated by his brethren, but he found favor in the eyes of Potiphar. Moses may be despised by the Hebrews, but he received kindly treatment in the house of Jethro. Rather than Elijah should starve by the brook Cherith, the Lord commanded the ravens to feed him. Our supplies are sure, though at times they may come from strange quarters.

"And he said, Give unto the people, that they may eat" (v. 42). In the preceding miracle this same trait is manifest: nothing is there said of Elisha partaking of the pottage, nor even of the young prophets in his charge, but rather "the people." Such liberality will not go unrewarded by God, for He has promised "Give, and it shall be given unto you" (Luke 6:38). Such was the case here, for the very next thing recorded after his "Pour out for the people that they may eat" (v. 41) is the receiving of these twenty loaves. And what use does he now make of them? His first thought was not for himself, but for others. We must not conclude from the silence of this verse that the prophet failed either to perceive the hand of God in this gift or that he neglected to return thanks unto Him. Had the Scriptures given a full and detailed account of such matters, they had run into many volumes instead of being a single one. According to the law of analogy we are justified in concluding that he did both. Moreover, what follows shows plainly that his mind was stayed upon the Lord.

The situation which confronted Elisha is one that in principle has often faced God's people. What the Lord gives to me is not to be used selfishly but is to be shared with others. Yet sometimes we are in the position where what is on hand does not appear sufficient for that purpose. My supply may be scanty and the claims of a growing family have to be met: if I contribute to the Lord's cause and minister to His servants and people, may not my little ones go short? Here is where the exercise of *faith* comes in: lay hold of such promises as Luke 6:38 and 2 Corinthians 9:8, act on them and you shall prove that "the liberal soul shall be made fat" (Prov. 11:25). Especially should the ministers of Christ set an example in this respect: if they be close handed it will greatly hinder their usefulness. Elisha did not scruple to make practical use of what was designed as an offering to the Lord, as David did not hesitate to take the "shewbread" and give to his hungry men.

Fourth, *its opposition*. "And his servitor said, What! should I set *this* before an hundred men?" (v. 43). Ah, the servant of God must not expect others to be equally zealous in exercising a gracious spirit or to cooperate with him in the works of faith, no not even those who are his assistants—none can walk by the faith of another. When Luther announced his intention of going to Worms even his dearest brethren sought to dissuade him. But was not such an objection a natural one? Yes, but certainly not spiritual. It shows how shallow and fleeting must have been the impression made on the man by the previous miracles. It was quite in keeping with what we read of this "servitor," Gehazi, elsewhere. His language expressed incredulity and unbelief. Was he thinking of himself? Did he resent his master's generosity and think, *We* shall need this food for ourselves? And this, after all the miracles he had seen God work through Elisha! Ah it takes something more than the witnessing of miracles to regenerate a dead soul, as the Jews made evident when the Son of God wrought in their midst.

Fifth, *its means*: faith in God and His Word. "He said again, Give the people that they may eat: for thus saith the Lord, They shall eat and shall leave thereof" (v. 43). Where there is real faith in God it is not stumbled by the unbelief of others, but when it stands in the wisdom of men it is soon paralyzed by the opposition it encounters. When blind Bartimaeus began to cry out, "Jesus, thou Son of David, have mercy on me," and many charged him that he should hold his peace, "he cried the more a great deal" (Mark 10:48). On the other hand, one with a stony-ground hearer's faith endureth for awhile, "for when tribulation or persecution ariseth because of the Word, by and by [quickly] he is offended" (Matt. 13:21). When Elisha had first said, "Give unto the people, that they may eat" it was the language of faith. Verse 41 seems to show that the people had been seeking the prophet in the extremity of their need. His own barrel of meal had probably run low, and it is likely he had been praying for its replenishment. And here was God's answer— yet in such a form or measure as to further test his faith! Elisha saw the hand of God in this gift and counted upon His making it sufficient to meet the needs of the crowd. Elisha regarded those twenty loaves as an "earnest" of greater bounties.

Do *we* regard such providences as "a token for good" or are we so wrapped up in the token itself that we look no further? It was a bold and courageous faith in Elisha: he was not afraid the Lord would put him to confusion and cause him to become a laughingstock to the people. At first his faith was a general (yet sufficient) one in the character of God. Then it met with a rebuff from Gehazi, but he refused to be shaken. And now it seems to us that the Lord rewarded His servant's faith by giving him a definite word from Himself. The way to get more faith is to use what has already been given us (Luke 8:18), for God ever honors those who honor Him. Trust Him fully and He will then bestow assurance. The minister of Christ must not be deterred by the carnality and unbelief of those who ought to be the ones to strengthen his hands and cooperate with him. Alas, how many have let distrustful deacons to quench their zeal by the difficulties and objections which they raise. How often the children of Israel opposed Moses and murmured against him, but "by faith he endured as seeing Him who is invisible" (Heb. 11:27).

Sixth, *its antitype*. There is no doubt whatever in our minds that the above incident supplies the Old Testament foreshadowment of our Lord's miracle in feeding the multitude, and it is both interesting and instructive to compare and contrast the type with its antitype. Note then the following parallels. First, in each case there was a crowd of hungry people. Second, Elisha took pity on them, and Christ had compassion on the needy multitude (Matt. 14:14). Third, a few "loaves" formed the principal article of diet, and in each case they were "barley" ones (John 6:9). Fourth, in each case, the order went forth "give [not 'sell'] the people that they may eat" (cf. Mark 6:37). Fifth, in each case an unbelieving attendant raised objection (John 6:7). Sixth, Elisha fed the crowd through his servant (v. 44) and Christ through His apostles (Matt. 14:19). Seventh, in each case a surplus remained after the people had eaten (v. 44 and cf. Matt. 14:20). And now observe wherein Christ has "the preeminence." First, He fed a much larger company: over 5,000 (Matt. 14:21) instead of 100. Second, He employed fewer loaves: 5 (Matt. 14:17) instead of 20. Third, He supplied a richer feast, fish as well as bread. Fourth, He wrought by His own power.

Seventh, *its meaning*. It will suffice if we just summarise what we have previously dwelt upon. 1. The servant of God who is faithful in giving out to others will not himself be kept on short rations. 2. The more such an one obtains from God, the more should he impart to the people: "Freely ye have received, freely give." 3. God ever makes His grace abound unto those who are generous. 4. A true servant of God has implicit confidence in the Divine character. 5. Though he encounters opposition he refuses to be stumbled thereby. 6. Though other ministers ridicule him, he acts according to God's Word. 7. God does not fail him, but honors his trust. —AWP

DOCTRINE OF SAINTS' PERSEVERANCE
10. Its Benefits

It has been pointed out on a previous occasion that what has been engaging our attention is far more than a subject for theological debate: it is full of practical value. It must be so, for it occupies a prominent place in the Divinely-inspired Scriptures which are "profitable for doctrine" (2 Tim. 3:16), and that, because it is "the doctrine which is according to godliness" (1 Tim. 6:3)—revealing the standard of piety and actually promoting piety in the soul and life of him who receives it by faith. Everything revealed in the Word and all the activities of God have two chief ends in view: His own glory and the good of His people. And as we draw to the close of this series it is fitting that we should seek to set before readers some of the benefits which are conferred by a believing apprehension of this truth, some of the blessed effects it produces and fruits it yields. We somewhat anticipated this aspect of our subject by what we said under its Blessedness (in the Jan. and Feb. 1942 issues), yet as we then did little more than generalise it behooves us now to more definitely particularise.

In attempting to describe some of the benefits which this doctrine affords we shall be regulated by whether we are viewing it from the Divine side or the human, for as we have sought to make clear in the preceding articles, the perseverance of the saints in holiness and obedience is the direct effect of the continued operations of Divine grace and power within them, and those operations are guaranteed by the promises of the everlasting covenant. Viewed from the Divine side, perseverance in the faith and in the paths of righteousness is itself a gift, a distinct gift from God: "who shall also confirm you unto the end" (1 Cor. 1:8). Absolutely considered God's preservation of His people turns upon no condition to be fulfilled by them, but depends entirely on the immutability and invincibility of the Divine purpose. Nevertheless, God does not preserve His people by mere physical power and without their concurrence, as He keeps the planets steadfast in their orbits. No, rather does He treat them throughout as moral agents and responsible creatures, drawing them with the cords of love, inclining their hearts unto Himself, rendering effectual the motives He sets before them and the means which He requires them to use.

The infallible certainty of the Divine operations on behalf of and within His saints and the mode of their working cannot be insisted upon too emphatically or repeated too often. On the one hand, the crown of honor and glory must be ascribed to the King Himself; and on the other hand, the response and concurrence or loyalty of His subjects is to be made equally plain. God preserves His people by renewing them in the inner man day by day (2 Cor. 4:16), by quickening them according to His Word, by granting them fresh supplies of grace, and also by moving them to heed His warnings and respond to His exhortations; in a word, by working in them both to will and to do of His good pleasure (Phil. 2:13). Thus our portrayal of some of the benefits and fruits of this doctrine will be governed by our viewpoint: whether we trace out what follows faith's appropriating of the Divine promises or what follows from faith's appropriation of the Divine precepts. God has promised to carry forward in sanctification and complete in glorification the work begun in regeneration, yet not without requiring us to perform the duties of piety and avoid everything contrary thereto.

1. Here is cause *for adoring God*. The doctrine set forth in this series most certainly redounds more to the glory of God than does the contrary one, which leaves our

everlasting felicity in uncertainty. It exemplifies God's *power*, whereby He not only restrains our external foes from overthrowing our salvation, but also by fixing the wavering disposition of our wills that we do not cease from the love of and desire after holiness. Also His *truth* in the promises of the Covenant, on which we securely rely, being assured that He who gave them will certainly make the same good. His *goodness*, whereby He patiently bears with our weakness and dullness, so that when we fall into sin, He does not cast us off, but by His loving chastenings recovers us through moving us to renewed repentance. His *holiness*, when because of our folly we trifle with temptation for a season, disregarding His warnings, He makes us conscious of His displeasure by withholding tokens of His favor and declining an answer to our prayers, bringing us to confess and forsake our sins, that fellowship with Him may be restored and that peace and joy may again be our portion.

2. Here is *peace for the soul* in a world of strife and where men's hearts fail them for fear of the future. This is evident if we consider the opposite. In themselves believers are weak and unstable, unable to do anything as they ought. They have no strength of their own to keep themselves in the love of God, but carry about with them a body of sin and death. They are continually exposed to temptations which ensnare the wisest and overthrow the strongest. Suppose then they had received no guarantee of the unchangeableness of God's purpose, no infallible word of the continuance of His love, no pledge that He will keep and secure them by the working of His mighty power, no declaration that unfailing supplies of His Spirit and grace shall be vouchsafed them, no assurance that He will never leave them nor forsake them, no revelation of an Advocate on high to plead their cause and of the sufficiency of His mediation and the efficacy of His intercession. But rather that they are left to their own fidelity: and in consequence some of the most eminent saints have apostatized from the faith, that thousands have utterly fallen out of God's love and favor, and so been cast from His covenant, from whence few have ever recovered; and all confidence and peace will be at an end, and fear and terror fill their place.

How vastly different is the teaching of the Word from what we have supposed above. There we find God, as it were, saying to His people: I know your weakness and insufficiency, your dullness and darkness, how that without My Son and continual supplies of His Spirit you can do nothing. The power and rage of your indwelling sin is not hidden from Me, and how with violence it brings you into captivity against your desires. I know that though you believe, yet you are frequently made to groan over your unbelief, and that you are then ready to fear the worst. And when in that case Satan assaults and tempts, seeking to devour you; that first he acts like a serpent, attempting to beguile and ensnare, and then as a lion to terrify. But be not ignorant of his devices: resist him steadfast in the faith: take unto you the whole armor of God, watch night and day that ye be not seduced by him, and you shall overcome him by the blood of the Lamb. "Fear thou not, for I am with thee: be not dismayed, for I am thy God: I will strengthen thee, yea I will help thee, yea I will uphold thee with the right hand of My righteousness" (Isa. 41:10). Though you may be tripped up, ye shall not utterly fall. Though you be fearful, My kindness shall not be removed from you. So be of good cheer, and run with patience the race that is set before you.

3. Here is *solid comfort* for the saints in a day of declension, when there is a great "falling away" of those who once appeared to run well. Though what is termed

"organised Christianity" be a demonstrated failure, though corporate Christendom be now in ruins, though ten thousands have apostatised yet let the saints be fully assured that God has and will reserve to Himself a remnant who bow not the knee to Baal; and therefore may those who have the living God for their "refuge" confidently exclaim "Therefore will not we fear though the earth [the most stable and ancient establishments] be removed, and though the mountains [the leaders and most towering professors] be carried [by the winds of false doctrine] into the midst of the sea"—the masses of the wicked: Isaiah 57:20. When many of the nominal disciples of Christ "went back and walked no more with Him," He turned to the apostles and said "Will ye also go away?" Whereupon Simon Peter as their spokesman answered "Lord, to whom shall we go? Thou hast the words of eternal life" (John 6:66-68). Thus it was then, has been throughout the centuries, and will be unto the end of time. The sheep are secure, while the goats turn aside and perish.

Observe how Paul emphasizes this very note in 2 Timothy 2. Hymeneus and Philetus eminent men in the church had apostatised, and by their defection and false teaching had overthrown the doctrinal faith of some; yet says the apostle, This is no reason why the real children of God should be made to quake and imagine that their end is uncertain. "Nevertheless the foundation of God standeth sure, having this seal: the Lord knoweth them that are His; and, let every one that nameth the name of Christ depart from iniquity" (v. 19). Note the two sides of that "seal," preserving the balance of Truth: on the one side there is a cordial— those who are built upon the foundation of God's unchanging purpose and love shall not be prevailed against; on the other there is a warning—trifle not with "iniquity," whether it be doctrinal or practical, but "depart" from it. Similarly John assures believers who might be shaken at seeing certain in their assemblies being seduced by the antichrists of that day, but such were only *unregenerate* professors (1 John 2:19), and therefore that the regenerate, held in the hand of Christ, shall not be overcome by deceivers.

4. Here is *ground for holy confidence*. The Lord knows how difficult is the task assigned His people and how deep is the sense of their own insufficiency. He knows too that nothing more enervates their hearts and enfeebles their hands than doubts and fears, and therefore has He made absolute promise to those who hear His voice and follow Him that "they shall never perish" (John 10:29). It was this which armed Joshua to the battle: "There shall not a man be able to stand before thee all the days of thy life; as I was with Moses, so I will be with thee: I will not fail thee nor forsake thee." And from thence the Lord drew an argument—the very opposite of that which the legalistic Arminian infers—namely, "Be strong and of a good courage" (Josh. 1:5, 6). Such a promise would not make a Joshua reckless or lax, whatever effect it might have upon a self-righteous freewiller. No, rather would it produce a holy confidence, which prompted to the use of lawful means and gave assurance of God's blessing thereon. Such a confidence causes its possessor to trust in the Lord with all his heart and lean not unto his own understanding.

Such encouragement is conveyed and such confidence is engendered by the Divine declaration "the righteous shall hold on his way" (Job 17:9). As the young believer contemplates the likely length of the journey before him and the difficulties of the road which has to be trod, he is apt to give way to despair; but if his faith lays hold of this promise that he shall certainly reach the desired goal, new strength will be imparted to his feeble knees and increased resolution to his fainting heart. It is the confidence that by continuing to plod along the weary traveler will reach home, which causes him to take courage and refuse to give in. It is the assurance of success which is to the right-minded and best stimulus of labor. If the Christian be persuaded that the world shall not overcome him, that sin shall not slay him, that Satan shall not triumph over him, then will he take unto him the shield of faith and the Sword of the Spirit and fight like a man and be more than conqueror. As it has been truly said "This is one of the reasons why British troops have so often won the fight: because the drummer boys know not how to beat a retreat and the soldiers refused to believe in the possibility of defeat."

5. Here is *consolation for us in the severest trials*. Let us illustrate this point from the case of Job, for it is difficult to conceive one more acute and extreme than his. You know how severe, how many, and how protracted were those afflictions. You know how far Satan was permitted to proceed with him. You know how his wife turned against and his so-called friends tantalised him. His cup of trouble was indeed filled to the brim, yet we find him looking above his afflictions and censorious critics, exclaiming "He knoweth the way that I take: when He hath tried me I shall come forth as *gold*" (23:10). Weigh well those words and bring to mind the situation of the one who uttered them. Observe that there was no doubt or uncertainty in his mind about the issue of his afflictions: it was not "I fear I shall perish in the furnace," for he refused to allow those fiery trials to turn him into a skeptic. Nor did he merely cherish a faltering hope that things might possibly be well with him at the end, and say "I *may* come forth as gold." No, there was the undoubting, positive conviction "I shall"!

Ah, my reader, Job saw "the bright light in the cloud" (37:21). He drew comfort from what assured Cowper when he wrote those lines—

> *"Judge not the Lord by feeble sense,*
> *But trust Him for His grace:*
> *Behind a frowning providence,*
> *He hides a smiling face."*

Job knew that God maketh "all things work together for good to them that love Him, to them who are the called according to His purpose" (Rom. 8:28), and therefore he knew there could be no possibility of his perishing in the fires. And why was there no doubting as to the outcome of his trials? Because he could say "For I know that *my Redeemer* liveth" and therefore could he add "and though after my skin worms destroy this body, yet in my flesh *shall I* see God" (19:25,26). That was the ground of his confidence— nothing in himself. That was what caused him to triumphantly exclaim "I shall come forth as gold." Cheer up fellow believer: the process may be painful, but the end is sure; the path may be rough and you may feel faint, but the prospect is entrancing and certain.

6. Here is *cause for praise*. Why should I be found still holding on my way when so many who made a bright profession and who appeared to make much faster progress in spiritual things than I did, have long ago dropped out of the race, and have gone right back into the world? Certainly not because I was any better by nature. No, I freely ascribe all the glory unto God who has so graciously ministered unto me and continued to work in me; who has been so longsuffering and recovered me when I strayed. O

what thanks are due unto Him. How often have I had occasion to say "He restoreth my soul" (Psa. 23:3)—as He did Abraham's, Jacob's, Peter's. Thus I may say with David "I will sing of the mercies of the Lord *forever*" (Psa. 89:1). Not today or tomorrow, but for "forever"; not only when I come to the brink of the Jordan, but after I have passed safely through it, the high praises of His faithfulness shall be the theme of my song throughout eternity.

7. Here is *a powerful incentive to confirm Christians* in their spiritual lives and to spur them unto the duties of piety. This is evident from what regeneration works in them. All the arguments drawn from the possibility of the apostasy of saints are derived from the terror of dreadful threatenings and the fear of eternal punishment; whereas those taken from the assurances conveyed by the everlasting covenant breathe nothing but the sweetness of grace. Since the children of God have received "the spirit of adoption, whereby they cry Father, Father" (Rom. 8:15), they are more powerfully drawn by the cords of love than by the scourge of horror. Moreover since all acceptable obedience springs from gratitude, then that which most effectually promotes gratitude must be the most powerful spring of obedience, and as to whether a grace bestowed by the Lord is perpetual or one which may be lost is likely to inspire the deepest gratitude, we leave to the judgment of our readers. The more firmly be secured the reward of duty, the more diligent shall we be in performing duty.

8. Here is *an incentive to practical godliness*. If Christian perseverance is one of continuance in the path of obedience and holiness, then will the saints make diligent use of the aids which God has provided for them and eschew the contrary. Especially will they be encouraged to ask for and seek after the grace which God has promised. As it is a sight and sense of Christ's being crucified because of *my* heinous sins which produces evangelical repentance (Zech. 12:10), so it is a realisation of the immutability of God's purpose, the unchangeableness of His love, and the preciousness of His promises which strengthen faith and inflame love to serve and please Him. This twofold doctrine of Divine preservation and perseverance in holiness supplies effectual motives unto piety. Negatively, it removes discouragements by letting us know that our denials of self, mortifications of the flesh and efforts to resist the Devil, are not in vain (1 Cor. 15:58; Gal. 6:9). Positively, it places upon us the most powerful obligations to live unto God, to show forth His praises, and adorn the doctrine we profess (2 Cor. 7:1).

9. Here we are shown *the need of continual diligence* in order to persevere unto the end. But, says the Arminian, I would have concluded the very opposite, since final perseverance be guaranteed. That is due to his misconception. God has declared "The righteous shall hold on his way": not become slack and sit down, still less that he will forsake it for the way of the ungodly. That very promise is the best means of producing the desired result. If a man could be definitely assured that in a certain line of business he would make a fortune, would such assurance cause him to refuse that business or lead him to lie in bed all day? No, rather would it be an incentive to diligence in order to prosper. Napoleon believed he was "the man of destiny": did that conviction freeze his energies? No, the very opposite. God's promising a thing unto His children causes them to pray for the same with greater confidence, earnestness and importunity. God hath promised to bless our use of lawful means and therefore we employ them with diligence and expectation.

10. Here is *a truth to humble us*. Admittedly it has been wrested by Antinomians and perverted unto the feeding of a spirit of presumption. But it is "ungodly men" and not the saints who turn the grace of our God into lasciviousness (Jude 4). Different far is the effect of this truth upon the regenerate. It works in them a sense of their own insufficiency, causing them to look outside of themselves for help and strength. So far from rendering them slothful, it deepens their desires after holiness and makes them seek it more earnestly. As the Christian realises "Thou hast commanded us to keep Thy precepts diligently," he is moved to pray "O that my ways were directed to keep Thy statutes diligently...Make me to go in the path of Thy commandments, for herein do I delight" (Psa. 119:4,5,35). The more he is taught of the Spirit the more will he cry "Hold Thou me up, and I shall be safe" (Psa. 119:117). —AWP

SPIRITUAL GROWTH OR CHRISTIAN PROGRESS
1. Introduction
The name which is usually given to our subject by Christian writers is that of "Growth in Grace" which is a Scriptural expression, being found 2 Peter 3:18. But it appears to us that, strictly speaking, growing "in grace" has reference to but a single aspect or branch of our theme: "that your *love* may abound yet more and more" (Phil. 1:9) treats of another aspect, and "your *faith* groweth exceedingly" (2 Thess. 1:3), with yet another. It seems then that "spiritual growth" is a more comprehensive and inclusive term and more accurately covers that most important and desirable attainment "may grow up into Him in *all* things, which is the Head, even Christ" (Eph. 4:15). Let it not be thought from this that we have selected our title in a captious spirit or because we are striving after originality. Not so: we have no criticism to make against those who may prefer some other appellation. We have chosen this one simply because it seems more fitly and fully describe the ground which we hope to cover. Our readers understand clearly what is connoted by "physical growth" or "mental growth," nor should "spiritual growth" be any the less intelligible.

The subject which is to be before us is a "deeply important" one. First, that we may understand aright the Spirit's teaching thereon. There seems to be comparatively few who do so, and the consequence is that the Lord is robbed of much of the praise which is His due, while many of His people suffer much needless distress. Because so many Christians walk more by sense than by faith, measuring themselves by their feelings and moods rather than by the Word, their peace of mind is greatly destroyed and their joy of heart much decreased. Not a few saints are seriously the losers through misapprehensions upon this subject. Scriptural knowledge is essential if we are to better understand ourselves and diagnose more accurately our spiritual case. Many exercised souls form quite an erroneous opinion of themselves because of failure at this very point. Surely it is a matter of great practical moment that we should be able to judge aright of our spiritual progress or retrogression, that we may not flatter ourselves on the one hand or unduly depreciate ourselves on the other.

Some are tempted in one direction, some in the other—depending partly on their personal temperament and partly on the kind of teaching they sat under. Many are inclined to think more highly of themselves than they ought to, and because they have obtained considerably increased intellectual knowledge of the Truth imagine they have made a proportionate spiritual growth. But others with weaker memories and who acquire a mental grasp of things more slowly, suppose this to signify a lack of spirituality. Unless our thoughts about spiritual growth be formed by the Word of God we are certain to err and jump to a wrong conclusion. As it is with our bodies, so it is with our souls. Some suppose they are healthy while suffering from an insidious disease; whereas others imagine themselves to be ill when in fact they are hale and sound. Divine revelation and not human imagination ought to be our guide in determining whether or not we be "babes, young men, or fathers"—and our natural age has nothing to do with it.

It is deeply important that our views should be rightly formed, not only that we may be able to ascertain our own spiritual stature, but also that of our fellow Christians. If I long to be made a help and blessing to them then obviously I must first be capable of deciding whether they be in a healthy or unhealthy condition. Or, if I desire spiritual counsel and assistance then I shall meet with disappointment unless I know whom to go to. How can I regulate my course and suit my converse with the saints I contact if at a loss to gauge their religious caliber? God has not left us to our own erring judgment in this matter, but has supplied rules to guide us. To mention but one other reason which indicates the importance of our subject: unless I can ascertain wherein I have been enabled to make spiritual progress and wherein I have failed, how can I know what to pray for, and unless I can perceive the same about my brethren how can I intelligently ask for the supply of what they most need?

Our subject is a very mysterious one. Physical growth is beyond human comprehension. We know something of what is essential in order to it, and the thing itself may be discovered, but the operation and process is hidden from us: "As thou knowest not what is the way of the spirit, nor how the bones do grow in the womb of her that is with child, even so thou knowest not the works of God who maketh all" (Eccl. 11:5). How much more so must spiritual growth be incomprehensible. The beginning of our spiritual life is shrouded in mystery (John 3:8), and to a considerable extent this is true also of its development. God's workings in the soul are secret, indiscernible to the eye of carnal reason and imperceptible to our senses. "The things of God knoweth no man" save to whom the Spirit is pleased to reveal them (1 Cor. 2:11,12). If we know so little about ourselves and the operation of our faculties in connection with natural things, how much less competent are we to comprehend ourselves and our graces in connection with that which is supernatural.

The "new creature" is from above, whereof our natural reason has no acquaintance: it is a product supernatural and can only be known by revelation supernatural. In like manner, the spiritual life received at the new birth *thrives* as to its degrees, unperceived by our senses. A child, by weighing and measuring himself, may discover he has grown, yet he was not conscious of the process while growing. So it is with the new man: it is "renewed day by day" (2 Cor. 4:16) yet in such a hidden way that the renewing itself is not felt, though its effects become apparent. Thus there is no good reason to be disheartened because we do not *feel* that any progress is being made or to conclude there is no advance because such feeling is absent. "There are some of the Lord's people in whom the essence and reality of holiness dwell, who do not perceive in themselves any spiritual growth. It should therefore be remembered that there is a real growth in grace where it is not perceived. We should judge of it not by what we experience of it in ourselves, but by the Word. It is a subject for *faith* to be exercised on" (S.

E. Pierce). If we desire the pure milk of the Word and feed thereon, then we must not doubt that we duly "grow thereby" (1 Peter 2:3).

To quote again from Pierce: "Spiritual growth is a mystery and is more evident in some than in others. The more the Holy Spirit shines upon the mind and puts forth His life-giving influences in the heart, so much the more sin is seen, felt and loathed, as the greatest of all evils. And this is an evidence of spiritual growth, namely, to hate sin as sin and to abhor it on account of its contrariety to the nature of God. The quick perception and insight which we have of inherent sin, and our feeling of it, so as to look on ourselves as most vile, to renounce ourselves and all we can do for ourselves, and look wholly and immediately to Christ for relief and strength, are growth in grace, and a most certain evidence of it." How little is the natural man capable of understanding that! Having no experience of the same, it sounds to him like a doleful delusion. And how the believer needs to beg God to teach him the truth about the same. As we can know nothing whatever about the new birth save what God has revealed in His Word, so we can form no correct comprehension about spiritual growth except from the same source.

Our subject is not only mysterious but it is also a difficult one. This is due in part to Satan's having confused the issue by inventing such plausible imitations that multitudes are deceived thereby, and knowing this the conscientious soul is troubled. Under certain influences and from various motives people are induced to suddenly and radically reform their lives, and their absence from the grosser forms of sin accompanied by a zealous performance of the common duties of religion, is often mistaken for genuine conversion and progress in the Christian life. These are the "tares" which so closely resemble the wheat they are often indistinguishable until the harvest. Moreover, there is a work of the Law, quite distinct from the saving effects wrought by the Gospel, which in its fruits both external and internal cannot be distinguished from a work of grace except by the light of Scripture and the teaching of the Spirit. The terrors of the Law have come in power to the conscience of many an one, producing poignant convictions of sin and horrors of the wrath to come, issuing in much activity in the works of righteousness; but resulting in no faith in Christ, and no love for Him.

Again: spiritual progress is difficult to discern because growth in grace is often not nearly so apparent as first conversion. In many cases conversion is a radical experience of which we are personally conscious at the time and of which a vivid memory remains with us. It marked a revolutionary change in our life. It was when we were relieved of the intolerable burden of guilt and the peace of God which passeth all understanding possessed our souls. It was a being brought out of the awful and total spiritual darkness of nature into God's marvelous light, whereas spiritual growth is but the enjoying further degrees of that light. It was that tremendous change from having no grace at all to the beginnings of grace within us, whereas that which follows is the receiving of additions of grace. It was a spiritual resurrection, a being brought from death unto life, but the subsequent experience is only renewings of the life then received. For Joseph to be suddenly translated out of prison to sit upon the throne of Egypt, second only to Pharaoh, would affect him far more powerfully than to have any new kingdoms added to him later, such as Alexander had. At first everything in the spiritual life is new to the Christian; later he learns more perfectly what was then discovered to him, yet the effect made is not so perceptible and entrancing.

Further: the spiritual life or nature communicated at regeneration is not the only thing in the Christian: the principle of sin still remains in the soul after the principle of grace has been imparted. Those two principles are at direct variance with each other, engaged in a ceaseless warfare as long as the saint is left in this world. "For the flesh lusteth against the spirit, and the spirit against the flesh: and these are contrary the one to the other; so that ye cannot do the things that ye would" (Gal. 5:17). That fearful conflict is apt to confuse the issue in the mind of its subject, yea, it is certain to lead the believer to draw a false inference from it unless he clearly apprehends the teaching of Scripture thereon. The discovery of so much opposition within, the thwarting of his aspirations and endeavors, his felt inability to wage the warfare successfully, makes him seriously to doubt whether holiness has been imparted to his heart. The ragings of indwelling sin, the discovery of unsuspected corruptions, the consciousness of unbelief, the defeats experienced, all appear to give the lie direct to any spiritual progress. *That* presents an acute problem to a conscientious soul.

Our subject is both a *complex and comprehensive* one. By which we mean that this is a tree with many branches, which bears a different manner of fruits according to the season. It is a subject into which various elements enter, one that needs to be viewed from many angles. Spiritual growth is both upward and downward, and it is both inward and outward. An increased knowledge of God leads to an increased knowledge of self, and as one results in higher adoration of its Object, the other brings deeper humiliation in its subject. These issue in more and more inward denials of self and abounding more and more outwardly in good works. Yet this spiritual growth needs to be most carefully stated, lest we repudiate the completeness of regeneration. In the strictest sense, spiritual growth consists of the Spirit's drawing out what He wrought in the soul when He quickened it. When a babe is born into this world it is complete in parts though not in development: no new members can be added to its body nor any additional faculties to its mind.

There is a growth of the natural child, a development of its members, an expansion of its faculties, with a fuller expression and clearer manifestation of the latter, but nothing more. The analogy holds good with a babe in Christ. "Though there are innumerable circumstantial differences in the cases and experience of the called people of God, and though there is a growth suited to them, considered as 'babes, young men and fathers,' yet there is but *one common life* in the various stages and degrees of the *same* life carried on to its perfection by the Holy Spirit until it issues in glory eternal. The work of God the Spirit in regeneration is eternally complete. It admits of no increase nor decrease. It is one and the same in all believers. There will not be the least addition to it in Heaven: not one grace, holy affection, desire or disposition then, which is not in it now. The whole of the Spirit's work therefore from the moment of regeneration to our glorification is to draw out those graces into act and exercise which He hath wrought within us. And though one believer may abound in the fruits of righteousness more than another, yet there is not one of them more regenerated than another." (S. E. Pierce)

The complexity of our subject is due in part to both the Divine and the human elements entering into it, and who is competent to explain or set forth their meeting-point! Yet the analogy supplied from the physical realm again affords us some help. Absolutely considered, all growth is due to the Divine operations, yet relatively there are certain conditions which we must meet or there will be no growth—to name no other, the partaking of suitable food is an essential prerequisite; nevertheless that will not nourish unless God be pleased to bless the same. To insist that there are certain conditions we must meet, certain means we must use in order to our spiritual progress, is not to divide the honors with God, but is simply pointing out the *order* He has established and the connection He has appointed between one thing and another. In like manner there are certain hindrances which we must avoid, or growth will inevitably be arrested and spiritual progress retarded. Nor does that imply that we are thwarting God, but only disregarding His warnings and paying the penalty of breaking those laws which He has instituted.

The very complexity of our subject increases the difficulty before the one attempting to expound the same, for as is the case with so many other problems presented to our limited intelligence, it involves the matter of seeking to preserve a due balance between the Divine and the human elements. The operations of Divine grace and the discharge of our responsibility must each be insisted upon, and the concurring of the latter with the former, as well as the superabounding of the former over the latter be proportionately set forth. In like manner our contemplation of spiritual growth upward must not be allowed to crowd out that of our growth downward, nor must our deeper loathing of self be suffered to hinder an increasing living upon Christ. The more sensible we are of our emptiness, the more we must draw upon His fullness. Nor is our task rendered easier when we remember these articles fall into the hands of very different types of readers, who sit under varied kinds of ministry—the one needing emphasis upon a different note from another.

That there *is* such a thing as spiritual growth is abundantly clear from the Scriptures. In addition to the passages alluded to in the opening paragraph we may quote the following. "They go from strength to strength" (Ps. 84:7). "The path of the just is as the shining light, that shineth more and more unto the perfect day" (Prov. 4:18). "Then shall we know if we follow on to know the Lord" (Hos. 6:3). "But unto you that fear the Lord shall the Sun of Righteousness arise with healing in His wings, and ye shall go forth and *grow up* as calves of the stall" (Mal. 4:2). "And of his fullness have all we received, and grace for grace" (John 1:16). "Every branch in Me that beareth fruit He purgeth it that it may bring forth more fruit" (John 15:2). "But we all, with open face beholding as in a glass the glory of the Lord, are changed into the same image from *glory to glory* as by the Spirit of the Lord" (2 Cor. 3:18). "Increasing in the knowledge of God" (Col. 1:10). "As ye have received of us how ye ought to walk and to please God, so ye abound more and more" (1 Thess. 4:1). "He giveth more grace (James 4:6).

The above list might be extended considerably, but sufficient references have been given to show that not only is such a thing as spiritual growth clearly revealed in the Scriptures, but that it is given a prominent place therein. Let the reader duly observe the *variety* of expressions which are employed by the Spirit to set forth this progress or development—thereby preserving us from too circumscribed a conception by showing us the many-sidedness of the same. Some of them relate to what is internal, others to what is external. Some of them describe the Divine operations, others the necessary acts and exercises of the Christian. Some of them make mention of increased light and knowledge, others of increased grace and strength, and yet others of increased conformity to Christ and fruitfulness. It is thus that the Holy Spirit has preserved the balance and it is by our carefully noting the same that we shall be kept from a narrow and one-sided idea of what spiritual growth consists of. If due attention be paid to this varied description we shall be kept from painful mistakes, and the better enabled to test or measure ourselves and discover what spiritual stature we have attained unto.

From what has been pointed out in the last few paragraphs it will be seen that this is an intensely *practical subject*. It is no small matter that we should be able to arrive at the clear apprehension of what spiritual growth actually consists of, and thereby be delivered from mistaking for it mere fantasy. If there be conditions which we have to comply with in order to the making of progress, it is most desirable that we should acquaint ourselves with the same and then translate such knowledge into prayer. If God has appointed certain means and aids, the sooner we learn what they are and make diligent use of them the better for us. And if there be other things which act as deterrents and are inimical to our welfare, the more we are placed upon our guard the less likely we are to be hindered by them. And if Christian growth has many sides to it this should govern our thinking and acting thereon, that we may strive after a fitly-proportioned and well-rounded Christian character, and grow up into Christ not merely in one or two respects but "in *all* things" that our development may be uniform and symmetrical. —AWP

(continued from back page)

commandments I must be conversant with them and in order to perceive their breadth and specific application unto any problem or decision confronting me, I must "meditate therein day and night." Meditation stands to reading as mastication does to eating. Prosperity eludes the dilatory and careless.

"That thou mayest observe to do according to all that is written therein." *This* must be the dominating motive and object. God's Word is to be appropriated and masticated—fed and meditated upon—first and foremost, day in and day out. Not for the purpose of understanding its prophecies or obtaining an insight into its mysteries, but in order to learn God's will for me, and having learned it to conform thereto. God's Word is given to us chiefly not to gratify curiosity or to entertain our imagination, but as "a lamp to our feet and a light unto our path" (Psa. 119:105) in this dark world. It is a Rule for us to walk by: it is a heavenly Standard for the regulation of all our conduct. It points out the things to be avoided, the things which would harm us. It tells of the things to be followed and practiced, the things which are for our good, our peace. It contains not only good advice, but is clothed with Divine authority, commanding implicit and unqualified obedience.

"For then—if we feed on the Word, if we constantly meditate upon its precepts and promises, if we render to it entire obedience—shalt thou make thy way prosperous and then thou shalt have good success." The promise is emphatic, unqualified, sure. If then this new year is not a prosperous one for me the fault is entirely my own: it will be because I have failed to meet the conditions prescribed in the context. Turn to 2 Chronicles 20:20 and see how well Jehoshaphat understood the secret of prosperity. Mark what occasioned the prosperity of Hezekiah (2 Chron. 31:20,21). Compare Job 36:11. Ponder all that precedes the last clause of Psalm 1:3. "But whoso looketh into the perfect law of liberty and continueth therein, he being not a forgetful hearer, but a doer of the work, this man *shall be blessed* in his deed" (James 1:25). —AWP

(continued from front page)
success" (Josh. 1:8). Here is the positive side, the making known the conditions which regulate and determine prosperity, as the repeated "then" plainly intimates. The passage begins at verse 5, and the whole of verses 5-8 should be attentively weighed. Let us first anticipate an objection by asking the question "was it written for his sake alone" (Rom. 4:23)? Undoubtedly those words had a special reference to Joshua himself, yet that they have a wider bearing is clear from other passages, and that they have a general application to God's children today is definitely established by the New Testament. But as some of our readers have come under the influence of those who would rob the Christian of his rightful portion, under the pretext of "rightly dividing the Word of Truth," we must labour the point.

Note then how unhesitatingly David appropriated these words of the Lord to Joshua when he spoke to his son, for he emphatically assured him that if Divine grace enabled him to "keep the Law of the Lord his God" taking heed to "fulfill the statutes and judgments" of it, "*then* shalt thou prosper" (1 Chron. 22:12,13). But more pertinently still, observe how the apostle expressly appropriates the promise of Joshua 1:5 "I will never leave thee nor forsake thee" and insists that it belongs equally to the whole household of faith, immediately adding "so that *we* may boldly say, The Lord is *my* Helper" (Heb. 13:5,6). That precious promise of God, then, belongs as truly *to me* as it did to Joshua of old. Are not the needs of believers the same in one age as in another? Is not God affected alike unto all of His children: does He not bear to them the same love? If He would not desert Joshua, He will not desert you! Consequently, if I would ascertain the laws which will determine my prosperity, I must pay attention to those which regulated *his*.

"This Book of the Law shall not depart out of thy mouth." It was the Rule given to act by. In Joshua's case it furnished him with Divine authority for his conduct in the governing of Israel. In our case we may give these words a spiritual meaning. God's Word is our appointed food: thus the "mouth" speaks to us of feeding upon it. In verse 6 God says, "Be strong and of a good courage," and in verse 7 adds, "only be thou strong and very courageous that [in order that] thou mayest observe to do according to all the Law." Obedience to God calls for firmness, resolution, boldness. Without it we shall yield unto temptations to compromise, being intimidated by the ridicule and opposition of our fellows. How, then, is this strength and courage to be obtained? By feeding on the Word, being "nourished up in the words of faith" (1 Tim. 4:6), having the Law of the Lord continually in our "mouth." This is the interpretation made by the apostle; appropriate that promise "I will never leave thee" and then, says he, every believer may confidently declare "The Lord is *my* Helper, and I will *not fear* what man shall do unto me" (Heb. 13:6). There is the proof that feeding on the Word imparts strength and courage.

"But thou shalt meditate therein day and night." Only thus will its injunctions be fixed in the memory: only thus shall we be able to ascertain our duty: only thus shall we discern the rightful application of the Divine precepts to all the varied details of our daily lives. It is entirely our own fault if we be ignorant of God's "mind" in connection with any situation confronting us. God's will for us is revealed in His Word, and "a good understanding have all they that do His commandments" (Psa. 111:10). The more I am regulated by the Divine Rule, the more shall I be preserved from the "mistakes" or folly which characterises those who follow a course of self-pleasing. But in order to *do* God's

. (continued on proceeding page)

VOL. XXIII.　　　　　FEBRUARY, 1944.　　　　　NO. 2

STUDIES ɪɴ ᴛʜᴇ SCRIPTURES

"Search the Scriptures." John 5:39.

Publisher and Editor—Aʀᴛʜᴜʀ W. Pɪɴᴋ,
27 Lewis Street,
Stornoway, Isle of Lewis,
Scotland.

OUR RIGHTEOUS REDEEMER

Does such a title have somewhat of a strange sound to the ear of the reader? Is that adjective unfamiliar in such a connection? Probably the great majority of us are far more accustomed to such expressions as "our loving Redeemer" and "our gracious Redeemer," or even "our mighty Redeemer." We confess that to the best of our recollection we have never heard this particular expression used, nor do we remember ever coming across it in our reading. Our employment of it here is not because we are striving after originality, nor is it coined for the purpose of alliteration. No, rather is such an appellation required by the teaching of Scripture. In fact, if we carefully observe where the Holy Spirit has placed the emphasis it is incumbent upon us that we should conform our terminology thereto. Test your memory and see how many passages you can recall where either "loving" or "gracious" is used as an adjective in connection with Christ. If memory fails, consult a concordance, and then perhaps you will be surprised that neither of them occurs a single time! Now test your memory with the word "righteous" and see how many passages come to mind where the Lord Jesus is referred to as such.

In Isaiah 53:11 Christ is referred to as "My righteous Servant," in Jeremiah 23:5 as "a righteous Branch," and in the next verse as "the Lord our righteousness." In Malachi 4:2 as "the Sun of righteousness," in Luke 23:47 as a "righteous Man," in 2 Timothy 4:8 as "the righteous Judge." In Hebrews 7:2, 3 He is seen as the antitypical Melchizedek or "King of righteousness"; while in 1 John 2:1, as our Advocate with the Father, He is termed "Jesus Christ the righteous." In addition, we find the same Greek word (dikaios) rendered "just" in the following passages: in Matthew 27:19 Pilate's wife sends a warning to her husband saying "Have thou nothing to do with this just [righteous] Man"; while in verse 24 of the same chapter Pilate himself declared "I am innocent of the blood of this just Person." In Acts 3:14 and James 5:6 He is denominated "the Just," and in Acts 7:52 and 22:14 "the Just One"; while in 1 Peter 3:18 we have the well-known words "Christ also hath once suffered for sins, the Just for the unjust"—actually rendered "the righteous for the unrighteous" by the American R.V. When Zechariah predicted His entry into Jerusalem, riding on the back of an ass, he said, "Behold, thy King cometh to thee, He is just," and in Revelation 19:11, where He is depicted on a white horse, it is said "in righteousness He doth judge and make war."

(continued on back page)

IMPORTANT NOTICES

Please advise promptly of change in address, otherwise copies will be lost in the mails.

We are glad to send a sample copy to any of your friends whom you believe would be interested in this publication.

This magazine is published as "a work of faith and labour of love," the editor and his wife gladly giving their services free. There is no regular subscription price, as we do not wish the poor of the flock to be deprived. This does not mean that those looking for something for nothing may "help themselves." Those getting this Magazine, who are financially able and who receive spiritual help from its pages, are expected to gladly contribute towards its expenses; otherwise, their names are dropped from our lists.

Will those forwarding International Money Orders please have them made out to us at Stornoway, Isle of Lewis, Scotland. Checks (Cheques-Eng.) made out on U.S.A. Banks are not negotiable here, so please do not send them.

CONTENTS

THE PRAYERS OF THE APOSTLES
2. Romans 1:8-12

We shall not take up Paul's prayers in their chronological order but according as they are found in his epistles in our present-day Bible. The Thessalonian epistles were written before the Roman, but as Romans (because of its theme and importance) rightly comes first we shall begin with those of his prayers recorded therein. Opinion is divided as to whether the verses before us chronicle a particular prayer actually offered by Paul at that time, or whether he is here informing them how he was wont to remember them at the throne of grace. It appears to us the distinction is such a fine one that it makes little practical difference which view be adopted: personally we incline to the former concept. This epistle was taken down by an amanuensis (16:22), and as the apostle dictated the words "to all that be in Rome beloved of God" (v. 7) his heart was immediately drawn out in thanksgiving that some of His elect were to be found even in the capital of the Roman empire, yea, in "Caesar's household" (Phil. 4:22).

The position of Paul was one of some delicacy, being a stranger to the saints at Rome. No doubt they had often heard of him—at first as a dangerous person. When assured of his conversion, and learning that he was the apostle to the Gentiles, probably they wondered why he had not visited them, especially when he had been so near to Rome as Corinth. So he now makes known his deep personal interest in them. They were continually upon his heart and in his prayers. How his "I thank my God through Jesus Christ for you all" would draw out their affections unto the writer of this epistle! How it would move them to read with warmer interest what he now sent to them! Nothing more endears one Christian to another than to know he is remembered by him before the throne of grace. As one of our readers recently wrote: "I prize the prayers of God's dear saints more than I would all the riches of the world. The latter would only prove a curse, while the former reaches to blessings in the highest heaven and lays me even lower before God's holy throne."

"First, I thank my God, through Jesus Christ for you all, that your faith is spoken of throughout the whole world" (v. 8). There are five things here which claim our attention. First, *the manner*, or method, of Paul's praying: the first note struck is one of praise. This is made very emphatic: "*First* I thank my God" takes precedence of the "make request" of verse 10. Thus we see how blessedly the apostle practiced what he preached: "In every thing by prayer and supplication *with thanksgiving* let your requests be made known unto God" (Phil. 4:6). Thanksgiving ought to have a prominent place in our prayers: to say the least, it is due unto God. As one of the Puritans expressed it, "It is rent due Him for the mercies received." It is an effective means of strengthening faith, for it puts the heart into a more suitable frame to petition Him for further favors. It is conducive to joy in the Christian life: "I *thank* my God upon every remembrance of you, always in every prayer of mine for you all, making request with *joy*" (Phil. 1:3,4). Nothing is more calculated to dispel a spirit of gloom from the soul than the cultivation of gratitude and praise. The same will encourage and cheer our fellow-Christians: piety is not commended by sadness and sourness.

The above example is so far from being exceptional that it rather indicates the usual custom of the apostle. It is blessed to observe how frequently Paul blended thanksgiving with petitions: let the reader compare 1 Corinthians 1:4; Ephesians 1:16; Colossians 1:3; 1 Thessalonians 1:2; Philemon 4; and remember, this has been recorded for our learning. Does not failure at this very point go far to explain why so many of our prayers remain unanswered?—if we have not owned the goodness and grace of God for previous mercies can we expect Him to continue bestowing them upon the ungrateful. Praise and petitions, thanksgiving and requests, should ever be conjoined: Colossians 4:2. But it was much more than this, something nobler and more selfless which we see here in the apostle. His heart was continually drawn out in gratitude to God for the wondrous things *He* had done for His people, and this emboldened him to seek further blessings for them.

Second, *the One whom Paul invoked*: termed here "my God." It is indeed blessed to observe how the apostle regards the Deity: not as an absolute, infinitely-removed, unrelated One. There is no formality, no sense of remoteness, no uncertainty: instead, God was a living and personal reality to him: "my God." This was an avowal of *Covenant* relationship. The grand covenant promise is "I will be to them a God, and they shall be to Me a people" (Heb. 8:10), which looks back to Jeremiah 24:7; 31:33; and that in turn has its roots in Genesis 17:7 and Exodus 6:7. It was on that ground Moses and the children of Israel sang on the farther shores of the Red Sea, "The Lord is my strength and song, and He is become my salvation: He is *my God*" (Ex. 15:2). It was for that reason David exclaimed "O God, Thou art my God" (Ps. 63:1). In like manner we find that Caleb (Josh. 14:8), Ruth (1:16), Nehemiah (6:14), Daniel (9:4,19) and Jonah (2:6) owned Him as "my God" in avowal of the covenant relationship.

"My God": this was expressive of a *personal* relationship. He was his God by eternal election, having loved him with an everlasting love. He was his God by redemption, having purchased him with precious blood. He was his God by regenerating power, having communicated to him spiritual life and stamped the Divine image upon his heart, making him manifestly His own dear child. He was his God by personal choice, for when revealed to him and in him he had surrendered to His claims, saying, "What wilt thou have me to do?" By bestowing upon him His own nature and by the apostle's own acceptance, God had become his everlasting Portion, his all-satisfying Inheritance. "My God": the One who had shown such sovereign and signal mercy unto him. It was also an *assured* relationship, there was no doubting, hesitation or uncertainty. Paul could say with Job, "I have heard of Thee by the hearing of the ear, but now mine eye seeth Thee" (42:5). And it was a *practical* relationship: "whom I serve" (v. 9).

Now put the two parts together: "I thank—my God." What other collocation can there be! Is not such a God worthy of thanks? And if I know Him personally as *my* God, will not, must not, thanksgiving issue spontaneously from my heart and lips. This it is which both opens the meaning of and gives due force to the opening word: "First, I thank my God." It is not the "first" of enumeration, but of emphasis, of spiritual order. If God Himself be mine, then everything that is pure, holy, lovely, satisfying, is mine. If that glorious fact, that infinitely grand truth, be the subject of constant meditation and adoration, then my heart will not be cold and dull, nor will my mouth be paralysed when I draw near to the throne of grace. It is not an absolute and unrelated Deity whom I approach, but "my God." And that blessed and blissful relationship is to be duly acknowledged by the Christian when he bows the knee before Him. So far from being the language of presumption, it be wicked presumption, insulting unbelief, to deny it.

Third, *the ground of approach*: "through Jesus Christ." How thankful is the writer (and the reader too, if regenerate) for this clause. Though God be "my God" yet He ever remains the ineffably Holy One and how can I, conscious of pollution and utter unworthiness, think of approaching Infinite Purity? Ah, there is the blessed answer, the all-sufficient provision to meet my need: I may obtain access to the thrice holy God "through Jesus Christ." But suppose my assurance be dampened and through sad failure in my walk I no longer enjoy the conscious relationship of His being "my God," how can I now give thanks to Him? And again, the answer is "through Jesus Christ." As it is written, "By him [Jesus Christ] therefore, [because of the merit and efficacy of His sanctifying blood, see previous verse], let us offer the sacrifice of praise to God *continually*, that is, the fruit of our lips giving *thanks* to his name" (Heb. 13:15). Whatever my case may be, however burdened with a sense of guilt and defilement, it should not only keep me away from the throne of grace, but it must not deter me from giving thanks—for Jesus Christ and God's provision of Him.

Grammatically the "through Jesus Christ" is connected with the giving of thanks, but theologically or doctrinally there is a double thought. God is "my God" through Jesus Christ: as He declared to His beloved disciples, "I ascend unto My Father, and your Father, and to My God, and your God" (John 20:17)—*your* God because *My* God. And I give thanks unto "My God" "through Jesus Christ," for it is both the duty and the privilege of the regenerate, who are members of the holy priesthood, "to offer up spiritual sacrifices acceptable to God by Jesus Christ" (1 Peter 2:5). Not only is there no approach to God save "through Jesus Christ" the alone Mediator between God and men, but our worship is acceptable to God only through His merits (Col. 3:17). This too must be the subject of the believer's constant meditation and adoration, for only thus will the blessed assurance of "my God" be maintained in the heart. Jesus Christ changes not: His mediation changes not: however deeply despondent I may be by my sense of unworthiness as I approach the Throne, let me turn to and believingly ponder the infinite worthiness of Jesus Christ, and I shall "*thank* my God."

"First, I thank my God through Jesus Christ." Upon these words the late Handley Moule most beautifully said, "My God": it is the expression of an indescribable appropriation and reverent intimacy...it is the language of a personality wherein Christ has dethroned self in His own favor...And this holy intimacy, with its action in thanks and petition, is all the while 'through Jesus Christ,' the Mediator. The man knows God as my 'God' and deals with Him as such, never out of that Beloved Son who is equally one with the believer and with the Father, no alien medium, but the living point of unity." Just in proportion as that is realised in the soul, just in proportion as faith be mixed with the declarations of the Word thereon, will there be liberty and freedom, holy "boldness," as we draw near the Throne. Only thus will the Christian enjoy his birthright and live up to his blood-bought privilege; and only thus will God be honored by the praise and thanksgiving which must issue from such an one.

Fourth, *the subjects* of Paul's thanksgiving: "for you all." This will appear strange to the natural man, who is wrapped up so much in self. The carnal mind is quite incapable of appreciating the motives which actuate and the principles which regulate those who are spiritual. Here is the apostle thanking God for those whom he had never met! They were not the fruits of his own labors, yet he rejoices over them. How that condemns the narrow-minded bigotry and sectarian exclusiveness which has brought such a blight upon Christendom. Though these saints at Rome were not his own sons in the Gospel, though he had never met them in the flesh, and as far as we know received any communication from them, yet he praises God for them. It was because of what *He* had wrought in them, because they were trees of His planting, the products of His "husbandry" (1 Cor. 3:9). This too is for our instruction: do not expect the assurance of "my God" unless you have a love unto and pray for "all saints" (Eph. 6:18).

Fifth, *the occasion* of his thanksgiving: "that your faith is spoken of throughout the whole world." This good tiding was spread abroad by travelers from Rome, the capital, telling of the humble reliance of the saints there on the Lord Jesus and their loving allegiance to Him. Wherever the apostle went this blessed information was given him. It was not only that these people had believed the Gospel, but that their faith was of such a character as to be everywhere spoken of, and Paul's thanksgiving for them was the recognition and acknowledgment that He was the Giver of their faith. His notification of the same was not to induce complacency, but to quicken them to answer to the testimony borne to them and the expectations awakened thereby. Again we would remark, how blessed to behold the apostle praising God for what His grace had wrought in others. What an insight it does give us into his character. What a spirit of love unto the brethren was here revealed. What gratitude and devotion unto his Master. What an example for the servant of Christ today when tidings are received of the fruits of the Spirit in distant places.

Ere passing on to the next verse let us seek to make application unto ourselves of what has been before us. It was not the doubting and unbelief of these Roman saints, but their faith which was noised abroad. Is *our* faith known to others and talked about? Does it evoke praise and thanksgiving unto God? Theirs was no formal and lifeless faith, but a vigorous and fruitful one, which compelled others to take notice of. It was a faith which transformed their character and conduct. Lest it be thought we have read into our verse more than is there, we refer the reader to 16:19—"your *obedience* is come abroad to all." The two declarations are to be placed side by side, for the one explains and amplifies the other. If our faith be not productive of obedience, such as others will take note of, there is something seriously wrong with us. We regard, then, the word "faith" in verse 8 as a generic expression for the graces of the Spirit, but the employment of this specific term was probably a prophetic rebuke of Romanism, in which the chief thing lacking is saving faith!

"For God is my Witness, whom I serve with my spirit in the Gospel of His Son, that without ceasing I make mention of you always in my prayers" (v. 9). "For God is my Witness": the opening "For" signifies, One above knows how much you are on my heart. This was an act of worship, a due acknowledgment of God's omniscience. It was a reverent appeal to Him as the Searcher of hearts (cf. 2 Cor. 1:23; Gal. 1:20). "Whom I serve": am at His entire disposal, subject to His orders. "With my spirit": not hypocritically, from greed or formally; but from the very depths of my being—willingly, heartily, joyously. "In the Gospel of His Son" is the counterpart of "a servant of Jesus Christ...separated unto the Gospel of God" (v. 1). "That without ceasing I make mention of you always in my prayers" made known his constancy. His rejoicing over and praying for them was no evanescent spasm but an enduring thing. That his "without ceasing" was no exaggeration he had called upon God as his Witness. Though in a flourishing condition, they still needed praying for.

We cannot do the saints a greater kindness or exercise our love for them in a more practical and effective way than by praying for them. Yet we do not regard the verses before us as establishing a precedent for Christians or ministers to *proclaim abroad* their praying. To parade our piety is but a species of pharisaism. Praying is not a thing to advertise; as it is a secret exercise before God it should—as a rule—be kept secret from men. True, there are exceptions: as when believers are in trouble or isolated it is a comfort for them to know they are being remembered before the Throne. Paul's mentioning of his praying was to inform the saints that his not having visited them (v. 13) was due to no indifference on his part, to assure them they had a constant place in his affections, and pave the way for his coming to them by acquainting them of his deep solicitude for them.

"Making request, if by any means now at length I might have a prosperous journey by the will of God to come unto you" (v. 10). His love for them made him desirous of meeting them, and he prays that God would make this possible. Let it be duly noted that he refused to take matters into his own hands and act upon an inward urge. Instead, he subordinates his own longings and impulses to the will of Him he served. This is very striking and blessed. Paul did not consider what many would regard as "the Spirit's prompting" a sufficient warrant: he must first be assured—by His providences—that this journey was ordered by his Master. Accordingly he spread his case before God, committing the matter to His decision and pleasure.

Observe that there was no "claiming," still less demanding, but an humble and submissive "request"—"if possible" or "if it may be." This was an acknowledgment that God is the Orderer of all events: Romans 11:36. His "now at length" shows that he was exercised about the timing of this journey and visit. "To everything there is a season and a time to every purpose under the heaven" (Eccl. 3:1). It is of great practical importance for us to heed that fact, for it means the difference between success or failure in our undertakings. Unless we "rest in the Lord and wait patiently for Him" (Ps. 37:7) only confusion and trouble will ensue. We agree with Charles Hodge that the "prosperous journey" signified "that his circumstances should be so favorably ordered that he might be able to execute his long-cherished purpose of visiting Rome." It is blessed to note that a little later, yea before this epistle was completed, he was given Divine assurance of his request being granted: Romans 15:28, 29. The "journey" itself is described in Acts 27 and 28: after a most trying and hazardous voyage, he arrived at Rome a prisoner in chains! Yet see Acts 28:30, 31 for the measure of liberty accorded him.

"For I long to see you, that I may impart unto you some spiritual gift, to the end ye may be established" (v. 11). This is not a part of his prayer, yet it is intimately connected with it, for it makes known what prompted his "request" or the reason why he was so desirous of seeing them. His was the "longing" of spiritual affection, as a comparison with Philippians 2:26 and 2 Timothy 1:4 shows, where the same Greek word occurs. It tells how strong was his desire to visit them, and how real and commendable his subjection to the will of God. We see here the heart of an under-shepherd with his burning zeal, yet at the same time his blessed submission to the chief Shepherd. It was not a pleasure trip or to obtain variety in his labors, but to be made a blessing to these saints which Paul sought. Though their faith was well spoken of, yet he wished them to be stablished, strengthened, settled (1 Peter 5:10). To expound to them the Way more perfectly, to add to their spiritual light and joy, to open to them more fully the unsearchable riches of Christ was his object. Pastors, be not content with seeing sinners converted: seek their growth and establishment.

"That is, that I may be comforted together with you by the mutual faith both of you and me" (v. 12). This was to avoid giving offence, lest they should feel he was reflecting upon their immaturity. "Shall we call this a sentence of fine tact: beautifully conciliatory and endearing? Yes, but it is also perfectly sincere. True tact is not only the skill of sympathetic love, but not the less genuine in its thought because that thought seeks to please and to win. He is glad to show himself as his disciples' brotherly friend: but then he first *is* such, and enjoys the character, and has continually found and felt his own soul made glad and strengthened by the witness for the Lord which far less gifted believers bore, as he and they talked together" (H. Moule). It is beautiful to see Paul employing the passive form: "that ye may be established" (v. 11)—not "that I may establish you;" he hides himself by expressing the result. Equally gracious is his "that I may be comforted together with you"—contact with kindred minds refreshes, and "he that watereth [others] shall be watered also himself" (Prov. 11:25). —AWP

THE MISSION AND MIRACLES OF ELISHA
14. The Tenth Miracle

The healing of Naaman is the best known one of all the wonders wrought through Elisha, for it has been made the subject of numerous sermons in the past, supplying as it does a very striking typical picture of salvation. Not in all its varied aspects—for salvation is many-sided—but as portraying the condition of him who is made its subject, his dire need because of the terrible malady of which he was the victim, the sovereign grace which met with him, the requirements he had to comply with, his self-will therein, and how his reluctance was overcome. Yet there is not a little in this incident which is offensive to our supercilious age, inclining present-day preachers to leave it alone, so that much that has been said about it in the past will be more or less new unto the present generation. As it has pleased the Holy Spirit to enter into much more detail upon the attendant circumstances of this miracle, this will require us to give it a fuller consideration.

It is their *typical* import which renders the Old Testament Scriptures of such interest to us upon whom the ends of the ages are come: "For whatsoever things were written aforetime were written for *our* learning" (Rom. 15:4). That which is set before us more abstractly in the epistles is rendered simpler of understanding by means of the concrete and personal illustrations supplied under the previous dispensations, when figures and symbols were employed more freely. Noah and his family in the ark preserved from the flood which swept away the world of the ungodly, the Hebrews finding security under the blood of the Pascal lamb when the angel of death slew all the first-born of the Egyptians, healing being conveyed by faith's look at the brazen serpent on the pole, the cities of refuge affording asylum to the manslayer who fled thither for refuge from the avenger of blood, are so many examples of simple yet graphic prefigurations of different aspects of the redemption which is found in Christ Jesus. Another is before us here in 2 Kings 5.

Before taking up the spiritual meaning of what is recorded of Naaman, there is one thing mentioned about him deserves separate notice, and we will look at it now so that our main line of thought may not be broken into later on. In the opening verse of our chapter it is stated that Naaman was "a great man with his master and honorable because by him the Lord had given deliverance ['victory'] unto Syria." This teaches us that there can be no success in any sphere of life unless God gives it, for "the way of man is not in himself, it is not in man that walketh to direct his steps" (Jer. 10:23), still less to insure their outcome. "Except the Lord build the house, they labor in vain that build it [as was made evident when God brought to nought the lofty ambitions of those erecting the tower of Babel!], except the Lord keep the city the watchman waketh but in vain" (Ps. 127:1)— as Belshazzar discovered, when the Medes surprised and overcame his sentinels and captured Babylon.

Not only can there be no success in any human undertaking unless the Lord is pleased to prosper the same, but He exercises His own sovereignty in the instruments or agents employed in the carrying out of His purposes, whether it be in the communicating of blessings or the execution of judgments. It is therefore to be duly observed that it was not because Naaman was a good man that the Lord caused his military efforts to thrive; so far from it, he was an idolator, a worshiper of Rimmon. Moreover, not only was he a stranger to God spiritually but he was a leper, and therefore ceremonially unclean, shut out by the Mosaic law. From which we may learn that when the Most High is pleased to do so, He makes use of the wicked as well as the righteous— a truth which needs pressing on the attention of the world today. Temporal success is far from being an evidence that the blessing of God rests upon either the person or the nation enjoying the same. All men are in God's hands to employ as and where He pleases—as truly so in the political and military realms as in the churches.

First, *its subject*. Six things (the number of man) are here recorded about Naaman. 1. He was "captain of the host of the king of Syria." In modern language this would be,

Commander-in-chief of the king's army. Whether or not he had risen from the ranks we cannot be sure, though the reference to his "valor" suggests that he had been promoted from a lower office. Whether that be so or no, he now occupied a position of prominence, being at the summit of his profession. 2. He was "a great man with his master." It has been by no means always the case that the head of the military forces was greatly esteemed by his master. History records many instances where the reigning monarch has been jealous of the popularity enjoyed by the general, fearful in some cases that he would his powerful influence against the interests of the throne. But it was quite otherwise in this case, for as the sequel goes on to show, the king of Syria was warmly devoted to the person of his military chieftain. 3. "And honorable." Far from the king's slighting Naaman and keeping him in the background, he stood high in the royal favor. Naaman had furthered the interests of his kingdom, securing notable victories for his forces, and his master was not slow to show his appreciation and reward his valorous general. The brilliant exploits of many a brave officer have passed unnoticed by the powers that be: but not so here. 4. His military success is here directly ascribed to God, for our passage goes on to say "by him the Lord had given deliverance unto Syria." The blessing of Heaven had attended him and crowned his efforts, and therein he was favored above many. Not that this intimated he personally enjoyed the approbation of God, but that Divine providence made use of him in accomplishing His will. 5. He was naturally endowed with qualities which are highly esteemed among men, being possessed of great bravery and fortitude, for we are told, "he was also a mighty man in valor"—daring and fearless—and thus well equipped for his calling.

It might well be asked, What more could any man desire more? Did he not possess everything which is most highly prized by the children of this world. Was he not what they would designate "the darling of fortune," having all that the human heart could wish. He had, as the votaries of mammon express it, "made good in life." He occupied a most enviable position. He was possessed of those traits which were admired by his fellows. He had served his country well and stood high in the king's regard and favor. Even so there was a dark cloud on his horizon. There was something which not only thoroughly spoiled the present for him, but took away all hope for the future. For, 6. "he was a *leper*." Here was the tragic exception. Here was that which cast its awful shadow over every thing else. He was the victim of a loathsome and incurable disease. He was a pitiful and repulsive object, with no prospect whatever of any improvement in his condition.

Yes, my reader, the highly-privileged and honored Naaman was a leper, and as such he portrayed what *you* are, and what *I* am by nature. God's Word does not flatter man: it lays him in the dust—which is one reason why it is so unpalatable unto the great majority of people. It is the Word of truth, and therefore instead of painting flattering pictures of human nature, it represents things as they actually are. Instead of lauding man it abases him. Instead of speaking of the dignity and nobility of human nature, it declares it to be *leprous*—sinful, corrupt, depraved, defiled. Instead of eulogising human progress, it insists that "every man at his best estate is altogether vanity" (Ps. 39:5). And when the Holy Scriptures define man's attitude toward and relationship with God, they insist that "there is none righteous, no not one, there is none that understandeth, there is none that seeketh after God" (Rom. 3:10,11). They declare that we are His enemies by our wicked works (Col. 1:21), and that consequently we are under the condemnation and curse of God's law, and that His holy wrath abideth on us (John 3:36).

The Word of Truth declares that by nature all of us are spiritual lepers, foul and filthy, unfit for the Divine presence: "being alienated from the life of God" (Eph. 4:18). Ah, my reader: you may occupy a good position in this world, even an eminent station in the affairs of this life; you may have "made good" in your avocation and wrought praiseworthy achievements judged by human standards: you may be "honorable" in the sight of your fellows, but how do you appear in the eyes of *God*—a leper, one whom His law pronounces unclean, one who is utterly unfit for His holy presence. *That* is the first outstanding thing; the dominant lesson taught by our present passage. As it was with Naaman, so it is with you: a vast difference between his circumstances and his condition. There, was the horrible and tragic exception: "a great man— but a *leper*"! There was a worm gnawing at his vitals: a deathbed at his feast, a ghastly thing which cast its baneful shadow over all his fair prospects.

We would not be faithful to our calling were we to glide over that in God's Word which is distasteful to proud flesh and blood. Nor would we be faithful to our readers if we glossed over their frightful and fatal natural condition. It is in their souls' interests they should face this humiliating and unpleasant fact: that in God's sight they are spiritual lepers. But we must individualise it. Hast thou, my reader, realised this fact in thine *own case*? Hast thou seen thyself in God's light? Art thou aware that thy soul is suffering from a disease that neither you nor any human being can cure? It *is* so, whether you realise it or not. The Scriptures declare that from the sole of thy foot to the crown of thy head there is no soundness in thee, yea, that in the sight of the Holy One, thou art a mass of "wounds and bruises, and putrefying sores" (Isa. 1:6). Only as you penitently accept that Divine verdict is there any hope for you.

All disease is both the fruit and the evidence of sin, as was plainly intimated unto Israel. Under the Levitical law God might well have required separate purifications for every form of disease. But He did not, and thereby He displayed His tenderness and mercy, for such a multiplicity of ceremonial observances to have been required would have constituted an intolerable burden. He therefore singled out one disease to be a standing object-lesson, and *that* such an one could not fail to be a fit representation and most effective symbol of sin. This disease was white leprosy, described with much minuteness of detail in Leviticus 13 and 14. Leprosy, then, was not only a real but a typical disease, adumbrating in a most solemn and striking manner that fearful malady sin, with which we are infected from the centre to the circumference of our beings. While it be true that the type is only intelligible in the light of its antitype, the shadow in the presence of its substance, yet the former is often an aid to the understanding of the latter.

That the disease of leprosy *was designed* to convey a representation of the malady of sin appears from these considerations. First, the ceremonial purification whereby the stain of leprosy was cleansed pointed to the Lord Jesus as making atonement for the cleansing of His people. Second, it was not a physician but the high priest who was the person specifically appointed to deal with the leper. Third, there was no prescribed remedy for it: it could only be cured by a direct miracle. Fourth, the leper was cut off from the dwelling place of God and the tabernacle of His congregation, being put "outside the camp." Thus it will be seen from these circumstances that leprosy was removed from the catalogue of ordinary diseases, and had stamped upon it a peculiar and typical character. It was a visible sign of how God regarded the sinner: as one unsuited to the presence of Himself and His people. How unspeakably blessed then, to discover that, though not the first He performed, yet the first individual miracle of Christ's recorded in the New Testament is His healing of the leper (Matt. 8:2-4).

For the particular benefit of young preachers and for the general instruction of all we will close this article with an outline. 1. Leprosy has an *insignificant beginning*. To the non-observant eye it is almost imperceptible. It starts as "a rising, a scab, or bright spot" (Lev. 13:2). It is so trivial that usually no attention is paid to it. Little or no warning is given of the fearful havoc it will work. Was it not thus with the entrance of sin into this world? To the natural man the eating of the forbidden fruit by our first parents appears a very small matter, altogether incommensurate with the awful effects it has produced. The unregenerate discern not that sin is deserving of and exposes them to eternal destruction. They regard it as a trifle, unduly magnified by preachers.

2. Leprosy is *inherited*. It is a communicable disease. It poisons the blood, and so is readily transmitted from parent to child. It is so with sin. "By one man sin entered into the world, and death by sin, and so death passed upon all men, for that all sinned" (Rom. 5:12). None has escaped this dreadful entail. "Behold, I was shapen in iniquity, and in sin did my mother conceive me" (Ps. 51:5) is equally true of every member of Adam's race. None is born spiritually pure: depravity is communicated in every instance from sire to son, from mother to maid. Human nature was corrupted at its fountain head and therefore all the streams issuing therefrom are polluted.

3. Leprosy *works insidiously* and almost imperceptibly, for it is a disease which is attended by little pain: only in its later stages, when its horrible effects discover themselves, is it unmistakably manifest. And thus it is with that most awful of all maladies. Sin is subtle and sly, so that for the most part its subjects are quite unconscious of its workings. Hence we read of "the deceitfulness of sin" (Heb. 3:13). It is not until the Spirit convicts, that one is made aware of the awfulness and extent of sin, and begins to feel "the plague of his own heart" (1 Kings 8:38). Yes, it is not until a person is born again that he learns his very nature is depraved. Only as the sinner grows old in sin does he discover what a fearful hold his lusts have upon him.

4. Leprosy *spreads* with deadly rapidity. Though it begins with certain spots in the skin which are small at first, they gradually increase in size: slowly but surely the whole body is affected. The corruption extends inwardly while it spreads outwardly, vitiating even the bones and marrow. Like a locust on the twig of a tree, it continues eating its way through the flesh, till nothing but the skeleton is left. This is what sin has done in man—it has corrupted every part of his being, so that he is totally depraved. No faculty, no member of his complex constitution has escaped defilement. Heart, mind, will, conscience—spirit and soul and body—are equally poisoned. "I know that in me, that is in my flesh, dwelleth no good thing" (Rom. 7:18).

5. Leprosy is *highly infectious*. Inherited inwardly, contagious outwardly. The leper communicates his horrible disease to others wherever he goes. That is why he was quarantined under the Mosaic Law, and when he saw anyone approaching he was required to give warning by crying, "Unclean, unclean." The analogy continues to hold good. Sin is a malady which is not only inherited by nature, but it is developed by association with the wicked. "Evil communications *corrupt* good manners" (1 Cor.

15:33). That is why the righteous are bidden, "Enter not into the path of the wicked, and go not in the way of evil men. Avoid it [as a plague], pass not by it, turn from it, and pass away" (Prov. 4:14-15)—such repetition bespeaks our danger and intimates how slow we are to be warned against it. "Shun profane and vain babblings...their word will *eat* as doth *a canker*" (2 Tim. 2:16,17).

6. Leprosy is *peculiarly loathsome*. There is nothing more repellent to the eye than to look upon one on whom this awful disease has obtained firm hold. Except with the most callous, despite one's pity, he or she is obliged to turn away from such a nauseating sight with a shudder. Under Judaism there was no physician who ministered to the leper, and hence it is said of his putrefying sores that "they have not been closed, neither bound up, neither mollified with ointment" (Isa. 1:6). The leper may well appropriate to himself the language of Job, "All my inward [or 'intimate'] friends abhorred me, and they whom I love are turned against me" (19:19). All of which is a figure of how infinitely more repellent is the sinner in the sight of Him who is "of purer eyes than to behold evil and canst not look on iniquity" (Hab. 1:13).

7. Leprosy is a *state of living death*. First the joints become relaxed, then dislocated, and then an eye falls out, or the fingers and toes are shed, and even limbs fall off, until the whole body becomes a horrible mess of dissolution and decay. It is a state of daily and progressive death. As one has said, "The leper is a walking sepulcher." And this is precisely what sin is: a state of spiritual death—a living on the natural side of existence, but dead to all things spiritual. Thus we find an apostle declaring "she that liveth in pleasure is dead while she liveth" (1 Tim. 5:6). The natural man is "dead in trespasses and sins" (Eph. 2:1): alive sin-ward and worldward but dead Godward.

8. Leprosy was *dealt with by banishment*. No leper was allowed to remain in the congregation of Israel. The terms of the Mosaic law were most explicit: "he shall dwell alone; without the camp shall his habitation be" (Lev. 13:46). In the centre of the camp was Jehovah's abode and around His tabernacle were grouped His covenant people. From them the leper was excluded. How rigidly that was enforced may be seen from the fact than even Miriam the sister of Moses (Num. 12:10-15), and Uzziah the king (2 Kings 15:5) were not treated as exceptions. The leper was deprived of all political and ecclesiastical privileges, dealt with as one dead, excluded from fellowship. It is a visible sign of how God regarded the sinner, for sin shuts out from His presence: see Isaiah 59:2; 2 Thessalonians 1:9.

9. Leprosy makes its victim *an object of shame*. It could not be otherwise. Robbing its subject of the bloom of health, replacing it with that which is hideous. Excluding him from God and His people, placing him outside the pale of decency. Consequently the leper was required to carry about with him every mark of humiliation and distress. The law specified that "his clothes shall be rent, and his head bare, and he shall put a covering upon his upper lip, and shall cry, Unclean, unclean" (Lev. 13:45). What a spectacle! What a picture of abject misery! What a solemn portrayal of the natural man! Sin has marred the features of God's image, in whose likeness man was originally made, and stamped upon him the marks of the devil.

10. Leprosy is *incurable* so far as man is concerned. One really stricken with this disease was beyond all human aid. The outcome was inevitably fatal. Medical science was helpless before its advance. In like manner sin is beyond human cure; it can neither be eradicated nor ameliorated. No power of will or effort of mind can cope with it.

Neither legislation nor reformation is of any avail. Education and culture are equally impotent. Sooner can the Ethiopian change his skin or the leopard his spots than those do good who are accustomed to do evil (Jer. 13:23).

But what is beyond the power of man is possible with God. Where the science of the ages stands helpless the Savior manifests His sufficiency. "He is able also to save them to the uttermost that come unto God by Him" (Heb. 7:25). To the leper He said, "I will, be thou clean, and immediately his leprosy was cleansed" (Matt. 8:3). Blessed, thrice blessed is that! In view of the ten points above, how profoundly thankful every Christian should be that "the blood of Jesus Christ God's Son *cleanseth* us from *all* sin" (1 John 1:7). —AWP

N.B. This magazine is still being sent to at least three families of those who heard the editor preach for four hours and three quarters on "The Healing of Naaman" in Philadelphia, USA December 31ˢᵗ, 1925.

DOCTRINE OF SAINTS' PERSEVERANCE
11. Conclusion

It now remains for us to gather up a few loose ends, to summarise what has been before us, make a practical application of the whole, and our present task is completed. Not that we have said anything like all that could be said thereon; yet we have sought to set before the reader the principal aspects of this subject and to preserve a due balance between the Divine and human sides of it—God's operations in connection therewith and the Christian's concurrence therein. Much of the opposition which has been raised against what is termed "the dangerous tendency" of this truth arose from a defective view of the same, through failure to apprehend that the perseverance of the saints exhibited in the Scriptures is their *continuance in faith and holiness*: that the One who has made infallible promise they shall reach the desired goal has also decreed they shall tread the one path which leads to it, that the means as well as the end are ordained by Him, and that He moves them to make diligent use of those means and blesses and makes effectual their labor in the same.

That for which we have contended throughout these chapters is steadfastness in holiness, constancy in believing, and in bringing forth the fruits of righteousness. Saving faith is something more than an isolated act: it is a spiritual dynamic, a principle of action, which continues to operate in those who are the favored subjects of it. This is brought out very clearly and decisively in the great Faith chapter. In Hebrews 11 the Holy Spirit sets before us the faith of Abel, of Enoch, of Noah, of Abraham and Sarah, Isaac and Jacob, and after describing various exercises and fruits of the same, declares "these all died in faith" (v. 13), not one of them apostatised from the same. The "faith" spoken of, as the context shows, was both a justifying and sanctifying one, and those who had received the same from God not only lived by it but died in it. Theirs was a faith which wore and lasted, which overcame obstacles and triumphed over difficulties, which endured to the end. True, the patriarchs had to wrestle against their natural unbelief, and, as the inspired records show, more than once they were tripped up by the same, yet they continued fighting and emerged conquerors.

The Christian is required to continue as he began. He is to daily own his sins to God and he is daily to renew the same acts of faith and trust in Christ and His blood which he exercised at the first. Instead of counting upon some past experience, he is to maintain a present living on Christ. If he continues to cast himself on the Redeemer, putting his salvation wholly in His hands, then He will not, cannot, fail him. But in order to cast myself upon Christ I must be *near* Him; I cannot do so while following Him "afar off." And to be near Him, I must be in separation from all that is contrary to Him. Communion is based upon an obedient walk (John 15:10): the one cannot be without the other. And for the maintenance of this, I must continue to "show the *same* diligence" I did when first convicted of my lost estate, when I perceived that sin was my worst enemy, that I was a rebel against God and His wrath upon me, and when I fled to Christ for refuge, surrendering myself to His lordship and trusting entirely to the sufficiency of His sacrifice to save me from my sins — their dominion, their pollution, and their guilt.

"Show the same diligence to the full assurance of hope unto the end" (Heb. 6:11). The selfsame earnestness and pains which actuated my heart and regulated my acts when I first sought Christ must be continued unto the end of my earthly course. This means persevering in a holy life, in the things which are appointed by and are pleasing to God, and unto this the servants of God are to be constantly urging the saints. "Ministerial exhortation unto duty is needful unto those who are sincere in the practice of it, that they may abide and continue therein" (J. Owen). In no other way can the "full assurance of hope" (a confident expectation of the issue or outcome) be Scripturally maintained. The Christian has to be constant in giving "the same diligence" to the things of God and the needs of his soul as he did at the outset. "He said, *to the end*, that they might know they had not reached the goal, and were therefore to think of further progress. He mentioned diligence that they might know they were not to sit down idly, but to strive in earnest." And who think you, my reader, was the author of that quotation? None other than John Calvin! How grievously has Calvinism been perverted and misrepresented.

"That ye be not slothful, but followers of them who through faith and patience inherit the promises" (Heb. 6:12). The apostle here warns against the vice which is the antithesis of the virtue previously enjoined, for slothfulness is the opposite of diligence. The indolence dehorted is in each of us by nature, for spiritual laxity is not something peculiar to those of a lazy disposition. The evil principle of the "flesh" remains in every Christian and that principle hates and therefore is opposed to the things of God. But the flesh must be resisted and the desires of the "spirit" or principle of grace heeded. When conscious of this indisposition unto practical holiness, this native enmity against the same, the believer must pray with renewed earnestness "draw me, we will run after Thee" (Song of Sol. 1:4), "Order my steps in Thy Word, and let not any iniquity have dominion over me" (Ps. 119: 133). It is this which distinguishes the true child of God from the empty professor: his wrestling with the Lord in secret to enable him to press forward in the race set before him.

"But followers of them who through faith and patience inherit the promises." The immediate reference is to the patriarchs who, by continuing steadfast in the faith, persevering in hope amid all the trials to which they were subjected, had no entrance into the promised blessings. Their faith was far more than a notional one: it was influential and practical, causing them to live as "strangers and pilgrims" in this scene (see Heb. 11:13). The word for "patience" here is usually rendered "longsuffering. " It is a grace which makes its possessor refuse to be daunted by the difficulties of the way or be so discouraged by the trials and oppositions encountered as to desert the course or forsake the path of duty. It is just such faith and patience which are required of the saint in every age, for there never has been and never will be any journeying to Heaven on "flowery beds of ease." If the continued exercise of such graces was required of the patriarchs—persons who were so high in the love and favor of God—then let not us imagine they may be dispensed with in *our* case. The things promised are not obtained "*for* faith and patience," but they are entered into "through" them.

Assurance of final perseverance neither renders needless wariness and care (1 Cor. 10:12), nor the unwearied use of the appointed means of grace (Gal. 6:9). We must distinguish sharply between confidence in Christ and a weakening of the security of the flesh. The teaching that carnal security and presumption is no bar to eternal glory is a doctrine of the Devil. David prayed "Teach me, O Lord, the way of Thy statutes, and I shall keep it unto the end" (Ps. 119:33). Upon it Spurgeon said, "The end of which David speaks is the end of life, or the fullness of obedience. He trusted in grace to make him faithful to the utmost, never drawing a line and saying to obedience 'Hitherto shalt thou go but no further.' The end of our keeping the Law will come only when we cease to breathe: no good man will think of marking a date and saying, 'It is enough, I may now relax my watch, and live after the manner of men.' As Christ loves us to the end so must we serve Him to the end. The end of Divine teaching is that we may serve to the end" (Treasury of David, Vol. 6). O for more of this well-balanced teaching.

When faith and the spirit of obedience are inoperative the features of the new birth are under a cloud, and when we have no evidence of regeneration we lack any warrant to entertain the assurance of eternal happiness. The man who gives free rein to the flesh and takes his fill of the world gives the lie to his profession that he is journeying to Heaven. It is the glory of the Gospel that while it announces mercy unto the chief of sinners, yet if any be encouraged by this to persist in a course of evil-doing it pronounces his doom. The Gospel encourages hope, but it also promotes holiness; it imparts peace, but it also inculcates godly piety; it cherishes confidence, yet not by looking back to conversion but forward to the desired haven. It justifies the expectation of preservation, but only as we persevere in the path of duty. While it declares emphatically that the believer's continuance in and maintenance of his faith depend wholly on something extraneous to himself or his present case, yet with equal clearness it insists that the believer's perseverance is carried on and perfected by his use of all the appointed means.

It is freely granted that many of the objections which are made against this subject apply most pertinently to the Antinomian perversion of it, for hyper-Calvinists have been guilty of presenting this truth in such an unguarded and one-sided manner as to virtually set a premium on loose walking. They have dwelt to such an extent upon the Divine operations as to quite crowd out human responsibility, picturing the Christian as entirely passive. Others who were quite unqualified to write on such a theme have given much occasion to the enemies of the Truth by their crudities, representing the security of the believer as a mechanical thing, divorcing the end from the means, ignoring the safe-guards by which God Himself has hedged about this doctrine, and prating about "once saved, always saved" no matter what the daily walk may be. Nevertheless such abuses do not warrant anyone in repudiating the doctrine itself and opposing the teaching of Scripture thereon, for there is nothing in the Word of God which has the slightest tendency to make light of sin or countenances loose living, but rather everything to the contrary.

When expressing his hatred of the truth of the eternal security of Christ's sheep, John Wesley exclaimed "How pleasing is this to flesh and blood," which is the very thing it is *not*. Such a doctrine can never be agreeable to fallen human nature. Depraved man is essentially proud, and hence any scheme of perseverance accomplished by the strength of man's own will power is pleasing to the vanity of his mind; but a perseverance dependent upon the faithfulness and power of God, a perseverance which is not the result of any human sufficiency but rather of the merits and intercession of Christ, is most unpalatable unto the self-righteous Pharisee. Only the one who has been given to feel the prevailing power of indwelling sin, who has discovered that his own will and resolutions are wholly incompetent to cope with the corruptions of his heart, who has proved by painful experience that he is completely "without strength" and that apart from Christ he can do nothing, will truly rejoice that none cam pluck him out of the Redeemer's hand. As only the consciously sick will welcome the Physician, so none but those who realise their own helplessness will really find the doctrine of Divine preservation acceptable to them.

Moreover, *the duties inculcated* by this doctrine are most repugnant to flesh and blood. Subjection to Christ's authority and the daily taking of His yoke upon us is a requirement very far from welcome to those who wish to please themselves and follow their own devices. The standard of piety, the spirituality of God's Law, the nature of holiness, the insistence that we must keep ourselves unspotted from this world, are directly contrary to the inclinations of the natural man. That we must discipline our affections, regulate our thoughts, mortify our carnal appetites, cut off a right hand and pluck out a right eye, are certainly not good news to the unregenerate, especially when God insists that such mortification is never to be remitted but continued until mortality be swallowed up of life. No, it is impossible that fallen man will ever be pleased with a doctrine of perseverance in *denying self*, taking up his cross daily and following a holy Christ who is despised and rejected by this world. Thus it will abundantly appear from all that has been said, how baseless and pointless is the Arminian objection that the preaching of this doctrine encourages laxity and makes for licentiousness.

How can it be supposed that the proclamation of this blessed truth will lead to carelessness and carnality when we lay it down as a fundamental maxim that no one has any shadow of reason to consider himself interested in the blessing of perseverance except as he has and gives clear evidence that he is inwardly conformed to God and outwardly obedient to His commands? Yet it must be allowed, no matter how carefully and proportionately the doctrine of Scripture be set forth by God's servant, there will always be those ready to wrest to their own destruction. If the Lord Jesus was falsely charged with "perverting the nation" (Luke 23:2), His ministers must not expect immunity from similar criminations. If the apostle Paul was slanderously reported of teaching "Let us do evil, that good may come" (Rom. 3:8), we must not be surprised if the enemies of God should falsify our assertions and draw erroneous inferences from them. Yet this must not deter us from proclaiming all the counsel of God or keeping back anything that would be profitable to His people (Acts 20:27,20).

And now to make practical application of all that has been before us. 1. How earnest should sinners be of becoming Christians. In Christ alone is salvation and safety to be found. Security of person and of estate is the principal concern of men in this world, but security of soul has little or no place in the thoughts of the majority. How fearful to be in imminent danger of death and eternal punishment, and how alarming the condition of those indifferent to their everlasting welfare. Where there is an underground shelter which is out of range of artillery and below the reach of falling bombs, how eagerly will the sane turn thither when the siren sounds. "The name of the Lord is a strong tower, the righteous runneth into it and is safe" (Prov. 18:10). O let every reader who has not yet done so make haste into his closet, fall upon his knees and rise not till he has committed himself wholly unto Christ for time and eternity. Halt no longer between two opinions. The wrath of God is upon thee, and there is but one way of escape: then flee for refuge to the hope set before you in the Gospel (Heb. 6:18). Christ stands ready to receive you if will throw down your weapons of warfare.

2. How diligently you should examine whether or no you are in Christ, the place of eternal security. You should *know* whether or not you have complied with the requirements of the Gospel, whether or not you have closed with Christ's gracious offer therein, whether spiritual life has come to your soul, whether you have been made a new creature in Christ. These things may be known with definite certainty. Put these questions to your soul. Had I sincere resolution to forsake my wicked way when I came to Christ? Did I relinquish all dependence upon my own works? Did I come to Him empty-handed, resting on His promise "him that cometh to Me I will in no wise cast out"? Then you may be assured on the infallible Word of God that Christ received you, and you are most grievously insulting Him if you doubt it. Do you value Christ above all the world? Do you desire to be conformed more and more to His holy image? Is it your earnest endeavor to please Him in all things, and is it your greatest grief and confession to Him when you have displeased Him? Then these are the sure marks of every one who is a member of His mystical Body.

3. How jealously we should watch over and seek to protect this tree of God's planting, from the winds of false doctrine and the pests which would fain destroy it. If we are to do so then we must give due attention to that injunction, "Keep thy heart with all diligence, for out of it are the issues of life" (Prov. 4:23). We must make conscience of everything which is harmful to godliness. We must walk in separation from the world and have "no fellowship with the unfruitful works of darkness." We must feed daily upon the Word of God, for otherwise growth is impossible. We must have regular recourse to the throne of grace, not only to obtain pardoning mercy for the sins committed but to find grace to help for present needs. We must make constant use of the shield of faith for there is no other defense against the fiery darts of Satan. A good beginning is not sufficient: we must press forward unto the things before. A small leak will eventually sink a ship if it be not attended to: many a noble vessel now lies wrecked upon the rocks.

4. How we should beware of wresting this doctrine. Let none encourage themselves in carelessness and fleshly indulgence through presuming upon their security in Christ. It is those who "hear" (heed) His voice and that "follow" Him to whom He has made promise "they shall never perish" (John 10:27,28). The ones of whom the Lord

has declared "They shall not depart from Me" are those to whom He said "I will put My fear in their hearts" (Jer. 32:40), but He gives no such assurance to those who trifle with Him. God has promised a victory to His people, but that very promise implies a warfare: victories are not gained by neglect and sloth. When Divine grace brings salvation to a soul it teaches him to deny "ungodliness and worldly lusts" and to "live soberly, righteously and godly in this present world" (Titus 2:12), and if it is not so teaching me, then I am a stranger to saving grace. There is nothing which has so much forwarded the Arminian error of apostasy as the scandalous lives of professing Christians: see that your life gives the lie to it.

5. How we must ascribe all the glory unto God. If thou hast stood firm while others have been swept away, if thou hast held on thy way when many who accompanied thee at the beginning have forsaken the paths of righteousness, if thou hast thrived when others have withered, it is due entirely to the distinguishing mercy and power of God. "Who maketh thee to differ, and what hast thou that thou didst not receive" (1 Cor. 4:7): thou hast no cause whatever to boast. "But the Lord is faithful, who shall stablish you and keep you from evil" (2 Thess. 3:3): if the Lord, then not myself. It is true we "will" and do, but it is God who worketh both in us (Phil. 2:13). Our sufficiency is of Him and not of ourselves, and due acknowledgment should be made of this; and it *will be* by real saints. "Not unto us, O Lord, not unto us, but unto Thy name give glory, for thy mercy, for Thy truth's sake" (Ps. 115:1).

6. How we should magnify the grace of God. The mind is incompetent to perceive how much we are beholden to the Lord for His interest in and care of us. As His providence is virtually a continual creation, an upholding of all things by His 'power, without which they would lapse back again into nonentity: so the Christian's preservation is like a continual regeneration, a maintenance of the new creation by the operations of the Spirit and the bestowing fresh supplies of grace. It was the realisation of this fact that moved David to acknowledge of God, "Which holdeth our soul in life and suffereth not our feet to be moved" (Ps. 66:9). As Charnock well said, "It is a standing miracle in the world that all the floods of temptation shall not be able to quench this little heavenly spark in the heart, that it shall be preserved from being smothered by the streams of sin which arise in us, that a little smoking flax shall burn in spite of all the buckets of water which are poured upon it." Thus God perfects His strength in our weakness. "O give thanks unto the Lord, for His goodness, for His mercy endureth forever" (Ps. 106:1).

7. How compassionate we should be unto weaker brethren. The more thou art mindful of the Lord's upholding hand, the more compassionate wilt thou be unto those with feeble knees. "If a man be overtaken in a fault, ye which are spiritual restore such a one in the spirit of meekness, considering thyself lest thou also be tempted" (Gal. 6:1). Call to mind how patiently the Lord hast borne with thee. Remember how ignorant thou wast but a short time ago, and expect not too much from babes in Christ. Has not the Lord often recovered thee when thou didst wander? Have not thy brethren still occasion to bear with many blemishes in thee? If so, wilt thou be hyper-critical and censorious toward them! Despise not small grace in any, but seek to encourage, to counsel, to help. Christ does not break the bruised reed, nor must we. —AWP

SPIRITUAL GROWTH OR CHRISTIAN PROGRESS
2. Its Root

Before attempting to define and describe what the spiritual growth of a Christian consists of we should first show what it is that is capable of growth, for spiritual growth necessarily supposes the presence of spiritual life: only a regenerated person can grow. Progress in the Christian life is impossible unless I be a Christian. We must therefore begin by explaining what a Christian is. To many of our readers this may appear quite superfluous, but in such a day as this, wherein spiritual counterfeits and delusions abound on every side, when so many are deceived on the all-important matter, and because this magazine is read by such widely-different classes, we deem it necessary to follow this course. We dare not take for granted that all our readers are Christians in the Scriptural sense of that term, and may it please the Lord to use what we are about to write to give light to some who are yet in darkness. Moreover, it may be the means of enabling some real Christians, now confused, to see the way of the Lord more clearly. Nor will it be altogether profitless, we hope, even to those more fully established in the faith.

Broadly speaking there are three kinds of "Christians": preacher-made, self-made, and God-made ones. In the former are included not only those who were "sprinkled" in infancy and thereby made members of a "church" (though not admitted to all its privileges), but those who have reached the age of accountability and are induced by some high-pressure "evangelist" to "make a profession." This high-pressure business is in different forms and in varying degrees, from appeals to the emotions to mass hypnotism whereby crowds are induced to "come forward." Under it countless thousands whose consciences were never searched and who had no sense of their lost condition before God were persuaded to "do the manly thing," "enlist under the banner of Christ," "unite with God's people in their crusade against the devil." Such converts are like mushrooms: they spring up in a night and survive but a short time, having no root. Similar too are the vast majority produced under what is called "Personal work," which consists of a species of individual "buttonholing," and is conducted along the lines used by commercial travelers seeking to make a "forced sale."

The "second" class is made up of those who have been warned against what has just been described above, and fearful of being deluded by such religious hucksters they determined to "settle the matter" directly with God in the privacy of their own room or some secluded spot. They had been given to understand that God loves everybody, that Christ died for the whole human race, and that nothing is required of them but faith in the Gospel. By saving faith they suppose that a mere intellectual assent to or acceptance of such statements as are found in John 3:16; Romans 10:13 is all that is intended. It matters not that John 2:23, 24 declares that "many *believed* in His name…but Jesus did not commit Himself unto them," that "many believed on Him, but because of the Pharisees they did not confess Him lest they be put out of the synagogue, for they loved the praise of men more than the praise of God" (John 12:42,43)—which shows how much their "believing" was worth. Imagining that the natural man is capable of "receiving Christ as a personal Saviour" they make the attempt, doubt not their success, go on their way rejoicing, and none can shake their assurance that they are now real Christians.

"No man can come unto Me except the Father which has sent Me draw him" (John 6:44). Here is a declaration of Christ's which has not received even mental assent by the vast majority in Christendom. It is far too flesh-abasing to meet with acceptance from those who wish to think that the settling of a man's eternal destiny lies entirely within his own power. That fallen man is wholly at the disposal of God is thoroughly unpalatable to an unhumbled heart. To come to Christ is a spiritual act and not a natural one, and since the unregenerate are dead in sins they are quite incapable of any spiritual exercises. Coming to Christ is the effect of the soul's being made to feel its desperate need of Him, of the understanding's being enlightened to perceive His suitability for a lost sinner, of the affections being drawn out so as to desire Him. But how can one whose natural mind is "enmity against God" have any desire for His Son?

God-made Christians are a miracle of grace, the products of Divine workmanship (Eph. 2:10). They are a Divine creation, brought into existence by supernatural operations. By the new birth we are capacitated for communion with the Triune Jehovah, for it is the spring of new sensibilities and activities. It is not our old nature made better and excited into spiritual acts, but instead, something is communicated which was not there before. That "something" partakes of the same nature as its Begetter: "that which is born of the Spirit is spirit" (John 3:6), and as He is holy so that which He produces is holy. It is the God of all grace who brings us "from death unto life," and therefore it is a principle of grace which He imparts to the soul, and it disposes unto fruits which are well pleasing unto Him. Regeneration is not a protracted process, but an instantaneous thing, to which nothing can be added nor from it anything taken away (Eccl. 3:14). It is the product of a Divine fiat: God speaks and it is done, and the subject of it becomes immediately a "new creature."

Regeneration is not the outcome of any clerical magic nor does the individual experiencing it supply ought thereto: he is the passive and unconscious recipient of it. Said Truth incarnate: "Which were born not of blood [heredity makes no contribution thereto, for God has regenerated heathens whose ancestors have for centuries been gross idolators] nor of the will of the flesh [for prior to this Divine quickening the will of that person was inveterately opposed to God] nor of the will of [a] man [the preacher was incapable of regenerating himself, much less others] but of God" (John 1:13)—by His sovereign and all-mighty power. And again Christ declared, "The wind bloweth where it listeth and thou hearest the sound thereof [its effects are quite manifest] but canst not tell whence it cometh and whither it goeth [its causation and operation are entirely above human ken, a mystery no finite intelligence can solve] so is every one that is born of the Spirit" (John 3:8)—not in certain exceptional cases, but in *all* who experience the same. Such Divine declarations are as far removed from most of the religious teaching of the day as light is from darkness.

The word "Christian" means "an *anointed* one," as the Lord Jesus is "The Anointed" or "The Christ." That was one of the titles accorded Him in the Old Testament: "The kings of the earth have set themselves and the rulers taken counsel together against the Lord and against His anointed" or "Christ" (Ps. 2:2 and cf. Acts 2:26,27). He is thus designated because "God anointed Jesus of Nazareth with the Holy Spirit" (Acts 10:38), for induction into His office and enduement for the discharge thereof. That office has three branches, for He was to act as Prophet, Priest and Potentate. And in the Old Testament we find this foreshadowed in the anointing of Israel's prophets (1 Kings 19:16), their priests (Lev. 8:30) and their kings (1 Sam. 10:1; 2 Sam. 2:4). Accordingly it was upon entrance into His public ministry the Lord Jesus was "anointed," for at His baptism "the heavens were opened unto Him" and there was seen "the Spirit of God descending like a dove and lighting upon Him," and the Father's voice was heard saying "This is My beloved Son in whom I am well pleased" (Matt. 3:16,17). The Spirit of God had come upon others before that, but never as He now came upon the incarnate Son, "For God giveth not the Spirit by measure unto Him" (John 3:34), for being the Holy One there was nothing whatever in Him to oppose the Spirit or grieve Him, but everything to the contrary.

But it was not for Himself alone that Christ received the Spirit, but to share with and communicate unto His people. Hence in another of the Old Testament types we read that "The precious ointment upon the head, that ran down upon the beard, upon Aaron's beard, that ran down to the skirts of his garments" (Ps. 133:2). Though all Israel's priests were anointed, none but the high priest was so upon the *head* (Lev. 8:12). This foreshadowed the Saviour being anointed not only as our great High Priest but also as the Head of His church, and the running down of the sacred unguent to the skirts prefigured the communicating of the Spirit to all the members, even the lowliest, of His mystical Body. "Now He who…hath anointed us is God, who hath sealed us and given us the earnest of the Spirit in our hearts" (2 Cor. 1:22). "Of his [Christ's] fulness have all we received" (John 1:16).

When the apostles "were all filled with the Holy Spirit and began to speak with other tongues as the Spirit gave them utterance" on the day of Pentecost, and some mocked, Peter declared "This is that which was spoken by the prophet Joel" and concluded by affirming that Jesus had been by the right hand of God exalted and "having received of the Father…*He* hath shed forth *this*" (Acts 2:33). A "Christian" then is an anointed one because he has received the Holy Spirit from Christ "the Anointed." And hence it is written "But ye have an Unction [or "anointing"] from the Holy One," that is, from Christ; and again, "the Anointing which ye have received of Him abideth in you" (1 John 2:20,27), for just as we read of "the Spirit descending and *remaining* on Him" (John 1:33) so He abides with us "forever" (John 14:16).

This is the inseparable accompaniment of the new birth. The regenerated soul is not only made the recipient of a new life, but the Holy Spirit is communicated to him, and by the Spirit he is then vitally united to Christ, for "he that is joined to the Lord is one Spirit" (1 Cor. 6:17). The Spirit comes to indwell so that his body is made His temple. It is by this anointing or inhabitation the regenerate person is sanctified or set apart unto God, consecrated to Him, and given a place in that "holy priesthood" which is qualified "to offer up spiritual sacrifices acceptable to God by Jesus Christ" (1 Peter 2:5). Thereby the saint is sharply distinguished from the world, for "If any man have not the Spirit of Christ, he is none of His" (Rom. 8:9). The Spirit is the identifying mark or seal: as it was by the Spirit's descent on Christ that John recognised Him (John 1:33) and "Him hath God the Father *sealed*" (John 6:27), so believers are "sealed with that Holy Spirit." (Eph. 1:13)

But since the individual concerned in regeneration is entirely passive and at the moment unconscious of what is taking place, the question arises, how is a soul to ascertain whether or no he has been Divinely quickened? At first sight it might appear that no satisfactory answer can be forthcoming, yet a little reflection should show that this must be far from being the case. Such a miracle of grace wrought within a person cannot long be imperceptible to him. If spiritual life be imparted unto one dead in sins its presence must soon become manifest. This is indeed the case. The new birth becomes apparent by the effects it produces, namely, spiritual desires and spiritual exercises. As the natural infant clings instinctively to its mother, so the spiritual babe turns unto the One who gave it being. The authority of God is felt in the conscience, the holiness of God is perceived by the enlightened understanding, desires after Him stir within the soul. His wondrous grace is now faintly perceived by the renewed heart. There is a poignant consciousness of that which is opposed to the glory of God, a sense of our sinnership such as was not experienced formerly.

The natural man [albeit he is as a fallen creature by the first birth] receiveth not the things of the Spirit of God, for they are foolishness unto him, neither can he know them, because they are spiritually discerned" (1 Cor. 2:14). By no efforts of his own, by no university education, by no course of religions instruction can he obtain any spiritual or vital knowledge of spiritual things. They are utterly beyond the range of his faculties. Self-love blinds him: self-pleasing chains him to the things of time and sense. Except a man be born again he cannot see the kingdom of God. He may obtain a notional knowledge of them, but until a miracle of grace takes place in his soul he cannot have any spiritual acquaintance with them. Fishes could sooner live on dry ground or birds exist beneath the waves than an unregenerate person enter into a vital and experimental acquaintance with the things of God.

The first effect of the spiritual life in the soul is that its recipient is convicted of its impurity and guilt. The conscience is quickened and there is a piercing realisation of both personal pollution and criminality. The illumined mind sees something of the awful malignity of sin, as being in its very nature contrary to the holiness of God, and in its essence nothing but high-handed rebellion against Him. From that arises an abhorrence of it as a most vile and loathsome thing. The demerit of sin is seen, so that the soul is made to feel it has grievously provoked the Most High, exposing him to Divine wrath. Made aware of the plague of his heart, knowing himself to be justly liable to the awful vengeance of the Almighty, his mouth is stopped, he has not a word to say in self-extenuation, he confesses himself to be guilty before Him; and henceforth that which most deeply concerns him is, What must I do to be saved? in what way may I escape the doom of the Law?

The second effect of the spiritual life in the soul is that its recipient becomes aware of the suitability of Christ unto such a vile wretch as he now discovers himself to be. The glorious Gospel now has an entirely new meaning for him. He requires no urging to listen to its message: it is heavenly music in his ears, "good news from a far Country (Prov. 25:25). Nay, he now searches the Scriptures for himself to make sure that such a Gospel is not too good to be true. As he reads therein of who the Saviour is and what He did, of the Divine incarnation and His death on the cross, he is awed as never before. As he learns that it was for sinners, for the ungodly, for enemies that Christ shed His blood, hope is awakened within his heart and he is kept from being overwhelmed by his burden of guilt and from sinking into abject despair. Desires of an interest in Christ spring up within his soul, and he is resolved to look for salvation in none other. He is convinced that pardon and security are to be found in Christ alone if so be that He will show him favor. He searches now to discover what Christ's requirements are.

A Christian is not only one "anointed" by the Spirit, but he is also one who is *a disciple* of Christ (see Matt. 28:19 margin and Acts 11:26), that is, a learner and follower of Christ. His terms of discipleship are made known in Luke 14:26-33. Those terms a regenerate soul is enabled to comply with. Convicted of his lost condition, having learned that Christ is the appointed and all-sufficient Saviour for sinners, he now throws down the weapons of his rebellion, repudiates his idols, relinquishes his love of and friendship with the world, surrenders himself to the Lordship of Christ, takes His yoke upon him, and thereby finds rest unto his soul; trusting in the efficacy of His atoning blood, the burden of guilt is removed, and henceforth his dominant desire and endeavor is to please and glorify his Saviour. Thus *regeneration* issues in and evidences itself by *conversion*, and genuine conversion makes one a disciple of Christ, following the example He has left us. —AWP

(continued from back page)

might be—not put into a capacity of acquiring a righteousness of our own, but—made the righteousness of God in Him" (2 Cor. 5:21). Here we have the double imputation of our sins to Christ and of His righteousness to us. Observe that we are not here said to be made righteous, but "righteousness" itself, and not righteousness only, but "the righteousness *of God*," which is the utmost that language can reach unto. And in the self-same manner that Christ was "made sin" we are made "righteousness." Christ knew not actual sin, but upon His mediatorial interposition on our behalf, He was regarded and dealt with as a guilty person. We likewise are destitute of all legal righteousness, yet upon our receiving Christ and believing on His name, we are viewed and treated by the Divine majesty as righteous creatures. Both were by imputation: amazing exchange! So as to utterly exclude the idea that any inherent righteousness is in view, it is expressly said "we are made the righteousness of God *in Him*": as the sin imputed to Christ is inherent in us, so the righteousness by which we are justified is inherent in Him.

By the Divine plan of redemption the claims of the Law were fully satisfied. There was nothing in all its sacred injunctions which Christ did not perform, and nothing in its awful threatenings which He did not sustain. He fulfilled all its precepts by an unspotted purity of heart and the most perfect integrity of life. He exhausted the whole curse when He hung upon the cross, abandoned by God, a bleeding Victim, for the sins of His people. His obedience conferred higher honour upon the Law than it could possibly have received from an uninterrupted compliance by Adam and all his posterity. The perfections of God which were dishonoured by our rebellion, are glorified in our redemption. In redemption God appears inflexibly just in exacting vengeance, and inconceivably rich in showing mercy. "The sword of justice and the scepter of grace has each its due exercise, each its full expression" (James Hervey). The interests of holiness are also secured for where redemption is received by faith it kindles in the heart an intense hatred of sin and the deepest love and gratitude unto God. —AWP

(continued from front page)

It hardly requires to be pointed out that, in all of the above passages, the Father's "Fellow" and Equal is viewed in His official character, as the God-man Mediator. It is equally evident that those verses intimate that the Lord Jesus is righteous in His person, in the administration of His office, in the discharge of the great commission given to Him. Before His incarnation it was announced "righteousness shall be the girdle of His loins and faithfulness the girdle of His reins" (Isa. 11:5), and Christ Himself affirmed by the Spirit of prophecy "I have preached righteousness in the great congregation" (Psa. 40:9). There was no fault or failure in His performing of the honourous and momentous task committed to Him, as His own words to the Father prove: "I have glorified Thee on the earth, I have finished the work which Thou gavest Me to do" (John 17:4). God's owning of Christ as "My righteous Servant" signifies that He excellently executed the work entrusted to Him: as the Holy Spirit declares, He "was faithful to Him that appointed Him" (Heb. 3:2), and when the Father rewarded Him He said, "Thou lovest righteousness and hatest wickedness" (Psa. 45:7).

But further: Christ is the righteous Redeemer of his people because their righteousness is *in Him*. He wrought out a perfect righteousness for them, which, upon their believing in Him, is imputed or reckoned to their account, and therefore is He designated "the Lord our righteousness" (Jer. 23:6). Christ was righteous not as a private Person, not for Himself alone, but for us sinners and our salvation. Throughout He acted as God's righteous Servant and as His people's righteous Sponsor. He lived and died that all the infinite merits of His obedience might be made over to them. In the justifying of His sinful people God neither disregarded nor dishonoured His Law: instead He has "established" it (Rom. 3:31). The Redeemer was "made under the Law" (Gal. 4:4) and its strictness was not relaxed nor was one iota of its requirements abated in connection with Him. Christ rendered to the Law a personal, perfect and perpetual obedience, and therefore did He "magnify the Law and make it honourable" (Isa. 42:21). Consequently God is not only gracious but "just" at the very moment He is "the Justifier of him which believeth in Jesus" (Rom 3:26), because Jesus satisfied every requirement of righteousness in the stead and behalf of all who trust in Him.

In the righteous Redeemer, then, we find the answer to the question, How can those who have no righteousness of their own and who are utterly unable to procure any, become righteous before God? How can I, who am a mass of corruption, draw nigh unto the ineffably Holy One and look up into His face in peace? By coming to God as unrighteous, acknowledging my inability to remove my unrighteousness, offering nothing to palliate or propitiate Him. By reaching forth the beggar's hand and thankfully receiving the righteousness *He* has provided. Because we were unable to reach up to the holy requirements or righteousness of the Law, God has brought down His righteousness to us: "I bring near My righteousness" (Isa. 46:13). That righteousness was brought near to sinners when the Word became flesh and tabernacled among men. It is brought near to us now in the Gospel, "for therein is the righteousness of God revealed from faith to faith" (Rom. 1:17), a righteousness which God imputes to all who believe and then deals with them according to its deserts, and which will constitute their beauteous array when they enter the celestial courts.

"For He [God] hath made Him [Christ] to be sin for us, who knew no sin, that we

. *(continued on proceeding page)*

VOL. XXIII.   MARCH, 1944.   NO. 3

STUDIES ɪɴ ᴛʜᴇ SCRIPTURES

" Search the Scriptures." John 5:39.

Publisher and Editor—Arthur W. Pink,
27 Lewis Street,
Stornoway, Isle of Lewis,
Scotland.

WISDOM FOR THE WISE

"He giveth wisdom unto the wise" (Dan. 2:21). These words may seem almost puzzling to some: if already wise, why should wisdom be given to such? Others may be discouraged: if wisdom be given only to the wise, then I am cut off, for I am an ignoramus, a veritable dunce. If by that you mean (as the world does) uneducated and unsophisticated, that may be quite true—possibly due in part to slackness in failing to improve your opportunities when young. But if you signify, one who is conscious of spiritual dullness, having a felt lack of capacity to enter into Divine things, such a consciousness is a hopeful sign. The word "wise" is used in Scripture in connection with two very different characters: those who are "wise in their own conceits" (Prov. 26:12; Isa. 5:21) and those who are so in the estimation of God. The former are fools in *His* sight; the latter are dunces in their *own* valuation. It is much to be thankful for when we have been made aware of our spiritual ignorance and stupidity, if it induces us to cry with Job, "That which I see not teach Thou me."

The setting and occasion of our opening text is as follows. Nebuchadnezzar had a dream and though it had gone from him its effects deeply impressed him, and he longed to discover its meaning. Accordingly he summoned before him the magicians and astrologers, demanding that they not only tell him his dream but its interpretation also. The demand was unreasonable, preposterous, nevertheless death was to attend their failure—a sentence which extended also to Daniel and his fellows (Dan. 2:14). Whereupon Daniel went in and requested "that he would give him time," assuring him that "he would show the king the interpretation"

(v. 16). Then Daniel acquainted his companions with the situation, and asked them to join him in desiring "mercies of the God of heaven concerning this secret" (v. 18). Prayer was their sole recourse; and it was enough. Their petition was answered: "then was the secret revealed unto Daniel in a night vision," and he "blessed the God of heaven" (v. 19), saying "Blessed be the name of God for ever and ever: for wisdom and might are His…He giveth wisdom unto the wise and knowledge to them that know understanding."

Limiting ourselves first to the above, we learn *who* are the "wise" and *how* their wisdom is manifested. This incident is indeed a striking one. At the time of its occurrence

(continued on back page)

IMPORTANT NOTICES

Please advise promptly of change in address, otherwise copies will be lost in the mails.

We are glad to send a sample copy to any of your friends whom you believe would be interested in this publication.

This magazine is published as "a work of faith and labour of love," the editor and his wife gladly giving their services free. There is no regular subscription price, as we do not wish the poor of the flock to be deprived. This does not mean that those looking for something for nothing may "help themselves." Those getting this Magazine, who are financially able and who receive spiritual help from its pages, are expected to gladly contribute towards its expenses; otherwise, their names are dropped from our lists.

Will those forwarding International Money Orders please have them made out to us at Stornoway, Isle of Lewis, Scotland. Checks (Cheques-Eng.) made out on U.S.A. Banks are not negotiable here, so please do not send them.

CONTENTS

THE PRAYERS OF THE APOSTLES

3. Romans 15:5-7

The verses we are about to consider supply another illustration of how the apostle was wont to mingle prayer with instruction. He had just issued some practical exhortations, and now he breathes a petition to God that He will make the same effectual. In order to enter into the spirit of this prayer it will be necessary to attend closely to its setting: the more so because not a few are very confused about the present-day bearing of the context. The section in which the passage before us is found begins at 14:1 and terminates at 15:13. In it the apostle gave directions relating to the maintenance of Christian fellowship and the mutual respect with which believers are to regard and treat one another, even where they are not entirely of one accord in matters pertaining to minor points of faith and practice. Those who see not eye to eye with each other on things where no doctrine or principle is involved, are to dwell together in unity, bearing and forbearing in a spirit of meekness and love.

In the Christian company at Rome, as in almost all the then churches of God beyond the bounds of Judea, there were two classes clearly distinguished from each other. The one was composed of Gentile converts and the more enlightened of their Jewish brethren, who (rightly) viewed the institutions of the Mosaic law as annulled by the new and better covenant. The other class comprised the great body of Jewish converts, who, whilst they believed in the Lord Jesus as the promised Messiah and Savior, yet held that the Mosaic law was not and could not be repealed, and therefore continued zealous for it—not only observing its ceremonial requirements themselves but desirous of imposing the same on the Gentile Christians. The particular points here raised were abstinence from those "meats" which were prohibited under the old covenant, and the observance of certain "holy" days connected with the feasts of Judaism. The epistle of Hebrews had not then been written, and little explicit teaching given on the subject. Until God over-threw Judaism in A.D. 70 He tolerated the slowness of understanding on the part of many Jewish Christians.

It can be easily understood, human nature being what it is, the evil tendencies which such a situation threatened, and how real was the need for the apostle to address suitable exhortations unto each party, for differences of opinion are liable to lead to alienation of affections. The first party mentioned above were in danger of despising the other, looking down upon them as narrow-minded bigots, as superstitious. On the other hand, the second party were in danger of judging harshly of the first, viewing them as latitudinarians, lax, or as making an unjust and unloving use of their Christian liberty. The apostle therefore made it clear that, where there is credible evidence of a genuine belief of saving Truth, where the grand fundamentals of the Faith are held, then such differences of opinion on minor matters should not in the slightest degree diminish brotherly love or mar their spiritual and social fellowship together. A spirit of bigotry, censoriousness, and intolerance is utterly foreign to Christianity.

The particular controversy which existed in the apostle's time and the ill feelings it engendered have long since passed away, but the principles in human nature which gave rise to them are as powerful as ever. In companies of professing Christians there are diversities of endowment and acquirements (some have more light and grace than others), and there are differences of opinion and conduct, and therefore the things here recorded will, if rightly understood and legitimately applied, be found "written for our learning." It is through *failure* to understand exactly what the apostle was dealing with that the most childish and unwarrantable applications have been made of the passage, many seeming to imagine that if their fellow-Christians refuse to walk by *their* rules, they are guilty of acting uncharitably and of putting a stumbling block in their way. We know of a sect who deems it sinful for a married woman to wear a wedding ring, and of another who considers it wrong for a Christian man to shave. We know of Christian organizations who exclude from their fellowship any who smoke; and all of these people *condemn* those who decline to conform to their ideas.

Now not only are the cases just mentioned entirely foreign to the scope of Romans 14 and 15, but they involve an evil which it is the bounden duty of God's servants to resist and denounce. That such cases as the ones we have alluded to *are* in no wise analogous to what the apostle was dealing with should be clear to any one who attentively considers these simple facts. Under Judaism certain meats were Divinely prohibited and designated "unclean" (Lev. 11:4-8 etc.), but such a prohibition has been Divinely removed (Acts 10:15; 1 Tim. 4:4), hence there is no parallel in abstaining from things which *God* has *never* forbidden. If some people wish to do so, if they think well to deprive themselves of some of the things which God has given us richly to enjoy (1 Tim. 6:17), that is their privilege; but when they demand that others should do likewise out of respect to their ideas, they exceed their rights and attack the God-given liberty of their brethren.

But there are not a few who go yet farther. They not only insist that others should walk by the rule *they* have set up (or accept the particular interpretation of certain scriptures which they give *and* the specific application of the term "meat" which they make) but stigmatise as "unclean," "carnal," and "sinful" the conduct of those differing from them. This is a very serious matter, for it is a manifest and flagrant commission of that which this particular portion of God's Word expressly reprehends. "Let not him that eateth not judge him that eateth...who art thou that judgest another man's servant...why dost thou judge thy brother?...let us not therefore judge one another any more" (Rom. 14:3,4,10,13)! Thus the very ones who are so forward in judging their brethren are condemned by God! It is surely significant that there is no other portion of Holy Writ which so strongly and so repeatedly forbids passing judgment on others as this chapter to which appeal is so often (wrongly) made by those who condemn their fellows for things which Scripture has not prohibited.

One of the grand blessings won for us by the fierce battle of the Reformation was *the right of private judgment*. For a thousand years Romanism had filched this fundamental blessing from Christendom. Not only was the Word of God withheld, but no man was at liberty to form any ideas on spiritual things for himself: he must perforce receive his doctrines and have every department of his life ordered by the pope and his agents. If any one dared to shake off such shackles, he was anathematised, and if he remained firm in refusing such bondage, he was cruelly tortured and then murdered by those religious tyrants. But in the mercy of God, Luther and his fellows defied Rome, and by Divine providence the Holy Scriptures were restored to the common people, translated into their own language, and every man then had the right to pray directly to God for enlightenment and to form his own judgment of what His Word taught. Alas that such an inestimable privilege is now so little prized, and that the vast majority of non-Romanists (few of them are entitled to be called "Protestants") are too indolent to search the Scriptures for themselves, preferring to accept their views from others.

It was because many of those who enjoyed this dearly-bought privilege had such little courage or wisdom to resist modem encroachments on personal spiritual liberty, that those who sought to lord it over their brethren have made so much headway during the last two or three generations. And once again the whirlwind has followed the "sowing of the wind" and that spirit which was allowed to domineer in the churches is now being more and more adumbrated in the world. Under the plea of "necessary War measures" liberties have been rudely sacrificed. Private homes forced to lodge strangers, and now the wives and mothers themselves threatened with being "directed" into factories, even though it means the break-up of their homes. We refrain from any comment on such a procedure, but merely call attention to what has become a prominent sign of the times; and we do so because of its pertinence to our present subject—the invading of the rights of conscience, the right each man has to interpret the Word according to the light God has given him.

Almost a century ago, when commenting on Romans 14 John Brown said, "It is to be hoped, notwithstanding much that still indicates, in some quarters, a disposition to exercise over the minds and consciences of men an authority and an influence which belongs only to God, that the reign of spiritual tyranny—the worst of all tyrannies—is drawing to a close. Let us determine neither to exercise such domination, nor to submit to it even for an hour. Let us 'call no man master,' and let us not seek to be called masters by others. One is our Master, who is Christ the Lord, and we are His fellow-servants. Let us help each other, but leave Him to judge us. He only has the capacity, as He only has the authority, for so doing." Let us heed that apostolic injunction "Stand fast therefore in the liberty wherewith Christ hath made us free, and be not entangled again with the yoke of bondage" (Gal. 5:1), refusing to heed the "Touch not, taste not, handle not...after the commandments and doctrines *of men*" (Col. 2:21,22).

"Him that is weak in the faith receive ye, but not to doubtful disputations" (Rom. 14:1). The reference is not to one of feeble faith, beset by doubts, but rather to one who is imperfectly instructed in the Faith, who has not yet grasped the real meaning of Christian liberty, who was still in bondage to the prohibitions of Judaism. Notwithstanding his lack of knowledge, receive him into your affections, treat him kindly: cf. Acts 28:2 and Philemon 15-17 for the force of "receive." He was neither to be excommunicated from Christian circles nor looked upon with contempt because he had less light than others. "But not to doubtful disputations" means, that he is not to be disturbed about his own conscientious views and practices, nor on the other hand is he to be allowed to pester his brethren by seeking to convert them to his views. There is to be mutual forbearance and amity between believers. "Each Christian has, and ought to have, the judgment of discretion, and should have his senses exercised to the discerning between good and evil, truth and error," (Matthew Henry).

But does the above verse mean that no effort is to be made to enlighten one who has failed to lay hold of and enter into the benefits Christ secured for His people? Certainly not. Rome may believe that "Ignorance is the mother of devotion," but not so those who are guided by the Word. As Aquila and Priscilla took Apollos unto them and "expounded unto him the way of God more perfectly" (Acts 18:26), so it is both the duty and privilege to pass on to fellow-Christians the light God has given us. Yet that instruction must be given humbly and not censoriously, in a spirit of meekness and not contention. Patience must be exercised: "he that *winneth* [not 'browbeateth'] souls is wise." The aim should be to enlighten his mind rather than force his will, for unless the conscience be convicted, uniformity of action would be mere hypocrisy. A spirit of moderation must temper zeal and the right of private judgment must be fully respected: "Let every man be fully persuaded in his own mind." If we fail to win him it would be sinful to attribute it to his mulishness.

Space will allow us to single out only one other weighty consideration: "The kingdom of God is not meat and drink; but righteousness and peace, and joy in the Holy Spirit" (v. 17). "The kingdom of God" or the Gospel dispensation does not consist of such comparative trivialities as using or abstaining from meat and drink (or jewelry and tobacco)—it gives no rule either one way or another. The Jewish religion consisted much in such things (Heb. 9:10), but Christianity of something infinitely more important and valuable. Let us not be guilty of the sin of the Pharisees who paid tithes of "mint and anise" but "omitted the weightier matters of the Law—judgment, mercy and faith" (Matt. 23:23). "You give a false and degrading view of Christianity by these contentions, leading men to think that freedom from ceremonial restrictions is its great privilege, while the truth is, justification, peace with God, and joy in God, produced by the Holy Spirit, are the characteristic privileges of the children of the kingdom" (John Brown).

But another principle is involved here, a most important and essential one, namely, *the exercise of brotherly love*. Suppose I fail to convince my weaker brother, and he claims to be stumbled by the allowing myself in things he cannot conscientiously use, then what is my duty? If he be unable to enter into the breadth of Christian liberty which I perceive and exercise, how far does the law of Christian charity require me to forgo my liberty and deny myself of that which I feel free before God to use? That is not an easy question to answer, for there are many things which have to be taken into consideration. If it were nothing but a matter of deciding between pleasing myself and *profiting* my brethren, there would be no difficulty, but if it is merely a matter of yielding to their whims, where is the line to be drawn? We have met some who consider it wrong to drink tea or coffee because it is injurious. The one who sets out to try and please everybody is likely to end by pleasing nobody.

A sharp distinction is to be drawn between moderation and abstinence. To be "temperate in all things" (1 Cor. 9:25) is a dictate of prudence—to put it on the lowest ground. "Let your moderation be known to all men" (Phil. 4:5) is a Divine injunction. It is not the use but the abuse of many things which mark the difference between innocence and sin. But because many abuse certain of God's creatures, that is no sufficient reason why others should altogether shun them. As Spurgeon once said, "Shall I cease to use knives because some men cut their throats with them?" Shall, then, my wife remove her wedding ring because certain people profess to be "stumbled" at the sight of one on her finger? Does love to them require her to become fanatical? Would it really make for their profit, their edification, by conforming to their scruples? or would it not be more likely to encourage a spirit of self-righteousness. We once lived for two years in a small place where there was a church of these people, but we saw little signs of humility in those who were constantly complaining of pride in others.

There are many thousands of professing Christians (by no means all of them Romanists) who would consider they grievously dishonored Christ if they partook of any animal meat on Friday: how far would the dictates of Christian love require me to join with them in such abstinence were I to reside in a community where these people preponderated! Answering for himself, the writer would say, it depends on their viewpoint. If it was nothing more than a sentiment, he would probably yield; though he would endeavor to show them there was nothing in Scripture requiring such abstinence. But if they regarded it as a virtuous thing, as being necessary to salvation, he would unhesitatingly disregard their wishes, otherwise he would be encouraging them in fatal error. Or, if they said he too was sinning by eating animal meat on Friday, then he would deem it an unwarrantable exercise of brotherly love to countenance their mistake, and an unlawful trespassing upon his Christian liberty.

It is written, "Give none offence, neither to the Jews, nor to the Gentiles, nor to the church of God" (1 Cor. 10:32), yet like many another precept that one cannot be taken absolutely without any qualification. For example, if I be invited to occupy an Arminian pulpit it would give great offence should I preach upon unconditional Election, yet would that warrant my keeping silent thereon? Hyper-Calvinists do not like to hear about man's responsibility, but should I therefore withhold what is needful to and profitable for them? Would brotherly love require this of me? None more pliable and adaptable than he who wrote "Unto the Jews I became a Jew, that I might gain the Jews...To the weak became I as weak, that I might gain the weak" etc. (1 Cor. 9:20-22), yet when Peter was to be blamed because he toadied to those who condemned eating with the Gentiles, he "*withstood him* to the face" (Gal. 2:11,12), and when false brethren sought to bring them into bondage, he refused to have Titus circumcised (Gal. 2:3-5).

Another incident much to the point before us is found in connection with our Lord and His disciples. "The Pharisees and all the Jews, except they wash their hands oft, eat not, holding the tradition of the elders. And when they come from the market, except they wash, they eat not" (Mark 7:3,4). First a "tradition," this had become a religious practice, a conscientious observance, among the Jews. Did then our Lord then bid His disciples respect their scruples and conform to their standard? No, indeed; for when the Pharisees "saw some of His disciples eat bread with defiled [ceremonially defiled], that is to say, with unwashen hands, they found fault" (v. 2). On another occasion Christ Himself was invited by a certain Pharisee to dine with him, "and He went in and sat down to meat. And when the Pharisee saw it, he marveled that He had *not* first washed before dining" (Luke 11:37,38). Even though He knew it would give offence, Christ declined to be bound by *man-made* laws!

But we must draw to a close. The exercise of Christian charity is an essential duty, yet it is not to override everything else, any more than God has not exercised love at the expense of righteousness. The exercising of love does not mean that the Christian himself is to become a non-entity, a mere straw blown hither and thither by every current of wind he encounters. He is never to please his brethren at the expense of displeasing God. Love is not to oust liberty. The exercise of love does not require the Christian to yield principle, to wound his own conscience or to become the slave of every fanatic he meets. It *does* enjoin the curbing of his own desires and seeking the good, the profit, the edification, of his brethren, but *not* the subscribing to their errors and depriving him of the right of personal judgment. There is a balance to be preserved here: a happy medium between the cultivation of unselfishness and becoming the victim of the selfishness of others. —AWP

THE MISSION AND MIRACLES OF ELISHA
15. Tenth Miracle - part 2

In the preceding article our attention was confined to the *subject* of this miracle, namely Naaman the Syrian, who was stricken with the horrible disease of leprosy—a striking type of the natural man, corrupted by sin, unfit for the presence of a holy God. The most fearful thing of all was, that leprosy was incurable by the hand of man. Naaman was quite incapable of ridding himself of his terrible burden. No matter what plan he followed, what attempts he made, no help or relief was to be obtained from self-efforts. Have you realised the truth of this, in its typical imports, my reader: that there is no deliverance from sin, no salvation for your soul by anything that *you* can do? Nor was there any physician in Syria who could effect a cure: no matter what fee he offered, what quack he applied to, none was of any avail. And such is the case of each of us by nature. Our spiritual malady lies deeper than any human hand can reach unto: our condition is too desperate for any religious practitioner to cure. Man can no more deliver himself, or his fellows, from the guilt and defilement of sin than he can create a world.

Most solemnly was the fact shadowed forth under the system of Judaism. No remedy was provided for this fearful disease under the Mosaic Law: no directions were given to Israel's priesthood to make use of any application, either outward or inward. The leper was shut up entirely to God. All the high priest of the Hebrews could do was to examine closely the various symptoms of the complaint, have the leper excluded from his fellows, and leave him to the disposal of the Lord. Whether the sufferer was healed or not, whether he lived or died, was wholly to be decided by the Almighty. So it is in grace. There is no possible salvation for any sinner except at the hands of *God*. There is no other possible alternative, no other prospect before the sinner than to die a wretched death and enter a hopeless eternity unless distinguishing mercy intervenes, unless a sovereign God is pleased to work a miracle of grace within him. It is entirely a matter of *His* will and power. Again we ask, do you realise that fact my reader? God is your Maker, and He is the Determiner of your destiny. You are clay in His hands to do with as He pleases.

Second, *its contributor.* "And the Syrians had gone out by companies and had brought away captive out of the land of Israel a little maid, and she waited on Naaman's wife" (2 Kings 5:2). In one of the many seasons in which the name of Jehovah was blasphemed among the heathen, through the unfaithfulness of His ancient people, a little Jewish maid was taken captive by the Syrians. In the dividing of the spoils she fell into the hands of Naaman the commander of the Syrian forces. Observe the series of contrasts between them. He was a Gentile, she a hated Jewess. He was a "great man," she but "a little maid." He was "Naaman," she was left unnamed. He was "captain of the host of Syria," while she was captive in the enemy's territory. But he was a leper; while strange to say, she was made a contributing instrument unto his healing. It has ever been God's way to make use of the despised and feeble, and often in circumstances which seemed passing strange to human wisdom. Let us take note how this verse teaches us a most important lesson in connection with the mysteries of Divine providence.

"And had brought away captive out of the land of Israel a little maid." Visualize the scene. One fair morning the peace of Samaria was rudely broken. The tramp of a hostile army was heard in the land. A cruel foe was at hand. The Syrians had invaded the country, and Heaven was silent. No scourge from God smote the enemy: instead, he was suffered to carry away some of the covenant people. Among the captives was "a little maid." Ah, that may mean little to us today, but it meant much to certain people at that day. A home was rendered desolate! Seek to enter into the feelings of her parents as their young daughter was ruthlessly snatched from them. Think of the anguish of her poor mother, wondering what would become of her. Think of her grief-stricken father in his helplessness, unable to rescue her. Endeavor to contemplate what would be the state of mind of the little girl herself as she was carried away by heathen to a strange country. Bring before your mind's eye the whole painful incident until it lives before you.

Do you not suppose, dear friend, that both the maid and her parents were greatly perplexed? Must they not have been sorely tried by this mysterious providence? Why, O why? must have been asked by them a hundred times. Why had God allowed the joy of their home to be shattered? Passing strange, if the maiden reflected at all, must she have thought her lot. Why was she, a favored daughter of Abraham, now a servant in Naaman's household? Why this enforced separation from her parents? Why this cruel captivity? Such questions she might have asked at first, and asked in vain. Ah, does the reader perceive the point we are leading up to? It is this: God had a good reason for this trial. He was shaping things in His own unfathomable way for the outworking of His good and wise purpose. There is nothing happens in this world by mere chance. A predestinating God has planned every detail in our lives. Our "times are in *His* hand" (Ps. 31:15). He "hath determined the times before appointed, and the bounds of their habitation" (Acts 17:26). What a resting place for our poor hearts does that grand truth supply!

It was God who directed that this "little maid" of Israel should become a member of Naaman's household. And why? That she might be a link in the chain which ended not only in the healing of his leprosy, but also most probably in the salvation of his soul. Here then is the important lesson for us to take to heart from this incident. Here is the light which it casts upon the mysterious ways of God in providence: He has a wise and good reason behind each of the perplexing and heart-exercising trials which enter our lives. The particular reason for each trial is frequently concealed from us at the time it comes upon us—if it were not, there would be no room for the exercise of faith and patience in it. But just as surely as God had a good reason for allowing the happiness of this Hebrew household to be darkened, so He has in ordering whatever sorrow has entered your life. It was *the sequel* which made manifest God's gracious design; and it is for the sequel you must quietly and trustfully wait. This incident is among the things recorded in the Old Testament "for our learning, that we through patience and comfort of the Scriptures might have hope" (Rom. 15:4).

"And she said unto her mistress, Would God my lord were with the prophet that is in Samaria, for he would recover him of his leprosy" (v. 3). This is surely most striking and blessed. It had been natural for this young girl to have yielded to a spirit of enmity against the man who had snatched her away from her own home, to have entertained hatred for him, and to have been maliciously pleased that he was so afflicted in his body. The Fall not only alienated man from God but it radically changed his attitude toward his fellows—evidenced at a very early date by Cain's murder of his brother Abel. Human depravity has poisoned every relationship: in their unregenerate state God's own people are described as "hateful and hating one another" (Titus 3:3). But instead of cherishing ill feelings against her captor this little maid was concerned about his condition and solicitous about his welfare. Apparently she had been brought up in the nurture of the Lord, and the seeds planted by godly parents now sprang up and bore fruit in her young life. Beautiful is it to here behold grace triumphing over the flesh.

How this little maid puts us to shame! How sinfully have we conducted ourselves when the providence of God crossed our wills and brought us into situations for which we had no liking! What risings of rebellion within us, what complaining at our circumstances. So far from being a blessing to those we came into contact, we were a stumbling block unto them. Has not both writer and reader much cause to bow the head in shame at the recollection of such grievous failures! Was not this child placed in uncongenial circumstances and a most trying situation? Yet there was neither murmuring against God nor bitterness toward her captor. Instead, she bore faithful testimony to the God of Israel and was moved with compassion toward her leprous master. What a beautiful exemplification of the sufficiency of Divine grace! She remembered the Lord in the house of her bondage and spoke of His servant the prophet. How we need to turn this into earnest prayer, that we too may "glorify the Lord in the fires" (Isa. 24:15).

No position would seem more desolate than this defenceless maiden in the house of her proud captors, and no situation could promise fewer openings for usefulness. But though her opportunities were limited she made the most of them. She despised not the day of small things, but sought to turn it to advantage. She did not conclude it was useless for her to open her mouth, nor argue that an audience of only one person was not worth addressing. No, in a simple but earnest manner she proclaimed the good news that there was salvation for even the leper, for the very name "Elisha" meant "the salvation of God." These lines will be read by more than one who is now serving as a kitchen maid. Is there not here a word for them? Not that we suggest for a moment they should assume the office of preachers or speak frequently about spiritual things to their mistress. Nevertheless, if you have a compassionate regard for her good and look to the Lord for guidance, He may well be pleased to give you a "word in season" for her, and make the same fruitful.

"And one went in and told his lord, saying, Thus and thus said the maid that is of the land of Israel" (v. 4). A very incidental and apparently trivial statement is this, yet being a part of God's eternal Truth it is not to be passed over lightly and hurriedly. We are ever the losers by such irreverent treatment of the Word. There is nothing meaningless in that Holy Volume: each single verse in it sparkles with beauty if we view it in the right light and attentively survey it. It is so here. First, this verse informs us that the little maid's words to her mistress did not pass unheeded. Well they might have done, humanly speaking, for it would be quite natural for those about her—a mere child, a foreigner in their midst—to have paid no attention unto her remarks. Even had they done so, surely such a statement as she had made must have sounded like foolish boasting. If the best physicians in Syria were helpless in the presence of leprosy, who would credit that a man of another religion, in despised Samaria, should be able to heal him! But strange as it may seem, her words *were* heeded.

Second, in this we must see the hand of *God*. "The hearing ear and the seeing eye, the Lord hath made both of them" (Prov. 20:12)—true alike both physically and spiritually. Yet how little is this realised today, when the self-sufficiency of man is proclaimed on every side and the operations of the Most High are so much ignored. The professing Christian is asked "who maketh thee to differ?" (1 Cor. 4:7). All around us are those who pay no heed to the declarations of Holy Writ and who perceive no beauty in Christ that they should desire Him. Who then has given to thee an ear that responds to the Truth and an eye that perceives its Divine origin? And every real Christian will answer, the God of all grace. As it was the Lord who opened the heart of Lydia that she "took unto her [Greek] the things which were spoken" (Acts 16:14), so He caused those about her to listen unto the words of this little maid. Ah, my reader, make no mistake upon this point: the most faithful sermon from the pulpit falls upon deaf ears unless the Holy Spirit operates, whereas the simplest utterance of a child becomes effectual when God is pleased to so apply the same.

Third, this made manifest the effect of the maid's words upon her mistress. She communicated it to another, and this other went in and acquainted the king of the same.

Thus verse 4 reveals to us one of the links in the chain that eventually drew Naaman to Elisha and resulted in his healing. It also shows how that our words are heard and often reported to others, thereby both warning and encouraging us of the power of the tongue. This will be made fully manifest in the Day to come. Nothing which has been done for God's glory will be lost. When the history of this world is completed God will make known before an assembled universe what was spoken for Him (Mal. 3:16; Luke 12:3).

Finally, we are shown here how God is pleased to make use of "little" and despised things. A maid in captivity—who had supposed *her* to do service for the Lord? Who would be inclined to listen to her voice? Her age, her nationality, her position were all against her. Yet because she improved her opportunity and bore witness to her mistress, her simple message reached the ears of the king of Syria. The Lord grant us to be faithful wherever He has placed us.

"And the king of Syria said, Go to, go, and I will send a letter unto the king of Israel" (v. 5). Here also we must see the hand of the Lord. Had He not wrought upon him too the message had produced no effect on his majesty. Why should that monarch pay any attention to the utterance of a kitchen maid? Ah, my reader, when God has a design of mercy He works at both ends of the line: He not only gives the message to the messenger, but He opens the heart of its recipient to heed it. He who bade Philip take a journey into the desert, also prepared the Ethiopian eunuch for his approach (Acts 8:26-31). He who overcame Peter's scruples to go unto the Gentiles, also inclined Cornelius and his household to be "present before God, to hear all things that were commanded him of God (Acts 10:33). "The king's heart is in the hand of the Lord, as the rivers of water: He turneth it whithersoever He will" (Prov. 21:1): strikingly did that receive illustration here. Yet though God wrought, in the instance now before us it did not please Him to remove the king's infirmities.

Third, *its misapprehension.* "Go to, go, and I will send a letter unto the king of Israel." As will appear in the sequel, the Lord had a reason for suffering the king to act thus. Poor Naaman was now *misdirected* by the carnal wisdom of his master. The little maid had said nothing about "the king of Israel," but had specified "the prophet that is in Samaria." It had been much better for the leper to have heeded more closely her directions, then had he been spared needless trouble. Yet how true to life is the typical picture here presented. How often is the sinner, who has been awakened to his desperate condition, wrongly counseled and turned aside to cisterns which hold no water! Rarely does an exercised soul find relief at once. More frequently his experience is like that of the old woman in Mark 5:26 who tried "many physicians" in vain, before she came to Christ; or like the prodigal son when he "began to be in want" and went and joined himself to a citizen of the far country and got nothing better than "the husks that the swine did eat" (Luke 15:14,15), ere he sought unto the Father.

"And he departed, and took with him ten talents of silver, and six thousand pieces of gold, and ten changes of raiment" (v. 5). It has been computed that the value of these things would be at least seventy thousand dollars or fifteen thousand pounds. The Hebrew maid had said nothing of the need for silver and gold, but knowing nought of the *grace* of God Naaman was prepared to pay handsomely for his healing. Again we exclaim, how true to life is this typical picture. How many there are who think the "gift of God" may be purchased (Acts 8:20), if not literally with money, yet by works of righteousness and religious performances. And even where that delusion has been removed, another equally erroneous often takes its place: the idea that a heavily-burdened conscience, a deep sense of personal unworthiness, accompanied by sighs and tears and groans, is the required qualification for applying to Christ and the ground of peace before God. Fatal mistake: "without money and without price" (Isa. 55:1) excludes all frames, feelings and experiences, as truly as it does the paying of a papish priest to absolve me.

Fourth, *its foil*. "And he brought the letter to the king of Israel, saying, Now when this letter is come unto thee, behold I have therewith sent Naaman my servant to thee, that thou mayest recover him of his leprosy. And it came to pass, when the king of Israel read the letter that he rent his clothes and said, am I God to kill and to make alive, that this man doth send unto me to recover a man of his leprosy? Wherefore consider, I pray you, and see how he seeketh a quarrel against me" (vv. 6,7). How this made manifest the apostate condition of Israel at that time and shows why God had moved the Syrians to oppress them! There was some excuse for the king of Syria acting as he did, for he was a heathen; but there was none for the king of Israel. Instead of getting down on his knees and spreading this letter before the Lord, as a later king of Israel did (Isa. 37:14), he acted like an infidel; instead of seeing in this appeal an opportunity for Jehovah to display His grace and glory, he thought only of himself.

What a contrast was there here between the witness of the little maid and the conduct of the king of Israel. Yet his meanness served as a foil to set off her noble qualities. She was in lowly and distressing circumstances, whereas he was a monarch upon the throne. Yet she was concerned about the welfare of her master, while he thought only of himself and kingdom. She had implicit confidence in God and spoke of His prophet, whereas neither God nor His servant had any place in the his mind. Some may think from a first reading of verse 7 that the king's language sounds both humble and pious, but a pondering of it indicates it was but the utterance of pride and unbelief. Knowing not the Lord, he saw in this appeal of Benhadad's nothing but a veiled threat to humiliate him and he was filled with fear. Had he sought unto God, his terror had soon been quieted and a way of relief shown him; but he was a stranger to Him, and evidenced no faith even in the idols he worshiped. Yet this made the more illustrious the marvel of the miracle which followed.

Perhaps the Christian reader is tempted to congratulate himself that there is nothing searching for him in verse 7. If so, such complacency may be premature. Are you quite sure, friend, that there has been *no* parallel in your past conduct to that of Israel's king? Were you never guilty of the thing wherein he failed? When some heavy demand was made upon you, some real test or trial confronted you, did you never respond by saying, I am not sufficient for this: it is quite beyond my feeble powers? Possibly you imagined that was a pious acknowledgment of your weakness, when in reality it was a voicing of your unbelief. True, the Christian is impotent in himself; so too is the non-Christian. Is then the saint no better off than the ungodly? If the Christian continues impotent, the fault is his. God's grace is sufficient and His strength is made perfect in our weakness. Feeble knees and hands which hang down bring no glory to God. He has bidden us "Be strong in the Lord and in the power of His might" (Eph. 6:10). Then cease imitating this defeatist attitude of Israel's king, and "be strong in the grace that is in Christ Jesus" (2 Tim. 2:1). —AWP

THE DOCTRINE OF RECONCILIATION

1. Introduction

Three considerations have influenced us in the selection of this theme. First, a desire to preserve the balance of Truth. In order to do this it is desirable that there should be an alternation between and a proportionate emphasis upon both the objective and the subjective sides of the Truth. After we had completed our exposition of the doctrine of Justification we followed the same with a series on the doctrine of Sanctification: the former treats entirely of the righteousness which Christ has wrought or procured for His people, being something wholly outside of themselves and independent of their own efforts; whereas the latter speaks not only of the perfect purity which the believer has in Christ, but also of the holiness which the Spirit actually communicates to the soul and which is influential on his conduct. Then we took up the doctrine of Predestination which is concerned entirely with the sovereignty of God, and therefore we followed that with a series of man's Impotency and the Saints' Perseverance, where the principal emphasis was upon human responsibility. It will be well for us now to turn our attention back again to the Divine operations and the wondrous provisions of Divine grace for the recovery of rebels against God.

Second, because of a felt need of again bringing conspicuously before our readers "the cross of our Lord Jesus Christ." It is His sacrificial work which is prominent yea dominant in the reconciling of God to His people. It was by the shedding of Christ's precious blood that God was placated and His wrath averted. It was by Christ's being chastised that peace has been made for us. And it is by the preaching of the Cross that our awful enmity against God is slain and that we are moved to abandon our vile warfare against Him. As it is upwards of twelve years since we completed the rather lengthy series of articles we wrote upon the Atonement, under the title "The Satisfaction of Christ," it seems high time that we once more contemplated the greatest marvel and miracle of all history, namely, the Lamb of God being slain for the redemption of sinners. The doctrine of reconciliation has much to do with what took place at Calvary, yea apart from *that* no reconciliation with God had been possible. It is therefore a subject which should warm the hearts of the saints and bow them in adoration at the feet of the Redeemer.

Third, because it treats of an aspect of the Gospel which receives scant attention in the modern pulpit. Nor has it ever, so far as we have been able to ascertain, been made very prominent. This doctrine has failed to command the notice which it merits even from God's own servants and people. Far less appears to have been preached on it than on either justification or sanctification: for one book written on this subject probably fifty have been published on either of the others. Why this should be is not easy to explain: it is not because it is more obscure or intricate—in our judgment, much to the contrary. Certainly it is of equal importance and value, for it treats of an aspect of our relationship and recovery to God as essential as either of the others. Our need of justification lies in our failure to keep the Law of God; of sanctification, because we are defiled and polluted by sin, and therefore unfit for the presence of the Holy One; our reconciliation, because we are alienated from God, rebels against Him, with no heart for fellowship with Him. Though the terms justify and sanctify occur more frequently in the New Testament than does "reconcile," yet the correlative "God of peace" and other expressions must also be duly noted.

Not only has this doctrine been more or less neglected, but it has been seriously perverted by some and considerably misunderstood by many others. Both Socinians (who repudiate the Tri-unity of the Godhead and the Atonement of Christ) and Arminians deny the twofoldness of reconciliation, declaring it to be only on one side. They insist that it is man who is alienated from God, and so in need of reconciliation, that God never entertained enmity toward His fallen creatures, but has ever sought their recovery. They argue that since it was man who made the breach by departing from his Maker, he is the one who needs to be reconciled and restored to Him. They refuse to allow that sin has produced any change in God's relationship or attitude unto the guilty, yea so far from doing so that His own love moved Him to take the initiative and provide a Saviour for rebels, and that He now beseeches them to throw down the weapons of their opposition, assuring them of a Father's welcome when they return unto Him.

Such is the view of the Plymouth Brethren. In his work "The Ministry of Reconciliation" C. H. Macintosh (one of the most influential of their early men) declares: "We often hear it said that 'the death of Christ was necessary in order to reconcile God to man.' This is a pious mistake, arising from inattention to the language of the Holy Spirit and indeed to the plain meaning of the word 'reconcile.' God never changed, never stepped out of His normal and true position. He abides faithful. There was, and could be, no derangement, no confusion, no alienation, so far as He was concerned; and hence there could be no need of reconciling Him to us. In fact it was exactly the contrary. Man had gone astray; he was the enemy, and needed to be reconciled...Wherefore, then, as might be expected, Scripture never speaks of reconciling God to man. There is no such expression to be found within the covers of the New Testament." This is something he calls a "point of immense importance," and consequently all who have succeeded him in that strange system have echoed his teaching: how far it is removed from the Truth will be shown (D.V.) in the articles that follow.

Some hyper-Calvinists are also much confused on this doctrine. Through failing to see that God's being reconciled to sinners who believe concerns His *official* relationship and not His essential character, they have demurred at the expression "a reconciled God," supposing it connotes some charge within Himself. They argue that since God has loved His elect with an everlasting love (Jer. 31:3) and that since He changes not (Mal. 3:6), it is wrong for us to suppose that reconciliation is anything more on our side only. They insist that to speak of God's being reconciled unto us implies an alteration either in His affections or purpose, and that neither of these can stand with His immutability. To speak of God's first loving His people, then hating them, and then again loving them, appears to them as imputing fickleness to Him. So it would be if these predictions of God were made of Him considered in the *same character* and relationship. But they are not. As their Father God has loved His people with an unalterable love, but as the Moral Governor of this world and the Judge of all the earth He has a legal enmity against those who trample His Law beneath their feet.

The following question was submitted to Mr. J. C. Philpot: "What is meant by 'a reconciled God,' an expression which some of the Lord's children, even great and good men, have made use of? I believe that the Lord Jehovah from all eternity foresaw the fall, and provided means to save those whom He had chosen in Christ, consistent with all His attributes, holiness, justice, etc. Now, as love was the moving cause, how can the word 'reconcile' be correctly used in respect of God? Does it not imply a change? If it does, how can it be correctly used in reference to God?" His answer thereto appears in the March 1856 issue of "The Gospel Standard," and though it will make a rather lengthy quotation, yet we might be doing him an injustice not to give it in full.

"We do not consider the expression 'A reconciled God' strictly correct. The language of the New Testament is not that God is reconciled to us, but that we are reconciled to God. 'And all things are of God, who has reconciled us to Himself by Jesus Christ, and hath given to us the ministry of reconciliation; to wit, that God was in Christ, reconciling the world to Himself, not imputing their trespasses to them; and hath committed unto us the word of reconciliation. Now, then, we are ambassadors for Christ, as though God did beseech you by us: we pray you, in Christ's stead, be ye reconciled to God.' (2 Cor. 5:18-20). And again: 'And having made peace through the blood of His cross, by Him to reconcile all things unto Himself; by Him, I say, whether they be things in earth or things in heaven. And you, that were sometime alienated and enemies in your mind by wicked works, yet now hath He reconciled in the body of His flesh through death, to present you holy and unblameable and unreprovable in His sight,' (Col. 1:20-22). See also Romans 5:10.

"The very nature of God, His very being and essence, is to be unchanging and unchangeable, as James beautifully speaks: 'With Him there is no variableness, neither shadow of turning.' But reconciliation on God's part to us, would seem to imply a change of mind, an alteration of purpose in Him, and is therefore, so far, inconsistent and incompatible with the unchangeableness of the Divine character. It is also, strictly speaking, inconsistent, as our correspondent observes, with the eternal love of God, and seems to represent the atonement as influencing His mind, and turning it from wrath to love, and from displeasure to mercy and grace. Now, the Scripture represents the gift of Christ, and consequently the sufferings and blood-shedding for which and unto which He was given, not, as the procuring *cause*, but as the gracious *effect* of the love of God. 'Herein is love, not that we loved God, but that He loved us, and sent His Son to be a propitiation for our sins' (1 John 4:10). See also John 3:16, Romans 8:32, 1 John 4:9.

"But though the Scripture speaks of reconciliation, not of God to man, but of man to God, and that through the blood of the cross alone (Col. 1:20); yet it holds forth, in the plainest, strongest language, a real and effective 'sacrifice,' 'atonement,' and 'propitiation,' offered to God by the Lord Jesus; all which terms express or imply an actual satisfaction rendered to God for sin, and such a satisfaction, as that without it there could be no pardon. It is especially needful to bear this in mind, because the Socinians and other heretics who deny or explain away the atonement, insist much on this point, that the Scripture does not speak of a reconciled God. Therefore, though we do not believe that the atonement produced a change in the mind of God, so as to turn Him from hatred to love, for He loved the elect with an everlasting love, (Jer. 31:3), or that it was a price paid to procure His favor, still, there was a sacrifice offered, a propitiation made, whereby, and whereby alone, sin was pardoned, blotted out, and forever put away.

"By steadily bearing these two things in mind, we shall be the better prepared to understand in what reconciliation through the blood of the cross consists. Against the persons of the elect there was, in the mind of God, no vindictive wrath, no penal anger (Isa. 27:4); but there was a displeasure against their sins, and so far with them for their sins. So God was angry with Moses (Deut. 1:37), with Aaron (Deut. 9:20), with David (2 Sam. 11:27; 1 Chron. 21:7), with Solomon (1 Kings 11:9) for their personal sins, though all of them were in the covenant of grace, and loved by Him with an everlasting love. Thus the Scriptures speak of the anger and wrath of God, and of that wrath being turned away and pacified (Isa. 12:1; Ezek. 16:63), which it could only be by the blood of the Lamb.

"Again, sin is a violation of the justice of God, a breaking of His holy Law, an offence against His intrinsic purity and holiness, which He cannot pass by. Adequate satisfaction must, therefore, be made to His offended justice, or pardon cannot be granted. Now, here we see the necessity and nature of the sufferings and obedience, blood-shedding and death of the Lord Jesus, as also why reconciliation was needed, and what reconciliation effected. By the active and passive obedience of the Son of God in the flesh, by His meritorious life and death, by His offering Himself as a sacrifice for sin, a full and complete satisfaction was rendered to the violated justice of God, the Law was perfectly obeyed and everlasting righteousness brought in. Satisfaction being rendered to His infinite justice, now God can be 'just and yet the Justifier of him which believeth in Jesus.' Now the jarring perfections of mercy and justice are harmonised and reconciled, so that mercy and truth meet together, righteousness and peace kiss each other. Now God can not only be gracious, but 'faithful and just to forgive us our sins and to cleanse us from all unrighteousness.' There is, then, no such reconciliation of God as to make Him love those whom He did not love before, for He loved the elect from all eternity in Christ, their covenant-head; but a breach being made by the fall, and sin having, as it were, burst in to make a separation between God and them (Isa. 59:2), that love could not flow forth till satisfaction was made for sin, and that barrier removed, which it was in one day (Zech. 3:9). And not only so, but the persons of the elect were defiled with sin (Ezek. 16:5,6), and therefore needed washing, which they were in the blood of the Lamb (Rev. 1:5 etc.). In this way not only was the reconciliation of the Church effected, but she, the bride and spouse of Christ, was brought near unto God, from whom sin had separated her.

"But reconciliation has a further aspect. It comprehends our reconciliation to God not merely as a thing already effected by the blood-shedding of God's dear Son, but as a present experience in the soul. The apostle says 'By whom we have now received the atonement' (margin, reconciliation: Rom. 5:11); and again, 'we pray you, in Christ's stead, be ye reconciled to God' (2 Cor. 5:20), that is, by receiving into your hearts the reconciliation already made by His blood. It is with reference to this experience that much is spoken in the Scriptures which has led to the idea of 'a reconciled God.' Thus the Church complains of God's being angry with her (Isa. 12:1), of being 'consumed by His anger and troubled by His wrath' (Ps. 90:7), of His 'shutting up in anger His tender mercies' (Ps. 77:9), and again of His 'turning away from the fierceness of His anger and causing it to cease' (Ps. 85:3,4), of His 'not keeping anger forever' (Ps. 103:9), of His being pacified (Ezek. 16:63) of His 'anger being turned away' (Ps. 78:38; Hosea 14:4). All these expressions are the utterance of the Church's experience. When God's anger is sensibly felt in the conscience He is viewed as angry, and His wrathful displeasure is dreaded and deprecated; when He manifests mercy this anger is felt to be removed, to be turned away; and it is now as if He were reconciled to the sinner.

"Putting all these things together we seem to arrive at the following conclusions: 1. That it is not God who is reconciled to the Church, but that it is the Church which is reconciled to God. 2. That this reconciliation was effected by the incarnation, obedience, sacrifice and death of the Lord Jesus. 3. That till this reconciliation be made experimentally known the awakened conscience feels the anger of God on account of sin. 4. That when the atonement is received and the blood of Christ sprinkled on the conscience, then the soul is really and truly reconciled to God." —*J.C. Philpot*

What satisfaction this reply gave to the original inquirer, or how lucid it appears to our readers (even after a second or third perusal), we know not, but to us it seems a strange medley, lacking in perspicuity and betraying confusion of thought in the mind of its composer. First, Mr. Philpot considered that the language of the New Testament does not warrant the expression "A reconciled God." Second, he felt that to affirm a reconciliation on God's part to us would imply an alteration of purpose in Him and as though the Atonement changed His mind "from displeasure to mercy and grace." Then he evidently feared he was coming very close to the ground occupied by the Socinians; so, third, he allowed that the work of Christ was both a "sacrifice" and a "propitiation." But "a propitiation" is the very thing which is needed to *conciliate* one who is offended! To aver there was "rendered to God for sin an actual satisfaction, and such a satisfaction as that without which there could be no pardon," is only another way of saying that God was alienated and needed placating before He could be reconciled to His enemies.

In his next paragraph he virtually or in effect contradicts what he had advanced in the previous one, for he expressly declares "Against the persons of the elect there was in the mind of God no vindictive wrath, *no penal anger*." Then wherein lay the need of a "propitiation"? "Penal" means "relating to punishment": if there was no judicial anger on God's part as Governor and Judge and if His elect were not exposed to the punishment of the Law because of their sins, then why the sacrifice of Christ for them? Clearly Mr. P. felt the shoe pinching him here, for in his next paragraph he brings in the violation of the justice of God and the "satisfaction" this required. Yet toward the end he wavers again by saying "sin having, as it were, burst in to make a separation between God and them." Why such hesitating qualification? sin *did* cause a breach on both sides, and the one Party needed to be "propitiated," and the other "converted" before the breach could be healed. Our purpose in quoting form C.H. Mackintosh and J.C. Philpot (whose writings served to mould the views of many thousands) is to demonstrate the need for a Scriptural exposition of this doctrine.

N. B. We are glad to say that in his last years Mr. Philpot was granted a clearer grasp of the truth, as appears from his helpful exposition of Ephesians 2. —AWP

SPIRITUAL GROWTH OR CHRISTIAN PROGRESS
3a. Its Necessity

We commenced our last by pointing out that none can possibly make any progress in the Christian life unless he first be a Christian, and then devoted the remainder to defining and describing what a "Christian" is. It is indeed striking to note that this title is used by the Holy Spirit in a *twofold* way: primarily it signifies an "anointed one," subordinately it denotes "a disciple of Christ." Thereby we have brought together in a truly wonderful manner both the Divine and the human sides. Our "anointing" with the Spirit is God's act, wherein we are entirely passive; but our becoming "disciples of

Christ" is a voluntary and conscious act of ours, whereby we freely surrender to Christ's lordship and submit to His sceptre. It is by the latter that we obtain evidence of the former. None will yield to the flesh-repellent terms of Christian "discipleship" save those in whom a Divine work of grace has been wrought; but when that miracle *has* occurred, conversion is as certain to follow as a cause will produce its effects. One made a new creature by the Divine miracle of the new birth desires and gladly endeavors to meet the holy requirements of Christ.

Here, then, is the root of spiritual growth: the communication to the soul of spiritual life. Here is what makes possible Christian progress: a person's becoming a Christian—first by the Spirit's anointing and then by his own choice. This twofold signification of the term "Christian' is the principal key which opens to us the subject of Christian progress or spiritual growth, for it ever needs to be contemplated from both the Divine and the human sides. It requires to be viewed both from the angle of God's operations and from that of the discharge of our responsibilities. The twofold meaning of the title "Christian" must also be borne in mind under the present aspect of our subject, for on the one hand progress is neither necessary nor possible, while in another very real sense it is both desirable and requisite. God's "anointing" is not susceptible of improvement, being perfect; but our "discipleship" is to become more intelligent and productive of good works. Much confusion has resulted from ignoring this distinction, and we shall devote the remainder of this article to the negative side, pointing out those respects in which progress or growth *does not* obtain.

1. Christian progress does not signify advancing in God's favor. The believer's growth in grace does not further him one iota in God's esteem. How could it, since He is the Giver of his faith and the One who has "wrought all our works in us" (Isa. 26:12)! God's favorable regard of His people originated not in anything whatever in them, either actual or foreseen. God's grace is absolutely free, being the spontaneous exercise of His own mere good pleasure. The cause of its exercise lies wholly within Himself. The *purposing* grace of God is that good will which He had unto His people from all eternity: "Who hath saved us and called us with a holy calling, not according to our works, but according to His own purpose and grace which was given us in Christ Jesus before the world began" (2 Tim. 1:9). And the *dispensing* grace of God is but the execution of His purpose, ministering to His people: thus we read "God *giveth* grace," yea that "He giveth more grace" (James 4:6). It is entirely gratuitous, sovereignly bestowed, without any inducement being found in its object.

Furthermore, everything God does for and bestows on His people is *for Christ's sake*. It is in nowise a question of their deserts, but of Christ's deserts or what He merited for them. As Christ is the only Way by which we can approach the Father, so He is the sole Channel through which God's grace flows unto us. Hence we read of "the grace of God, and the gift of grace [namely, justifying righteousness] by one man, Jesus Christ" (Rom. 5:15); and again, "the grace of God which is given you by Jesus Christ" (1 Cor. 1:4). The love of God toward us is "in Christ Jesus our Lord" (Rom. 8:39). He forgives us "for Christ's sake" (Eph. 4:32). He supplies all our need "according to His riches in glory by Christ Jesus" (Phil. 4:19). He brings us to Heaven in answer to Christ's prayer (John 17:24). Yet though Christ merits everything for us, the original cause was the sovereign grace of God. "Although the merits of Christ are the (procuring) cause of our salvation, yet they are not the cause of our being ordained to salvation. They are the cause of purchasing all things decreed unto us, but they are not the cause which first moved God to decree those things unto us" (Thos. Goodwin, Puritan)

The Christian is not accepted because of his "graces," for the very graces (as their name connotes) are bestowed upon him by Divine bounty, and are not attained by any efforts of his. And so far from these graces being the reason why God accepts him, they are the *fruits* of his being "chosen in Christ before the foundation of the world" and, decretively, "blessed with all spiritual blessings in the heavenlies in Christ" (Eph. 1:3,4). Settle it then in your own mind once for all, my reader, that growth in grace does not signify growing in the favor of God. This is essentially a Papish delusion, and though a creature-flattering it is a horribly Christ-dishonoring one. Since God's elect are "accepted in the Beloved" (Eph. 1:6) it is impossible that any subsequent change wrought in or attained by them could render them more excellent in His esteem or advance them in His love. When the Father announced concerning the incarnate Word "this is My beloved Son [not "with whom" but] *in whom* I am well pleased," He was expressing His delight in the whole election of grace, for He was speaking of Christ in His federal character, as the last Adam, as Head of His mystical body.

The Christian can neither increase nor decrease in the favor of God, nor can anything he does or fails to do alter or affect to the slightest degree his perfect standing in Christ. Yet let it not be inferred from this that his conduct is of little importance or that God's dealings with him have no relation to his daily walk. While avoiding the Romish conceit of human merits, we must be on our guard against Antinomian licentiousness. As the moral Governor of this world God takes note of our conduct, and in a variety of ways makes manifest His approbation or disapprobation: "No good thing will He withhold from them that walk uprightly" (Ps. 84:11), yet to His own people God says "your sins have withholden good things from you" (Jer. 5:25). So too as the Father He maintains discipline in His family, and when His children are refractory He uses the rod (Ps. 89:30-33). Special manifestations of Divine love are granted to the obedient (John 14:21,23), but are withheld from the disobedient and the careless.

2. Christian progress does not denote that the work of regeneration was incomplete. Great care needs to be taken in stating this truth of spiritual growth lest we repudiate the perfection of the new birth. We must repeat here in substance what was pointed out in the first article. When a normal child is born into this world naturally the babe is an entire entity, complete in all its parts, possessing a full set of bodily members and mental faculties. As the child grows there is a strengthening of its body and mind, a development of its members and an expansion of its faculties, with a fuller use of the one and a clearer manifestation of the other; yet no new member or additional faculty is or can be added to him. It is precisely so spiritually. The spiritual life or nature received at the new birth contains within itself all the "senses" (Heb. 5:14) and graces, and though these may be nourished and strengthened, and increased by exercise yet not by addition, no, not in Heaven itself. "I know that whatsoever God doeth it shall be forever: nothing can be put to it, nor anything taken from it" (Eccl. 3:14). The "babe" in Christ is just as truly and completely a child of God as the most matured "father" in Christ.

Regeneration is a more radical and revolutionizing change than glorification. The one is a passing from death unto life, the other an entrance into the fullness of life.

The one is a bringing into existence of "the new man which after God is created in righteousness and true holiness" (Eph. 4:24), the other is a reaching unto the full stature of the new man. The one is a translation into the kingdom of God's dear Son (Col. 1:13), the other an induction into the higher privileges of that kingdom. The one is the begetting of us unto a living hope (1 Peter 1:3), the other is a realisation of that hope. At regeneration the soul is made "a new creature" in Christ, so that "old things are passed away, behold, all things are become new" (2 Cor. 5:17). The regenerate soul is a partaker of every grace of the Spirit, so that he is "complete in Christ" (Col. 2:10), and no growth on earth or glorification in Heaven can make him more than "complete"!

3. Christian progress does not procure a title for Heaven. The perfect and indefeasible title of every believer is in the merits of Christ. His vicarious fulfilling of the Law, whereby He magnified and made it honorable, secured for all in whose stead He acted the full reward of the Law. It is on the all-sufficient ground of Christ's perfect obedience being reckoned to his account that the believer is justified by God and assured that he shall "reign in life" (Rom. 5:17). If he lived on earth another hundred years and served God perfectly it would add nothing to his title. Heaven is the "purchased possession" (Eph. 1:14), purchased for His people by the whole redemptive work of Christ. His precious blood gives every believing sinner the legal right to "enter the holiest" (Heb. 10:19). Our title to glory is found alone in Christ. Of the redeemed now in Heaven it is said, "they have washed their robes and made them white in the blood of the Lamb: *therefore* are they before the throne of God and serve Him day and night in His temple" (Rev. 7:14,15).

It has not been sufficiently realised that God's pronouncement of justification is very much more than a mere sense of acquittal or non-condemnation. It includes as well a positive imputation of righteousness. As James Hervey so beautifully illustrated it: "When yonder orb makes his first appearance in the east, what effects are produced? Not only are the shades of night dispersed, but the light of day is diffused. Thus it is when the Author of salvation is manifested to the soul: He brings at once pardon *and acceptance*." Not only are our filthy rags removed, but "the best robe" is put upon us (Luke 15:22), and no efforts or attainments of ours can add anything to such a Divine adornment. Christ not only delivered from death, but purchased life for us; He not only put away our sins, but merited an Inheritance for us. The most mature and advanced Christian has nought to plead before God for his acceptance than the righteousness of Christ: *that*, nothing but that, and nothing added to it, as his perfect title to Glory.

4. Christian progress does not make us meet for Heaven. Many of those who are more or less clear on the three points considered above are far from being so upon this one, and therefore we must enter into it at greater length. Thousands have been taught to believe that when a person has been justified by God and tasted the blessedness of "the man whose transgression is forgiven, whose sin is covered," that much still remains to be done for the soul before it is ready for the celestial courts. A widespread impression prevails that after his justification the believer must undergo the refining process of sanctification, and that for this he must be left for a time amid the trials and conflicts of a hostile world; yea so strongly held is this view that some are likely to take exception to what follows. Nevertheless, such a theory repudiates the fact that it is the new-creative work of the Spirit which not only capacitates the soul to take in and enjoy

spiritual things now (John 3:3,5), but also fits it experimentally for the eternal fruition of God.

One had thought that those laboring under the mistake mentioned above would be corrected by their own experience and by what they observed in their fellow Christians. They frankly acknowledge that their own progress is most unsatisfactory to them, and they have no means of knowing when the process is to be successfully completed. They see their fellow Christians cut off apparently in very varied stages of this process. If it be said that this process is completed only at death, then we would point out that even on their death-beds the most eminent and mature saints have testified to being most humiliated over their attainments and thoroughly dissatisfied with themselves. Their final triumph was not what grace had made them to be in themselves, but what Christ was made to be unto them. If such a view as the above were true, how could any believer cherish a desire to depart and be with Christ (Phil. 1:23) while the very fact that he was still in the body would be proof (according to this idea) that the process was not yet complete to fit him for His presence!

But, it may be asked, is there not such a thing as "progressive sanctification"? We answer, it all depends upon what is signified by that expression. In our judgment it is one which needs to be carefully and precisely defined, otherwise God is likely to be grossly dishonored and His people seriously injured by being brought into bondage to a most inadequate and defective view of Sanctification as a whole. There are several essential and fundamental respects in which sanctification is *not* "progressive," wherein it admits of no degrees and is incapable of augmentation, and those aspects of sanctification need to be plainly stated and clearly apprehended *before* the subordinate aspect be considered. First, every believer was decretively sanctified by God the Father before the foundation of the world (Jude 1). Second, he was meritoriously sanctified by God the Son in the redemptive work which He performed in the stead of and on the behalf of His people, so that it is written "by one offering He hath *perfected forever* them that are sanctified" (Heb. 10:14). Third, he was vitally sanctified by God the Spirit when He quickened him into newness of life, united him to Christ, and made his body His temple.

If by "progressive sanctification" be meant a clearer understanding and fuller apprehension of what God has made Christ to be unto the believer and of his perfect standing and state in Him, if by it be meant the believer living more and more in the enjoyment and power of that, with the corresponding influence and effect it will have upon his character and conduct; if by it be meant a growth of faith and an increase of its fruits, manifested in a holy walk, then we have no objection to the term. But if by "progressive sanctification" be intended a rendering of the believer more acceptable unto God, or a making of him more fit for the heavenly Jerusalem, then we have no hesitation in rejecting it as a serious error. Not only can there be no increase in the purity and acceptableness of the believer's sanctity before God, but there can be no addition to that holiness of which he became the possessor at the new birth, for the new nature he then received is essentially and impeccably holy. "The babe in Christ, dying as such, is as capable of as high communion with God as Paul in the state of glory" (S. E. Pierce).

Instead of striving after and praying that God would make us more fit for Heaven, how much better to join with the apostle in "Giving thanks unto the Father who *hath made us meet* to be partakers of the inheritance of the saints in light" (Col. 1:12), and then seek grace to walk suitably unto such a privilege and dignity! *That* is for the saints to "*possess* their possessions" (Obad. 17); the other is to be robbed of them by a thinly-disguised Romanism. Before pointing out in what the Christian's meetness for Heaven consists, let us note that Heaven is here termed an "Inheritance." Now an inheritance is not something that we acquire by self-denial and mortification (a papish concept), nor purchased by our own labors or good works; rather is it that to which we lawfully succeed in virtue of our relationship to another. Primarily, it is that to which a child succeeds in virtue of his relationship to his father, or as the son of a king inherits the crown. In this case, the Inheritance is ours in virtue of our being *sons of God*.

Peter declares that the Father hath "*begotten us* unto a living hope...*to* an inheritance incorruptible and undefiled and that fadeth not away" (1 Peter 1:4). Paul also speaks of the Holy Spirit witnessing with our spirit that we are the children of God, and then points out: "and if *children*, then *heirs*; heirs of God and joint-heirs with Christ" (Rom. 8:16,17). If we inquire more distinctly, what is this "inheritance" of the children of God? the next verse (Col. 1:13) tells us: "it is the kingdom of God's dear Son." Those who are joint-heirs with Christ must share His kingdom. Already He has made us "kings and priests unto God" (Rev. 1:6), and the inheritance of kings is a crown, a throne, a kingdom. The blessedness which lies before the redeemed is not merely to be subjects of the King of kings, but to sit with Him on His throne, to reign with Him forever (Rom. 5:17; Rev. 22:4). Such is the wondrous dignity of our inheritance: as to its *extent*, we are "joint-heirs with" Him whom God "hath appointed Heir of all things" (Heb. 1:2). Our destiny is bound up with His. O that the faith of Christians would rise above their "feelings," "conflicts," and "experiences" and possess their possessions.

The Christian's title to the Inheritance is the righteousness of Christ imputed to him: in what, then, consists his "meetness"? First, since it be meetness for the Inheritance, they must be *children* of God, and this they are made at the moment of regeneration. Second, since it is "the Inheritance of saints," they must be *saints*, and this too they are the moment they believe in Christ, for they are then sanctified by that very blood in which they have forgiveness of sins (Heb. 13:12). Third, since it is an Inheritance "in light," they must be made *children of light*, and this also they become when God called them "out of darkness into His marvelous light" (1 Peter 2:9). Nor is that a characteristic only of certain specially favored saints; "ye are *all* the children of light" (1 Thess. 5:5). Fourth, since the Inheritance consists of an everlasting kingdom, in order to the enjoyment of it we must have *eternal life*, and that too every Christian possesses: "he that believeth on the Son of God hath everlasting life" (John 3:36).

"For ye are all the children of God by faith in Christ Jesus" (Gal. 3: 26): are they children in name, but not in nature? What a question! it might as well be supposed they have a title to the Inheritance and yet be without meetness for it, which would be saying that our sonship was a fiction and not a reality. Very different is the teaching of God's Word: it declares we become His children by being born again (John 1:13). And regeneration does not consist in the gradual improvement or purification of the old nature, but the creation of a new one. Nor is becoming children of God a lengthy process at all, but an instantaneous thing. The all-mighty Agent of it is the Holy Spirit, and obviously that which is born of *Him* needs no improving or perfecting. The "new man" is itself "created in righteousness and true holiness" (Eph. 4:24) and certainly *it* cannot stand in need of a "progressive" work to be wrought in him! True, the old nature opposes all the aspirations and activities of this new nature, and therefore as long as the believer remains in the flesh he is called upon "through the Spirit to mortify the deeds of the body"; yet in spite of the painful and weary conflict, the new nature remains uncontaminated by the vileness in the midst of which it dwells.

That which qualifies the Christian or makes him meet for Heaven is the spiritual life which he received at regeneration, for that is the life or nature of God (John 3:5; 2 Peter 1:4). That new life or nature fits the Christian for communion with God, for the presence of God—the same day the dying thief received it, he was with Christ in Paradise! It is true that while we are left here its *manifestation* is obscured, like the sunbeam shining through opaque glass. Yet the sunbeam itself is not dim, though it appears so because of the unsuitable medium through which it passes; but let that opaque glass be removed, and it will at once appear in its beauty. So it is with the spiritual life of the Christian: there is no defect whatever in the life itself, but its manifestation is sadly obscured by a mortal body; all that is necessary for the appearing of its perfections is deliverance from the corrupt medium through which it now acts. The life of God in the soul renders a person meet for glory: no attainment of ours, no growth in grace we experience, can *fit* us for Heaven any more than it can *entitle* us to it. —AWP

(continued from back page)

their prayer "So teach us to number our days that we may apply our hearts unto Wisdom" (Psa. 90:12). "Rebuke a wise man and he will love thee" (Prov. 9:8)—it is the self-important fool who fails to see that the rebuke was designed for his good. "Give instruction to a wise man and he will be yet wiser" (Prov. 9:9)—treasuring up the instruction and turning it to profit. "A wise man feareth and departeth from evil" (Prov. 14:16)—knowing that as it is dangerous to play with fire, so to dally with temptation. "The way of life is above to the wise" (Prov. 15:24)—his affections set upon things in Heaven is what marks his course.

"The Lord's voice crieth unto the city, and the man of wisdom shall see Thy name" (Micah 6:9), which means that when God is speaking loudly in judgment (as He is today) the one endowed with spiritual wisdom will discern the intent of the Divine dispensations and set his own house in order—this is clear from the remainder of the verse: "hear ye the rod, and Who hath appointed it." Another mark of the "wise" man is that he dug deep and "built his house upon a rock" (Matt. 7:24), which signifies that he is a *doer* of the Word and not a hearer only. The "wise" virgins were those who "took oil in their vessels with their lamps" (Matt. 25:4)—who had grace in their hearts as well as a Christian profession on their lips. "Let no man deceive himself: if any man among you seemeth to be wise in this world, let him become a fool, that he may be wise" (1 Cor. 3:18)—renounce proud reason and come before God as a little child to be taught by Him. The wise "redeem the time" (Eph. 5:16). "Who is a wise man and endowed with knowledge among you? let him *show* out of a good conversation [deportment] his works with meekness of wisdom" (James 3:13). —AWP

(continued from front page)

Daniel was but a young man, and so far as Scripture informs us he had never previously received a prophetic "vision" from God! Yet such was his confidence in the Lord that he tells the king, without any hesitation or qualification, that if allowed time he *would* (not "might" or that he "hoped to") tell him both his dream and its signification. It should also be duly noted that Daniel and his fellows had no specific promise they could plead before God, no detail in His Word which exactly suited their present emergency, and therefore they fell back upon the general "desiring mercies" from Him. We may also point out that this happened at a time when Israel's spirituality was at an exceedingly low ebb, when the Divine judgments were heavy upon that nation, when many of her sons were in captivity in a heathen land. Nevertheless, Daniel had no fear that God would suffer him to be confounded or put to confusion. In childlike assurance he bowed the knee before Him and obtained that which he sought.

No, my reader, He never puts to confusion those who fully trust Him—He would not be *God* if He did. He has pledged Himself to honour those who honour Him, and as nothing more honours Him than genuine faith in Himself, He always rewards it wherever it be found. The trouble today is that the majority of professing Christians are so occupied with natural "means" that direct dealings with God is crowded out. The wisdom of Daniel then appears, first, in his implicit confidence in the Lord's sufficiency: that it was a simple matter for Him to do what had baffled all the "wise men" of Babylon. Second, in his counting upon God's "mercies": he laid hold of that fact that He is of tender compassion, and this encouraged him in the hour of dire need. Third, in spreading his case before Him, and expecting an answer, as is unmistakably clear from his confident language unto Nebuchadnezzar. It is the faith which *expects* from God that is not disappointed. Such was the faith of Abraham: "I and the lad will go yonder and worship, and *come again* [notwithstanding Isaac's being slain] to you" (Gen. 22:5 and cf. Heb. 11:19). Such was the faith of Elisha (2 Kings 4:3). Such was the faith of Paul (Acts 27:25).

And unto *that* "wise" man God gave more "wisdom" as He "giveth more grace" unto the humble (James 4:5). And this striking and blessed incident has been recorded for our learning: to show us what spiritual wisdom is, how it acts, and what it obtains. Natural knowledge puffs up its possessor, and the more he has the more self-sufficient he deems himself. But it is the very opposite with spiritual wisdom: the more God bestows of that upon His child, the more ignorant and stupid he feels himself to be, and the more dependent upon the Holy Spirit does he become. Then it is that he really values that precious promise "If any of you lack wisdom, let him ask of God, that giveth to all liberally and upbraideth not; and it *shall be* given him" (James 1:5). The truly "wise" person will not only greatly prize such a promise, but he will daily *make use* of it, mixing faith therewith, pleading it before the throne of grace, and obtaining answers of peace. As it is "when I am weak [in myself], then am I strong" (2 Cor. 12:10), so it is when we (spiritually speaking) conduct ourselves as "babes" that God reveals unto us what is hidden from the worldly wise and prudent (Matt. 11:25).

Let us now widen our scope and take notice of some of the marks of the spiritually "wise." "O that they were wise, that they understood this, that they would consider their latter end" (Deut. 32:29). The "wise," then, are those who solemnly ponder their future, who are seriously concerned about where they will spend eternity; and therefore is it

. (continued on proceeding page)

VOL. XXIII.   APRIL, 1944.   NO. 4

STUDIES ɪɴ ᴛʜᴇ SCRIPTURES

" Search the Scriptures." John 5:39.

Publisher and Editor—Arthur W. Pink,
27 Lewis Street,
Stornoway, Isle of Lewis,
Scotland.

IGNORANCE AND KNOWLEDGE

"Thou knowest not what evil shall be upon the earth" (Eccl. 11:2). These words enunciate a broad principle which is of general application, intimating our ignorance of future providences. But they also have a more specific meaning, as may be seen from their setting. The context contains an exhortation unto generosity, cultivating acts of benevolence. For the husbandman to cast bread-corn, which he could ill spare, upon a marshy soil, especially if covered by waters; might seem improvident and unwise, but assurance is given him that he shall find it again after many days: the autumn harvest will vindicate his springtide faith and labor. From this a practical application is made: "Give a portion to seven and also to eight." Do not selfishly hoard up what God has so freely bestowed on you, but distribute a goodly proportion among those who are not so well provided for. Consider the poor and needy and minister to their wants: think not it will all be wasted upon them and come to nought.

But unbelief may object, The outlook is far from being propitious and therefore I should lay up more and more against my own "rainy day." The miser says, I know not what the future has in store for me, so it is the part of prudence to accumulate whilst I may. No, says our passage, we should reason the very opposite: "*For* thou knowest not what evil shall be upon the earth." Since thou knowest not how calamitous the times may shortly be, then do all possible in the present and you will not be the loser in the future. The instability of human affairs and the possibility that our riches may soon take to themselves wings and fly away, furnishes a sound reason why we should do as much good with them as we can while we have them, and leave the outcome with God. He will not suffer the liberal soul to starve. He who has been wisely charitable to the indigent is likely to be the recipient of most kindness if an evil day should come upon him; but the miser makes no friends and is left alone when misfortune strikes.

The exhortations of Ecclesiastes 11:1,2 are by no means to be restricted unto the disbursement of temporal charity: they have also a spiritual import, with a particular application unto the minister of the Gospel. As Faith is needed by the farmer in order to the discharge of his duties, so it is with the evangelical husbandman. He must not be discouraged by the lack of response he meets with and the absence of immediate fruitage to his labours. If he be faithful in casting the

(continued on back page)

IMPORTANT NOTICES

Please advise promptly of change in address, otherwise copies will be lost in the mails.

We are glad to send a sample copy to any of your friends whom you believe would be interested in this publication.

This magazine is published as "a work of faith and labour of love," the editor and his wife gladly giving their services free. There is no regular subscription price, as we do not wish the poor of the flock to be deprived. This does not mean that those looking for something for nothing may "help themselves." Those getting this Magazine, who are financially able and who receive spiritual help from its pages, are expected to gladly contribute towards its expenses; otherwise, their names are dropped from our lists.

Will those forwarding International Money Orders please have them made out to us at Stornoway, Isle of Lewis, Scotland. Checks (Cheques-Eng.) made out on U.S.A. Banks are not negotiable here, so please do not send them.

CONTENTS

THE PRAYERS OF THE APOSTLES

4. Romans 15:5-7

Under the New Covenant there is no longer any distinction in the sight of God between different kinds of "meat" nor of the sacred "days" set apart for religious exercise that obtained under the Jewish economy. Some of the early Christians perceived this clearly, others either did not or would not acknowledge such liberty. This difference of opinion bred dissensions and disrupted fellowship. To remove this evil and to promote good the apostle laid down certain rules which may be summed up thus. First, "let every man be fully persuaded in his own mind" (14:5) and not blindly swayed by the opinions or customs of others. Second, be not censorious and condemn not those who differ from you (v. 13). Third, be not occupied with mere trifles, but concentrate on the essentials (v. 17). Fourth, follow after those things which make for peace and mutual edification (v. 19) and quibble not over matters which are to no profit. Fifth, make not an ostentatious display of your liberty, nor exercise the same to the injury of others (vv. 19-21).

There is great variety and diversity among the saints. This is true of their natural make-up, temperament, manner, and thus in their likeableness or unlikeableness. It also holds good spiritually: Christians have received varying degrees of light, measures of grace, and different gifts. One reason why God has ordered things thus is to try their patience, give opportunity for the exercise of love, and occasion to display meekness and forbearance. All have their blemishes and infirmities. Some are proud, others peevish; some are censorious and others backboneless, and in various ways difficult to get on with. Opinions differ and customs are by no means uniform. Much grace is needed if fellowship is to be maintained. If the rules mentioned above had been rightly interpreted and genuinely acted upon through the centuries many dissensions had been prevented and much that has marred the Christian testimony in public avoided.

"We then that are strong ought to bear the infirmities of the weak and not please ourselves" (15:1). The "then" is argumentative, pointing a conclusion drawn from the principles laid down in the foregoing chapter—for some understanding of which the preceding article was necessary. Let it be duly noted that the pronouns are in the *plural* number: it was not so much individual differences of opinion and conduct, with the personal ill feelings they bred, which the apostle had been reprehending, but rather the development of the same collectively into party spirit and sectarian prejudice, so that the Christian company would be rent asunder—this too must be borne in mind when making a present-day application. The "weak" here signifies those who had a feeble grasp of that freedom which Christ has obtained for His people, as a reference to 14:1 makes clear; the "strong" those who have a better apprehension of the extent of their Christian privileges from the restrictions which had been imposed by the ceremonial law and the traditions of men— such as the austerities of the Essenes.

The Greek word here rendered "bear" signifies "to take up." It was used of porters carrying luggage, assisting travelers. It is found again in Galatians 6:2, only the apostle there mentions "burdens" rather than infirmities: see also Luke 14:27, Romans 11:18. This term also helps to determine the interpretation of what is in view, and thus fixes the proper application. We are not here enjoined to bear *with* the petty whims or scruples of one another, but to render practical aid to those who lag behind the rest. A "burden" is something which is apt to cause its carrier to halt or faint by the way, incapacitating him in his pilgrimage. The strong are bidden to help these weak ones. As charity requires us to ascribe their weaknesses to lack of understanding, it becomes the duty of the better instructed to seek to *enlighten* them. No doubt it would be easier and nicer to leave them alone, but we are "not to please ourselves." Apparently it was at this point the Gentile believers had failed, for while the Jewish Christians were aggressive in seeking to impose their view on others, the Gentiles seem to have adopted a negative attitude.

It is ever thus: fanatics and extremists are not content to deprive themselves of things which God has not prohibited, but are zealous in endeavoring to press their will upon all, whereas others who use them temperately are content to mind their own business and leave in peace those who differ from them. Christians who drink wine and smoke tobacco in moderation do not go about seeking to induce others to do the same, yet many of their brethren who are total abstainers take it upon them to pester these with their fads and say the most uncharitable things about those who refuse to adopt their whims. It is not the use of wine but the intemperate abuse of the same which Scripture forbids: see John 2:1-11; Ephesians 5:18; 1 Timothy 3:8. It was the ex-pharisees "which believed" who insisted that "it was necessary to circumcise" converted Gentiles and "to command them to keep the law of Moses" (Acts 15:5) and thereby bring them into bond-age, a thing which the apostle Paul steadfastly resisted and condemned.

In the passage before us the Roman saints were exhorted to cease maintaining their negative attitude, however much easier and more congenial it might be to continue in the same. "And not to please ourselves" (v. 1) signifies not an abstention from something they liked, but the performing of a duty which they disliked, how men do turn the things of God upside down! This is quite evident from the preceding part of the verse, where the "strong" (or better instructed) were bidden to "bear the infirmities of the weak": how would their abstaining from certain "meats" be a compliance with *such* an injunction? No, it was not something they were told to forgo out of respect for others' scruples, but a *bearing* of their "infirmities," a rendering assistance to their fellow-pilgrims (Gal. 6:2) which they were called upon to do. And how was this to be done? Well, *what were* their "infirmities"? Why, self-imposed abstinences because of ignorance of the Truth. Thus it was the duty of the Gentile Christians to expound unto their Jewish brethren "the way of God more perfectly" (Acts 18:26).

Try and place yourself in *their* position, my reader. Imagine yourself to be Lydia or the Philippian jailor. All your past life had been in the darkness and idolatry of heathenism, when unsought by you the sovereign grace of God opened your heart to receive the Gospel. You are now a new creature in Christ Jesus, and have been enabled to perceive your standing and liberty in Him. Living next door to you, perhaps, is a family of converted Jews. All their past lives they have read the Scriptures and worshiped the true God, and though they have received Christ as the promised Messiah and as their personal Savior, yet they are still in bondage to the restrictions of the Mosaic Law. You marvel at their dullness, but consider it none of your concern to interfere. And now you receive a copy of this Epistle and ponder 15:1. You now see that you *have* a duty toward your Jewish sister and brother, that God bids you make the effort to pass on to her or him the light He has granted you. The task is distasteful: perhaps so, but we are "not to please ourselves"!

That what we have sought to set forth above brings out, or at least points to, the real meaning of verse 1 is unequivocally established by the next verse. "Let every one of us please his neighbor for his good to edification" (Rom. 15:2). This is obviously the amplification in positive form of the negative clause in the verse before. To "edify" a brother—here called "neighbor" according to Jewish terminology!—is to build him up in the Faith, and the appointed means for *that* is to instruct him by and enlighten him with the Truth. It should be carefully noted that this "pleasing of our neighbor" is no mere yielding to his whims, but an industrious effort to promote his knowledge of Divine things, particularly in the privileges which Christ has secured for him. It may prove a thankless task, but it "ought" to be undertaken, for concern for his good requires it. If he resents your efforts and insults you, *your* skirts are clear and you have the satisfaction of knowing that you have honestly attempted to discharge your duty.

"For even Christ pleased not Himself; but as it is written, The reproaches of them that reproached Thee fell on Me" (v. 3). This supplies further proof of the soundness of our interpretation of the previous verses. The meaning of "we…ought…not to please ourselves" is placed beyond all uncertainty by what is here said of our Lord. In His case it signified something vastly different than *abstaining* from things that He *liked*, and certainly the very opposite of attempting to ingratiate Himself in the esteem of men by flattering their prejudices. No, rather was Christ in all things regulated by the Divine Rule: not His own will, but the will of His Father was whatever governed Him. Not attempting to obtain the approval of His fellows, but rather seeking of their "good" and the "edification" of His brethren was what uniformly actuated Him. And in the exercise of such disinterested charity, so far from being appreciated for the same, He brought upon Himself "reproaches." And if the disciple follows His example he must not expect to fare any better.

In his closing remarks on Romans 14, Charles Hodge pointed out: "It is often necessary to assert our Christian liberty at the expense of incurring censure and offending good men, in order that right principles of duty may be preserved. Our Savior consented to be regarded as a Sabbath-breaker and even a 'winebibber' and 'friend of publicans and sinners'; but wisdom was justified of her children. Christ did not in those cases see fit to accommodate His conduct to the rules of duty set up and conscientiously regarded as correct by those around Him. He saw that more good would arise from a practical disregard of the false opinion of the Jews as to the manner in which the Sabbath was to be kept and as to the degrees of intercourse which was allowed with wicked men, than from concession to their prejudices." Better then to give offence or incur obloquy than sacrifice principle or disobey God.

"For whatsoever things were written aforetime were written for our learning, that we through patience and comfort of the Scriptures might have hope." This statement seems to be made for a double reason. First, to inform the saints that though the Mosaic law was abrogated and the Old Testament treated of a past dispensation, yet they must not conclude therefrom that it was now out of date. The uniform use which the New Testament writers made of it, frequently appealing to it in proof of what they advanced, proves otherwise: all of it is intended for our instruction today, and the examples of piety contained therein will stimulate us—see James 5:10. Second, a prayerful pondering of the Old Testament will nourish that very grace which will most need to be exercised when complying with the foregoing exhortations—"patience," in dealing with those who differ from us; it will minister "comfort" to us if we are reviled for performing our duty.

"Now the God of patience and consolation grant you to be like-minded one toward another according to Christ Jesus." By his example the apostle here teaches us that if we are to discharge this duty acceptably unto God we must have recourse unto *prayer*. He alone can grant success in it, and unless His aid be definitely and earnestly sought, failure is almost certain to be the outcome. There are few things which the majority of people more resent than to have their religious beliefs and ways called into question. Something more is involved than an imperfectly-informed understanding: there is prejudice of heart to be overcome as well, for 'convince a man against his will, and he is of the same opinion still.' Moreover much grace is required on the part of the one who undertakes to deal with the mistaken scruples of another, lest, acting in the energy of the flesh, he gives place to the Devil, sowing seeds of discord and causing "a root of bitterness" to spring up, and thus makes matters worse rather than better. Such grace needs to be personally and fervently sought.

There is a zeal which is not according to knowledge. There is an ardor which is merely of nature and not prompted by the Holy Spirit. If then it should become my duty to pass on to a brother a measure of that light which God has granted me and which I have reason to believe he does not enjoy, I need to ask help from Him for the execution of such a task. I need to ask Him to impress my heart afresh with the fact that *I* have nothing but what I received from Him (1 Cor. 4:7) and to beg Him to subdue the workings of pride, that I may approach my brother in a humble spirit. I need to ask for wisdom, that I may be guided in what to say. I need to ask for love that I may truly seek the good of the other. I need to be shown when it is the right time to approach him. Above all, I need to ask that God's glory may be my paramount concern. Furthermore, I need to pray that it may please God to go before me and prepare the soil for the seed, that He will graciously meeken the heart of my brother, remove the prejudice, and make him receptive to the Truth.

Observe the particular character in which the apostle addressed the Deity: as "the God of patience and consolation." He eyed those attributes in God which were most suited to the petition he presented, namely, that He would grant "like-mindedness" where there was a difference in judgment and mutual forbearance was called for. It was the grace of patience that was needed among dissenting brethren: "consolation" too was required to bear the infirmities of the weak: as another has said, "If the heart be filled with the comforts of the Almighty it will be as oil to the wheels of Christian charity." The Father is here contemplated as "the God of patience and consolation" because He is the Author of these graces, because He requires the exercise of the same in us (Eph. 5:1), and because we are to constantly seek from Him the quickening and strengthening of them. In the preceding verse we are shown that "patience and comfort" are conveyed to believing souls through the Scriptures: they are, as it were, the conduit-pipe; but here we are taught that God Himself is the Fountain-head of the same.

Consider now *the mercy sought*: that the God of patience and consolation would "grant you to be like-minded one to another." As Charles Hodge rightly pointed out, like-mindedness here "does not signify unanimity of opinion but harmony of feeling." This should be apparent to those who possess no knowledge of the Greek: how can "babes" in Christ be expected to have the same measure of light on spiritual things as mature Christians! No, the apostle's petition went deeper than that the saints might see eye to eye on every detail—which is neither to be expected nor desired in this life: it was that affection one toward another might obtain, even where difference of opinion upon minor matters persisted. The thing requested was, that quarreling should cease, all ill feelings be set aside, patience and forbearance be exercised, and mutual love prevail. It was that such a state of unity might obtain that notwithstanding difference of view, they might enjoy together the delights and advantages of Christian fellowship.

"According to Christ Jesus" (v. 5). The margin gives "after the example of": this is certainly included, yet not to be restricted thereto. We regard this like-mindedness "according to Christ Jesus" as having a threefold force. First, according to the *precept*, command, or law of Christ: "By this shall all men know that ye are My disciples, if ye have love one to another" (John 13:35); "bear ye one another's burdens, and so fulfil the law of Christ" (Gal. 6:2). Second, according to His *example*. Remember how He bore with the dullness and bickering of His disciples. Remember how He stooped to wash their feet. Third, by making Him "the Centre" of their unity: "Agree in the Truth, not in any error. It was a cursed concord and harmony of those who were of one mind to give their power and strength to the Beast (Rev. 17:13): that was not a like-mindedness *according* to Christ, but *against* Christ" (Matthew Henry). Thus, "according to Christ Jesus" signifies in a Christian manner. Let the reader ponder carefully Philippians 2:2-5, for it furnishes an inspired comment on our present verse.

Yet there is such a fullness in the words of Scripture that the threefold meaning of "according to Christ Jesus" given above by no means exhausts their scope. They need also to be considered in the light of what immediately precedes and pondered as a part of this prayer. The apostle is making request that God would cause this Christian company (composed of such different elements as believing Jews and Gentiles) to be "likeminded," which, of course, implies that they were not so—Titus 3:3 describes what we are by nature. Observe the blessing sought, however desirable, was not something to be claimed, but which it was prayed that God would "grant": by adding "according to Christ Jesus" we may therefore understand those words as the ground of appeal—grant it according to the *merits* of Christ. Finally, we may also regard this clause as a plea: grant it for the *honor* of Christ—that unity and concord may obtain for the glory of His name.

"That ye may with one mind, one mouth glorify God, even the Father of our Lord Jesus Christ" (v. 6). This is *the grand end* in view: that such brotherly love may be exercised, such mutual forbearance shown, such concord and unity maintained, that the spirit of worship be not quenched. The One who will not receive from me an offering while I be alienated from my brother (Matt. 5:23,24) will not accept the praise of a company of believers where there are divisions among them. Something more than coming together under the same roof and joining in the same ordinance is required (1 Cor. 11:18-20). There cannot truly be "one mouth" unless there first be "one mind." Tongues which are used to backbite one another in private cannot blend together in singing God's praises. The "Father" is mentioned here as an emphatic reminder of the *family* relationship: all Christians are His children, and therefore should dwell together in peace and amity as brethren and sisters—"of *our* [not 'the'!] Lord Jesus Christ" intensifies the same idea.

"They may be divided in their dietary views; this in itself is a small matter; but they must not be divided in their worship and praise of God. For the patient and comforted mind can join in praise with those from whom there is dissent of opinion. This is true Christian union" (James M. Stifler). "Wherefore receive ye one another, as Christ also received us to the glory of God" (v. 7). This is not an exhortation to one class only, but to the "strong" and the "weak" alike. They are here bidden to ignore all minor differences, and inasmuch as Christ accepts all who genuinely believe His Gospel whether they be Jews or Gentiles, so are we to receive into fellowship and favor all whom He has received. "If He accepts men in all their weakness and without any regard to their views about secondary things, well may we" (Stifler). Thereby is God glorified, and for this we should pray and act. —AWP

THE MISSION AND MIRACLES OF ELISHA

16. Tenth Miracle - part 3

In the previous chapter we emphasized the secret operations of God in inclining one and another to pay attention to the message of the little Hebrew maid: He it was who gave the hearing ear to both Naaman's wife and the king of Syria. Perhaps some have remarked, But such was not the case with the king of Israel! No, it was not, for so far from sharing her confidence and cooperating with her effort, he was skeptical and antagonistic. Therein we may perceive God's sovereignty. He does not work in all alike, being absolutely free to do as He pleases. He opens the eyes of some, but leaves others in their blindness. This is God's high and awful prerogative: "Therefore hath He mercy on whom He will have mercy, and whom He will He hardeneth" (Rom. 9:18). This is what supplies the key to God's dealings with men and which explains the course of evangelical history. Clearly is that solemn principle exemplified in the chapter before us, and we should be unfaithful as an expositor if we—as so many now do—deliberately ignored it.

"And it came to pass when the king of Israel had read the letter that he rent his clothes, and said, Am I God to kill and to make alive; that this man doth send unto me to recover a man of his leprosy?" (2 Kings 5:7). So utterly sceptical was Jehoram that he deemed it not worth while to send for Elisha and confer with him. The prophet meant nothing to Israel's unbelieving king, and therefore he slighted him. Perhaps this strikes the reader as strange, for the previous miracles Elisha had wrought must have been well known. One had thought his restoring of a dead child to life had thoroughly authenticated him as an extraordinary man of God. But did not the Lord Jesus publicly raise a dead man to life, and yet within a few days both the leaders of the nation and the common people clamored for His crucifixion! And is it any different in our day? Have we not witnessed providential marvels, Divine interpositions both of mercy and judgment, and what effect have they had on our evil generation? Jehoram's conduct is easily accounted for: "the carnal mind is enmity against God" (Rom. 8:7), and that enmity evidenced itself by slighting His accredited servant.

"And it was so, when Elisha the man of God had heard that the king of Israel had rent his clothes, that he sent to the king, saying, Wherefore hast thou rent thy clothes? let him come now to me, and he shall know that there *is* a prophet in Israel" (v. 8). The slighted Elisha pocketed his pride and communicated with the king, rightly concluding that his own feelings were not worth considering where the glory of God was concerned. "Naaman came into the land of Israel, expecting relief from a prophet of the God of Israel, and Elisha would by no means have him go back disappointed, lest he should conclude that Jehovah was like the gods of the nations, and as unable to do good or evil as they were. On the contrary he would have it known that God had 'a prophet in Israel' by whom He performed such cures as none of the heathen prophets, priests, or physicians could effect; and which were far beyond all the power of the mightiest monarchs" (Thomas Scott). The "counsel of the Lord it shall stand" whatever devices were in Jehoram's heart to the contrary (Prov. 19:21).

"The righteous are bold as a lion." Elisha not only rebuked the king for his unbelieving fears but summarily gave him instructions concerning Naaman. However unwelcome might be his interference, that deterred him not. The real servant of God does not seek to please men, but rather to execute the commission he has received from on high. It is true that the prophets, like the apostles, were endowed with extraordinary powers, and therefore they are not in all things models for us today; nevertheless the Gospel minister is not to cringe before any one, still less is he to take orders from human authorities. It is his duty to denounce unbelief and to proclaim that the living God is ever ready to honor Him and work wonders in response to genuine faith. As God overruled the king of Syria's misdirecting of Naaman, so He now overcame the skepticism of the king of Israel by moving him to respond to Elisha's demand—thereby demonstrating that the words of the little maid were no idle boast and her confidence in God no misplaced one.

"So Naaman came with his forces and with his chariot and stood at the door of the house of Elisha" (v. 9). Naaman before the prophet's abode may be regarded as a picture of the natural man in his sins, not yet stripped of his self-righteousness, nor aware that he is entirely dependent on Divine mercy, having no title or claim to receive any favor at God's hand. The fact that he was seated in a chariot mitigated his terrible condition not one iota. No matter how rich the apparel that covered his body, though it might hide from human view his loathsome disease, it availed nothing for the removal of it. And as the valuables he had brought with him could not procure his healing, neither can the cultivation of the most noble character nor the performance of the most praiseworthy conduct in human esteem merit the approbation of God. Salvation is wholly of Divine grace and cannot be earned by the creature: "Not by works of righteousness which we have done, but according to His mercy He saved us by the washing of regeneration and renewing of the Holy Spirit; which He shed on us abundantly through Jesus Christ our Savior" (Titus 3:5,6).

However much it might be in accord with the principles and sentiments which regulate fallen human nature, there was surely something most incongruous in the scene now before us. Here was a poor creature stricken with a most horrible disease, and yet we behold him seated in a chariot. Here was one smitten by a malady no physician could heal, surrounded by official pomp. Here was one entirely dependent upon the Divine bounty, yet whose horses were laden with silver and gold. Do we not behold in him, then, a representative not only of the natural man in his sins, but as filled with a sense of his own importance and bloated with pride! Such is precisely the case with each of us by nature. Totally depraved though we be, alienated from God, criminals condemned by His holy Law, our minds at enmity against Him, dead in trespasses and sins, yet until a miracle of grace is wrought within and the tumor of our pride is lanced, we are puffed up with self-righteousness, refuse to acknowledge we deserve naught but eternal punishment, and imagine we are entitled to God's favorable regard.

Not only does Naaman here fitly portray the self-importance of the natural man while unregenerate, but as hinted above he also adumbrates the fact that the sinner imagines he can gain God's approbation and purchase his salvation. The costly things which the Syrian had brought with him were obviously designed to ingratiate himself in the eyes of the prophet and pay for his cure. The following such a policy was of course quite natural, and therefore it types out what is the native thought of every man. He supposes that a dutiful regard of religious performances will obtain for him the favorable notice of God, that his fastings and prayers, church-attendance and contributing to its upkeep, will more than counterbalance his demerits. Such an insane idea is by no means confined to Buddhists and Romanists but is common to the whole human family. It is for this reason we have to be assured, "By grace are ye saved, through faith, and that not of yourselves, it is the gift of God, not of works, lest any man should boast" (Eph. 2:8,9). Spiritually speaking, every man is bankrupt, a pauper, and salvation is entirely gratis, a matter of charity.

"But the natural man receiveth not the things of the Spirit of God, for they are foolishness unto him, neither can he know them because they are spiritually discerned" (1 Cor. 2:14). This is true alike of the most cultured and the thoroughly illiterate. No amount of education or erudition fits one for the apprehension of spiritual things. Man is blind, and his eyes must be opened, before he can perceive either the glory of God and His righteous claims or his own wretchedness and deep needs. Not until a miracle of grace humbles his heart will he betake himself unto the Throne of Grace in his true character, not until the Holy Spirit works effectually within him will he come to Christ as an empty-handed beggar. It is recorded that a famous artist met with a poor tramp and was so impressed with his woe-begone appearance and condition that he felt he would make an apt subject for a drawing. He gave the tramp a little money and his card and promised him a sovereign if he would call at his house on the following day and sit while he drew his picture. The next morning the tramp arrived, but the artist's intention was defeated: the tramp had washed and shaved and so spruced himself that he was scarcely recognisable!

Similarly does the natural man act when he first attempts to respond to the Gospel call. Instead of coming to the Lord just as he is in all his want and woe, as one who is lost and undone, he supposes he must first make himself more presentable by a process of reformation. Thus he busies himself in amending his ways, improving his conduct, and performing pious exercises, unaware that Christ "came not to call the righteous, but sinners to repentance"—to take their place in the dust before Him. What we have just been dwelling upon receives striking illustration in the chapter before us. Instead of sending Naaman direct to Elisha, Benhadad gave him a letter of introduction unto the king of Israel; and instead of casting himself on the mercy of the prophet, he sent a costly fee to pay for the healing of his commander-in-chief. We have seen the futility of his letter—the effect it had upon its recipient; now we are to behold how his lavish outlay of wealth produced no more favorable response from Elisha, for Naaman had to learn the humiliating truth that where Divine grace is concerned the millionaire stands on precisely the same level as the pauper.

Fifth, *its requirement.* "And Elisha sent a messenger unto him, saying, Go and wash in Jordan seven times, and thy flesh shall come again to thee, and thou shalt be clean" (v. 10). As the representative of Him who deigned to wash the feet of His disciples, the minister of the Gospel must not decline the meanest service nor despise the poorest person. Elisha has set us an example of both, for he scorned not to minister to the physical needs of Elijah by washing his hands (3:11), and refused not to help the impoverished widow (4:2). On the other hand, the servant of Christ is to be no sycophant, toadying to those of affluence, nor is he to feed the pride of the self-important. From the sequel it is evident Naaman considered that he, as a "great man," was entitled to deference, and probably felt that the prophet ought to consider a favor or honor was now being shown him. But, officially, Elisha was an ambassador of the King of kings, and with becoming dignity he let Naaman know that he was at no man's beck and call, though he failed not to inform him of the way in which healing was to be obtained.

"And Elisha sent a messenger unto him, saying, Go and wash in Jordan seven times, and thy flesh shall come again to thee, and thou shalt be clean." Here we see no servile obeisance nor owning of the mightiness of Naaman. The prophet did not even greet him, nor so much as go out of his house to meet him in person. Instead, he sent him a message by a servant. Ah, my reader, God is no respecter of persons, nor should His ministers be. Incalculable harm has been wrought in churches by pastors pandering to those in high places, for not only are the haughty injured thereby, but the lowly are stumbled, and in consequence the Holy Spirit is grieved and quenched. God will not tolerate any parading of fleshly distinctions before Him: "that *no* flesh should glory in His presence" (1 Cor. 1:29) is the unrepealable decision. The most eminent and gifted of this world are due no more consideration from the Most High than the street-sweeper, for "there is no difference: all have sinned and come short of the glory of

God" (Rom. 3:22). All alike have broken the Law, all alike are guilty before the supreme Judge, all alike must be saved by sovereign grace if they be saved at all.

But there is another way in which we may regard the prophet's conduct on this occasion: not only did he maintain his official dignity, but he evidenced personal humiliation and prudence, having his eye fixed on the glory of God. It is not that he was indifferent to Naaman's welfare: no, the fact that he sent his servant out to him with the needful directions evidenced the contrary. But Elisha knew full well that the all-important thing was not the messenger, but the message. It mattered nothing who delivered the message— himself or his servant, but it mattered everything that the God-given word should be faithfully communicated. Elisha knew full well that Naaman's expectation lay *in himself*, so like a true "man of God" he directed attention away from himself. What a needed lesson for us in this creature-exalting day. How much better would preachers serve souls and honor their Master if, thus hidden, they occupied them with the Gospel instead of with themselves. It was in this self-effacing spirit that Paul rebuked the creature-worshipping Corinthians when he said "who then is Paul and who is Apollos, but ministers by whom ye believed?" (1 Cor. 3:5). So too our Lord's forerunner who styled himself "the voice [heard but not seen!] of one crying in the wilderness" (John 1:23).

What was the force of "Go wash in Jordan seven times"? Let us give first a general answer in the words of another. "When Naaman stood with his pompous retinue, and with all his silver and gold at the door of Elisha, he appears before us as a marked illustration of a sinner building on his own efforts after righteousness. He seemed furnished with all that the heart could desire, but in reality all his preparations were but a useless encumbrance, and the prophet soon gave him to understand this. 'Go wash' swept away all confidence in gold, silver, raiment, retinue, the king's letter, everything. It stripped Naaman of everything, and reduced him to his true condition as a poor defiled leper needing to be washed. It put no difference between the illustrious commander-in-chief of the hosts of Syria, and the poorest and meanest leper in all the coasts of Israel. The former could do nothing less; the latter needed nothing more. Wealth cannot remedy man's ruin, and poverty cannot interfere with God's remedy. Nothing that a man has done need keep him out of heaven; nothing that he can do will ever get him in. 'Go wash' is the word in every case."

But let us consider this "Go wash" more closely and ponder it in the light of its connections. As one stricken with leprosy, Naaman pictures the natural man in his fallen estate. And what is his outstanding and distinguishing characteristic of such? Why, that he is a depraved creature, a sinner, a rebel against God. And what is sin? From the negative side, it is failure to submit to God's authority and be subject to His Law; positively, it is the exercise of self-will, a determination to please myself; "we have turned every one to *his own way*" (Isa. 53:6). If then a sinner inquires of God's servant the way of recovery, what is the first and fundamental thing which needs to be told him? Why this: that self-will and self-pleasing must cease, that he must submit himself to the will of God. And that is only another way of saying that he must be *converted*, for "conversion" is a turning round, a right-about-face. And in order to conversion, *repentance* is the essential requisite (Acts 3:19), and in its final analysis "repentance" is taking sides with God against myself, judging myself, condemning myself, bowing my will to His.

Again, sin is not only a revolt against God, but a deification of self: it is a determination to gratify my own inclinations; it is saying, "I will be lord over myself." That was the bait which the Serpent dangled before our first parents when he tempted Eve to eat of the forbidden fruit: "Ye shall be as *gods*" (Gen. 3:5). Casting off allegiance to God, man assumed an attitude of independency and self-sufficiency. Sin taking possession of his heart, he became proud, haughty, self righteous. If, then, such a creature is to be recovered and restored to God, it must necessarily be by a process of *humbling him*. The first design of the Gospel is to put down human pride, to lay man low before God. It was predicted by Isaiah when speaking of Gospel times "The lofty looks of man shall be humbled and the haughtiness of men shall be bowed down" (2:11). And again, "every mountain shall be made low and the crooked shall be made straight" (40:4); and therefore did our Lord begin His sermon on the mount by saying, "Blessed are the poor in spirit, for theirs is the kingdom of heaven" (Matt. 5:3). That was the basic truth which the prophet pressed upon Naaman: that he must abase himself before the God of Israel.

"Go wash in Jordan seven times" was but another way of saying to the conceited Syrian, "God resisteth the proud, but giveth grace unto the humble. Submit yourselves therefore to God...Cleanse your hands ye sinners and purify your hearts ye double minded. Be afflicted and mourn and weep: let your laughter be turned to mourning and your joy to bitterness. Humble yourselves in the sight of the Lord, and He shall lift you up" (James 4:6-10). Naaman must come down from off his high horse and take his proper place before the Most High. Naaman must descend from his "chariot" and evidence a lowly spirit. Naaman must "wash" or "bathe" as the word is often translated, in the waters of the Jordan; not once or twice but no less than seven times, and thus completely renounce self. And the requirement which God made of Naaman, my reader, is precisely the same as His demand upon you, upon me: pride has to be mortified, self-will relinquished, self-righteousness repudiated. Have we complied therewith? Have we renounced self-pleasing and surrendered to the Divine scepter? Have we given ourselves to the Lord (2 Cor. 8:5) to be ruled by Him? If not, we have never been savingly converted.

In its ultimate significance, the "Go wash in Jordan seven times" had a typical import, and in the light of the New Testament there is no difficulty whatever in perceiving what that was. There is one provision, and one only, which the amazing grace of God and the wondrous love of His Son has made for the healing of spiritual lepers. It is that blessed "Fountain" which has been opened for sin and for uncleanness (Zech. 13:1). That holy "Fountain" had its rise at Calvary, when from the pierced side of Christ "forthwith came there out blood and water" (John 19:34). That wondrous "Fountain" which can cleanse the foulest was provided at the incalculable cost of the crucifixion of Immanuel, and hence the washing in "Jordan" which ever speaks of death. Here, then, dear friend, is the evangelical significance of what has been before us. If you have been made conscious of your depravity, ready to deny self, willing to humble yourself into the dust before God, here is the Divine provision: a bath into which by faith you may plunge, and thereby obtain proof that "the blood of Jesus Christ God's Son cleanseth us from all sin" (1 John 1:7). If by grace you have already done so, then join the writer in exclaiming, "Unto Him that loved us and washed us from our sins in His own blood...to Him be glory and dominion forever. Amen" (Rev. 1:5,6). —AWP

THE DOCTRINE OF RECONCILIATION
2. Its Distinctions

Before taking up our subject in a positive and constructive manner it seems advisable that we should endeavor to remove a misapprehension under which a number of our readers are laboring, and which requires to be cleared up before they will be in a fit condition to weigh without bias and thus be enabled to receive what we hope to present in later articles. It is for their special benefit this one is composed, and we trust that other friends will kindly bear with us if they find it rather wearisome to follow a labored discussion of that which presents no difficulty to *them*. To enter into a consideration of this particular point at such an early stage in the series will oblige us to somewhat infringe upon other aspects of our subject which will be taken up later (D.V.), but this appears necessary if we are to "clear the decks for action," or to change the figure, if we are to rid the ground of superfluous encumbrances and fit it for a sowing of the seed.

That which presents a difficulty to those who have been brought up in some Calvinistic circles is, how can God be said to be *reconciled* to His elect, seeing that He has loved them with an everlasting and unchanging love? Much of our opening article was devoted to a particular answer to such an inquiry, but as we deem that answer far from being a satisfactory one, we shall here confine ourselves to its elucidation. To us it appears that the explanation furnished by Mr. Philpot was confused and faulty, and that it was so through failure to distinguish between things that differ—hence the title we have accorded this article. If we are to avoid becoming hopelessly muddled on this point we must discriminate sharply between what the elect are as viewed only in the eternal purpose of God, and what they are *in themselves by nature*. And further, we must carefully differentiate between God considered as their Father and God considered as the Moral Governor and *Judge* of all mankind.

That it may appear we do not advance anything in the remainder of this article which clashes with or deviates from the teaching of sound theologians in the past, we will make brief quotations from four of the best-known Puritans. "We are actually justified, pardoned and reconciled when we repent and believe. Whatever thoughts and purposes of grace God may have towards us from eternity, we are under the fruits of sin till we become penitent believers" (T. Manton). In his treatise on "The Work of the Holy Spirit in our Salvation" Thomas Goodwin (book 2, beginning of chapter 1) points out: "There are two different states or conditions which the elect of God, who are saved, pass through, between which regeneration is the passage. The one is their first state in which they are born: a state of bondage to sin, and obnoxious to instant damnation whilst they remain in it...The other of grace and salvation, therefore oppositely to the former state."

"God does hate His elect in some sense before their actual reconciliation. God was placable before Christ, appeased by Christ. But until there be such conditions which God hath appointed in the creature, he hath no interest in this reconciliation of God, and whatsoever person he be in whom the condition is not found, he remains under the wrath of God, and therefore in some sense under God's hatred" (Stephen Charnock, vol. 3, p. 345). When writing on "The Satisfaction of Christ" John Owen said: "This then is what we ascribe to the death of Christ, when we say that as a sacrifice we were reconciled to God or that He made reconciliation for us. Having made

God our Enemy by sin, Christ by His death turned away His anger, appeased His wrath, and brought us into favor again with God." How far Mr. Philpot digressed from the teaching of these men we must leave his friends to judge for themselves. But we appeal now to an infinitely higher authority, namely, the Word of God.

Nothing is more plainly taught in Scripture than that all men without exception are before actual regeneration in a like state and condition, and occupy *the same* standing or status before the Divine Law. Whatever distinguishing design God has purposed in Himself to afterward effect as a change in His own elect by the operations of His free grace, until those operations take place they are in precisely the same case as the non-elect. "We have before proved both Jews and Gentiles that they are all under sin"—guilty, beneath sentence of condemnation. "There is none righteous, no not one"—not one who has met the requirements of the Divine Law. "That every mouth may be stopped and all the world may become guilty before God"— that is, obnoxious to the Divine judgment. "There is no difference, for all have sinned and come short of the glory of God" (Rom. 3:9,10,19,22,23). The condition and position of every one relative to the Law is one and the same before his regeneration and justification, and the decree of God concerning any difference that is yet to be made in some in nowise modifies that solemn fact. This is one chief reason why the Gospel is to be preached to every creature.

The Scriptures are equally explicit in describing the effects and consequences of lying under God's wrath. Before conversion the elect equally with the non-elect are in a state of alienation from God (Eph. 4:18), and therefore none of their services or performances can be acceptable to Him. He will receive naught at their hands: "he who turneth away his ear from hearing the Law [an in the case with every unregenerate soul], even his prayer shall be abomination" (Prov. 28:9). They are all under the power of the Devil (Col. 1:13), who rules at his pleasure in the children of disobedience (Eph. 2:2). They are "without Christ...having no hope, and without God in the world" (Eph. 2:12). They are under the curse or condemning power of the Law (Gal. 3:13). They are "children in whom is no faith" (Deut. 32:20) and therefore utterly unable to do a single thing which can meet with God's approval, for "without *faith* it is impossible to please God" (Heb. 11:6). They are therefore "ready to perish" (Deut. 26:5).

"He that believeth not the Son shall not see life, but the wrath of God abideth on him" (John 3:36). What could be plainer than that? Is not an elect soul an *unbeliever* until the moment God is pleased to give faith unto him? Assuredly: then equally sure is it that he is also under the wrath of God so long as he remains an unbeliever. Not only so, but the Word of God solemnly declares that the elect are "by nature the children of wrath even as others" (Eph. 2:3), and no Papish priest can make them otherwise by sprinkling a few drops of "holy water" upon them. But "children of wrath" they could not be had they come into this world in a justified and reconciled state. No person can be in two contrary states at the same time: obnoxious to wrath, and yet God at peace with him; under the guilt of sin, and yet justified. Wrath is upon them from the womb (because of their sinning in Adam), and that wrath remains on them so long as they continue unbelievers. Though they were (in God's purpose) in Christ from eternity, that did not prevent them being in Adam in time, and suffering the penal effects of his fall.

There is an appointed hour in their earthly history when the elect pass from under the penal wrath of God and are justified by Him and reconciled to Him. Justification is an act of God, an act *in time*, an external act. It is an act of God in a way of judicial process—His declaration as supreme Judge. It is opposed to condemnation, the granting a full discharge therefrom (Rom. 8:33-35). It is not an internal decision in God, which always remains in Him, and effects no change in the *status* of the person justified; but is a temporal act of His power which makes a relative change in the person's standing before Him. It is upon the person's believing in Christ that God justifies him and that he passes from a state of guilt and alienation to one of righteousness and reconciliation: he that believeth on Him is not condemned (that is, he is justified), but he that believes not is condemned already (John 3:18). "He that believeth on Him that sent Me hath everlasting life [by regeneration], and shall not come into condemnation, but is *passed from* death unto life"—i.e. the life of justification (John 5:24).

If persons are justified in a proper sense by faith, then they are not justified from eternity, for we believe in time, not eternity. That we *are* justified by faith, is the doctrine of the Gospel, as is apparent from the whole current of God's Word. To cite but one verse: "Knowing that a man is not justified by the works of the Law, but by the faith of Jesus Christ [that is, by the faith of which He is the Object], even we have believed in Jesus Christ that we might be justified by the faith of Jesus Christ" (Gal. 2:16). That the apostle is there speaking of being justified in the sight of God, and not merely in the court of conscience, is beyond all doubt to any that will duly and fairly consider the scope of the Holy Spirit in that passage. Being justified by faith in Jesus Christ is there placed in opposition to being "justified by the works of the Law," which shows that something more fundamental than our own assurance is in view. "By the deeds of the Law shall no flesh be justified in His sight" (Rom. 3:19) makes it clear that none can obtain sentence of acquittal in the court of Divine adjudication by their own deeds. It is before God and not in the believer's consciousness that justification takes place.

"And the Scripture foreseeing that God would justify the heathen [Gentiles] through faith, preached before the Gospel unto Abraham, saying, In thee shall all nations be blessed" (Gal. 3:8). It is to be noted that there are two words here which lie directly against justification before believing: that God *would* justify the heathen—which must needs respect time to come; and "*shall* all nations be blessed" or justified—a "shall be" cannot be put for a thing already done. To this agrees "in the Lord *shall* all the seed of Israel be justified" (Isa. 45:25): by union with Christ through faith shall they be pronounced righteous. Again; "For as by one man's disobedience many *were* made sinners, so by the obedience of One *shall* many be made righteous" (Rom. 5:19). Upon which the Puritan William Bridge said, "It is remarkable that when the Holy Spirit speaks of Adam's sin condemning his posterity, He speaks of it as already past; but when He speaks of Christ's righteousness for the justification of sinners He changes to the future tense—as if He purposely designed to prevent our thoughts running after justification before believing."

What has been said above about the justification of God's elect upon their believing, holds equally good concerning His reconciliation to them when they throw down the weapons of their warfare against Him. Not only was their reconciliation decreed from everlasting but peace was actually made by Christ when He shed His blood (Col. 1:20); nevertheless, reconciliation itself is not effected until the Holy Spirit has so wrought within them as to bring about their conversion. This is conclusively established by the following passages: "For if, when we were enemies we were [judicially] reconciled to God by the death of His Son, much more being [actually] reconciled, we shall be saved by His life. And not only so, but we also joy in God through our Lord Jesus Christ, by whom we have *now* received the reconciliation" (Rom. 5:10,11)—that "now" would be meaningless if we were reconciled only in the eternal decree of God: what God decreed *for* us is here "received" *by* us! So again, "And you that were some-time alienated and enemies in your mind by wicked works, yet NOW hath He reconciled" (Col. 1:21).

It would obviate considerable misunderstanding if it were clearly perceived that the everlasting love of God toward His elect is mainly an act of His will, the exercise of His good pleasure, the purpose of His grace, whereby He determined to do certain things for them and instate them in glory in His own good time and way. But that purpose *effects nothing* for them nor puts anything into them—for *these* there must be external acts of God's power making good His purpose. From all eternity God determined to make this earth, yet six thousand years ago it existed not! He had ordained a final Day of Judgment but it has not yet actually arrived. God has purposed that in and through Christ He will justify and save certain persons, but they are not thereby justified because God has purposed it. It is true they *will be* in due time, but not before they have been enabled to believingly appropriate the atoning work of Christ in their behalf. We must therefore draw a line between the absolute certainty of the fruition of anything God has eternally purposed, and its actual accomplishment or bringing it to pass in His appointed time.

What has been pointed out in the last paragraph should make it easier for the reader to grasp that God's eternal love unto His own (which is an imminent act of His will or good pleasure, entirely within Himself) does not exempt them from coming beneath His anger (which is not any passion in God, but the outward visitation of His displeasure) because of sin; nor does it prevent their lying beneath the dispensations of His judicial wrath, until by some interpositions of His grace in time, when He actually changes their personal state (by regeneration) and legal status (by justification), freeing them from condemnation and instating them into His favor. In other words, much may occur in the interval between God's eternal purpose and the actual working out of the same—though nothing which can in anywise jeopardise His purpose, and nothing that was not foreseen when He framed it.

But it is objected by hyper-Calvinists, If the elect were not justified in Christ from all eternity, then when God pronounces them just there is an alteration in His will and love toward them. Not so. God is no more mutable because He justifies His people in time, than He is because He regenerates them in time. God is no more chargeable with change of purpose when He produces a change in a person's standing upon his believing, than He is when He produces a change in a person's condition by the miracle of the new birth. All the change is in the creature. Though God absolutely decrees, and that from everlasting, to regenerate, to justify and to reconcile all His chosen, with the alteration of His *governmental attitude* toward them which that involves, yet this argues not the least shadow of change in God Himself when at the predestinated hour that great change is effected. Do but distinguish between the grace decreeing and the power of God executing, and all is plain. "Whom He did predestinate, them He also called, and whom He called, them He also justified" (Rom. 8:30) —the calling and justifying are the *fruits* of His electing love.

But again it is objected, The elect are designated "sheep" before they believe (John 10:16), and in God's esteem they are then in a justified state. Answer: they are called "sheep" according to the immutability of the Divine decree, which cannot be frustrated, and on that account God calls "things which be not as though they were" (Rom. 4:17), nevertheless, that verse affirms they "be not"—that is, they have no actual existence. They are "sheep" in the purpose of God, but not so as touching *the accomplishment* of the same until they be regenerated. Paul was a sheep in the decree of God even when he was wolf-like in preying upon the flock of Christ. Surely none will say he was actually a sheep whilst he was "breathing out threatenings and slaughters against the disciples of the Lord" (Acts 9:1). From the decree of God we may safely conclude the certainty of its accomplishment, but to argue that a thing is *actually* accomplished because Divinely foreordained is a most foolish and dangerous way of reasoning.

The love of God's purpose and good pleasure has not the least inconsistency with those hindrances to the peace and friendship of God which sin has interposed, for though the holiness of His Law, the righteousness of His government and the veracity of His Word, stood in the way of His taking a *sinner* into friendship and fellowship with Himself, until full satisfaction has been made to His broken Law and insulted Majesty; nevertheless His love determined and His wisdom devised a way whereby His sovereign good will should recover His people, and that, without sullying the Divine character to the slightest degree, yea, in magnifying those attributes which sin had affronted. God's love has proven efficacious by the means He devised "that His banished be not expelled from Him" (2 Sam. 14:14).

From all that has been pointed out above it should be quite evident that this doctrine of reconciliation does not teach that God loved and hated His elect at the same time and in the same respect. He loved them in respect of the free purpose of His sovereign will; but His wrath was upon them in respect of His violated Law and provoked justice by their sin. But His love gave Christ to satisfy for their sins and to redeem them from the curse of the Law, and in due time He sends His Spirit to regenerate them, which lays the foundation for their conversion and restoration to Him.

The following distinctions must, then, be kept steadily in mind: 1. Between God's looking upon His elect in the purpose of His grace and as under the sentence of His Law: though the elect are born under the dispensation of His wrath, yet it is not executed upon them personally. 2. Between there being no change in God and a change in His outward dealings with us. 3. Between God's purpose concerning His elect in eternity and the accomplishment of that purpose in a time state. 4. Between God's viewing the elect in Christ their Covenant-Head and as the depraved descendents of fallen Adam: in the one cause, as "His dear children" in the other; as being "by nature the children of wrath." 5. Between God's unchanging love for us as our Father, and His official displeasure as our moral Governor and Judge. This distinction is illustrated in the case of Christ: He was the Beloved of the Father and never ceased to be so, yet Divine wrath was visited upon Him at the cross. He was dealt with not as the Son (as such) but as the Surety of His guilty people, by the Father, not as such, but as the supreme Judge. —AWP

SPIRITUAL GROWTH OR CHRISTIAN PROGRESS
3b. Its Necessity

In reply to what was said in our last it may be asked, if the regeneration of Christians be complete, if their essential sanctification be effected, if they are already fitted for Heaven, then why does God still leave them here on earth? why not take them to His own immediate presence as soon as they be born again? Our first answer is, there is no "if" about it. Scripture distinctly and expressly affirms that even now believers are "complete in Christ" (Col. 2:10), that He has "perfected forever them that are sanctified" (Heb. 10:14), that they are "made meet for the inheritance of the saints in light" (Col. 1:12), and more than "complete," "perfect" and "meet" none will ever be. As to why God—generally, though not always!—leaves the babe in Christ in this world for a longer or shorter period: even if no satisfactory reason could be suggested that would not invalidate to the slightest degree what has been demonstrated, for when any truth is clearly established a hundred objections cannot set it aside. However, while we do not pretend to fathom the mind of God, the following consequences are more or less obvious.

By leaving His people here for a season, opportunity is given for: 1. God to manifest His keeping power: not only in a hostile world, but sin still indwelling believers. 2. To demonstrate the sufficiency of His grace: supporting them in their weakness. 3. To maintain a witness for Himself in a scene which lieth in the Wicked One. 4. To exhibit His faithfulness in supplying all their need in the wilderness before they reach Canaan. 5. To display His manifold wisdom unto angels: 1 Corinthians 4:9; Ephesians 3:10. 6. To act as "salt" in preserving the race from moral suicide: by the purifying and restraining influence they exert. 7. To make evident the reality of their faith: trusting Him in sharpest trials and darkest dispensations. 8. To give them an occasion to glorify Him in the place where they dishonored Him. 9. To preach the Gospel to those of His elect yet in unbelief. 10. To afford proof they will serve Him amid the most disadvantageous circumstances. 11. To deepen their appreciation of what He has prepared for them. 12. To have fellowship with Christ, who endured the cross before He was crowned with glory and honor.

Before showing why Christian progress is necessary, let us remind the reader once more of the double signification of the term "Christian," namely, "an anointed one" and "a disciple of Christ," and how this supplies the principal key to the subject before us, intimating its *twofoldness*. His "anointing" with the Holy Spirit is an act of God, wherein he is entirely passive, but his becoming a "disciple of Christ" is a voluntary act of his own, wherein he surrenders to Christ's Lordship and resolves to be ruled by His scepter. Only as this is duly borne in mind shall we be preserved from error on either side, as we pass from one aspect of our theme to another. As the double meaning of the name "Christian" points to both the Divine operations and human activity, so in the Christian's progress we must keep before us the exercise of God's sovereignty and the discharge of our responsibility. Thus from one angle growth is neither necessary nor possible, from another it is both desirable and requisite. It is from this second angle we are now going to view the Christian, setting forth his obligations therein.

Let us illustrate what has been said above on the twofoldness of this truth by a few simple comments on a well-known verse: "So teach us to number our days that we may apply our hearts unto Wisdom" (Ps. 90:12). First, this implies that in our fallen condition we are wayward at heart, prone to follow a course of folly; and such is our present state by nature. Second, it implies the Lord's people have had a discovery made to them of their woeful case, and are conscious of their sinful inability to correct the same; which is the experience of all the regenerate. Third, it signifies an owning of this humiliating truth, a crying to God for enablement. They beg to be "taught," which means far more than to be shown how, namely, to be "*so* taught" as to be actually empowered. In other words, it is a prayer for enabling grace. Fourth, it expresses the end in view: "that *we* may apply our hearts unto Wisdom"—perform our duty, discharge our obligations, conduct ourselves as "Wisdom's children." Grace is to be improved, turned to good account, traded with.

We all know what is meant by a person's "applying his *mind*" to his studies, namely, that he gathers in his wandering thoughts, focuses his attention on the subject before him, concentrates thereon. Equally evident is a person's "applying his *hand*" to a piece of manual labor, namely, that he get down to business, set himself to the work before him, earnestly endeavor to make a good job of it. In either case there is an implication: in the former that he has been given a sound mind, in the latter that he possesses a healthy body. And in connection with both cases it is universally acknowledged that the one *ought* to so employ his mind and the other his bodily strength. Equally obvious should be the meaning of and the obligation to "apply our *hearts* unto Wisdom": that is, diligently, fervently, earnestly make Wisdom our quest and walk in her ways. Since God has given a "new heart" at regeneration, it is to be thus employed. If He has quickened us into newness of life then we ought to grow in grace. If He has made us new creatures in Christ we are to progress as Christians.

Because this article will be read by such widely-different classes of readers and we are anxious to help all, we must consider here the objection which will be made by hyper-Calvinists, for the removal of which we quote the renowned John Owen. "It will be said that if not only the beginning of grace, sanctification, and holiness be *from God*, but the carrying of it on and the increase of it also be from Him, and not only so in general, but that all the actings of grace, and every act of it, be an immediate effect of the Holy Spirit, then what need is there that *we* should take any pains in this thing ourselves, or use our own endeavors to grow in grace and holiness as we are commanded. If God worketh all Himself in us, and without His effectual operation in us we can do nothing, there is no place left for our diligence, duty, or obedience.

"Answer. 1. This objection we must expect to meet withal at every turn. Men will not believe there is a consistency between God's effectual grace and our diligent obedience; that is, they will not *believe* what is plainly, clearly, distinctly, revealed in the Scripture, and which is suited unto the experience of all that truly believe, because they cannot, it may be, comprehend it within the compass of carnal reason. 2. Let the apostle answer this objection for this once: 'His Divine power hath given unto us all things that pertain unto life and godliness, through the knowledge of Him that hath called us to glory and virtue; whereby are given unto us exceeding great and precious promises, that by these ye might be partakers of the Divine nature, having escaped the corruption that is in the world through lust' (2 Peter 1:3,4). If all things that pertain unto life and godliness, among which doubtless is the preservation and increase of grace, be given unto us by the power of God; if from Him we receive that Divine nature, by virtue whereof our corruptions are subdued, then I pray what need is there of any endeavors of our own? The whole work of sanctification is wrought in us, it seems and that by the power of God: we therefore, may let it alone and leave it unto Him whose it is, whilst we are negligent, secure and at ease. Nay says the apostle, this is not *the use* which the grace of God is to be put unto. The consideration of it is, or ought to be, the principal motive and encouragement unto all diligence for the increase of holiness in us. For so he adds immediately: 'But also for this cause' [Greek] or because of the gracious operations of the Divine power in us; 'giving all diligence, add to your faith virtue,' etc. (v. 5).

"These objectors and this apostle were very diversely minded in these matters: what they make an insuperable discouragement unto diligence in obedience, that he makes the greatest motive and encouragement thereunto. 3. I say, from this consideration it will unavoidably follow, that we ought continually to wait and depend on God for supplies of His Spirit and grace without which we can do nothing: that God is more the Author by His grace of the good we do than we are ourselves (not I, but the grace of God that was with me): that we ought to be careful that by our negligences and sins we provoke not the Holy Spirit to withhold His aids and assistances, and so to leave us to ourselves, in which condition we can do nothing that is spiritually good: these things, I say, will unavoidably follow on the doctrine before declared; and if any one be offended at them it is not in our power to render them relief."

Coming now more directly to the *needs-be* for spiritual growth or Christian progress. This is not optional but obligatory, for we are expressly bidden to "Grow in grace and in the knowledge of our Lord and Saviour Jesus Christ" (2 Peter 3:18)— grow from infancy to the vigor of youth, and from the zeal of youth to the wisdom of maturity. And again, to be "building up yourselves on your most holy faith" (Jude 20). It is not sufficient to be grounded and established in the faith, for we must grow more and more therein. At conversion we take upon us the yoke of Christ, and then His word is "learn of Me," which is to be a lifelong experience. In becoming Christ's disciples we do but enter His school: not remain in the kindergarten but to progress under His tuition. "A wise man will hear and increase learning" (Prov. 1:5), and seek to make good use of that learning. The believer has not yet reached Heaven: he is on the way, journeying thither, fleeing from the city of destruction. That is why the Christian life is so often likened unto a *race*, and the believer unto a runner: "forgetting those things which are behind and reaching forth unto those things which are before, I press toward the mark for the prize" (Phil. 3:13,14).

1. Only thus is the Triune God glorified. This is so obvious that it really needs no arguing. It brings no glory to God that His children should be dwarfs. As sunshine and rain are sent for the nourishment and fructification of vegetation, so the means of grace are provided that we may increase in our spiritual stature. "As new born babes, desire the sincere milk of the Word that ye may grow thereby" (1 Peter 2:2)—not only in the intellectual knowledge of it, but in a practical conformity thereunto. This should be our chief concern and be made our principal business: to become better acquainted with God, to have the heart more occupied with and affected by His perfections, to seek after a fuller knowledge of His will, to regulate our conduct thereby, and thus "show forth the praises of Him who hath

called us out of darkness into his marvelous light" (1 Peter 2:9). The more we evidence our sonship, the more we conduct ourselves as becometh the children of God before a perverse generation, the more do we honor Him who has set His love upon us.

That our spiritual growth and progress *is* glorifying unto God appears plainly from the prayers of the apostles, for none were more concerned about His glory than they were, and nothing occupied so prominent a place in their intercession as this. As we hope to allude to this again in later articles, one or two quotations must here suffice. For the Ephesians Paul prayed, "that ye might be filled with all the fulness of God" (3:19). For the Philippians "that your love may abound yet more and more, in knowledge and in all judgment...being filled with the fruits of righteousness" (1:9-11). For the Colossians, "that ye might walk worthy of the Lord unto all pleasing, being fruitful in every good work and increasing in the knowledge of God" (1:10,11). From which we learn that it is our privilege and duty to obtain more spiritual views of the Divine perfections, begetting in us an increasing holy delight in Him, making our walk more acceptable. There should be a growing acquaintance with the excellency of Christ, advancing in our love of Him, and the more lively exercises of our graces.

2. Only thus do we give proof of our regeneration. "Herein is My Father glorified, that ye bear much fruit: *so* shall ye be My disciples" (John 15:8). That does not mean we become the disciples of Christ as a result of our fruitfulness, but that we make manifest we *are* His by our fruitbearing. They who bear no fruit have no vital union with Christ, and like the barren fig tree, are under His curse. Very solemn is this, and by such a criterion each of us should measure himself. That which is brought forth by the Christian is not to he restricted unto what, in many circles, is called "service" or "personal work," but has reference to that which issues from the exercise of all the spiritual graces. Thus: "Love your enemies, bless them that curse you, do good to them that hate you and pray for them which despitefully use you and persecute you; that ye may be the children of your Father which is in heaven" (Matt. 5:44,45), that is, that you may *make it evident* to yourself and fellows that you have been made partaker of the Divine nature.

"Now the works of the flesh are manifest, which are these etc. ...But the fruit of the spirit is love, joy, peace, longsuffering, goodness, gentleness, faith, meekness, temperance" (Gal. 5:19,22,23). The reference is not directly to what the Holy Spirit produces, but rather to that which is borne of the "spirit" or new nature of which He is the Author (John 15:16). This is evident from its being set over against the "works of the flesh" or old nature. It is by means of this "fruit," these lovely graces, that the regenerate make manifest the presence of a super-natural principle within them. The more such "fruit" abounds, the clearer our evidence that we have been born again. The total absence of such fruit would prove our profession to be an empty one. It has often been pointed out by others that what issues from the flesh are designated "works," for a machine can produce such; but that which the "spirit" yields is *living* "fruit" in contrast from "dead works" (Heb. 6:1; 9:14). Thus, fruit-bearing is necessary in order to evidence the new birth.

3. Only thus do we certify that we have been made partakers of an effectual call and are among the chosen of God. "Brethren, give diligence to make your calling and

election sure" (2 Peter 1:10) is the Divine exhortation—one which has puzzled many. Yet it should not: it is not to secure it Godward (which is impossible), but make it more certain to yourselves and your brethren. And how is this to be accomplished? Why, by acquiring clearer and fuller evidence of the same: by spiritual growth, for growth is the proof that life is present. This interpretation is definitely established by the context. After enumerating the bestowments of Divine grace (vv. 3,4), the apostle says, now here is your responsibility: "And besides this, giving all diligence, add to your faith [by bringing it into exercise] virtue; and to virtue, knowledge; and to knowledge, temperance; and to temperance, patience; and to patience, brotherly kindness; and to brotherly kindness, love" (vv. 5-7). Faith itself is ever to be operative, but according to different occasions and in their seasons let each of your graces be exercised, and in proportion as they are, the life of holiness is furthered in the soul and there is a proportionate spiritual growth—cf. Colossians 3:12, 13.

4. Only thus do we adorn the doctrine we profess (Titus 2:10). The Truth we claim to have received into our hearts is "the doctrine which is according to godliness" (1 Tim. 6:3), and therefore the more our daily lives be conformed thereto, the clearer proof do we give that our character and conduct is regulated by *Heavenly* principles. It is by our fruits we are known (Matt. 7:16), for "every good tree bringeth forth good fruit." Thus, it is only by our being "fruitful in every good work" (Col. 1:10) that we make it manifest that we are the "trees of the Lord" (Ps. 104:16). "Now are ye light in the Lord, walk as children of light" (Eph. 5:8). It is not the character of our walk which qualifies us to become the children of light, but which demonstrates that we are such. Because we are the children of Him who is light (1 John 1:5) we must shun the darkness. If we have been "sanctified in Christ Jesus" (1 Cor. 1:2) then only that should proceed from us which "becometh saints" (Eph. 5:3). The more we progress in godliness, the more we adorn our profession.

5. Only thus do we experience more genuine assurance. Peace becomes more stable and joy abounds in proportion as we grow in grace and in the knowledge of our Lord and Saviour Jesus Christ, and become more conformed practically to His holy image. It is because so many become slack in using the means of grace and are so little exercised about growing up into Christ "in all things" (Eph. 4:15) that doubts and fears possess their hearts. If they do not "give all diligence to add to their faith" (2 Peter 1:5) by cultivating their several graces, they must not be surprised if they are far from being "sure" of their Divine calling and election. It is "the diligent soul" and not the dilatory, who "shall be made fat" (Prov. 13:4). It is the one who makes conscience of obedience and keeps Christ's commandments who is favored with love-tokens from Him (John 14:21). There is an inseparable connection between our being "led [forward] by the Spirit of God"—which intimates our voluntary occurrence—and His "bearing witness with our spirit" (Rom. 8:14,16).

6. Only thus are we preserved from grievous backsliding. In view of much that has been said above this should be quite obvious. The very term "backsliding" denotes failure to make progress and go forward. Peter's denial of Christ in the high priest's palace was preceded by his following Him "afar off" (Matt. 26:58), and that has been recorded for our learning and warning. The same principle is illustrated again in connection with the awful fall of David. Though it was "at the time when kings go forth to battle," he was selfishly and lazily taking his ease, and while so lax succumbed to temptation (2 Sam. 11:1,2).

Unless we "follow on to know the Lord" and learn to make use of the armor which He has provided, we shall easily be overcome by the Enemy. Only as our hearts are kept healthy and our affection set upon things above shall we be impervious to the attractions of this world. We cannot he stationary: if we do not grow, we shall decline.

7. Only thus shall we preserve the Cause of Christ from reproach. The backsliding of His people makes His enemies to blaspheme—how many have taken occasion to do so from the sad case of David! When the world sees us halting, it is gratified, being bolstered up in their idea that godliness is but a pose, a sham. Because of this, among other reasons, Christians are bidden to "be blameless and harmless, the sons of God, without rebuke in the midst of a crooked and perverse nation, among whom ye shine as lights in the world" (Phil. 2:15). If we go backward instead of forward—and we *must* do one or the other—then we greatly dishonor the name of Christ and fill His foes with unholy glee. Rather is it "the will of God that with well-doing we may put to silence the ignorance of foolish men" (1 Peter 2:15). The longer they remain in this world, the more apparent should be the contrast between the children of light and those who are the subjects of the Prince of darkness. Very necessary then, from many considerations, is our growth in grace. —AWP

(continued from back page)

Christendom, however much they may yet increase in their severity, yet "we know that all things work together for good to them that love God" (Rom. 8:28).

"Surely I know that *it shall be well* with them that fear God." This is the knowledge of faith and not of reason. It is the assurance that fills the soul of him who rests with implicit confidence on the Divine promises. God has said to His covenant people "I will not turn away from them to do them good" (Jer. 32:40). He has not, [even] in the darkest hours of history. When His wrath burst upon the antediluvians, shelter was provided for Noah and his family in the ark. When the long-protracted drought was upon Samaria with its attendant famine, the Lord provided for Elijah by the brook Kerith, and later in the home of the Zarephath widow. When Jezebel determined to stamp out the worship of Jehovah and slew His prophets, one hundred of them were hid in caves and fed with bread and water (1 Kings 18:13). When the Dragon "persecuted the woman" which brought forth the Man child, "a place was provided for her in the wilderness." And when the Serpent sought to destroy her with a flood of water, "the earth helped" her by opening its mouth and swallowing up the flood (Rev. 12:13-16).

But let due attention be paid to the description here given of those to whom this assurance belongs: "I know that it shall be well with them that *fear God*, which fear before Him." The added clause renders it most emphatic, that there may be no mistaking their identification. It is not merely those who make a religious profession and associate themselves with His saints, but only the ones who genuinely fear God. To "fear God" is to have a reverential awe of His authority, a filial veneration of His majesty, a heart realization of His omniscience and omnipresence, a soul subjection to His scepter. Those who fear God are regulated by His revealed will, have respect to His commandments, are afraid of displeasing Him. Those who fear God will not trifle with Him or deliberately act the part of hypocrites. Concerning them, and them only may it be said, "*Surely* I know it shall be well with them"—well for time and for eternity. —AWP

. *(continued on proceeding page)*

(continued from front page)

Bread of life upon the human "waters" (see Rev. 17:15), particularly "*thy Bread*"—those portions you have personally received from God and which have proved a blessing to your own soul—the sure promise is "thou shalt find it again after many days." Therefore be not slack or exclusive but "give a portion to seven and also to eight," for if you prayerfully seek opportunities and carefully observe the openings Providence makes you will be brought into touch with hungry souls. There is many a starved sheep wandering about today who will deeply appreciate the ministrations of one of Christ's shepherds.

Not only so, but "for thou knowest not what evil shall be upon the earth" supplies a further incentive to fidelity. Things are indeed bad enough today, but the shrewdest is quite incapable of foreseeing how much worse they may become. When the restraining hand of God is removed, lawlessness abounds with increasing rapidity and intensity. When the sluice-gates are open wickedness floods the whole land, carrying everything before it. When God speaks in judgment to a nation and it refuses to heed His voice His judgments increase in severity, as did His plagues upon Egypt of old. Therefore it is the part of wisdom to redeem the time and make the most of the privileges which are ours to-day. Work while it is called day, for the night cometh when no man can work (John 9:4). Since we have no guarantee about the future "upon the earth" utilise to the full the present.

"Thou knowest not what evil shall be upon the earth." A generation ago there were men with spiritual discernment who seeing the trend of things then, gave warning that "evil men and seducers shall wax worse and worse." Those with anointed eyes perceived the blight which had attacked the churches, the decay of vital godliness and family worship, the children growing up without any religious and little moral instructions. They knew that such an awful "falling away" must result in fearful consequences. Even statesmen and unregenerate leaders with natural acumen had dark forebodings of what lay ahead for the world: "Men's hearts failing them for fear and for looking after those things which are coming on the earth" (Luke 21:26). But who among the most foreseeing, or even the most pessimistic, would have believed that things should come to the awful pass they now have!—the Spirit largely withdrawn, morality almost disappeared, the lower classes getting things more and more under their control, the whole world in a state of chaos, the vials of God's wrath being poured out on the earth. And the end is not yet, not has the worst by any means been reached. The next generation will reap a still more horrible harvest from what is now being sown.

Black indeed is the outlook for this poor world. But over against this "thou *knowest not* what evil shall be upon the earth," let us place "Yet surely *I know* that it shall be well with them that fear God" (Eccl. 8:12). Glorious contrast! Blessed assurance! No matter what may yet come "upon the earth" it shall not harm the saints. Though it may overturn their carnal plans and unpleasantly affect their circumstances, yet it shall not injure their souls. Rather will such temporal afflictions be sanctified unto them, to the drawing of their affections more and more unto things above, thereby causing them to regard more lightly and hold more loosely the things that perish. The plagues which God sent upon Egypt eventuated in the deliverance of His people from the house of bondage. The casting of the Hebrews into Babylon's furnace issued in the burning off of their bonds. However long protracted the Divine judgments upon an apostate

(Continued on preceding page)

VOL. XXIII.   MAY, 1944.   NO. 5

STUDIES in the SCRIPTURES

" Search the Scriptures."   John 5:39.

*Publisher and Editor—*ARTHUR W. PINK,
27 Lewis Street,
Stornoway, Isle of Lewis,
Scotland.

THE PATH OF DUTY
Part A

Occasionally we receive a letter from one of our readers who is confronted with what he regards as a perplexing situation, involving perhaps the stirring of his nest and a change of circumstances, expressing himself as very concerned to know what is "God's will" for him. Our first reaction is to wonder how far the inquirer has been *accustomed* to make conscience of pleasing God. If the inquirer (or the reader) is only exercised about the Divine will when some pressing situation or emergency faces him, it is a bad sign, betraying a sad state of soul and making it doubtful whether such an one has been truly converted. Just as being very religious on the Sabbath but thoroughly worldly through the week is to have "a form of godliness" but "denying the power thereof" (2 Tim. 3:5), so for me to be very solicitous about ascertaining and performing the will of God when some crises arises but to have little regard what He has appointed during the general course of my life, is to place a big question-mark against the genuineness of my Christian profession.

The Most High is not at our beck and call, to be made use of only when we are in difficulty. Those who are indifferent to His honour and glory while things are going smoothly and pleasantly for them, are not likely to receive light and help from Him when they feel disposed to make an accommodation of Him in the evil day. Scripture is too plain upon this matter to be misunderstood: "he that turneth away his ear from hearing the Law, even his prayer shall be abomination" (Prov. 28:9). Of the hypocrite it is said "will God hear his cry when trouble cometh upon him" (Job 27:9). No, He certainly will not. "Because I have called, and ye refused; I have stretched out My hand, and no man regarded; but ye have set at nought all My counsel…I also will laugh at your calamity…then shall they call upon Me, but I will not answer…For that they hated knowledge and did not choose the fear of the Lord…Therefore shall they eat of the fruit of [having] their own way" (Prov. 1:24-31). Compare Micah 3:4; Zechariah 7:13.

But in sharp contrast from the class mentioned above there are those who *have sought* to walk with God and avoid those things which are displeasing to Him, and when some difficulty arises, a parting of the ways suddenly confronts them, an important decision has to be made, they are anxious to know "what is God's will" for them.

(continued on back page)

IMPORTANT NOTICES

Please advise promptly of change in address, otherwise copies will be lost in the mails.

We are glad to send a sample copy to any of your friends whom you believe would be interested in this publication.

This magazine is published as "a work of faith and labour of love," the editor and his wife gladly giving their services free. There is no regular subscription price, as we do not wish the poor of the flock to be deprived. This does not mean that those looking for something for nothing may "help themselves." Those getting this Magazine, who are financially able and who receive spiritual help from its pages, are expected to gladly contribute towards its expenses; otherwise, their names are dropped from our lists.

Will those forwarding International Money Orders please have them made out to us at Stornoway, Isle of Lewis, Scotland. Checks (Cheques-Eng.) made out on U.S.A. Banks are not negotiable here, so please do not send them.

CONTENTS

THE PRAYERS OF THE APOSTLES
5. Romans 15:13

In his preceding prayer the apostle had made request that the God of patience and consolation would grant the saints at Rome to be "like-minded one toward another, according to Christ Jesus" (v. 5) so that amity and concord might prevail among them. He had followed this by reminding them that the Redeemer's mission embraced not only the Jews but also the Gentiles: that the eternal purpose of God respected an elect portion from both parts of the human race (vv. 8-9). In support of which statement he made quotation of no less than four Old Testament passages, taken respectively from the Law, the Psalms, and the Prophets (which were the principal sections into which the Divine oracles were divided, see Luke 24:44), each of which foretold that the Gentiles would take their place alongside of the Jews in worshiping the Lord. Thus the Hebrew Christians need have no hesitation in welcoming believing Gentiles into their midst. The apostle then concluded this section of his epistle, by again supplicating the Throne of grace on their behalf, thereby evidencing his deep solicitude for them, and intimating that God alone could impart the grace necessary for obedience to the injunctions given them.

Vital instruction is to be obtained by attending closely to the connection between the verse which is to be before us and those which immediately precede. In the context Paul had cited a number of Old Testament passages which announced the salvation of the Gentiles and their union with believing Jews. Now the prophecies of Scripture are to be viewed in a threefold manner. First, as proofs of their Divine inspiration, demonstrating as they do the omniscience of their Author in unerringly forecasting things to come. Second, as so many revelations of the will of God, announcements of what He has eternally decreed, and which must therefore come to pass. Third, as possessing a moral and practical bearing upon us: where they are predictions of judgment, they are so many *threatenings* and therefore warnings of the objects to be avoided and the evils to be shunned—as the foreannounced destruction of the Papacy bids us have nought to do with that detestable system; but where they consist of predictions of Divine blessing, they are so many *promises* for faith to lay hold of and for hope to anticipate before their actual fulfillment. It is in this third respect Paul is viewing them.

Here the apostle shows us what *use* we are to make of the Divine promises, namely, turn them into believing prayer, requesting God to make them good. As God draws near to us in promise, it is our privilege to draw near unto Him in petition. Those prophecies were so many infallible assurances that God intended to show mercy unto the Gentiles; no sooner had Paul quoted them than he bowed his knees before their Giver, thereby teaching the Roman saints, and us, how to turn the promises to practical account, instructing them *what* to ask for. In like manner when he would have the Ephesian saints beg God to enlighten their understandings, that they might know the great things of the Gospel, he set them an example by praying for that very thing (1:17,18). So here; it was as though he said "Thou hast promised that the Gentiles should hope in Thee [v. 12]. Thou art 'the God of hope,' then graciously work in these saints so that they 'may abound in hope through the power of the Holy Spirit,' and that they too may from my example be constrained to supplicate Thee and plead this promise to the same end for the attainment of this very blessing."

That the reader may have a more definite view of the connection we will now quote the verse before our prayer: "And again, Isaiah saith, There shall be a Root of Jesse and He that shall rise to reign over the Gentiles: in Him shall the Gentiles trust." That is taken from one of the great Messianic prophecies, recorded in Isaiah 11. Whatever may or may not be its ultimate accomplishment Paul was moved to make known unto us that that prediction was even then receiving fulfillment. Literally the Greek reads, "in Him shall the Gentiles *hope*," and it is thus rendered correctly in the Revised Version. Though intimately connected, as Hebrews 11:1 shows, there is a real difference between faith and hope. Faith is more comprehensive in its range, for it believes all that God has said concerning the past, present, and future— the threatenings as well as the promises; but hope looks solely to a *future good*. Faith has to do with the *Word* promising, hope is engaged with the *thing* promised. Faith is a believing that God will do as He has said, hope is a confident looking forward to the fulfillment of the promise.

Having sought to point out the instructive connection between the apostle's prayer and the verses immediately preceding, a word now on its *remoter context*. This prayer concludes that section of the epistle begun at 14:1, in which the apostle had labored to remove what threatened to produce an unhappy division in the company of the Roman saints. Without taking sides and expressly declaring which was in the wrong, he had laid down broad and simple principles for each to act upon, so that if their conduct was regulated thereby, Christian love and Christian liberty would alike be conserved. He set before them the example of their Master, and then showed that both Jews and Gentiles were given equal place in the Word of Prophecy. Now, to borrow the lovely language of Moule, "He clasps them impartially to his own heart in this precious and pregnant benediction, beseeching for both sides, and for all their individuals, a wonderful fullness of those blessings, in which most speedily and most surely, the spirit of their strife would expire." The closer a company of Christians are drawn to their Lord, the closer they are drawn to one another.

"Now the God of hope fill you with all joy and peace in believing, that ye may abound in hope, through the power of the Holy Spirit." The "God of hope" is both the Object and the Author of hope. He is the One who has prepared the blessings which are to be the objects of our hope, who has set them before us in the Gospel, and who by the power of the Spirit enables us to understand and believe the Gospel, which awakens motives and sets in action principles that ensure hope. The burden of Paul's prayer was that the saints might abound in this spiritual grace, and therefore he addressed the Deity accordingly. As Matthew Henry points out, "It is good in prayer to fasten upon those names, titles and attributes of God which are most suitable to the errand we come upon and will best serve to encouragement concerning it." A further reason why the apostle thus addressed the Deity appears from the preceding verse, where it was announced of the Lord, "in Him shall the Gentiles hope." More literally our verse reads, "Now the God of that [or 'the'] hope"—the One who is the Inspirer of all expectations of blessing.

This expression "the God of [that] hope" had special pertinency and peculiar suitability unto the *Gentiles*—who are mentioned by name no less than four times in the verses immediately preceding. Its force is the more apparent if we consider it in the light of Ephesians 2:11,12, where Gentile believers are reminded that in time past they "were without Christ [devoid of any claim upon Him], being alienated from the commonwealth of Israel and strangers from the covenants of promise, having *no hope* and without God in the world"—without any knowledge of Him, without a written revelation from Him. But the incarnation of Christ had radically altered this. The grand design of His mission was not restricted to Palestine but was worldwide, for He shed His atoning blood for sinners out of all peoples and tribes; and upon the triumphant conclusion of His mission commissioned His servants to preach the Gospel to all nations. Hence the apostle had reminded the Roman saints that God said, "rejoice ye Gentiles with His people." He had now become *to them* "the God of hope."

Unless God had revealed Himself in the Word of Truth we should be without any foundation of hope, but the Scriptures are windows of hope to us. This is evident from the 4th verse of our chapter: "For whatsoever things were written aforetime were written for our learning, that we through patience and comfort of the Scriptures might have *hope.*" Thus the God of hope is revealed in His living oracles with the design of inspiring hope. If we would be filled with faith, joy, and peace, it must be by believing what is presented to us in Holy Writ. Before we have any true inward grounds of hope, God Himself as revealed in the Bible must be our confidence. It was by searching it that the apostle discovered there was hope for the Gentiles, and so may the most burdened heart find solid consolation therein if he will search and believe its contents. Every Divine promise is calculated to inspire the believer with hope. Therein is to be found a sure foundation to rest upon.

Let us now consider the petition the apostle here presented unto the God of hope: it was that He would "fill you with all joy and peace in believing." This is to be considered first in its local bearing. The phrase "in believing" looks back to those blessed portions of the Old Testament which had just been quoted: it was a prayer that God would graciously enable those saints to lay hold of such promises and conduct themselves in harmony therewith. "In the fulfillment of that promise [v. 12] Christ came, and preached salvation to those who were near and to those who were afar off (Eph.

2:17). As both classes had been thus kindly received by the condescending Savior and united into one community, they should receive and love each other as brethren, laying aside all censoriousness and contempt, neither judging nor despising one another" (C. Hodge). In other words, the apostle longed that both alike should be occupied with Christ.

Let faith and hope be duly operative, and joy and peace would displace discord and strife. "Let that prayer be granted, in its pure depth and height, and how could the 'weak brother' look with quite his old anxiety on the problems suggested by the dishes at a meal and by the dates of the Rabbinic calendar? And could 'the strong' bear any longer to lose his joy in God by an assertion, full of self, of his own insight and liberty? Profoundly happy and at rest in the Lord, whom they embrace by faith as their Righteousness and Life, and whom they anticipated in hope as their coming Glory; filled through their whole consciousness by the indwelling Spirit with a new insight into Christ, they would fall into each other's embrace, in Him. They would be much more ready when they met to speak 'concerning the King,' than to begin a new stage of their not very elevating discussion. How many a church controversy now as then, would die of inanition, leaving room for living truth, if the disputants could only gravitate, as to their always most beloved theme, to the praises and glories of their redeeming Lord Himself!" (H. Moule).

As our Lord's prayer in John 17 was not confined to His then disciples but reached forward to "them also which should believe" (v. 20), so this prayer of Paul's is suited to all the children of God. "The God of hope fill you with all joy and peace in believing." Let it be duly noted that Paul did not hesitate *to ask for* these particular blessings. We make that remark because we very much fear that some of our readers are well-nigh afraid to cry unto God for such things: but they need not be. Fullness of spiritual joy does not unfit its possessor to live his life in this world, nor does fullness of peace produce presumption and carnal security. If such experiences were "dangerous," as Satan would fain have us conclude, the apostle would not have sought them on behalf of his fellow Christians. From his making request for these very blessings we learn they are eminently *desirable* and furnished warrant for us to supplicate for the same, both for ourselves and our brethren.

The example which the apostle has here set before us evidences that it is not only desirable for Christians to be filled with joy and peace, but that such a delightful experience is *attainable*. "We *may* be filled with joy and peace in believing, and may abound in hope. There is no reason why we should hang our heads and live in perpetual doubt. We may not only be somewhat comforted, but we may be full of joy; we may not only have occasional quiet, but we may dwell in peace, and delight ourselves in the abundance of it. These great privileges are attainable or the apostle would not have made them the subject of prayer…The sweetest delights are still grown in Zion's gardens, and are to be enjoyed by us; and shall they be within our reach and not be grasped? Shall a life of joy and peace be attainable, and shall we miss it through unbelief? God forbid. Let us as believers resolve that whatsoever of privilege is to be enjoyed we *will* enjoy it" (C. H. Spurgeon).

Once again we appeal to the context, for clear proof is found there that it *is* God's revealed will for His saints to be a *rejoicing* people. In verse 10 the apostle cites a verse from the Old Testament which says, "Rejoice ye Gentiles with His people." Israel had been given no monopoly of joy: those whom God had purposed to call from out the Nations would also share therein. If there was joy for Israel when redeemed from the house of bondage and led through the Red Sea, much more so is there for those delivered from the power of Satan and translated into the kingdom of God's dear Son. Observe that the passage quoted is not in the form of a promise, but is a specific precept: regenerated Gentiles are expressly bidden *to* "rejoice." Nor did the apostle stop there. As though anticipating our slowness to enter into our privileges, he added, "And again, Praise the Lord, all ye Gentiles" (v. 11)—not merely the most eminent among them but all alike. Where there is praise there is joy, for joy is a component part of it. Thus one who professes to be a Christian and at the same time complains that he is devoid of joy and peace, acknowledges that he is failing to obey these precepts.

"The God of hope fill you with all joy and peace" intimates three things. First, that there are degrees of these blessings. A few Christians there are who enjoy them fully, but the great majority (to their shame) experience but a taste thereof. Each of us should look to God for the fullest communication of these privileges. Second, the breadth of the apostle's words, as also his "that ye may *abound* in hope," manifest how his heart was enlarged toward the saints and what comprehensive supplies of grace he sought for them. Third, that it is thus we honor God in prayer: by counting on the freeness of His grace. There is no straitness in Him, and there should be none in us. Since we are coming to Heaven's King, let us "large petitions with us bring." Has He not given us encouragement to do so? Having given His beloved Son for us and to us "how shall He not with Him also freely give us all things"! Has He not invited us to "drink, yea, drink *abundantly*" (Song of Sol. 5:1): then let our requests be in accord with His invitation and not approach Him as though He were circumscribed like unto ourselves.

That the apostle prayed for these blessings indicated they are not only desirable and attainable, but also that it is *incumbent upon us* to enter into possession of them. We cannot now attempt proof, but will here state the fact that, the things we may ask God for or to give us are, at the same time, obligations upon ourselves. Privileges and duties cannot be separated. It is the bounden *duty* of the Christian *to be joyous* and peaceful. If any should question that statement we would ask him to consider the opposite: surely none would affirm that it is a spiritual duty to be miserable and full of doubts! We do not at all deny that there is another side to the Christian's life, that there is much both within and without the believer to make him mourn. Nor is that at all inconsistent. The apostle avowed himself to be "sorrowful," yet in the very same breath he added "yet alway rejoicing" (2 Cor. 6:10). Most assuredly those who claim to be accepted in the Beloved and journeying unto everlasting bliss, bring reproach upon Him whose name they bear and cause His Gospel to be evil spoken of, if they are doleful and dejected and spend most of their time in the slough of despond.

But to proceed one step further. The apostle here made known *how* these most desirable and requisite blessings may be *obtained*. First, they are to be sought in prayer, as is evident from Paul's example. Second, they can only be attained as the heart is occupied with "the God of hope," that is, a promising God, for the things we are to hope for are revealed in His promises. Third, these blessings come to us "*in believing*," in faith's laying hold of the things promised. "Fill you with all joy and peace in believing." Many seek, though vainly, to reverse that order. They will not believe God till they feel they have joy and peace, which is like requiring flowers before the bulb has been set in the ground. But how can I have joy and peace while engaged in such a conflict—mostly a losing one—with indwelling sin? Answer: you cannot successfully oppose indwelling sin if you are joyless and full of doubts, for "the joy of the Lord is your *strength*" (Neh. 8:10)! There is no genuine joy and peace except "in believing," and in exact proportion to our faith will be our joy and peace.

"That ye may abound in hope." This clause informed the Roman saints, and us, the reason why the apostle made the above request, or the design he had in view for them. Established as to the past, joyous in the present, he would have them to be confident as to the future. The best is yet to be, for as yet the Christian has received but an "earnest" of his inheritance, and the more he is occupied with the Inheritance itself the better equipped he will be to press forward to it, through all difficulties and obstacles, for "*hope*" is one of the most powerful motives or springs of action: Hebrews 6:11, 12. In our day some of the Lord's people need to be informed that the word "hope" has quite a different meaning in Scripture from what it is accorded in human speech. On the lips of most people "hope" signifies little more than a bare wish, and often with considerable fear it will *not* be realised, being nothing better than a timid and hesitant desire that such may be obtained. But in Scripture (see e.g. Rom. 8: 25; Heb. 6:18,19) "hope" signifies a firm expectation and confident anticipation of the things God has promised. As joy and peace increase "in believing" so too does hope.

"Through the power of the Holy Spirit": the Father is the Giver, but the Spirit is the Communicator of our graces. Though it is the Christian's duty to be filled with joy and peace in believing and to abound in hope, yet it is only by the Spirit's enablement such can be realised. Here, as everywhere in the Word, we find the kindred truths of our accountableness and dependency intimately connected. The joy, peace, and hope here are not carnal emotions or natural acquirements but spiritual graces, and therefore they must be Divinely imparted. Even the promises of God will not produce these graces unless they be Divinely *applied* to us. Note that it is not merely "through the operation" but "the *power* of the Holy Spirit," for there is much in us which opposes! Nor can they be increased or even maintained by us in our own strength— though they *can* be decreased by us, through grieving the Spirit. They are to be sought by prayer, by eyeing the promises, and by looking for the enablement of the Holy Spirit. That "hope" is but a vain fancy which is not fixed upon God and inwrought by Him: "remember the word unto Thy servant upon which *Thou* hast caused me to hope" (Ps. 119:49). —AWP

THE MISSION AND MIRACLES OF ELISHA
17. Tenth Miracle - part 4

In our last chapter we dwelt mainly upon *the requirement* which was made upon Naaman when he reached the prophet's abode: "Go and wash in Jordan seven times," seeking to supply answers to—why was he so enjoined? what was the implication in his case? what beating has such a demand upon men generally today? what is its deeper significance? We saw that it was a requirement which revealed the uselessness and worthlessness of Naaman's attempt to purchase his healing. We showed that it was a requirement which demanded the setting aside of his own will and submitting himself to the will of Israel's God. We pointed out that it was a requirement which insisted that he must get down off his high horse (descend from his chariot), humbling and abasing himself. We intimated that it was a requirement which, typically, pointed to that amazing provision of the grace of God for spiritual lepers, namely, the "Fountain which has been opened for sin and for uncleanness" (Zech. 13:1), and by which alone defilement can be cleansed and iniquities blotted out.

"But Naaman was wroth and went away, and said, Behold, I thought, he will surely come out to me, and stand, and call on the name of the Lord his God, and strike his hand over the place, and recover the leper" (2 Kings 5:11). In his own country he was a person of consequence, a "great man," commander-in-chief of the army, standing high in the favor of the king. Here in Israel the prophet had treated him as a mere nobody, paying no deference to him, employing a servant to convey his instructions. Naaman was chagrined: his pride was wounded, and because his self-importance had not been ministered to, he turned away in a huff. Elisha's "Go and wash in Jordan seven times" was not intended to signify the means of cure, but was designed as a *test* of his heart, and strikingly did it serve its purpose. It was a call to humble himself before Jehovah: it required the repudiation of his own wisdom and the renunciation of self-pleasing; and that is at direct variance with the inclinations of fallen human nature, so much so that no one ever truly complied with this just demand of God's until He performed a miracle of grace in the soul.

Even the most humiliating providences are not sufficient in themselves to humble the proud heart of man and render him submissive to the Divine will. One had thought that a person so desperately afflicted as this poor leper, would have been meekened and ready to comply with the prophet's injunction. Ah, my reader, the seat of our moral disease lies too deep for external things to reach it. So fearful is the blinding power of sin that it causes its subjects to be puffed up with self-complacency and self-righteousness and to imagine they are entitled to favorable treatment even at the hands of the Most High. Aye, does not that very spirit lurk in the hearts of the regenerate! and not only lurk there, but at times moves them to act like Naaman! Has not the writer and the Christian reader never come before the Lord with some pressing need and sought relief at His hands, and then been angry because He responded to us in quite a different way from what we expected and desired? Have we not had to bow our heads for very shame as He gently reproved us with His "doest thou well to be angry?" (Jonah 4:4). Yes, there is much of this Naaman spirit in each of us that needs to be mortified.

"Behold, I *thought*" said Naaman. Herein he supplies a true representation of the natural man. The sinner has his own idea of how salvation is to be obtained. It is true that opinions vary when it comes to the working out of detail, yet in all the world over, fallen man has his own opinion of what is suitable and needful. One man thinks he must perform some meritorious deeds in order to obtain forgiveness. Another thinks the past can be atoned for by turning over a new leaf and living right for the future. Yet another, who has obtained a smattering of the Gospel, thinks that by believing in Christ he secures a passport to Heaven, even though he continues to indulge the flesh and retain his beloved idols. However much they may differ in their self-concocted schemes, this one thing is common to them all: "*I thought*," and that "I thought" is put over against the Word and way of God. They prefer the way that "seemeth right" to them: they insist on following out their own theorisings: they pit their prejudices and presuppositions against a "thus saith the Lord." Reader, you perceive here the folly of Naaman, but have you seen the madness of setting *your* thoughts against the authority of the living God!

And what was it that this foolish and haughty Syrian "thought"? Why this: "he will surely come out *to me*, and stand, and call on the name of the Lord his God, and strike his hand over the place, and recover the leper." He was willing to be restored to health, but it must be in his own way—a way in which his self-respect might be retained and his importance acknowledged. He desired to be healed provided he should also be duly honored. He had come all the way from Syria to be rid of his leprosy, but he was not prepared to receive cleansing in the manner of God's prescribing. What madness! What a demonstration that the carnal mind is enmity against God! What proof of the fearful hold which Satan has over his victims until a stronger One delivers them from his enthralling power! Naaman had now received what the king of Israel had failed to give him—full directions for his cure. There was no uncertainty about the prescription nor of its efficacy, would he but submit to the same: "Go and wash in Jordan seven times and thou *shalt* be clean." But he felt slighted: such instructions suited not his inclinations; the Divine requirement accorded not with the conceits of his unhumbled heart.

What right had Naaman, a leper, to either argue or prescribe? He was a petitioner and not a legislator: he was suing for a favor, and therefore was in no position to advance any demands of his own. If such was the case and situation of Naaman, how infinitely less has any depraved and guilty sinner the right to make any terms with God! He is a criminal, justly pronounced guilty by the Divine Law. Mercy is his only hope, and it is therefore for God to say in what way mercy is to be shown him and how salvation is to be obtained. For this reason the Lord says not only "Let the wicked *forsake his way*," but also adds "and the unrighteous man his *thoughts*" (Isa. 55:7). Man must repudiate his own ideas, abandon his own prejudices, turn away from his own schemes and reject his own preferences. If we are to enter the kingdom of Heaven we must "become as little children" (Matt. 18:3). Alas, of the vast majority of our fellows it has to be said, that they, "going about to establish their own righteousness, have not submitted themselves unto the righteousness of God" (Rom. 10:3). They "*will not* come to Christ that they might have life" (John 5:40).

"In Naaman's mind all was arranged. He pictured the scene to himself, and made himself the foremost figure in the group—the Gentile idolator waited on by the prophet of God. The incongruity of this he did not then see. We see it. God would visit him in grace, but as one who had no ground of his own to stand on. As a sinner He could meet him. As a leper He could heal him. As the captain of the hosts of the king of Syria He would not receive him. What place has a sinner before God save that of one to whom *mercy* can be shown? What place is suited to the leper save that *outside* the camp? Naaman has to learn his place. He may be wroth with the prophet, but he cannot move him. Before him he is only a leper, whatever he may appear before others. Learning his place, he has to learn his vileness. He imagined Elisha would have struck his hand over the place. A sign, a scene, he expected—not a mere word. He did not know what a defiling object he was. The priest looked on the leper to judge whether he was leprous or not. He touched him only when he was clean (Lev. 14). Of Naaman's leprosy there was no doubt, for he had come to be healed of it. To touch him ere he was clean would only have defiled the prophet! But further, if he had been able to touch him, and so have healed him, would not man have thought there was virtue in the prophet? By sending him to the Jordan to wash, it would be clearly seen the cure was direct from God. Man has no virtue in himself—he can only be the channel of God's grace to others. *God* must have *all* the glory of the cure, and Naaman must be taught his own condition and vileness" (C. E. Stuart).

"Are not Abana and Pharpar, rivers of Damascus, better than all the waters of Israel? may I not wash in them, and be clean? So he turned and went away in a rage" (v. 12). Naaman was incensed not only because he thought that insufficient respect had been shown to his own person, but also because he felt his country had been slighted. If it was merely a matter of bathing in some river, why could not those of his own land have sufficed? This was tantamount to dictating unto Jehovah, for it was the word of His prophet he now challenged. Shall the beggar insist on his right to choose what form the supply of his need must take! Shall the patient inform the physician what remedy will be acceptable to him! Is the guilty culprit to have the effrontery to dictate to the judge what shall be done to him! Yet a worm of the earth deems himself competent to pit his wits against the wisdom of the Ancient of Days. A Hell-deserving sinner is impudent enough to draw up terms on which he considers Heaven is due him. But if we are to be cleansed, it can only be by the way of God's appointing and not by any of our own devising.

"He thinks this too cheap, too plain, too common, a thing for so great a man to be cured by; or he did not believe it would at all effect the cure, or, if it would, what medicinal virtue was there in Jordan more than in the rivers of Damascus? But he did not consider (1) That Jordan belonged to Israel's God, from whom he was to expect the cure, and not from the gods of Damascus; it watered the Lord's land, the holy land, and in a miraculous cure, relation to God was much more considerable than the depth of the channel or the beauty of the stream. (2) That Jordan had more than once before this obeyed the commands of Omnipotence: it had of old yielded a passage to Israel, and of late to Elijah and Elisha, and therefore was fitter for such a purpose than those rivers which had only observed the common law of their creation, and had never been thus distinguished; but above all, Jordan was the river *appointed*, and if he expected a cure from the Divine power he ought to acquiesce in the Divine will, without asking why or wherefore. It is common for those that are wise in their own conceits to look with contempt on the dictates and prescriptions of Divine wisdom, and to prefer their own fancies before them" (Matthew Henry).

"So he turned and went away in a rage." How true to life: how accurate the picture! The flesh resents the humbling truth of God and hates to be abased. And let us say here for the benefit of young preachers who are likely to read these lines: you must expect some of *your* hearers to turn from you in anger if you faithfully minister the Word of God in its undiluted purity. It has ever been thus. If the prophets of the Lord incensed their hearers, can you expect your message will be palatable to the unregenerate? If the incarnate Son of God had to say, "Because I tell you the Truth, you believe Me not" (John 8:45), can you expect the Truth to meet with a better welcome from your lips? If the chief of the apostles declared "for if I yet pleased men I should not be the servant of Christ" (Gal. 1:10), do you expect to be popular with them? There is but one way to avoid displeasing your hearers, and that is by unfaithfulness to your trust, by carnal compromise, by blunting the sharp edge of the Sword of the Spirit, by keeping back what you know will prove unacceptable. In such an event, God will require their blood at your hand and you will forfeit the approbation of your Master.

"So he turned and went away in a rage." In this we may see the final effort of Satan to retain his victim ere Divine grace delivered him. The rage of Naaman was but the reflection of his whom he had hitherto served and who was now furious at the prospect of losing him. It reminds us of the case recorded in Luke 9. A father of a demon-possessed child had sought for help from the apostles, which they had been unable to render. As the Savior came down from the mount the poor father approached Him and He gave orders "bring thy son to Me," and we are told "and as he was yet *a coming*, the devil threw him down, and tear him" (v. 42). But Jesus rebuked the unclean spirit, and healed the child, and delivered him again to his father. It is frequently thus: the conflict which is waged in the soul is usually sorest just before peace is found. Lusts rage, unbelief seeks to wax supreme, the truth of sovereign grace when first apprehended is obnoxious, to be told our righteousnesses are as filthy rags stirs up enmity. Satan fills the soul with rage against God, against His truth, against His servant. Often that is a hopeful sign, for it at least shows that the sinner has been aroused from the fatal sleep of indifference.

"And his servants came near and spake unto him, and said, My father, if the prophet had bid thee do some great thing, wouldest thou not have done it? how much rather then, when he saith to thee, Wash, and be clean"? (v. 13). Let us consider first the surface teaching of this verse. This gentle remonstrance was "a word spoken in season." Had Naaman remained calm and reasonable he should have perceived that what was required of him was simple and safe, and neither difficult nor dangerous. Had the prophet prescribed some laborious and lengthy task, or ordered a drastic operation or painful remedy, probably Naaman had complied without a murmur, so why not do so when no other sacrifice was demanded of him but the humbling of his pride? "When sinners are under serious impressions, and as yet prejudiced against the Lord's method of salvation, they should be reasoned with in meekness and love, and persuaded to make trial of its simplicity" (T. Scott). If it is necessary to rebuke their petulence and point out to them the foolishness of their proud reasoning, we should make it evident that our rebuke proceeds from a desire for their eternal welfare.

"It is a great mercy to have those about us that will be free with us, and faithfully tell us our faults and follies, though they be our inferiors. Masters must be willing to hear reason from their inferiors: Job 31:13, 14. As we should be deaf to the counsel of the ungodly though given by the greatest and most venerable names, so we should have our ears open to good advice, though brought to us by those who are much below us: no matter who speaks, if it be well said. The reproof was modest and respectful: they call him 'father'—for servants must honor and obey their masters with a kind of filial affection" (Matthew Henry). Alas, how far has our socialistic and Bolshevistic generation departed from the sound teaching of our Puritan forebears! How few ministers of the Gospel now proclaim the Divine injunction "Let as many servants as are under the yoke count their own masters worthy of all honor, that the name of God and His doctrine be not blasphemed" (1 Tim. 6:1).

It may be those servants had heard quite a lot from the Hebrew maid of the wondrous miracles that had been wrought by Elisha, and hence they were very desirous that Naaman should try out his directions. Or, perhaps it was because they were deeply devoted to their master, holding him in high esteem, and felt he was forsaking his own mercies by permitting his wounded vanity to now blind his better judgment. At any rate, they saw no sense in coming all the way from Syria and now leaving Samaria without at least making a trial of the prophet's prescription. Such are the suggestions made by the commentators to explain the ground and spring of this action of Naaman's attendants. Personally, we prefer to look higher and see the power of the Most High in operation, working in them both to will and to do if His good pleasure, employing them as one more link in the chain which brought about the accomplishment of His purpose; for "of Him and through Him and to Him, are *all* things: to whom be glory for ever. Amen" (Rom. 11:36).

What has been before us here is in full accord with the other things already contemplated. It seemed quite unlikely that any serious attention should be paid to the simple statement of the captive Hebrew maid, but God saw to it that her words did not fall to the ground. It appeared very much as though Naaman's mission was blocked when the sceptical king of Israel failed to co-operate therein, but God moved Elisha to intervene and caused his royal master to carry out his order. And now that Naaman himself turned away from the prophet in a rage, it certainly looked as though the quest would prove unsuccessful. But that could not be. The Almighty had decreed that the Syrian *should* be healed of his leprosy and brought to acknowledge that the God of Israel was the true and living God; and all the powers of evil could not prevent the fulfillment of His decree. Yet accordingly as He is generally pleased to work, so here, He used human instruments in the accomplishing of His purpose. It may be concluded that, naturally and normally, those attendants had kept their place and distance, and would not have dared to remonstrate with their master while he was in such a rage. Behold the secret power of God working within them, subduing their fears, and moving them to appeal unto Naaman.

The "little maid" was not present to speak to her august master and plead with him to further his best interests. The prophet of the Lord had issued his instructions, only for them to be despised. What, then, shall Naaman return home unhealed? No, such a thing was not possible. He was to learn there was a God in Israel and that He had thoughts of mercy toward him. But he must first be abased. Mark, then, how God acted. He moves in a mysterious way His wonders to perform—oftentimes unperceived and unappreciated by us. He inclines his own followers to admonish Naaman and show him the folly of his proud reasoning. Remarkable and significant is it to observe the particular instruments the Lord here employed. It was first the *servant* maid whom He used to inform Naaman that there was a prophet in Israel by whom he could obtain healing. Then it was through his "servant" that Elisha gave the Syrian the needed instructions. And now it was his own *servants* who prevailed upon him to heed those instructions. All of this was intended for the humbling of the mighty Naaman. And, we may add, for *our* instruction: we must take the servant's place and have the servant spirit if we would hope for God to employ us.

See here too the amazing patience and longsuffering of the Lord. Here was one who was wrothful against His faithful prophet: what wonder then had He struck him down in his tracks. Here was a haughty creature who refused to humble himself and, in effect, impudently dictated to God how he should receive healing. Had he been on his knees supplicating the Divine favor, his attitude had been a becoming one; instead, he turns his back upon God's servant and moved away in a rage. Yet it was *then* that God acted: not against him, but *for* him, so that where sin abounded, grace did much more abound. And why? Because sovereign mercy had ordained him a vessel unto honor from all eternity. Let the Christian reader join with the writer in looking back to the past, recalling when we too kicked against the pricks. How infinite was the forbearance of God toward us! Though we had no regard for Him, He had set His heart upon us, and perhaps at the very time when our awful enmity against Him was most high-handedly operative He moved some one of comparative obscurity to reason with us and point out to us the folly of our ways and urge us to submit to God's holy requirements. —AWP

THE DOCTRINE OF RECONCILIATION
3. Its Need

The word reconciliation means to unite two parties who are estranged. It denotes that one has given offence and the other has taken umbrage or is displeased thereby, in consequence of which there is a breach between them. Instead of friendship there is a state of hostility existing, instead of amity there is enmity, which results in separation and alienation between them. This it is which makes manifest the need for peace to be made between the estranged parties, that the wrong may be righted, the cause of the displeasure be removed, the ill-feeling cease, the breach be healed and reconciliation accomplished. The parties at variance are man and God. Man has grievously offended the Most High. He has cast off allegiance to Him, revolted from Him, despised His authority, trampled upon His commandments. The enormity of such an offence it is impossible for us to fully conceive. The heinousness of it can only be measured by the exalted dignity of the One against whom it is committed. It has been committed against the Almighty, against One who is infinite in majesty, infinite in excellency, infinite in His sovereign rights over the creature of His own hands; and therefore it is an offence of *infinite* magnitude and turpitude.

The original offence was committed by Adam in Eden, but that fearful transgression can only be rightly understood as we recognize that Adam acted there not as a private individual but as a public person. He was Divinely constituted to be not only the father but also the federal head of the human race. He stood as the legal representative of all mankind, so that in the sight of the Divine Law what *he* did *they* did, the one transacting on the behalf of the many. The whole human race were placed on probation in the person of the first man. His trial was their trial. While he stood they stood. While he retained the approbation of God and remained in fellowship with Him, they did the same. Had he survived the trial, had he fitly discharged his responsibility, had he continued in obedience to God, his obedience had been reckoned to their account, and they had entered into the reward which had been bestowed upon him. Contrariwise, if he failed and fell, they failed and fell in him. If he disobeyed God his disobedience is imputed unto all those whom he represented, and the just but fearful curse pronounced upon him falls likewise on all for whom he transacted.

What has just been pointed out by us above, was amplified at some length in our articles on the Adamic Covenant, which appeared in this magazine some ten years ago, but as many of our present readers have never seen them it will be necessary for us now to give a brief summary of what was then said. The legal relation between Adam and his posterity may be illustrated thus. God did not deal with mankind as with a field of corn, where each stalk stands upon its own individual root; but He dealt with it as a tree, all the branches of which have one common root and trunk. If you strike with an axe at the root of a tree, the whole tree falls—not only the trunk, but also the branches and even the twigs on the branches: all wither and die. So it was with Adam in Eden. God permitted Satan to lay the axe at the root of humanity and when he fell all his posterity fell with him. At one fatal stroke Adam was severed from communion with his Maker, and as the consequence "death passed upon all men." This is not a theory of human speculation but a fact of Divine revelation.

That Adam *was* the federal head of the human race, that he *did* act and transact in a representative character, and that the judicial consequences of his act was imputed to all those for whom he stood, is clearly taught in Romans 5. "Wherefore as by one man sin entered into the world, and death by sin, and so death passed [as a capital sentence] upon all men, in whom all sinned" (v. 12). "Through the offence of one many be dead" (v. 15). "The judgment was by one to condemnation" (v.16). "By one man's offence death reigned" (v.17). "By the offence of one judgment came upon all men to condemnation" (v. 18). "By one man's offence many were made [legally constituted] sinners" (v. 19). Such repetition and emphasis intimates the basic importance of the truth here revealed, and also hints at our slowness or rather reluctance to receive the same. The meaning of these declarations is too plain for any unprejudiced mind to misunderstand: it pleased God to deal with the human race as *represented* in and by Adam: "in Adam all die" (1 Cor. 15:22). There is the plainly-revealed fact, and they who deny it make God a liar.

Here, then, we learn what is the formal ground of man's judicial condemnation before God. The popular idea of what it is which renders man a sinner in the sight of Heaven is altogether inadequate and erroneous. The prevailing conception is that a sinner is one who commits and practices sin. It is true that this is the *character* of the sinner, but it certainly is not that which primarily *constitutes* him such before the Divine Law. The truth is that every member of our race enters into this world a guilty sinner, alienated from God, before ever he commits a single transgression. It is not only that he possesses a depraved nature but that he is directly "under condemnation," the curse of the broken Law resting upon him, and from God he is "estranged from the womb" (Ps. 58:3). We are legally constituted sinners neither by what we are nor by what we are doing, but by the disobedience of our federal head, Adam. Adam acted not for himself alone, but for all who were to spring from him, so that his act, was forensically, our act.

Here also is the only key which satisfactorily opens to us the meaning of human history and explains the universal prevalence of sin. The human race is suffering for the sin of Adam, or it is suffering for nothing at all: there is no escape from that alternative. This earth is the scene of a grim and awful tragedy. In it we behold misery and wretchedness, strife and hatred, pain and poverty, disease and death on every side. None escape the fearful entail. That "man is born unto trouble as the sparks fly upward" is an indisputable fact. But what is the *explanation* of it? Every effect must have a previous cause. If we are not being punished for Adam's sin, then, coming into this world we are "children of wrath" (Eph. 2:3), beneath the Divine judgment, corrupt and defiled, on the broad road which leadeth to destruction, *for nothing at all*! Who would contend that this was better, more satisfactory, more illuminative, than the Scriptural explanation of our ruin? Genesis 3 alone explains why human history is written in the ink of blood and tears.

The objection that such an arrangement is unjust is invalid. The principle of *representation* is a fundamental one in human society. The father is the legal head of his children during their minority: what he does binds the family. A business house is held responsible for the transactions of its agents. Every popular election illustrates the fact that a constituency will act through its representative and be bound by his acts. The heads of a state are vested with such authority that the treaties they make are binding upon the whole nation. This principle is so basic it cannot be set aside. Human affairs could not continue nor society exist without it. This is the method by which God has acted all through. The sins of the fathers are visited upon the children: the posterity of Canaan were cursed for the single transgression of their parent (Gen. 9), the whole of his family stoned for Achan's sin (Josh. 7). Israel's high priest acted on behalf of the whole nation. One acting for others is a basic principle both of human and Divine government.

Finally, let it be pointed out that the sinner's *salvation* is made to depend upon this very same method. Beware, then, my reader, of quarrelling with the justice of this principle of representation—the one standing for the many. On this principle we were wrecked, and by this principle only can we be rescued. If on the one hand, the disobedience of the first Adam was the judicial ground of our condemnation, on the other hand the obedience of the last Adam is the legal basis on which God justifies sinners. The substitution of Christ in the place of His people, the imputation of their sins to Him and of His righteousness to them, is the central fact of the Gospel. But the principle of being saved by what Another has done is only possible on the ground that we were lost through what another did. The two stand or fall together. If there had been no Covenant of Works there would have been no Covenant of Grace: if there had been no death in Adam there had been no life in Christ. The Christian knows that such an arrangement is just because it is part of the revealed ways of Him who is infinitely holy and righteous.

Here, then, is the Divinely revealed fact: "by the offence of one judgment came upon all men to condemnation" (Rom. 5:19). Here is cause of humiliation which few think about. We are members of an accursed race, the fallen children of a fallen parent, and as such we enter this world "alienated from the life of God" (Eph. 4:18), exposed to His judicial displeasure. In the day that Adam fell the frown of the Most High came upon His children. The holy nature of God abhorred the apostate race. The curse of His broken Law descended upon all of Adam's posterity. It is only thus we can account for the universality of human depravity and suffering. The corruption of human nature which we inherit from our first parents is a great evil, for it is the source of all our personal sins. For God to allow this transmission of depravity is to inflict a *punishment*. But how can God punish all, unless all were guilty? The fact that all *do* share in this common punishment is proof that all sinned in Adam. Our depravity and misery are not, as such, the infliction of the Creator, but are the retribution of the Judge.

If we now repeat some of the statements made above it is that the reader may not form a wrong conception or draw a false conclusion. We are very far from teaching here that the human race is suffering for an offence in which they had no part, that innocent creatures are being condemned for the action of another which could not fairly be laid to their account. Let it be clearly understood that God punishes none for Adam's sin (if considering him as a private person), but only for *his own* sin *in* Adam. The whole human race had a federal standing in Adam. Not only was each of us seminally in his loins when God created him, but each of us was legally represented by him when God made with him the Covenant of Works. Adam acted and transacted in that Covenant as a public person, not simply as a private individual, but as the surety and sponsor of his race. The very fact that we continue breaking the Covenant of Works and disobeying the Law of God demonstrates our oneness with Adam under that Covenant. Our complicity with Adam in his rebellion is evidenced every time that we personally sin against God.

It is nothing short of downright hypocrisy for us to murmur against the justice of this arrangement or constitution while we follow in the steps of Adam. If we have nothing to do with him and are not in bondage through him, why do we not repudiate him—refuse to sin, break the chain, stand out in opposition to him, and be holy? This brings us to the second chief count in the fearful indictment against us. We take sides with Adam: we perpetuate his evil course: we make him are exemplar. The life of the unregenerate is one unbroken curse of rebellion against God. There is no genuine submission to Him, no concern for His glory, no disinterested love for Him. Self-will is our governing principle and self-pleasing our goal. Whatever religious deference may apparently be shown God, it is rendered out of self-interest—either to curry favor with Him, or to appease His anger. The things of time and sense are preferred before Him, the lies of Satan are heeded rather than the Word of Truth, and instead of humbling ourselves before Him because of our original offence in Eden, we multiply transgressions against Him.

However unpalatable it may be to proud flesh and blood, the fact is that the natural man is engaged in a warfare against God. He hates the things God loves, and loves the things He hates. He scorns the things God enjoins and pursues the things He has forbidden. He is a rebel against the Divine government, refusing to be in subjection to the Divine will. The moment his own will is crossed by the dispensations of Providence he murmurs. He is unthankful for the mercies of which he is the daily recipient, and less mindful of the Hand that so freely ministers to him than the horse or the mule to the one who feeds him. He continually growls at his lot, constantly grumbles at the weather, and is a stranger to contentment. In short "the carnal mind is enmity against God and is not subject to the Law of God, neither indeed can be" (Rom. 8:7). "The natural man receiveth not the things of the Spirit of God, for they are foolishness unto him" (1 Cor. 2:14)—contrary to his corrupted mind, at variance with his vitiated desires. "There is none that seeketh after God" (Rom. 3:11).

There is then a breach—a real, a broad, a fearful breach—between God and man. In the very nature of the case it cannot be otherwise. That breach has been made by sin. God is holy, so holy that He is "of purer eyes than to behold evil and canst not look on iniquity" (Hab. 1:13). Sin has given infinite offence unto God, for it is that "abominable thing" which He hates (Jer. 44:4). Sin is a species of spiritual anarchy, a defiance of the triune Jehovah: it is a saying in actions "Let us break Their bands, and cast away Their cords from us" (Ps. 2:3)—let us disregard the Divine laws and be lords of ourselves. Not only is sin highly obnoxious to the infinitely-pure nature of God, but it is flagrant affront to His government, being rebellion against it, and therefore as the moral Rector of the universe He declares His displeasure against the same. "For the wrath of God is revealed from heaven against all ungodliness and unrighteousness of men" (Rom. 1:18)—an open display of which was made of old when the flood swept the earth clean of His enemies.

Here then is the black background which discovers to us the *need for* reconciliation: "your iniquities have separated between you and your God, and your sins have hid His face from you" (Isa. 59:2). He is displeased with us and His justice cries out for our destruction. "They rebelled and vexed His Holy Spirit: therefore He was turned to be their *Enemy*" (Isa. 63:10). Unspeakably solemn is that, the terrible import of which is utterly beyond our powers to conceive. That the great I Am, the Creator and Sustainer of the universe has become man's "Enemy," so that His anger burns against him. This was evidenced at the beginning, for right after God had arraigned the guilty culprits in Eden, we are told that "He *drove out* the man, and He placed cherubims at the east of the garden of Eden, cherubim and a flaming sword which turned every way, to keep the way of the tree of life" (Gen. 3:24). Man was now cut off from access to the One whom he had so grievously offended and turned to be his Enemy. And man is also at enmity with Him.

How little is it realised that there is an immeasurable gulf between God and the sinner. And little wonder that so few have even the vaguest idea of the same. All human religion is an attempt to gloss over this fearful fact. And with exceedingly rare exceptions the religion of present-day Christendom is but a studied effort to hide the awful truth that man has forfeited the favor of God and is barred from His holy presence, yea that "the Lord is *far from* the wicked" (Prov. 15:29). The religion of the day proceeds on the assumption that God is favorably disposed even unto those who spend most of their time trampling His commandments beneath their feet: that providing they will assume an outwardly devout demeanor, they have but to petition Him and their supplications are acceptable unto Him. Priests and parsons who encourage such a delusion are but throwing dust in the eyes of the people: "the sacrifice of the wicked is an abomination unto the Lord" (Prov. 15:8).

The religion of our day deliberately ignores the fact of *sin*, with its terrible implications and consequences. It leaves out of sight that sin has radically changed the original relationship which existed between God and His creatures. It conceals the truth that man is outlawed by God and is "far off" (Eph. 2:12,13) from Him. It tacitly denies that "they that are in the flesh cannot please God" (Rom. 8:8), that He "heareth not sinners" (John 9:31). Yea it insists that they *can* please Him with their hypocritical piety and sanctimonious playacting. But the Holy One cannot be deceived by their pretences nor bribed by their offerings. Nor can they so much as draw nigh unto Him while they despise and reject the One who is the only Way of approach to Him. Make no mistake upon this point, my reader: until that awful breach which sin has made be healed, you can have no fellowship with God; until He be reconciled to you and you to Him, He will accept nought at your hands nor can you obtain audience with Him. Unless reconciliation be effected you will be "punished with everlasting destruction from the presence of the Lord"(2 Thess. 1:9).

The need for reconciliation is unmistakable. A fearful breach exists, brought about by the entrance of sin, and continued by the perpetuation of sin. That breach radically altered the relationship of God to man and of man to God. Not only had man now forfeited His favor, but he had incurred His wrath. God could no longer view him with approbation, but instead regarded him with detestation. While man ceased to be a loyal and loving subject, becoming a rebellious outlaw. And "what fellowship hath righteousness with unrighteousness? And what communion hath light with darkness?" None: they are opposites, the one antagonistic to the other. That breach between God and man, between righteousness and unrighteousness, will be demonstrated in the distance between Heaven and Hell. Therefore did Christ represent Abraham as saying to Dives in the place of torment, "Between us and you there is a *great gulf* fixed, so that they which would pass from hence to you cannot; neither can they pass to us" (Luke 16:26). It is only by God's reconciliation to us and of our reconciliation to God the fearful breach can be healed. How that is effected we hope to show in future articles. —AWP

SPIRITUAL GROWTH OR CHRISTIAN PROGRESS
4. Its Nature

We have now arrived at what is really the most important part of our subject, but which is far from being the easiest to handle. If we are to be preserved or delivered from erroneous views at this point it is very necessary that we should form a right concept of what spiritual growth is *not* and what it actually *is*. Mistaken ideas thereon are widely prevalent and many of God's own people have been brought into bondage thereby. There are those who have made little or no advancement in the school of Christ that fondly imagine they have progressed considerably, and are very hurt if others do not share their opinion; nor is it any simple task to disillusion them. On the other hand, some who have grown considerably know it not, and even conclude they have gone backward; nor is it any easy matter to assure them they have been needlessly disparaging themselves. In either ease the mistake is due to measuring themselves by the wrong standard, or in other words, through ignorance of what spiritual growth really consists of.

If the reader met a half dozen people out of as many different sections of Christendom whom he is warranted in regarding as children of God, and asked them to define for him their ideas of spiritual growth, he would probably be surprised at the diversity and contrariety of the answers given. As the reception of one part of the Truth prepares us to take in another, so the admittance of error paves the way for the coming in of more. Moreover, the particular denomination to which we belong and the distinctive form of *its* "line of things" (2 Cor. 10:16) has a powerful effect in determining the type of Christians reared under its influences—just as the nature of the soil affects the plants growing in it. Not only are his theological views cast into a certain mold and his concept of the practical side of Christianity largely determined thereby, but his devotional life and even his personal demeanor are also considerably affected by the same. Consequently there is much similarity in the "experience" of the great majority belonging to that particular company. This is largely the case with all the principal evangelical denominations, as it is also with those who profess to be "outside all systems."

Just as a trained ear can readily detect variations of inflection in the human voice and locate by a person's speech and accent which part of the country he hails from, so one with wide interdenominational associations has little difficulty in determining, even from a brief talk on spiritual things, which sect his companion belongs to: no label is necessary, his affiliation is plainly stamped upon him. And if in the course of the conversation he should ask his acquaintance to describe what he considered to be a mature Christian, his portrayal would naturally and necessarily be shaped by the particular ecclesiastical type he was best acquainted with. If he belonged to one particular group, he would picture a sombre and gloomy Christian; but if to a group at the opposite pole, a confident and joyous one. The kind most admired in some circles is a deep theologian; in others, the one who decries "dry doctrine" and is occupied chiefly with his subjective life. Yet another would value neither theology nor experience, considering that the soul's contemplation of Christ was the beginning and end of the Christian life; while still others would regard as eminent Christians those who were most zealous and active in seeking to save sinners.

In attempting to describe the character of Christian progress, or as it is more frequently termed, growth in grace, we shall therefore seek to avoid a mistake often made thereon by many denominational writers—a mistake which has had most injurious effects on a large number of their readers. Instead of bringing out what the Scriptures teach thereon, only too often they related their own experiences; instead of treating the essentials of spiritual growth, they dwelt upon circumstantials; instead of delineating those general features which are common to all who are the subjects of gracious operations, they depicted those exceptional things which are peculiar only to certain types—the neurotic or melancholy. This is much the same as though artists and sculptors took for their models only those with unusual deformities, instead of selecting an average specimen of humanity. True, it would be a human being that was imaged, yet it could convey only a misrepresentation of the common species. Alas that, in the religious as well as the physical realm, a freak attracts more attention than a normal person.

We shall not then relate our own spiritual history. First, because we are not now writing to satisfy the unhealthy curiosity of a certain class of readers who delight in perusing such things. Second, because we regard the private experience of the Christian as being too sacred to expose to the public view. It has long seemed to us that there is such a thing as spiritual unchastity: the inner workings of the soul are not a fit subject to be laid bare before others—"The heart knoweth his own bitterness, and a stranger doth not intermeddle with his joy" (Prov. 14:10). Third, because we are not so conceited as to imagine that our own particular conversion and the ups and downs of our Christian life are of sufficient importance to narrate. Fourth, because there are probably some features about our conversion and some things in our subsequent spiritual history which have been duplicated in very few other cases, and therefore they would only be calculated to mislead others if they should look for a parallel in themselves. Finally, because as intimated above, we deem it more honoring to God and far more helpful to souls to confine ourselves to the teaching of His Word on this subject.

But before proceeding we must anticipate an objection which is almost certain to be brought against what has been said in the last paragraph. Did not the apostle Paul describe *his* conversion! And may not, should not, we do so too? Answer: first, Paul is the only New Testament writer who gave us any account of his conversion or related anything of his subsequent experiences. It would be a reversal of all sound reasoning to make an exception into a rule or conclude that an isolated case established a precedent. The very fact that Paul's case stands alone, indicates it is *not* to be made an example of. Second, his experience was not only exceptional but unique: the means used was a supernatural appearance to him of the ascended Christ, so that he had a physical sight of Him and heard His voice with his natural ears—a thing which none has done since. Third, the account of his conversion was not made to intimate Christian friends, nor before a local church when applying for membership: but instead before his enemies (Acts 22), and Agrippa— virtually his judge—when making defence for his life. Thus the circumstances were extraordinary and afford no criterion for ordinary cases. Finally, his experience on the Damascus road was necessary to qualify him for the apostolic office: Acts 1:22; 1 Corinthians 15:8, 9 and cf. 2 Corinthians 12:11).

Once more it seems advisable to take up first the negative side of our subject ere turning to the positive. So many mistaken notions now hold the field that they need uprooting if the ground is to be prepared: or to drop the figure, if the minds of many are to be fitted to take in the Truth. Our readers differ so much in the type of ministry they have sat under, and some of them have formed such fallacious views of what spiritual growth consists of, that if we now described the principal elements of Christian progress, one and another would probably consider, according to what they have imbibed, that we had omitted the most important features. We shall therefore devote the remainder of this article to pointing out as many as possible of those things which, though often regarded as such, are *not* essential parts of spiritual growth, in fact no part thereof at all. Though this may prove rather wearisome to some, we would ask them to bear with us and offer up a prayer that it may please God to use the paragraphs which follow to the enlightenment of those who are befogged.

1. *Weight of years.* It is often considered that spiritual growth is to be measured by the calendar, that the length of time one has been a Christian will determine the amount of progress he has made. Certainly it ought to do so, yet in fact it is frequently no index at all. God often pours contempt on the distinctions made by men: out of the mouths of "babes and sucklings" has He perfected praise (Matt. 21:16)! It is generally supposed that those with snowy locks are much more spiritual than young believers, yet if we examine what is recorded of the closing years of Abraham, Isaac, David, Hezekiah and others of Israel's kings, we find reason to revise or qualify such a conclusion. True, some of the choicest saints we have ever met were "patriarchs" and "mothers in Israel," yet they have been exceptions rather than the rule. Many Christians make more real progress in piety the first year than in the next ten that follow.

2. *Increasing knowledge.* We must distinguish between things that differ, namely, a knowledge of spiritual things and actual spiritual knowledge. The former can be

acquired by the unregenerate: the latter is peculiar to the children of God. The one is merely intellectual and theoretical; the other is vital and effectual. One may take up "Bible study" in the same way as another would the study of philosophy or political economy. He may pursue it diligently and enthusiastically. He may obtain a familiarity of the letter of Scripture and a proficiency in understanding its terms, far in advance of the hard-working Christian who has less leisure and less natural ability; yet what is such knowledge worth if it affects not the heart, fails to transform the character and make the daily walk pleasing to God! "Though I understand all mysteries and all knowledge…and have not love, I am nothing" (1 Cor. 13:2). Unless our "Bible study" is conforming us, both inwardly and outwardly, to the image of Christ, it profits us not.

3. *Development of gifts*. An unregenerate person taking up the study of the Bible may also be one who is endowed with considerable natural talents, such as the power of concentration, a retentive memory, a

persevering spirit. As he prosecutes his study his talents are called into play, his wits are sharpened and he becomes able to converse fluently upon the things he has read, and he is likely to be sought after as a speaker and preacher; and yet there may not be a spark of Divine life in his soul. The Corinthians grew fast in gifts (1 Cor. 1:4,7), yet they were but "babes" and "carnal" (3:2,3), and needed to be reminded of the "more excellent way" of love to God and their brethren. Ah, my reader, you may not have the showy gifts of some, nor be able to pray in public as others, but if you have a tender conscience, an honest heart, a forbearing and forgiving spirit, you have that which is far better.

4. *More time spent in prayer*. Here again, to avoid misunderstanding, we must distinguish between things that differ: natural prayer and spiritual. Some are constitutionally devotional and are attracted by religious exercises, as others are by music and painting; and yet they may be total strangers to the breathings of God's Spirit in their souls. They may set aside certain parts of the day for "a quiet time with God" and have "a prayer list" as long as their arm, and yet be utterly devoid of the spirit of grace and supplications. The Pharisees were renowned for their "long prayers." The Mohammedan with his "praying mat," the Buddhist with his "praying wheel," and the Papist with his "beads," all illustrate the same principle. It is quite true that growth in grace is ever accompanied by an increased dependence upon God and a delighting of the soul in Him, yet that does not mean that we can measure our spirituality by the clock—by the amount of time we spend on our knees.

5. *Activity in service*. In not a few circles this has been and still is made the test of one's spirituality. As soon as a young person makes a Christian profession he is set to work, either in the Sunday school, the Christian endeavor society, or taking part in open-air meetings. It matters not how ill-qualified he is, lacking as yet (in many instances) even a rudimentary knowledge of the fundamentals of the faith, nevertheless he is required or at least expected to engage forthwith in some form of what is plausibly termed "service for Christ." But the Epistles will be searched in vain for a warrant for such things: they contain not so much as a single injunction for young believers to engage in "personal work." On the contrary they are enjoined to obey their parents in the Lord (Eph. 6:1) and the young women are to be "keepers at home" (Titus 2:5). Many have reason to lament "*they* [not God!] made me the keeper of the vineyards, but mine own vineyard [spiritual graces] have I not kept" (Song of Sol. 1:6).

6. *Happy feelings*. Considerable allowance needs to be made for both temperament and health. Some are naturally more vivacious and emotional than others, of a more lively and cheerful spirit, and consequently they engage in singing rather than sighing, laughter than weeping. When such people are converted they are apt to be more demonstrative than others, both in expressing gratitude to the Lord and in telling people what a precious Saviour is theirs. Yet it would be a great mistake to suppose that they had received a larger measure of the Spirit than their more sober and equable brethren and sisters. A shallow brook babbles noisily but "still waters run deep"—yet there are exceptions here, as the Niagara Falls illustrate. Increasing holiness is not to be gauged by our inward comforts and joy, but rather by the more substantial qualities of faith, obedience, humility and love. When a fire is first kindled there is more smoke and crackling, but after, though the flame has a narrower compass, it has more heat.

7. *Becoming more miserable*. Yet, strange as it may sound to some of our readers, there are not a few professing Christians who regard *that* as one of the principal elements of spiritual growth. They have been taught to regard assurance as presumption and Christian joy as lightness, if not levity. Should they experience a brief season of peace "in believing," they are fearful that the Devil is deceiving them. They are occupied mostly with indwelling sin, rather than with Christ. They hug their fears and idolize their doubts. They consider that the slough of despond is the only place of safety, and are happiest when most wretched. That is by no means an exaggerated picture, but sadly true to a certain type of religious life, where longfacedness and speaking in whispers are regarded as evidences of a "deep experience" and marks of piety. True, the more light God gives us the more we perceive our sinfulness, yet, though humbled thereby, the more thankful should we be for the cleansing blood.

8. *Added usefulness*. But God is sovereign and orders His providences accordingly. Unto one He opens doors, unto another He closes them, and to His good pleasure we are called upon to submit. Some streams He replenishes, but others are suffered to dry up: thus it is in His dealings with His people—by providing or withholding favorable openings for them to be of spiritual help to their fellows. It is therefore a great mistake to measure our growth in grace and our bringing forth of good fruit by the largeness or smallness of our opportunities of doing good. Some have larger opportunities when young than when they become older, yet if the hearts of the latter are right, God accepts the will for the deed. Some that have the most grace are stationed in isolated places and are largely unknown to their fellow Christians, yet the eye of God sees them. Shall we say that the flowers on the mountain side are wasted because no human eye admires them or that the songs of birds in the forests are lost on the air because they regale not the ears of men!

9. *Temporal prosperity*. Though it is shared by few of our fellow ministers, yet it is the firm conviction of this writer that, as a general rule, temporal adversity and straitened circumstances in the present life of a Christian is a mark of God's displeasure; an evidence that he has choked the channel of blessing: see Psalm 84:11; Jeremiah 5:25; Matthew 6:33, and compare the January cover-page article. On the other hand we should certainly be drawing an erroneous conclusion if we regard the flourishing affairs of an unregenerate professor as a proof that the smile of Heaven rested upon him; rather would it be the case of one who was being fattened for the "day of slaughter"

(James 5:5). Many such an one receives his good things in this world, but in the world to come is tormented in the flame (Luke 16:24,25). Even among God's own people there may be those who yield to a spirit of covetousness, and in some cases the Lord gratifies their carnal desires, but "sends leanness into their souls" as He did with Israel of old.

10. *Liberality in giving*. We do not believe any heart can remain selfish and miserly where the love of God has been shed abroad in it, but rather that such an one will esteem it a privilege as well as duty to support the cause of Christ and minister to any brother in need, according as God has prospered him, yet it is a very misleading standard to judge a person's spirituality by his generosity: 1 Corinthians 13:3. For some years we lived in districts where the principal denominations taught insistently that the church's spirituality was manifested by the amount it contributed to missions; yet while numbers of them raised very considerable sums, vital godliness was mostly conspicuous by its absence. Millions of pounds have recently been given to the "Red Cross society" by those making no Christian profession at all! Never were the coffers of the churches so full as they are today, and never were the churches so devoid of the Spirit's unction and blessing! — AWP

(continued from back page)

I must. Thereby a multitude of considerations are reduced to a simple and single issue.

What has been pointed out above may be summed up thus: God's "mind" or "will" for me ever lies in my treading *the path of duty*. And that there may be no misunderstanding, let us here define our terms. What is *duty*? The word means "due to," that which I am required to render unto another. The performance of duty is to discharge my obligations Godwards and manwards: loving Him with all my heart and strength and my neighbour as myself. It is to render that service which I am naturally or morally bound to perform unto others. More particularly, it is the execution of my responsibilities in the place which I occupy, whether in the home, the church, or the world. The *ground* of our duty is the Divine command, which is the sole determiner of human responsibility. The *end* of our duty is the glory of God, the pleasing of Him in the task He has allotted. The *present reward* of duty is a good conscience, the peace and satisfaction of mind in knowing I have done what is right. The *path* of duty is the course which Divine providence brings me into and which the Divine precepts have marked out for me.

It is by the providence of God each of us is black or white, male or female, a man of one or of five talents. Yet it is our responsibility to trade with those talents, and if they be put to a good use, more will be entrusted to us. Yet while the providence of God is often an *index*, it is *not the rule* to walk by—for *that* we must turn to the Word. It is in the Scriptures, and there alone, the path of duty is defined for us. Therein it is termed "the path of Thy commandments" (Psa. 119:35), which we need to pray that God will "make us go in," for by nature we are not disposed thereto, being born "like a wild ass's colt" (Job 11:12). Thus the path of duty is that of full obedience to God. It is "The way of holiness" (Isa. 35:8) in contrast from "the course of this world" (Eph. 2:2), which is one of *expediency* or choosing what seems easiest and pleasantest. It is "the way of wisdom" (Prov. 4:11) in distinction for the by-ways of folly. May Divine grace cause us to persevere therein. —AWP

(continued from front page)

It appears to us that frequently these souls needlessly perplex themselves by the way in which they frame their question. It has long seemed to us that confusion of thought is betrayed by those who inquire "How am I to ascertain God's mind for me when I have to choose between two alternatives?" Yea, that something more than faulty terminology is involved, is evident from the sequel which immediately follows. So far as our own observation goes the questioner fails to arrive at any clear and decisive answer, being left in a state of doubt and distress, which is neither honouring to God nor comforting for His bewildered child.

Much confusion would be avoided and much uncertainty prevented by asking "Is this, or would that be, *according to the Scriptures*?" for God's "will" or "mind" is made known in His Word. *That* is the Rule, the sure and sufficient Rule we are to walk by, and not inward impressions of His secret will. Perhaps the reader replies, "Yes, I know the will of God is revealed in His Word on all spiritual and eternal matters, but it is about temporal things, the affairs of this life, which I am exercised about and over which I often find myself at an uncertainty." But that should not be, dear friend. God's Word is given to us for the express purpose of being "a lamp unto our feet and a light unto our path" (Psa. 119:105), that is, our path in and through this world, which, because of its separation and alienation from God, is "a dark place" (2 Peter 1:19). It is wrong, quite unwarrantable, for us to mentally draw a line between spiritual and temporal matters as though they belonged to separate departments of our life.

The present spiritual life of the Christian is lived out in this world, and it is to actuate and regulate him in all his varied concerns: "whether therefore ye eat or drink, or whatsoever ye do, do all to the glory of God" (1 Cor. 10:31). A spiritual life is very much more than elevated contemplations, ecstatic feelings, or being engaged only in distinctly devotional exercises—that is the erroneous view taken of it by those who shut themselves up in monasteries and convents. A spiritual life is not a nebulous and mystical thing, but something intensely practical. A spiritual life is to be maintained and exercised by the Christian in the schoolroom, the home, the workshop, as well as in the House of prayer. It is to dominate him in all his relations, in every association with his fellows, setting before them an example of piety, honesty, unselfishness, helpfulness. In other words, the whole of his conduct is to be ordered by the precepts of Holy Writ, and not by the dictates of self-pleasing, nor by the customs of the world or the whims of "public opinion."

In His Word God has given us rules which are pertinent to every aspect of our sojourn down here, which are to control every detail of our complex lives, so that there is no need for us to wonder "Is this right"? or "Is that wrong"? We are not left to our own erring judgment nor that of our fellows, for the Lord has supplied us with an unfailing chart and compass to direct us in our voyage to the better Land. The Scriptures not only announce explicit precepts enjoining obedience in detail but they also enunciate broad principles applicable to every sphere or situation in which Divine providence may place us. Therefore the one question for the saint to be constantly occupied about is, What does Holy Writ require of me? am I acting in accord with *its* teachings? Is my motive in harmony with what it demands? Would I be acting contrary to the Divine Rule if I entered upon such and such a course, adopted this or that fashion or followed a certain policy because my competitors do so or because my employer insists

(Continued on preceding page)

VOL. XXIII.   JUNE, 1944.   NO. 6

STUDIES ɪɴ ᴛʜᴇ SCRIPTURES

" Search the Scriptures." John 5:39.

Publisher and Editor—Arᴛʜᴜʀ W. Pɪɴᴋ,
27 Lewis Street,
Stornoway, Isle of Lewis,
Scotland.

THE PATH OF DUTY
Part B

In our last we pointed out (1) that God's will for us is revealed in His Word; (2) that His Word is to regulate all our ways and control all our conduct; (3) that no matter what situation we be in or what emergency may arise, God's Word is all-sufficient as a lamp unto our feet and a light unto our path; (4) that it therefore follows, the path of duty is defined for us in the Divine commandments. Yet there are some who say that they find it more difficult to *discern* their duty than to actually *perform* it once their duty is clearly perceived. But this should not be. That is tantamount to saying they have no light on their path, that they are in darkness, and surely that is a sad acknowledgement from anyone who professes to be a "child of light" (Eph. 5:8). Did not the Savior declare "he that followeth Me shall not walk in darkness, but shall have the light of life" (John 8:12). If then I find myself in darkness, must not the fault be entirely mine? Then should I not examine myself and seek to discover the reason of it?—"is there not a cause"! Was it because I yielded to the pleasing of self and ceased to "follow" Him who is the Light? If so, my duty is plain I must humbly and penitently confess my failure to God and have the wrong put right, or my darkness will deepen.

Perhaps some reader replies, What you have said above hardly covers my case. The perplexity which confronts me is this: I find myself at the parting of the ways, and I am not clear whether I should turn to the right hand or to the left. My situation has drastically changed: the death of a loved one, the calling-up of my employer, or some other war emergency, has suddenly altered my circumstances. I have to make a decision, and what is for the best I am at a loss to discover. What am I to do? "Trust in the Lord with all thine heart, and lean not unto thine own understanding. In all thy ways acknowledge Him, and He shall direct thy paths" (Prov. 3:5,6). Confer not with flesh and blood, for if you consult your Christian friends the probability is that no two will offer the same counsel, and you will be more perplexed than ever. Go to the Lord Himself, acknowledge His Proprietorship over you, mix faith with this promise of His, turn it into definite and earnest prayer and *expect* an answer of peace from Him, trusting Him for the same.

Consider the case of Eliezer in Genesis 24. His master bade him journey from Canaan to Mesopotamia in search for a wife for his son Isaac. If ever a man was

(continued on back page)

IMPORTANT NOTICES

Please advise promptly of change in address, otherwise copies will be lost in the mails.

We are glad to send a sample copy to any of your friends whom you believe would be interested in this publication.

This magazine is published as "a work of faith and labour of love," the editor and his wife gladly giving their services free. There is no regular subscription price, as we do not wish the poor of the flock to be deprived. This does not mean that those looking for something for nothing may "help themselves." Those getting this Magazine, who are financially able and who receive spiritual help from its pages, are expected to gladly contribute towards its expenses; otherwise, their names are dropped from our lists.

Will those forwarding International Money Orders please have them made out to us at Stornoway, Isle of Lewis, Scotland. Checks (Cheques-Eng.) made out on U.S.A. Banks are not negotiable here, so please do not send them.

CONTENTS

THE PRAYERS OF THE APOSTLES
6. Romans 15:33

"Now the God of peace be with you all. Amen." The "God of peace": contrary to the general run of the commentators, we regard this Divine title as expressing, first of all, what God is *in Himself*, that is, as abstracted from relationship with His creatures and apart from His operations and bestowments. He is Himself the Fountain of peace. Perfect tranquility reigns in His whole Being. He is never ruffled in the smallest measure, never perturbed by anything, either within or without Himself. How could He be? Nothing can possibly take Him by surprise, for "Known unto God are all His works from the beginning of the world" (Acts 15:18). Nothing can ever disappoint Him, for "of Him, and through Him, and to Him, are all things" (Rom. 11:36). Nothing can to the slightest degree disturb His perfect equanimity, for He is "the Father of lights, with whom is no variableness, neither shadow of turning" (James 1:17). Consequently perfect security ever fills Him: that is one component element of His essential glory. Ineffable peace is one of the jewels in the diadem of Deity.

Living as we now are in a war-torn and war-weary world, let us for a season gird up the loins of our minds and endeavor to contemplate something vastly different, something infinitely more excellent, namely, the One who is a total Stranger to unrest and disquietude, One who enjoys undisturbed calm, "the God *of peace*." It seems strange that this glorious excellency of the Divine character is so little dwelt upon by Christian writers. The sovereignty of God, the power of God, the holiness of God, the immutability of God, have frequently been made the theme of devout pens; but the peace of God Himself has received scarcely any attention. Numerous sermons have been preached upon "the God of Love" and "the God of all grace," but where shall we find any on "the God of *peace*," except it be as the reconciled God? Yet only once in all the Scriptures is He specifically designated "the God of love," and only once "the God of all grace," yet five times over is

He addressed or referred to as "the God of peace." As such a perpetual calm characterises His whole Being: He is infinitely blessed in Himself.

The names and titles of God make known to us His Being and character, and it is by meditating upon each one of them in turn, by mixing faith therewith, by giving all of them a place in our hearts and minds, that we are enabled to form a better and fuller concept of who He is and what He is in Himself, His relationship unto and His attitude toward us. God is the Fountain of all good, the Sum of all excellency. Every grace and virtue we perceive in the saints are but so many scattered rays which have emanated from Him who is Light. We not only do Him a great injustice but we are largely the losers ourselves if we habitually think and speak of God according to *only one* of His titles, be it "the Most High" on the one hand, or "our Father" on the other. Just as we need to read and ponder *every* part of the Word if we are to become acquainted with God's revealed will and be "thoroughly furnished unto all good works," so we need to meditate upon and make use of *all* the Divine titles if we are to form a well-rounded and duly-balanced concept of His perfections and realise what a God is ours—His absolute sufficiency for us.

"The God of peace." According to the usage of this expression in the New Testament and in view of the teaching of Scripture as a whole concerning the Triune Jehovah and peace, we believe it will be best opened up to the reader if we make use of the following outline. This title "the God of peace" tells us, first of all, what He is essentially, namely, the Fountain of peace. Second, it announces what He is economically or dispensationally, namely, the Ordainer or Covenanter of peace. Third, it reveals what He is judicially, namely, the Provider of peace—a reconciled God. Fourth, it declares what He is paternally, namely, the Giver of peace to His children. Fifth, it proclaims what He is governmentally, namely, the Orderer of peace in the churches, and in the world. The meaning of these terms will become plainer and simpler, we trust, as we fill in our outline.

First, "the God of peace" tells us what He is *essentially*, that is, what God is in Himself. As pointed out above, peace is one of grand perfections of the Divine nature and character. We regard this title as referring not so much to what God is absolutely, nor only to the Father, but to the *Triune* Jehovah. First, because there is nothing in the context or in the remainder of the verse which requires us to limit this prayer to any particular person in the Godhead. Second, because we should ever take the terms of Scripture in their widest latitude and most comprehensive meaning when there is nothing obliging us to restrict their scope. Third, because it is a fact, a Divinely-revealed truth, that the Father, the Son, and the Holy Spirit are alike "the God of peace." Nor could there be any force to the objection that since *prayer* is here made unto "the God of peace" we are obliged to regard the reference as being to the Father, for in Scripture prayer is also made to the Son and to the Spirit. True, the reference in Hebrews 13:20 is to the Father, for He is there distinguished from "our Lord Jesus," but since no such distinction is made here, we decline to make any.

That this title belongs to the Father scarcely needs any arguing, for the opening words of the salutation found at the beginning of most of the New Testament epistles will readily occur to the reader: "Grace to you and peace from God our Father" (Rom. 1:7; 1 Cor. 1:3 etc.)—"grace" from Him as He is "the God of all grace" (1 Peter 5:10), "peace" from Him as He is "the God of peace." The added words of that salutation "and the

Lord Jesus Christ" establishes the same fact concerning the Son, for grace and peace could not proceed from Him unless He were also the Fountain of both. It will be remembered that in Isaiah 9:6 He is expressly denominated "the Prince of peace," which coming immediately after His other titles there,—"The mighty God, The everlasting Father"—shows that He is "the Prince of peace" in His essential Person. In 2 Thessalonians 3:16 Christ is designated "the Lord of peace," Hebrews 7:2 tells us He is the "King of peace," typed out as such by Melchizedek the priest-king. In Romans 16:20 the apostle announced, "the God of peace shall bruise Satan under your feet shortly," and in the light of Genesis 3:15 there can be no doubt that the reference is immediately unto the incarnate Son.

Less is explicitly revealed in Scripture concerning the Person of the Holy Spirit, because He is not presented to us objectively, like the Father and the Son, inasmuch as He works within and indwells the saints. Nevertheless, clear and full proof is given in the Sacred Oracles that He is *God*, co-essential, coequal, and co-glorious with the Father and the Son. It is a most serious mistake to conclude from theologians referring to Him as "the third Person" of the Godhead that He is in any wise inferior to the other Two, as a careful examination of Scripture and a comparison of one passage with another will demonstrate. If in Matthew

28:19 and 2 Corinthians 13:14 He is mentioned after the Father and Son, in Revelation 1:4, 5 He is named (as "the seven Spirits,"—the Spirit in His fullness) before Jesus Christ, while in 1 Corinthians 12:4-6 and Ephesians 4:4-6 He is named *before* both the Son and the Father—such variation of order manifesting Their co-equality. Thus, as co-equal with the Father and the Son the Holy Spirit must also be "the God of peace," which is evidenced by His communicating Divine peace to the hearts of the redeemed. When He descended from heaven on our baptized Savior, it was in the form of a "dove" (Matt. 3:16)—the bird of peace.

Second, "the God of peace" announces what He is *dispensationally*, in the economy of redemption, namely, the Ordainer or Covenantor of peace. This is clear from Hebrews 13:20, 21 where the apostle prays, "Now the God of peace that brought again from the dead our Lord Jesus, that great Shepherd of the sheep, through the blood of the everlasting covenant, make you perfect in every good work to do His will." It was specifically as "the God of peace" that the Father delivered our Surety from the tomb, "through the blood of the everlasting covenant," that is, on the ground of that blood which ratified and sealed the great Compact which had been made between Them before the foundation of the world. Reference is made to that Compact in Psalm 89:3, where the allusion is to the antitypical David or "Beloved," as verses 27, 28 conclusively prove. In His foreviews of the entrance of sin into the world, with the fall of His elect in Adam, and the breach that made between Him and them, alienating the One from the other, God graciously purposed to effect a reconciliation and secure a permanent peace on a righteous basis, a basis which paid homage to His authority and honored His Law.

A "covenant" is a mutual agreement between two parties, wherein a certain work is proposed and a suitable reward promised in return. In the Everlasting Covenant the two parties were the Father and the Son. The task assigned the Son was that He should become incarnate, render unto the Law a perfect obedience in thought and word and deed, and then endure its penalty on behalf of His guilty people, thereby offering unto the offended God (considered as Governor and Judge) an adequate atonement, satisfy-ing His justice, magnifying His holiness, and bringing in an everlasting righteousness. The reward promised was that God would raise from the dead the Surety and Shepherd of His people, exalting Him to His own right hand high above all creatures, conform-ing them unto the image of His Son, and having them with Himself in glory forever and ever. The Son's voluntary compliance with the proposal appears in His "Lo, I come to do Thy will, O God," and all that He did and suffered was in fulfillment of His cov-enant agreement. The Father's fulfillment of His part of the contract, in bestowing the promised reward, is fully revealed in the New Testament. The Holy Spirit was the Witness and Recorder of that Covenant.

Now that everlasting Compact is expressly designated "the Covenant *of peace*" in Isaiah 54:10, Ezekiel 34:25 and 37:26. In that Covenant Christ stood as the Repre-sentative of His people, transacting in their name and on their behalf, holding all their interests dear to His heart. In that Covenant, in compliance with the Father's will and from His wondrous love for them, Christ agreed to enter upon the most exacting en-gagement and to undergo the most fearful suffering, in order that they might be deliv-ered from the judicial wrath of God and have peace with Him, that there might be perfect amity and concord between God and them. That engagement was faithfully discharged by Christ and the peace which God eternally ordained has been effected, and in due course the Father brings each of His elect into the good of it. It is to that same Eternal compact that Zechariah 6:12, 13 alludes: "the counsel of peace shall be between them Both" (v. 13). That "counsel of peace" or mutual good-will was this "Covenant of peace," and the "between Them Both," between "The Man whose name is the Branch" and Jehovah "the Lord of hosts" (v. 12); and the "counsel" concerned Christ's building of the Church (Eph. 2:21) and His exaltation to the throne of glory.

Third, "The God of peace" reveals what He is *judicially*, namely, the Provider of peace, a reconciled God. That which is to here engage our attention is the actual out-working and accomplishment of what has been before us in the last division. Of old God said concerning His people "For I know the thoughts that I think toward you, saith the Lord: thoughts of peace and not of evil, to give you an expected end" (Jer. 29:11). Yes, despite their apostasy from Him in the Adam Fall, despite the guilt that rested upon them for their legal participation therein, and despite their own multiplied trans-gressions against Him, there had been no change in His everlasting love for them. A real and fearful breach had been made, and as the Moral Governor of the universe God would not ignore it; nay, as the Judge of all the earth His condemnation and curse rested upon them. Nevertheless His heart was toward them and His wisdom found a way whereby the horrible breach might be healed and His banished people restored to Himself, and that not only without compromising His holiness and justice but by glori-fying the one and satisfying the other. God determined to put away their sins and se-cure reconciliation.

"When the fullness of the time was come, God sent forth his Son, made of a woman, made under the Law, to redeem them that were under the Law" (Gal. 4:4,5). It was in order to carry out what had been agreed upon in the Everlasting Covenant that God sent forth His Son. It was in order to provide an adequate compensation to His Law that God's Son was made of a woman, that in our nature He should satisfy the requirements of the Law, put away our sins and bring in everlasting righteousness. It was in order to redeem His people from the curse of the Law that the Son lived and died and rose again. It was in order to make peace with God, to placate His wrath, to secure an equitable and stable peace that Christ obeyed and suffered. In the redemptive work of His Son, God provided peace. At His birth, the heavenly hosts, by anticipation, praised God, saying, "Glory to God in the highest, and on earth peace, good will toward men" (Luke 2:14). And at His death, Christ "made peace [between God and His people] through the blood of His cross" (Col. 1:20), reconciling God (as the Judge) to them, establishing perfect and abiding amity and concord between them.

Fourth, "the God of peace" declares what He is *paternally*, namely, the Giver of peace unto His children. This goes beyond what has been pointed out above. Before the foundation of the world God ordained there should be mutual peace between Himself and His people. As the immediate result of Christ's mediatorial work, peace was made with God and *provided* for His people. Now we are to consider how the God of peace makes them the actual participants of this inestimable blessing. By nature they are utter strangers to it, for "there is no peace, saith my God, to the wicked" (Isa. 57:21). How could there be when they are engaged continually in active hostility against God? They are without peace, in their conscience, in their minds, or in their hearts. As God has indissolubly united holiness and happiness, so sin and wretchedness are inseparably connected. Just so long as men are found fighting against God, breaking His Law, and being lords unto themselves, it has to be said "The way of peace have they not known" (Rom. 3:17).

Before the sinner can be reconciled to God and enter into participation of the peace which Christ has made with Him, he must cease his rebellion, throw down the weapons of his warfare, and yield to His rightful authority. But for that a miracle of grace must be wrought in him by the Holy Spirit. As the Father ordained peace, as the incarnate Son made peace, so the Holy Spirit brings us into the same. He convicts us of our awful sins, and makes us willing to forsake them. He communicates faith to the heart whereby we savingly believe in Christ: then "being justified by faith we have peace with God" (Rom. 5:1) objectively— we are brought into His favor. But more: we enjoy peace subjectively. The intolerable burden of guilt is removed from the conscience and we "find rest unto our souls." Then it is we know the meaning of that word "The peace of God which passeth all understanding shall keep your hearts and minds through Christ Jesus" (Phil. 4:7). By His Spirit, through Christ, the Father has now actually bestowed peace upon His believing child, and in proportion as his mind is stayed on Him, by trusting in Him, he will be kept in perfect peace (Isa. 26:3).

Fifth, "The God of peace" proclaims what He is *governmentally*, namely, the Orderer of peace in the churches and in the world. Though each Christian has peace with God, yet he is left in a world which lieth in the Wicked one. Though the Christian has the peace of God in his heart, yet the flesh remains, causing a continual conflict within, and, unless restrained, breaking forth into strife with his brethren. Therefore unless God was pleased to put forth His restraining power upon that which seeks to disturb and disrupt the believer's calm, he would enjoy little or no tranquillity within or rest from without. Our responsibility is "as much as lieth in" us to "live peaceably with all men" (Rom. 12:18); God's gracious interventions—so far as He deems it to be for His own glory and our good—is to make all men live peaceably with us. For illustrations of this aspect of the Divine administration see Genesis 35:5; Exodus 34:24; Leviticus 26:6; 1 Chronicles 22:9; 2 Chronicles 17:10; Psalm 147:14; Proverbs 16:7; 1 Corinthians 14:33.

"Now the God of peace *be with you all*. Amen." By that petition we understand the apostle made request that God would, in this particular character or excellency make Himself *manifest* among them, that His felt presence should thus be known in their midst. Were it not for the overruling providence of the Lord, His people would have no rest at any time in this world. But He rules in the midst of His enemies (Ps. 110:2) and gives them a considerable measure of peace from their foes. This shows us that we ought to be constantly looking to God for His peace. If we seek it not, but grow self-confident and secure, trials and assaults are likely to arise from every quarter. Our only security is in God, and our duty is constantly to ask peace of Him in the midst of a world of trouble. Peace is a blessing which the churches greatly need, for without it there can be neither spiritual prosperity nor happiness. Thus we ought to regularly beseech God to maintain peace not only in the Christian circle with which we may be connected, but with companies of the redeemed all over the world. We ought to "pray for the peace of [the spiritual] Jerusalem" as our chief joy (condensed from R. Haldane).

By clear implication this prayer "Now the God of peace *be with you all*" implies that the saints must conduct themselves in harmony therewith, that amity and concord must prevail among them, so that there be no such grievous failure on their part as would offend God and cause Him to withdraw such a beneficent manifestation of His presence from them. Philippians 4:9 makes known the conditions of our enjoying the manifested presence of the God of peace: "these things which ye have both learned and received, and heard, and seen in me, DO, *and* the God of peace shall be with you." That is, the leading of a holy life and the faithful performance of duty are the necessary prerequisites. As the individual believer experimentally enjoys the peace of God in proportion as he casts every care upon Him and maintains a spirit of thanksgiving (Phil. 4:6,7), so a corporate company of believers must be in subjection to Divine authority and maintain a Scriptural discipline if they would enjoy the God of peace in their midst.

A parallel passage is, "Be perfect [sincere and upright], be of good comfort, be of one mind, *live in peace*, and the God of love and peace shall be with you" (2 Cor. 13:11). Upon which C. Hodge well said, "The existence of love and peace is the condition of the presence of the God of love and peace. He withdraws the manifestations of His presence from the soul disturbed by angry passion, and from a community torn by dissension. We have here the familiar Christian paradox. God's presence produces love and peace, and we must have love and peace in order to have His presence. God gives what He commands. God gives, but we must cherish His gifts. His agency does not supersede ours, but mingles with it, and becomes one in our consciousness. We work out our own salvation, while God works in us. Our duty is to yield ourselves to the operation of God. ...It is vain for us to pray for the presence of the God of love and peace unless we strive to free our hearts from all evil passions." AWP

We thank our friends who responded to the request at the foot of page 4 of the February issue: God has graciously answered and raised up many new readers. But our circulation is still much below what it was a few years ago.

THE MISSION AND MIRACLES OF ELISHA
18. Tenth Miracle - part 5

That to which we devoted much of our attention in previous meditations was *the requirement* made upon Naaman, because that demand and his compliance therewith is the hinge on which this miracle turns, as the response made by the sinner to the call of the Gospel settles whether or not he is to be cleansed from his sin. This does not denote that the success or failure of the Gospel is left contingent upon the will of men, but rather announces that *order of things* which God has instituted: an order in which He acts as Moral Governor and in which man is dealt with as a moral agent. In consequence of the fall, man is filled with enmity against God and is blind to his eternal interests. His will is opposed to God's and the depravity of his heart causes him to forsake his own mercies. Nevertheless, he is still a responsible creature, and God treats him as such. As His Moral Governor, God requires obedience from him, and in the case of His elect He obtains it, not by physical compulsion but by moral persuasion, not by mere force but by inclining them to free concurrence. He does not overwhelm by Divine might, but declares, "I drew them with cords of a man, with bands of love" (Hosea 11:4).

What has just been pointed out above receives striking illustration in the incident before us. When God's requirement was made to Naaman, it pleased him not: he was angry at the prophet and rebellious against the instructions given him. "Go and wash in Jordan seven times" was a definite test of obedience, calling for the surrender of his will unto the Lord. Everything was narrowed down to that one thing: would he bow before and submit to the authoritative Word of God? In like manner every person who hears it is tested by the Gospel today. The Gospel is no mere "invitation" to be heeded or not as men please, and grossly dishonoring to God is it if we consider it only as such. The Gospel is a Divine proclamation, demanding the throwing down of the weapons of our warfare against Heaven. God "now *commandeth* all men everywhere to repent" (Acts 17:30). And again we are told, "And this is His *commandment*: that ye believe on the name of His Son Jesus Christ" (1 John 3:23). The Gospel is "for faith obedience" (Rom. 1:5) and Christ is "the Author of eternal salvation unto all them that obey Him" (Heb. 5:9). To those "that *obey not* the Gospel" the Lord Jesus will come in flaming fire, taking vengeance (2 Thess. 1:7-8). If men will not bow to Christ's scepter, they shall be made His footstool.

It was this very obedience that Naaman was reluctant to render: so much so that he was on the point of returning to Syria unhealed. Yet that could not be. In the Divine decree he was marked out to be the recipient of God's sovereign grace. As yet Naaman might be averse from receiving grace in the way of God's appointing, and the Devil might put forth a supreme effort to retain his victim; but whatever be the devices of the human heart or the malice of his Enemy, the counsel of the Lord must stand. When God has designs of mercy toward a soul, He sets in operation certain agencies which issue in the accomplishment of His purpose. The flesh may resist and Satan may oppose, but it stands written "Thy people *shall* be willing in the day of Thy power" (Ps. 110:3). That "day" had now arrived for Naaman, and speedily was this made manifest. It pleased God to exercise His "power" by moving the Syrian's servants to remonstrate with him and by making effectual their expostulation. "My father" they said, "if the prophet had bade thee do some great thing, wouldst not thou have done it? how much rather then when he saith to thee, Wash and be clean. *Then* went he down" and did as Elisha ordered.

"Then went he down and dipped himself seven times in Jordan, according to the saying of the man of God" (2 Kings 5:14). "Then went he *down*": that was something which *he* had to do, and until he did it there was no cleansing for him. The sinner is not passive in connection with God's blotting out his iniquities, but active. He has to repent (Acts 3:19), and believe in Christ (Acts 10:43) in order to obtain forgiveness of his sins. It was a *voluntary* act on the part of Naaman. Previously he had been unwilling to comply with the Divine demand, but the secret power of God had wrought in him—by means of the pleading of his attendants—overcoming his reluctance. It was an act of *self-abasement.* "He went down and dipped" signifies three things: he descended from his chariot, he waded into the waters, he was submerged beneath them, and thus did he own his vileness before God. No less than "seven times" must he plunge into that dark stream, thereby acknowledging his *total* uncleanness. A person only slightly soiled may be cleansed by a single washing, but Naaman must dip seven times to make evident how great was his defilement. The "seven times" also intimated that God required *complete* submission to His will: nothing short of full surrender to Him is of any avail.

"Then went he down and dipped himself seven times in Jordan, according to the saying of the man of God." It is of deep importance that we grasp the exact purport of this second clause, otherwise we shall miss one of the principal lines in this Gospel picture. Note well then that it was *not* "according to the pleading of his attendants"— the last thing mentioned in the context. Had Naaman acted simply to please *them*, he might have dipped himself in Jordan seventy times and been no better off for it. Nor does it read "according to the saying of *Elisha*," for it looks infinitely higher than that. "According to the saying of the man of God" signifies, according to the declaration of God Himself through His prophet. Naaman heeded the Word of God and rendered "faith obedience" (Rom. 1:5) to it. Repentance is not sufficient to procure cleansing: the sinner must also believe. And this is what Naaman now did: his heart laid hold of the Divine promise, "Go and wash in Jordan seven times, and thy flesh *shall* come again to thee and thou *shalt* be clean." He believed that "shalt" and acted upon it. Have you done similarly, my reader? Has your faith definitely appropriated the Gospel promise "Believe on the Lord Jesus Christ and thou shalt be saved"? If not, you will never be saved until it has. Faith is the indispensable requirement, for "without faith it is impossible to please God" (Heb. 11:6).

"And his flesh came again like unto the flesh of a little child, and he was clean" (v. 14). Of course it did: it could not be otherwise, for "He is *faithful* that promised" (Heb. 10:23). None has ever laid hold of a Divine promise and found it to fail him, and none ever will. That which has been spoken through the prophets and apostles is the Word of Him "that cannot lie" (Titus 1:2). He cannot falsify His Word. He cannot depart from it, alter it, or break it. "Forever, O Lord, Thy Word is settled in heaven" (Ps. 119:89). Forever, too, is it settled on earth: "My covenant will I not break, nor alter the thing that has gone out of My lips" (Ps. 89:34). God has *promised* to receive, welcome, own, justify, preserve, and bring to Heaven, all who will take Him at His simple Word: who will rely upon it unconditionally and without reservation, setting to their seal that He is true. The warrant for us to believe lies in the promise itself, as it did for Naaman. The promise says, "you *may;*" the promise says, "you *must;*" the promise says, "you are shut up to me" (Gal. 3:23). And I—I say, "Lord, I believe." Faith is a taking God at His Word—His undeceiving and infallible Word—and trusting in Jesus Christ as my Savior. If you have not already done so, delay no longer, but trust Him now, and wash in that "Fountain" which has been opened "for sin and for uncleanness" (Zech. 13:1).

"And his flesh came again like unto the flesh of a little child and he was clean." Let it be duly noted that there was no lengthy interval between the faith-obedience of Naaman and his healing, in fact no interval at all. There was no placing of him upon probation before his disease was removed: his cleansing was instantaneous. Nor was his cleansing partial and effected only by degrees: he was fully and perfectly healed there and then, so that not a single spot of his leprosy remained. And that is exactly what the glorious gospel of God announces and promises: "the blood of Jesus Christ His Son cleanseth us from *all* sin" (1 John 1:7). The moment a sinner claims Christ as His own, His perfect righteousness is placed to his account. The moment any sinner really takes God at His Word and appropriates the Gospel promise, he is—without having to wait for anything further to be done for him or in him—entitled to and fit for Heaven, just as was the dying thief. If he be left here another hundred years he may indeed enter into a fuller understanding of the riches of Divine grace, but he will not become one iota fitter for Glory. "Giving thanks unto the Father, which *hath* made us meet [not is now doing so] to be partakers of the Inheritance of the saints in light" (Col. 1:12).

"And he returned to the man of God, he and all his company, and came and stood before him—and he said, Behold now I know that there is no God in all the earth but in Israel; now therefore, I pray thee, take a blessing of thy servant" (v. 15). When a work of grace is wrought upon a person it is soon made evident by him. Mark the radical and blessed transformation which had been produced in Naaman's heart as well as in his body. He might have hastened back at once to Syria, but he did not. Previously he had turned his back upon Elisha in a rage, but now he sought his face in gratitude. Formerly he had despised the "waters of Israel" (v. 12), now he acknowledged the God of Israel. All was completely changed. The proud and haughty Syrian was humbled, terming himself the prophet's "servant." The bitterness of his legalistic heart which had resented a way of deliverance that placed him on the same level as paupers had received its death wound. The enmity of his carnal mind against God and his hatred of His prophet, together with his leprosy, were all left beneath Jordan's flood, and he emerged a new creature—cleansed and lowly in heart. No longer does he expect the prophet to seek him out and pay deference to him: instead he at once betook himself to Elisha and honored him as God's servant—a lovely figure of a saved sinner desiring fellowship with the people of God.

Sixth, *its sequel.* Let us look more closely at the actions of the cleansed Naaman. First, he "returned to the man of God." Nor did he seek him in vain: this time he came forth in person, there being no longer any occasion to communicate through his servant. Second, Naaman was the first to speak, and he bore testimony to the true and living God: "Behold, now *I know* there is no God in all the earth but in Israel." He had listened to no lectures on evidences of the Divine existence, nor did he need to; effectively is a soul taught when it is made partaker of saving grace. Naaman was as sure now as Elisha himself that Jehovah is God, and He alone. Third, this testimony of Naaman's was not given in private to the prophet, but openly before "all his company." Have you, my reader, made public profession of your faith? "I am not ashamed of the Gospel of Christ" (Rom. 1:16): does a like witness issue from your lips, or are you attempting to be a "secret disciple" of His? Fourth, Naaman now wished to bestow a present on Elisha as an expression of his gratitude: are you ministering to the temporal needs of God's servants?

Yes, my reader, where a work of Divine grace has been wrought its subject soon makes the same evident to those around him. One who has fully surrendered to God cannot hide the fact from his fellows; nor will he wish to. A new life within cannot but be made manifest in a new life without. When Zaccheus was made a partaker of God's so-great salvation he gave half his goods to the poor and made fourfold restitution to those he had robbed (Luke 19:8). When Saul of Tarsus was converted he at once said, "Lord, what wilt *Thou* have me to do?" and henceforth a walk of loving obedience unto Him marked the grand transformation. No sooner was the Philippian jailor made savingly acquainted with Christ than he who had made fast in the stocks the feet of the sorely-beaten apostles "washed their stripes" and, after being baptised "brought them into his house and set meat before them" (Acts 16). Is it thus with you? Does your everyday conduct testify what Christ has done for you? or is your profession only like unto a leafy tree without any fruit on it?

"But he said, As the Lord liveth, before whom I stand I will receive none. And he urged him to take it; but he refused" (v. 16). Naaman was now taught the *freeness* of God's grace—just as Joseph (type of Christ as the Bread of Life) gave orders for the sacks of his brethren to be filled with corn and their money to be returned and placed in their sacks (Gen. 42:25). When God gives to sinners, He gives freely. It was for a truly noble reason then that Elisha declined the blessing from Naaman's hand: he would not sully or compromise the blessed truth of Divine grace. "He would have Naaman return to Syria with this testimony, that the God of Israel had taken nothing from him but his leprosy! He would have him go back and declare that his gold and silver were useless in dealing with One who gave all for nothing" (Things New and Old). God delights in being the Giver: if you wish to please Him, continue coming before Him as a receiver. Listen to David, "What shall I render unto the Lord for all His benefits? I will *take* the cup of salvation and *call* upon His name" (Ps. 116:12,13)—in other words, he would "render" to Him by receiving more!

By his response Elisha showed Naaman that the servant of God looks upon the wealth of this world with holy contempt. "Gratitude to the Lord will dictate liberality to the instruments of His mercies. But different circumstances will render it necessary for them to adopt different measures. The 'man of God' will never allow himself to covet any one's gold or silver, or apparel; but be content with daily bread, and learn to trust for tomorrow. Yet sometimes he will understand that the proffered kindness is the Lord's method of supplying his necessities, that it will be fruit abounding to the benefit of the donor, and that there is a propriety in accepting it as a token of love; but as others, the gift will be looked on as a temptation, and he will perceive that the acceptance of it would degrade his character and office, dishonor God, and tend exceeding to the injury of the giver. In this case he will decidedly refuse it. This is particularly to be adverted to in the case of the great, when they first turn their thoughts to religious subjects. From knowledge of the world, they are apt to suspect all their inferiors of mercenary designs, and naturally suppose that ministers are only carrying on a trade like other men; while the conduct of too many so-called confirms them in the sentiment. There is but one way of counteracting this prejudice, and that is by evidencing a disinterested spirit, and not asking anything, and in some cases refusing to accept favors from them, until they have attained a further establishment in the faith; and by always persevering in an indifference to every personal interest" (T. Scott).

"And Naaman said, Shall there not then, I pray thee, be given to thy servant two mules' burden of earth? for thy servant will henceforth offer neither burnt offering nor sacrifice unto other gods, but unto the Lord" (v. 17). Once the true God is known (v. 15) all false ones are repudiated. Observe carefully his "be given" and "thy servant." He does not offer to purchase this soil, nor does he as "captain of the hosts" of Syria's victorious army demand it as a right. Grace had now taught him to be a *recipient* and conduct himself as a *servant*. Beautiful is it to see the purpose for which he wanted this earth: it was not from a superstitious veneration of the soil, but that he might honor God. This exhibits, once more, the great and grand change which had been wrought in Naaman. His chief concern now was to be a worshiper of the God of all grace, the God of Israel, and to this end he requests permission to take home with him sufficient soil of the land of Israel to build an altar. And is not the application of this unto ourselves quite apparent. When a soul has tasted that the Lord is gracious, the spirit of worship possesses him, and he will reverently pour out his heart's adoration unto Him.

The order of Truth we have been considering is deeply instructive. First, we have a cleansed leper, a sinner saved by grace, (v. 14). Then an assured saint: "I know" (v. 15), and now a voluntary worshiper (v. 17). That is the unchanging order of Scripture. No one that ignores the cleansing blood of Christ or "the washing of water by the Word" (Eph. 5:26) can obtain any access to the thrice holy God. And none who doubts his acceptance in the Beloved can offer unto the Father that praise and thanksgiving which are His due, and therefore believers are bidden to "draw near with a true heart in full assurance of faith, having our hearts sprinkled from an evil conscience" (Heb. 10:22). As we have passed from one detail to another we have sought to make definite application unto ourselves. Let us do so here. Naaman was determined to erect an altar unto the Lord in his own land. Reader, are you the head of a household? and do you claim to be a Christian? Then suffer this question: Have you erected an "altar" in your home? Do you gather the family around you each day and conduct worship? If not, you have good reason to call into question the genuineness of your profession. If God has His due place in your *heart*, He will have it in your *home*.

"In this the Lord pardon thy servant, that when my master goeth into the house of Rimmon to worship there, and he leans on my hand and I bow myself in the house of Rimmon: when I bow down myself in the house of Rimmon the Lord forgive thy servant in this thing" (v. 18). This presents a real difficulty, for as the verse reads it quite mars the typical picture and seems utterly foreign to all that precedes. It is true that Naaman was a converted heathen, yet he had himself acknowledged that "there is no God in all the earth but in Israel," so however great his previous ignorance, he was now enlightened. His desire to erect an altar unto

Jehovah would appear to quite preclude the idea that he should in the next breath suggest that he play the part of a temporiser and compromiser and then presumptuously count on the Lord's forgiveness. One who is fully surrendered to the Lord makes no reservation: he cannot, for His requirement is "thou shalt worship the Lord thy God and *Him only* shalt thou serve"; and again, "touch not the unclean thing, and I will receive you." And still more difficult is it for us to understand Elisha's "Go in peace" (v. 19) if he had just been asked to grant a dispensation for what Naaman himself evidently felt to be wrong.

Is there then any legitimate method of removing this difficulty? Though he does not adopt it himself, Thomas Scott states that many learned men have sought to establish an alternative translation: "In this thing the Lord pardon thy servant: that when my master *went* into the house of Rimmon to bow down himself there, that I bowed down myself there—the Lord pardon thy servant in this thing." We do not possess sufficient scholarship to be able to pass judgment on this rendition, but from what little we do know of the Hebrew verb (which has no present tense) it strikes us as likely. In this case, Naaman's words look backward, evidencing a quickened conscience, confessing a past offense; rather than forward and seeking a dispensation for a future sin. But if that translation be a cutting of the knot rather than an untying of it, then we must suppose that Elisha perceived that Naaman was convinced that the thing he anticipated was not right, and so instead of rebuking him, left that conviction to produce its proper effect, assured that in due course when his faith and judgment matured he would take a more decided stand against idolatry.

Space prevents our taking up, seventh, the *meaning* of this miracle, so we must postpone it for the next. —AWP

THE DOCTRINE OF RECONCILIATION

3b. Its Need

In our last, we dwelt chiefly upon the fearful breach which the entrance of sin made between the thrice Holy One and His fallen and rebellious creatures. In this we must point out some of the consequences and evidences of that breach, thereby showing in more detail the urgency of the sinner's case. By his act of disobedience in Eden, man invaded God's right of sovereignty, spurning as he did His authority, throwing off the yoke of submission, determining to be his own lord. The outcome of such revolt we are not left to guess at: it is plainly made known in the Scriptures: by his fearful offence man lost the favor and friendship of God and incurred His holy displeasure and righteous indignation. The Creator became the punishing Judge. Our first parents were promptly arraigned and sentence was passed upon the guilty culprits. Man had fallen into sin and the Divine wrath now fell upon him. God drove man out of Paradise and unsheathed the flaming sword (Gen. 3:24), thereby making it manifest that Heaven and earth were at variance. As the result of the fall sin became man's delight and henceforth he was an enemy to all holiness and consequently of the Holy One.

1. Fallen man became separated from God. It is easy to write or read those words, but who is competent to fathom their fearful import! Separated from God, the Fountain and Giver of all blessedness! Cast out of His favor. Severed from communion with Him. Cut off from the enjoyment of Him. Devoid of His life, of His holiness, of His love. Such is the terrible and inevitable consequence of sin. Sin snapped the golden cord which had united man to his Maker. Sin broke the happy relationship which origi-

nally existed between man and his rightful Lord. Sin made a breach between its committer and the Holy One. Not only did sin conduct man to a guilty distance from God, but sin necessarily placed God at a holy distance from man. God will not suffer those who are hostile to Him and offensive to His absolute purity to dwell in His presence. Therefore do we read that "God spared not the angels that sinned, but cast them down to Hell, and delivered them into chains of darkness, to be reserved unto judgment" (2 Peter 2:4). They were banished from Heaven, excluded from the company of the Most High, imprisoned in the place of unutterable woe.

God had plainly made known unto our federal head the penalty of his disobedience: "But of the tree of the knowledge of good and evil thou shalt not eat of it, for in the day that thou eatest thereof, thou shalt surely die" (Gen. 2:17). Thus at the very beginning of human history the Lawgiver announced that "the wages of sin is death"—death spiritual, death judicial, death eternal if pardon be not obtained. And death is not annihilation but separation. Physical death is the separation of the soul from the body, expulsion from this earth. So spiritual death is the separation of the soul from God, expulsion from His favor. In that tragic yet hope-inspiring parable of the prodigal son our Lord represented the sinner as being in "the far country," a "great way off" from the Father's house (Luke 15:13,20), and when he returned in penitence the Father said, "this My son was dead [separated from Me] and is alive again [restored to Me]; he was lost and is found." When Christ as the Substitute and Surety of His people bore their sins in His own body on the Tree (1 Peter 2:24) He received the wages of sin, crying to God "why hast Thou *forsaken* Me!"

But the death inflicted upon Adam and all whom he represented was also judicial. Fallen man is a malefactor, dead in Law, lying under its sentence, a criminal in chains of guilt, held fast in fetters until the day of execution, unless he obtains a pardon from God. If no pardon be obtained, then he shall be cast into "the lake which burneth with fire and brimstone," and that is expressly denominated "the second death" (Rev. 21:8), because it is a being "punished with everlasting destruction from the presence of the Lord" (2 Thess. 1:9). Man then, every man while unregenerate, is living "without God in the world," "far off" from Him (Eph. 2:12,13). Being "dead in trespasses and sins" he is cut off from God, having no access to Him. He is a "castaway" from the Divine presence. God will have no commerce with him, nor receive any offering at his hands. He is outside the kingdom of God, and cannot enter it save by the new birth (John 3:5). He is born into the world "alienated from the life of God" (Eph. 4:18). When the Lord came down upon Sinai Israel was not suffered to draw near Him (Ex. 19): sin had imposed an effectual barrier.

2. Fallen man became an object of abhorrence to God. Once more we use language the meaning of which no mortal is capable of fully entering into. It is not that we have employed terms which the case does not warrant, for we have but paraphrased the words of Holy Writ. Nor can it be otherwise if God be what Scripture affirms and if man has become what he is represented therein. God is light (1 John 1:5) and man is "darkness" (Eph. 5:8). God is holy, man totally depraved. God is our rightful Lord and King, man is an insurrectionist, a defiant rebel. God is immaculately pure, man a loathsome leper. If man saw himself as he appears to the Divine eye or even as he is portrayed by the Divine pencil, it would be evident that he *must be* an object of repugnance unto Him who sits enthroned on high. "From the sole of the foot even unto the

head there is no soundness in it, but wounds and bruises, and putrifying sores: they have not been closed, neither bound up, neither mollified with oil" (Isa. 1:6). What a repulsive object! yet that is precisely what you and I (by nature) look like unto the eye of God.

"Thou hatest all workers of iniquity" (Ps. 5:5). In this Psalm God's alienation from and detestation of the wicked is set forth in six steps. First, He has no delight in them: "Thou art not a God that hath pleasure in wickedness" (v. 4). Second, they cannot reside in His presence "neither shall evil dwell with Thee" (v. 4). Third, they have no status before Him: "the foolish shall not stand in Thy sight" (v. 5). Fourth, they are obnoxious to Him: "Thou hatest all workers of iniquity" (v. 5). Fifth, He will pour upon them the fury of His indignation: "Thou shalt destroy them that speak leasing" or "lies" (v. 6). Sixth, they will for all eternity be abhorred by Him: "The Lord will abhor the bloody and deceitful man" (v. 6). None would be shocked at such frightful declarations as these if he had anything like an adequate conception of the exceeding sinfulness of sin and of the infinite holiness of God. Though they are scarcely ever heard from any pulpit today, whether we believe them or not, they are the words of Him who cannot lie and throughout eternity their verity will be borne amply witness to.

"Thou hatest all workers of iniquity." Not merely their evil works, but the workers themselves; not some of the most notorious of the workers but *all* of them. My reader, if you are out of Christ, still unregenerate, whether you be a Britisher, an American, or an Australian, you are an object of God's hatred. Rightly did C. H. Spurgeon point out from these words, "It is not a little dislike, but thorough hatred which God bears to workers of iniquity. To be hated of God is an awful thing. O let us be very faithful in warning the wicked around us, for it will be a terrible thing for them to fall into the hands of an angry God…How forcible is the word 'abhor' (in the next verse). Does it not show us how powerful and deep-seated is the hatred of the Lord against the workers of iniquity!" It is the very nature of righteousness to hate unrighteousness. Those who are so corrupt and abominable *must* be loathed by One who is ineffably holy. It is the very perfection of the Divine character to hate the totally depraved.

3. Fallen man came under the condemnation and curse of the Divine Law. "It is written, Cursed is every one that continueth not in all things which are written in the Book of the Law to do them" (Gal. 3:10). Those words are a quotation from Deuteronomy 17:26—a verse which contains the conclusion of the maledictions pronounced upon the disobedient of the context, being really the sum and substance of them all. It is the solemn declaration that those who have despised God's authority and trampled His commandments beneath their feet are exposed to the Divine displeasure and to condign punishment as the expression of that displeasure. The "curse of the Law" is that sentence and penalty which is due unto sin. Sin and the curse are inseparable; wherever the one is, the other must be. Hence the unrestricted "every one" and that not only for multiplied transgressions but for a single offence. The Divine Law is perfect, and demands perfect and perpetual conformity to it. A single transgression brings down upon its perpetrator the Divine curse, as was evidenced in Eden, and in consequence of our representative participation therein, all of us entered this world under the maledictions of God's Law.

"Cursed is every one…" Those solemn words, so little known, so faintly apprehended even by those who are acquainted with them, reveal the fearful situation of every soul out of Christ: they are under sentence of execution. Their position is identical with the convicted murderer in the condemned cell, awaiting the dread summons of vindictive justice. If you be unregenerate, my reader, at this very moment you are under sentence of death: "condemned already." Since the curse of the Law falls upon men for a single sin, then what must be the punishment that will be meted out upon those with multiplied transgressions to their account! "The curse of the Lord is in the house of the wicked" (Prov. 3:33). That unspeakable malediction rests upon all that he has and all that he does. "Cursed shalt thou be in the city and cursed shalt thou be in the field. Cursed shalt be thy basket and thy store," (Deut. 28:17). Nay, God has said "I will curse your blessings: yea, I have cursed them already" (Mal. 2:2). To those out of Christ He will yet say "Depart from Me ye cursed into everlasting fire" (Matt. 25:41).

4. Fallen man came under the wrath of God. This follows inevitably from what has already been pointed out. Since a rebel against the Divine government is necessarily an object of abhorrence unto his holy Lord, since he has come beneath the curse and condemnation of the Divine Law, justice cries aloud for vengeance. The Maker of heaven and earth is no indifferent Spectator of the conduct of His creatures.

He was not of Adam's. The father and head of the race was summoned before His judgment bar, fairly tried, justly condemned, and made to experience the beginnings of God's wrath, for the full measure thereof is reserved for the transgressor in the next life. As the consequence of their sin and fall in the person of their representative all of Adam's posterity are "by nature the children of wrath" (Eph. 2:3)—not only defiled and corrupt, but the objects of God's judicial indignation. "The children of wrath": those words should be to the ungodly reader as the handwriting on Belshazzar's wall (Dan. 5:5, 6)—they should blanch his countenance, trouble his thoughts, and make his knees smite together.

This fearful expression "the children of wrath" is more forceful than many conclude. In the previous verse we read of "children of disobedience," which means more than disobedient children, for such may the regenerate be. It means such as are addicted to disobedience, who make a trade of it. So "children of wrath" signifies more than to be liable to wrath: it connotes the objects of God's wrath, wholly devoted thereto, born to it as their portion and heritage—the corruptions of their nature being its fuel. When the angels sinned the wrath of God was visited upon them (2 Peter 2:4), thereby evidencing that no natural excellence in the creature can exempt it from the judgment of God. Further demonstrations of His wrath were given when the flood was sent to drown the antediluvian world, when fire and brimstone destroyed Sodom and Gomorrah, and when Pharaoh and his hosts were overwhelmed at the Red Sea. And the execution of God's wrath upon you, my unsaved reader, is hourly drawn nearer. Ignorance cannot shield you from it. Outward privileges will not save you from it. Nor will a mere profession of religion. The only way of deliverance is for you to "*flee from* the wrath to come" by betaking yourself to Christ for refuge.

"God is angry with the wicked every day" (Ps. 7:11), on which Spurgeon remarked: "He not only detests sin, but is angry with those who continue to indulge in it. We have no insensible and stolid God to deal with. He can be angry, nay, He is angry today and every day with you, ye ungodly and impenitent sinners. The best day that ever dawned on a sinner brings a curse with it. Sinners may have many feast days, but not safe days. From the beginning of the year even to its ending, there is not an hour in which God's oven is not hot and burning in readiness for the wicked, who shall be as stubble." And on the words of the verse which immediately follows—"If He turn not, He will whet His sword" —that faithful preacher declared: "What blows are those which will be dealt by that long uplifted arm! God's sword has been sharpening upon the revolving stone of our daily wickedness, and if we will not repent, it will speedily cut us to pieces. Turn or burn is the sinner's alternative."

5. Fallen man is the subject and slave of Satan, under a more terrible bondage than ever the Hebrews were to Pharaoh, for it is a bondage of the soul. Yet this is justly inflicted. At the beginning our first parents preferred Satan's lie to God's truth, and therefore did He allow Satan to obtain dominion over them. Yet with each of his descendants it is a willing bondage therein: as the Jews desired Barabbas rather then Christ, so we entered this world with a nature that is in harmony with Satan's. Yes, without a single exception, every member of our race is born so depraved that he voluntarily serves and obeys the arch-enemy of God. There are but two spiritual kingdoms in this world: that of Christ's (Col. 1:13) and that of Satan's (Matt. 12:26), and every human being is a subject of the one or the other. Those who have not come to Christ and surrendered to His sceptre are ruled by Satan and are fighting under his banner against God. Therefore when Paul was sent forth to preach the Gospel it was in order to open the eyes of men "to turn them from darkness to light and from the power of Satan unto God" (Acts 26:18).

The Devil is the sinner's master, as he was the Christian's before Divine grace regenerated him: "And you hath He quickened who were dead in trespasses and sins. Wherein in time past ye walked according to the course of this world, according to the Prince of the power of the air, the spirit that now worketh in the children of disobedience" (Eph. 2:1,2). He not only tempts from without but dominates them from within. As God worketh in His people "both to will and to do of His good pleasure" (Phil 2:13) so the devil operates in the hearts of his subjects to perform his fiendish pleasure. He "put into the heart" of Judas to betray Christ (John 13:2). He made Pilate and Herod condemn Him to death, for it was "their hour and the power of darkness" (Luke 22:53). He "filled the heart" of Ananias to lie to the Holy Spirit (Acts 5:3). Yet each of them acted freely and according to the inclinations of his own evil nature. Satan's subjects render him a voluntary and cordial obedience: "ye are of your father the Devil, and the lusts [desires] of your father ye will [determine to] do" (John 8:44).

6. Fallen man is under the reigning power of sin. This "abominable thing" which God hates has entered the human constitution like a deadly poison that has completely corrupted our whole being. Sin has full dominion and undisputed sway over the human soul. The mind makes no opposition to it, for it is sin's "servant" (John 8:34) and not "captive." It exerts a determining power on the will. Sin so reigns in the heart of the unregenerate that it directs their affections and controls all the motives and springs of their actions, causing them to walk after their own evil imaginations and devisings. As the air is the native element of the birds, so sin is the natural element of fallen man. "Abominable and filthy is man, who drinketh in iniquity like water" (Job 15:16). Like a parched traveler in the desert who craves water, seeks after it, and greedily swallows it when found, so is iniquity unto the sinner.

The course of the natural man is described as "serving divers lusts and pleasures" (Titus 3:3), as "bringing forth evil fruits" (Matt. 7:17), as yielding his members "servants to uncleanness and to iniquity" (Rom. 6:19). The service rendered by the unregenerate to sin is a whole-hearted one, voluntary, and cordial. Man is in love with sin, preferring darkness to light, this world to Heaven. His lusts are his idols. Therefore does he persist in sin despite all pleadings, warnings, threatenings, chastisements. While he is unregenerate he does nothing but sin in thought and word and deed. Solemn it is to think that every one is in continual remembrance with God, set in the light of His countenance, recorded in that book which will be opened in the day of judgment. Not one of them is pardoned, or can be, while he is out of Christ. So much guilt lies upon his soul as is sufficient to sink it into the lowest Hell, and *will* do so unless blotted out by atoning blood.

7. Fallen man hates God. "The carnal mind is enmity against God, and is not subject to the Law of God"—and so inveterate is that "enmity" it is at once added—"neither indeed can be" (Rom. 8:7). We may not believe it, or be conscious of it, but there is the Divinely-revealed fact. God is an Object of aversion unto the natural man. The language of the hearts of sinners unto the Almighty is, "Depart from us: we desire not the knowledge of Thy ways" (Job 21:14). They do not hate Him as their Provider and Preserver, but as a Being who is infinitely holy and who therefore hates sin and is "angry with the wicked every day." They detest Him as a sovereign Being, who dispenses His favors according to His absolute pleasure. They abominate Him as the Moral Governor of the world, demanding obedience to His Law, and pronouncing cursed all who break it. They abhor Him as the Judge, who shall yet cast all His enemies into the Lake of Fire. Proof of this was furnished when God became incarnate and was manifested unto men: they *crucified* Him!

"Can two walk together except they be agreed?" (Amos 3:3). Obviously not; then how much less could rebels dwell together with a holy God for all eternity! For *that* reconciliation must be effected. But how is peace possible? How are alienated sinners to be restored to friendship with God without Him denying His own perfections? Some grand provision must be made whereby the wrath of God is appeased, whereby His Law is magnified, His honor vindicated, His justice satisfied. Some wondrous redemption is imperative if sinners are to be delivered from that dreadful state of enmity, darkness, and slavery into which the Fall conducted them. Some marvel of wisdom and miracle of grace is necessary if those so "far off" are to be "made nigh," if the unholy are to be made holy, if those dead in sin are to be quickened into newness of life. Some unique Mediator is indispensable if the breach between an offended God and offended creatures is to be healed: a Mediator who is capable of conserving the interests and promoting the glory of God, and who also can win the hearts of those in revolt. The *needs-be* for reconciliation is crystal clear; the *effectuation of it* is the grand subject of the Gospel, the wonder of angels, and will be the theme of the song of the redeemed throughout the unending ages of the future. —AWP

SPIRITUAL GROWTH OR CHRISTIAN PROGRESS

4b. Its Nature

All sound teaching, like the safest method of reasoning, proceeds from the general to the particular, and therefore we shall attempt to show the principles from which spiritual growth issues and the main lines along which Christian progress advances, before we enter into a detailed analysis of the same. God first gave Israel His Law, and then because "His commandment is exceeding broad" (Ps. 119:96)—supplied amplification through the Prophets and a still more specific explication of its contents through Christ and His apostles. Spiritual growth is the development of spiritual life, and spiritual life is communicated to a sinner at the new birth, so the more clearly we are enabled to understand the nature of regeneration, the better prepared shall we be to perceive the character of spiritual growth. Admittedly regeneration is profoundly mysterious, but there are at least two things which afford help thereon: the fact that it is a "renewing" (Titus 3:5), and that it is a real and radical (though not complete or final) reversal of what happened to us at the fall. The old creation gives us some idea of the new creation, and the order in which the former was wrecked prepares us to grasp the order in which the latter is effected.

The natural man is a composite being, made up of spirit and soul and body. The "spirit" seems to be the highest part of his nature, being that which capacitates for God-consciousness or the knowledge of God—He being "spirit": John 4:24. The "soul" or ego appears to be that which, expressing itself through the body, constitutes what is termed our "personality," and is the seat of self-consciousness, and by it man has communion with his fellows. The body or physical organism is that which provides the soul with a habitation in this world, and it is the seat of sense-consciousness, being that through which man has contact with material things. The order of Scripture is "spirit and soul and body" (1 Thess. 5:23), but man with his customary perversity invariably reverses it and speaks of "body, and soul and spirit." How that reveals what fallen man has degenerated into: the body, which he can see and feel, and which occupies most of his concern, comes first in his consideration and estimation! His "soul" receives little thought and still less care, and as to his "spirit" he is unaware that he has any.

"And God said, Let *Us* make man in *Our* image, after Our likeness" (Gen. 1:26). God is triune, there being three persons in one and indivisible Divine essence. And it was in the image of the Triune God that man was made, as the plural pronouns plainly connote. Thus man was made a triune creature. His "spirit" which is the intellectual principle and highest part, was capacitated for communion with God and was designed to regulate (by its wisdom) the soul, in which resides the emotional nature or the "affections." The soul in turn was to regulate the body, as it received through the physical senses information of the external world. But at the fall man reversed the order of his creation: making a "god" of his belly, he henceforth became enslaved to the lower world, and the soul instead of directing the physical mechanism became to a large extent the lackey of its senses and demands. Communion with God being severed, the spirit no longer functioned according to its distinctive nature, and though not extinguished, was dragged down to the level of the soul.

What has just been pointed out should be clearer to the reader by pondering it in the light of Genesis 3. In assailing Eve, Satan made his attack upon her *spirit*—the principle which receives from God—for he first called into question the Divine prohibition (v. 2) and then, replying to her objection, assured her "ye shall not surely die," and added as an inducement "in the day ye eat thereof, then your eyes shall be opened, and ye shall be as gods, knowing good and evil" (vv. 4,5)—thereby seeking to weaken her faith, and flatter her ambition by promising greater wisdom. Hearkening to his lies, the woman was "deceived" (1 Tim. 2:14). Her judgment became beclouded through doubting God's threat, and once the light of God in her spirit was lost, all was lost. Her affections became corrupted, so that she now "desired" or lusted after the forbidden fruit—not by the prompting of her spirit, but by the solicitation of her physical senses: and her will became depraved, so that she "took" thereof.

Now, from the experimental side of things, regeneration is the initial work of God in reversing the effects of the fall, for its favored subject is then "renewed in knowledge, after the image of Him that created him" (Col. 3:10): that is to say, spiritual perception is restored to him, so that he now has again what he lost in Adam—a vital, powerful, direct knowledge of God. In consequence of this he is brought back again into communion with God, restored to a conscious fellowship with Him. One aspect of this mysterious but blessed work is brought before us in Hebrews 4:12, where we are told "the Word of God is quick and powerful, and sharper than any two-edged sword, piercing even to the dividing asunder of soul and spirit." We understand that last clause to signify that the regenerated person's "spirit" is now freed from its immersion into the soul and is raised to its own superior level, being placed *en rapport* (brought into harmony with) God Himself. Thus Paul declares "I serve [God] with my *spirit*" (Rom. 1:9)—not "soul"; and "my spirit prayeth" (1 Cor. 14:14). In distinction therefrom "purified your *souls* [affections] in obeying the Truth" (1 Peter 1:22).

Though the above may sound recondite and, being new to our readers, somewhat difficult to grasp, yet it should we think be more or less clear that in order for us to answer to what God has wrought in us, in order to live as becometh Christians, the body should take second place to the soul, and be ruled thereby: and the soul in turn be subordinated to the spirit, which is to be enlightened and controlled by God. Unless the body be made subservient to the soul, man lives his life on the same level as the animals; and unless the Christian's "affections" and emotions be regulated by wisdom from the spirit, he lives on the same plane as the unregenerate. "Seek ye first the kingdom of God and His righteousness, and all these things shall be added unto you" (Matt. 6:33). That means, make the things of the spirit your paramount concern, and your lower interests will be automatically subserved. If the mind or spirit be "stayed on God," the soul will enjoy perfect peace, and the soul at rest will act beneficently on the body. Thus, in proportion as our lives accord with what took place in us at the new birth will be our spiritual growth and prosperity.

Nothing but a knowledge of God can satisfy the spirit of man, as nought but His love can content the soul. Man's supreme happiness consists in the exercise of his noblest parts and faculties on their proper objects, and the more excellent those objects be, the more real and lasting pleasure do they give us in the knowledge and love of them. Thus it is that, when God has designs of mercy toward an individual, He begins by shining upon his understanding and attracting his heart unto Himself. As that work of grace proceeds, that individual is enabled to perceive something of "the deceitfulness of sin" (Heb. 3:13), how it has deluded him into vainly imagining that the things of time and sense could afford him satisfaction, until he discovers that (to use the figurative language of the prophet) he has "spent his money for that which is not bread" and labored for that which satisfieth not (Isa. 55:2). Therefore does God say unto him, "hearken unto Me, and eat ye that which is good, and let your soul delight itself in fatness." Until God becomes our "Portion" the soul is left with an aching void.

Here, then, is what occurs at regeneration: God "hath given us an understanding that we may know Him that is true" (1 John 5:20)—and this He does by quickening the "spirit" in us. And again we read "For God who [in connection with the first creation: Gen. 1:3] commanded the light to shine out of darkness, hath [in His work of the new creation] shined in our hearts, to give the light of the knowledge of the glory of God in the face of Jesus Christ" (2 Cor. 4:6). Thus, Christian progress must consist in our advancing in a personal and experimental knowledge of God, and consequently when the apostle prayed for the spiritual growth of the Colossians he made request that they might be "increasing in the knowledge of God" (1:10). Simultaneously with this communication of a supernatural knowledge of Himself, the "love of God is shed abroad in our hearts by the Holy Spirit" (Rom. 5:5) and therefore spiritual growth consists of a deeper apprehension and fuller enjoyment of that love with a more complete response thereto; and hence, when making request for the same on behalf of the Ephesians, Paul prayed that they might "know the love of Christ which passeth knowledge" (3:19).

It is not our immediate design to give as full a description as our present light affords of the precise nature of regeneration, but only to point out those of its principal elements which the better enables us to grasp what spiritual growth consists of. We will therefore mention but one other feature of the new birth, or that which is at least an inseparable adjunct of it, namely, the impartation of *faith*. Nor shall we now attempt to define what faith is: sufficient for the moment to acknowledge it is a blessed "gift of God" (Eph. 2:8), in nowise originating in the exercise of the human will, but communicated by "the operation of God" (Col. 2:12), and therefore it is a supernatural principle, active in its favored recipient, bringing forth fruit after its own kind, and thereby evidencing its Divine source. It is "by faith, not by sight" (2 Cor. 5:7) the Christian walks: as said the apostle "the life which I now live in the flesh, I live by the faith of the Son of God [He being its Object], who loved me and gave himself for me" (Gal. 2:20). This it is which distinguishes all the regenerate from the unregenerate, for the latter are "children in whom is no faith" (Deut. 32: 20 and cf. 2 Thess. 3:2,3).

The Christian life begins by the exercise of a God-given faith, namely, an act whereby we receive Christ as our own personal Saviour (John 1:12). We are "justified by faith," and by Christ "have access by faith into this grace [i.e. accepted into God's favor] wherein we stand" (Rom. 5:1,2). We are "sanctified by faith" (Acts 26:18), that is, made actual participants of the ineffable purity of Christ. Through the Spirit we "wait for the hope of righteousness by faith" (Gal. 5:5 and cf. 2 Tim. 4:8). It is by "the shield of faith," and that alone, we are "able to quench all the fiery darts of the wicked" (Eph. 6:16). It is "through faith and patience" that we "inherit the promises" (Heb. 6:12). It was by faith that the Old Testament saints "obtained a good report" (Heb. 11:2) and wrought such wonders, as the remainder of that chapter demonstrates. It is by faith we successfully resist the Devil (1 Peter 5:9) and overcome the world (1 John 5:4). From all of which it is very evident that the measure of our Christian progress will be very largely determined by the extent to which this principle be kept healthy and remains operating in us.

To sum up what has been pointed out above: regeneration is both a "renewing" and a "new creation." As a "renewing" it is a continual process, as 2 Corinthians 4:16 clearly shows. This aspect of it is a partial reversal of and recovery from what happened to us at the fall. It is a Divine quickening, which necessarily presupposes an entity or faculty already existing, though in need of being made alive or revived. This "renewing" is of the inner man, which includes both spirit and soul or "the mind" and "heart." It is an initial and radical act, followed by a repeated but imperceptible process whereby the nobler or immaterial parts of our beings are elevated or refined. This does not mean that "the flesh" or evil principle in us undergoes any improvement, but that our faculties are spiritualised; and thus spiritual growth will consist of the mind being more and more engaged with Divine objects, the affections being increasingly set upon things above, the conscience becoming more tender, and the human will made more amenable to the Divine, and thereby the inner man more and more conformed to the holy image of Christ.

But regeneration is something more than a "renewing" or quickening of parts and faculties already in existence: it is also a "new creation," the bringing into existence of something which did not exist before, the actual bestowment of something to the sinner in addition to all that he had as a natural man. That "something" is variously designated in Scripture (and by theologians) according to its different relations and aspects. It is termed "life" (1 John 5:12), yea life "more abundantly" (John 10:10) than unfallen Adam enjoyed. It is named "spirit" because "born of the Spirit" (John 3:6) and therefore is to be distinguished from our natural spirit; and "the spirit of power and of love and of a sound mind" (2 Tim. 1:7). It is called "the earnest of the Spirit" (2 Cor. 1:22), being a token or firstfruits of what will be ours when glorified; and "grace" (Eph. 4:7) as an inward principle. Theologians designate it "the new nature," and many allude to it under the composite term of "the Christian's graces," which is warranted by John 1:16, and is probably the easiest for us to comprehend. Considered thus, spiritual growth may be said to be the development of our graces: the strengthening of faith, the enlarging of hope, the increasing of love, the abounding of peace and joy: see 2 Peter 1:3 and carefully note verses 5-8.

Thus far we have been dwelling almost entirely upon the internal aspect of our theme, so we will now quote one verse which directs attention to the external side. "For we are His workmanship, created in Christ Jesus unto good works, which God hath before ordained that we should walk in them" (Eph. 2:10). Here is the response which we are required to make unto the new birth. God's purpose in our new creation or regeneration is that we should "walk in good works," that we may make manifest the spiritual root which He then implanted by bearing spiritual fruit. Such was the design of Christ in dying for us: to "purify unto Himself a peculiar people, zealous of good works" (Titus 2:14). From which it plainly follows that, the more zealous we are of good works and the more steadfastly we walk in them, the more do we rightly answer to what God has wrought in us. Now the performance of our daily duties are so many "good works," if they be done from faith's obedience to God's requirements and with an eye to His approbation and glory. Hence the more faithfully and conscientiously we discharge our obligations toward God and toward our fellows, the more true Christian progress are we making.

All that has been before us above receives simplification when it is viewed in the light of *conversion* and its proper sequel. Regeneration is entirely the work of God, wherein we are passive, but conversion is an act of ours; the one being the effect and consequence of the other. The word "conversion" means to turn around, it is a right-about-face. It is a turning from the world unto God, from Satan unto Christ, from sin unto holiness, from being absorbed with the things of time unto devotion to our eternal interests. At regeneration we received a super-natural knowledge of God, and as the consequence, in His light we see ourselves as depraved, lost and undone. At regeneration we received a nature which is "created in righteousness and true holiness" (Eph. 4:24), and as a consequence we now hate all unrighteousness and sin. At regeneration we were given an understanding that we might know Him that is true (1 John 5:20) and our response is to yield ourselves unto His dominion and trust in His atoning blood. At regeneration we received Divine "grace" as an indwelling principle, and the effect is to make us willing to deny ourselves and take up our cross and follow Christ. The proper sequel to such a conversion is that we steadfastly adhere to the surrender we then made of ourselves unto the Lord Jesus, and the more we do so, such will be our spiritual progress. —AWP

(continued from back page)

fall down and worship the golden image he had set up, the three Hebrews rightly refused to do so; and when a later king issued an idolatrous edict, Daniel disregarded it; and in each case God vindicated their fidelity to Him. It is never right to do wrong, no matter who commands it, or what may be the emergency.

"Let every soul be subject unto the higher powers. For there is no power but of God: the powers that be are ordained of God. Whosoever therefore resisteth the power, resisteth the ordinance of God, and they that resist shall receive to themselves damnation" (Rom. 13:1,2). Is that an exhortation which requires *unqualified* submission to the governing power of a country? Does it signify that it is not permissible for the Christian to make any resistance unto magistrates, no matter what may be the nature of the laws they enact? Some have insisted this inspired injunction is to be taken without any modification. They point out it was given to Christians in the days of Nero, requiring them to be fully obedient unto the Roman emperors even though their edicts were destructive of Christianity itself. But such an understanding of these verses is quite untenable, failing as it does to leave any place for the superior claims of *God*. Children are commanded "obey your parents in *all* things" (Col. 3:20), yet if they ordered to *steal* it would be the child's duty to disobey them!

The duty of obedience to those in authority is enforced by Holy Writ: see 1 Peter 2:13, 14. The civil government (whatever its form) is a Divine institution, and therefore to resist magistrates in the exercise of their lawful authority is disobedience to God. Yet since their authority is only a delegated one, delegated by God Himself, then they *transcend* their rights if they require anything which is inconsistent with our obedience to God; and when such a case arises it becomes the Christian's duty to disobey them. The "power" to which Christians are bidden to be subject is a righteous and benevolent one, and not an iniquitous and malevolent one: "he is the minister of God to thee *for good"* (Rom. 13:4), but he ceases to be "the minister of God to thee" if he demands what is evil. Wives are Divinely ordered to be "subject to their own husbands in everything" (Eph. 5:24), yet if they forbade their wives to read the Scriptures it would be their duty to disobey them. Wherever human law conflicts with the Divine "we must obey *God* rather than men" clearly defines our duty. (*D. V. to be continued*). —AWP

(continued from front page)

assigned a difficult task it was this one. But his duty was clear, for obedience to his master required him to enter upon this quest. Accordingly we find him setting out on his mission. But observe how he acted. When he arrived at the outskirts of the city of Nahor, he made his camels to kneel down by the well, and then he said "O Lord God of my master Abraham, I beseech Thee send me good speed this day" (v. 12). It was the hour when the maidens came to draw water from the well, so Eliezer asked the Lord to give him a sign whereby he might "know" which of them was the appointed wife for Isaac (v. 14). And the Lord did not fail him, but honored his faith. In the sequel we find Eliezer bowed in worship and saying, "Blessed be the Lord God of my master Abraham, who hath not left destitute my master of His mercy and His truth: I being *in the way* [of duty] the Lord *led* me" (v. 27). And that is recorded for our instruction and encouragement.

Do not act hastily or impulsively, for God says "He that believeth shall not make haste" (Isa. 28:16). But some reader may reply "I am obliged to make a prompt decision in the matter before me." Even so, if you have been living as becometh a child of God, there ought to be no difficulty: "the light of the body is the eye: if therefore thine eye be single, thy whole body shall be full of light" (Matt. 6:22). That is a figurative way of saying, if you have an undivided heart, if your dominant aim be the pleasing of God, then your mind will be illumined and able to perceive clearly the path of duty. Perplexity is occasioned by conflicting interests swaying me, when opposing motives seek to actuate me, when the pleasing of self comes into competition with the glorifying of God. Keep steadily in view that the thing you have to decide is not which is the easier or most congenial path—the right hand or the left—but which is my *duty*?

Perhaps you reply, but that is my difficulty: how am I to decide *what is* my duty? Well, ponder the *negative* side: it is never right to do wrong, and therefore it can never be the Christian's duty to do anything which God's Word forbids, nor can it ever be his duty to enter into any position which would prevent him doing what Scripture enjoins. For example, if one alternative be going into debt my duty is plain, for Scripture says "Owe no man anything" (Rom. 13:8); or if it be to enter into a partnership or any other union with an unbeliever, God's Word forbids it: "Be ye not unequally yoked together" (2 Cor. 6:14); or if a worldly employer requires me to do work on the Sabbath day, then he is asking me *to sin* by breaking the fourth commandment; or if a Christian mother be ordered to enter a position wherein she could no longer care for her little ones, her duty would be clear, for "train up a child in the way he should go" (Prov. 22:6) is a privilege and responsibility which she cannot delegate unto others.

But suppose the *Government* should demand from me what is against my conscience, as the performing of manual labor on the Sabbath, does not Scripture itself bid me "be subject unto the higher powers?" God's people most certainly ought to be models of law-abiding citizens: righteous and merciful in all dealings with their fellows, doing unto others as they would be done by. They are Divinely enjoined to "render tribute to whom tribute is due," and thus to pay their taxes promptly and unmurmuringly. Nevertheless they must ever remember *God's* claims upon them, and never allow the fear of man to prevent their meeting His claims. We are to submit unto the Government so long as its requirements do not clash with the demands of God, but no further. When the king of Babylon issued a decree that all in his dominions should

(Continued on preceding page)

VOL. XXIII.   JULY, 1944.   NO. 7

STUDIES in the SCRIPTURES

" Search the Scriptures." John 5:39.

Publisher and Editor—ARTHUR W. PINK,
27 Lewis Street,
Stornoway, Isle of Lewis,
Scotland.

THE PATH OF DUTY
Part C

"And an highway shall be there, and a way, and it shall be called The way of holiness; the unclean shall not pass over it, but it shall be for those: the wayfaring men, though fools, shall not err therein" (Isa 35:8). This is a most blessed though little-understood prophecy and promise. The figure used in the first part of the verse is simple and should occasion no difficulty. It is that of a specially-made road through a wild country or trackless desert, provided for the use of pilgrims and travelers. The making known of the will of God unto us is here likened to the casting up of a clearly defined highway through a strange land. The reference is to the state of the Gentile world at the time the Israelitish seer made this prediction. During the days of the Jewish theocracy, the heathen nations were in spiritual darkness and ignorance, being without any written revelation from God. But the incarnation of Christ would entirely alter that awful state of affairs. The people which sat in darkness would see "great light" (Isa 42:6, 7; Mat 4:15, 16). The glorious Gospel would be preached to all nations and the Highway of salvation—the Way which leadeth unto Life, the "way of peace have they not known" (Rom 3:17)—would be clearly revealed unto them.

This Divinely-provided highway through the world is here denominated "the way of holiness." It is so designated because it is appointed by a holy God and brings us to a holy Heaven. It is so designated because it stands out in sharp contrast and separation from all the by-ways of sin. It is expressly said, "the unclean shall not pass over it" (Isa 35:8): the unconverted, the impenitent, the unbelieving have no access to it. Only those who have been cleansed by the atoning blood of Christ have any title to walk in this way, as they are the only ones with any desire to tread the same. Those who traverse this "way of holiness" are termed the "wayfaring men." The Hebrew for this compound "wayfaring" is literally "to go on in the way," which is more informative than the English rendition. It tells us that only those persons who are possessed with a true desire and firm determination will walk therein. The grand requirement for its treader, and that which ensures success therein, is a *heart* for this "way"—that is, the possession of a love of holiness.

The "wayfaring man" is here termed a "fool." It is generally considered that two things are connoted thereby. First, what he is in himself naturally considered. We are

(continued on back page)

IMPORTANT NOTICES

Please advise promptly of change in address, otherwise copies will be lost in the mails.

We are glad to send a sample copy to any of your friends whom you believe would be interested in this publication.

This magazine is published as "a work of faith and labour of love," the editor and his wife gladly giving their services free. There is no regular subscription price, as we do not wish the poor of the flock to be deprived. This does not mean that those looking for something for nothing may "help themselves." Those getting this Magazine, who are financially able and who receive spiritual help from its pages, are expected to gladly contribute towards its expenses; otherwise, their names are dropped from our lists.

Will those forwarding International Money Orders please have them made out to us at Stornoway, Isle of Lewis, Scotland. Checks (Cheques-Eng.) made out on U.S.A. Banks are not negotiable here, so please do not send them.

CONTENTS

THE PRAYERS OF THE APOSTLES
7. Romans 16:25-27

Perhaps by this time, some of our readers are feeling rather disappointed at the method we have followed in the previous articles, considering it had been more profitable had we made it our principal concern to show in more detail how these breathings of the apostles' souls bear upon, or should bear upon, the prayer life of believers today. Yet judging from letters so far to hand, others are grateful that we are endeavouring— in keeping with the title of this magazine—to give an interpretation, as well as an application, of these precious portions of Holy Writ: we shall try to pay attention to both. The more closely we examine the wide range of the recorded prayers of the apostles, the more are we impressed by their deep importance — doctrinally, as well as experimentally—their great variety, their extensive scope: and the more do we feel convinced that they need to be approached and dealt with *expositionally*, as well as devotionally and practically. There has been far too much lazy generalizing of the Truth, and far too little painstaking and detailed instruction.

The passage before us is a case in point, though we admit it is rather an exceptional one, occurring as it does in what many regard as the profoundest epistle in the New Testament. We wonder how many of our readers will obtain, even after a careful reading and rereading of our present passage, any clear-cut and intelligent conception of the contents of this prayer: its scope or its subject. We wonder how many of them could supply satisfactory answers to the following questions: 1. Why is the Deity here addressed as, "Him that is *of power* to stablish you"? 2. What is the force of "according to *my* Gospel"? 3. What is signified by "the *preaching* of Jesus Christ"? 4. What is this "mystery" which "was kept secret since the world began"?

5. How harmonise "kept secret" with "but now is made manifest by the Scriptures of the *prophets*?" 6. Why "according to the commandment of the *everlasting*

God"? 7. What is the special force of "to God *only wise*"? Is there not a real need here for the *teacher!*

One has but to honestly face and carefully ponder those questions to at once be conscious of his dire need of wisdom from Above. At any rate, that is the feeling of this writer. That the central subject of these verses is something especially profound seems very obvious. That they contain Truth of the deepest importance which reader and writer alike should be sensible of. But if their meaning be not apparent from a cursory perusal, neither can it be conveyed to others through a hurriedly prepared article. Prayer and study, study and prayer, are called for, and *they* demand the exercise of faith and patience—graces in which the present generation of Christians are sadly deficient. While we believe it has pleased God to grant us some insight into the contents of this portion of His Word (of which the reader must be the judge), yet we are far from concluding we shall ever plumb such depths in this life. May it please the gracious Spirit to now shine upon our benighted understandings, that in His light, we may see light.

In his repeated studyings of our passage, this writer has long felt that before he was ready to work out its details, he must first ascertain what is its principal subject. Before he is prepared to weigh or even consider what is the burden of this prayer, he must seek to discover what is its leading theme. In setting about that task, full consideration has to be given unto the particular Epistle in which it is found and the distinctive subject of that Epistle. Each separation detail has to be pondered in its relation to the whole; after which parallel passages have to be sought and their aid made use of. That calls for impartial investigation, focused attention, laborious and persevering effort, and above all, humbly seeking wisdom from God. The task of the expositor is no light one, which is why there are so few such, for probably never a generation more detested hard work and mental toil than ours.

In his commentary upon this epistle, John Brown summarised his remarks on these verses by saying, they are "one of the most magnificent doxologies in the New Testament—a worthy devotional peroration to such a doctrinal discussion." This is not only a sublime prayer, but it is also one of the greatest doctrinal passages contained in Holy Writ. If on the one hand it rises to unsurpassed heights of devotion, on the other, it conducts us to the profoundest subject of Divine revelation. This is more or less evident from the terms used in our passage. It speaks not only of a "mystery," but of "the mystery"—that which includes and is the sum of all others. The principal theme of the epistle is here epitomised as affording the special ground for the praise not offered to God. In Romans, the Gospel is expounded (see Rom 1:1, 9, 16) in a more formal and systematic form than elsewhere in the Word: in the body of the epistle, we are shown the blessings it conveys to those who believe it; in this doxology, we are taught how the Gospel originated.

"Now to Him that is of power to stablish you" (Rom 16:25). This is not a petitionary prayer, but an adoration of Deity. No request is made for the saints, but God is exalted before them. The apostle begins reminding us of the excellency and sufficiency of the Divine power. He had concluded his introduction to this epistle by affirming "the Gospel of Christ...is the power of God unto salvation to every one that believeth" (Rom 1:16), and now he points out that the believer is equally dependent upon God's power for his establishment. Christians cannot establish themselves, nor can their ministers establish them. The one and the other may use the appointed means, but they cannot ensure success—God alone can make them effectual unto any of us. But blessed be His name, HE *can* do so, for "God *is* able to make all grace abound toward you; that ye, always having all sufficiency in *all* things, may abound to every good work" (2Co 9:8). It is to be duly noted that the word "able" includes disposition, as well as capacity: He *can,* He *will*— cf. Rom 4:21; Eph 3:20, etc.

The Greek word translated "stablish" (*sterizo*) is rendered, "set steadfastly" in Luke 9:51 and "strengthen" in Luke 22:32 and Revelation 3:2. It means to thoroughly establish, to make us rooted, grounded, and settled in the faith (Col 1:23; 2:7), both in our hearts (1Th 3:12) and walk (2Th 2:17). This is a duty incumbent upon us, for we are expressly bidden "stablish your hearts" (Jam 5:8). But because we are not sufficient for the performance of such a task, God has most graciously made promise: "But the Lord is faithful (though we are unfaithful), who shall stablish you and keep *you* from evil" (2Th 3:3). Though it be our privilege and obligation to study the Word, to grow in grace and in the knowledge of the Lord Jesus, yet so strongly are our hearts influenced by sin, so dull our understanding, and feeble our love, it requires the working of God's power to preserve us. Not only were we unable to bring ourselves into the Faith, we cannot continue in it without Divine strength. Because of our proneness to apostatise, the subtlety and strength of our spiritual enemies, the world in which we live, God's power alone can keep us—cf. Jud 24.

"According to my Gospel" (Rom 16:25). Here we are shown *what it is* in which Christians are "stablished" or "established," namely the Gospel. Romanists are established in human tradition; thousands of so-called Protestants are established in errors equally fatal; but God's own people are established in the Truth—an inestimable favour, especially in such a day as this, when God has given up the vast majority in Christendom to "believe a lie" (2Th 2:11). But more: this clause not only makes known unto us the spiritual sphere in which Christians are established, but also the *means* which the Holy Spirit employs in this gracious work. Only as our hearts are Divinely enabled to cleave unto the grand substance of the Gospel are we kept from being "tossed to and fro, and carried about with every wind of doctrine, by the sleight of men, *and* cunning craftiness, whereby they lie in wait to deceive" (Eph 4:14). Third, this clause signifies: established according to this Divine rule—brought into accord with it both inwardly and outwardly, so that there is no swerving from it in belief or practice: cf. Rom 6:17 margin.

"According to my Gospel" (Rom 16:25). First, this is to be regarded as a discriminative expression: the Gospel I have proclaimed in contradistinction from the false gospel of the Judaisers. None of the other apostles makes any reference to a spurious gospel, but Paul particularly warned the Corinthians against "another gospel" (2Co 11:4) and to the Galatians he wrote, "But though we, or an angel from heaven, preach any other gospel unto you than that which we have preached unto you, let him be accursed" (Gal 1:8)—my Gospel, then, in opposition to all counterfeits, for none other can avail for the salvation of the soul. Second, because Paul was the preeminent expounder of it, his first epistle being devoted to an unfolding of its grand contents. The term "Gospel" occurs scores of times in his writings, yet excepting 1st Peter, it is found nowhere else in the Epistles. Third, because a special dispensation of the Gospel was committed unto him for the Gentiles (Gal 2:7; Eph 3:2). Finally, it accords with the special fervour which marked him: *"my* God shall" (Phi 4:19), "Christ Jesus *my* Lord" (Phi 3:8).

"And the preaching of Jesus Christ" (Rom 16:25). As Robert Haldane pointed out, "This phrase is not the mere repetition of the same thing—as the former. It is indeed the same truth, but from a different point of view. In the one it is considered as good news, in the other as the publication of the truth about Jesus Christ: we are to be established according to what the apostle taught concerning *Him.* " Perhaps it would be more to the point to say, this clause is subjoined to the former in order to inform us what is the substance and contents of the Gospel. Jesus Christ is the grand Object and theme of all true evangelical ministry. The *"preaching* of Jesus Christ" is very much more than making a frequent use of His name in our discourses, or even telling of His wondrous love and work for sinners. It is first and foremost the magnifying of His unique Person, the making known of who He is—the God-man. Second, it is the opening up of His mediatorial office, in which He serves as Prophet, Priest and Potentate. Third, it is a proclamation of His wondrous redemption. Fourth, it is the enforcing of His claims and the holding up of the perfect example He has left us.

"According to the revelation of the mystery, which was kept secret since the world began" (Rom 16:25). This is both an explanation and amplification of the foregoing. The glorious Gospel of Christ is no invention of human wit, but is the wondrous product of the consummate wisdom of God. As J. Evans (Matthew Henry's commentary) well said of the Gospel: "It has in it an inconceivable height and such an unfathomable depth as passes knowledge. It is a mystery, which the angels desire to look into and cannot find the bottom of. And yet, blessed be God, there is as much of this mystery made plain as will suffice to bring us to heaven, if we do not wilfully neglect so great salvation." The Gospel not only infinitely surpasses man's skill to originate, but he could have no knowledge whatever of it, until God was pleased to publish the same. Nor was it any provision of His, devised in time, to meet some unforeseen calamity, no mere improvised remedy for sin, but that which engaged the Divine mind before heaven and earth was created.

Mention is made in the N. T. of "the mysteries of the kingdom of heaven" (Mat 13:11) and of "the mysteries of God" (1Co 4:1). It refers to the yet future restoration and salvation of Israel as a "mystery" (Rom 11:25) and of the resurrection and bodily transformation of the saints as a "mystery" (1Co 15:51). We read also of "the mystery of iniquity" (2Th 2:7), which is in horrible contrast from "the mystery of godliness" (1Ti 3:16). There is also "the mystery of the seven stars" in the right hand of Christ and "the seven golden candlesticks" among which He walks (Rev 1:20 and 2:1), by which we understand His local churches; "the mystery of God" (Rev 10:7), which many regard as His ways in Providence, particularly His governance of this world; and "mystery Babylon the great, the mother of harlots, etc." (Rev 17:5), which the Puritans viewed as Romanism. That which is before us in Romans 16:25 is, we believe, elsewhere termed "the mystery of His will" (Eph 1:9), the "great mystery" of Christ and His Church (Eph 5:32), "the mystery of the Gospel" (Eph 6:19), "the mystery of God (the Spirit), and of the Father, and of Christ" (Col 2:2).

According to the usage of this word in the New Testament, a "mystery" is a concealed truth over which a veil was cast. It concerns something which transcended the powers of man to conceive, and therefore beyond his ability to invent. It related to something, which was undiscoverable by the human mind, beyond human knowledge until Divinely revealed. In recent years, those known as dispensationalists have substituted the term "secret," but we deem it a faulty alternative. It is true these "mysteries" were "secrets" impenetrable by finite sagacity till brought to light by God, but they are still designated "mysteries" after their revelation! Even now they are made known to us there remains a *mysterious* element, which is beyond our ken. "Behold, I shew you a mystery; We shall not all sleep" (1Co 15:51 and cf. 1Th 4:17)—before the Holy Spirit made such disclosures, who ever imagined a whole generation of God's people would enter Heaven without passing through the portals of death! "Great is the mystery of godliness: God was manifest in flesh" (1Ti 3:16)—yet now the miracle of the virgin birth has been recorded, there remains about the Divine incarnation that which is beyond our understanding. The Divine mysteries, therefore, are addressed to *faith* and not to reason.

In seeking to frame a definition of the grand "mystery" of our passage, we will first appropriate the help supplied by the clauses, which have already been before us. It is something "according to" which the God of power is to stablish His people. Contributory thereto, or as the means He employs in connection therewith, is what Paul styles "my Gospel"—i.e. that which he had expounded at length in this very epistle, the heart or central object of which is, "the preaching of Jesus Christ." Next, we observe, this mystery "was kept secret since the world began," by which we understand that it was: hidden from all the wise men of this world (1Co 2:8), that the O.T. saints had not such light upon it as Christians are now favoured with (1Pe 1:10; Col 1:26), and that even the holy angels were not permitted to enter into its wondrous contents until the same was actualised historically (1Pe 1:11; Eph 3:10). Further, we are told that this mystery is now "made known to all nations for the obedience of faith" (Rom 16:26)— for Jew and Gentile alike to give up themselves to Christ to be accepted (by God) through Him, to be ruled by Him.

Turning now to parallel passages, we find that this mystery has to do with that which "Eye hath not seen, nor ear heard, neither have entered the heart of man, the things which God hath prepared for the that love Him. But God *hath revealed them* unto us (especially in the N.T.) by His Spirit: for the Spirit searcheth all things (proof of His omniscience), yea, the deep things of God" (1Co 2:7-10). This intimates the transcendent sublimity of its contents. "The mystery of His will" (Eph 1:9) declares its origin and hints at its selective nature. "The mystery of Christ" (Eph 3:4) signifies Christ *mystical,* for it is His Body in which believing Jews and Gentiles are made "fellowheirs" (Eph 3:6), which tells of its international scope. Colossians 1:26,27 speaks of "the riches of the glory of this mystery," which announces the plenitude of its bestowments. 1 Timothy 3:16 shows us the outworking of it centered around the incarnation, justification, and exaltation of God the Son.

This grand mystery was, we believe, what is designated in other passages "the Everlasting Covenant" (Heb 13:20), which concerned the Divine plan of redemption or the amazing scheme, whereby lost and depraved sinners might be everlastingly saved to the glory of God. This seems clear not only from the other passages referred to above, but more especially from the whole of 1 Corinthians 2. There, Paul affirmed that his paramount concern was to preach "Jesus Christ, and Him crucified" (1Cor 2:2), disdaining the devices of rhetoric in so doing, yet "speak[ing] the wisdom of God in a mystery" (1Cor 2:7): a message so unworldly, so incredible, so exacting that none but the Holy Spirit could open human hearts to savingly receive it. And here, for the moment, we must pause. —AWP

THE MISSION AND MIRACLES OF ELISHA

19. Eleventh Miracle

The eleventh miracle of Elisha is so closely connected, and so intimately bound up with the tenth, that it will scarcely be out of place for us to bring forward the final division of the foregoing and use it as the introduction to this one. Though we dwelt at more than customary length on the healing of Naaman, and pointed out much as we went along that was typical in connection with the same, yet there still remains several details of interest which deserve separate notice, and unto them we now turn. First, the cleansing of Naaman supplied a striking display of *the sovereignty of God.* This was emphasised by the Lord Jesus in His first public discourse in the synagogue at Nazareth, when He reminded His hearers, "And many lepers were in Israel in the time of Eliseus (Elisha) the prophet; and none of them was cleansed, saving Naaman the Syrian" (Luk 4:27). It is ever thus with Him whose thoughts are so different from and whose ways are so high above ours that, when acting in the freeness of His grace, He passes by others and singles out the most unlikely to be the recipients of His high favours (1Co 1:26-29).

Second, the cleansing of Naaman afforded a blessed foreshadowment of the Divine mercy reaching out unto *the Gentiles,* for Naaman was not an Israelite, but a Syrian; nevertheless, he was made to learn the humbling lesson that if Divine grace was to be extended to him, such grace proceeds from the God of Abraham. That was why he must wash in the Jordan: the waters of "Abana and Pharpar" (2Ki 5:12) were of no avail—he must wash in one of *Israel's* streams! This truth is written large across the pages of Holy Writ. The harlot of Jericho was to be spared when her city was destroyed, but it could only be by her heeding the instructions of the two Hebrew spies. The widow of Zarephath was preserved through the famine, but it was by receiving Elijah into her home. The Ninevites were delivered from impending wrath, but at the preaching of Jonah. The king of Babylon received a dream from God, but for its interpretation, he must turn to Daniel. To the Samaritan adulteress, Christ declared "salvation is of the Jews" (Joh 4:22). Then let us heed the warning of Romans 11:18, 25.

Third, the cleansing of Naaman provided a full adumbration of "the way of salvation" or what is *required of the sinner* in order to his cleansing. First, we have a picture of how fallen man appears in the eyes of the thrice holy God—a leper, one condemned by His Law, a loathsome object, unfit for the Divine presence, a menace to his fellows. Then we behold his self-righteousness and self-importance, as he came expecting to purchase his healing, and was angry at the prophet's refusal to show him deference. Next, we learn of the demand made upon him: he must descend from his chariot, and go and wash seven times in the Jordan. There must be the setting aside of his own thoughts and desires, the humbling of proud self, the acknowledgement of his total depravity, full surrender to God's authority and faith's laying hold of the promise "and the flesh shall come again to thee and thou shalt be clean" (2Ki 5:10). Finally, we behold the immediate and complete transformation: "and his flesh came again like unto the flesh of a little child" (2Ki 5:14) with a corresponding change of heart and conduct toward Elisha and his God.

Ere passing from this most fascinating incident, one further word on the particular waters into which Naaman was required to dip. It was not in the river Kishon, nor the pool of Bethesda, but the Jordan. Why? The answer to that question reveals the striking accuracy of our type. As leprosy (emblem of sin) was in question, the *curse* must be witnessed to. Sin has called down the curse of the One against whom it has raised its defiant head (Gen 3). The curse is God's judgment upon sin, and that judgment is *death*. It is this, of which the Jordan ever speaks. It was not because its waters possessed any magical properties or healing virtue: the very name Jordan means "judgment." Those who heeded our Lord's forerunner "were all baptized of him in the river of Jordan, confessing their SINS" (Mar 1:5)—immersion beneath its waters was the acknowledgement that death was their due. Therefore did the Saviour allude to His death as a "baptism" (Luk 12:50), for at the cross, He was overwhelmed by the judgments of God (Psa 42:7; 88:7), and when a sinner believes the Gospel and appropriates Christ as his Substitute, God regards him as having passed through His judgment of sin, so that he can now say, "I am crucified with Christ" (Gal 2:20), and in his baptism as a believer, there is a symbolical showing forth of that fact.

The miracle which is to now to engage our attention is of quite another order, the differences between them being most striking. We will, therefore consider, first, its *contrasts*. The subject of the foregoing miracle was a heathen idolater, now it is the prophet's own servant. The one sought unto the prophet for relief; the other pursued the relieved one and virtually demanded tribute from him. There we behold Elisha teaching Naaman the grand truth of the freeness of Divine grace, here we see Gehazi casting a dark cloud over the same. In the one, Naaman is represented as expressing deep gratitude for his recovery and urging the man of God to receive a present at his hands; in the other, the avaricious Gehazi is portrayed as coveting that which his master so nobly refused. There it was a poor creature healed of his leprosy; here it is one being smitten with that dread disease. There we behold the goodness of God acting in a way of mercy; here we see His severity acting in holy justice. The former closes with the recipient of Divine grace returning home as a devout worshipper; the latter ends with a pronouncement of God's cure on the transgressor and on his seed forever.

Second, its *subject*. The one on whom this solemn miracle was wrought is Gehazi, the servant of Elisha. He has come before us several times previously, and nowhere was he seen to advantage. First, when the woman of Shunem sought unto the man of God on behalf of her dead son and cast herself at his feet, "Gehazi came near to thrust her away" (2Ki 4:27) and his master bade him, "Let her alone." Then the prophet instructed his servant to go before him and lay his staff upon the face of the child (2Ki 4:29). Elisha could successfully smite the waters of Jordan with Elijah's mantle because "the spirit of Elijah" rested upon him (2Ki 2:15), but being devoid of the Spirit, the prophet's staff was of no avail in the prayerless hands of Gehazi (2Ki 4:31). In 2 Kings 4:43, we behold his selfishness and unbelief: "What, should I set this before an hundred men?" when Elisha was counting upon God to multiply the loaves. Thus, his character and conduct is all of a piece and in keeping with his name, which significantly enough means, "Denier."

Third, its *occasion*. "But Gehazi, the servant of Elisha the man of God, said, Behold, my master hath spared Naaman this Syrian, in not receiving at his hands that which he brought: but, *as* the LORD liveth, I will run after him, and take somewhat of him" (2Ki 5:20). It will be remembered that before Naaman left Syria for the land of Samaria that he provided himself with a costly treasure, consisting of "ten talents of silver and six thousand *pieces* of gold, and ten changes of raiment" (2Ki 5:5). No doubt, a part of this was designed for travelling expenses for the retinue of servants who accompanied him, but the major portion of it, he evidently intended to bestow upon his benefactor. But Elisha had firmly refused to receive anything (2Ki 5:15, 16), and so he was now returning home with his horses still laden with the treasure. This was more than the covetous heart of Gehazi could endure, and he determined to secure a portion of it for himself. The honour of Jehovah and the glory of His grace counted nothing with him.

Every word in the above verse repays careful attention. It opens not with the usual "And," but the ominous "But," intimating the solemn contrast between the two miracles. Gehazi is here termed not only "the servant of Elisha," but "of Elisha the man of God"—the added words bring out the enormity of his sin. First, they call attention to the greatness of the privilege he had enjoyed being in close attendance on so pious a master. This rendered the more excuseless his wicked conduct, for it was not the act of an ignorant person, but of one well instructed in the ways of righteousness. Second, it emphasises the enormity of his offence, for it reflected seriously on the official character of the one who employed him. The sins of those in the sacred office, or of those associated with them therein are far graver than those of others. But Gehazi had no concern for the glory of God, so he cared nothing for the reputation of Elisha.

What has just been pointed out above definitely refutes one of the widespread delusions of our day, namely, that it is their unfavourable surrounding which is responsible for the degenerate conduct of so many of the present generation: social improvement can only be effected by improving the wage and homes of the poor. And is the behaviour of the rich any better? Is there less immorality in the west-end of London than in the east? It is drunken and thriftless people who makes the slums, and not the slums which ruin the people. God's Word teaches it is "out of the heart" of fallen man (Mar 7:21-23), and not from his faulty environment that proceeds all which defiles human nature. Nor it is any more warrantable for any person to attempt throwing the blame for his downfall on being obliged to mingle with evil characters. Gehazi was isolated from all bad companions placed in the most favourable circumstances, dwelling with a "man of God," but his soul was depraved! While "the heart of the sons of men is fully set in them to do evil" (Ecc 8:11), the Gospel and not better "social amenities" is their only remedy.

Neither his close association with the man of God nor the witnessing of the miracles performed by him effected any change within Gehazi. The state of his heart is revealed by each expression recorded in 2 Kings 5:20, "Behold, my master hath spared Naaman." Incapable of appreciating the motives, which had actuated Elisha, he felt that he had foolishly missed a golden opportunity. Gehazi regarded Naaman as legitimate prey, as a bird to be plucked. Contemptuously, he refers to him as *"this* Syrian." There was no pity for the one who had been such a sufferer, and no thankfulness that God had healed him. He was determined to make capital out of the situation: "I will run after him, and take somewhat of him." His awful sin was deliberately premeditated. What was worse, he made use of an impious oath: *"as* the LORD liveth, I will run after him." There was no fear of God before his eyes: instead, he defiantly took His holy name in vain.

"So Gehazi followed after Naaman. And when Naaman saw *him* running after him, he lighted down from the chariot to meet him, and said, *Is* all well?" (2Ki 5:21). It is solemn to observe that God put no hindrance in the ways of him who had devised evil. He could have moved Naaman to quicken his pace and so out-distance Gehazi. But He did not: an indication that He had given him up to his heart's lusts. It is ever a signal mark of Divine mercy when the Lord deigns to interfere with our plans and thwart our carnal designs. When we purpose doing anything wrong and a providential obstacle blocks us, it is a sign that God has not yet abandoned us to our madness. The graciousness of Naaman in alighting from his chariot and the question he asked gave further evidence of the change, which had been wrought in him.

Fourth, its *aggravation.* "And he said, All *is* well. My master hath sent me saying, Behold, even now there be come to me from mount Ephraim two young men of the sons of the prophets: give them, I pray thee, a talent of silver, and two changes of garments" (2Ki 5:22). Here we see the wicked Gehazi adding sin to sin, thereby treasuring up to himself "wrath against the day of wrath" (Rom 2:5). First, his greedy heart cherished a covetous desire, then he deliberately and eagerly (as his "running" shows) proceeded to realise the same, and now he resorts to falsehoods. Liars can tell a plausible tale, especially when asking for charity. The thievish knave pretended it was not for himself, but for others in need that he was seeking relief— ever a favourite device employed by the unscrupulous when seeking to take advantage of unwary victims. Worse still, he compromised his master by saying *he* had sent him. To what fearful lengths will a covetous heart carry its subjects!

"And Naaman said, Be content, take two talents. And he urged him, and bound two talents of silver in two bags, with two changes of garments, and laid *them* upon two of his servants; and they bare *them* before him" (2Ki 5:23). Naaman was quite unsuspicious. He not only complied with Gehazi's request, but gave him more than he asked for. After the prophet's firm and repeated refusals to accept ought at his hands, he should have been more on his guard. There is a warning here for us to beware of crediting every beggar we encounter, even though he be a religious one. There have ever been religious leeches who consider the righteous are legitimate prey for them to fatten upon. Whilst it is a Christian duty to relieve the genuinely poor, and there are few such today, yet we are not to encourage idleness, nor suffer ourselves to be deceived by those with a smooth tongue: *investigate* their case.

"And when he came to the tower he took *them* from their hand and bestowed *them* in the house: and he let the men go, and they departed" (2Ki 5:24). He took pains to carefully conceal his ill-gotten gains in a "secret place" (margin), no doubt congratulating himself of his shrewdness—reminding us of the hiding themselves of our first parents (Gen 3:8) and of Achan (Jos 7:21). "But he went in, and stood before his master" (2Ki 5:25). Pretending to be a faithful and dutiful servant, he now appeared before Elisha to await his orders—the most untruthful and dishonest often assume a pious pose in the company of the saints! "And Elisha said unto him, Whence comest thou, Gehazi?" An opportunity was thus given him to confess his sins, but instead of so doing, he added lie to lie: "And he said, Thy servant went no whither." There was no repentance, but a daring brazening of it out.

Fifth, its *justice.* "And he said unto him, Went not mine heart *with thee* when the man turned again from his chariot to meet thee? *Is it* a time to receive money, and to receive garments, and olive-yards and vineyards, and sheep and oxen, and menservants and maidservants? The leprosy therefore of Naaman shall cleave unto thee, and unto thy seed for ever. And he went out from his presence a leper *as white* as snow" (2Ki 5:26, 27). Though Christians are not endowed with the extraordinary powers of the prophets, yet if they be truly walking with God, they will discern a liar when he confronts them (1Co 2:15). Elisha put his finger on the worst feature of the offence, "*Is it* a time to receive money"! and thus, sully God's free grace. From the words that follow, Elisha indicated that he knew how Gehazi designed to use the money— intending to leave his service and set up as a farmer. His punishment was a condign one: he had coveted something of Naaman's—he should have that which would henceforth symbolically portray the polluted state of his soul.

Sixth, its *significance.* Space obliges us to abbreviate. That Gehazi fully deserved the frightful punishment which was visited upon him, and that the form it took was a case of what is termed 'poetic justice' will be evident to every spiritual mind: nevertheless, there was a severity of dealing with him which is more noticeable than in other cases. Nor is the reason far to seek. God was incensed at his having so grievously compromised the display of His free grace. The Lord is very jealous of His types. Observe how He moved Joseph to restore the money to the sacks of his brethren when they came to obtain food from Egypt (Gen 42:25): because he was there foreshadowing Christ as the Bread of life—given to us "without money and without price" (Isa 55:1). The failure of Moses was far more than a losing of his temper: it was a marring of a blessed type. Note "smite the rock" in Exodus 17:6, but only *"speak"* to it in Numbers 20:8—Christ was to be "smitten" (Isa 53:4) but once! As Moses suffered premature death for his fault, so Gehazi was smitten with leprosy for his.

Seventh, its *lessons*. We can but mention three. First, there is a sharply-pointed example here of the bitter fruits borne by the nourishing of a covetous spirit, and a fearful exemplification of that word, "For the love of money is the root of all evil: which while some coveted after, they have erred from the Faith, and pierced themselves through with many sorrows" (1Tim 6:10). How we need to pray, "Turn away mine eyes from beholding vanity (Psa 119:37). Second, there is a most solemn warning against putting a stumbling block in the way of a babe in Christ. Naaman had only recently come to know Jehovah as "the God of all grace" and that was another reason why He dealt so severely with Gehazi, *see* Matthew 18.6! Third, there is a searching test for those of us who are engaged exclusively in God's service, though delivered from the love of money, we may *seek* the good opinion and praise of men.—A.W.P.

THE DOCTRINE OF RECONCILIATION

4. Its Author

This doctrine of Reconciliation presents to our view that which is both indescribably horrible, and also, that which is inexpressibly blessed. The background of it is formed by the fearful calamity of Eden, when the entrance of sin into the world involved the ruination of our race and its alienation from God. The sin of Adam (and of ours in him) was a revolt against God's authority, a contempt of His government, a declaration of war against Him. Man is a rebel, an outlaw, an enemy of God, cut off from access to Him. This has already been before us in previous articles. Now we turn to contemplate the blessed contrast wherein God determined to deliver a part of Adam's descendants from the effects of the fall, and this in such a way that His absolute sovereignty, His free grace, His inexorable justice, unsearchable wisdom, ineffable holiness, all-mighty power, infinite goodness and rich mercy, might be equally honoured. This is actually accomplished in the saving of His elect by Jesus Christ.

The Author of reconciliation is God. More distinctly, it is God the Father, for there is an *order* of the Divine Persons in this work, as in all others. "But to us there is but one God, the Father, *of* whom are all things, and we in Him; and one Lord Jesus Christ [the alone Mediator] *by* whom are all things, and we by him" (1Co 8:6). "God [the Father], who created all things by Jesus Christ" (Eph 3:9): as that was the order of their operation in connection with the old creation, so it is with regard to the new creation—the Father has effected reconciliation by the death of His Son (Rom 5:10). Distinct offices are ascribed to each of the Eternal Three. The Father is the Deviser, the Son transacts the part of Mediator, being the One by whom the work of reconciliation is performed; the Holy Spirit is the Recorder of the Father's plan, and of the satisfaction offered by the Son and of the peace He has made, and is also the One who sheds abroad Their love in the hearts of the redeemed.

The order pointed out above is still more observable in connection with our approach to God: it is *through* Christ and *by* the Holy Spirit that we have access *unto* the Father (Eph 2:18). All the spiritual blessings we have in Christ are expressly attributed unto the Father (Eph 1:3), by no means the least of which is reconciliation. Our election is ascribed particularly unto the Father (Eph 1:3, 4) and so is our regeneration (Jam 1:17, 18). It is the Father who has made us meet to be partakers of the inheritance of the saints in light, having delivered us from the power of darkness, and translated us into the kingdom of His dear Son (Col 1:13). In accord with this Divine order, we find the opening salutation in the Epistles is, "Grace unto you and peace from God the Father, and the Lord Jesus Christ." Hence the Father is due the same honour and love from us for the sending of His Son, as the Son is for His willingness in being sent. Scripture represents the Father as the One directly wronged by sin, for we are told that Jesus Christ is "an Advocate with the Father" (1Jo 2:1).

1. *His will.* When accountable creatures rebel against their Maker and King, they cut themselves off from all right to claim any blessing or benefit at His hands, for they deserve nothing from Him but wrath and punishment. If they be recovered from the ruin which they have brought upon themselves, and are made partakers of Divine salvation, it is solely from the good pleasure of His will, and must be in a way that does not injure any of His perfections; but if they be left to suffer the direful consequences of their apostasy, God is in no wise unjust, for He inflicts no more upon them than they deserve. When a large company of the angels and their chiefs, under Satan's lead, conspired against the Most High, proudly aspiring to a higher position than had been allotted them, God promptly cast them down from their exalted estate, banished them from His presence, and doomed them to suffer everlasting woe (2Pe 2:4). He had not a thought of mercy toward those celestial creatures when they revolted against Him.

In view of that unspeakably solemn example, it ought to be unmistakeably clear to each of us that God might, without the slightest stain upon His own honour, without any unbecoming severity, have left the whole of Adam's guilty race to suffer eternal destruction, for certainly they had no more clarity upon His favour than had the fallen angels. That He did not immediately consign the entire family of fallen mankind to irremediable woe, was due alone to His imperial will: that He was pleased to appoint a remnant of them to obtain salvation and eternal glory, is to be attributed solely to His sovereign and amazing grace. That such a concept is no invention of harsh theologians: but is plainly taught in the Word of God, is clear from His own declarations, "Having predestinated us unto the adoption of children by Jesus Christ to Himself, according to the good pleasure of His will, to the praise of the glory of His grace" (Eph 1:5, 6); "Who hath saved us, and called *us* with an holy calling, not according to our works, but according to His own purpose and grace." (2Ti 1:9).

"Having made known unto us the mystery of His will, according to His good pleasure which He hath purposed in Himself" (Eph 1:9). The "mystery" refers to "the everlasting covenant" in which God arranged and provided for the recovery and salvation of His people who fell in Adam. In proof of which assertion, we cite 1 Corinthians 2:7: "But we speak the wisdom of God in a mystery, *even* the hidden *wisdom*, which God ordained before the world unto our glory," amplified in 1 Corinthians 2:9, 10. Now that which is germane to our present design is, that God "purposed in Himself" or resolved to reconcile some of the sons of men to Himself, even though they had become guilty rebels against Him, and this purpose He purposed "before the world began" (2Ti 1:9). One portion or aspect of that purpose is expressly stated in what immediately follows: "That in the dispensation of the fulness of times [this Christian era] He might gather together in one all things in Christ, both which are in heaven, and which are on earth, *even* in Him" (Eph 1:10). Sin alienates and separates, but the putting away of sin by Christ healed the breach between God and man, between believing Jews and Gentiles, and between them and the holy angels. *Now* "the whole family in heaven and in earth (Eph 3:15) is one—see Revelation 5:11, 12.

The restoration and reconciliation of His guilty and alienated people is attributed to God's "good pleasure," whereof no reason is given save that He "purposed [it] in Himself"—which means that the idea was suggested by none other, and that no external motive influenced Him. There was necessity put upon Him for this resolution: without the least dishonour to Himself, He might have destroyed the entire apostate race, yea, and have been glorified in their destruction. He who was able out of stones "to raise up children unto Abraham" (Mat 3:9), could have consigned Adam and Eve to eternal woe before they produced any children, and have made a new pair from the dust of the ground. There was nothing whatever in the creature that moved God to show mercy unto him. But there is another concept conveyed by this expression— namely, the certainty and powerful efficacy of what He has decided upon, God cannot possibly be disappointed in the accomplishment of His purpose, for none can overthrow it; nor will He ever alter it. "My counsel shall stand, and I will do all My pleasure" (Isa 46:10); "For I am the Lord, I change not (Mal 3:6).

Here is sure and solid comfort for the spiritually-awakened sinner. That simple fact that God is merciful in His nature is not sufficient: Satan knows *that,* but such knowledge affords him no peace! But the Divine assurance *will* "shew mercy" (Exo 33:19) opens a real door of hope. Suppose that Christ had died, and there had been no Gospel revelation and proclamation of the Divine purpose of His death? The mere knowledge of His crucifixion avails me nothing, unless I am assured that it was the will of God to accept Christ's death in lieu of the death of believing sinners: "By the which will we are sanctified through the offering of the body of Jesus Christ once *for all*" (Heb 10:10). The "will" of God is not only the foundation of the "mystery" or plan of redemption, but it is also its *blessedness*. This is the very pith and preciousness of the Gospel: that it is the revealed will of God to save and accept every sinner who puts his or her trust in the atoning blood of Christ. "Who gave Himself for our sins, that He might deliver us from [the corruption and doom of] this present evil world, according to the will of God and our Father" (Gal 1:4).

2. *His love.* A few may be surprised that we should distinguish between the will and love of God, but probably a far greater number will wonder why any explanation should be required from us for so doing. Yet John Owen in his "Arguments against Universal Redemption" (chapter 8, paragraph 5) said, "The eternal love of God towards His elect is nothing but His purpose and good pleasure—a pure act of His will, whereby He determines to do such and such things for them in His own time and way." And again, in his "Vindiciae Evangelicae" (chapter 29), after referring to John 3:16 and other passages, "Now the love of God is an eternal free act of His will, His purpose." Such a cold and bare definition may suit philosophers and metaphysicians, but it will scarcely appeal to the hearts of the regenerate. When Scripture affirms that Christ is the "Son of His love" (Col 1:13, see margin), we are surely to understand something more than that the Son is merely the Object on which the Divine will is set. Rather do we believe, with many others, that the Son is the Darling of the Father's heart. How, too, are we to understand the Saviour's representation of the Father in His welcome of the returning prodigal: He "ran, and fell on his neck, and kissed him" (Luk 15:20)!

While we are far from believing that God's unfathomable love in anywise resembles ours, as an emotion or passion, subject to fluctuation, yet we refuse to regard it as a mere principle. When the voice of the Father audibly declared, "this is My beloved Son in whom I am well pleased," He gave expression to the language of deep and warm affection. When the Lord Jesus affirmed, "The only-begotten Son (a term of endearment) which is in the bosom of the Father, He hath declared Him" (Joh 1:18), we grant that He employed an anthropomorphism (ascribing to God what pertains properly to man); nevertheless, we cannot allow that it was a mere figure of speech devoid of real meaning. "God *is* love" (1Jo 4:8), and no refinements of the most eminent theologians must be suffered to rob us of the blessedness and preciousness of that fundamental truth. All things issue from the will of God (Eph 1:11), but Scripture nowhere tells us that all things proceed from God's love. The non-elect are the subjects of His will, but they are not the objects of His love. Thus there is a clear distinction between the two things.

We greatly prefer the statement of Thomas Goodwin. Near the beginning of his massive work on "Christ the Mediator," he shows what was done by God the Father from all eternity in connection with our salvation. First, He points out His eternal purpose and grace, and then enquires, "If you would further know, What should be the reason of this strange *affection* in our God (i.e. exercised unto those who had rebelled against Him): why the Scripture gives it: our God being *love,* even love itself." Love is an essential perfection in God's very nature, and as it has pleased Him, to exercise the same unto His elect. It is an act of His will, yet not of His will absolutely considered, but of "the good pleasure of His will" toward them. All the acts of God unto His people in Christ, all the blessings which He has bestowed upon them in Christ, all His thoughts concerning them, all the operations of His grace in them, and the workings of His providence for them, all the manifestations of His kindness and mercy unto them, proceed from His *love* for them. Love is the fountain from which flows every stream of His goodness unto them.

The wondrous love of God for His people can only be known by its blessed manifestations toward them. As the effects which it produces discovers to us the nature of the cause which produces them, so the love which God bears unto His elect is revealed by His acts unto them and bestowments upon them. God's love for us does not commence when we first respond to His gracious overtures unto us through the Gospel, nor even when He capacitates us to respond by first quickening us into newness of life, for His very calling of us out of darkness into His own marvellous light proceeds from His love for us. Nor did God's love for the Church begin when Christ died for her and put away her sins, for it was because God so loved her that He gave up His beloved Son to die in her room and stead. "I have loved thee with an everlasting love" (Jer 31:3) is God's own ringing declaration. Therefore it was in love that He "predestinated us unto the adoption of children by Jesus Christ unto Himself" (Eph 1: 4, 5), which is the foundation of all our blessings. Nor did our fall in Adam produce the slightest change of God's love unto His elect.

Though our sin in Eden did not quench God's love for His people, nor even chill it to the slightest degree, yet that horrible disobedience of theirs raised such formidable obstacles from the holiness of His nature and the righteousness of His government, yea opposed such a barrier against us as appeared to all finite intelligences an insuperable one to prevent the exercise of God's compassion unto His guilty and corrupted people. In a word, the Law of God with its inexorable demand for satisfaction, seemed to effectually prevent the operation and manifestation of His love toward its transgressors. Consider carefully an example on the human plane. Darius was induced to sign a decree that if any person asked a petition during the next thirty days from any save himself, he should forfeit his life (Dan 6). Daniel himself defied that decree, making supplication of his God as aforetime. His watchful enemies promptly reported this to the king and demanded that Daniel should be cast into the den of lions. Darius was displeased with himself "and *set* his heart on Daniel to deliver him: and he laboured till the going down of the sun to deliver him" (Dan 6:14). But in vain: the honour of his law barred the outflow of his love; justice triumphed over mercy.

Consider still another case. Absalom committed a grievous offence against his father, for he sought to rob him of his sceptre and wrest the kingdom from his hands, and furthermore, murdered another of his sons. His attempt to gain the kingdom failed, and he fled the country, and remained an exile for three years. David mourned for his son every day and "longed to go forth unto Absolom" (2Sa 13:39), but the honour of his throne clearly prohibited such an action. When Joab perceived "that the king's heart *was* toward Absalom" (2Sa 14:1) and that he knew not how to make an advance toward him without disgracing his character and government, he decided to further his own plans. Accordingly, the unscrupulous Joab resorted to guile and employed a woman to speak to David, pleading that Absalom's crime might be pardoned, his attainder reversed, and be released from banishment. Strangely enough, she reminded the king that God "doth He *devise means*, that His banished be not expelled from Him" (2Sa 14:14). But such a task of restoring his son without sullying his own honour was quite beyond David. The best he could devise was, "Let him turn to his own house, and let him not see my face" (2Sa 14:24).

3. *His wisdom.* Where the wit of Darius completely failed before the requirements of human law, the wisdom of God gloriously triumphed over the obstacles interposed by the Divine Law. Where the wit of David could contrive nothing better than a wretched compromise, for which he later paid dearly, the omniscience of Deity found a way whereby His banished sons are restored and which redounds unto His everlasting honour. In pursuance of His gracious design to recover and reconcile His elect from their fall and alienation, the love of God set His consummate wisdom to work in contriving the fittest means for accomplishing the same. Hence, it is that we read in connection with God's grand purpose concerning our salvation, that He "worketh all things after the counsel of His own will" (Eph 1:11). "He works all by counsel to effect and bring to pass what His will is pitched upon, and the stronger His will is in a thing, the deeper are His counsels as to it" (Thomas Goodwin). —AWP

SPIRITUAL GROWTH OR CHRISTIAN PROGRESS
4c. Its Nature

In our last we sought to show the principles from which spiritual growth issues and the main lines along which Christian progress advances, pointing out that spiritual growth is the development of the spiritual life communicated at regeneration. In this, we shall proceed from the general to the particular, seeking to set out in some detail what that development actually consists of.

1. Spiritual growth consists of an increase in spiritual knowledge.

God works in us as rational creatures, according to our intelligent nature, so that nothing is wrought in us unless knowledge paves the way. We cannot speak a language, unless we have some understanding of the same. We cannot do work with an implement or machine, nor play on a musical instrument, until we have a knowledge of them. The same obtains in connection with spiritual things. We cannot worship intelligently or acceptably an unknown God. He must first reveal Himself and be known by us, for we could not love or trust One with whom we had no acquaintance. Therefore, does God's Word declare, "They that know Thy Name will put their trust in Thee" (Psa 9:10). It cannot be otherwise: once God is revealed to us as living reality, the heart at once confides itself to Him, as being infinitely worthy of its fullest reliance and dependence. It is spiritual ignorance of God, which lies at the foundation of all our distrust of Him, and therefore, of all our doubts and fears: "Acquaint now thyself with Him and be at peace" (Job 22:21).

The Christian life begins in knowledge, for "the new *man* is renewed in knowledge" (Col 3:10). "This is life eternal, that they might know Thee the only true God, and Jesus Christ, whom Thou hast sent" (Joh 17:3). There has been much difference of opinion among commentators as to the scope of those words. When we wrote thereon some twenty years ago, we adopted the view of the majority of Christian writers, namely, a declaration of the way and means by which eternal life is obtained: just as the words that follow "this is the condemnation" in John 3:19 do not define the character of that condemnation, but rather tell us the *cause* of it. While we still believe in the legitimacy and soundness of the interpretation we gave formerly, yet mature reflection would not restrict the meaning of John 17:3 to that explanation, but would also understand it to signify that "eternal life" (of which we now have, but the promise and earnest) or everlasting bliss and glory will consist of an ever-increasing knowledge of the Triune God, as revealed in the person of the Mediator.

This knowledge does not consist in theological thoughts or metaphysical speculations about the Godhead, but in such a spiritual understanding of Him as causes us to believe in the Lord God, to cast our souls upon Him, and be centered in Him as our everlasting Portion. "The renewed understanding is raised up and enlightened with a supernatural life, so that what we know of the Lord is by intuitive knowledge, which the Holy Spirit is most graciously pleased to give. Hence, believers are said to be called out of darkness into marvellous light, and Paul says, 'ye were sometimes darkness, but now are ye light in the Lord.' As the knowledge of the Father, Son and Spirit, is reflected upon the renewed mind in the person of Christ, so it is received into the heart" (S. E. Pierce). This spiritual apprehension of God is such as no outward means can of themselves convey: no not even the reading of the Word or hearing it preached. In addition thereto, God by His own light and power conveys to the human spirit such an effectual discovery of Himself as radically affects the understanding, conscience, affections and will, reforming the life.

As the Christian life begins in spiritual knowledge, so it is increased thereby: "But grow in grace and *in* the knowledge of our Lord and Saviour Jesus Christ" (2Pe 3:18), upon which we quote again from the excellent Pierce, "I conceive that by *grace* here all those faculties, graces, habits and dispositions, which are wrought in us by the Holy Spirit, are to be understood. And to have our spiritual faculties, graces, habits and dispositions exercised distinctively and supernaturally on their proper objects and subjects *is* to 'grow in grace.' What follows in the text is explanatory: 'and in the knowledge of our Lord and Saviour Jesus Christ.' He is the Object on which all our graces are to be exercised. He is the life of all our graces. Therefore, growing into a greater knowledge of Him, and the Father's love in Him, is to 'grow in grace,' for hereby all our graces are quickened, strengthened, exercised and drawn forth to the praise of God." While we do not think that exhausts the meaning of 2 Peter 3:18, yet such an interpretation is borne out by the second verse of the epistle: "Grace and peace be multiplied unto you *through* the knowledge of God, and of Jesus our Lord"—not by the knowledge of God alone, nor of the Lord Jesus alone, but of God in Christ the Mediator, which is also the force of John 17:3.

One of the ways by which we may ascertain what spiritual growth consist of is by attending to the recorded prayers of the apostles, and noting what it was they made request for. Being very eminent themselves in grace and holiness, it was their earnest desire that the churches and particular individuals to whom their epistles were addressed, might increase and greatly flourish in those Divine bestowments. Accordingly, in his prayer for the Ephesians, we find Paul petitioning that the Father of glory would give unto them "the spirit of wisdom and revelation in the knowledge of Him," that the eyes of their understanding might be enlightened that they might know what is the hope of His calling (Eph 1:17, 18). It should be obvious that in asking for successful favours for those saints, there was no implication that they were entirely devoid of them, or that he sought the initial bestowment of them—any more than John 20:31 signifies the Fourth Gospel was addressed to unbelievers (Eph 1:16 proves otherwise), or that his first Epistle was sent to Christians lacking in assurance: rather does 1 John 5:13 connote "that ye may have a clearer and fuller knowledge that eternal life is yours."

No, in making those petitions on behalf of the Ephesian saints, Paul requested that a larger degree of heavenly light might be furnished unto their minds, that they might have a more spiritual apprehension of the One with whom they had to do, of His wondrous perfections according to the revelation He has made of Himself in the Word, and of his varied relationships to them. It was that they might discern the wonders of His grace and power toward, in, and for them. It was that they might have an enlarged conception and perception of their vivification when they were in a state of death in sin. In like manner, he prayed that the love of the Philippian saints might "abound yet more and more in knowledge and *in* all judgment" (Phi 1:9). So for the Colossians, that they might be "increasing in the knowledge of God" (Col 1:10), which is to be taken in its fullest sense: increasing in the knowledge of God in the manifestation He has made of Himself in creation, in providence, in grace; the knowledge of God in His three Persons, in His Christ the Mediator, in His Law, in His Gospel; in the knowledge of His holy will.

This knowledge of God, which distinguishes the regenerate from the unregenerate, which the apostle solicited on behalf of his converts, and which is the basic element in all real Christian progress, is something vastly different from and superior to the mere possession of a correct opinion about God or any speculative view concerning Him. It is a supernatural and saving knowledge. A merely theoretical knowledge of God is inoperative and ineffectual, but an experimental acquaintance with Him is dynamical and transforming. It is a knowledge, which deeply affects the heart, producing reverential awe, for "the fear of the LORD is the beginning of wisdom" (Pro 9:10). It is such a knowledge as strengthens the Christian's graces and calls them forth into lively exercise. Since that Divine light and power is communicated to the saint by the Spirit through the Scriptures, it causes him to search and ponder them as he never did previously, and to mix faith with what he reads and takes in. It is such a knowledge as promotes holiness in the heart and piety in the life. It is a knowledge which produces obedience to the Divine commandments, as 1 John 2:3, 4 plainly teaches. Yet there can be no such knowledge of God except as He is apprehended through Christ (2Co 4:6).

Such a knowledge of God lies at the foundation of every thing else in the spiritual life, being both essential and introductory. Without such a knowledge of God, we cannot know ourselves, how to order our lives in this world, nor what awaits us in the world to come: until made acquainted with Him who is light (1Jo 1:5), we are in complete darkness. Calvin evinced the profundity of his spiritual insight by commencing his renowned "Institutes" in saying, "True and substantial wisdom primarily consists of two parts: the knowledge of God and the knowledge of ourselves." Without a spiritual and personal knowledge of God, we cannot perceive the infinite evil of sin and the fearful havoc it has wrought in us: it is only in His light that we "see light" (Psa 36:9) and discover the horribleness and totality of our depravity. Then it is that we both behold and feel ourselves to be just as God has described us in His Word. Equally so it is only by such a knowledge of God that we can appreciate the Divinely-provided remedy: either in discovering wherein it consists or realising our dire need of the same. "The way of the wicked *is* as darkness" (Pro 4:19).

From all that has been pointed out above, we may see how completely dependent the Christian is upon God: no spiritual progress is possible, except as He continues to shine upon us. Neither a powerful intellect, the artificial aids of philosophy, nor a thorough training in logic, can contribute one iota unto a spiritual apprehension of Divine things. True, they are of use in enabling the teacher to discourse thereon, to express himself more readily and fluently than the illiterate, but as to discovering to him Divine truth, they are of no value whatever. The reason of this is evident: celestial things are high above the reach of carnal reason, and therefore, it can never attain unto an acquaintance with their true nature. Heavenly grace is required for an entrance into heavenly things, and the meanest capacity is as susceptible to heavenly grace as the most capacious mind. Moreover, the things of God are addressed to *faith,* and that is a grace of which the unregenerate, be he the most accomplished savant, is utterly devoid. Divine mysteries are hidden from the naturally wise and prudent, but they are supernaturally revealed to spiritual babes (Mat 11:25)—revealed by the Holy Spirit through a Divinely-imparted faith.

An uneducated Christian may not be able to enter into the subtle niceties of theological metaphysics, he may not be competent to debate the Truth with ingenious objectors, but he is capable of understanding the character and perfections of God, the person and work of Christ, the mysteries and wonders of redemption, so as to obtain such a gracious view thereof as to excite in his mind a holy adoration of the Father and a love for and joy in the Redeemer. And such a knowledge, and that alone, will stand us in stead in a time of trial, the hour of temptation, or the article of death. Yet it is only as the Holy Spirit is pleased to give fresh light and life to the believer's mind by bringing home anew by His own unction and efficacy, what is already known, that he can increase in the spiritual knowledge thereof. What God has revealed in His Word must be applied again and again by the Spirit if it is to be operative in us and bear fruit through us. The believer is as much dependent upon God for an increase of spiritual knowledge as he was for the first reception of it, and constantly does he need to bear in mind that humbling word, "without Me ye can do nothing" (Joh 15:5).

If we added nothing to the last paragraph, we should present a most unbalanced view of this point, conveying the impression that we had no responsibility in the matter. As there is a radical difference between the Christian and the non-Christian, so there is between our first spiritual knowledge of God and our increase in the same. "But grow in grace and *in* the knowledge of Our Lord" (2Pc 3:18) is a Divine exhortation, intimating both our privilege and our duty. We are required to make a diligent use of the means God has provided, for He places no premium on slothfulness. Though we are dependent upon the Spirit to apply the Truth to us, yet that does not signify it will make no difference whether or not we keep the things of God fresh in our minds by daily meditation upon them. Only God can bring His Word home to our hearts in living power, nevertheless we must pray, "quicken Thou me according to Thy Word" (Psa 119:25). Moreover, it is our obligation to abstain from whatever would grieve the Spirit and thereby weaken the assurance, which enables us to say "*my* Father" and "*my* Redeemer." If we increase not in the knowledge of God, the fault is ours.

2. Spiritual growth consists of a deeper delight in spiritual things and objects.

This is ever the accompaniment and effect of spiritual knowledge—affording us another criterion by which we may test the kind of knowledge we have. A merely speculative knowledge of Divine things is cold and lifeless, but a spiritual and experimental acquaintance with them affects the heart and moves the affections. One may accept much of God's Word (through early training) in a traditional way, and even be prepared to contend for the same against those who oppose it, yet it will avail nothing when the Devil assails him. Hence, we are told that when the Wicked one is revealed, whose coming is after the working of Satan, with all power and signs and living wonders, God permits him to work "with all deceivableness of unrighteousness in them that perish," and His reason for this is stated to be: "because they received not *the love of* the Truth that they might be saved" (2Th 2:10). At best, they had only a letter acquaintance with the Truth: it was never enshrined in their affections. But different far is it with the regenerate: each of them can say with the Psalmist, "O how love I Thy Law! it *is* my meditation all the day" (Psa 119:97).

Spiritual delight necessarily follows spiritual knowledge, for an object cannot be appreciated any further than it is apprehended and known. Spiritual knowledge of spiritual things imparts not only a conviction of their verity and a certainty of their reality, but it also produces the soul's adherence to them, the cleaving of the affections unto them, a holy joy in them, so that they appear inexpressibly blessed and glorious unto those granted a discovery of the same. But not having been admitted into the secret thereof, the unregenerate can form no true concept or estimate of the Christian's experience, and when he hears him exclaiming of the things of God, "More to be desired are they than gold, yea, than much fine gold: sweeter also than honey and the honeycomb" (Psa 19:10), he can but regard such language as wild enthusiasm or fanaticism. The natural man lacks both the power to discern the beauty of spiritual things and a palate to taste their sweetness. Nor is the believer's relish for God's Word confined unto the promises and comforting portions: he also declares, "I will delight myself in Thy *commandments,* which I have loved" (Psa 119:47).

The more the believer advances in a spiritual acquaintance with the excellency and beauty of heavenly things, the more solid satisfaction do they afford his mind. The more the Christian enters into the importance and value of God's eternal Truth, the more his heart is drawn out unto the glorious objects revealed therein. The more he actually tastes that the Lord is gracious (1Pe 2:3), the more will he delight himself in Him. The more light he is granted upon the sublime mysteries of the Faith, the more will he admire the wondrous wisdom which devised them, the power which executed them, the grace which conveyed them. The more he realises the Scriptures are the very Word of God Himself, the more he is awed by their solemnity and impressed with their weightiness. The more the ineffable perfections of Deity are revealed to his spirit, the more will he exclaim, "Who is like unto Thee, O Lord, among the gods [or "mighty ones"]? who is like Thee, glorious in holiness, fearful in praises, doing wonders?" (Exo 15:11). And the more his heart is occupied with the person, the office, and the work of the Redeemer, the more will he enter into the experience of him who said, "I count all things but loss for the excellency of the knowledge of Christ Jesus my Lord" (Phi 3:7, 8).

It is true that, through slackness and folly, the believer may to a considerable extent lose his relish for spiritual things, so that his reading of the Word affords him little satisfaction and delight. One who eats and drinks unwise upsets his stomach, and then the palate no longer finds the choicest food agreeable to him. It is thus spiritually. If the believer be out of communion with God and turns to the world for satisfaction, he loses his appetite for the heavenly manna. Wherefore we are bidden to "lay apart all filthiness and superfluity of naughtiness, and receive with meekness the engrafted Word" (Jam 1:21), there must be this "laying apart" before there can be an appreciative reception of the Word. So again, 1 Peter 2:1 shows us there are certain lusts which have to be mortified if we are to "as new-born babes, *desire* the sincere milk of the Word, that ye may grow thereby" (1Pe 2:2). If such exhortations be duly heeded, and the Word of Christ dwells in us richly, then shall we be found "singing with grace in your hearts to the Lord" (Col 3:16) with an ever-deepening joy in Him. —AWP

WELCOME TIDINGS

The time has again come round when, according to our custom for many years past, we seek to give some account of our stewardship unto those who send us gifts to be used in this written ministry, and to encourage our prayer helpers to continue their support at the Throne of Grace. Their supplication have not been in vain, and as we survey the pile of appreciative letters before us, we can but exclaim, "What hath God wrought!" (Num 23:23), for certain none but *He* could multiply our poor loaves and fishes in such a day as this. It is good to recognise His hand as it works in providence; it is still better when our hearts are duly affected thereby, and we are brought to bow before Him in wonderment and worship. More words of cheer have been received than formerly, and we can but make a brief selection here and there.

"I read with trembling heart your treatment of Matthew 7:21-23. I do not at all think that you are too exacting or severe: you could not be faithful were you less so. I feel so much the hypocrisy of my soul that I need continual such warnings" *(Victoria)*.

"Thank you for the valuable Biblical expositions in your paper, which have been very helpful to me personally and to the members of the 'Bible Study Class'" *(New South Wales)*.

"We have received great help and blessing from the Studies, and I give the Lord all the glory and thank and pray daily for you both that He will bless and keep you" *(South Australia)*.

"I am again grateful for the Studies which have come to hand satisfactorily. They are particularly searching and for that reason most profitable" *(New Zealand)*.

"I look upon it as a special favour shown me from the Most High that ever the Studies came into my hands, and that I am still receiving them. I hope you will long be able to send forth the good Seed, and that it may bring forth fruit to the glory of God, and that in ministering to others, you may be blessed" *(New Zealand)*.

"Only eternity will reveal what Studies have meant to me. They have strengthened my faith and been a real spiritual blessing during the past years of fellowship with you in the deep things of God. So many times I find I am savourless salt and a cumberer of the ground, and then sitting with you at the feet of our Lord, my heart is encouraged as you lead me on to know Him and to rejoice in God my Saviour" *(Canada)*.

"I always look forward for the Studies to arrive: they are a source of great comfort and consolation to me in this barren wilderness. How sad that so few in this day appreciate anything of this nature" *(Canada)*.

"It is a very precious magazine to me, and has been so helpful in many ways. In a day of such confusion it is good to hear a voice proclaiming what *the Lord* says" *(Canada).*

"I wish to take this opportunity to express my thanks to God for the blessings received through your written ministry. It has not only helped me in my preaching, but especially so in my own personal life. How thankful I am that you have been led to deal with the practical side of the Scriptures. In no one else's works that I have ever read am I so exercised and probed by the Word as by yours" *(U.S. Pastor).*

"We are grateful to Almighty God for sparing you thus far to carry on the work of the Studies" *(Canadian Pastor).*

"The Lord bless your witness. It is greatly needed: but it cannot fail of His blessing" *(English Pastor).*

"Again I write to thank you for your Studies, which are most valuable as expositions of God's Word, and most helpful spiritually. They are strong meat, which is a vital need in these days" *(English Rector).*

"Your Studies in the Scriptures have been blessed greatly to my soul, and through my dark days have been a great comfort to me. So do not think it amiss for you, as God's servant, to know that many a refreshing drink has been received through the furtherance of God's Word by your labours" *(Helpless shut-in).*

"Your Studies come to me regular. I receive much help in reading them. I used to think old age was a time of rest and freedom from temptations and trials. I now find my mistake: I am in the furnace of afflictions as much as I ever was. God shows me where I am, and I am so glad He does. I have no fault to find: His goodness and mercy have followed me all the days of my life" *(Very aged Pilgrim).*

"We have enjoyed every article and especially those on the Sermon on the Mount, which have been very instructive as well as searching, and they must be if we are to get any real benefit from them. In these trying times, one needs messages that *lead* to heart searching and deeper piety" *(California).*

"We are indeed thankful to Him that by His enabling grace, you were able to complete, and to read, yet another year of the Studies. They have provided, as always, most of the spiritual food and drink outside of the Word itself. Not only do we ourselves owe much to the Studies, but delight in seeing others to whom we have introduced it grow in the knowledge of Him" *(Pennsylvania).*

"I can't tell you how much some of the articles, I think I might say, most of them, have meant to me. They have been a source of strengthening, refreshing and reviving in the midst of these distressing times. What a mercy to have our minds directed to One above and beyond it all, and our affections centered upon Him who controls all. Surely He is worthy of our highest praise" *(North Carolina).*

"The ever blessed things set forth in the Studies are the choicest things I get. Your comments on 'Dagon Destroyed' speak my mind exactly. May God's good blessings continue with you and direct you in the fullness of His will" *(Montana).*

"The Studies have again been of great benefit to my soul. The series on the Sermon on the Mount have been especially illuminating, very searching; and I hope that after I have applied them to my own heart and mastered them in some degree, to be able to give them to the believers here" *(San Salvador).*

"I want to thank you for sending me 'Studies in the Scriptures,' which I have received at irregular intervals during the past year. They have been very helpful to me.

I was particularly edified by the balance of truth in the exposition of the Sermon on the Mount. I had the privilege of introducing my friend—to the magazine and I know he, too, rejoiced in the sound teaching contained therein" *(One in the Middle East Forces)*.

"Long may you both be spared to carry on with the publication of the Studies: they bring comfort to many a starved heart" *(Scotland)*.

"I feel the Studies humble me and trust they will prove a blessing. They always give a sense of the greatness and holiness of God" *(Scotland)*.

"Thanks for the magazines. I never but feel refreshed reading them. How very thankful we should be in the midst of a dark generation that such is written and studied in our day" *(Scotland)*.

"I find the articles as profitable as at any time during the last sixteen years, and take it as an outstanding mercy of God that such help is afforded to His people in such dark days as these. I thank you personally for your 'labour of love,' and may God's blessing rest upon you and the magazine" *(Itinerant preacher)*.

"You are enabled to go deep into the subjects, and they search me very much; in fact, I have to leave off sometimes to pray. I feel that I come very short of being what I should be. But what a blessing to have a Throne of Grace to go to!" *(England)*.

"Your magazines come like a breath from another world" *(New reader)*.

"I thank our God that both you and your dear wife have been enabled to carry on this great work for another year: may you be spared, strengthened and guided to continue this ministry for many years. I say this sincerely my dear Christian friend: your writings are most stimulating, your solemn warnings and frequent spurs are also just the kind of spiritual medicine one needs to continually take lest we neglect and come short" *(England)*.

(continued from back page)

book for instruction. He dare not move a pace until he has received directions therefrom. His daily prayer is, "Order my steps in Thy Word" and "make me to go in the path of Thy commandments; for therein do I delight" (Psa 119:133, 35). So stupid does he feel himself to be, yes, even though he has a M.A. or D.D. degree—that he cries, "Teach me, O LORD, the way of Thy statutes" (Psa 119:33). It is not light *on* the Word he needs, for God's Word is itself light (Psa 119:105), but light *from* the Word, and therefore, does he beg God, "Give me understanding" (Psa 119:73) and illuminate my sin-darkened heart. Thus and thus only does he perceive and walk in the path of duty.

"The wayfaring men, though fools, shall not err *therein*" (Isa 35:8). Note well, it is something else and something better than *"need not* err therein" as so frequently misquoted: namely, "shall not." Just so long as he remains a "fool" in his own esteem, and no longer, will he be kept from making mistakes or wandering off into the by-paths of folly. So long as he is conscious that he "lacks wisdom," he will "ask of God" (Jam 1:5). So long as he is conscious of his ignorance, will he value his Guidebook and seek counsel therefrom. So long as he is kept aware of his stupidity, will he pray for enlightenment. And so long as *that* be the case, he *will* progress in the way of holiness. But as soon as pride is allowed to work, a spirit of independency and self-sufficiency will take possession of his heart, and though he may still "read the Bible" perfunctorily or as a duty, he will no longer consult it anxious for light on his path, and soon he *will* "err therein," for "God resisteth the proud, but giveth grace unto the humble" (Jam 4:6). —AWP

(continued from front page)

expressly told that among those called of God, there are "not many wise men after the flesh," and if it be inquired why this is so, the inspired answer is, "God hath chosen the foolish things of the world to confound the wise;" and His reason for that is, "that no flesh should glory in His presence" (1Co 1:26, 27, 29). In order to magnify the riches of His sovereign grace, God has singled out from among men the weak, the base, mere "nonentities" or "nobodies" (as is the force of the Greek rendered "things which are not" in 1 Corinthians 1:28) to be the recipients of His highest favours. The great majority of His people are "the poor of this world" (Jam 2:5): poor in its material riches, poor in mental equipment, poor in what the world terms, "natural advantages." Second, the term "fool" describes the wayfaring man as he appears unto the unregenerate, because of his spirituality: the one who seeks to please God rather than self, to live for eternity, rather than time, is a madman in their eyes.

"The wayfaring men, though fools, shall not err therein" (Isa 35:8). The two significations given above of the term, "fool," do not in our judgment exhaust or reach its principal meaning here. There is many a natural dolt who deems himself very wise, many a man of one talent who considers himself fully qualified to hold a position which calls for a person of five talents. Ignorance by no means excludes egotism. The "fool" in the verse before us is not necessarily one whose mentality is of poor quality, nor one who is crazy in the esteem of his fellows; rather, is it a person who has been made a fool in his *own eyes*. When a miracle of grace is wrought in the soul, that person is humbled into the dust, his self-complacency and self-sufficiency receives its death wound, he is stripped of his peacock feathers. Not only does he perceive that his righteousness or best performances are "filthy rags" in the sight of God, not only does he feel himself to be "without strength" when it comes to doing what God requires of him, but his wisdom appears folly, and all his education and erudition worthless—so far as obtaining a knowledge of Divine things is concerned.

While it be true that "not many wise men after the flesh" (1Co 1:26) are called by God out of darkness into His marvelous light, yet it does not say "not *any*." There are a few of great natural abilities, of eminent mental endowments, of keen intellectual acumen, who are snatched as brands from the burning. And the change produced in them by regeneration is as radical and marked as it is in the conversion of the most dissolute character. Such an one was Saul of Tarsus, brought up at the feet of Gamaliel, and blessed with most remarkable intellectuality. Yet, he became as "a little child," acknowledging he was not sufficient of himself "to think any thing as of himself" (2Co 3:5). In other words, he became a "fool" in his own estimation (1Co 3:18), and therefore, one who deeply realised his need of being taught of God. And that is true in every case where regeneration takes place. Its subjects are made conscious of their ignorance. Concerning spiritual things, they feel themselves to be utter dunces, and therefore, their earnest cry to the Lord is, "That which I see not teach Thou me" (Job 34:32).

Here, then, is the Divinely-defined character of the man who treads "The way of holiness" (Isa 35:8). He is a "wayfaring man," one who has been given a *heart* for this way, who *desires* to tread it. And second, he is a "fool" in his own estimation and valuation: who feels himself totally insufficient to make any progress in this way. Consequently, he is the one who instinctively and sincerely turns constantly to his Guide-

(Continued on preceding page)

VOL. XXIII.   AUGUST, 1944.   NO. 8

STUDIES ɪɴ ᴛʜᴇ SCRIPTURES

" Search the Scriptures."   John 5:39.

Publisher and Editor—Aʀᴛʜᴜʀ W. Pɪɴᴋ,
27 Lewis Street,
Stornoway, Isle of Lewis,
Scotland.

THE PATH OF DUTY
Part D

In our last we sought to show that in order to tread the path of duty or "way of holiness" there must be, first, a desire for it: one must be a "wayfaring man"—that is, a man with a heart for that way, a love of holiness. Second, there must be a sense of our insufficiency: one must be a "fool" in his own estimation—that is, a person possessed of an humble spirit, conscious of his own stupidity. Third, there must be a turning to God's Word for light on our path, for instruction therein, for that Word is the sole Rule of conduct, our Guidebook from earth to heaven. Obviously, the measure in which the first two things mentioned operate and are really dominant in me will determine the success I shall have in obtaining from the Scriptures the directions I so sorely need, and without which I am certain to "err" in the path of duty. If my desire for light from God wanes, or if I cherish confidence in my own wisdom or "common sense" then, though I may still read the Bible in a formal manner, yet I shall no longer "search the Scriptures daily" (Act 17:11) in a spirit of earnest and prayerful inquiry.

"My son, if thou wilt receive My words, and hide My commandments with thee; So that thou incline thine ear unto wisdom [which you profess to feel the need of], *and* apply thine heart to understanding; Yea, if thou criest after knowledge [of God's will], *and* liftest up thy voice for understanding [of thy duty]: If thou seekest her as silver and searchest [the Scriptures] for her as *for* hid treasures [sparing no pains]; *Then* shalt thou understand the fear of the Lord [which is 'the beginning of knowledge': Pro 1:7] and find the knowledge of God" (Pro 2:1-5). It is not to the careless and halfhearted that the promise is made. It is not to the one who is content to please the Lord in merely a general way that "the secret of the Lord" is revealed. It is not to the prayerless that wisdom and spiritual discernment are vouchsafed. He who is largely indifferent to the holy claims of God upon him in times of prosperity, must not expect Him to show the way out of difficulty when a day of adversity overtakes him. It is those who are out and out for God and who walk by the precepts of His Word who have light on their path.

Let us call attention to one other spiritual grace, which is essential if we are to recognise the path of duty and then walk therein: "The *meek* will He guide in Judgment: and the *meek* will He teach His way" (Psa 25:9). Meekness is not to be confounded with humility,

(continued on back page)

IMPORTANT NOTICES

Please advise promptly of change in address, otherwise copies will be lost in the mails.

We are glad to send a sample copy to any of your friends whom you believe would be interested in this publication.

This magazine is published as "a work of faith and labour of love," the editor and his wife gladly giving their services free. There is no regular subscription price, as we do not wish the poor of the flock to be deprived. This does not mean that those looking for something for nothing may "help themselves." Those getting this Magazine, who are financially able and who receive spiritual help from its pages, are expected to gladly contribute towards its expenses; otherwise, their names are dropped from our lists.

Will those forwarding International Money Orders please have them made out to us at Stornoway, Isle of Lewis, Scotland. Checks (Cheques-Eng.) made out on U.S.A. Banks are not negotiable here, so please do not send them.

CONTENTS

THE PRAYERS OF THE APOSTLES
8. Romans 16: 25-27

The parallels between Romans 16:5-27 and 1 Corinthians 2 are more or less obvious. In the one the apostle adores "Him that is of power to stablish you according to my Gospel and the preaching of Jesus Christ." In the other, he averred that he had "determined not to know any thing among you, save Jesus Christ, and Him crucified" (1Co 2:2) and affirmed his preaching had been "in demonstration of the Spirit and of power" (1Co 2:4). In the former, he declares that his preaching had been "according to the revelation of the mystery, which was kept secret since the world began" (Rom 16:25). And in the latter, he affirms, "But we speak the wisdom of God in a mystery, *even* the hidden *wisdom*, which God ordained before the world unto our glory" (1Co 2:7). There, he announces the mystery "now is made manifest, and by the Scriptures of the prophets" (Rom 16:26). Here, he quotes one of the Prophets and adds, "But God hath revealed *them* [the inconceivable things of the previous verse] unto us by His Spirit" (1Co 2:10). In the doxology, he ascribes glory unto "God only wise;" in the doctrinal passage, he expressly mentions "the wisdom of God" (1Co 2:7). Thus, one passage serves to interpret the other.

"And now is made manifest." What is? Why, the grand "mystery" mentioned in the previous verse. And how is it "made manifest"? Why by his "gospel and the preaching of Jesus Christ." With this declaration of the apostle's should be closely compared his earlier one: "But now the righteousness of God without the Law is *manifested*" (Rom 3:21); and that in turn takes us back to the thesis of this epistle: "For I am not ashamed of the Gospel of Christ: for it is the power of God unto salvation to everyone that believeth; to the Jew first, and also to the Greek. For therein is the righteousness of God *revealed* from faith to faith" (Rom 1:16, 17). In the N.T. era (the "now" of our text and of Rom 3:21), there has been a fuller and more glorious manifestation of God than there was in all the preceding eras. And that in a twofold sense: both in the degree of light given and those who received it. God was wondrously made known to Israel, yet nothing like He was when He became incarnate and tabernacled among men. God's perfections were exhibited in His Law, yet how much clearer are they irradiated by His Gospel!

Perhaps nothing more strikingly portrays the contrast between the two dispensations in connection with the manifestation of the Divine excellency than placing side by side what is recorded in Exodus 32 and a statement made in 2 Corinthians 4. In the former, we find Moses making request of Jehovah: "I beseech Thee, shew me Thy glory" (Exo 33:18). Let the reader look up verses 19 to 22 and then ponder the Lord's response: "thou shalt see My back parts: but My face shall not be seen" (Exo 33:23)—how well may a person be known by a passing glance of his "back parts"! That was characteristic and emblematic of the O.T.[1] economy. Now set over against that this most precious passage: "For God, who commanded the light to shine out of darkness, hath shined in our hearts, to *give* the light of the knowledge of the glory of God in *the face* of Jesus Christ" (2Co 4:6)! "The only begotten Son, which is in the bosom of the Father, He hath declared *Him*" (John 1:18)—revealed Him, made Him known, fully told Him forth.

But there is another sense in which the "mystery" is "now made manifest," as it was not previously, namely, in the more extensive promulgation of it. Under the former economy, the Psalmist declared, "He sheweth his word unto Jacob, his statutes and his judgments unto Israel. He hath not dealt so with any nation: and *as for his* judgments, *they* have not known them. Praise ye the LORD." (Psa 147:19, 20). For more than half the present span of human history, the heathen world was left in darkness—for from the tower of Babel (Gen 11) onwards, God "suffered all nations to walk in their own ways" (Act 14:16), so that they were deprived of even the outward means of grace. But after His resurrection, the Saviour bade His ambassadors, "Go ye therefore and teach *all* nations, baptizing them in the name of the Father, and of the Son, and of the Holy Ghost." (Mat 28:19), in accord with which He gave a special commission unto Saul of Tarsus to bear His name "before the Gentiles" (Act 9:15), and by and through the Gospel—which he proclaimed the contents of the grand mystery—were heralded abroad far and wide.

That to which reference has been made receives express mention in all of the leading passages where this Mystery is in view. In our present one, it is specifically declared that it is "made known to all nations" (Rom 16:26). In 1 Corinthians 2:8, we learn that in the past, it was that which "none of the princes of this world knew," but which God had revealed unto the Corinthian saints (1Co 2:10). In Ephesians 3:8, the **O.T.** – Old Testament apostle averred it had been given him to "preach among the Gentiles the unsearchable riches of Christ," which in the light of verses 2 to 5, signifies that therein was contained the very substance of the mystery. In Colossians 1:25-27, he alludes again to the special dispensation God had given him unto *the Gentiles* in connection with the mystery, which he there speaks of as "Christ in you [or 'among you'], the hope of glory." While in what may perhaps be termed the classic passage of 1 Timothy 3:16, one of the items comprising the mystery is that it should be "preached unto the Gentiles."

The prominent place accorded "the Gentiles" in these passages has led some of the more extreme dispensationalists to draw an erroneous conclusion, arguing that the mystical Body of Christ is pre-eminently Gentilish, that the O.T. saints have no place in it, and that it not only had no begun-historical existence before the call of the apostle Paul, but that no other reference to it is to be found outside of his epistles. We shall not turn aside to refute this error, but would simply call attention to the fact that O.T. Prophecy clearly foretold that Christ should be "a light of the Gentiles" (Isa 42:6,7; 49:6), while the Saviour Himself announced "other sheep I have, which are not of this fold. . . and there shall be one fold, *and* one Shepherd" (Joh 10:16), and Caiaphas prophesied that He should "gather together in one the children of God that were scattered abroad" (Joh 11:52). It is not the simple purpose to call Gentiles into the Church, nor to make them "joint-heirs" with the Jews, but rather the whole plan of redemption, which made that possible, that the "mystery" is concerned with.

"...And by the Scriptures of the prophets, according to the commandment of the everlasting God, made known to all nations for the obedience of faith:" (Rom 16:26). We will consider the subordinate clause first. This "commandment" respects the three things mentioned in the previous verse: it was by Divine appointment that this Gospel, this preaching of Jesus Christ, this revealed mystery, should be made known. The word rendered, "commandment" may mean "decree," and then the reference is to Psalm 2:7 and those passages where the decree is declared, such as, "all the ends of the earth have seen the salvation of our God." (Psa 98:3); it may mean law or "statute," in which case the reference is to the words of our Lord, "Go ye therefore and teach all nations"—that was indeed the commandment of the everlasting God, both as the Father spake in Him and as He "is over all, God blessed forever" (Rom 9:5). The reason for and the special propriety of, here styling Deity "the *everlasting* God," lies in the dominant subject of this passage—namely, "the mystery" or "the everlasting covenant," in which was centralised His "eternal purpose" (Eph 3:11), which respected the salvation of His elect (2Ti 1:9), concerning which God "promised [to Christ] before the world began" (Tit 1:2).

We regard the clause "and by the Scriptures of the prophets" (Rom 16:26) as looking back first to the "mystery" of the previous verse; second, as being linked to this, the "but now is made manifest;" and third, as connected with the final clause of this verse. The mystery or *everlasting covenant* was the subject of

O.T. revelation (2Sa 23:5; Psa 89:34; Isa 55:3), yet for the most part its wondrous contents were couched in obscure figures and mysterious prophecies. It is by means of the antitypes of those figures, and the fulfilment of those prophecies, that such light has been cast upon what was so heavily veiled throughout the old economy, that the parable they contained has been explained and their symbols interpreted, so, that what was for many generations dark is "now made manifest." Israel's prophets announced the grace that should come unto us and "searched diligently" (1Pe 1:10) in connection therewith, yet Peter himself needed a special vision (Act 10) to convince him that salvation was designed for the Gentiles. Thus, the O.T. credits the New, and the N.T. illuminates the Old: what was latent in the one is now patent in the other.

"Made known to all nations for the obedience of faith." This is the immediate design of the Gospel, the preaching of Jesus Christ, the revelation of the mystery, the commandment of the everlasting God: it is that all who read and hear the same should both believe and obey it, receive and be governed by it. Though saving faith and evangelical obedience may be distinguished, yet they are inseparable, the one never existing without the other. As we said in the foregoing article, the Gospel commands us to give up ourselves to Christ, to be accepted through Him, and to be ruled by Him, for He is "the Author of eternal salvation unto all them that obey Him" (Heb 5:9). Unspeakably solemn is it to know that He will yet come "in flaming fire taking vengeance on them that know not God, and that obey not the Gospel" (2Th 1:8). Only that faith is of any value, which produces sincere and loving obedience, and only that obedience is acceptable to God, which issues from faith in His incarnate Son. The design of the Gospel is to bring us to both. Faith is the vital principle, obedience its necessary product; faith is the root, obedience is the fruit.

"To God *only wise be* glory" (Rom 16:27). The reason why the apostle here adores the Deity thus leads unto a wide and wondrous subject, which we trust will grip the reader, as much as it has the writer. Though we propose to devote the balance of this article to a consideration of the same, we shall not now attempt a complete outline of it, for in the perfect timing of His providence (it is quite without design on our part), this glorious attribute of God's and the exercise thereof will come before us in our current articles on the doctrine of Reconciliation—to which we suggest the reader should turn after completing this one. It is in the grand mystery to which the apostle had alluded in the previous verses, in the constitution and outworking of the everlasting covenant, that the consummate *wisdom of God* is so illustriously and pre-eminently displayed, and which drew out the apostle's heart to give praise for this Divine excellency. O that wisdom may be given us to hold up to view this perfection of Him whose "understanding is infinite" (Psa 147:5).

"To God only wise." He is the only wise Being essentially, superlatively, eternally: cf. 1Ti 1:17, Jude 25. God is wise not by communication from another, but originally and independently; whereas the wisdom of the creature is but a ray from "the Father of lights." The wisdom of God is seen in all His ways and works, yet in some, it appears more conspicuously than in others. "O LORD, how manifold are Thy works! in wisdom hast Thou made them all: the earth is full of Thy riches" (Psa 104:24)—the reference being to His works in creation. The same adoring exclamation may be made of His works *in providence,* wherein He regulates all the complicated affairs of the universe and governs this world so that all things are made to redound unto His glory and work together for good to His people. But it is the marvelous plan of redemption, which may well be called the masterpiece at His wisdom. That is indeed "the wisdom of God in a mystery, *even* the hidden *wisdom,* which God ordained before the world unto our glory:" (1Co 2:7), containing as it does "the deep things of God" (1Co 2:10). So many were the problems to be solved (humanly speaking), so many the ways and means required, so great the variety of its exercise, that it is designated "the *manifold* wisdom of God" (Eph 3:10).

The consummate wisdom of God appears in devising a salvation for sinners, which otherwise had baffled forever the understanding of all finite intelligences. He contrived a way where they could have found none. Both the design of the Everlasting Covenant and the means ordained to be used are most worthy of God. "The mystery of His *will*" (Eph 1:9) is the foundation of it. "I will have mercy on whom I will have mercy" (Rom 9:15). "In whom also we have obtained an inheritance, being predestinated according to the purpose of Him who worketh all things after the counsel of His own will" (Eph 1:11). As one of the Puritans expressed it, "His will set His wisdom to work." During recent years, Christian writers when treating of God's so-great salvation, have thrown most of their emphasis upon the *grace* which provided it and the *power* which effectuates it, and comparatively little attention has been given to *the wisdom* which planned it. God determined to work in a most glorious manner, and the end and the means were equally admirable. So grand and marvellous is the work of redemption, that when the angels were sent as ambassadors extraordinary to bring tidings of peace unto the world, they burst forth in that moving adoration, "Glory to God in the highest" (Luk 2:14).

The supreme end which God had in view was His own glory; the subordinate end, the recovery of His lapsed and ruined people. By the "Glory of God," it is meant the manifestation of Himself in the exercise of His attributes, the display of His perfections. In all the works of God, His excellencies are evidenced; but as some stars shine more brightly than others, so His perfections are more manifest in certain of His works; and as there is one heavenly body—which far surpasses all the planets—so the work of redemption greatly exceeds in wonder all the marvels of creation. It is here that wisdom and goodness, righteousness and mercy, holiness and grace, truth and peace, love and power, are united in their highest degree and beauty. Upon that account the apostle uses the expression, "the *glorious* Gospel of the blessed God" (1Ti 1:11), it being (as one has expressed it), "the unspotted mirror wherein the great and wonderful effects of Deity are set forth." It is the glorious work of redemption, which evokes the praise and thanksgiving of all the inhabitants of Heaven: Rev 5:12, 13.

In contemplating the possibility of redemption, the very attributes of God seem to be divided, and so, *against it.* Mercy was inclined to save; whereas, justice demanded the death of the transgressor. The majesty of God seemed to render it unworthy of His exalted greatness that He should treat with defiled dust. The veracity of God required the infliction of the penalty, which He had denounced against disobedience: the honour of His truth must be preserved. The holiness of God appeared to utterly preclude any advance toward depraved creatures. Yet the love of God was set upon them. But how could it flow forth without compromising His other perfections? What finite intelligence could have found a solution to such a problem! Suppose that the problem had been submitted to the angels, and after due deliberation, they had recognised that a *mediator* was necessary to heal the breach which sin had made, to reconcile God to sinners and sinners to God. Suppose such a thing we say, and *where* was a suitable mediator to be found? Consider the qualifications he must possess.

In order to be eligible for such an undertaking, a mediator must be able to touch equally both extremes: he must be capable of the sentiments and affections at both the parties he would reconcile; he must be a just esteemer of the rights and injuries of the one and the other. But for that, he must possess the *nature* of both, so that he has in himself a common interest in both. Moreover, he must have sufficient merit as to secure the reward for many. But such an one was not to be found, either in heaven or in earth. Yet this absence did not defeat Omniscience: God determined to provide one, and that none other than His own Son. But how could that be! seeing He was possessed of the Divine nature only? Suppose *that* question had been submitted to the celestial spirits: had they not been forever at a loss to unravel the difficulty? Suppose further that God had made known to them that His Son should become incarnate, taking unto Himself human nature, the Word becoming flesh. Would they not still have been completely baffled, asking, How can such a prodigy be?

Admire then and adore the amazing *wisdom* of God in ordaining a Mediator fully qualified to reconcile God to men, and men to God. Marvel at such an exercise of omniscience that devised the virgin birth, whereby the Son became partaker of our nature without contracting the least iota of its defilement, whereby He was Immanuel both by nature and by office, whereby He was a fit Daysman (Job 9:33) to lay His hand on each of the estranged parties, whereby He had both zeal for God and compassion for men, and whereby He might serve as a Substitute on behalf of the guilty and make full satisfaction to the Divine justice in their stead. Moreover, Divine wisdom resolved this difficulty in such a way that so far from the glory of the Son being tarnished by the incarnation, it has been enhanced thereby—for He receives throughout the endless ages of eternity such a revenue of praise from His redeemed that the holy angels are incapable of rendering Him, while they themselves have been afforded additional grounds for adoring Him.

Consider also the *compass* of the Divine wisdom in taking occasion from the sin and fall of man to bring more glory to God and to raise man to a more excellent state. Sin, in its own nature, hath no tendency to good; it is not an apt medium, it hath no proper efficacy to promote the glory of God: so far is it from a direct contributing to it that, on the contrary, it is the most real dishonour to Him. But as a black background in a picture, which in itself only defiles, when placed by art, sets off the lighter colours and heightens their beauty, so the evil of sin, considered absolutely, obscures the glory of God, yet by the overruling disposition of His providence, serves to illustrate His name and to make it more glorious in the esteem of reasonable creatures. Without the sin of man, there had been no place *for* the most perfect exercise of God's goodness. Happy fault, not in itself, but by the wisdom and marvellous counsel of God, to be repaired in a way so advantageous that the salvation of the earth is the wonder of heaven.

"The wisdom of God appears in ordaining such contemptible and, in appearance, opposite means, to accomplish such glorious effects. The way is as wonderful as the work. That Christ dying on the cross, a reputed malefactor, should be made our everlasting righteousness; that descending to the grave, He should bring up a lost world to life and immortality, is so incredible to our narrow understandings that He saves us and astonishes us at once. In nothing is it more visible that the thoughts of God are far above our thoughts and His ways above our ways as heaven is above the earth (Isa 55:8). It is a secret in physic to compound the most noble remedies of things destructive to nature, and thereby, make one death victorious over another: but that eternal life should spring from death, glory from ignominy, blessedness from a curse, is so repugnant to human sense that to render the belief of it easy, it was foretold by many prophets, that when it came to pass, it might be looked on as the effect of God's eternal counsels" (W. Bates, *The Harmony of the Divine Attributes,* 1680).

"To God only wise, be glory through Jesus Christ for ever. Amen" (Rom 16:27). The Greek is somewhat complex and the R.V.[2] gives, more literally, "To the only wise God, through Jesus Christ, to whom be the glory forever. Amen." As each translation is equally legitimate,[3] we adopt them both, for each is in perfect harmony with other passages. The thought conveyed by the A.V. is: our adoration of God is possible only through the *mediation of* Jesus Christ. The concept expressed by the R.V. is: it is in and through Jesus Christ that God is superlatively *manifested* as both infinite in might and omniscient in knowledge. "Christ the power of God and the wisdom of God" (1Co 1:24): in and by the person and work of Christ are these Divine perfections supremely displayed—He is "The Image of the invisible God" (Col 1:19), "the Brightness [or 'outshining'] of His glory" (Heb 1:3). The *Object* of this doxology is the omnipotent and omniscient God; the *subject* which gives rise to it is the "mystery" or "Everlasting Covenant;" the *substance* of it is "be glory forever;" the *medium* of it, "Jesus Christ." —AWP

THE MISSION AND MIRACLES OF ELISHA
20. Twelfth Miracle

We have entitled this series of articles, "The Mission and Miracles of Elisha," and as we pointed out in our Introductory paper, much the larger part of what is recorded of the life of this prophet is devoted to a description of the miracles performed by him and the circumstances or occasions which gave rise to them. Excepting that which occupied our attention in the first two or three articles, when we contemplated the preparing and enduing of him for his work, very little indeed has been said about Elisha's mission or ministry up to the point we have now reached in his history. Yet here and there, brief hints have been given us of that which engaged most of his energies. Those hints centre around the several brief mentions made of "the sons of the prophets" and the relation which Elisha sustained to them, a further reference to whom is found in the passage, which is now to be before us. As we pointed out under the previous series on Elijah, Israel had fallen on bad times and their spirituality was at a low ebb. Idolatry was rampant and God's judgments fell frequently upon them—in the form of suffering the surrounding nations to invade their land (1Ki 20:1, 26; 22:1; 2Ki 1:1; 5:2).

From the brief allusion made to them, it would seem that Elisha devoted much of his time and attention to the training of young preachers, who were formed into schools and designated "the sons of the prophets"—which in the Hebrew language would emphasise the nature of their calling and contain no reference to their ancestry. There was one group of them at Bethel and another at Jericho (2Ki 2:3, 5) and yet another at Gilgal (2Ki 4:38). It is from the last reference we learn that Elisha was wont to sojourn with them for a season and preach or lecture to them, as their "sitting before him" signifies (Deu 33:3; Luk 2:46; 10:39); and from the repeated mention of "the people" in this connection (2Ki 4:41, 42) we gather that these seminaries also served as more general places of assembly whither the pious in Israel gathered together for the worship of Jehovah and to receive edification through His servant. That Elisha acted as rector or superintendent of these schools is evident from the young prophets owning him as "*thou* man of God" (2Ki 4:40) and "master" (2Ki 6:5).

First, *its connection.* "And the sons of the prophets said unto Elisha, Behold now, the place where we dwell with thee is too strait for us" (2Ki 6:1). By means of the opening "And" the Holy Spirit has linked together the miracle recorded at the end of chapter 5 and the one we are now to consider. As in previous instances, it points both comparisons and contrasts. Each miracle concerned those who were intimately connected with Elisha—in the one case, his personal attendant; in the other, his students. Each occurred at the same place—in the immediate vicinity of the Jordan. Each was occasioned by dissatisfaction with the position its subjects occupied—the one reprehensible, the other commendable. But there, it was the unfaithful Gehazi; while here, it was the devoted sons of the prophets. In the one, Gehazi took matters into his own hands; in the other, they deferentially asked permission of their master. In the former, an act of theft was committed; in the latter, a borrowed article was recovered. In that, a curse descended upon the guilty one; in this, an article was retrieved from the place of judgment.

Second, *its occasion.* "And the sons of the prophets said unto Elisha, Behold now, the place where we dwell with thee is too strait for us" (2Ki 6:1). There does not appear to us to be anything in this verse, which justifies the conclusion that some have drawn from it, namely, that these young men were discontented with their quarters and lusted after something more congenial. Charity always requires us to place the best construction on the projects and actions of our fellows. The motives which prompt them lie beyond our purview, and therefore, are outside of our province; and actions are to be condemned only when it is unmistakably clear that they are evil in their nature or tendency. Had these students given expression to a covetous desire, surely Elisha had reproved them; certainly, he would not have encouraged their plan, as the sequel shows he did.

We are not told which particular school of the prophets this one was, but from its proximity to the Jordan, there can be little doubt that it was the one situated either at Jericho or Gilgal—most probably the latter, because the reference in 2 Kings 4:38 seems to indicate that it was there that Elisha made his principal headquarters. This appears to be confirmed by the language used by the students, "where we *dwell* with thee" (2Ki 6:1)—they had said, "sojourn" had he been merely on a temporary visit to them. From their statement, we gather that under the superintendency of Elisha, their school had flourished, that there had been such an increase of their numbers, the accommodation had become too cramped for them. Accordingly, they respectfully called the attention of their master to what seemed a real need. It is to be observed that they did not impudently take matters into their own hands and attempt to 'spring a surprise' upon Elisha, but becomingly pointed out to him the exigency of the situation.

"Let us go, we pray thee, unto Jordan, and take thence every man a beam, and let us make us a place there, where we may dwell" (2Ki 6:2). Had their desire for more spacious quarters proceeded from carnal ambition, they had aspired to something more imposing than a wooden building; nor is it at all likely that in such a case, they had volunteered to do the work themselves—rather had they suggested going around with collecting cards, soliciting gifts from the people, so that they might have the money to hire others to erect a more commodious seminary for them. "They were humble men who did not affect that which was gay or great. They did not speak of sending for cedars, and marble stones and curious artificers, but only of getting every man a beam, to run up a plain hut or cottage with. It becomes the sons of the prophets, who profess to look for the great in the *other* world to be content with mean things in *this*" (Matthew Henry). Alas, that Protestants have so often aped the Romanists in making a show before the world.

"And he answered, Go ye" (2Ki 6:2), which he surely had not done if they had become discontented with their humble quarters and were lusting after some thing more agreeable to the flesh. That reply of Elisha's was something more than a bare assent to their proposal or permission for them to execute the same; it was also a real testing of their hearts. Those who are accustomed to judge harshly of others might infer that these young men had grown tired of the strict discipline which Elisha must have enforced, and had found irksome the pious and devotional type of life he required from them, and that this idea of making for the Jordan was but a cover for their determination to get away from the man of God. In such a case, they had promptly availed themselves of his grant, bidden him farewell, and promptly taken their departure.

But we may learn something more from this answer, "Go ye": it gives us a sidelight on the prophet's own character, manifesting as it does his *humility.* He at once perceived the reasonableness of their request and concurred with them therein, whereas a proud and haughty man had quickly resented any suggestion coming from those under his charge or care. Thus, an important practical lesson is here inculcated: superiors ought not to deem themselves above receiving and weighing ideas from their inferiors, and when discerning the wisdom of the same and recognising they could be carried out to advantage, should not hesitate to adopt them. It is the mark of a little mind, and not of a great one, which considers it has a monopoly of intelligence and is independent of help from others. Many a man has paid dearly for disdaining the counsel of his wife or employees.

"And one said, Be content, I pray thee, and go with thy servants" (2Ki 6:3). Very blessed is this, revealing as it does the happy relations, which existed between them and of the veneration and love these students had for their master. Such meekness and graciousness on the part of superiors, as we have alluded to above, is not unappreciated by their inferiors. Right nobly did they respond to the test contained in Elisha's "Go ye," by begging him to accompany them on their expedition. And how such a request on their part refutes the evil inference which some might draw from their original proposal—jumping to the conclusion that they were tired of Elisha's company and merely devised this plan as a pretext to get away from him. A warning to us not to surmise evil of our fellows, giving point to Christ's admonition, "Judge not according to the appearance, but judge righteous judgment" (Joh 7:24).

Third, *its location*: the Jordan. "And he answered, I will go. So he went with them" (2Ki 6:3,4). And a good thing it was that he did so, as the sequel shows. "And when they came to Jordan, they cut down wood" (2Ki 6:4). Very commendable was this. But how unlike the pampered and spoiled young people of our generation who have been encouraged to expect that some one else will do everything for them, that they should be waited on hand and foot by their seniors. These young men were willing and ready to put their own shoulder to the work. They did not seek to shelter behind a false conception of their sacred calling and indulge a foolish pride or papish-like exaltation of their office by concluding that such a thing was beneath their dignity, considering themselves far too superior to engage in manual labour. No, instead of hiring others to do it, they performed the task themselves.

"But as one was felling a beam, the axe head fell into the water: and he cried and said, Alas, master! for it was borrowed" (2Ki 6:5). An accident now happened. In one sense, it is perfectly true that there are no accidents in a world that is presided over by the living God; but in another sense, it is equally true that accidents *do* occur in the human realm. This calls for a defining of our term: what is an accident? It is when some effect is produced or some consequence issues from an action *undesigned* by its performer. From the Divine side of things, nothing occurs in this world, but what God has ordained; but from the human side, many things result from our action, which were not intended by us. It was no design of this man that he should lose the head of his axe: that he did so was accidental on his part.

Fourth, its *purpose:* To recover a borrowed article. "And he cried and said, Alas, master! for it was borrowed." How strange that such a thing should happen while in the performance of duty! Yet the Lord had a wise and good reason for permitting the same, and mercifully prevented the death of another (Deu 19:5). It is to be duly noted that he did not regard Elisha as being too great a man to be troubled about such a trifling matter, but as an honest person deeply concerned over the loss, and assured of his master's sympathy, he at one informed him. His "alas" seems to denote that he regarded his loss as final and had no expectation it would be retrieved by a miracle. The lesson for us is plain: even though (to our shame) we have no faith, of His showing Himself strong on our behalf, it is ever our duty and privilege to spread before our Master everything that troubles us.

"Not one concern of ours is small
If we belong to Him,
To teach us this, the Lord of all
Once made the iron to swim" – *John Newton.*

Fifth, *its means.* "And the man of God said" (2Ki 6:6)—observe the change from verse 1: not simply "Elisha" here, because he was about to act officially and work a miracle. "Where fell it?": this was designed to awaken hope in him. "And he shewed him the place. And he cut down a stick and cast *it* in thither; and the iron did swim" (2Ki 6:6). There was no proportion between the means and the end—to demonstrate the power was of God! The Hebrew word for "stick" is a generic one. It is rendered "tree" 162 times, being the same word as in Exodus 15:25; Deuteronomy 21:22— quoted in Galatians 3:13! It is also translated "wood" 103 times, as in Genesis 6:14, the shittim "wood" used in connection with the frame and furniture of the Tabernacle, and in verse 4 of our passage. Evidently, it was a small tree or sapling Elisha cut down, and the above references make clear its typical import.

Sixth, *its meaning.* The incident which has been before us may, we consider, be justly regarded as broadly illustrating what is portrayed by the Law and the Gospel. It serves to give us a typical picture of the sinner's ruin and redemption. As the result of being dissatisfied with the position God originally assigned us—subjection to His authority—we (in Adam) appropriated what was not ours, and in consequence suffered a fearful fall. The inanimate iron falling into the Jordan—the place of "judgment"—is an apt figure of the elect in their natural state: dead in trespasses and sins, incapable of doing ought for their deliverance. The way and means which God took for our recovery was for Christ to come right down to where we were, and to be "cut off" (Dan 9:26), yea, "cut off out of the land of the living" (Isa 53:8), enduring Judgment on our behalf, thereby recovering us to God (1Pe 3:18).

This incident may also be taken as informing the believer *how lost blessing* may be restored to him. Are there not among our readers some who no longer enjoy the liberty they once had in prayer or the satisfaction they formerly experienced in reading the Scriptures? Are there not some who have lost their peace and assurance, and are deeply concerned of being so deprived? If so, the Devil will say the loss is irrecoverable and you must go mourning the rest of your days. But that is one of his many lies.

This passage reveals how your situation may be retrieved. 1. Acquaint your Master with your grief (2Ki 6:5): unbosom yourself freely and frankly unto Him. 2. Let His "Where fell it?" (2Ki 6:6) search you. Examine yourself, review the past, ascertain the place or point in your life where the blessing ceased, discover the personal *cause* of your spiritual loss, judge yourself for the failure and confess it, acknowledging the blame to be entirely yours. 3. Avail yourself and make us of the means for recovery: cast in the "stick" or "tree" (2Ki 6:6): that is, plead the merits of Christ's cross (1Pe 2:24). 4. Stretch forth the hand of faith (2Ki 6:7), that is, count upon your Master's infinite goodness and grace, *expect* His effectual intervention, and the lost blessing shall be restored to you.

This incident may also be viewed as making known to us how we may *grow in grace.* 1. There must be the desire and prayer for spiritual expansion (2Ki 6:1)—a longing to enter into and possess the "large place" (Psa 118:5) God has provided for us. 2. The recognition that to enter therein involves effort from us (2Ki 6:2), labour on our part. 3. Seek the oversight of a servant of God in this (2Ki 6:3) if he be available. 4. Observe very carefully the particular place to which we must betake ourselves if such spiritual enlargement is to be ours. It is "the Jordan" and that speaks of *death*: we can only enter into an enriched spiritual experience by dying more and more unto the flesh, that is, by denying self, and mortifying our lusts (Rom 8:13; Col 3:5). 5. Expect to encounter difficulties (2Ki 6:5). 6. Use the appointed means (2Ki 6:6) for overcoming the obstacle of the flesh (Gal 6:14). 7. Stretch forth the hand of faith (2Ki 6:7) and appropriate what God has given us in Christ.

Seventh, *its lessons.* 1. See the value of requesting our Master's presence even when about to engage in manual labour. 2. Be conscientious about borrowed articles—*books* for example! We should be more careful about things loaned us than those which are our own. 3. Despise not those engaged in manual labour: Elisha did not. 4. Let not the servant of God disdain what may seem trifling opportunities to do good. 5. Remember your Father cares for His people in their minutest concerns. 6. Is anything too hard for Him who made the iron to swim? 7. What encouragement is here for us to heed, Philippians 4:6! —AWP

SPIRITUAL GROWTH OR CHRISTIAN PROGRESS
4d. Its Nature
3. Spiritual growth consists of a greater love for God.

When pointing out the various aspects of regeneration (in the June article) we quoted Romans 5:5: "the love of God is shed abroad in our hearts by the Holy Ghost which is given unto us." Contrary to the commentators, we do not regard the reference there as being to God's love for His people, but rather one of the blessed effects or consequents of the same. First, because the scope and unity of the whole context requires such an interpretation. In Romans 5:1-11, the apostle enumerates a sevenfold result of our being justified by faith: we have peace with God (v. 1), we are established in His favour (v. 2), we rejoice in hope (v. 2), we are enabled to benefit from trials (vv. 3, 4), we have a hope that fails not (v. 5), our hearts are drawn out to God (v. 5), we are assured of final preservation (vv. 6-10). Second, the relation of the second half of verse 5 ("because") to the first leads to the same conclusion: it is *our* love to God which furnishes evidence that our hope is a valid one. Third, God's love for us is in Himself, and though manifested unto us could scarcely be said to be "shed abroad in our hearts." Verse 8 clearly distinguishes His love toward us.

By nature, the elect have not one particle of love for God: nay, their very minds are enmity against Him. But He does not leave them forever in that fearful state. No, having from eternity set His heart upon them, He has determined to win their hearts unto Himself. And how is that accomplished? By shedding abroad His love in their hearts, which we understand to denote by communicating from Himself a spiritual principle of love, which qualifies and enables them to love Him. Faith is His gift to them (Eph 2:8), and the evidence of that principle being in them is that they now believe and trust in Him. Hope is also His gift to them (2Th 2:16), for prior to regeneration, we had "no hope" (Eph 2:12), and the evidence of that principle being in us is that we have a confident expectation of the future. In like manner, love is also a Divine gift, and the evidence of that principle being in an individual is that he now loves God, loves His Christ, loves His image in His people. Note how in Romans 5, we have the Christian's faith (v. 1), hope (vv. 4, 5) and love (v. 5)—which are the three great dynamics and regulators of the Christian life.

This Divine virtue which is communicated to the hearts of all Christians is that which moves their affections to cleave unto God in Christ as their supreme Good. It is designated "the love of God" because *He* is the Bestower of it, because He is the Object of it, and because He is the Increaser and Perfecter of it. It is first stirred unto action or drawn out to God when the soul apprehends His love for him, for "We love Him, because He first loved us" (1Jo 4:19), for so long as we feared His wrath we hated Him. This particular grace is the one which most affects the others: if the heart be kept right, the head will not go far wrong; but when love cools, every grace languishes. Hence, we find the apostle praying for the Ephesian saints, that they might be "rooted and grounded in love" (Eph 3:17). As the Christian grows, he learns to love God not only for what He has done for him, but chiefly for what He is in Himself—the infinitely glorious One, the Sum of all perfection. Yet our love for Him is easily chilled— through the heart's being turned unto other objects. In fact, of all our graces, this one is the most sensitive and delicate and needs the most cherishing and guarding: Mat 24:12; Rev 2:5.

The force of what has just been pointed out appears in that exhortation, "Keep yourselves in the love of God" (Jud 1:21). Negatively, that means, avoid everything which would chill and dampen it: careless living soon dulls our sense of God's love. Eschew whatever would grieve the Spirit or thereby give Him occasion to convict us of our sins and occupy us with our waywardness, instead of taking the things of Christ and showing them unto us (Joh 16:14). Shun the embraces of the world, keeping yourselves from idols (1Jo 5:21). Positively, it signifies: use the appointed means for keeping your affections warm and lively, set on things above. Familiarise yourself with God's holy Word, regarding it as a series of letters from your heavenly Father. Cultivate communion with Him by prayer and frequent meditations on His perfections. Keep up a fresh sense of His love for you, sunning your soul in the enjoyment of it. Above all, adhere strictly to the path of obedience. When the Lord Jesus bade us "continue ye in My love", He at once went on to explain how we may do so: "If ye *keep* My commandments ye *shall* abide in My love; even as I have kept My Father's commandments and abide in His love" (Joh 15: 9, 10, cf. 1Jo 5:3).

A deeper and increasing love for God is not to be ascertained so much by our consciousness of the same as by the evidences it produces. There are many who sing and talk about how much they love Christ, but their walk gives the lie to their avowals. On the other hand, there are some who bemoan the feebleness of their love and the coldness of their affections, whose lives make it manifest that their hearts beat true to Him. Feelings are no safe criterion in this matter: it is conduct which is the surest index to it. Moreover, it must be borne in mind that the holiest saint who ever walked this earth, who enjoyed the most intimate fellowship with the Lord, would be the first to acknowledge and bewail the inadequacy of his affection for Him whose love passeth knowledge. Nevertheless, there *is* such a thing as a growing love for God in Christ, and the same is demonstrated by a stronger bent of soul toward Him, the mind being more stayed upon Him, the heart enjoying more communion with Him and greater delight in Him, and the conscience increasingly exercised in our care to please Him. The more we are spiritually engaged with God's love for us, the more will our affections to Him be inflamed.

4. Spiritual growth consists of the strengthening and enlarging of our faith.

Faith is the gift of God (Eph 2:8), by which is signified that it is a spiritual prin-ciple, grace or virtue which He communicates to the hearts of His elect at their regen-eration. And as His "talents" are bestowed upon us to trade with, to profit by and increase, so the principle of faith is given us to *use* and employ to the glory of God. Its first act is to believe Christ, to trust in Him, and as Colossians 2:6 bids us, "As ye have therefore received Christ Jesus the Lord, *so* walk ye in Him." That is a most compre-hensive and summarised exhortation, and would require many details in order to fur-nish a full explanation of it. For example, it might be pointed out that the Christian is called upon to walk humbly, dependently, submissively or obediently; yet all of these are included in faith itself. Faith is a humbling and self-emptying grace, for it is the stretching forth of the beggar's hand to receive God's bounty. Faith is an acknowledgement of my own insufficiency and need, a leaning upon One who is mighty to save. Faith is also an act of the will, whereby it surrenders to the authority of Christ and receives Him as King to reign over our hearts and lives. Thus, though there is much more in it than this, yet the prime and essential force of Colossians 2:6 is: as ye became Christians at the first by an act of faith in Christ Jesus the Lord, *continue* trusting in Him and let your life be regulated by faith—"walk" denotes progress or going forward.

In Hebrews 10:38, we are told "now the just shall live by faith." A very elemen-tary statement is that, yet one which is turned into a serious error the moment we tamper with or change its pronoun. We are not justified *because of* our faith, but be-cause of the imputed righteousness of Christ, but that righteousness is not actually reckoned to our account until we believe—instrumentally we are "justified by faith" (Rom 5:1). Nor are the justified bidden to "live *upon* their faith," though many vainly attempt to do so. No, the believer is to live upon Christ, yet it is only by *faith* he can do so. Let us be as simple as possible: I break my fast with food, yet I partake of that food by means of a spoon. I feed myself, yet it is the food and not the spoon I eat. It was said of Esau *"by* thy sword shalt thou live" (Gen 27:40), not *on* thy sword—he could not eat *it*. Esau would live on what his sword brought in. The Christian makes a serious blun-der when he attempts to live upon the faith he fancies he can find or feel within himself; rather is he to feed upon the Word, and this he does only so far as faith is operative—as faith lays hold of and appropriates its holy and blessed contents.

"Now the just shall live by faith" (Heb 10:38) may well be regarded as the text of the sermon which follows immediately in the next chapter, for in Hebrews 11, we are shown at great length and in considerable variety of detail how the O.T. saints exercised that God-given principle, how they lived by faith, and wrought great wonders by it. Nothing is there said of their courage, zeal, patience, but all their works and triumphs are attributed to *faith:* the reason for this being that their courage, zeal and patience were the fruits of faith. As it was with them, so it is with us: we are called to "walk by faith" (2Co 5:7), and the extent to which we do so will determine the measure of success or failure we have in our Christian lives. As the Lord Jesus declared unto the two blind beggars who besought His mercy, "According to your *faith* be it unto you" (Mat 9:29) and to the father of the demon-possessed child, "all things *are* possible to him that believeth" (Mar 9:23). If we are straitened it is not in God but in ourselves, for He ever responds to reliance in and counting upon His intervention. He has expressly promised to honour those who honour Him, and nothing honours Him more than a firm and childlike faith in Him.

"The life which I now live in the flesh, I live by the faith of the Son of God, who loved me, and gave Himself for me" (Gal 2:20). Such a testimony from the chief of the apostles shows us the place which faith has in the Christian life. This expression "the faith of the Son of God" signifies that He is the grand *Object* of faith, the One on whom it is to be exercised—which should help the reader to the better understanding of "the love of God" in Romans 5:5 and our remarks thereon. The Christian's is essentially a life of faith, and in proportion as his faith is not operative does he fail to live the Christian life. A life of faith consists of faith being engaged with Christ, drawing on Him, receiving from Him the supply of every need. The life of faith begins by looking to Christ, trusting in Him, relying wholly upon Him as our righteousness before God, and it is continued by looking to and trusting in Him for everything else. Faith is to look to Christ for *wisdom,* that we may be able to understand all that He has revealed concerning God, ourselves, salvation, our various duties. Faith is to lay hold of His precepts and appropriate His promises. But more especially, faith is to look to Christ for *strength* to perform His precepts acceptably. As we have no righteousness of our own, so no strength; we are as dependent upon Him for the one as for the other, and each is obtained from Him *by faith.*

But at this most vital point, many of the Lord's people have been grievously misled. Under the guise of debasing the creature and exalting Divine grace, they have been made to believe that they are quite helpless in this matter: that as God alone is the Imparter of faith, so He alone is the Increaser of it, and that they have to meekly submit to His Will, as to the measure of faith He bestow, or as to what He withholds from them. The consequence is that so far from their faith increasing, they are for the most part, left to spend their remaining days on earth in a state full of doubtings and fears. And what is still worse, many of them feel *no blame* or reproach for the feebleness of their faith, but instead, blatantly attribute it to the sovereignty of God. If such people rebuked a godless drunkard for his intemperance, they would be justly shocked were he to reply, "God has not given me grace to overcome my thirst;" and yet, when they are reproved for their unbelief, they virtually charge God with it, by saying that He has not granted them a larger measure of faith. What wicked slander! What a horrible misuse of the truth of God's sovereign grace. The blame is theirs, and they should honestly acknowledge it and penitently confess it before Him.

It is perfectly true that God is the Increaser, as well as the Giver of faith, but it certainly does not follow from this that *we* have no responsibility in the matter. The littleness and weakness of my faith is entirely my own fault: due not to God's unwillingness to give me more, but to my sinful failure to *want* what He has already given me! to my not crying earnestly unto Him, "Lord, Increase our faith" (Luk 17:5), and to my woeful neglect in making a proper use of the means He has appointed for my obtaining an increase of it. When the disciples were filled with terror of the tempest and awoke their Master, saying "carest Thou not that we perish" (Mar 4:38), He reproved them for their unbelief, saying "Why are ye fearful? O ye of little faith?" (Mat 8:26): *that* was far from inculcating the deadly delusion that they had no responsibility concerning the measure and strength of their faith! On another occasion, He said to His disciples, "O fools, and slow of heart, to believe" (Luk 24:25), which plainly signified that they were to blame for their lack of faith and were to be admonished for their unbelief.

If I have surrendered myself to the Lordship of Christ and trusted in Him as an all-sufficient Saviour, then Christ is *mine*, and I may *know* He is mine upon the infallible authority of God's Word. Since Christ *is* mine, then it is both my privilege and duty to obtain an increasing knowledge of and acquaintance with Him, through the Scriptures. It is my privilege and duty to "trust in Him at *all* times" (Psa 62:8), to make known to Him my every need and to count upon Him to graciously supply the same. It is my privilege and duty to make full use of Christ, to live upon Him, to draw from His fulness (Joh 1:16), to freely avail myself of His sufficiency to meet my every want. It is my privilege and duty to store up His precepts and promises in my memory, that the one may direct my conduct and the other support my soul. It is the office of faith to obtain from Him strength for the former and comfort from the latter, *expecting* Him to make good His word, "Ask, and it shall be given you; seek, and ye shall find; knock, and it shall be opened unto you:" (Mat 7:7). It is my privilege and duty to "mix with faith" (Heb 4:2) every recorded sentence that fell from His sacred lips, and according as I do so shall I be "nourished up" (1Ti 4:6)—my faith will be fed, thrive, and become stronger.

But if on the other hand, I walk by sight, if I constantly take my eyes off their proper Object, and am all the time looking within at my corruptions, I shall go backward and not forward. If I am more concerned about my inward comforts than I am about my outward walk in the pleasing of Christ, in earnestly seeking to follow the example He has left me, then the Holy Spirit will be grieved and will cease taking of the things of Christ and showing them unto me. If I form the habit of attempting to view the promises of God through the darkened and thick lens of my difficulties, instead of looking at my difficulties in the light of God's promises, then defeat—rather than victory—will inevitably follow. If I turn my eyes from my allsufficient Saviour and am occupied with the winds and waves of my circumstances, then like Peter of old, I shall begin to sink. If I do not make it my daily and diligent business to resist the workings of unbelief in my heart and cry out to Christ for strength to enable me so to do, then faith will surely suffer an eclipse, and the fault will be entirely my own. If I neglect feeding upon "the words of faith and of good doctrine" (1Ti 4:6), then my faith will necessarily be weak and languishing.

We say again that the Christian life is a life of *faith*, and just so far as the believer is not actuated by this spiritual principle, does he fail at the most vital point. But let it be said very emphatically that a life of faith is not the mystical and nebulous thing which far too many imagine, but an intensely practical one. Nor is it the monoply of men like George Muller and those who go forth to preach the Gospel in foreign lands without any guaranteed salary or belonging to any human organisation, trusting God alone for the supply of their every need; rather is it the birthright and privilege of *every* child of God. Nor is it a life made up of ecstasies and rapturous experiences, lived up in the clouds: no, it is to be worked out on the common level of everyday life. The man or the woman whose conduct is regulated by the Divine precepts and whose heart is sustained by the Divine promises, who performs his or her ordinary duties as unto the Lord, looking to Him for wisdom, strength and patience for the discharge thereof, and who counts upon His blessing on the same, is living a life of faith as truly as is the most zealous and self-sacrificing preacher.

It is true we must be on our guard against unwarrantably exalting the means and making them a substitute for the Lord Himself. The doctrine, the precepts and the promises of Scripture are so many windows through which we are to behold *God*. It is our privilege and duty to look to Him for His blessing upon the means, and since He has appointed the same to count upon His sanctifying them to us, expecting Him to make them effectual. But we must conclude our remarks upon this point by mentioning some of the *evidences* of a deepening and increasing faith. It is a proof of a stronger and larger faith when the soul is more established in the Truth, when there is a steadier confidence in God, and when we make a greater use of His promises. When we are less influenced and affected by what other professing Christians believe, resting our souls alone on a "thus saith the LORD" (1Co 2:5). When we live more out of ourselves and more upon Christ. When many of His unregenerate disciples are turning away from Christ and He says, "Will ye also go away"? and we can answer, "to whom shall we go? Thou has the words of eternal life" (Joh 6:66-69). When we have become conscientious and diligent in the performing of our duties, for faith is shown by its works (Jam 2:17, 18).

5. Spiritual growth consists of advancing in personal piety.

Our space is nearly exhausted, but this article would be sadly incomplete if we omitted all reference to progress in practical godliness. As various aspects of this will come before us (D.V.)[4] under the next branch of our subject, there is the less need now to enter into much detail. As the Christian obtains an enlarged spiritual apprehension of God's perfections, not only is his heart increasingly affected by His wondrous goodness and grace, but he is more and more awed by His high sovereignty and ineffable holiness, so that he has a deeper reverence for Him and His fear a larger place in his heart, ever exerting a more potent influence in his approaches to Him and on his deportment and conduct. In like manner, as the Christian becomes better acquainted with the personal offices and work of Christ, he obtains not only a fuller realisation of how much he owes to Him and what he has in Him, but he is made more and more conscious of what is due unto Him and what becomes one who is a follower of the Lord till glory. The better he realises that he is "not his own, but bought with a price," the more will he resolve and endeavour to glorify God in Christ "in (his) body, and in (his) spirit, which are God's" (1Co 6:19, 20), longing more ardently for the time when he will be able to do so without let or hindrance. —AWP

THE DOCTRINE OF RECONCILIATION
4b. Its Author

In our last we were only able to barely mention that the *wisdom* of God was engaged in the salvation of His people. Before we attempt to illustrate this particular aspect, let us point out that it was in His character of *Judge* that the Father then acted. It is most important that this should be recognised, yea, essential if we are to view our subject from the correct angle, for reconciliation was entirely a judicial procedure. In Hebrews 12:23, God the Father is expressly spoken of as "the Judge of all," which is an official title. He it was who passed sentence upon sinning Adam and all whom he represented as a federal head. None but "the Judge of all" could have "made Christ to be sin" for His people, or them to be "the righteousness of God in Him" (2Co 5:21). "*It is* God that justifieth" (Rom 8:33): that is, it is the Father as "the Judge of all" who actually and formally pronounces righteous in His sight the sinner who believes on Christ. It is on this twofold ground that the apostle there argues the irreversibility of our justification: that the sentence of justification is pronounced by the Supreme Judge, and that, on the basis of the full satisfaction which has been made to Him by Christ.

We closed our last by calling attention to the fact that the determination of the Father to recover His lapsed people is described as "the purpose of Him who worketh all things after the *counsel* of His own will" (Eph 1:11), which signifies there was an exercise of His infinite understanding in devising how that resolve should be made good to His own glory. To speak after the manner of men, the Father consulted with Himself, called His omniscience into play, and drew up a plan in which His "*manifold wisdom*" (Eph 3:10) is exemplified. That many-sided plan is termed "the mystery" because it has to do with "the deep things of God" (1Co 2:7, 10). "There is variety in the mystery and mystery in every part of the variety. It was not one single act, but a variety at 'counsels' met in it: a conjunction of excellent ends and means" (Charnock). What those excellent ends and means were, we shall now try to set forth, yet knowing full well that our utmost efforts can convey only a most inadequate and fragmentary idea of what will be our wonderment and admiration for all eternity. God's consummate and manifold wisdom is seen.

1. In Love's triumph over the Law. We begin here because it the better links up with the closing paragraphs of our last and the opening one of this. Continuing that line of thought, be it said, the solution to the problems raised by sin and the harmonization of Love and Law is termed a "mystery," because it transcends human reason and can only be known by Divine revelation. It is called "the hidden wisdom" of God, because it remained an impenetrable secret until He was pleased to disclose it. No discovery of it was made in creation. Though "the heavens declare the glory of God and the firmament showeth His handiwork," yet they gave no indication it is His will to show mercy unto rebels: rather does the universe exhibit an inexorable reign of law. If a devoted mother gives her child medicine from the wrong bottle, the result will be the same as if an enemy poured poison down its throat. Break one of Nature's laws, even in ignorance, and no matter how deep our regret, there is no escaping the penalty. Divine Love has triumphed over the Law not by trampling upon it, but by fully meeting its demands and rendering it honourable. Divine wisdom contrived a way in which there was no compromise between Love and Law, but each was given fullest expression.

The way in which God has dealt with what to human wit appears insoluable, both manifests His perfect wisdom and greatly redounds to His glory. He has dealt with the problem raised by sin by taking it into the court of His Law and settling it on a righteous basis. The needs-be for that is evident. Sin is far too great an evil for man to meddle with and every attempt he assays in that direction only makes bad matters worse— as appears in both the social and international spheres. Still more is this the case when man attempts to treat with God: his very efforts to remove sin do but aggravate it, and any attempt to approach God in spite of it only serves to increase his guilt. None but God is capable of dealing with sin, either as a crime or as pollution, as that which is a dishonour to Him, or as it is, a barrier to our access to Him. Moreover, as sin is too great an evil for us to deal with, so righteousness is too high for the fallen creature to reach unto, yea too high for holy creatures to bring down to us. Only God Himself can bring near His righteousness (Isa 46:13).

Yes, God has dealt with the momentous issue raised by sin by taking it into the court of His Law. For fallen man to have taken it there would have inevitably meant the losing of his case, for he is a transgressor of the Divine statute and a moral bankrupt, utterly unable to make any reparation for his offence. But His consummate wisdom enabled the Judge of all to deal with it in such a manner that the honour of His Law has been maintained unimpeached, and yet, the case has been settled on a basis equally favourable to God and that sinner! Settled in such a way that the wondrous love of God is free to flow forth unto His elect, children of disobedience though they be in themselves, without ignoring or condoning their disobedience, and so that His love remains a *holy* love. It is on that judicial settlement that an all sufficient and final answer has been furnished to man's anguished and age-long questions, "How then can man be justified with God? or how can he be clean that is born of a woman?" (Job 25:4); "Wherewith shall I come before the LORD"? (Mic 6:6).

2. In exercising two Contrary principles in Redemption. This is an achievement worthy of Omniscience. God is love, nevertheless, He is "light' (1Jo 1:5) as well: not only is He full of kindness and benevolence, but He is immaculately pure and holy. God is abundant in mercy, but He is also just and "will by no means clear *the guilty*" (Exo 34:7). Here then are two of the Divine perfections moving in opposite directions: how can such contraries be reconciled? Love goes out unto the prodigal, but Light cannot look upon iniquity (Hab 1:13). Mercy would fain spare the offender, but justice demands his punishment. Grace is ready to bestow a gratuitous salvation, but righteousness insists that the defaulter cannot be released till he has "paid the uttermost farthing" (Mat 5:26). Shall then the tenderness of the Father yield to the severity of the Judge? or shall the rights of the Judge give place to the desire of the Father? Each must be satisfied. But how? Admire and adore that wondrous wisdom which devised a means whereby, "Mercy and truth are met together; righteousness and peace have kissed each other." (Psa 85:10).

It is said God loves the sinner, but hates his sin. Yet that provides no solution to the problem, for the question still returns, Will God sink His love to the sinner in His hatred of his sin? or allow His love for the sinner to override His hatred of his sin? God has sworn, "the soul that sinneth, it shall die" (Eze 18:4); but He has also sworn, "I have no pleasure in the death of the wicked; but that the wicked turn from his way and live" (Eze 33:11). The oath of justice and the oath of pity appear irreconcilable: must then one yield to the other? No, both must stand. But how? In redemption, God has manifested two opposite perfections at the same time, and in one action, in which there is shown supreme hatred of sin and superlative love of the sinner. Justice and mercy has alike maintained its ground without compromise, yea, has issued from the conflict honourable and glorious. Divine wisdom contrived plan whereby God has punished transgression without scourging the transgressors, and has repaired the ruin of the sinner without condoning his sin.

3. In appointing a suitable Mediator. Clearly, this was the first step necessary in order to a solution of the intricate problems to which we have alluded. The fall of man placed him at an immeasurable *distance* from God—"your iniquities have separated between you and your God" (Isa 59:2). Not only so, but the fall produced an infinite moral *difference,* man becoming polluted and a hater of God, God Himself ineffably holy and at legal enmity with man. Such a breach appeared unbridgeable. For on the one hand, it became not the glory of His nature, nor the honour of His government, for God to make any direct advance towards rebellious subjects; and on the other hand, man had no desire to be restored to His image or favour, and even if he had, was barred from any access to Him. Thus, all intercourse between God and men was at an end; an impassé was created; an utterly hopeless situation seemed to exist. "For our God is a consuming fire" (Heb 12:29), and who was there that could interpose himself between Him and us? But Divine wisdom provided a means and remedy, decreeing there should be a Mediator who would bridge the distance and heal the difference between them, affecting a mutual reconciliation.

But where was such an one to be found? that was capable of laying his hand upon both (Job 9:33)? He must be entirely clear of any participation in the offence. He must, on account of his personal excellence, stand high in the esteem of the injured One. He must be a person of exalted dignity if the weight of his mediation was to bear any proportion to the magnitude of the crime and the value of the favour he would confer. He must be able to fully maintain the interests and subserve the honour of God. He must also possess a tender compassion towards the wretched offenders or he would not cordially interest himself on their behalf. And to give greater fitness to such a procedure, it would be eminently proper that he should be intimately related to each of the parties. But where was one with so many and so necessary qualifications to be found? There was no creature worthy of so high office and so honourable an undertaking, no, not "in heaven, nor in earth, neither under the earth" (Rev 5:3). None but Omniscience had ever thought of appointing God's own beloved and co-equal Son to take upon Him our nature.

4. In the union of such diverse natures in the person of Christ. It was necessary that the Mediator should be a *Divine* person in order that He might be independent and not the mere creature of either party; in order that He might reveal the Father (Joh 1:18; 14:9), in order to render unto the Law an obedience He did not owe for Himself (as all creatures do) and be one of infinite value; and in order that He might be capacitated to administer the realms of providence and grace, which are committed to Him as Mediatorial Prince (Mat 28:18; Joh 17:2). None other than God can forgive sins, impart eternal life, restore the fallen creature to true liberty, or bestow the Holy Spirit. Yet it was equally necessary that the Mediator should be *Man*: in order that He might truly represent men as "the last Adam" (1Co 15:45), in order that He might be "made under the law" (Gal 4:4) to obey it, in order that He could suffer its death-penalty, and in

order that, in His glorified humanity, He might be Head of the Church. He was to be "the Apostle and High Priest" (Heb 3:1): God's Apostle unto us, our "High Priest" with God, for He must both pacify God's wrath and remove our enmity.

But how furnish the Son for His office? How become partaker of human nature without contracting its corruption? How unite Godhood and manhood, the Infinite with the finite, Immortality with mortality, Almightiness with weakness? How produce such a union that the two natures were perfectly wedded in one Person and yet preserve their distinctness, conjoined yet not confounded? so that the Deity was not changed into flesh, nor flesh transformed into God? Before the Word's becoming flesh, must we not exclaim, "O the depth of the riches both of the wisdom and knowledge of God! (Rom 11:33). By that unique and wondrous union, Christ was fitted to be "the Mediator of a better covenant" (Heb 8:6). There was nothing that belonged to Deity, which He did not possess, and nothing that pertained to humanity but He was clothed with (Rev 1:5-8). He had the nature of Him that was offended by sin, and of him that offended. "As sin was our invention (Ecc 7:29), so Christ alone is God's, and therefore is He called 'The Wisdom of God' (1Co 1:24), which is not spoken of Him essentially as Second Person, but as Mediator, because in Him, God's wisdom to the utmost is made manifest" (Thomas Goodwin).

5. In constituting Christ the federal Head of His people. "When God in wisdom had found a suitable Person, yet since this must be His only Son, here was a greater difficulty to be overcome: how to give Him for us" (Thomas Goodwin). To satisfy both the requirements of His justice and the abundance of His mercy, God determined that a full satisfaction should be made unto His Law, and such a satisfaction than if was thereby more honoured than if it has never been broken, or the whole race damned. In order thereto, He appointed that Christ should serve as the Surety and Substitute of His people. He must stand as their Representative and both fulfil all righteousness for them and endure the curse in their stead, so that they might be legally reckoned to have obeyed and suffered in Him. By transferring their guilt to the Surety, God both punishes sin and pardons the sinner. In the same stupendous Sacrifice, God has upheld the claims of His Law and lavished His kindness on His people. "The depths of God's *love* are seen here, as of His wisdom before, in not sparing His own Son, but exposing Him to all the rigours of justice, which would not make the least abatement" (Thomas Goodwin).

Christ then was made the "Surety of a better testament" (Heb 7:22). There could be no thought of reconciliation between a holy God and polluted rebels until sin had been put away and everlasting righteousness brought in; and as our Surety, the Lord Jesus accomplished both. But O my reader, marvel at and stand in awe before what that involved. It involved that He who was in the form of God should take upon Him the form of a Servant. The Lord of angels should be laid in a manger. That the Maker of the universe should not have where to lay His head. That He should be constantly engaged in doing good and injuring none, yet be cast out by the world and deserted by His own followers. That the Lord of glory should be condemned as a malefactor, His holy face fouled by the vile spittle of men and His back scourged by them. That the King of kings should be nailed hand and foot to a convict's gibbet. That the Beloved of the Father should be smitten and forsaken by Him. Such contraries transcend the wit of man and could never have been invented by him. Must we not exclaim, "O LORD, how great are thy works! and thy thoughts are very deep." (Psa 92:5)!

6. In overruling sin to our gain. What a marvel of Divine wisdom is this: that God has not only removed the reproach, which the entrance of it brought upon His government, but that He made sin to be the foil for a greatest and grandest display of His perfections; and that He has not only devised a plan whereby His people are completely recovered from all the dire consequences and effects of the fall, but that they obtain a vastly superior inheritance than was the portion of unfallen Adam. God would have His people not only saved from Hell, but also brought to Heaven, yet in such a way should be most to the honour of Himself and of His Son. The apostle speaks of "the salvation which is in Christ Jesus *with eternal glory*" (2Ti 2:10)—not only salvation, but a glorious one: one that is to the glory of Him who contrived it, of Him who purchased it, of Him who applies it, and of them who enjoy it. What a truly amazing thing is this that shame should be the path to glory, that fallen sinners are enriched by the Redeemer's poverty, that those grovelling in the mire of sin should be advanced to the highest dignities by Christ's making Himself "of no reputation" (Phi 2:7)!

What honour it brings to God's wisdom not only to restore fallen men, but to make the fall issue in their superior excellence. If they had only been restored to their forfeited estate and the enjoyment of that happiness which they had lost, it had been a remarkable triumph of grace, but to make them "joint-heirs with Christ" (Rom 8:17) and partakers of His glory (Joh 17:24) leaves us lost in amazement. It is a mystery of nature that the corruption of one thing is made to minister to the generation of another (as the bones of animals fertilize vegetation), but it is a grander mystery of grace that our fall in Adam should occasion a nobler restitution. Innocence was not our last end: a superior felicity awaits us on High. Human nature is raised to a far higher degree of honour than had man retained his innocency, for through redemption and regeneration, the elect are vitally united to the God-man Mediator and made members of His Body. The devil's empire is overthrown by the very same nature as he overthrew (Gen 3:15; Rom 16:20)!

7. In winning rebels unto Himself. Having contemplated — something of the wisdom and love of the Father, the willingness and work of the Son, here we are to behold (more distinctively) the power and grace of the Holy Spirit. When He first draws near to the elect in their unregenerate state, He finds them in a most deplorable condition: their understandings darkened by sin, their hearts filled with enmity toward God, their wills steeled against Him. Not only have they no regard for His glory, but they are without any desire for His so-great salvation, yea, positively and strongly averse to it. Here too are obstacles which need removing, obstacles so formidable that nothing short of omniscience and omnipotence could overcome the same. How shall captives be delivered who are thoroughly satisfied with their prison? How shall slaves be freed who are in love with their bonds? Particularly, how shall that be effected while treating them as rational and responsible beings, without offering violence to their wills and reducing them to mere machines?

Some may regard the above as a very exaggerated statement of the case, supposing that a complete solution is found by presenting the Gospel to them. But Scripture teaches, and experience and observation verifies it, that the natural man has no eyes capable of beholding the beauty of the Gospel, and that his heart is so desperately wicked he will not receive the Saviour that it offers him. How then are such creatures to be saved from themselves? How shall those who detest holiness be brought to desire it? the dead in sins made to walk in newness of life? That such a miracle *is* performed we know, but *how* it is wrought, we know not. Christ Himself declares it is a mystery as inscrutable to man as the workings of the wind (Joh 3:8). All we know is that life, light, love are supernaturally communicated, by which the unwilling are made willing—not by compelling them to do what they abhor, but by sweetly overcoming their aversion. "With *lovingkindness* [not by mere physical power] have I *drawn* thee" (Jer 31:3).

8. In making our holiness and happiness conserve each other. This is yet another of the marvels of God's wisdom: that He has contrived that the same Gospel, which secures our everlasting felicity, shall also promote our present purity. The sanctity of God is not compromised by His clemency of sinners, for the Redeemer is Himself both the principle and pattern of holiness unto all who are saved by Him. Moreover, the same grace to send His Son to die for us gives the Holy Spirit to renew us according to the Divine image; and thereby, make us meet for communion with Him. What a wonder of Divine wisdom to so highly exalt those who are so utterly unworthy in themselves and yet, at the same time, effectually humble them that they cry, "Not unto us O LORD, not unto us, but unto Thy name give glory, for Thy mercy, *and* for Thy truth's sake" (Psa 115:1)! God's lovingkindness unto His people neither loosens the bonds of duty, nor breaks that relation in which they stand to Him as their sovereign Lord and Governor. The Gospel does not permit its beneficiaries to return hatred for love, nor contempt for benefit, but lays them unto deeper obligations of gratitude to obedience. Those chosen to salvation are also "predestinate[d] to be conformed to the image of His [God's] Son" (Rom 8:29). The law of faith requires us to submit to Christ's scepter, as well as depend upon His sacrifice. —AWP

(continued from back page)

first step is taken in obedience to His will, He indicates the next one, and the more we yield ourselves to His governance, the clearer light shall we have both within and without. "A good understanding have all they that *do His commandments*" (Psa 111:10) because obedience to God delivers from the deceptions of the flesh and the delusions of Satan. That "good understanding" enables us to apply the general rules of Scripture to the varied details of our complex lives. That "good understanding" preserves us from making foolish mistakes. Because that "good understanding" is formed by obedience to the Divine commandments, it keeps us from acting according to selfish, worldly and carnal motives. And thus, it is that He *"leads [us]* in the way of righteousness" (Pro 8:20).

One question and we must conclude. Suppose I *failed* at a certain point to render obedience unto the clearly-revealed will of God, and instead in pursuing the path of duty, turned aside into the way of self-pleasing, and now I am eating the fruit of my own folly. Suppose I find that my way has become "hedge[d] up...with thorns" (Hos 2:6), so that I know not how to extricate myself. What am I to do? What steps must the backslider take in order to recovery? Why, humbly *confess* the sin to God and go back to the very point where you forsook the path of obedience. Abraham was called to sojourn in the land of Canaan, but when a famine arose, he forsook it and "went down into Egypt to sojourn there" (Gen 12:10)—where he got into serious trouble. But later, he went "unto the place where his tent had been at the *beginning*. . . Unto the place of the altar which he had made there at the first" (Gen 13:3, 4). Do thou likewise: "Remember therefore from whence thou art fallen, and repent, and do the *first* works"

(continued from front page)

for they are quite distinct qualities. This is clear from the words of the Saviour who said, "Take My yoke upon you and learn of Me; for I am meek and lowly in heart:" (Mat 11:29)—the Greek word here rendered "lowly" is translated "humble" in James 4:6 and 1 Peter 5:5. There should be no difficulty in discovering the force of this word. To go no further than the verse quoted (Psa 25:9): the fact that "meekness" is required in order to our being "guided" and "taught" suggests that it signifies a pliant and receptive heart. As humility is the opposite of pride and self-sufficiency, so meekness is the opposite of self-will and stubbornness. It is not the natural virtue which we are here treating of, for *that* very often approximates closely to weakness, but the spiritual grace of meekness, which is bold as a lion before an enemy, is submissive and obedient before God.

This lovely grace, like all others, appears in its full perfection in the Lord Jesus. Seen in His readiness to be the Covenant-head of His people, in His willingness to assume our nature, in His being subject to His parents during the days of His childhood, in His submitting to the ordinance of baptism, in His entire subjection to the Father's will, in the whole course of His obedience. Seen when He was "led [not 'dragged' 'or driven,' but 'led' unresistingly] as a lamb to the slaughter" (Isa 53:7). Thus, it should be evident that there is a real difference between true humility and meekness. Not only are they distinct, but they are not always operative in the same person. One may be humble and yet far from being meek. One may have a real sense of his own ignorance and stupidity, pray to God for light and wisdom, search His Word for the needed direction, and then when those directions are received *disregard* them because unacceptable. Unless our wills be truly yielded to God's, when His will crosses ours, then we shall decline to heed the same.

It appears to the writer that what has just been pointed out serves to expose the sophistry of those who imagine that it is a more difficult matter to ascertain their duty, than to perform the same once it is perceived. Both experience and observation reveal the contrary. God's Word is not ambiguous, but written in simple language for simple souls. True, it treats of the profoundest mysteries, which transcend the grasp of every finite intelligence; nevertheless, where it describes the way of holiness and defines what God requires from us, it uses terms so plain that misunderstanding is excuseless. Nor is it because our Guidebook is inadequate: it furnishes full directions and presents a sufficient solution to every practical problem, which may occasion us difficulty. It is the *obedience* which is difficult to flesh and blood, because our Rule so often demands that which is contrary to our natural inclinations. It is because so many fear that to follow the right course would involve them in unpleasant consequences, that they so often turn from it. That is why the Saviour said, "If ye *know* these things, happy are ye if ye *do* them" (Joh 13:17). We all know various things, which should be done, but are slow to perform, because the flesh in us finds them distasteful.

"The way of the righteous *is made plain*" (Pro 15:19). The "righteous" man is he whose heart is right with God and whose conduct is regulated by the "Word of Righteousness." And since his heart be right toward God, he heeds those rules given him for the ordering of his steps: see Proverbs 4:23, 27. Do not expect God to reveal to you the whole path of duty in a moment: rather does He make known one step at a time. As the

(Continued on preceding page)

VOL. XXIII.   SEPTEMBER, 1944.   NO. 9

STUDIES IN THE SCRIPTURES

" Search the Scriptures."   John 5:39.

Publisher and Editor—ARTHUR W. PINK,
27 Lewis Street,
Stornoway, Isle of Lewis,
Scotland.

TO THE UNSAVED

As one who has been called to declare "all the counsel of God," it is our bounden duty to keep back nothing which may prove profitable. We dare not assume that all of our readers have actually passed from death unto life; and therefore, we are required to address ourselves, occasionally at least, to those who are yet under the condemnation and wrath of a sin-hating God, especially unto such as mistakenly suppose they have been reconciled to Him. Though our chief design and effort is to provide spiritual nourishment for those who are in Christ; yet, we cannot altogether ignore the ones who are yet strangers to Him. The more so that, in this generation, there are so few who are seriously attempting to expose empty professors unto themselves, and make it plain that many of those who fondly believe they are journeying Heavenwards are entertaining a false hope—that instead of their hope being fixed upon the Rock, it rests upon nothing but a foundation of sand. Is that the case with *you,* dear friend?

"Ye cannot serve the LORD: for HE is an holy God; He is a jealous God; He will *not forgive* your transgressions nor your sins" (Jos 24:19). Those words bring before us an essential and fundamental aspect of the Truth, which is rarely proclaimed today, and which multitudes who sit under modern "evangelism" (?) are quite unacquainted with. The view which now so widely obtains is, that nothing is easier and simpler than the obtaining of the forgiveness of our sins. Millions of people have been assured by the blind leaders of the blind, that all which is required from them is that they believe the Gospel and receive Christ as their personal Saviour. It matters nothing what be the state of their hearts, what be their concept of God's character, what be their attitude to His Law. It matters not that they regard sin as trifle, are thoroughly carnal and in love with the world, and have no realisation of their deep need: so long as they "accept Christ" all is well with them. Nor does it matter how unchanged are their future lives—all is now well with them forever. So Satan would have them think.

"Ye cannot serve the LORD." What is signified by *serving* the Lord? It means that I recognise His claims upon me, that I own His authority, that I unreservedly submit myself to His will. It means that I take the place and discharge the obligations of a servant, and a servant is one who is at the disposal of his master, who does as he tells him, who seeks to please him and promote his interests. Perhaps the reader is saying in

(continued on back page)

IMPORTANT NOTICES

Please advise promptly of change in address, otherwise copies will be lost in the mails.

We are glad to send a sample copy to any of your friends whom you believe would be interested in this publication.

This magazine is published as "a work of faith and labour of love," the editor and his wife gladly giving their services free. There is no regular subscription price, as we do not wish the poor of the flock to be deprived. This does not mean that those looking for something for nothing may "help themselves." Those getting this Magazine, who are financially able and who receive spiritual help from its pages, are expected to gladly contribute towards its expenses; otherwise, their names are dropped from our lists.

Will those forwarding International Money Orders please have them made out to us at Stornoway, Isle of Lewis, Scotland. Checks (Cheques-Eng.) made out on U.S.A. Banks are not negotiable here, so please do not send them.

CONTENTS

THE PRAYERS OF THE APOSTLES

9. 1 Corinthians 1: 4-7

The original Corinth was the chief city of ancient Greece, not only in authority, but in wealth and grandeur, and, we may add, in luxury and licentiousness—the temple of Venus being situated there. It was entirely destroyed by the Roman consul Mummius, 120 B.C., and as one writer expresses it, "its inhabitants were dispersed, and the conqueror carried with him to Rome the richest spoils that ever graced the triumphs of a Roman general." For a century after that, it lay desolate in ruins. But Julius Caesar perceiving the military importance and commercial possibilities of its location determined to rebuild it, and for that purpose sent thither a colony, consisting chiefly of freed men. Justus (Act 18:7), Crispus and Gaius (1Co 1:14), Fortunatus and Achaicus (1Co 16:17) are all names of Roman origin. That colony, however, was little more than the nucleus of the new city. Merchants flocked thither from all parts, and many Jews were drawn to it by the lure of commerce. Art, literature, and luxury revived. The Isthmian games were again celebrated there.

The new Corinth was made the capital of Achaia. Under the fostering care of Augustus Caesar, Corinth regained much of its ancient splendour, and by A.D. 50 had reached a pre-eminence, which made it the glory of Greece. But it was a material and carnal glory, for it was a centre of voluptuousness. Yet, where sin abounded, grace did much more abound, for God had ordained that this place of gross wickedness should witness some of the grandest triumphs of the cross of Christ. From that viewpoint, it is easy to perceive how well situated Corinth was to be a centre from which the Gospel might be diffused. Not only was it the political capital of Greece, the seat of its commercial and intellectual life, a place of concourse of many citizens and nations, but it was a place from which influences of many kinds emanated in all directions. To the city, Paul was sent. Though an ambassador of the King of kings, he was attended by no retinue, and his approach was entirely unheralded and unaccompanied.

A complete stranger to the place, Paul sought out two of his own countrymen who were employed in the same craft in which he was proficient—Aquila and his wife Priscilla—lodging and working with them in tent making (Act 18:1-3). On the Sabbaths, he went to the synagogue, where he reasoned with and persuaded both Jews and Greeks. A little later, his hands were strengthened by Silas and Timothy joining him, and he testified to the Jews that Jesus is the Christ. But they opposed and blasphemed. Nothing daunted Paul, as he shook his raiment and said to them, "Your blood be upon your own heads: I am clean: from henceforth I will go unto the Gentiles" (Act 18:6). The Lord honoured his decision, first saving Crispus, the chief ruler of the synagogue and all his house, and the "many of the Corinthians hearing, believed and were baptized" (Act 18:8). But they were only the firstfruits: a larger harvest was to be gathered. "Then spake the Lord to Paul in the night by a vision, Be not afraid, but speak, and hold not thy peace: For I am with thee, and no man shall set on thee to hurt thee: for *I have* much people in this city." (Act 18:9, 10).

They were the Lord's people, be it noted, even though yet in a state of nature, dead in trespasses and sins—His, by sovereign and eternal election. "And he continued there a year and six months, teaching the Word of God among them." (Act 18:11). Richly were his labours blest, and the many monuments of Divine grace that were raised up constituted the foundation—members of the Church of God at Corinth. After the apostle's departure, trouble arose in the assembly and various evils broke out. It must be remembered that the membership of this church was a heterogeneous one, that many of them had been reared in heathendom, that they were surrounded by all the incentives to see indulgence, plied on every hand by vain philosophers, and that at this time, part of the N.T. was in circulation. Judaisers had propagated error and sowed the seeds of dissension and a strong party spirit was at work, threatening breach in their ranks. Not only was a schismatic spirit at work, but considerable carnality prevailed and serious moral disorders were marring their Christian testimony.

Among the evils which obtained in the Corinthian church were cliques and factions, the violation of the seventh commandment in various forms and the remissness of the assembly to exercise discipline in such matters; a disorderly and unbrotherly spirit in their meetings—women being allowed to enter the congregation with uncovered heads and to speak in public; exercising the gifts of prophesy and speaking in tongues without regard to order and edification; the debasing of the Lord's Supper into a common meal; brother going to law against brother before heathen magistrates, and some of them having become disaffected unto himself. Tidings of these things had reached the apostle's ears, and though this epistle was written in answer to certain more specific inquiries, he had received from them (1Co 7:1), he improved the opportunity in reply to take up all those things which needed correction. Though there were some things in this epistle, which concerned local, evanescent and special matters, yet fundamental doctrine and much that is of lasting importance was as interweaved.

It is most blessed to see how the apostle commenced his letter to them. He had much more to say of blame than of praise, yet after the opening address and salutation, he tells them, "I thank my God always on your behalf" (1Co 1:4). Before directly charging them with their disorderly conduct, he first assured them of the place which they had in his affections. Though now absent from them, yet they held a warm place in his heart, being constantly remembered before the throne of grace—a lesson here for those engaged in the pastoral office, that when called of God to occupy another place in His vineyard, they are not to forget those they left in their former field of service. The "thank my God *always* on your behalf" tells us that Paul did not regard prayer as a spiritual luxury, to be enjoyed only on rare and special occasions, but rather that it was a regular practice with him, a duty which he constantly discharged; and that, not only in seeking fresh supplies of grace for himself, but on the behalf of others also. Prayer has rightly been termed, "the pulse of the Christian's life," intimating as it does his health or sickliness.

Once more, we find the apostle referring to the One unto whom he returned thanks as "my God." Though we sought to bring out the force of that expression on a former occasion, yet it may be well for us to summarise the same here. Paul did not regard Deity as absolute and infinitely removed, but as a living and personal reality, to Whom he was intimately related. "My God" was an avowal of His *covenant* relationship, for the grand Covenant promise was, "I will be to them a God and they shall be to Me a people." "My God" was expressive of *personal* relationship: He was his God by eternal election, by redemption and by regenerating power, when He communicated life to him and stamped the Divine image upon his heart, thereby making him manifestatively His own dear child. "My God" was an acknowledgement of his own personal *choice,* for he had consciously and voluntarily taken God to be his absolute Lord, supreme Good, and everlasting Portion. "My God" was a confession of *practical* relationship; "whose I am and whom I serve"—the One who has shown me such abundant mercy, who will keep that which I have committed unto Him, who will supply all my need, to whose glory all my talents and energies are devoted.

Such a God was an Object of fervent adoration. His goodness must be acknowledged, and Paul was continuously engaged in that holy exercise: "I thank my God always *on your behalf* for the grace of God which is given you by Jesus Christ" (1Co 1:4). In this, the apostle has set all of us an example: "Be ye followers of me" (1Co 11:1). If we do not emulate him in this blessed practice, then most certainly we shall suffer loss. Yea, is not their failure at this particular point one reason why some of the Lord's people find it so difficult to obtain assurance that "the grace of God" has been given *them* by Jesus Christ? Is it not because they were not, and are not, truly thankful when they have reason to believe He has bestowed His grace *others?* Is there no tendency to be too much occupied with our own spiritual interests? God will not prosper self-centeredness. It is not without reason that the Lord has bidden His people "look not every man on his own things, but every man also on the things of others" (Phi 2:4). There is such a thing as spiritual selfishness, as well as natural. Then let us seek to heed that exhortation, "rejoice with them that do rejoice…" (Rom 12:15).

"I thank my God always on your behalf." That word "always" is very blessed when we call to mind the attendant circumstances: it points an important practical lesson for us. There had been various changes in the Corinthian assembly during the apostle's absence, and none of those changes had been for the better, but there had been no alteration or lessening of Paul's affections *for them.* There had been that among them which must have dampened his joy, but he had not allowed it to chill his love. He gave thanks for them now as frequently as he had done formerly: yes, even though some of these had become disaffected unto him. And does not the writer and the reader need to keep close watch over his heart that he suffers not any change in the condition of his brethren to diminish his love for them? True, it may call for a variation of the expression (as in Paul's case: see 1Co 4:21), for love must ever be faithful and the form taken by its outward manifestation is to be regulated by what the good of its object requires, yet there is to be no lessening of its fervour.

Though Paul could not assure the Corinthians, "I thank my God through Jesus Christ for you all, that your faith is spoken of throughout the whole world" (Rom 1:8), yet he did adore Him for having effectually called them, "I thank my God always on your behalf *for the grace* of God, which is given you by Jesus Christ" (1Co 1:4). And does not that inculcate another important lesson for us, namely, that we are not to despise the bruised reed, nor the smoking flax. True, we shall thank God most ardently for those who most evidently resemble His Son, yet we must not fail to thank Him *also* for those in whom (as yet) we can but faintly discern Him. If the name of Christ be fragrant to us, we shall rejoice wherever it is poured forth, and if His image be precious to us, we should own it in whomsoever we behold it—just as if His Gospel be prized by us, we shall be glad by whomsoever it be preached. Though as yet Christ's image can only be faintly detected in His babes, yet if we see it at all, we have infallible assurance that He who has begun a good work in them will assuredly complete the same (Phi 1:6).

It was that particular truth which sustained the apostle's heart at this very time (1Co 1:8). At least three years had passed since he had left Corinth, during which time he had laboured hard in other fields, but he recalls with gratitude and joy how graciously and wondrously God had wrought in their notoriously wicked city. That was what upheld him when he learned of the sad disorderly among them. "I thank my God always on your behalf for the grace of God, which is given you by Jesus Christ"—his memory went back to the "day of the espousals." Instead of being wholly absorbed with and weighted down of their sad failures, Paul held fast to the fact and kept foremost in his mind the truth that they had been both the objects and recipients of the sovereign and invincible grace of God. Since that grace had not been earned by them, but "given by Jesus Christ," he knew it could not be forfeited; yea, that they would "grow in grace and in the knowledge of their Lord and Saviour," and careful reading of the second epistle which he, later, sent to this same church shows how blessedly his confidence was justified and his hope realised.

The apostle then did not begin this epistle by rebuking the Corinthians for their waywardness, but instead, by enumerating certain things, which evidenced them to be the special objects of Divine favour. We are to see in this not only a lovely exemplification of the apostle's own magnanimity and graciousness, but also important instruction as to how any servant of God is to proceed in his dealings with those— particularly his own children in the Gospel who have wandered out of the way. He must first seek to reach and melt their hearts with a renewed sense of God's goodness to them, for only then will they be capable of perceiving the exceeding sinfulness of sin and the dishonour done Him by a disorderly walk on the part of those who bear His name. By calling to remembrance the "day of their espousals," Paul not only sought to recall them to the marvel of Divine mercy in bringing them out of darkness into the marvellous light, but also to remind them that *he* had been the favoured instrument used by God to their conversion. And therefore, as he was their spiritual "father" (1Co 4:15), they should the more readily attend to the message he was about to give them.

The "grace of God" has reference first to His free and sovereign favour, and then to the blessings which issue therefrom—as we speak of "receiving favours" from a person. It was in this second sense the apostle used the term when he thanked God for the grace which had been given to the Corinthians. Observe how careful he was to honour the Saviour by according Him His due place as Mediator: "the grace of God which is given you *by Jesus Christ.*" God's grace was first given to His elect *in* Christ before the foundation of the world (2Ti 1:9), and then it is given them *by* Christ at their regeneration and throughout their Christian course (Joh 1:14-16)—all the grace of God flows to us through the Redeemer. It was, first, for the grace of God by Jesus Christ that had been bestowed on the Corinthians at their conversion, then "That in every thing ye are enriched *by Him*, in all utterance and in all knowledge" (1Co 1:5). The same truth is emphasised here, gifts and attainments being expressly ascribed to Christ. Thus, all ground for self-gratulation and boasting was removed, and the honour was placed where it rightfully belonged. There was no pandering to the creature here, but an humbling of him.

"Enriched by Him in all utterance, and in all knowledge." The order of those two things may strike us strange: if so, it is through failure to understand the particular kind of utterance and knowledge to which the apostle alluded. The reference was not to what is ordinary, but extraordinary, not to the graces which the Spirit imparts, but to His gifts. At the beginning of this dispensation, there were not only officers extraordinary (apostles and prophets), but there were gifts extraordinary, and as successors were not appointed for the former, so a continuance of the latter was never intended. In the early days of this era, the Holy Spirit made His presence evident by sensible signs: Acts 2:1-4; 10:44-46; extraordinary gifts and signs being given in fulfillment of Christ's promise (Mar 16:17, 18) for the establishing of Christianity and the infantile state of the Church, certifying the truth of the Gospel (Heb 2:4), Divinely attesting the doctrine taught by the apostles and evidencing God's approval of the same. We term these miraculous works of the Spirit extraordinary so as to distinguish them from His ordinary ones or those gifts and graces, which He has communicated to Christians all through this age.

Those supernatural gifts were designed to arrest the attention of outsiders (1Co 14:22), to command a hearing for the apostles, to authenticate the Gospel in heathen countries. Of all the churches of God that we read of in the N.T., that at Corinth seems to have abounded most in these gifts, and to have abused them most—despising those of their number who had not their particular gift, and those without envying those who had them. The gift of "utterance" included "prophesying" or speaking by Divine afflatus, but more especially referred to a miraculous endowment, which enabled its possessor to speak in divers languages (1Co 12:10; 14:4, 5). The gift of "knowledge" was a supernatural endowment for interpreting the prophesies and strange tongues (1Co 12:10; 14:26). In the body of the epistle, Paul acquainted them with the excellency of those gifts and how they were to be used. They were from the Spirit (1Co 12:4, 8), they were given for mutual profit (1Co 12:7), they were to be exercised in an orderly manner for edification (1Co 14:26-33); while he also pointed out to them something still more desirable and excellent—the "way" to exercise *love* (1Co 13).

Though these gifts were to render them more serviceable, they were not sanctifying ones (1Co 13:2). Though the Corinthians had been plenteously endowed therewith, yet spiritually, they were only babes (1Co 3:1). Though through their pride and forwardness, those gifts had been much abused, yet the apostle adores God for the communicating of them. They were the purchase of Christ (Eph 4:8) and the fruit of

His ascension (Act 2:33). Though the apostle could not (as yet) rejoice at the fruits of the Spirit being borne by them, yet he lets them know he returned thanks for the extraordinary gifts bestowed on them. That too was calculated to have a conciliatory effect on the Corinthians and dispose them to heed what followed. So far from depreciating those gifts as valueless, because they had not made a better use of them, Paul traces them to God as their Source, and Jesus Christ as their Bestower. Thus, there was no flattering of them, because they were in possession of the same, but a magnifying of Him to whom they were indebted—compare 1 Corinthians 4:7!

Though these extraordinary gifts no longer obtain, yet there are others distinguishable from spiritual graces—natural endowments, intellectual capacity, readiness of speech, etc. While those special gifts and the natural talents we have mentioned are far inferior to spiritual graces, yet from the example of the apostle here with reference to the former, we may learn valuable lessons concerning the latter. First, the one as much as the other, is the gift of God and is to be thankfully acknowledged as such. Grace is the most excellent thing of all, yet add gifts thereto, and it becomes more excellent. I was the temple, which sanctified the gold, nevertheless, the gold beautified the temple. It is grace which sanctifies gifts, yet gifts adorn and render its possessors more useful. Second, the possessors of them have no reason to be puffed up thereby, nor to look down upon those who have them not, for it is God who maketh one to differ from another. Third, we should not disparagingly contrast gifts with graces: Paul did not. If there be a danger on the one hand, there is no less so on the other: one may be as proud of his faith or love, as another with his utterance or knowledge.

After all that has been brought out above on 1 Corinthians 1:4 and 5, there is the less need for us to say much on what follows. "Even as the testimony of Christ was confirmed in (or "among") you" (1Co 1:5). The "Testimony" of Christ signifies the Gospel; in 1 Corinthians 2:1, it is termed "the Testimony of God"—the former referring to its grand Object; the latter, to its gracious Author. Mention is made of this Testimony being "confirmed," as a proof it did not come to them in the letter only, but also in Divine power. In other words, it was an evidence they had savingly received the Gospel (compare Col 1:6). The Gospel had been accepted by a God-given faith and was firmly established in their conviction and affections. If we translate "confirmed *among* you," then the allusion is to the miraculous gifts, which had been imparted to them (compare Heb 2:4). The opening "even as" looks back to both verses 4 and 5: as your conversion and as your endowment with these gifts proceeded from the grace of God by Jesus Christ, equally so did this "confirmation."

"So that ye come behind in no gift; waiting for the coming of our Lord Jesus Christ" (1Co 1:7). This confirms the *double* meaning we have given to the previous verse. The Gospel had been so confirmed "among" them that no church was more plenteously endued with gifts. It had been so confirmed "in" them that it produced this blessed fruit—they were eagerly awaiting the Redeemer's return. The reference is to the expectation they cherished of Christ's second advent, the promise of which was connected with the resurrection, His people, and the consummation of His kingdom. So generally was Christ's return the "blessed hope" of all the early Christians, they were characterised as those "who loved His appearing" (2Ti 4:8)—how much more so should *we,* now that this glorious event is two thousand years nearer! The gifts and graces of the Spirit are but the "firstfruits" (Rom 8:23), and they should make us yearn for the coming of Christ when we shall enter fully into the inheritance He purchased for us. —AWP

THE MISSION AND MIRACLES OF ELISHA

21. Thirteenth Miracle

In the incident which is to be before us, we behold Elisha discharging a different line of duty. No longer do we see him engaged in ministering to the young prophets, but instead, we find him faithfully rendering valuable assistance to his sovereign. Once more the lust of blood or booty moved the king of Syria to war against Israel. Following the advice of his military counsellors, he decided to encamp in a certain place through which the king of Israel was wont to pass, expecting to catch him and his retainers. God acquainted Elisha with his master's peril, and accordingly the prophet went and warned him thereof; and heeding the same, the king was preserved from the snare set for him. It is required of us that, as we have opportunity, we "do good unto all men" (Gal 6:10). True, the Christian is not endowed with the extraordinary gifts of an Elisha; nevertheless, he has a responsibility toward his king or ruler. Not only is he Divinely commanded to "Honour the King" (1Pe 2:17), but "I exhort therefore, that, first of all, supplications, prayers, intercessions, and giving of thanks, be made for all men; for kings, and for all that are in authority" (1Ti 2:1, 2). Coming now to our miracle.

First, its *connection.* "Then the king of Syria warred against Israel, and took counsel with his servants, saying, In such and such a place shall be my camp" (2Ki 6:8). Clearly, the opening "Then" bids us pay attention to the connection. From a literary viewpoint, we regard our present incident as the sequel to what is mentioned in 2 Kings chapter 5, taking chapter 6 verses 1 to 7 as a parenthesis, thereby emphasising the base ingratitude of the Syrian monarch for the miraculous healing of his commander-in-chief in the land of Israel. There he had written a personal letter to Israel's king (2Ki 5:5, 6) to recover Naaman from his leprosy; but here he has evil designs upon him. That he should invade the land of Samaria so soon after such a signal favour had been rendered to him, aggravated his offence and made the more manifest his wicked character. It is wrong for us to return evil for evil, for vengeance belongeth alone unto the Lord; but to return evil for good is a sin of double-dyed enormity—yet how often have we treated God thus!

But there is another way in which this opening "Then" may be regarded; namely, by linking it unto the typical significance of what is recorded in 2 Kings 6:1-7. We suggested a threefold application of that miracle. First, as supplying a picture of the sinner's redemption. Viewing it thus, what is the next thing we should expect to meet with? Why, the rage of the Enemy, and this is adumbrated by the attack of the king of Syria. Second, that miracle may also be regarded as showing the Christian how a lost blessing is to be retrieved. And when the believer has peace, joy, assurance restored to him, what is sure to follow? This, "Then the king of Syria warred against Israel." Nothing so maddens Satan as the sight of a happy saint— blessed is it to see in what follows how his evil designs were thwarted. Third, that miracle can also be viewed as portraying how the Christian may grow in grace—by mortifying his members which are upon the earth. And if he does, and enters into an enlarged spiritual experience, then he may expect to be an object of the Enemy's renewed assaults; yet he shall not be overcome by him.

"Then the king of Syria warred against Israel." Yes my reader, there were *wars* in those days: human nature has been the same in each generation and in all countries. So far from war being a new thing, the history of nations—both ancient and modern, civilized and uncivilized—is little more than a record of animosities, intrigues, and fightings. "Their feet are swift to shed blood" (Rom 3:15), is one of the solemn indictments which God has made against the whole human family. There is no hint anywhere that Benhadad had received any provocation from Israel: it was just his own wicked greed and bloodthirstiness which moved him. And this, in spite of a serious defeat he had suffered on a previous occasion (1Ki 20:1, 26-30). "The heart of the sons of men is fully set in them to do evil" (Ecc 8:11) and nothing can stop them from executing their desires and devices, but the restraining hand of God. Neither solemn warnings nor kindly favours—as this man had recently received—will soften their hearts, unless the Lord is pleased to sanctify the same unto them.

"Then the king of Syria warred against Israel, and took counsel with his servants"—not asked counsel of the Lord, for he was a stranger to Him. We are glad to see no mention is made here of Naaman: it was with his "servants" rather than "the captain of the host" (2Ki 5:1) he now conferred. Fain would we hope that it was *against* the remonstrance of Naaman, rather than with his approval the king now acted. Yet what daring impiety to attack a people whose God wrought such marvels! If he was impressed by the healing of the general, the impression speedily faded. "Saying, in such and such a place shall be my camp." From the sequel, it would appear that this particular "place" was one through which the king of Israel had occasion to frequently pass; thus, he evidently laid a careful ambush for him there. Thus, it is with the great Enemy of our souls: he knows both our ways and our weaknesses always, and where he is most likely to gain an advantage over us. But carefully as he made his plans, this king reckoned without the Most High.

Second, its *occasion.* "And the man of God sent unto the king of Israel saying, Beware that thou pass not such a place; for thither the Syrians are come down" (2Ki 6:9). Yes, the king of Syria had left the living God out of his calculations: He is fully acquainted with the thoughts and intention of His enemies and, with the utmost ease, can bring them to naught. The methods which He employs in providence are as varied as His works in creation. On this occasion, He did not employ the forces of nature, as He did at the Red Sea when He overthrew Pharaoh and his hosts. Nor did He bid the king of Israel engage his enemy in battle and enable him to vanquish him. Instead, He prompted His servant to give his royal master warning and made the same effectual unto him. The lesson for us is important. God does not always use the same method in His interpositions on our behalf. The fact that He came to my relief for deliverance in a certain manner in the past is no guarantee that He will follow the same course or use the same means now—this is to lift our eyes above all secondary causes to the Lord Himself.

Observe that it was "the man of God"—not merely "Elisha"—who were with this warning: "Surely the Lord GOD will do nothing, but He revealeth His secret unto His servants the prophets" (Amo 3:7). Thus it was in his official character that he went to the king with this Divine message. Just previously, he had used his extraordinary powers to help one of his students; here, he befriended his sovereign. Whatever gift God has bestowed on His servants, it is to be used for the good of others—one of their principal duties is to employ the spiritual knowledge they have received in *warning* those in peril. How merciful God is in warning both sinners and saints of the place of danger! How thankful we should be when a man of God puts *us* on our guard against an evil which we suspected not! How many disastrous experiences shall we be spared if we heed the cautions given us by the faithful messengers of Christ. It is at our peril and to our certain loss if—in our pride and self-will—we disregard their timely, *"Beware* that thou pass not such a place" (2Ki 6:9).

The course which the Lord took in delivering the king of Israel from the ambush set for him may not have flattered his self-esteem, any more than Timothy's was when Paul bade him *"flee* youthful lusts;" yet, we may perceive the wisdom of it. God was enforcing the king's responsibility: He gave him fair warning of his danger; if he disregarded it, then his blood was on his own head. So it is with us. The particular locality of peril is not named. The Syrian had said, "In such and such a place shall be my camp," and "Beware that thou pass not such a place" was the prophet's warning. That the king would identify it in his mind is clear from the sequel; yet, as there is nothing meaningless in Scripture, there must be a lesson for us in its *not* being specifically named. We are plainly informed in the Word that our arch-foe lies in wait to ensnare us (1Pe 5:8). Sometimes a particular danger is definitely described, at others it is (as here) more generally mentioned—that we may ever be on our guard, pondering "the path of *our* feet" (Pro 4:26).

Though Satan may propose, God will both oppose and dispose. Ere passing on to the sequel, let us link up what has just been before us with the typical teaching of the previous miracle—as the opening "Then" of 2 Kings 6:8 and the connecting "And" of verse 9 require—and complete the line of thought set out in our third paragraph above. When a sinner has been delivered from the power of darkness and translated into the kingdom of God's dear Son, he at once becomes the object of the Devil's enmity; but God has graciously made provision for his security and prevents the Enemy from ever completely vanquishing him. Likewise, when a believer has been enabled to regain his peace and joy, Satan will renew his efforts to encompass his downfall; but his attempts will be foiled, for since the believer is now in communion with God, he has light on his path and clearly perceives the place to be avoided. So also when by means of mortification, the Christian enjoys an enlarged spiritual experience, Satan will lay a fresh snare for him; but it will be in vain, for such an one will receive and *heed* Divine warning.

"And the king of Israel sent to the place which the man of God (not "Elisha"!) told him and warned him of, and saved himself there, not once nor twice" (2Ki 6:10). Here we see the king's skepticism (compare 2Ki 5:7): he had some respect for the prophet's message or he had disregarded it; yet, he had not full confidence therein or he had not "sent" to investigate. It was well for him that he went to that trouble, for thereby, he obtained definite corroboration and found the caution he had received was no groundless one.

Ah, my reader, the warnings of God's servants are not idle ones, and it is our wisdom to pay the most serious heed to them. But alas, while most of our fellows will pay attention to warnings against physical and temporal dangers, they are deaf concerning their spiritual and eternal perils. There is a real sense in which *we* are required to emulate Israel's king here: we are to follow no preacher blindly, but *test* his warnings, investigating them in the light of Scriptures, "Prove all things; hold fast that which is good" (1Th 5:21) and thereby we shall obtain Divine corroboration.

"Therefore the heart of the king of Syria was sore troubled for this thing; and he called his servants, and said unto them, Will ye not shew me which of us is for the king of Israel?" (2Ki 6:11). It never crossed his mind that it was the Lord who was thwarting him. Being a stranger to Him, God had no place in his thoughts, and therefore, he sought a natural explanation. Instead of recognising that God was on the side of Israel, and blaming himself, he was chagrined at the failure of his plan, suspected there was a traitor in his camp, and sought a scapegoat.

"And one of his servants said, None, my lord, O king: but Elisha the prophet that is in Israel telleth the king of Israel the words that thou speakest in thy bedchamber" (2Ki 6:12). Even the heathen are not in entire ignorance of God: they have sufficient light and knowledge of Him to render them "without excuse" (Rom 1:19, 20; 2:14, 15)—much more so is this the case with unbelievers in Christendom. This verse also shows how the spirituality and power of a true servant of God is recognised even by his enemies. The spokesman here may have been one of those who formed the retinue of Naaman when he came to Elisha and was healed of his leprosy. Yet observe there was no recognition and owning of *God* here. There was no acknowledgement that He was the One who revealed such secrets unto His servants, no terming of Elisha "the man of God," but simply "the prophet that is in Israel"—he was regarded merely as a *"seer"* possessing magical powers. Neither God nor His servant is accorded His rightful place by any, save His own people.

Third, its *location,* namely, Dothan, which was to the west of Jordan, in the northeast portion of Samaria. Significantly enough, Dothan means "double feast" and from Genesis 37:16 and 17, we learn it was the place where the flocks were fed. "And he said, Go and spy where he is, that I may send and fetch him. And it was told him, saying, Behold he is in Dothan" (2Ki 6:13). Even now the Syrian monarch was unwilling to recognise that he was fighting against Jehovah, but determined to remove this obstacle in the way of a successful carrying out of his campaign—even though that obstacle was a "prophet." God allowed him to have his own way up to this point, that he might discover he was vainly flinging himself against the bosses of His buckler and made him feel his own impotency. Typically, this verse illustrates the persistency of our great Adversary, who will not readily accept defeat. As the Syrian now sought to secure the one who had come between him and his desired victim, the Devil makes special efforts to silence those who successfully warn the one he would fain take captive.

"Therefore sent he thither horses and chariots, and a great host [of infantry]: and they came by night, and compassed the city about" (2Ki 6:14). That he had some realisation of the power Elisha wielded is evident by the strength and silence of the force, he now sent forth to take him prisoner; yet, that he did not deem him to be invincible is shown by the plan he put into operation. Though the wicked are rendered uneasy by the stirrings of conscience and their conviction that they are doing wrong and following a course of madness; yet, they silence the one and treat the other as vain superstitions, and continue in their sin career. The surrounding of Dothan "by night" illustrates the truth that the natural man prefers the darkness to the light, and typically signifies that our Adversary follows a policy of stealth and secrecy, ever seeking to take us unawares—especially when we are *asleep.*

Fourth, its *subject.* "And when the servant of the man of God was risen early, and gone forth, behold, an host compassed the city both with horses and chariots. And his servant said unto him, Alas, my master! how shall we do?" (2Ki 6:15). Notice its subject is termed a servant—not of "Elisha," but "of the man of God." It is in such small, but perfect details that the devout student loves to see the handiwork of the Holy Spirit, evidencing as it does the *verbal* inspiration of the Scriptures—God guiding each penman in the selection of every word He employed. This man, the successor of Gehazi, was new in the prophet's service, and therefore, was he now tested and taught. When a young believer throws in his lot with the people of God, he will soon discover they are hated by the world; but he is called upon to share their reproach. Let not his older brethren expect too much from him while he is young and inexperienced: not until he has learned to walk by faith will he be undaunted by the difficulties and perils of the way.

"Alas my master! how shall we do?" See here a picture of a young, weak, timid, distracted believer. Is not the picture true to life? Cannot all of us recall its exact replica in our own past experience? How often have we been nonplussed by the trials of the way and the opposition we have encountered. Quite likely, this "young man" (see 2Ki 6:17) thought he would have a smooth path in the company of the man of God, and yet here was a situation that affrighted him. And did we never entertain a similar hope? and when our hope was not realised, did we never give utterance to an unbelieving "Alas! how shall we do?"—shutting God completely out of our view, with no hope of deliverance, no expectation of His showing Himself strong on our behalf? If memory enables us to see here a past representation of our self, then let compassion cause us to deal leniently and gently with others who are similarly weak and fearful.

It should be borne in mind that the young believer has become, constitutionally, more fearful than unbelievers. Why so? Because his self-confidence and self-sufficiency has been shattered. He has become as "a little child," conscious of his own weakness. So far so good: the great thing now is for him to learn *where* his strength lies. It should also he pointed out that Christians are menaced by more numerous and more formidable foes than was Elisha's servant, "For we wrestle not against flesh and blood, but against principalities, against powers, against the rulers of the darkness of this world, against spiritual wickedness in high places." (Eph 6:12). Well might we tremble and be more distrustful of ourselves were we more conscious of the supernatural beings opposing us. "And he answered, Fear not: for they that be with us are more than they that be with them" (2Ki 6:16). A realisation of *that* will dispel our doubts and quieten our fears. "Greater is He that is in you, than he that is in the world" (1Jo 4:4).

Fifth, its *means.* "And Elisha *prayed,* and said, LORD, I pray Thee, open his eyes that he may see" (2Ki 6:17). How blessed is this! "Thou wilt keep him in perfect peace, whose mind is stayed on Thee: because he trusteth in Thee" (Isa 26:3). There was no trepidation on the part of Elisha: perfect peace was his, and therefore could he say, "Fear not" to his trembling companion. Note there is no scolding of his affrighted servant, but instead, a turning to the Lord on his behalf. At first, the writer was puzzled at the "*Elisha* prayed" rather than the "man of God;" but pondering the same brought out a precious lesson. It was not in his official character that he prayed, but simply as a personal believer—to show *us* that God is ready to grant the petition of a child of His who asks in simple faith and unselfish concern for another.

Sixth, its *marvel.* "And the LORD opened the eyes of the young man; and he saw: and, behold, the mountain was full of horses and chariots of fire round about Elisha." (2Ki 6:17). Proof was this of his "they that be with us are more than they that be with them" (2Ki 6:16): the invisible guard was now made visible in the eyes of his servant. Blessed illustration is this, that "The angel of the LORD encampeth round about them that fear Him, and delivereth them (Psa 34:7) and of "Are they [the "angels" of the previous verse] not all ministering spirits, sent forth to minister for them who shall be heirs of salvation?" (Heb 1:14)! Doubtless, the angels took the form of "horses and chariots" on that occasion because of the Syrian horses and chariots which "encompassed Dothan" (2Ki 6:14)—what could horses of flesh and material chariots do against celestial ones of fire! That they were personal beings is clear from the "they" of verse 14; that they were angels may also be gathered from a comparison with Hebrews 1:7 and 2 Thessalonians 1:7,8.

Seventh, its *meaning*. Here we are shown how to deal with a young and fearing Christian. "The strong ought to bear the infirmities of the weak" (Rom 15:1). Many of God's little ones are living far below their privileges, failing to apprehend the wondrous provisions which God has made for them. They are walking far too much by sight, occupied with the difficulties of the world and those opposing them. First, such are not to be browbeaten or upbraided; that will do no good, for unbelief is not removed by such a method. Second, their alarm is to be quieted with a calm and confident "Fear not," backed with "for they that be with us are more than they that be with them" and "If God be for us, who can be against us?" (Rom 8:31)!—showing their fears are needless. Third, definite prayer is to be made for the shrinking one, that the Lord will operate on and in him—for God alone can open his spiritual eyes to see the sufficiency of His provision for him. —AWP

SPIRITUAL GROWTH OR CHRISTIAN PROGRESS

5. Its Analogy

An "analogy" is an agreement or correspondence in certain respects between things which otherwise differ. And just as it is often an aid to obtaining the force of a word by considering its synonyms, so it frequently helps us to a better understanding of a subject or object to compare it with another, and ascertain the analogy between them. This method was frequently used by our Lord in His public teaching, when He likened the "Kingdom of heaven" to considerable variety of things. The same principle is illustrated by the figurative names which Scripture gives to the people of God. For example, they are called "sheep"—and that not only because of the relation which they sustain to Christ as their Shepherd, but also because there are many resemblances between the one and the other—God having designed that in different respects this animal more than any other should shadow forth the nature and character of a Christian. Much valuable instruction is obtained by tracing out those resemblances. The same Divine wisdom which designated our Saviour both "the Lamb" and "the Lion" was exercised in selecting the various objects and creatures after which His children are figuratively named, and it behoves us to follow out the analogy between them and learn the lessons they are intended to impart.

"That they might be called trees of righteousness, the planting of the LORD, that He might be glorified" (Isa 61:3). Both in the O.T. and in the New, this similitude is used of the saints. The Psalmist declared, "I *[am]* like a green olive tree in the house of God" (Psa 52:8) and affirmed "The righteous shall flourish like a palm tree: he shall grow like a cedar in Lebanon. Those that be planted in the house of the LORD shall flourish in the courts of our God." (Psa 92:12, 13). Our Saviour employed the same figure when He said, "Every good tree bringeth forth good fruit" (Mat 7:17) and again,

"Either make the tree good, and his fruit good; or else make the tree corrupt, and his fruit corrupt: for the tree is known by his fruit" (Mat 12:33)—thus, every passage where "fruit" is mentioned is also an extension of the same emblem. In Romans 11, the apostle Paul likened the nation of Israel unto "a good olive tree" and Christendom unto "a wild olive tree" (verses 24, 17) in connection with their testimony before the world. The Saviour Himself was termed "the Branch of the Lord" and as One who should grow before Him "as a tender plant, and as a root out of a dry ground" (Isa 4:2; 53:2), while He resembled Himself and His people in communion with Him unto "the true Vine" (Joh 15:1).

Now it should be obvious from the frequency with which this similitude is used in the Scriptures that it must be a peculiarly instructive one. Some of the more prominent resemblances are quickly apparent. For example, their *attractiveness.* How the countryside and the mountain slopes are beautified by the trees! And what so lovely in the human realm as those who bear the image of Christ and show forth His praises! They may be despised by the unregenerate, but to an anointed eye, God's children are "the excellent" of all the earth (Isa 4:2), and how they be regarded by Him whose workmanship they are is revealed in those words, "his *beauty* shall be as the olive tree" (Hos 14:6). So too their *usefulness.* Trees provide a habitation for the birds, shade for the earth, nourishment for the creature, material for building, fuel for the relief of man against the cold. Many too are the uses, which God makes of His people in this world. Among other things predicated of them, they are "the salt of the earth" (Mat 5:13)— preserving the body politic from going to utter putrefaction.

Before turning to that which bears most closely upon our present theme, it should be particularly noted that it is not wild, but cultivated trees, which is the similitude used. "Blessed is the man that trusteth in the LORD...For he shall be as a tree *planted* by the waters" (Jer 17:7,8). Observe how frequently this word "planted" occurs: "which the LORD hath planted" (Num 24:6), and compare Psalm 92:13, 14; 104:16; Isaiah 61:3. They are the property of the Heavenly Husbandman (Joh 15:1; 1Co 3:7-9) and the objects of His care. This it is which gives such solemn force to our Lord's words, "Every plant, which My heavenly Father hath not planted, shall be rooted up" (Mat 15:13). This figure of the saints being "planted" by God— transferred from one soil or position to another—has at least a threefold reference. First, to God's eternal decree, when He took them out of the creature mass and chose them in Christ (Eph 1:3-5). Second, to their regeneration, when He lifts them out of the realm of death and makes them "new creatures in Christ" (2Co 5:17). Third, to their translation, when they are removed from earth and planted in His celestial Paradise. But it is the *growth* of "trees" we must now consider.

1. They have the principle of growth *within themselves.* Trees do not grow spontaneously and immediately from external furtherances, but from their own seminal virtue and radical sap. And it is thus with the spiritual growth of the Christian. At regeneration, a Divine "seed" is planted in his heart (1Pe 1:23; 1Jo 3:9), and that "seed" contains within itself a living principle of growth. We cannot define that "seed" more closely than to say that the new life or spiritual nature which has been communicated to the one born again, is that which distinguishes the living children of God from the lifeless profession all around them. The latter may from external influences—such as the appeals and exhortations of preachers, the example of Christians, the natural con-

victions produced from reading the Word—be induced to perform all the outward duties of Christianity, but since their works issue not from a principle of spiritual life in the soul, they are not the fruits of holiness. That spiritual principle or Divine grace imparted is described by Christ as "the water" which He gives and which becomes within its possessor "a well of water springing up into everlasting life" (Joh 4:14). Thus it is the nature of Christians to grow, as it is trees with the seminal principle within them to do likewise. "The tree yielding fruit, whose seed was in itself" (Gen 1:12)—first reference to "trees"!

2. They must be *watered from above.* Though trees have within themselves a vital principle, yet they are not independent of provision from the Creator, being far from self-sustaining. Their growth is not something inevitable by virtue of their own seminal power—for in a protracted drought, they wither and decay. Hence, when Scripture speaks of the growth of trees, it is careful to ascribe it unto God's watering of them. "For I will pour water upon him that is thirsty, and floods upon the dry ground," which is interpreted by: "I will pour my spirit upon thy seed, and my blessing upon thine offspring: And they shall spring up as among the grass, as willows by the water courses" (Isa 44:3, 4); "I will be as the dew unto Israel: he shall grow as the lily, and cast forth his roots as Lebanon" (Hos 14:5). Only as God waters vegetation will it thrive or even survive. It is so, spiritually. The Christian is not self-sufficient and independent of God. Though he has a nature capable of growth, if left to itself that nature would die, for it is only a *creature* even though a "new creature." Hence the believer needs to be "renewed in the inner man day by day" (2Co 4:16).

3. They grow *silently and imperceptibly.* The development of the small sapling into the towering tree is a process veiled in secrecy. "So is the kingdom of God, as if a man should cast seed into the ground; And should sleep, and rise night and day, and the seed should spring and grow up, he knoweth not how (Mar 4:26, 27). The growing of the tree cannot be discerned by the keen eye, except by the consequences and effects of it. It is equally thus with spiritual growth: it is unrecognisible to either ourselves or others. No matter how closely we observe the workings of our hearts, or how introspective becomes our viewpoint, we cannot perceive the actual process. It is seen only by Him of whom it is wrought. Nevertheless, it is made manifest by its effects and fruits—in the case of some, more clearly than others. But though the process be secret, the *means* are plain: in the case of trees—nourishment from the soil, moisture from the clouds, light and heat from the sun. So with the Christian: "Meditate on these things; give thyself wholly to them; that thy profiting *may appear* to all" (1Ti 4:15)—that thy spiritual growth may be evident to those about thee.

4. They grow *gradually.* In the case of some trees, it is a very sad experience; with others, maturity is reached more quickly. Hence, in the passage, the growth of believers is likened unto that of "a cedar" (Psa 92:12); whereas in another—where a recovered backslider is in view—it is said, "he shall grow as the lily" (Hos 14:5). But in the majority of cases, the development of spiritual life in the saints is a protracted process, being carried on by degrees, or as the prophet expressed it, "For precept must be upon precept, precept upon precept; line upon line, line upon line; here a little, and there a little" (Isa 28:10). Our spiritual growth is produced and promoted by the gracious, wise, patient, and faithful operations of the Holy Spirit. No real Christian is ever satisfied with his growth: far from it, for he is painfully conscious of what little progress

he has made and how far short of God's standard he comes. Nevertheless, if he uses the appointed means and avoids the hindrances, he *will* grow. But let us now endeavour to present the analogy more closely.

First, the growth of a tree is *upward*. The vital principle within it is drawn out unto the sun above, attracted by its rays. Though rooted in the earth, its nature is to move toward heaven, slowly but surely lifting its head higher and higher. Thus, the growth of a tree is ascertained first and may be measured by its *upward progress*. And does not the analogy hold good in the spiritual realm? Is it not thus with the saint? It is the very nature of that new life which he received at regeneration to turn unto its Giver. The first evidence of that life being imparted to the soul is his seeking unto God in Christ. The need of Him is now felt; His suitability is now perceived, and the heart is drawn out unto Him. As yet, he may not be able to intelligently articulate the newborn desire in his heart, yet if that desire were put into Scriptural language, it would be expressed thus: "As the hart panteth after the waterbrooks so panteth my soul after Thee, O God" (Psa 42:1), for none else can now satisfy the newly-created thirst within him. In view of our last two articles, there is the less need for us to develop this point at length.

The higher the top of the tree reaches toward heaven, the further from the earth does it move. Ponder that, my reader, for it is a parable in action. Before regeneration, thy heart was wholly set upon this world and what it provides for its devotees. But when your heart was supernaturally illumined, and you beheld "the light of the knowledge of the glory of God in the face of Jesus Christ" (2Co 4:6), the spell was broken, and you could no longer be content with the perishing baubles which hitherto enthralled you. True, the "flesh" may still lust after them, and if you yield to their solicitations, your peace and joy will be dampened; and for a season, disappointment and sorrow will be your portion. Yet there is that within you now that is no longer contented with childish toys and that seeks after the One who bestowed that new nature. It is the normal thing for that spiritual life to grow, and if it does not, you are living far below your privileges. Such upward growth will consist of stronger yearnings after God, more constant and frequent seekings unto Him, a closer acquaintance of Him, a warmer love for Him, more intimate communion with Him, fuller conformity to Him, and a deeper joy in Him.

As the believer grows Godward, His glory becomes more and more his concern, and the pleasing of Him in all his ways the main business of his life—so that he performs even common duties with an eye increasingly upon Him. Our personal experimental knowledge of God increases by our "following on" to know Him (Hos 6:3), for the more we seek to *do* His will, the better we come to understand (Joh 7:17), and admire the same. Truth is then sealed on the mind, the understanding is more quickened in the fear of the Lord, and our relish of God's ways is intensified. Holy acts become holy habits, and what at first was difficult and irksome, becomes easy and pleasant. The more we "exercise ourselves unto godliness" (1Ti 4:7), the more are we admitted into its secrets. From a dim perception of spiritual mysteries, we gradually attain unto "all riches of full assurance of understanding" (Col 2:2) of them. The more we are weaned from the world, the keener relish do we have for spiritual things and the sweeter do they become to our taste. As God is better known, our love for Him increases, and we set a higher esteem on Him, a greater delight in Him is experienced, and more and more the heart pants after a full fruition of Him in glory.

Not that the believer ever reaches a point where he is satisfied with his knowledge of God or pleased with his love for Him. There could be no more lamentable proof of spiritual deadness and fatal self-deception than a set complacent view of our love for God. On the other hand, equally unwarrantable is it to conclude we are not children of God at all, because our love for Him is so feeble and faulty. It is not the love of a natural son for his father which constitutes him his child—though filial love is the proper effect of that relationship. An exalted conception of the character of a parent and of the sacredness of the relationship will render an affectionate child dissatisfied with himself and cause him to declare, "I reproach myself daily that I love my father so little, and I can never repay him as I ought." That would be the language of filial relation. Yet he would not be warranted in arguing, "Because I do not love him as I ought, I cannot be his child; or because I love him so little, I question it very much if he loves me at all." Then why reason thus in connection with a heavenly Father! Summing up this aspect, we may say that the upward growth of a believer is expressed in his heavenly-mindedness and the measure in which his affections are set upon things above.

Second, the growth of a tree is *downward.* It takes a firmer hold of soil. More particularly is that the case in hot countries—for there, the taproot of a tree has to penetrate deeper and deeper into the earth in order to find needed moisture. An allusion to this aspect of our analogy is found in Hosea 14:5 where the Lord promises Israel that He shall "cast forth (or, better, "strike"—see margin) his roots as Lebanon"—that is, as the cedars of Lebanon struck their roots deeper into the mountain slopes—compare "his smell as Lebanon" in the next verse, where the obvious reference is to the fragrant aroma of cedars. The spiritual counterpart of this is found in such expressions as, "being rooted and grounded in love" (Eph 3:17), and "continue in the faith, grounded and settled" (Col 1:23), the two things being brought together in "rooted and built up in him and stablished in the faith" (Col 2:7)—which all speak in language of our present similitude.

As the believer grows spiritually, he takes a firmer grip upon Christ: *"Lays hold on eternal life"* (1Ti 6:12), no longer touching merely "the hem of His garment" (Mat 14:36). He becomes more settled in his knowledge and enjoyment of the Saviour's love and is established more securely in the Faith, so that he is less liable to be "tossed to and fro, and carried about with every wind of doctrine, by the sleight of men, and cunning craftiness, whereby they lie in wait to deceive" (Eph 4:21). The young sapling has but a shallow and feeble grip on the ground and, therefore, is in greater danger of being uprooted by storms and gales; the older tree, which has survived the hostile winds, has taken deep root and is more secure. So it is spiritually: the young Christian is susceptible to erroneous teachings, but those who are mature and established in the Truth discern and refuse human fables. The more we are rooted in the love of Christ, governed by the fear of God, and have His Word dwell richly in us, the less shall we be swayed by the fear of man, the customs of the world, or the assaults of Satan.

But more specifically: the downward growth of a Christian consists of increasing *humility,* or becoming more and more out of love with himself. And this of necessity, for in exact ratio to his real growth Godward, will be his growth downward. The more we grow upward—that is, the more we take into our renewed minds spiritual apprehensions of the perfections of God, the excellency of the Mediator and the merits of His work—the more are we made conscious of what is due the One and the Other, and the more deeply do we feel what a poor return we have made unto Them. If it be something deeper and more influential than a merely speculative or theoretical knowledge of the Father and the Son, if instead we be granted an experimental, vital and affecting knowledge of Them, then shall we be made thoroughly ashamed of ourselves, wholly dissatisfied with our love, our devotion, our conformity to Their image. Such knowledge will humble us into the dust, making us painfully sensible of the coldness of our hearts, the feebleness of our graces, the leanness of our souls, and the corruptions which still indwell us.

The more a tree grows downward, the deeper its roots become embedded in the earth; the more firmly is it fixed and the stronger it becomes, having a greater power to resist the force of the tempest. It is neither the height nor the girth of the tree, but the depth of its roots and its clinging to the ground which gives it stability and security. So it is, spiritually. For the believer to grow downward is for him to have less and less confidence in and dependence upon himself: "When I am weak, then am I strong" (2Co 12:10); for a consciousness of my weakness causes me to turn more and more unto God and cling to Him. "O our God wilt Thou not judge them? for *we have no might* against this great company that cometh against us; neither know we what to do: but our eyes *are upon Thee*" (2Ch 20:12)—that was the language of one who had grown downward! —AWP

THE DOCTRINE OF RECONCILIATION
5. Its Arrangement

In our last, we dwelt upon God's decision to redeem and reconcile fallen rebels: His love originating, His will determining, and His wisdom planning the outworking of the same. In illustrating how the Divine wisdom found a solution to all the formidable problems which stood in the way, we unavoidedly anticipated somewhat the ground which we hoped to cover in future articles. That Divine decision and scheme was "eternally purposed in Christ Jesus our Lord" (Eph 3:11)—for God's purpose to reconcile and His provision for the same are inseparable. That purpose respected not simply the exercise of mercy unto His lapsed people, but also the exercise of it in such a way that His Law was honoured. Yet it must not be suppposed that God was under any moral necessity of saving His people, or that redemption was an expedient to deliver the Divine character from reproach on account of the strictness of the Law in condemning *all* transgressors—no atonement was provided for the fallen angels! Rather has redemption vindicated the Law, and that in such a way that *no* transgressor is exempted from suffering its curse—either in himself or in a Substitute.

Reconciliation has been procured by the incarnate Son, the Lord Jesus Christ, for He is the grand and all-sufficient Provision of God for the accomplishing of His purpose. But it was effected by the Lord Jesus in fulfilment of *a Covenant agreement:* unless *that* be clearly perceived, we are without the principal knowledge to the understanding of this stupendous undertaking. There was a time when Christians generally were well instructed in Covenant truth; but alas, a generation has grown up the great majority of which have heard nothing or next to nothing thereon. It will therefore be necessary for us to proceed slowly in connection with this fundamental aspect of our subject and enter into considerable detail—for we do not ask the reader to receive ought from our pen, until clearly convinced it is in full accord with, and has the definite backing of, God's Word. A few of our readers are more or less familiar with what we shall advance, yet it will do them no harm to have brought before them again the foundation on which faith should rest, and to ponder the proofs which we now bring forward.

The great majority of our readers know that "it is the blood [and that alone, plussed by nothing from us] that maketh an atonement for the soul" (Lev 17:11), but we wonder how many of them have pondered and grasped the purport of that blessed and remarkable statement, "The God of peace, that brought again from the dead our Lord Jesus, that great Shepherd of the sheep, through *the blood of the everlasting covenant"* (Heb 13:20). That implies first, that there was a covenant-agreement between God and our Lord Jesus; second, that it was a covenant made with Him as the Head of His people, "that great Shepherd of the sheep;" third, that Christ performed the condition of the covenant; fourth, that it was as the One propitiated and reconciled to God that Christ here acted; fifth, that it was in fulfilment of covenant promise that God raised Christ; sixth, that Christ's blood was the meritorious ground on which He (and all the saints in Him) was delivered from the prison of the grave; seventh, that hereby the Church has Divine assurance of its complete redemption and salvation. We cannot dwell upon these points, but would request careful weighing of them as introductory to what follows.

Three things are necessary in order to make a "covenant": the parties, the terms, the agreement. A "covenant" is a solemn pact or contract in which there are certain "articles" or conditions to be performed, in return for which performance an agreed reward is promised and assured. It is a mutual agreement in which one party guarantees a stipulated return for the other's fulfillment of the work he has pledged himself to undertake; it is an agreement entered into voluntarily by both parties (see Mat 26:15). The two parties in "the everlasting covenant" were the Father and the Son—the Holy Spirit concurring therein, being the Witness thereto, and agreeing to co-operate the same. In Scripture, the Father is represented as taking the initiative in this matter, proposing to His Son the terms of the covenant. The Father posed a federal transaction, in which the Son should take upon Him the Mediatorial office and serve as the Head of His people, thereby assuming and charging their liabilities and bringing in an everlasting righteousness for them. The Son is represented as freely and gladly consenting thereto.

It needs to be pointed out and emphatically insisted upon that there was not so circumstanced and antecedently to His susception of the Mediatorial office that He could not have avoided the humiliation and sufferings which He endured. We shall explain later the precise meaning of His words, "My Father is greater than I" (Joh 14:28); "Neither came I of myself, but He sent me (Joh 8:42); "This commandment [to lay down His life] have I received of my Father" (Joh 10:18)—sufficient now to point out they have no reference, ever to His condition and position prior to the Covenant, for He then enjoyed absolute equality with the Father in every way. The Son might have resigned the whole human race to the dire consequences of their apostasy and have remained Himself everlastingly blessed and glorious. It was by His own voluntary consent that He entered into covenant engagement with the Father: in that free consent lay the excellency of it. It was His willing obedience and personal merits, which gave infinite value to His oblation. Behind that willingness lay His love for the Father and His love for the Church.

On the other hand, it is equally true that though the Son had pitied, yea so loved the elect (foreviewed as fallen), that He was willing to become their Surety and Substitute, yet He could not have redeemed them without the Father's acceptance of His sacrifice: the Father, too, must consent to such an undertaking. Thus, there must be a mutual agreement between them. The relation which Christ assumed to His people and the work He did for them presupposes the Father's willingness therein. Ere passing on it must also be pointed out that in consenting to become Mediator and Servant—and as such, in subjection to the Father— the Son did not surrender any of His perfections, nor relinquish any of His Divine rights; but He agreed to assume an inferior office, and for a season, to be subordinate to the Father's will—and this, for the glory of the whole Godhead and the salvation of His people. After He became incarnate, He was still in possession of His essential glory, though He was pleased to veil it in large measure from men and make Himself of "no reputation" in the world.

Before adducing proof-texts of the covenant made between the Father and the Son, let us call attention to a number of passages, which clearly *imply it* and which otherwise are not fully intelligible. Take Christ's very first recorded utterance after He became incarnate: "wist ye not that I must be about My Father's business?" (Luk 2:49)— did not that intimate He had entered this world with a clearly defined and Divinely designed task before Him? "I came down from heaven, not to do Mine own will, but the will of Him that sent Me" (Joh 6:38) is even more explicit: such subordination of one Divine person to another argues a mutual agreement between Them—and that, for some unique end. "Say ye of Him, whom the Father hath sanctified, and sent into the world, Thou blasphemest; because I said, I am the Son of God?" (Joh 10:36): observe carefully the *order* of the two verbs: Christ was "sanctified" by the Father—that is, set apart and consecrated to His Mediatorial office—*before* He was "sent" into the world! "Other sheep I have...them also I *must* bring" (Joh 10:16)—why "must" unless He was under definite engagement so to do?

That Christ went to the cross in fulfillment of a covenant-agreement may be gathered from His own words: "truly the Son of man goeth, as it was determined" (Luk 22:22), with which should be linked, "Of a truth against Thy holy child Jesus, whom Thou hast anointed, both Herod and Pontius Pilate, with the Gentiles, and the people of Israel, were gathered together, for to do whatsoever Thy hand and Thy counsel *determined before* to be done" (Act 4:27,28). When you stand before the cross and gaze by faith upon its august sufferer, recognise that He was there fulfilling the compact into which He entered with the Father before the world was. His blood shedding was necessary—"ought not Christ to have suffered these things"! (Luk 24:26). He asked—because of the relation He sustained to His people and their Surety. He was pledged to secure their salvation in such a way as glorified God and magnified His Law, for that had been Divinely "determined" and mutually agreed upon in the everlasting Covenant. Had not Christ died, there had been no atonement, no reconciliation to God; equally true is it that, had there been no covenant, Christ had never died!

Every passage where Christ owns the Father as *His* "God" witnesses to the same truth. When Jehovah established His covenant with Abraham, He promised "I will...be a *God* unto thee, and to thy seed" (Gen 17:7); and therefore, when He "remembered His covenant with Abraham, with Isaac and with Jacob" (Exo 2:24) and revealed Himself to Moses at the burning bush preparatory to delivering His people from Egypt, He declared Himself to be, "The LORD God of your fathers, the God of Abraham, the God of Isaac, and the God of Jacob...this is My name for ever, and this is My memorial to all generations" (Exo 3:15)—this is My covenant title and the guarantee of My covenant faithfulness. So too, the grand promise of the new covenant is, "I...will be their God" (Jer 31:33 and compare Heb 8:10). If then the Father had entered into covenant with His Son, we should expect to find Him owning Him as *His God* during the days of His flesh. And this is exactly what we *do* find, "My *God,* My *God,* why hast Thou forsaken Me" (Mat 27:46; Mar 15:34) was not only a cry of agony, but an acknowledgement of covenant relationship. "I ascend to My Father, and your Father, and to My God, and your God" (Joh 20:17). So also after His ascension, He declared, "Him that overcometh will I make a pillar in the Temple of *my God*...and I will write upon Him the Name of my God, and the name of the city of my God" (Rev 3:12).

Turning to the Epistles, we find many passages which presuppose the Father's covenant with Christ before creation on behalf of His people. "Who hath saved us...according to His own purpose and grace, which was *given us in Christ Jesus* before the world began" (2Ti 1:9). Even at that time, if time it may be called, there was a federal relationship subsisting between Christ and the Church—though it was not made fully manifest until He became incarnate. That subsisting relationship formed the basis of the whole economy of Divine grace toward them after the Fall, as it was the ground on which God pardoned the O.T. saints and bestowed spiritual blessings upon them. "In hope of eternal life, which God, that cannot lie, promised before the world began" (Tit 1:2). Does not that "promised" imply an agreement? that God made promise to Christ as the Covenant Head and to His people in Him! Christ was "*faithful* to Him that appointed Him" (Heb 3:2): as "obedience" implies a precept, so "faithfulness" connotes *a trust,* and a trust wherein only has engaged himself to perform that trust according to directions given him.

Passing now from indirect allusions to what is more specific, we begin with Psalm 89:3. "I have made a covenant with My Chosen, I have sworn unto David My Servant." The immediate allusion is to the historical David, but the spiritual reference is to David's Son and Lord. This is clear from many considerations. First, the striking and lofty manner in which this Psalm opens, intimates that its leading theme must be one of great weight and value. "I will sing of the mercies of the LORD forever: with my mouth will I make known Thy faithfulness to all generations. For I have said, Mercy shall be built up for ever: Thy faithfulness shalt Thou establish in the very heavens (Psa 89:1,2). Such language denotes that no ordinary or common "mercies" are in view, but those which, when apprehended, fill the hearts of the redeemed with holy songs and cause them to magnify the fidelity of Jehovah as nothing ever does. Thus, such an introduction should prepare us to expect a Divine revelation of extreme importance and blessedness.

Second, "I have made a covenant with my chosen" [same word as 'mine elect' in Isa 42:1], I have sworn unto David (which means 'beloved') my servant" (Psa 89:3). In the following passages, it may be seen that Christ is expressly referred to as "David" by the prophets: Jeremiah 30:9; Ezeziel 34:23; 37:24; Hosea 3:5—and let it be duly borne in mind that all those predictions were made long after the historical David had passed away from this scene. "Thou spakest in vision to thy Holy One, and saidest, I have laid help upon One that is mighty, I have exalted One chosen out of the people [compare Deu 18:15]. I have found David my Servant, with my holy oil have I anointed him" (Psa 89:19,20). Who can doubt that a greater than the son of Jesse is here before us? But more: God goes on to say, "I will make him my first born, higher than the kings of the earth...My covenant shall stand fast with him" (Psa 89:27,28)—does not that establish beyond a doubt the identity of the One with whom Jehovah made the covenant! Such declarations pertain to no merely human being.

Third, the covenant *promises* here made establish the same fact. "His seed will I make to endure for ever, and His throne as the days of heaven" (Psa 89:29)—the throne of the historical David perished over two thousand years ago! That this promise was to be fulfilled in Christ is clear from Luke 1:31-33, where it was said to Mary, thou "shalt call his name Jesus. He shall be great, and shall be called the Son of the Highest: and the Lord God shall give unto him the throne of his father David: and he shall reign over the [spiritual] house of Jacob for ever and of his kingdom, there shall be no end." Another proof that it is not the typical David who is viewed in this Psalm appears in, "If his children forsake my Law...then will I visit their transgression with the rod" (Psa 89:30, 32). Had it been the successor of Saul who was the subject of this Psalm, it had said "If *he* shall break my Law...I will visit *his* transgression with the rod"—as he *was* sorely chastised for so grievously wronging Uriah. No, it is Christ and His spiritual children who are referred to, and it is because of God's covenant with Him that He casts them not off (see Psalm 89:33-36).

Fourth, in Acts 13:34, Paul proved the resurrection of Christ thus: "As concerning that he raised him up from the dead, now no more to return to corruption, he said on this wise, I will give you the sure mercies of David." But wherein did that quotation from Isaiah 55:3 provide proof? By the resurrection of Christ, the "sure mercies of David" are confirmed unto His children: if they are in possession of them, then Christ must have risen! That word of Paul's looks back beyond Isaiah 55 to Psalm 89, which, as we have seen, begins thus: "I will sing of the mercies of the LORD for ever." The principal mercies are, "I have made a covenant with my Chosen...Thy seed will I establish for ever, and build up thy throne to all generations" (Psa 89:3,4). Here then are "the sure mercies of David": that God has covenanted to raise up Christ and set Him at His own right hand from whence, on His Mediatorial throne, He communicates those mercies to His seed. All doubt on this point is removed by Peter's avowal that through David, God had sworn that "Of the fruit of his loins...He would raise up Christ to sit on His throne" (Act 2:30 and see verse 33).

On Psalm 89:3, 4, the immortal Toplady said, "Do you suppose that this was spoken to David in his own person only? No, indeed; but to David as the type, figure, and forerunner of Jesus Christ. 'I have sworn unto David my servant'— unto the Messiah, who was typified by David, unto My co-equal Son, who stipulated to take upon Himself 'the form of a servant.' 'Thy seed'—all those that I have given unto Thee in the decree of election; all those whom Thou shalt live and die to redeem. Those 'will I establish forever,' so as to render their salvation irreversible and not inadmissible. And build up Thy Throne'—Thy Mediatorial throne, as King of saints and covenant Head of the elect. 'To all generations'—there shall always be a succession of favoured sinners to be called and sanctified, in consequence of Thy federal 'obedience unto death,' and every period of time shall recompense Thy covenant sufferings with an increasing revenue of converted souls, until as many as were ordained to eternal life shall be gathered in." (Author of that precious hymn, "Rock of Ages".) —AWP

(continued from back page)

16:13). No one has any difficulty in understanding what it signifies to "*serve* mammon." It is to make material riches my dominant quest, to make the acquirement of them my supreme aim, to devote all my powers to the securing of them. Equally plain is what is included in the "*serving* of God." It means putting Him first in our hearts and lives. It means for all our faculties and energies to be devoted to an ascertaining and then a *doing* of whatever He requires. It means the rendering to Him of an unqualified and loving obedience. And that necessarily involves the renunciation of all objects which are opposed to Him and abstaining from whatever He has forbidden. To allow any lust to reign in us is to depose God from the heart.

"He will *not forgive* your transgressions nor your sins." Solemn, unspeakably solemn words. How faintly any of us realise what it means for one to pass out of time into eternity with his transgressions *unforgiven*. "Ye shall die in your sins" (Joh 8:24) said Christ—not to avowed infidels—but the religious professors of His day. And why? Because they refused to take His "yoke" upon them, because they declared, "We will not have this man to reign over us" (Luk 19:14). Nor does death purge away sins, for after death, "the judgment" (Heb 9:27). Yes, eternal, inexorable, unbearable judgment—suffering the wrath of a holy and jealous God. Then "Beware of Him, and obey His voice, provoke Him not; for He will *not pardon* your transgressions" (Exo 23:21). Something more than believing is necessary: Christ is "the Author of eternal salvation unto all them that *obey* Him" (Heb 5:9). And how and where is the obedience of a sinner to begin? Just here: "Let the wicked forsake his way [of self-pleasing] and the unrighteous man his thoughts [of being saved in any other manner]: and let him return unto the LORD [from whom he revolted in Adam], and He will have mercy upon him; and to our God, for He will abundantly pardon (Isa 55:7).

What we have set forth above is not the Gospel, but it *is* the necessary background of it. The Divine Law reveals my duty and condemns me for my utter failure in discharging it. The Law makes known the just demands of God upon me and my woeful falling short of meeting the same. Not until I am personally convicted of my sinful failure, not until my heart sincerely repents for that failure, am I experimentally fit for the Gospel. But more so, there must be wrought in me a genuine desire to serve God, to give up myself wholly to His righteous requirements, and accompanying this must be the realisation of my own insufficiency, that I "cannot." Then, and only then, will the Gospel be music to my soul, for it tells first of how my awful guilt may be blotted out, and second, of how strength may be obtained for the discharge of duty. The Gospel exempts not the believer from the service of God, but binds him to it, for when we savingly believe the Gospel, we not only receive from God, but we "give ourselves" to Him (2Co 8:11, 12). Have *you* done so, my reader? Have you *really*, or is Satan deceiving you into thinking you have? —AWP

(continued from front page)

his heart, "But I have no desire to be a 'servant' of the Lord in that sense, all I want is to be assured that my sins are pardoned and that I am secured from Hell." If so, you are wanting something you will never obtain, for serving the Lord and obtaining His forgiveness of transgressions are inseparably connected. But do you realise what is implied by your assertion that you have no desire to serve the Lord? It signifies you are quite satisfied with your present master and decline to leave his service. Your present master is Satan and *his* servant you are. There are but two Masters over the sons of men: the Lord and the Devil—and if we are not serving the former, we are the latter.

"Ye *cannot* serve the LORD." Why? "For He is an *holy* God; He is a jealous God" (Jos 24:19). That presents a view of the Divine character, which only too many pulpits guiltily conceal. God is not only good and ready to pardon, but He is ineffably pure and cannot look on sin without displeasure. He is not only merciful and gracious, but He will tolerate no rivals, and requires that we love *Him* with all our heart and strength. Nor is that aspect of the Divine character restricted to the revelation, which He made of Himself at Sinai: the earth quaked at Calvary, thick darkness overshadowed the Cross, and the holiness of God was evidenced as He "spared not His own Son" (Rom 8:32). In the N.T., the call goes forth, "Wherefore we receiving a kingdom which cannot be moved, let us have grace, whereby we may serve God acceptably, with reverence and godly fear; for our God is a consuming fire" (Heb 12:28, 29). Ah, my reader, the glib manner and easy complacency with which so many talk of pardon and their assurance of it, proceeds from dullness of conscience rather than from strength of faith. They have never felt in their souls the exceeding sinfulness of sin, the holiness of Him with whom they have to do. Had they done so, their cry would be, "Behold, I am vile;" (Job 40:4) "Woe is me! for I am undone" (Isa 6:5).

"Ye cannot serve the LORD: for He is an holy God." Serving God is a very different matter from what the world thinks. The natural man imagines that he may devote the greater part of his time to the pleasing of himself, and then that he may appease God by assuming a pious air on the Sabbath. But He will not be imposed upon by any such mockery. To all such He says, "Ye adulterers and adulteresses, know ye not that the friendship of the world is enmity with God? Whosoever therefore will be a friend of the world is the enemy of God" (Jam 4:4)—spiritual adultery is illicit intercourse, setting our affections upon the creature rather than the Creator, devoting to them what belongs only to Him: our lusts, inveigling the soul from God. God will not accept the homage of a *divided heart.* That was made crystal clear by the Lord Jesus: "No man can serve two masters: for either he will hate the one, and love the other; or else he will hold to the one, and despise the other" (Mat 6:24). There we learn that service must proceed from *love.* God will not accept a legal service, which is rendered from dread, nor from a mercenary spirit, which seeks gain therefrom. He must be served freely and gladly.

The Devil deceives many into being satisfied with a superficial change and half reformation. They make a religious profession, persuading themselves they are trusting in the finished work of Christ, and yet continue in love with the world and to indulge the flesh. It is a fatal mistake to think we can divide our hearts between God and the world, to serve Him and our lusts. "Ye cannot serve God and mammon" (Mat 6:24; Luk

(Continued on preceding page)

VOL. XXIII.   OCTOBER, 1944.   NO. 10

STUDIES IN THE SCRIPTURES

" Search the Scriptures." John 5:39.

Publisher and Editor—ARTHUR W. PINK,
27 Lewis Street,
Stornoway, Isle of Lewis,
Scotland.

SERVANTS OF GOD

The Christian bears a twofold fundamental relationship to God: he is a "son" and he is a "servant"— the one speaks of privilege, the other expresses his duty. The one complements the other, and we should preserve a balance in our thinking upon them. The Christian was made a son; he made himself a servant. He was a son from all eternity in the purpose of God, he became so actually at his regeneration. He was an enemy by nature and practice, but at conversion, he renounced the service of sin and Satan and took upon him the yoke of Christ, to henceforth own Him as his alone Lord and Master. Thus, we become God's servants by free contract, by a voluntary act of our own, by "giving ourselves" unto the Lord (2Co 8:11, 12), to be controlled and directed by Him, to live now so as to honour and please Him in all things. Such unreserved dedication of ourselves unto God is our "reasonable service" (Rom 12:1). It is due God as His creatures, for He made us. It is due Him as our Preserver and Provider, for we are dependent on Him for every breath that we draw. It is due Him by right of redemption, for the Christian is not his own—free to please himself—but has been bought with a price (1Co 6:19, 20): he is the purchased property of Christ.

God's rights over us are unmistakable and absolute, but He will have them acknowledged by our own consent; and therefore, we only become His servants professedly and truly when we yield ourselves "unto God, as those that are alive from the dead," and our members (of both soul and body) "as instruments of righteousness unto God" (Rom 6:13), which was done at conversion, when we disowned sin, recognised the high claims of Christ, and received Him as our Lord and Master. Henceforth, we carry ourselves as His "servants" just in proportion as we live under a sense of our surrender to and dedication of ourselves to Him; or in other words, just so far as we now make the performing of His revealed will and the giving of pleasure to Him the chief business of our lives, for a "servant" is one at the command of his master. The motive-springs of such service is gratitude unto Him for as He died and suffered for us, with a realisation of the obligations this imposed upon us—for He will only be served out of *love*. "What doth the LORD thy God require of thee, but to fear the LORD thy God, to walk in all his ways, and to love him, and to serve the LORD thy God with all thy heart and with all thy soul" (Deu 10:12).

(continued on back page)

IMPORTANT NOTICES

Please advise promptly of change in address, otherwise copies will be lost in the mails.

We are glad to send a sample copy to any of your friends whom you believe would be interested in this publication.

This magazine is published as "a work of faith and labour of love," the editor and his wife gladly giving their services free. There is no regular subscription price, as we do not wish the poor of the flock to be deprived. This does not mean that those looking for something for nothing may "help themselves." Those getting this Magazine, who are financially able and who receive spiritual help from its pages, are expected to gladly contribute towards its expenses; otherwise, their names are dropped from our lists.

Will those forwarding International Money Orders please have them made out to us at Stornoway, Isle of Lewis, Scotland. Checks (Cheques-Eng.) made out on U.S.A. Banks are not negotiable here, so please do not send them.

CONTENTS

THE PRAYERS OF THE APOSTLES

10. 2 Corinthians 1: 3-5

The communication of news in ancient times was a much slower business than it is today. How long an interval elapsed between Paul's sending of his first epistle to the Corinthian church and his obtaining tidings from them we cannot be sure, but probably at least a year passed before he learned how they had received his communication and what effects, under God, it had produced in them. During that suspense, he appears to have been in a state of unusual depression and anxiety. The fierce opposition he encountered in Asia, where he was "pressed out of measure" (2Co 1:8) and the deep concern which he had for them, affected his peace of mind (2Co 7:5). His first epistle had been sent from Ephesus, where he had expected to remain until the following Pentecost (1Co 16:8), evidently hoping by then to hear from them. From Ephesus, he proposed to pass unto Macedonia and from thence to Corinth (1Co 16:5-7). But desiring to learn what had been their reactions to his letter, before he came to them, he sent Timothy (1Co 4:17; 16:10), commissioning him to set things in order and bidding them to respond peacefully to his counsels.

A little later on, the apostle sent Titus to Corinth in order to ascertain how matters were progressing, with instruction to return and make a report unto himself, for the manner and measure in which they had responded to his exhortations would regulate to a considerable extent his future movements. A momentous issue was at stake: the interests of the Gospel in an important city, the prosperity of a church which he had planted, and the honour of his Master's name were involved. Deeply exercised, he had left Ephesus and come unto Troas on his way to Macedonia, where it seems he had arranged for Titus to meet him and make his report. But in this he was disappointed (2Co 2:13), and having no rest in his spirit, he pressed forward to Macedonia. There too, peace was denied him, for "he had no rest," being troubled on every side—"without were fightings, within were fears" (2Co 7:5). Then it was that God relieved his suspense by the arrival of the eagerly-awaited Titus, who brought him a most favourable report, assuring him that his epistle had accomplished most of what he desired (2Co 7:6-16); and thereby, the heart of the apostle was greatly comforted.

Learning that the Corinthians had received his admonitions in Christian meekness, that they had been brought to repentance and had dis-fellowshipped the incestuous person (2Cor 7:9; 2:6), and that the major portion of the assembly had expressed the warmest affection for him (2Co 1:14; 7:7), he at once sent this second epistle to them. The news brought by Titus not only greatly relieved his mind, but also filled him with gratitude to God. On the other hand, the boldness and influence of the false teachers there had increased, as had their charges against himself, and their determined efforts to undermine his apostolic authority (2Co 10:2; 11:2-6, 12-15), moved him to indignation. This it is which explains the sudden change from one subject to another and the noticeable variation of tone in this second epistle. To the obedient section of the church, Paul wrote in the tenderest affection, commending their penitence, assuring them he had forgiven and forgotten. But when he turns to the corrupters of the Truth among them, he strikes a note of severity which is not heard elsewhere in his epistles.

"Blessed be God, even the Father of our Lord Jesus Christ [for the Greek is the same as in Ephesians 1:3 and 1 Peter 1:3, and the three passages are uniformly so translated in the Revised Version], the Father of mercies and the God of all comfort" (2Co 1:3). This is an ascription of praise, for "Blessed be" signifies "Adored be." The Father is here adored under a threefold appellation, each of which views Him as related to us in Christ—that is, to Christ as the covenant Head and His elect in Him. As the first will come before us again in Ephesians 1:3, we reserve our remarks upon it until we come (D.V.[1]) to that verse. The three titles are most intimately related, the one depending upon the other. He "the Father of mercies" unto His people, because He is the God and Father of their Head; and because He is "the Father of mercies" unto them, He is also their "God of all comfort." This threefold designation is worthy of our devoutest and closest meditation. "I do not know of anything more conducive to a wholesome spiritual edification than an acquaintance with God in the titles by which He has been pleased to reveal Himself to His people in His blessed Book. It is thus He delights to communicate His comforts and consolations to their exercised hearts" (T. Bradbury, 1830).

"The Father of mercies." Though it be blessedly true that God is "plenteous in mercy" (Psa 86:5), yet this title conveys more than the idea that He is our most merciful Father: it also connotes that these mercies issue from His very nature and that they are therefore both His offspring and His delight. The Hebrews used the word "father" for the author or first cause of anything, as Jabal is termed "the father of such as dwell in tents" and Jubal as "the father of all such as handle the harp and organ" (Gen 4:20, 21)—that is, the originator or founder of such. For the same reason God is called "the Father of spirits" (Heb 12:9), because He is the Begetter of them. In James 1:17, He is designated "the Father of lights," as He is the Author of all gifts coming down to us from above. There is a manifest allusion there to the sun which is the author and giver of light unto all the planets, and may therefore be termed the "father" or first original of light unto the earth. God is appropriately termed, "the Father of mercies"—for but for Him none of our mercies would have any existence. He sustains the same relation to His "mercies" as a father does to his dear children.

There is thus at least a threefold reason why God is here styled, "the Father of mercies." First, it is as "the God and Father of our Lord Jesus Christ" that He is such unto us: thus, it is *covenant* mercies which are here in view. Second, to signify that He is so far from begrudging these unto us that "mercies" are regarded as the Father's offspring, as proceeding from His nature; and therefore, are His *delights* (Mic 7:18). Third, because of its pertinency to the case of the Corinthians. It was His mercy which had moved the apostle to deal so faithfully with them in his first letter, for little as we may realise it, and still less as we may prize it, it is a great mercy when we are rebuked for our faults—instead of being abandoned by God. It was a further signal mercy, which caused the Corinthians to be convicted by Paul's rebukes, for the most faithful admonitions are ignored by us, unless God is pleased to sanctify them unto us: only in His light can we see ourselves. It was an additional mercy which wrought in them a godly sorrow, which caused them to mourn for their sins and put right what was wrong, for it is the goodness of God which leads us to repentance (Rom 2:4).

"And the God of all comfort." This is an excellency peculiar to the true and living God. None of the false gods of heathendom have such a quality ascribed to them; rather are they represented as being cruel and ferocious, and consequently, they are regarded—even by their worshippers—as objects of dread. But how different is the Lord God: "As one whom his mother comforteth, so will I comfort you" (Isa 66:13) He declared. What a revelation of the Divine character is that! Though inconceivable in majesty, all-mighty in power, inflexible in justice, yet he is also infinite in tenderness. How this should draw out our love for Him. How freely should we seek unto Him for relief in times of stress and sorrow. But alas, how slow most of us are in turning to God for consolation; how readily and eagerly do we seek unto the creature for the assuaging of our grief. Many believers seem to be as reluctant to go out of themselves to God alone for comfort, as unbelievers are to go out of themselves to Christ alone for righteousness. Yea, are there not some who, in a petulant and rebellious mood, say by their actions, "my soul refused to be comforted" (Psa 77:2)—despising their own mercies.

"The God of all *comfort.*" That term has come to have a narrower meaning than its derivatives, connoting little more today than consolation or soothing. Our English word is formed from the Latin *can fortis,* "with strength." Divine comfort is the effect produced by His "mercies." Every genuine comfort is here traced back to its source: He is "the God of *all* comfort" (2Co 1:3). In its lower sense, "comfort" is the natural refreshment that we obtain, under God, from the creature: we say "under God"—for apart from *His* blessing of them to us, we can derive no enjoyment and no benefit even from temporal mercies. In its higher signification, "comfort" has reference to support under trials. It is a Divine strengthening of the mind when there is a danger of our being overwhelmed by fear or sorrow. "This is my comfort in my affliction: for thy word hath *quickened* me" (Psa 119:50). Blessed is it to remember how often the Holy Spirit is termed, in relation to God's people, "The Comforter." Sometimes He makes use of our fellow-Christians to administer a spiritual cordial to our fainting hearts, as Paul was comforted by the coming of Titus to him (2Co 7:6).

It is inexpressibly solemn to consider that it was in precisely these characters of "the Father of mercies, and the God of all comfort" that Christ was *deserted by Him.* It was as our Surety and not as His beloved Son (regarded such) that the Judge of all the earth dealt with Him in holy severity and exorable justice, crying, "Awake, O sword, against my shepherd, and against the man that is my fellow, saith the LORD of hosts: smite the shepherd" (Zec 13:7). This is why that, amid all the indignities and inhumanities inflicted upon Him by *men,* He "opened not His mouth" (Isa 53:7); but when the Father of mercy withdrew from Him the light of His countenance and His comforts were withheld, He broke forth into that mournful lamentation, "My God, my God, why hast *thou* forsaken me?" And it is just because God sustained not the characters to the Saviour on the cross, that He bears these relations to us. If it ever be remembered by us that our cup is sweet because His was bitter, then God communes with us, because He forsook Christ—that we are enlightened, because He passed through those fearful hours of darkness.

"Who comforteth us in all our tribulation, that we may be able to comfort them which are in any trouble, by the comfort wherewith we ourselves are comforted of God" (2Co 1:4). The immediate reference is to the experiences through which the apostle had recently passed. He had occasion to personally adore God as "the Father of mercies, and the God of all comfort" (2Co 1:3), since he had been proving Him as such, for He had comforted *him* in all his trouble. Yet, he graciously and tenderly associates the Corinthians with himself, for they too had sorrowed and been comforted (2Co 7:9, 13). How striking is the difference between these verses and those which occupied us on the last occasion. Then the apostle could only thank God for their endowments (1Co 1:4-7), for he could not rejoice in their condition; but now he adores Him for the grace which makes all things work together for good unto His own and causes their very troubles to issue in their profit. There he had termed the One addressed "not God," but here it is "the Father of mercies, and the God of all comfort" who he adored. Only as we pass through the fires, do we obtain a fuller experimental knowledge of God and become more intimately acquainted with Him.

"Who comforteth us in all our tribulation." The soul is more capable receiving Divine comfort at such a season, for the things of time and sense that cease to charm it. Moreover, the Lord manifests more tenderness to His people on such occasions: "If ye be reproached for the name of Christ, happy are ye; for the spirit of glory and of God resteth upon you" (1Pe 4:14). God has various designs in bringing His people into trouble and sustaining them under it: for their growth, for a fuller discovery of Himself to them, for them to learn the sufficiency of His grace.

But another reason is here alluded to: "That we may be able to comfort them which are in any trouble, by the comfort wherewith we ourselves are comforted of God" (2Cor 1:4). The favours which He bestows upon us are intended to be made useful unto others. If I have found the Lord "a very present help in trouble" (Psa 46:1), it is both my privilege and duty to witness unto my troubled brethren as to *how* I was enabled to overcome temptations, found the Divine promises in support, and obtained peace in Christ while in the midst of tribulation. The best place of training for the pastor is not a seminary, but the school of adversity; spiritual lessons can only be learned in the furnace of affliction.

This principle receives its highest exemplification in the person of a blessed Redeemer. "Wherefore in all things it behoved him to be made like unto his brethren, that he might be a merciful and faithful high priest in things pertaining to God, to make reconciliation for the sins of the people" (Heb 2:17). It is clear from those words that in order to the perfecting of character to serve in that office, He must know first hand what actual trial and sorrow are. The "merciful" here signifies to lay to heart the miseries of His people, and to care for them so as to sustain and relieve their distresses. Yet it is not His mercifulness in general which is in view (for He possessed that both as God and man), but rather that which is drawn forth by the memory of the temptations and sufferings through which He passed. It is the exercise of mercifulness and faithfulness in His priestly work on high as excited and called into exercise by a sense of the afflictions He experienced on earth to which the apostle refers. Not only "merciful," but "faithful" also, in His constant care and attention to the needs of His weak and weeping people here below. Filled with compassion toward them, He is ever ready to support and sustain, strengthen and cheer them.

"For in that he himself hath suffered being tempted, he is able to succour them that are tempted" (Heb 2:18). Having trod the same path as His suffering people, He is qualified to enter into their afflictions. He is not like the holy angels who never experienced poverty or pain. No, during the season of His humiliation, He knew what weakness and exhaustion were (Joh 4:6), what the hatred and persecution of enemies entailed, what it was to be misunderstood and then deserted by those nearest to Him. Then how well fitted is He *to* sympathise with His suffering Church! Ponder such a passage as Psalm 69:1-4 and then ask yourself, Is not the One who passed through such trials capacitated to enter into the exercises of His tried people? "The remembrance of *His own* sorrows and temptations makes Him mindful of the trials of His people, and ready to help them" (M. Henry). The same heart beats within the Lord Jesus today as when He shared the grief of Mary and Martha by the grave of Lazarus, for His sympathies have not been impaired by His exaltation to heaven (Heb 13:8). O what a Saviour is ours: the all-mighty God, the all-tender Man!

"For we have not an high priest which cannot be touched with the feeling of our infirmities; but was in all points tempted like as we are, yet without sin" (Heb 4:15). Christ's being "tempted" must not be restricted to the evil solicitations of Satan. It includes the whole of His condition, circumstances, and course during the days of His flesh, when He suffered the pangs of hunger, had not where to lay His head, encountered reproach and shame, endured the contradiction of sinners against Himself. Thereby, He was prepared for the further discharge of His priestly office, fitted to be affected with a sense of our weakness, and to suffer with us. Though so high above us, He is yet one with us in everything except our sins, and concerning them also, He is our Advocate with the Father. We too are tempted (tried) in many ways, but there is One who consoles with us, yea, who is afflicted in all our afflictions and who helpeth our infirmities. But in remembering this, forget not that *He* had to cry, "I looked for some to take pity, but there was none; and for comforters, but I found *none*" (Psa 69:20).

"Who comforteth us in all our tribulation, that we may be able to comfort them which are in any trouble, by the comfort wherewith we ourselves are comforted of God" (2Co 1:4). One can enter more fully and closely into the grief of another if he has passed through identical circumstances. The Israelites were reminded of this when the Lord said, "Also thou shalt not oppress a stranger: for ye *know the heart of* a stranger, seeing ye were strangers in the land of Egypt" (Exo 23:9). Thus it was with the apostle Paul. God's design in so afflicting him was that he might be the better qualified to minister unto other afflicted souls. For an outline of his afflictions, see 2 Corinthians 11:24-30; yet so wondrous had God sustained him, he said, "I am filled with comfort,

I am exceeding joyful in all our tribulation" (2Co 7:4). God comforts by stilling the tumult of our mind, by assuaging the grief of our heart, and by filling the soul with peace and joy believing; and this, that we may be the comforters of others. Are some of us experiencing *less* of His consolations now, because in the past, we failed to seek out the sorrowing and cheer them?

"For as the sufferings of Christ abound in us, so our consolation also aboundeth by Christ" (2Co 1:5). The Christian must expect sufferings in the world, and such sufferings as non-Christians are free from. Faithfulness in Christ instead of exempting him from the same will rather intensify them. This is not always pointed out by preachers. It is true there is peace and joy to those who take Christ's yoke upon them, and such peace and joy as the worldling knows nothing of; yet it is also true that each one who enlists under His banner will be called upon to "endure hardness, as a good soldier of Jesus Christ" (2Ti 2:3), and that they "must through much tribulation enter into the kingdom of God" (Act 14:22). Therefore, it is but honest and right that the recruiting-sergeants of the Gospel should bid those who are contemplating taking upon them a Christian profession to "sitteth…down first, and counteth the cost" (Luk 14:28, 31) and faithfully warn them that "all that will live godly in Christ Jesus shall suffer persecution" (2Ti 3:12). To be forewarned is to be forearmed, and those properly forearmed will *not* think it "strange" when the "fiery trial" comes upon them (1Pe 4:12).

Verse 5 supplies a confirmation of the preceding one, its force being: we *are* able to comfort others *for* our consolation is equal to our sufferings. In particular afflictions to which the apostle here alluded, are termed "the sufferings of Christ," because they are the same in kind (though rarely if ever so in degree) as He experienced at the hands of men, and because of our union with Him and in order to be conformed to His image, we are required (in our measure) to have "fellowship" (Phi 3:10) therein. They are also termed, "the sufferings of Christ," because they are what His followers willingly endure for his sake" (Phi 1:29): since He is despised and rejected of the world, if we go forth unto Him without the camp, it must inevitably entail "bearing reproach" (Heb 13:13). It may be well to point out that some Christians through their folly, fanaticism, haughtiness, and other things—bring upon themselves needless suffering, but Christ gets not glory from them. But it is more necessary in this day to warn His people against a temporizing and compromising spirit, which seeks to *escape* "the sufferings of Christ "at the price of unfaithfulness to Him.

"So our consolation also aboundeth by Christ." Here is rich compensation. As union with Christ is the source and cause of the "sufferings," so it is of "consolation" (Joh 16:33)—as it will be of our glorification (Rom 8:17, 30; 2Ti 2:12. This it is which makes and marks the great difference between believers and unbelievers. Alienation from Christ does not exempt from suffering, but it cuts off from the only source of real consolation; and there, "the sorrow of the world worketh death" (2Co 7:10). There is a due proportion between the sufferings and the consolation, and if we would experience more of the latter, we must have more of the former, and for that, we must respond more faithfully to the light He has given us. God regulates the supply according to the trial and suits His dispensations unto our needs. The more the world frowns on us, the more His smile is enjoyed by us. If material effects be taken away, He supplies spiritual ones. If our bodies be cast into prison, our souls will enjoy more of Heaven. He graciously provides a sweetening tree for every Marah (Exo 15:23). —A.W.P.

THE MISSION AND MIRACLES OF ELISHA
22. Fourteenth Miracle

First, *its connection.* That which engaged our attention on the last occasion grew out of the determination of Benhadad to again wage war on Israel. After taking counsel with his servants, the Syrian laid an ambush for the king of Israel, but they had reckoned without Jehovah. He revealed to His servant the prophet the danger menacing his royal master, and accordingly, he went and acquainted him with the same, who, attending to the warning, was delivered from the trap set for him. The heart of the king of Syria was sore troubled at this thwarting of his design, and suspecting a traitor in his own camp made inquiry. Whereupon one of his attendants informed him that nothing could be concealed from the prophet that was in Israel, and that *he* had put the intended victim on his guard. After sending out spies to discover the whereabouts of Elisha and learning that he was in Dothan, the king of Syria sent a formidable force, consisting of "horses and chariots" and a "great host" of footmen to take him captive, determining to remove this obstacle from his path.

The miracle we are about to consider is a *double* one, and strictly speaking, comprises the fourteenth and fifteenth of the series connected with our prophet. But the record is so brief and the two miracles are so closely related that they scarcely admit of separate treatment, and therefore, instead of taking them singly we propose to consider them conjointly, viewing the second as the counterpart or complement of the former. It is a miracle which stands out from the last one which occupied our notice. That concerned the opening of eyes; this, the closing of them. There but a single person was involved; here, a great host of men were concerned. In the one, it was the prophet's own servant who was the subject of it; here, it was the soldiers who have been sent to take him captive. In the former, he wrought in response to an urgent appeal from his attendant; in the other, he acted without any solicitation. They both occurred at the same place. They were both wrought in answer to Elisha's prayer. They are both recorded for our learning and comfort.

In connection with the preceding miracle, Elisha had prayed to his Master for Him to open the eyes of his servant, and we are told, "And the LORD opened the eyes of the young man; and he saw: and, behold, the mountain was full of horses and chariots of fire round about Elisha" (2Ki 6:17). That the prophet himself already saw this celestial convoy is clear: it was his own vision of them which moved him to ask that his servitor might also behold them. We may deduce the same from the immediate sequel. So far from being in a panic at the great host of Syrians, which had come to take him captive, Elisha calmly stood his ground. "The wicked flee when no man pursueth: but the righteous are bold as a lion" (Pro 28:1), for since God be for them, who can be against them? There was no need for him to cry unto the Lord for deliverance, for Divine protection was present to his view. Therefore, he quietly waited till the enemy actually reached him before he acted.

Ere passing on, let us offer a further remark upon this celestial guard which was round about Elisha. That it was composed of personal beings is clear from the pronoun, "*they* that be with us are more than they that be with them" (2Ki 6:16). That they were angelic beings is evident from several passages: "Who maketh his angels spirits; his ministers a flaming fire" (Psa 104:4). At His second advent, we are told "the Lord Jesus shall be revealed from heaven with his mighty angels, In flaming fire taking vengeance on them that know not God, and that obey not the gospel of our Lord Jesus Christ" (2Th 1:7, 8). The ministry of angels is admittedly a mysterious subject, one about which we know nothing, save what it hath pleased God to reveal to us. Yet it is a subject which holds by no means an inconspicuous place in Holy Writ. It would be outside our present scope to explore it at large; rather, must we confine ours to that aspect of it which is here presented unto us.

Angels are not only God's messengers sent on missions of mercy, but they are also His soldiers, commissioned both to guard His people, and execute judgment on His enemies. They are designated, "the heavenly *host"* (1Ki 22:19; Luk 2:13)—the Greek word meaning "soldiers"—or as we would term them, "men of war," the militia of Heaven. In full accord with that conclusion, we find the Saviour reminding His disciples that "more than twelve legions of angels" (Mat 26:53) were at His disposal, should He but ask the Father for protection against the armed rabble that had come to arrest Him. It was a host of them, in the form of fiery horses and chariots (compare Psalm 68:17) who here encamped around Elisha, ready to fight for him. How mighty the angels are, we know: one, called "the destroyer" (Exo 12:23, compare 2Sa 24:16) slew all the firstborn of the Egyptians, while another slew one hundred and eighty-five thousand Assyrians in a night (2Ki 19:35). That their operations continue in this Christian era is plain from such passages as Act 12:7; Heb 1:14; Rev 7:1, 15:1; Mat 24:31, etc.

"And when they came down to him, Elisha prayed unto the LORD and said, Smite this people, I pray thee, with blindness" (2Ki 6:18). The "they" looks back to the armed host mentioned in verse 14. Formidable as was the force sent to slay him, or at least take him captive, yet the prophet stood ground and calmly waited their approach. And well he might. Could he say, "I will not be afraid of ten thousands of people, that have set themselves against me round about" (Psa 3:6), and again, "Though an host should encompass about me, my heart shall not fear" (Psa 27:3)! And should not this confidence and courage be the Christian's? "The clearer sight we have of sovereignty and power of heaven, the less shall we fear the calamities of earth" (M. Henry). Perhaps the reader says, If I were favoured with an accurate view of protecting angels round about me, I would not fear physical danger in human enemies. Ah my friend, is not that tantamount to a confession that you are walking by sight? and may we not apply to you those words, "Blessed are they that have not seen, and yet have *believed"* (Joh 20:29).

Why, think you my reader, has God chronicled here that which assures the heart of His servant of old? Is this nothing more than a registering of a remarkable incident in ancient history? Is *that* how you read and understand the sacred Scriptures? May we not adopt the language used by the apostle in connection with a yet earlier incident and say, "Now it was not written for his sake alone...But for us also" (Rom 4:23, 24)? Most certainly we also, for later on in that very epistle, we are expressly informed, "For whatsoever things were written aforetime were written for *our* learning, that we through patience and comfort of the scriptures might have *hope"* (Rom 15:4). God recorded that sight of those protecting angels for our faith to lay hold of and remember that if faith is to stand us in good stead in the hour of emergency, it must be regularly nourished by the Word; if it be not, then the terrors of earth will be real to us and the comforts of heaven unreal. Unless faith appropriates that grand truth, "If God be for us, who can be against us?" we shall neither have peace ourselves, nor be qualified to quieten the fears of others.

Second, *its means.* "And when they came down to him, Elisha prayed unto the LORD" (2Ki 6:18). That needs to be pondered and interpreted in the light of the previous verse, or we are likely to miss its beauty and draw a false inference. Very lovely was the prophet's conduct on this occasion. The presence of those horses and chariots of fire round about Elisha was virtually a sign that God had delivered these Syrians into his hands: he had only to speak the word and the angels had destroyed them. But he bore his enemies no ill will. Had our present verse stood by itself, we might have concluded that the prophet was asking in self-defence, begging the Lord to protect him from his foes, but it opens with the word, "And" and in the light of the one preceding, we are obliged to revise our thought. It is quite clear that Elisha was in no personal danger, so it could not have been out of any concern for his own personal safety that he now sought unto God. Yet, though he calmly awaited their approach, he did not meet his enemies in his own strength, for prayer is an acknowledgement of insufficiency.

"Elisha prayed unto the LORD, and said, Smite this people, I pray thee, with blindness" (2Ki 6:18). At first glance, it seems strange that he is referred to here by his personal name, rather than as "the man of God," which the Holy Spirit generally uses when he was about to work a miracle; yet the variation in this place is neither fortuitous nor meaningless. It points a blessed lesson for *us,* showing as it does the readiness of the Lord to hearken to the requests of His people. Though we do not possess the extraordinary powers of a prophet, yet it is our privilege to ask God to confuse and confound those of our natural enemies who seek our harm, and to subdue our spiritual ones. This incident has been recorded for our instruction and comfort, and one of the things we are to learn therefrom is that prayer avails to render our enemies impotent. Another lesson we should draw from it will be evident if we link up this verse with the preceding one, wherein we see another of Elisha's requests granted: success in prayer should encourage and embolden us to ask further favours from God.

Going back again for a moment to Elisha's situation. This petition of his was neither because he felt he was in any personal danger, nor did it proceed from any spirit of malice which he bore his enemies: then *what* was it that prompted the same? Does not the miraculous healing of Naaman supply the answer to our question! When the king of Israel had rent his clothes in dismay, the man of God assured him that the king of Syria "shall know there is a prophet in Israel" (2Ki 5:7, 8), and when Naaman was recovered of his leprosy, he sought unto the man of God, and before all his own retinue, testified "now I know that there is no God in all the earth, but in Israel" (2Ki 5:15). And now this heathen monarch had sent his forces to take the prophet prisoner! Very well, then, if he was not yet convinced that it was the true and living God whom Elisha served, he should receive further proof. It was *Jehovah's glory* which prompted Elisha's request. Weigh that well my reader, for everything depends upon the motive which inspires our petitions, determining whether or no we shall receive an answer. True and acceptable prayer rises above a sense of personal need, having in view the honour of God's name—keep before you 1 Corinthians 10:31.

"And he smote them with blindness, according to the word of Elisha" (2Ki 6:18). That was an exact reversal of what took place under the foregoing miracle: there the prophet's servant was enabled to see what was invisible to others (2Ki 6:17); but here, the Syrian soldiers were rendered incapable of seeing what was visible to others. But let us behold in this miracle the willingness of our God to respond to the cries of His own, that He is a prayer-hearing and prayer-answering God. If we self-distrustfully refuse to encounter foes in our own strength, if we confidently ask God to render their efforts impotent, and if we do so with His glory in view, we may be assured of His gracious intervention. No matter what may be our need, how drastic the situation, how urgent our case, how formidable our adversary, while simple faith is exercised, and the honour of God be our aim, we may count upon His showing Himself strong on our behalf. "For I am the LORD, I change not" (Mal 3:6): He is the same now as He was in Elisha's day.

Third, *its mercy*. "And Elisha said unto them, This is not the way, neither is this the city: follow me, and I will bring you to the man whom ye seek. But he led them to Samaria" (2Ki 6:19). He did not abandon them to their blindness and leave them to themselves: contrast Genesis 19:11, when God was dealing in wrath. Had they not been blinded, probably they would have identified the prophet by his attire; but being strangers to him, they would be unable to recognise him by his voice. Spiritually that illustrates the fundamental difference between the goats and the sheep: the former are incapable of distinguishing between teachers of Truth and of error; not so the latter, for they "know not the voice of strangers" but "will flee from him" (Joh 10:5). But exactly what did Elisha signify by those statements? It is lamentable to find one commentator, in whose notes there is generally that which is sound and good, saying, "The prophet intended to deceive the Syrians, and this might lawfully be done, even if he had meant to treat them as enemies, in order to his own preservation; but he designed them no harm by such deception."

Apart from such a view giving the worst possible interpretation to the prophet's language, such an observation as the above is most reprehensible. It is never right to do wrong, and no matter what may be our circumstances, for us to deliberately lie is to sin both against God and our fellows. Such an explanation as the above is also absurd on the face of it. Elisha was in no personal danger at all, and now these Syrians were blinded, he could have walked away unmolested by them had he so pleased. "This is not the way"—whitherto. He could not mean to "Dothan," for they were already there and must have known it. "I will bring you to the man whom ye seek": and who was that? Why, ultimately and absolutely, the king of Israel, for whom their master has laid an ambush (note verse 11!)—Elisha being merely an obstacle who had hindered him. One who had just obtained from God such an answer to prayer, and who was now showing mercy to his enemies, would scarce lie to them!

Fourth, *its counterpart*. "And it came to pass, when they were come into Samaria, that Elisha said, LORD, open the eyes of these men, that they may see. And the LORD opened their eyes, and they saw; and, behold, they were in the midst of Samaria" (2Ki 6:20). Here was still further proof that Elisha harboured no malice against these Syrians and that he intended them no harm. Though they had hostile designs against him, yet he now uses his interest with the Lord on their behalf. Most gracious was that. What an example for every servant of God: "In meekness instructing those that oppose themselves" (2Ti 2:25). Instead of cherishing ill will against those who are unfriendly to us, we should seek their good and pray to the Lord on their behalf. How this incident reminds us of a yet more blessed example: when the Lord of glory in the midst of His sufferings made intercession for His crucifiers (Isa 53:12; Luk 23:34). A further miracle was now wrought in answer to Elisha's intercession, showing us once more the mighty power of God and His willingness to employ the same in answer to the petitions of His people. Note how Elisha made good his promise: he led them to the man they really sought, for the next person mentioned is "the king of Israel"!

Fifth, *its accompaniment.* "And the king of Israel said unto Elisha, when he saw them, My father, shall I smite them? shall I smite them?" (2Ki 6:21). Very solemn is this and in full accord with his character: the Lord did not open *his* eyes—consequently, he was blind to the working of His goodness and incapable of appreciating the magnanimous spirit, which had been displayed by the prophet. Here we see what man is by nature: fierce, cruel, vindictive. Such are we and all of our fellows as the result of the fall: "Living in malice and envy, hateful, and hating one another" (Tit 3:3). It is nought, but the restraining hand of God which prevents our fellows from falling upon us. Were that Hand completely withdrawn, we should be no safer in a 'civilized country' than if we were surrounded by savages or cast into a den of wild beasts. It is not sufficiently realised by us that God's restraining power is upon those who hate us: "For I am with thee, and no man shall set on thee to hurt thee" (Act 18:10).

"And he answered, Thou shalt not smite them: wouldest thou smite those whom thou hast taken captive with thy sword and with thy bow? set bread and water before them, that they may eat and drink, and go to their master" (2Ki 6:22). Observe how Elisha kept full control of the situation, even though now in the royal quarters—something which every servant of God needs to heed, exercising the authority which Christ has given him. Note too how this verse teaches that mercy is to be shown unto prisoners of war—or taking it in its wider application, how that kindness is to be extended unto our enemies. And this, mark it well, occurred under the O.T. economy! The Divine Law commanded its subjects, "If thine enemy be hungry, give him bread to eat; and if he be thirsty, give him water to drink" (Pro 25:21 and see also Exo 23:4, 5), much more so under the dispensation of grace are we required to "overcome evil with good." (Rom 12:21).

Sixth, *its sequel.* Elisha had his way and the king, "And he prepared great provision for them: and when they had eaten and drunk, he sent them away, and they went to their master" (2Ki 6:23a), that he might learn anew that our times, the success or failure of our plans, our health and our lives, are in the hand of the living God, and that He is not only infinite in power, but plenteous in mercy. The sequel was, "*So* the bands of Syria came no more into the land of Israel" (2Ki 6:23b). God honoured the magnanimity of His prophet and rewarded the obedience of his royal master by exempting the land from any further depredations from these savage bands.

Seventh, *its meaning.* May we not see in the above incident another lovely Gospel picture, viewing the graciousness of Elisha unto those who had gone to take him captive as a shadowing forth of God's mercy unto elect sinners? First, we are shown what they are by nature: at enmity with His servant. Second, we behold them as the subjects of His servant's prayers—that they may be granted a sense of their wretched condition. Third, in answer thereto they are duly brought to realise their impotency—who so consciously helpless as the blind! Fourth, they were moved to follow the instructions and guidance of God's servant. Fifth, in due course, their eyes were opened. Sixth, they were feasted with "great provision" at the King's own table. Seventh, the picture is completed by our being given to behold them as *changed* creatures coming no more on an evil errand into Israel's land.

But is there not also an important spiritual meaning and lesson here for Christians?—one which has been pointed out in the course of our remarks; namely, How we are to deal with those who seek to injure us. Negatively, we are to harbour no malice against such, nor to take vengeance upon them even should Providence deliver them into our hands. Positively, we are to ask the Lord to nullify their efforts and render them powerless to injure us. But more, we are also to pray that God will open their eyes, and treat them kindly and generously: see Matthew 5:44. —A.W.P.

SPIRITUAL GROWTH OR CHRISTIAN PROGRESS

5b. Its Analogy

Near the close of our last, we stated that increasing *humility* is that in a Christian which corresponds to the downward growth of a tree. As the upward growth of a tree is accompanied by its becoming more deeply rooted in the ground, so the Christian's acquaintance with, love for, and delight in God issues in a deeper self-depreciation and self-detestation. If the knowledge we have acquired of the Truth, or if what we term our "Christian experience" has made us think more highly of ourselves and better pleased with our attainment and performances, then that is a sure proof we are completely deceived, imagining we have made any real growth upward. The grand design of the Scriptures is to exalt God and humble man, and the more we experimentally or spiritually know God, the less we shall think of ourselves and the lower place shall we take before Him. The knowledge which "puffeth up" is merely an intellectual or speculative one, but that which the Spirit imparts causes its recipient to feelingly own that I "knoweth nothing yet" as I "ought to know" (1Co 8:2).

The more the soul converses with God and the more it perceives His Sovereignty and majesty, the more will he exclaim with Abraham, "which am but dust and ashes" (Gen 18:27). The more the believer is granted a spiritual view of the Divine perfections, the more will he acknowledge with Job, "I abhor myself, and repent in dust and ashes" (Job 42:6). The more the saint apprehends the ineffable holiness of the Lord, the more will he declare with Isaiah, "Woe is me! for I am undone; because I am a man of unclean lips" (Isa 6:5). The more he is occupied with the perfections of Christ, the more will he find with Daniel, "my comeliness was turned in me into corruption, and I retained no strength" (Dan 10:8). The more he discerns that exalted spirituality of God's Law and how little his inner man is conformed thereto, the more will he groan in concert with Paul, "O wretched man that I am! who shall deliver me from the body of this death?" (Rom 7:24). In God's light, we see ourselves, discover the horrible corruptions of our very nature, mourn over the plague of our own heart (1Ki 8:38), and marvel at the continued long sufferance of God unto us.

The truly humble person is not the one who *talks most* of his own unworthiness, and is frequently telling of how such and such an experience abased him into the dust. "There are many that are full of expressions of their own vileness, who yet expect to be looked upon as eminent saints by others as their duty, and it is dangerous for any so much as to hint the contrary or to carry it toward them any otherwise than as if we looked upon them as some of the chief of Christians. There are many that are much in crying out their wicked hearts and their great shortcomings and unprofitableness, and speaking of themselves as though they looked on themselves as the meanest of the saints; who yet, if a minister should seriously tell them the same things in private, and should signify that he feared they were very low and weak Christians and that they had reason solemnly to consider of their great barrenness and unprofitableness and falling so much short of many others, it would be more than they could digest. They would think themselves highly injured and there would be danger of a rooted prejudice in them against such a minister" (J. Edwards).

The same writer defined evangelical humility as the "sense that a Christian has of his own utter insufficiency, despicableness and odiousness, with an answerable frame of heart." That answerable frame of heart consists of being "poor in spirit" (Mat 5:3), a sense of deep need, a realisation of sinfulness and helplessness. The natural man compares himself with his fellows and prides himself that he is at least as good as his neighbours. But the regenerate person measures himself by the exalted standard which *God* has set before him and which is perfectly exemplified in the example Christ has left him that he should "follow his steps" (1Pe 2:21), and as he discovers how lamentably he falls short of that standard and how "far off" he follows Christ, he is filled with shame and contrition. This empties him of self-righteousness and causes him to depend wholly on the finished work of Christ. It makes him conscious of his weakness and fearful that he will suffer a sad fall, and therefore, he looks above for help and cries, "Hold thou me up, and I shall be safe" (Psa 119:117). Thus, the truly humble person is the one who lives most outside of himself on Christ.

This brings us to those oft-quoted, but we fear, little-understood words: "Grow in grace" (2Pe 3:18). Growth in grace is only too frequently confused with the development of the Christian's *graces*. That is why we selected a different title for these articles than the one commonly accorded the subject. Growth in grace is but one aspect or part of spiritual growth and Christian progress. When a minister asked a simple countryside woman what was her concept of "growing in grace," she replied, "A Christian's growth in grace is like the growth of a cow's tail." Puzzled at her reply, he asked for an explanation. Whereupon she said, "The more a cow's tail grows, the nearer it comes to the ground; and the more a Christian grows in grace, the more does he take his place in the dust before God." Ah, she had been taught from above what many an eminent theologian and commentator is unacquainted with. Growth in grace is a growth *downward:* it is the forming of a lower estimate of ourselves, it is a deepening realisation of our nothingness, it is a heartfelt recognition that we are not worthy of the least of God's mercies.

What is it to enter into a personal experience of saving grace? Is it not a feeling my deep *need* of Christ and the consequent perception of His perfect suitability to my desperate case?—to be acutely conscious that I am "sick" in soul and the betaking of myself to the great "Physician." If so, then must not any advancement in grace consist of an intensification of the same experience, a clearer and fuller realisation of my need of Christ? And such growth in grace results from a closer acquaintance and fellowship with Him: "Grace and peace be multiplied unto you through the knowledge of God, and of Jesus our Lord" (2Pe 1:2)—that is, a vital, practical, effectual knowledge of Him. In His light we see light: we become better acquainted with ourselves, more aware of our total depravity, more conscious of the workings of our corruptions. Grace is favour shown unto the undeserving, and the more we grow in grace, the more we perceive our undeservingness, the more we feel our need of grace, the more sensible we are of our indebtedness to the God of all grace. Thereby are we taught to walk with God and to make more and more use of Christ.

Every Christian reader will agree that if ever there was one child of God who more than others "grew in grace," it was the apostle Paul, and yet observe how he said, "Not that we are sufficient of ourselves to *think any thing* as of ourselves; but our sufficiency is of God" (2Co 3:5); and again, "But by the grace of God I am what I am" (1Co 15:10). What breathings of humility were those! But we can appeal to an infinitely higher and more perfect example. Of the Lord Jesus, it is said that He was "*full* of grace and truth" (Joh 1:14), and yet He declared, "Take my yoke upon you, and learn of me; for I am meek and lowly in heart: and ye shall find rest unto your souls" (Mat 11:29). Does the reader detect a slip of the pen in the last sentence? Since Christ was "full of grace and truth," we should have said, *"therefore* (and not 'yet'). He declared, 'Learn of me; for I am meek and lowly in heart'"—the latter was the evidence of the former! Yes, so "meek and lowly in heart" was He that, though the Lord of glory, He declined not to perform the menial task of washing the feet of His disciples! And in proportion, as we learn of Him, shall *we* become meek and lowly in heart. Hence, "and in the knowledge of our Lord and Saviour Jesus Christ" is explanatory of "grow in grace" in 2 Peter 3:18.

True humility dwells only in a heart which has been supernaturally enlightened of God and which has experimentally learned of Christ, and the more the soul learns of Christ, the more lowly will it become. Even in natural things, it is the novice, and not the servant, who is the most conceited. A smattering of the arts and sciences fills its youthful possessor with an exalted estimate of his wisdom, but the further he prosecutes his studies, the more conscious will he become of his ignorance. Much more so is this the case with spiritual things. An unregenerate person who becomes familiar with the letter of the Truth imagines he has made great progress in religion; but a regenerate person—even after fifty years in the school of Christ—deems himself a very babe in spirituality. The more a soul grows in grace, the more does he grow out love with himself. In one of his early epistles, Paul said, "I am the least of the apostles" (1Co 15:9); in a later, "who am less than the least of all saints (Eph 3:8); in one of his last, "sinners, of whom I am chief" (1Ti 1:15)!

Third, trees grow *inwardly,* which brings us to what is admittedly the hardest part of our subject. We have never made a study of botany, and even though we had, it is doubtful if it would stand us in much stead on this point. That there must be an inward growth of the tree is obvious, though, exactly what it consists of is another matter. Yet that need not surprise us, for the analogy holds good here, too, is not this uncertainty just what we should expect? Is not the inward growth of a Christian that aspect of his progress which is the most difficult to define, describe, and still more so, to put into practice? Unless the tree grows inwardly, it would not grow in any other direction, for its outward growth is but the development and manifestation of its vital or seminal principle. We must fall back then on general principle and exercise a little common sense, and say: the inward growth of a tree consists of an increase of its sap, a resisting of that which would injure, and the toughening of its tissues.

The sap is the vital juice of all plants, and its free circulation, the determined of its health and growth. The analogy of this in the Christian is the grace of God communicated to his soul, and his spiritual progress is fundamentally determined by his receiving fresh supplies of grace. At regeneration, God does not impart to us a supply of grace sufficient for the remainder of our lives: instead, He has made Christ to be the grand Fountain of all grace, and we are required to continue betaking ourselves to Him for fresh supplies. The Lord Jesus has issued a free invitation: "If any man thirst, let him come unto me, and drink" (Joh 7:37), which must not be restricted to our first approach. As long as the Christian remains on earth, he is as needy as when he drew his first spiritual breath, and his need is supplied in no other way than by his coming to Christ daily for fresh supplies of His grace. Christ is "full of grace" and that fulness is *available* for His people to draw from (Heb 4:16). "He giveth more grace...unto the humble" (Jam 4:6)—that is, to those who "thirst," who are conscious of their need and who present themselves as empty vessels to be replenished.

But there is another principle which operates and regulates our obtaining further supplies of grace: "For unto everyone that hath shall be given, and he shall have abundance" (Mat 25:29, compare Luk 8:18). The context shows that the one who "hath" is he who has traded with what had been bestowed upon him—in other words, the way to obtain more grace, is to make a right and good *use* of what we *already* have—why should Christ give more if we have not improved what He previously communicated? Faith becomes stronger by exercising it. And *how* does the Christian make a good use of grace? By heeding that all-important injunction, "Keep thy heart with all diligence; for out of it are the issues of life." (Pro 4:23). *This* is the great task which God has assigned unto each of His children. The "heart" signifies the whole inner man—the "hidden man of the heart" (1Pe 3:4). It is that which controls and gives character to all that we become and do. The man is what his heart is, for "as he thinketh in his heart, so is he" (Pro 23:7). To guard and garrison the heart is the grand work God has appointed us: the enablement is His, but the duty is ours.

Negatively, the keeping of the heart with all diligence signifies, excluding from it all that is opposed to God. It means the keeping of the imagination free from vanity, the understanding from error, the will from perverseness, the conscience clear from all guilt, the affections from being inordinate and set on evil objects, the inner man from being dominated by sin and Satan. In a word, it means, to *mortify* the "flesh" within us, with all its affections and lusts: to resist evil imaginations, nipping them in the bud, to strive against the swellings of pride, the workings of unbelief, to swim against the tide of the world, to reject the solicitations of the Devil. This is to be our constant concern and ceaseless endeavour. It means to keep the conscience tender unto sin in its first approach. It means looking diligently after its cleansing when it has been defiled. For all of this, much prayer is required, earnest seeking of God's assistance. His supernatural aid, and if it be sought trustfully, it will not be sought in vain, for it is the grace of God which teaches us *to deny* "ungodliness and worldly lusts" (Tit 2:11, 12).

Positively, the keeping of our hearts with all diligence signifies the cultivation of our spiritual graces—called "the fruit of the spirit" (Gal 5:22, 23). For the health, vigour, exercise, and manifestation of those graces, we are accountable. They are like so many tender plants which will not thrive, unless they are given much attention. They are like so many tendrils on a vine which must be lifted from trailing on the ground, pruned and sprayed, if they are to be fruitful. They are like so many saplings in the nursery which need rich soil, regular watering, and the warmth of the sun, if they are to thrive. Go carefully over the ninefold list given in Galatians 5:22, 23, and then honestly ask the question, What sincere effort am I really making to cultivate, to foster, to develop those graces? Compare, too, the sevenfold list of 2 Peter 1:5-7 and put to yourself a similar inquiry. When your graces are lively and flourishing and Christ draws near, you will be able to say, "My beloved is gone down into his garden, to the beds of spices, to feed in the gardens, and to gather lilies" (Son 6:2). God esteems nothing so highly as holy faith, unfeigned love, and filial fear—compare 1 Peter 3:4 and 1 Timothy 1:5.

"Man looketh on the outward appearance, but the LORD looketh on the heart" (1Sa 16:7). Is that sufficiently realised by us? If it is, then we are making it our chief concern to keep our hearts with all diligence. "My son, give me thine *heart*" (Pro 23:26): until *that* be done, God will accept nothing from you. The prayers and praises of our lips, the offerings and labours of our hands, yea, a correct outward walk, are things of no value in His sight—unless the heart beats true to Him. Nor will He accept a divided heart. And if I *have* really given Him my heart, then it is to be *kept* for Him, it must be devoted to Him, it must be suited to Him. Ah, my reader, there is much head religion, much hand religion—busily engaged in what is termed, "Christian service," and much feet religion—rushing around from one meeting, "Bible Conference," "Communion," to another, but where are those who make conscience of keeping their *hearts!* The heart of the empty professor is like "the vineyard of the man void of [spiritual] understanding," namely, "all grown over with thorns, and nettles had covered the face thereof" (Pro 24:30, 31).

A very few words must suffice upon the third aspect of inward growth. In the case of a tree, this consists in the toughening of its tissues or strengthening of its fibres—apparent from the harder wood obtained from an older one than from a sapling. The spiritual counterpart of that is found in the Christian attaining unto more firmness and fixedness of character, so that he is no longer swayed by the opinions of others. He becomes more stable, so that he is less emotional and more rational, acting not from sudden impulse, but from settled principle. He becomes wiser in spiritual things, because his mind is increasingly engaged with the Word of God and his eternal concerns; and therefore, more serious and sober in his demeanour. He becomes confirmed in doctrine; and therefore, more discerning and discriminating in whom he hears and what he reads. Nothing can move him from allegiance to Christ, and having bought the Truth, he refuses to sell it (Pro 23:23). He is not afraid of being called a bigot, for he has discovered that "liberality" is emblazoned prominently as the Devil's banner.

Fourth, the growth of a tree is *outward,* seen in the spreading of its bough, and the multiplication of its branches. We have purposely devoted a great space unto those aspects of our subject, on which we felt the reader most needs help. This one almost explains itself: it is the *daily walk* of the believer, his external conduct, which is in view. If the Christian has grown upward—that is, if he has obtained an increased vital and practical knowledge of God in Christ; if he has grown downward—that is, if he has become thoroughly aware of his total depravity by nature and learned to have "no confidence in the flesh" (Phi 3:3) to effect any improvement in himself; if he has grown inwardly, obtained fresh supplies of grace from Christ and has diligently used the same striving against indwelling sin, and by resolutely resisting his carnal and worldly lusts, and if he has improved that grace by diligently cultivating his spiritual graces in the garden of his heart; then that upward, downward and inward growth will be (not simply "ought to be"), *must be,* clearly and unmistakably shown in his outward life.

And how will that upward, downward and inward growth be manifested by the Christian outwardly? Why, by a life of *obedience* to his Lord and Saviour. Out of love and gratitude unto the One who suffered and did so much for him, he will sincerely endeavour to please Him in all his ways. Realising that he is not his own, but bought with a price, he will make it his highest aim and earnest endeavour to glorify God in his body and in his spirit (1Co 6:19, 20). The genuineness of his desire to please God, and the intensity of his purpose to glorify Him, will be evidenced by the diligence and constancy with which he reads, meditates upon, and studies His Word. In searching the Scriptures, his main quest will not be to occupy his mind with its mysteries, but rather, to obtain a fuller knowledge of God's *will for him;* and instead of hankering after an insight into its typology or its prophecies, he will be far more concerned in how to become *more proficient* in performing God's will. It is in the light of His Word he longs to walk; and therefore, it is His precepts and promises, His warnings and admonitions, His exhortations and aids, he will most lay to heart.

One of the N.T. exhortations is, "We beseech you, brethren, and exhort you by the Lord Jesus, that as ye have received of us how ye ought to walk and to please God, so ye would *abound more and more*" (1Th 4:1). One of its prayers is, "That ye might be filled with the knowledge of his will in all wisdom and spiritual understanding; That ye might walk worthy of the Lord *unto all pleasing*, being fruitful in every good work" (Col 1:9, 10). One of its promises is, "God is able to make all grace abound toward you; that ye, always having all sufficiency in all things, *may abound* to every good work" (2Co 9:8). And one of its examples is, "And they [the parents of John the Baptist] were both righteous before God, walking in *all* the commandments and ordinances of the Lord *blameless*" (Luk 1:6). In the light of those verses—each of which treats with outward growth—our duty and privilege is clear: what God requires from us and the sufficiency of His enablement for the same. —A. W. P.

THE DOCTRINE OF RECONCILIATION

5b. Its Arrangement

A solemn covenant was entered into between the Father and the Son before ever the world was. A compact was made wherein the Father assigned the Son to be the Head and Saviour of His elect, and wherein the Son consented to act as the Surety and Sponsor of His people. There was a mutual agreement between them, of which the Holy Spirit was both the Witness and Recorder. It was therein that the Son was appointed unto the Mediatorial office, when He was "set up" (or "anointed" as the Hebrew signifies), when He was "brought forth" from the eternal decree (Pro 8:23, 24) and given a covenant subsistence as the God-man. It was then that Christ as a lamb, without blemish and without spot, "Who verily was foreordained before the foundation of the world" (1Pe 1:18-20). It was then that every thing was arranged between the Father and the Son, concerning the redemption of the Church. It is this which throws such a flood of light upon many passages in the N.T.—which otherwise are shrouded in mystery.

As the One more especially offended (1Jo 2:1), the Father is represented as taking the initiative in this matter: "I have made a covenant with my chosen" (Psa 89:3), yet the very fact that it was a "covenant" necessarily implied the willing concurrence of the Son therein. Before the covenant was settled, there was a conference between them. As there was a conferring together of the Divine Persons concerning our creation (Gen 1:26), so there was a consultation together over our reconciliation, as to how peace could be righteously made between God and His enemies, and as to how their enmity against Him might be slain; and thus, we are told, "and the counsel of peace shall be between them both" (Zec 6:13). The terms which the Father proposed unto the Son may be gathered from the office He assumed and the work He performed—for the relation into which He entered and the task He discharged were but the actual fulfilling of the conditions of the covenant. The Son's acceptance of those terms, His willingness in entering its office and discharging its duties, is clearly revealed in both Testaments.

This covenant was made by the Father with Christ on behalf of His people. "Thy seed will I establish for ever" follows immediately after Psalm 89:3. So again, "My covenant shall stand fast with him. His seed also will I make to endure for ever" (Psa 89:28, 29). In the next verses, His seed are termed, "his children;" and should they be unruly, God says, "Then will I visit *their* transgression with the rod. Nevertheless my lovingkindness will I not utterly take from *him*" (Psa 89:32, 33)—showing their covenant oneness with Him. The elect were committed to Christ as a charge or trust, so that He is held accountable for their eternal felicity. "Of them which thou gavest me have I lost none." (Joh 18:9)! Since the covenant was made with Christ as the Head of the elect, it was virtually made with them in Him, they having a representative concurrence therein.

The terms of the covenant may be summed up thus. First, it was required that Christ should take upon Him the form of a Servant, be made in the likeness of men, and act as the Surety of His people. Second, it was required of Him that He should render a full and perfect obedience to the Law; and thereby, provide the meritorious means of their justification. Third, it was required of Him that He should make full satisfaction for their sins, by serving as their Substitute and having visited upon Him the entire curse of the Law. In consideration of His acceptance of those terms, the Father promised Him adequate supports; and on fulfillment of the task prescribed, specified reward were promised Him. Let us briefly amplify these points. Little needs to be said on the first—for it should be clear to the reader that in order for the Son to render obedience to the Law, He must become a subject of it and be under its authority. Equally evident is it that to be the Substitute of His people and suffer the penalty of their sins, He must become partaker of their nature—yet without sharing its defilement.

It was required from our Surety that He should comply in every respect with the precepts of the Divine Law. Such obedience was required of man originally under the Adamic covenant, and since the nature of God and His relation to the creature changes not, that requirement holds good for ever. If then a Surety engages to discharge all the obligations of God's elect, then He must necessarily meet that requirement on their behalf—which is only another way of saying that He would thereby provide or bring in an everlasting righteousness for them. "There was no possibility that man could obtain happiness, unless this obedience was performed by him, or by another whom the Law should admit to act in his name. 'If thou wilt enter into life, keep the commandments' (Mat 19:17) is the answer which the Law returns to the sinner who asks what he shall do to inherit eternal life. It is evident the same obedience was required from our Saviour when acting as our federal Head" (J. Dick).

The Father required from our Surety full satisfaction for the sins of His people. Since they had broken the Divine Law, its penalty must be inflicted — either on them or on One who was prepared to suffer in their room. But before the penalty could be inflicted, the guilt of the transgressors must be transferred to Him: that is to say, their sins must be judicially imputed to Him. To that arrangement, the Holy One willingly consented, so that He who "knew no sin" was legally "made sin" for His people. God laid on Him the iniquities of them all; and therefore, the sword of Divine justice smote Him and exacted satisfaction. Without the shedding of blood, there was no remission of sins: the blotting out of transgression, procuring for us the favour of God, and the purchase of the heavenly inheritance, required the death of Christ.

The Son's free acceptance of those terms is revealed in Psalm 40. All the best of the commentators from Calvin to Spurgeon have expounded this Psalm throughout of Christ as the Head of His Church. Its opening verses contain His personal thanksgiving for deliverance from death and the grave, but in His new song, He makes mention of "*our* God" (Psa 40:3)—His people sharing His glorious triumph. In Psalm 40:5, Christ owns Jehovah as "my God" and speaks of His thoughts to "*us-ward*"—that is, to the elect as one with Himself. But it is in Psalm 40:6-10 we have that which is most germane to our present subject—a passage quoted in Hebrews 10, and which looks back to the far distant past. The force of "Sacrifice and offering thou didst not desire" (Psa 40:6) is given us in, "For it is not possible that the blood of bulls and of goats should take away sins" (Heb 10:4). "Mine ears hast thou opened" (Psa 40:6) speaks in the type of Exodus 21:5, 6 and tells of our Lord's readiness to serve and His love to His Father and His children. "A body hast thou prepared me" (Heb 10:5) announces the Son's coming into this world, equipped for His arduous undertaking.

"Then said I": when alternatives had been discussed and it was agreed that animal sacrifices were altogether inadequate for satisfying Divine justice, "Lo, I come": willingly of Mine own volition—from the ivory palaces to the abodes of misery. Those words signified His cheerful acceptance of the terms of the covenant. "In the volume [or 'head'] of the book, it is written of me" (Psa 40:7; Heb 10:7): thus, it was recorded at the very beginning of the Divine decrees—of which the Scriptures are a faithful transcript—that I should make My advent to earth. Thus, it was registered by the Holy Spirit who witnessed My solemn engagement with the Father so to do. Thus, it was formally and officially inscribed that in the fulness of time, I should become incarnate and accomplish a purpose which lay beyond the capacity of all the holy angels. "I delight to do thy will, O my God" (Psa 40:8) tells us first of the object for which He came—to make good the Father's counsels; second, His freeness and joy therein; third, the character in which He acted—as covenant Head: "My God."

"I delight to do thy will, O my God" (Psa 40:8). Herein consists the very essence of obedience: the soul's cheerful and loving devotion to God. Christ's obedience, which is the righteousness of His people, was pre-eminent in this quality. Notwithstanding unparalleled sorrows and measureless griefs, our Lord found delight in His work: "Who for the joy that was set before him endured the cross, despising the shame" (Heb 12:2). "Yea, thy law is within my heart" (Psa 40:8), He declared. No mere outward and formal subjection to the Divine will was His. That Law which is "holy, and just, and *good*" (Rom 7:12) was enshrined in His affections. "O how love I thy law!" (Psa 119:97), He averred. The Law did not have to be "written" on *His* heart, as it has on ours (Heb 8:10), for it was one with the holiness of His nature. Then what a horrible crime for any to speak disparagingly of or want to be delivered from that Law which Christ loved!

The two things—the Father's proposing the terms of the covenant and the Son's free acceptance of them—are brought together in a striking, yet rarely considered passage: "And their nobles [the Hebrew is in the singular number] shall be of themselves, and their governor shall proceed from the midst of them; and I will cause him to draw near, and he shall approach unto me: for who is this that engaged his heart to approach unto me? saith the LORD" (Jer 30:21). That is one of the great Messianic prophecies, and it is closely parallel with Psalm 89:19, 20, 27. In it, we see the Father taking the initiative, and equally so the Son's cheerful compliance. The Son is to become incarnate, for He was to "proceed from the midst of" the people of Israel. He was to be the "Governor," and in order thereto is seen "approaching" the Father, or voluntarily presenting Himself to serve in that capacity. His free consent and heartiness so to act appears in His, "that engaged his heart to approach unto me? saith the LORD" (Jer 30:21).

We cannot now enter into the connections of the above verse, but if the reader compares verse 9 of the same chapter and ponders what follows, he will find confirmation of our interpretation. There, the Father announced, "But they shall *serve* the LORD their God, *and* David their king, whom I will raise up [not from the grave, but exalt to office, as in Deu 18:15, Luk 1:69, etc.] unto them." That can be meant of none other than Christ, the antitypical David, for "serve" includes rendering Divine homage (Mat 4:10), and worship will never be performed to the resurrected son of Jesse. Now it is the antitypical David—the Father's "Beloved"—who is the King and Governor of the spiritual Israel and to whom Divine honours are paid. And He is the One who before earth's foundation was laid, "engaged his heart" (Jer 30:21)—or as the Hebrew signifies, "became a *surety* in his heart" (for so the word is rendered in Gen 44:32, Pro 6:1, etc.), and *that* is the ground of the covenant which follows: "And ye shall be my people, and I will be your God" (Jer 30:22).

Before looking at some of the assurances made by the Father of adequate assistance to His incarnate Son in the discharge of His covenant engagement, we must consider more closely *the office* in which He served, In previous articles, we pointed out the needs for a Mediator—if God and His people were to be reconciled in a way that honoured His Law—as we also intimated His consummate wisdom in such an arrangement, and showed the perfect fitness of Christ for such an office. As the Mediator, He was to serve as our Surety and also fulfill the functions of Prophet, Priest, and King. As the Mediator, He was "set up" or "anointed" from the beginning (Pro 8:23)—that is, when given a covenant subsistence as such before God, in which He acted all through the O.T. era. The prophets (equally with the apostles) were *His* ministers; and therefore, the Spirit who spoke in them is termed, "the Spirit of Christ" (1Pe 1:11). In Zechariah 1:11, 12 and 3:2, we find Him interceding: and in anticipation of the incarnation, He appeared as "man" (Jos 5:13, 14; Dan 12:6, 7).

Christ is Mediator in respect of His person, as well as office. Only then could He be the Representative of God unto us, the Image of the invisible God, the One in whom He is seen (Joh 14:9), the light of whose glory shines in His face (2Co 4:6). It must ever be remembered that it was a Divine person who became flesh, and it is equally necessary to insist that the whole of His mediatory work is inseparably founded on the exercise of *both* of His natures. It is quite unwarrantable to predicate certain things of His Divine nature, and others of His human, for though not confounded, there is perfect oneness between them. It was the God-man who was tempted, suffered and died, "the *Lord's* death" (1Co 11:26). This is indeed a subject beyond human comprehension; nevertheless, though "great is the mystery of godliness," yet it is "without controversy" (1Ti 3:16) unto all those who bow to the all-sufficient authority of Divine revelation and receive the same as "little children" (Mat 18:3).

As the Mediator Christ became the Father's "servant" (Isa 42:1; Phi 2:7). Yet in so doing, He ceased not to be a Divine person, but rather the God-man in whom "dwelleth all the fulness of the Godhead bodily." (Col 2:9). As our Surety, Christ became subordinate to the Father's will; nevertheless, He still retained all His Divine perfections and prerogatives. When the Holy Spirit announced that unto us a Child should be born and a Son given, He was careful to declare that such an One was none other than "The mighty God" (Isa 9:6). When the Father brought His First begotten into the world, He gave orders, "Let all the angels of God *worship* him." (Heb 1:6). Yet as our Surety and the Father's Servant, He was "sent" into the world, received "commandment" from His Father and became "obedient" unto death. Retaining as He did His Divine perfections, He could rightly say, "I and my Father are one" (Joh 10:30), co-equal and co-glorious, yet, as the Servant, "My Father is greater than I" (Joh 14:28), not essentially so, but officially; not by nature, but by virtue of the place which He had taken. This distinction throws a flood of light upon many passages.

To be Himself "the true God" (1Jo 5:20) and yet subject to God, owning Him as "My God;" to be the Law-Giver, and yet "under the law" (Gal 4:4), to be One with the Father and yet inferior to Him, to be "The Lord of glory" (1Co 2:8) and yet *made...both Lord and Christ*" (Act 2:36) are, according to all human reason and logic, inconsistent properties; nevertheless, Scripture itself expressly predicates these very things of one and the same Person, yet looked at in *different relationships*! In the days of His flesh, Christ was "over all, God blessed for ever" (Rom 9:5), yet as our Surety, "the head of Christ is God" (1Co 11:3). While walking this earth as the Man of sorrows, the disciples beheld His glory "as of the only begotten of the Father" (Joh 1:14), yet as our Substitute, He was "crucified through weakness" (2Co 13:4). As God manifest in flesh, He both laid down His life and took it again (John 10:18); but as our Shepherd, God "brought again from the dead our Lord Jesus" (Heb 13:20). There is perfect harmony amid wondrous variety.

Christ's entrance into covenant engagement was entirely voluntary on His part: there existed no prior obligation, nor was there any authority by which He could be compelled to it. As the Father's "Fellow," He was subject to no law and acknowledged no superior, supreme dominion was His, and He "thought it not robbery to be equal with God" (Phi 2:6). But having freely entered into the covenant and agreed to fulfill its terms, the Son became officially subordinate to the Father, and as our Surety, He sent Him "into the world" (Joh 3:17), and as our Surety, He was "anointed...with the Holy Ghost and with power" (Act 10:38), was "delivered...up for us all" (Rom 8:32), was raised from the dead (Act 2:24), was given "all power...in heaven and in earth" (Mat 28:18), was elevated to the right hand of the Majesty on high (Heb 1:3), was exalted "to be a Prince and a Saviour, for to give repentance to [the spiritual] Israel, and forgiveness of sins" (Act 5:31), and was "ordained of God to be the Judge of quick and dead" (Act 10:42). Thus, the very passages over which "Unitarians" have stumbled and broken their necks, speak of Christ not in His essential Person, but in His mediatorial office: the former giving value to the latter, the latter endearing the former to our hearts. —A.W.P.

(continued from back page)

our constant concern to glorify Him, or we are not His servants, but rather the servants of our lusts and the bond slaves of Satan.

What an inestimable privilege, what a high honour to be the servants of the Lord of glory! "Happy are thy men, happy are these thy servants, which stand continually before thee and that hear thy wisdom" (1Ki 10:8) exclaimed the queen of Sheba as she beheld those who waited upon Solomon. But one infinitely greater than Solomon is our Master, even Immanuel. He is no hard taskmaster (like the Egyptians) demanding that we make bricks without providing us with straw. No, His yoke is easy and His burden light (Mat 11:30). It is a blessed thing to serve Him, and His service is freedom—the only genuine freedom there is. The service of Satan is captivity (2Ti 2:26), for though he and his emissaries may declare it is and promise us "liberty," yet all who heed his lies are "brought in bondage" (2Pe 2:19), for the service of sin is drudgery, slavery, tyranny. Not only is Christ's service honourable and blessed, but it is richly recompensed both now and hereafter: "If any man serve me, him will my Father honour" (Joh 12:26) with peace of conscience, contentment of mind, joy of heart. And in the day of rewards, He shall say, "Well done, thou good and faithful servant...enter thou into the joy of thy Lord" (Mat 25:21).

A few words now upon the spirit and character of our service: *1) It must be in "newness of spirit"* (Rom 7:6), for that which proceeds from the flesh is "dead works" (Rom 7:5). Our serving God is to express the new relation into which His wondrous grace has brought us and issue from the enablement of the new power He has communicated to us, the indwelling Holy Spirit. *2) It must be rendered from love.* It was so with the Lord of glory: "That the world may know that I love the Father; and as the Father gave me commandment, even so I do" (Joh 14:31). In like manner, according to their much lower stature, it is said of His servants, "the love of Christ constraineth us" (2Co 5:14). *3) It must be with cheerfulness:* "Serve the LORD with gladness" (Psa 100:2), whether it be in the kitchen or in the workshop. As Spurgeon says, "He is our Lord, and therefore He is to be served: He is our gracious Lord, and therefore to be served with joy." *4) It must be in a spirit of filial fear,* owning the Lord's authority over us, venerating His majesty. Nehemiah prayed that the ear of the Lord might be attentive to the "prayer of thy servants, who desire to fear thy name" (Neh 1:11) and David could say, "Stablish thy word unto thy servant, who is devoted to thy fear" (Psa 119:38), while of the perfect Servant, it is recorded that He "was heard in that he feared" (Heb 5:7). *5) With serenity of mind,* and not in a slavish spirit of dread, either of God or man. "That we being delivered out of the hand of our enemies, might serve him without fear [of His despising our poor efforts if they be sincere, or of the consequences from our fellows], In holiness and righteousness before him, all the days of our life" (Luk 1:74, 75). *6) Without partiality:* no license is given us to pick and choose, "Whatsoever he saith unto you, do it" (Joh 2:5, compare Mat 28:20). *7) Dependently:* Definitely, earnestly, daily waiting upon Him for enabling wisdom and strength: see Hebrews 12:28 and 4:16. — A.W.P.

(continued from front page)

God has joined these two things inseparably together: "Them that love me, and keep my commandments" (Exo 20:6). The Lord Jesus enforced the same truth: "If ye love me, keep my commandments" (Joh 14:15). "Ye are my friends [all others are His enemies], if ye do whatsoever I command you" (Joh 15:14). But Christ did more: He *exemplified* this truth in His own blessed person and perfect life: He voluntarily "took upon him the form of a servant" (Phi 2:7) and manifested His entire subjection to God by becoming "obedient" to Him: an obedience without any reserve or limit, for He "became obedient unto death, even the death of the cross" (Phi 2:8). Thus, a "servant" is known chiefly by his *obedience*: "Know ye not, that to whom ye yield yourselves servants to obey, his servants ye are" (Rom 6:16). Of Christ the Father declared, "Behold my servant, whom I uphold; mine elect, in whom my soul delighteth" (Isa 42:1). And why did the Father find such "delight" in Him? Because He loved righteousness and hated wickedness (Psa 45:7), because He could say "I do always those things that please him" (Joh 8:29). And it is only as the Christian conducts himself as an *obedient* "servant" that he has fellowship with Christ, follows the example He has left him, and gives his Redeemer "delight."

"For unto me the children of Israel are servants; they are my servants whom I brought forth out of the land of Egypt: I am the LORD your God" (Lev 25:55). Mark it well, my reader: it was not only Moses and Aaron, or even the priests and Levites who were His "servants," but *all* the Israelites who had been redeemed from the house of bondage; and they were "servants" because He was the Lord their God. "Lord" and "servant" are correlative terms, as are husband and wife, parent and child. This holds good in the N.T. era as truly and fully as it did in the Old: all who have been genuinely converted and brought to receive Christ as their Lord are His servants. This was foretold of old: "Also the sons of the stranger, that join themselves to the LORD, *to serve him*, and to love the name of the LORD, to be his servants" (Isa 56:6). "Not with eyeservice, as menpleasers; but as the servants of Christ, doing the will of God from the heart" (Eph 6:6). "Ye turned to God from idols to serve the living and true God" (1Th 1:9). "Not using your liberty as a cloak of maliciousness, but as the servants of God" (1Pe 2:16). Even in Heaven, the saints shall still sustain this relationship and character: "His servants shall serve him" (Rev 22:3).

We have designedly added passage to passage in the last paragraph, because in some religious circles a "servant of Christ" is limited unto a minister of the Gospel, while in other sections of Christendom, "Christian service" is restricted to certain special activities which only a small number engage in, such as a Sunday School Class, tract distributing, speaking in the open air, engaging in "personal work." Thus, it is implied and actually believed by many that one may be a real Christian, and yet, not a "servant" of Christ at all. That is indeed a serious misconception, yea, a fatal delusion. It is indeed true that one may be a real Christian without engaging in any of the forms of "service" just mentioned, for they were quite unknown two centuries ago! But in the sense we have pointed out in the preceding paragraphs, unless I am consciously and conscientiously serving the Lord, then I am not a Christian at all. Lip patronage will not satisfy Christ, nor will the performing of tasks to which He has never called us. We must do the things *He* has commanded, render obedience to Him out of love, make it

(Continued on preceding page)

VOL. XXIII.   NOVEMBER, 1944.   NO. 11

STUDIES ɪɴ ᴛʜᴇ SCRIPTURES

"Search the Scriptures." John 5:39.

Publisher and Editor—Aʀᴛʜᴜʀ W. Pɪɴᴋ,
27 Lewis Street,
Stórnoway, Isle of Lewis,
Scotland.

THE HIDDEN MANNA

"To him that overcometh will I give to eat of the hidden manna" (Rev 2:17). This is one of the seven promises in Revelation 2 and 3 made to the overcomers, which is one of the many designations accorded the children of God in the Word of Truth, though probably one of those which most of these are least familiar with. The first time the word occurs in the N.T., it is used of the Lord Jesus (Luk 11:22), where He is portrayed as the One stronger than Satan, overcoming him and dividing his spoils--a representation of what He does for His elect at their conversion, when He delivered them from the power of Satan. The next time this word is found in the N.T. it is again in connection with Christ: "Be of good cheer; I have overcome the world" (Joh 16:33)--we are to take courage and consolation from that fact, for since He overcame the world for His people, and since they are both legally and vitally one with Him, God has ordained they shall participate in His victory. The word occurs again in connection with Christ as "the Lion of the tribe of Judah," where we are told He "hath prevailed [overcome] to open the book" (Rev 5:5)—perhaps the title-deeds to that Inheritance.

"To him that overcometh"--the enemies of his salvation. The Christian is a warrior, engaged in a life and death fight, and though he receives many wounds in the conflict and is often thrown down by his adversaries, yet he gets up again, renews the struggle, and in the end, comes out victorious. "Him that overcometh" is in contrast from those who are overcome--like the unbelieving Israelites who were overthrown in the wilderness, like the many of John 6:66 who were offended at Christ's doctrine and who "went back and walked no more with Him," like Demas who made a promising start and accompanied Paul for a while, but of whom he had to say, he "hath forsaken me, having loved this present world" (2Ti 4:10). It is not enough to engage in warfare against sin and Satan, the flesh and the world; we must persevere therein unto the end. The overcomer is the one who cleaves to Christ and adheres to the Truth, who refuses to be deterred by the difficulties of the way, the assaults of his enemies, the allurements of false teachers.

Four things are necessary in order for anyone to be an overcomer. First, he must be supernaturally regenerated, for the task involved is much too arduous for mere nature to succeed in: "For whatsoever is born of God overcometh the world" (1Jo 5:4). It

(continued on back page)

IMPORTANT NOTICES

Please advise promptly of change in address, otherwise copies will be lost in the mails.

We are glad to send a sample copy to any of your friends whom you believe would be interested in this publication.

This magazine is published as "a work of faith and labour of love," the editor and his wife gladly giving their services free. There is no regular subscription price, as we do not wish the poor of the flock to be deprived. This does not mean that those looking for something for nothing may "help themselves." Those getting this Magazine, who are financially able and who receive spiritual help from its pages, are expected to gladly contribute towards its expenses; otherwise, their names are dropped from our lists.

Will those forwarding International Money Orders please have them made out to us at Stornoway, Isle of Lewis, Scotland. Checks (Cheques-Eng.) made out on U.S.A. Banks are not negotiable here, so please do not send them.

CONTENTS

THE PRAYERS OF THE APOSTLES

11. 2 Corinthians 12: 7-10

So many aspects of the Truth are brought before us and so many lines of thought are suggested by these verses that we must dispense with an introduction and consider, first, the *occasion* of this prayer. This is discovered to us in the immediate context. As we have pointed out in a previous article, false teachers had appeared at Corinth and had succeeded in sowing the seeds of dissension in the assembly there. The saints were in danger of being turned away from Christ by having their confidence in Paul undermined by the misrepresentations of his enemies. This had obliged him to engage in the distasteful task of vindicating himself--presenting the grounds which he had for claiming spiritual authority over them and for asserting his apostolic powers. So repugnant was this to his feelings, that he apologized for thus speaking of himself and begged them to bear with him (2Co 11:1), pointing out it was solely for their good that he now appeared to indulge in self-laudation.

Paul's enemies had insisted that he was greatly inferior to the Eleven, yea, that he was not an apostle at all, since he lacked the all-essential qualifications stated in Acts 1:21, 22--he had neither been one of the favoured band who were most closely associated with Christ during His public ministry, nor had he been a witness with them of His resurrection. That was an exceedingly grave charge, for if Paul was not a Divinely-called apostle, he had no authority to take the oversight of the churches and regulate their concerns. This obliged him to indulge in what seemed like boasting and to affirm, "I was not a whit behind the very chiefest apostles" (2Co 11:5). Previously, he had openly acknowledged his personal unworthiness to be numbered of their company (1Co 15:9), but now he was compelled to point out that in authority, knowledge, and effective grace, none of them excelled him, and then spread before them his credentials (2Co 11:22-33).

It is very blessed and touching to see the nature of the proofs Paul advanced to show he was a *true* minister of the Gospel. He boasts not of the success of his labours, the souls that had been saved under his preaching, or the number of churches he had planted, but mentions rather the opposition he had met with, the persecutions encountered, the sufferings he had gone through. He shows to them as it were the *scars* he had received "as a good soldier of Jesus Christ" (2Ti 2:3). He demonstrated he was a real servant of His by calling attention to the reproaches, the ignominy, the cruel treatment he had received. It was his sufferings, and his patient endurance of them, that made manifest that he was a genuine minister of Christ (compare Gal 1:10). Though great indeed was that honour attached to his office, yet the faithful discharge of it entailed that which no impostor, no self-seeker, no hireling would continue to meekly bear.

In chapter 11, the apostle had first met his opponents on their own ground and by comparing himself with them, had answered the fool according to his folly (Pro 26:5). Then he had demonstrated that he was a genuine officer of Him who is "despised and rejected of men" (Isa 53:3). But now he comes to that which was peculiar to himself and relates an experience which far excelled any that the other apostles had been favoured with. He continues his apology, but in an altered tone: "It is not expedient for me doubtless to glory. I will come to visions and revelations of the Lord" (2Co 12:1). To have "seen" the Lord was one of the requisites of valid apostleship (1Co 9:1), and Paul *had* done so by a heavenly vision (Act 26:19). Moreover these Corinthians were probably aware that he had been the subject of a vision which especially concerned *them* (Act 18:9, 10). But over and above these, he now went on to relate an experience which afforded superlative evidence of the favour of God to him as an apostle.

"I knew a man in Christ above fourteen years ago (whether in the body, I cannot tell; or whether out of the body, I cannot tell: God knoweth;) such an one caught up to the third heaven...How that he was caught up into Paradise, and heard unspeakable words, which it is not lawful for a man to utter" (2Co 12:2, 4). This was an experience unparalleled in the recorded history of men-- an honour and privilege which far exceeded that bestowed upon any other mortal. It is impossible for us to adequately conceive of the extraordinary favour that was here granted the beloved apostle. He was personally transported to Paradise, translated to the Father's House, permitted an entrance into the Palace of the Sovereign of the universe. For a brief season, he was taken to be with "the spirits of just men made perfect" (Heb 12:23). There was the glorified Lamb upon the Throne, and he would hear the seraphim exclaiming before Him, "'Holy, holy, holy is the LORD of hosts" (Isa 6:3). It is useless to indulge in speculation and impious to give rein to our imagination--we can but wonder and worship.

"Of such an one will I glory: yet of myself I will not glory, but in mine infirmities. For though I would desire to glory, I shall not be a fool; for I will say the truth: but now I forbear, lest any man should think of me above that which he *seeth* me to be, or that he heareth of [not 'from'!] me" (2Co 12:5, 6). That is exquisitely lovely. Paul had indeed a just ground for insisting upon the higher favour which God had shown him above all others, but inasmuch as it was gratuitous, implying no personal worthiness, he forbore. Had he glorified it had not been as a "fool" or empty boaster, but according to truth, to fact; but he restrained himself because he desired others not to think too highly of him! He preferred that men should judge him by what they saw and heard, and not esteem him by the special revelations God had given him! It was his "infirmities" he would glory in, for weakness, sustained by grace, is all that any saint may boast of in himself.

"And lest I should be exalted above measure through the abundance of the revelations, there was given to me a thorn in the flesh, the messenger of Satan to buffet me, lest I should be exalted above measure" (2Co 12:7). Having stated in the preceding verse that he did not wish others to think of him more highly than they should, he now tells us what means God used to prevent *himself* from so doing. The apostle was in danger of being unduly elated by the extraordinary manifestation of the Divine favour he had received. This is quite understandable--for one who had visited Paradise itself and then to be suddenly returned to this world of woe, required a heavy ballast to keep his ship on an even keel. The "third heaven" was too dizzy a remembrance to be safely borne by one who had to walk again on earth--and that, in a body of sin and death. The Lord knew this and graciously dealt accordingly, bestowing upon him that which kept him humble.

By nature, Paul was just as proud and foolish as all other men, and if his heart was kept lowly, it was not by his own unaided fidelity to the Truth, but because of the faithfulness of his Master who dealt so wisely with him. We must distinguish between the *cause* and the *occasion* of pride--the former is the evil nature or principle from which it proceeds; the latter, the object on which it fastens and which it perverts to its use. The "pride of life" (1Jo 2:16) can feed on anything, turning temporal mercies and even spiritual gifts and graces into poison. Pride was the main ingredient in the sin of our first parents--aspiring to be as God. There is pride in every sin, since it is a lifting up of the creature against the Creator. We are shown how God regards and abominates pride in Proverbs 6:16-19, where seven things are mentioned which the Lord hates, and the list is headed with "a proud look" (Pro 6:17)! The great work of grace is the subduing of our pride.

The celestial revelations which Paul had received had no tendency whatever in themselves to produce or promote pride, but like all other things, they were capable of being abused by indwelling sin. Therefore, lest he should be spiritually proud, become vain and self-confident regarding himself as a special favourite of Christ, there was given to Paul "a thorn in the flesh" (2Co 12:7). That it is termed a "thorn" intimates it was something that was painful; that it was a bodily affliction is signified by the words, "in the flesh"; that it remained within him is seen from his prayer that it might "depart"; and that Satan aggravated it appears from the next clause of the verse. So far from proposing to join the numerous company of the curious who have indulged in all manner of speculations as to precisely what this "thorn" consisted of, we are frank to say we have no idea of its nature, nor have we the least desire to be wise above what God has revealed.

Personally, we admire the Divine wisdom in restraining the apostle from being more explicit, for the general statement is better suited to a far wider application. Human nature being what it now is--had the Holy Spirit made known the specific character of this particular "thorn in the flesh"--certain afflicted and querulous souls would be most apt to say: Paul might "glory" in *his,* but if he had the painful distress which is *mine,* he would have sung another tune. Suppose the apostle had mentioned any certain physical disorder—say, inflamed eyes-those free from it, but having another (say, the gout) would consider that *their* "thorn" was much harder to endure. But since God has wisely left it undefined, each afflicted saint may take comfort from the possibility that his affliction is identical with Paul's. Whatever in our persons or our circumstances serves to *mortify* our pride may be regarded as our "thorn in the flesh."

Instead of vainly conjecturing exactly what Paul's "thorn in the flesh" consisted of, let us draw comfort from the blessed fact that it was (not "sent" but) *"given"* him—that is, by God, as a Divine favour! It is thus that we should regard each painful trial as a merciful bestowal from God, the design of which is to hide pride from us. But this word "given" also connotes Paul's *acceptance* of the same, that he meekly and thankfully regarded it as from the Lord. This "thorn" he also speaks of as "the messenger of Satan to buffet me" (2Co 12:7), the cases of Job and his boils, the woman of Luke 13:16, and the demon possessed, show that the Devil is given the power to cause bodily affliction. In Paul's case, Satan desired to disqualify him from his work, but the Lord overruled him and made him render the apostle a good service. This should teach us to look above Satan and seek from God the reason why He has permitted him to afflict us.

"Lest I should be exalted above measure." Paul not only accepted the painful affliction as a gift from the Lord, but he also perceived *why* it was given him. And so should each Christian in like circumstances, and until he does so, he should humbly continue waiting on the Lord saying, "show me *wherefore* Thou contendest with me" (Job 10:3 and compare 2Sa 21:1, Job 6:24). If the reader has a "thorn in the flesh" and seeks enlightenment from above, he too may discover the needs-be for it. In Paul's case, it was to humble him to hide pride from him; and is not *that* usually God's chief design in His disciplinary dealings with *us*! In the apostle's case, it was not for correction, but for prevention. Such may have been God's merciful design towards you—perhaps He turned a wealthy relative against you to will his money elsewhere, or has withheld business prosperity from you—lest you be "puffed-up." How effective Paul's "thorn" was appears from the fact that for fourteen years, he never mentioned his rapture into Paradise, and would not have done so now but for exceptional circumstances.

"For this thing I besought the Lord thrice, that it might depart from me" (2Co 12:8). The "thorn" did not make him fret and fume, but caused him to pray. This brings us, second, to *the Object* of his prayer—namely, the Lord Jesus, as the next verse plainly shows. A decisive proof is this of the Godhead of Christ and also a clear intimation that petitions may be addressed to Him, as well as to the Father. Prayer was made to *Him* in Acts 1:24 and 4:24. As Stephen was being stoned, he cried, "Lord Jesus, receive my spirit" and begged Him not to lay this sin to the charge of his slayers (Act 7:59, 60). When he was the persecuting Saul of Tarsus, Ananias told the Lord that he had authority from the chief priests "to bind all that call on thy name" (Act 9:10-14). That it was the common practice of the primitive saints to invoke the Saviour's name is very evident from 1 Corinthians 1:2. There was a special propriety in Paul, here addressing Christ, for *He* is the One who admits into Paradise (Act 7:59, Rev 1:18).

But let us consider next, *his petition*: "I besought the Lord thrice that it might depart from me." We, regard this request as being made before he had any perception of why the Lord had afflicted him, and also of manifesting his native kinship with us. Thorns are far from pleasant, and we desire their prompt removal. Nor is it wrong for us to do so—we should not be rational and sentient creatures if we did not shrink from suffering. For us to ask for deliverance from pain and trouble is not sinful, neither is it spiritual. Then *what is it?* Why, *natural,* the exercise of that instinct of self-preservation with which the Creator has endowed us. But it becomes sinful when we insist on deliverance, insubordinate to the Divine will. In Paul's case, and in many others, we see how grace triumphed over nature, the heart gladly acquiescing in the Lord's design.

Some have argued from the example of Christ in Gethsemane and Paul's case here that we ought never to ask God more than thrice for any particular thing, and that if it be not then granted, we must desist. But such an idea is contrary to the many Scriptures where *importunity* in asking is inculcated—for example, in Isaiah 62:7, Luke 11:8; 18:7. God is often pleased to test our faith and patience, for "the LORD wait, that he may be gracious" (Isa 30:18). The repeated request for deliverance shows how heavily the burden pressed upon Paul, as well as indicating how human he was—a man of "like passions as we are" (Jam 5:17). But as God's dear Son learned obedience by the things which He suffered—so also, on the behalf of Christ, it was given His most eminent servant to tread a similar path and be perfected by a special process of affliction.

Fourth, *the answer he received:* "And he said unto me, My grace is sufficient for thee: for my strength is made perfect in weakness." (2Co 12:9). God's answer is not always in kind, and a mercy for us that it is not. How little are we able to perceive what would be for our good: "We know not what we should pray for as we ought" (Rom 8:26). Often we ask for temporal things, and God gives us spiritual; we ask for deliverance, and He grants patience—He answers not according to our will, but our wealth or profit. Hence, we must not be disheartened if our requests be not literally answered—sometimes God answers by reconciling our minds to humiliating trials. "My grace is sufficient for thee" (2Co 12:9)—to support under the severest and most protracted affliction, to enable the soul to lie submissively as clay in the hands of the Potter, to trust His wisdom and love, to be assured that He knows what is best for us.

"My grace": It is Mediatorial grace, the grace given to Christ as the covenant Head of His people (Joh 1:16). It is the Head speaking to a member of His Body. It is not inherent grace or the new nature, but freshly imparted, quickening grace. "My grace *is* sufficient"—not simply "will prove to be." What he knew theoretically, he was now to learn experimentally. A grace that can save a hell-deserving sinner must be sufficient for the petty trials of this life! He who gives the "thorn" also gives grace to bear it. Grace is given not only to resist temptations and strengthen graces, but also endure trials—yet it must be definitely and diligently sought (Heb 4:16). "In the day when I cried thou answeredst me, and strengthenedst me with strength in my soul" (Psa 138:3). "For my strength is made perfect in weakness," in supporting earthen vessels under the buffetings of Satan—*His* strength was demonstrated when frail women voluntarily went to the stake!

Fifth, Paul's *improvement thereof:* "Most gladly therefore will I rather glory in my infirmities that the power of Christ may rest upon me" (2Co 12:9). That was more than a sullen submission or even a meek acquiescence. The "rather" points a contrast from the removal of the thorn: To glory on account of infirmities went far beyond resignation in suffering—namely, a *rejoicing*—and to this, *we* should aspire and pray. "Souls that are rich in grace can bear burdens without a burden," said a Puritan. Here is a test by which we may ascertain the measure or degree of grace we have—not by our speculative knowledge, but by the ease with which we bear afflictions, the cheerfulness of our spirits under persecution. When the apostles had been beaten, they departed "rejoicing that they were counted worthy to suffer shame for his name" (Act 5:40, 41).

"Therefore I take pleasure in infirmities, in reproaches, in necessities, in persecutions, in distresses for Christ's sake: for when I am weak, then am I strong" (2Co 12:10). This goes further than the foregoing verse—it was because I "took pleasure" in His infirmities that he gloried in them; and it was because they were the occasion of manifesting the power of Christ to uphold and work through one so frail, that he was glad of them. What nature recoils from an enlightened faith accepts and delights in, for the sake of the ulterior blessing—another example of where God can bring a clean thing out of an unclean, and also where He can make both the wrath of man and the enmity of the Serpent to praise Him! In the same way, though on a lower plane, David said, "It is good for me that I have been afflicted: that I might learn thy statutes" (Psa 119:71). By "the power of Christ," Paul triumphed over all obstacles.

What is meant by "when I am weak, then am I strong"? This needs to be correctly defined, for there is a weakness which does not result in strength, yea, a Christian's consciousness of weakness. There are those who are constantly talking about their inability and bemoaning their helplessness, and their ends! But he who has a true and spiritual sense of his insufficiency to do anything as he ought, is the one who is most earnest in crying to the strong for strength and, other things being equal, the one who is most active in appropriating His strength. To be "weak" is to be emptied of self—but to be at the time occupied with our inability, is to be absorbed with self. To be spiritually "weak" is to be conscious that I "lack wisdom," and that makes me "ask of God" (Jam 1:5); to feel my unbelief, and beg for an increase of faith.

Some *say* they are *"weak"* and then contradict their words by the way they act. Others are *happy* over the very realisation of their impotency—which is like one smitten with a stroke rejoicing in his paralysis as such. It needs to be steadily borne in mind that "hands which hang down, and the feeble knees" (Heb 12:12; Isa 35:3) bring no glory to God. 2 Kings 5:7 illustrates—*that* was not the language of humility and piety, but of unbelief and pride! My insufficiency is but a privative negative thing and is nothing to boast about—a consciousness thereof is only of value when it moves me to turn unto and lay hold of the Lord's sufficiency—2 Corinthians 3:5 gives *both* sides! The complement to, "for without me ye can do nothing." (Joh 15:5) is "I *can* do all things through Christ which strengtheneth me" (Phi 4:13 and compare Eph 6:10, 2Ti 2:1). —A.W.P.

THE MISSION AND MIRACLES OF ELISHA
23. Fifteenth Miracle

The passage which is now to engage our attention is much longer than usual, beginning as it does at 2 Kings 6:24 and running to the end of chapter 7. The whole of it needs to be read at a sitting, so as to perceive its connection, its unity, and its wonders. In it, there is a striking mingling of light and shade: The dark background of human depravity and the bright display of the prophet's faith, the exercise of God's justice in His sore judgments upon rebellious and wayward people, and the manifestation of His amazing mercy and grace. In it, we are shown how the wrath of man was made to praise the Lord, how the oath of a wicked king was made to recoil on his own head, how scepticism of his courtier was given the lie, and how the confidence of Elisha, his Master's word was vindicated. In it, we behold how the wicked was taken in his own craftiness, or to use the language of Samson's parable, how the eater was made to yield meat and how poor outcast lepers became the heralds of good news.

Truth is indeed stranger than fiction. Were one to invent a story after the order of the incident narrated in our present portion, critical readers would scorn it as being too far-fetched. But those who believe in the living and omnipotent God that presides over the affairs of this world, so far from finding anything here which taxes their faith, bow in adoration before Him who has only to speak and it is done, to will a thing and it is accomplished. In this case, Samaria was besieged by a powerful enemy, so that its inhabitants were completely invested. The situation became drastic and desperate, for there was a famine so acute that cannibalism was resorted unto. Yet under these extreme circumstances, Elisha announced that within twenty-four hours, there would be an abundance of food for everyone. His message was received with incredulity and scorn. Yet it come to pass, just as he had said, without a penny being spent, a gift being made, or a blow being struck—the investing Syrians fleeing in panic and leaving their vast stores of food to relieve the famished city.

We begin our examination of this miracle by considering, first, *its reality.* After our remarks above, it may strike the reader that it is quite an unnecessary waste of effort to labour a point which is obvious, and offer proof that a miracle *was* wrought on this occasion. The writer had thought so, too, had he not after completing his own meditations thereon, consulted several volumes on the O.T., only to find that this wonder is not listed among the miracles associated with Elisha. Even such a work as "The Companion Bible"—which supplies what is supposed to be a complete catalogue of the miracles of Elijah and Elisha—*omits* this one. We offer no solution to this strange oversight, but since other writers have failed to see in 2 Kings 7 one of the marvels of our prophet, we feel that we should present some of the evidence—which, in our judgment, furnishes clear proof that a supernatural event *was* wrought on this occasion, and that we are fully warranted in connecting it with him on whom Elijah's mantle fell.

The first thing that we would take note of is that when the people were in such desperate straits, and the king was so beside himself that he rent his clothes and swore that the prophet should be slain that very day, we are told, "But [contrastively] Elisha sat in his house, and the elders sat with him" (2Ki 6:32), which suggests to us that they had waited upon the Lord and had received assurance from Him of His intervention in mercy. Second, that the prophet *was* in communion with and in possession of the secret of the Lord, is borne out by the remaining words of the verse, where he tells his companions of Jehoram's evil intention and announces the approach of his agent before he arrived. Next, we find the prophet plainly declaring that an abundant supply of food would be provided on the morrow (2Ki 7:1), and he did so in his official character as "the man of God" (2Ki 7:2 and repeated in 2Ki 7:17, 19!)—which, as we have seen in previous articles, is the title that is always accorded him when God was about to work mightily through him or for him in answer to his prayers.

Consider, too, the circumstances. "And there was a great famine in Samaria: and, behold, they [the Syrians] besieged it, until an ass's head was sold for fourscore pieces of silver, and the fourth part of a cab of dove's dung for five pieces of silver." (2Ki 6:25). Nevertheless, the prophet declared that there should suddenly be provided sufficient food for all; and the sequel shows it came to pass just as he had predicted.

Nothing short of a miracle could have furnished such an abundant supply. The manner in which that food was furnished clearly evidenced the supernatural, as an impartial reading of 2 Kings 7:6, 7 will make clear—for it was their *enemies* who were made to supply their tables! Finally, if ye give due weight to the "according to the word of the LORD" and "as the man of God had said" in 2 Kings 7:16, 17 and link with 2 Kings 4:43, 44—where another of his miracle is in view and so referred to—the demonstration is complete.

Second, *its occurrence.* This was the terrible shortage of food in the city of Samaria, due to its being invested by an enemy, so that none of its inhabitants could go forth and obtain fresh supplies. "And it came to pass after this, that Benhadad king of Syria gathered all his host, and went up, and besieged Samaria" (2Ki 6:24). Strange as it may at first seem and sound to the reader, we see here one of the many internal evidences of the Divine inspiration of the Scriptures. This will appear if we quote the last clause of the very immediately preceding: "So the bands of Syria came *no more* into the land Israel" (2Ki 6:23). Had an impostor written this chapter, attempting to palm off upon us a pious forgery, he surely would not have been so careless as to place in immediate juxtaposition two statements, which a casual reader can only regard as flat contradiction. No; one who was inventing a story had certainly made it read consistently and plausibly. Hence, we arrive at the conclusion that this is no fictitious narrative from the pen of a pretender to inspiration.

"So the bands of Syria came no more into the land of Israel [of which 'Samaria' was a part; as verse 20 shows]. And it came to pass after this, that Benhadad king of Syria gathered all his host, and went up, and besieged Samaria" (2Ki 6:23, 24). Now the placing of those two statements side by side is clear intimation to us that the Scriptures need to be read closely and carefully—that their terms require to be properly weighed, and that failure so to do will inevitably lead unto serious misunderstanding of their purport. It is because infidels only skim passages here and there, and are so poorly acquainted with the Word, that they charge it with being "full of contradictions." But there is contradiction here, and if it presents any "difficulty" to us, it is entirely of our own making. The first statement has reference to the freebooting and irregular "bands"—which had, from time to time, preyed on the Samaritans (compare "companies" of 2 Kings 5:2), what we would term today, "commando raids"; where 2 Kings 6:24 speaks of organized war, a "mass invasion," Benhadad gathering together "*all* his hosts."

"And it came to pass after this, that Benhadad king of Syria gathered all his host, and went up, and besieged Samaria" (2Ki 6:24). The opening clauses far more than a historical time-mark—properly understood, it serves to bring out the character of this man. The introductory—"And"—bids us link his action here with what is recorded in the context. In the remote context (chapter 5), we saw how that God graciously healed

Naaman of his leprosy. Naaman was a commander-in-chief of this man's army and had been sent by him into Samaria to be cured of his dread disease. But so little did the Syrian monarch appreciate that signal favour, shortly after he assembled an increased force of his band and "warred against Israel" (2Ki 6:8). His plan was to capture Jehoram, by being foiled by Elisha, he sent his men to capture the prophet. In that too, it failed, for in answer to Elisha's prayer, they were smitten with blindness—though instead of taking advantage of their helplessness, he later prayed for their eyes to be opened, and after having them feasted, sent them home to the master, who had returned to Syria.

"And it came to pass after *this* "—not that Benhadad repented of his former actings, nor that he was grateful for the mercy and kindness which had been shown his soldiers; but that he "gathered all his hosts and went and besieged Samaria." Not only was this base ingratitude against his human benefactors, but it was blatant defiance against Jehovah Himself. Twice the Lord had manifested His miracle-working power, and that in grace, on his behalf; and here was his response. Yet we must look further if we are to perceive the deeper meaning of "it came to pass after this," for we need to answer the question, Why did the Lord suffer this heathen to invade Israel's territory? The reply is also furnished by the context. Benhadad was not the only one who had profited by God's mercies in the immediate past—the king of Israel had also been Divinely delivered from those who sought his life. And how did *he* express his appreciation? Did he promptly institute a religious reformation in his dominions and tear down the altars which his wicked parents had set up? No, so far as we are informed, he was quite unmoved and continued in his idolatry.

It is written, "the curse causeless shall not come" (Pro 26:2). When God afflicts a people, be it a church or a nation, it is because He has a controversy with them—if they refuse to put right what is wrong. He chastises them. God, then, was acting in judgment on Samaria when He commissioned the Syrians to now enter their land in full force. "O Assyrian, the rod of mine anger, and the staff in their hand is *mine* indignation. I will send him against an hypocritical nation" (Isa 10:5, 6). So again, at a later date, the Lord said of Nebuchadnezzar, "Thou art *my* battle axe and weapons of war: for with (or "by") thee will I break in pieces the nations, and with thee will I destroy kingdoms" (Jer 51:20). It is in the light of such passages as these that we should view the activities of Hitler and Mussolini! Though God's time to completely cast off Israel had not come in the days of Jehoram, yet He employed Benhadad to grievously afflict his kingdom.

"And there was a great famine in Samaria: and, behold, they besieged it, until an ass's head was sold for fourscore pieces of silver, and the fourth part of a cab of dove's dung for five pieces of silver" (2Ki 6:25). Troubles seldom come singly, for God means to leave us without excuse if we fail to recognise *whose* hand it is which is dealing with us. Benhadad chose his hour to attack when Israel was in sore tribulation, which serves also to illustrate Satan's favourite method of assaulting the saints—like the fiend that he is—he strikes when they are at their lowest ebb, coming as the roaring lion when their nerves are already stretched to the utmost, seeking to render them both praiseless and prayerless while lying on a bed of sickness, or to instill into their minds doubts of God's goodness in the hour of bereavement, or to question His promises when the meal has run low in their barrel. But since "we are not ignorant of his devices" (2Co 2:11), we should be on our guard against such tactics.

"And there was a great famine in Samaria" (2Ki 6:25). It needs to be pointed out in these days of skepticism and practical atheism that the inhabitants of earth are under the government of something infinitely better than "fickle fortune"—namely, in a world which is ruled over by the living God. Goodly harvests, or the *absence* of them, are not the result of chance nor the effect of a blind fate. In Psalm 105:16, we read that God "called for a famine upon the land: he brake the whole staff of bread." And, my reader, when *He* calls for a "famine," neither farmers nor scientists (so-called) can prevent or avert it. We have read in the past of "famines" in China and in India, but how faintly can we conceive of the awful horrors of one! As intimated above, the Lord called for this famine on Samaria, because the king and his subjects had not taken to heart His previous chastisements of the land for their idolatry—when a people refuse to heed the rod, then He smites more heavily.

"And there was a great famine in Samaria: and, behold they besieged it." (2Ki 6:25). Their design was not to storm but to starve the city, by throwing a powerful military cordon around it, so that none could either go out or come in. "And as the king of Israel was passing by upon the wall, [probably taking stock of his defences and seeking to encourage the garrison] there cried a woman unto him saying, Help, my lord, O king" (2Ki 6:26). And well she might, for these were now deprived of the bare necessities of life, with a slow but painful death by starvation staring them in the face. Ah, my reader, how little we really value the common mercies of this life until they are taken from us! Poor was man; she turned to lean upon a broken reed, seeking relief from the apostate king, rather than making known her need unto the Lord. There is no hint anywhere in the narrative that the people betook themselves unto the Throne of grace.

"And he said, If the LORD do not help thee, whence shall I help thee? out of the barnfloor, or out of the winepress?" (2Ki 6:27). That was not the language of submission and piety, but, as the sequel shows, of derision and blasphemy. His language was that of anger and despair—the Lord will not help, I cannot, so we must perish. Out of the abundance of his evil heart his mouth spake. Calming down a little, "And the king said unto her, What aileth thee? And she answered, This woman [pointing to a companion] said unto me, Give thy son, that we may eat him to day, and we will eat my son to morrow. So we boiled my son, and did eat him: and I said unto her on the next day, Give thy son, that we may eat him: and she hath hid her son." (2Ki 6:28, 29)—which shows the desperate conditions which then prevailed and the awful pass to which things had come. Natural affection yielded to the pangs of hunger. This too must also be regarded as a most solemn example of the Divine justice, and vengeance on idolatrous Israel.

It must be steadily borne in mind that the people of Samaria had cast off their allegiance to Jehovah and were worshipping false gods, and therefore, according to His threatenings, the Lord visited them with severe judgments. They were so blockaded by the enemy that all ordinary food supplies failed them, so that in their desperation, they were driven to devour the most abominable offals and even human flesh. Of old, the Lord had announced unto Israel, "And if ye will not for all this hearken unto me, but walk contrary unto me; Then I will walk contrary unto you also in fury; and I, even I, will chastise you seven times for your sins. And ye shall eat the flesh *of your sons*" (Lev 26:28, 29). And again, "The LORD shall bring a nation against thee...and he shall besiege thee...and thou shalt eat the fruit of thine own body, the flesh of thy sons and of thy daughters, which the LORD thy God hath given thee, in the siege, and in the straitness" (Deu 28:49-53)—more completely fulfilled at the destruction of Jerusalem in A.D. 70. No words of God's shall fall to the ground: His *threatenings*—equally with His promises—are infallibly certain of fulfilment!

How few there are in Great Britain today who realise that but for the infinite mercy of God, the people in these Isles had, but three years ago, been reduced to sore straits. We too were besieged—both by sea and air—and only sovereign God prevented our merciless enemies from totally succeeding in cutting off our principal food supplies. We are not unmindful of the kindness and help of the U.S.A., and the still nobler   generosity of Canada, but all their loans and gifts had been useless if they failed to cross the ocean—in that case, long before now the spectre of famine had stalked our cities. Nor are we unmindful of our intrepid Royal Navy, nor the brave men who manned our merchant ships. But *Who* was it that imparted such courage to them that—again and again after their ships had been torpedoed and themselves left to spend awful days in an open boat—as soon as they were rescued, volunteered to man other ships and went forth afresh to bring in vital supplies? There is a human side to it, and we greatly admire the same; but there is also a Divine side to it, and we have reminded ourselves of it.

Though they recognise not the hand of the Lord in deliverance, the people of Britain now breathe easier since they believe that the submarine menace has been mastered, and we now have full control of the air. But multiplied weapons, both of defence and of offence, are no security against the displeasure of Him whom we continue to defy, with our Sabbath ploughing, harvesting, pleasuring, and many other things. Agriculture may be organized here on a scale it never has been before, yet that guarantees neither crops nor weather to gather them. Of old, God said unto Israel, "*I have smitten you with blasting and mildew: when your gardens and your vineyards and your figtrees, and your olive trees increased,* the palmerworm devoured them: yet have ye not returned unto Me. I have sent among you the pestilence after the manner of Egypt; your young men have I slain with the sword...yet have ye not returned unto Me, saith the Lord" (Amo 4:9, 10). The Almighty has a thousand weapons in His armoury by which He can slay us, Will our nation remain deaf to His continued warnings until His patience is exhausted? It looks very much like it.

"And it came to pass, when the king heard the words of the woman, that he rent his clothes; and he passed by upon the wall, and the people looked, and, behold, he had sackcloth within upon his flesh" (2Ki 6:30). According to the customs of those days and the ways of Oriental people, this was the assumption of the external garb of a penitent; but what was it worth while he renounced not his idols? Not a particle in the eyes of Him who cannot be imposed upon by any outward shows. It was a pose which the king adopted for the benefit of his subjects, to signify that he felt deeply for their miseries; yet he lamented not for his *own* iniquities, which were the procuring cause of the calamity. Instead of so doing, the very next verse tells us that he took an awful oath that Elisha should be promptly slain. "Rend your *heart* and not your garments" (Joe 2:13) is ever the Divine call to those under chastisement, for God desireth truth (reality) in "the inward parts" (Psa 51:6).

As it is useless to wear sackcloth when we mourn not for our sins, so it is in vain to flock to church on a "day of prayer" and then return at once to our vanities and idols. In the past, Israel complained, "Wherefore have we fasted, say they, and thou seest not? wherefore have we afflicted our soul, and thou takest no knowledge? Behold, in the day of your fast ye find pleasure, and exact all your labours." And God made them answer by saying, "Behold, in the day of your fasting, ye find *pleasure* and things wherewith ye grieve others...ye fast not as this day to make your voice heard on High" (Isa 58:3, 4). Thus, there is such a thing as not only praying, but fasting; and yet, for God to pay no attention to it. At a later date, He said to them, "When ye fasted and mourned...did ye at all fast unto me, even to me? Should ye not *hear* the words which the LORD hath cried by the former prophets"! (Zec 7:5, 7). While a nation tramples upon the Divine commandments, neither prayer and fasting, nor any other religious performances, are of any avail with Him who says, "Behold *to obey* is better than sacrifice" (1Sa 15:22). There must be a turning away from sin before there can be any real turning unto God. —A.W.P.

THE DOCTRINE OF RECONCILIATION
5c. Its Arrangement

Upon the Son's cheerful acceptance of the terms proposed to Him concerning the federal undertaking He was to engage in, the Father in turn bound Himself to do certain things for and unto the Son. This it was which constituted the very essence of that compact which was made by Them, for a covenant is an agreement between two parties who come under mutual engagements. Something is to be done by one party, in consequence of which the other party binds himself to do another thing in return. As there must be two parties to covenant, so there must be two parts in a covenant; a condition and a promise. It is the performing of the condition or terms of the covenant—the work of service specified—which gives the first party the right to the promised reward. Having already shown what Christ consented to do, we turn now to consider what the Father promised to bestow. First, He agreed to make all needful preparation for the incarnation of His Son. Second, to give Him all requisite assistance in the performing of His work. Third, to bestow upon Him a meet reward.

The promise to make all needful preparation for the incarnation of His Son comprehended the whole of the Father's providences or governance of this world from the creation of man until Christ began His public ministry: "But Jesus answered them, My Father worketh hitherto [now], and I work" (Joh 5:17). The Father's "work" included the ordering of human history, and particularly, His dealings with Abraham and his descendants, and the separation of Israel from the rest of the nations—for it was from Israel that Christ, according to the flesh, would issue. The Father's "work" included the giving of a written revelation, in which the covenant was made known and the advent of His Son promised, so that an expectation of His appearing was created and a foundation was laid for His mission. The Father's "work" also involved the "preparation of a body for His Son, which was accomplished by the miracle of the virgin birth. When "the fulness of the time was come [when all the necessary preparations were completed], God sent forth his Son, made of a woman" (Gal 4:4).

The Father promised to give His Son all requisite help for the performing of His work. First, in order for the discharge of His mediatorial office, there was that which *fitted Him* thereto. "And there shall come forth a rod out of the stem of Jesse, and a

Branch shall grow out of his roots: And the spirit of the LORD shall rest upon him, the spirit of wisdom and understanding, the spirit of counsel and might, the spirit of knowledge and of the fear of the LORD" (Isa 11:1, 2). Upon which the Puritan Charnock said, "All the gifts of the Spirit should reside in Him as in a proper habitation, perpetually. The human nature being a creature could not beautify and enrich itself with needful gifts; this promise of the Spirit was therefore necessary, His humanity could not else have performed the work it was designed for. So that the habitual holiness residing in the humanity of Christ was a fruit of this eternal covenant. Though the Divine nature of Christ, by virtue of its union, might sanctify the human nature, yet the Spirit was promised Him, because it is His proper office to continue those gifts, which are necessary for any undertaking in the world; and the personal operations of the Trinity do not interfere. It might also be because every person in the Trinity should plainly have a distinct hand in our redemption."

The Father, then, furnished and equipped Christ for His arduous work by a plentiful effusion of the graces and gifts of the Holy Spirit. Thus, He declared, "Behold my servant, whom I uphold; mine elect, in whom my soul delighteth; I have put my spirit upon him" (Isa 42:1). Those promises were fulfilled at His baptism, when the Spirit descended upon Him (Mat 3:16), for it was then that "God anointed Jesus of Nazareth with the Holy Ghost and with power" (Act 10:38). This was freely owned by the Saviour Himself, for in the synagogue, He read, "The Spirit of the Lord is upon me, because he hath anointed me to preach the gospel to the poor; he hath sent me to heal the brokenhearted, to preach deliverance to the captives, and recovering of sight to the blind, to set at liberty them that are bruised," and then declared, "This day is this scripture fulfilled in your ears" (Luk 4:18, 21). So too we find Him acknowledging, "I cast out devils by the Spirit of God..." (Mat 12:28).

Second, the Father promised to invest His Son with a threefold office. In order to the saving of His people, it was most requisite that whatever Christ did, He should act by the authority of the Father, by a commission under the broad seal of Heaven. Accordingly, He said, "I will raise them up a Prophet from among their brethren" (Deu 18:15, 18 and see Act 3:22). Christ did not run without being sent: It was God who anointed Him to preach. Again, "So also Christ glorified not himself to be made an high priest [He did not intrude Himself into that office]; but he that said unto him, Thou art my Son, to day have I begotten thee (Heb 5:5)—Christ was "*made* an high priest for ever after the order of Melchisedec" (Heb 6:20). So also God the Father invested Him with the royal office: "Yet have I set ['anointed'] my king upon my holy hill of Zion" (Psa 2:6), "Behold, the days come, saith the LORD, that I will raise unto David a righteous Branch, and a King shall reign and prosper" (Jer 23:5), for "The Father loveth the Son, and hath given all things into his hand" (Joh 3:35); and therefore, hath He made Him "higher than the kings of the earth." (Psa 89:27).

Third, the Father promised Christ strength, support and protection to execute the great work of redemption. His undertaking would be attended with such difficulties that creature power, though unimpaired by sin, would have been quite inadequate for it. It was to be performed in human nature, and *that* had failed in a much easier task, even when possessed of untainted innocence. Therefore did the Father assure Him of help and succour, to carry Him through all the obstacles and dangers, trials and opposition He would meet with. "Behold my servant, whom I uphold...I the LORD have called thee in righteousness, and will hold thine hand, and will *keep thee*, and give thee for a covenant of the people, for a light of the Gentiles" (Isa 42:1, 6). "The work of redemption was so high and so hard that it would have broken the hearts and the backs of all the glorious angels and mighty men on earth, had they entered on it; therefore, the Father engaged Himself to stand close to Jesus Christ and mightily assist and strengthen Him in all His mediatoral administrations" (T. Brooks, Puritan).

Christ is said to be "the son of man whom thou [God the Father] madest strong for thyself" (Psa 80:17), for He had sworn, "mine arm also shall *strengthen* him" (Psa 89:21). It is blessed to see how that the Redeemer, in the days of His flesh, acknowledged these promises. "I was cast upon thee from the womb: thou art my God from my mother's belly" (Psa 22:10). "Listen, O isles, unto me; and hearken, ye people, from far; The LORD hath called me from the womb; from the bowels of my mother [see Mat 1:21, 22] hath he made mention of my name. And *he* hath made my mouth like a sharp sword; in the shadow of his hand hath he hid me, and made me a polished shaft; in his quiver hath he hid me" (Isa 49:1, 2). "The Lord GOD hath given me the tongue of the learned… For the Lord GOD *will help* me…and I know that I shall not be ashamed" (Isa 50:4, 7). In unshaken confidence, when His enemies were conspiring against Him, and His friends were on the point of forsaking Him, He declared, "yet I am not alone, because the Father is with me" (Joh 16:32).

Those promises of the Father were the support of His soul in the hour of His supreme crisis: His heart laid hold of them, acted faith on them, and received comfort and strength therefrom. "Preserve me, O God: for in thee do I put my trust" (Psa 16:1), was His petition and plea. "I gave my back to the smiters, and my cheeks to them that plucked off the hair: I hid not my face from shame and spitting. *For* the Lord GOD will help me; therefore shall I not be confounded: therefore have I set my face like a flint, and I know that I shall not be ashamed." (Isa 50:6, 7). When He was denounced by the Jews and condemned by Pilate, He consoled Himself with the assurance, "He is near that justifieth me; who will contend with me? let us stand together: who is mine adversary? let him come near to me" (Isa 50:8). "I have set the LORD always before me: because he is at my right hand, I shall not be moved. Therefore my heart is glad, and my glory rejoiceth: my flesh also shall rest in hope. For thou wilt not leave my soul in hell; neither wilt thou suffer thine Holy One to see corruption. Thou wilt shew me the path of life: in thy presence is fulness of joy; at thy right hand there are pleasures for evermore" (Psa 16:8-11). In the prospect of death, He rejoiced in the sure knowledge of resurrection.

Fourth, the Father promised Him a glorious reward. First, a glory for Himself *personally,* as the God-man Mediator. As He was to endure the cross, so He was also to receive the crown. The enduring of the cross was a covenant engagement on His part, and the bestowing of the crown was a covenant engagement on the Father's part. That was plainly borne witness to by His prophets, for the Spirit in them "testified beforehand the sufferings of Christ, *and* the glory that should follow" (1Pe 1:11). That glory consisted in His being fully invested with His priestly and royal offices. As it was with that type, so with the Antitype. David was anointed incipiently and privately before he slew Goliath (1Sa 16:13), but formally and publicly after his victories (2Sa 5:12). The antitypical David was indeed "anointed with the Holy Spirit" at the Jordan, but not until after He had triumphed over sin, Satan, and the grave, did God anoint Him "with the oil of gladness above thy fellows" (Heb 1:9) and publicly make Him to be "both Lord and Christ" (Act 2:36).

"The solemn inauguration into all His offices was after His making reconciliation: making an end of sin, bringing in everlasting righteousness and thereby shutting up all prophecy and vision, because all the prophecies tended to Him and were accomplished in Him; and then as manifesting Himself the most holy, He was to be anointed—i.e. fully invested in all the office of Prophet, Priest and King (Dan 9:24). The compact ran thus: Do this, suffer death for the vindication of the honour of My Law, and Thou shalt be Priest and King forever. He could not, therefore, be solemnly installed until He had performed the condition on His part (for the promise was made to Him, considered as Mediator or God-man); then it was that He was advanced, for the ground of His exaltation is pitched wholly upon His sufferings. Therefore, God hath given Him a glory as a just debt due to the price paid, the sufferings undergone, and the obedience yielded to the mediatory Law" (S. Charnock). Hence, it is that the general assembly of Heaven say, with a loud voice, "Worthy is the Lamb that was slain to receive power, and riches, and wisdom, and strength, and honour, and glory, and blessing" (Rev 5:12).

Subsidiary to that glorious investiture was the Father's promise to *raise* Christ from the dead. "He asked life of thee, and thou gavest it him, even length of days for ever and ever" (Psa 21:4). Beautifully does that link up with Psalm 102:23-27—quoted by the apostle in Hebrews 1:12 as the words of the Father to the Son. In Psalm 102:23, 24, we hear the incarnate Son saying, "He shortened my days. I said, O my God, take me not away in the midst of my days"—to which the Father made answer, "Thy years are throughout all generations...But thou art the same, and thy years shall have no end" (verse 27). So again, He received assurance, "He shall prolong his days!" (Isa 53:10). The Father made promise that the One who had been bruised by Him and whose soul He had made "an offering for sin" should have a glorious deliverance and should reign in life. It was in fulfilment of such promises as these that "The God of peace [the reconciled One], that brought again from the dead our Lord Jesus, that great shepherd of the sheep, through the blood of the everlasting covenant" (Heb 13:20).

In like manner, subsidiary to Christ's glorious investiture of His full priestly and kingly offices was His *ascension,* for though He was born King and acted as Priest at the cross when He "offered Himself to God" and "made intercession for the transgressors," yet not until He had completely performed His part of the covenant could He enter into His rightful reward. Accordingly, we find promise of ascension made unto Him. It was clearly implied in "I will make Him My Firstborn, higher than the kings of the earth" (Psa 89:27). It was revealed in, "Who shall ascend into the Hill of the Lord? or who shall stand in His Holy Place?" answered by, "Lift up your heads, O ye gates; and be ye lift up, ye everlasting doors; and the King of glory shall come in" (Psa 24:3, 7). It was plainly announced in "Thou hast ascended on high, thou hast led captivity captive" (Psa 68:18). It was such promises as these the Saviour had in mind when He said "Ought not Christ to have suffered these things, and to enter into his glory?" (Luk 24:26).

"Behold, my servant shall deal prudently [consequently], he shall be exalted and extolled, and be very high" (Isa 52:13). The 53rd of Isaiah—that wondrous chapter in which we have so solemnly, so strikingly, and so evangelically depicted, the vicarious sufferings of Christ—closes with that blessed promise of the Father: *"Therefore* will I divide him a portion with the great, and he shall divide the spoil with the strong; because he hath poured out his soul unto death" (Isa 53:12). The similitude used there is taken from the honouring of military conquerors who, having in fight defeated and rooted their enemies, gained a great victory; and in consequence, are suitably rewarded by their princes—being exalted by them and given a share of the spoils or fruits of war. It was as though God the Father said: This My incarnate and successful Son shall receive such honour, glory, renown, and riches after His toils and conflicts as are meet for His triumphs. He shall have a glorious recompense for all His humiliation and sufferings at the hands of men, for His opposition from Satan and for His enduring of My wrath—for nothing less is due Him. The fulfillment of Isaiah 53:12 is seen in Ephesians 4:8, Colossians 2:15, etc.

"The obedience of Christ bears to these blessings not only the relation of antecedent to consequent, but of merit to reward; so that His obedience is the cause: and the condition being fulfilled by virtue of obedience, He has a right to the reward" (H. Witsius, the Dutch Puritan). That is the precise force of the "Therefore" in the above verse, as it is also in "Thou lovest righteousness, and hatest wickedness [a summary of His work of obedience]: therefore God, thy God, hath anointed thee with the oil of gladness above thy fellows (Psa 45:7). It was not only that justice required it, but the covenant fidelity of the Father was involved therein—hence His assurance, "But my faithfulness and my mercy shall be with him: and in my name shall his horn be exalted" (Psa 89:24). Thus also the N.T.: Christ "became obedient unto death, even the death of the cross. *Wherefore* God also hath highly exalted him, and given him a name which is above every name" (Phi 2:8, 9). It was Christ's meriting the reward for *Himself* which was the ground of His meriting life and glory for *us*.

"Therefore let all the house of Israel know assuredly, that God hath made that same Jesus, whom ye have crucified, both Lord and Christ" (Act 2:36). That was the whole burden or theme of Peter's pentecostal sermon, the grand truth proclaimed therein and enforced by Scripture, that He—whom the Jews had vilified—God had glorified. Having faithfully fulfilled the terms of the everlasting covenant, the Saviour was elevated to dominion and empire over the world. God's exaltation of Him in His human nature to His own right hand (Isaiah 33), was a full confirmation and demonstration of what He had acquired by His death. He made Him "both Lord and Christ," seating "Messiah the Prince" (Dan 9:25) upon the throne of the universe. This is an economical Lordship, a dispensation committed to Him as God-man by the Father—just as He has "given him authority to execute judgment also" (Joh 5:27). The One whom His enemies crowned with thorns, God has "crowned with glory and honour" (Heb 2:9). He must be received by us as "Lord" before we can have Him for our "Christ": He must have the throne of our hearts, if we are to receive His benefits.

It was promised Christ that "He shall have dominion also from sea to sea, and from the river unto the ends of the earth...Yea, all kings shall fall down before him: all nations shall serve him. For he shall deliver the needy when he crieth; the poor also, and him that hath no helper" (Psa 72:8, 11, 12). As of this in consequence of, "The LORD [the Father] said unto my Lord, Sit thou at my right hand, until I make thine enemies thy footstool...The LORD hath sworn, and will not repent, Thou art a priest for ever after the order of Melchizedek" (Psa 110:1, 4); that is, a *royal* Priest—"he shall be a priest upon his throne" (Zec 6:13). A regal inheritance was assured Him. Not only has He acquired the mundane inheritance forfeited by the first Adam, but as the risen Redeemer declared, "All power is given unto me in heaven and in earth" (Mat 28:18), for the Father "hath appointed [Him] heir of all things" so that now He is "upholding all things by the word of his power" (Heb 1:2, 3), wielding the sceptre of universal dominion. The "government" is upon "*His* shoulder" (Isa 9:6).

It was promised that a blessed harvest should crown His undertaking, that He should reap the fruit of His sufferings. "The pleasure of the LORD shall prosper in his hand" (Isa 53:10). What that signifies is intimated in such passages as the following: "I will preserve thee, and give thee for a covenant of the people, to establish the earth, to cause to inherit the desolate heritages; That thou mayest say to the prisoners, Go forth" (Isa 49:8, 9). "Behold, thou shalt call a nation that thou knowest not, and nations that knew not thee shall run unto thee because of the LORD thy God, and for the Holy One of Israel; for he hath glorified thee" (Isa 55:5). "And the Gentiles shall come to thy light, and kings to the brightness of thy rising" (Isa 60:3). To the One who came forth from Bethlehem, it was promised, "now shall he be great unto the ends of the earth" (Mic 5:2, 4). How fully these promises have yet been fulfilled or how much longer human history must yet continue we do not profess to know, but even now, "angels and authorities and powers" are "subject unto him" (1Pe 3:22). — A.W.P.

SPIRITUAL GROWTH OR CHRISTIAN PROGRESS
6. Its Seasonableness

"To every thing there is a season, and a time to every purpose under the heaven...He hath made every thing beautiful in his time" (Ecc 3:1, 11). If the whole of these eleven verses be read consecutively, it will be seen that they furnish a full outline of the many and different experiences of human life in this world—each aspect of man's varied career and his reactions thereto being stated. That which is emphasised in connection with all the mutations and vicissitudes of life, is that they are all ordained and regulated by God, according to His unerring wisdom. Not only has He appointed a time to every purpose under heaven, but has made "every thing beautiful *in* his time." Nothing is too early, nothing too late; everything is perfectly coordinated, and, as we learn from the N.T., made to "work together for good to them that love God, to them who are the called according to his purpose" (Rom 8:28).

There is a predestined time when each creature and each event shall come forth, how long it shall continue, and in what circumstances it shall be—all being determined by the Lord. This is true of the world as a whole, for God "worketh all things after the counsel of his own will" (Eph 1:11). This earth has not always existed. God was the One who decided when it should spring into being, and He created it by a mere fiat: "For he spake, and it was done; he commanded, and it stood fast" (Psa 33:9). Nor will it last forever, for the hour is coming when its very elements "shall melt with fervent heat, the earth also and the works that are therein shall be burned up up" (2Pe 3:10). How far distant, or how near, that solemn hour is, no creature has any means of knowing; yet the precise day for it is unchangeably fixed in the Divine decree.

The same grand truth which pertains to the whole of creation applies with equal force to all the workings of Divine Providence. The beginning and the end, and the whole intervening career, of each person has been determined by his Maker. So too the rise, the progress, the height attained, and the entire history of each nation has been foreordained of God. "For of him, and through him, and to him, are all things: to whom be glory for ever. Amen" (Rom 11:36). A nation is but the aggregate of individuals comprising it, and though its corporate life be much longer than of any one generation of its members, yet it is subject to the same Divine laws. Each kingdom, each empire, has its birth and development, its maturity and zenith, its decline and death. The Egyptian had; so had the Babylonian, Medo-Persian, Grecian and Roman.

What is stated in Ecclesiastes 3:1, 11 holds good of things in the spiritual realm; equally so with those in the material sphere—though we are more apt to forget this in connection with the former than with the latter. It is a fact that in the Christian life, "To every thing there is a season, and a time to every purpose under the heaven" (Ecc 3:1). How can it be otherwise, seeing that the God of creation, the God of providence, and the God of all grace is one. It is true there is much in the Divine operations, both in Providence and in Grace—which is profoundly mysterious, for "great things doeth he, which we cannot comprehend" (Job 37:5). Yet not a little light is cast upon those higher mysteries, if we seek to observe the ways and workings of God *in Nature.* How often the Lord Jesus made us of that principle, directing the attention of His hearers unto the most familiar objects in the physical realm.

Again and again, we find the Divine Teacher using the things growing in the field to illustrate and adumbrate the things which are invisible and to inculcate lessons of spiritual value. "*Consider* the lilies" (Mat 6:28; Luk 12:27). Not only look upon and admire them, but receive instruction therefrom. "Learn a parable of the fig tree" (Mat 24:32; Mar 13:28). Yes, *learn* from it—ponder it, let it inform you about spiritual matters. When Christ insisted on the inseparable connection there is between character and conduct, He employed the similitude of a tree being known by its fruit. When He urged the necessity of new hearts in ordering for the reception of new covenant blessings, He spoke of new bottles for new wine. When He revealed the essential conditions of spiritual fruitfulness, He mentioned the vine and its branches. Yes, there is much in the material world from which we may learn valuable lessons on the spiritual life.

Take the seasons which God has appointed for the year and how each brings forth accordingly. The coldness and barrenness of the winter gives place to the warmth and fertility of the spring, while the vegetables and fruit which sprout in the spring and grow through the summer are matured in the autumn. Each season has its own peculiar features and characteristic products. The same principle is seen operating in a human being. The life of man is divided into distinct seasons or stages: Childhood, youth, maturity and old age. And each of those stages is marked by characteristic features: The innocence and shyness of (normal) children, the zeal and vigour of youth, the stability and endurance of maturity, the experience and wisdom of old age—and each of these distinctive features is "beautiful in [its] time."

Not only has God appointed the particular seasons when each of His creatures shall come forth and flourish, but we are obliged to *wait* His set time for the same. If we sow seeds in the winter, they will not germinate. Plants which sprout in the spring cannot be forced, but have to wait for the Summer's sun. So it is in the human realm. "To every thing there is a season, and a time to every purpose under the heaven." We cannot put old heads on young shoulders, and though our moderns are attempting to do so, their efforts will not only prove unsuccessful but issue in disastrous consequences. As everything is "beautiful in his time," they are incongruous and unseemly *out* of season. "When I was a child, I spake as a child...I thought as a child: but when I became a man, I put away childish things" (1Co 13:11).

In the light of what has been said, it is both interesting and instructive to ponder the ways of God with His people during the O.T. and N.T. eras. Much of that which obtained under the Mosaic dispensation was suited to that infantile period and was "beautiful in his time," but now that "the fulness of time" has come, such things would be quite out of place. During that kindergarten stage, God instituted an elaborate ritual which appealed to the senses, and instructed by means of pictures and symbols. There was the colourful tabernacle, the priestly vestments, the burning of incense, the playing of instruments. They were all invested with a typical significance, but when the Substance appeared, there was no further need of them. They had become obsolete, and to bring forward such things into Christian worship—as Rome does—is an unseasonable lapsing back to the nursery stage.

All that has been pointed out above is most pertinent to the spiritual growth of the individual Christian—and particularly to the several *stages* of his development or progress, and if duly attended to, should preserve from many mistaken notions and erroneous conclusions. As the year is divided into different seasons, so the Christian life has different stages, and as there are certain features which more or less characterise the year's seasons, so there are certain experiences, more or less peculiar to each stage in the Christian life, and a search of the year's seasons is marked by a decided *change* in what the garden and the orchard then brings forth, so there is a variation and alteration in the graces manifested and the fruits borne by the Christian during the several stages through which he passes; but "everything is beautiful in his time"—as it would be incongruous out of its season.

Now though, the earth's seasons are four in number, yet only three of them are concerned with fertility or production. The analogy pertains spiritually: In the Christian life, there is a spring, a summer, and an autumn—the "winter" is when his body has been committed to the grave in sure and certain hope of resurrection, awaiting the eternal Spring. Thus, we should expect to find that the more explicit teaching of the N.T. divides the spiritual life of the saint on earth into three stages; and such is indeed the case. In one of his parables of the kingdom of God, Christ used the similitude of a man casting seed into the ground (a figure of preaching the Gospel), saying "For the earth bringeth forth fruit of herself; first the blade, then the ear, after that the full corn in the ear" (Mar 4:28): *There* are the three stages of growth. In like manner, we find the apostle grading those to whom he wrote into three classes—namely, "fathers," "young men," and "little children" (1Jo 2:13).

Nothing which lives is brought to maturity immediately in this lower world. Instead, everything advances by gradual growth and orderly progress. God indeed created Adam and Eve in their full perfection, but He does not regenerate us into our complete stature in Christ. All the parts and faculties of the new man come into being at the new birth, but time is needed for their development and manifestation. Moreover, as natural talents are not bestowed uniformly—to some being given five, to others two, and to yet others only one (Mat 25:15), so God bestows a greater measure of grace to one of His people than to another. There is therefore a great difference among Christians—all are not of one stature, strength, and growth in godliness. Some are "sheep" and others, but "lambs" (Joh 21:15, 16). Some are "strong"; others are "weak" (Rom 15:1). Some are but "babes"; others are of "full age" (Heb 5:13, 14). Nevertheless, each brings forth fruit "in his season" (Psa 1:3).

If more attention were paid unto the principles, which we have sought to enunciate and illustrate above, some of us would be preserved from forming harsh judgments of our younger brethren and sisters and from criticizing them, because they do not exercise those graces and bear those fruits which pertain more to the stage of Christian maturity. One would instantly perceive the folly of a farmer who complained, because his field of grain bore no golden ears during the early months of spring. Equally senseless and sinful is it to blame a babe in Christ, because he has neither the mature judgment nor the patience of an experienced and long-tried believer. To that statement, every spiritual reader will readily assent; yet, we very much fear that some of these very persons are guilty of the same thing in another direction: *Self-ward*—reproaching themselves in later life, because they lack the glow and ardour, and the zeal and zest which formerly characterised them.

Some older Christians look back and compare themselves with the days of their spiritual youth, and then utter hard things against themselves, concluding that so far from having advanced, they have retrograded. In certain cases, their lamentations are justifiable, as with Solomon. But in many instances, they are not warrantable—being occasioned by a wrong standard of measurement and through failing to bear in mind the seasonableness or unseasonableness of certain fruits at particular times. They complain now because they lack the liveliness of earlier days, when they had warmer affections for Christ and His people, more joy in reading the Word and prayer, more zeal in seeking to promote the good of others, more fruit for their labours. They complain that though they now spend more time in using the means of grace, others who are but spiritual babes appear to derive far greater benefit, though less diligent in duties than they are.

In some cases where conversion has been more radical and clearly marked, growth is more easily perceived, but where conversion itself was a quiet and gradual experience, it is much more difficult to trace out the subsequent progress that is made. As the Christian obtains more light from God, he becomes increasingly aware of his filth, and by apprehensions of his decrease, he will increase in humility. As spiritual wisdom increases, he measures himself by *higher* standard—and thus, becomes more conscious of his comings short thereof. Formerly, he was more occupied with his outward walk, but now he is more diligent in seeking to discipline his heart. In earlier years, there may have been more fervour in his prayers; but now, his petitions should be more spiritual. As the Christian grows spiritually, his desires enlarge, and because his attainments do not keep pace, he is apt to err in his judgment of himself: "There is that maketh himself poor, yet hath great riches" (Pro 13:7)!

Young Christians are generally more enthusiastic and active, yet the zeal is not always according to knowledge, and at times, it is unseasonable through neglecting temporal affairs for spiritual. A young Christian is ready to respond to almost any plausible appeal for money, but a mature one is more cautious before he acts, lest he should be supporting enemies of the Truth. The older Christian may not perform some duties with the same zest as formerly, yet with more conscience—quality rather than quantity is what now more concerns him. As we grow older, greater and more difficulties are encountered, and the overcoming of them evidences that we have a larger measure of grace. Particular graces may not be as conspicuous as previously, and yet the exercise of new ones be more evident (2Pe 1:5-7). Measure not your growth by any one part of your life, nor by any single aspect of it, but by your Christian career as a whole.

It is by no means a simple matter to accurately classify believers as to which particular form they belong to in the school of Christ, either concerning ourselves or others, for spiritual growth is rarely *uniform*—though it ought to be so. Some Christians are weak and strong at one and the same time, in different respects, as both experience and observation show. Some have better heads than hearts, while others have sounder hearts than heads. So they are weak in knowledge, ignorant and unsettled in the Faith, who nevertheless put to shame their better-instructed brethren by their love and zeal, and their walk and fruitfulness. Others have a good understanding of the Truth, but are veritable babes when it comes to putting it into practice. Solomon was endued with great wisdom, but ruined his testimony through yielding to fleshly lusts. "A Christian should labour for a good heart well-headed, and a head well-hearted" (T. Manton, 1620-1677).

Again, it needs to be borne in mind that there are great differences in the same Christian at sundry times, yea, within a single season, so that the three stages of spiritual growth may coincide in a single saint. The maturest "father" in some respects may be as weak as a new born "babe" in other regards, and tempted as violently as the "young men." The case of the godliest man is not always uniform. One day, he may be rapt into the holy mount to behold Christ in His glory, and the same evening, be tossed with winds and waves, and in his feelings like a ship on the point of sinking. Now he may, like Paul, be caught up into Paradise and favoured with revelations, which he cannot express to others, and anon be afflicted with a thorn in the flesh, the messenger of Satan to buffet him. Calms and storms, peace and troubles, combats and conquests, weakness and strength, alternate in the lives of God's people—yet in each, they may bring forth fruit which is "beautiful in his time" (Ecc 3:11).

All that has been dwelt upon above may appear unto some of our readers as being so elementary and obvious that there was really no need to point out the same. Though that be the case, there are others who at least require to be reminded thereof. It is not so much our knowledge, but the *use* we make of it that counts the most, and often our worst failures issue not from ignorance, but from acting contrary to the light we have. A due recognition of the seasonableness or unreasonableness of particular spiritual fruits in the Christian life will preserve from many wrong conclusions. On the one hand, it should keep him from expecting to find in a spiritual babe those fruits and developed graces which pertain unto a state of maturity; and on the other hand, he who regards himself as a "father" in Christ must vindicate that estimation by banding forth far more than do young Christians. — A.W.P.

TO AMERICAN READERS

In order to give a double opportunity for at least one of each issue of the "Studies" to reach those of our U.S.A. and Canadian friends, who kindly take two or more copies, we have, for the last four years, sent the same with a two weeks' interval between mailings, so that the second lot could go by a different convoy. But now that conditions on the Atlantic are reported to be much improved, we shall cease so doing, and during 1945 D.V., post two of each issue in the same envelope—no doubt that will be more acceptable. Yet *prayer* will still be needed that it may please God to protect your copies as they cross the ocean.

(continued from back page)

can be lost—all of it, we believe, will be feasted upon at the marriage supper of the Lamb, when He shall say "eat, O friends; drink, yea, drink abundantly, O beloved" (Son 5:1). "To him that overcometh will I give to eat of the hidden manna" (Rev 2:17). We shall hear from Christ's own lips the secrets of His life as He sojourned for thirty-three years in this world of sin, making known to us more fully the depths of humiliation into which He descended for us and the perfections He exercised—hidden from the eyes of men—as He endured the contradiction of sinners against Himself.

Third, the historical reference (Exo 16:33, 34 and compare Heb 9:4) shows that the literal "hidden manna" consisted of a "pot" of manna which was laid "up before the LORD" to be "kept for your generations." It was designed as a testimony and memorial of God's grace unto His people. In its anti-typical fulfilment, this points, we believe, to the unfolding of His secret providences—which the Lord will make to us in Heaven, when we shall be able to *understand* (with amazement, awe, and adoration) what now we only *believe*—namely, that all His dealings with us were ordered by perfect love and unerring wisdom; and also to the blessed workings of His grace in and through us. "Then they that feared the LORD spake often one to another: and the LORD hearkened, and heard it, and a book of remembrance was written before him *for them* that feared the LORD, and that thought upon his name" (Mal 3:16), and the next verse seems to more than hint that the contents of that book will be made known and enjoyed "in that day" when the Lord of hosts makes up His jewels.

We conceive that each one of the redeemed will be given the holy privilege of making his or her personal contribution to this unfolding of God's wondrous ways with us in providence and in grace—there will be no Divine restriction, "let your women keep silence in heaven," for all the consequences of the Fall will be obliterated and the sisters as well as the brethren will then be "as the angels of God in heaven" (Mat 22:30). This writer believes that each one of the blood-bought company will say, in turn, "Come and hear, all ye that fear God, and I will declare what he hath done for *my* soul" (Psa 66:16)—not only in regeneration, but in all that followed. O what a testimony each of them will then bear to God's amazing grace and patience! What a witness each will give to God's unfailing faithfulness and goodness in supplying every need as he crossed the Wilderness of Sin! How blessed it will be to hear one and another relate God's wondrous answers to prayer—then there will be none of the scepticism which we fear there would be now were we to relate some of the miracles God has wrought in response to our feeble petitions. Everything which redounds to the glory of God will then be made known to the whole of His family. —A.W.P.

(continued from front page)

is the new nature, energised by the Holy Spirit, which qualifies for victory. Second, he must be endowed with a supernatural principle, otherwise his native unbelief would make defeat inevitable and certain: "This is the victory that overcometh the world, even our faith" (1Jo 5:4)—God's gift, but our use of it. It is by the exercise of this grace that we obtain strength for the conflict and incentives to persevere. Third, he must have recourse to that which will heal his wounds and prevail before God as his plea: "And they overcame him by the blood of the Lamb" (Rev 12:11). That blood gives the believer the right to claim enablement for his repelling of every attack of Satan's. Fourth, he must "hold fast the confidence and the rejoicing of the hope firm unto the end" (Heb 3:6).

For the encouragement of the Christian engaged in this fierce conflict the Lord has graciously made known the reward awaiting him, and the more his faith lays hold of the same and his hope anticipatively enjoys it, the more incentive will he have to continue fighting, or (changing the figure) to "run with patience the race that is set before us" (Heb 12:1). It was thus our great Exemplar nerved Himself: "Who for the joy that was set before him endured the cross" (Heb 12:2). In our judgment, these promises to the overcomer supply an intimation of wherein the blessedness of the heavenly state consists, such as is to be found nowhere else in the Scriptures. As they draw nearer the end of their pilgrimage the Lord's people should project their thoughts more and more unto what awaits them on High. The worn-out *worldling* seeks satisfaction in living over again in his mind those "pleasures of sin" (Heb 11:25) which engaged him in the past, but the veteran saint will rather contemplate those "pleasures for evermore" which are at God's right hand (Psa 16:11). A part of what those "pleasures" consist of is intimated in Revelation 2:17.

"To him that overcometh will I give to eat of the hidden manna" (Rev 2:17). Here is a part of the spiritual entertainment which Christ has provided for His friends in glory. It seems to denote three things. First, as the manna was the food which God supplied from Heaven for His people of old, nourishing and sustaining them throughout their wilderness journey, it must be regarded as a figure of the written word which is the Christian's spiritual staff of life. And since the Word of God "liveth and abideth for ever" (1Pe 1:23), does not the *"hidden* manna" (Rev 2:17) point to the inexhaustible riches of Divine wisdom, which are stored up in it, and of which we have at present, but a fragmentary knowledge. We cannot think that any of that treasure will be lost to us—rather, do we conclude it will be made known and afford part of our delectation on High. Now we know the marvels of Divine inspiration and revelation "in part," but then shall we know them in full. 2 Corinthians 12:7 shows that Heaven is the place of "the abundance of the revelations."

As the risen Christ expounded the Scriptures to His disciples and opened their understandings to understand them (Luk 24:27, 45), will not the glorified Saviour do the same for us (Heb 13:8)!

Second, the "manna" which God gave to Israel in the wilderness was also a manifest type of the incarnate Son, the "bread of life"—which is given to us, because broken for us (Joh 6:35, 48). Therefore, the "hidden manna" (Rev 2:17) refers, we conclude, to "In whom are *hid* all the treasures of wisdom and knowledge" (Col 2:3) in Him, of which I now have but the faintest conception, and to the "many things which Jesus did" that have not been recorded on any earthly scroll (Joh 21:25), and also to much that was precious about Him—which was never cognised even by His apostles. Nothing of this

(Continued on preceding page)

VOL. XXIII.   DECEMBER, 1944.   NO. 12

STUDIES in the SCRIPTURES

" Search the Scriptures."   John 5:39.

Publisher and Editor—Arthur W. Pink,
27 Lewis Street,
Stornoway, Isle of Lewis,
Scotland.

A WORD TO PARENTS

One of the most terrible tragedies of this war is that hundreds of thousands of our sailors, soldiers and airmen are going forth into active service without any saving acquaintance with God in Christ, and the great majority of them without even an intellectual knowledge of Him. Many of them grew up without attending the "churches," and the few who went there heard, for the most part, nothing of God's just claims upon them, nothing about the exceeding sinfulness and infinite guilt of sin—little about how Divine forgiveness of sins may be obtained, and nothing about the everlasting punishment in the Lake of Fire (Rev 20:14, 15) which awaits all who die with their sins unpardoned. What is still more pathetic (in the judgment of the writer) is that the great majority of these young men received no Scriptural and spiritual instruction in the *homes* where they were reared. As children, they listened to the jazz of the radio, rather than the songs of Zion; they saw their parents reading the Sunday newspapers rather than the Word of God; and never was the voice of prayer heard in the family circle. How far is any country entitled to be called "Christian" where the vast majority of its homes are Pagan.

But let us turn now to a very much smaller and more favourable circle. Let us contemplate the homes of "church members." The fathers and mothers "belong to" some denomination, and occasionally, perhaps on each Lord's Day, attend "Divine service"—mostly because their parents before them were accustomed so to do. Yet apart from for this single exception, there is nothing to distinguish them from "respectable" neighbours who make no formal profession at all. No family worship is conducted in these homes, and even on the Sabbath Day, the conversation is of the work from morn to night. The parents—while very solicitous about the bodily welfare of their children—act toward them as though they had *no soul*. True, some of them sent their little ones to the "Sunday school" where they were amused and entertained, and knew little more of Holy Writ at the finish than they did at the beginning; but that was a shelving of their responsibility and not a discharging of it.

Narrow the circle still further, and it is indeed a tiny one, and take the homes of those which charity requires us to regard as Christian ones. Here there is indeed a noticeable difference, but in only too many cases, it is merely a negative one. Here,

(continued on back page)

IMPORTANT NOTICES

Please advise promptly of change in address, otherwise copies will be lost in the mails.

We are glad to send a sample copy to any of your friends whom you believe would be interested in this publication.

This magazine is published as "a work of faith and labour of love," the editor and his wife gladly giving their services free. There is no regular subscription price, as we do not wish the poor of the flock to be deprived. This does not mean that those looking for something for nothing may "help themselves." Those getting this Magazine, who are financially able and who receive spiritual help from its pages, are expected to gladly contribute towards its expenses; otherwise, their names are dropped from our lists.

Will those forwarding International Money Orders please have them made out to us at Stornoway, Isle of Lewis, Scotland. Checks (Cheques-Eng.) made out on U.S.A. Banks are not negotiable here, so please do not send them.

CONTENTS

THE PRAYERS OF THE APOSTLES

12. 2 Corinthians 13:14

"The grace of the Lord Jesus Christ, and the love of God, and the communion of the Holy Ghost, be with you all. Amen." (2Co 13:14). This threefold invocation is familiarly known as the Christian Benediction. The O.T. formula of blessing was authorised to be used in the assemblies of Israel: "Speak unto Aaron and unto his sons, saying, On this wise ye shall bless the children of Israel, saying unto them, The LORD bless thee, and keep thee: The LORD make his face shine upon thee, and be gracious unto thee: The LORD lift up his countenance upon thee, and give thee peace. And they shall [thus] put my name upon the children of Israel; and I will bless them." (Num 6:22-27). But there is nothing to indicate that God required the Benediction of 2 Corinthians 13:14 to be employed in the Christian churches; yet there is certainly nothing to show that it is incongruous to do so. As a fact, it has been made wide use of; and that, because of its deep importance doctrinally and because of its appropriateness, for those words are both a confession of the Christian faith and a declaration of Christian privilege.

The Benediction contains a brief summary of *the Christian doctrine of God*. We say the *Christian* doctrine of God, in contradistinction from not only the horrible delusions of the idolatrous heathen, but also from the inadequate conception of Deity which obtained in Judaism. By the Christian doctrine of God, we mean the revelation which is given of Him in the N.T. more particularly. And that brings us to ground where we need to tread very carefully, lest we disparage or underestimate what was revealed of Him in the O.T. If on the one hand, we must guard against the fearful error that the God of the O.T. is a very different character from the God of the New; on the other hand, we need to be careful that we do not too fully read the clearer teaching of the New into the Old, or at any rate, conclude that those under the legal dispensation perceived the same significance in some of those things in their Scriptures, which we now interpret in the brighter light of the evangelical economy. Such statement as "the darkness is past, and the true light now shineth" (1 Jo 2:8) needs to be remembered in this connection.

It has been erroneously and blasphemously asserted by German neologians and their Anglo-Saxon echoers, who deny the real inspiration of the Scriptures that Jehovah was but a tribal God, and that what is said of Him in the O.T. is but the views which the Hebrews entertained of Him. But it is greatly to be feared that many who reject such a Satanic crudity as that, and who regard the O.T. as being equally the Word of God with the New, nevertheless hold the idea (with varying degrees of consciousness) that the revelation which we have of the Divine character in the latter, is much to be preferred above the delineation given thereto in the former. But such is a serious misconception. The severity of God appears as plainly in the book of Revelation as it does in Joshua; in fact, the vials of His wrath are more fearful in their nature than the plagues which He inflicted upon Egypt and Canaan. On the other hand, the goodness of God, as made known in the Epistles, in no wise surpasses His benevolence as depicted in the Psalms. The God of Sinai and of Calvary are one and the same, as He is also the Author of both the Law and the Gospel.

In saying that we need to be careful not to read too fully into the O.T. Scriptures the clearer teaching of the New, we mean that while we who ever have the completed Word of God in our hands, and are thereby enabled, recognise more plainly that the substance of the truth of the Triunity of God is found in the earlier Books. Yet it has to be granted that there is no statement in them, which is quite as explicit as say, Matthew 28:19, and certainly, it is much to be doubted if the Jewish *nation* as such recognised that there were three distinct Persons in the Godhead. The grand truth made known under the old economy was rather the *unity* of God: "Hear, O Israel: The LORD our God is one LORD" (Deu 6:4) in sharp contrast from the polytheism of the idolatries of the heathen. On the other hand, we have no doubt that individual saints in these times had a saving knowledge of the Triune God, yet not so fully perhaps as we have. "As God afforded a clearer manifestation of Himself at the advent Christ, the three Persons became better known" (John Calvin), especially in the covenant offices and distinct operations.

"The path of the just is as the shining light, that shineth more and more unto the perfect day" (Pro 4:18). It is to be remarked that those words have a corporeate fulfilment as well as a personal: they apply to the Church collectively, as well as individually. The light of Divine revelation brought forth "here a little, and there a little" (Isa 28:10, 13) and shone not in meridian splendour until Immanuel Himself tabernacled among men. The degree in which the doctrine of the Trinity was made known in the O.T. Scriptures no doubt bore a proportion to the discovery of other mysteries of the Faith. It was definitely revealed from the beginning, yet hardly with the same explicitness and perspicuity as now. "God, who at sundry times and in divers manners spake in time past unto the fathers by the prophets, Hath in these last days spoken unto us by his Son" (Heb 1:1, 2). This is the first contrast given in that epistle, the theme of which is the superiority of Christianity over Judaism. Until the former era God's revelation of Himself was fragmentary and incomplete, but in this final dispensation, His mind and heart have been fully told, only there, it was through such instruments as "the prophets"; now it is by the Person of His Own Son.

The Christian revelation comes to us through the Lord Jesus Christ. God is manifested in and by the incarnate Son, for as He can only be approached through the

Mediator, so He can only be vitally and savingly known in Him. It was the grand mission of Christ as the Prophet of His Church to make known the character and perfections of God. That is signified by His title, "The Word." "In the beginning was the Word, and the Word was with God, and the Word was God… And the Word was made flesh, and dwelt among us, (and we beheld his glory, the glory as of the only begotten of the Father,) full of grace and truth" (Joh 1:1, 14). A "word" is a medium of manifestation. I have in my mind a thought, yet others know it not. But the moment I clothe that thought in words, it becomes cognisble. Words then make objective unseen thoughts. This is precisely what the Lord Jesus has done: He has made manifest the invisible God. A "word" is also a means of communication. It is by my words that I transmit information to others. By words I express myself, make known my will, and impart knowledge. So Christ, as the Word, is the Divine Transmitter, expressing to us God's full mind and will, communicating to us His life and love.

A "word" is also a means of revelation. By his words, a speaker or writer exhibits both his intellectual caliber and his moral character. "Out of the abundance of the heart, the mouth speaketh" (Mat 12:34), and our very language betrays what we are within. By our words, we shall be justified or condemned in the Day to come, for they will reveal and attest what we were and are. And Christ, as the Word, reveals the attributes and perfections of God. How fully Christ has revealed God! He displayed His power and illustrated His patience, He manifested His wisdom and exhibited His holiness, He showed forth His faithfulness and demonstrated His righteousness, He made known His grace and unveiled His heart. In Christ, and nowhere else, is God fully and finally told out. That is why He is designated, "Who is the image of the invisible God" (Col 1:15), for He has set before our eyes and hearts a visible, tangible and cognisable representation of Him. Though "no man hath seen God at any time," yet "the only begotten Son, which is in the bosom of the Father, he hath declared him" (Joh 1:18), that is, He has faithfully and fully told Him out, the word for "declared" is rendered "told" in Luke 24:35.

There was an infinite suitability that He who was in the bosom of the Father, even when He walked this earth, should declare Him, for only One who was His "fellow," His co-equal, was capacitated to tell Him forth. So perfectly did Christ reveal Him that at the close of His ministry, He said unto Philip, "he that hath seen me hath seen the Father" (Joh 14:9), and to Him He affirmed, "I have manifested thy name unto the men which thou gavest me out of the world…And I have declared unto them thy name" (Joh 17:6, 26). By the "name" of God is meant all that He is in a manifestative and communicative way. For what God is essentially in His absoluteness, in His ineffable majesty, in His incomprehensible boundlessness, in His self-existing essence, as three in one and one in three, the infinite Jehovah, cannot be made fully known to any finite intelligence, however spiritual, no, not unto eternity. It is in His love to His Church, in His covenant relationship to His people in Christ, in His everlasting delight to them in His Beloved, as the Medium and Mediator of all union and communion with them, that He has been graciously pleased to reveal and make Himself known.

That in and by and through the Lord Jesus Christ, *God is revealed* unto us is the testimony of the chief of the apostles when he declared Him to be "the brightness of his [the Triune God's] glory, and the express image of his person" (Heb 1:3), where he was certainly speaking of Christ as the God-man, that is, of the Son as incarnate, as the same verse goes on to show: "when he had by himself purged our sins" (Heb 1:3). By that blessed statement, we understand that through Christ, a clear and full exhibition has been made of the Father's personality, and that in the Mediator, all the glory of the Godhead is realised and manifested, so as for it to be reflected on the Church and hereby to be known and enjoyed, and so as for God to be glorified. A manifestation consists in revealing, so our Lord revealed and made known the "name" of God. He did so by His incarnation, by His holy life, by His magnifying of the Law, by His preaching, by His miracles, by His sufferings and death, by His triumphant resurrection, by His ascension. He did so by His Spirit, for it was more than an external manifestation of God which Christ made unto His own, namely, an internal, by supernatural revelation, just as He "opened he their understanding, that they might understand the scriptures" (Luk 24:45).

That which we have dwelt upon at such length above is, that if the Benediction sets before us, in summarised form, the Christian doctrine of God, it is to the Lord Jesus we are especially indebted for that revelation; not exclusively in the letter of it, but supremely so in the spirit thereof. It is because this is not sufficiently realised, even by many of God's dear people, and also because we find the subject so fascinating, that instead of entering at once into a detailed exposition of 2 Corinthians 13:14 or even of offering some more definite remarks upon the Holy Trinity, we deemed it best to make clear what we owe to our Redeemer in making known to us the character of God Himself and the relations which He sustains to us. As He averred, "All things are delivered unto me of my Father: and no man knoweth the Son, but the Father; neither knoweth any man the Father, save the Son, and he to whomsoever the Son will *reveal him*" (Mat 11:27). As none can approach unto the Father except by Christ's mediation, so none can have any vital and spiritual knowledge of Him except by Christ's supernatural revelation of Him to the soul.

When our Lord declared, "he that hath seen me hath seen the Father" (Joh 14:9), He uttered words with a far deeper significance than appears on their surface. Locally they were spoken more by way of reproof, for Philip had said unto Him, "Lord, shew us the Father, and it sufficeth us" (Joh 14:8). To which the Saviour replied, "Have I been so long time with you, and yet hast thou not known me, Philip?" My life, My teaching, My works, reveal plainly enough who I am. And then He added, "he that hath seen me hath seen the Father; and how sayest thou then, Shew us the Father?" (Joh 14:9). But it is to be remembered that the Spirit was not then given as He now is, and that the hearts of these apostles were sore troubled (verse 1) at the prospect of His death and His subsequent departure from them. But in its deeper meaning, "he that hath seen me" refers not to any physical sight of Him, but he that has been granted a spiritual view of Him with the eyes of a Divinely-enlightened understanding, such an one is enabled to recognise His *oneness* with the Father, and to exclaim, "my Lord and my God" (Joh 20:28).

The two things we have mentioned above are brought together in that familiar statement, "For God, who commanded the light to shine out of darkness, hath shined in our hearts, to give the light of the knowledge of the glory of God in the face of Jesus Christ" (2Co 4:6). First, the clearest revelation of that God is and what He is, is made in the person of Christ, so that those who refuse to see God in the Redeemer lose all true knowledge of Him. Second, as the glory of God is spiritual, it can only be spiritually discerned. Only in God's light can we see Him who is light, and therefore God must shine in our hearts to give us a real and experimental knowledge of Himself, for such knowledge of Him is not by mental apprehension, nor that which one man can communicate to another. Our reception of that light is not the result of our will or any effort put forth by us, but is the immediate effect of a Divine fiat, as when at the beginning of this world God said, "Let there be light: and there was light" (Gen 1:3). God created light, and He awakens the dead souls of His elect, thereby calling them out of darkness into His own marvellous light, whereby they behold Himself shining in the perfection of grace and truth in the face or person of Jesus Christ. Nothing but the exercise of Omnipotence can produce a miracle so wondrous and so blessed. God shines in our hearts by the power and operation of the Holy Spirit.

Here then is found the answer to that all-important question, How may I obtain a better, deeper, fuller and more influential knowledge of God? By the heart's occupation with the Lord Jesus. By studying and meditating upon all that is revealed in Holy Writ concerning His wondrous person and work. By realizing my complete dependency upon the Holy Spirit and begging Him to take of the things of Christ and show them unto me (Joh 16:14); and therefore, by abstaining from everything which grieves the Spirit and would (morally) hinder Him from performing this office work of His. Nothing can make up for or take the place of personal intercourse with the Redeemer. It is only as we behold, with the eyes of faith and love, the glory of the Lord in the mirror of the Lord that we are "changed into the same image from glory to glory, even as by the Spirit of the Lord" (2Co 3:18). Then let us emulate the apostle and make it our chief ambition and endeavour "that I may know him" (Phi 3:10), for in knowing Him, we arrive at the knowledge of the triune God.

The Christian Benediction stands closely linked with both the baptism of Christ and the baptismal formula which He gave to His disciples. The former presents to us a most remarkable scene, for it was there that the three Persons of the Godhead were openly manifested together, in connection with that which gave a symbolical showing forth of the work of redemption. John the Baptist had come preaching repentance toward God and faith in His Lamb who should take away the sin of the world, while he also made definite mention of the Holy Spirit (Mat 3:11). When the Saviour presented Himself for baptism at the hands of His forerunner in the Jordan, He came as our Surety acknowledging that death was His due, and it was there He entered upon that path which was to terminate at the cross. As He rose from that symbolical grave, the heavens were opened and the Spirit of God in form as a dove descended and alighted upon Him, thereby anointing Him for His priestly work (Act 10:38). At the same time, the Father's voice was audibly heard saying, "This is my beloved Son, in whom I am well pleased" (Mat 3:17). "Therefore doth my Father love me, because I lay down my life, that I might take it again" (Joh 10:17), and here, while emblematically pledging Himself so to do, the Father attested His pleasure in Him and the acceptance of His offering.

Christ's reception of the Spirit at the Jordan was the equipment for His messianic ministry. And as He was sent, and anointed by the Spirit, so He commissions and endows His ambassadors: "As my Father hath sent me, even so send I you. And when he had said this, he breathed on them, and saith unto them, Receive ye the Holy Ghost:" (Joh 20:21, 22). After which He gave them the great commission: "All power is given unto me in heaven and in earth. Go ye therefore, and teach all nations, baptizing them [after they had been taught and become disciples or Christians] in the name of the

Father, and of the Son, and of the Holy Ghost:" (Mat 28:18-20). Baptism into "the name" means baptism unto God, and the name of God in the new covenant is "the Father, and of the Son, and of the Holy Ghost", the Triune God being now fully revealed. That was the culmination and consummation of Christ's teaching concerning God. He ordained that rite for all time to be the initiating avowal of faith for all who would enter His kingdom. It is the inspired formula with which all believers are to be received into Christian fellowship, for it sets forth the fundamental doctrine of the Christian Church. It is both the basis of all Christian doctrine and the general confession of the Christian Faith. — A.W.P.

THE MISSION AND MIRACLES OF ELISHA

24. Fifteenth Miracle – Part 2

"Then he said, God do so and more also to me, if the head of Elisha the son of Shaphat shall stand on him this day" (2Ki 6:31). This was the language of hatred and fury. Refusing to own that it was his own impenitency and obduracy which was the procuring cause of the terrible straits to which his kingdom was now reduced, Jehoram turned an evil eye on the prophet and determined to make a scapegoat of him. As though the man of God was responsible for "the famine," Israel's apostate king took a horrible oath that he should be promptly slain. He was well acquainted with what had happened in the reign of his parents, when in answer to the words of Elijah, there had been no rain on Samaria (1Ki 17:1), and he probably considered that his own desperate situation was due to Elisha's prayers. Though just as Ahab declined to recognise that the protracted drought was a Divine judgment upon his own idolatry, so his son now ignored the fact that it was his personal sins that had called down the present expression of Divine wrath.

This solemn and awful incident should be viewed in the light of that Divine indictment, "the carnal mind is enmity against God" (Rom 8:7)–and that, my reader, is true of *your* mind and of *my* mind by nature. You may not believe it, but He before whose omniscient eye your heart is open, declares it to be so. You may be quite unconscious of your awful condition, but that does not alter the fact. If you were better acquainted with the true God, made sensible of His ineffable holiness and inexorable justice, and realised that it was *His* hand that smites you when your body suffers acute pain or when your circumstances are most distressing, you might find it easier to discover how your heart really beats toward Him and the ill-will you bear Him. True, that fearful "enmity" does not always manifest itself in the same way or to the same degree–for in His mercy, God often places His restraining hand upon that wicked and prevents the full outbursts of their hostility and madness. But when that restraining hand is removed, their case is like that described in Revelation 16:10, 11: "They gnawed their tongues for pain, And blasphemed the God of heaven because of their pains and their sores, and repented not of their deeds."

And why do we say that Jehoram's conduct on this occasion made manifest "the enmity of the carnal mind against God"? Because, while he was unable to do Jehovah any injury directly, he determined to visit his spite upon Him indirectly, by maltreating His servant. Ah my reader, there is important, if solemn, instruction for us in that. Few people realise the *source* from which proceeds the bitterness, the opposition made against, the cruel treatment meted out to many of the ministers of the Gospel. As true representatives of the Holy One, they are a thorn in the side of the ungodly. Though they do them no harm, but instead desire and seek their highest good, yet are they detested by those who want to be left alone in their sins. Nothing recorded in human history more plainly and fearfully displays the depravity of fallen man and his alienation from God than his behaviour toward the most faithful of His servants, supremely manifested when the Lord of glory took upon Him the form of a servant and tabernacled among men. It was just because He made known and revealed the character of God as none else ever did, that man's hatred of and enmity against Him was so inveterately and fiercely exhibited.

"But Elisha sat in his house, and the elders sat with him" (2Ki 6:32). This verse also needs to be pondered in the light of other Scriptures. For example: "Whoso hearkeneth unto me shall dwell safely, and shall be quiet from fear of evil" (Pro 1:33). The one who truly fears the Lord, fears not man, and his heart is preserved from those trepidations which so much disturb the rest and so often torment the wicked. No, "He shall not be afraid of evil tidings", he shall neither have alarming anticipations of such, nor be dismayed when they actually arrive. And why not? "His heart is fixed, trusting in the LORD" (Psa 112:7). Rumours do not shake him, nor does he quake when they are authenticated. For he is assured that his "times" are in the hand of the Lord (Psa 31:15). And therefore, is he kept in peace. In the light of all that is recorded of him, who can doubt that Elisha and his companions had been on their knees before the Throne of grace, and now calmly awaited events. That is the holy privilege of the saints in seasons of acutest stress and distress: To "rest in the LORD, and wait patiently for him" (Psa 37:7).

"And the king sent a man from before him" (2Ki 6:32). This man was dispatched post-haste ahead of Jehoram, either to announce his awful decision or to put it into actual execution. Had the king paused to reflect, he should have realized that it was one thing to form such a determination, but quite another to carry it out. Had not Benhadad, only a short time previously, sent a "great host" not only of footmen, but of "horses and chariots" against this servant of the Lord (2Ki 6:14), only for them to discover their impotency against him! But when a soul (or a people) is abandoned of the Lord, he is given up to a spirit of madness, so that not only does God have no place in his thoughts, but he is no longer capable of acting rationally, rationality and spirituality are closely connected. "But ere the messenger came to him, he [Elisha] said to the elders, See ye how this son of a murderer hath sent to take away mine head? look, when the messenger cometh, shut the door, and hold him fast at the door: is not the sound of his master's feet behind him?" (2Ki 6:32).

"And while he yet talked with them, behold, the messenger came down unto him: and he said, Behold, this evil is of the LORD; what should I wait for the LORD any longer?" (2Ki 6:33). We confess we do not find it easy to ascertain the precise force of this verse, not even its grammatical meaning. The first sentence is clear, for the "while he yet talked" evidently refers to what Elisha was saying to the elders. The difficulty is to discover the antecedent of the "And *he* said": the nearest is the "him" or Elisha; yet, certainly *he* would not say the proposed murder of himself ("this evil") was "of the Lord" ordered by Him. The next is "the messenger", but the prophet had given definite orders that *he* was not to be admitted, nor would this agree with what follows in 2 Kings 7:1, 2. We, therefore, regard the second sentence as recording the words of the king himself, who had followed immediately on the heels of his messenger, thus the more remote, but *principal*, antecedent of verses 30, 31: just as we understood "the man whom ye seek" as meaning Jehoram, rather than Elisha (2Ki 6:19).

But what did the king signify by "*this* evil is of the LORD"? (2Ki 6:33). We certainly do not concur with M. Henry and Scott that he referred to the siege and famine, for not only is the grammar of the passage against such a view, but it is in direct opposition to everything else which is recorded of this son of Jezebel. He did not believe in Jehovah at all, and therefore, his language must be regarded as that of derision and blasphemy. The context shows he was in a towering rage, that he regarded Elisha as being in some way responsible for the present calamity, and that he was determined to put a sudden end to his life. Fully intending to execute his murderous design, he now burst in on the prophet and said, "This evil is of the LORD." Those were the words of contemptuous mockery: you profess to be a servant of an all-powerful Jehovah, let's see what He can do for you now, behold me as His executioner if you please. "What should I wait for the LORD any longer?" (2Ki 6:33). Jehovah has no place in *my* thoughts or plan: the situation is hopeless, so I shall waste no more time, but slay you and surrender to Benhadad and take my chance.

"Then Elisha said" (2Ki 7:1). "Then" looks back to all that has been before us in the last ten verses of 2 Kings 6. "Then": when "all the hosts of Syria" were besieging Samaria; "then": when there was a great famine and things had come to such an extreme pass that the people were paying immense prices for the vilest of offals, and mothers were consuming their own infants. "Then": when the king of Israel had sworn that the prophet should be beheaded this very day; "then": when the king in a white heat of passion entered Elisha's abode to carry out his murderous intention. "Then", *what*? The prophet gave way to abject despair and broke forth in bitter lamentations of murmuring rebellion? No indeed. Then what? Elisha flung himself at the king's feet and pleaded with him to spare his life? Very far from it: such is not the way the ambassadors of the King of kings conduct themselves in a crisis. Instead, "Then Elisha said, [calmly and quietly] Hear ye the word of the LORD" (2Ki 7:1). To what import?–that His patience is exhausted, that He will now pour out His wrath and utterly consume you? No, the very reverse; the last thing they could have expected him to say.

"Then Elisha said, Hear ye the word of the LORD; Thus saith the LORD, To morrow about this time shall a measure of fine flour be sold for [as little as] a shekel, and two measures of barley for a shekel, in the gate of Samaria." (2Ki 7:1). This brings us, third, to *the announcement* of the amazing miracle which was about to be wrought. In view of the next verse, it is quite clear that the prophet addressed himself to the king and those who had accompanied him. It was as though he said, I have listened to the derisive and insulting words which you have spoken of my Master; now hear ye that *He* has to say! And what was His message on this occasion? This: He is about to have mercy upon your kingdom. He is on the point of working a miracle within the next twenty-four hours–which will entirely reverse the present situation, so that not only will the Syrians depart, but there shall be provided an abundant supply of food, which will fully meet the needs of your people; and that, without a blow being struck or your royal coffers being any the poorer.

Admire here the remarkable *faith* of Elisha. "Then": when things were at their lowest possible ebb, when the situation was desperate beyond words, when the outlook appeared to be utterly hopeless. Mark the implicit confidence of the prophet in that dark hour. He had received a message of good tidings from his Master, and he hesitated not to announce it. Ah, but put yourself in his place, my reader, and remember that he was a man "of like passions" with us; and therefore, liable to be cast down by an evil heart of unbelief. It is a great mistake for us to look upon the prophets as super-human characters. In this case–as in all parallel ones–God was pleased to place His treasure in an "earthen vessel," that the glory might be *His*. Elisha was just as liable to the attacks of Satan as we are. For all we know to the contrary and reasoning from the law of analogy, it is quite likely that the Enemy of souls came to him at that time with his evil suggestions and said, May you not be mistaken in concluding that you have received such a word as this from the Lord? Nay, you *are* mistaken, your own wish is father to the thought: you are deluded into imagining that such a thing can be.

Those who are experimentally acquainted with the conflict between faith and unbelief, who are frequently made to cry out, "Lord, I believe; help thou mine unbelief" (Mar 9:24) will have little difficulty in following us in what has just been said. They who know something from first-hand acquaintance of the tactics of the Devil, and the methods of his assaults, will not deem our remarks above as far-fetched. Rather, will they concur that it is more than likely Elisha was hotly assailed by the Adversary at this very time. Would he not pose too as an angel of light, and preach a little sermon to the prophet, saying. A holy God is now acting in judgment righteously scourging the idolatrous Jehoram; and therefore, you must certainly be mistaken in supposing He is about to act in a way of mercy. At any rate, exercise prudence, wait a while longer lest you make a fool of yourself: it would be cruel to raise false hopes in the starving people! But if so, Elisha heeded him not, but being strong in faith, he gave glory to God. It was just such cases as this that the apostle had in mind when he mentioned the faith of "the prophets" in Hebrews 11:32.

Ah, my reader, Elisha was assured that what he had received was "the Word" of Him "that cannot lie" (Tit 1:2), and no matter how much opposed it was to common sense and to all outward appearances, he firmly took his stand upon it. The "faith of God's elect" (Tit 1:1) is no fiction but a glorious reality. It is something more than a beautiful ideal to talk about and sing of. It is a Divine gift, a supernatural principle, which not only overcomes the world, but survives the "fiery trial" (1Pe 4:12), yea, issues therefrom refined. Elisha was not to put to confusion. That Divine "word", though perhaps quite unexpected and contrary to his own anticipation, was faithfully and literally fulfilled; and remember that this is recorded for *our* learning and consolation. We, too, have in our hands the Word of Truth, but do we have it in our hearts? Are we really relying upon its promises, no matter how unlikely their accomplishment may seem to carnal reason? If so, we are resting upon a sure foundation, and we too shall have our faith vindicated and God will be glorified through and by us.

But let us look higher now than Elisha's faith in that Divine word to the One who gave it him. It was the Lord manifesting Himself as "the God of all grace" (1Pe 5:10) to those who were utterly unworthy. In their dire extremity, the Lord had mercy upon them and remembered they were the seed of Abraham; and therefore, He would not entirely destroy them. He turned an eye of pity on the starving city and promised them speedy relief from the awful famine. How truly wonderful is His mercy! He was saying, "How shall I give thee up, Ephraim? how shall I deliver thee, Israel? how shall I make thee as Admah? how shall I set thee as Zeboim? mine heart is turned within me, my repentings are kindled together" (Hos 11:8). But that mercy rested on a righteous basis, there was a handful of salt in Samaria which preserved it from destruction, the prophet and "the elders." Rightly was Elisha styled by a later king, "the chariot of Israel, and the horsemen thereof" (2Ki 13:14), for his presence in their midst was a better defence than a multitude of infantry and cavalry, a queen feared the prayers of Knox far more than any arm of flesh.

And may not what has just been pointed out provide a ray of hope for us in this, spiritually speaking, dark night? Of old Israel was reminded, "For what nation is there so great, who hath God so nigh unto them, as the LORD our God is in all things that we call upon him for?" (Deu 4:7). Has not *that* been true of Britain the past four centuries as of no other people? God has shown us favours, granted us privileges, such as no other nation in the world has enjoyed. And we, like Israel of old, have evilly requitted Him and abused His great benefits. For years past, His judgments have been upon us; and like Israel again, we have sadly failed to bow to His rod and turn from our sins. And now we are passing through the greatest crisis of our history, and our people after still impenitent. But thank God we have a king and queen who are radically different from Jehoram and his mother Jezebel. If God was so reluctant to abandon Israel, may He not continue to show us mercy, and for the sake of the little "salt" still left in our midst, spare us from destruction? Time will tell, but we are not left without hope.

"Then a lord on whose hand the king leaned answered the man of God, and said, Behold, if the LORD would make windows in heaven, might this thing be?" (2Ki 7:2). Here was the response that was made to Jehovah's word through His prophet: instead of being received with thanksgiving and tears of gratitude, it met with a contemptuous sneer. The courtier's language expressed the scepticism of carnal reason. Unbelief dared to question the Divine's promise, illustrative of the unregenerate's rejection of the Gospel. This man argued from what he could *see*: as no possible relief was visible, he scorned its probability, or rather certainty. "And he [Elisha] said, Behold, thou shalt see it with thine eyes, but shalt not eat thereof" (2Ki 7:2). Let it be noted that the prophet wasted no breath in reasoning with this sceptic. It is not only useless, but most unbecoming for a servant of the Lord to descend to the level of such objectors. Instead, he simply affirmed that this man *should* witness the miracle but be unable to share in its benefits. God Himself will yet answer that sceptics of this age, as He did that one, with condign judgment. Such will be the doom of unbeliever: they shall *see* the redeemed feasted at the marriage supper of the Lamb, yet not partake thereof (Mat 8:11, 12). — A.W.P.

THE DOCTRINE OF RECONCILIATION

5d. Its Arrangement

Consider now Christ's relation to the covenant. 1. He is the very *substance* of it: "I will preserve thee, and give thee for a covenant of the people" (Isa 49:8): as His our "propitiation" (1Jo 2:1, 2) and "peace" (Eph 2:14), so He is our covenant. 2. He is the *Witness* of the covenant (Isa 55:3, 4) for He saw, heard and testified it all; and therefore, He is termed, "the faithful and true witness" (Rev 3:14). 3. He is "the *prince* of the covenant" (Dan 11:22 and compare 8:11, 25), called "Messiah the Prince" (Dan 9:25), because He is given the royal right to administer it. 4. He is "the *messenger* of the covenant" (Mal 3:1), acting as God's "Apostle" to us (Heb 3:1) and our Redeemer Representative before God. 5. He is the *"surety"* of the covenant–"testament" is the same Greek word (Heb 7:22, 26), because He engaged Himself to discharge the obligations of His people, its covenantees. 6. He is "the *mediator* of a better covenant" (Heb 8:6), because He stands between and serves both parties, God and His people. 7. He is the *Testator* of the covenant (Heb 9:16, 17), because He has sealed it with His blood.

Consider its various and descriptive designations. 1. It is an "everlasting covenant" (Heb 13:20), because it was entered into before all worlds, and because its blessings shall be administered and enjoyed in perpetuity. 2. It is a "covenant of salt" (Num 18:19; 2Ch 13:5), because it is incorruptible, inviolable, perpetual; because its provisions seasoneth us and makes all our services savoury to God (compare Col 4:6). 3. It is a "covenant of...peace" (Isa 54:10), for therein, Christ engaged to pacify the Divine Judge, remove the infirmity of His people, and effect a mutual reconciliation. 4. It is a "new covenant" (Jer 31:31), for it secures for His people a new standing before God, makes them new creatures in Christ, and puts a new song in their mouths. 5. It is a "covenant...of life" (Mal 2:5), for by its terms, life is promised, restored, and given more abundantly. 6. It is a "holy covenant" (Luk 1:72), manifesting the ineffable purity of God in all its arrangements. 7. It is a covenant "of promise" (Eph 2:12), both to Christ and His seed.

In view of what has just been pointed out, well may we adopt the language of Octavius Winslow and say, "This covenant must be *rich* in its provisions of mercy, seeing it is made by Jehovah Himself, the Fountain of all holiness, goodness, mercy and truth, whose very essence is 'Love.' It must be *glorious*, because the second Person in the blessed Trinity became its Surety. It must be *stable*, because it is eternal. It must meet all the circumstances of a necessitous Church, because it is 'ordered in all things.' It must be *sure*, seeing its administration is in the hands of an infinitely glorious Mediator, who died to secure it, rose again to confirm it, and ever liveth to dispense its blessings as the circumstances of the saints require." To which might be added, it must be *inviolable*, since the eternal God is its Author, and the precious blood of Christ has sealed it. And therefore, it should be "all my salvation, and all my desire" (2Sa 23:5), for what more could I ask or wish!

Returning now to the covenant *promises* which the Father made unto the Mediator. In addition to those considered in our last, Christ was assured of a "*seed*." "When thou shalt make his soul an offering for sin, he shall see his seed" (Isa 53:10). In the previous verses, we are shown what was required from Christ in the discharge of His covenant engagements. Here, we have revealed the reward which the Father bestowed upon Him because of His fidelity. In the last three verses of this wonderful chapter, we also behold the prophet replying to the Jews, who regarded the cross as the "stumblingblock," being scandalized at the idea of their Messiah suffering such an ignominious death. But it is here pointed out that Christ's crucifixion is not to be accounted an infamy to Him, because it was the very means ordained by God, whereby He propagated unto Himself a spiritual seed. He had Himself pointed out, "Except a corn of wheat fall into the ground and die, it abideth alone: but if it die, it bringeth forth much fruit" (Joh 12:24).

Observe well that in Isaiah 53:10, it was promised Him, "He shall see his seed" which, coming immediately after, "when thou shalt make his soul an offering for sin" clearly implied His resurrection. Accordingly, this is more explicitly stated in what at once follows: "He shall prolong His days." The figure is used again in the next verse: "He shall see of the travail of his soul, and shall be satisfied" (Isa 53:11). "A woman when she is in travail hath sorrow, because her hour is come: but as soon as she is delivered of the child, she remembereth no more the anguish, for joy that a man is born into the world" (Joh 16:21), considering her sufferings to be more than recompensed by the happy issue of them. So the Redeemer deems Himself richly rewarded for all His pains by the children which are His, as the result of His dying travail: He is "satisfied" (Isa 53:11) and "rejoiceth" (Luk 15:7; Mat 18:13) as each one of them is brought forth.

"This seed" which was promised Christ, occupies a prominent place in the great Covenant Psalm–the 89th. There we hear the Father saying, "I have made a covenant with my chosen [or "elect", Isa 42:1], I have sworn unto David my servant, *Thy seed* will I establish for ever" (Psa 89:3, 4). And again, "I will make him my firstborn, higher than the kings of the earth. My mercy will I keep for him for evermore, and my covenant shall stand fast with him. His seed also will I make to endure for ever" (Psa 89:27-29). In the verses that follow, His "seed" are termed His "children," and assurance is given that though they be wayward and the rod be visited upon their transgressions, yet God's covenant faithfulness shall be seen in their preservation (Psa 89:31-36). In the Cross Psalm, it was declared, "A seed shall serve him; it shall be accounted to the Lord for a generation" (Psa 22:30). It was to be a perpetual seed: "His name shall endure for ever: His name shall be continued as long as the sun" (Psa 72:17).

Christ then was assured by the Father from the beginning of the success of His undertaking and promised a seed which should bear His image, serve Him, and show forth His praises. "I will bring thy seed from the east, and gather thee from the west; I will say to the north, Give up; and to the south, Keep not back: bring my sons from far, and my daughters from the ends of the earth" (Isa 43:5, 6). Though they be born into this world in a state of unregeneracy, God promised they should be born again and savingly drawn to embrace Christ as their Lord and Saviour: "Thy people [said the Father to the Mediator, see verse 1] shall be willing in the day of thy power, in the beauties of holiness from the womb of the morning: thou hast the dew of thy youth" (Psa 110:3). Yet again, Christ is represented as saying, "Behold I and the children whom the Lord hath given me [quoted by the apostle of Christ in Hebrews 2:13] are for signs and for wonders in Israel, fror the Lord of hosts which dwelleth in mount Zion" (Isa 8:18).

As there are two parts of the covenant, so the elect were given to Christ in a twofold manner. As He was to fulfill the terms of the covenant, they were entrusted to Him as a *charge*; but in fulfilment thereof, the Father promised to Christ to bestow them upon Him as a *reward*. The elect are to be regarded first, as those who were beloved of the Father before time began. They are designated God's "own elect" (Greek of Luke 18:7), which signifies both His delight with and singular propriety in them. He chose them before all others, He preferred them above all others, and set His heart upon them. As such, the Father gave them to Christ as God-man Mediator, "set up" in the Divine councils; and therefore, having a real subsistence, as a choice expression of His love for Him. Second, they are to be regarded as God foreviewed them under their defection in Adam, and as such, God gave them as a charge to Christ to be raised up from all the ruins of the fall, and also as a reward for His work on their behalf. The twofoldness of Truth needs ever to be borne in mind.

Viewed as *fallen*, the elect were given to Christ as a *charge* for whose salvation He was held responsible. They were committed to Him as "prisoners" (Isa 49:9), whose lawful discharge He must obtain. They were committed to Him as desperate patients, whom He must bind up and heal (Isa 61:1). They were committed to Him as strayed and *lost sheep* (Isa 53:6), whom He must seek out and bring into the fold (Joh 10:16). God placed His elect in the hands of the Mediator and made them His care. How graciously and tenderly He discharged His trust appears in that touching word, "He shall feed his flock like a shepherd: he shall gather the lambs with his arm, and carry them in his bosom, and shall gently lead those that are with young" (Isa 40:11). It appears again in that wonderful word, "And when he hath found it [the lost sheep], he layeth it on his shoulders, rejoicing" (Luk 15:5). Finally, it was evidenced at the moment of His arrest: "If therefore ye seek me, let these go their way: That the saying might be fulfilled, which he spake, Of them which thou gavest me have I lost none" (Joh 18:8, 9).

On the fulfilment of His covenant engagement that people were given to Christ as His *reward,* as the fruit of His travail, as the trophies of His glorious victory over sin, Satan and death, as His crown of rejoicing in the day when all the inhabitants of the universe shall be assembled together, as His beloved and glorious Bride when the marriage of the Lamb is come. In contemplation of this, God made certain promises to the Surety concerning them. He promised to bestow upon them the gift of eternal life. "Paul, a servant of God, and an apostle of Jesus Christ, according to the faith of God's elect, and the acknowledging of the truth which is after godliness, in hope of eternal life which God, that cannot lie, *promised* before the world began" (Tit 1:1, 2). As the elect then had no actual existence, that promise must have been made in their name to the Surety. That particular promise virtually included *all* the benefits which Christ procured for His people, for as "eternal death" contains the essence of all evils, so "eternal life" contains the essence of all blessings.

"The LORD commanded the blessing, even life for evermore" (Psa 133:3); "This is *the* promise that he hath promised us, even eternal life" (1Jo 2:25), how perfect is the harmony between the two Testaments! If we break up that promise into its component parts we may say that, first, God promised to *regenerate* His people or bestow upon them a spiritual nature which delights in His Law: "I will put my laws into their mind, and write them in their hearts" (Heb 8:10). Second, He promised to *justify* them, the negative part of which is to remit their transgressions: "For I will be merciful to their unrighteousness, and their sins and their iniquities will I remember no more" (Heb 8:12). Third, He promised to *sanctify* them: "Then will I sprinkle clean water upon you, and ye shall be clean: from all your filthiness, and from all your idols, will I cleanse you" (Eze 36:25). Fourth, He promised to *preserve* them: "I will not turn away from them, to do them good; but I will put my fear in their hearts, that they shall not depart from me" (Jer 32:40). Fifth, He promised to *glorify* them: "they shall obtain joy and gladness, and sorrow and sighing shall flee away" (Isa 35:10).

Finally, God made promise *of the Holy Spirit* to Christ. What we are now to contemplate is admittedly one of the deep things of God; and therefore, requires to be handled with prayerful concern and godly caution. But if on the one hand, we are certain to err should we deviate one iota from the Scriptures; on the other hand, it is to the glory of God and His Christ and to the needful instruction of our souls that faith humbly receives *all* that is revealed to us in Holy Writ. Now Scripture teaches not only that the Spirit of the Lord rested upon Christ (Isa 11:1, 2) during the days of His earthly ministry, that God put His Spirit upon Him to furnish Him for His great work (Isa 42:1), that He was anointed with the Spirit in order to preach the Gospel (Isa 61:1) and work miracles (Act 10:38; Mat 12:28), but the oracles of Truth make it very clear that Christ received the Spirit in another manner and for a different purpose after His ascension to heaven, namely, that to the God-man Mediator has been given the *administration* of the Spirit's activities and operations; and this, both in the sphere of grace Churchward, and in the sphere of providence world-ward.

In John 7:39, we read that "Holy Ghost was not yet given; because that Jesus was not yet glorified," but He was both promised to Christ (Psa 45:7) and by Christ. Let us seek to attentively consider some of His statements concerning the Holy Spirit's relation unto Himself. "But the Comforter, which is the Holy Ghost, whom the Father will send *in my name*" (Joh 14:26), the force of which is intimated in "Whatsoever ye shall ask the Father in my name, he will give it you" (Joh 16:23). Again, "But when the Comforter is come, whom *I will send* unto you from the Father" (Joh 15:26), which is parallel with Christ's being "sent" by Him (Joh 3:17). And again, "It is expedient for you that I go away: for if I go not away, the Comforter will not come unto you; but if I depart, I will send him unto you" (Joh 16:7). Such repetition argues both the importance of this truth and our slowness to receive it.

To the writer, three things are clear concerning the above passages. First, each was spoken by the God-man Mediator, for they were the utterances of the Word made flesh. Second, from John 7:39 and 16:7, it is apparent that the advent of the Spirit was dependent upon the ascension of Christ. Third, from His repeated "whom I will send unto you" (Joh 15:26), we learn that in this present era, the activities of the Spirit are regulated by the will of the Lord Christ. That the Spirit is at the economical disposal of the Redeemer was evidenced after His resurrection and before His ascension, for to the apostles He said, "Peace be unto you: as my Father hath sent me, even so send I you" (Joh 20:21); and then we are told, "And when he had said this, he breathed on them, and saith unto them, Receive ye the Holy Ghost" (Joh 20:22 and compare Gen 2:7). And as He was on the point of leaving them, the Saviour said, "Behold, I *send* the promise of my Father upon you" (Luk 24:49), which was duly accomplished ten days later.

In Acts 2, when Peter explained the supernatural phenomena of the day of Pentecost, he said, "This Jesus hath God raised up, whereof we all are witnesses. Therefore being by the right hand of God exalted, and having *received* of the Father the promise of the Holy Ghost, *he* hath shed forth this, which ye now see and hear" (Act 2:32, 33), the glorified Saviour hath poured forth this effusion of the Spirit's gifts. On which the Puritan Thomas Goodwin, after quoting Psalm 45:7 and explaining it by Acts 2:36, said on verse 33, "which 'receiving' is not to be only understood of His bare and single receiving the promise of the Holy Spirit for us, by having power given Him to shed Him down upon them, as God had promised, though this *is* a true meaning of it; but further, that He had received Him first as poured forth on Himself, and so shed Him forth on them, according to that rule that whatever God doth unto us by Christ, He first doth it unto Christ" (Vol. 4, page 121). It was the Saviour's outpouring of the Spirit's gifts which demonstrated He had been "made both Lord and Christ" (verse 36).

From the passages quoted above, it seems plain that upon the completion of His covenant work, the Father bestowed the Spirit on Christ to administer from His mediatorial throne. In full accord with that, we hear the Lord Jesus saying from heaven, "These things saith he that *hath* the seven Spirits of God" (Rev 3:1), that is, "hath" to administer the Holy Sprit in the plentitude of His power and the diversity of His manifestations, compare the seven-branched candlestick in Exodus 25:30, 31 and the sevenfold gift of the Holy Spirit to Christ in the days of His flesh (Isa 11:1, 2). On the words, "He that hath the seven Spirits of God" (Rev 3:1), Thomas Scott says, "that is, the Divine Saviour, through whom the Holy Spirit, in the variety and abundance of His precious gifts and graces *was communicated* to all the churches." So again, in Revelation 5:6, we read, "I beheld, and, lo, in the midst...stood a Lamb as it had been slain, having seven horns [compare Matthew 28:18] and seven eyes, which are the seven Spirits of God sent forth into all the earth", here it is Christ exercising His governmental power and administering the Spirit toward the world, as in Revelation 3:1, it was toward the Church. Thus, if on the one hand, none other ever suffered such ignominy as did the Mediator; on the other hand, none other ever has received or ever will such marks of honour as He has. — A.W.P.

SPIRITUAL GROWTH OR CHRISTIAN PROGRESS

6b. Its Seasonableness

The leading principle which we sought to enunciate and illustrate in our last, namely, fruit suitable to the season, receives exemplification in that statement, "A word spoken in due season, how good is it!" (Pro 15:23): A word of sympathy to one in trouble, of encouragement to the despondent, of warning to the careless. Hence, we find the minister of Christ exhorted, "Preach the word; be instant in season, out of season; reprove, rebuke, exhort with all longsuffering and doctrine" (2Ti 4:2), by the "in season, out of season," we understand, at stated times and as opportunity occurs. The same principle was exemplified by the Baptist when he said, "Bring forth therefore fruits meet for repentance" (Mat 3:8), praising God for His mercies at that time would have been unseasonable; rather was godly sorrow for the abuse of them called for. There is "a time to weep, and a time to laugh" (Ecc 3:4).

Fruitfulness is an essential quality of a godly person, but his fruit should be *seasonable.* A time of suffering calls for self-examination, confession, and the exercise of patience. A season of testing and trial requires the exercise of faith and courage. When blest with revivings and spiritual prosperity, holy joy and praise are becoming. It is written, "Therefore will the LORD wait, that he may be gracious...blessed are all they that wait for him" (Isa 30:18), wait for the time He has appointed for the development and manifestation of particular graces. Unseasonable graces are like untimely figs, which are never full flavoured. Most of us are too impatient. "No chastening for the *present* seemeth to be joyous, but grievous... nevertheless *afterward* it yieldeth the peaceable fruit of righteousness unto them which are *exercised* thereby" (Heb 12:11), exercised in conscience as to what has given occasion for the chastisement, exercising faith for the fulfilling of this promise, and patience while awaiting the same.

As we turn now to look at the characteristics which mark the three stages of the Christian life, it must be borne in mind, (1) We are not to understand that what is predicated of the "fathers" in nowise pertains to the "babes," but rather that the particular grace ascribed abounds in the former more eminently. (2) That what is said of each of the three may, in different respects, belong to a single Christian, so that "young men" who are "strong" may in another way, be as weak as the "babes." (3) We must not lose sight of God's liberty in apportioning His grace as and when He pleases: He works not uniformly, and causes some of His people to make much more rapid progress than others during the earlier years of their Christian lives, while others who seem slow at the start overtake and pass them at a later stage.

"I write unto you, little children ["teknia"], because your sins are forgiven you for his name's sake" (1Jo 2:12). "I write unto you, fathers, because ye have known him that is from the beginning. I write unto you, young men, because ye have overcome the wicked one. I write unto you, little children ["paidia"], because ye have known the Father" (1Jo 2:13). This is the classical passage on the present aspect of our theme, though its force is somewhat obscured through the translators making no distinction between the two different Greek words they have rendered "little children." The passage of 1 John 2:12 pertains to the whole of the "called" family of God, irrespective of growth attainment, for every believer has had his sins forgiven him for Christ's sake. The word used there for "little children" is a term of *endearment*, and was employed by Christ in John 13:33 when addressing the apostles, and occurs again in this epistle in 1 John 2:28; 3:7, etc.

Only in 1 John 2:13 are believers graded into three distinct classes according to the degrees of their spiritual progress: "fathers," "young men," and "little children", or preferably, "babes," to mark the distinction from the word used in verse 12. That is the order of dignity and responsibility: had it been the order of *grace,* it had been "babes, young men and fathers." As someone has said, "If Christ were to enter a Christian gathering for the purpose of showing forth His favour, He would commence with the youngest and feeblest one present; but if to judge the works of His servants, He would begin with the maturest saint." For example, Christ appeared many times after His resurrection: He ended by manifesting Himself to the apostle Paul, but with whom did He begin?, with Mary Magdalene out of whom He had cast seven demons!

The same principle is illustrated in the parable of the "pence" (grace), beginning with the eleventh-hour labourer; but reversed in the parable of the "talents," where *responsibility* is in view.

As we are writing on the subject of spiritual progress, or as most writers designate it, "growth in grace", we propose to inverse the order of 1 John 2:13 and consider first the spiritual *babes*. If anyone should consider we are taking an unwarrantable liberty with the Word in so doing, we would appeal to Mark 4:28, where our Lord spoke of, "first the blade, then the ear, after that the full corn in the ear." And now as we seek to grapple more closely with our present task, we have to acknowledge we experience considerable difficulty in attempting to set forth with any measure of definiteness what it is which specially marks the spiritual "babe" in contrast from the "young men" and "fathers"; or if others prefer, that which distinguishes the "blade" from the "ear," and "the full corn in the ear." But if we cannot satisfy our readers, we trust that we may be kept from confusing any of them.

In view of the vastly superior conditions which obtained in the days of the apostles, illustrated by such passages as Acts 2:44, 45; 11:19-21; 1 Corinthians 12:8-

11, it is not to be supposed that many of the features which marked that glorious period will be reproduced in a "day of small things" (Zec 4:10), such as we are now living in. The line of demarcation between the Church and the world was much more plainly drawn then than it is now; the contrast between lifeless and living professors more easily perceived, and so on. Therefore, it is reasonable to conclude that the distinct stages of the Christian life and the different forms which believers occupied in the school of Christ, were then more plainly marked; and though the difference be one of degree rather than of kind, yet that very difference renders it the more difficult for us to describe or identify the several grades.

In his most excellent "Letters on Religious Subjects," John Newton has three pieces entitled, "Grace in the Blade," "Grace in the Ear," "Grace in the Full Corn." He began his second piece by saying, "The manner of the Lord's work in the hearts of His people is not easily traced, though the fact is certain and the evidence demonstrable from Scripture. In attempting to explain it, we can only speak in *general,* and are at a loss to form such a description as shall take in the immense variety of cases which occur in the experience of believers." It is just because so many preachers have failed to take into their account that "immense variety of cases," and instead, have pictured the experience of conversion as though it were cast in a *uniform* mould, that numbers of their hearers and readers have been much stumbled, fearing they were never truly converted because their experience differed widely from that described by the preacher.

George Whitefield (1714-1770) states, "I have heard of a person who was in a company with fourteen ministers of the Gospel, some of whom were eminent servants of Christ, and yet not one of them could tell the time when God first manifested Himself to their soul." Then he went on to say to his hearers and readers, "We do not love the pope, because we love to be popes ourselves, and set up our own experience as a standard to others. Those that had such a conversion as the Philippian jailor or the Jews on the day of Pentecost may say, You are not Christians at all because you had not the like terrible experience. You may as well say to your neighbour, You have not had a child, for you were not in labour all night. The question is, whether a real child is born: not how long was the preceding pain, but whether it was productive of the new birth and whether Christ has been formed in your hearts"!

Some are likely to object to what is said above and say, Though the circumstantials of conversion may vary in different cases, yet the essentials are the same in all: the Law must do its work before the soul is prepared for the Gospel, the heart must be made sensible of its sickness before it will betake itself unto the great Physician. Even though that should be the experience of many of the saints, yet the Holy Spirit is by no means tied down to that order of things, nor do the Scriptures warrant any such restricted view. Take the cases of Peter and Andrew his brother and the two sons of Zebedee (Mat 4:18-22), and there is nothing in the sacred narrative to show that *they* went through a season of conviction of sin before they followed Christ! Nor was there in the case of Matthew 9:9. Zaccheus was apparently attracted by mere curiosity to obtain a sight of the Lord Jesus, and a work of grace was wrought in his heart immediately, and he "received him *joyfully*" (Luk 19:6)!

Let us not be misunderstood at this point. We are neither casting any reflection upon those ministers who preach the Law by which a knowledge of sin is obtained

(Rom 3:20), nor disparaging the importance and necessity of conviction of sin. Rather, are we insisting that God is perfectly free to work as He pleases, and that I have no Scriptural reason to doubt the reality of my conversion, simply because my heart was then melted by a sense of God's wondrous *love,* rather than awed by a discovery of His holiness or terrified by a realization of His wrath; and that I have no warrant to call into question the genuineness of another's conversion, merely because it was not cast in a certain mould. The all-important thing is whether the subsequent walk evidences that I have passed from death unto life. In Zechariah 12:10, "mourning" *follows,* and not precedes, a saving looking upon Christ! There are some who taste the bitterness of sin more sharply after conversion than they did before.

Now as the Holy Spirit is pleased to use different means in connection with the converting of souls, so also there is real variety in the experiences of those newly brought to a saving knowledge of the Truth. On the other hand, as there are certain essentials found in every genuine conversion, the turning from sin, self, the world unto God in Christ, receiving Him as our personal Lord and Saviour and then following Him in the path of obedience, so there are certain characteristics in babes in Christ which distinguish them from the "young men" and "fathers." And the very name by which they are designated more largely defines those characteristics. As infants or little children, they are largely creatures of impulse, swayed by their emotions more than regulated by judgment. Feelings play large part in their lives. They are very impressionable, easily influenced, and largely unsuspecting, believing readily whatever is told them by those who have their confidence.

"I write unto you, little children, because ye have known the Father" (1Jo 2:13). *That* is the distinguishing mark which none other than that Holy Spirit has given of the spiritual infant. It is a statement which needs to be particularly taken to heart and pondered by some of our readers, for it plainly signifies that unless *we* "know the Father," we are not entitled to regard ourselves as being His children. In the natural life, the very first thing which babes and young children discover is an acknowledgement, in their infantile way, of their parents, aiming to call them by their names ("papa" and "mamma") in distinguishing them from others. And thus, it is also spiritually the distinguishing act of babes in Christ to acknowledge God to be their *Father,* and this they do by expressing, in their way, their attachment to Him, their delight in Him, and their dependence on Him, lisping out His name in their praises and petitions before the throne of grace.

What we have just pointed out is agreeable to such passages as these: "Thou shalt call me, My father; and shalt not turn away from me" (Jer 3:19) "I am a father to [the spiritual] Israel, and Ephraim is my first-born...Is Ephraim my dear son? is he a pleasant child?...I will surely have mercy upon him, saith the LORD" (Jer 31:9, 20). In the first formal instruction which the Lord Jesus gave to His young disciples, He bade them, "After this manner therefore pray ye: *Our Father* which art in heaven" (Mat 6:9). How can we approach Him with any confidence or freedom unless we view Him in this blessed relation? If we have been reconciled to Him by Jesus Christ, then God *is* our Father, and "because ye are sons, God hath sent forth the Spirit of his Son into your hearts, crying, Abba, Father"! (Gal 4:6), and that spirit causes its possessor to come in a holy familiarity and childlike manner to God, and evidences itself in desire to honour and please Him.

Not only would it be misleading to our minds for the young convert (even though old in years) to be likened unto a "little child" (Mat 18:2-5) unless there was a *real resemblance,* and thus, a propriety in employing this figure, but it would also be a strange departure from one of the well-established "ways" of God, namely, His having so wrought in the first creation as to strikingly foreshadow His works in the new creation, the natural having been made to adumbrate the spiritual. We see that principle and fact illustrated in every direction. As in the natural, so in the spiritual: there is a begetting (Jam 1:18), a conception or Christ being formed in the soul (Gal 4:19), a birth (1Pe 1:23), and that birth evidenced by a "cry" (Rom 8:15), and the newborn babe desiring "the sincere milk of the word" (1Pe 2:2), so there are many features in common between the natural and the spiritual infant.

Little children are far more regulated by their affections than by their understanding, and the young Christian is much taken with the love of God, the grace of the Lord Jesus, and the comforts of the Holy Spirit. He delights greatly in his own experience, and to hear the experience of others. As the natural child is timorous and easily scared, so the young Christian as quickly alarmed, as was evidenced by the fearing disciples on the storm-swept sea, to whom the Saviour said, "O ye of *little* faith." As the digestive system of a youngster is feeble, so the babe in Christ needs to be fed on "milk" rather than "strong meat" (Heb 5:12-14). "I have yet many things to say unto you, but ye cannot bear them now" (Joh 16:12). Owing to an undeveloped understanding, babes in Christ are not "established" in the Faith: "Be no more *children*, tossed to and fro, and carried about with every wind of doctrine" (Eph 4:14).

"A young convert is much taken with his own importunity in prayer with his own enlargements and affections (they being very warm and lively), with the multitude of means and the much time he spends in the use of and observance of them; whereas, a believer of longer standing and greater measure of spiritual growth values those discoveries which the Holy Spirit gives him in prayer and inward converse with the Lord, of the Father's free love, and the Son's personal, particular, and prevalent intercession on his behalf: and he is more taken with those, than with his own fervour and supplications...The 'babes' in Christ are particularly affected with a sense and enjoyment of pardoning mercy and calling God 'Father.' Hence, the blessings of pardon of sin, peace with God, the spirit of adoption, and an advancement in and an increased spiritual perception of these precious realities, must be a growth in grace such as is quite suited to their spiritual stature and circumstances" (S. E. Pierce). —A.W.P.

OUR ANNUAL LETTER

"If any man speak, let him speak as the oracles of God; if any man minister, let him do it as of the ability which God giveth: that God in all things may be glorified through Jesus Christ, to whom be praise and dominion for ever and ever. Amen" (1Pe 4:11). Those words define the principal duty of Christ's servant: the Rule by which he must work, the enablement by which he is furnished, and the grand end he must ever keep in view, the glory of God. He is to speak not according to any human system, nor after his own fancies, but in undeviating harmony with the Word of God. If God is to be glorified, it must be by enforcing and opening up the teaching of Holy Writ, for God has magnified His Word above all His name (Psa 138:2), that is, above any other revelation He has made of Himself. During our first pastorate, we wrote on the inside-page of our Bible, "Ye shall not add unto the word which I command you, neither shall ye diminish ought from it" (Deu 4:2). To which we then added Exodus 4:12; Isaiah 51:16; 55:11, and for many years, it was our practice to read them immediately before entering the pulpit.

But for the past ten years, we have been denied the holy privilege of preaching orally; and therefore, we are very thankful to find a place is given us in the above verse. As we seek to "minister" to God's people by means of our pen, we can only do so "as of the ability which God giveth" (1Pe 4:11), and that it is our privilege and duty to seek. Not to lean unto our own understanding, but to ask wisdom from Above: wisdom to discern "the present truth" (2Pe 1:12), what is most seasonable today; wisdom to preserve the balance, to minister appropriately to such widely different classes of readers. Yet our aim must be the same now as when our voice was employed: "That God in all things may be glorified" (1Pe 4:11); that our writings may extol the Triune Jehovah, and be of such a tendency as to promote holiness in the lives of our readers; that self may be mortified and Christ exalted.

It is only by heeding the rules laid down in 1 Peter 4:11 that Christ's servant will be preserved from being either a self-seeker or a man-pleaser, two of the principal snares which beset him. If his message be according to the Divine Oracles, temptations to speculation or to adopt novelties will be nipped in the bud. If he labours according to "the ability which God giveth," he will, on the one hand, be kept in the place of humble dependence, ever seeking fresh supplies of grace; and on the other hand, he will do with his "might," whatsoever his "hand findeth to do" (Ecc 9:10). If he be regulated by this paramount motive, "that *God* in all things may be glorified" (1Pe 4:11), he will neither seek the smiles of men, nor fear their frowns. Instead of being in bondage to "what will people think and say of me," his only concern will be the approbation of the One he serves.

"That God in all things may be glorified through Jesus Christ" (1Pe 4:11). If that be kept conscientiously and constantly before the mind and heart of the minister of the Gospel, it will not only preserve him from self-seeking and men-pleasing, but it will also exert a disciplinary effect on his character and conduct. It will be a means of delivering him from slackness and slovenliness, from laziness and lethargy. He will not go into the pulpit unprepared, to preach a sermon which cost him no hard labour. And if his pen be employed, it will not scribble down the first things which enter his mind. Instead, he will "study to show himself approved unto God, a *workman* that needeth not to be ashamed." While others are sleeping, he will be pouring over the Word or pouring out his heart unto God. He will preach or write to the very best of his "ability." There is an old adage, "If a thing be worth doing, it is worth doing *well*,"and surely, anything done unto the Lord and in His Name is entitled to our utmost endeavours.

"That God in all things may be glorified." Unless *that* be the editor's grand aim in the publishing of this magazine, then far better that it should now cease and he fade out into silence. The years are passing swiftly by and most of our life on earth is already behind us. The days in which we are living are much too solemn for trifling. Not only is there everything in the profane world which makes against holy living, but there is little now left in the professing world that fosters it. Judging from the many letters we receive, an increasing number of God's people are becoming more and more dependent upon the printed page for spiritual food. It comforts us to know that God's glory is bound up in the good of His people; and therefore, the most effectual way to minister unto *them* is to be governed by 1 Peter 4:11. As the private Christian can only glorify God as his motives and actions are regulated by the teaching of Holy Writ, so the public servant of God can only glorify Him as his ministry is devoted to an explaining and enforcing of the Divine Oracles. Thus our course is plain.

If the editor of this little magazine be governed by 1 Peter 4:11, then his course is not only plain, but his task is greatly simplified. If he had to 'think up' subjects as secular writers, then he might often be at a loss for a suitable and profitable theme for his pen; but with the inexhaustible Word of God to turn to, with its endless variety of spiritual riches available, with the Holy Spirit to instruct him, there is no need or excuse why he should ever 'run out' of material. Had any other textbook been ours, after penning so many thousands of pages on its contexts, we should indeed be worried over how to find something new for our readers. To the praise of God's grace, we can say that, so far from feeling it a wearisomeness or strain, we have had more joy in preparing this year's issues than ever before. God *does* hear the prayers of His people on our behalf!

As many of our readers have never seen the earlier volumes, we repeat here what has been said in the past, and ask the friends to kindly *refrain* from addressing us as "Rev." Though an ordained minister of the Gospel for upwards of thirty years, we have never felt we could accept any such title. The word occurs but once in the Scriptures: "Holy and reverend is HIS Name" (Psa 111:9); and in view of that verse, it seems to us most impious, a relic of popery, to so address any worm of the earth. We condemn not our brethren who feel otherwise, but simply ask friends to please respect our scruple of conscience.

During the earlier years of publishing this magazine, when we were also active in oral ministry, preaching five or six times a week for years, we often inserted several articles in an issue from the pens of God's servants of the past; and hence, it was necessary to append the name of each author. But since all doors have been closed against us, through our refusal to join any particular denomination and limit our activities thereto, instead of remaining "the Lord's free man", our energies have been undivided and more time became available for writing; until this year, every article in the "Studies" has been from our own pen. If we are spared, this will likely be the case, more or less in the future, so we shall no longer obtrude our initials at the close of each article. Will readers therefore please note that, henceforth, all unsigned articles are by the editor.

Throughout another year, the Lord has favoured us both with health and strength and freely supplied our every need. Though there is much lost ground to be recovered, we are thankful to say our 1944 circulation has shown a welcome increase. Once again, we close with a credit balance. Our principal trial now is, and will likely be, the difficulty of getting the magazine printed. Printers are short staffed, handicapped by the absenteeism of workmen, and tempted to do temporary work for the Government at high rates. We are always prompt in forwarding manuscript. We thank our readers for being patient, especially those abroad, and ask them to make *this* a definite matter of prayer. We hope to continue the present series of articles in 1945, and that the 1944 bound volume will be available by the end of January, at 5/6 post paid ($1.25). Commending you all to God and the Word of His grace, Yours by Divine mercy. — *A.W. and Vera E. Pink*

(continued from back page)

more firmly in the sovereignty of Divine grace than did the apostle Paul, yet his belief therein did not hinder him from saying, "Brethren, my heart's desire and prayer to God for Israel is, that they might be saved" (Rom 10:1). And we have but to read through the book of Acts to see how such a desire and prayer was expressed in constant and earnest efforts after this Salvation.

If the "Articles of Faith" subscribed to by the reader have bred in his heart a spirit of apathy, so that he or she assumes a more or less fatalistic attitude toward the eternal interests of those nearest and dearest unto them, then that is proof positive there is something radically defective about those "Articles," for the teaching of the Scriptures inculcates the very opposite spirit. Concerning their children, Christian parents are expressly bidden to "bring them up in the nurture and admonition of the Lord" (Eph 6:4), and that involves considerably more than "taking them to church" with them on the Sabbath, or even having them join in family worship each day. It signifies to give them such instruction that they shall become acquainted with the Lord, to train them *for Him*, to make known His claims upon them, to explain to them His Law and to preach to them His Gospel; and to relinquish not their efforts until each of them shall voluntarily avow with Ruth, "thy people shall be my people, and thy God my God" (Rut 1:16).

It is indeed true that *you* cannot save your offspring, but it is both your privilege and duty to seek to be an *instrument* therein. The minister of the Gospel cannot save any in his congregation, but his knowledge of that does not deter him from seeking of God an appropriate message, putting forth his best endeavours in preparing that message for the pulpit, supplicating the blessing of Heaven thereon, and then delivering that message earnestly and expectantly. It has pleased God "by the foolishness of preaching to save them that believe" (1Co 1:21), and there requires not to be a congregation before there can be "preaching," nor a "consecrated building" for it to be done in. As Philip rode in the chariot with the eunuch, he "preached unto him Jesus" (Act 8:35). Thus, one may "preach" to a single individual! Let it be noted that Philip preached the Saviour to that Ethiopian out of Isaiah 53, and there is no more suitable passage in the whole Word of God for *you*, Christian father, to "preach" Christ from to your son or daughter. Once they leave your home, they may never again hear "the Gospel of Christ," so make the most of your present opportunity.

A personal testimony and we conclude. The father of the writer was an exceptionally busy business man, so busy that for over thirty years, he never had more than three consecutive days' holiday. He was a corn merchant, and after returning from market, attended to much of the clerical work in person, so that for years, he did not cease till 11:50 Saturday night. Yet he did not lie in bed Sabbath mornings, but took his children to hear God's Word preached. He did not send us to "Sunday school" while he took a nap in the afternoon, but gathered us around him and spent a couple of hours in reading to us from the Scriptures, from *Fox's Book of Martyrs,* Bunyan's *Pilgrim Progress,* etc. Every day, he conducted family worship, and when we were too little to sit up for the evening, our godly mother took us around her knees and prayed with us. Those are sacred memories. "Them that honour me I will honour" (1Sa 2:30), my parents honoured Him, and He honoured them by calling their firstborn into the ministry. — A.W.P.

(continued from front page)

there are no "Sunday" newspapers or world literature to grieve the eye. Here, the radio is silent during the Sabbath. Here, the whole family attend Divine service, perhaps morning and evening; and in the interval, there is a discussing of the sermon and the general conversation is on spiritual lines. In some of these homes, God is honoured with family worship and an attempt is made to familiarize the children with the letter of Scripture. So far so good. But suppose the oldest boy is called to the colours, will he leave home knowing in theory at least what he must do to be saved? Will he, at camp, and later, perhaps lying wounded in a hospital thousands of miles from home, have the memory of father and mother kneeling with him ere he parted from them, as they earnestly committed him into the hands of the Lord? If not, then his parents failed him at the most crucial point.

Some who read this magazine are likely to have sons and daughters who have not yet quite reached the "calling up" age. Perhaps only a year or two is now left before they too will be required to leave home, joining the forces or one of the services. If so, it is high time you seriously took stock of the situation, and diligently sought help from above to redeem the time. You have not fulfilled the whole of your duty toward your offspring by sheltering them from the grosser elements of the world, by providing them with wholesome food, by sending them to a good school. Those things concern time: What about *eternity*? Are you setting before the children an example of piety, which will give them to feel it is real and not a pose? Is your Christian character winsome or depressing and chilling? Do they take knowledge of you that you have "been with Jesus" (Act 4:13)? Can they perceive that your affections are set upon things above and that "the joy of the LORD is your strength" (Neh 8:10)? Does your general demeanor in the home commend Christ to them?

Have you had a heart-to-heart talk with your son or daughter? Do they know that their eternal welfare is your deepest concern? Have you encouraged them to read the Word of God for themselves in private, and told them of the need for asking God to give them an understanding of it? Have you explained to them the Gospel of the grace of God, so that they are quite clear Christ is the sinner's only Saviour? You may have prayed much *for* them in secret, have you ever prayed *with* them singly? These are duties you cannot legitimately transfer to a minister of the Gospel, nor should you desire to do so. They are duties and privileges which devolve upon *you* toward the fruit of your bodies. You may be deeply conscious of your weakness and unworthiness, but it is just *such* instruments that God is pleased to use, that the glory may be His. A broken prayer that is watered with tears is often more effectual than the most orthodox sermon.

Do you say, But the salvation of my children is not in *my* hands: God alone can save them. If that be an attempt to evade your responsibility by hiding behind the truth of Predestination, then such a rejoinder (pious as you may deem it) is of the Devil. Predestination is none of *your* concern. The *physical* well-being of the children was not in *your* hands, yet the knowledge of that did not hinder you from using all appointed means, and asking God's blessing on the same. If you be a hyper-Calvinist, bear with us for a moment, dear friend. It was no cold and fatalistic Christ who, when He, behind the city of Jerusalem, "wept over it" (Luk 19:41). It was no hard and dry doctrinaire who declared, "I am made all things to all men, that I might by all means save some" (1Co 9:22). If *your* belief of Election is hindering you from doing everything in your power to direct your offspring to Christ, you have an erroneous concept of that blessed truth. None ever believed

(Continued on preceding page)

I completed these 12 Pink Books on May 14 2023. It was a Blessing to study under A W Pink for several years now.

I will begin the last of his writings on May 16 2023. God willing.

These are scattered in seperate Booklets. They end in 1952 - when he died, the same year I was born.

May our Lord Jesus richly bless all Christians.

CPSIA information can be obtained
at www.ICGtesting.com
Printed in the USA
JSHW021226030221
11497JS00001B/1

9 781589 602243